MEDIEVAL ENGLISH LITERATURE

D. C. Heath and Company

Lexington, Massachusetts   Toronto

MEDIEVAL ENGLISH LITERATURE

Thomas J. Garbáty
The University of Michigan

ACKNOWLEDGMENTS

NITA SCUDDER BAUGH: "The Debate of the Body and Soul," from *A Worcestershire Miscellany*, edited by Nita Scudder Baugh. Reprinted by permission of the author.

J M DENT & SONS LTD.: "Lanval," from *Lays of Marie de France and Other French Legends*, translated by Eugene Mason. Everyman's Library. Reprinted by permission of J M Dent & Sons Ltd.

E. P. DUTTON & CO., INC.: "Lanval," from the book *Lays of Marie de France and Other French Legends*, translated by Eugene Mason. Everyman's Library. Reprinted by permission of E. P. Dutton & Co., Inc.

EARLY ENGLISH TEXT SOCIETY: *Robert of Brunne's Handlyng Synne*, edited by F. J. Furnivall, and *Mandeville's Travels*, edited by P. Hamelius, reprinted by permission of the Council of the Early English Text Society.

OXFORD UNIVERSITY PRESS: From *The Works of Sir Thomas Malory*, edited by Eugène Vinaver, 2nd ed. 1967, © Eugène Vinaver 1967. Reprinted by permission of Oxford University Press.

PENGUIN BOOKS LTD.: Geoffrey of Monmouth: *The History of the Kings of Britain*, translated by Lewis Thorpe (Penguin Classics, 1966) pp. 51–52, 54–56, 146–48, 212–14, 222–25, 229–33, 237–41, 251–53, 257–61, 264–65, 284. Copyright © Lewis Thorpe, 1966. Reprinted by permission of Penguin Books Ltd.

RUSSELL & RUSSELL: Walter Hoyt French and Charles Brockway Hale, Editors. *The Middle English Metrical Romances* [1930] (New York: Russell & Russell, 1964). Reprinted with the permission of Russell & Russell, Publishers.

SIDGWICK & JACKSON LTD.: From *Early English Lyrics*, edited by E. K. Chambers and F. Sidgwick. Reprinted by kind permission of Sidgwick & Jackson Ltd.

SMITH COLLEGE: "The Wedding of Sir Gawain and Dame Ragnell," from *Smith College Studies in Modern Language*, edited by Laura Sumner. Reprinted by permission of The Trustees of the Smith College.

In Memory of
Albert C. Baugh, MacEdward Leach, Harold Stine
Teachers, Scholars,
Friends

PREFACE

"And gladly wolde he lerne and gladly teche."

The primary purpose of this volume is to increase the pleasure, and facilitate the process, of learning and teaching the literature of medieval England. Teachers and learners, authors and readers, we cannot function without each other. If this book, like a literary Noah's ark, ensures the continuity of creative thought and brings us together to a heightened awareness of the past, it will have done its job.

A period reader, I feel, ought to reproduce the spirit of the times and the vitality which engaged the individual writers. It should be able to recapture the tensions, griefs, and joys of daily living which nurtured the art that mirrored nature. Of course, an anthology, a "gathering of flowers" according to the Greek sense, is nothing new. After all, the *Florilegium* was a part of medieval education. But a "garland" for this period, with its implied cohesiveness and organic whole, has long been missing from our shelves.

Perhaps it is too demanding to require that this kind of work should have a life of its own, or that it should be a surrogate as close as possible in temperament to the time it represents. But such, I hope, is this book; in covering medieval English literature from the years 1100 through 1500, I have endeavored to arrange a garland with no dead twigs or broken strands. Although for the most part the works are in Middle English, examples of Old English, Anglo-Latin, and Anglo-Norman literature are also included in translation, since no medieval English anthology would be representative without them.

The complexity of this period of letters, often considered esoteric, an era cruel and violent but also charitable, courtly, and virile, always deeply devout, demands a logical, uncomplicated approach. The obstacles to communication on all levels—philosophic and social, as well as linguistic—must be reduced to a minimum. My intention to make the teaching of literary history as easy as possible has been accomplished in two ways. First, the reader will note a lengthy General Introduction, which is not literary history as such, but which, as one of the major unifying features of the book, places almost every work into a specific medieval framework. Through it students can appreciate the roles that individual forces like the Church, the aristocracy, the middle class, and the development of language itself, played in the evolution of various genres. The General Introduction puts medieval English literature in perspective, and cross-references will continually look back to it from the text. Such an essay is an innovative feature among medieval collections.

The second factor is linguistic. It will be seen that every work in verse has its own marginal gloss, while the prose sections have their translations in footnotes. This method has proved to be the most convenient way for students to read Middle English, but I have avoided making the translation too easy. The same word, or a closely related form, is not translated more often than once every forty lines, or about once a page. If students, therefore, do not see their word translated on the right-hand margin, let them hunt, and learn in the process.

The book is organized so that it can be approached in many different ways, depending on the inclination of the instructor. Here this reader does pioneering work. The Table of Contents shows one way of organization, that of type or genre. Critics have found this a convenient method, and the fact that Middle English literature for the greater part falls into such groupings is already seen by Chaucer's *Canterbury Tales*, a collection of most medieval literary types. Thus I have grouped the genres, with the first seven connected either through evolution in narrative style or through process of oral transmission. Each genre has a brief explanatory headnote, cross-references to the General Introduction, and a short bibliography. The works within the genre are placed in chronological order.

The Appendixes provide other arrangements. For the linguist there is a table of contents according to dialects, for the folklorist another table organizing the works into motifs and recurrent themes. There is another organization of the contents according to their "modes" (Courtly, Popular, Religious, or combined, whatever the intended audience or purpose may have been), and of course one table in the book arranges all the works in chronological order, as they always appear within each separate table. The instructor, if he or she wishes, can trace the development of courtly-heroic literature, or see the overlapping of religious and popular intent in various works. The folklorist or the Arthurian scholar can follow similar motifs through a number of texts. In fact, I have often attempted to include the same story or figure as seen in various genres: Horn in romance and ballad, Caradoc in lyric and fabliau, similar Arthurian motifs in chronicle and epic matter. In this way, the book truly has a teaching life of its own. The Appendixes may guide you into methods of instruction that I myself cannot foresee.

Although this anthology is not primarily intended as a philological reader, a guide to Middle English spelling and pronunciation is included, and brief paragraphs on the outstanding scribal and dialectal idiosyncracies of specific works are to be found at the head of the annotations for each item. These, with the addition of the index and arrangement according to dialects in the Appendixes, should provide sufficient material so that this book can be used for a Middle English philology or history of the language course.

Finally, each work has its own brief introduction, as well as relevant bibliographical material. I have stressed full and informative annotations, historical and critical, in the footnotes, having myself regretted their occasional lack in other collections. I would rather be embarrassed by riches than by poverty.

Instructors will find ninety percent of what they expect to be here. Obviously, the longest works (Alliterative *Morte Arthure*, Layamon's *Brut*, etc.) could only be included in parts, but the reader will find a large selection of complete romances and of longer works like *The Owl and the Nightingale*, *Pearl*, and many others. From Chaucer I have included *Sir Thopas*, the *Miller's Tale*, and the *Complaint to His Purse*, as the best examples of a type. They are not meant to be representative of Chaucer, but they may put Chaucer into perspective, show his greatness in relief, and entice the student into a Chaucer course.

It remains, finally, to account for the debt which I owe to a select group of people. This book, as a friend once said, has touched many lives and has drawn its own energy from all of us. For personal and professional support in this project, I thank Herbert Addison, Herman Makler, and Lloyd Scott. To Mrs. Albert C. Baugh, I am grateful for much special information and the use of her edition of the *Disputisoun between the Body and Soul*. Professor Donald Sands read the prospectus and gave me valuable advice in regard to contents and the nature of the Appendixes. Professor John Reidy, Consulting Editor of the *Middle English Dictionary*, read the complete manuscript and made a study of the glosses, the linguistic apparatus, and the general information of the introduction and notes, also suggesting emendations of the texts. His wisdom and unusual, wide-ranging knowledge is evident on almost every page of this book. Also, it is a truth universally to be acknowledged that without a good copy editor there are few good books. I am lucky in having the best. The laurels of final publication must undoubtedly go to my good friend Virginia Brinkley. She guided me like the Pearl maiden, if not to the New Jerusalem, at least toward a book in print. To Holt Johnson of D. C. Heath I am grateful for the many weary hours he spent among Owls, Loathly Ladies, Green Knights and others, getting the book ready for the press. In fact, to all of the above must go a large part of the credit for any success this work may have. Unfortunately, what mistakes remain are due, alas, only to me.

In principio, I gained the original stimulus and love for the Middle Ages from my parents. Through them I perceived the period as I have tried to show it here, in "huge cloudy symbols of a high romance." In the end, however, no person but my wife Elsbeth can fully share with me the intense satisfaction in the completed project, after having endured with me the *agonia* of the process. For both of us my years of enforced absence in the charmed forests of medieval Logres have not been without vitalizing rewards; still I am thankful that I may return again to the less charming and gothic, but preferred red brick halls of Ann Arbor.

Thomas J. Garbáty

CONTENTS

THE LYRIC _____631

ALLEGORICAL AND RELIGIOUS VERSE _____675

MEDIEVAL ENGLISH LITERATURE

ORKNEY
ISLANDS

John o'Groats

ATLANTIC

SCOTTISH
GAELIC

Aberdeen

NORTH SEA

Celtic Language Groups

OCEAN

Dun-
fermline
Firth of Forth

Bannock-
burn Edinburgh

Clyde R.

Berwick

CHEVIOT
HILLS

ROMAN WALL

Tyne R.

Carlisle

MULL OF GALLOWAY

NORTHERN

Whitby

ISLE OF
MAN

IRISH SEA

York

Humber

IRISH
GAELIC

ANGLESEY

HOLYHEAD
ISLAND

Wakefield

Hampole

Grimsby

Lincoln

THE
WASH

Dublin

Chester

Nottingham

WEST
MIDLAND

Bourne

Ely

Bury
St. Edmunds

Coventry

Severn R.

Leo-
minster
Malvern
Mon-
mouth

Areley
Warwick

EAST

Cambridge

ANGLO-
IRISH

ST. GEORGE'S CHANNEL

Wye R.

WELSH

MIDLAND

Oxford

Gloucester

London R.

Thames

Caerleon-
on-Usk

Swansea

Malmesbury

Bath

Canterbury

Dover

SOUTH
EASTERN

Bristol Channel

Glaston-
bury

Winchester

Salisbury Southampton

Hastings

SOUTH WESTERN

Exeter

Portisham

ISLE OF
WIGHT

Tintagel Camelford

CORNISH

ENGLISH CHANNEL

CHANNEL ISLANDS

Barfleur

Rouen

Seine R.

Bayeaux

COTENTIN

FRANCE

Mont St. Michel

N

BRITAIN & IRELAND

Approximate Middle English Dialect Boundaries
and Place Names Mentioned in the Literature

0   50   100 Miles

50   100   150 km.

ASPECTS OF MEDIEVAL ENGLISH LITERATURE

THE GENERAL PERSPECTIVE

Although our colleagues the historians may, without too much fear of arousing a professional outcry, cite the period between classical times and the Renaissance as the Middle Ages, such a broad grouping is impossible for us as students and critics of English literature. Even before the cultural and political shock occasioned by the Norman Conquest in 1066 (that is, already under the reign of Edward the Confessor), French influence was strongly felt at the English court, and the traditional Anglo-Saxon ways were changing. The trauma of the Conquest ended a period in English letters, and for almost a hundred years the native tradition was dormant. Thus we must divide English literature into that of the Anglo-Saxon period, Old English (c. 700–1050), and the poetry and prose of the Middle Ages, Middle English (c. 1150–1500). Medieval England also produced Latin and French literature, which will be mentioned briefly below. These productions, especially the latter, were most abundant in the two centuries after the Norman invasion, after which the precedence of Anglo-Norman letters again gave way to English. The break between Old English and Middle English literature was marked, therefore, by a change in language and in cultural temperament.

Old English, the bane of graduate students, is a much more difficult tongue to master than Middle English. As an offshoot from the West Germanic linguistic family, Old English lacks any of the numerous French loanwords which link Middle English with Modern English. It is an inflected language, ruled by the stern precepts of case and gender. A previous knowledge of German is of great benefit to the student of Old English, and, in fact, a certain amount of Prussian discipline is required to attain a reading ability in it. That there can be great delight and pleasure in this, however, is a fact for which many of us can vouch.

The poetic principle underlying Old English verse is that of alliteration, seen in the example from *The Battle of Brunanburg*. Two half-lines are linked by alliteration, with one or two metrically stressed syllables alliterating in the first half-line, but normally only one in the second half-line. Any vowel can alliterate with another. A consistent pattern, or group of patterns, in this was first shown convincingly by Eduard Sievers (who gave his name to "Sievers types"), although other theories, using musical notation, have been advanced, the most recent by J. C. Pope being based on the idea

1

of isochronism. To scan or "siever" a line of Old English verse implies correctly reading the beat. And this strong intonation of the mighty Anglo-Saxon line mirrors the mood which the verse often expresses. Old English lives in the present. The verbs have no future tense, and no past beyond the immediate one. The temperament of the versifier is a realistic one, matter-of-fact, unromantic, serious, and often sad.

And if we were to paint the Old English panorama with very broad strokes (achieving thereby an admittedly generalized picture), we would see a society of Germanic seriousness. The Old English poet refused to exaggerate, except when he told of the exploits of his hero. With rare exceptions, he did not splash his colors, but drew in light and shade, often a monochrome gray. The dreariness of Grendel's mere, the darkness of Hrothgar's hall, the solitary melancholy of the Wanderer or the icy nights endured by the Seafarer, and the hopeless battle of Maldon—all these could be the product of an eighteenth-century author's "hypochondria," or the "gray disease," did not the other side of this Germanic seriousness show up as strongly: loyalty to the lord, the spirit of the comitatus, unflinching, even desperate, courage in defeat—in short, rigorous adherence to the tribal code of existence.

The finest of the Old English secular poems—the *Beowulf*, the elegiac lyrics of the Exeter Book, such as the *Wanderer*, the *Seafarer*, and *Deor's Lament*, and many others—stress the most sterling qualities in the relationship of man to man: loyalty and friendship. The code is to endure, to keep the proverbial "stiff upper lip." In the *Wanderer* we find these lines:

> . . . I know it for truth
> that there is for an earl a noble custom
> that he bind fast his heartmood,
> guard his feeling, whatever his thoughts.

For the heroic, tribal society, which Old English literature in certain aspects presents, the close relationship between chief and thane was an absolute necessity. The lord, the *winedrihten*, represented life, security, home. His housecarls, the comitatus, pledged to live and die with him. Woe to the retainer who returned from battle without his chieftain! The full agony of the lordless man, the outcast, the wanderer, is difficult to measure today, but the theme of social alienation was one of the main motifs of Old English poetry. The code could be broken only at the expense of the broken man.

Even the religious poetry, such as that of the Cædmonian school, was influenced by the martial epic thunder of the secular verse. The *Genesis* and *Exodus* stories are told in warlike terms, and the relationship between the battle poems of *Brunanburg* and *Maldon* is easily seen. In that most beautiful of Old English religious lyrics, the *Dream of the Rood*, Christ is a young warrior who embraces the cross, fearless and stouthearted. Thus we can say also that, with the exception of the purely religious writings, most Old English verse shows a strong courtly flavor. The deeds that the scop, or bard, recites are noble and heroic; and except for a number of spells, charms, and gnomic tags, which might have been used by the serf for his crops and in his daily life, the Old English literature which has come down to us was written to be recited in the hall.

How different, though, is the panorama of Middle English literature! If we were to view the period from the height of the twentieth century back through the ages, somewhat as William Langland, perhaps, looked down from his Malvern Hills, we would indeed see a vast and fair field, full of the most diverse folk imaginable. We would sample the literature of many social classes, from the castle to the barnyard and field and later to the town.

Whereas in the perhaps more democratic Old English society every man, whether of low or high estate, pursued an occupation necessary to the group, the feudal period saw the rise of a leisure class and an audience of women. Both factors controlled the new type of courtly secular entertainment. The code continued, but now it was chivalric. The knight, under the laws of French *courtoisie* or English *gentilesse*, endured the agony of alienation, of years of physical hardship and frustration, not so much for his sovereign lord as for his sovereign lady—who could as easily have been a haughty and cruel Guinevere to her Lancelot as a patient and loyal Rymenhild to her Prince Horn. The ladies of the castle were more interested in the gentle behavior of young men toward their sex, in the description of clothing (which the poet of *Sir Gawain and the Green Knight* has mastered almost beyond perfection), and in deeds of adventure than they would have been in the gory, anatomic description of Beowulf's fight with Grendel or the flow of beer in the mead hall.

Thus our view of the field of folk will show us much courtly, knightly adventure. But at the same time, in another part of the area, we can see the games, the songs, and the festivals of the middle and lower classes. Havelok the Dane puts the shot at the fair in Lincoln and wins the prize. Jack the holy-water clerk seduces his maid on Midsummer Day; and as her girdle grows larger, she assures us plaintively again and again (indeed, it seems she protests too much), "Thought I on no guile." The love expressed in the lyric *Alisoun* is earthy and warm, quite different from the cold courtly-love ritual often expressed elsewhere. The Middle English secular song gives us a unique picture of spring and May and the gay country life outdoors. But the panorama also includes pithy, Brueghel-like vignettes of less bucolic tavern carousing. The Rabelaisian descriptions in *Piers Plowman* of the Seven Deadly Sins, especially Gluttony, are unsurpassed in this period for realistic detail.

Later, and in the far distance toward the north, we can see the rise of the towns, the Corpus Christi plays of the merchant classes, the guilds. We listen to the ballads of wandering tinkers and minstrels, the folklore of the Middle Ages with its romantic heroes, Robin Hood, Johnie Cock, Edward, and Lord Randall, drawn from the outlaw tradition and the sensational affairs of isolated northern hamlets. It is true, as Kenneth Sisam has said, that Middle English added romance to literature, not only in the long courtly and chivalric narrative poems of that name, but in the whole imaginative sweep of the era.

Romance and also humor, both for the most part absent in Old English literature, were granted us in the Middle Ages. But the field of folk would not be complete without the inclusion of the numerous religious figures and their record. Their presence was felt everywhere as they mingled with their secular brothers. In the middle ground, toward the west, we might notice a benign and gentle confessor, smiling at three young ladies, sisters wishing to become anchoresses. He is writing their rule, restricting their household pets to a single cat, but allowing them to dangle their bare feet in the sun on a hot summer's day. A man who knows the world and its temptations, but also the tenderness of his young wards and the limits of their endurance, he is the kindly unknown author of the *Ancrene Riwle*. Without looking too closely, we see the friars, Dominicans and Franciscans, everywhere mixing with the crowds in the market and at the fairs. The Dominicans are preachers, their stories, *exempla*, spiced with worldly interest; to the Franciscans we owe many lyrics, mostly religious, though they occasionally slipped into less spiritual themes. Much maligned were the friars, the butt of many jokes and of Chaucerian satire (and not without reason in later times); but they were the source and inspiration of some of our finest songs, as well as of the broadest medieval humor. Vanity of vanities saith the Preacher! But man can yet be saved. For, again toward the north, we see the mystics, the ascetics, lost in meditation, forbearance, and ecstasy. There, for one, is the hermit Richard Rolle of Hampole, an artist in prose, surrounded by his disciples, a rapt group of religious ladies, to many of whom it seemed that they sat in the presence of a saint.

There is so much to see, so many colors and such varied life. These are the times, indeed, which gave rise to the concept of "Merrie England," a phrase as joyful in tone as it is misleading from a closer view. Certainly, to understand the period we cannot afford to regard it only from a distant perspective, from the top of our Malvern Hills. We must descend into the crowd and live with it. But this we can do today only by reading the works themselves, so that the old authors may talk to us directly. Such evidence has always been more valid than the hearsay of modern literary critics, necessary and elucidating as these may be.

As we read, we shall notice especially that the Middle English epoch seemed to bind together a common European literary heritage and tradition, folklore motifs and recurring ideas, to produce, in spite of the babel of dialects and the differentiation of courtly, religious, or bourgeois modes and style, quite a remarkable pattern of cohesiveness. Yet it is also self-evident from the kaleidoscope of life which we see in medieval English literature (Middle English, Anglo-Norman, and Anglo-Latin) that this was not a monolithic period. There was evolution and development, as in all ages of mankind.

LANGUAGE AND ITS RELATIONSHIP
TO THE LITERARY EVOLUTION OF THE PERIOD

Perhaps the most valid background against which to view the progressive changes in Middle English literature is that of the development of the English language. Although in the Middle Ages language did not symbolize national consciousness to the extent that it does today (or that it did for the French schoolmaster in Daudet's *La Dernière Classe*), nevertheless in the years following the Conquest French and English literary productions did mirror their respective national interests. And since the French language was adopted by the upper class, both Norman and Saxon, whereas English remained the language of the common folk of both nationalities, it is natural that the secular literature of entertainment in the years after the Conquest would be written in Anglo-Norman and would represent the interests of the leisure class.

In his efficient but ruthless domination of the country, William the Conqueror achieved one of the fastest and most radical linguistic changes the history of language has ever known. After eliminating 90 percent of the Saxon nobles, he married his Norman cadets to their widows, which was his right by feudal law. The Saxon wives perforce learned the tongue of their new husbands, and the few English nobles who were spared the sword because of their neutrality or allegiance to the Conqueror's cause also spoke French in order not to be totally isolated from the court. On the other hand, the common soldier from Poitiers or Limousin, who sought land, money, or adventure, often settled in the Saxon villages or farms, married the miller's daughter, and learned English so as to communicate with his wife, and her sisters and her cousins and her aunts. The linguistic division in the years after the Conquest was therefore a social and economic one, rather than one of nationality, though, since to the victor belong the spoils, power (and therefore nobility) was in the hands of the Normans.

We cannot speak of a "return of the English language" (as we do, for instance, of the "return of King Arthur"), because the English language never died. It continued side by side with Norman French, but mainly in oral transmission. The miller's daughter, whatever her other assets, could not read, and she did not have the leisure to listen to nor the means to reward a minstrel. Therefore little was written for her, with the few exceptions of religious tracts, sermons, and stories.

On the other hand, the Norman nobility, from the king on down, much preferred their southern duchy to the fog and drizzle of England, and for years they felt no need to learn the language or customs of the natives. William thought Normandy important enough to leave the duchy to his eldest son Robert; Henry I spent most of his time in France; and Richard the Lion-hearted, in the spirit of the *courtoisie* for which he is famous, is said to have remarked that the English were dogs, good for nothing but taxes. What need, then, to learn the barbaric Saxon tongue?

Thus we have a period of Anglo-Norman literature, quite prolific, though even today somewhat neglected and worthy of more intensive exploration. Its productions included material on religious themes, and the important histories by Gaimar (*Estorie des Engles*, c. 1150, which describes part of the Havelok story) and Wace (*Roman de Brut*). Both of these were adaptations of Geoffrey of Monmouth's Anglo-Latin *Historia Regum Britanniae*, which contains the germ of the Arthurian legends, Wace's being by far the more successful. The Norman spirit seemed to be an eminently practical one (though one cannot call it prosaic by any definition), and Anglo-Norman literature produced little in the way of lyric poetry. We do, however, have a modest collection of verse romances.

One of the most famous of these Anglo-Norman poets who wrote in the spirit of romance and the chivalric code was Marie de France (fl. 1175), the author of the famous Breton *lais*. We know little about her except that she was of Norman birth and royal blood and resided in England. "Marie ai nom, si sui de France" ("My name is Marie, and I am of France") is her laconic introduction in *Ysopet*. Attempts by scholars to identify her with the abbess of Shaftesbury, sister of Henry II, remain theory only. Her influence on English literature was great, since several of her lais were adapted in English (as, for example, *Lanval*) and she inspired many native stories of the type, such as *Sir Orfeo*. The Breton lais are short narratives, concisely organized, with much Celtic magic. The stories perhaps originated in Wales or in Cornwall and then migrated by oral transmission to Brittany. Since Wace's *Brut* influenced Marie, her lais are important for their many Arthurian motifs and analogies; but as artistic entities in themselves, they are not easily surpassed in medieval literature. It has been said that the Breton lai is to the romance what the modern short story is to the novel, and in some aspects this holds true. The lais were probably composed to be recited or sung without interruption; hence, whereas the romances are long-winded, discursive, and episodic, the lais are plotted, pointed, and short. Poe's theory that only the short poem can keep up an intensity of mood is here verified.

Though the Bretons were noted in England for their storytelling powers, the lai became a genre of verse rather than a specific product of Brittany. The origin of the term was therefore soon obscured, although, as we see by Chaucer's *Franklin's Tale* and *Wife of Bath's Tale* two hundred years after Marie, interest in the type remained.

The earliest Breton lai which survives, however, is not one by Marie, but the Anglo-Norman *Lai du Cor* (*Lay of the Horn*) by Robert Biket. It treats the old motif of the Chastity Test, this time in Arthur's court and at Arthur's expense. The only one in the group not a cuckold is the renowned Welsh hero Caradoc, who appears in a similar episode in the ballad called *The Boy and the Mantle* and is also mentioned in the lyric *Annot and Iohon.*

But if Anglo-Norman was the language of entertainment for the elite, Latin continued as the international tongue of the scholar. No work that was considered truly important by its creator, of serious tone and benefit to the world at large, could be trusted to the vernacular, French or English. The linguistic fear expressed by Pope's "Such as Chaucer is will Dryden be" was not new in the eighteenth century. Thus Anglo-Latin literature thrived from Old English times to Milton. For our purposes we need mention only two chronicles among the mass of theological, scientific, encyclopedic material produced in England by Latin writers of the period.

The first, William of Malmesbury's *Gesta Regum Anglorum* (c. 1125) needs only brief treatment. His history merges into imagination and fantasy, and his digressions, hints of forgotten songs and stories, add a romantic flavor to the usual dull chronicle style. In fact, some of his episodes served as raw material for later poetic treatment, as in the ballad *Sir Aldingar.* And it is also this element of romance which makes Geoffrey of Monmouth's very important work *Historia Regum Britanniae* (1137) worth our attention. Geoffrey wrote history and literature. In its outline of the Arthurian story—the first detailed one—and its legends of Lear, Gorboduc, and many others, the *History of the Kings of Britain* became the most influential chronicle in the Middle Ages. The author, a Welshman seeking preferment in the Church, always refers to "a little black book" sent by his friend Walter, archdeacon of Oxford, as his source. In the Middle Ages it did not do to invent one's own stories. Certainly the greatest creative genius of the epoch, Geoffrey Chaucer, rarely invented a narrative; and when he did, he tried very hard to hide the fact. The appeal was to authority and source in those dogmatic times. But Geoffrey of Monmouth's source, the black book, is unknown, and there is serious doubt that it ever existed. Geoffrey was an artist who fused old legends and matter from oral tradition to produce a literary work. Is it chronicle, epic, or romance? The Arthurian stories, the matter of romance, are derived from the chronicles of Nennius and Bede, but epic matter from Virgil also appears. Geoffrey's work is, therefore, a grand coalition of types, and its prestige continued for centuries until it was finally supplanted by the fatal magnitude of Malory's *Morte Darthur*.

This strange situation of a trilingual literature continued until a series of political disruptions loosened England from her French ties. Even in spite of this, the native tradition would in time have pushed itself to the surface. In any nation, the original tongue will survive, no matter how effective the cover of later cultures. Even the American Indian languages survive, albeit in isolated groups except for their widespread usage in geographical designations.

In 1204 King John Lackland earned his nickname by losing Normandy. Statesmen pay a high price when their actions are governed by emotion. John fell in love with the daughter of a powerful French vassal, and, to support his suit, attacked her family. They in turn appealed to Philip Augustus, who, as king of France, was John's overlord in Normandy, and a council of the peers was called. When John did not appear before this gathering, he was declared in contempt of court, and Normandy was forfeited to the French crown. The claim was quickly consolidated with military victories, and the old home was lost. No longer could the English king and the Norman nobility vacation for a lifetime in the south. Slowly lands were exchanged among brothers and cousins on both sides of the Channel. As political ties were loosened, so were those of family. In 1244 the separation of French and English nobility was completed by the Decree of the Two Masters. Louis IX, faced with an insurrection of his vassals who drew help from their English lands and retainers, stated that a double allegiance was impossible; those who wanted to stay in France could do so only at the sacrifice of their English estates and titles. Henry III reciprocated, and there was an end to the interlocking nobility of the two nations. Norman nobles were now in England to stay; and, like it or not, their contact with the English increased.

And so they attempted to speak to the miller and his daughter, at first hesitatingly, in a strange, macaronic language containing more French words than English. It was the eternal humorous, frustrating problem of the immigrant's painstaking attempts to learn the tongue of his new home. The studies of Jespersen and Baugh based on the *Oxford English Dictionary* show that more French words entered the English vocabulary in the years 1250–1400 than at any other time. For when the immigrant is at the same time the conqueror, the elite, or if he becomes for some reason the social arbiter, his foreign intrusions will be regarded as *en vogue* and will be accepted into the language. The numerous ethnic terms in the New York City dialect serve as a kind of parallel, even if the Pennsylvania Dutch phrase "Die Kuh is over the fence gejumped" has not gone into General American.

Thus English secular literature of entertainment was again recorded for the pleasure of wealthy patrons, and when in 1300 the author of the romance *Arthur and Merlin* says he has written it in English because many nobles no longer understand French, we know that the native language has been reestablished. What a loss it would have been for English letters (and what a gain for French literature) had Chaucer, a court poet, written fifty years before he did! But King Alfred, the father of English prose, might have scratched his head in puzzlement, trying to decipher this new English which was so different from the old. In many ways, of course, it was much simpler. Recorded literature will transfix a language, will brake its development; while oral transmission, on the other hand, will hasten change, always in the direction of greater facility in pronunciation and simplicity of grammar. Thus Middle English lost inflections and genders and many of its strong verbs were weakened. But if the language was streamlined in this fashion, it also achieved much greater diversity according to the geography of the country. We usually identify four or five different dialects, of which the easiest to recognize are the Southern (for example, in *The Owl and the Nightingale*, voicing of initial *f*, the present participle ending *-inde*) and the Northern (for example, in Barbour's *Bruce*, *a* for *o* in other dialects, as *haly*, *knaw*; *qu* for *wh*; the present participle ending in *-and*). Chaucer's dialect is considered to represent that of London; and the East and West Midland dialects have their own variations. Travelers in those days had difficulty communicating with one another, for not only their pronunciation but also their vocabulary might differ in the extreme. William Caxton, who more than any other single man finally achieved through his press a certain uniformity of language, illustrates the plight of an editor as late as 1490:

> . . . And that comyn englysshe that is spoken in one shyre varyeth from a nother. In so moche that in my dayes happened that certayn marchauntes were in a shippe in tamyse, for to have sayled over the see into zelande, and for lacke of wynde, thei taryed atte forlond, and wente to lande for to refreshe them. And one of theym named Sheffelde, a mercer, cam in to an hows and axed for mete; and specyally he axyd after egges. And the goode wyf answerde, that she coude speke no frenshe. And the marchaunt was angry, for he also coude speke no frenshe, but wolde have hadde egges, and she understode hym not. And thenne at laste a nother sayd that he wolde have eyren. Then the good wyf sayd that she understod hym wel. Loo, what sholde a man in thyse dayes now wryte, egges or eyren? Certaynly it is harde to playse every man by cause of dyversite and chaunge of language.

But it is just this development of the English language, or rather its ever-greater use for varied genres of literature, that has given us the frame for dividing the vast period of Middle English into separate chronological categories. The late Alois Brandl, longtime Ordinarius for Anglistik at the University of Berlin, set up the following still quite valid divisions in his essay *Mittelenglische Literatur* (1893).

The first period, from the beginning to 1250, was, as we have seen, a time little devoted to secular literary entertainment in English, since this was the prerogative of Anglo-Norman. The Church did not write for gain as did the minstrels, who produced for French-speaking patrons. Thus the early Middle English literature, meant for the common folk, was religious in temper, biblical and instructive. Brandl calls this the Period of Religious Record.

From 1250 to 1350, that is, in the years when the Norman nobility was learning English, we get a mixture of religious and secular entertainment. Along with moralistic, devotional, and mystical writing, we find such romances as *Havelok* and *Horn*. This, then, is the Period of Religious and Secular Literature.

The flowering of Middle English literature, however, occurred in the third period—a brief one, 1350–1400: the Period of Great Individual Writers. The linguistic climate is now settled, and our foremost medieval authors appear: Chaucer; the Pearl Poet, author of *Sir Gawain and the Green Knight*; the author of *Piers Plowman* (William Langland?); Wycliffe; and Gower. The court had fully accepted English by this time, and French was spoken only at such modish places as the cloister of Stratford atte Bowe, which Chaucer's Prioress attended. French of Paris was to her unknown; fifty years before, she would have scorned to speak English!

However, the fourth period, that of Imitation or Transition, shows a general decline of inspiration, caused in part by the overwhelming fame of Chaucer—one can imitate much in Chaucer, but not his genius. Lydgate produced his volumes of verse at this time and fully acknowledged his debt to "his master, Geoffrey." The Scottish Chaucerians, like Henryson, showed somewhat more vitality than the English ones. In general, the fifteenth century, marked as it was by internal wars and dissension, proved a slough for English letters. Yet there were bright spots: the century did, for instance, produce the great comic dramatist of the *Second Shepherds' Play*, and also Thomas Malory, considered by many the finest prose writer since Alfred. With these works in drama and prose, English literature looked ahead to the Elizabethan Renaissance.

There have been some exceptions to Brandl's first category. The native tradition in secular literature was not altogether quiescent; and even the didactic, religious prose of this early period included some examples of astonishingly undogmatic humaneness, common sense, and even wit. For our purposes we need mention only three works here: *The Owl and the Nightingale* (c. 1195), Layamon's *Brut* (c. 1205), and the nuns' guide, known as the *Ancrene Riwle* (c. 1200).

Perhaps because of the influence of the old English court at Winchester, the native tradition revived early in the South. The North was silent for centuries, while Southern is the dialect of that unique and delightful example of "debate" literature *The Owl and the Nightingale*. The debate, an outgrowth of medieval scholasticism (for example, Abelard's *Sic et Non*), was not a new genre. Alcuin's *Conflictus Veris et Hiemis* is an example from the eighth century, and the *tensouns* of the troubadours were popular in Provence. The medieval mind, which saw all issues concerning earth and heaven as in stark opposition and taught them by clearly defined contrasts, loved to discuss the values of each. Thus we have debates ranging from those between hand and eye, body and soul, cook and baker, sheep and wool, to those on the more crucial issues discussed by the Oxford Union today.

The Owl and the Nightingale is the first of its type in English. It draws from English tradition, quotes proverbs from King Alfred, and employs a verse line which could be scanned according to Sievers. The language is early Middle English with few French loanwords. More French, on the other hand, is the rhymed octosyllabic couplet, as rhymed verse in general is of French influence, having its origins in Church Latin. But the poem is characterized by a humor similar to that of Chaucer, colloquial and idiomatic, rather than the seriousness of the legal style usually employed by the debate. The Nightingale is quick, witty, sarcastic; the Owl replies slowly, gathering the full ammunition for heavy blasts. The judge is to be Nicholas of Guildford, who is lauded exceedingly in the poem but who, like Hamlet, lacks advancement. He may well be the author, and though some critics feel no man would sing his own praises to such an extent in his own work, this seems tenuous reasoning. On the other hand, if he was the author, he shows dubious sense in attacking prospective patrons for their nepotism.

Critics have also looked for allegory in this quarrel, which has borrowed much from the beast fable. Thus the Nightingale is seen to represent Youth and the Owl, Age; or the debate is said to be one of Gaiety versus Gravity, Art versus Philosophy, the new critics versus the old clergy, or amorous, courtly poetry versus didactic poetry. But perhaps this pleasant avian argument was simply intended to be a lively debate between an owl and a nightingale.

The poem is a good piece of work for any period of Middle English literature, even the third; that it was written in the first is truly remarkable. The author is a realist: he knows his birds; he knows his people. The Owl is the English brown owl; its nest is disorderly with the picked bones of small animals. The Nightingale hides in the bush but would challenge the Owl if it had a sword. This is Chaucerian humor in the twelfth century; but then no wonder: the twelfth century, in France as well as England, was a fecund period of literary, artistic, and scholarly renaissance.

If *The Owl and the Nightingale* has some French elements, Layamon's *Brut* has almost none at all. It is English in tone, vocabulary, content, and alliterative line. Nationalistic in spirit, it bears the native tradition proudly. The author, a country priest from Worcestershire, painstakingly ruled out French loanwords, though his sources (aside from Bede's *Ecclesiastical History*) were probably the Arthurian chronicles of Wace and an Anglo-Norman translation of Geoffrey of Monmouth. Layamon also drew heavily on Welsh material, since he lived near the Severn in the Cymric-English borderland. In Worcestershire, which harbored several Celtic linguistic islands (see Herbert Pilch, *Layamon's "Brut"* [Heidelberg, 1960]), Welsh stories and legends circulated widely, and Layamon was in constant touch with the Welsh people and their literary heritage. He consciously used Cymric tales as raw material for his great work. But for Layamon, language and national spirit were one. The Arthurian story, told here for the first time in English, controls about one-third of this vast (sixteen-thousand-line) chronicle of the history of England from Brutus, the mythical Trojan founder, until 689, with the final defeat of the Briton Cadwallader in the Welsh mountains. And the Arthurian story is a pronouncedly English one. In Geoffrey of Monmouth, Arthur was a world conqueror; in Wace, he was a feudal, courtly king; but in Layamon, Arthur is an Englishman, and he reasserts the English spirit. Yet we have, in the author of the *Brut*, the strange paradox of a backward-looking English poet celebrating the history of his people's hereditary enemies.

In many ways the *Brut* is an English epic in the Old English tradition. Its use of alliteration, compound epithets, and kennings (see *The Battle of Brunanburg*, this volume, p. 49, l. 2n, and p. 51, ll. 61–62n), its description of feasts, of boasting before battle, and of battles themselves, its concept of the comitatus and of the rule of fate—all this is in the Anglo-Saxon literary temper. Indeed, the *Brut* is a propagandistic book, with its attempt to throw off the Norman cultural yoke. But its literary aspects also show unusual strength: the author does not intrude; the story moves at its own momentum, and the characters speak directly. It is the technique of Chrétien de Troyes, of Marie de France, one which gives life to letters and richness to language. The *Brut*, therefore, has been called by some the greatest English work before Chaucer and a most important influence on later Arthurian literature. As a link with the past, as an example of the continuity of language and the native tradition, this epic is of vital interest for us. Behind it, in the far background, we feel the stoic courage of Harold's comitatus on the hill at Senlac; and in the losing battle against Norman military and cultural might, there is an echo of the grizzled old warrior's admonition in *Maldon*: "May our spirit be the stronger, our hearts the keener, our courage the greater, as our might lessens."

Quite different in temper and purpose is the *Ancrene Riwle*, which is an example of the native tradition in prose. Whereas poetry shows an emotional approach to literature, prose must appeal primarily to the intellect; the latter, therefore, will indicate the flow of culture better than the former. The *Ancrene Riwle*, or rule for anchoresses, stands in the tradition of the religious prose of Ælfric and Wulfstan, and is for R. W. Chambers, in his famous essay *On the Continuity of English Prose*, one of the building blocks of literature from Alfred to Rolle, Malory, and More. The rule was written as a guide for three wealthy sisters, tentatively identified by Hope Emily Allen as Emma, Gunilda, and Christina, former ladies-in-waiting to Queen Maud, wife of Henry I. In 1135 the abbot of Westminster granted them the hermitage of Kilburn. This identification, however, is much too early and, though quite pleasant, can no longer be accepted. We know that several treatises that influenced the *Riwle* were not composed before the middle of the twelfth century, and other factors militate against an early date. The work achieved great popularity, and many later versions, less personal and directed at a larger community, appeared under the title *Ancrene Wisse*. Scholars date our version of the *Riwle* at c. 1200.

The circumstances surrounding the origin of the treatise and the contents themselves might seem plain, dusty, unpromising in the extreme for students of literature. But indeed nothing could be further from the truth. The eight books of the *Ancrene Riwle*, six connected with the inner life and two with domestic affairs, show us an author keenly aware of the frailty of his young charges. He writes with compassion and excellent common sense. His style is homey and his illustrations of flatterers, backbiters, and gossiping women often whimsical and full of humor. His wise counsel constitutes chiefly, not a "rule" in the orthodox religious sense, but a way of life best fitted for the three young women, who were used to an easier road than the one they chose to follow. Thus the eighth book is of great interest for us because it deals with the little things of domestic life. How many servants could attend the sisters? How much cattle could they own, and why not more? Where could yeast be gotten when it ran out? The more we read the *Riwle*, the greater our admiration for the writer. He must have been well trained in the classical Old English prose style, learned, wise in the knowledge of mankind, benevolent—a good friend and an ideal confessor.

After Layamon the alliterative long line suffers eclipse for a hundred and fifty years. The native tradition seems to have slumbered, or else it evolved in oral transmission only. Apparently it survived in the country—which will normally show more conservative tendencies, culturally or linguistically, than will the more populated cities. When the Old English line, though not the vocabulary, reappeared, it was in the middle of the fourteenth century, in the North and Northwest, as part of a greater force of literary vitality. This is the movement which we call the Alliterative Revival.

For some reason, perhaps the rawer climate, the more somber temperament of the people, or just the greater distance from the London court and its French influence, the North was linked to the Old English tradition in more than just the alliterative line. The literature of Scotland, Yorkshire, and even the Northwest Midlands seems more restrained, less romantic, than that of the South, with a greater seriousness in both secular and religious writing—the North playing a leading part in the latter type especially. The early Scots show this in marked fashion. John Barbour's *Bruce* (1376) is an earnest account of the battle of Robert Bruce and his great lieutenant Douglas against the English. The author, archdeacon of Aberdeen, calls his long poem a romance. In its adventurous episodes, it comes close to this type; but in its authentic incidents and its highly patriotic character, its celebration of "Scotland the Brave," it is more important as the beginning of Scottish literature and of a vigorous nationalistic spirit. This intensity of the Scots ranged at times into a kind of social Darwinism. Thus *The Testament of Cresseid* by the Scottish Chaucerian Robert Henryson is a cruel epilogue to the humane story of the English master, Geoffrey Chaucer. And perhaps no more concise illustration of this "sea change" between English and Scottish verse can be found than in two ballads on the same theme, the English *Three Ravens*, exemplifying love and loyalty, and the cynical, stark (though undoubtedly more lyrical) Scottish *Twa Corbies*, where the atavistic vestiges of the Old English birds of prey, found in *Beowulf* and the *Wanderer*, make their somber reappearance.

If the alliterative line stayed in oral production, it also changed in nature and became simplified, just as the language did. In 1350 we can no longer scan the half-line, for the whole becomes a unit of thought. Chaucer scorned this Northern phenomenon: "But trusteth wel, I am a Southern man,/I can not geste—rum, ram, ruf—by lettre," says his Parson; but as Kenneth Sisam remarked, the alliterative poets found a master key to the dialects, and thereby overcame one of the greatest factors inhibiting a wider understanding and transmission of vernacular verse throughout England.

Thus not only some of the finest but also some of the most popular works of the fourteenth century belong to the Alliterative Revival. We need mention only the two productions of the Pearl Poet included here: *Sir Gawain and the Green Knight* and the *Pearl*. It is unfortunate that the author of *Gawain*, perhaps the best romance in Middle English, also seems to have taken undue pride in the range of his vocabulary, certainly the largest "word hoard" of his contemporaries. Almost every line contains a new word. The joy of reading *Sir Gawain and the Green Knight* in the original is, therefore, often limited to philology courses. The very opening lines predict that the pages of the glossary will be well thumbed, worn, and blackened by the time the semester is over:

> Siþen þe sege and þe assaut watz sesed at Troye,
> Þe borȝ brittened and brent to brondez and askez,
> Þe tulk þat þe trammes of tresoun þer wroȝt,
> Watz tried for his tricherie, þe trewest on erthe;
> Hit watz Ennias þe athel, and his highe kynde,
> Þat siþen depreced prouinces, and patrounes bicome
> Welneȝe of al þe wele in þe west iles. . . .

Gawain is a courtly romance in the highest sense of the word. The poet is conversant with architecture and fashions, with gowns and personal adornments. Well versed in the art of hunting, he describes the hue and cry, the capture, and the rewards to the hounds. He is a master storyteller, weaving several Arthurian legends, Irish folk-tales, shrewd human psychology, realistic yet highly poetic descriptions of cold and winter, sex, and suspense into one of the most marvelous narratives to come out of the Middle Ages.

Was he also the author of the *Pearl*? We must believe so, on the basis of dialect and of the fact that both poems are found in the same manuscript (British Library. Cotton Nero A.x). But we see two sides of the man through his works: while *Gawain* is out-going, worldly, the *Pearl*, on the other hand, is introspective, spiritual—one of the most sensitive of religious allegories, which has been widely interpreted along theo-logical lines. But the *Pearl* is most beautiful and touching if we see it as what it claims to be: a song of mourning, an attempt at self-consolation. The author has lost a pearl in the grass. As he visits the spot in his grief, he sleeps and dreams he sees a two-year-old child, whom he recognizes as his Pearl. She tells him that in reality she is not lost, but rather saved by the Heavenly Bridegroom, and her home is the New Jerusalem. The dreamer wakes—not happy, perhaps, but at peace.

Although the Alliterative Revival produced some literature meant purely for entertainment—the Alliterative *Morte Arthure*, for example—it appears that the move-ment was very much occupied with moral and religious themes, as we shall see below. A didactic purpose predominates; even in *Gawain* there is more than a hint of the power of spiritual intercession. And in many cases this ethical instruction is combined with themes of social protest, both qualities being aimed to reach, not the establish-ment obviously, but the poor and the troubled lower classes. Thus linguistic vehicle and theme came to be symbiotic in nature. The author would write, not in French rhyme or style, but in a native form, a traditional line, one with which the folk were familiar and at ease. And thus, too, the link between the literature of the Period of Religious Record, which, with its strong Old English characteristics, was aimed mainly at the common man, and the rather earnest, instructive intent of some of the later alliterative poems is not wholly tenuous.

This happy combination of functional language and style, of theme, and of direc-tion, resulting in a great popular appeal, is best seen in that major dream-vision allegory of the fourteenth century, *The Vision of William Concerning Piers the Plowman*, usually called simply *Piers Plowman*. One of the few non-Northern pieces, it is in the dialect of the Southwest Midlands. The author, a certain William Langland, was a Shropshire man with a view of life in many ways as melancholy as that of the later Shropshire Lad. Langland, sitting atop his Malvern Hills, has several dreams, all of them concerned with man's search for salvation in allegorical form. The main char-acter, Piers, or Peter, the Plowman, runs the gamut of symbol, from the good Christian to the Samaritan to Christ himself. He is the one unifying figure in what, through three revisions called the A, B, and C versions, is too often an episodic work. The strength of the poem lies in the first two versions. The picture of the "fair field full of folk," a microcosm of fourteenth-century life, is a lively one of beggars and courtiers, friars and villeins, guildsmen and palmers. High up in the distance is the tower of Truth, representing God, down below the dungeon of Falsehood, representing the Devil. Holy Church, in the form of a lady, calls the sleeper and urges him to work with the others. When he asks her how he might achieve salvation, she replies that this is done through Truth, and through helping the poor. Much of *Piers Plowman* concerns the vices of mankind: corruption, guile, bribery; and in the second vision of William, we have a robust, even somewhat coarse description of the Seven Deadly Sins personified. With the autobiographical references to Langland and his wife, the earthy tavern scenes, and the realistic general descriptions of medieval daily life, *Piers Plowman* is an important social document; and in many ways it proves to be a counterpart, albeit much more austere and unsmiling, to Chaucer's *Canterbury Tales*.

Piers Plowman was not meant to be funny; its humor is only incidental to its purpose, and its irony is often heavy-handed. The vision of Piers is essentially a gloomy one; the past is lost, the present ridden by care, the future dim and doubtful. Langland, like Arnold, wandered "between two worlds, one dead, the other powerless to be born."

Underlying the whole poem is the theme of the second vision, the search for Saint Truth, with whom only Piers, the simple plowman, is acquainted. And the pilgrimage to the shrine of this saint, the continual quest for a spiritual answer to temporal questions, **the affirmation of faith and appeal to God,** is the source and integral element of much of medieval literature. The influence of Holy Church on all literary productions of the time, secular or spiritual, was constant, pervasive, and often controlling. For better or for worse, in a negative as well as a positive fashion, Ireland and Rome helped to direct the course of medieval literary history.

THE CHURCH AND ITS INFLUENCE
ON THE DEVELOPMENT OF LITERARY GENRES

In many ways the organization of medieval English society consisted of various systems or institutions which worked together as blocks to build the complete structure. Thus politically we have the feudal code, socially the system of chivalry and the ways of the **urban bourgeois** and the country folk, economically the guild system, spiritually the Church. There were other such institutions, of course, all with set rules, behavior motifs, traditions, even dogmas; and all of them were interrelated. In literature these social blocks were represented by what might be called *modes*—courtly, popular (or bourgeois), and spiritual—as against specific literary *genres*; and like the institutions, the modes were never pure, but an amalgamation of different influences. Yet of all the medieval institutions, only the Church has survived; and it has done so with a basically medieval character, feudal and hierarchical. The reason for this must lie in the fact that the Church alone was able to adapt, to adjust to new forces, dangers, and developments, in what under the circumstances can truly be called a miraculous fashion. The proof lies in the literary productions of the period: by tracing the course of religious action and reaction, we gain what little knowledge we have of lost literary origins, we perceive clues to forgotten songs, and we understand the motivating force behind many secular productions.

From Old English times through the Middle Ages, the Church pursued a zigzag course, at times condemning secular literature outright, at times utilizing it for its own purposes. The famous Alcuin, abbot of Tours and educator of Charlemagne, writing to the monks of Lindisfarne in the late eighth century and inquiring after their customs, posed the rather grumpy question "Quid Hinieldus cum Christo?" (that is, "What do the lays of the pagan king Ingeld have to do with Christ, King of Kings?") The story of Ingeld is alluded to in *Beowulf* and *Widsith*; we gather from this that it was not unusual for the religious brothers to entertain themselves in the refectory with traditional popular legends. But Alcuin felt that God's little acre of Lindisfarne was too narrow in scope to hold two kings: Caesar and God could not share the same temple. Yet a hundred years earlier, Saint Aldhelm had evidently thought they could. William of Malmesbury described in the twelfth century how the saint had stood in marketplaces and on bridges playing his harp and singing popular songs, lyrics now lost, enticing thereby the crowds to whom he then revealed God's good news.

Certainly we can state categorically that in these early years the life of letters depended on the life of the Church. In the seventh and eighth centuries, the great monasteries of Whitby, Wearmouth, and Jarrow produced such men as Cædmon and Bede and later Cynewulf; to these monasteries and their libraries we also owe the survival of the *Beowulf* manuscript. In these places of peace and repose and of humane and spiritual thought, learning flourished; in the scriptoria were heard the constant scratching of quills and the hum of the murmuring scribes. But the Danes uprooted the Church, and learning withered. King Alfred in the ninth century could only muse over the empty monasteries and the ignorant monks. Under the weight of the "various and manifold businesses of this kingdom," he started a system of education. Yet it needed the health of the Church to prosper, and this had to wait until the tenth century, with the monastic reform or so-called Benedictine Renaissance led by Dunstan, archbishop of Canterbury, Æthelwold, bishop of Winchester, and Oswald, archbishop of York.

As with Alcuin's question, it is often through the expressed anger of the Church in these early years that we know of the existence of secular songs. Two peculiar "graveyard episodes" could be cited as examples. Robert Mannyng of Brunne in his *Handlyng Synne* retells the old story of the Dancers of Kölbigk (Colbek) in Germany, an incident which occurred on Christmas Eve of the year 1020. Mannyng transfers the happening to England. When twelve gay young people caroling around the church (the word *carol* meant "ring dance" and did not acquire religious connotations until the fifteenth century) disturbed the priest at mass, he cursed them, that they might not break the ring or stop dancing for a twelvemonth. Alas, the curse was only too effective! His own daughter was among the dancers, and when her brother attempted to free her from the ring, he was able to pull away only her arm. The daughter and her companions continued dancing, unwearied, day and night, in cold and rain, without food and drink, the whole long year. This is a typical *exemplum*, an interesting, occasionally somewhat macabre tale with a moral: Together, the chants of Orpheus and Gregory can produce only discord. "Tempora mutantur, nos et mutamur in illis!"

Other evidence of early popular lyrics is mentioned by Giraldus Cambrensis in his *Gemma Ecclesiastica*: the embarrassing plight of a parish priest in Worcestershire. The poor man was kept awake all night by a love song outside his window in the churchyard, with the continually repeated refrain "Swete lamman dhin are" ("Sweet lover, thy favor"). Next morning, through lack of sleep perhaps, he committed the Freudian slip of singing "Swete lamman dhin are" for the Dominus Vobiscum of the Mass. The church did not fall in, nor was the priest struck by lightning, as the congregation undoubtedly expected; but the uproar was unpleasant enough for Bishop Northall (1184–90) to pronounce a curse and excommunication on anyone in his diocese who in the future sang these verses.

Indeed, the Church could do little at first but ban and excommunicate. The songs of the goliards (after the fictitious Bishop Golias), scurrilous drinking and love songs, mostly in Latin, sung by wandering students (*scholares vagantes*), were especially anathema. Officially, the ecclesiastical authorities did not care for revelry during these solemn times. In 1207 Innocent II issued a ban on maskings in church at Christmas, since occasional flings like the Feast of Fools and of the Ass had in the past been suffered. The miracle plays, to be discussed more fully below, were at first religious dramatizations performed in the sanctuary; but popular ebullience and horseplay could not be controlled even there, and the plays were cast out into the marketplace. Needless to say, this change of venue did little to rehabilitate them, so that the learned, urbane, and truly genial Bishop Grosseteste of Lincoln was forced in 1255 to order his clergy to take effective measures against the miracles.

But with the coming of the friars, one of the most important and influential specifically religious occurrences in the Middle Ages, alternate forces and solutions were brought into play. The Dominicans, stern, fervent, hypnotic, were the first to reach England in 1221. They were the friar-preachers, who drew the populace, as Saint Aldhelm had done, in the markets and squares during village festivals with anecdotes, exempla, and often secular stories, always turning the Devil's work into God's word. Certainly the mission spirit has always proved successful for the Church. The friars mingled with the people and, until corruption infected even the institution of the mendicant orders in later years, shared their hardships in food and lodging. Yet for the history of literature, the appearance of the Franciscans (1224) was more important. The Friars Minor, habited in gray, devoted to vows of poverty, not only produced some of our finest religious lyrics but also contributed to the mass of secular songs: very often they wrote spiritual verses adapted to popular tunes, or interpreted folk lyrics in religious terms.

The *joculatores Dei*, or "God's minstrels," as Saint Francis called his followers, were translators and composers. They changed Latin songs into English, and they wrote lyrics in which the line between the expression of a spiritual love and a carnal one is fine indeed. The cross-fertilization of religious and secular love lyrics is therefore apparent. Neither the friars nor the regular clergy seemed to be above enjoying vernacular, worldly songs—the five hundred years since Alcuin had done painfully little to change human nature. In order to combat the flames of hell with spiritual ardor, the Irish Franciscan bishop of Ossory, Richard de Ledrede (1317–60) rewrote some sixty French and English carnal songs, keeping the popular tunes and substituting pious Latin words. And this effort was directed, not at the lay congregation, but at his own clergy! How familiar they were with the "devilish" songs is shown by the bishop's action of placing the first line of the popular lyric before the religious verse, thus reminding his all-too-worldly spiritual helpers of the tune they were to sing. In his method, obviously patient, and his nature, probably kindly, Richard de Ledrede reminds one of the author of the *Ancrene Riwle*.

Sometimes this process of pouring new wine into old bottles proved too laborious, and churchmen utilized the powerful gift of medieval allegory to reinterpret common verses. The lines of a now-forgotten lyric, "Atte **wrastlinge** my lemman I ches/And atte ston-casting I him forless," which probably refer to an athletic match at a country fair (similar to the episode in *Havelok the Dane*), are shown by a preacher in a thirteenth-century sermon to be symbolic: by wrestling with the Devil, the world, and the flesh, we choose our spiritual lover, Christ; we lose him by casting stones because of our stony hearts. Allegory was the alchemical philosopher's stone of the Church which turned rock into gold, carnal elements into spiritual. Whether the process was convincing to a country audience, untrained in metaphysical reasoning, is debatable. For us, however, these incidents are important, since they provide the few clues we have to lost literature and forgotten lore.

Truly, it is one of the pathetic ironies of history that the friars, who in the beginning were earnest and altruistic in their actions and contributed so much to the flowering of literature, should have later, when the orders had degenerated and were harboring all too many scoundrels, called forth against themselves such a vast outpouring of satirical verse in the fourteenth century. For decades the friars were central to English letters. They acted on the world until they themselves became too worldly, and the world reacted against them.

In many other ways, too, the Church attempted to woo the large group of unsophisticated folk. Why should the Devil have all the best stories? The clergy produced saints' lives which were just as sensational as the worst accounts of secular mayhem and appealed to the same morbid, titillating feelings as they did. Whatever the ingenious tortures, the awesome dangers, that the saint experienced, his end was a happy one, because his trauma ended in spiritual bliss. But along with such stories as those of Saint Catherine or Saint Cecelia, there were others more normal, adventurous, and even exploratory, like that of the voyage of Saint Brendan (1121).

There were often whole books of moral stories, the exempla mentioned above, from which the preacher could choose every Sunday in order to illustrate his text. Thus, if a country parson wanted to expound on the saying "Radix malorum est cupiditas" ("Avarice is the root of all evil"), he might choose Chaucer's *Pardoner's Tale* of the three revelers who sought Death and found it in a pot of gold. Robert Mannyng of Brunne (Bourn in Lincolnshire), a canon of the Gilbertine order, was one of the most successful authors of exempla, aside from the friars and John Gower in his later *Confessio Amantis*. Brunne's *Handlyng Synne* (1303) was written "for þe luf of symple men/Þat strange Inglis can not ken." His style is lively, uncomplicated, and direct; and his stories, always told for the purpose of turning "lewde [ignorant] men" from the ways of the world, give us one of the most varied, amusing, and detailed pictures of medieval daily life.

Perhaps the best example of the aforementioned alchemical process is the most popular collection of stories to be found in the Middle Ages, the *Gesta Romanorum*. Originally this work was a gathering of highly entertaining narratives in Latin, which reached undoubtedly into the far Orient for their sources: classical legends, patristic accounts, biblical apocrypha—in sum, the well of Eastern and Western folklore. The work was composed in England sometime in the late thirteenth century and was translated into English from Anglo-Latin in the fifteenth century. Very much about it, certainly, is obscure, including the author of the English version and the date of the original. What is certain is that the anthology of stories, all of them set in Roman times, found widespread use among monks and parsons as a source of illustrative texts. Each narrative is followed by an allegorical interpretation, but the link between story and moral is slim indeed. The reader who has enjoyed a lusty tale is often vastly surprised at the spiritual depth of the narrative when this is pointed out to him in the detailed moral interpretation tacked on at the end. We can say, therefore, that the episodes in the *Gesta* could in a way be classed as exempla, but originally they were not so. They are further proof that the Church often utilized secular stories for spiritual aims, finding this method much more effective than to condemn the tales outright. The importance of the *Gesta Romanorum* must be stressed: it contains the whole account of Apollonius of Tyre; and it is the source of several of Boccaccio's novellas and in-directly of Shakespeare's *Merchant of Venice*, *King Lear*, and *Pericles*, Chaucer's *Man of Law's Tale*, and Gower's story of Constance.

With this wide influence of the Church on all forms of literature, it is not surprising to note, finally, that the earliest Middle English secular lyric of which we have evidence, the burden or refrain of a dance song, comments on a religious chant. Thomas of Ely in the twelfth century recalls how King Canute, being rowed on the river near the monastery of Ely, heard the monks within singing. Delighted by their song, the king composed verses which proved very popular but of which we have only the following four lines:

Merye sungen the muneches binnen Ely
Þa Cnut King rew þer by:
"Roweþ knites, noer þe land,
And here we þes muneches sæng."

The religious mood pervaded all literature, spiritual and secular, courtly and popular. But again, if any one part of the nation seemed to show a concentration of moral themes in verse and prose, it was definitely the North. The austere temper of this segment of the country has already been discussed above. In the fourteenth century, temper and times combined to produce literary works of a more reflective, spiritually searching nature. The period was filled with events which shook the foundations of society. In 1348 occurred the Great Plague, which ravaged mainly the poor, attacking the villages and farms. Labor was in short supply; workers demanded higher wages and moved to the towns. The social system, long thought to be immutable, was breaking down. In 1381 the Peasants' Rebellion erupted in violence and hate; the Commons in Parliament felt their power; and at the end of the century the king himself was deposed. Political progress some might have thought it, but not the author of *Piers Plowman*, or the more conservative elements in the country. All this was food for deep thought: change brought but sorrow; the only stability lay in God's kingdom, in eternal per-manence. The Alliterative Revival, as we have noted, had definite religious undertones: *Piers Plowman* saw corruption and shallowness among God's own servants, and looked to the past with yearning. The *Pearl* was an escape into mystical dreams, and even the courtly *Sir Gawain and the Green Knight* is, in its total effect, an extended orison to the Virgin Mary.

Escape toward inner reflection proved to many in this period the only solution, and the fourteenth century is the age of the great English mystics. Certainly the foremost of these was Richard Rolle, again a native of the North country, hermit of Hampole. Born in 1300 near York, he studied at Oxford but was disillusioned with scholasticism and returned home. While in meditation, he suddenly felt a "merry and unknown heat" within him, and realized it was of divine origin. Fashioning a hermit's cowl from his father's rain hood and a gown from his sister's kirtles, he ran off in a fit of ecstasy (which his family thought was madness) and was taken in by the Dalton family. There he lived as a solitary and wrote works in a beautifully cadenced prose style. Later in life he retired to Hampole in the south of Yorkshire, surrounded by a group of adoring, pious ladies, nuns and recluses, who worshiped him as a saint, although he was never canonized. In 1349 he died, probably of the plague.

We have seen how the Church, or at least the divine fervor of the author, was not controlled by literary mode. Mystical, moral, didactic, courtly types—all felt the spiritual influence. But Richard Rolle did not write for the villein in the fields or the shoemaker in the town. It was important for the spiritual authorities to reach these, the common folk, who did not have the time, learning, or inclination to pore laboriously over letters. They had to be drawn by less rarefied methods. The answer lay of course in pageantry, in the religious dramatizations of the guilds which we know as miracle plays (because originally they depicted miracles of saints). Robert Dodsley, in 1744, first called these dramatic sequences mystery cycles, after the French *mystère*, "scriptural play," from Latin *mysterium*, originally "religious truth." Since the Middle English word for "guild" was also *mystery* (altered from Latin *ministerium*, "service"), the term has always been connected with the guild cycles because of erroneous etymology. In the Middle Ages, however, the dramas were known as miracles or Corpus Christi plays.

Originally these "plays" started as extensions (*tropes*) of the Easter service, in the church itself. Thus the very authority which had vigorously rooted out the remnants of Roman drama and the low comedy (which was often unadulterated obscenity) of the mimes gave impetus to a new form and fostered it until it no longer seemed to serve a spiritual purpose. In the church service of around the year 900 we find these famous words:

Quem quaeritis in sepulchro, o Christicolae?
Jesus Nazarenum crucifixum, o caelicolae.
Non est hic, surrexit sicut praedixerat!
Ite, nuntiate, quia surrexit de sepulchro.

Whom do you seek in the sepulcher, O Christians?
The crucified Jesus of Nazareth, O heavenly ones.
He is not here, he has risen as he foretold!
Go, proclaim that he has risen from the tomb.

They were attached to the Mass, which really allowed for no further changes. However when the words were added to the office of matins, the trope was lengthened. The dialogue was sung antiphonally by choir members who took the parts of the angels and the Christians. This, according to literary historians, is the germ of modern drama. Soon the Christmas service and then Epiphany, with their wealth of tableau material— the shepherds, the manger scene, the gift-bearing Magi—were likewise adorned. With more dialogue, more "actors," the "stage" of the choir became too cramped. The nave increased the space of the "boards" for a while, but soon even this was not enough. Church drama finally ended up on the church porch; from there it left holy ground altogether. It seemed the clergy first lost some control over the action in these plays and later of the production itself. Humorous byplay crept in, burlesque, secular love songs, and unspiritual primping on the part of Mary Magdalene. The size of the ensemble got out of hand. Apocryphal scenes were produced, and the Old Testament was heavily mined for episodes. The greater the popular appeal, the more nervous the Church seemed to become. All productions were finally transferred to the marketplaces and the streets, and there they stayed until the Renaissance. Needless to say, the edict of Bishop Grosseteste in 1255 was ineffective.

According to most recent authorities it was in the 1370s, for the observance of Corpus Christi Day, that there occurred in England a new start with the great guild cycles, the miracle or mystery plays. Yearly a group or sequence of biblical plays was performed on this holiday. We know that in York the different guilds acted on floats or pageant wagons, repeating the same performance at several points in the city, sometimes as often as fourteen times, from dawn till dusk. It should be stressed that the guilds were themselves organizations with a strong religious foundation, and Church backing, especially as the plays later enhanced an important festival, was unquestioned. Yet the secular municipal authorities also saw in these pageants solid advertising for their city, and Mammon was not forgotten. The guilds took pride in competition, commissioning from their ranks expert clerical dramatists (for the Church would hardly relinquish control of these plays) and actors. Only later, in the fifteenth century, when the financial burdens became too severe and the novelty had worn off, do we find them attempting to shake off what had come to seem an onerous duty. The great cycles were that of York (forty-eight plays), dating to before 1378, and the Wakefield group known as the Towneley Plays, which contained at least thirty-four productions, to one of which, the *Second Shepherds' Play* by the famous Wakefield Master, we shall return below. Of lesser artistic merit is the Chester cycle, which, however, seems oddly enough to have had the longest run. Finally we can mention the Ludus Coventriae, the least of the four—a group which does not reflect negatively on the dramatic vigor of the city of Coventry, since the plays were never performed there but are of unknown origin and mistakenly named, their dialect being that of Norfolk. That the provenance of these great religious dramatic cycles was in the North of England would seem to be consistent with the deep moral commitment found in the literature of this geographic section. However, it must be pointed out that there were also plays in the South, but these may have been more efficiently suppressed by the reformed Church.

If the influence of clerical authority on popular entertainment was direct and practical, the relationship of Church dogma to the courtly romances and aristocratic literature in general was much more subtle and therefore in many ways more interesting. Secular entertainment of the nobility (the courtly games of "Holly versus Ivy," "Flower versus Leaf," and especially the stories of the long romances) involved generally all aspects of the chivalric institution, which was based on the three principles of devotion to God, service to the lord, and courtesy toward women. With the first two the Church did not quarrel; the third caused trouble. The Church did not recognize woman as being worthy of devotion. She was the daughter of Eve, who caused the fall of man; and she symbolized devilish carnality, worldly desire, and greed. Yet the true knight, the servant of Christ, worshiped his "sovereign lady" in a manner known as "courtly love," which saw woman as the highest example of spiritual and physical good, an exalted creature who, being ideal herself, raised her lover to superior heights. Thus arises a strange paradox, all the odder when we consider the social status of medieval woman: all too often she was considered chattel who came with the land. As MacEdward Leach once said, in the Middle Ages a young man married a fief and had a wife thrown in! Marriage was a political and economic contract; love was a matter of coincidence after conjugal consummation.

Whence, then, came the ideas of love (as contrasted with sexual desire) which we find in such romances as *King Horn*, *Havelok*, and the Arthurian cycle? It seems that in certain ways society and Church combined, in spite of themselves, to raise the status of women. The first must be traced to Provence in southern France. In the twelfth century, Provençal troubadours produced lyric poems known as *chansons* or *canzones*, which described an ideal relationship between knight and highborn lady. Often this woman was married, sometimes the wife of the lover's feudal lord and therefore his "sovereign mistress." The love described by the troubadours was neither platonic nor purely sensual, but a mixture of both, and, in theory at least, sometimes adulterous. The treatise by the French chaplain Andreas Capellanus, *De Arte Honesti Amandi*, is usually cited as the standard textbook on courtly love, though it is often inconsistent and more dully philosophical than practical. We know that this literary fashion was in vogue at the courts of Eleanor of Aquitaine and Marie of Champagne. In fact, Andreas mentions several mock legal cases of love affairs which the ladies at the court of Marie debated and judged: the lovers testified, the evidence was gathered, the rules were applied. In all, there could have been no more delectable pastime for the lady judges.

It does seem that the social prominence of the lady compared to the lover, often a cadet knight at the court, made such a situation of respect and honor, even love, possible. The troubadours expressed their feelings in a hyperbolic, rarefied fashion. Love ennobled them; its joy was of a mystical nature. The distance, hauteur, even cruelty, of the lady only inflamed desire. Although in the past scholars have indulged in romantic speculation of "what really happened," seeing the Provençal courts as the centers of sexual games, of cults of venery among the wealthy, some modern critics have severely questioned whether the amorous dreams of the troubadours were ever put into practice. There is little proof that courtly love was ever more than a literary fashion, even if the normal peccadilloes of any leisure class were committed. Though Western literature shows no evidence of this tradition before the advent of the troubadours, we do have knowledge of Arabic love poetry, showing similar strains, which could easily have reached southern France through Spain and especially the Catalan dialect, linguistically related to Provençal. Yet certainly Arabic society was not known to be especially amoral or licentious.

That the Church looked at all this courtly folderol with a jaundiced eye can well be imagined. But whatever other influences there may have been on the poetry of courtly love, the Church itself, long before the twelfth century, prepared the groundwork for the veneration of woman. The cult of the Virgin must be considered one of the most important influences on courtly and chivalric medieval literature. Sometime in the fourth century, interest in the Virgin Mary seemed to be developing in ecclesiastical ritual. The idea of a mother cult is an ancient one, and literary folklorists have drawn parallels between the worship of the Mother of God and the Pan-Mediterranean devotion to the Magna Mater, the White Goddess. Remnants of these rituals can still be seen in Rome and Capri, and the prehistoric Mesolithic figures of the "fat woman" found on Malta point to similar ceremonies. All of these perhaps find their source in originally matriarchal societies.

In 656 at the Council of Toledo, Mary was awarded special favors, and the ideal of perpetual virginity was emphasized. The Cistercians adopted Mary as their special protector, and in the tenth century the Ave Maria was added to prayers. The Virgin became the intercessor between man and God, and as such she entered both religious and secular literature in the Middle Ages. Mary redeemed womankind. She remained always the final argument against the often virulent anti-feminist attacks of the times. Lyrics devoted to the Virgin Mary increased in popularity and must be classed among our finest medieval religious songs. Justly famous is the haunting *I Sing of a Maiden*, which has received so much critical attention. Then there also appeared a large group of stories devoted to miracles which Mary performed to save individuals from mortal danger, even death. Chaucer's *Prioress's Tale* is the most famous of these "miracles of the Virgin," a specific literary genre.

But of greatest interest is the confusion which developed between courtly and religious language, between secular and spiritual love. And here the influence of one on the other becomes obscure. Certainly the cult of the Virgin preceded the appearance of courtly-love poems in England, yet the amorous, at times even sensual language of the religious lyrics addressed to Mary, and even of those to Christ, must be of courtly origin. The songs directed to Mary, in fact all invocations to Mary, were written by men, monks or friars who borrowed the vocabulary of the secular love songs. Thus the words *sovereign mistress*, *lady*, *love*, *physical and spiritual savior*, *mercy*, *queen*, *prayer*, came to have double meanings, and were applicable in both religious and secular terms. The "Queen of Love" could have as easily been Venus (worshiped in the courtly-love ritual) as Mary, and so could the "Mother of the God of Love." The language was often consciously confused. One of the finest literary examples of how authors played with the double entendre of courtly, religious, and even economic phrases is that brilliant satire by Geoffrey Chaucer, the *Complaint to His Purse*.

So we can say that the Church both motivated in part and utilized in part the courtly tradition. Without fear of any opprobrium, the mid-thirteenth-century Franciscan friar Thomas of Hales could write this love song for a nun:

A mayde Cristes me bit yorne
Þat ich hire wurche a luve-ron,
For whan heo myhte best ileorne
To taken on oþer soþ lefmon
Þat treowest were of alle berne
And best wyte cuþe a freo wymmon.
Ich hire nule nowiht werne:
Ich hire wule teche as ic con.

A maid of Christ asked me eagerly
That I write for her a love song,
By means of which she might best learn
How to gain a true lover
Who would be the truest of all knights
And could best protect a noble woman.
I will in no way deny her this:
I will teach it to her as well as I can.

The man that the friar describes is a "knight" of perfect qualities, rich and powerful. If she will become his "lover," she will receive such apparel from him as neither king nor emperor could give. He is full of "fin amur," and the wedding gift of this Heavenly Bridegroom, Christ, is virginity.

Aside from such clerical participation in the love poetry of the times, the Church was also involved in furthering the creation and propagation of certain romances. These long poems dealt mainly with adventure, rather than amorous escapades, the name *romance* describing the Latin-descended language (French) in which they were originally written. A large segment of the adventures in the Arthurian cycle describes the Grail quest; and the stories of Lancelot, Galahad, Percival, the Fisher King, and the Grail knights were often deeply imbued with a mystical intensity, the participants appearing as true ascetics. Such romances were of course quite acceptable, as contrasted to the Lancelot-Guinevere and Tristram-Isolde legends, which the Church disliked and vigorously opposed.

Many of the early English romances are based on French sources or originals. Yet the *chansons de geste*, those great stories of Charlemagne, Roland, and Turpin, had only a limited appeal in England—perhaps, as A. C. Baugh supposed, because of nationalistic rivalries. The militant action in the Charlemagne epics is always in defense of the faith and recounts the struggles of the Franks against the Saracens in Spain. Christianity is everywhere victorious and the crusading fervor evident in most of these poems. It was an act of devotion, a religious observance of a kind, for the minstrel to sing them and for an audience to listen. As Baugh has noted, "judged by both choice of subject and treatment the English Charlemagne romances seem, with one or two exceptions, to be a group in which the missionary spirit is made to work through minstrel recitation."[1]

---

1. Albert C. Baugh, et al., *A Literary History of England*, 2d ed. (New York, 1967), Vol. I, Kemp Malone and Albert C. Baugh,   *The Middle Ages*, pp. 188–89.

Furthermore, the interesting theory of Joseph Bédier casts additional light on the activity of the Church in fostering the legends of the Charlemagne group. Bédier noticed that in many of the chansons de geste a specific church or cloister figured prominently as the location important in the life of the hero. Also many of these religious sites, like the town of Blaye in the Pyrenees near Roncesvalles, which claimed the tomb of Roland, were in possession of weapons, relics, or other memorials. Checking these churches on the map, Bédier found that they were all located on the great pilgrimage routes of Europe, those leading to Aix la Chapelle, the shrine of Saint James of Compostela in Galicia, and others. He concluded, in his famous work *Les Légendes épiques* (2d ed., Paris, 1914–21), that the monks hired minstrels or jongleurs, supplied them with the "historical facts," and asked them to compose the long poems, in which the hero and the location were played up, as advertisement for the churches. Thus a minstrel might join a group of pilgrims as they approached the monastery and entice them to visit the place by singing a chanson de geste and pointing out the historical interest of the spot. The churches profited thereby through gifts and benefices.

Bédier's theory cannot, of course, account for the origin of all, or even most, of the chansons. Some scholars also have argued pettily that Bédier put the cart before the horse: the churches did not invent stories and heroes in order to fit them, opportunistically, to relics or weapons already in their possession, but the stories were in existence in oral tradition long before the composition of the clerical poems. The churches, therefore, only utilized already existing traditions for their own purposes. Such pedantic quarrels do not benefit the scholarly cause. And if Bédier's evidence is valid for even a half dozen of the chansons de geste, which were widely imitated later with or without mention of a specific church, it is enough to establish his theory as one of the most influential views concerning their origin. In the main, it shows the importance of scholarly research by the medievalist, the literary historian: painstaking examination of all the evidence is fundamental—small clues lead to big answers.

Support for Bédier from another source could be inferred from the *Penitential* of Thomas of Cobham, which describes various sins and the penance exacted for them. One of these sins was listening to minstrels, of whom there were three types. First, there were those who disrobed and were guilty of immodest behavior and gestures: "These shall be damned." Here there seems to be a reference to the mimes, of whom nudity was expected in the Roman burlesque shows, especially during the festival of the Floralia. When Rome fell in 476, the Church closed the theaters—as another purist clergy was to do again twelve hundred years later—and the mimes took to the road, coming at an early date to England, where they found rocky soil and foggy bottoms. The second class of minstrels satirized prominent people and sang scurrilous songs behind their backs: "They also shall be damned." These undoubtedly were the goliards, the *scholares vagantes*. The third class included those minstrels who played musical instruments, and these were again divided into classes. There were those who sang licentious songs appealing to the lower instincts of their audience: "They shall be damned." And there were those who sang of the lives of saints and the exploits of princes: "These only shall be saved." It was therefore a meritorious act for a church or monastery to sing the praises of princes and heroes, especially of those who fought in the cause of Christ. For that, the clerical authors, or their hired poets, could not be damned.

In this, as in many other ways, the Church shifted, adapted, countered, and embraced secular literature, courtly and popular. At the same time it directed its own religious verse and prose toward all segments of medieval society. And this was a necessity, because Middle English literature was addressing itself to a heterogeneous audience and represented, certainly much more than do the extant Old English remnants, the interests of all the social classes.

SOCIETY AS REFLECTED BY THE SPECTRUM OF MIDDLE ENGLISH LITERATURE

It is interesting that an age which only in its later years developed a socially viable middle class should in England from an early period reflect definite popular elements in its literature. The English yeoman and his bow of yew were a strong force to be reckoned with in war, the last argument of kings, at Crécy in 1346 and at Poitiers in 1356, long before the rest of Europe considered military action anything but a gentleman's game. And since war making is one function of the executive branch of government, the freeborn Englishman soon earned the right to speak his political piece, up to a point.

Unquestionably, the early literature reflected mainly aristocratic tastes. But in an age of almost universal illiteracy, the reliance on oral transmission, whether by minstrels in noble halls or wandering singers in town and country, produced a paucity of texts. The more popular the work, the less important the manuscript, since the minstrel who added it to his repertoire would rely on his memory alone. Many manuscripts of a moral nature have survived because the libraries of religious houses guarded these carefully; therefore we must not suppose to be always applicable the generally accepted rule that the more numerous the extant texts of a work, the greater was its contemporary appeal.

The leisure class listened to the chivalric romances, which in the years before 1300 were always in verse, a mnemonic device necessary for oral production. The subjects of this genre of adventurous literature were grouped into three classes or "matters of romance," according to Jean Bodel in his *Chanson des Saisnes*:

N'en sont que trois materes a nul home entendant,
De France, et de Bretaigne, et de Rome la grant.

*There are only three matters for any knowledgeable man,
Of France, and of Britain, and of Rome the great.*

The Matter of France comprised the cycles of Charlemagne and his Peers, the Doon of Mayence, and William of Orange; that of Britain told the story of Arthur and the Round Table; and that of Rome included all classical legends, of Troy and Thebes and Alexander the Great. To these three "matters" a fourth must be added, which is of greater interest for us because it included many popular elements and became an organic part of oral literary evolution. This was the Matter of England, which comprised the romances of *Havelok*, *King Horn*, *Athelston*, *Guy of Warwick*, *Bevis of Hampton*, and *Richard Coeur de Lion*. Here are stories which concerned English events and locality and included native elements in style and vocabulary. *Havelok the Dane* and *King Horn* are very early; the latter (c. 1250) even contains many Old English elements. That the oldest romances in England play up native heroes must speak for the nationalistic interest of those first nobles to accept the English language as their own. By this time the great period of the French romances, the twelfth-century renaissance, had passed; and many of our English poems, adapted from the French originals (especially those of the master Chrétien de Troyes), are warmed-over fare.

In fact, the genre of romance generally fits well the lines of T. S. Eliot in *Gerontion*: they multiplied variety "in a wilderness of mirrors." In the epics the hero retains some part of his personality, but in the romance we meet the same man again and again. He is, of course, a "noble" type, gracious, courteous, brave, generous, debonaire, and handsome—Lancelot, Gawain, Tristram, Galahad, Erec, or Kay. And he appeals to the ladies—as G. K. Anderson remarked, the romance in general is a kind of "feminized" form of the old heroic literature. The only thing the hero changes, for the sake of variety, is his "grey flannel suit"; at times he jousts in black armor, at times in green, at times in white. The epic keeps to some sort of logic: although Beowulf is a superman, he owes his success to his own hands and strength, with the exception of the fight with Grendel's dam. But the worthy of romance is aided by magic. The former superman is now a ladies' man in desperate straits, and supernatural powers come to his aid.

Somewhat more clearly defined in characterization and plot were the Breton lais, which have been discussed above. However, it may not be unfair to comment that as long as English literature of this genre was unoriginal, was adapted from the French, remained in the hands of the noble establishment, and reflected the tastes of the chivalric code, it often lacked vitality and interest.

The oral transmission of courtly literature did little to further originality, since the minstrels were tied to common romance motifs. Evolution did occur, as we shall see below; but it was not until a wider literacy lessened the need for poetry's mnemonic aid, enabling these works to be written in prose, that we begin to find room for variation, stylistic originality, and the expression of personal creative power. Though the first prose romances were quite humdrum, the fifteenth-century *Morte Darthur* of Thomas Malory is an example in point. Malory inherited the stories, the tradition of the great French Arthurian romances; but he changed the genre, achieving a new form, a kind of carte blanche of unlimited possibilities, freed from all traditional ties. Malory could have translated French into English, but he did more. He transfigured episodic plots and a serpentine style into compact stories told in a vigorous, terse language. Malory is one of the masters of English prose. Using the material of the twelfth-century aristocratic genre, and himself identifying with the knightly class, he nevertheless wrote an adventure story for all England. In the chapters on the Fisher King and on Lancelot's tragic Unasked Question, and in the last book of Lancelot and Guinevere, Malory expressed heights of spiritual joy, depths of worldly sorrow. His work remains one of the fountainheads of our literary heritage.

Ironically, scholarship has always been more concerned with the negative achievements of this man. Malory's life was sensational, to be sure—if it was his life at all. He has been identified as the rapist, robber of monasteries, rebel, gang leader, inveterate convict, escapee, and recidivist who ended up in Newgate Prison and composed the *Morte* in the dungeon with sources borrowed from the nearby Greyfriars Library (said to have been founded by Dick Whittington, "thrice lord mayor of London"). A sensational, romantic story, well fitted to the plots of his literary product! Indeed, Malory's life of rampant fifteenth-century criminality would be an interesting counterpart to that high chivalric code which is the motive for the similarly violent action of his heroes. In the *Morte* Malory asks his readers to pray for the soul of the "knight prisoner." Today literary historians have attempted to cleanse Malory of his sins by identifying him with another man. The campaign to rehabilitate the "Ill-Framed Knight" (as W. Matthews calls his book on Malory [Berkeley, Calif.: 1966]) is carried on with vigor.

Equally mysterious is the author of an earlier prose work, the famous *Travels* of Sir John Mandeville. This fantastic travelogue to exotic places starts off as a quiet guide to the Holy Land; but as it reaches farther and farther into the mysterious Orient, it surpasses the limits of contemporary experience and stands revealed to modern readers as an overt, if glorious, fraud. Tales of Prester John (culled undoubtedly from the somewhat more realistic accounts of Marco Polo), of the Old Man of the Mountain and his Assassins, of the Cyclops, and many others fascinated readers who had lost the sense of romance in their own society and dreamed the eternal romantic vision of far-off places, foreign shores, and bizarre customs. Thus Mandeville's *Travels*, told with an earnest, even deadpan expression of absolute truth, satisfied a longing for escape, in the same way as had the early courtly romances toward an ethical, chivalric realm. But the moral tenor of society had changed. The journey toward escape had become a necessarily longer one—and it is even longer today. The writer of the *Travels*, in fact, never did get away. According to one source, he was a physician of Liège, called John of Burgundy, who on his deathbed confessed to being an English knight, John de Mandeville, a count of Monfort. He had had to flee his country because of a murder. Recent evidence does seem to show that the author of the *Travels* may have been an Englishman, but the work was composed in French between 1366 and 1371. Its popularity soon caused it to be translated into many languages, including English; but the author knew only two at most. He traveled in fancy, and composed the work from his study.

 A drastic shift away from courtly and fantastic literature toward the popular, bourgeois, and practical never did occur, because already in the earliest romances we can find these elements side by side. Noble society could not exist in a vacuum; it needed and depended on the folk. That the English establishment came to realize this was part of its political strength. England soon developed a national consciousness; and the unpatronizing admiration and respect for the common man, his common sense, shrewdness, humor, and robust vitality, is one of the most sympathetic traits of Middle English literature.

Thus whereas *King Horn* deals only with the usual stereotyped romance activities (albeit not with the courtly gloss of later works), *Havelok the Dane* has a definite earthy flavor. The ways of king and countryman, noble and peasant, are intertwined. Prince Havelok flees his native Denmark with a fisherman named Grim after his life has been threatened by a former trusted counselor of his dead father the king. Settling in Lincolnshire, in Grimsby (a town seal still shows the names of Havelok, Grim, and Goldboro, Havelok's wife), Havelok fishes and sells at the market with the rest of the family. Later he works as a cook for the earl of Lincoln, and is liked for his good nature rather than any prowess with lance or sword. He grows to be big and strong, a champion at the country fair. Through a series of adventures in love and war, he later regains his kingdom. It has been conjectured that *Havelok*, as well as perhaps *Horn*, goes back to some earlier Old English folk legend, some lost Anglo-Saxon chanson de geste. Though the poems represent a definitely aristocratic genre, *Havelok* especially appeals to popular taste and could not have been written by an author whose views and range of experience were alien to the bourgeois temper.

That refined palates in the Middle Ages were also capable of enjoying the spiciest fare is seen by the popularity of that class of literature known as the *fabliaux*. If *Havelok* was an example of a courtly frame heavily charged with folk elements, the fabliaux were just the opposite: a folk and middle-class frame which often utilized courtly themes for purposes of humor, later even satire and parody. Originally these short, bawdy, and very funny poetic stories may have been found in the Latin literature of the *vagantes*, though many originated in the Orient and are found in that cosmopolitan source book the *Gesta Romanorum*. We meet a heavy concentration of them in Old French but very few examples in English. A half dozen, the most brilliant, are by Chaucer: the stories of the Miller, the Reeve, the Summoner, the Friar, the Merchant, and the Shipman. Undoubtedly, some were recited orally by minstrels, and memory obviated the need for expensive parchment. The Church also would have frowned on such items—who knows what some religious palimpsests still hide today? But then, the French sense of values has traditionally been different from the English.

That the fabliaux were bourgeois comedy was the long-accepted theory of Joseph Bédier. Recently, however, Per Nykrog strongly argued against this view, stating that it is impossible to separate the fabliaux from the courtly milieu. The stories were written for an aristocratic audience and reflected its views. The comic force of the fabliaux presupposed among their listeners a knowledge of courtly literature, and the humor of what was essentially a courtly burlesque resided in the continual reversal of the elements of courtly love: carnality for sentiment, lower class for nobility, and so forth. The laughter of the gentles, therefore, was directed downward. Cunning middle-class lovers, hardworking horned husbands, worldly, opportunistic clergy, sexy young wives—frustrated or not—carried on in eternal triangles and vicious circles. Normally there was no waste of words: situations and fast-paced action controlled the whole.

Before Chaucer, we must regard *Dame Sirith* (1250) as the most important fabliau in English. It is an old story with Oriental analogues and sources; the laughing witch, the weeping bitch, the boy and the girl. The plot is simple: young clerk loves young married woman (courtly love among the folk). Young wife refuses her favors, and clerk hires old bawd, Dame Sirith, for help. The madam takes her bitch, rubs spice in its eyes, and parades it in front of the lady, explaining that the dog was her daughter, magically caninized (and now eternally weeping) for having refused a lover. In panic the wife accedes, and all but the dog are happy. Dialogue does much for the humor here, though one cannot say that the plot is especially inspiring. Yet the student of comparative literature must be on his guard: Dame Sirith and her weeping bitch appear again and again, in many guises.

The court poet Geoffrey Chaucer (1340–1400), the master writer of England before Shakespeare, has the surest control over his medium. The *Miller's Tale* is unsurpassed, even by Boccaccio in the *Decameron*. For the tale of Robin the Miller is more than a dirty, traveling-salesman joke. At a time when courtly love had passed its boulevard days (if indeed these ever existed) and even its literary reflection had dulled, the story of the rich carpenter and his roomer, "hende Nicholas," of dandyish Absolon and wild young Alisoun (fair of body as a weasel), Noah's ark, the Flood, and the red-hot poker must have come as a brisk blast of invigorating fresh air to the languid lords and ladies for whom Chaucer read his works. Here is the beginning of antiromance and the antichivalric hero. The whole courtly-love ritual—the precious phrases, the impossible, searing physical tests to be passed, the deliciously (and odoriferously) cruel mistress— all fall (and quite violently, too) into the bourgeois milieu. What a wild parody this is! It is no less a work of genius than Chaucer's famous satire of romance, *Sir Thopas*. Courtly and popular literary modes are here combined, as happened so often in Middle English literature, and the upper class delighted in seeing their own foibles through the cracks in middle-class morality.

Another important group of folk stories is the genre known as *beast epic* or *fable*. The ultimate source of these, too, is to be sought in the Orient; but of course the type has been known from Aesop, to La Fontaine, to the Indian coyote stories of the Great Plains, to Mickey Mouse and Tom and Jerry today. Peasant wit and cunning are always embodied in Reynard the fox, stupidity and avaricious hunger in Ysengrim the wolf. The very popular thirteenth-century French *Roman de Renart* occurs in English only in Caxton's version, *Reynard the Fox* (1481), Chaucer's *Nun's Priest's Tale*, and the poem called *The Fox and the Wolf*, included here. The beast epic first appeared in the Low Countries sometime in the twelfth century. From there it spread widely, and though we have little extant evidence, it seems the type was quite popular in England. The environment for these folktales is the farm, or the village and barnyard. The mock-heroic action often takes place *in medias res*, in the midst of the peasant chores. Dogs bark, chickens scrabble, Ysengrim is pursued with hue and cry by Hodge and Stubbs, armed with cudgels. The common people in all their moods, their uncompli- cated worries and naïve pleasures, are represented in animal terms. The tales are indeed bucolic compared to the jungle of our twentieth-century *Animal Farm!*

Thus parody of standard procedure, courtly traditions, and heroic ways appeared in fabliau and beast epic when the original sap had run dry. The more bombastic the speech of Chauntecleer the cock, the lovelier the description of Pertelote's plumage, the more ridiculous the whole aristocratic mood becomes in retrospect. *Don Quixote* not only satirized the romances but marked their termination; in the eighteenth century, Mackenzie's *Man of Feeling* did the same, whether consciously or not, for the sentimental fashion. With Chaucer, too, there was a termination, and a new beginning.

Chaucer, beyond any society and yet part of all, was able to express this perspective totally in his literature. All genres were the tools of his craft: the masterpiece *Troilus and Criseyde* is courtly in tone, but essentially realistic. The *Canterbury Tales*, especially the General Prologue and the "links," is a view of all life from his Aldgate window, but the satirical thrust penetrates both high and low, courtly and common. In this general unifying aspect of his work, which attains an almost complete yet interrelated assortment of all types and styles, Chaucer, as artist and critic, has tapped an essential quality of Middle English literature: there are many units, but few independent ones; modes merge and genres influence one another. As will be explained more fully below, there seems to be a kind of organic totality in the literature of this age which other periods do not attain.

If the above statements have any validity, they can be tested by a genre which best fits the requirements of emotional spontaneity and the absence of intellectual strictures: lyric song. An intense feeling of joy, a kind of bubbling rapture, is felt in the Middle English lyrics. When England sang, the forests murmured in reply. It is hard to find Continental analogues for these songs of spring (*Lenten Is Come with Love to Town*), of the country maiden Alisoun, and of the longing that becomes poignant when the nightingales sing. Though the motif of the *reverdie*, the coming of spring, was a universal European one, it seems to have been employed more artistically in England than elsewhere. Chaucer's opening in the General Prologue of the *Canterbury Tales* and in the *Legend of Good Women* is as effective, in spite of repeated traditional use, as that famous round *Sumer Is Icumen In*. But what seems to separate the English secular lyric most sharply from its French, Provençal, and German counterparts is its constant use of folk themes, its descriptions of lower-class country amusements, and finally its direct approach to physical desire.

The theory, commonly held in the past, that in the absence of any Old English lyric or extant native tradition, the songs of the troubadours were the source of Middle English lyric has been countered by objective critics who point out a radical difference in style and mood. The Provençal chansons followed a strict rhetoric and form: they were all highly polished, artificial poetic exercises which lacked even an imitation of natural feeling, and the love they expressed was a tortured, hopeless one, with the lover enjoying his suffering and coldly analyzing his passion. Present-day scholarship sees the probable origin of the Middle English lyric in Latin love songs and in poems of the type found among the *Carmina Burana*, which were not national but European in provenance and wide in their influence. As the international language of the medieval student, Latin not only moved the dusty scholastic thought of intellectual tomes but served as the fresh, uninhibited conveyance of youthful exuberance and joy.

Yet the problem of the Middle English lyric is further complicated, as we have seen in the section on Church influence, by the variety of its types. In the main, English song is popular in tone and was probably composed by poets of the bourgeois class, who might have included minstrels or even clerics. There is too much knowledge of the little things taking place on the side during the Midsummer Day dance, too much intimate detail of the serving maid's holiday, for us to doubt that the author of many of these lyrics was personally involved, if indeed he was not himself Jankyn, the ubiquitous amorous holy-water clerk.

There were, however, certain songs which must definitely be classed among folk literature. These seem to show remnants of very old and forgotten rituals, chants, expressions of fertility cults, which were passed down through generations by word of mouth until they were transcribed in an idle moment, perhaps by some young friar daydreaming in the sun. The seductive little *Irish Dancer* and the *Maiden in the Moor Lay*, about a girl who lay seven nights by a well in order to conceive, are poems of this type found in the Rawlinson Fragments, a small, narrow manuscript of scribbled parchment. Wellings and ritual dances are folk customs, part of the subconscious prehistoric heritage of the people. Their preservation may be proof of lost incantations and religious lyrics in Old English times.

The other side of the stylistic spectrum is the courtly language of the so-called Harley Lyrics. If the theory of Provençal troubadour origin merits any attention, it is due to these lovely verses of British Library MS. Harleian 2253. In many of them we find the typical appeals for mercy (*rew*) of the lover, who is in the maid's power and brought to woe. The mistress is compared to sapphire, garnet, diamond, jasper, coral, and emerald. Her complexion is as red as the rose, or lily-white. We have known the phrases from childhood, since they are part of the eternal fairy-tale tradition, undoubtedly transferred in the Middle Ages from the stereotyped clichés of romance. The author of the Harley Lyrics was a man bred in courtly ways and familiar with the chivalric code. There is no need, however, to see more than an indirect influence of the French troubadour tradition in these poems; for instance, we have noted above, pp. 22–23, how often the amatory vocabulary and mood was transferred to many of the religious songs. These lyrics, to Christ, on his Passion, or to Mary, Queen of Heaven, sorrowing for her Son, outnumber by far the preserved secular poems. The Middle English lyric, therefore, is a genre in which the three modes, courtly, popular, and religious, are confluent.

With the ballad we enter the realm of pure folklore. It has been questioned whether these narrative songs should be treated as a medieval type, since most of our texts come from manuscripts of the sixteenth century and later. But the thirteenth-century poems *Judas* and *Twelfth Day* show definite ballad characteristics in tempo of dramatic development, and the Danish ballads (which folklorists claim as the source of many of our traditional English and Scottish songs) were composed about 1200. There is also evidence from *Piers Plowman* that the stories of Robin Hood and the now-forgotten songs of Randolph, earl of Chester, were popular in the fourteenth century. The ballad is, therefore, definitely a medieval genre, even though the state in which we see most examples of it today is a later one.

The form of the ballads changed through the decades (perhaps centuries) in which they were passed down by word of mouth until they were finally recorded, somewhat as a phrase whispered into the ear of a child at one end of the line during the party game of "telephone" changes in oral transmission. This is the folk process of literary evolution. No doubt the original ballad makers were individuals of the same temper as the authors of some of the lyrics: members of a culturally homogeneous group, with rich traditions and poetic genius. The romantic "communal origin" theory of the Grimm brothers was that "das Volk dichtet" ("the people as a group compose");

this idea, however, not only lacked the evidence of field work but was somehow influenced by a Rousseau-like dream that if one savage is noble, how nobly creative a coterie of savages must have been! Modern scholars are more empirical: they know the people did not compose or create. They did, however, re-create according to their individual tastes, understanding, and inclination. This is the reason for the sea change between the English *Three Ravens* and the Scottish *Twa Corbies*.

The sensations of the small town, the isolated rural hamlet, the mountain community, were ballad subjects: incest, murder, rape, adultery, fratricide, patricide, betrayal, robbery—common human failings. Still, not often did a young man murder his father on the advice of his mother (*Edward*) or a young girl dispatch her fiancé by feeding him poisoned eels (*Lord Randal*). Today, the tabloid newspapers would scream out the news in black headlines; in the Middle Ages a nurse, tinker, blacksmith, teacher, or minstrel composed a ballad. The events of *Edward* happened, at some time. And certain ballad singers in our own Smoky Mountains today believe they know who Edward was: someone related to their third cousins in the valley. The ballads were real, and are so even now. The folk own them; and because the situations are timeless in their horror, their love, their universal human passions, ballads are alive today in England, Scotland, and America. Yet the more specifically "medieval" the subjects, the more vulnerable they were to extinction; and Robin Hood is today dead in oral transmission, whereas Barbara Allen, that undying femme fatale, lives on in over seventy versions of her story.

But here again, modes and even genres merge. Many of the ballads are close to lyrics (*The Unquiet Grave*, *The Twa Corbies*), and the line between the two groups is a fine one. Narrative poems sometimes evolved into pure lyric moods. At one time the story of *On Top of Old Smoky* was an extended one, and we believe most ballads were originally much longer. But the folk were not interested in motive or detail. The story "leaped" over these, and "lingered" on the action alone, which became central. This is the reason so many ballads end with the frustrating question Why? This Why? teases us, but it does not disturb the artistry, the poetic power. Rather, these are enhanced; and often a subjective, unspecific lyricism or a dramatic power replaces the more prosaic detailed narrative.

Most of the ballads treat nonaristocratic themes. Sometimes, as in the Border Ballads, they relate the excitement of cattle raids into the "debatable land" between England and Scotland; at other times they recount old fairy legends. Many are "drifters" brought in by mariners from Scandinavia. Few ballads are religious in nature, surprisingly enough; but there is some evidence that certain of them were composed by minstrels specifically for noble entertainment. Thus even in a genre that is definitely of folk origin, the courtly mode intrudes. Such ballads as *The Boy and the Mantle* and *Hind Horn* were adapted from the romances. In fact, ballad style in general shows the phrasing of romance cliché: "red-roan steed," "lily-white hand," "sewing a silken seam." Knights and fair ladies appear often, almost as if the folk yearned to hear about princes charming, satin and silk, gold and silver, and all the precious trappings of a luxury which they could never hope to attain.

Yet if it seems at times as though there were no pure, unadulterated expressions of the middle-class spirit, we need only mention the comedy of the miracle plays. One would hardly think of the Crucifixion as a theme for humor! But in the play of the York cycle performed by the pinners and painters, the Roman soldiers take their task most seriously, in a grotesque, even macabre manner. The crucifiers huff and puff as they bore the holes in the cross. The body is too short! No, the cross is wrongly marked! Why gab? Pull the lad so he fits! Lift him up, let's see! Ow! The weight! My back is broken! This may seem tasteless today, but the biblical stories were all treated in a similar manner. Did the audience laugh? Were they shocked by the paradox of raucous action and solemn event? The psychology of the medieval mind still holds some mysteries. At any rate, there is no doubt that the people were entertained and that they understood. Many a carpenter knew the frustration of an inexact measurement. How easy those Romans had it, with their Procrustean solution!

Less bloody but just as unpleasant are the medieval wives. Mrs. Noah refuses to enter the ark; she had intended to go to town. Noah could at least have told her what he was planning, and she won't go without her cousins and friends. Pilate's wife is a coddled and conceited coquette in these alliterative dramas, and her husband knows how to please her with wine and kisses.

But the purest fun is to be seen in the Mak episode of the Wakefield Master's *Second Shepherds' Play*. The sheep stealer Mak is undoubtedly the most brilliantly conceived antihero in all the mystery plays; his theft and his later outrageous trick (in which his cantankerous wife Jill helps) of passing off the sheep as his child in the cradle, takes up 637 lines of a total 754. It is obvious where the center of audience interest lay in this play about the adoration of the shepherds, and the Wakefield Master knew the meaning of box-office success. He also knew the meaning of hunger, cold, and the general grim poverty of the rural lower classes. The social protest found in the opening lines of the *Second Shepherds' Play* ought not to be overlooked. In the fifteenth century certain literary phenomena could occur which would have been deemed impossible in the thirteenth: a rogue for a hero, secular slapstick and the enjoyment of one of the Deadly Sins in a religious play, condemnation of the wealthy, and a work of entertainment pointed at and written for the poor.

There was, then, a subtle change in social direction over the centuries—as there had to be, with the more varied audience that developed as the bourgeoisie in the towns grew in political and cultural power. The appearance of Mak was an example of an important factor in this trend toward an increasingly popular literature as the Middle Ages waned. The interest in and development of the genial and likeable rogue as a type, a creation of conscious artistry, may have had its roots in the need to satisfy a new class of spectators, but it also ran directly parallel to an occurrence of literary evolution known in folklore as "the decline of the hero," or "epic degeneration." We know, as will be explained further below, that narrative verse, orally transmitted, evolved into different genres. And in this process the original epic and romance hero, whether an Arthur, a Charlemagne, or even a Robin Hood, parted with his magnificence and invincibility, became humanized, and finally lost his heroic balance altogether. He moved out of literary focus. In many stories the hero is replaced, not by another worthy, but by a group of lesser, yet more interesting, "lieutenants": Gawain and Lancelot; Roland and Oliver; Little John, Will Scarlet, and Friar Tuck. Arthur, savior of Britain, becomes a doddering cuckold, killed by his bastard son—

nephew. Robin Hood is clubbed by Little John, half drowned by Friar Tuck (all in fun), overcome or tricked by potters, pinners, tanners, and tinkers, and finally murdered by his cousin, the prioress of Kirklees.

The folk were sharp critics and hard masters of the literature they developed. They rejected any alien, artificial stylistic elements; they toppled the great off their pedestals and pulled them down to their own level. In many ways it can be said that Middle English literature was organic, that it developed continually. And it did so, from all sources, ever in the direction of an increased democratic awareness.

THE WEB AND CONTINUITY
OF MIDDLE ENGLISH LITERATURE

It remains now to draw the threads together and see the total picture. What may be called the "web" of Middle English literature, that widespread intertexture of various forces influencing one another, has been noted several times above. In the romance, the lyric, the drama, and elsewhere, religious and secular points of view, or modes, often cross and lose their separate identity. Courtly and popular modes are similarly related. The unity of thought thus expressed is a reflection of the medieval mind. More so than his progeny in later centuries, the man of the Middle Ages was born into a mold which unified all classes, of which the integral parts were a deep religious faith in spite of clerical corruption, strict adherence to the various codes of social conduct, and a loyalty to the political establishment. The disruptions in the fourteenth century were at first only the exceptions which proved the rule. In the fifteenth century, one of anarchy and turmoil, these exceptions became the rule itself; literature lost its homogeneous quality and went into a period of decline or transition.

Another factor which contributed greatly to the building of the web of Middle English literature and especially to its continuity was the source and method of its transmission. The origin of much that was produced can be found in age-old, standard, and universal motifs, stemming from Oriental, Germanic, and Celtic folklore, which were fused in English verse and prose tale. Since the delivery was at first by word of mouth, certain changes took place in the narrative process. Literary folklorists have therefore originated the theory of "oral narrative evolution," which, though it presents problems and must be approached with care and intelligence, is of great interest and in many ways sound.

The theory of oral narrative evolution rests on two premises. The first states that every period in the societal development of man has created a type of literature peculiarly adapted to it. Thus the Primitive Age produces the single *motifs*, which are combined into the *folktale* during the Barbaric Age. In the Heroic Age of warlike tribal organizations, whether in western Europe, Greece, or America among the Indians, an *epic* type of literature is formulated, concentrating on a powerful hero, a loyal comitatus, family feuds, wars, and revenge. In English certain short heroic poems or lays (perhaps the *Waldere*, certainly the *Finnsburg* fragment) and the *Beowulf* epic fall into this category. In the Feudal Age, the epic disappears and the *romance* takes its place, as more representative of a courtly, chivalric society of leisure, which included a female audience. The *ballad* comes into its own with the rise of the middle class at the end of this period.

The second premise suggests that all these genres are somehow linked in their development through oral transmission and the above-mentioned motifs. Narrative verse is therefore seen as a continuum. A theoretical progression can be stated as in the paragraphs that follow, which will consider in more detail the links in this evolutionary chain.

In the beginning was the archetypal motif, the root of all story. Thousands of these have been collected and classified by Stith Thompson in his important *Motif-Index*—to name just a few: the Male Cinderella, the Exile and Return, the Wicked Stepmother, the Patient Wife (the Penelope motif), Potiphar's Wife (the Wooing or Amorous Lady), the Loathly Lady, Prince Charming, the Chastity Test or Token. We know these motifs from the tales of the Grimm brothers or from those our grandmothers told.

In narrative verse the motifs, along with historical incidents, were formed into short epic lays, which in turn were the raw material for the longer epics. It was thought in the past that the epics—*Beowulf*, the *Odyssey*, the *Iliad*—were combinations of separate lays strung together. The famous French literary historian Léon Gautier theorized that Germanic *cantilenae* were the framework of the French epics, the chansons de geste; but this idea is too simplistic and outdated, especially as no *cantilenae* have been found. The epic is part of the evolutionary process. Created by one individual, it no doubt drew on past traditions, legends, and lays, but these were artistically transfigured by the poet.

However, between epic and romance there appears to be a break in the chain. The two have always been contrasted in character, style, and story. The epic hero is an individual; the romance hero, a type. Epic action is realistic, the romance story contains many supernatural elements. Then, too, the epic motifs are different in nature from those of romance, none of the magic items or miraculous tests being found in the older verse. So we cannot say that the romance grew out of the epic directly, if at all, even though these two long, popular, adventurous types of poetic narrative do seem to be connected in some manner.

Some scholars have therefore postulated for English oral narrative evolution a missing link, in the form of an Old English chanson de geste. The French epical poems of this type (for example, *The Song of Roland*) were composed in the ninth and tenth centuries and later; and their belligerent themes, combined with the courtly-love ideas of the troubadours, seem to have found their way into a new form, the medieval romance. This process may have worked in England also, and the post-*Beowulf* heroic poems *The Battle of Maldon* and *The Battle of Brunanburg*, both created in the tenth century, may be examples of such lost Old English chansons de geste.

It has been conjectured by G. K. Anderson (*Old and Middle English Literature from the Beginnings to 1485*) that some of the early, rawer Matter of England romances (*King Horn, Havelok the Dane*) can be traced to hypothetical native chansons de geste. But this theory, though interesting, suffers, like Gautier's on the *cantilenae*, from a lack of evidence.

Whereas in France the chansons were amalgamated with Provençal themes to form the romance, in England they may have been similarly combined with the chronicles of the twelfth century (for example, those of Geoffrey of Monmouth and William of Malmesbury). Though the chronicles were prose, and therefore could not be an organic part of narrative verse evolution, they may have acted as a catalyst, infusing fabulous elements and romantic imagination into martial epic realism. The tenth-century Old English poems combined with the influence of the later chronicles may have been the link between the epic and the Middle English romance.

As a parallel development to the romances, though not part of this specific line of oral evolution, we should name the Breton lais; the fabliaux, with their antiromance overtones; and the parodies.

Finally, the ballad occasionally evolved out of the romance, and this genre is therefore the end of the folkloric evolutionary chain. Various examples of the whole sequence and relationship might be schematized as follows:

Motif (Virility Test, Sluggish Younger Son)
↓
Folktale (*The Bear's Son Tale*)
↓
Historical incident (Hygelac's expedition c. 521, mentioned in *Beowulf*)
↓
Epic lay (*The Fight at Finnsburg*)
↓
Epic (*Beowulf*, eighth century)
↓
[Old English chanson de geste (*The Battle of Maldon*, tenth century)]
↓
[Chronicle (Geoffrey of Monmouth, twelfth century)]
↓
Romance (*King Horn*, thirteenth century)
↓
Ballad (*Hind Horn*, ? fifteenth century)

The problems in the theory of oral evolution are self-evident, and we would be remiss not to point these out. There is too much in the theory that remains unproved by evidence, and too little textual information is extant, for us to accept oral evolution as literary law. The idea must be approached objectively and critically. Thus scholars may rightfully point out that some ballads are proved to be older than certain romances, or that it is difficult to see how romances evolved out of epic literature. Critics also note that no matter what oral or popular features these works contain, most of them in their present state show the mark of individual artistic makers. Then, too, the development of the Arthurian story, to take a specific example, does not follow exactly the scheme outlined above. Though the Arthurian sequence contains some of the greatest puzzles in medieval literature, it may yet be seen as a guide to the folk process at work.

It seems that historical fact rests in the background of the legend. Geoffrey Ashe, in his study *The Quest for Arthur's Britain* (New York, 1968), shows considerable archaeological evidence for Arthur's actual existence, and even the distinct possibility that this real Arthur was buried in Glastonbury, the mythical Isle of Avalon. He was perhaps a rustic noble (Artorius) of romanized stock in the Southwest of England, who harassed the monasteries as well as the Saxon invaders, extorting levies from the former and beating the latter at Mount Badon. Welsh monastic tradition was unfriendly to Arthur and may have deprived him of notice in the records. The battle of Mount Badon, a Celtic victory over the Saxons, is first mentioned by Gildas (*De Excidio et Conquestu Britanniae*, c. 540), though the victor here is not Arthur but a certain romanized Celt called Ambrosius Aurelianus. Bede (*Historia Ecclesiastica Gentis Anglorum*, 731) repeats the historical tradition of Gildas, but with Nennius (*Historia Brittonum*, c. 880) legendary exaggeration is already at work: the battle chief here called Arthur himself kills 960 men. Thus it took about three hundred years for history to be changed into myth. If the *Beowulf* composition is to be dated at c. 725, the process of poetic and folkloric assimilation of factual events (Hygelac's raid, for instance) was somewhat shorter.

Arthurian motifs from Celtic (Welsh) stock appear in the imaginative chronicles of William of Malmesbury (1125) and the great work of Geoffrey of Monmouth (1100–55). Only after this was epical matter formed, with Wace's French verse translation the *Roman de Brut* (1155) and Layamon's important *Brut* (1205). Thus the chronology here is from factual happening to history to chronicle and thence to epic. Interwoven through all this matter is motif. We know that there was a Celtic Arthurian tradition, which may or may not have been connected with the Mount Badon incident, from the *Mabinogion*, a Welsh collection of tales. But for medieval Arthurian romance we must look across the Channel to France, to the magnificent works of Chrétien de Troyes in the twelfth century. What literary happenings occurred prior to Chrétien, and why the sea change, is a great mystery. Roger S. Loomis's theory of oral diffusion by Breton minstrels would account for the spread of the material in France and Italy, and also the difference in tone. There is some evidence, produced by the Italian scholar Pio Rajna, that the Arthurian cycle was known in Europe before Chrétien, as the sculpture on the early-twelfth-century cathedral of Modena seems to prove. But here as elsewhere, the link between epic and romance, although it undoubtedly exists, is veiled and obscure.

Thus the stages of folk evolution may take many forms. The fact that certain works show the imprint of individual makers should not worry us too much: hardly any medieval author, it seems, even such men of genius as Chrétien de Troyes or Geoffrey Chaucer, created his plots *sui generis*. Motifs, traditions, legends, were behind all, and these were passed down through the centuries.

Although the theory of oral transmission may not offer a completely satisfactory explanation of this process of folk evolution, there are, nevertheless, some solid facts about it which cannot be gainsaid. Stories containing similar plots, or motif chains, do evolve from one another. The romance of *King Horn* precedes the ballad *Hind Horn*; medieval tales and romances of Gawain's marriage with the Loathly Lady are the source of the later ballad on the subject. We have already pointed out that some of the Matter of England romances appear in shorter, more dramatic form in the ballads. As with language, oral transmission often produced ever more simplified forms, unless a poet consciously gathered shorter episodes into a larger whole. Thus one genre could change into another, and this is most easily noted in the case of romance and ballad. The dramatic, syncopated action of the stanzaic *Morte Arthur* makes this piece the most balladlike of longer English romances. And repetition of the same tags (short cliché phrases) and even longer sections, and a beginning *in medias res*—all ballad characteristics—are seen in *Athelston*.

This phenomenon need not surprise us. Not only are the motifs standard and universal but the formulas of structure, characterization, and stages of wooing are practically the same in all romances. The later ballad makers, therefore, had before them, not hundreds of different, individualized works, but a monolithic genre whose strict conventions they could not escape—although, of course, these traditions were adapted to new needs. In structure, for instance, the minstrel often starts with a bid for attention ("Listen lordings that be here!"), followed occasionally by flattery of his audience, thanks for the money he has received, and a prayer for the long life and prosperity of his listeners. Then the author of the romance speaks to the reciter ("Don't cut the story, or slight with words."). The minstrel refers to his authority, makes a short résumé of the story, and then develops it in a conventional fashion, in either a biographical or a plotted method. This is standard procedure, and so are the dramatis personae. There is the young hero, courageous and highborn, with a young friend who looks like him and to whom he is often mystically attached. There is the old friend, counselor to the hero's father the king, who gives advice (the father himself is often shadowy). The heroine, nobly born, is a Wooing Lady who falls in love with the hero and confides in a girl friend. The heroine's father and the evil False Steward or traitor (of the tribe of Ganelon) who belongs to her castle complete the roster of personages. From these integers the reader can easily work out the complete equation of plot. The first impetus, the falling in love, is followed by the first bar to the union. Since romance formulas fall into sets of three or seven, there is normally a second complication after the betrothal, in which the knight must prove himself. The third complication is the testing of faith (the Other Woman Test), followed by the climax: either a coming together or, in rare cases, tragedy. Although there are infinite variations on them, the formulas are ever the same; and similar schemes can easily be worked out for the ballad. "Plus ça change, plus c'est la même chose."

As MacEdward Leach used to state, narrative reflects the evolutionary growth of a people. The form and flesh of the story may change, but the basic plot is unchangeable. In no other period is this narrative continuity more visible and obvious than in Middle English. It is all the more true because the literature of medieval England acted as a clearinghouse for a cosmopolitan folklore. Ideas from Europe and Asia found their way onto the creative loom of this island until England became like Chaucer's whirling *House of Fame*:

Ne never rest is in that place
That hit nys fild ful of tydynges.

This is the web of medieval English literature. From Germanic sources we derive the beast fable, the Charlemagne romances, and many of our ballads. Celtic motifs are seen in the Breton lais, the Arthurian romances, and the story of Kulhwch and Olwen in the *Mabinogion*. The episodes in the *Gesta Romanorum*, the story of the Seven Sages of Rome, and the elements of the fabliaux come ultimately from Oriental lore. France contributed the code of courtly love in lyric and romance, though Arabic influence is also present here. The universal Latin spirit was alive in the lyric, in stories from postclassical Rome and the Ovidian tradition. All was woven into the English fabric.

And this is, too, the miracle of medieval man: he achieved a noumenal integrity out of phenomenal variety, one perspective out of many views. These he gathered at the Continental universities, in Paris, Bologna, Prague, and Vienna, on pilgrimages to Compostela, Aix, Rome, and Jerusalem, and on crusades to the Holy Land. Truly, a study of the Middle English record and a critical appreciation of its heritage should encourage the student to move out of national confinement into the broader discipline, greater freedom, and wider learning of a comparative European literature.

A SUMMARY OF MIDDLE ENGLISH SPELLING AND PRONUNCIATION

Inconsistency seems to be the rule in Middle English spelling (though not pronunciation); and exceptions to this guideline that are consistent in any specific work are scarce. The student who reads Middle English texts must be constantly alert and awake. One moment off guard, and the simplest word may slip past him unchallenged, to cause confusion and disturb the process of communication and sense. *Nosethirles*, for instance, are useless to the life function if they cannot be recognized as "nostrils." It is a good idea, therefore, to read the language aloud. Though the words look strange, they often sound familiar. (One must try to listen to the word without seeing an image of it.) At the same time that oral recitation facilitates understanding, it also imitates the medieval process of reading, which was rarely completely silent.

CONSONANTS

We are in luck here! Middle English consonants (with three exceptions, which we shall consider in a moment) look like ours today. However, unlike some in Modern English, *all* consonants are pronounced, as in German. ME *kniȝt, knicht* (Mod. Eng. *knight*) = $k + n + i + ch + t$. The omnipresent exception to the rule is silent initial *h* in French loanwords (for example, *honor*).

Initial *ch* is pronounced as in Mod. Eng. *church*; otherwise *ch* is pronounced as in German *nicht, Nacht* (with the back of the tongue against the roof [hard palate] or back [soft palate] of the mouth, and breathing out). Through the influence of Anglo-Norman scribes, *ch* is occasionally used for *k*: for example, *chnief* (Mod. Eng. *knife*).

Before *a, o,* and *u, c* was always pronounced *k*: *can, cold, curs*. Before *e* and *i(y) c* was always pronounced *s*: *celle, cite*. The consonant *gg* was pronounced either as *dg* in Mod. Eng. *bridge* (for example, *juggen*) or as *g* in Mod. Eng. *leg* (for example, *frogge*). The modern pronunciation, if the word exists, is a help not to be disregarded.

The three Middle English consonants different from Modern English are þ (*thorn*), ð (*crossed d* or *eth*), and ȝ (*yogh*). Both *thorn* and *eth* stand for voiced and voiceless *th*, though the second letter disappeared much earlier in manuscripts. The *thorn* is a survival of the old Saxon runic alphabet. Each letter stood for a word; and the thorn (a remnant of the Druid nature religion of thorn and ash) had, supposedly, magical properties. However this may be, it is wise to treat the letter with respect. In handwriting, þ was later corrupted to *y*, which printers often used to represent the sound of *th*. We thus get such oddities in the fifteenth century (as well as the twentieth) as "ye olde taverne," which makes no sense but sounds quaint and is good for the tourist trade.

The third letter, ȝ, is a peculiar chameleon which adapts itself to many situations. Initially, it has the sound of consonantal *y* (as in Mod. Eng. *yacht*), where in Modern English it is silent (for example, ME ȝ*if*, Mod. Eng. *if*) or hard (for example, ME ȝ*ive*, Mod. Eng. *give*). Medially it is pronounced like ME *ch*, where in Modern English it is silent *gh*: for example, ME *kniȝt*, *oȝt*, Mod. Eng. *knight*, *ought*. It even has the sound of final *s* in some scribal peculiarities (*watȝ* = *was*)! All in all, it seems best to play this letter by ear.

VOWELS

Alas, here we are in for trouble! But if the word *alas* was not pronounced "ehlayce," at least we are on the right track; for as in French and German (which are obviously good languages to know) Middle English vowels are pronounced phonetically.

The word-shattering and significant Great Vowel Shift of the fifteenth century fronted most vowels, relegated the study of Chaucer to special classes, and threw the eccentric English language into splendid isolation from other Continental tongues. But for all intents and purposes, the Great Vowel Shift applies only to long vowels. What we are concerned with, then, is determining whether a vowel was long or short. As a general rule, if the vowel or diphthong is long now, it was long then, and we can easily arrive at the Middle English pronunciation by tracing back through the individual changes that occurred:

Mod. Eng. *house* comes from OE *hūs*, ME *hous* (both pronounced to rhyme with Mod. Eng. *goose*).

Mod. Eng. *to* comes from ME *to* (pronounced like Mod. Eng. *toe*).

In phonetic notation these changes may be indicated thus:

[u] > [au]
[o] > [u]

Both of these changes are further explained below under *o* and *u*.

How do we recognize a Middle English long **vowel** when we see it? The rules are easy because they correlate with our modern spelling. Middle English indicates a long vowel by:

(a) doubling the vowel (ME *good*, pronounced like Mod. Eng. *goad*);
(b) following the vowel with one consonant plus final *e* (ME *name*, disyllabic [see below, p. 43], the *a* pronounced as in Mod. Eng. *ah!*);
(c) ending a monosyllabic word in the vowel (ME *go*), or ending a disyllabic word in the vowel as long as this is not final *e* (ME *into*), or ending a polysyllabic word borrowed from French in the vowel (ME *beaute*);
(d) in the Northern dialect alone, following the vowel with *i* (ME or Middle Scots *guid*, pronounced like Mod. Eng. *goo* + *d*).

In Middle English, therefore, the vowels are pronounced as follows:

a: short, as in German *Mann*; long, as in Mod. Eng. *father*.

e: short, as in Mod. Eng. *bed*; long, also spelled *ee* ($\bar{e}$), as in Mod. Eng. *there* (open, or slack, $\bar{e}$) or *they* (close, or tense, $\bar{e}$). If the modern spelling is *ee*, then the vowel was probably close in Middle English; if the modern spelling is *ea*, it was probably open. For example, ME *slepen*, *seken* (close $\bar{e}$) = Mod. Eng. *sleep*, *seek*; ME *heeth*, *yeer* (open $\bar{e}$) = **Mod. Eng.** *heath*, *year*. If the modern spelling is *e* (as in *complete*), there is no guide except etymological knowledge, I'm afraid. However, close $\bar{e}$ was more common, especially by Chaucer's time.

i(y): short, as in Mod. Eng. *hit*; long, as in Mod. Eng. *machine*. In Middle English, *i* and *y* were completely interchangeable spellings.

o: short, as in Mod. Eng. *or*; long ($\bar{o}$) as in Mod. Eng. *broad* (open $\bar{o}$) or *note* (close $\bar{o}$). If the modern pronunciation is $\bar{o}$ (as in *rode*, *road*), then the sound was probably open $\bar{o}$ in Middle English; if the modern pronunciation is a long *u* (as in *pool*), or if the modern spelling is *oo* (as in *blood*, *good*), then it was a close $\bar{o}$ in Middle English. For example, ME *hooly*, verb *rood* (open $\bar{o}$) = Mod. Eng. *holy*, *rode*; ME *roote*, *bone* (close $\bar{o}$) = Mod. Eng. *root*, *boon*.

u: short, as in Mod. Eng. *full*; long ($\bar{u}$), as in Mod. Eng. *food*. ME $\bar{u}$ was frequently spelled *ou*, *ow*, *ogh*; and if the spellings are used in the modern words today (*house*, *fowl*), then the Middle English vowel was $\bar{u}$. Otherwise—mainly in French loan-words—$\bar{u}$ was pronounced as in French *tu*. It is interesting to note that the short *u* from c. 1300 on was often spelled *o* next to *n*, *m*, or *i* (OE *sunu*, *hunig* = Mod. Eng. *son*, *honey*), because in the manuscripts, especially those in gothic script, the letters *n*, *m*, *i*, and *u* were hard to distinguish—as seen in the word ɪɪɪɪɪɪɪɪɪɪɪɪɪɪɪ (*minimum*).

The diphthongs are simpler; they are pronounced as follows:

ai, *ay*, *ei*, *ey*: as in Mod. Eng. *lie*, but transformed in Chaucer's period, c. 1380, into the sound of Mod. Eng. *day*. (We find this confusion still in Cockney and Australian English, as in the answer to the hospital query "Was he brought here to die?" "No, yesterday.")

ou, *ow*:[1] as in Mod. Eng. *grow*

au: as in Mod. Eng. *house*

ew: as in Mod. Eng. *knew*

oi, *oy*: as in Mod. Eng. *boy*

ou + *gh*: as in Mod. Eng. *fought* + ME noninitial *ch*

In Chaucer's time unaccented final *e* (and almost all final *e*'s were unaccented) was given a neutral pronunciation, like the *a* in *about* (as in French chanson singing, or the dialect of the Midi), unless it was swallowed by a following initial vowel (elision).

---

1. To tell whether the spelling *ou*, *ow* represents the long vowel $\bar{u}$ or the diphthong, think of the modern pronunciation if the word still exists. If it is the sound in *house*, *cow*, *now*, *found*, then it was the Middle English vowel $\bar{u}$; if the modern sound is that of *bought*, *sought*, *ought*, or that of *mow*, *crow*, *blow*, then it was the Middle English diphthong.

MISCELLANEOUS

1. Watch out for tricky *r*'s! The change (metathesis) of *r* around vowels is frequent and should not confuse the alert reader; *bridde* for *bird*, *bren* for *burn*, *arn* for *ran*, *þurgh* for *through*, and so forth. When the sly movements of this letter are recognized, they should cause little difficulty.

2. Negatives abound in Middle English. The more of them there are, the more emphatic the negative becomes. To facilitate this negative emphasis, the word *ne* contracts with verbs: *ne* + *was* = *nas*, *ne* + *wot* ("*knows*") = *not*, *ne* + *is* = *nis*, and so on. The grammarians of the eighteenth-century Age of Reason felt that two negatives make a positive, but what applies in electricity or the multiplication of negative numbers is not always apt in language. When a master sergeant shouts to recruits, "I don't like none of your negative attitudes!" only a pedantic fool would misunderstand his call for volunteers.

3. The interchange of *u* for *v* and *i* for *j* is common; thus we get *loue* for *love*. But in addition, in the Southern dialect *f* becomes *v* (*fox* = *vox*); so that, with the *u/v* interchange, a word like *Friday* in the Southern dialect goes through the following metamorphosis: *friday* > *vriday* > *uriday* (*uridawe*), and *from* becomes *urom*. In the interchange of *i* for *j* we find, for instance, *ioine* = *join*, *iolyf* = *jolly*.

4. Northern English often uses *qu* for *wh* (for example, *quene* = *when* [though in context it could also mean "queen"]), *quere* = *where*.

5. In the Midlands, *a* + nasal (*m*, *n*) often becomes *o* (for instance, *hond*, *lond*, *ond*, and the most common words *mon*, *con*).

Such dialectal variations as these, as well as any other **peculiarities**, will always be mentioned in the headnote of each selection in the present volume. Logically, the earlier works included here are much more difficult than the later. The former, indeed all of them, could have been normalized—that is, essentially abnormalized by being made consistent—thus producing a synthetic, fictitious, but easily digestible language. For many reasons it has seemed wise to avoid this.

Those students seriously interested in continuing this study may refer to the linguistic works in the bibliography below. In general, the marginal gloss and linguistic notes will be sufficient to make intelligent students literate in Middle English. And if the pronounciation slips at times, no matter. What is important, after all, is to be able to read the past.

SELECTED BIBLIOGRAPHY ON THE HISTORY OF MIDDLE ENGLISH LITERATURE AND LANGUAGE

Works relating to specific genres will be found under the genre introductions in the anthology.

Language

Baugh, A. C., and Cable, T. *A History of the English Language*. 3d ed. London, 1978.

Brook, G. L. *A History of the English Language*. Fair Lawn, N.J., 1958.

Clark, John W. *Early English*. New York, 1957.

Jespersen, O. *Growth and Structure of the English Language*. 9th ed., rev. New York, 1955.

Kurath, Hans, and Kuhn, Sherman, eds. *Middle English Dictionary*. Ann Arbor, Mich. 1954–. Herein abbreviated *MED*.

Marckwardt, A. H. *Introduction to the English Language*. New York, 1942.

Mossé, Fernand. *A Handbook of Middle English*. Trans. J. A. Walker. Baltimore, 1952.

Murray, James A. H.; Bradley, Henry; Craigie, W. A.; and Onions, C. T., eds. *Oxford English Dictionary*. Oxford, 1888–1928. Herein abbreviated *OED*.

Vising, J. *Anglo-Norman Language and Literature*. London, 1923.

Literature

Ackerman, Robert W. *Backgrounds to Medieval English Literature*. New York, 1966.

Anderson, George K. *Old and Middle English Literature from the Beginnings to 1485*. New York, 1966.

Baugh, A. C., and Malone, Kemp. *The Middle Ages*. Vol. I of *A Literary History of England*, ed. A. C. Baugh. 2d ed. 4 vols. New York, 1967.

Bennett, H. S. *Chaucer and the Fifteenth Century*. New York, 1961.

Chambers, E. K. *English Literature at the Close of the Middle Ages*. New York, 1961.

Chambers, R. W. *On the Continuity of English Prose from Alfred to More and His School*. Early English Text Society, 191. London, 1957.

Chaytor, H. J. *From Script to Print*. Cambridge, 1950.

Coulton, G. G. *Medieval Panorama*. 2d ed. 2 vols. London, 1961.

Gross, C. *The Sources and Literature of English History from the Earliest Times to about 1485*. 2d ed. London, 1915.

Hartung, Albert, E., ed. *A Manual of the Writings in Middle English, 1050–1500*. 4 vols. New Haven, 1972–.

Jackson, W. T. H. *The Literature of the Middle Ages*. New York, 1961.

———. *Medieval Literature, A History and a Guide*. New York, 1966.

Ker, W. P. *The Dark Ages*. New York, 1958.

———. *English Literature: Medieval*. London, 1912.

———. *Epic and Romance*. London, 1908.

Lewis, C. S. *The Allegory of Love*. New York, 1958.

Loomis, Roger Sherman. *Introduction to Medieval Literature Chiefly in England: A Reading List and Bibliography*. New York, 1949.

———, and Willard, Rudolph. *Medieval English Verse and Prose in Modernized Versions*. New York, 1948.

Matthews, William. *Later Medieval English Prose*. New York, 1963.

———. *Old and Middle English Literature*. Golden Tree Bibliographies. New York, 1968.

Severs, J. Burke, ed. *A Manual of the Writings in Middle English, 1050–1500*. 2 vols. New Haven, 1967–70.

Sisam, Kenneth. *Fourteenth Century Verse and Prose*. Oxford, 1955.

Taylor, H. O. *The Medieval Mind*. 2 vols. New York, 1919.

Thompson, Stith. *Motif-Index of Folk-Literature*. Bloomington, Ind., 1932–58.

Tout, T. F. *The Political History of England, 1216–1377*. London, 1905.

Waddell, H. J. *The Wandering Scholars*. New York, 1955.

Wells, J. E. *A Manual of the Writings in Middle English, 1050–1400*. Supplements i–ix. New Haven, 1916–51. A new edition, extended to 1500, ed. J. B. Severs (Vols. I, II) and A. E. Hartung is nearing completion.

EPIC-HEROIC LITERATURE

Heroic narrative poems which concern the martial adventures of an individual or a group of men in the prefeudal age, composed most often by an anonymous author who utilizes as his raw material ancient legends, myths, and folklore in addition to historical events, are usually called epics. Normally the central figure is the epic hero (Odysseus, Achilles Roland, Siegfried, Beowulf), an individual superior in physical and sometimes mental and ethical qualities who is meant to embody the noblest national traits. On the success or failure of this epic hero depended, usually, the fate of the hero's society or nation. We thus use the somewhat inaccurate term *national folk epics* for those poems which represent a specific nation: the Greek *Odyssey* and *Iliad*, the French *Chanson de Roland*, the German *Nibelungenlied*, the Finnish *Kalevala*, and so on.

The word *folk* is misleading if it is used to mean the source of epics. The folk did not compose these long poems, but furnished the legendary material (perhaps in the form of short lays, fragments, or simply traditions) from which a "maker" created his work. And since the English epic *Beowulf* deals with Scandinavian motifs, it cannot accurately be termed a national epic. *The Battle of Maldon*, *The Battle of Brunanburg*, and Layamon's *Brut*, on the other hand, are definitely epical poems, with the high style, heroic action, and Saxon–Celtic heritage necessary for a national genre.

REFERENCES

Campbell, A., ed. *The Battle of Brunanburh*. London, 1938.

Carpenter, R. *Folk Tale, Fiction, and Saga in the Homeric Epics*. Berkeley, Calif., 1946.

Chadwick, H. M. *The Heroic Age*. Cambridge, 1912.

Chadwick, H. M., and Chadwick, N. K. *The Growth of Literature*. Cambridge, 1932.

Dickins, B. *Runic and Heroic Poems of the Teutonic Peoples*. Cambridge, 1915.

Haber, T. B. *A Comparative Study of the Beowulf and the Aeneid*. Princeton, 1931.

Klaeber, F., ed. *Beowulf* 3d ed. Lexington, Mass., 1950.

Lawrence, W. W. *Beowulf and the Epic Tradition*. Cambridge, Mass., 1928.

Raglan, F. R. S. *The Hero: a Study in Tradition, Myth, and Drama*. London, 1936.

Sedgefield, W. J., ed. *The Battle of Maldon and Short Poems from the Saxon Chronicle*. Boston, 1904.

Schlauch, M., trans. *The Saga of the Volsungs*. New York, 1949.

Whitelock, D. *The Audience of "Beowulf."* London, 1951.

Epic-heroic literature is treated in the General Introduction of this volume, pp. 1–2, 10–11, 34–37.

THE BATTLE OF BRUNANBURG

Found in the *Anglo-Saxon Chronicle* (the Parker Chronicle, Corpus Christi College, Cambridge, MS. 173, folios 1–32) under the year 937.

The poem recounts the victory of Æthelstan over the Scot Constantine, the Strathclyde Welsh, and the Norwegians. The site of the battle may possibly have been the Solway Firth.

   The beginning of the Old English original is given below, followed by a translation of the complete poem.

from THE ANGLO-SAXON CHRONICLE

An DCCCCXXXVII

Hēr Æðelstān cyning,   eorla drihten,
beorna bēahgifa,   and his brōðor ēac,
Ēadmund æðeling,   ealdorlangne tīr
geslōgon æt sæcce   sweorda ecgum
[5] ymbe Brunanburh: bordweall clufon,
hēowon heaðolinde   hamora lāfum,
eaforan Ēadweardes;   swā him geæðele wæs
fram cnēomāgum,   ðæt hī æt campe oft
wið lāðra gehwæne   land ealgodon,
[10] hord and hāmas.   Hettend crungon,
Scotta lēode   and scipflotan,
fæge feollon: feld dennode
secga swāte,   siþþan sunne ūpp
on morgentīd,   mære tungol,

---

1. *Hēr*: The *Anglo-Saxon Chronicle* entries always start with "In this year. . . ."

[1b.] *éorlă dríhtĕn*, a Sievers "A" line (see above, p. 1).

2. *ring-giver*: a kenning (a compound noun used metaphorically) for "king."

[2b.] *ǎnd hǐs bróðor ēac*, a Sievers "B" line.

[3b.] *éaldŏrlàngnĕ tîr*, a Sievers "E" line, with the second syllable "resolved."

5. The shield wall, a stationary defensive device in which frontline troops remained behind their shields and repelled the attack, was used by the Saxons at Hastings.

6. *war-linden*, *leavings of hammers*: kennings for "shield," "swords," respectively.

[8a.] *frǎm cnéomǎgǔm*, a Sievers "C" line.

[9b.] *lánd éalgòdŏn*, a Sievers "Da" line.

49

[15] glād ofer grundas,   Godes candel beorht,
ēces Drihtnes,   oð sīo æðele gesceaft
sāh tō setle.   Ðær læg secg monig
gārum agēted,   guma Norðerna
ofer scyld scoten,   swylce Scyttisc ēac
[20] wērig wīges sæd.   Wesseaxe forð
andlangne dæg   ēoredcystum
on lāst legdon   lāðum ðēodum;
hēowon hereflȳman   hindan ðearle
mēcum mylenscearpum.   Myrce ne wyrndon
[25] heardes handplegan   hæleða nānum,
ðāra ðe mid Anlāfe   ofer ēargebland
on lides bōsme   land gesōhton,
fæge tō gefeohte.   Fife lāgon
on ðām campstede,   cyningas geonge
[30] sweordum āswefede,   swylce seofone ēac
eorlas Anlāfes,   unrīm herges
flotena and Scotta. . . .

In this year Æthelstan king,   lord of earls,
ring-giver of men,   and his brother too,
Eadmund the noble,   lifelong glory
gained in battle   with the edges of swords
5 near Brunanburg.   They cleft the shield wall,
hewed the war-linden   with the leavings of hammers,
those sons of Edward.   Thus noble blood urged them,
inherited from kinsmen,   that they often in battle
against all enemies   defended their land,
10 their hoard and their homes.   The enemy died,
the Scottish people   and the sailors,
fell fated.   The field became dark
with the blood of warriors,   after the sun
in the morning,   that great star,
15 rose over earth,   the bright candle of God,
of the eternal Lord,   until that noble creation
again sank to earth.   There lay many a man
injured by spears,   a warrior of the Northmen
shot over his shield,   as also a Scot
20 sad and weary of war.   The West Saxons onward
all day long   with their troops
pursued   the hostile people.

[15b.] *Gódes cándĕl bèorht*, a Sievers "Db" line, with the second
syllable "resolved."

They cut the battle fugitives   severely from behind
with sharp-ground swords.   The Mercians did not refuse
²⁵ hard hand-play   to any warriors
of those that with Anlaf   over the ocean
in the bosom of ships   sought this land,
fated in fight.   Five lay
on that war-field,   young kings
³⁰ stilled with swords,   as also seven
earls of Anlaf,   and uncounted soldiers
of the shipmen and Scots.   There was put to flight
the chief of the Northmen,   compelled by force
to the prow of his boat   with a small band.
³⁵ The ship hastened to sea,   the king went out
on the dark flood,   saved his life.
Likewise the old man   escaped in flight
north to his home,   Constantine,
the hoary warrior: he dared not exult
⁴⁰ in the joining of swords!   He was bereft of his kin,
deprived of his friends   on that battleground;
they were slain in the fight,   and he left his son
on the slaughter-place   torn with wounds,
the young man in combat.   He needed not boast,
⁴⁵ this gray-haired soldier,   of the clashing of swords,
the evil old man,   not Anlaf either.
With their army remnants   they could not laugh
that in the war-work   they were superior,
in the battleplace,   in the conflict of banners,
⁵⁰ the meeting of spears,   the encounter of men,
the exchange of weapons,   which they on the slaughter-fields
with Edward's   sons fought out.
Went then the Northmen   in their nailed boats,
the dreary spear-survivors   on the rushing sea,
⁵⁵ over the deep water   to seek Dublin,
Ireland again   in shame.
Also then the brothers   both together,
king and noble,   sought their home,
the West Saxon land,   exultant in fight.
⁶⁰ They left behind them   to share the corpses
the dark-coated   swarthy raven,

24–25. An example of *litotes* (an affirmative expressed by its negative opposite). See also ll. 39, 44, 47.

60–65. The raven, eagle, hawk, and wolf were the traditional "beasts of battle" or slaughter animals, battlefield scavengers, who appear in many Anglo-Saxon poems, for example,

Beowulf, Wanderer. See also the ballad *Twa Corbies* (this volume, p. 496).

61–63. *dark-coated, horn-beaked, gray-coated, white-tailed*: examples of the *compound epithet*, very popular in Anglo-Saxon verse.

horn-beaked,   and the gray-coated
eagle, white-tailed,   to possess the carrion,
the greedy war-hawk   and that gray wild beast,
65 the wolf in the forest.   Never was slaughter the greater
on this island,   never yet
a people cut down   before this
with the edges of swords,   as books tell us,
old wisemen,   since eastward hither
70 the Angles and Saxons   had come up
over the broad waters,   had sought Britain,
the proud war-smiths,   conquered the Welsh,
the earls, eager for glory,   had seized this land.

from BRUT

Layamon

DATE: c. 1189–1205. ◆ MANUSCRIPTS: British Library Cotton Caligula A. ix (c. 1250), British Library Cotton Otho C. xiii (c. 1270). The dialect is Southwest Midland (Worcestershire), but impure. ◆ EDITION: Sir Frederick Madden, *Laȝamons Brut*, or *Chronicle of England* (London, 1847). This is a diplomatic text of the two MSS, with a modern English paraphrase. A new edition is that of G. L. Brook and R. F. Leslie, Vol. I, Early English Text Society, 250 (London, 1963 [for 1961]), Vol. II, Early English Text Society, 277 (London, 1978). The version used here is that of Madden's rendition of Cotton Caligula A. ix, but corrected for obvious errors. Occasionally, when lines are missing from this MS, they are added from Cotton Otho C. xiii.

The contemporary pronunciation of the author's name, in spite of the traditional spelling, was probably closer to *Lawman*. The spelling and general characteristics tend to be quite conservative. (1) Southern initial *f* is voiced to *v* (and thus appears in this version most often as *u*); *u* and *v* are in most cases interchanged: *uall = fall*, *luuest = lovest*. (2) Another Southern characteristic is the interchange of *u* for *i*: *hull = hill*, *furst = first*, *fust = fist*. (3) The Old English inflections of pronouns and adjectives are kept to a great extent: *heo*, "they," *heom*, "them," *hine*, "himself," "him" accusative, *hire*, "her," *wit*, "we two," and so on. (4) Infinitives end in *-en* or *-ien*; the relative pronoun is *þe* or *þa* (the latter may also mean "when," "then"). (5) The spelling *eo*, representing a rounded *e*, is very common in Southern and Southwest Midland. Later London and East Midland dialects would have an *e* in corresponding position: *feole = fele*, *weore = were*. (6) The fricative, spelled elsewhere *gh* or *ȝ*, is here usually *h*.

This epic-chronicle of the history of Britain from its founding by the mythical Brutus (whose ancestor was the Trojan Aeneas) to 689, when Cadwallader retreated before the Saxons into the Welsh mountains, is a poem of over 16,000 long lines, written by Layamon, a secular priest living in Worcestershire. It shows the Old English poetic survival in vocabulary, tone, and metrical structure, though its theme is the glory of Celtic Britain rather than of Saxon England. Layamon used as his sources Bede's *Ecclesiastical History of the English People* and, very extensively, Wace's Anglo-Norman *Roman de Brut*, in addition to folklore and legends surrounding the story of Arthur, with whose campaigns one-third of the *Brut* deals.

Layamon's Introduction (vss. 1–67)

An preost wes° on leoden,°	Laȝamon wes ihoten;°	*priest was/land/called*
he wes Leouenaðes sone,°	liðe° him° beo drihten;°	*son/gracious/to him/be (the) Lord*

---

1. Layamon was a secular priest, living on the land, i.e., not a monk in orders.

he wonede° at Ernleȝe	at æðelen are chirechen°	*lived/a noble church*
vppen Seuarne staþe,°	sel þar° him þuhte,°	*upon Severn's shore/pleasant there/ (it) seemed*
⁵ on fest° Radestone,	þer° he bock radde.°	*near/where/books read*
Hit com° him on mode°	and on his mern þonke°	*it came/in mind/deep thought*
þet° he wolde° of Engle°	þa æðelæn tellen,°	*that/would/English/the noble (deeds) tell*
wat heo° ihoten weoren,°	and wonene° heo comen°	*what they/were/whence/came*
þa° Englene° londe°	ærest ahten°	*that/of (the) English/(the) land/ first possessed*
¹⁰ æfter þan flode°	þe° from drihtene° com,	*the flood/that/God*
þe al her a-quelde°	quic° þat he funde,°	*here destroyed/alive/found*
buten Noe° and Sem,°	Japhet and Cham,°	*except Noah/Shem/Ham*
and heore° four wiues	þe mid heom weren° on archen.°	*their/with them were/ark*
Laȝamon gon° liðen°	wide ȝond þas leode,°	*began to/travel/widely through the land*
¹⁵ and bi-won° þa æðela boc°	þa he to bisne nom.°	*got/noble book/as source took*
He nom þa Englisca° boc	þa makede seint Beda;°	*English/made Saint Bede*
an oþer he nom on Latin	þe makede seinte Albin,°	*Albinus*
and þe feire Austin°	þe fulluht broute hider° in;	*fair Augustine/baptism brought here*
boc he nom þe þridde,°	leide° þer amidden,°	*third/laid (out)/among them*
²⁰ þa makede a Frenchis clerc,	Wace wes ihoten,	
þe wel couþe° writen,°	and he hoe ȝef° þare° æðelen°	*knew how to/write/it gave/to the/ noble*
Ælienor° þe wes Henries quene,	þes heȝes° kinges.	*Eleanor/the high*
Laȝamon leide þeos boc°	and þa leaf wende;°	*these books/leaves turned*
he heom leofliche° bi-heold,°	liþe him beo drihten;	*with pleasure/beheld*
²⁵ feþeren° he nom mid fingren°	and fiede° on boc-felle,°	*pen/fingers/wrote/parchment*
and þa soþere word°	sette to-gadere,°	*true words/together*
and þa þre° boc	þrumde° to are.°	*three/compressed/one*

---

3. *Ernleȝe:* the village of King's Areley, near Bewdley, Worcestershire.

5. Radstone takes its name from the cliff of reddish sandstone over the Severn at Redstone Ferry, which links Asteley and Areley. It is there that Layamon read the Mass or the Bible.

16. The Venerable Bede's *Ecclesiastical History* (*Historia Ecclesiastica Gentis Anglorum*), translated into Old English in the reign of King Alfred.

17. Albinus, abbot of Saint Augustine's monastery at Canterbury (who died in 732), was a source for Bede, though none of his works survive.

18. Saint Augustine died in 604. Layamon seems confused about his sources. He did not know that Bede originally wrote in Latin and, in fact, did not follow Bede too closely. The mention of authorities was a medieval tradition, a ritual necessary to

convince the reader that what he was about to read had the mark of distinguished authors.

20. Wace was the most important source for Layamon. The Anglo-Norman *trouvère*, author of the *Roman de Brut* (translated c. 1155 from Geoffrey of Monmouth's *Historia Regum Britanniae*), was a vital poet who inspired Layamon to compose his epic-chronicle in verse. The English writer, however, contributed several independent sections, which will be pointed out below. It will be recalled that he had access to, and used, many Welsh chronicle sources (see above, p. 10).

21–22. Eleanor, duchess of Aquitaine, later queen of France, finally wife of Henry II of England (1154–89), was one of the foremost medieval patrons of literature at her court of Aquitaine, where noble troubadours celebrated the joy of *l'amour courtois*.

Nu biddeð° Laȝamon   alcne æðele mon,°   *now prays/each noble man*
for þene almiten° Godd,   *the (love of) almighty*
30 þet þeos° boc rede,°   and leornia° þeos runan,°   *this/reads/learns/sayings*
þat he þeos soðfeste° word   segge° to sumne,°   *true/say/together*
for his fader saule°   þa hine° forð brouhte,°   *father's soul/him/brought*
and for his moder° saule   þa hine to monne iber,°   *mother's/(be a)* **man bore**
and for his awene° saule   þat hire° þe selre° beo.   *own/it/better*

Amen.

The Murder of King Gracien (vss. 12243–330)

35 Iwarð° þe king Gracien   gumene° forduðest;°   *became/of men/most wicked*
al he for-uerde° þis lond;°   þa leoden° him° weoren laðe;°   *destroyed/land/the people/to him/ were hateful*

þa riche he for-uerde;   þa wræcche° he drof of ærde;°   *poor/drove from (the) land*
ne durste° þa riche þeines°   nowhær° him cumen to-ȝeines,°   *not dared/thanes/nowhere/oppose*
ah° alle heo hine fluȝen°   and alle heo hine bibuȝen.°   *but/they him fled/avoided*
40 Þa° weoren in Æst Ængle°   æðele iborene cheorles,°   *then/East Anglia/noble-born men*
twene ibroðeren,°   itwinnes° heo weoren;   *two brothers/twins*
þe oðer° hehte° Eðelbald   and þe oðer Ælfwald.   *one/was called*
Heo isehȝen on feole studen°   hou þe king þis lond fordude;°   *saw in many places/destroyed*
þas° cheorles heom bi-þohten°   whæt° heo don mihten,°   *those/considered/what/do might*
45 and speken heom ful stille°   þat þene° king heo walden quellen,°   *spoke together very secretly/the/ would kill*
and senden° in Æst Ængle   wide ȝeond þan° londe,   *sent/widely throughout the*
and sumnede° on ærde°   seouen° hundred cheorles,   *gathered/in (the) land/seven*
and seiden° þurh alle þing°   þat heo walden bi-sechen° þene king,   *said/everywhere/seek*
and bidden° hine mildce,°   þurh° þene milde Godd,   *pray/mercy/through*
50 þat he þurh his mihte   heolde heom° to rihte.°   *govern them/justly*
Ah Ælfwald and his broðer   al heo þuhten oðer;°   *thought differently*
heo uerden swiðe warliche°   mid wunsumme lades,°   *traveled very warily/with pleasant looks*

and ælc bær an honde°   ænne saȝel° stronge,   *each bore in hand/a staff*
and bisiden° heo gunnen heongen°   cniues° swiðe longe   *beside/did hang/knives*

35–78. Gracien (in Geoffrey of Monmouth called Gratianus Municeps) was a freedman dispatched with two legions to Britain by the Roman emperor Maximian to defeat the Picts and Scots. After driving these to Ireland, he became (according to Geoffrey of Monmouth) emperor of Britain in 407, but in a few months he was slain. Maximian (evidently the historical Magnus Maximus [cf. below, p. 126, n. 16]), however, was killed in 388. We have here, therefore, a typical example of fact and fiction confused and interwoven, which was one of the principal characteristics of both Geoffrey and Layamon. In Geoffrey's sixth book this incident is treated in one line: "Catervis factis, plebs in eum irruerent et interficerent." Wace added the tearing of the king's body by the people; Layamon expanded the story from lost traditions and folklore. The incident bears certain resemblances to the mysterious murder of William Rufus, son of William the Conqueror.

⁵⁵ vnder heore barme°   to scilden° heom wið hærme,°
their breast|shield|from harm

and swa° heo forð ferden°   alle i-sunde,°
so|traveled| in safety

and vmben are° mile   heo ræsten ane° while,
about a|rested a

and auer ælcne° hired-gume°   feire° heo igrætten,°
ever each|courtier|courteously| greeted

and mildeliche° þurh alle þing   fræineden whær° weoren þe king,
mildly|asked where

⁶⁰ and hiredmen° heom tahten°   whær heo hine finden mæhten,°
courtiers|showed|find might

whær he wes° in anne wude°   in ane wilderne,°
was|a forest|wilderness

æfter° ane bare;°   he hine° a-bohte° ful sære.°
(i.e., hunting)|boar|it|paid for| greviously

Þa cheorles wenden° to þan wuden°   and warliche heom hudden,°
went|wood|themselves hid

alle bute tweien;°   toward þan kinge heo weoren beien,°
except two|were (going) both

⁶⁵ and iuunden° þene king   þær° he wes an slæting,°
found|where|a-hunting

and him to cleopeden°   quickere stæuene,°
called|(in a) lively voice

"Hiderward,° lauerd° king;   we þe° wulleð° cuðen° a wunderlic° þing,
come here|lord|to you|wish to|make known|wondrous

of ane swulche° bare   þe her° is bi-halues,°
one such|that here|aside

vnder ane berȝe°   þer° he burh hafueð i-chosen,°
hill|where|lair has chosen

⁷⁰ ne iherde° we næuere° on liue°   tellen° of swulche° swine,
not heard|never|earth|tell| such (a)

ȝif þu þider wult riden°   þer he þe abideð."°
if you there will ride|you awaits

Þer fore wes þe king glad   and þiderwærd° wes swiðe ræd,°
for that|quickly ready

and þa cheorles him biuoren°   beien to-gædere.°
before|together

Þa cheorles up þreowen,°   þene king heo icneowen,°
started|knew

⁷⁵ and heo hine niðer setten°   and al hine to-heowen.°
down struck|cut to pieces

Þus Gratien þe king   for ut° an slæting.
went out

Sone hit° wes ouer al° iseid°   þat þe luðere° king wes dæd;°
soon it|everywhere|said|evil|dead

þa weoren° inne Bruttene°   blissen inowe.°
was|Britain|joy enough

The Birth of Arthur (vss. 18686–19067)

Fulle seouen nihte°   þe king mid° his cnihten°
fully seven nights (i.e., a week)| with|knights

⁸⁰ bilæi þene° castel;   his men þer hafeden sorȝen;°
besieged the| had sorrow

ne mihte° he of þan eorle°   naþing iwinnen,°
not might|from the earl|nothing win

and alle þa° seouen nihte   ilaste° þat selliche feoht.°
those|lasted|wondrous fight

Þa iseh° Vðer king   þat him° ne spedde° naðing,
when saw|for him|succeeded

ofte he hine biþohte°   whæt° he don mahte,°
considered|what|do might

79–82. According to Wace, Gorlois, duke of Cornwall, who was holding the castle, hoped for help from Ireland and held out doggedly.

⁸⁵ for Ygærne him° wes swa leof°   æfne alse° his aȝen lif,°   *to him|was so dear|even as|own life*
and Gorlois him wes on leoden°   monnen° alre° lædest,°   *earth|of men|all|most hateful*
and ælches weies° him wes wa°   a þissere° weorlde-riche,°   *every way|woe|in this|world*
for he ne mihte beon wurðe°   na þing of his wille.   *have*
Þa° wes mid þan kinge   an ald mon swuðe hende;°   *then|old man very wise*
⁹⁰ he wes a swiðe° riche þein°   and ræh on ælche dome;°   *very|thane|skillful in every counsel*
he was ihaten° Vlfin;   muche wisdom wes mid him.   *called*
Þe king bræid° up his chin   and bisah an° Vlfin;   *turned|looked at*
swiðe° he murnede;°   his mod° wes iderued.°   *greatly mourned|mind|troubled*
Þa quað° Vðer Pendragun   to Ulfin þan cnihte,°   *said|knight*
⁹⁵ "Ulfin, ræd° me summe ræd°   oðer ich° beo° ful raðe dæde;°   *(i.e., give)|some counsel|or I|shall be|very quickly dead*

swa swiðe me longeð°   þat ne mai i noht libben°   *I yearn|not live*
after þere° faire Ygærne;   þis word halt° me° derne,°   *for the|keep|for me|secret*
for Ulfin þe leoue,°   aðele° þine lare,°   *beloved|noble|counsels*
lude° and stille,   don ich heom wulle."°   *loud|them will*
¹⁰⁰ Þa andswarede° Ulfin   þan kinge þet spac° wið him,   *answered|that spoke*
"Nu ihere° ich muche seollic°   ænne° king suggen.°   *now hear|strangeness|a|say*
Þu luuest° Ygærne   and halst hit° swa deorne;°   *you love|keep it|secret*
þe wifmon° is þe° to° leof   and hire lauerd° al to lað;°   *woman|to you|too|her lord|hateful*
his lond° þu forbernest°   and hine blæð wurchest,°   *land|burn up|him poor make*
¹⁰⁵ and þrattest° hine to slænne°   and his cun° to fordone.°   *threaten|slay|kin|destroy*
Wenest° þu mid swulche hærme°   to biȝeten° Ygærne?   *think|such harm|obtain*
Þenne heo sculde° don   swa° ne deð na wifman,°   *she should|as|does no woman*
mid æie vnimete°   halden° luue swete.°   *fear immense|hold|sweet*
Ah ȝif° þu luuest Ygærne   þu sculdest hit halden° derne,   *but if|keep*
¹¹⁰ and senden° hire sone°   of seoluere° and of golde,   *send|soon|silver*
and luuien° hire mid liste°   and mid leofliche bihæste.°   *love|guile|dear promises*
Þa ȝet hit weore° a wene°   whar° þu heo mihtes aȝe,°   *would be|doubt|whether|her might possess*

for Ygærne is wel idon,°   a swiðe treowe wimmon;°   *chaste|true woman*
swa wes hire moder°   and ma° of þan kunne.°   *mother|more|her kin*
¹¹⁵ To soðe° ich þe suggen,   leofest alre° kinge,°   *truly|of all|kings*
þat oðere weies° þu most agunnen°   ȝif þu hire wult°   *otherwise|must begin|wish to|win*
awinnen.°
For ȝurstendæi° me com° to   an æremite° wel idon,°   *yesterday|came|hermit|good*
and swor bi his chinne   þat he wuste° Merlin,   *knew*
whar° he ælche nihte°   resteð vnder lufte,°   *where|each night|(the) sky*
¹²⁰ and ofte he him spæc° wið   and spelles° him talde,°   *spoke|stories|told*

---

91. Ulfin, called Ulfin de Ricaradoch in Geoffrey, appears in Welsh as Ulfin of Caer Caradoc (modern Salisbury).

94. *Pendragun:* "Chief dragon," the title given to British and Welsh chieftains (from the figure on their battle standard) in supreme command of power.

117–86. Wace states this incident in seven lines; Layamon has expanded it in a romantic fashion.

and ʒif we mihte° Merlin   mid liste biwinnen,°   *might/with cunning win*
þenne mihtest þu þine iwille°   allunge° biwinne."   *will/wholly*
Þa wes Vðer Pendragun   þa softer an° his mode,°   *the easier in/mind*
and andsware red.°   "Vlfin, þu hauest wel isæd.°   *answer gave/said*
[125] Ich þe° ʒiue an honde°   þritti solh° of londe,   *you/promise/thirty plows*
þat þu Merlin biwinne   and don° mine iwille."   *do*
Vlfin ʒeond° þat folc wende°   and sohte° al þa uerde,°   *throughout/went/searched/host*
and he vmbe stunde°   þene° æremite funde,°   *in a while/the/found*
and an hiʒinge°   brohte° hine to þan° kinge,   *in haste/brought/the*
[130] and þe king him sette an hond°   seouen sulʒene° lond,   *promised/seven plows (of)*
ʒif he mihte bringen°   Merlin to þan kinge.   *bring*
Þe æremite gon° wende°   in þene west ænde,°   *started to/go/the western parts*
to ane wilderne,°   to ane wude muchele,°   *a wilderness/forest great*
þer° he iwuned hafde°   wel feole wintre,°   *where/lived had/very many winters*
[135] and Merlin swiðe° ofte   þer inne sohte.°   *very/sought*
Sone° þe armite° com in   þa ifunde° he Mærlin,   *as soon as/hermit/then found*
vnder ane treo stonden,°   and sære° him° gon° longen°   *tree standing/greatly/for him/began to/long*

þene æremite he isæh cume,°   alse while wes° his iwune,°   *saw coming/as often was/custom*
he orn° him to-ʒænes,°   beiene heo uæineden þas;°   *ran/toward/both they rejoiced therefore*

[140] heo clupten,° heo custen°   and cuðliche° speken.°   *embraced/kissed/in friendly fashion/spoke*

Þa sæide° Merlin,   muchel wisdom wes mid him,   *said*
"Sæie þu,° mi leofe freond,°   wi° naldest° þu me suggen,°   *say you/dear friend/why/would not/tell*

þurh nanes cunnes° þinge,   þat þu wældest° to þan kinge.   *through no kind (of)/wanted (to go)*

Ah ful ʒare ich hit° wuste,   anan swa° ich þe miste,°   *but very readily I it/as soon as/you missed*

[145] þat þu icumen weore°   to Vðere kinge,   *come were*
and what þe king þe wið spæc   and of his londe° þe bæd,°   *land/offered*
þat þu me sculdest° bringe   to Vðer kinge.   *should*
And Vlfin þe sohte   and to þan kinge brohte,
and Vðer Pendragun   forð rihtes° anan°   *immediately/then*
[150] sette him an honde   þritti solh of londe,
and he sætte þe an honde°   seoue sulhʒene° lond.   *promised you/seven plows (of)*
Vther is of-longed°   æfter° Ygærne þere hende,°   *yearns/for/the fair*
wunder ane swiðe,°   after Gorloises wiue.°   *wonderously much/wife*
Ah longe° is æuere°   þat ne° cummeð° nauere,°   *(as) long (as)/ever/not/will be/never*

---

125. A plow-land was a land measure after the Norman Conquest, based on the quantity that could be tilled by a team of eight oxen in one year.

143. *nanes cunnes þinge:* i.e., "anything at all."
154. *æuere:* i.e., "eternity."

155 þat he heo° biwinne,   bute° þurh mine ginne,°   *her/except/stratagem*
for nis° na wimmon treowere°   in þissere° worlde-riche.°   *(there) is not/no woman truer/this/*
world

And neoðeles° he scal aзe°   þa hende Yзærne;   *yet/shall possess*
on hir° he scal streonen°   þat° scal wide sturien;°   *her/beget/(him) that/rule*
he scal streonien hire° on   ænne swiðe sellichne mon.°   *beget her/a/wondrous man*
160 Longe beoð° æuere   dæd° ne bið° he næuere;°   *is/dead/will be/never*
þe wile þe° þis world stænt°   ilæsten° scal is worðmunt,°   *while/stands/last/his glory*
and scal inne Rome   walden° þa þeines.°   *rule/thanes*
Al him° scal abuзe°   þat wuneð° inne Bruttene;°   *to him/bow/live/Britain*
of him scullen gleomen°   godliche singen,°   *shall minstrels/goodly sing*
165 of° his breosten° scullen æten°   aðele scopes;°   *from/breast/eat (i.e., be nourished)/*
noble poets

scullen of his blode°   beornes beon° drunke;   *blood/knights be*
of his eзene° scullen fleon°   furene gleden;°   *eyes/fly/fiery sparks*
ælc° finger an° his hond°   scarp stelene brond;°   *each/on/hand/(shall be a) sharp*
steel sword

scullen stan° walles   biuoren° him to-fallen;°   *stone/before/fall*
170 beornes scullen rusien,°   reosen heore mærken.°   *fall/sink their banners*
Þus he scal wel longe   liðen зeond londen,°   *travel through (the) lands*
leoden biwinnen,°   and his laзen° sette.   *people conquer/laws*
Þis beoð þa tacnen° of þan sune°   þe° cumeð° of Uðer   *these are the signs/the son/that/*
Pendragune   *shall come*
and of Yзærne.   Þes speche° is ful derne,°   *this speech/secret*
175 for зet næt° hit neoðer°   Yзærne no° Uðer,   *knows not/neither/nor*
þat of Vðere Pendragune   scal arisen swilc° a sune,   *arise such*
for зet he beoð unstreoned,   þa° sturieð° al þa þeoden.°   *that/shall rule/people*
"Ah lauerd,"° quoð° Merlin,   nu° hit is iwille° þin°   *lord/said/now/will/your*
þat forð I scal fusen°   to uerde° þas° kinges;   *depart/host/of the*
180 þi word ich wulle heren°   and nu ich wulle wende,°   *will obey/go*
and faren° ich wulle for þire lufe°   to Vthere Pendragune,   *travel/your love*
and habben þu scalt° þat lond   þat he þe° sette an hond."°   *have you shall/you/promised*
Þus heo þa ispecken;°   þæ æremite gon° to weopen;°   *they then spoke/the hermit began/*
weep

deorliche° he hine custe;°   þer° heo gunnen° dælen.°   *affectionately/him kissed/then/began*
to/part

185 Merlin ferde riht suð;°   þat lond him wæs ful cuð;°   *went straight south/was well known*
forð riht° he fusde°   to þes° kinges ferde.°   *immediately/departed/the/host*
Sone swa° Vðer hine isæh,°   swa° he him to-зeines bæh,°   *as soon as/saw/so/approached*
and þus quað Vðer Pendragune,   "Mærlin, þu ært wilcume.°   *are welcome*
Her ich° sette þe an honde   al þene ræd° of mine londe,°   *here I/the counsel/land*

160–77. Geoffrey of Monmouth prophesies, "In ore populorum celebrabitur, et actus ejus cibus erit narrantibus" ("Arthur will be celebrated among the people and his deeds told far and wide"). Layamon obviously knew of the traditional prophecies of Merlin concerning Arthur.

190 and þat° þu me ræde°   to muchere neode."°   *if|advise|in great need*
Vther him talde°   al þat he walde,°   *told|would*
and hu° Ygærne him wes° on leoden°   wimmonnen° leofest,°   *how|was|earth|of women|dearest*
and Gorlois hire lauerd   monnen° alre° laðest.°   *of men|all|most hateful*
"And buten° ich habbe þinne° ræd   ful raðe° þu isihst° me   *unless|have your|very quickly|see|*
    dæad,°   *dead*
195 for ich lang° so swiþe°   after° Gorloys his wifue."°   *long|greatly|for|wife*
Þa andswerede° Merlin,   "Let nu cume° in Vlfin,   *answered|come*
and bitæc° him an° honde   þritti sulȝene° lond,   *grant|in|thirty plows (of)*
and bi-tæc þan æremite   þat° þu him bihete,°   *what|promised*
for nulle° ich aȝæn na° lond,   neouðer seoluer na° gold,   *not will|own no|neither silver nor*
200 for ich am on rade°   rihchest° alre° monnen,°   *in counsel|richest|of all|men*
and ȝif° ich wilne° æhte°   þenne wursede° ich on crafte.   *if|wished for|possessions|would*
                                                                 worsen

Ah° al þin iwille°   wel scal° iwurðen,°   *but|your will|shall|turn out*
for ich con swulcne leche-craft°   þe leof° þe° scal° iwurðen, *know such magic|pleasant|for you|*
                                                                 (it) shall

þat al scullen° þine gareres°   iwurðen swulc þas eorles,°   *shall|appearance|become like the*
                                                                 earl's
205 þi speche, þi dede°   imong þere duȝeðe,°   *behavior|among the people*
þine hors and þine iwede,°   and al swa þu scalt ride.   *clothes*
Þenne° Ygærne þe scal iseon°   a mode° hire scal° wel beon;° *when|see|in mind (i.e., heart)|her*
                                                                 (it) shall|be

heo lið° inne Tintaieol°   uaste bituned.°   *she lies|Tintagel|fast enclosed*
Nis° nan cniht swa wel iboren°   of nane° londe icoren°   *(there) is not|no knight|born|from*
                                                                 no|chosen

210 þe mid strengðe° of Tintaieol   þe ȝeten mihten un-tunen,° *by force|gates might open*
buten heo weoren ibirsted°   mid° hungere and mid þurste.   *they were burst|with*
Þat is þat sode°   þat ich þe sugge° wulle;   *the truth|tell*
þurh° alle þinge° þu scalt beon   swulc° þu eorl weore,°   *through|things|as if|were*
and ich wulle beon iwil del°   swulc him is° Brutael,   *every bit|like*
215 þat is a cniht swiðe herd;°   he is þeos° eorles stiward.° *very hardy|the|steward*
Jurdan is his bur-cniht;°   he is swiðe wel idiht;°   *knight of the chamber|dressed*
ich wulle makien anan°   Ulfin swulc is° Jurdan.   *make then|like*
Þenne bist° þu lauerd,°   and ich Brutael þi stiward,   *are|lord*
and Ulfin Jurdan þi bur-cniht,   and we scullen faren nu°   *go now|tonight*
    to niht;°
220 faren þu scalt bi ræde   wuder swa° ich þe læde.°   *where|lead*
Scullen nu to nihte   half hundred cnihten
mid speren° and mid scelden°   beon abuten° þine telden,°   *spears|shields|around|tents*
þat nauere° nan quik° mon°   ne cumen° þer aneosten,°   *never|alive|man|not come|near*

---

208. *Tintaieol:* a castle on the north coast of Cornwall, the   Ruins of the castle may still be seen at Tintagel Head.
home of Gorlois and later of King Mark of the Tristram legend.

and ʒif þer auer æi° mon cume   þat his hæued° him° beon   *ever any|head|from him|cut off*
    bi-numen,°

225 for þa° cnihtes scullen suggen,°   selen° þine beornen,°   *the|say|good|men*
þat þu° ært ilete blod°   and restest þe° on bædde."°   *you|let blood (i.e., bled)|yourself|
    bed*

Þas° þingges forð rihte°   þus weoren idihte.°   *these|immediately|arranged*
Forð ferde° þe king,   næs° hit cuð° na þing,°   *went|was not|it known|at all*
and ferden° forð mid him   Vlfin and Merlin;   *went*
230 heo tuʒen riht þen wæi°   þa° in to Tintaieol læi;°   *they proceeded straight (on) the way|
    that|led*

heo comen° to þas castles ʒæte°   and cuðliche° cleopeden,°   *came|gate|in friendly fashion|
    called*

"Vndo þis ʒæt essel;°   þe eorl is icumen° here,   *bolt|come*
Gorlois þe læuerd,°   and Britael his stiward,   *lord*
and Jurdan þe burcniht;   we habbeoð ifaren° al niht."°   *have traveled|night*
235 Þe ʒæteward° hit cudde° ouer al,°   and cnihtes urnen   *gatekeeper|made known|everywhere|
    uppen wal°   ran upon (the) wall*
and speken° wið Gorlois   and hine icneowen° mid iwis.°   *spoke|him knew|indeed*
Þa cnihtes weoren swiðe whæte°   and wefden° up þa castles   *alert|raised*
    ʒæte,
and letten° hine binnen° fare,   þa læsse wes þa heore° care;   *let|within|less was then their*
heo wenden° mid iwisse   to habben muchel blisse.°   *thought|have much joy*
240 Þa hædden° heo mid ginne°   Merlin þer wið inne,   *had|(a) trick*
and heo Vðer þene° king   wið inne heore walding,°   *the|power*
and ledde þer mid him   his gode þein° Ulfin.   *good thane*
Þis tidinde com biliue°   in to þan° wife   *news came quickly|the*
þæt hire° læuerd wes icumen   and mid him his þreo   *her|three men*
    gumen.°
245 Vt° com Yʒærne   forð to þan eorle°   *out|earl*
and þas word seide°   mid wunsume wurde,°   *these words said|pleasant speech*
"Wilcume,° læuerd,   monne me° leofest,°   *welcome|to me|dearest*
and wilcume Jurdan   and Britael is al swa;°   *also*
beo ʒe mid isunde°   to-dæled° from þan kinge?"   *are you in safety|parted*
250 Þa quæð° Vðer ful iwis°   swulc° hit weore Gorlois,   *said|very truly|as if*
"Muchel° þat monkun°   þæt is mid° Vther Pendragun,   *great|multitude|with*
and ich æm° bi nihte   bi-stole° from þan fihte,°   *I am|night stolen|fight*
for æfter þe ic° wes of-longed;°   wilfmonne,° þu ært° me   *for you I|longing|of women|are|
    leofuest.°   dearest*
Buð° in to bure°   and let° mi bed makien,°   *go|chamber|order|made*
255 and ich me wulle ræsten°   to þissere nihte uirste°   *myself will rest|for this night's space*
and alle dai to mærwe°   to blissien mire duʒeðe."°   *tomorrow|gladden my people*

230-42. Wace states simply that Uther was well received by
the enemy, who recognized him as Gorlois.

Ygærne beh° to bure   and lætte° bed him° makien;   *went/ordered/for him*
wes þat kinewurðe° bed   al mid palle° ouer bræd.°   *kingly/noble cloth/covered*
Þe king hit wel° bihedde°   and eode° to his bedde,   *with joy/looked at/went*
260 and Ygærne læi adun°   bi Uðere Pendragun.   *lay down*
Nu wende° Ygærne ful iwis   þat hit weoren° Gorlois;   *now thought/was*
þurh neuere nænes cunnes° þing   no icneou heo° Vðer   *through never no kind (of)/not knew*
      þene king.   *she*
Þe king hire wende° to   swa wapmon sculde° to wimmon°   *turned/as men should/women*
      do
and hæfde him° to done°   wið leofuest wimmonne,°   *had/do/of women*
265 and he streonede° hire on   ænne selcuðne mon,°   *begot/a marvelous man*
kingen° alre kenest°   þæ æuere com to monnen,°   *of kings/all bravest/that ever/men*
and he wes on ærde°   Ærður ihaten.°   *earth/Arthur called*
Nuste noht° Ygærne   wha° læie on° hire ærme,°   *knew not not at all/who/in/arms*
for æuere heo wende ful iwis   þat it weoren þe eorl Gorlois.

The Fairy Gifts to Arthur (vss. 19252–69)

270 Þe time com þe wes icoren,°   þa° wes Arður iboren.°   *came that was chosen/when/born*
Sone swa° he com an eorðe°   aluen hine iuengen;°   *as soon as/on earth/elves him*
                                                              received

heo bigolen° þat child   mid galdere swiðe° stronge;   *they enchanted/with magic very*
heo ȝeuen° him mihte°   to beon bezst° alre° cnihten;°   *gave/might/be best/of all/knights*
heo ȝeuen him an oðer þing,   þat he scolde° beon riche king; *should*
275 heo ȝiuen° him þat þridde,°   þat he scolde longe libben;° *gave/the third/live*
heo ȝifen° him, þat kine-bern,°   custen° swiðe gode,°   *gave/king's son/virtues/good*
þat° he wes mete-custi°   of alle quikemonnen;°   *so that/most generous/men alive*
þis þe alue° him ȝef,°   and al swa° þat child iþæh.°   *elves/gave/thus/thrived*

The Plot against Uther Pendragon (vss. 19634–805)

Nu sæiden Saxisce° men   in heore som runen,°   *now said Saxon/their common*
                                                              council
280 "Nime° we six cnihtes,°   wise men and wihte,°   *take/knights/brave*
and hæweres witere,°   and senden° we to hirede;°   *spies clever/send/court*
læten heom uorð liðen°   an° almes monnes° wisen,°   *let them forth travel/in/beggars'/*
                                                              guise
and wunien an° hirede   mid° heȝe þan° kinge,   *dwell at/with/the high*
and æuer ælche dæie°   þurh-gon° al þa duȝeðe,°   *ever each day/pass through/the crowd*

270–78. This section is missing completely in Wace. The elves here are quite similar to the *Märchen-feen* in such a tale as that of Dornröschen (Sleeping Beauty) and may be traced to Norse mythology, where the Norns often attended the birth of a child. *Aluen* (l. 271) is cognate with the Nibelungen dwarf-king Alberich and the Shakespearean Oberon.

285 and gan° to þas° kinges dale°   swulc° heo weoren vn-hale,° *go/the/dole/as if/they were infirm*
    and imong þan wracchen°   harcnien ȝeorne,° *among the poor/listen carefully*
    ȝif mon mihte° mid crafte,   a° dæi oðer° a nihte,° *if one might/by/or/night*
    inne Winchæstres tun°   cumen° to Vðer Pendragun, *Winchester town/come*
    and mid morð-spelle°   þene° king aquellen;° *murder/the/kill*
290 þenne weoren° heore iwil°   allunge iwurðen;° *would be/will/wholly done*
    þenne weoren heo care-læse°   of Costantines cunne."° *careless/Constantine's kin*
    Nu wenden° forð þa cnihtes   al bi dæies lihten,° *traveled/daylight*
    on ælmes monnes° claðes,°   cnihtes forcuðest,° *beggars'/clothes/most wicked*
    to þas kinges hirede,   þer° heo hærm wrohten.° *where/harm wrought*
295 Heo eoden° to þære° dale   swulc heo weoren un-hale, *went/the*
    and hærcneden ȝeornen°   of° þas kinges hærme, *listened eagerly/concerning*
    hu me þæne° king mihte   to dæðe idihte.° *how one the/death put*
    Þa imetten° heo enne° cniht,   from þan kinge he com riht;° *then met/a/came straight*
    he wes° Vðeres mæi,°   and monnen° him leofuest.° *was/relation/of men/to him dearest*
300 Þas swiken° þer heo sæten°   on longen° þere streten,° *these traitors/sat/along/the street*
    cleopeden° to þan cnihte   mid cuðliche worden,° *called/friendly words*
    "Lauerd,° we beoð wracche° men   a þissere° weorlde-riche;° *lord/are poor/in this/world*
    while° we weoren on londe°   for gode° men iholden,° *formerly/in (the) land/good/held*
    a þat° Sæxisce men   setten° us a-dune,° *until/set/down*
305 and al bi-ræiueden° us   and ure æhten° binomen° us. *robbed/our possessions/took from*
    Nu we beden° singeð   for Vðer kinge; *beads (i.e., prayers)*
    ælche° dæie on° a mæl°   ure mete° trukeð,° *every/at/meals/meat/is lacking*
    ne cumeð naucre° inne ure disc°   neoþer flæs na° no fisc,° *nor comes never/dish/neither meat nor/fish*

    no nanes cunnes drænc°   buten° water scenc,° *nor no kind (of) drink/except/draught*

310 buten water clæne,°   for þi° we beoð þus lænc."° *clean/therefore/lean*
    Þis iherde° þe cniht;   aȝæn° he eode forð riht,° *heard/again/immediately*
    and com to þan kinge   þer he lai on bure,° *in chamber*
    and seide° to þan kinge,   "Lauerd, beo þu° on sunde,° *said/be you/health*
    her ute° sitteð six men   iliche° on heouwen;° *here outside/alike/appearance*
315 alle heo beoð iferen°   iscrudde mid° heren.° *are companions/dressed in/hair shirts*

    While heo weoren   a þissere worlde-richen
    god-fulle þeines°   mid goden° afcolled;° *worthy thanes/goods/well provided*

---

285. The king's dole was a daily custom of giving food to beggars. Most monasteries observed a similar practice.

288. Winchester was the old capital of England, where Alfred the Great held his permanent court. Since Uther was a British (i.e., Celtic) king, before the Saxon victory, there is an obvious anachronism here: Arthur, if he had any historical validity, would have been a Celtic chieftain who won one of the few victories against the Saxons at Mount Badon.

291. Constantine II (according to Geoffrey of Monmouth) was brother of Aldroenus, king of Brittany. The archbishop of London requested his coming to Britain with two thousand men, and he was chosen king. He had three sons: Constans, Aurelius Ambrosius, and Uther Pendragon. Constantine was killed by an unknown Pict. Oddly, the chroniclers Gildas (*De Excidio et Conquestu Britanniae*, c. 540) and Bede name a Roman, or Romanized Celtic leader, Ambrosius Aurelianus, as the victor at Mount Badon over the Saxons.

312. Uther is seriously ill at Saint Albans.

nu habbeoð° Sæxisce men	isæt hom° to grunden,°	*have/put them/ground*
þat° heo beoð on weorlde°	for wracchen ihalden;°	*so that/world/beggars held*
320 no raccheoð° heo to borde°	buten bræd ane,°	*nothing have/at table/but bread alone*
no to heore **drencches**°	bute° water scenches.°	*for their drinks/but/draughts*
Þus heo leodeð° heore lif°	inne þire leode,°	*lead/life/among your people*
and heore beoden biddeð°	þat Godd þe lete° longe libben."°	*beads pray/you let/live*
Þa quað° Vðer þe king,	"Let heom° cumen hider° in;	*said/them/here*
325 ich° heom wulle scruden°	and ich heom wulle ueden,°	*I/will clothe/feed*
for mines drihtenes lufe,°	þa wille þa° ich liuie."°	*my Lord's love/while/live*
Comen° into bure,	beornes° þa swikele;°	*(they) came/men/the treacherous*
þe king heo lette feden,°	þæ° king heom lette scruden,°	*them ordered fed/the/clothed*
and nihtes° hom læiden°	ælc° on his bedde,	*at night/home lay/each*
330 and ælc on his halue°	heoʒede ʒeorne°	*part/spied eagerly*
hu heo mihten þene° king	mid morðe aquellen;°	*they might the/with murder kill*
ah ne° mihten heo þurh naþing°	aquellen Vðer þene king,	*but not/nothing*
ne° þurh nane° crafte	cumen° to him ne mahten.°	*nor/no/come/might*
Þa iwærð hit° in ane° time	þe ræin him gon rine;°	*happened it/one/rain it did rain*
335 þa cleopede þer a læche°	þer° he læi° on bure	*physician/where/lay*
to ane° bur-cnihte°	and hahte hine° forð rihtes°	*a/knight of the chamber/ordered him/immediately*
irne° to þere welle	þe° wes on væst° þere halle	*to run/that/near*
and setten þere ænne ohte swain°	to biwiten heo wið° ræin.	*a good man/protect it from*
For þe king ne mai on duʒeðe°	bruken° nanes drenches,	*profitably/enjoy*
340 buten cald° welles stræm,°	þat him° is iqueme,°	*cold/water/to him/pleasant*
þat is to° his ufele°	aðelest° alre° drencche.°	*for/sickness/best/of all/drinks*
Þas speche uorð rihtes°	iherden þas° six cnihtes;°	*this speech/immediately/heard the/knights*
to° harme heo weoren wiþte,°	and ut wenden° bi-nihte°	*for/were prompt/out went/at night*
forð to þere° welle,	þer ho° hærm wrohten.°	*the/they/wrought*
345 Vt heo droʒen sone°	amppullen scone,°	*drew quickly/phials fair*
ifulled° mid attere,°	weten° alre° bitterest;	*filled/poison/of liquids/all*
six amppullen fulle	heo ʒeoten i þan° welle;	*threw in the*
þa wes° þa welle anan°	al mid attre bi-gon.°	*then was/immediately/poison infected*
Þa weoren ful bliðe°	þæ swiken on heore liue,°	*very happy/life*
350 and forð heo iwenden,°	ne dursten° heo þer bilæfen.°	*went/not dared/remain*
Þa comen þer forð rihtes	tweien° but-cnihtes;	*two*
heo beren on° heore honde°	twæie bollen° of golde.	*carried in/hands/two bowls*

---

318. *to grunden :* i.e., "down."

320. Boards were temporary tables set on trestles, rather than the permanent "tables dormant" used by Chaucer's Franklin. The bread referred to here is probably the "trencher bread," a flat, round loaf which served as a plate on which were heaped meat and gravy. The trencher bread left over from feasts in the hall was usually given to beggars at the gate. Since it was soaked with meat juices, it was undoubtedly most nutritious and palatable.

Heo comen to þare° welle   and heore bollen feolde;°   *the/filled*

aȝæin° heo gunnen wende°   to Vðer þan kinge;   *again/did return*

355 forð in to þan bure   þer he læi on bedde.

"Hail seo þu,° Vðer;   nu° we beoð icumen her,°   *be you/now/are come here*

and we habbeoð° þe ibroht°   þat° þu ær° bedde,°   *have/brought/what/before/asked for*

cæld° welle water;   bruc° hit on wunne."°   *cold/receive/joy*

Vp aras° þe seocke° king   and sat on his bedde;   *arose/sick*

360 of þan watere he dronc,°   and sone° he gon° sweten;°   *drank/soon/began to/sweat*

his heorte gon° to wakien;°   his neb bigon° to blakien,°   *heart began/weaken/face began/ became pale*

his wombe° gon to swellen;°   þe king gon to swelten.°   *stomach/swell/die*

Næs° þer nan° oðer ræd;°   þer wes Vðer king dæd;°   *was not/no/counsel/dead*

alle heo iwurðen dede°   þat drunken° of þan watere.   *were dead/drank*

Arthur Battles the Forces of Colgrim (vss. 20046–189)

365 Þer liðen to-somne°   alle Scotleode.°   *came together/Scottish people*

Peohtes° and Sæxes°   siȝen heom° to-gæderes,°   *Picts/Saxons/merged/together*

and moniennes cunnes° men   uuleden° Colgrimen.   *many kinds (of)/followed*

Forð he gon° fusen°   mid vnimete verde°   *began to/travel/with (a) huge host*

to-ȝaines° Arðure,   aðelest° kingen;°   *against/noblest/of kings*

370 he þohte° to quellen°   þe king on° his þeoden,°   *thought/kill/in/land*

and his folc ualden,°   uolden° to grunden,°   *cut down/felled/ground*

and setten° al þis kine-lond°   an° his aȝere hond,°   *set/kingdom/in/own hand*

and fallen° to þan grunde°   Arður þene ȝunge.°   *fell/the ground/the young*

Forð wende° Colgrim,   and his ferde° mid him,   *went/army*

375 and wende mid his ferde   þat° he com° to anc° watere;   *until/came/a*

þat water is ihaten° Duglas;°   duȝeðen hit aquelle.°   *called/Douglas/people it destroyed*

Þer com Arður him aȝein,°   ȝaru° mid his ferde;   *toward/ready*

in ane brade° forde   þa ferden° heom° imetten,°   *broad/the armies/each other/met*

fastliche on-sloȝen°   snelle° heore kempen;°   *vigorously hewed/brave/their champions*

380 feollen° þa uæie,°   uolden° to grunde;   *fell/fated/felled*

þer wes muchel blod gute;°   balu° þer wes riue;°   *was much blood shed/woe/abounding*

brustlede scæftes;°   beornes° þer ueollen.°   *splintered (were) shafts/men/fell*

---

364. Uther was poisoned at Saint Albans, and a hundred of his men with him, according to Geoffrey of Monmouth.

367. In Geoffrey of Monmouth (who calls him Colgrin) Colgrim is a Saxon who came from Germany and conquered the northern part of Britain from the Humber to Caithness. After the death of Octa and Eosa, Colgrim was the leader of the Saxons.

376. The river Douglas is near Wigan, in Lancashire.

377–429. The battle description is very reminiscent of the Anglo-Saxon poems *The Battle of Maldon* and *The Battle of Brunanburg*. The *uæie*, "fated ones" (l. 380), recall the OE *fæge*, whose death is controlled by *wyrd* (cf. Mod. Eng. *weird*; see also below, p. 954, l. 385*n*). The atmosphere is more pagan than Christian—typical, of course, of war descriptions in general.

379. *kempen:* Cf. 1, 608*n*.

Þat isæh° Arður;   on mode him° wes unneðe.°   *saw/mind he/uneasy*
Arður hine biðohte°   whæt° he don mahte,°   *considered/what/do might*
385 and thehte hine° a bacward°   in enne uald° brade.   *withdrew/backward/a plain*
Þa wenden° his feond°   þat he flæn walde;°   *thought/enemy/flee would*
þa wes glad Colgrim   and al his ferde mid him;
Heo° wende þat Arður   mid arhredðe° weore afallæd° þere,   *they/fear/had retreated*
and tuȝen° ouer þat water   alse° heo wode weoren.°   *rushed/as if/mad were*
390 Þa° Arður þat isah,°   þat Colgrim him° wes swa neh°   *when/saw/to him/so near*
and heo weoren beien°   bihalues° þan wateren,°   *both/on the same side of/water*
þus seide° Arður,   aðelest kingen,   *said*
"Iseo ȝe,° mine Bruttes,°   here us bihalfues°   *see you/Britons/beside*
ure iuan uulle,°   Crist heom aualle,°   *our foe foul/them destroy*
395 Colgrim þene stronge,   ut° of Sæx-londe.°   *out/(the) land of the Saxons*
His cun i° þisse londe°   ure ælderne aqualden;°   *kin in/land/forefathers killed*
ah nu° is þe dæi icumen°   þe drihten haueð idemed,°   *but now/day come/that (the) Lord has appointed*

þat he scal° þat° lif leosen°   and leosien° his freonden,°   *shall/(i.e., his)/life lose/lose/ friends*

oðer° we sculle dæde beon;°   ne muȝe° we hine quic iseon;°   *or/shall dead be/not must/him alive see*

400 scullen Sæxisce° men   sorȝen ibiden,°   *shall Saxon/sorrow have*
and we wreken wurhliche°   ure wine-maies."°   *avenge worthily/kinsmen*
Vp bræid°Arður his sceld°   foren to° his breosten,°   *raised/shield/before/breast*
and he gon° to rusien,°   swa° þe runie° wulf,   *began/rush/as/howling*
þenne° he cumeð of holte°   bi-honged° mid snawe,°   *when/comes from (the) wood/ covered/snow*
405 and þencheð° to biten   swulc deor° swa him likeð.   *thinks/such animals*
Arður þa cleopede°   to leofe° his cnihten,°   *then called/dear/knights*
"Forð° we biliue,°   þeines ohte,°   *forward (go)/quickly/thanes good*
alle somed° heom to;   alle we sculleð wel don."   *together*
And heo uorð hælden°   swa þe hæȝe wude,°   *forth rushed/high forest*
410 þenne wind wode°   weieð hine mid mæine.°   *fierce/heaves it with might*
Fluȝen° ouer þe woldes°   þritti þusend° sceldes,   *flew/fields/thirty thousand*
and smiten a° Colgrimes cnihtes   þat° þa eorðe aȝæn quehte;°   *smote on/so that/earth again shook*
breken braden speren,°   brustleden° sceldes;   *broken (were) broad spears/splin- tered (were)*

feollen Sæxisce men,   folden° to grunden.°   *felled/ground*
415 Þat isah Colgrim;   þer uore° wa° wes him,   *therefore/woe*
þe alre° hendeste mon°   þe ut of Sexlonde° com.°   *of all/fairest man/(the) land of the Saxons/came*

Colgrim gon° to flænne°   feondliche swiðe,°   *began/flee/very quickly*

393–401. Arthur's hortatory speech is standard in Old English   is the poetic description of Arthur's "rush."
epic poetry; cf. *Maldon*. This passage is unique to Layamon, as

and his hors hine bar° mid hæhзere° strengðe	*carried/great*
ouer þat water deope° and scelde° hine wið dæðe.°	*deep/saved/from death*
420 Saxes° gunnen sinken;° sorзe° heom wes зiueðe.°	*Saxons/started to sink/sorrow/ given*
Arður wende° his speres ord° and for-stod° heom þene uord;°	*turned/point/hindered/(from) the ford*
þer adruncke Sexes° fulle seoue° þusend.	*drowned Saxons/fully seven*
Summe° heo gunnen wondrien,° swa doð° þe wilde cron°	*some/wander/does/crane*
i þan moruenne,° þenne his floc° is awemmed,°	*in the moor/flight/impaired*
425 and him haldeð after° hauekes° swifte;	*pursue/hawks*
hundes° in þan reode° mid reouðe° hine imeted;°	*hounds/reeds/mischief/meet*
þenne nis° him neouðer god,° no þat lond no° þat flod;°	*is not/neither (any) good/not the land nor/water*
hauekes hine smiteð;° hundes hine biteð;	*tear*
þenne bið° þe kinewurðe foзel° fæie on° his siðe.°	*is/royal bird/fated in/time*
430 Colgrim ouer feldes° flæh him° biliues,°	*fields/fled/quickly*
þat° he com to Eouerwic,° riden swiðe sellic;°	*until/York/riding very strenuously*
he wenden° into burзe° and faste heo biclusde;°	*went/town/it enclosed*
hafuede° he binnen° ten þusend monnen,°	*had/within/men*
burh-men mid þa bezste,° þe him bihalues° weoren.°	*townsmen of the best/on his side/were*
435 Arður halde after° mid þritti þusend cnihten,	*pursued*
and ferde riht° to Eouerwic mid folke swiðe sellic.°	*went straight/numerous*

Arthur Describes Childric (vss. 20825–98)

Þa loh° Arður ludere stefene,°	*then laughed/(with a) loud voice*
"Iþonked wurðe drihtene,° þe° alle domes waldeð,°	*thanked be God/that/judgments governs*
þat Childric þe stronge is sad° of mine londe.°	*tired/land*
440 Mi lond he hafeð° to-dæled° al his duзeðe-cnihtes;°	*has/divided among/retainers*
me seoluen° he þohte° driuen° ut° of mire leoden;°	*myself/thought/to drive/out/my country*
halden° me for hæne,° and habben° mine riche°	*(he) holds/base/has/kingdom*
and mi cun° al for-uaren,° mi uole° al fordemed.°	*kin/destroyed/folk/put to death*
Ah° of him bið iwurðen° swa bið° of þan voxe,°	*but/(it) has turned out/as (it) is/the fox*
445 þenne he bið baldest° ufen an° þan walde,°	*when/boldest/over/field*
and hafeð his fulle ploзe° and fuзeles inoзe;°	*play/fowl enough*

---

431. Eoforwicceastre was the Old English name for York, where Colgrim sought refuge and was besieged by Arthur.

439. Childric (Cheldric in Geoffrey of Monmouth and Wace) may have been the Cerdic of the Anglo-Saxon chronicles. Bringing troops from Germany to help Colgrim and his brother Baldulf, he landed with six hundred ships at Albany and harried the country.

444–59. Madden believes this description of a fox hunt to be one of the earliest in literature, along with those of *The Owl and the Nightingale* and *Sir Gawain and the Green Knight*.

for wildscipe° climbið and cluden° iseched°	*wildness/rocky cliffs/seeks*
i° þan wilderne;° holȝes him wurcheð;°	*in/wilderness/holes he digs*
faren° wha swa auere° fare,° naued° he næuere nænne° kare;	*come/whoever/(may) come/has not/ never no*
450 he weneð° to beon of duȝeðe° baldest alre° deoren.°	*thinks/be in might/of all/animals*
þenne siȝeð° him to segges° vnder beorȝen,°	*come/hunters/hills*
mid hornen,° mid hunden,° mid haȝere stefenen;°	*with horns/hounds/loud voices*
hunten þar talieð,° hundes þer galieð;°	*huntsmen there halloo/yelp*
þene° vox driueð ȝeond° dales and ȝeond dunes;°	*the/through/hills*
455 he ulih° to þan holme° and his hol iseched;	*flees/hill*
i þan uirste ænde° i þan holle wendeð;°	*furthest end/hole (he) turns*
þenne is þe balde uox° blissen° al bideled,°	*fox/of bliss/deprived*
and mon° him to-delueð° on ælchere heluen;°	*men/dig out/each side*
þenne beoð° þer forcuðest° deoren° alre pruttest.°	*will be/most wretched/of animals/all proudest*
460 Swa wes° Childriche, þan strongen° and þan riche;	*so was/strong*
he þohten° al mi kinelond° setten° an his aȝere hond,°	*thought/kingdom/to set/own hand*
ah nu ich habbe hine idriuen° to þan bare dæðe,°	*now I have him driven/death*
whæðer swa° ich wulle don,° oðer slæn oðer ahon.°	*whatsoever/will do/either slay or hang*
Nu ich wulle ȝifen° him grið° and leten° hine me secken° wið;	*give/peace/let/speak*
465 nulle° ich hine slæ no° ahon, ah his bode° ich wulle fon;°	*will not/slay nor/prayer/receive*
ȝisles° ich wulle habben° of hæxten° his monnen,°	*hostages/have/highest/men*
hors and heore wepnen,° ær heo heonne wenden;°	*their weapons/before they hence go*
and swa heo scullen wræcchen° to heoren scipen liðen,°	*shall (as) wretches/their ships turn*
sæilien° ouer sæ° to sele° heore londe;	*sail/sea/good*
470 and þer wirðliche° wunien on° riche,	*worthily/live in*
and tellen tidende° of Arðure kinge,	*tell news*
hu° ich heom° habbe ifreoied,° for mines fader saule,°	*how/them/freed/my father's soul*
and for mine freo-dome° ifrouered þa° wræcchen."	*freedom/solaced the*

The Return and Ravages of Childric (vss. 20955–21011)

Sone swa° heo a lond comen,° þat folc° heo asloȝen;°	*as soon as/they to land came/folk/ slew*
475 þa cheorles° heo uloȝen;° þa tileden° þa corðen;	*the men/drove off/that tilled/land*
heo hengen° þa cnihtes° þa biwusten° þa londes,	*hanged/knights/defended*
alle þa gode° wiues heo stikeden mid cnifes;°	*good/stabbed with knives*
alle þa maidene° heo mid morðe aqualden;°	*maidens/murder killed*
and þaie ilærede° men heo læiden° on gleden.°	*the learned/laid/fire*

474–501. The fierce description of Childric's ravages is   479. *ilærede men:* i.e., "clerks."
Layamon's own. The English poet had a gift for, and perhaps
pleasure in, frightening and realistic details.

480 Alle þa heorede-cnauen°   mid clibben° heo a-qualden;   *hired men|clubs*
heo velledden° þa castles;   þat lond heo a-wæsten;°   *destroyed|laid waste*
þa chirechen° heo for-barnden;°   baluw wes on° folke;   *churches|burned down|woe was among*

þa sukende° children   heo adrenten° inne wateren.°   *suckling|drowned|(the) water*
Þat orf° þat heo nomen°   al heo sloʒen;°   *the cattle|took|slaughtered*
485 to heore° inne ladden°   and suden° and bradden;°   *their|inns led| boiled|roasted*
al heo hit° nomen   þat heo neh° comen.   *it|near*
Alle dæi° heo sungen°   of Arðure þan° kinge,   *day|sang|the*
and sæiden° þat heo haueden°   hames biwunnen,°   *said|had|homes won*
þæ scolden heom i-halden°   in heore onwalden;°   *that (they) should them hold|power*
490 and þer heo wolden wunien°   wintres and sumeres.°   *would dwell|summers*
And ʒif° Arður weoren swa kene°   þat he cumen wolde°   *if|were so bold|come would*
to fihten° wið Childrichen,°   þan strongen° and þan richen,°   *fight|Childric|strong|rich*
heo wolden of his rugge°   makien ane brugge,°   *back|make a bridge*
and nimen° þa ban° alle   of aðele° þan kinge,   *take|bones|noble*
495 and teien° heom to-gaderc°   mid guldene teʒen,°   *tie|together|golden lies*
and leggen i þare° halle-dure,°   þer æch mon sculde uorð faren,°   *lay (them) in the|hall door|where each man should forth go*
to wurðscipe° Childrich,   þan strongen and þan riche.   *honor*
Þis wes al heore gome,°   for Arðures kinges° sceome,°   *game|King Arthur's|shame*
ah° al hit iwarð° on oðer°   sone° þer after;   *but|turned out|otherwise|soon*
500 heore ʒelp° and heore gome   ilomp° heom seoluen° to scame;°   *boast|turned|themselves|shame*
and swa deð° wel iwære°   þe mon þe° swa ibereð.°   *does|everywhere|that|acts*

The Battle of Bath (vss. 21291–422)

Þa isæh° Arður,   aðelest° kingen,°   *when saw|noblest|of kings*
whar° Colgrim at-stod°   and æc stal wrohte,°   *where|stood fast|again (a) stand made*

þa clupede° þe king,   kenliche lude,°   *then called|keenly loud*
505 "Balde° mine þeines,°   buhʒeð° to þan hulles.°   *bold|thanes|move|the hills*
For ʒerstendæi wes° Colgrim   monnen° alre kennest;°   *yesterday was|of men|all boldest*
nu him° is al swa þere gat,°   þer° he þene hul wat;°   *now he|as the goat|where|the guards*
hæh uppen° hulle   fehteð mid hornen,°   *high upon|(he) fights with horns*
þenne° comeð þe wlf° wilde   touward hire winden.°   *when|wolf|him approaching*
510 Þeh° þe wulf beon ane,°   buten ælc imane,°   *though|be alone|without any herd*
and þer weoren° in ane loken°   fif° hundred gaten,°   *were|a fold|five|goats*

502–67. The battle of Bath, identified wrongly by some critics as the famous Celtic victory over the Saxons at Mount Badon in Berkshire, occurred, according to Madden, at Lansdownhill near Bath, c. 520. Colgrim, Baldulf, and Childric attacked Arthur; the first two were killed, but Childric escaped, to be slain later by Duke Cador of Cornwall on the Isle of Thanet. Arthur's speech, ll. 505–30, is original with Layamon.

þe wulf heom° to iwiteð°   and alle heom abiteð.°   *them/goes/bites*
Swa ich wulle° nu to dæi°   Colgrim al fordemen;°   *so I will/today/destroy*
ich am wulf and he is gat;   þe gume scal° beon fæie.'"°   *man shall/fated*
515 Þa ȝet cleopede° Arður,   aðelest kingen,   *called*
"Ȝurstendæi wes Baldulf   cnihten° alre baldest;   *of knights*
nu he stant° on hulle   and Auene bi-haldeð,°   *stands/Avon beholds*
hu ligeð i° þan stræme°   stelene fisces;°   *how lie in/stream/steel fishes*
mid sweorde bi-georede°   heore sund° is awemmed;°   *sword armed/their health/ destroyed*

520 heore scalen wleoteð°   swulc gold-faȝe sceldes;°   *scales float/like gold-tinted shields*
þer fleoteð° heore spiten°   swulc° hit spæren° weoren.   *float/fins/as if/it spears*
Þis beoð seolcuðe° þing   isiȝen° to þissen londe,°   *is (a) marvelous/come/this land*
swulche deor an° hulle,   swulche fisces in walle.°   *such animals on/stream*
Ȝurstendæi wes þe kaisere°   kennest alre° kingen;   *emperor/of all*
525 nu he is bicumen hunte,°   and hornes him fulieð;°   *become (a) hunter/follow*
flihð° ouer bradne wæld,°   beorkeð° his hundes;°   *flies/broad field/bark/hounds*
he hafeð bihalues Baðen°   his huntinge bilæfued;° it   *has beside Bath/deserted*
freom° his deore° he flieð,°   and we hit scullen° fallen,°   *from/deer/flees/shall/cut down*
and his balde ibeot°   to nohte ibringen,°   *boast/naught bring*
530 and swa we scullen brukien°   rihte bi-ȝæten."°   *enjoy/(our) rights gained*
Efne þan worde°   þa þe king seide,°   *even (with) these words/that/said*
he bræid hæȝe° his sceld   forn to° his breosten;°   *raised high/before/breast*
he igrap his spere° longe;   his hors he gon° spurie.°   *grasped/spear/began to/spur*
Neh° al swa° swiðe°   swa° þe fuȝel fliȝeð°   *nearly/as/swift/as/bird flies*
535 fuleden° þan kinge   fif° and twenti þusend°   *followed/five/thousand*
whitere monnen,°   wode° under wepnen,°   *brave men/fierce/arms*
hælden° to hulle   mid hæhȝere° strengðe,   *rushed/great*
and uppen Colgrime smiten,°   mid swiðe smærte biten.°   *smote/very smart blows*
And Colgrim heom þer hente°   and feolde þa Bruttes° to grunde;°   *received/felled the Britons/ground*
540 i þan uormeste ræse°   fulle° fif hundred.   *first rush/fell*
Þat isæh Arður,   aðelest kingen,
and wrað him iwræðed°   wunder ane swiðe,°   *was angered/wondrously much*
and þus cleopien° a-gon,°   Arður þe hæhȝe° man,   *to cry/began/great*
"War beo ȝe,° Bruttes,   balde mine beornes?°   *where are you/men*
545 Her stondeð° us biuoren°   vre ifan° alle icoren;°   *here stand/before/our foes/chosen*
gumen° mine gode,°   legge we° heom° to grunde."   *men/good/let us lay/them*
Arður igrap his sweord riht,°   and he smat ænne Sexise cniht,°   *rightly/smote a Saxon knight*
þat° þat sweord þat wes° swa god°   æt þan toþen at-stod,°   *so that/was/good/at the teeth stopped*

---

514. *fæie*: Cf. above, ll. 377–429n and below, p. 954, l. 385n.

517. The Avon here is the river flowing through Bath and Bristol into the Bristol Channel, not to be confused with the Avon River of Shakespeare fame, flowing into the Severn.

524. Childric never had the title of *kaiser* (Latin *caesar*, German *Kaiser*) or "emperor"; Layamon probably means "chieftain" or "leader."

and he smat enne oðer,°   þat wes þas° cnihtes broðer,   *another/the*
550 þat his halm° and his hæfd°   halden° to grunde;   *helmet/head/fell*
þene þridde dunt° he sone ȝaf°   and enne° cniht atwa° clæf.°   *the third blow/quickly gave/a/in two/clove*

Þa weoren° Bruttes   swiðe ibalded,°   *then were/greatly emboldened*
and leiden o° þan Sæxen°   læȝen° swiðe stronge,   *laid on/Saxons/laws*
mid° heore speren° longe   and mid sweoreden° swiðe stronge.   *with/spears/swords*
555 Sexes° þer uullen°   and fæie-sih° makeden,°   *Saxons/fell/fated journey/made*
bi hundred bi° hundred   hælden to þan grunde,   *(and) by*
bi þusund° and bi þusend   þer feollen æuere in° þene grund.   *thousand/fell ever on*
Þa iseh° Colgrim   wær° Arður com° touward him,   *when saw/where/came*
ne mihte° Colgrim for° þan wæle°   fleon a nare° side;   *not might/because of/slaughter/flee on no*

560 þer fæht° Baldulf   bi-siden° his broðer.   *fought/beside*
Þa cleopede° Arður   ludere stefne,°   *called/(in a) loud voice*
"Her ich cume,° Colgrim,   to cuððen° wit° scullen ræchen;°   *I come/(a) land/we two/grasp*
nu° wit scullen þis lond dalen°   swa þe° bið° alre laððest."°   *now/land share/to you/will be/most unpleasant*

Æfne° þan worde   þa þe king sæide,°   *even/said*
565 his brode swærd° he up ahof°   and hærdliche adun sloh,°   *broad sword/raised/strongly down cut*

and smat Colgrimes hælm°   þat he amidde° to-clæf,°   *helmet/in the middle/split*
and þere° buren° hod°   þat hit° at þe breoste° at-stod.   *the/chain-mail/hood/it/breast*

The Founding of the Round Table (vss. 22719–986)

Her mon mai arcdc°   of Arðure þan° king,   *here one may tell/the*
hu° he twelf ȝere°   seoðen wuneden° here,   *how/twelve years/afterwards lived*
570 inne griðe° and inne friðe,°   in alle uæȝernesse.°   *peace/prosperity/fairness*
Na° man him ne faht° wið,   no° he ne makede° nan un-frið;°   *no/not fought/nor/made no strife*
ne mihte nauere° nan man   bi-þenchen° of blissen,°   *might never/think/joys*
þat weoren° in ai þeode,°   mare° þan i° þisse;   *were/any land/more/in*
ne mihte nauere mon cunne°   nan swa muchel wunne°   *know/none so much joy*
575 swa wes mid° Arður   and mid his folke here.   *as was with*
Ich° mai sugge° hu hit iwarð,°   wunder þæh° hit þunche.°   *I/say/it happened/wondrous though/seem*

---

555. *fæie-sih:* "fated journey," a kenning for "death." The old English poetic tradition is pervasive in the *Brut*.

562. *wit:* OE nominative of the 1st person dual = we two.

568–701. The story of the Round Table is one of the most important of Layamon's additions to Wace and Geoffrey of Monmouth. Wace mentions very briefly that Arthur created "la Runde Table," at which all sat as equals. The story behind this short statement is perhaps one of the tales "dunt Bretun dient meint fable" ("of which the Bretons tell many a fable"), which circulated in popular tradition in the 12th century and were known by Layamon.

Hit wes in ane° ȝeol-dæie°   þat Arður in Lundene° lai;   *on a/Yule Day/London*
þa° weoren him to i-cumen°   of° alle his kinerichen,°   *then/come/from/kingdom*
of Brutlonde,° of Scotlonde,   of Irlonde, of Islonde,°   *Britain/Iceland*
580 and of al þan londe°   þe° Arður hæfede an honde,°   *lands/that/controlled*
alle þa hæxte þeines,°   mid horsen° and mid sweiens.°   *the highest thanes/horses/men*
Þer weoren seouen knigene sunes°   mid seouen hundred   *seven kings' sons/knights*
    cnihten° icumen,
wið uten° þan hired°   þe herede° Arðure.   *besides/retainers/belonged to*
Ælc hafede an heorte°   leches heȝe;°   *each had in heart/thoughts proud*
585 and lette° þat he weore°   betere° þan his iuere.°   *believed/was/better/companions*
Þat folc° wes of feole° londe;   þer wes muchel onde,°   *folk/many/envy*
for þe an hine talde hæh,°   þe oðer muche herre.°   *one himself felt high/higher*
Þa bleou mon þa bemen°   and þa bordes bradden;°   *blew men the trumpets/tables spread*
water me brohte an uloren,°   mid guldene læflen,°   *men brought on floor/golden bowls*
590 seoððen claðes soften,°   al of white seolke.°   *then cloths soft/silk*
Þa sat Arður adun,°   and bi him Wenhauer° þa quene;   *down/Guinevere*
seoððen sete° þa eorles°   and þer after þa beornes,°   *sat/earls/barons*
seoððen þa cnihtes,°   al swa° mon heom dihte.°   *knights/as/them directed*
Þa heȝe iborne°   *people* þene mete beoren,°   *highborn/the food carried*
595 æfne° forð rihten°   þa to þan cnihten,   *ever/forthright*
þa touward þan þæinen,°   þa touward þan sweinen,°   *thanes/young men*
þa touward þan bermonnen,°   forð at þan borden.°   *porters/tables*
Þa duȝeðe wærð iwraðð;°   duntes° þer weoren riue;°   *company became angry/blows/rife*
ærest° þa laues heo weorpen°   þa while þa° heo ilæsten,°   *first/loaves they threw/while/lasted*
600 and þa bollen seoluerne°   mid wine iuulled,°   *bowls silver/filled*
and seoððen þa uustes°   uusden° to sweoren.°   *fists/went/necks*
Þa leop° þer forð a ȝung mon°   þe ut° of Winet-londe com,°   *leaped/young man/out/came*
he wes iȝefen° Arðure   to halden to ȝisle,°   *given/hold as hostage*
he wes Rumarettes sune,   þas° kinges of Winette.   *the*
605 Þus seide° þe cniht þere   to Arðure kinge,   *said*
"Lauerd° Arður, buh raðe°   into þine bure,°   *lord/go quickly/chamber*
and þi quene mid þe,°   and þene mæies cuðe,°   *you/relatives known*

---

577. *ȝeol-dæie:* Yule Day, or Christmas, seems to have been a traditional time in romance and story for an adventure to occur (cf. *Sir Gawain and the Green Knight*). *in Lundene lai:* The verb *lie* normally signifies a stay away from home. Chaucer uses it in the General Prologue to the *Canterbury Tales,* "In Southwerk at the Tabard as I lay," when he describes the evening at the Tabard Inn before the pilgrimage starts. Since Winchester was the traditional capital, Arthur (who in Geoffrey of Monmouth, Wace, and Layamon leads a rather peripatetic existence, rushing from battle to battle and country to country) "lay" in London. The lore of the court at Caerleon and Camelot came from other sources.

591. On Guinevere, see l. 1021n.

592–93. The knights were seated by rank, the highest near Arthur, the lowest "below the salt" at the end, the salt cellar being set in the middle of the table and dividing it.

599. They threw the trencher bread at one another (cf. l. 320n).

602. *Winet-londe:* Gwynedd, in northwest Wales.

604. *Rumarettes . . . kings:* i.e., "the son of Rumaret, the King."

and we þis comp scullen to-delen°   wið þas uncuðe
   kempen."°
   Æfne þan worde°   he leop to þan borde,
610 þer leien° þa cniues°   bi-foren° þan leod-kinge;°
þreo cnifes° he igrap°   and mid þan anæ° he smat°
i þere swere° þe cniht   þe ærest bigon° þat ilke fiht,°
þat° his hefued i° þene flor°   hælde° to grunde.°
Sone° he sloh° ænne oðer,°   þes° ilke þeines° broðer;
615 ær° þa sweordes comen,°   seouene he afelde.°
Þer wes fæht swiðe græt;°   ælc mon oðer° smat;
þer wes muchel blod gute;°   balu° wes an hirede.°

Þa° com þe king buȝen°   ut of his buren,°
mid° him an hundred beornen°   mid helmen° and mid
   burnen;°
620 ælc bar° an his riht hond°   whit stelene brond.°

Þa cleopede° Arður,   aðelest° kingen,°
"Sitteð, sitteð swiðe,°   elc° mon bi° his liue,°
and wa swa° þat nulle° don,°   he scal° for-demed° beon.°

Nimeð° me þene ilke mon   þa° þis feht ærst bigon
625 and doð wið/ðe° an his sweore°   and draȝeð hine° to ane
   more,°
and doð hinc in an ley uen;°   þer he scal liggen.°
And nimeð al his nexte cun°   þa ȝe maȝen iuinden,°
and swengeð of þa hafden°   mid breoden° eouwer
   sweorden;°
þa wifmen° þa ȝe maȝen ifinden°   of his nexten cunden,°
630 kerueð° of hire neose°   and heore wlite ga° to lose,°

and swa ich wulle° al fordon°   þat cun þat he of com.
And ȝif° ich auere mare°   seoððen ihere°
þat æi° of mine hirede,°   of heȝe na° of loȝe,°

of° þissen° ilke slehte°   æft sake arere,°

---

fight shall undertake/foreign warriors
even (with) these words/the
where lay/knives/before/land's king
three knives/grasped/one/smote
the neck/began/same fight
so that/head on/floor/fell/ground
quickly/slew/another/the/thane's
before/swords came/killed
was (a) fight very great/another
much blood shed/destruction/among (the) people
then/hurrying/chamber
with/men/helmets/chain mail

carried/right hand/(a) white steel sword
called/noblest/of kings
quickly/each/on/life
whoever/will not/do/shall/put to death/be
take/that
put (a) rope/neck/drag him/a moor

low fen/lie
nearest kin/you may find
cut off the heads/broad/your swords

women/find/nearest kin
carve/their noses/their beauty (let) go/loss
so I will/destroy
if/ever more/after hear
any/retainers/high nor (i.e., or)/low
because of/this/slaughter/again strife raise

---

608. *comp:* The term for the area of combat came to be transferred to the combat itself. Thus from Latin *campus,* "field," originated German *Kampf,* and, by way of Anglo-Norman, English *camp, campaign,* and *encampment.* The Central French pronunciation gave us *champion.* The translation of the Latin word itself into English *field,* German *Feld,* shows similar martial characteristics, as in *field marshal, Feldmarschall, Feldwebel,* for example. *Kempen,* "warriors," has the same etymology as *comp.*

622–37. Arthur's vengeance on those who disturbed his feast has epic savagery. Only with Chrétien de Troyes did the softer influence of romance prevail in the description of Arthur and the Round Table.

635 ne sculde° him neoðer gon fore,°   gold ne na gærsume,°
not should/neither go for (i.e., ransom)/*nor no treasure*

hæh° hors no hære scrud,°   þat he ne sculde beon ded,°
fine/nor war garment (i.e., armor)/*dead*

oðer° mid horsen° to-draȝen;°   þat is elches° swiken laȝen.°
or/horses/drawn apart/of every/traitor (the) *law*

Bringeð þene halidom°   and ich wulle swerien° þer on;
the relics/swear
swa ȝe scullen, cnihtes,°   þe weoren° at þissen fihte,
knights/that were
640 eorles° and beornes,°   þat ȝe hit breken° nulleð.
earls/barons/it break
Ærst sweor Arður,   aðelest kingen,
first swore
seoððen sworen° eorles,   seoððen sweoren° beornes,
then swore/swore
seoððen sweoren þeines,   seoððen sweoren sweines,°
country men
þat heo nauere° mare   þe sake nulde° arere.
they never/would not
645 Me nom° alle þa dede°   and to leirstowe° heom ladden.°
they took/dead/burial place/them carried

Seoððen me bleou bemen°   mid swiðe murie dremen;°
blew trumpets/merry sound
weoren° him° leof° weoren him læð,°   elc þer feng° water and clæð,°
were (it)/*to him/pleasant/unpleasant/received/cloth*
and seoððen adun seten,°   sæhte to borden,°
down sat/reconciled at table
al for Arðure° æiȝe,°   aðelest kingen.
of Arthur/fear
650 Birles° þer þrungen;°   gleomen° þer sungen;°
cupbearers/thronged/minstrels/sang
harpen° gunnen° dremen;°   duȝeðe wes on selen.°
harps/began to/resound/ (the) *host was in joy*

Þus fulle° seoueniht°   wes þan hirede idiht.°
fully/seven nights (i.e., *a week*)/*the company maintained*

Seoððen hit seið° in þere° tale   þe king ferde° to Cornwale;°
says/the/went/Cornwall
þer him com° to anan°   þat wæs° a crafti weorc-man,°
came/then/ (one) *that was/skillful workman*

655 and þene king imette°   and feiere° hine grætte,°
met/courteously/greeted
"Hail seo þu,° Arður,   aðelest kinge.°
be you/of kings
Ich æm þin aȝe mon;°   moni lond° ich habbe° þurh-gan;°
am your own man/many lands/have/traveled through

ich con° of treo-werkes°   wunder feole craftes.°
know/woodwork/wondrous many skills

Ich iherde suggen°   bi-ȝeonde sæ neowe tidende,°
heard tell/beyond (the) *sea new tidings*

660 þat þine cnihtes   at þine borde° gunnen fihte;°
table/fight
a° midewinteres dæi°   moni þer feollen,°
on/day/fell
for heore muchele mode°   morð-gomen wrohten,°
great pride/murder-play wrought
and for heore hehȝe cunne°   ælc° wolde° beon° wið inne.°
high lineage/each/wanted to/be/inside

Ah° ich þe° wulle wurche°   a bord swiðe hende,°
but/you/make/very excellent

---

647. *weoren . . . læð:* i.e., "whether he would or not."

665	þat þer maȝen setten° to sixtene hundred and ma,°	*sit/more*
	al turn abuten,° þat° nan° ne beon wið uten,°	*about/so that/none/outside*
	wið uten and wið inne, mon to-ȝæines° monne.	*facing*
	Whenne þu wult° riden° wið þe þu miht° hit leden,°	*wish to/ride/might/carry*
	and setten° hit whar° þu wulle° after þine iwille,°	*set/where/wish/will*
670	and ne dert° þu nauere adrede° to þere worlde longen°	*need/fear/world's end*
	þat æuere æine modi° cniht at þine borde makie° fiht,	*any proud/(will) make*
	for þer scal° þe hehȝe beon æfne° þan loȝe."°	*shall/even/low*
	Timber me lete biwinnen° and þat beord bi-ginnen;°	*men ordered brought/table begun*
	to feouwer wikene uirste° þat werc° wes iuorðed.°	*in four weeks' time/work/finished*
675	To ane heȝe° dæie þat hired° wes isomned,°	*a feast/court/gathered*
	and Arður him seolf° beh° sone° to þan borde	*himself/came/soon*
	and hehte° alle his cnihtes to þan borde forð rihtes.°	*called/immediately*
	Þo° alle weoren iseten° cnihtes to heore mete,°	*when/seated/their food*
	þa spæc° ælc wið oðer, alse° hit weore° his broðer;	*then spoke/as if/were*
680	alle heo seten abuten,° nes° þer nan wið uten.	*around/was not*
	Æuereælches cunnes cniht° þere wes swiðe wel idiht;°	*every kind (of) knight/placed*
	alle heo weoren° bi ane,° þe hehȝe and þa laȝe;°	*were/equal/the low*
	ne mihten° þer nan ȝelpen° for° oðere kunnes scenchen°	*not might/boast/of/another kind (of) drink*
	oðer° his iueren° þe° at þan beorde weoren.	*than/companions'/that*
685	Þis wes þat ilke° bord þat Bruttes° of ȝelpeð,	*same/Britons*
	and sugeð° feole cunne lesinge° bi° Arðure þan kinge.	*tell/kinds (of) lies/about*
	Swa deð auer alc° mon þe oðer luuien con;°	*so does ever each/love can*
	ȝif° he is him° to leof,° þenne wule° he liȝen,°	*if/to him/too dear/will/lie*
	and suggen on° him wurð-scipe° mare þenne° he beon wurðe,°	*say about/praise/more than/is worth*
690	ne beo° he no° swa luðer mon° þat his freond° him wel° ne on.°	*not be/never/wicked (a) man/friend/good/does*
	Æft° ȝif on uolke° feond-scipe arereð°	*again/among folk/enmity appears*
	an æuer æi° time bitweone twon monnen,°	*at ever any/between two men*
	me con bi þan læðe° lasinge° suggen,	*the hated (one)/lies*
	þeh° he weore° þe bezste° mon þe æuere æt° at borde;	*though/were/best/ate*
695	þe mon þe him weore lað° him cuðe° last finden.°	*hostile/could (he)/find*
	Ne° al soh ne° al les° þat leod-scopes° singeð,	*(it is) not/truth nor/lie/minstrels*
	ah þis is þat soððe° bi Arðure þan kinge.	*the truth*
	Nes næuer ar swulc° king, swa duhti þurh° alle þing;°	*never before such (a)/doughty through/things*
	for þat soðe stand a° þan writen° hu hit° is iwurðen,°	*truth stands in/writing/how it/happened*
700	ord from° þan ænden,° of Arðure þan kinge,	*from beginning/to end*
	no mare no lasse° buten alse° his laȝen° weoren.	*less/but as/laws*

---

666. The Round Table evidently was hollow in the middle, with the knights sitting on the inside and outside, facing each other. The "inside" of the original table (cf. l. 663) referred to the places at the head, the "outside" to those at the end.

Arthur's Host Departs from Southampton (vss. 25525–48).

Þer comen seilien sone°   ȝeond þa sæ° wide   *came sailing soon/over the sea*
scipes uniuoȝe°   to þas° kinges folke;   *ships numerous/the*
þe king þat folc beide°   ȝeond þa scipen° longe;   *folk distributed/ships*
705 bi þusend° and bi þusend   to þan° scipen þrasten;°   *thousand/the/(they) thronged*
þe uader weop a þene sune,°   suster° a þene broðer,   *father wept over the son/sister*
moder° a þa dohter,°   þa° þa duȝeðe sturede.°   *mother/daughter/when/army departed*

Weder stod on° wille;   wind wex° an honde;°   *weather stood at/increased/momently*
ankeres heo° up droȝen;°   drem wes on uolken.°   *anchors they/drew/joy was among folk*

710 Wunden° into widen° sæ   þeines wunder bliðe;°   *traveled/wide/thanes wondrous happy*

scipen þer forð þrungen;°   gleomen° þer sungen;°   *pressed/minstrels/sang*
seiles° þer tuhten;°   rapes° þer rehtten;°   *sails/(they) pulled up/ropes/righted*
wederen° alre° selest;°   and þa sæ sweuede.°   *weather/of all/(was) best/slept*

Arthur Fights the Giant of Brittany (vss. 25641–26146)

To Barbe-fleot° at Costentin   þer com muchel moncun° in,   *Barfleur/came (a) great multitude*
715 of° alle þan londe°   þa° Arður hafde an honde.°   *from/the lands/that/controlled*
Swa sone° swa heo mihten,°   ut° of scipe heom rehten;°   *as soon/they might/out/ship they moved*

þe king his folc hehte°   herberwe° isechen,°   *folk commanded/lodging/to seek*
an badien° þe king wolde°   þat° his folc come.   *and tarry/would/until*
Nes° he þere buten ane niht°   þa° com him to an hende cniht;°   *was not/but one night/when/fair knight*
720 he talde tidinge°   Arðure° þan kinge;   *told news/to Arthur*
he seide° þat þer wes icumen°   a scaðe liðe,°   *said/was come/monster hateful*
of westward Spaine,   wel reordi feond,°   *(a) very loathsome fiend*
and inne Brutaine°   bisi° wes to harme;   *Brittany/busy*
bi þere sæ° side   þet lond° he weste wide;°   *the sea/that land/wasted widely*
725 nu hit° hatte° Munt Seint° Michel;   þat lond welde° wide.   *now it/is called/Mont Saint/(he) controls*

"Lauerd° king," queð° þe cniht,   "to soðe° ich þe cuðe her riht,°   *lord/said/truly/I you inform here right*
he hafueð inome° þine maȝe°   mid hahliche strenðe,°   *has taken/relative/with great force*

---

714. Barfleur, near Cap Barfleur, on the Cotentin peninsula near Cherbourg, was the site of heavy combat during another allied invasion in 1944.

721. In a few copies of Wace the giant is named Dinabruc.

725. Mont-Saint-Michel, off the northern coast of Brittany near Avranches, is a cliff on what is at high tide an island town. At low tide the island is surrounded by quicksand, which makes an approach difficult, and the tide is said to rise with incredible speed. Connected today by an auto causeway with the mainland, the mount is a famous tourist attraction.

heȝe wimmon iboren,°   Howeles° dohter icoren;° *noble woman born|Hoel's|daughter chosen*

Eleine° wes ihaten,°   aðelest° maidenen.° *Helena|(she) was called|noblest|of maidens*

730 To þan munte° he heo uerede,°   aðelest maidene;° *mount|her carried|of maidens*

nu fulle feowertene niht°   þe feond heo hafueð ihalden° þer; *fully fourteen nights|held*

nute° we on liue°   þeh° he heo nabbe° to wife. *know not|in life| whether|have not*

Alle he makeð him to mete°   þa° men þa he igripeð,° *his food|the|captures*

ruðeren,° hors, and þa scep,°   gæt and þa swin eke;° *cattle|sheep|goats|swine also*

735 al þis lond he wule for-fare°   buten þu afeollen ure° kare; *will destroy|unless you allay our*

lond and þas leode,°   a° þe is ure neode."° *this people|ever|need*

Ȝet þe cniht seide   to þan uolc-kinge,° *folk king*

"Isihst° þu, lauerd, þe munt   and pene wude° muchele, *see|the forest*

þer wuneð° þe scaðe inne   þa scendeð° þas leode. *where lives|harms*

740 We habbeð° wið him iuohten°   wel feole siðen,° *have|fought|many times*

bi sæ and bi londe;   þes leoden° he amærde;° *this people|destroyed*

ure scipen° he aseingde;°   þat folc he al adrente;° *ships|sank|drowned*

þeu° þat feuhten a° þan londe,   þeo° he adun leide;° *those|fought in|them|down struck*

we habbeoð idriuen° þat swa° longe   þat we hine læteð ane,° *have suffered|so|him let alone*

745 faren° hou swa° he wule,°   after° iwille him;° *to do|as|wishes|according to|his desire*

þis lond° cnihtes ne durren°   wið him mare na° fehten."° *land's|not dare|no more|fight*

Arður þis iherde,°   aðelest alre° kinge;° *heard|of all|kings*

he cleopede° him to þene eorl Kæi,°   þe° wes his stiward° and his mæi,° *called|earl Kay|that|steward| kinsman*

Beduer° eke to him he cleopede;   he wes þes° kinges birle.° *Bedevere|the|cupbearer*

750 He hæhte heom° forð riht°   beon° al war tu midder-niht° *commanded them|immediately|to be| ready at midnight*

mid alle heore wepne°   to wenden° wið þan kinge, *their weapons|go*

þat° na mon° under Criste   of heore uare° nuste,° *so that|no man|journey|knew not*

buten° Arður þe king   and þa tweien° cnihtes mid him, *except|two*

and heore sweines° sixe,   ohte° men and wihte,° *men|sturdy|brave*

755 and þe cniht þe radde°   hit þan° kinge heom ladde.° *advised|to the|led*

To þere° midnihte   þa men weoren aslepe,° *at|were asleep*

Arður forð him wende,°   aðelest alre kinge. *went*

Bi-foren rad° heore lod-cniht   þat° hit was dæiliht;° *before rode|guide until|daylight*

728–29. According to Geoffrey of Monmouth, Hoel I was king of Brittany, the son of King Boudicius and Arthur's sister Anna; Helena was his niece. Geoffrey contradicts himself by saying that Arthur's sister Anna had only two sons, Gawain and Modred, by her husband, King Loth of Lodonesia, and later making Hoel the son of Boudicius and the sister of Aurelius Ambrosius, Arthur's uncle; this would make Hoel Arthur's cousin instead of nephew. (It is useless, however, to attempt to follow Arthurian genealogy too closely; incest, intermarriage, remarriage, and so on, complicate, bastardize, and becloud the issue.) The close personal relationship of Arthur with Gawain and Modred is typical of the uncle-nephew bond (perhaps originating from prehistoric matrilineal societies) found in folklore: Charlemagne-Roland, Mark-Tristram, and so forth (cf. Tacitus, *Germania*, XX).

heo lihten of° heore steden°   and rihten° heore iweden.°   *they dismounted|steeds|righted|clothes*

760 Þa iseȝen° heo nawiht feorren°   a muchel fur smokien°   *then saw|not far|great fire smoking*

uppen ane hulle°   mid sæ ulode bi-uallen,°   *upon a hill|flood surrounded*

and an oðer hul þer wes swiðe heh;   þæ° sæ hine° bifledde° ful neh;°   *was very high|the|it|flowed around| very near*

þer uuen on° heo iseȝen a fur   þat wes muchel and swiðe stor.°   *upon|strong*

Þæ cnihtes þa tweoneden°   to whaþere° heo faren mihten,°   *knights then doubted|which|approach might*

765 þet° þe eotend war° neore°   of þeos° kinges fore.°   *so that|giant aware|would not be| the|coming*

Þa nom him to rede°   Arður þe ræȝe°   *advised|bold*

þat heo sculden somed faren°   aneosten þan ane furen,°   *should together go|near the one fire*

and ȝif° hine þer funden°   a-quellen° hine to deðen.°   *if|found|kill|death*

Forð þe king wende°   þat° he com aneuste;°   *went|until|came near*

770 noht° he þer ne funde°   bute° a muchel fur þer berninde.°   *nothing|found|but|burning*

Arður eode abute°   and his cnihtes bi his siden;°   *went around|side*

na whit° heo ne funden   quikes° uppen wolden°   *nothing|alive|earth*

buten þat fur muchele   and ban vnimete,°   *bones countless*

bi atlinge° heom° þuhte°   þritti uoðere.°   *estimation|to them|(it) seemed| thirty loads*

775 Arður þa nuste   nenne red godne,   *no counsel good*

and bi-gon him° to speken°   to Beduer his eorle,   *began|speak*

"Beduer, far biliue°   a-dun of þissen° hulle,   *go quickly|down from this*

and wend þe° ouer þat water deope°   mid allen° þine iwede,°   *go you|deep|with all|clothes*

and mid wisdome°   wend to þan fure,°   *caution|fire*

780 and bi-halues þe iga°   and bihald ȝeorne°   *aside you go|look carefully*

ȝif þu miht a-finden°   oht° of þan feonden.°   *might find|anything|fiend*

And ȝif þu hine miht of-ȝiten°   on aiȝes cunnes wisen,°   *perceive|in any kind (of) way*

wend adun° stille   þat cume° to þan watere,   *down|(you) come*

and seien° me þer sone°   what þu i-seȝen habbe.°   *tell|soon|seen have*

785 And ȝif hit ilimpeð swa°   þat þu liðen° to þan fure,   *it happens so|approach*

and þe feond° þe of-ȝite°   and þu to fuse,°   *fiend|perceives|goes*

hafe° mine godne horn   þe al mid golde is ibon,°   *take|adorned*

and blawe° hine mid maine°   swa° mon scal° for neode,°   *blow|strength|as|shall|need*

and fus° þe to þan feonde   and bigin° to fihten,°   *approach|begin|fight*

790 and we þe scullen fusen° to   swa we hit swiðest° maȝen don.°   *shall come|as quickly as we it|may do*

And ȝif þu hine ifindest°   aneouste° þan fure,   *him find|near*

and þu al un-aȝeten°   aȝein miht iwende,°   *unnoticed|return*

þenne for-beode ich° þe,   bi þine bare life,   *forbid I*

þat þu nauere° wið þene scucke°   feht no° biginne."   *never|the monster|fight not*

795 Beduer iherde°   what his lauerd° him° seide;°   *Bedevere heard|lord|to him|said*

his wepnen° he on him dude°   and forð him iwende,°   *weapons|put|he went* and up a-stæh° þene munt°   þe° is unimete.°   *climbed/mount/that/huge*

He bar an° his honde°   ænne gære° swiðe stronge,   *carried in/hand/a spear*

ænne sceld an° his rugge°   irust° al mid golde,   *a shield on/back/decorated*

800 hælm° an his hafde°   hehne° of stele;°   *helmet/head/high/steel*

his bodi wes bifeong°   mid fæire° are° burne;°   *covered/fair/a/coat of mail*

he hafde° bi his side   enne brond° al of stele;   *had/a sword*

and forð he gon steppen,°   stið imainede eorl,°   *did step/(the) powerful, strong earl*

þat° he com fusen°   an neouste° þan° furen,   *until/approaching/near/the*

805 and he under ane treo°   gon him at-stonden.°   *a tree/stop*

Þa° iherde he wepen°   wunder ane swiðen,°   *then/(one) weeping/wondrously much*

wepen and weinen°   and wanliche iberen.°   *wailing/woefully lamenting*

Þa þe cniht wende°   þat hit þe eotend weoren,°   *knight thought/giant was*

and he an-bursten agon°   swulc° weore° a wilde bar,°   *enraged became/as if/(he) were/boar*

810 and forȝæt° sone   þat° his lauerd him sæide.°   *forgot/what/told*

His sceld he bræid° on breoste;°   his spere° he igrap° faste,   *raised/breast/spear/grasped*

and an neoste° gon° fuse°   touward þan fure;   *near/began to/approach*

he wende to finden°   þene feond sturne,°   *find/fierce*

þat he fehten° mihte   and fondien° hine seolue.°   *fight/prove/himself*

815 Þa fond° he þer ane quene°   quecchen mid° hafde,   *found/woman/shaking her*

heor-lockede wif°   weop° for hire wei-sið,°   *gray-haired woman/(who) wept/her wretchedness*

wanede° hire siðes°   þat heo wæs° on liues,°   *deplored/time/she was/alive*

þat set° bi þan furc   mid reolichen ibere,°   *sat/with piteous cries*

and sæt° and biheold æuere°   ænne burinæsse,°   *sat/regarded ever/grave*

820 and hire ȝeddes sæide°   ȝeomere stefne,°   *words said/(with) doleful voice*

"Wale Eleine,°   wale deore° maide,   *alas Helena/dear*

wale þat ich þe uedde,°   þat ich þe uostredde;°   *I you fed/fostered*

wale þat þæ wald-scaðe°   here þe haueð° þus for-uare;°   *the monster/has/destroyed*

wale þat ich wes iboren;°   mine leomen° he haueð   *was born/limbs/broken to pieces*
   to-broken."°

825 Þa bi-sæh° þat wif abuten°   whar° þe eotend come buȝen;°   *looked/around/where/should come*

bi-seh a° þene eorl Beduer   þa icumen° wes þer.   *(she) saw/that come*

Þa sæide þat wif hore°   þer° heo sæt bi fure,°   *hoary/where/(the) fire*

"Whæt ært þu, fære whit,°   ært° þu angel, ært cniht;   *what are you, fair man/are*

beoð° þine feðer-heomen°   ihaneked° mid golden?   *are/wings/behung*

830 Ȝif° þu ært of heuene,°   þu miht° isund° faren heonene,°   *if/heaven/might/in safety/go hence*

and ȝif þu ært eorðlic° cniht,   ærm° þu iwurðest° forð riht.°   *earthly/wretched/will be/immediately*

For nu anan cumeð° þe scaðe   þe alle þine leomen wule°   *now soon comes/will/pull apart*
   to-draȝen,°

---

797. In Wace, Bedevere must cross by boat because of high tide.

þeh° þu weore stel° al he þe awalt° iwildel.°	though/steel/will destroy/every bit
He uerde° to Brutaine° to aðelest° alre° bolde,°	went/Brittany/noblest/of all/ mansions
835 to Howeles° castle, hæh mon° inne Brutene;°	Hoel's/great man/Brittany
þa ȝaten° alle he to-brac° and binnen° he gon wende.°	the gates/broke in pieces/inside/go
He nom þare° halle wal and helden hine° to grunde;°	took the/threw it/ground
þæs bures dure° he warp adun° þat° heo to-barst a uiuen;°	the chamber door/threw down/so that/it burst into five (pieces)
he funde i° þan buren° fæirest alre bruden.°	found in/chamber/maidens
840 Eleinen wes ihaten,° aðelest° kunnen,°	Helena was (she) called/of noblest/ race
Howeles dohter,° hæh mon of Brutene,	daughter
Arðures maȝe,° of swiðe heȝe cunne.°	kinsman/very noble family
Ich wes hire uoster-moder° and feire heo° uostredde.	foster-mother/well her
Þer þe eotend unc ifeng° forð mid him seoluen,°	us took/himself
845 and hire bar° a lutel wile,° fiftene mile,°	carried/short space/mile
into þisse wilde wude,° hider° to þissen ilke stude;°	forest/here/this same place
þus he us dihte° to-dæi a seouen nihte.°	treated/a week ago
Sone° swa° he hider com,° swa° he þat maide inom;°	as soon/as/came/so/took
he wolde° mon-radene° habben° wið þan° maidene.	wanted to/carnal intercourse/have/ the
850 Ælde° næfde° heo na mare° buten° fiftene ȝere;°	age/had not/no more/than/years
ne° mihte þat maiden his mone i-þolien;°	not/force endure
anan° swa he lai hire mide,° hire lif° heo losede sone,°	as soon/with/life/lost quickly
and her° he heo bi-burede,° burden° alre hendest,°	here/buried/of maids/all fairest
Eleine min aȝen° uoster,° Howelles dohter.	my own/foster child
855 Þa° he hafde° þis idon° swa° me seoluen° inom;°	when/had/done/also/myself/(he) took
a uolden° he me laiden° and lai mid me seoluen;	on (the) ground/laid
nu hafeð° he mine ban° alle ladliche a-brokene,°	has/bones/loathsomely broken
mine leomen al to-leðed;° mi lif me° is a-laðed.°	wrenched/to me/odious
Nu ich habbe þe itald° hu° we beoð° her ilæd;°	have you told/how/are/made to come
860 flih° nu swiðe,° lest he þe ifinde;°	flee/quickly/find
for ȝif he cumeð a-bolȝen° mid° his balu ræsen,°	enraged/with/baleful rush
nes° he° neuere° iboren þe maȝen stonden° þe biuoren."	was not/(i.e., the man)/never/that may stand/before
Efne° þissen° worden° þa þat wif seide,°	even/with these/words/woman said
Beduer° heo gon° hirten° mid hendeliche° worden.	Bedevere/began to/comfort/kind
865 "Leofe moder, ich æm mon° and cniht° æm wel idon,°	dear mother, I am (a) man/(a) knight/very brave
and ich þe° wule suggen° þurh° soðe° mine worden,	to you/say/through/true
næs° nan kempen iboren° of nauer nare burden°	was not/no champion born/no woman

---

844. *unc:* OE accusative of the 1st person dual "us two" (cf.
l. 562*n* and below, p. 225, l. 1703*n*).

þat mon ne mæi° mid strenðe°   stupen hine° to grunde,   *may/strength/throw him*
and hore° þe an alde wifmon;°   swiðe lutle beoð° þine   *(that cannot) rape/old woman/little*
    mæhten;°   *are/powers*
870 ah hafuen° nu swiðe godne dæi,°   and ich wulle faren°   *but have/good day/will go/way*
    minne wæi."°
Adun him ferde° Beduer   to his duʒeðe-kinge,°   *went/host-king*
and talde° him hu he hafde kare   and hu he hafde al ifare,°   *told/fared*
and what þat wif alde   of þan° maidene him talde,   *the*
and hu þe eotend ælche° dæi   bi þan alde wiue° lai.   *giant each/woman*
875 Þer heo heom bi-twenen°   heolden heore runen,°   *they them between/held their counsel*
hu heo mihten taken° on   þat þe scucke° weore° fordon.°   *might carry/monster/would be/*
                                                              destroyed

Þeo° while com þe eotende faren°   and fusden° to his fure;°   *in a/giant approaching/went/fire*
he bar uppen° his rugge°   burðene grete,°   *upon/back/(a) burden great*
þat weore twælf° swine   iteied to-somne,°   *was twelve/tied together*
880 mid wiðen° swiðe grete   y-wriðen° al to-gadere.°   *twigs/wound/together*
Adun° he warp° þe dede swin°   and him seolf° sæt þer bi;   *down/threw/dead swine/himself/sat*
his fur° he beten° agon°   and muchele treowen læiden° on;   *fire/mend/began to/much wood laid*
þa° six swin he to-droh°   and euere° he to° þan wiue loh,°   *then/pulled apart/ever/at/smiled*
and sone umbe° while   he lai bi þan wife,°   *in a/woman*
885 ah he nuste° noht° þan tidende°   þat comen° to° his wife-   *knew not/not at all/outcome/would*
    þinge.°   *result/from intercourse*
He droh ut° his gleden;°   his flæsce° he gon breden,°   *drew out/embers/flesh/did roast*
and þa° six swin he gon æten° alle   ær° he arise of selde;°   *the/eat/before/arose from (his) seat*
al biwaled on axen,°   wanliche weoren° þa sonden;°   *smeared with ashes/woeful were/*
                                                              viands

and seoððen° he gon ræmien°   and raxlede swiðe,°   *then/roar/stretched greatly*
890 and adun lai bi þan° fure   and his leomen strahte.°   *the/limbs stretched*
Lete we nu þene° eotend bi-lafuen°   and atlien° to þan kinge.   *let us now the/let be/return*
Arður at þan watere   his wapnen nom an honde,°   *weapons took in hand*
and þe eorl° Beduer,   god° cniht wis° and war,°   *Bedevere/good/wise/prudent*
and þe þridde wes Kæi,°   þes° kinges stiward° and his mæi.°   *third was Kay/the/steward/kinsman*
895 Ouer þan watere heo comen,°   iwepned° mid þan bezsten,°   *came/weaponed/best*
and stiʒen° up þan hulle°   mid allen° heore maine,°   *climbed/hill/all/might*
þat° heo comen fusen°   a-neuste° þan furen,°   *until/approaching/near/fire*
þer° þe eotende lai and slæp°   and þa quene° sæt and weop.°   *where/slept/woman/wept*
Arður hine teh°   bi-siden° his iferen,°   *himself drew/beside/companions*
900 for-bad heom bi heore leomen   and bi heore bare liuen,°   *lives*
þat nan° neoren° swa kene°   þat heom neh° comen,°   *none/would not be/so bold/near/*
                                                              would come

buten° he iseʒen°   þat hit ned weoren.°   *unless/saw/it necessary was*
Beduer at-stod him° þere   and Kæi his iuere.°   *remained/friend*

---

869. The sense of this line is obscure.

Arður gon° stepen vorð,° stið imoded° kempe,°	*began to/step forth/brave-minded/ warrior*
905 þat he com° to þan ulette° þer þe feond° lai and slæpte.°	*came/place/fiend/slept*
Æuere° wes Arður ærhðe° bideled;°	*ever/in fear/lacking*
þet° wes sutel° þer on,° sellic þah° hit þunche;°	*that/plain/in/wondrous though/ seemed*
for Arður mihte° þere þene eotende al to-hæuwe,°	*might/have cut apart*
slan° þene scucke þer he lai and slapte;°	*slain/slept*
910 þa° nolde° Arður on slepen° na wiht° hine areppen,°	*then/would not/sleep/in no way/him touch*
leste he an uferre daჳe° up-bræid iherde.°	*on (a) future day/blame heard*
Þa cleopede° Arður anan,° aðelest° kingen,°	*called/at once/noblest/of kings*
"Aris,° aris, feond-scaðe,° to þine fæie-siðe;°	*arise/fiend-monster/death journey*
nu wit° scullen delen° þene dæd° of mire maჳen."°	*we two/shall avenge/death/my kins- woman*
915 Ær þe king hæfde° þæs ful isæide,°	*had/this fully said*
þe eotend° up a-sturte° and igrap° his mucle° clubbe,	*giant/jumped/grasped/great*
and wende mid þan dunten° Arður al to-driuen,°	*thought with the blow/to destroy*
ah° Arður bræid heჳe° his sceld buuen° his hælme,°	*but/raised high/shield above/helmet*
and þe eotend smat° þer an ouenan° þat° al he gon° to-scenen.°	*struck/above/so that/it began/shiver*
920 And Arður him swende to° an hiჳende° mid his sweorde,°	*struck/hastily/sword*
and þen° chin him° of-swipte° mid alle þan cheuele,°	*the/from him/cut off/jaw*
and sturte him° biaften ane treo° þe° þer stod aneouste,°	*jumped/behind a tree/that/stood near*
and þe eotend smat after biliue° and noht hine ne hutte,°	*quickly/not hit*
ah he þat treo smat þat al his clubbe to-draf.°	*broke*
925 And Arður aneouste° þat treo bieorn° abute,°	*thereupon/ran around/about*
and swa Arður and þe scucke° biurnen° hit þreie° a-buten.°	*monster/ran around/three times/ about*
Þa wes þe eotend heui° swiðe° and Arður wes swiftre,°	*heavy/very/swifter*
and of-toc° þene eotend and up ahof° his gode brond,°	*overtook/raised/good sword*
and þat þih° him of-smat,° and eotend adun wæt.°	*the thigh/cut off/down fell*
930 And Arður at-stod° and biheold;° þa gon to spekene° þe ueond,°	*stood/beheld/speak/fiend*
"Lauerd,° lauerd, ჳef° me grif;° wha is° þat me fihteð° wið?	*lord/give/peace/who is (it)/fights*
Ne wende ich° þat na° man a þissere weorlde-richen°	*I/no/in this world*
me mihte þus lehtliche° aleggen° mid fehte,°	*easily/defeat/fight*

908–11. Wace says that Arthur hoped to surprise the giant and steal his club, but the giant noticed his approach. Layamon's depiction of Arthur's generosity and honor here is in stark and amusing contrast to the king's treatment of the women after the Round Table fight.

921. The motifs of two stories are confused here. Arthur, in Geoffrey of Monmouth, had previously fought on Mount Arvaius (Snowdon) a giant Retho, who had made a coat from the beards of kings he had slain. He challenged Arthur to rip off his own beard and send it to him, or else meet him in single combat. Arthur took up the challenge and won, taking the giant's beard and coat. In Layamon, the giant of Mont-Saint-Michel is confused with Retho, though Arthur mentions a giant Riun in l. 954. It is interesting to trace the development of these two incidents in Geoffrey of Monmouth, Layamon, and the Alliterative *Morte Arthure*.

bute hit Arður weore,°	aðelest alre° Brutte,°	were/of all/Britons
935 and neoðeles° næs° ich nauere°	of Arður afæred sære.''°	nevertheless/was not/never/afraid greatly
Þa him° sæide° Arður,	aðelest kingen,	to him/said
"Ich æm° Arður þe king	Bruttene deorling.°	am/Britons' darling
Tel me of þine cunne°	and whar beo heore beonste,°	kin/where is their dwelling
and wha þe° weore on uolde°	fader oðer moder ihalde,°	to you/earth/father or mother accounted
940 and of wulche londe°	þu° art iliðen hidere,°	from which land/you/come here
and whi þu mine maʒe°	a-ualled hafuest° mid morðe.''°	kinswoman/killed have/murder
Þa andswarede° þe feond	þer° he læi° and biheold,	answered/where/lay
"Al þis ich wulle don°	and þine treoðe under-fon,°	will do/pledge loyalty to you
wið þat° þu me lete liuien°	and mine leomen hælen.''°	if/let live/limbs heal
945 Arður hine iwraððede°	wunder ane swiðe,°	became angered/wondrously much
and he Beduer° cleopede,	balde° his kempe,°	Bedevere/bold/warrior
"Ga° aneouste, Beduer,	and hefd° him binim° her°	go/(the) head/cut off/here
and fere hit° forð mid þe°	adun of þisse munte.''°	carry it/you/mount
Beduer aneouste com°	and his hafued° him binom,°	came/head/cut off
950 and swa heo þeonene ferden°	adun to heore iferen.°	so they thence went/companions
Þo° sat þe king adun	and hine° gon to resten,°	then/himself/rest
and þas word seide,°	Arður þe sele,°	these words said/good
"No uæht° ich nauere feht non°	uppen° þissere uolden,°	not fought/none (such)/upon/earth
buten þa° ich sloh þene° king Riun	uppen þan° munte of Rauinite.''	except when/slew the/the
955 Scoððen° heo uorð wenden°	and to þere uerde comen;°	then/forth went/the army came
þa þe° þat hafd iseʒe,°	sellic° heom° þuhte,°	they/head saw/wondrous/to them/ (it) seemed
whar weore under heuene°	swulc hafed ikenned.°	heaven/such (a) head begotten
Howel° of Brutaine°	beh° to þan° kinge,	Hoel/Brittany/came/the
and þe king him seide°	al of þan maidene.	told
960 Þa wes° Howel sari°	and sorhful an heorte° for þi,°	then was/sad/sorrowful at heart/ therefore
and nom° al his feren°	and ferde° to þan munte,	took/friends/went
þer þat Brutisce° maide	bibured° læi on eorðe.°	British/buried/in earth
He lette° þer areren sone°	ane chireche° swiðe faire,	had/built soon/a church
a scinte Marie nomen,°	drihtenes° moder,	in Saint Mary's name/(the) Lord's
965 and seoððen he ʒæf nome° þan° hulle°	ær° he þonne wende,°	gave (a) name/to the/hill/before/ thence went
and hehte hine Æleine Tunbel;°	nu° hit hæhte° Munt Seint Myhhel.°	called it Helena's Tomb/now/is called/Michel

---

954. *Riun, Rauinite:* probably the giant Retho and Mount Arvaius mentioned in Geoffrey. With metathesis of *r*, we would have the word *Rauaius* (Ravaius), which is undoubtedly the same as Layamon's *Rauinite*. Wace also has the story of the giant of Mount Snowdon; but Malory, like Layamon, confuses him with the giant of Mont-Saint-Michel.

966. The story of Helena's Tomb is part of the history of the abbey of Mont-Saint-Michel.

The Battle with Lucius Hiberius (vss. 27424–89)

Æfne þan worde° þa sturede þa uerde,°	*even (with) these words/then moved the host*
bi þusend° and bi þusende heo þrunggen to-somne;°	*thousand/they thronged together*
ælc° king of his folke ȝarkede ferde.°	*each/prepared (an) army*
970 Þa hit° al was iset° and ferden° isemed,°	*when it/readied/armies/set in order*
þa weoren þar riht italde° fulle° fiftene ferden;	*were there rightly counted/fully*
twein° kinges þere æuere° weoren ifere,°	*two/ever/companions*
feouwer eorles° and a duc° dihten heom to-gadere,°	*four earls/duke/grouped themselves together*
and þe kæisere° him seolf° mid° ten þusend kempen.°	*emperor/himself/with/warriors*
975 Þa gon° þat folc° sturien;° þa eorðen° gon to dunien;°	*began/folk/to move/earth/resound*
bemen° þer bleowen;° bonneden° ferden;	*trumpets/blew/assembled*
hornes þer aqueðen° mid hæhȝere stefnen;°	*resounded/loud voice*
sixti þusende bleowen to-somne.	
Ma° þer aqueðen of Arðures iueren,°	*more/troops*
980 þene° sixti þusende segges° mid horne;°	*than/knights/horns*
þa wolcne° gon to dunien, þa eorðe° gon to biuien.°	*sky/earth/tremble*
To-somne heo heolden° swulc° heouene wolde uallen;°	*charged/as if/heaven would fall*
ærst° heo lette fleon to° feondliche swiðe°	*first/fly off/terribly quickly*
flan° al swa° þicke swa° þe snau adun° ualleð;	*arrows/as/as/snow down*
985 stanes° heo letten seoððen° sturnliche winden;°	*stones/let then/fiercely fly*
seoððen speren chrakeden;° sceldes brastleden;°	*spears shattered/shields clashed*
helmes to-helden;° heȝe° men uellen;°	*helmets rolled/noble/fell*
burnen° to-breken;° blod ut ȝeoten;°	*chain mail/broke to pieces/blood out flowed*
ueldes falewe wurðen;° feollen° here-mærken.°	*fields brown became/fell/battle standards*
990 Wondrede ȝeond° þat wald° iwundede cnihtes° ouer al;°	*wandered over/field/wounded knights/everywhere*
sixti hundred þar weoren to-tredene mid horsen;°	*trampled by horses*
beornes° þer swelten;° blodes at-urnen;°	*knights/died/blood/ran out*
stræhten after stretes° blodie stremes;°	*flowed over paths/bloody streams*
balu wes on uolke;° þe burst° wes vnimete.°	*woe was among (the) folk/ slaughter/boundless*

967–99. The battle with Lucius Hiberius, in Geoffrey of Monmouth procurator of the Roman Republic, probably took place at Saussy near Langres in the Champagne. The vexed question of identifying the site of this battle, called in the Latin of Geoffrey *Siesia*, in Layamon *Sosie*, and in the Alliterative *Morte Arthure* (as well as in Malory) *Sessoyne*, has been thoroughly reviewed in two recent articles: William Matthews, "Where Was Siesia-Sessoyne?" and Hans E. Keller, "Two Toponymical Problems in Geoffrey of Monmouth and Wace: Estrusia and Siesia," both in *Speculum*, Vol. 49, No. 4 (Oct., 1974). Wace praises Lucius, a man of valor, between thirty and forty years old, born in Spain. Lucius attacks Arthur, rather unwillingly, with an army of pagans and Romans divided by thirties, forties, on up to thousands, into horse and foot. Arthur is decisively victorious though Bedevere is killed, as is Lucius. Wace's account is even more spirited than Layamon's.

995 Swa° al swa° sugge∂ writen°   þæ° wite3en° idihten,°   *so/also/say (the) writings/that/*
                                                               skillful men/composed

þat wes þat þridde mæste uiht°   þe auere° wes here idiht;°   *the third greatest fight/that ever/*
                                                               fought

þeo° at þan° laste   nuste° nan kempe°   *so that/the/knew not/no warrior*
whæm° he sculde° slæn on°   and wham° he sculde sparien;°   *whom/should/strike/whom/spare*
for no icneou na° man o∂er° þere   for° vnimete° blode.   *not recognized no/another/because*
                                                               of/(the) quantity (of)

Arthur's Dream (vss. 27992–28199)

1000 Þa com° þer in are tiden°   an oht mon riden,°   *then came/once/noble man riding*
and brohte tidinge°   Ar∂ure þan° kinge   *brought news/to Arthur the*
from Moddrede his suster sune;°   Ar∂ure he wes wilcume,°   *sister's son/was welcome*
for he wende° þat he brohte   boden swi∂e gode.°   *thought/news very good*
Ar∂ur lai alle longe niht°   and spac° wi∂ þene 3eonge cniht;° *night long/spoke/the young knight*
1005 swa nauer° nulde° he him sugge°   so∂ hu hit ferde.°   *so never/would not/tell/truth (of)*
                                                               how it happened

Þa° hit wes dæi a mar3en°   and du3e∂e° gon° sturien,°   *when/day in (the) morning/(the)*
                                                               company/began to/stir

Ar∂ur þa up aras°   and strehte° his ærmes;°   *arose/stretched/arms*
He aras up and adun° sat   swule° he weore° swi∂e seoc.°   *down/as if/were/sick*
Þa axede hine° an° uæir° cniht,   "Lauerd,° hu hauest þu   *asked him/(i.e., the)/fair/lord/have*
    iuaren to-niht?"°   *you fared tonight*
1010 Ar∂ur þa andswarede,°   a mode him° wes une∂e,˘   *answered/mind he/uneasy*
"To niht a mine slepe°   þer ich læi on bure,°   *sleep/where I lay in chamber*
me imætte˘ a sweuen;˘   þer uore° ich ful sari æm.°   *I dreamed/dream/therefore/very*
                                                               grieved am

Me imette° þat mon° me hof°   uppen arc° halle;   *dreamed/men/raised/upon a*
þa° halle ich gon bi-striden°   swulc ich wolde riden;°   *the/did bestride/would ride*
1015 alle þa lond þa° ich ah°   alle ich þer ouer sah,°   *lands that/possessed/overlooked*
and Walwain° sat biuoren° me;   mi sweord° he bar an   *Gawain/before/sword/bore in hand*
    honde.°

Þa com Moddred faren° þere   mid unimete uolke;   *approaching*
he bar an his honde   ane wiax° stronge;   *a battle-ax*
he bigon° to hewene°   hardliche˘ swi∂e,   *began/hew/strongly*
1020 and þa postes for-heou° alle   þa heolden° up þa halle. *cut down/held*

1000–103. The prophetic dream of Arthur is entirely an invention of Layamon. It is one of the most important additions to Wace, who states only that Arthur, after hearing of Modred's treason, divides his army, assigning Hoel the protection of France and Burgundy and returning himself with the rest to Britain.

1002. Modred had been left in charge of Britain by Arthur, his uncle (see. ll. 728–29n). He was also the protector of Guinevere (see l. 1021n).

1016. Gawain was a nephew of Arthur (see ll. 728–29n). The interchange of *w* for *g* (the Anglo-Norman sound for that of Central French) is common, and often both spellings were accepted in English: e.g., *Gawain-Wawain, Guinevere-Wenheuer* (l. 1021), *warden-guardian, warranty-guarantee.*

Þer ich iseh Wenheuer eke,°	wimmonnen° leofuest° me;°	*saw Guinevere also/of women/ dearest/to me*
al þere muche° halle rof°	mid hire honden heo° to-droh;°	*the great/roof/her hands she/pulled down*
þa halle gon° to hælden°	and ich hæld to grunden,°	*began/tumble/fell/(the) ground*
þat° mi riht° ærm to-brac;°	þa seide° Modred, 'Haue þat!'	*so that/right/broke to pieces/said*
1025 Adun ueol° þa halle	and Walwain gon to ualle,°	*fell/fall*
and feol a° þere eorðe;°	his ærmes brekeen beine,°	*fell on/earth/broke both*
and ich igrap mi sweord leofe°	mid mire leoft° honde	*grasped/dear/my left*
and smæt of° Modred° is hafd°	þat hit wond° a þene ueld.°	*smote off/from Modred/his head/ rolled/field*
And þa quene ich al to-snaðde°	mid deore° mine sweorede,°	*cut to pieces/dear/sword*
1030 and seoððen° ich heo° adun sette°	in ane swarte putte.°	*then/her/cast/black pit*
And al mi uolc riche°	sette° to fleme,°	*folk powerful/(were) put/flight*
þat nuste° ich under Criste	whar heo bicumen weoren.°	*knew not/where they gone were*
Buten° mi seolf° ich gon atstonden°	uppen ane wolden,°	*but/myself/stand/plain*
and ich þer wondrien° agon°	wide ȝeond° þan moren;°	*to wander/began/widely through/ moors*
1035 þer ich isah gripes°	and grisliche fuȝeles.°	*griffins/grisly birds*
Þa com an guldene leo°	liðen° ouer dune,°	*golden lion/approaching/downs*
deoren° swiðe hende°	þa ure drihten maked;°	*animal/fair/our Lord made*
þa leo me orn° foren to°	and iueng° me bi þan midle,°	*ran/toward/took/middle*
and forð hire° gun° ȝeongen°	and to þere sæ wende.°	*she/began to/travel/sea turned*
1040 And ich isæh þæ vðen°	i° þere sæ driuen,°	*saw the waves/in/driving*
and þe leo i þan ulode°	iwende° wið me seolue;°	*flood/went/myself*
þa wit° i sæ comen	þa vðen me hire° binomen;°	*we two/came/from her/took away*
com° þer an fisc liðe°	and fereden° me to londe;°	*came/fish approaching/carried/land*
þa wes° ich al wet	and weri of sorȝen° and seoc;	*then was/weary from sorrow*
1045 þa gon° ich iwakien,°	swiðe° ich gon to quakien;°	*began/to awaken/greatly/quake*
þa gon ich to biuien°	swulc ich al fur burne.°	*tremble/(with) fire burned*
And swa° ich habbe° al niht°	of mine sweuene swiðe iþoht;°	*so/have/night/much thought*
for ich what to iwisse°	agan° is al mi blisse;°	*know with certainty/gone/joy*
for a° to° mine liue°	sorȝen ich mot driȝe;°	*forever/in/life/must endure*
1050 wale° þat ich nabbe° here	Wenhauer° mine quene."	*alas/have not/Guinevere*
Þa andswarede° þe cniht,	"Lauerd, þu hauest un-riht;°	*answered/knight/lord, you do wrong*
ne sculde me nauere sweuen°	mid sorȝen arecchen;°	*not should men never dream/ interpret*
þu ært° þe riccheste mon°	þa rixleoð° on londen°	*are/man/reigns/earth*

1021. Guinevere was Arthur's wife, who betrayed him for the love of Modred. (The traditional love affair of Lancelot and Guinevere occurs first in Chrétien de Troyes.)

1025. Gawain was killed by Modred at Richborough when the landing of Arthur was resisted.

1027. The "dear sword" is the magic weapon called Calibeorne by Layamon, Caliburn by Geoffrey of Monmouth.

1035. Griffins were monsters half lion, half eagle.

and þe alre° wiseste   þe wuneð° under weolcne.°   *of all/that lives/heaven*
1055 ȝif hit weore° ilimpe°   swa° nulle° hit ure drihte,   *if it were/to happen/as/will not*
þat Modred þire suster sune°   hafde° þine quene inume,°   *your sister's son/had/taken*
and al þi kineliche° lond   isæt an° his aȝere hond,°   *royal/put in/own hand*
þe þu him° bitahtest°   þa° þu to Rome þohtest,°   *to him/entrusted/when/thought*
        (to go)

and he hafde al þus ido°   mid° his swikedome,°   *done/with/treachery*
1060 þe° ȝet þu mihtest þe awreken°   wurðliche° mid wepnen,°   *then/might yourself avenge/*
        worthily/weapons

and æft° þi lond halden°   and walden° þine leoden,°   *again/hold/rule/people*
and þine feond fallen°   þe þe° ufel unnen,°   *enemies fell/to you/evil did*
and slæn heom° alle clane°   þet° þer no bilauen nane."°   *slay them/clean/so that/not remain*
        none

Arður þa andswarede,   aðelest° alre kinge,°   *noblest/kings*
1065 "Longe bið æuere°   þat no wene ich° nauere   *(as) long (as) is ever/thought I*
þat aeuere Moddred mi mæi,°   þat man his° me° leouest,°   *kinsman/is/to me/dearest*
wolde° me biswiken,°   for alle mine richen,°   *would/betray/kingdom*
no° Wenhauer mi quene   wakien on þonke,°   *nor/weaken in thought*
nulleþ° hit biginne°   for nane° weorld-monne."°   *would not/begin/no/man in the*
        world

1070 Æfne þan worde° forð riht°   þa andswarede þe cniht,   *even (with) these words/immedi-*
        ately

"Ich sugge þe soð, leofe° king,   for ich æm þin° vnderling;   *tell you truth, dear/am your*
þus hafeð° Modred idon;°   þine quene he hafeð ifon,°   *has/done/taken*
and þi wunliche° lond   isæt an his aȝere hond;   *fair*
he is king and heo° is quene;   of þine kume° nis° na wene;°   *she/coming/(there) is not/no thought*
1075 for no weneð heo° nauere to° soðe   þat þu cumen° aȝain   *think they/in/will come*
        from Rome.
Ich æm þin aȝen° mon   and iseh þisne° swikedom,   *own/saw this*
and ich æm icumen° to þe seoluen°   soð þe to suggen;°   *come/yourself/tell*
min hafued beo° to wedde°   þat isæid° ich þe habbe   *my head be/pledge/said*
soð buten lese°   of leofen° þire quene   *without lie/dear*
1080 and of Modrede þire suster sune,   hu° he hafueð Brutlond°   *how/has Britain/from you/taken*
        þe° binume."°
Þa sæt° hit al stille   in Arðures halle;   *sat (i.e., was)*
þa wes þer særinæsse°   mid sele° þan° kinge;   *sorrow/good/the*
þa weoren Bruttisce° men   swiðe vnbalde uorþæn.°   *were British/very downcast therefore*
Þa umbe stunde°   stefne° þer sturede;°   *in a while/voices/stirred*
1085 wide° me mihte iheren°   Brutten iceren,°   *widely/hear/Britons clamor*
and gunne° to tellen°   a feole cunne spellen°   *begin/tell/in many kinds (of)*
        speeches

hu heo wolden for-deme°   Modred and þa° quene,   *would destroy/the*
and al þat moncun for-don°   þe mid Modred heolden.°   *multitude kill/held*
Arður þa cleopede,°   hendest° alre Brutte,°   *then called/fairest/Britons*
1090 "Sitteð adun° stille,   cnihtes inne halle,   *down*

and ich eou° telle wulle° spelles vncuðe.°	*you/will/discourse strange*
Nu to-mærȝe þenne° hit dæi° bið and drihten hine° sende,	*now tomorrow when/day/(the) Lord it*
forð ich wulle buȝe° in toward Bruttaine,°	*travel/Britain*
and Moddred ich wulle sclan ° and þa quen for-berne,°	*slay/queen burn*
1095 and alle ich wulle for-don þa biluueden þen° swikedom.	*that approved the*
And her° ich bileofuen° wulle me leofuest° monne,°	*here/leave/dearest/of men*
Howel, minne° leofue mæi, hexst° of mine cunne,°	*Hoel, my/highest/kin*
and half mine uerde° ich bilæfuen° a þissen ærde°	*army/leave/this land*
to halden al þis kine-long° þa ich habbe° a mire hond.°	*kingdom/have/my hand*
1100 And þenne þas þing beoð° alle idone aȝan° ich wulle° to Rome,	*when these things are/back/will (go)*
and mi wunliche lond bitæche° Walwaine,° mine mæie,	*land entrust/to Gawain*
and iuorþe° mi beot seoððe° bi mine bare life;	*carry out/threat then*
scullen° alle mine feond° wæi-sið° makeȝe.''°	*shall/enemies/death journey/make*

The Last Battle (vss. 28450–651)

Þa wes hit° itimed° þere þat° Merlin seide while,°	*then was it/come to pass/what/said before*
1105 ''Ærm° wurðest° þu, Winchæstre,° þæ eorðe þe scal forwalȝe;''°	*wretched/will be/you, Winchester/ the earth you shall swallow*
swa° Merlin sæide,° þe witeȝe° wes mære.°	*so/said/that (a) prophet/great*
Þa° quene læi° inne Eouwerwic,° næs° heo næuere° swa sarlic;°	*the/lay/York/was not/she never/ sorrowful*
þat wes Wenhauer° þa quene, særȝest° wimmonne.°	*Guinevere/saddest/of women*
Heo iherde suggen° soððere worden,°	*heard tell/true words*
1110 hu° ofte Modred flah,° and hu Arður hine bibah;°	*how/fled/him pursued*
wa° wes hire þere° while þat heo wes on life.°	*woe/her the/alive*
Ut° of Eouerwike° bi nihte° heo iwende°	*out/York/night/went*
and touward Karliun tuhte° swa swiðe° swa heo mahte,°	*Caerleon traveled/as quickly/might*
for heo nolde° Arþur more ise° for al þan worle-riche;°	*would not/see/the world*
1115 þider heo brohten° bi nihte of hire cnihten tweiȝe,°	*there her brought/knights two*
and me° hire hafd bi-wefde° mid ane hali rifte,°	*men/head covered/with a holy veil*
and heo wes þer munechene,° kare-fullest° wife.°	*(a) nun/most sorrowful/woman*
Þa nusten° men of þere quene war° heo bicumen weore;°	*knew not/where/gone was*
no feole ȝere seoððe° nuste° hit mon to soðe°	*not many years after/knew not/one in truth*
1120 whaðer° heo weore° on deðe° and ou° heo hinne wende,°	*whether/were/dead/how/hence departed*

1104. At this point Arthur has besieged and taken Winchester, killed all the inhabitants, and burned the town.   **1113.** Caerleon was later associated with Arthur's court.

whaðer heo here seolf° weore   isunken° in þe watere.   *herself/sunk*
Modred wes i Cornwale°   and somnede cnihtes° feole;   *in Cornwall/gathered knights*
to Irlonde he sende°   a-neoste° his sonde;°   *sent/quickly/messengers*
to Sex-londe° he sende   aneouste° his sonde;   *(the) land of the Saxons/then*
1125 to Scotlande he sende   aneouste his sonde;
he hehten heom° to cume° alle anan°   þat wolde lond   *ordered them/come/quickly/would*
    habben,°   *land have*
oðer seoluer oðer° gold   oðer ahte° oðer lond;   *either silver or/possessions*
on ælchere wisen°   he warnede° hine seoluen,°   *in every way/protected/himself*
swa deð ælc witer mon°   þa neode° cumeð uuenan.°   *does every wise man/that need/upon*
1130 Arður þat iherde,   wraðest° kinge,°   *angriest/of kings*
þat Modred wæs° i Cornwale   mid muchele monweorede,°   *was/(a) great army*
and þer wolde abiden°   þat° Arður come riden.°   *abide/until/came riding*
Arður sende sonde   ȝeond° al his kine-londe;°   *throughout/kingdom*
and to cumen° alle hehte°   þat quic° wes on° londe,   *come/ordered/alive/in (the)*
1135 þa to uihte oht weoren,°   wepnen° to beren,°   *fight brave were/weapons/bear*
bote° he were swike°   and mid Modred heolde;°   *unless/(a) traitor/held*
þaie° he habbe° nolde   þeh hii comen° wolde,   *these/have/though they come*
and wah swa° hit for-sete°   þat þe king hete,°   *whoever/neglected/commanded*
þe king hine wolde a folden°   quic al for-bernen.°   *in (this) world/burn*
1140 Hit læc° toward hirede,°   folc vnimcte,°   *they moved/the host/folk innumerable*
ridinde° and ganninde°   swa þe rim° falleð adune.°   *riding/walking/snow/down*
Arður for° to Cornwale   mid unimete ferde.°   *traveled/(an) immense army*
Modred þat iherde   and him toȝeines heolde°   *toward went*
mid vnimete folke;   þer weore monie uæie;°   *many fated*
1145 uppen° þere Tanbre°   heo tuhten to-gadere;°   *upon/Camel/they clashed together*
þe stude° hatte° Camelford;   euer mare° ilast° þat ilke   *place/is called/evermore/lived/same*
    weorde.°   *word*
And at Camelforde wes isomned°   sixti þusend,°   *were gathered/thousand*
and ma° þusend þer to;   Modred wes heore ælder.°   *more/was their leader*
Þa þiderward gon° ride   Arður þe riche,°   *then there did/powerful*
1150 mid unimete folke,   uæie þah° hit weore.   *though*
Uppe þere° Tambre   heo tuhte to-somne,°   *upon the/clashed together*
heuen° here-marken,°   halden° to-gadere,   *raised/battle standards/rushed*
luken sweord° longe,   leiden o° þe helmen;°   *joined swords/hewed on/helmets*
fur ut sprengen;°   speren brastlien;°   *fire out sprang/spears cracked*
1155 sceldes gonnen scanen,°   scaftes° to-breken;°   *shields did shiver/shafts/break to*
          pieces

1124. Modred was evidently allying himself with all of Arthur's former enemies: Scots, Irish, and Saxons.

1144. *uæie:* Cf. above, ll. 379–429n.

1145–46. In Geoffrey of Monmouth the battle takes place "ad flumen Cambula," which in Wace is called Camblan, Tanbre, or Tamble; later it is referred to as Alan or Camel, the name the river bears today. It rises from the Cornish Heights two miles north of Camelford, in the parish of Lanteglos, and flows into Towan Bay below Padstow. According to Madden, the local traditions of Camelford confirm the story of Arthur's last battle.

þer faht° al to-somne   folc vnimete.   *fought*

Tambre wes on flode°   mid vnimete blode;°   *flooded/with (an) immense (amount of) blood*

mon° i þan fihte non° þer ne mihte°   ikenne nenne kempe,°   *men/the fight none/not might/recognize no warriors*

no wha dude wurse° no wha bet,°   swa° þat wiðe° wes imenged;°   *nor who did worse/better/so/conflict/mingled*

1160 for ælc sloh° adun riht,°   weore° he swein° weore he cniht.   *each slew/aright/were/man (or)*

þer wes Modred of-slaʒe°   and idon of lif-daʒe;°   *slain/done with (his) life*

and alle his cnihtes   islaʒe° in þan fihte.   *slain*

þer weoren of-slaʒe   alle þa snelle,°   *the brave*

Arðures hered-men°   heʒe° and lowe,   *followers/high*

1165 and þa Bruttes° alle   of Arðures borde,°   *Britons/table*

and alle his fosterlinges°   of feole kineriches,°   *dependents/many kingdoms*

And Arður forwunded°   mid wal-spere brade;°   *greatly wounded/slaughter-spear broad*

fiftene he hafde°   feondliche wunden;°   *had/grievous wounds*

mon° mihte i þare lasten°   twa glouen iþraste.°   *one/in the least/two gloves thrust*

1170 þa nas° þer na mare°   i þan fehte° to laue,°   *was not/no more/fight/remaining*

of twa hundred þusehd monnen°   þa° þer leien° to-hauwen °   *men/that/lay/cut down*

buten° Arður þe king ane°   and of his cnihtes tweien.°   *except/only/knights two*

Arður wes for-wunded   wunder ane swiðe;°   *wondrously much*

þer to him com° a cnaue°   þe° wes of his cunne;°   *came/young man/that/kin*

1175 he wes Cadores sune,°   þe eorles° of Cornwaile.°   *son/earl's/Cornwall*

Constantin hehte° þe cnaue;   he wes þan° kinge deore.°   *was called/to the/dear*

Arðure him lokede on°   þer° he lai on folden°   *looked at/where/ground*

and þas word seide°   mid sorhfulle heorte,°   *these words said/sorrowful heart*

"Costætin, þu° art wilcume;°   þu weore Cadores sone;°   *Constantine, you/welcome/son*

1180 ich° þe° bitache° here   mine kineriche,   *I/to you/entrust*

and wite° mine Bruttes   a to þines° lifes,   *defend/ever in your*

and hald° heom° alle þa laʒen°   þa habbeoð istonden a°   *keep/for them/laws/have stood in/ days*
mine daʒen,°

and alle þa laʒen gode°   þa bi° Vðeres daʒen stode.°   *good/in/stood*

And ich wulle uaren° to Aualun,°   to uairest° alre°   *will fare/Avalon/ fairest/of all/ maidens*
maidene,°

1157. A crossing over the Camel is today called Slaughter Bridge.

1172. In Malory the surviving knights are Sir Lucan and Sir Bedevere; but the latter, in these earliest sources, was already killed at the battle of Saussy. In the Welsh Triads (short lists of three persons, objects, or things for the purpose of cataloging folk heroes, wise sayings, and the like, as a mnemonic device for bards) there are some Arthurian motifs, among them the *three* knights who survived the battle of Camelbord: Morvran ab Tegid, because he was so ugly that all thought him a hellish demon; Sandde Bryd Angel, because of his fairness; and Glewlwyd Gavaelvawr, because of his enormous size.

1175–76. *Cadores . . . eorles:* i.e., "Son of Cador, the earl." Constantine III, king of Britain after Arthur, in 542, was the son of Arthur's close friend Cador (Craddoc), duke of Cornwall, who had distinguished himself at York against Baldulf and at the Isle of Thanet, where he was mentioned in dispatches, and who was one of the commanders at the battle of Saussy. Constantine's appearance on the battlefield at Arthur's death and the king's words to him regarding the future of Britain are final epic similarities to *Beowulf*, in which the young warrior Wiglaf is entrusted by the dying king with the welfare of his people.

¹¹⁸⁵ to Argante þere quene, aluen swiðe sceone,°	*elf very beautiful*
and heo scal° mine wunden makien° alle isunde,°	*she shall/make/sound*
al hal° me makien mid haleweiȝe drenchen.°	*whole/healing draughts*
And seoðe° ich cumen° wulle to mine kineriche,	*then (afterwards)/come*
and wunien° mid Brutten° mid muchelere wunne."°	*dwell/Britons/much bliss*
¹¹⁹⁰ Æfne þan worden° þer com of se wenden°	*even (with) these words/from (the) sea approaching*
þat wes° an sceort bat liðen,° sceouen° mid vðen,°	*was/small boat approaching/moving/with (the) waves*
and twa wimmen° þer inne, wunderliche idihte,°	*women/wondrously arrayed*
and heo nomen° Arður anan° and aneouste hine uereden;°	*they took/quickly/then him carried*
and softe hine adun leiden° and forð gunnen heo liðen.°	*down laid/did they depart*
¹¹⁹⁵ Þa wes hit iwurðen° þat Merlin seide whilen,°	*then was it come to pass/before*
þat weore° unimete care° of° Arðures forð-fare.°	*(there) would be/boundless sorrow/concerning/departure*
Bruttes ileueð ȝete° þat he bon° on liue,°	*believe yet/is/alive*
and wunnien° in Aualun mid° fairest alre aluen,°	*dwells/with/elves*
and lokieð euere° Bruttes ȝete whan° Arður cumen liðe.°	*await ever/(the time) when/shall come again*
¹²⁰⁰ Nis° nauer° þe mon iboren,° of nauer nane burde icoren,°	*(there) is not/never/man born/no woman chosen*
þe cunne° of þan soðe° of Arðure sugen° mare.	*can/the truth/say*
Bute while wes° an witeȝe° Mærlin° ihate;°	*but formerly (there) was/prophet/(that) Merlin/was called*
he bodede° mid worde,° his quiðes weoren° soðe,	*prophesied/words/sayings were*
þat an Arður sculde° ȝete cum Anglen° to fulste.°	*should/come English (i.e., Britons/help*

1184–85. The Isle of Avalon, also mentioned in Geoffrey, was the place where Caliburn was forged. It is sometimes called the Isle of Apples, ruled over by Morgan la Fay, the mysterious fairy sister of Arthur, who seems here to be confused with Argante. In folklore, Avalon has often been identified with Glastonbury, the site of Arthur's tomb (cf. below, p. 118, l. 879*n*). The name Avalon was thought at one time to originate from *aval*, derived from Irish *ablach*, "rich in apple trees," and in the Welsh texts the island is called *ynys avallach*. Apples were common in fairy lore, and a visitor had to remain in the enchanted land if he ate one. It seems, however, that since *aval* is a ghost word, *ynys avallach* meant "island of Avallach," Avallach being the proper name of the ruler.

1204. The legend of Arthur's return is similar to that of other national heroes, specifically Friedrich Barbarossa, who sits in the Kyffhäuser mountains until the ravens cease flying about it. Charlemagne is said to live on in the Untersberg, near Salzburg. In fact, whole armies continue to slumber inside the mountains with their leaders (cf. below, p. 118, l. 879*n*).

from THE ALLITERATIVE MORTE ARTHURE

DATE: c. 1370–80. ❧ MANUSCRIPT: Lincoln Cathedral A 5.2, transcribed by Robert of Thornton, 1430–40. The dialect was originally Northwest Midland, but it was changed first by a Southern scribe, second by the Northern Yorkshire forms of Thornton. ❧ EDITIONS: E. Brock, Early English Text Society, 8 (London, 1871); Mary M. Banks, *Morte Arthure* (London, 1900); Erik Björkman, *Morte Arthur* (Heidelberg, 1915) which has been used here; Valerie Krishna, *The Alliterative Morte Arthure* (New York, 1976). One might also refer to the critical work by William Matthews, *The Tragedy of Arthur* (Berkeley, Calif., 1960), which has a full and excellent bibliography.

Although the text of the Alliterative *Morte Arthure* was originally from the Northwest Midlands, it was copied by a Northern scribe, and the dialect reflects this. (1) *Qwen* is occasionally used for *when*. (2) The word *til(l)* is used for *to*. (3) The letter ʒ (transcribed *z*) often stands for final *s*. (4) In weak verbs (those without a root-vowel change in the preterite forms), *-id, -yd* (*callid, kyllyd*) is used for the past participle, and *-ande* (*wepande*) for the present participle. (5) The present singular ending of verbs is *-es, -is* (*-ys*), *-ez* (the ancestor of our modern form), in contrast with Southern *-eth*; the present plural ending is either the same or Midland *-en, -e*. (6) The Northern *ā* for Southern *ō* should be noted: *haldes = holdes, twa = two*. (7) The verb *shall* appears as *sall*, with *sulde* in the preterite, though *schall* with *sholde* is also found. (8) *Full* can normally be translated as "very." (9) The interchange of *u/v* should be especially noted, as in *seluyn, vp*.

The Alliterative *Morte Arthure*, a poem of 4346 lines, is one of the most vigorous and outstanding works of the Alliterative Revival. Drawing on the Arthurian material in Geoffrey of Monmouth and Wace and on the cycle of Alexander the Great, the author (identified on tenuous grounds by some critics as a Scot, Huchown of the Awle Ryale [Royal Court]) narrates Arthur's expedition to Europe after the demand of a Roman senator, ambassador of the procurator Lucius Hiberius, that he pay tribute. He campaigns in France, Italy, and Rome; while in Viterbo, he accepts the Roman surrender and the pope's offer to make him emperor. Recalled to Britain by news of Modred's treason, he vanquishes his enemy but is himself killed and buried at Glastonbury.

Arthur's campaign is in the manner of Edward III's conquest of France; the heroism of Arthur is everywhere stressed, and the temper of the work is martial. Thus, although it treats a matter of romance, the poem is epic in nature, and has been classed as such by R. W. Chambers. The fantasy of romance is replaced by the force and spirit of epic: sometimes brutal, at other times lyric, but always heroic in a national sense. The Alliterative *Morte Arthure* is the direct source for Book V of Thomas Malory's *Morte Darthur*.

The Roman Messenger Comes to Arthur on New Year's Day
(vss. 26–123)

Qwen° that the kynge Arthur, by conqueste hade wonnyn°	*when/won*
Castells and kyngdoms and contreez° many,	*countries*
And he had couerede° the coroun° of the kythe° ryche,	*won/crown/country*
Of all that Vter° in erthe aughte° in his tyme,	*Uther/controlled*
5 Orgayle° and Orkenay and all this° owte-iles,°	*Argyll/these/outer islands*
Irelande vttirly,° as Occyane rynnys,°	*completely/ocean flows*
Scathyll° Scottlande by skyll he skyftys° as hym lykys,°	*dangerous/organizes/he likes*
And Wales of were° he wane° at hys wille,	*in war/won*
Bathe° Flaundrez and Fraunce fre til° hym seluyn;°	*both/free to/self*
10 Holaund and Henawde° they helde of° hym bothen,	*Hainault/held allegiance to*
Burgoyne° and Brabane° and Bretayn° the lesse,	*Burgundy/Brabant/Britain*
Gyan° and Gothelande° and Grace° the ryche.	*Guienne/Jutland/Grasse*
Bayon° and Burdeux he beldytt full° faire,	*Bayonne/built very*
Turoyn° and Tholus° with toures° full hye;°	*Touraine/Toulouse/towers/high*
15 Off Peyters° and of Prouynce° he was prynce holdyn,°	*of Poitiers/Provence/called*
Of Valence and Vyenne,° off value so noble,	*Vienne*
Of Eruge° and Anyon,° thos erledoms ryche.	*?Auvergne/Anjou*
By conqueste full cruell þey knewe hym fore° lorde	*for*
Of Nauerne° and Norwaye and Normaundye eke,°	*Navarre/also*
20 Of Almayne,° of Estriche° and oþer ynowe;°	*Germany/Austria/others enough*
Danmarke he dryssede° all by drede° of hym seluyn,	*controlled/fear*
Fra° Swynn° vnto Swetherwyke,° with his swerde kene.°	*from/? Zwin/Sweden/sword sharp*
Qwenn he thes dedes° had don, he doubbyd° hys knyghtez,	*these deeds/dubbed*
Dyuysyde dowcherys° and delte° in dyuerse remmes;°	*established duchies/separated/divers realms*
25 Mad° of his cosyns kyngys ennoyntede°	*made/anointed*
In kythes,° there° they couaitte,° crounes to bere.°	*lands/where/desired/wear*
Whene he thys rewmes° hade redyn° and rewlyde° the 'pople,°	*realms/traversed/ruled/people*
Then rystede° that ryall° and helde þe rounde tabyll;	*rested/king*
Suggeourns° þat seson° to solace° hym seluen,°	*sojourns/season/entertain/self*
30 In Bretayn þe braddere,° as hym beste lykes;	*greater*
Sythyn° wente into Wales with his wyes° alle,	*then/knights*

---

4. Uther Pendragon is Arthur's father (*cf.* above, p. 57), l. 94*n*).

5. Argyll, in western Scotland, and the Orkney Islands off the northeastern tip of Scotland, were both considered wild sections with truculent inhabitants (*cf. Scathyll Scotlande*, l. 7).

11. *Bretayn the lesse:* i.e., Brittany; cf. *Bretayn þe braddere*, i.e., Great Britain, l. 30.

16. Valence and Vienne are both in the Rhone valley of southern France.

22. Swynn is either Zwin, a bay in the North Sea between Zealand and Flanders (now silted up), or the present Sluis, where the naval battle between England and the French-Genoese fleet occurred in 1340.

Sweys° into Swaldye   with his swifte houndes, — *moves*
For to hunt at þe hartes   in thas hye laundes,° — *those highlands*
In Glamorgan with glee,   thare gladchipe° was euere,° — *where happiness/ever*
35 And thare° a citee° he sette,°   be° assentte of his lordys, — *there/city/established/by*
That Caerlyon° was callid,   with curius walles, — *Caerleon*
On the riche reuare,°   þat rynnys so faire, — *great river*
There he myghte semble° his sorte°   to see,° whenn hym — *assemble/company/at (his) throne*
    lykyde.
Thane° aftyre at Carelele°   a Cristynmesse° he haldes,° — *then/Carlisle/Christmas/celebrates*
40 This ilke kyde° conquerour   and kende hym for° lorde, — *same famous/proclaimed himself as*
Wyth dukez and dusperes°   of dyuers rewmes, — *peers*
Erles and ercheuesqes°   and oþer ynowe, — *archbishops*
Byschopes and bachelers   and banerettes nobill,
Þat bowes to his banere,   buske° when hym lykys. — *make ready*
45 Bot° on the Cristynmesdaye,   when the knightes were all — *but/assembled*
    semblyde,°
That comlyche° conquerour   commaundez° hym seluyn, — *fair/commands*
Þat ylke a° lorde sulde lenge°   and no lefe° take, — *each/should remain/leave*
To° the tende° day fully   ware° takyn to þe ende. — *till/tenth/were*
Thus on ryall° araye   he helde his rounde table, — *in royal*
50 With semblant° and solace°   and selcouthe metes;° — *pomp/entertainment/rare food*
Was neuer syche noblay°   in no manys° tyme — *such ceremony/man's*
Mad in mydwynter   in þa weste marchys.° — *the western marches*

  Bot on the newȝere° daye,   at þe none euyne,° — *New Year/high noon*
As the bolde° at the borde°   was of brede seruyde,° — *hero/table/with roast served*
55 So come° in sodanly°   a senatour of Rome, — *came/suddenly*
Wyth sexten° knyghtes in a soyte°   sewande° hym one.° — *sixteen/group/following/alone*
He saluȝed° the souerayne   and the sale° aftyr, — *saluted/hall*
Ilke a° kynge aftyre kynge,   and mad his enclines;° — *each/bows*
Gaynour° in° hir degre°   he grette° as hym lykyde,° — *Guinevere/according to/rank/ greeted/he liked*

60 And syne° agayne to þe gome°   he gaffe vp° his nedys:° — *then/man/presented/business*
"Sir Lucius Iberius,   the louerd° of Rome, — *lord* (i.e., *procurator*)
Saluz the° as sugett°   vndyre his sele ryche;° — *greets you/subject/seal powerful*
It es° credens,° sir kynge,   with cruell° wordez, — *is/letter of introduction/stern*
Trow° it for no trufles,°   his targe es° to schewe!° — *believe/joke/arms mean/show*

---

32. *Swaldye:* perhaps the present Swansea in the county of Glamorgan, southeastern Wales.

36. Caerleon-upon-Usk in Monmouthshire, two miles from Newport, was called by the Romans Isca Silurum.

39. Carlisle here is probably a mistake for Caerleon.

41. *Dusperes* (also *douzepers, duzseperez, dusszeperis*), from the Twelve Peers of Charlemagne, came to mean any group of noble knights.

43. Bachelors were candidates who had not yet achieved a rank or station in the arts or the military; bannerets had the privilege of leading a company under their own banners.

53. Adventures usually started on New Year's Day at Arthur's court; cf. *Sir Gawain and the Green Knight*.

64. The arms are those on the seal.

65 Now in this newȝers daye   with notaries sygne°   *signatures*
    I make the somouns° in sale   to sue for þi landys,   *summons*
    That on Lammesse° daye   thare be no lette founden,°   *Lammas/delay found*
    Þat thow bee redy° at Rome   with all thi rounde table   *you be ready*
    Appere° in his presens   with thy price° knyghtez,   *to appear/noble*
70 At pryme of the daye,   in° payne of ȝour lyvys,   *on*
    In þe kydde Capytoile   before þe kyng selvyn,°   *himself*
    When he and his senatours   bez sette° as them lykes,   *are seated*
    To ansuere anely,° why thow   ocupyes the laundez,°   *answer alike/lands*
    That awe° homage of alde°   till° hym and his eldyres;°   *owe/old/to/forebears*
75 Why thow has redyn° and raymede°   and raunsound° þe   *overridden/plundered/extorted/*
      pople°   *people*
    And kyllyde doun his cosyns,   kyngys ennonttyde!°   *anointed*
    Thare° schall thow gyffe rekkynynge°   for all thy round   *there/give reckoning*
      table,
    Why thow art rebell to Rome   and rentez° them wytholdez.   *tributes*
    Ȝiff° thow theis° somouns wythsytte,°   he sendes thie thies° *if/this/disregard/you these*
      wordes:
80 He sall° the seke° ouer þe see°   wyth sexten kynges,   *shall/seek/sea*
    Bryne Bretayn° þe brade°   and bryttyn° thy knyghtys   *burn Britain/great/destroy*
    And brynge the bouxsomly° as a beste°   with brethe,   *obediently/beast/violence, where*
      whare° hym lykes,
    That thow ne° schall rowte ne ryste°   vndyr the heuene°   *not/assemble nor rest/heaven*
      ryche,
    Þof° thow for reddour° of Rome   ryne° to þe erthe.   *though/fear/run*
85 For if thow flee into Fraunce   or Freselaund owþer,°   *Friesland anywhere*
    Þou sall be fechede° with force   and forfette° fore euer.   *fetched/counted guilty*
    They fadyr mad fewtee,°   we fynde in oure rollez,   *your father made fealty*
    In the regestre of Rome,   who so ryghte lukez:°   *looks*
    Withowttyn more trouflynge°   the trebute we aske,   *trifling*
90 That Iulius Cesar wan°   wyth his ientill° knyghttes."   *won/noble*

     The kynge blyschit on° the beryn°   with his brode eghen,°   *looked at/knight/fierce eyes*
    Þat full brymly° for breth°   brynte° as the gledys;°   *very angrily/fury/burned/embers*
    Keste colours as° kynge   with crouell lates,°   *(his face) changed color like (a)/*
                                                                    grim looks

    Luked as a lyon   and on his lyppe bytes.
95 The Romaynes for radnesse°   ruschte° to þe erthe,   *fright/fell*
    Fore ferdnesse° of hys face,   as° they fey° were;   *for fear/as if/fated*
    Cowchide° as kenetez°   before þe kynge seluyn,   *cowered/hounds*
    Because of his contenaunce   confusede them semede.°   *they appeared*

---

67. Lammas (*hlāfmæsse*, "bread feast") Day is August 1.   **96.** *fey:* See above, p. 65, ll. 379–429n.
70. Prime was the period 6–9 A.M.

Arthur Feasts the Senator (vss. 166–258)

Now er° they herberde° in hey° and in oste holden°	*are/lodged/quickly/quarters kept*
[100] Hastyly wyth hende° men within thees heghe° wallez;	*friendly/high*
In chambyrs with chympnes° þey chaungen° þeire wedez,°	*fireplaces/change/clothes*
And sythyn° the chauncelere° þem fecchede° with cheualrye° noble.	*then/chancellor/fetched/chivalry*
Sone° þe senatour was sett,° as hym wele semyde,°	*soon/seated/to him well seemed*
At þe kyngez ownn borde;° twa° knyghtes hym seruede,	*table/two*
[105] Singulere sothely,° as Arthure hym seluyn,°	*most excellently in truth/self*
Richely on þe ryghte haunde° at the rounde table,	*hand*
Be **resoun**° þat þe Romaynes ware° so ryche holden,°	*by reason/were/important held*
As of þe realeste° blode,° þat reynede in° erthe.	*most royal/blood/reigned on*
There come° in at þe fyrste course, befor þe kynge seluen,°	*came/himself*
[110] Bareheuedys,° þat ware bryghte, burnyste° with syluer,	*boars' heads/adorned*
All with taghte° men and town° in togers full° ryche,	*expert/practiced/togas very*
Of saunke reall° in suyte,° sexty° at ones;°	*blood royal/company/sixty/once*
Flesch fluriste° of fermyson° with frumentee° noble,	*fattened/in the closed season/ frumenty*
Therto wylde° to wale° and wynlyche bryddes,°	*game/choice/pleasant birds*
[115] Pacokes° and plouers in platers of golde,	*peacocks*
Pygges of porke-despyne,° þat pasturede neuer;	*porcupine*
Sythen herons in hedoyne,° hyled° full faire;	*sauce/covered*
Grett° swannes full swythe° in silueryn chargeoures,°	*great/quick/silver platters*
Tartes of Turky: taste whan þem lykys!°	*when they like*
[120] Gumbaldes graythely,° full gracious to taste,	*dainties suitable*
Seyne bowes° of wylde bores° with þe braune° lechyde,°	*then thighs/boars/flesh/cut in pieces*
Bernakes° and botures° in baterde° dysches;	*barnacle geese/bitterns/embossed*
Þareby braunchers° in brede,° bettyr was neuer,	*young hawks/roasted*
With brestez of barowes,° þat bryghte ware to schewe.°	*pigs/behold*
[125] Seyn come þer sewes sere,° with solace° þerafter,	*soups various/pleasure*
Ownde° of azure all ouer and ardant þem semyde;°	*rippling/shining they seemed*
Of° **ilke a**° leche° þe lowe° launschide° full hye,	*from/each/strip of jelly/flame/ leaped*
Þat all ledes° myghte lyke, þat lukyde° þem apone;°	*men/looked/upon*
Þan° cranes and curlues,° craftyly° rosted,	*then/curlews/skillfully*
[130] Connygez° in cretoyne,° colourede full faire,	*rabbits/spiced broth*
Fesauntez enflureschit° in flammande° siluer,	*pheasants decorated/gleaming*
With dariells endoride,° and daynteez ynewe;°	*pastries glazed/enough*

---

113. Frumenty was wheat boiled in milk.

Þane° clarett and Creette° clergyally rennen°	then/Cretan (wine)/skillfully flowed
With condethes° full curious, all of clene° siluyre;	pipes/pure
135 Osay and algarde and oþer° ynewe,	others
Rynisch° wyne and Rochell,° richere was neuer;	Rhenish/La Rochelle
Vernage of Venyce vertuouse° and Crete	fine
In faucetez of fyn° golde: fonode° who so lykes!	fine/taste
The kynges cope-borde° was closed in° siluer,	wine table/covered with
140 In grete° goblettez ouergylte,° glorious of hewe;°	great/gilded over/hue
There was a cheeffe buttlere,° a cheualere° noble,	cupbearer/knight
Sir Cayous° þe curtaise,° þat of cowpe° sernede,	Kay/courteous/cup
Sexty cowpes of suyte° fore° þe kyng seluyn,°	after another/before/himself
Crafty° and curious, coruen° full faire,	skillful/carved
145 In euerilk a° party pyghte° with precyous stones,	every/part decorated
That nan enpoyson sulde goo° preuely° þerundyre,	no poison should go/secretly
Bot° þe bryght golde for brethe° sulde briste° al to peces,°	but/anger/burst/pieces
Or ells° þe venym sulde voyde° thurghe° vertue of þe stones;	else/disappear/through
And the conquerour hymseluen, so clenly° arayede,	brightly
150 In colours of clene° golde cledde,° wyth his knyghttys,	shining/dressed
Drissid° with his dyademe on his deesse° ryche,	arrayed/dais
Fore° he was demyde° þe doughtyeste þat duellyde° in erthe.	for/thought/dwelled
Thane° þe conquerour kyndly carpede° to þose lordes,	then/spoke
Rehetede° þe Romaynes with realle speche:°	encouraged/royal speech
155 "Sirs, bez° knyghtly of contenaunce and comfurthes° 3our seluyn:°	be/comfort/selves
We knowe noghte° in þis countre° of curious metez,°	not/country/foods
In thees barayne° landez bredes non oþer;°	barren/roasts none either
Forethy° wythowttyn feynynge° enforce 3ow° þe more,	therefore/pretense/try you
To feede 3ow° with syche feble,° as 3e° before fynde!"	yourself/such inferior (food)/you
160 "Sir," sais þe senatour, "so Criste motte° me saue,	may
There ryngnede° neuer syche realtee° within Rome walles.	reigned/royalty
There ne es° prelatte, ne pape,° ne prynce in þis erthe,	not is/nor pope
That he ne myghte be wele payede° of° þees pryce° metes!"	well pleased/with/prize
Aftyre theyre welthe° þey wesche° and went vnto chambyre,	pleasure/washed

---

133–37. The wines listed here were common and occur also in the Introduction to *Piers Plowman* as being "called" and sold in the streets of London; *clarett*: wine flavored with honey, *osay*: Alsatian wine, *algarde*: Spanish wine, *vernage*: Italian white wine.

141–142. The famous Seneschal, Sir Kay, is here Butler ("bottler," i.e., cupbearer) to Arthur, a position held in most sources by Sir Lucan.

146. In the noted porcelain collection of the Topkapi Serail Museum in Istanbul is a set of yellow china, presented as a gift to a former sultan, which was said to be able to change color under the influence of poison. Chemists say it is entirely possible for a glaze to be made to react to a specific poison, such as perhaps arsenic, though not to all poisons: the material would corrode but not shatter. On the other hand, in the Middle Ages, stones had magical properties which cannot be measured by present scientific standards.

165 Þis ilke kydde° conquerour   with knyghtes ynewe.   *same famous*
Sir Waywayne° þe worthye   Dame Waynour° he ledys;°   *Gawain/Guinevere/leads*
Sir Owghtreth on þe toþer syde,   of Turry was louerd.°   *lord*
Thane spyces vnsparyly°   þay spendyde° thereaftyre,   *unsparingly/distributed*
Maluesye° and muskadell,°   þase meruelyous° drynkes,   *malmsey/muscatel/those marvelous*
170 Raykede ful rathely°   in rossete° cowpes   *moved very quickly/russet*
Till° all þe riche° on rawe,°   Romaynes and oþer.   *to/worthies/one after another*
Bot the soueraingne sothely,°   for solauce° of hym seluen,°   *truly/pleasure/self*
Assingnyde° to þe senatour   certaygne° lordes,   *assigned/certain*
To lede to his leuere,°   whene he leue° askes,   *lodging/leave*
175 With myrthe and with melodye   of mynstralsy noble.
     Thane þe conquerour to concell°   cayres° thereaftyre   *council/goes*
Wyth lordes of his lygeaunce,°   þat to hym selfe langys;°   *allegiance/belong*
To þe geauntes toure°   iolily° he wendes,°   *Giant's Tower/happily/goes*
Wyth justicez and iuggez°   and gentill° knyghtes.   *judges/noble*
180 Sir Cador of Cornewayle   to þe kynge carppes,°   *speaks*
Lughe on° hym luffly°   with lykande lates:°   *laughed at/pleasantly/cheerful manner*

"I thanke Gode of° þat thraa,°   þat vs þus thretys!°   *for/battle/threatens*
Ʒow moste° be traylede,° I trowe,°   bot ʒife° ʒe trett° bettyre: *must/dragged (as punishment)/believe/unless/negotiate*

Þe lettres of sir Lucius   lyghttys myn herte.°   ***lighten my heart***
185 We hafe° as losels° liffyde°   many longe dayes,   *have/worthless men/lived*
Wyth delyttes in this lande,   with lordchipez° many,   *estates*
And forelytenede° the loos,°   þat we are laytted:°   *lessened/renown/formerly sought*
I was abaischite,° be° oure Lorde,   of oure beste bernes,°   *ashamed/by/knights*
Fore gret dule° of deffawte°   of dedez° of armes.   *great sorrow/weakness/deeds*
190 Now wakkenys° þe were,°   wyrchipe° be Cryste!   *awakens/war/worshiped*
And we sall° wynn it agayne   be wyghtnesse° and strenghe."°   *shall/bravery/strength*

Arthur Bids Farewell to Guinevere (vss. 693–735)

Nowe he takez hys leue°   —and lengez° no langere°—   *leave/delays/longer*
At° lordez, at lege-men,°   þat leues° hym byhynden.   *of/liege men/(he) leaves*

---

166. Gawain was the son of King Loth of Lodonesia and Anna, daughter of Uther Pendragon, Arthur's sister. Gawain's relationship to Arthur, that of nephew to uncle, was especially close in medieval romance (cf. above, p. 77, ll. 728–29n). Guinevere was Arthur's wife. (The forms *Waywayne* and *Waynour* alternate with *Gawain* and *Guinevere*, according to the needs of alliteration. The interchange of *w* with *g* was seen in Anglo-Norman and Central French words; English borrowed from both French dialects, e.g., *warden* and *guardian*, *reward* and *regard*.)

167. Sir Owghtreth of Turry has not been identified.

178. The Giant's Tower may be a place name in Wales (cf.

Dylan Thomas's poem *In the White Giant's Thigh*) rather than the home of a real giant. In Geoffrey of Monmouth, the Giant's Ring is found on Mount Killaraus in Ireland.

180. Sir Cador, duke of Cornwall, is an important man in Arthur's retinue. In Layamon's *Brut* he is active in the Saxon defeat after the battle of Bath and on the Isle of Thanet; but he is headstrong and at times a liability in Arthur's Continental campaign. In the battle with Lucius Hiberius, at Saussy (see above, pp. 84–85), Cador distinguishes himself by his valiant conduct. Arthur at his death gives the English crown to Cador's son Constantine (cf. ll. 892–93).

192–234. Arthur's departure is the poet's invention.

And seyne° þat worthilyche wy°   went vnto chambyre   *then/worthy man*
195 For to comfurthe° þe qwene,   þat in care lenges;°   *comfort/remains*
Waynour waykly°   wepande° hym kyssiz,   *Guinevere weakly/weeping*
Talkez to hym tenderly   with teres ynewe:°   *tears enough*
    "I may wery° the wye,   thatt this werre mouede,°   *curse/war started*
That warnes° me wyrchippe°   of my wedde lorde;   *forbids/good company*
200 All my lykynge° of lyfe   owt of lande wendez,°   *love/departs*
And I in langour am lefte,   leue ȝe,° for euere!°   *if you leave/ever*
Why ne° myghte I, dere lufe,°   dye° in ȝour armes,   *not/dear love/die*
Are° I þis destanye of dule°   sulde drye° by myne one?"°   *before/sorrow/must bear/myself alone*

    "Grefe þe noghte,° Gaynour,°   fore° Goddes lufe of hewen,°   *grieve you not/Guinevere/for/heaven*
205 Ne gruche° noghte my ganggynge:°   it sall° to gude° turne.   *nor begrudge/going/shall/good*
Thy wonrydez° and thy wepynge   woundez myn herte,°   *grief/my heart*
I may noghte wit° of þis woo,°   for all þis werlde ryche;°   *know/woe/world*
I haue made a kepare,°   a knyghte of thyn awen,°   *guardian/your own*
Ouerlynge° of Ynglande   vndyre thy seluen,°   *steward/self*
210 And that es° sir Mordrede,   þat þow° has mekyll° praysede,   *is/you/greatly*
Sall be thy dictour,° my dere,   to doo whatt the lykes."°   *agent/want*
    Thane° he takes hys leue   at ladys in chambyre,   *then*
Kysside them kyndlyche°   and to Criste beteches,°   *kindly/commits (them)*
And then cho swounes full swythe,°   when he hys swerde aschede,°   *she swoons very suddenly/sword demanded*
215 Sweyes° in a swounyng,°   swelte as cho walde.°   *falls/faint/as if she would die*
He pressed to his palfray°   in presance of lordes,   *horse*
Prekys of° the palez°   with his prys° knyghtes,   *spurs from/palace/prize*
Wyth a reall rowte°   of þe rounde table,   *royal company*
Soughte° towarde Sandwyche: cho sees hym no more!   *headed*
220   Thare° the grete ware gederyde°   wyth galyarde° knyghtes,   *there/great host gathered/lusty*
Garneschit° on þe grene felde°   and graythelyche° arayede;   *garnished/field/wondrously*
Dukkes and duzseperez°   daynttely° rydes,   *peers/expertly*
Erlez of Ynglande   with archers ynewe:
Schirreues° scharply   schiftys° the comounes,°   *sheriffs/control/commons*
225 Rewlys° before þe ryche°   of the rounde table,   *command/powerful (men)*
Assingnez° ilke a° contree°   to certayne lordes,   *assigns/each/district*

---

210. Modred was the second son of King Loth of Lodonesia and Arthur's sister, and therefore, like Gawain, Arthur's nephew.

219. Here and in Malory, Sandwich is named as the assembly point of the army; in all other sources it is Southampton.

223. The prominent reference to archers here, and in the later sea battle against Modred, signals the importance of this fighting force of yeomen in British battle strategy of the time—especially against the heavy and cumbersome chivalry of France, as at Crécy and Poitiers.

220–34. This is a vigorous description of a medieval expeditionary force on the move, with the packing of duffel bags, tents, chests, and so on. We may imagine that William the Conqueror's army in 1066 was in similar turmoil before embarkation.

In the southe on þe see-banke:° saile when þem° lykes!°	*seacoast/they/want to*
Thane bargez them° buskez° and to þe baunke° rowes,	*for themselves/(they) prepare/shore*
Bryngez blonkez° on bourde° and burlyche helmes;°	*horses/board/noble helmets*
230 Trussez° in tristly° trappyde stedes,°	*pack/reliably/steeds with trappings*
Tenntez and othire toylez° and targez° full ryche,	*cloths/shields*
Cabanes° and clathe-sekkes° and coferez° full noble,	*portable huts/clothes-bags/coffers*
Hukes° and haknays° and horsez of armez;°	*horses/hackneys/war-horses*
Thus they stowe in the stuffe of full steryn° knyghtez.	*stern*

Arthur Fights the Giant of Mont-Saint-Michel (vss. 933–1191)

235 Than ferkez° this folke and on fotte lyghttez,°	*then move/foot alight*
Festenez° theire faire stedez° o ferrom bytwenne;°	*fasten/steeds/at a distance*
And thene the kynge kenely° comandyde hys knyghtez,	*sharply*
For to byde with theire blonkez° and bowne° no forthyre:°	*horses/go/farther*
"Fore° I will seke° this seynte° by my selfen one°	*for/seek/saint/self alone*
240 And mell° with this mayster-mane,° þat this monte ȝemez;°	*deal/ruler/mount guards*
And seyn sall ȝe° offyre,° aythyre° aftyre oþer,	*then shall you/make offering/one of you*
Menskfully at° Saynt Mighell° full° myghtty with° Criste!"	*honorably to/Michael/very/in*
The kyng coueris° þe cragge wyth cloughes° full hye,°	*reaches/chasms/high*
To the creste of the clyffe he clymbez on lofte;°	*high up*
245 Keste° vpe hys vmbrere,° and kenly he lukes,°	*cast/visor/looks*
Caughte of° þe colde wynde, to comforthe° hym seluen;°	*breathed in/comfort/self*
Two fyrez he fyndez, flawmande° full hye,	*flaming*
The fourtedele a furlange° betwene þus he ferkes!°	*fourth of a furlong/travels*
The waye by þe welle-strandez° he wandyrde hym one,°	*well streams/by himself*
250 To wette° of þe warlawe,° whare þat° he lengez;°	*learn/warlock/where/dwells*
He ferkez° to þe fyrste fyre, and euen° there he fyndez	*goes/right*
A wery wafull wedowe,° wryngande hire° handez	*weary woeful widow/wringing her*
And gretande° on a graue grysely teres,°	*weeping/terrible tears*
New merkyde on molde,° sen° myddaye it semede:°	*made in earth/since/seemed*
255 He saluȝede° þat sorowfull° with sittande° wordez	*greeted/sorrowful (one)/pleasant*
And fraynez° aftyre the fende° fairely° thereaftyre.	*asks/fiend/graciously*
Thane° this wafull wyfe vnnwynly° hym gretez,°	*then/unhappily/greets*
Couerde° vp on hire knees and clappyde hire handez;	*got*
Said: "Careful careman,° thow carpez to° lowde:	*wretched man/you speak too*

235–493. Compare the description of Arthur's fight with the giant of Mont-Saint-Michel in Geoffrey of Monmouth (this volume, pp. 133–35) and in Layamon's *Brut* (this volume, pp. 76–85). The giant has captured, raped, and killed Helena, the niece of Hoel, king of Brittany. Arthur tells Kay and Bedevere that he wishes to go alone to seek a saint on the mount and sets out to avenge his kinsman Hoel.

248. A furlong (i.e., a "furrow long") is one-eighth of a mile; thus Arthur proceeds 165 feet.

252–342. In Geoffrey of Monmouth and in Layamon, it is Bedevere who talks with the old woman.

260 May ʒone° warlawe wyt,°   he worows° vs alle.   *if that|hears|would tear to pieces*
　　Weryd worthe° þe wyghte ay,°   that þe° thy° wytt refede,°   *cursed be|man ever|you|of your|*
　　　　　　　　　　　　　　　　　　　　　　　　　　　　　robbed

　　That mas° the to wayfe° here   in þise° wylde lakes!°   *makes|wander|these|streams*
　　I warne the, fore wyrchipe°   þou wylnez aftyr° sorowe.   *honor|wish for*
　　Whedyre buskes° þou, berne?°   vnblysside° þow semes!   *whither go|knight|unblessed*
265 Wenez° thow to britten° hym   with thy brande ryche?°   *think|destroy|sword powerful*
　　Ware° thow wyghttere° than Wade   or Wawayn owthire,°   *were|stronger|Gawain either*
　　Thow wynnys no wyrchipe,   I warne the before;
　　Thow saynned the vnsekyrly,°   to seke to° þese mountez!   *blessed yourself badly|for*
　　Siche sex° ware to symple,°   to semble° with hym one;   *six such|few|fight*
270 For and° thow see hym with syghte,   the seruez° no herte,°   *if|avails|courage*
　　To sayne the sekerly,°   so semez hym huge!   *surely*
　　Thow art frely° and faire   and in thy fyrste flourez,°   *noble|flower*
　　Bot° thow art fay,° be° my faythe,   and þat fele° me   *but|doomed|by|much|sorrows*
　　　　forthynkkys.°
　　Ware syche fyfty° on a felde°   or on a faire erthe,°   *fifty such|field|plain*
275 The freke walde° with hys fyste   fell ʒow° at ones.°   *monster would|you|once*
　　Loo!° here the duchez dere°   —to daye was cho° takyn—   *lo|duchess dear|she*
　　Depe doluen° and dede,°   dyked° in moldez!°   *deep dug|dead|buried|earth*
　　He hade morthirede° this mylde,°   be° myddaye war   *murdered|mild (one)|when|was*
　　　　rongen,°   　　　　　　　　　　　　　　　　　　*rung*
　　Withowttyn mercy on molde,   I not° whatt it mente: *know not*
280 He has forsede° hir and fylede,°   and cho es fay leuede;°   *raped|dishonored|is **dead left***
　　He slewe hir vnslely°   and slitt hir to þe nauyll,°   *roughly|navel*
　　And here haue I bawmede° hir   and beryede° þeraftyr;   *embalmed|buried*
　　For bale of° þe botelesse°   blythe be I neuer!   *misery over|what is without remedy*
　　Of alle þe frendez cho hade,   þere folowede none aftyre,
285 Bot I, hir foster-modyr°   of fyftene wynter;°   *foster-mother|winters*
　　To ferke of° this farlande°   fande sall° I neuer,   *from|promontory|attempt*
　　Bot here be founden° on felde,°   til I be fay leuede!"   *found|ground*
　　　　Thane answers sir Arthure   to þat alde° wyfe: *old*
　　"I am comyn fra° þe conquerour,   curtaise° and gentill,°   *from|courteous|noble*
290 As one of þe athelest°   of Arthur° knyghtez,   *noblest|Arthur's*
　　Messenger to þis myxen,°   for mendemente° of þe pople,°   *filth|help|people*
　　To mele° with this maister-man,°   that here this mounte   *deal|ruler|guards*
　　　　ʒemez;°
　　To trete° with this tyraunt   for tresoun° of landez   *treat|treason*
　　And take trew° for a tym,°   to bettyr may tide."°   *truce|time|until a better time*
295　　"ʒa,° thine wordis are bot waste,"   quod° this wif thane,°   *yes|said|then*
　　"For bothe landez and lythes°   full° lyttill by he settes,°   *people|very|he accounts*

---

266. Wade was the father of Wayland the Smith. According
to the early English poem *Widsith*, Wade, who ruled the
Hælsings, was a giant, son of a woman who lived in the sea.

276. Helena, duchess of Brittany, Hoel's niece.

Of rentez ne° of rede° golde rekkez° he neuer; *tribute nor/red/cares*
For he will lenge° owt of lawe,° as hym selfe° likes, *remain/lawless/he*
Withouten licence of lede,° as lorde in his awen.° *man/own (right)*
300 Bot he has a kyrtill° on, kepide° for hym seluen,° ***tunic**/kept/self*
That was sponen° in Spayne with° specyall byrdez,° *spun/by/young women*
And sythyn garnescht° in Grece full graythly togedirs;° *then decorated/excellently together*
It es hydede° all with hare° hally° al ouere *covered/hair/wholly*
And bordyrde with the berdez° of burlyche° kyngez, *beards/strong*
305 Crispid° and kombide,° that kempis° may knawe° *curled/combed/men/know*
Iche° kynge by his colour, in kythe there° he lengez.° *each/country where/dwells*
Here the fermez° he fangez° of fyftene rewmez,° *tributes/receives/realms*
For ilke° Esterne-ewyn,° howeuer that it falle, *each/**Easter Eve***
They send it hym sothely° for saughte° of þe pople *truly/security*
310 Sekerly° at þat seson° with certayne knyghtez, *surely/season*
And he has aschede° Arthure all þis aughte wynntter.° *demanded of/these eight winters*
Forthy erdez° he here, to owttraye° hys pople, *therefore lives/destroy*
Till þe Bretons kynge haue burneschte° his lyppys *shaved*
And sent his berde to that bolde° wyth his beste berynes;° *bold (one)/knights*
315 Bot thow hafe° broghte þat berde, bowne the° no forthire,° *unless you have/go you/farther*
For it es butelesse° bale, thowe biddez oghte elles;° *without remedy/await nothing else*
For he has more tresour° to take, when hym lykez,° *treasure/he likes*
Than euere aughte° Arthure or any of hys elders.° *ever owned/forebears*
If thow hafe broghte þe berde, he bes° more blythe, *will be*
320 Thane þow gafe° hym Burgoyne° or Bretayne° þe more;° *(if) you gave/Burgundy/Britain/ greater*

Bot luke° now for charitee,° þow chasty° thy lyppes, *but look/heaven's sake/(that) you control*

That the no wordez eschape,° what wonder so° betydez;° *escape/whatever wonder/(may) happen*

Luke þi presante be priste° and presse° hym bott lytill, *ready/urge*
For he es° at his sowper,° he will be sone greuyde.° *is/supper/quickly angered*
325 And° þow my concell doo,° þow dos of° thy clothes *if/counsel follow/put off*
And knele° in thy kyrtyll and call hym thy louerd.° *kneel/lord*
He sowppes° all þis seson° with° seuen knaue childre,° *sups/time/on/boy babes*
Choppid in a chargour° of chalke-whytt° syluer *dish/chalk-white*
With pekill° and powdyre of precious spycez *pickle*
330 And pyment° full plenteuous of Portyngale° wynes; *spiced, honeyed drink/Portugal*
Thre balefull birdez° his brochez° þey turne, *three miserable girls/spits*
Þat byddez° his bedgatt,° his byddynge° to wyrche;° *await/going to bed/will/do*
Siche foure° scholde° be fay° within foure hourez, *four such/should/doomed*

---

297. *rede golde:* Cf. below, p. 183, l. 47*n*.

300–20. In Geoffrey of Monmouth the beard-garment story concerns the giant Retho who is killed by Arthur on Mount Arvaius (also called Mount Erith or Mount Aravia; cf. *montez*

of Araby, l. 477), which has been identified as Mount Snowdon or Eryri in Wales. The confusion of the two stories is also in Layamon.

Are° his fylth ware° fillede,   that his flesch ȝernes."°   *before/lust were/desires*

335 "Ȝa,° I haue broghte þe berde," quod° he,   "the bettyre   *yes/said/I am the happier*
me lykez;°

Forthi will I boun me°   and bere° it my seluen;   *make myself ready/carry*

Bot, lefe,° walde þow° lere° me   whare° þat lede lengez,°   *dear/if you would/tell/where/man stays*

I sall alowe þe,° and I liffe,°   oure Lorde so me helpe!"   *shall praise you/live*

"Ferke° fast to þe fyre," quod cho,°   "that flawmez° so   *go/she/flames/high*
hye;°

340 Thare fillis° þat fende hym:°   fraist° when the lykez!°   *there stuffs/fiend himself/seek (him)/like*

Bot thow moste seke° more southe,   sydlynngs° a lyttill,   *must scout/aside*

For he will hafe sent° hym selfe   sex° myle large."°   *scent/six/miles distant*

To þe sowthre° of þe reke°   he soghte° at þe gayneste,°   *south/smoke/scouted/most profitably*

Sayned° hym sekerly   with certeyne° wordez,   *crossed/certain*

345 And sydlynngs° of þe segge°   the syghte had he rechide,°   *from the side/man/reached*

How vnsemly° þat sott°   satt sowpande° hym one.°   *ugly/fool/supping/by himself*

He lay lenand° on lange,°   lugande vnfaire,°   *leaning/full length/resting grossly*

Þe thee° of a manns lymme°   lyfte vp by þe haunche;   *thigh/limb*

His bakke° and his bewschers°   and his brode lendez°   *back/buttocks/broad loins*

350 He bekez° by þe bale-fyre°   and brekless hym semede;°   *bakes/bonfire/without breeches he seemed*

Þare ware rostez full ruyde°   and rewfull° bredez,°   *roasts very raw/terrible/roast meats*

Beerynes° and bestaile°   brochede togeders,°   *men/beasts/spitted together*

Cowle° full cramede°   of crysmede childyre,°   *tub/crammed/with confirmed babes*

Sum° as brede° brochede;   and hierdez° þam tournede.°   *some/roast/young women/them turned*

355   And þan° this comlych° kynge,   bycause of his pople,°   *then/fair/people*

His herte bledez° for bale°   one bent,° whare he standez.   *heart bleeds/sorrow/on field*

Thane° he dressede on his schelde,°   schuntes° no lengere,°   *then/slung/shield/delays/longer*

Braundescht° his brode swerde°   by þe bryghte hiltez,   *brandished/sword*

Raykez° towarde þe renke°   reghte° with a ruyde° wille   *turns/man/straight/hardy*

360 And hyely hailsez° þat hulke°   with hawtayne° wordez: *proudly greets/monster/haughty*

"Now, all-weldand° Gode,   þat wyrscheppez vs alle,°   *all-powerful/all of us worship*

Giff the° sorowe and syte,°   sotte, there thow lygges,°   *give you/misery/where you lie*

For the fulsomeste freke,°   that fourmede° was euere!°   *most horrible monster/created/ever*

Foully thow fedys the,°   þe fende haue thi saule!°   *feed yourself/soul*

365 Here es cury vnclene,°   carle,° be° my trowthe,°   *is cooking unclean/lout/by/troth*

Caffe° of creatours° all,   thow curssede wriche!°   *refuse/creatures/wretch*

Because that þow killide has   þise° cresmede childyre,   *these*

Thow has marters made   and merked° out of lyfe,   *destroyed*

Þat here are brochede on bente   and brittenede° with thi   *cut up*
handez,

370 I sall merke° þe thy mede,°   as þou has myche serfede,°   *give/reward/much deserved*

Thurghe° myghte of seynt Mighell,° þat þis monte ȝemes.°	*through/Saint Michael/mount guards*
And for this faire ladye, þat þow has fey leuyde°	*dead left*
And þus forcede° on foulde° for fylth° of þi selfen,°	*raped/ground/lust/your own*
Dresse° the now, dogge-sone,° the deuell° haue þi saule!	*prepare/dog's son/Devil*
375 For þow sall dye° this day thurghe dynt° of my handez!"	*die/blow*
Than glopnede° þe gloton° and glorede vnfaire,°	*was frightened/glutton/glared wildly*
He grennede° as a grewhounde° with grysly tuskes;°	*snarled/greyhound/terrible fangs*
He gapede, he groned faste, with grucchande latez°	*growling manner*
For grefe° of þe gude° kynge, þat hym with grame gretez.°	*fear/good/anger greets*
380 His fax° and his foretoppe° was filterede° togeders	*hair/forelock/matted*
And owte of his face come° ane° halfe fote large;°	*grew/a/foot long*
His frount° and his forheuede,° fully° was it ouer	*face/brow/all*
As þe fell° of a froske,° and fraknede° it semede,°	*skin/frog/spotted/seemed*
Huke-nebbyde° as a hawke, and with a hore berde,°	*hook-nosed/gray beard*
385 And herede° to þe eyghn-holes° with hyngande° browes;	*hairy/eye holes/hanging*
Harske° as a hunde-fisch,° hardly° who so lukez,°	*harsh/dogfish/sharply/looks*
So was þe hyde of þat hulke hally° al ouer.	*completely*
Erne° had he full huge and vgly to schewe,°	*ears/behold*
With eghne° full horreble and ardauunt° for sothe;°	*eyes/glittering/truly*
390 Flatt-mowthede as a fluke° with fleryande° lyppys,	*flounder/grinning*
And þe flesche in his fortethe° fowly° as a bere.°	*front teeth/ugly/bear*
His berde was brostly° and blake,° þat till° his brest rechede;°	*bristly/black/to/reached*
Grassede° as a mereswyne° with corkes° full° huge,	*fat/dolphin/carcass/very*
And all falterde° þe flesche in his foule lippys,	*trembled*
395 Ilke wrethe° as a wolfe-heuede,° it wraythe° owtt at ones!°	*each fold/wolf's head/twisted/once*
Bullenekkyde° was þat bierne° and brade° in the scholders,	*bullnecked/fellow/broad*
Brok-brestede° as a brawne° with brustils° full large,	*badger-breasted/boar/bristles*
Ruyd° armes as an ake° with rusclede° sydes,	*rough/oak/wrinkled*
Lym° and leskes° full lothyn,° leue ȝe° for sothe:	*limb/loins/hideous/believe you*
400 Schouell-fotede° was þat schalke° and schaylande° hym semyde°	*shovel-footed/fellow/crooked-legged/he seemed*
With schankez vnschaply, schowand togedyrs;°	*shoved together*
Thykke theese° as a thursse° and thikkere in þe hanche,°	*thighs/giant/haunch*
Greesse-growen° as a galte,° full gryslych° he lukez.	*fat/pig/grisly*
Who þe lenghe° of þe lede° lelly accountes,°	*length/man/accurately measures*
405 Fro° þe face to þe fote he was lange fyfe fadom.°	*from/long five fathoms*
Thane stertez° he vp sturdely on two styffe° schankez,	*then jumps/strong*
And sone° he caughte hym a clubb all of clene yryn.°	*quickly/himself/pure iron*
He walde hafe° kyllede þe kynge with his kene wapen,°	*would have/sharp weapon*
Bot° thurghe þe crafte° of Cryste ȝit° þe carle° failede,	*but/power/yet/churl*
410 The creest° and the coronall,° þe claspes of syluer,	*crest/diadem*
Clenly° with his clubb he crasschede° doune at onez.	*strongly/crashed*

The kynge castes vp his schelde° and couers hym faire,°	*shield/well*
And with his burlyche brande° a box° he hym reches;°	*strong sword/blow/fetches*
Full butt° in þe frunt° the fromonde° he hittez,	*plain/forehead/monster*
415 That° the burnyscht blade to þe brayne rynnez;°	*so that/slices*
He feyede° his fysnamye° with his foule hondez°	*wiped/face/hands*
And frappez° faste at hys face fersely° þeraftyre.	*strikes/fiercely*
The kyng chaungez° his fote, eschewes° a lyttill,	*moves/retreats*
Ne° had he eschapede° þat choppe, cheuede had° euyll;	*not/escaped/would have occurred*
420 He folowes in fersly and a dynte festeness°	*blow delivers*
Hye° vpe on þe hanche with his harde wapyn,	*high*
That he hillid° þe swerde halfe a fote large;°	*sank in/foot deep*
The hott blode° of þe hulke° vnto° þe hilte rynnez,°	*blood/monster/onto/flows*
Ewyn° into þe inmette° the gyaunt he hyttez,	*even/intestines*
425 Iust° to þe genitales and jaggede þam° in sondre.°	*right/ripped them/asunder*
Thane he romyede° and rarede,° and ruydly° he strykez	*screamed/roared/harshly*
Full egerly at Arthure and on the erthe hittez,	
A swerde-lenghe° within þe swarthe° he swappez° at ones,	*sword length/grass/cuts*
That nere swounes° þe kynge for swoughe° of his dynttez.	*almost faints/rush*
430 Bot ȝit the kynge sweperly° full swythe° he byswenkez,°	*quickly/fast/retaliates*
Swappez in with the swerde, þat it þe swange brystedde;°	*loins burst*
Bothe þe guttez and the gorre° guschez owt at ones,	*gore*
Þat all englaymez° þe gresse° on grounde, þer° he standez.	*becomes slimy/grass/where*
Thane he castez the clubb and the kynge hentez,°	*grabs*
435 On þe creeste of þe cragg he caughte hym in armez,	
And enclosez hym clenly, to cruschen° hys rybbez;	*crush*
So harde haldez° he þat hende,° þat nere his herte brystez.°	*holds/man/heart bursts*
Þane þe balefull bierdez° bownez° to þe erthe,	*woeful maidens/fall*
Kneland° and cryande,° and clappide þeire handez:	*kneeling/crying*
440 "Criste comforthe ȝone° knyghte and kepe° hym fro sorowe	*comfort that/keep*
And latte° neuer ȝone fende° fell hym o° lyfe!"	*let/fiend/destroy his*
Ȝitt es° þe warlow° so wyghte,° he welters° hym vnder,	*is/warlock/strong/throws*
Wrothely þai wrythyn° and wrystill togederz,°	*angrily they twist/wrestle together*
Welters° and walowes° ouer within þase° wilde buskez,°	*turn/roll/those/bushes*
445 Tumbellez and turnes faste and terez þaire wedez,°	*tear their clothes*
Vntenderly fro° þe toppe þai tiltin° togederz,	*from/fall*
Whilom° Arthure ouer and oþerwhile° vndyre,	*sometimes/other times*
Fro þe heghe° of þe hyll vnto þe harde roche;°	*top/rock*
They feyne° neuer, are° they fall at þe flode merkes.°	*give up/before/seashore*
450 Bot Arthur with ane anlace° egerly smyttez°	*a dagger/eagerly smites*
And hittez euer in° the hulke vp to þe hiltez.	*into*
Þe theeffe at° þe dede-thrawe° so throly° hym thryngez,°	*in/death throes/vigorously/fights*
Þat three rybbys in his syde he thrystez° in sundere.°	*thrusts/asunder*

Then sir Kayous þe kene°   vnto þe kynge styrtez,°   *bold/comes*

⁴⁵⁵ Said: "Allas! we are lorne,°   my lorde es confundede,°   *lost/brought to ruin*

Ouerfallen with° a fende,   vs° es full hapnede!°   *attacked by/to us/bad luck*

We mon° be forfetede° in faith   and flemyde° for euer."   *must/lost/put to flight*

    Þay hafe° vp hys hawberke þan°   and handilez° þervndyre   *raise/armor then/feel*

His hyde° and his haunche eke,°   on heghte° to þe schuldrez,°   *skin/also/up/shoulders*

⁴⁶⁰ His flawnke° and his feletez°   and his faire sydez,   *flank/rib muscles*

Bothe his bakke° and his breste   and his bryghte° armez.   *back/fair*

Þay ware fayne,° þat þey fande°   no flesche entamede°   *were happy/found/wounded*

And for þat journee° made joye,   þir gentill° knyghttez.   *day's work/these noble*

    "Now, certez,"° sais Sir Bedwere,°   "it semez, be° my   *certainly/Bedevere/seems, by*
    Lorde!

⁴⁶⁵ He sekez seyntez bot selden,°   þe sorere° he grypes,°   *seeks saints but seldom/harder/grips*

Þat þus clekys° this corsaunt°   owt of þir heghe° clyffez,   *seizes/saint/high*

To carye forthe siche° a carle,°   at close° hym in siluere.   *such/fellow/enclose (as a relic)*

Be Myghell,° of syche a makk°   I hafe myche° wondyre,   *Michael/fellow/have much*

That euer owre soueraygne° Lorde   suffers° hym in heuen;°   *sovereign/allows/heaven*

⁴⁷⁰ And° all sayntez be syche,   þat seruez oure Louerd,   *if*

I sall° neuer no seynt bee,°   be my fadyre sawle!"°   *shall/be/father's soul*

    Thane bouredez° þe bolde kynge   at Bedvere° wordez: *laughed/Bedevere's*

"Þis seynt haue I soghte,   so saue me owre Louerd!

Forthy brayd° owtte þi brande°   and broche° hym to þe   *therefore pull/sword/pierce*
herte!

⁴⁷⁵ Be sekere° of this sergeaunt,°   he has me sore greuede.°   *make sure/armed man/greatly troubled*

I faghte noghte° wyth syche a freke°   þis° fyftene wyntyrs,   *fought not/fellow/these*

Bot in þe montez° of Araby   I mett syche anoþer;   *mount*

He was þe forcyere° be ferre,°   þat had I nere° funden:°   *stronger/far/almost/found out*

Ne° had my fortune bene° faire,   fey° had I ben° leuede.°   *not/been/dead/would I have been/left*

⁴⁸⁰ Onone° stryke of° his heuede°   and stake it thereaftyre,   *quickly/off/head*

Gife° it to thy hanseman,°   fore° he es wele° horsede;   *give/servant/for/is well*

Bere° it to sir Howell,°   þat es in herde bandez,°   *carry/Hoel/hard bonds (of sorrow)*

And byd hym herte hym° wele,   his enmy° es destruede;°   *take heart/enemy/destroyed*

Syne° bere it to Bareflete   and brace° it in yryne°   *then/enclose/iron*

⁴⁸⁵ And sett it on the barbycane,°   biernes° to schewe.°   *barbican/knights/show*

My brande and my brode schelde°   apon° þe bent lyggez,°   *broad shield/upon/field lies*

On þe creeste° of þe cragge,   thare° fyrste we encontrede,°   *crest/where/met*

And þe clubb þarby,°   all of clene° iren,   *by it/pure*

---

465. "However hard his grip, he will not seek such saints often." Bedevere is following up with a joke Arthur's ruse to be alone (see l. 239).

477. Cf. ll. 300–20n.

484. Barfleur, where Arthur landed in France, is on the Cotentin peninsula, near Cherbourg.

485. The barbican was the outermost fortification wall of a stronghold.

þat many Cristen° has kyllyde   in Constantyne landez;   *Christians*
490 Ferke° to the farlande°   and fetche me þat wapen°   *go/promontory/weapon*
And late° us founde till° oure flete,°   in flode° þare it lengez.°   *let/turn toward/fleet/sea/lies*
If thow wyll° any tresour,°   take what the lykez;°   *you desire/treasure/you like*
Haue I° the kyrtyll° and þe clubb,   I coueite noghte elles "°   *as long as I have/tunic/desire*
                                                                                       nothing else

Arthur's Army Crosses the Alps (vss. 3084–133)

When þe kyng Arthure   hade lely° conquerid   *honorably*
495 And the castell couerede°   of þe kythe° riche,   *won/province*
All þe crowell° and kene°   be craftes° of armes,   *hard/bold (men)/by might*
Captayns and constables,   knewe hym for lorde.
He deuysede° and delte°   to dyuerse° lordez   *granted/distributed/divers*
A dowere° for þe duchez°   and hir dere childire;°   *endowment/duchess/dear children*
500 Wroghte wardaynes° by wytte°   to welde° all þe londez,°   *made governors/wisdom/rule/lands*
That he had wonnen of werre°   thorowe° his weise°   *won in war/through/hardy*
      knyghtez.
    Thus in Lorayne he lenges°   as lorde in his awen,°   *remains/own (right)*
Settez lawes in the lande,   as hym° leefe thoghte;°   *to him/good seemed*
And on þe Lammese-day°   to Lucerne he wendez,°   *Lammas Day/goes*
505 Lengez thare° at laysere°   with lykynge inowe.°   *there/leisure/pleasure enough*
Thare his galays ware graythede,°   a full gret° nombyre,   *ships were prepared/very great*
All gleterand° as glase°   vndire grene hyllys   *glittering/glass*
With cabanes° couerede   for kynges anoyntede,   *cabins*
With clothes of clere° golde   for knyghtez and oþer;°   *pure/others*
510 Sone° they stowede theire stuffe   and stablede þeire horses,   *quickly*
Strekes streke° ouer þe strem°   into þe strayte londez.°   *take course straight/water/narrow*
                                                                                       passes

Now he moues his myghte   with myrthes° of herte°   *joy/heart*
Ouere mowntes° so hye,°   þase meruailous° wayes;   *over mountains/high/those marvelous*
Gosse° in by Goddarde,°   the garett° he wynnys,   *goes/Saint Gotthard/watchtower*
515 Graythes° the garnison°   grisely wondes.°   *inflicts on/defenders/grisly wounds*
When he was passede the heghte,°   than° the kyng houys°   *height/then/stops*
With his hole batayle,°   behaldande° abowte,   *whole army/looking*
Lukande one° Lumbarddye,   and one lowde° melys:°   *looking on/aloud/speaks*
"In 3one lykande° londe   lorde be I thynke."°   *that pleasant/I mean to be*
520   Thane° they cayre° to Combe°   with kyngez anoyntede,   *then/move/Como*

---

489. The Constantine lands are the Cotentin peninsula.
494–95. Metz in Lorraine has been captured by Arthur.
499. The duchess of Lorraine is pardoned; the duke languishes in prison in Dover Castle.
504. Cf. l. 67n.

511. Arthur evidently uses the ships to transport his army over the Lake of Lucerne. He then heads over the Saint Gotthard pass.
520. Como is on Lake Como. Arthur's route was probably via Bellinzona and Lugano to Como.

That was kyde of° þe coste,°   kay° of all oþer.   *famous on/coast/key*
Sir Florent and sir Floridas   þan fowndes° before   *go*
With freke° men of Fraunce   well a° fyve hundreth;°   *bold/a good/hundred*
To þe cete vnsene°   thay soghte° at þe gayneste°   *city unseen/they reached/most*
                                                          quickly

525 And sett an enbuschement,°   als° þem selfe° lykys.°   *ambush/as/they/desire*
Thane ischewis° owt of þat cete   full sone be° þe morne   *ride/in*
Skathele discouerours,°   skyftes° theire horses;°   *dangerous scouts/move*
Than skyftes þes skouerours°   and skippes° on hyllis,   *these scouts/jump*
Diskoueres° for skulkers,   that they no skathe lymppen;° *spy/harm undergo*
530 Pouerall° and pastorelles°   passede on aftyre   *poor people/shepherds*
With porkes to pasture   at° the price ʒates;°   *through/noble gates*
Boyes in þe subarbis°   bourden° full heghe°   *suburbs/had their fun/great*
At° a bare synglere,°   that to þe bente rynnys.°   *with/wild boar/field runs*
Thane brekes° oure buschemennt°   and the brigge° wynnes, *breaks out/ambush/bridge*
535 Brayedez° into þe burghe°   with baners displayede,   *storms/town*
Stekes° and stabbis thorowe,   that° them aʒayne-stondes;° *pierces/(them) that/withstand*
Fowre stretis,° or° þay stynte,°   they stroyen° fore euere.° *four streets/before/stop/destroy/*
                                                               forever

Now es° the conquerour in Combe   and his courte holdes   *is*
Within þe kyde castell   with kynges enoynttede;°   *anointed*
540 Reconsaillez° the comouns,°   þat to þe kyth lengez,° *reconciles/common people/land*
                                                             belong

Comfourthes° þe carefull°   with knyghtly wordez;°   *comforts/unhappy*
Made a captayne kene°   a knyghte of hys awen;°   *bold/own*
Bot° all þe contre° and he   full sone° ware accordide.° *but/country/soon/in agreement*

Modred's Treason and the Sea Battle (vss. 3456–711)

Thane° rysez the riche° kynge   and rawghte° on his wedys,° *then/great/put/garments*
545 A reedde acton° of rosse,°   the richeste of floures,° *red aketon/rose color/flowers*
A pesane° and a paunson°   and a pris girdill;°   *chest-neck armor/stomach armor/*
                                                              precious belt

And on he henttis° a hode°   of hewe full° riche,   *throws/hood/hue very*
A pauys° pillion-hatt,   þat pighte° was full faire   *Pavian/decorated*
With perry° of þe Oryent   and precyous stones;°   *pearls*
550 His gloues gayliche° gilte   and grauen by° þe hemmys, *gaily/embroidered on*

---

544. After the capture of Rome, Arthur has had a dream that is interpreted to mean impending disaster (cf. Laymon's *Brut*, this volume, pp. 85–88).
545. The aketon was a heavy, lined coat worn under the chest armor.

548. The pillion hat was shieldlike.

With graynes° of rubyes,   full gracious to schewe;°   *chips/behold*
His bede grehownde° and his bronde°   and no byerne elles,°   *greedy greyhound/sword/man else*
And bownnes° ouer a brode mede°   with breth° at his herte;°   *walks/broad meadow/anger/heart*
Furth° he stalkis° a stye°   by þa° still euys,°   *forth/walks (on)/path/the/border lanes*

555 Stotays° at a hey strette,°   studyande° hym one.°   *stops/main road/in study/alone*
Att the surs° of þe sonne°   he sees there commande,°   *rising/sun/coming*
Raykande° to Rome-warde   the redyeste° wayes   *traveling/shortest*
A renke° in a rownde cloke   with righte rowmme° clothes,   *man/full*
With hatte and with heyghe schone,°   homely and rownde;   *high shoes*
560 With flatte ferthynges° the freke°   was floreschede° all ouer,   *farthings/fellow/decorated*
Manye schredys and schragges°   at his skyrttes hynnges,°   *tatters/hang*
With scrippe° ande with sclawyn°   and skalopis° inewe,°   *bag/pilgrim's mantle/scallop shells/enough*

Both pyke° and palme,   alls° pilgram hym scholde.°   *staff/as/he should*
  The gome graythely° hym grette°   and bade gode morwen;°   *man graciously/greeted/good morning*
565 The kyng lordelye hym selfe   of langage° of Rome,   *in language*
Of Latyn corroumppede° all,   full louely° hym menys:°   *corrupted/kindly/addresses*
"Whedire wilnez thow, wye,°   walkande° thyn one?°   *whither will you (go), man/walking/alone*

Qwhylls° þis werlde es o werre,°   a wathe° I it holde;   *while/is at war/danger*
Here es ane enmye° with oste°   vndire ȝone° vynes,   *an enemy/host/those*
570 And° they see the, forsothe,°   sorowe the betyddes;°   *if/you, truly/will befall*
Bot ȝif° thow hafe° condethe°   of° þe kynge selfen,°   *unless/have/safe conduct/from/himself*

Knaues will kill the   and keppe at° thow haues;   *keep what*
And if þou halde° þe hey waye,°   they hente° the also,   *stay on/highway/seize*
Bot if thow hastyly hafe helpe   of his hende° knyghttes."   *good*

575 Than karpes° sir Cradoke°   to the kynge selfen: *then says/Craddock*
"I sall forgyffe° hym my dede,°   so me Gode helpe.   *shall forgive/death*
Onye grome° vndire Gode,   that on this grownde walkes,   *any man*
Latte° the keneste° come,   that to þe kyng langes,°   *let/boldest/belongs*

558–63. The description fits that of a typical pilgrim, or palmer. The round cloak is like that of Chaucer's Friar, which was "rounded as a bell." The farthings (lit., "small pieces") were the signs or souvenirs of the various spots the palmer had visited: common ones were scallop shells symbolic of Saint James of Compostela in Galicia (Spain), palms (which gave him his name) from Jerusalem, and silver keys representing Rome. The scrip was his begging bag. The picture is very similar to that of the palmer in *Piers Plowman* (cf. this volume, p. 709; see also below, p. 168, l, 1037*n*).

566. The "corrupted Latin" is Vulgar or "monk's" Latin, the contemporary international language of Europe, as differentiated from classical Latin. It may also be a reference to the Latin spoken by Romanized Britons. Chaucer was aware that the later Romans spoke a Latin different from the classical; in the *Man of Law's Tale* (B 519) he says of the Roman Custance, "A maner Latyn corrupt was hir speche."

575. Sir Craddock is the famous hero Caradoc Briebras (Karaducs Briebraz) found in the works of Chrétien de Troyes. He plays a chief part in Biket's *Lay of the Horn* and the ballad *The Boy and the Mantle* (this volume, pp. 334–39, and pp. 497–504): and his name also occurs in the lyric *Annot and Iohon* (this volume, pp. 642–44). He is known in the folklore of Wales and Brittany.

I sall encountire hym as knyghte,   so Criste hafe my sawle!° *soul*
580 For thow may noghte reche° me   ne areste° thy selfen, *not touch/nor arrest (me)/self*
Þoff° þou be richely arayede   in full riche wedys; *though*
I will noghte wonde° for no werre,   to wende whare me likes, *fear/go where I like*
Ne° for no wy of this werlde,   þat wroghte° es on erthe. *not/created*
Bot° I will passe in pilgremage   þis pas° vnto Rome, *but/way*
585 To purchese me° pardonne   of the pape° selfen *myself/pope*
And of° paynes of purgatorie   be plenerly assoyllede.° *from/fully absolved*
Thane° sall I seke sekirly°   my souerayne° lorde, *then/seek truly/sovereign*
Sir Arthure of Inglande,   that auenaunt byeryn,° *adventurous warrior*
For he es in this empire,   as athell° men me telles, *noble*
590 Ostayande° in this Oryente°   with awfull° knyghtes." *campaigning/eastern region/ awesome*

"Fro qwyn° come þou, kene man,"   quod° þe kynge thanne,° *from where/said/then*
"That knawes° kynge Arthure   and his knyghttes also? *knows*
Was þou euer in his courte,   qwylls he in kyth° lengede?° *native land/dwelled*
Thow karpes° so kyndly,   it comforthes myn herte;° *speak/comforts my heart*
595 Well wele° has þou wente,°   and wysely þou sechis,° *very well/come/search*
For þou art Bretowne bierne,°   as by thy brode speche."° *British man/broad speech*
"Me awghte° to knowe þe kynge,   he es my kydde louerd,° *I ought/famous lord*
And I was calde° in his courte   a knyghte of his chambire; *called*
Sir Craddoke was I callide°   in his courte riche, *called*
600 Kepare° of Karlyon°   vndir the kynge selfen. *guardian/Caerleon*
Now am I cachede° owtt of kyth   with kare at my herte, *chased*
And that castell es cawghte°   with vncowthe ledys."° *captured/by foreign men*
Than the comliche° kynge   **kaughte° hym in armes,** *fair/embraced*
Keste of° his ketill-hatte°   and kyssede hym full sone,° *threw off/helmet/very soon*
605 Saide: "Welcom, sir Craddoke,   so Criste mott° me helpe! *may*
Dere cosyn° of kynde,°   thowe coldis° myn herte, *dear cousin/natural/make cold*
How faris it in Bretaynne°   with all my bolde berynns?° *Britain/knights*
Are they brettende° or brynte°   or broughte owt of lyue?° *beaten/burned/life*
Ken° þou me kyndely,   whatt caase es° befallen; *tell/chance is*
610 I kepe° no credens° to crafe,°   I knawe the° for trewe."° *need/assurance/ask/you/true*
"Sir, thi wardane° es wikkede   and wilde of° his dedys,° *warden/in/deeds*
For he wandreth° has wroghte,°   sen° þou awaye passede. *misfortune/caused/since*
He has castells encrochede°   and corownde° hym seluen, *captured/crowned*
Kaughte° in all þe rentis°   of þe rownde tabill;° *taken/revenue/table*
615 He devisede° þe rewme°   and delte° as hym° likes, *divided/realm/distributed/he*
Dubbede of þe Danmarkes°   dukes and erlles,° *Danes/earls*
Disseueride° þem sondirwise°   and cites° dystroyede; *scattered/many ways/cities*

---

602. *vncowthe:* Cf. below, p. 160, l. 733*n*.
611. The "warden" is Modred.

616. It was especially dastardly of Modred to dub Danish knights, because they were the traditional enemy of England.

Of Sarazenes° and Sessoynes° appon sere halues°		*Saracens/Saxons/upon many sides*
He has semblede° a sorte° of selcouthe berynes,°		*assembled/army/foreign knights*
⁶²⁰ Soueraynes° of Surgenale and sowdeours° many,		*chiefs/mercenaries*
Of Peyghtes° and paynymms° and prouede knyghttes		*Picts/pagans*
Of Irelande and Orgaile,° owtlawede berynes;		*Argyll*
All thaa° laddes are knyghttes, þat lange° to þe mowntes,°		*those/belong/mountains*
And ledynge° and lordechippe has, alls° them selfe° likes.°		*rule/as/they/like*
⁶²⁵ And there es sir Childrike° a cheftayne holdyn,°		*Childric/chieftain recognized*
That ilke° cheualrous man, he chargges° thy pople;°		*same/oppresses/people*
They robbe thy religeous° and rauische thi nonnes°		*monks/nuns*
And redy ryddis° with his rowtte° to rawnsone° þe pouere.°		*ready rides/gang/rob/poor*
Fro Humbyre to Hawyke he haldys° his awen°		*holds/own*
⁶³⁰ And all þe cowntre° of Kentt be couenawnte entayllide,°		*country/by covenant entailed*
The comliche castells, that to the corown langede,		
The holttes° and the hare-wode° and the harde bankkes,		*forests/gray wood*
All þat Henguste° and Hors° hent° in þeire tyme.		*Hengist/Horsa/captured*
Att Southampton on the see° es seuen skore schippes,		*sea*
⁶³⁵ Frawghte° full of ferse° folke owt of ferre° landes		*filled/fierce/far*
For to fyghte with thy frappe,° when þow° them assailles.		*host/you*
Bott ȝitt° a worde witterly,° thow watt noghte° þe werste:°		*but yet/truly/know not/worst*
He has weddede Waynore° and hir his wieffe° holdis,		*Guinevere/wife*
And wonnys° in the wilde bowndis° of þe weste° marches		*lives/bounds/western*
⁶⁴⁰ And has wroghte hire° with wenchel,° as wittnesse tellis.		*got her/child*
Off° al þe wyes° of þis worlde woo° motte hym° worthe,°		*of/men/woe/to him/happen*
Alls wardayne vnworthye, women to ȝeme!°		*guard*
Thus has sir Modrede merrede° vs alle!		*hurt*
Forthy° I merkede° ouer thees mowntes, to mene° þe the sothe."°		*therefore/traveled/tell/truth*
⁶⁴⁵ Than the burliche° kynge for brethe° at his herte°		*noble/anger/heart*
And for this botelesse bale° all his ble chaungede.°		*sorrow without remedy/color changed*
"By þe rode,"° sais þe roye,° "I sall° it revenge;		*cross/king/shall*
Hym sall repente full rathe° all his rewthe werkes!"°		*very quickly/wicked deeds*

---

620. *Surgenale:* ? South Wales.

622. Men of Ireland, Argyll, and Denmark and also the Picts are grouped together with paynims and Saracens, all "outlawed men" (cf. *Scathyll Scottlande*, l. 7). It does not seem possible, therefore, that the author of the poem was himself a Scot, as has been at times supposed. As l. 623 notes, all of Modred's followers are "men of the mountains" (including the men of South Wales, l. 620). The mountainous areas of Great Britain were the historical and natural breeding grounds for nationalistic and rebellious activity against the established order. Paynims and Saracens (i.e., Moslem infidels) never invaded England, of course, except in romance (cf. *King Horn*), but they are named by the author to point up Modred's indiscriminate choice of evil allies. In Geoffrey of Monmouth, paynims are

identified with pagan Saxon invaders. Both works undoubtedly show the influence of the Crusades on literature.

625. This Childric is obviously not the Saxon chief slain by Cador (cf. l. 180n) on the Isle of Thanet, but another, allied with Modred. Already killed in vs. 2960, he reappears at this point through a confusion in the poem and is killed in the final battle of Camblam.

629. *Fro Humbyre to Hawyke:* from the river Humber to Hawick on the Teviot, in southern Scotland.

630. To "entail" in property law is to grant lands inalienably in perpetuity.

633. Hengist and Horsa were Jutish invaders of Britain, c. 449–50 (cf. below, p. 137, n. 56).

All wepande° for woo he went to his tentis;   *weeping*

650 Vnwynly° this wyesse° kynge he wakkenyss° his beryns,   *joyless/wise/wakens*
Clepid in° a clarioune° kynges and othire,°   *called on/bugle/others*
Callys them to concell° and of þis cas° tellys: *council/matter*
"I am with treson° betrayede for all my trewe dedis,°   *treason/true deeds*
And all my trauayle es tynt,° me tydis° no bettire;   *labor is lost/befalls*

655 Hym sall torfere betyde,° þis° tresone has wroghte,°   *sorrow befall/(who) this/done*
And I may traistely° hym take, and° I am trew louerd;°   *surely/if/lord*
This es Modrede, þe man, that I moste traystede,°   *trusted*
Has my castells encrochede° and corownde° hym seluen°   *captured/crowned/self*
With renttes° and reches° of the rownde table;   *revenue/riches*

660 Has made all hys retenewys° of renayede wrechis°   *retinue/renegade wretches*
And devysed° my rewme° to dyverse° lordes,   *distributed/realm/divers*
To sowdeours° and to Sarazenes° owtt of sere londes.°   *mercenaries/Saracens/many lands*
He has weddyde Waynore and hyr to wyefe° holdes,   *wife*
And a childe es eschapede,° the chaunce° es no bettire.   *begotten/luck*

665 They hafe semblede° on the see seuen schore° schippis,   *have assembled/score*
Full of ferrom° folke, to feghte° with myn one.°   *foreign/fight/my own*
Forthy to Bretayne° the brode° buske vs byhouys,°   *Britain/great/travel we must*
For to brettyn° þe berynne,° that has this bale raysede.°   *vanquish/warrior/caused*
Thare° sall no freke° men fare, bott° all on fresche horses,   *there/bold/except*

670 That are fraistede° in fyghte and floure° of my knyghttez: *proved/flower*
Sir Howell° and sir Hardolfe here sall beleue°   *Hoel/remain*
To be lordes of the ledis,° that here to me lenges;°   *people/belong*
Lokes° into Lumbardye, þat thare no lede chaunge,°   *look/men change (allegiance)*
And tendirly to Tuskayne° take tente alls° I byde;°   *attentively of Tuscany/care as/bid*

675 Resaywe° the rentis° of Rome, qwen þay° are rekkenede;°   *receive/tributes/when they/due*
Take sesyn° the same daye, that laste was assygnede,°   *control/assigned*
Or ells° all þe ostage° withowttyn þe wallys   *else/hostages*
Be hynggyde hye appon hyghte° all holly° at ones."°   *hanged high upon height/wholly/ once*

Nowe bownes° the bolde kynge with his beste knyghtes,   *prepares*
680 Gers° trompe° and trusse° and trynes° forth aftyre;   *calls for/trumpet/packing/goes*
Turnys thorowe° Tuskayne, taries bot° littill,   *through/tarries but*
Lyghte noghte° in Lumbarddye, bot when þe lyghte failede;   *stops not*
Merkes° ouer the mowntaynes full mervaylous° wayes,   *travels/marvelous*
Ayres thurghe Almaygne° evyne at the gayneste;°   *journeys through Germany/most quickly*

685 Ferkes° into Flawndresche° with hys ferse° knyghttes.   *travels/Flanders/fierce*
Within fyftene dayes his flete° es assemblede,   *fleet*
And thane° he schoupe hym° to schippe and schowntes° no lengere,°   *then/takes himself/delays/longer*
Scherys° with a scharpe wynde ouer þe schyre° waters;   *cuts/bright*
By þe roche° with ropes he rydes on ankkere.°   *rocks/at anchor*

690 Thare the false men fletyde° and one flode lengede,° *floated/on sea remained*

With chefe° chaynes of chare° chokkode togedyrs,° *excellent/loading chains/thrown together*

Charggede° evyn chekefull° of°cheualrous knyghtes; *filled/cheek to cheek/with*

And in þe hynter° one heghte° helmes° and crestes, *rear/on high/helmets*

Hatches with haythen° men hillyd ware° thare vndyre, *heathen/covered were*

695 Prowdliche purtrayede° with payntede clothys,° *proudly portrayed/cloths*

Iche a° pece° by pece prykkyde tyll° oþer, *each/piece/fastened to*

Dubbyde° with dagswaynnes° dowblede° they seme;° *lined/(coarse cloth)/doubled/seem*

And thus þe derfe Danamarkes° had dyghte° all theyre schippys, *fierce Danes/decorated*

That° no dynte° of no dart° dere° them ne schoulde.° *so that/blow/arrow/damage/not should*

700 Than° the roye° and þe renkes° of the rownde table *then/king/knights*

All ryally° in rede° arrayes his schippis. *royally/red*

That daye ducheryes° he delte° and doubbyde° knyghttes, *duchies/granted/dubbed*

Dresses° dromowndes° and dragges° and drawen° vpe stonys; *prepares/large sailboats/rafts/drew*

The toppe-castells he stuffede with toyelys,° as hym lykyde,° *equipment/he liked*

705 Bendys bowes of vys° brothly° þareaftyre; *screws/quickly*

Tolowris° tentyly° takell they ryghtten,° *weapon fitters/carefully/prepare*

Brasen hedys full brode° buskede° on flones,° *brazen heads very broad/fastened/arrows*

Graythes° for garnysons,° gomes° arrayes, *prepares/defenders/men*

Grymc gaddcs° of stele,° glywes° of iryn,° *grim hooks/steel/bands/iron*

710 Stiʒttelys° steryn° one steryne° with styffe° men of armes. *stations/stern (men)/stern/strong*

Mony lufliche launce° appon lofte° stonndys,° *many (a) fair lance/aloft/stands*

Ledys° one leburde,° lordys and oþer,° *men/lee/others*

Pyghte° payvese° one porte, payntede scheldes,° *place/large shields/shields*

One hyndire° hurdace° one highte° helmede knyghtez. *rear/wicker defense/high*

715 Thus they scheften fore schotys° on thas schire strandys,° *prepare for shots/those bright beaches*

Ilke schalke° in his schrowde,° full scheen° ware þeire wedys.° *each man/coat/shining/garments*

The bolde kynge es° in a barge and abowtte rowes, *is*

All bare-heuvede° for besye° with beueryn° lokkes,° *bareheaded/zeal/beaver-colored/locks*

And a beryn° with his bronde° and ane° helme betyn° *knight/sword/a/hammered*

720 Mengede with° a mawntelet° of maylis° of siluer, *attached to/mantle/mail*

690–799. The sea battle is supposedly drawn after the naval engagement of Winchelsea, 1350.

695. The painted cloth served both as decoration and as protection against weather, arrows, and so forth.

704. The castles were the ship's fortifications built on stem or stern (cf. Mod. Eng. *forecastle*).

705. *bowes of vys:* "crossbows."

706. *tolowris:* Cf. Mod. Eng. *toolers.*

Compaste° with a coronall°   and couerde full riche,   *encircled/coronet*
Kayris° to yche a° cogge,°   to comfurthe° his knyghttes: *moves/each/ship/comfort*
To Clegys and Cleremownde   he cryes one lowde:°   *aloud*
"O Gawayne! O Galyran!   thies gud° mens bodyes."   *(by) these good*
725 To Loth and to Lyonell   full louefully° he melys°   *kindly/speaks*
And to sir Lawncelot de Lake   lordliche° wordys: *(in) lordly*
"Lat° vs couere° þe kythe,°   the coste° es owre owenn,°   *let/recover/country/coast/own*
And gere° them brotheliche blenke,°   all ȝone blod-hondes,°   *make/quickly blench/those*
                                                                         bloodhounds

Bryttyn° them within bourde°   and brynne° them   *smash/aboard/burn/thereafter*
     þareaftyre,°
730 Hewe down hertly°   ȝone heythen tykes!°   *heartily/heathen curs*
Thay° are harlotes halfe,°   **I hette ȝow myn honnde!"°**   *they/(on the) rascal's side/wager*
                                                                         you my hand

Than he coueres° his cogge   and caches on° ankere,°   *regains/fastens/anchor*
Kaughte° his comliche helme°   with þe clere° maylis;   *took/comely helmet/bright*
Buskes° baners on brode,°   betyn of gowles,°   *runs up/unfurled/embroidered with*
                                                                         gules
735 With corowns° of clere golde,   clenliche° arraiede;   *crowns/brightly*
Bot þare° was chosen° in þe chefe°   a chalke-whitte° mayden   *but there/set/chief/chalk-white*
And a childe in hir arme,   þat chefe es of hevyne:°   *heaven*
Withowtten changynge in chace,°   thies ware° þe cheefe   *alteration in battle/were*
     armes
Of Arthure þe auenaunt,°   qwhylls° he in erthe lengede.°   *adventurous/while/lived*
740   Thane° the maryners mellys°   and maysters° of schippis. *then/seamen shout/masters*
Merily° iche a° mate   menys till° oþer;   *merrily/each/speaks to*
Of° theire termys° they talke,   how þay ware tydde,°   *in/jargon/things were happening*
Towyn° trvssell° one trete,°   trvssen° vpe sailes,   *tow/furled sail/on trestle/trussed*
Bet bonettez° one brede,°   bettrede° hatches;   *spread bonnets/abroad/battened*
745 Brawndeste° brown stele,   braggede in trompes;°   *brandished/blew on trumpets*
Standis styffe° on the stamyn,°   steris° on aftyre;°   *sturdily/stem/steer/thereupon*
Strekyn° ouer þe streme,°   thare stryvynge° begynnes,   *take course/water/where fighting*
Fro° þe wagande° wynde   owt of þe weste rysses,°   *after/blowing/rises*
Brethly bessomes° with byrre°   in beryns° sailles.   *quickly rushes/vigor/men's*
750 With hir° bryngges one burde°   burliche cogges,°   *it/alongside/noble*
Qwhylls þe bilynge° and þe beme°   brestys° in sondyre;°   *prow/beam/bursts/asunder*
So stowttly þe forsterne°   on þe stam° hyttis,   *fore-stern/stem*

723–26. Clegys, a knight of the Round Table and leader of a band of knights in Arthur's army, traced his lineage back to Brutus, legendary founder of Britain. He cannot be further identified. A romance by Chrétien de Troyes (*Cligés*) and a late-14th-century romance in English (*Sir Cleges*) bear his name. Galeron of Galowey (Galway), a knight of the Round Table, in Malory joins Agravain and eleven others in the plot against Lancelot du Lac, also of the Round Table, son of King Ban of Benwick (Bayonne or Beaune). On Loth, see l. 166*n* and l. 210*n.* Lyonell was a nephew of Lancelot. Cleremownde has not been identified.

734. Gules is in heraldry the color red.

736. The chief is the upper part of the heraldic field.

744. A bonnet was an extra piece of canvas, normally furled but attached to the foot of the foresail when the wind was moderate.

Þat stokkes° of þe stere-burde°   strykkys° in peces.°   *stocks/steerboard/shatters/pieces*
Be than° cogge appon° cogge,   krayers° and oþer,°   *at that/upon/barks/others*
755 Castys crepers° on crosse,°   als° to þe crafte langes.°   *boarding hooks/across/as/pertains*
Thane was hede-rapys° hewen,°   þat helde vpe þe mastes;   *head ropes/cut*
Thare was conteke full kene°   and crachynge° of schippys,   *conflict very sharp/crashing*
Grett° cogges of kampe°   crassches° in sondyre,   *great/battle/crash*
Mony kaban° was clevede,°   cabills° destroyede,   *many (a) cabin/cut up/cables*
760 Knyghtes and kene° men   killide the berynes,°   *bold/warriors*
Kidd° castells were corven°   with all theire kene wapen,°   *famous/cut apart/keen weapons*
Castells full comliche,   þat coloured ware faire.
Vpcydes eghelynge°   þay ochen° þareaftyre,   *upwards cutting/hacked*
With þe swynge of þe swerde°   sweys° þe mastys;   *sword/sways*
765 Ovyrefallys° in þe firste°   frekis° and othire,   *fall over/at that time/knights*
Many frekke° in þe forchipe°   fey es byleuede.°   *(a) warrior/foreship/dead is left*
Than brothely° they bekyre°   with boustouse° tacle,   *then vigorously/attack/fierce*
Brusches° boldlye on burde°   brynyede° knyghtes,   *rush/board/byrnied*
Owt of botes on burde°   was buskede° with stonys,   *boats one ship/attacked*
770 Bett° down of° þe beste,°   brystis° the hetches;°   *beaten/by/best (men)/burst/hatches*
Som gomys° thourghegyrde°   with gaddys° of yryn,°   *men/gored through/points/iron*
Gomys gayliche clade°   englaymes° the wapen,   *gaily clothed/make bloody*
Archers of Inglande   full egerly schottes,°   *eagerly shoot*
Hittis thourghe° þe harde stele°   full hertly dynnttis.°   *through/steel/hearty blows*
775 Sonne hotchen° in holle°   the heþenne° knyghtes,   *quickly stagger/hull/heathen*
Hurte thourghe þe harde stele,   hele° they neuer.   *heal*
Than they fall to þe fyghte,   foynes° with sperys,°   *thrust/spears*
All the frekkeste on frownte,°   þat to þe fyghte langes;°   *boldest in front/is fitting*
And ilkon° treschely   fraystez° theire strenghes,°   *each one/prove/strength*
780 Were° to fyghte in þe flete°   with theire fell wapyn.°   *war/fleet/fierce weapons*
Thus they dalte° þat daye,   thire dubbide° knyghtes,   *dealt/these dubbed*
Till all þe Danes ware dede°   and in þe depe throwen.°   *were dead/sea thrown*
    Than Bretons brothely°   with brondis° they hewen,°   *Britons harshly/swords/hewed*
Lepys° in vpone lofte°   lordeliche berynes;°   *leap/aloft/lordly knights*
785 When ledys° of owt-lonndys°   leppyn° in waters,   *men/foreign lands/leap*
All oure lordes one lowde°   laughen° at ones.°   *aloud/laughed/once*
Be thane° speris° ware spronngen,°   spalddyd° schippys.   *at that time/spears/thrown/split*
Spanyolis spedily°   sprentyde° ouer burdez;°   *Spaniards quickly/jumped/ overboard*

All þe kene men of kampe,   knyghtes and oþer,
790 Killyd are colde dede   and castyn ouer burdez.
Theire swyers sweyftly°   has þe swete leuyde,°   *squires swiftly/blood shed*

---

755. Arthur uses the tactics of the Roman navy, first ramming the enemy ships and then, with boarding or grappling hooks, boarding them to fight what was essentially a land war.

761. See l. 704*n*.

768. A byrnie was a coat of mail.

	Heþen heuande° on hatche	in þer hawe° ryses,	*hewing/enclosure*
	Synkande° in þe salte see°	seuen hundrethe° at ones.	*sinking/sea/hundred*
	Thane° sir Gawayne the gude,°	he has þe gree wonnen,°	*then/good/honor won*
795	And all þe cogges grete°	he gafe° to his knyghtes,	*ships great/gave*
	Sir Geryn and sir Grisswolde	and othir gret lordes;	
	Garte° Galuth a gud gome,°	girde of þaire hedys.°	*made/game/cut off their heads*
	Thus of° þe false flete	appon° þe flode happenede,°	*to/upon/sea (it) happened*
	And thus þeis feryne° folke	fey are beleuede.°	*this foreign/left*

Arthur's Death (vss. 4224–346)

800	Þat persayfes° oure prynce	and presses to° faste,	*perceives/to (him)*
	Strykes into þe stowre°	by strenghe° of hys handis,	*tumult/strength*
	Metis° with sir Mordrede,	he melis vnfaire:°	*meets/speaks harshly*
	"Turne, traytoure vntrewe,°	þe tydys° no bettyre;°	*untrue/you awaits/better (fate)*
	Be gret° Gode, thow sall dy°	with dynt° of my handys!	*by great/you shall die/stroke*
805	The schall rescowe° no renke°	ne reches° in erthe!''	*rescue/man/nor riches*
	The kyng with Calaburn°	knyghtly hym strykes,	*Caliburn*
	Þe cantell° of þe clere schelde°	he kerfes° in sondyre°	*edge/bright shield/cuts/asunder*
	Into þe schuldyre° of þe schalke°	a schaftmonde large,°	*shoulder/man/palm's length*
	Þat þe schire rede blode°	schewede° on þe maylys.°	*so **that**/bright **red blood**/showed/ mail*
810	He schodirde° and schrenkys°	and schontes bott° lyttill,	*shuddered/shrinks/hesitates **only***
	Bott schokkes° in scharpely	in his schene wedys;°	*but rushes/fair garments*
	The felone with þe fyn swerde°	freschely° he strykes,	*fine sword/vigorously*
	The felettes° of þe ferrere° syde	he flassches° in sondyre,	*rib muscles/far/cuts*
	Thorowe jopown° and jesserawnte°	of gentill mailes.°	*through **tunic**/jacket armor/noble mail*
815	The freke fichede° in þe flesche	an halfe fotte large:°	*man struck/foot deep*
	That derfe dynt° was his dede,°	and dole° was þe more,	*hard blow/death/grief*
	That euer þat doughtty sulde° dy,	bot° at Dryghttyns° wylle!	*doughty (**man**) should/except/ God's*
	Ʒitt° with Calyburn his swerde	full° knyghttly he strykes,	*yet/very*
	Kastes° in° his clere schelde	and coueres hym° full faire;°	*moves vigorously/under/himself/well*
820	Swappes of° þe swerde-hande,	als° he by glentes,°	*cuts off/as/glances*
	Ane° inche fro° þe elbowe	he ochede° it in sondyre,	*an/from/hacked*

792–93. Probably whole fortifications, with men in them, were pushed overboard.

796–97. Geryn (in Geoffrey of Monmouth Gerrin of Chartres), one of the Twelve Peers of Gaul, supported Arthur in his campaigns against Lucius Hiberius. Grisswolde has not been identified. Galuth was Gawain's sword.

800. At this point the aged Sir Marrok (see ll. 842–43*n*) is having to retreat before Modred's attack, and Arthur rushes in to help him.

806. Caliburn, or Excalibur, is Arthur's famous sword, which in Malory is received from and returned to the Lady of the Lake.

814. The jupon or gypon was the tunic worn under the hauberk or breast armor; the jesseraunte was a jacket stiffened with metal plates in the lining.

Þat he swounnes° on þe swarthe°	and on swym° fallis,	*faints/grass/in swoon*
Thorowe bracer of brown stele°	and þe bryghte mayles,	*steel*
That the hilte and þe hande	appon° þe hethe ligges.°	*upon/heath lies*
825 Thane frescheliche° þe freke	the fence° vpe rerys,°	*then fiercely/shield/raises*
Brochis° hym in with the bronde°	to þe bryghte hiltys,	*strikes/sword*
And he brawles° on the bronde	and bownes° to dye.	*squirms/turns*
"In faye,"° says þe feye° kynge,	"fele me forthynkkes,°	*faith/doomed/much I regret*
That euer siche° a false theefe	so faire an ende haues."°	*such/has*
830 Qwen° they had fenyste° þis feghte,°	thane was þe felde wonnen,°	*when/finished/fight/field won*
And the false folke in þe felde	feye° are byleuede.°	*dead/left*
Till° a foreste they fledde	and fell in the greuys,°	*to/woods*
And fers feghtande° folke	folowes them aftyre;	*fierce fighting*
Howntes° and hewes down	the heythen tykes,°	*hunts/heathen dogs*
835 Mourtherys° in the mowntaygnes°	sir Mordrede° knyghtes;	*murders/mountains/Modred's*
Thare chapyde° neuer no childe,°	cheftayne° ne oþer,	*there escaped/knight/chieftain*
Bot they choppes them down in the chace,	it chargys° bot littyll.	*costs*
Bot when sir Arthure anon°	sir Ewayne he fyndys,	*then*
And Errake þe auenaunt°	and oþer grett° lordes,	*adventurous/great*
840 He kawghte° vp sir Cador	with care at his herte,°	*raised/heart*
Sir Clegis, sir Cleremonde,	þes clere° men of armes,	*those famed*
Sir Lothe and sir Lyonell,	sir Lawncelott and Lowes,	
Marrake and Meneduke,	þat myghty ware° euer;	*were*
With langoure° in the launde°	thare he layes them togedire,°	*sorrow/open plain/together*
845 Lokede° on theyre lighames,°	and with a lowde steuen°	*looked/bodies/loud cry*
—Alls lede° þat liste noghte° lyfe	and loste had his myrthis°	*as man/cared not for/joy*
Then he stotays° for° made,°	and all his strenghe° faylez,	*staggers/as if/mad/strength*
Lokes° vpe to þe lyfte°	and all his lyre chaunges;°	*looks/sky/countenance changes*
Downne he sweys° full swythe°	and in a swoun° fallys,	*sways/quickly/swoon*
850 Vpe he coueris° on kneys°	and kryes full often:	*gets/knees*
"Kyng comly° with crowne,	in care am I leuyde;°	*fair/left*
All my lordchipe° lawe° in lande°	es° layde vndyre!	*lordly following/low/earth/is*
That me has gyfen gwerdons°	be° grace of hym seluen,°	*given rewards/by/themselves*
Mayntenyde° my manhede°	be myghte of thine° handes,	*maintained/manhood/(i.e., their)*
855 Made me manly on molde°	and mayster° in erthe;°	*earth/master/(the) land*

---

823. The bracer protected the inner arm from the bow string.

838–39. Ewayne (Ywain in Geoffrey of Monmouth, and the hero of *Yvain* [or *Le Chevalier au Lyon*] by Chrétien de Troyes) was the son of Urian, king of Moray, and nephew of Loth, king of Lodonesia. Errake is identical with Geraint of the *Mabinogion* and with the hero of *Erec et Enide* by Chrétien. Both knights were members of the Round Table.

840. See l. 180*n*.

842–43. Marrake (Marrok, Marrys de la Roche, Mauruc) was an older knight active in all of Arthur's wars. Malory identifies him with a knight turned into a werewolf by his wife, an odd confusion with *Bisclaveret*, a lai by Marie de France. Meneduke of Mentoche was a knight of Lancelot's kin. Lowes has not been identified.

In a tenefull tym°	this torfere° was reryde,°	*woeful time/sorrow/arisen*
That for a traytoure has tynte°	all my trewe° lordys.	*are lost/true*
Here rystys° the riche blude°	of the rownde table,	*rests/great blood*
Rebukkede with° a rebawde,°	and rewthe° es the more!	*cut down by/scoundrel/pity*
860 I may helples° on hethe	house° be myn one°	*helpless/live/alone*
Alls° a wafull wedowe,°	þat wanttes° hir beryn.°	*like/woeful widow/misses/lord*
I may werye° and wepe°	and wrynge myn° handys,	*grieve/weep/my*
For my wytt and my wyrchipe°	awaye es for euer.	*honor*
Off° all lordchips I take	leue to° myn ende;	*of/leave till*
865 Here es þe Bretons blode°	broughte owt of lyfe,	*Britons' blood*
And now in þis journee°	all my joy endys!"	*day's work*
Thane relyes° þe renkes°	of all þe rownde table,	*then rally/knights*
To þe ryall roy°	thay° ride þam alle;°	*royal king/they/all of them*
Than° assembles full sone°	seuen score knyghtes,	*then/very quickly*
870 In sighte to þaire souerayne,°	þat was vnsownde leuede.°	*of their sovereign/wounded left*
Than knelis° the crownede kynge	and kryes on lowde:°	*kneels/aloud*
"I thanke þe,° Gode, of thy grace,	with a gud° wylle,	*you/good*
That gafe° vs vertue° and witt,	to vencows þis beryns,°	*gave/power/vanquish these warriors*
And vs has grauntede° þe gree°	of theis gret° lordes!	*granted/victory/over these great*
875 He sent vs neuer no schame,	ne schenchipe in° erthe,	*nor dishonor on*
Bot° euer ȝit° þe ouerhande°	of all oþer kynges:	*but/yet/upper hand*
We hafe° no laysere° now,	þese lordys to seke,°	*have/time/seek*
For ȝone laythely ladde°	me lamede° so sore.°	*that loathsome fellow/lamed/greatly*
Graythe vs° to Glaschenbery,°	vs gaynes non oþer;°	*let us go/Glastonbury/avails nothing else*
880 Thare we may ryste vs° with roo°	and raunsake° oure wondys.°	*rest ourselves/peace/mend/wounds*
Of° þis dere° day-werke°	þe Dryghtten° ne louede,°	*for/good/day's work/Lord/loved*
That vs has destaynede° and demyd°	to dye in° oure awen."°	*destined/judged/die among/own*
Thane they holde at° his heste°	hally at ones°	*to/request/all together*
And graythes° to Glasschenberye	þe gate° at þe gayneste;°	*proceed/(on the) road/most direct*
885 Entres þe Ile of Aueloyne,°	and Arthure he lyghttes,°	*Avalon/alights*
Merkes° to a manere° there,	for myghte he no forthire.°	*travels/dwelling/further (go)*
A surgyn° of Salerne°	enserches° his wondes,°	*surgeon/Salerno/searches/wounds*
The kyng sees be asaye°	þat sownde° bes° he neuer,	*(the) attempt/sound/will be*
And sone to his sekyre° men	he said theis wordes:	*faithful*

---

879. Glastonbury, founded according to legend by Joseph of Arimathea in Somersetshire, is the site of Arthur's tomb. His supposed bones were found by the monks of Glastonbury Abbey in 1191. The result of this identification (which according to the archaeological evidence presented in Geoffrey Ashe's *Quest for Arthur's Britain* [cf. above, p. 37] may very possibly be a correct one) served the purpose of the Plantagenet kings and shattered the nationalistic belief of the Welsh that Arthur would return from the Isle of Avalon to lead them to victory. In fact, Glaston-bury was identified as the Isle of Avalon from this date (cf. above, p. 91, ll. 1184–85n and l. 1204n).

887. Salerno's medical school, originating from the Benedictine physician-monks of Monte Cassino, was the oldest in Europe and influenced the founding and teaching of many others, especially that of Bologna. It flourished from the 11th to the 13th centuries.

890 "Doo calle° me a confessour   with Criste° in his armes;   *have called/(i.e., the Host)*
I will be howselde° in haste,   what happe so betyddys;°   *given the Host/whatever may happen*
Constantyn my cosyn°   he sall° the corown bere,°   *cousin/shall/crown wear*
Alls° becommys hym of kynde,°   ȝife° Criste will hym thole.°   *as/by nature/if/permit*
Beryn, fore° my benyson,°   thow berye ȝone° lordys,   *knight (i.e., Constantine), for/ blessing/you bury those*

895 That in bataille° with brondez°   are broghte owt of lyfe;   *battle/swords*
And sythen merke° manly   to Mordrede° children,   *then go/Modred's*
That they bee sleyghely° slayne   and slongen° in watyrs;   *be prudently/thrown*
Latt° no wykkyde wede° waxe   ne wrythe on this erthe;   *let/wicked weed*
I warne fore thy wirchipe,   wirke° alls I bydde!   *do*

900 I foregyffe° all greffe,°   for Goddez lufe° of heuen,°   *forgive/injury/love/heaven*
Ȝif Waynor hafe wele wroghte,°   wele hir betydde!"°   *Guinevere has well done/(may) good her befall*

He saide, "In manus" with mayne°   on molde,° whare° he ligges,°   *strength/earth/where/lies*
And thus passes his speryt,°   and spekes° he no more.   *spirit/speaks*
The baronage of Bretayne° thane,   beschopes° and othire,°   *Britain/bishops/others*
905 Graythes them° to Glaschenbery   with gloppynnande hertes °   *travel/grieving hearts*
To bery thare° the bolde kynge   and brynge to þe erthe,   *there*
With all wirchipe° and welthe,°   þat any wy scholde.°   *honor/wealth/man should*
Throly° belles thay° rynge   and Requiem syngys,   *vigorously/they*
Doss messes° and matyns   with mournande° notes: *say masses/mourning*
910 Relygeous° reueste°   in theire riche copes,   *high priests/vested*
Pontyficalles° and prelates   in precyouse wedys,°   *pontiffs/garments*
Dukes and dusszeperis°   in theire dule-cotes,°   *peers/mourning dress*
Cowntasses knelande°   and claspande° theire handes,   *countesses kneeling/wringing*
Ladys languessande°   and lowrande° to schewe;°   *grieving/sorrowful/behold*
915 All was buskede° in blake,°   birdes° and othire,   *dressed/black/maidens*
That schewede° at the sepulture°   with sylande teris;°   *appeared/sepulcher/streaming tears*
Was neuer so sorowfull a syghte   seen in theire tyme!
    Thus endis kyng Arthure   as auctors alegges,°   *authors declare*
That was of Ectores° kynne,   the kynge° son of Troye,   *Hector's/king's*
920 And of sir Pryamous,° the prynce,   praysede in erthe;   *Priam*
Fro thethyn° broghte the Bretons°   all his bolde eldyrs°   *from thence/Britons/ancestors*
Into Bretayne the brode,°   as þe Bruytte° tellys.   *great/Brut*

---

892. *Constantyn:* Cf. l. 180n.

902. *"In manus":* Latin, "Into Thy hands (I commend my spirit" [Luke 23:46]).

908–10. A requiem was a dirge sung or mass celebrated for the repose of the dead. Matins was the service beginning at midnight. Copes were long ecclesiastical mantles worn in processions.

919–20. *Kynge . . . Troye:* i.e., "son of the king of Troy."

Hector, Trojan hero and oldest son of Priam, king of Troy, was of the same race as Arthur's ancestor Brutus, the mythical founder of Britain (cf. l. 922n.).

922. *Bruytte:* A Brut was, more or less, a history of Britain, according to the *MED*. Brutus (not to be confused with Caesar's assassin) was the first king of the Britons, a great-grandson of Aeneas (cf. Geoffrey of Monmouth, this volume, pp. 124–25).

THE CHRONICLE

Long accounts of historical and pseudo-historical matter appeared early in England, both in Latin and in the vernacular, in prose and in verse. The Anglo-Latin Gildas, in *De Excidio et Conquestu Britanniae* (c. 540), and Nennius, in *Historia Brittonum* (c. 800) deal with British kings, but both are overshadowed by the monumental and, considering the times, historically valid *Historia Ecclesiastica Gentis Anglorum* written by Bede in 731. King Alfred translated Bede and also started (c. 900) the Old English *Anglo-Saxon Chronicle*, which recounted the wars with the Danes and the vicissitudes of political life up to the disastrous reign of King Stephen in the year 1154. In the twelfth century much fiction was mixed with fact in the *Gesta Regum Anglorum* of William of Malmesbury (c. 1125) and Geoffrey of Monmouth's great Arthurian chronicle *Historia Regum Britanniae* (c. 1136). Though some critics include Layamon's *Brut* (c. 1205) and Barbour's *Bruce* (1316–95) in the genre of verse chronicle in English, they are better classified as epic and Scottish literature, respectively. Bede's account and the description of Alfred's wars in the *Anglo-Saxon Chronicle* can be accepted as fairly accurate, but the influence of romance literature, folklore, and legends seriously attenuates the "authority" of the twelfth-century chronicles. The *Chronica Majora* of Matthew Paris, the greatest of the thirteenth-century historians of the monastery of Saint Albans, deserves special mention.

REFERENCES

Bede, *History of the Church of England*. Trans. T. Stapleton. 2 vols. Oxford, 1929.

Garmonsway, G. N., trans. and ed. *The Anglo-Saxon Chronicle*. Everyman's Library, No. 624. New York, 1953.

Giles, J. A. *The Works of Gildas and Nennius*. London, 1841.

Plummer, C., ed. *Bede's Historia Ecclesiastica Gentis Anglorum*. 2 vols. Oxford, 1896.

Potter, K. R., ed. *William of Malmesbury, The Historia Novella*. Nelson's Medieval Classics. London, 1955.

Tatlock, J. S. P. *The Legendary History of Britain: Geoffrey of Monmouth's "Historia Regum Britanniae" and Its Early Vernacular Version*. Berkeley, Calif., 1950.

Thorpe, Lewis, trans. *Geoffrey of Monmouth, The History of the Kings of Britain*. Baltimore, 1966.

The chronicle is treated in the General Introduction of this volume, pp. 6–7, 36–37.

from HISTORY OF THE KINGS OF BRITAIN
Geoffrey of Monmouth

DATE: 1136–39. ✦ MANUSCRIPTS: Over 186 Latin MSS are extant today, from the 12th century and later. These can be found in the Cambridge University Library (MS. 1706), Trinity College, Cambridge (MS. 1125), Berne Stadtbibliothek (MS. 568, N.I. 8), Leyden University Library (MS. B.P.L. 20), the Bibliothèque Nationale in Paris (f. lat. 6233), and elsewhere. The language is Anglo-Latin. ✦ EDITIONS: Acton Griscom, *The Historia Regum Britanniae of Geoffrey of Monmouth* (London, 1929), which lists the number of MSS and which uses that of Cambridge University; Edmond Faral, *La Légende Arthurienne* (Paris, 1929), III, 64–303, which uses the Trinity College, Cambridge, MS. with variants; Jacob Hammer, *Geoffrey of Monmouth, Historia Regum Britanniae* (Cambridge, Mass., 1951). The translation of Sebastian Evans, revised by Charles W. Dunn, *Histories of the Kings of Britain by Geoffrey of Monmouth* (New York, 1958), has been standard in the past. A modern translation with excellent introduction is the one used here: Lewis Thorpe, *Geoffrey of Monmouth, The History of the Kings of Britain* (Baltimore, 1966).

Geoffrey of Monmouth was born around 1100, probably near Monmouth and Caerleon-upon-Usk in the southern part of Wales. From 1129 to 1149 Geoffrey may have been one of the Augustinian canons of the college of Saint George at Oxford. Walter, archdeacon of Oxford, from whom Geoffrey received the "ancient book written in the British language" which he translated, was provost of this college. In 1151, Geoffrey became bishop elect of Saint Asaph in Flintshire, and as a necessary step toward taking office he was ordained priest the next year at Westminster; but probably never occupied his see. He died in 1155.

The *History of the Kings of Britain* was written at Oxford between 1136 and 1139 and dedicated to Robert, earl of Gloucester, natural son of King Henry I, and to Waleran, count of Mellent, son of Robert de Beaumont, with a view to preferment. Geoffrey's *History* is mainly fictitious, and his sources are unknown. The stories of the conquests and campaigns of two of his heroes, Brutus, founder of Britain, and Belinus, the conqueror of Rome, are overshadowed by the last, those of Arthur; and it is as the originator of the Arthurian romantic legend in Europe that Geoffrey is justly famous. His work was translated into French by the Norman Wace and thence into English by Layamon. A comparison of the narrative development of certain of the Arthurian episodes in Geoffrey, Layamon, and the Alliterative *Morte Arthure* is of interest.

For the rest of British history, Geoffrey used Bede, Nennius, and Gildas, but his "history" is more in the style and nature of the romance, with flights of descriptive fancy and accounts of adventure, than a dry chronicle of facts.

from BOOK I

from CHAPTER I

Epistle Dedicatory to Robert, Earl of Gloucester

Whenever I have chanced to think about the history of the kings of Britain, on those occasions when I have been turning over a great many such matters in my mind, it has seemed a remarkable thing to me that, apart from such mention of them as Gildas[1] and Bede[2] had each made in a brilliant book on the subject, I have not been able to discover anything at all on the kings who lived here before the Incarnation of Christ, or indeed about Arthur and all the others who followed on after the Incarnation. Yet the deeds of these men were such that they deserve to be praised for all time. What is more, these deeds were handed joyfully down in oral tradition, just as if they had been committed to writing, by many peoples who had only their memory to rely on.

At a time when I was giving a good deal of attention to such matters, Walter, Archdeacon of Oxford,[3] a man skilled in the art of public speaking and well-informed about the history of foreign countries, presented me with a certain very ancient book written in the British language. This book, attractively composed to form a consecutive and orderly narrative, set out all the deeds of these men, from Brutus, the first King of the Britons, down to Cadwallader,[4] the son of Cadwallo. At Walter's request I have taken the trouble to translate the book into Latin, although, indeed, I have been content with my own expressions and my own homely style and I have gathered no gaudy flowers of speech in other men's gardens.[5] If I had adorned my page with high-flown rhetorical figures, I should have bored my readers, for they would have been forced to spend more time in discovering the meaning of my words than in following the story.

I ask you, Robert, Earl of Gloucester,[6] to do my little book this favour. Let it be so emended by your knowledge and your advice that it must no longer be considered as the product of Geoffrey of Monmouth's small talent. Rather, with the support of your wit and wisdom, let it be accepted as the work of one descended from Henry, the famous King of the English;[7] of one whom learning has nurtured in the liberal arts and whom his innate talent in military affairs has put in charge of our soldiers, with the result that now, in our own lifetime, our island of Britain hails you with heartfelt affection, as if it had been granted a second Henry.

· · · · ·

---

1. Gildas (c. 547) in his *De Excidio et Conquestu Britanniae*, a short history of Britain, mentions the Celtic victory at Mount Badon.

2. Geoffrey of Monmouth uses Bede's *Historia Ecclesiastica Gentis Anglorum* (*Ecclesiastical History of the English People*) quite extensively. The Venerable Bede (673–735) completed his history in 731 at the monastery of Jarrow. Already in his lifetime he was famous throughout Europe as a historian, Bible commentator, and natural philosopher.

3. Geoffrey several times refers to the ancient book which his friend Walter presented him as the source of his *History*. The book no longer exists, and there is debate on whether it ever did. Perhaps Geoffrey gained much of his information from oral transmission or lost Welsh chronicles.

4. Cadwallader, the Cliedvalla of Bede's *Historia*, died c. 689.

5. Geoffrey refers to the *Flores* or *Florelegium*, which were compilations of quotable phrases, sections of distinguished rhetoric, and purple passages used by writers of the time and incorporated into their works. Many classical allusions and "proofs" of wide reading can be attributed to these books.

6. Robert, earl of Gloucester (d. 1147), illegitimate son of Henry I, was a great patron of the arts and supported the chroniclers William of Malmesbury, Henry of Huntingdon, and Geoffrey of Monmouth.

7. Henry I of England, son of William the Conqueror.

CHAPTER III

The Early Years of Brutus

After the Trojan war, Aeneas[8] fled from the ruined city with his son Ascanius and came by boat to Italy. He was honourably received there by King Latinus, but Turnus, King of the Rutuli, became jealous of him and attacked him. In the battle between them Aeneas was victorious. Turnus was killed and Aeneas seized both the kingdom of Italy and the person of Lavinia, who was the daughter of Latinus.

When Aeneas' last day came, Ascanius was elected King. He founded the town of Alba on the bank of the Tiber and became the father of a son called Silvius. This Silvius was involved in a secret love-affair with a certain niece of Lavinia's; he married her and made her pregnant. When this came to the knowledge of his father Ascanius, the latter ordered his soothsayers to discover the sex of the child which the girl had conceived. As soon as they had made sure of the truth of the matter, the soothsayers said that she would give birth to a boy, who would cause the death of both his father and his mother; and that after he had wandered in exile through many lands this boy would eventually rise to the highest honour.

The soothsayers were not wrong in their forecast. When the day came for her to have her child, the mother bore a son and died in childbirth. The boy was handed over to the midwife and was given the name Brutus. At last, when fifteen years had passed, the young man killed his father by an unlucky shot with an arrow, when they were out hunting together. Their beaters drove some stags into their path and Brutus, who was under the impression that he was aiming his weapon at these stags, hit his own father below the breast. As the result of this death Brutus was expelled from Italy by his relations, who were angry with him for having committed such a crime. He went in exile to certain parts of Greece; and there he discovered the descendants of Helenus,[9] Priam's son, who were held captive in the power of Pandrasus, King of the Greeks. After the fall of Troy, Pyrrhus,[10] the son of Achilles, had dragged this man Helenus off with him in chains, and a number of other Trojans, too. He had ordered them to be kept in slavery, so that he might take vengeance on them for the death of his father.

When Brutus realized that these people were of the same race as his ancestors, he stayed some time with them. However, he soon gained such fame for his military skill and prowess that he was esteemed by the kings and princes more than any young man in the country. Among the wise he was himself wise, and among the valiant he too was valiant. All the gold and silver and the equipment which he acquired he handed over to his soldiers.[11] In this way his fame spread among all peoples. The Trojans began to flock to him and to beg him to become their leader, so that they might be freed from their subjection to the Greeks. They said that this could easily be done, for they had now increased in number in the country to

---

8. Aeneas, a Trojan leader, with his son Ascanius (who was later to succeed him as king of Italy), left Troy after its fall to the Greeks and came eventually to Latium in Italy. King Latinus of Latium first opposed Aeneas but then gave him his daughter Lavinia in marriage. Turnus, who had been betrothed to Lavinia, turned against Aeneas but was defeated (cf. Virgil, *Aeneid*; XII).

9. Helenus was the son of Priam, king of Troy, and his queen, Hecuba. He was captured by the son of Achilles (Neoptolemus,

or Pyrrhus) and finally married Andromache, his former sister-in-law, the widow of Hector.

10. Neoptolemus, called Pyrrhus because of his blond hair.

11. Brutus, like the heroic chieftains of the epics (e.g., Hrothgar in *Beowulf*), dispenses gifts to his followers after battle. Generosity was the sign of a good king in the heroic period, as was "largesse" later in feudal times (cf. below, p. 341, n. 5).

such an extent that there were reckoned to be seven thousand of them, not counting the women and children.

What is more, there was a certain nobly-born youth in Greece called Assaracus who favoured their faction. He was the son of a Trojan mother, and he had the greatest faith in them, thinking that with their help he could resist the persecution of the Greeks. His own brother was harassing Assaracus, on account of three castles which his dying father had given him, and was trying to take these away from him by alleging that he was the son of a concubine. This brother was Greek on both his father's and his mother's side, and he had persuaded the King and the other Greeks to support his case. When Brutus saw how many men he now had, and realized that the castles of Assaracus were there for him to take, he agreed without misgiving to the request of the Trojans.[12]

from BOOK VI

CHAPTER III

The Stupid Britons

Next the Romans gave the pusillanimous Britons some firm advice. They left behind them models showing how weapons could be constructed; and they recommended that towers should be built overlooking the water at intervals along the sea-coast of the southern shore, where the Britons kept their shipping, for it was there that barbarian attacks were most to be feared.[13]

However, it is easier for a kite to be made to act like a sparrow-hawk than for a wise man to be fashioned at short notice from a peasant. He who offers any depth of wisdom to such a person is acting as though he were throwing a pearl among swine.

The moment the Romans said good-bye and went away, apparently never to return, the enemies whom I have mentioned[14] reappeared once more from the ships in which they had sailed off to Ireland. They brought with them other companies of Scots and Picts, with Norwegians, Danes and all the rest whom they had under command, and seized the whole of Albany up to the Wall. Once the departure of those who had supported the Britons became known, and the fact that they had sworn never to return, the invaders pressed on even more confidently than before with their devastation of the island. In opposition to them, slow-witted peasants were posted on the top of the walls, men useless in battle, who were unable even to run away for the very palpitation of their bellies, and who shook with fear through the days and nights, on top of their stupid perches. Mean-

---

12. Later Brutus becomes the leader of the Trojans. After many battles he defeats Pandrasus and receives permission to lead the Trojans out of Greece. His voyage to different places parallels in several ways that of Odysseus. He is told by the goddess Diana in a temple on a deserted island that he will found a second Troy in an island beyond the sea. After passing the Pillars of Hercules (Straits of Gibraltar), Brutus joins with another party of Trojans and lands in Aquitaine in southern France, where he fights Goffar, king of the Aquitanians. He is victorious, ravages the country, and founds the city of Tours, but leaves for Totnes in Britain because his reinforcements in France are dwindling. Gogmagog and other giants attack him in Britain, but he overcomes them and builds his capital, Troja

Nova or Trinovantum on the Thames, where he dies and is buried. His sons are Locrinus, Kamber, and Albanactus, the first of these giving his name to Loegria or Logres, the regions of England south of the Humber later to be governed by Arthur.

13. After 407 more and more Roman legions were withdrawn to Italy. The Romanized Britons had relied on the Roman army for support against the northern Picts and Scots (Irish Celts who had settled in Scotland), and they were poorly prepared to defend themselves. At this point the Romans attempted to train them and made ready to turn the defense of the island over to the native inhabitants.

14. Guanius, leader of the Huns, and Melga, king of the Picts.

while the enemy continued to ply their hooked weapons, dragging the miserable *plebs*[15] down from the walls with them, so that they were dashed to the ground. The very suddenness of the death they endured was a stroke of luck to those who were killed in this way, for by their immediate execution they avoided the miserable torments which awaited their brothers and their children.

Oh, how God avenges himself for past sins! Alas for the absence of so many warlike soldiers through the madness of Maximianus.[16] If only they had been there in this great disaster! No people could have attacked them whom they would not have driven away in flight. This was made clear enough as long as they remained there. In those days they occupied Britain in all tranquillity and, what is more, they added far-distant realms to their own power. Thus it is when a kingdom is handed over to the safe-keeping of its peasantry.

What more can I say? Cities were abandoned,

and the high Wall too. For the inhabitants banishments, dispersions which were even more desperate than usual, pursuits by the enemy, and more and more bloody slaughters followed fast upon each other. Just as sheep are torn apart by the wolves, so were the wretched *plebs* maltreated by their enemies. Once more the miserable remnants sent letters to Agicius, the general commanding the Roman forces, to convey the following appeal: "To Agicius, three times consul, come the groans of the Britons." There followed a short introduction, and then they continued their complaints as follows: "The sea drives us into the hands of the barbarians, and the barbarians drive us into the sea. Between the two of them, we have two deaths to choose from: we can either be drowned or have our throats cut." For all this, the messengers returned sadly home, to explain to their fellow-citizens their lack of success, for they had received no promise of help.

from BOOK IX

CHAPTER I

The Crowning of Arthur

After the death of Utherpendragon,[17] the leaders of the Britons assembled from their various provinces in the town of Silchester[18] and there suggested to Dubricius,[19] the Archbishop of the

City of the Legions, that as their King he should crown Arthur, the son of Uther. Necessity urged them on, for as soon as the Saxons heard of the death of King Uther, they invited their own

---

15. Latin, "common people."

16. Maximianus, according to Geoffrey a Roman senator (but historically a Spaniard, Magnus Maximus, who usurped the purple), came to Britain (according to Geoffrey on the advice of Mauricius, son of Caradoc, duke of Cornwall) in order to use its troops. In 383 he crossed the Channel to conquer Gaul. In the process he took with him many legions stationed in Britain, bleeding the island of its finest fighting men, and the troops thus withdrawn were not replaced by Rome. According to Geoffrey, Maximianus had been made king of Britain after marrying the daughter of the British king Octavius. Later Arthur claims kinship with Maximianus, as emperor of Rome and a former king of Britain (cf. p. 132).

17. Uther (called Uther Pendragon [cf. above, p. 57, l. 94*n*] after his standard, two golden dragons fashioned in the likeness

of a dragon-shaped meteor) was killed with a hundred followers at Saint Albans, after the Saxons had polluted a well whose water was meant to cure him of his illness (cf. the account in Layamon's *Brut*, this volume, pp. 62–65).

18. Silchester in Hampshire, ten miles south of Reading, was the Roman Calleva Atrebatum, mentioned by Nennius as the site of one of Arthur's victories. The Twentieth Legion was stationed there for three hundred years.

19. Dubricius, archbishop of Caerleon-upon-Usk in Monmouthshire (Urbs Legionum, "City of the Legions," being a Latinization of Cair Legion, i.e., Caerleon, originally Kaerusc), after crowning Arthur at Silchester, becomes a papal legate; late in life he resigns his archbishopric and retires as a hermit (cf. p. 130).

countrymen over from Germany, appointed Colgrin[20] as their leader and began to do their utmost to exterminate the Britons. They had already over-run all that section of the island which stretches from the River Humber to the sea named Caithness.[21]

Dubricius lamented the sad state of his country. He called the other bishops to him and bestowed the crown of the kingdom upon Arthur. Arthur was a young man only fifteen years old; but he was of outstanding courage and generosity, and his inborn goodness gave him such grace that he was loved by almost all the people. Once he had been invested with the royal insignia, he observed the normal custom of giving gifts freely to everyone. Such a great crowd of soldiers flocked to him that he came to an end of what he had to distribute. However, the man to whom open-handedness and bravery both come naturally may indeed find himself momentarily in need, but poverty will never harass him for long. In Arthur courage was closely linked with generosity, and he made up his mind to harry the Saxons, so that with their wealth he might reward the retainers who served his own household. The justness of his cause encouraged him, for he had a claim by rightful inheritance to the kingship of the whole island. He therefore called together all the young men whom I have just mentioned and marched on York.

As soon as this was announced to Colgrin, he assembled the Saxons, Scots and Picts, and came to meet Arthur with a vast multitude. Once contact was made between the two armies, beside the River Douglas, both sides stood in grave danger for their lives. Arthur, however, was victorious. Colgrin fled, and Arthur pursued him; then Colgrin entered York and Arthur besieged him there.

As soon as Baldulf, the brother of Colgrin, heard of the latter's flight, he came to the siege with six thousand troops, in the hope of freeing the beleaguered man. At the time when his brother had gone into battle, Baldulf himself had been on the sea-coast, where he was awaiting the arrival of Duke Cheldric, who was on his way from Germany to bring them support. When he was some ten miles distant from the city of York, Baldulf decided to take the advantage of a night march, so that he could launch an unexpected attack. Arthur heard of this and ordered Cador,[22] Duke of Cornwall, to march to meet Baldulf that same night, with six hundred cavalry and three thousand foot. Cador surrounded the road along which the enemy was marching and attacked the Saxons unexpectedly, so that they were cut to pieces and killed, and those who remained alive were forced to flee. As a result Baldulf became extremely worried at the fact that he could not bring help to his brother. He debated with himself how he could manage to talk with Colgrin; for he was convinced that by consulting together it would be possible for them to hit upon a safe solution—that is, if only he could make his way into his brother's presence.

Once Baldulf had come to the conclusion that no other means of access was open to him, he cut short his hair and his beard and dressed himself up as a minstrel with a harp. He strode up and down in the camp, pretending to be a harpist by playing melodies on his instrument.[23] No one suspected him and he moved nearer and nearer to the city walls, keeping up the same pretence all the time. In the end he was observed by the besieged,

20. Colgrin, the leader of the Saxons, and his brother Baldulf are later killed at the battle of Bath. Cheldric, another Saxon chieftain, after reinforcing Colgrin and Baldulf at Albany, survives the battle of Bath but is killed by Cador, duke of Cornwall (see n. 22) on the Isle of Thanet (cf. the account in Layamon's *Brut*, this volume, pp. 69–71).

21. Probably the Pentland Firth. (Caithness is the northernmost county of Scotland, in the tip opposite the Orkney Islands.)

22. Cador, one of the sturdiest and most impetuous of Arthur's supporters, later receives the challenge of Lucius Hiberius eagerly as a chance to achieve glory (see p. 98). He distinguishes himself at the battle of Saussy (see p. 84).

23. As a singer and teller of tales, Baldulf would have had easy access to many places; entertainers and pilgrims were welcome in every noble hall (cf. *King Horn*, this volume, p. 178, where the hero returns in similar disguise).

dragged up over the top of the walls on ropes and taken to his brother. When Colgrin set eyes on Baldulf he had the solace of embracing him and kissing him to his heart's desire, as though Baldulf had been restored to him from the dead. Finally, when, after exhaustive discussions, they had abandoned all hope of ever escaping, messengers returned from Germany to say that they had brought with them to Albany six hundred ships which were commanded by Cheldric and loaded with brave soldiery. When Arthur's advisers learned this, they dissuaded him from continuing the siege any longer, for if so large an enemy force were to come upon them they would all be committed to a most dangerous engagement.

CHAPTER XI

Arthur Fights Frollo

Arthur then[24] began to increase his personal entourage by inviting very distinguished men from far-distant kingdoms to join it. In this way he developed such a code of courtliness in his household that he inspired peoples living far away to imitate him. The result was that even the man of noblest birth, once he was roused to rivalry, thought nothing at all of himself unless he wore his arms and dressed in the same way as Arthur's knights. At last the fame of Arthur's generosity and bravery spread to the very ends of the earth; and the kings of countries far across the sea trembled at the thought that they might be attacked and invaded by him, and so lose control of the lands under their dominion. They were so harassed by these tormenting anxieties that they re-built their towns and the towers in their towns, and then went so far as to construct castles on carefully-chosen sites, so that, if invasion should bring Arthur against them, they might have a refuge in their time of need.

All this was reported to Arthur. The fact that he was dreaded by all encouraged him to conceive the idea of conquering the whole of Europe. He fitted out his fleets and sailed first of all to Norway, for he wished to give the kingship of that country to Loth, who was his brother-in-law.[25] Loth was the nephew of Sichelm the King of Norway, who had just died and left him the kingship in his will. However, the Norwegians had refused to accept Loth and had raised a certain Riculf to the royal power, for they considered that they could resist Arthur now that their towns were garrisoned. The son of this Loth, called Gawain,[26] was at that time a boy twelve years old. He had been sent by Arthur's brother-in-law to serve in the household of Pope Sulpicius, who had dubbed him a knight. As soon as Arthur landed on the coast of Norway, as I had begun to explain to you, King Riculf marched to meet him with the entire population of the country and then joined battle with him. Much blood was shed on either side, but in the end the Britons were victorious. They surged forward and killed Riculf and a number of his men. Once they were sure of victory, they invested the cities of Norway and set fire to them everywhere. They scattered the rural population and continued to give full license to their savagery until they had forced all Norway and all Denmark, too, to accept Arthur's rule.

---

24. I.e., having been settled in Britain for twelve years and having conquered all the outlying lands.

25. Loth, king of Lodonesia (Orkney) and Norway, was the husband of Anna, Arthur's sister. Geoffrey is in continual confusion on the matter of her marriage (cf. n. 28; also above, p. 77, ll. 728–29n), and as a result, so is the reader.

26. Gawain and Modred (see p. 137, as sons of King Loth and Anna, are the nephews of Arthur and thus in a kinship relationship which was the closest bond in medieval romance (cf. above, p. 77, ll. 728–29n).

As soon as he had subdued these countries and raised Loth to the kingship of Norway, Arthur sailed off to Gaul. He drew his troops up in companies and began to lay waste the countryside in all directions. The province of Gaul was at that time under the jurisdiction of the Tribune Frollo, who ruled it in the name of the Emperor Leo. The moment Frollo heard of the coming of Arthur, he marched out supported by the entire armed force which he had under command. He was determined to fight against Arthur, but in effect he could offer little resistance. The young men of all the islands which Arthur had subdued were there to fight at his side, and he was reported to have so powerful a force that it would hardly have been conquered by anyone. What is more, the better part of the army of the Gauls was already in Arthur's service, for he had bought them over by the gifts which he had given them. As soon as Frollo saw that he was having the worst of the fight, he quitted the battle-field without more ado and fled to Paris with the few men left to him.

There Frollo reassembled his scattered people, garrisoned the town and made up his mind to meet Arthur in the field a second time. Just as Frollo was considering how to strengthen his army by calling upon neighbouring peoples, Arthur arrived unexpectedly and besieged him inside the city. A whole month passed. Frollo grieved to see his people dying of hunger, and sent a message to Arthur to say that they should meet in single combat and that whichever was victorious should take the kingdom of the other. Being a man of immense stature, courage and strength, Frollo relied upon these advantages when he sent his message, hoping in this way to find a solution to his problem. When the news of Frollo's plan reached Arthur, he was immensely pleased; and he sent word back that he would be willing to hold the meeting that had been suggested. An agreement was come to on both sides and the two met on an island outside the city, the populace gathering to see what would happen to them.

Arthur and Frollo were both fully armed and seated on horses which were wonderfully fleet of foot. It was not easy to foretell which would win. For a moment they stood facing each other with their lances held straight in the air: then they suddenly set spurs to their horses and struck each other two mighty blows. Arthur aimed his lance with more care and hit Frollo high up on his chest. He avoided Frollo's weapon, and hurled his enemy to the ground with all his might. Arthur then drew his sword from the scabbard and was just hurrying forward to strike Frollo when the latter leapt quickly to his feet, ran forward with his lance levelled and with a deadly thrust stabbed Arthur's horse in the chest, thus bringing down both horse and rider. When the Britons saw their King thrown to the ground, they were afraid that he was dead and it was only with great self-control that they restrained themselves from breaking the truce and hurling themselves as one man upon the Gauls. Just as they were planning to invade the lists, Arthur sprang quickly to his feet, covered himself with his shield, and rushed forward to meet Frollo. They stood up to each other hand to hand, giving blow for blow, and each doing his utmost to kill the other. In the end Frollo found an opening and struck Arthur on the forehead. It was only the fact that he blunted the edge of his sword-blade at the point where it made contact with Arthur's metal helmet that prevented Frollo from dealing a mortal blow. When Arthur saw his leather cuirass and his round shield grow red, he was roused to even fiercer anger. He raised Caliburn[27] in the air with all his strength and brought it down through Frollo's helmet and so on to his head, which he cut into two halves. At this blow Frollo fell to the ground, drummed the earth with his heels and breathed his soul into the winds. The moment this was made known through-

---

27. Excalibur, Arthur's sword, made in the Isle of Avalon and presented him by the Lady of the Lake, who, in Malory, receives it back at Arthur's death.

out the army, the townsfolk ran forward, threw open their gates and surrendered their city to Arthur.

As soon as Arthur had won his victory, he divided his army into two and put one half under the command of Hoel,[28] ordering him to go off to attack Guitard, the leader of the Poitevins. With the other half Arthur busied himself in subduing the remaining provinces which were still hostile to him. Hoel soon reached Aquitania,[29] seized the towns of that region, and, after harassing Guitard in a number of battles, forced him to surrender. He also ravaged Gascony with fire and sword, and forced its leaders to submit.

Nine years passed. Once Arthur had subjected all the regions of Gaul to his power, he returned once more to Paris and held a court there. He called an assembly of the clergy and the people and settled the government of the realm peacefully and legally. It was then that he gave Neustria, now called Normandy, to his Cup-bearer Bedevere, and the province of Anjou to his Seneschal Kay. He gave a number of other provinces to the noblemen who had served him. Once he had pacified all these cities and peoples he returned to Britain just as spring was coming on.

CHAPTER XIV

Tourneys and Games

Invigorated by the food and drink which they had consumed,[30] they went out into the meadows outside the city and split up into groups ready to play various games. The knights planned an imitation battle and competed together on horseback, while their womenfolk watched from the top of the city walls and aroused them to passionate excitement by their flirtatious behaviour. The others passed what remained of the day in shooting with bow and arrows, hurling the lance, tossing heavy stones and rocks, playing dice and an immense variety of other games: this without the slightest show of ill-feeling. Whoever won his particular game was then rewarded by Arthur with an immense prize. The next three days were passed in this way. On the fourth day all those who in the office which they held had done Arthur any service were called together and each rewarded with a personal grant of cities, castles, archbishoprics, bishoprics and other landed possessions.

CHAPTER XV

The Roman Procurator Sends Emissaries to Arthur

Then the saintly Dubricius, who for a long time had wanted to live as a hermit, resigned from his position as Archbishop. David, the King's uncle, whose way of life had afforded an example of unblemished virtue to those whom he had instructed in the faith, was consecrated in his place.

---

28. Hoel I, king of Brittany, a son of Arthur's sister (cf. n. 25), fought with Arthur against the Saxons in England and the Romans in France.

29. Aquitaine, or Guyenne, the whole southern part of France, became famous in the 12th century under Eleanor, duchess of Aquitaine, whose court fostered the poetry of the troubadours (cf. above p. 54, l. 21n). Under Edward III and the Black Prince in the 14th century, Aquitaine belonged to England.

30. The knights had attended Arthur's state banquet on Whitsunday. In later romances (cf. *Sir Gawain and the Green Knight*), Arthur holds a plenary court and wears his crown five times a year; on these occasions an adventure has to occur before the banquet. The plenary court described here, and its ensuing interruption, is the start of this literary tradition.

At the same time Tebaus, the celebrated priest of Llandaff,[31] was appointed in the place of the holy Samson, Archbishop of Dol: this with the approval of Hoel, King of the Armorican Britons, to whom Tebaus' life and saintly habits had commended him. The bishopric of Silchester was given to Maugannius, that of Winchester to Diwanius and that of Alclud[32] to Eledenius.

While Arthur was distributing these benefices among his clergy, twelve men of mature years and respectable appearance came marching in at a slow pace. In their right hands they carried olive branches,[33] to show that they were envoys. They saluted Arthur and handed to him a communication from Lucius Hiberius. This letter read as follows:

"Lucius, Procurator of the Republic,[34] wishes that Arthur, King of Britain, may receive such treatment as he has deserved. I am amazed at the insolent way in which you continue your tyrannical behaviour. I am even more amazed at the damage which you have done to Rome. When I think about it, I am outraged that you should have so far forgotten yourself as not to realize this and not to appreciate immediately what it means that by your criminal behaviour you should have insulted the Senate, to which the entire world owes submission, as you very well know. You have had the presumption to disobey this mighty Empire by holding back the tribute of Britain, which tribute the Senate has ordered you to pay, seeing that Gaius Julius Caesar and other men of high place in the Roman State had received it for many years. You have torn Gaul away from that Empire, you have seized the province of the Allobroges[35] and you have laid hands on all the Islands of the Ocean, the Kings of which paid tribute to my ancestors from the first moment when the might of Rome prevailed in those regions. As a result the Senate has decreed that punishment should be exacted for

this long series of wrongs which you have done. I therefore order you to appear in Rome, so that you may submit yourself to your overlords and suffer the penalty of whatever sentence they may pass; and I appoint the middle of next August as the time for your coming. If you fail to arrive, I shall invade your territory myself and do my best to restore to the Roman State all that you have taken from it by your insane behaviour."

This letter was read aloud in the presence of the kings and the leaders. Arthur then withdrew with them to a gigantic tower near the entrance to the palace, to consider what ought to be done in the face of such a message. As they began to climb the stairs, Cador, Duke of Cornwall, who was a merry man, burst out laughing.

"Until now," he said to the King, "I have been afraid that the life of ease which the Britons have been leading might make cowards of them and soften them up during this long spell of peace. Their reputation for bravery on the battle-field, for which they are more famous than any other people, might well have been completely lost to them. Indeed, when it is obvious that men are no longer using their weapons, but are instead playing at dice, burning up their strength with women and indulging in other gratifications of that sort, then without any doubt their bravery, honour, courage and good name all become tainted with cowardice. For the past five years or thereabouts we have thought of nothing but these follies, and we have had no battle experience. It is precisely to free us from this sloth that God has stirred up the resentment of the Romans, so that they may restore our courage to what it used to be in the old days."

As Cador was saying this to them, and much more in the same strain, they reached their seats. When they had all sat down, Arthur made the following speech:

---

31. A city in Glamorganshire.

32. A city in Albany.

33. In Greece and Rome the olive branch was the traditional symbol of peace.

34. I.e., Rome.

35. The Allobroges have been identified with the Burgundians.

from CHAPTER XVI

Arthur's Speech

"You who have been my companions in good times and in bad, you of whose fortitude both in giving advice and in waging war I have had ample proof in the past, give me now your closest attention, every one of you, and in your wisdom tell me what you consider we should do on receiving such a letter as this. Anything which has been planned with great care by man in his wisdom is realized the more easily when the time for action arrives. It follows that we shall be able to bear this attack of Lucius with great equanimity if we have first of all worked out with one accord how we are best to resist him. For myself, I do not consider that we ought to fear his coming very much, seeing with what a trumped-up case he is demanding the tribute which he wants to exact from Britain. He says that he ought to be given it because it used to be paid to Julius Caesar and those who succeeded him. When these men landed with their armed band and conquered our fatherland by force and violence at a time when it was weakened by civil dissensions, they had been encouraged to come here by the disunity of our ancestors. Seeing that they seized the country in this way, it was wrong of them to exact tribute from it. Nothing that is acquired by force and violence can ever be held legally by anyone. In so far as the Roman has done us violence, he pleads an unreasonable case when he maintains that we are his tributaries in the eyes of the law. Since he presumes to exact something illegal from us, let us by a similar argument seek from him the tribute of Rome! Let him who comes out on top carry off what he has made up his mind to take! If the Roman decrees that tribute ought to be paid him by Britain simply because Julius Caesar and other Roman leaders conquered this country years ago,[36] then I decree in the same way that Rome ought to give me tribute, in that my ancestors once captured that city. Belinus,[37] that most glorious of the Kings of the Britons, with the help of his brother Brennius, the Duke of the Allobroges, hanged twenty of the noblest Romans in the middle of their own forum, captured the city and, when they had occupied it, held it for a long time. Similarly, Constantine,[38] the son of Helen, and Maximianus,[39] too, both of them close relations of mine, wearing the crown of Britain one after the other, each gained the throne of imperial Rome. Do you not agree, then, that it is we who should demand tribute of Rome? As for Gaul and the neighbouring Islands of the Ocean, we need send no answer, for when we snatched those lands from their empire they made no effort to defend them."

. . . . .

---

36. Julius Caesar landed in Britain in 55 B.C., but the first invasion was under Claudius, A.D. 43.

37. Belinus, king of Britain, and his brother Brennius, the ruler of Northumbria, became enemies after Belinus usurped parts of Northumbria. Brennius went to France, allied himself with the Allobroges and invaded Britain to fight his brother, but the two were reconciled, attacked Gaul, and invaded Italy; and after many battles the two brothers captured and plundered the city of Rome. It was Belinus who founded Kaerusc (Caerleon), the City of the Legions.

38. According to Geoffrey, Constantine I was the son of Constantius, a Roman senator and later king of Britain, and Helen, daughter of Coel, king of Britain. He is probably to be identified with Constantine the Great, son of the emperor Constantius Chlorus and Helena, a Balkan serving girl. Legends later made her father a British prince; Geoffrey raised him to king of Britain. We have here another instance of Geoffrey's ingenious combination of fact and fiction.

39. Cf. n. 16.

from BOOK X

CHAPTER III

Arthur and the Giant of Mont-Saint-Michel

Meanwhile[40] the news was brought to Arthur that a giant of monstrous size had emerged from certain regions in Spain. This giant had snatched Helena, the niece of Duke Hoel, from the hands of her guardians and had fled with her to the top of what is now called the Mont-Saint-Michel.[41] The knights of that district had pursued the giant, but they had been able to do nothing against him. It made no difference whether they attacked him by sea or by land, for he either sank their ships with huge rocks or else killed them with a variety of weapons. Those whom he captured, and they were quite a few, he ate while they were still half alive.

The next night, at two o'clock, Arthur came out from the tents without telling his companions, roused his Seneschal Kay and his Cup-bearer Bedevere and set out for the Mount. Being a man of such outstanding courage, he had no need to lead a whole army against monsters of this sort. Not only was he himself strong enough to destroy them, but by doing so he wanted to inspire his men.

When he came near to the Mount, they saw a fire gleaming on the top and a second fire ablaze on a smaller peak. Bedevere the Cup-bearer was ordered by the King to make his way to this second fire by boat. He could not have reached it in any other way, for the hill rose straight up from the sea. As Bedevere began to climb up to the summit, he heard a woman's scream come from above him. This terrified him at first, for he was afraid that the monster was there. His courage soon returned, however, and he drew his sword from its scabbard

and climbed up the hillside. On the top he could see nothing at all, except the great fire which he had observed before. Then he made out a newly-made tumulus nearby, and at its side an old woman who was weeping and wailing. The moment she saw him the old woman stopped weeping and began to speak to him instead. "Unhappy man!" said she. "What ill fortune has brought you to this spot? I pity you, for you are about to suffer death by the most unspeakable tortures. This very night a foul monster will destroy the flower of your youth. The most odious of all giants will come here. Cursed be his name! It is he who carried the Duke's niece off to this mountain. I have just buried her in this very spot. With her he brought me, her nurse. Without a moment's hesitation he will destroy you too, by some unheard-of form of death. How hideous the fate of my fairest nurseling was! When this foul being took her in his arms, fear flooded her tender breast and so she ended a life which was worthy of a longer span. Since he was unable to befoul with his filthy lust this child who was my sister soul, my second self, the joy and happiness of my life, in the madness of his bestial desire he raped me, against my will, as I swear by God and my own old age. Flee, my dear sir! Flee! If he comes, as he usually does, to have intercourse with me, he will find you here and tear you to pieces and destroy you miserably!"

Bedevere was as much moved as it is possible for a human being to be. He soothed the old woman with kind words, comforted her with the promise

---

40. Arthur had landed at Barfleur on the Cotentin peninsula near Cherbourg; and, after gathering his whole expeditionary force, he had proceeded to Brittany (see Layamon's *Brut*, this volume, pp. 76–83, and the Alliterative *Morte Arthure*, this volume, pp. 99–107).

41. See above, p. 76, l. 725*n*.

of speedy help and returned to Arthur to tell him all that he had discovered. Arthur grieved for the fate of the girl and ordered the other two to leave him to attack the monster alone. Should the need arise, they were to come to his assistance as smartly as they knew how and attack the giant in their turn. They then made their way to the taller of the two peaks. There they handed their horses over to their squires and began to clamber to the top, Arthur going on ahead.

At that moment the inhuman monster was standing by his fire. His face was smeared with the clotted blood of a number of pigs at which he had been gnawing. He had swallowed bits of them while he was roasting the rest over the live embers on the spits to which he had fixed them. The moment he saw the newcomers, nothing then being farther from his thoughts, he rushed to snatch up his club, which two young men would have found difficulty in lifting off the ground. The King drew his sword from its scabbard, held his shield in front of him and rushed forward at full speed to prevent the giant from seizing his club. The giant was quite aware of the advantage Arthur was hoping to gain. He took up his club and dealt the King such a mighty blow on his shield that he filled the shore in either direction with the reverberation of the impact and deafened Arthur's ears completely. The King grew white-hot in the fierceness of his rage. He struck the giant on the forehead with his sword and gave him such a blow that, although it was not mortal, all the same the blood ran down his face and into his eyes and prevented him from seeing. The giant had warded off the blow with his club and in this way had protected his forehead from a mortal wound. Blinded as he was by the blood which was gushing out, he rushed forward all the more fiercely. Just as a boar hurls itself at the huntsman, despite the latter's boar-spear, so the giant rushed against the King's sword. He

seized Arthur round the middle and forced him to the ground on his knees. Arthur gathered his strength and quickly slipped out of the giant's clutches. Moving like lightning, he struck the giant repeatedly with his sword, first in this place and then in that, giving him no respite until he had dealt him a lethal blow by driving the whole length of the blade into his head just where his brain was protected by his skull. At this the evil creature gave one great shriek and toppled to the ground with a mighty crash, like some oak torn from its roots by the fury of the winds. The king laughed with relief. He ordered Bedevere to saw off the giant's head and to hand it over to one of their squires, so that it might be carried to the camp for all to go and stare at.

Arthur said that he had not come into contact with anyone so strong since the time he killed the giant Retho on Mount Arvaius,[42] after the latter had challenged him to single combat. Retho had made himself a fur cloak from the beards of the kings whom he had slain. He sent a message to Arthur, telling him to rip his own beard off his face and when it was torn off send it to him. Since Arthur was more distinguished than any of the other kings, Retho promised in his honour to sew his beard higher up the cloak than the others. If Arthur would not do this, then Retho challenged him to a duel, saying that whoever proved the stronger should have the fur cloak as a trophy and also the beard of the man he had beaten. Soon after the battle began, Arthur was victorious. He took the giant's beard and the trophy too. From that day on, as he had just said, he had met nobody stronger than Retho.

When they had won their victory, as I have told you, the three returned to their tents with the head, just as dawn was succeeding to night. All their men crowded round them to gape at it and praise the man who had freed the country from

---

42. Arthur's previous fight with the giant Retho had taken place on Mount Arvaius (also Mount Aravia, Mount Erith), identified as Mount Snowdon or Eryri in Wales. In later versions the two fight stories are linked, and the beard garment is attributed to the monster of Mont-Saint-Michel (cf. Layamon's *Brut*, this volume, p. 82, and the Alliterative *Morte Arthure*, this volume, p. 102).

such a voracious monster. Hoel, however, grieved over the fate of his niece. He ordered a chapel to be built above her grave on the mountain-top where she had been buried. The peak took its name from the girl's burial place, and to this very day it is called Helena's Tomb.

CHAPTER IX

The Battle with Lucius Hiberius

Now at last they stood face to face with javelins raised, the Britons on this side and the Romans on that.[43] As soon as they heard the sound of the battle-trumpets, the legion commanded by the King of Spain and Lucius Catellus charged boldly at the division led by the King of Scotland and the Duke of Cornwall, but the latter stood firm, shoulder to shoulder, and the Roman force was not able to breach it. As the Roman legion persisted in its fierce attack, the division commanded by Gerin and Boso[44] moved up at the double. The Roman legion fought bravely, as has already been said, but this fresh division attacked it with a sudden cavalry charge, broke through and came into contact with the legion which the King of the Parthians[45] was directing against the division of Aschil, King of the Danes. Without a moment's delay the two forces met all along the line in a general mêlée, piercing each other's ranks and engaging each other in deadly combat. There ensued the most pitiable slaughter on both sides, with a bedlam of shouting and with men tumbling head foremost or feet first to the ground all over the place and vomiting forth their life with their heart's blood.

At first the Britons had the worst of it, for Bedevere the Cup-bearer was killed and Kay the Seneschal was mortally wounded. When Bedevere met Boccus, the King of the Medes,[46] he was run through by the latter's lance and fell dead inside the enemy lines. Kay the Seneschal did his utmost to avenge Bedevere, but he was surrounded by battalions of Medes and received a mortal wound. Nevertheless, brave soldier as he was, he cut a way through with the force which he was commanding, scattered the Medes and would have retreated to his own support-group with his line of battle unbroken, had he not come up against the legion of the King of Libya, whose counter-attack completely scattered the troops under Kay's command. Even then he fell back with a few men still alive and made his way to the Golden Dragon[47] with the corpse of Bedevere. How the Neustrians[48] grieved when they saw the body of their leader Bedevere slashed with so many wounds! The Angevins,[49] too, bewailed as they treated the wounds of their leader Kay in every manner they could think of.

This, however, was no moment for weeping and wailing, with the battle-lines meeting on both sides in a bath of blood and giving them little respite for lamentations of this sort before they were compelled to look to their own defence. Hyrelgas, the nephew of Bedevere, was greatly moved by his uncle's death. He gathered round him three hundred of his own men, made a sudden cavalry

---

43. See above, p. 84, ll. 967–99n.

44. Boso of Oxford and Gerin of Chartres, one of the Twelve Peers of Gaul, had previously been sent with Gawain to challenge Lucius Hiberius.

45. The Parthians were the inhabitants of an ancient country southeast of the Caspian Sea, now part of Iran.

46. The Medes were the inhabitants of Media, south of the Caspian Sea, now part of Iran. Both Media and Parthia were conquered by and allied with Rome, according to Geoffrey.

47. Arthur's standard, taken over from his father, Uther Pendragon (cf. n. 17). It was the battle flag around which stood the hard core of Arthur's retainers.

48. Inhabitants of Normandy, a province granted by Arthur to Bedevere.

49. Inhabitants of Anjou, a province granted by Arthur to Kay.

charge and rushed through the enemy lines to the spot where he had seen the standard of the King of the Medes, for all the world like a wild boar through a pack of hounds, thinking little of what might happen to himself, if only he could avenge his uncle. When he came to the place where he had seen the King, he killed him, carried off his dead body to his own lines, put it down beside the corpse of the Cup-bearer and hacked it completely to pieces. With a great bellow, Hyrelgas roused his fellow-countrymen's battalions to fury, exhorting them to charge at the enemy and to harass them with wave after wave of assault, for now a new-found rage boiled up within them and the hearts of their frightened opponents were sinking. They were drawn up, he shouted, in better order in their battalions than their enemies, fighting hand-to-hand as they were, and they were in a position to attack repeatedly and to inflict more serious losses. The Britons were roused by this encouragement. They attacked their enemy all along the line, and terrible losses were sustained in both armies.

Vast numbers fell on the side of the Romans, including Ali Fatima the King of Spain, Micipsa the Babylonian, and the Senators Quintus Milvius and Marius Lepidus. On the side of the Britons there died Holdin the Duke of the Ruteni, Leodegarius of Boulogne, and the three British leaders Cursalem of Caistor, Guallauc of Salisbury, and Urbgennius of Bath. The troops these men had commanded were greatly weakened and they drew back until they reached the battle-line of the Armorican Britons, which was commanded by Hoel and Gawain. However, this force burst into flame, as it were, rallied those who had been retreating, and compelled the enemy, who, a moment before, had been in pursuit, to withdraw in its turn. The Britons pressed on hard, hurling the fugitives to the ground and killing them. They did not pause in their slaughter until they reached the Emperor's own bodyguard. When he saw what disaster had overtaken his men, the Emperor hurried forward to give them support.[50]

CHAPTER XIII

Burial of the Slain

As soon as victory was assured, Arthur ordered the bodies of his leaders to be separated from the carcasses of the enemy. Once they were gathered together, he had these bodies prepared for burial with royal pomp and then they were carried to the abbeys of their own native districts and interred there with great honour. Bedevere the Cup-bearer was borne, with loud lamentations, by the Neustrians to Bayeux,[51] his own city, which his grandfather Bedevere I had founded. There he was laid to rest with all honour, beside a wall in a certain cemetery in the southern quarter of the city. Kay, who was mortally wounded, was carried away to Chinon, the town which he himself had built. Not long afterwards he died from his wound. As was fitting for a Duke of the Angevins, he was buried in a certain wood belonging to a convent of hermits not far from that town. Holdin, the Duke of the Ruteni, was carried to Flanders and laid to rest in his own city of Thérouanne.[52] At Arthur's command, the rest of the leaders and princes were borne to abbeys in the vicinity. He took pity on his enemies and told the local inhabitants to bury them. He ordered the body of

---

50. After a great slaughter, the issue being in doubt for a long time, Lucius Hiberius is finally slain, and Arthur is victorious.
51. In Malory, Bedevere survives the final battle of Camblam against Modred and, after some hesitation, returns Excalibur to the Lady of the Lake, on Arthur's command (see this volume,

pp. 856–57). The town of Bayeux in Normandy is famous for the detailed tapestry depicting the Norman invasion and victory at Hastings in 1066.
52. A village in Holland.

Lucius to be carried to the Senate, with a message that no other tribute could be expected from Britain.

Arthur spent the following winter in this same locality and found time to subdue the cities of the Allobroges. When summer came, he made ready to set out for Rome, and was already beginning to make his way through the mountains when the news was brought to him[53] that his nephew Mordred,[54] in whose care he had left Britain, had placed the crown upon his own head. What is more, this treacherous tyrant was living adulterously and out of wedlock with Queen Guinevere, who had broken the vows of her earlier marriage.

from BOOK XI

CHAPTER I

The Treason of Mordred

About this particular matter, most noble Duke, Geoffrey of Monmouth prefers to say nothing. He will, however, in his own poor style and without wasting words, describe the battle which our most famous King fought against his nephew, once he had returned to Britain after his victory; for that he found in the British treatise already referred to. He heard it, too, from Walter of Oxford, a man most learned in all branches of history.

As soon as the bad news of this flagrant crime had reached his ears, Arthur immediately cancelled the attack which he had planned to make on Leo, the Emperor of the Romans. He sent Hoel, the leader of the Bretons, with an army of Gauls, to restore peace in those parts; and then without more ado he himself set off for Britain, accompanied only by the island kings and their troops. That most infamous traitor Mordred, about whom I have told you, had sent Chelric,[55] the leader of the Saxons, to Germany, to conscript as many troops as possible there, and to return as quickly as he could with those whom he was to persuade to join him. Mordred had made an agreement with Chelric that he would give him that part of the island which stretched from the River Humber to Scotland and all that Hengist and Horsa had held in Kent in Vortigern's day.[56] In obedience to Mordred's command, Chelric landed with eight hundred ships filled with armed pagans.[57] A treaty was agreed to and Chelric pledged his obedience to the traitor Mordred as if to the King. Mordred had brought the Scots, Picts and Irish into his alliance, with anyone else whom he knew to be filled with hatred for his uncle. In all, the insurgents were about eighty thousand in number, some of them pagans and some Christians.

Surrounded by this enormous army, in which he placed his hope, Mordred marched to meet Arthur as soon as the latter landed at Richborough.[58] In the battle which ensued Mordred inflicted great slaughter on those who were trying to land. Auguselus,[59] the King of Albany, and Gawain, the

---

53. In the Alliterative *Morte Arthure* the message of Modred's treason is brought to Arthur by the famous Craddock in pilgrim's garb (see this volume, pp. 109–110).

54. Cf. n. 26.

55. This Chelric, a Saxon leader in league with Modred, must not be confused with the earlier Cheldric killed by Cador, duke of Cornwall (see n. 20).

56. Hengist and Horsa ("Stallion" and "Horse") were chieftains of the Jutes who according to Geoffrey came to Britain to help the king, Vortigern, repel the Picts (some sources say at the king's invitation). They landed in Britain at Ebbsfleet c. 449–50 and were granted the Isle of Thanet by Vortigern.

57. I.e., Saxon warriors. Normally the term is applied to Saracens in the romances; the author of *King Horn* has Saracens invading Britain, undoubtedly confusing them with Viking raiders (cf. above, p. 111, l. 622*n*).

58. Richborough is located in Kent near Sandwich and Thanet, close to the coast of the Strait of Dover.

59. The brother of Loth, king of Norway, Lodonesia, and Orkney.

King's nephew, died that day, together with many others too numerous to describe. Ywain,[60] the son of Auguselus' brother Urian, succeeded him in the kingship; and in the wars which followed he became famous because of the many brave deeds which he accomplished. In the end, but only with enormous difficulty, Arthur's men occupied the sea-shore. They drove Mordred and his army before them in flight and inflicted great slaughter on them in their turn. Profiting from their long experience in warfare, they drew up their troops most skilfully. They mixed their infantry with the cavalry and fought in such a way that when the line of footsoldiers moved up to the attack, or was merely holding its position, the horse charged at an angle and did all that they could to break through the enemy lines and to force them to run away.[61]

However, the Perjurer re-formed his army and so marched into Winchester on the following night. When this was announced to Queen Guinevere, she gave way to despair. She fled from York to the City of the Legions and there, in the church of Julius the Martyr,[62] she took her vows among the nuns,[63] promising to lead a chaste life.

CHAPTER II

The Death of Arthur

Now that he had lost so many hundreds of his fellow-soldiers, Arthur was more angry than ever. He buried his dead and then marched on the third day to the city of Winchester and laid siege to his nephew who had taken refuge there. Mordred showed no sign of abandoning his plans. He gave his adherents every encouragement he could think of, and then marched out with his troops and drew them up ready for a pitched battle with his uncle. The fight began and immense slaughter was done on both sides. The losses were greater in Mordred's army and they forced him to fly once more in shame from the battle-field. He made no arrangements whatsoever for the burial of his dead, but fled as fast as ship could carry him, and made his way towards Cornwall.

Arthur was filled with great mental anguish by the fact that Mordred had escaped him so often. Without losing a moment, he followed him to that same locality, reaching the River Camblam,[64] where Mordred was awaiting his arrival. Mordred was indeed the boldest of men and always the first to launch an attack. He immediately drew his troops up in battle order, determined as he was either to win or to die, rather than run away again as he had done in the past. From his total force of troops, about which I have told you, there still remained sixty thousand men under his command. From these he mustered six divisions, in each of which he placed six thousand, six hundred and sixty-six armed men. From those who were left over he formed one single division, and when he had assigned leaders to each of the others, he placed this last division under his own command.

---

60. Cf. above, p. 117, ll. 838–39n.

61. Arthur's troops were veterans of the wars against the Romans and used Roman battle tactics. Hannibal used a similar strategy at Cannae, in 216 B.C., sucking in the Roman infantry with a fluid and yielding front of his own troops of the line and then bringing his cavalry in from the wings to destroy the Roman flanks.

62. In Bede's *Ecclesiastical History* (I, 7), Julius is martyred by Diocletian and is described as "Legionum Urbis cives," the city being identified by some critics as Chester. Gildas has Julius a citizen of Carlisle; the confusion of Carlisle with Caerleon was a common one; cf. above, p. 94, l. 39n.

63. In Malory, Guinevere takes the veil in renunciation of and penitence for her love of Lancelot (who does not appear until the work of Chrétien de Troyes), which causes the dissolution of the Round Table and the eventual death of Arthur. Lancelot visits Guinevere before his own death (cf. this vol., pp. 838–41).

64. The river Camblam (today called the Camel) in Cornwall is close to Camelford, near the coast; Tintagel Head and the ruins traditionally known as King Arthur's castle are not far distant. Slaughter Bridge, on the river, is supposedly the site of the famous last battle (cf. above, p. 89, ll. 1145–46n).

As soon as they were all drawn up, he went round to encourage each of them in turn, promising them the possessions of their enemies if only they stood firm and were successful in battle.

On the other side, Arthur, too, was marshalling his army. He divided his men into nine divisions of infantry, each drawn up in a square, with a right and left wing. To each he appointed a commander. Then he exhorted them to kill these perjured villains and robbers who, at the request of one who had committed treason against him, the King, had been brought into the island from foreign parts to steal their lands from them. He told them, too, that this miscellaneous collection of barbarians, come from a variety of countries—raw recruits who were totally inexperienced in war— would be quite incapable of resisting valiant men like themselves, who were the veterans of many battles, provided always that they made up their minds to attack boldly and to fight like men.

While the two commanders were encouraging their men in this way in both the armies, the lines of battle suddenly met, combat was joined, and they all strove with might and main to deal each other as many blows as possible. It is heartrending to describe what slaughter was inflicted on both sides, how the dying groaned, and how great was the fury of those attacking. Everywhere men were receiving wounds themselves or inflicting them, dying or dealing out death. In the end, when they had passed much of the day in this way, Arthur, with a single division in which he had posted six

thousand, six hundred and sixty-six men, charged at the squadron where he knew Mordred was. They hacked a way through with their swords and Arthur continued to advance, inflicting terrible slaughter as he went. It was at this point that the accursed traitor was killed and many thousands of his men with him.

However, the others did not take to flight simply because Mordred was dead. They massed together from all over the battle-field and did their utmost to stand their ground with all the courage at their command. The battle which was now joined between them was fiercer than ever, for almost all the leaders on both sides were present and rushed into the fight at the head of their troops. On Mordred's side there fell Chelric, Elaf, Egbrict and Bruning, all of them Saxons; the Irishmen Gillapatric, Gillasel and Gillarvus; and the Scots and Picts, with nearly everyone in command of them. On Arthur's side there died Odbrict, King of Norway; Aschil, King of Denmark; Cador Limenich; and Cassivelaunus, with many thousands of the King's troops, some of them Britons, others from the various peoples he had brought with him. Arthur himself, our renowned King, was mortally wounded and was carried off to the Isle of Avalon,[65] so that his wounds might be attended to. He handed the crown of Britain over to his cousin Constantine, the son of Cador Duke of Cornwall: this in the year 542 after our Lord's Incarnation.

CHAPTER IX

Geoffrey's Sermon

You foolish people, weighed down by the sheer burden of your own monstrous crimes, never happy but when you are fighting one another, why have you so far weakened yourselves in domestic upsets that you, who need to submit far-distant kingdoms to your own authority, are

now like some fruitful vineyard which has gone sour and you cannot protect your own country, wives and children from your enemies? Keep on with your civil squabbling and forget what the Gospel says: "Every kingdom divided against itself shall be brought to desolation, and a house

---

65. Cf. above, p. 91, ll. 1184–85*n*.

divided against itself shall fall." Because your kingdom was divided against itself, because the lunacy of civil war and the smoke-cloud of jealousy obscured your mind, because your pride did not permit you to obey a single king, that is why you see your fatherland ravaged by the most impious heathens and your homesteads overturned one upon the other, all of which things those who come after you will lament in the future. They will see the cubs of the wild lioness occupy their castles, cities and other possessions. In their misery they will be driven forth from all of these, and only with the greatest difficulty will they ever recover the glory of their former estate, that is if they recover it at all![66]

from CHAPTER XIX

Of the Welsh

. . . As the foreign element around them became more and more powerful, they were given the name of Welsh instead of Britons: this word deriving either from their leader Gualo, or from their Queen Galaes, or else from their being so barbarous.[67]

The Saxons, on the other hand, behaved more wisely. They kept peace and concord among themselves, they cultivated the fields, and they re-built the cities and castles. They threw off completely the dominion of the Britons and under their leader Adelstan, who was the first among them to be crowned King, they ruled over the whole of Loegria.[68]

The Welsh, once they had degenerated from the noble state enjoyed by the Britons, never afterwards recovered the overlordship of the island. On the contrary, they went on quarrelling with the Saxons and among themselves and remained in a perpetual state of either civil or external warfare.[69]

CHAPTER XX

Geoffrey's Farewell

The task of describing their kings, who succeeded from that moment onwards in Wales, I leave to my contemporary Caradoc of Llancarfan. The kings of the Saxons I leave to William of Malmesbury and Henry of Huntingdon.[70] I recommend these last to say nothing at all about the kings of the Britons, seeing that they do not have in their possession the book in the British language which Walter, Archdeacon of Oxford, brought from Wales. It is this book which I have been at such pains to translate into Latin in this way, for it was composed with great accuracy about the doings of these princes and in their honour.

---

66. Geoffrey has throughout a very strong pro-British bias. His exhortation to the Welsh at the end is to remember the past and their place in history.

67. Geoffrey's fervor is more personally revealing than historically accurate: the word *Welsh* is derived from OE *welisc*, "Briton" or "foreigner" (cf. Latin *Volcae*, a Gallic tribe). German *welsch*, "foreign," from Germanic *walh*, "foreigner," and *Walloon* are related words.

68. *Loegria*: Cf. n. 12.

69. This and the following paragraph are an *explicit* found in the Berne and Harlech MSS. of the *Historia*, but not in Cambridge Univ. Lib. MS. 1706. Sebastian Evans divided the material as here, between the end of his Chap. XIX and Chap. XX.

70. The Welsh chronicler Caradoc of Lancarvan, in his *Vita Gildae* (c. 1130), describes the abduction of Guinevere (Gwenhwyfar) and her rescue by Arthur. The most famous work of William of Malmesbury (d. 1143), an important historian educated at Malmesbury Abbey, is the *Gesta Regum Anglorum*, a chronicle filled with folklore and entertaining stories in addition to history from 449 to 1127. The *Historia Anglorum* of Henry, archdeacon of Huntingdon (1084–1155), takes the history of England up to the year before his death.

THE ROMANCE

The word *romance* is derived from the adverb *romanice*, "Roman-like," as the dialect was called which developed from the Vulgar Latin spoken by Roman legions in the colonies. Later, this term was used for anything written in *romanice* or *romance* (i.e., the Romance languages, especially French) and it was specifically applied to the long narrative poems first produced in the twelfth century by the Frenchman Chrétien de Troyes. The romance became the most popular type of aristocratic literature in Europe, and it was normally recited by minstrels in noble halls. The common meter of the romances was the octosyllabic couplet, though after 1300 they were normally written in prose. The subjects, or "matters," of romance are usually divided into Arthurian British, Carolingian French, native English, and classical themes. Stories of heroic, chivalric adventure, usually fanciful and containing elements of the marvelous, make up the bulk of this genre. Love interest is often present, although frequently of secondary importance. Most romances are episodic, with stereotyped heroes and plots.

REFERENCES

Bédier, Joseph. *Les Légendes épiques.* 2d ed. Paris, 1914–21.

Billings, Anna Hunt. *A Guide to the Middle English Metrical Romances Dealing with English and Germanic Legends and with the Cycles of Charlemagne and of Arthur.* New York, 1901.

Capellanus, A. *The Art of Courtly Love.* Trans. J. J. Parry. New York, 1941.

French, Walter Hoyt, and Hale, Charles Brockway, eds. *Middle English Metrical Romances.* New York, 1964.

Gautier, Léon. *Les Épopées françaises.* Paris, 1878–92.

Hibbard, Laura A. *Mediaeval Romance in England.* New York, 1959.

Ker, W. P. *Epic and Romance.* London, 1908.

Loomis, Roger Sherman, ed. *Arthurian Literature in the Middle Ages.* London, 1959.

Sands, Donald, ed. *Middle English Verse Romances.* New York, 1966.

Weston, J. L. *From Ritual to Romance.* Cambridge, 1920.

The romance is treated in the General Introduction of this volume, pp. 12–13, 20–24, 25–26, 27–28, 35–39.

KING HORN

DATE: c. 1250. ◆ MANUSCRIPTS: British Library, Harleian 2253; Bodleian Library, Oxford, Laud Misc. 108; University Library, Cambridge, Gg.4.27.2. The dialect mixes Southern and Midland forms. ◆ EDITIONS: Walter Hoyt French and Charles Brockway Hale, *Middle English Metrical Romances* (New York, 1964); Joseph Hall, *King Horn* (Oxford, 1901), which is the standard three-text edition; Donald Sands, *Middle English Verse Romances* (New York, 1966).

Because of the Southern characteristics of the dialect, it is well to note the following textual points: (1) *v* and *u* are used for *f* (*verde = ferde*). (2) *u* is very often interchanged with *v* (*euel = evel, liuede = livede, vs = us, vre = ure*). (3) *u* often stands for Mod. Eng. *i* or *e* (*schup = ship*). (4) **OE** *heo* is often retained for *she*; *he* is also used for *she* as well as *they* (cf. ll. 1,743, 786), and *hi* and *hem* are used for *they* and *them*. (5) Metathesis of *r* (*vrne = run*) is occasionally found. (6) Negative contractions are, of course, quite common: for example, *nis, nas, nadde, nolde, nuste,* for *is not, was not, had not, would not, knew not.*

King Horn is the romancer's romance. It is, with *Havelok the Dane*, the first poem of this genre in English, some scholars dating it as early as 1225. The typical romance pattern, as outlined in the General Introduction, is followed here, including most of the clichés, stock characters, formulaic patterns, and motifs generally found in other works. *King Horn* is therefore a type, and as such it merits study. The story was very popular and found its way into the ballad (*Hind Horn*, this volume, p. 489) and the English prose romance of the 15th century (*King Ponthus and the Fair Sidone*). The central themes of *King Horn*, as also of *Havelok the Dane*, are the Exile and Return and the Male Cinderella motifs, a widespread combination very prevalent in Western folklore.

Alle beon he° bliþe°   be they/of cheer
Þat to my song lyþe.°   listen
A sang ihc° schal ʒou singe   song I
Of Murry þe Kinge.
⁵ King he was biweste°   in the west
So° longe so hit laste.°   as/he lived

1–2. Standard romance beginning, in which the minstrel addresses his audience. Such formulas are evidence of oral transmission.

4. The names Murry, Horn, Modi, and so forth, do not seem to refer to any known historical personages.

Godhild het° his quen;°   *was called/queen*
Faire ne miȝte non ben.°   *fairer not might none be*
He hadde a sone° þat het Horn,   *son*
¹⁰ Fairer ne miste° non beo° born,   *might/be*
Ne° no rein° vpon birine,°   *nor/rain/rain*
Ne sunne vpon bischine.°   *shine*
Fairer nis° non þane° he was,   *is not/than*
He was briȝt° so þe glas,   *bright*
¹⁵ He was whit° so þe flur,°   *white/flower*
Rose-red was his colur.
He was fayr and eke° bold,   *also*
And of fiftene winter° old.   *winters*
In none kingeriche°   *no kingdom*
²⁰ Nas° non his iliche.°   *was not/like*
Twelf feren° he hadde   *twelve companions*
Þat he alle wiþ him ladde.°   *led*
Alle riche mannes sones,
And alle hi° were faire gomes,°   *they/young men*
²⁵ Wiþ him for to pleie,°   *pass the time*
And mest° he luuede tweie;°   *most/liked two*
Þat on him° het Haþulf child   *the one he*
And þat oþer Fikenild.
Aþulf was þe beste,
³⁰ And Fikenylde þe werste.
Hit° was vpon a someres° day,   *it/summer's*
Also° ihc ȝou telle may,   *as*
Murri þe gode° King   *good*
Rod on° his pleing°   *rode in/sport*
³⁵ Bi þe se° side,   *sea*
Ase° he was woned° ride.   *as/accustomed to*
With him riden bote tvo;°   *rode only two*
Al to° fewe ware þo.°   *too/were they*
He fond° bi þe stronde,°   *found/shore*
⁴⁰ Ariued on his londe,°   *land*
Schipes fiftene
Wiþ Saraȝins kene:°   *Saracens fierce*
He axede° what hi soȝte°   *asked/sought*

10–16. These typical romance and courtly clichés were part and parcel of the genre and expected by the audience.

21. Twelve, from the number of Christ's disciples, was the normal number for retainers or bodyguards, as the Twelve Peers of Charlemagne in *Chanson de Roland*.

27–28. The typical faithful friend and treacherous villain; cf. Oliver and Ganelon. *child:* a term appearing before or after a proper name that indicates an aspirant to knighthood or a youth worthy, because of family and accomplishments, to be knighted.

42. No Saracens or paynims (cf. *payn*, l. 45) of course, ever landed in the British Isles (cf. above, p. 111, l. 622*n*). The sea raiders were probably originally Danes.

Oþer° to londe broȝte.°   or/brought
45 A payn° hit ofherde,°   pagan/heard
And hym wel sone answarede:°   very quickly answered
"Þi lond folk° we schulle slon,°   people/shall slay
And alle þat Crist luueþ vpon°   worship
And þe selue° riȝt anon,°   yourself/immediately
50 Ne° schaltu° to-dai henne gon."°   not/shall you/hence go
Þe Kyng aliȝte of° his stede,°   got off/steed
For þo° he hauede nede,°   of that/had need
And his gode kniȝtes° two;   knights
Al to fewe he hadde þo.°   then
55 Swerd° hi gunne° gripe   sword/began to
And togadere° smite.   together
Hy smyten° vnder schelde°   they smote/shield
Þat° sume° hit yfelde.°   so that/some/felt
Þe King hadde al to fewe
60 Toȝenes° so fele schrewe:°   against/many rascals
So vele miȝten yþe°   many might easily
Bringe hem þre° to diþe.°   them three/death
    Þe pains come° to londe   pagans came
And neme° hit in here honde:°   took/their hands
65 Þat folc hi° gunne quelle,°   they/kill
And churchen° for to felle:°   churches/raze
Þer ne moste libbe°   might live
Þe fremde ne° þe sibbe,°   strangers nor/kin
Bute° hi here laȝe asoke,°   unless/faith forsook
70 And to here° toke.°   theirs/went over
Of alle wymmanne,°   women
Wurst° was Godhild þanne;°   most miserable/then
For Murri heo weop sore°   she wept greatly
And for Horn ȝute° more.   yet
75 He° wente vt° of halle   she/out
Fram hire° maidenes alle   from her
Vnder a roche° of stone,   rock
Þer° heo liuede alone.   where
Þer heo seruede Gode
80 Aȝenes° þe paynes forbode:°   against/forbiddance
Þer he seruede Criste
Þat no payn hit° ne wiste:°   it/knew
Eure° heo bad° for Horn child   ever/prayed
Þat Jesu Crist him° beo° myld.   to him/be
85 Horn was in paynes° honde   pagans'

---

77. Hermits and recluses often found shelter in caves.

Wiþ his feren° of the londe.°   *companions/land*
Muchel° was his fairhede,°   *great/beauty*
For Ihesu Crist him makede.°   *created*
Payns him wolde slen,°   *would slay*
90 Oþer° al quic flen,°   *or/alive flay*
Ʒef° his fairnesse nere:°   *if/it were not for*
Þe children alle aslaʒe° were.°   *slain/would have been*
Þanne spak on admirad°—   *spoke an emir*
Of wordes he was bald,°—   *bold*
95 "Horn, þu° art wel kene,°   *you/very courageous*
And þat is wel isene;°   *seen*
Þu art gret° and strong,   *great*
Fair and euene long;°   *well proportioned*
Þu schalt waxe more
100 Bi fulle seue ʒere:°   *fully seven years*
Ʒef þu mote° to liue go°   *may/alive stay*
And þine feren also,
Ʒef hit so bifalle,°   *be*
Ʒe scholde° slen vs alle: *you should*
105 Þaruore° þu most° to stere,°   *therefore/must/boat*
Þu and þine ifere;°   *companions*
To schupe schulle° ʒe funde,°   *ship shall/hasten*
And sinke to þe grunde;°   *bottom*
Þe se° ʒou schal adrenche,°   *sea/drown*
110 Ne° schal hit us noʒt° of þinche;°   *nor/not/worry*
For if þu were aliue,
Wiþ swerd° oþer wiþ kniue,°   *sword/knife*
We sholden° alle deie,°   *should/die*
And þi fader deþ° abeie."°   *father's death/atone for*
115 Þe children hi broʒte° to stronde,°   *they brought/shore*
Wringinde here honde,°   *wringing their hands*
Into schupes borde°   *aboard*
At þe furste worde.°   *at once*
Ofte hadde Horn beo wo,°   *been sad*
120 Ac neure wurs° þan him° was þo.°   *but never more/he/then*
Þe se bigan to flowe,°   *rise*
And Horn child to rowe;
Þe se þat schup so fasste drof°   *drove*
Þe children dradde° þerof.   *feared*
125 Hi wenden to-wisse°   *believed certainly*

---

100. The number seven, as well as three and twelve, is standard in romances and ballads.

105–14. There are parallels to the setting adrift of unwanted persons, for example, in the exposure of Danae and Perseus, as well as in the Constance saga and Chaucer's *Man of Law's Tale* (cf. below, p. 195, ll. 519–22).

Of here lif to misse,°   *lose*
Al þe day and al þe niȝt°   *night*
Til hit° sprang dai-liȝt,°   *it/daylight*
Til Horn saȝ° on þe stronde   *saw*
130 Men gon° in þe londe.°   *walking/land*
"Feren," quaþ° he, "ȝonge,°   *companions/said/ young*
Ihc° telle ȝou tiþinge:°   *I/news*
Ihc here foȝeles° singe,   *hear birds*
And þat gras him springe.°   (*see*) *it growing*
135 Bliþe beo° we on lyue;°   *happy are/in life*
Vre° schup is on ryue."°   *our/shore*
Of° schup hi gunne° funde,   *off/began to*
And setten fout° to grunde;°   *set foot/ground*
Bi þe se side
140 Hi leten° þat schup ride:°   *let/ride (at anchor)*
Þanne° spak him° child Horn,   *then/spoke*
(In Suddene he was iborn):°   *born*
"Schup bi þe se flode,
Daies haue þu° gode°   *may you have/good*
145 Bi þe se brinke,
No water þe° nadrinke:°   *you/not sink*
Ȝef þu cume° to Suddenne,   *if you come*
Gret° þu wel of myne kenne,°   *greet/family*
Gret þu wel my moder,°   *mother*
150 Godhild, Quen° þe gode,   *queen*
And seie° þe paene° kyng,   *tell/pagan*
Jesu Cristes wiþering°   *enemy*
Þat ihc am hol° and fer°   *hale/hearty*
On þis lond ariued her:°   *here*
155 And seie° þat hei° schal fonde°   *say/they/feel*
Þe dent° of myne honde."°   *strength/hand*
Þe children ȝede° to tune,°   *went/town*
Bi dales and bi dune.°   *hills*
Hy metten° wiþ Almair King,   *they met*
160 (Crist ȝeue° him His blessing!)   *give*
King of Westernesse
(Crist ȝiue him muchel° blisse!).   *great*
He him spac° to Horn child   *spoke*
Wordes þat were mild:

---

142. Suddene has been identified by some as the Isle of Man, by others as part of southwestern Scotland. An obstacle to the latter identification is the island nature of Horn's home (see also l. 161*n*; cf. Walter Oliver, "King Horn and Suddene," *PMLA*, 46 (1931), 102–14).

157. *to tune:* i.e., "away."

161. Westerness is perhaps the Wirral district in Cheshire, or the Mull of Galloway. Or the words *Suddene* (l. 142) and *Westernesse* may refer only to countries in the south and the west; cf. the later *bi est*, also a vague term of direction.

165 "Whannes° beo ȝe,° faire gumes,°   *whence|you|youths*
    Þat her to londe beoþ icume,°   *are come*
    Alle þrottene,°   *thirteen*
    Of bodie swiþe kene?°   *very hardy*
    Bi God þat me makede,°   *created*
170 A swihc° fair verade°   *such a| group*
    Ne sauȝ ihc° in none stunde,°   *not saw I|no hour*
    Bi westene londe:°   *in western land*
    Seie me wat° ȝe seche."°   *what|seek*
    Horn spak here speche,°   *their speech*
175 He spak for hem° alle,   *them*
    Vor° so hit° moste biualle°   *for|it|had to be*
    He was þe faireste
    And of° wit þe beste.   *in*
        "We beoþ of Suddenne,
180 Icome° of gode kenne,   *come*
    Of Cristene blode,°   *Christian blood*
    And kynges suþe° gode.   *very*
    Payns° þer gunne° ariue   *pagans|did*
    And duden hem of lyue.°   *killed them*
185 Hi sloȝen° and todroȝe°   *they slew|tore apart*
    Cristene men inoȝe.°   *many*
    So° Crist me mote rede,°   *as|may counsel*
    Vs he dude lede°   *did put*
    Into a galeie,°   *rowboat*
190 Wiþ þe se° to pleie,°   *sea|strive against*
    Dai° hit is igon° and oþcr,°   *a day|passed|another*
    Wiþute° sail and roþer.°   *without|rudder*
    Vre° schip bigan to swymme   *our*
    To þis londes brymme°   *shore*
195 Nu þu miȝt° vs slen° and binde,   *now you might|slay*
    Ore honde° bihynde;   *our hands*
    Bute ȝef° hit beo° þi wille,   *but if|be*
    Helpe þat we ne spille."°   *die-*
        Þanne spak° þe gode° Kyng   *then spoke|good*
200 (I wis° he nas° no niþing):°   *indeed|was not|villain*
    "Seie° me, child,° what is þi name;   *tell|youth*
    Ne schaltu haue bute° game."°   *you shall have only|pleasure*
    Þe child him answerde,
    Sone so° he hit herde:°   *quickly when|heard*
205 "Horn ihc am ihote,°   *called*

165–73. The words of greeting, similar to the challenge of the Danish coast guard in *Beowulf*, are standard procedure in epic and romance.

Icomen vt° of þe bote,°	*come out/boat*
Fram° þe se side.	*from*
Kyng, wel mote þe tide."°	*may good befall you*
Þanne hym° spak þe gode King,	*to him*
210 "Wel bruc° þu þi neuening.°	*enjoy/name*
Horn, þu go wel schulle°	*shall*
Bi dales and bi hulle;°	*hills*
Horn, þu lude sune,°	*loud sound*
Bi dales and bi dune;°	*hills*
215 So schal þi name springe	
Fram kynge to kynge,	
And þi fairnesse	
Abute° Westernesse,	*round about*
Þe strengþe of þine honde	
220 Into eurech londe.°	*every land*
Horn, þu art so swete,°	*dear*
Ne° may ihc þe forlete."°	*not/I you lose*
Hom rod° Aylmar þe Kyng	*home rode*
And Horn mid° him, his fundling,°	*with/foundling*
225 And alle his ifere,°	*companions*
Þat were him° so dere,°	*to him/dear*
Þe Kyng com° into halle	*came*
Among his kniȝtes° alle:	*knights*
Forþ he clupede° Aþelbrus,	*called*
230 Þat was stiward° of his hus.°	*steward/house*
"Stiward, tak° nu here	*take*
Mi fundlyng for to lere°	*teach*
Of þine mestere°	*trade*
Of wude° and of riuere,°	*forest/river*
235 And tech° him to harpe	*teach*
Wiþ his nayles scharpe,	
Biuore° me to kerue,°	*before/carve*
And of° þe cupe serue.°	*from/to serve*
Þu° tech him of alle þe liste°	*you/wish*
240 Þat þu eure° of wiste,°	*ever/knew*
And his feiren° þou wise°	*companions/teach*
Into oþere seruise:°	*service*

210–14. Puns on *horn*, the musical instrument.

233. *mestere:* "mystery," i.e., "service" (cf. above, p. 19).

234. *of wude:* referring to hunting with hounds; *of riuere:* referring to hunting with hawks (possibly also to fishing).

237. Carving the roast before his lord was one of the duties of a squire; cf. Chaucer's Squire in the General Prologue of the *Canterbury Tales*. The head of the house still carves before guests in many English and American households, undoubtedly illustrating the survival of this medieval tradition.

	Horn þu underuonge°	take charge of
	And tech him of harpe and songe."	
245	Ailbrus gan° lere	did
	Horn and his yfere:°	companions
	Horn in herte laȝte°	heart stored
	Al þat he him taȝte.°	taught
	In þe curt° and vte,°	court/out
250	And elles° al abute,	elsewhere
	Luuede° men Horn child,	loved
	And mest° him louede° Rymenhild,	most/loved
	Þe Kynges oȝene doȝter,°	own daughter
	He was mest in þoȝte;°	(her) thought
255	Heo° louede so Horn child	she
	Þat neȝ° heo gan wexe wild:°	almost/become mad
	For heo ne miȝte° at borde°	might/table
	Wiþ him speke° no worde,	speak
	Ne noȝt° in þe halle	nor not
260	Among þe kniȝtes alle,	
	Ne nowhar° in non° oþere stede:°	nowhere/no/place
	Of folk heo hadde drede:°	fear
	Bi daie ne bi niȝte°	night
	Wiþ him speke ne° miȝte;	not
265	Hire soreȝe° ne hire pine°	her sorrow/pain
	Ne miȝte neure fine.°	never end
	In heorte° heo hadde wo,°	heart/sorrow
	And þus hire biþoȝte þo:°	she decided then
	Heo sende° hire sonde°	sent/messenger
270	Aþelbrus to honde,°	hand
	Þat he come hire to,	
	And also scholde° Horn do°	should/lead
	Al into bure,°	(the) bower
	For heo gan° to lure,°	began/look wan
275	And þe sonde seide°	said
	Þat sik° lai þat maide,	sick
	And bad° him come swiþe,°	bade/quickly
	For heo nas° noþing bliþe.°	was not/not happy
	Þe stuard° was in herte wo,°	steward/sad
280	For he nuste° what to do.	knew not
	Wat° Rymenhild hure þoȝte°	what/she decided
	Gret° wunder him° þuȝte,°	(a) great/to him/seemed
	Abute° Horn þe ȝonge°	about/young
	To bure for to bringe.	
285	He þoȝte vpon° his mode°	thought in/mind

Hit° nas for none gode:°
He tok° him anoþer,
Aþulf, Hornes broþer.
   "Athulf," he sede,° "riȝt anon°
290 Þu° schalt wiþ me to bure gon°
To speke wiþ Rymenhild stille°
And witen hure° wille.
In Hornes ilike°
Þu schalt hure biswike:°
295 Sore ihc me ofdrede°
He wolde° Horn misrede."°
Aþelbrus gan° Aþulf lede,°
And into bure wiþ him ȝede:°
Anon vpon° Aþulf child
300 Rymenhild gan wexe wild:°
He wende° þat Horn hit were
Þat heo hauede° þere:
Heo sette him on bedde;
Wiþ Aþulf child he wedde;°
305 On hire° armes tweie°
Aþulf heo gan leie.°
"Horn," quaþ° heo, "wel° longe
Ihc habbe þe luued stronge.°
Þu schalt þi trewþe pliȝte°
310 On myn hond her riȝt,°
Me to spuse° holde,°
And ihc þe lord° to wolde."°
   Aþulf sede on hire ire°
So stille° so hit were,°
315 "Þi tale nu° þu lynne,°
For Horn nis° noȝt° herinne.
Ne beo° we noȝt iliche:°
Horn is fairer and riche,°
Fairer bi one ribbe
320 Þane eni° man þat libbe:°
Þeȝ° Horn were vnder molde°
Oþer elles° wher he wolde°
Oþer henne° a þusend mile,°
Ihc nolde° him ne° þe bigile."°
325   Rymenhild hire biwente,°
And Aþelbrus fule° heo schente.°

it/no good (**purpose**)
took

said/immediately
you/go
in secret
know her
likeness
deceive
I am very afraid
she would/misguide
did/lead
went
quickly toward
become passionate
thought
she had

made love
in her/two
embrace
said/very
I have you loved deeply
troth plight
my hand here right
as spouse/to hold
(for my) lord/take
ear
as quietly/possible
talk now/stop
is not/not
not are/alike
powerful

than any/lives
though/ground
or else/wanted
hence/thousand miles
would not/nor/deceive
turned
foully/cursed

---

288. *broþer:* i.e., "friend," "brother-in-arms."
319–20. I.e., definitely, noticeably fairer (by additional qualities) than all other men. It is possible that Horn's fairness is being likened to that of Eve (Adam's rib), i.e., woman.

"Hennes° þu go, þu fule þeof,°   *hence/foul thief*
Ne wurstu° me° neure° more leof;°   *be/to me/never/dear*
Went vt° of my bur,°   *go out/bower*
330 Wiþ muchel° mesauentur.°   *great/ill fortune*
Schame mote þu fonge°   *may you receive*
And on hiȝe rode anhonge.°   *high cross hang*
Ne spek° ihc noȝt wiþ Horn: *spoke*
Nis he noȝt vnorn;°   *ugly*
335 Horn is fairer þane beo° he: *is*
Wiþ muchel schame mote þu deie."°   *die*
    Aþelbrus in a stunde°   *immediately*
Fel anon to grunde.°   *ground*
"Lefdi° min oȝe,°   *lady/own*
340 Liþe° me a litel þroȝe.°   *listen/while*
Lust° whi ihc wonde°   *hear/hesitated*
Bringe° þe Horn to honde.   *to bring*
For Horn is fair and riche,
Nis° no whar° his iliche.°   *(there) is not/nowhere/like*
345 Aylmar, þe gode° Kyng,   *good*
Dude° him on° mi lokyng,°   *put/in/charge*
Ȝef° Horn were her abute,°   *if/around*
Sore y° me dute°   *greatly I/suspect*
Wiþ him ȝe wolden° pleie°   *you would/make love*
350 Bitwex° ȝou selue tweie;°   *between/the two of you*
Þanne scholde wiþuten oþe°   *then should without question*
Þe Kyng maken° vs wroþe.°   *make/sorry*
Rymenhild, forȝef° me þi tene,°   *forgive/sorrow*
Lefdi, my Quenc,
355 And Horn ihc° schal þe° fecche,   *I/you*
Wham so hit recche."°   *no matter who cares*
    Rymenhild ȝef he cuþe°   *as she could*
Gan lynne° wiþ hire muþe.°   *did stop/mouth*
Heo makede hire wel bliþe;°   *she made herself very happy*
360 Wel° was hire° þat siþe.°   *good/to her/occasion*
"Go nu,"° quaþ° heo, "sone,°   *now/said/quickly*
And send him after none,°   *noon*
On a squicres wise.°   *guise*
Whane° þe Kyng arise   *when*
365 To wude° for to pleie,°   *(the) forest/enjoy himself*
Nis non° þat him biwreie.°   *none/betray*
He schal wiþ me bileue°   *remain*
Til hit° beo nir° eue,   *it/near*

---

358. I.e., "stopped talking."

To hauen° of him mi wille;   *have*
370 After ne recche° ihc what me telle."°   *not care/men say*
    Aylbrus wende° hire fro;°   *turned/her from*
    Horn in halle fond° he þo°   *found/then*
    Bifore þe Kyng on benche,
    Wyn° for to schenche.°   *wine/pour*
375 "Horn," quaþ he, "so hende,°   *gracious*
    To bure° nu þu° wende,°   *bower/you/go*
    After mete stille,°   *meal secretly*
    Wiþ Rymenhild to duelle;°   *stay*
    Wordes suþe° bolde,   *very*
380 In herte° þu hem° holde.   *heart/them*
    Horn, beo me wel trewe; °   *trust me well*
    Ne schal hit þe neure° rewe."°   *never/make sorry*
    Horn in herte leide°   *stored*
    Al þat he him seide;°   *told*
385 He ȝeode° in wel riȝte°   *went/right away*
    To Rymenhild þe briȝte;°   *fair*
    On knes° he him° sette,   *knees/himself*
    And sweteliche hure grette.°   *sweetly her greeted*
    Of° his feire siȝte°   *from/fair appearance*
390 Al þe bur gan° liȝte.°   *began/to shine*
    He spac° faire speche°—   *spoke/speech*
    Ne dorte° him no man teche.°   *needed/to teach*
    "Wel þu sitte and softe,
    Rymenhild þe briȝte,
395 Wiþ þine maidenes sixe
    Þat þe° sitteþ nixte.°   *to you/next*
    Kinges stuard° vre°   *steward/our*
    Sende° me into bure: *sent*
    Wiþ þe speke° ihc scholde:°   *you speak/I should*
400 Seie° me what þu woldest:°   *tell/would*
    Seie,° and ich° schal here.°   *say/I/hear*
    What þi wille were."
        Rymenhild vp gan stonde°   *did stand*
    And tok° him bi þe honde:°   *took/hand*
405 Heo° sette him on pelle°   *she/coverlet*
    Of wyn to drinke his fulle:°   *fill*
    Heo makede° him faire chere°   *made/entertainment*

---

390. It was thought that a person of royal blood could be recognized by the light shining from his body, though here the phrase may be meant symbolically. There is a similar motif in *Havelok the Dane* (cf. below, p. 197, l. 592n).

403–14. This is the motif of the Wooing Lady, also known as the Potiphar's Wife motif (cf. below, p. 344, n. 20). It is one of the central points in the Gawain–Loathly Lady stories (cf., for example, Chaucer's *Wife of Bath's Tale* and *The Wedding of Sir Gawain and Dame Ragnell*).

And tok him abute° þe swere.°   *about/neck*
Ofte heo him custe,°   *kissed*
410 So° wel so hire luste.°   *as/she liked*
"Horn," heo sede,° "wiþute strif,°   *said/without doubt*
Þu schalt haue me to° þi wif.°   *for/wife*
Horn, haue of° me rewþe,°   *on/pity*
And plist° me þi trewþe."°   *plight/troth*
415   Horn þo° him biþoзte°   *then/decided*
What he speke miзte.°   *might*
"Crist," quaþ° he, "þe wisse,°   *said/guide*
And зiue þe heuene° blisse   *heaven's*
Of° þine husebonde,°   *in/husband*
420 Wher° he beo° in londe.°   *whoever/shall be/land*
Ihc am ibore to° lowe   *born too*
Such wimman° to knowe.   *(a) woman*
Ihc am icome° of þralle°   *come/peasant (stock)*
And fundling bifalle.°   *(a) foundling become*
425 Ne° feolle hit° þe° of cunde°   *not/would it be/ for you/natural*
To spuse° beo° me° bunde.°   *as spouse/to be/to me/bound*
Hit nere° no fair wedding   *would not be*
Bitwexe° a þral and a king."   *between*
Þo gan° Rymenhild mislyke,°   *began to/be displeased*
430 And sore° gan to sike:°   *greatly/sigh*
Armes heo gan buзe:°   *wring*
Adun he feol iswoзe.°   *down she fell swooning*
Horn in herte° was ful wo,°   *heart/very sad*
And tok hire on° his armes two.   *her in*
435 He gan hire for to kesse°   *kiss*
Wel° ofte mid ywisse.°   *very/certainly*
"Lemman,"° he sede, "dere,°   *lover/dear*
Þin° herte nu þu stere.°   *your/now you guide*
Help me to kniзte°   *knighthood*
440 Bi al þine miзte,
To my lord þe King,
Þat he me зiue dubbing:
Þanne° is mi þralhod°   *then/thralldom*
I went° into kniзthod,°   *turned/knighthood*
445 And i schal wexe more,°   *become worthier*
And do,° lemman, þi lore."°   *follow/instruction*
Rymenhild, þat swete° þing,   *sweet*
Wakede of° hire swoзning.°   *from/swoon*
"Horn," quaþ heo,° "vel sone°   *she/right away*
450 Þat schal beon idone:°   *be done*
Þu schalt beo° dubbed kniзt   *be*
Are° come seueniзt.°   *before/a week*

Haue her° þis cuppe	*give here*
And þis ryng þervppe°	*also*
455 To Aylbrus þe stuard,°	*steward*
And se° he holde foreward.°	*see (that)/keep (his) pledge*
Seie ihc° him biseche,°	*say (that) I/beg*
Wiþ loueliche° speche.°	*loving/speech*
Þat he adun falle	
460 Bifore þe King in halle,	
And bidde þe King ariȝte°	*right then*
Dubbe þe to kniȝte.	
Wiþ seluer° and wiþ golde	*silver*
Hit° wurþ° him wel iȝolde.°	*it/will be/repaid*
465 Crist him lene spede°	*grant success*
Þin erende° to bede."°	*business/fulfill*
Horn tok° his leue,°	*took/leave*
For hit was neȝ° eue.	*almost*
Aþelbrus he soȝte°	*sought*
470 And ȝaf° him þat° he broȝte,°	*gave/what/brought*
And tolde him ful ȝare°	*quickly*
Hu° he hadde ifare,°	*how/fared*
And sede° him his nede,°	*told/need*
And bihet° him his mede.°	*promised/reward*
475 Aþelbrus also swiþe°	*quickly*
Wente to halle bliue.°	*immediately*
"Kyng," he sede,° "þu° leste°	*said/you/listen to*
A tale mid þe beste;°	*very good*
Þu schalt bere crune°	*wear (the) crown*
480 Tomoreȝe° in þis tune;°	*tomorrow/town*
Tomoreȝe is þi feste:°	*feast*
Þer bihoueþ° geste.°	*are necessary/festivities*
Hit nere° noȝt forloren°	*were not/not inappropriate*
For to kniȝti° child Horn,	*knight*
485 Þine armes for to welde;°	*wield*
God° kniȝt he schal ȝelde."°	*good/become*
Þe King sede sone,°	*quickly*
"Þat is wel idone.	
Horn me wel iquemeþ;°	*pleases*
490 God kniȝt him bisemeþ.°	*he promises to be*
He schal haue mi dubbing,	
And after, wurþ° mi derling.°	*become/favorite*
And alle his feren twelf°	*companions twelve*
He schal kniȝten° himself:	*knight*
495 Alle he schal hem° kniȝte	*them*
Bifore me þis niȝte."°	*night*
Til þe liȝt° of day sprang	*light*

Ailmar him° þuȝte lang.° — to him/seemed long
Þe day bigan to springe;
500 Horn com biuore° þe Kinge, — came before
Mid° his twelf yfere °— — with/companions
Sume hi° were luþere.° — some they/evil
Horn he dubbede to° kniȝte — as
Wiþ swerd° and spures briȝte;° — sword/spurs bright
505 He sette him on a stede whit:° — steed white
Þer nas° no kniȝt hym ilik.° — was not/like
He smot° him a litel wiȝt° — smote/stroke
And bed° him beon° a god kniȝt. — bade/be
   Aþulf fel a° knes þar° — on (his)/knees there
510 Biuore þe King Aylmar.
"King," he sede, "so kene,° — courageous
Grante me a bene:° — boon
Nu° is kniȝt Sire Horn — now
Þat in Suddenne was iboren:° — born
515 Lord he is of londe° — land
Ouer us þat bi him stonde;° — stand
Þin° armes he haþ and scheld° — your/shield
To fiȝte° wiþ vpon þe feld:° — fight/battlefield
Let him vs alle kniȝte
520 For þat is vre riȝte."° — our right
   Aylmar sede sone ywis:° — said quickly indeed
"Do nu þat° þi wille is." — what
Horn adun liȝte° — down stepped (from his horse)
And makede° hem alle kniȝtes. — made
525 Murie° was þe feste° — merry/feast
Al of faire gestes:° — festivities
Ac° Rymenhild nas noȝt° þer, — but/not
And þat hire° þuȝte° seue ȝer:° — to her/seemed/seven years (i.e., a
   long time)

After Horn heo° sente, — she
530 And he to bure° wente. — bower
Nolde° he noȝt go one:° — would not/alone
Aþulf was his mone.° — companion
Rymenhild on flore stod:° — floor stood
Hornes come° hire þuȝte god:° — coming/good
535 And sede, "Welcome, Sire Horn,
And Aþulf kniȝt þe biforn.° — knight you before (entering)
Kniȝt, nu is þi time
For to sitte bi me;
Do nu þat þu er° of spake:° — you before/spoke
540 To° þi wif° þu me take. — for/wife
Ef° þu art trewe° of dedes,° — if/true/deeds

Do nu ase° þu sedes.°   *as/said*
Nu þu hast wille þine,
Vnbind° me of° my pine."°   *release/from/pain*
545   "Rymenhild," quaþ° he, "beo° stille: *said/be*
Ihc wulle don° al þi wille,   *I will do*
Also hit mot bitide.°   *as it may chance*
Mid spere° i schal furst ride,   *with spear*
And mi kniȝthod° proue,   *knighthood*
550   Ar° ihc þe ginne° to woȝe.°   *before/begin/woo*
We beþ° kniȝtes ȝonge,°   *are/young*
Of o° dai al isprunge;°   *one/made*
And of vre mestere°   *calling*
So is þe manere.°   *custom*
555   Wiþ sume° oþere kniȝte   *some*
Wel for his lemman° fiȝte°   *lover/to fight*
Or° he eni° wif take: *before/any*
Forþi me stondeþ° þe more rape.°   *therefore I need/speed*
Today, so Crist me blesse,°   *(may) bless*
560   Ihc wulle do pruesse,°   *(deeds of) prowess*
For þi luue,° in þe felde   *love*
Mid spere and mid schelde.°   *shield*
If ihc come° to lyue,°   *come (through)/alive*
Ihc schal þe take to wyue."°   *wife*
565   "Kniȝt," quaþ heo, "trewe,
Ihc wene° ihc mai þe leue:°   *think/believe*
Tak nu her° þis gold ring: *take now here*
God him is þe dubbing,°   *good are its qualities*
Þer is vpon þe ringe
570   Igraue° Rymenhild þe ȝonge: *engraved*
Þer nis° non betere anonder° sunne   *is not/none better under*
Þat eni man of telle cunne.°   *can*
For my luue þu hit were,°   *wear*
And on þi finger þu him bere.°   *it bear*
575   Þe stones beoþ° of suche grace°   *are/power*
Þat þu ne° schalt in none° place   *not/no*
Of none duntes beon ofdrad,°   *blows be afraid*
Ne on bataille° beon amad,°   *nor in battle/confounded*
Ef þu loke þeran°   *you look thereon*
580   And þenke vpon þi lemman.
And Sire Aþulf, þi broþer,
He schal haue anoþer.

---

567. The ring is part of the Love Token motif. In some folktales, rings exchanged between lovers start to pinch if the partner is unfaithful. Shirts that become soiled, wine that is dulled, also appear.

	Horn, ihc þe biseche°	*you beg*
	Wiþ loueliche speche,°	*loving speech*
585	Crist ʒeue° god erndinge°	*(that) Christ give/success*
	Þe aʒen° to bringe."	*back*
	Þe kniʒt hire° gan° kesse,°	*knight her/began to/kiss*
	And heo° him to blesse.	*she*
	Leue at° hire he nam,°	*leave of/took*
590	And into halle cam:°	*came*
	Þe kniʒtes ʒeden° to table,	*went*
	And Horne ʒede to stable:	
	Þar° he tok° his gode fole,°	*there/took/good horse*
	Also blak so° eny cole.	*as black as*
595	Þe fole schok° brunie°	*shook/chain mail*
	Þat° al þe curt° gan denie.°	*so that/court/ to ring*
	Þe fole bigan to springe,	
	And Horn murie° to singe.	*merrily*
	Horn rod° in a while	*rode*
600	More þan a myle.	
	He fond o schup° stonde°	*found a ship/at anchor*
	Wiþ heþene honde:°	*heathen hounds*
	He axede° what hi soʒte°	*asked/they sought*
	Oþer° to londe broʒte.°	*or/land brought*
605	An hund° him gan° bihelde,°	*hound/did/look at*
	Þat spac° wordes belde:°	*spoke/bold*
	"Þis londe we wulleʒ° wynne,	*will*
	And sle þat° þer is inne."	*slay (all) that*
	Horn gan his swerd° gripe	*sword*
610	And on his arme wype:	
	Þe Sarazins° he smatte°	*Saracens/smote*
	Þat his blod hatte:°	*blood boiled*
	At eureche° dunte	*every*
	Þe heued of° wente;	*head off*
615	Þo gunne° þe hundes gone°	*then began/to rush*
	Abute° Horn alone:	*around*
	He lokede° on þe ringe,	*looked*
	And þoʒte on° Rimenilde;	*thought of*
	He sloʒ° þer on° haste	*slew/in*
620	On° hundred bi þe laste,°	*a/at least*
	Ne miʒte° no man telle°	*not might/count*

---

594. According to l. 505, Horn was knighted on a white steed, perhaps a special horse used for the ceremony. That his present war-horse is black may be a slip on the author's or minstrel's part. However, the interchange of colors, whether of the knight's armor or horse, on different days was a weak but typical method of variation in the romance, a genre too often filled with monotonous repetition.

602. *heþene honde*: a common epithet for pagans, especially Saracens.

Þat folc þat he gan quelle.°   *kill*
Of alle þat were aliue,
Ne miȝte þer non þriue.
625 Horn tok þe maisteres° heued,   *leader's*
Þat he hadde him° bireued,°   *from him/cut off*
And sette hit° on his swerde,   *it*
Anouen at° þan orde.°   *on top of/the point*
He verde hom° into halle,   *fared home*
630 Among þe kniȝte° alle,   *knights*
"Kyng," he sede,° "wel þu sitte,°   *said/(may) you stay*
And alle þine kniȝtes mitte.°   *with you*
To-day, after mi dubbing,
So i rod on° mi pleing,°   *for/pleasure*
635 I fond o schup rowe°   *floating*
Mid° watere al byflowe,°   *with/surrounded*
Al wiþ Sarazines kyn,
And none londisse° men,   *no native*
To-dai for to pine°   *harm*
640 Þe° and alle þine.   *you*
Hi gonne° me assaille: *did*
My swerd me nolde° faille: *would not*
I smot° hem alle to grunde,°   *smote/ground*
Oþer ȝaf hem diþes wunde.°   *or gave them death's wound*
645 Þat heued i þe bringe
Of þe maister-kinge.
Nu is þi wile iȝolde,°   *will repaid*
King, þat þu me kniȝti woldest."°   *knight would*
    A moreȝe þo° þe day gan° springe,   *one morning when/began to*
650 Þe King him rod° an huntinge.°   *he rode/a-hunting*
At hom lefte Fikenhild,
Þat was þe wurste moder° child.   *mother's*
Horn ferde° into bure°   *fared/bower*
To sen° auenture.°   *look for/adventure*
655 He saȝ° Rymenild sitte   *saw*
Also° he° were of witte.°   *as if/she/mad*
Heo° sat on þe sunne,   *she*
Wiþ tieres° al birunne.°   *tears/covered*
Horn sede, "Lef, þin ore;°   *dear, your favor*
660 Wi° wepestu° so sore?"°   *why/do you weep/greatly*
Heo sede, "Noȝt i ne° weþe°   *I only/weep*
Bute ase° i lay aslepe°   *because as/asleep*

---

624. I.e., "all were killed."
642. Swords often failed the hero at inappropriate times, for various reasons (cf. T. J. Garbáty, "The Fallible Sword: Inception of a Motif," *Journal of American Folklore*, 75 [1961], 58–59).

To þe se° my net i caste,   sea
And hit nolde noȝt° ilaste;°   not/stay whole
665 A gret fiss° at the furste°   great fish/right away
Mi net he gan to berste.
Ihc wene° þat ihc schal leose°   I believe/lose
Þe fiss þat ihc wolde cheose."°   choose
    "Crist," quaþ° Horn "and Seint° Steuene   said/Saint
670 Turne° þine sweuene.°   turn (to good)/dream
Ne° schal i þe biswike,°   not/betray
Ne° do þat° þe mislike.°   nor/what/displeases
I schal me° make þin owe°   myself/own
To holden° and to knowe   hold
675 For euerech oþere wiȝte,°   every/man
And þarto° mi treuþe° i þe pliȝte."°   thereto/troth/plight
Muchel° was þe ruþe°   great/sorrow
Þat was at þare truþe:°   their pledging
For Rymenhild weop ille,°   wept bitterly
680 And Horn let° þe tires stille.°   let (fall)/tears silent
"Lemman,"° quaþ he, "dere,°   lover/dear
Þu° schalt more ihere.°   you/hear
Þi sweuen schal wende,°   turn (to good)
Oþer sum° man schal vs schende.°   or some/harm
685 Þe fiss þat brak° þe lyne   broke
Ywis° he doþ° us pine:°   certainly/will cause/pain
Þat schal don° vs tene,°   cause/grief
And wurþ° wel sone isenc."°   will be/very soon seen
    Aylmar rod° bi Sture,   rode
690 And Horn lai in bure.
Fykenhild hadde enuye
And sede þes° folye:°   said these/false words
"Aylmar, ihc þe° warne,   you
Horn þe wule berne:°   will burn (i.e., kill)
695 Ihc herde whar° he sede,   heard where
And his swerd° forþ leide,°   sword/made ready
To bringe þe of lyue,°   kill you
And take Rymenhild to wyue.°   wife
He liþ° in bure°   lies/bower
700 Vnder couerture,°   sheets
By Rymenhild þi doȝter,°   daughter
And so he doþ wel ofte;
And þider þu° go al riȝt,°   thither (if) you/quickly
Þer þu him finde miȝt;°   might

---

689. *Sture:* the Mersey.

705	Þu do° him vt of londe,°	*cast/out from (the) land*
	Oþer he doþ þe schonde."°	*harm*
	Aylmar aȝen gan° turne	*back did*
	Wel modi° and wel murne.°	*angry/saddened*
	He fond° Horn in arme°	*found/(her) arms*
710	On Rymenhilde barme.°	*Rymenhild's bosom*
	"Awei° vt," he sede, "fule þeof,°	*away/foul thief*
	Ne° wurstu° me° neuremore leof!°	*not/are you/to me/nevermore dear*
	Wend° vt of my bure	*go*
	Wiþ muchel messauenture.°	*ill fortune*
715	Wel sone, bute° þu flitte,°	*unless/flee*
	Wiþ swerde ihc° þe anhitte.°	*I/strike on*
	Wend vt of my londe,	
	Oþer þu schalt haue schonde."°	*shame*
	Horn sedelede° his stede,°	*saddled/steed*
720	And his armes he gan sprede.°	*lay out (? over the horse)*
	His brunie° he gan lace	*chain mail*
	So° he scholde° into place.°	*as if/were going/battle*
	His swerd he gan fonge:°	*grasp*
	Nabod° he noȝt to° longe,	*not tarried/not too*
725	He ȝede° forþ bliue°	*went/immediately*
	To Rymenhild his wyue.	
	He sede, "Lemman derling,°	*darling*
	Nu° hauestu° þi sweuening.°	*now/you have/dream*
	Þe fiss° þat þi net rente,	*fish*
730	Fram° þe he me sente.	*from*
	Rymenhild, haue wel godne° day:	*very good*
	No leng abiden° i ne may.	*longer abide*
	In to vncuþe° londe,	*foreign*
	Wel more° for to fonde,°	*many more (adventures)/seek*
735	I schal wune° þere	*remain*
	Fulle seue ȝere.°	*fully seven years*
	At seue ȝeres ende,	
	Ȝef° i ne come ne sende,°	*if/nor send (a message)*
	Tak þe° husebonde:	*take yourself*
740	For me þu° ne wonde.°	*you/wait further*
	In armes þu me fonge,°	*take*
	And kes° me wel longe."	*kiss*
	He custe° him° wel a stunde,°	*they kissed/each other/a while*
	And Rymenhild feol° to grunde.°	*fell/ground*
745	Horn tok° his leue:°	*took/leave*
	Ne miȝte° he no leng bileue;°	*might/tarry*

---

733. *Uncouth* meant "unknown" or "foreign" (*cunnan*, "be able," "know"). It has been transferred to qualities or behavior which are foreign to our own ideas of dress and manners.

He tok Aþulf, his fere,°   *companion*
Al abute° þe swere,°   *about/neck*
And sede,° "Kniȝt° so trewe,°   *said/knight/true*
750 Kep° wel mi luue newe.°   *keep/love fresh*
Þu neure° me ne forsoke:°   *never/not forsake*
Rymenhild þu kep° and loke."°   *guard/look after*
His stede he gan bistride,
And forþ he gan° ride: *did*
755 To þe hauene° he ferde,°   *harbor/fared*
And a god schup° he hurede,°   *good ship/hired*
Þat him scholde londe°   *should land*
In westene° londe.   *western*
Aþulf weop° wiþ iȝe,°   *wept/eye*
760 And al þat him isiȝe.°   *saw*
Þe whyȝt him° gan stonde,°   *wind it/arise*
And drof tyl Hirelonde.°   *drove to Ireland*
To° lond he him° sette,   *on/himself*
And fot on° stirop sctte.   *foot in*
765 He fond° bi þe weie°   *found/way*
Kynges sones tweie;°   *sons two*
Þat on him° het° Harild,   *one he/was called*
And þat oþer Berild.
Berild gan him prcie°   *ask*
770 Þat he scholde him seie°   *tell*
What his name were
And what he wolde° þere.   *wanted*
"Cutberd," he sede, "ihc° hote,°   *I/am called*
Icomen vt° of þe bote,°   *out/boat*
775 Wel feor fram° biweste°   *very far from/the west*
To scche° mine beste."°   *seek/fortune*
Berild gan him° nier° ride   *to him/closer*
And tok him bi þe bridel:
"Wel beo þu,° kniȝt, ifounde;°   *are you/(i.e., met)*
780 Wiþ me þu lef° a stunde.   *stay*
Also mote° i sterue,°   *as may/die*
Þe King þu schalt serue.
Ne saȝ° i neure my lyue°   *saw/(in) my life*

---

758. *In western londe:* i.e., Ireland.

773. The resemblance of several incidents in Horn's story to the legend of Saint Cuthbert is striking. For example, Saint Cuthbert also was set adrift in a boat and landed in Galloway. Horn's use of the name here may further corroborate the theory of the minstrels' borrowing from saints' legends (cf. Irene P. McKeehan, "The Book of the Nativity of St. Cuthbert, *PMLA*, 48 [1933], 981–99; and above, p. 24).

775. Since Horn came from the east, *biweste* may refer to the kingdom of Westerness, or to Horn's original home, Suddene in Western Scotland (cf. l. 142*n*, 161*n*). But the author, minstrel, or scribe seems to have a predilection for blundering around the compass in odd directions (cf. ll. 953, 1337).

781. I.e., "on my life."

So fair kniȝt aryue."
785 Cutberd heo ladde° into halle,   *they led*
And he a kne° gan falle: *they on knee*
He sette him° a knewelyng°   *remained|kneeling*
And grette° wel þe gode° Kyng.   *greeted|good*
Þanne sede° Berild sone:°   *then said|quickly*
790 "Sire King, of him þu hast to done.°   *i.e., you must engage his service*
Bitak° him þi lond to werie.°   *take|guard*
Ne° schal hit° no man derie,°   *not|it|harm*
For he is þe faireste man
Þat eure ȝut° on þi londe cam."°   *ever yet|came*
795 Þanne sede þe King so dere:°   *dear*
"Welcome beo þu here.
Go nu,° Berild, swiþe,°   *now|quickly*
And make him ful bliþe,°   *very happy*
And whan° þu farst° to woȝe,°   *when|start|woo*
800 Tak° him þine gloue: *give (as a pledge)*
Iment° þu hauest to wyue,°   *(for when) intention|marry*
Awai he schal þe dryue.
For° Cutberdes fairhede°   *because of|fairness*
Ne schal þe neure° wel spede."°   *never|prosper*
805   Hit was at Cristesmasse,
Neiþer more ne lasse.°   *nor less*
Þer cam in at none°   *noon*
A geaunt suþe sone,°   *giant very suddenly*
Iarmed° fram paynyme,°   *armed|heathendom*
810 And seide þes ryme:°   *said this speech*
"Site° stille, Sire Kyng,   *sit*
And herkne° þis tyþyng:°   *hearken (to)|news*
Her buþ paens° ariued: *here are pagans*
Wel mo þane° fiue   *many more than*
815 Her beoþ° on þe sonde,°   *(they) are|beach*
King, vpon þi londe;°   *land*
On° of hem wile° fiȝte°   *one|them will|fight*
Aȝen þre kniȝtes:°   *against three knights*
Ȝef oþer° þre slen vre,°   *if (the) other|slay our (man)*
820 Al þis lond beo° ȝoure:°   *shall be|yours*
Ȝef vre on ouercomeþ ȝour þreo,°   *three*

799–804. An obscure passage. Perhaps Berild is being advised to give Horn his glove to insure that he will not interfere in Berild's wooing; Horn's handsomeness would otherwise prove too much competition.

805. Adventures often occurred at Christmas; see the similar episode in *Sir Gawain and the Green Knight*. Occasionally kings refused to start the meal until such a happening. In romances, at least, the pangs of hunger never lasted long.

814. I.e., "very many."

817–22. Wearisome and indecisive battles were often decided finally by single combat between champions.

Al þis lond schal vre beo.°   *ours be*
Tomoreӡe° be þe fiӡtinge,   *tomorrow*
Whane þe liӡt° of daye springe."   *light*
825   Þanne sede þe Kyng Þurston,
"Cutberd schal beo þat on,
Berild schal beo þat oþer,
Þe þridde° Alrid his broþer,   *third*
For hi beoþ° þe strengeste°   *they are/strongest*
830 And of armes þe beste.
Bute° what schal vs to rede?°   *but/help us*
Ihc wene° we beþ° alle dede."°   *I think/are/dead*
    Cutberd sat at borde°   *table*
And sede þes° wordes,   *said these*
835 "Sire King, hit° nis° no riӡte°   *it/is not/not right*
On wiþ þre to fiӡte:
Aӡen one hunde,°   *hound*
Þre Cristen° men to fonde.°   *Christian/take their chance*
Sire, i schal alone,
840 Wiþute° more ymone,°   *without/companions*
Wiþ mi swerd wel eþe°   *sword very easily*
Bringe hem þre° to deþe."°   *three of them/death*
    Þe Kyng aros amoreӡe,°   *in the morning*
Þat hadde muchcl sorӡe,°   *great sorrow*
845 And Cutberd ros of° bedde,   *rose from*
Wiþ armes he him schredde:°   *himself dressed*
Horn his brunie° gan° on caste,   *chain mail/did*
And lacede hit wel faste,
And cam° to þe Kinge   *came*
850 At his vprisinge.°   *rising*
"King," he sede, "cum° to felde,°   *come/(the) battlefield*
For to bihelde°   *behold*
Hu° we fiӡte schulle,°   *how/shall*
And togare° go wulle."°   *together/will*
855 Riӡt at prime tide°   *time*
Hi gunnen vt° ride,   *did out*
And funden° on a grene   *found*
A geaunt suþe kenc,°   *giant very fierce*
His feren° him biside   *companions*
860 Hore° deþ to abide.   *their*
    Þe ilke bataille°   *same force*
Cutberd gan assaille:
He ӡaf dentes inoӡe;°   *gave blows many*

---

855. Prime was the period 6–9 A.M., here probably 6 o'clock.

Þe kni3tes° felle iswo3e.°   *knights/swooning*
865 His dent he gan° wiþdra3e,°   *began to/withhold*
For hi were ne3 asla3e:°   *nearly slain*
And sede, "Kni3tes, nu 3e° reste   *now you*
One° while ef° 3ou leste."°   *a/if/wish*
Hi° sede hi neure° nadde°   *they/never/had not*
870 Of kni3te dentes so harde,
Bote° of þe King Murry,   *except*
Þat wes swiþe° sturdy.   *was very*
He was of Hornes kunne,°   *kindred*
Iborn° in Suddenne.   *born*
875   Horn him° gan to agrise,°   *he/shudder*
And his blod° arise.°   *blood/to rise*
Biuor him sa3° he stonde°   *saw/standing*
Þat° driuen° him of londe,°   *he that/had driven/land*
And þat his fader slo3;°   *father slew*
880 To him his swerd° he dro3.°   *sword/drew*
He lokede° on his rynge,   *looked*
And þo3te on° Rymenhilde.   *thought of*
Ho smot° him þure3° þe herte,°   *he smote/through/heart*
Þat° sore° him gan to smerte.°   *so that/greatly/hurt*
885 Þe paens,° þat er° were so sturne,°   *pagans/before/fierce*
Hi gunne awei vrne;°   *away run*
Horn and his compaynye
Gunne after hem° wel swiþe hi3e,°   *them/very quickly hasten*
And slo3en° alle þe hundes°   *slew/hounds*
890 Er hi here° schipes funde: *their*
To deþe° he hem alle bro3te;°   *death/brought*
His fader° deþ wel dere° hi bo3te.°   *father's/dearly/paid for*
Of alle þe Kynges kni3tes,
Ne scaþede° wer no wi3te,°   *not hurt/man*
895 Bute° his sones tweie°   *but/sons two*
Bifore him he sa3 deie.°   *die*
Þe King bigan to grete°   *weep*
And teres° for to lete.°   *tears/spill*
Me leiden° hem in bare°   *men laid/on bier*
900 And burden° hem ful 3are.°   *buried/very quickly*
    Þe King com° into halle   *came*
Among his kni3tes alle.
"Horn," he sede,° "i seie þe,°   *said/tell you*
Do as i schal rede° þe.   *advise*
905 Asla3en beþ° mine heirs,   *slain are*
And þu° are kni3t° of muchel pris,°   *you/knight/great worth*
And of grete° strengþe,   *great*
And fair o° bodie lengþe;   *of*

Mi rengne° þu schalt welde,°   realm/rule
910 And to spuse helde°   as spouse hold
    Reynild, mi doʒter,°   daughter
    Þat sitteþ on° þe lofte."°   in/upper room
        "O Sire King, wiþ wronge
    Scholte ihc hit vnderfonge,°   should I it accept
915 Þi doʒter, þat ʒe° me bede,°   you/offer
    Ower° rengne for to lcdc.°   your/rule
    Wel° more ihc schal þe serue,   much
    Sire Kyng, or° þu sterue.°   before/die
    Þi sorwe° schal wende°   sorrow/turn (to good)
920 Or seue ʒeres° ende: seven years'
    Wanne° hit is wente,°   when/gone
    Sire King, ʒef° me mi rente:°   give/reward
    Whanne° i þe doʒter ʒerne,°   when/desire
    Ne schaltu° me hire werne.°   shall you/her refuse
925 Cutberd wonede° þere   remained
    Fulle° seue ʒere   fully
    Þat to Rymenild he ne sente,
    Ne° him self ne wente.   nor
    Rymenild was in Westernesse
930 Wiþ wel° muchel sorinesse.°   very/grief
        A king þer gan° ariue   did
    Þat wolde° hire haue° to wyue;°   wanted/to have/wife
    Aton° he was wiþ þe King   agreed
    Of° þat ilke° wedding.   on/same
935 Þe daies were schortc,
    Þat° Rimenhild ne dorste°   so that/not dared
    Leten° in none° wise.   hesitate/no
    A writ he dude deuise;°   letter she did compose
    Aþulf hit dude write,
940 Þat Horn ne luuede° noʒt lite.°   loved/not (a) little
    Heo sende° hire sonde°   she sent/messenger
    To euereche londe,°   every land
    To seche° Horn þe kniʒt   seek
    Þer me° him finde miʒte.°   where men/might
945 Horn noʒt° þer of ne herde°   nothing/heard
    Til o° dai þat he ferde°   one/fared
    To wude° for to schete.°   (the) forest/shoot (i.e., hunt)
    A knaue° he gan imete.°   boy/meet
    Horn seden,° "Leue fere,°   said/dear comrade
950 Wat° sechestu° here?"   what/seek you

---

912. Women remained in solars or upper rooms.

"Kniȝt, if beo° þi wille,   (it) be
I mai þe sone° telle.   you quickly
I seche fram° biweste°   from/the west
Horn of Westernesse,
955 For a maiden Rymenhild,
Þat for him gan wexe wild.°   become passionate
A king hire wile° wedde   will
And bringe to his bedde:
King Modi of Reynes,
960 On° of Hornes enemis.   one
Ihc habbe walke wide,°   I have walked far
Bi þe se° side;   sea
Nis° he nowar ifunde.°   is not/nowhere found
Walawai° þe stunde!°   alas/the hour
965 Wailaway þe while!°   time
Nu° wurþ° Rymenild bigiled."°   now/will be/lost
Horn iherde° wiþ his ires,°   heard/ears
And spak° wiþ bidere tires:°   spoke/bitter tears
"Knaue, wel° þe bitide;°   (may) good/befall
970 Horn stondeþ° þe biside.   stands
Aȝen° to hure þu° turne,   back/her you
And seie° þat heo ne murne,°   say/mourn
For i schal beo° þer bitime,°   be/in time
A Soneday° bi pryme."   on Sunday
975 Þe knaue was wel bliþe°   very happy
And hiȝede° aȝen bliue.°   hastened/quickly
Þe knaue þere gan adrinke:°   did drown
Rymenhild hit° miȝte of þinke.°   it/regret
Þe see° him con ded° þrowe   sea/did dead
980 Vnder hire° chambre wowe.°   her/wall
Rymenhild undude° þe dure-pin°   unfastened/door bolt
Of þe hus þer heo° was in,   house where she
To loke° wiþ hire iȝe,°   look/eye
If heo oȝt° of Horn isiȝe:°   anything/saw
985 Þo fond° heo þe knaue adrent,°   then found/drowned
Þat he° hadde for Horn isent,°   she/sent
And þat scholde° Horn bringe.   should
Hire fingres he gan wringe.
    Horn cam° to Þurston þe Kyng,   came
990 And tolde him þis tiþing.°   story

---

953. Cf. l. 775n.

959. *Reynes*: perhaps Furness, in northern Lancashire.

981. In ballads often occurs the expression "He tirled at the pin," i.e., he attempted to shake loose the inner bolt from the outside.

Þo he was iknowe°   *informed*
Þat Rimenhild was his o3e,°   *own*
Of his gode kenne°   *good kin*
Þe King of Suddenne,
995 And hu° he slo3 in felde°   *how/slew/combat*
Þat° his fader quelde,°   *(him) that/father killed*
And seide,° "King þe wise,   *said*
3eld° me mi seruise:°   *reward/service*
Rymenhild help me winne.
1000 Þat° þu no3t° ne linne:°   *may/not/not hinder (me)*
And i schal do° to spuse°   *cause/to be married*
Þi do3ter° wel to huse:°   *daughter/in a worthy household*
Heo schal to spuse° haue   *as spouse*
Aþulf, mi gode fela3e,°   *friend*
1005 God° kni3t mid° þe beste   *good/among*
And þe treweste."°   *truest*
Þe King sede° so stille,°   *said/quietly*
"Horn haue nu° þi wille."   *now*
He dude writes sende°   *did letters send*
1010 Into Yrlonde°   *Ireland*
After kni3tes li3te,°   *knights agile*
Irisse° men to fi3te.°   *Irish/fight*
To Horn come ino3e°   *came many*
Þat to schupe dro3e.°   *on ship embarked*
1015 Horn dude him in þe weie°   *set out*
On° a god galeie.°   *in/galley*
Þe wind him gan° to blowe   *it began*
In a litel þro3e.°   *while*
Þe se° bigan to posse°   *sea/push*
1020 Ri3t° into Westernesse.   *right*
Hi strike seil° and maste   *they struck sail*
And ankere gunne° caste,   *anchor did*
Or eny° day was sprunge   *before any*
Oþer° belle irunge.°   *or/rung*
1025 Þe word bigan to springe°   *go around*
Of Rymenhilde° weddinge   *Rymenhild's*
Horn was in þe watere,
Ne mi3te° he come no latere.   *might*
He let his schup stonde,°   *ride at anchor*
1030 And 3ede° to londe.°   *went/land*
His folk he dude abide°   *made wait*

---

995. *felde*: Cf. above, p. 73, l. 608*n*.
1024. The canonical hours were rung by bells.

1028. I.e., he came just in time.

Vnder wude side.°   *at forest's edge*
Horn him° ʒede alone   *he*
Also° he sprunge of° stone.   *as if|from*
1035 A palmere he þar° mette,   *there*
And faire hine grette:°   *him greeted*
"Palmere, þu° schalt me telle   *you*
Al of þine spelle."°   *story*
He sede vpon° his tale: *in*
1040 "I come fram o° brudale;°   *from a|bridal feast*
Ihc° was at o wedding   *I*
Of a maide Rymenhild:
Ne° miʒte heo adriʒe°   *not|she refrain*
Þat heo ne weop° wiþ iʒe;°   *wept|eye*
1045 Heo sede þat heo nolde°   *would not*
Ben ispused° wiþ golde.°   *be married|gold (ring)*
Heo hadde on husebonde,°   *a husband*
Þeʒ° he were vt° of londe: *though|out*
And in strong halle,
1050 Biþinne° castel walle,   *within*
Þer° i was atte° ʒate,°   *where|at the|gate*
Nolde hi me in late.°   *let*
Modi ihote° hadde   *commanded*
To bure° þat me hire ladde:°   *bower|men her lead*
1055 Awai i gan° glide: *did*
Þat deol° i nolde abide.°   *sorrow|endure*
Þe bride wepeþ sore,°   *weeps greatly*
And þat is muche deole."°   *grief*
Quaþ° Horn, "So Crist me rede,°   *said|as Christ is my guide*
1060 We schulle chaungi wede:°   *shall exchange clothes*
Haue her° cloþes myne,   *here*
And tak° me þi sclauyne.°   *give|pilgrim's mantle*
Today i schal þer drinke
Þat° some hit° schulle of þinke."°   *so that|it|regret*
1065 His sclauyn he dude dun legge,°   *did down lay*
And tok° hit on his rigge,°   *put|back*
He tok° Horn his° cloþes: *took|Horn's*
Þat nere° him° noʒt loþe.°   *were not|to him|not displeasing*
Horn tok burdon° and scrippe°   *staff|bag*
1070 And wrong° his lippe.   *twisted*

1034. A reference to an ancient belief that the first men originated from stones, singly, and hence were solitary.

1037. Palmers were welcome guests at feasts and celebrations: their wide travels and exploits, real or imagined, entertained the residents and broke the winter monotony. A palmer's disguise was a common one (cf. Walter Scott's *Ivanhoe*, also above, p. 109, ll. 558–63n).

1052. To refuse visitors, beggars or otherwise, at a wedding showed the ungraciousness of the host.

He makede him° a ful chere,°   *made himself/ugly face*
And al bicolmede° his swere.°   *dirtied/neck*
He makede him vnbicomelich,°   *ugly*
Hes° he nas° neuremore° ilich.°   *as/was not/never before/like*
1075   He com° to þe gateward,°   *came/porter*
Þat him answerede hard:
Horn bad vndo softe°   *bade (him) open gently*
Mani tyme° and ofte,   *times*
Ne miȝte° he awynne°   *might/succeed*
1080   Þat he come þerinne.
Horn gan to þe ȝate turne
And þat wiket° vnspurne,°   *small gate/kick open*
Þe boye° hit scholde° abugge:°   *rogue/should/pay for*
Horn þreu° him ouer þe brigge°   *threw/drawbridge (into the water)*
1085   Þat his ribbes him° tobrake,°   *for him/broke to pieces*
And suþþe° com in atte gate.   *quickly*
He sette him wel loȝe,°   *quite low*
In beggeres rowe;
He lokede° him abute°   *looked/around*
1090   Wiþ his colmie snute,°   *dirty nose*
He seȝ° Rymenhild sitte   *saw*
Ase° heo° were of witte,°   *as if/she/mad*
Sore wepinge and ȝerne:°   *passionately*
Ne° miȝte hure° no man wurne.°   *not/her/stop*
1095   He lokede in eche halke:°   *each corner*
Ne seȝ he nowhar° walke   *nowhere*
Aþulf his felawe,°   *friend*
Þat he cuþe knowe.°   *as far as he knew*
Aþulf was in þe ture,°   *tower*
1100   Abute for to pure°   *look*
After his comynge,
Ȝef schup° him wolde° bringe.   *if ship/would*
He seȝ þe se° flowe   *sea*
And Horn nowar° rowe.   *nowhere*
1105   He sede vpon° his songe,   *said in*
"Horn, nu þu ert° wel longe.°   *now you are/staying too long*
Rymenhild þu me° toke°   *to me/entrusted*
Þat i scholde loke;°   *look after*
Ihc habbe ikept° hure eure;°   *I have guarded/ever*
1110   Com nu oþer neure:°   *never*

1082. Horn kicked in the wicket, the small door in the main gate that was opened when it was not necessary to let in horsemen.

1087–88. I.e., below the salt along the main table (cf. above, p. 72, ll. 592–93*n*).

I ne may no leng° hure kepe.   *longer*
For soreʒe° nu y wepe."°   *sorrow/I weep*
   Rymenhild ros of° benche,   *rose from*
Wyn° for to schenche:°   *wine/pour*
1115 After mete° in sale,°   *meal/hall*
Boþe wyn and ale.
On° horn he bar° anhonde,°   *a/she bore/in hand*
So laʒe° was in londe.°   *as custom/land*
Kniʒtes° and squier°   *knights/squires*
1120 Alle dronken° of þe ber,°   *drank/beer*
Bute° Horn alone   *but*
Nadde° þerof no mone.°   *he had not/share*
Horn sat vpon þe grunde;°   *ground*
Him° þuʒte° he was ibunde.°   *to him/(it) seemed/overcome (with*
                                                   emotion)

1125 He sede, "Quen° so hende,°   *queen/gracious*
To meward° þu wende;°   *toward me/turn*
Þu ʒef° vs wiþ þe furste: *serve*
Þe beggeres beoþ° of þurste."°   *are/thirsty*
   Hure horn heo leide adun,°   *she laid down*
1130 And fulde° him of a brun,°   *filled/brown (i.e., wooden bowl)*
His bolle of° a galun,°   *bowl with/gallon*
For heo wende° he were a glotoun.°   *thought/glutton*
He seide,° "Haue þis cuppe,   *said*
And þis þing° þervppe:°   *(i.e., bowl)/also*
1135 Ne saʒ° ihc neure, so ihc wene,°   *not saw/believe*
Beggere þat were so kene."°   *bold*
Horn tok hit° his ifere,°   *gave it/(to) his companion*
And sede, "Quen so dere,°   *dear*
Wyn nelle° ihc muche ne lite°   *wish not/nor little*
1140 Bute of cuppe white.
Þu wenest° i beo° a beggere,   *think/am*
And ihc am a fissere,°   *fisher*
Wel feor icome° bi este°   *very far come/eastward*
For fissen° at þi feste:°   *to fish/feast*
1145 Mi net liþ her bi honde,°   *lies here at hand*
Bi a wel fair stronde.°   *shore*
Hit haþ ileie° þere   *lain*
Fulle seue ʒere.°   *fully seven years*
Ihc° am icome to loke°   *I/see*

1113–16. Women often served the wine; cf. Wealtheow, Hrothgar's wife, who made the rounds with the mead cup in *Beowulf*.

1129–30. She put aside the white horn cup, reserved for guests of higher rank, and served him from the brown wooden bowl meant for the lower-ranking guests.

1142–55. Horn is referring to Rymenhild's dream (cf. ll. 662–68).

1150	Ef eni fiss° hit toke.°	*if any fish/took*
	Ihc am icome to fisse:	
	Drynke null° y of dyssh:°	*will not/I from bowl*
	Drink to Horn of horne:	
	Feor ihc am iorne."°	*traveled*
1155	Rymenhild him gan bihelde;°	*did behold*
	Hire heorte° bigan to chelde.°	*her heart/chill*
	Ne kneu° heo noȝt° his fissing,	*knew/not*
	Ne° Horn hymselue noþing:°	*nor (recognized)/himself not*
	Ac wunder° hire° gan þinke,°	*but strange/to her/(it) did seem*
1160	Whi he bad° to Horn drinke.	*bade*
	Heo fulde hire horn wiþ wyn,°	*wine*
	And dronk° to þe pilegrym.	*drank*
	Heo sede,° "Drink þi fulle,°	*said/fill*
	And suþþe þu° me telle	*quickly you*
1165	If þu eure isiȝe°	*ever saw*
	Horn vnder wude liȝe."°	*forest lie*
	Horn dronk of horn a stunde°	*while*
	And þreu° þe ring to grunde.°	*threw/(the) bottom*
	He seyde,° "Quen, nou seche°	*said/queen, now seek*
1170	Qwat hys° in þy drenche."°	*what is/drink*
	Þc Quen ȝede° to bure°	*went/bower*
	Wiþ hire maidenes foure.	
	Þo fond heo° what heo wolde,°	*then found she/wanted*
	A ring igrauen° of golde	*engraved*
1175	Þat Horn of hure hadde;	
	Sore hure dradde°	*greatly she feared*
	Þat Horn isterue° were,	*dead*
	For þe ring was þere.	
	Þo sente heo a damesele	
1180	After þe palmere;	
	"Palmere," quaþ° heo, "trewe,°	*said/true*
	Þe ring þat þu þrewe,	
	Þu seie whar° þu hit nome,°	*tell where/it got*
	And whi þu hider come."°	*hither came*
1185	He sede, "Bi Seint Gile,°	*Saint Gilles*
	Ihc habbe go° mani mile,°	*have gone/miles*
	Wel feor° bi ȝonde° weste	*very far/beyond*
	To seche my beste.°	*fortune*
	I fond Horn child stonde°	*about to go*
1190	To schupeward° in londe.°	*in a ship/somewhere*
	He sede he wolde agesse°	*would try*

1185. Saint Gilles was an 8th-century Athenian hermit whose shrine is near Nîmes.

To ariue in Westernesse.
Þe schip nam to þe flode°   *went out to sea*
Wiþ me and Horn þe gode;°   *good*
1195 Horn was sik° and deide,°   *sick/died*
And faire° he me preide:°   *kindly/asked*
'Go wiþ þe ringe
To Rymenhild þe ȝonge.'°   *young*
Ofte he hit custe,°   *kissed*
1200 God ȝeue° his saule° reste!"   *give/soul*
    Rymenhild sede at þe furste:°   *immediately*
"Herte, nu° þu berste,   *heart, now*
For Horn nastu° namore,°   *you have not/no more*
Þat þe° haþ pined° so sore."   *you/grieved*
1205 Heo feol on hire° bedde,   *her*
Þer° heo knif° hudde,°   *where/knife/had hidden*
To slc° wiþ King loþe°   *slay/hateful*
And hureselue° boþe   *herself*
In þat vlke niȝte,°   *same night*
1210 If Horn come ne miȝte.°   *not might*
To herte knif heo sette,
Ac° Horn anon° hire kepte.°   *but/quickly/caught*
He wipede þat blake of° his swere,°   *black off/neck*
And sede:° "Quen° so swete° and dere,°   *said/Queen/sweet/dear*
1215 Ihc° am Horn þin oȝe;°   *I/your own*
Ne canstu° me noȝt° knowe?   *can you/not*
Ihc am Horn of Westernesse;
In armes þu° me cusse."°   *you/kiss*
Hi custe° hem° mid ywisse,°   *they kissed/each other/certainly*
1220 And makeden° muche blisse.   *made*
    "Rymenhild," he sede, "y° wende°   *I/shall go*
Adun° to þe wudes ° ende: *down/forest's*
Þer beþ° myne kniȝtes°   *are/knights*
Redi° to fiȝte,°   *ready/fight*
1225 Iarmed° vnder cloþe;°   *armed/clothes*
Hi schulle° make wroþe   *shall/sorry*
Þe King and his geste°   *guests*
Þat come to þe feste:°   *feast*
Today i schal hem teche°   *them teach*
1230 And sore° hem areche."°   *greatly/strike*
    Horn sprong vt° of halle   *sprang out*
And let his sclauin° falle.   *robe*
Þe Quen ȝede° to bure°   *went/bower*
And fond° Aþulf in ture:°   *found/tower*
1235 "Aþulf," heo° sede, "be bliþe,°   *she/happy*
And to Horn þu go wel swiþe:°   *very quickly*

He is vnder wude boȝe,°   bough
And wiþ him kniȝtes inoȝe."°   many
   Aþulf bigan to springe°   jump
1240 For þe tiþinge:°   news
After Horn he arnde° anon,   ran (i.e., rode)
Also° þat hors miȝte gon.   as
He him ouertok ywis;°   overtook indeed
Hi makede suiþe muchel° blis.   very great
1245 Horn tok° his preie°   took/band
And dude him in þe weie.°   set out
He com° in wel sone:°   came/quickly
Þe ȝates° were vndone.°   gates/opened
Iarmed ful þikke°   very heavily
1250 Fram fote° to þe nekke,°   from foot/neck
Alle þat were þerin
Biþute° his twelf ferin°   except/twelve comrades
And þe King Aylmare,
He dude° hem alle to kare,°   caused/be sorry
1255 Þat at the feste were;
Here lif hi lete° þere.   their lives they lost
Horn ne dude° no wunder°   not exacted/fierce vengeance
Of° Fikenhildes false tunge.   for
Hi sworen° oþes holde,°   swore/oaths of loyalty
1260 Þat neure° ne scholde°   never/should (they)
Horn neure bitraie,
Þeȝ° he at diþe° laie.   though/death
Hi runge° þe belle   rang
Þe wedlak° for to felle;°   wedding/celebrate
1265 Horn him ȝede° with his°   he went/his (men)
To þe Kinges palais,
Þer was bridale suete,°   sweet
For riche° men þer ete.°   noble/feasting
Telle ne miȝte° tunge   might
1270 Þat gle° þat þer was sunge.   glee
   Horn sat on chaere,°   chair
And bad° hem alle ihere.°   bade/hear
"King," he sede,° "þu° luste°   said/you/listen to
A tale mid þe beste.°   very good
1275 I ne seie hit° for no blame: say it
Horn is mi name;
Þu me to kniȝt houe,°   knight raised
And kniȝthod haue proued:°   knighthood (I) have proved

1250. I.e., "from head to toe," the English translation of OF
cap à pie (Mod. Fr. *de pied en cap*, cf. Mod. Eng. *cap-a-pie*).

To þe,° King, men seide°   *you/said*
1280 Þat i þe bitraide;
Þu makedest° me fleme,°   *made/flee*
And þi lond° to reme;°   *land/leave*
Þu wendest° þat i wroȝte°   *believed/did*
Þat y° neure ne þoȝte,°   *what I/thought*
1285 Bi Rymenhild for to ligge;°   *lie*
And þat i wiþsegge.°   *deny*
Ne schal ihc° hit biginne,   *I*
Til i Suddene winne.
Þu kep hure° a stunde,°   *guard her/while*
1290 Þe while þat° i funde°   *while/attempt to come*
Into min° heritage,   *my*
And to mi baronage.
Þat lond i schal ofreche,°   *obtain*
And do° mi fader wreche.°   *shall/father avenge*
1295 I schal beo° king of tune,°   *be/(the) country*
And bere° kinges crune;°   *wear/crown*
Þanne° schal Rymenhilde   *then*
Ligge bi þe kinge."
    Horn gan° to schupe draȝe°   *did/ship start*
1300 Wiþ his Yrisse felaȝes,°   *Irish friends*
Aþulf wiþ him, his brother:
Nolde° he non° oþer.   *wanted not/no*
Þat schup bigan to crude,°   *make way*
Þe wind him bleu lude;°   *it blew loud*
1305 Biþinne° daies fiue   *within*
Þat schup gan ariue,
Abute middelniȝte.°   *about midnight*
Horn him ȝede wel riȝte;°   *he went right away*
He tok° Aþulf bi honde,°   *took/(the) hand*
1310 And vp he ȝede to londe.
Hi° founde vnder schelde°   *they/shield*
A kniȝt hende° in felde.°   *noble/combat*
O° þe shelde wes ydrawe°   *on/was drawn*
A croyȝ° of Ihesu Cristes lawe.°   *cross/religion*
1315 Þe kniȝt him aslepe° lay   *asleep*
Al biside þe way.
Horn him gan° to take°   *began/shake*
And sede,° "Kniȝt,° awake.   *said/knight*
Seie° what þu kepest?   *tell*
1320 And whi þu here° slepest?   *here*

1314. A cross on the shield normally signified the Crusader, soldier of Christ; here it probably only refers to the man's religion.

Me þinkþ° bi þine crois liȝte,°　　　　　　(it) seems to me/cross bright
Þat þu longest° to vre Driȝte.°　　　　　　belong/our Lord
Bute° þu wule° me schewe,°　　　　　　　unless/will/tell
I schal þe° tohewe,'"°　　　　　　　　　you/cut to pieces
1325　Þe gode° kniȝt vp aros;°　　　　　　good/arose
Of þe wordes him gros:°　　　　　　　he was very frightened
He sede, "Ihc° serve aȝenes° my wille　　　I/against
Payns ful ylle.°　　　　　　　　　　pagans very evil
Ihc was Cristene° a while:°　　　　　Christian/once
1330　Þo icom° to þis ille°　　　　　　then came/island
Sarazins blake,°　　　　　　　　　Saracens black
Þat dude° me forsake:°　　　　　　made/forsake (my faith)
On Crist ihc wolde bileue.°　　　　　would believe
On° him° hi makede° me reue,°　　　against/(i.e., Horn)/made/
　　　　　　　　　　　　　　　　watchman

1335　To kepe þis passage°　　　　　guard these straits
Fram° Horn þat is of age,　　　　from
Þat wunieþ° bieste,°　　　　　　lives/in the east
Kniȝt wiþ° þe beste;　　　　　　among
Hi sloȝe° wiþ here° honde　　　　slew/their
1340　Þe king of þis londe,°　　　　land
And wiþ him fele° hundred,　　　many
And þerof is wunder
Þat he ne° comeþ to fiȝte:°　　　not/fight
God sende° him þe riȝte,°　　　grant/right
1345　And wind him hider° driue,　　hither
To bringe hem of liue:°　　　　kill them
Hi sloȝen° Kyng Murry,　　　slew
Hornes fader,° king hendy.°　　father/gracious
Horn hi vt° of londe sente;　　out
1350　Tuelf felaȝes° wiþ him wente,　twelve friends
Among hem° Aþulf þe gode,　　then
Min oȝene° child, my leue fode:°　my own/dear son
Ef° Horn child is hol° and sund,°　if/hale/sound
And Aþulf biþute° wund—　　　without
1355　He° luueþ° him so dere,°　　(i.e., Horn)/loves/dearly
And is him so stere°—　　　to him such (a) guardian
Miȝte° i seon° hem tueie,°　　might/see/the two of them
For ioie° i scholde deie."°　　joy/should die
　　"Kniȝt, beo þanne bliþe,°　knight, be then happy
1360　Mest of alle siþe;°　　more than ever

1322. I.e., "that you are a Christian."
1337. Cf. l. 775n.
1353. Here *child* may mean merely "young," since in this instance the man does not know that Horn has been knighted (cf. ll. 27–28n).

Horn and Aþulf his fere°   companion
Boþe hi ben° here."   they are
To Horn he gan gon°   did go
And grette° him anon.°   greeted/quickly
1365 Muche ioie hi makede þere
Þe while hi togadere° were.   together
"Childre,"° he sede,° "hu habbe ȝe fare?°   children/said/how have you fared
Þat ihc° ȝou seȝ hit° is ful° ȝare.°   since I/saw it/very/long ago
Wulle° ȝe þis londe winne   will
1370 And sle° þat° þer is inne?"   slay/(those) that
He sede, "Leue Horn child,
Ȝut° lyueþ þi moder° Godhild;   still/mother
Of ioie heo° miste°   she/might have
If heo þe° aliue wiste."°   you/knew
1375   Horn sede on° his rime,°   in/speech
"Iblessed° beo þe time   blessed
I com° to Suddenne   came
Wiþ mine Irisse° menne: Irish
We schulle° þe hundes teche°   shall/hounds teach
1380 To speken vre° speche.°   speak our/speech
Alle we hem schulle sle,
And al quic° hem fle."°   alive/flay
Horn gan° his horn to blowe;   began
His folk hit gan iknowe;°   know
1385 Hi comen° vt of stere,°   came/stern
Fram° Hornes banere;°   from/banner
Hi sloȝen° and fuȝten,°   slew/fought
Þe niȝt° and þe vȝten;°   night/morning
Þe Sarazins cunde°   Saracens' kind
1390 Ne° lefde° þer non° in þende.°   not/left (they)/none/the end
Horn let wurche°   had built
Chapeles and chirche;
He let belles ringe
And masses let singe.°   sung
1395 He com to his moder° halle   mother's
In a roche° walle.   stone
Corn he let serie,
And makede feste° merie;   made feast
Murie lif° he wroȝte:°   merry life/led
1400 Rymenhild hit dere° broȝte.°   dearly/paid for

1380. I.e., "meet our terms."

1385–86. The banner was near the prow; the companies left the boat from the stern.

1388. *vȝten:* From OE *uht,*" early morning." In *The Fox and the Wolf* (this volume, p. 552, l. 265) we find the interesting term *houssong,* "matins."

1397. *serie:* probably a mistake for *ferie,* "carried."

Fikenhild was prut° on herte,°   *arrogant/heart*
And þat him dude smerte.°   *made trouble*
Ʒonge° he ʒaf° and elde°   *young/gave (money)/old*
Mid° him for to helde.°   *with/hold*
1405 Ston° he dude lede,°   *stones/did bring*
Þer° he hopede spede,°   *where/(it would) be useful*
Strong castel he let sette,°   *built*
Mid scc him biflette,°   *water it surrounded*
Þer ne miʒte liʒte°   *might land*
1410 Bute foʒel° wiþ fliʒte.°   *only bird/flight*
Bute whanne° þe se wiþdroʒe,°   *except when/sea receded*
Miʒte come men ynoʒe.°   *many*
Fikenhild gan wende°   *did intend*
Rymenhild to schende.°   *harm*
1415 To woʒe° he gan hure° ʒerne;°   *woo/her/passionately*
Þe Kyng ne dorste° him werne.°   *dared/refuse*
Rymenhild was ful of mode:°   *heartsick*
He wep teres° of blode.°   *she wept tears/blood*
Þat niʒt Horn gan swete°   *sweat*
1420 And heuie° for to mete°   *sorrowfully/dream*
Of Rymenhild his make°   *mate (that she)*
Into schupe° was itake:°   *ship/taken*
Þe schup bigan to blenche:°   *lurch*
His lemman scholde adrenche.°   *lover should drown*
1425 Rymenhild wiþ hire honde°   *her hand*
Wolde° vp to londe:°   *wanted/land*
Fikenhild aʒen° hire pelte°   *back/repelled*
Wiþ his swerdes° hilte.   *sword's*
    Horn him wok of slape°   *woke from sleep*
1430 So° a man þat hadde rape.°   *as/in a hurry*
"Aþulf," he sede,° felaʒe,°   *said/friend*
To schupe we mote draʒe.°   *must start*
Fikenhild me haþ idon vnder,°   *betrayed*
And Rymenhild to do wunder;°   *done treachery*
1435 Crist, for his wundes° fiue,   *wounds*
To-niʒt° me þuder° driue."   *tonight/thither*
Horn gan to schupe ride,
His feren° him biside.   *companions*
Fikenhild, or° þe dai gan springe,   *before*
1440 Al riʒt° he ferde° to þe Kinge,   *at once/fared*
After Rymenhild þe briʒte,°   *fair*
To wedden hire bi niʒte.
He ladde° hure bi° þe derke°   *led/in/dark*
Into his nywe werke.°   *new castle*
1445 Þe feste hi bigunne°   *feast they began*

Er þat° ros° þe sunne.   *before/rose*
Er þane° Horn hit wiste,°   *then/it knew*
Tofore° þe sunne vpriste,°   *before/rose*
His schup stod° vnder ture°   *stood/tower*
1450 At Rymenhilde bure.°   *Rymenhild's bower*
Rymenhild, litel weneþ heo°   *thinks she*
Þat Horn þanne° aliue beo.°   *then/is*
Þe castel þei ne° knewe,   *not*
For he° was so nywe.   *it*
1455 Horn fond sittinde° Arnoldin,   *found sitting*
Þat was Aþulfes cosin,°   *cousin*
Þat þer was in þat tide,°   *time*
Horn for tabide.°   *to await*
"Horn kniȝt,"° he sede, "kinges sone,°   *knight/son*
1460 Wel beo° þu to londe icome.°   *are/come*
Today haþ ywedde° Fikenhild   *wedded*
Þi swete° lemman Rymenhild.   *sweet*
Ne schal i þe° lie: *to you*
He haþ giled þe twie.°   *deceived you twice*
1465 Þis tur he let make°   *had made*
Al for þine sake.
Ne mai þer come inne
No man wiþ none° ginne.°   *no/siege mechanism*
Horn, nu° Crist þe wisse,°   *now/guide*
1470 Of Rymenhild þat þu ne misse."°   *lose*
    Horn cuþe° al þe liste°   *knew/cunning*
Þat eni° man of wiste.   *any*
Harpe he gan schewe,°   *did show*
And tok felaȝes° fewe,   *took friends*
1475 Of kniȝtes suiþe snelle°   *very agile*
Þat schrudde hem° at wille.   *disguised themselves*
Hi ȝeden° bi þe grauel°   *went/beach*
Toward þe castel;
Hi gunne murie° singe   *did merrily*
1480 And makede here gleowinge.°   *made their harping*
    Rymenhild hit gan ihere,°   *hear*
And axede° what hi were.   *asked*
Hi sede, hi weren° harpurs,   *were*
And sume° were gigours.°   *some/fiddlers*
1485 He dude° Horn in late°   *she did/let*
Riȝt° at halle gate,   *right*

1480. The Old English kenning for *harp* was *gleo-wudu,* "glee
(i.e., 'joy') wood."

He sette him° on þe benche,	*himself*
His harpe for to clenche.°	*grasp*
He makede Rymenhilde lay,°	*(a) song*
1490 And heo° makede walaway.°	*she/lamentation*
Rymenhild feol yswoȝe,°	*fell swooning*
Ne° was þer non° þat louȝe.°	*not/none/laughed*
Hit smot° to Hornes herte°	*it smote/heart*
So bitere° þat hit smerte.°	*bitter/hurt*
1495 He lokede on þe ringe	
And þoȝte on° Rymenhilde:	*thought of*
He ȝede vp to borde°	*table*
Wiþ gode suerdes orde:°	*good sword's point*
Fikenhildes crune°	*head*
1500 Þer he fulde adune,°	*cut off*
And al his men arowe°	*in a row*
He° dude adun° þrowe.	*they/down*
Whanne° hi weren aslaȝe,°	*when/they were slain*
Fikenhild he dude todraȝe.°	*tear to pieces*
1505 Horn makede Arnoldin þare°	*there*
King, after King Aylmare,	
Of al Westernesse	
For his meoknesse.°	*gentleness*
Þe King and his homage°	*vassals*
1510 Ȝeuen° Arnoldin trewage.°	*gave/tribute*
Horn tok Rymenhild bi þe honde°	*hand*
And ladde hure° to þe stronde,°	*led her/shore*
And ladde wiþ him Aþelbrus,	
Þe gode stuard° of his hus.°	*steward/house*
1515 Þe se° bigan to flowe,	*sea*
And Horn gan° to rowe.	*began*
Hi gunne° for to ariue	*began*
Þer° King Modi was sire.°	*where/lord*
Aþelbrus he makede þer king	
1520 For his gode teching:°	*stewardship*
He ȝaf° alle þe kniȝtes ore°	*gave/knights (his) favor*
For Horn kniȝtes lore.°	*counsel*
Horn gan for to ride;°	*(i.e., sail)*
Þe wind him bleu wel wide.°	*it blew very far*
1525 He ariuede in Yrlonde,°	*Ireland*
Þer he wo fonde,°	*sorrow found*

1526. The word *fonde* in the MS causes trouble: Horn found sorrow in Ireland perhaps because of the death of the king's sons, Harild and Berild, or the news of Rymenhild's forthcoming marriage with King Mody.

Þer he dude° Aþulf child   *made*
Wedden° maide Reynild.   *wed*
Horn com° to Suddenne   *came*
1530 Among al his kenne;°   *kin*
Rymenhild he makede° his quene;   *made*
So hit° miȝte° wel beon.°   *as it/might/be*
Al folk hem miȝte rewe°   *pity (for their troubles)*
Þat loueden° him so trewe.°   *loved/true*
1535 Nu ben° hi boþe dede,°—   *now are/dead*
Crist to heuene° hem lede!°   *heaven/lead*
Her° endeþ þe tale of Horn,   *here*
Þat fair was and noȝt vnorn;°   *not ugly*
Make we vs° glade eure° among,   *ourselves/ever*
1540 For þus him endeþ Hornes song.
Jesus, þat is of heuene king,
Ȝeue° vs alle His suete° blessing. AMEN.   *give/sweet*

EXPLICIT.

1527. Cf. l. 1353n.

HAVELOK THE DANE

DATE: c. 1285. ✦ MANUSCRIPT: Bodleian Library, Oxford, Laud Misc. 108, dated c. 1300–25. The dialect is Northeast Midland, with Northern and Southern elements. The poet probably lived in Lincolnshire. ✦ EDITIONS: W. W. Skeat, *Havelok the Dane*, Early English Text Society, ES 4 (London, 1868); W. W. Skeat, *The Lay of Havelok the Dane*, 2d ed., revised by Kenneth Sisam (Oxford, 1915); F. Holthausen, *Havelok*, 3d ed. (Heidelberg, 1928); W. H. French and C. B. Hale, *Middle English Metrical Romances* (New York, 1964); Donald Sands, *Middle English Verse Romances* (New York, 1966).

Although the dialect is in general from the Northeast Midlands, it contains a great mixture of Southern and Northern elements, the former caused by a Southern scribe, the latter by the Lincolnshire poet. In addition, an Anglo-Norman scribe seems to have had a hand in the transcription. Thus the following eccentricities should be closely watched: (1) Inorganic *h* before many vowels (*hold* = *old*, *his* = *is*) occurs very frequently. The scribe also omits *h* after *t* (*herknet*), or sometimes transposes it (*rith* = *riht*). Thus, as in other Southern pieces, the letter *h* should put the student on guard. (2) *W* often replaces *u* (*hw* for *hu* = *who*). (3) *Qu* stands for *wh*, a Northern feature. (4) ME yogh (ʒ) is completely replaced by *y* (*yeue* = *give*). (5) Finally, the constant interchange of *u* and *v* should be noted throughout (*euere* = *ever*, *hauen* = *have*, *vs* = *us*, and countless other examples).

The story of Havelok the Dane appeared first in the Anglo-Norman chronicle of Geoffrey Gaimer, *Estorie des engles* (1150), and was followed by the 12th-century Old English *Lai d'Havelok*. The present romance was the third version in the sequence, which ended with the short summary of Robert Mannyng of Brunne in his translation of Peter Langtoft's *Chronicle* (a. 1338). Thus the story, the motifs of the Male Cinderella and the Exile and Return, and the folk subjects were common and popular.

It is an essential part of the story of Havelok that he ruled over a combined kingdom of England and Denmark, and the Latin heading of the romance recalls this fact. The story alludes consciously to the Scandinavian ancestry of many northern English settlers and perhaps to the Danish line of kings starting with Canute. Certain specifically local Lincolnshire elements attached themselves to the plot (as Robert Mannyng, a Lincolnshire man, attested), and thereby the tale became part of the heritage of that section of England.

As contrasted with the courtly *King Horn* (with which it is often compared), *Havelok the Dane* has the rough epic energy and vigor reminiscent of *Beowulf* and the Scandinavian tradition. In meter, plotting, originality, and surprising bourgeois detail, *Havelok* is a good romance.

Incipit Vita Hauelok Quondam Rex Anglie Et Denemarchie

Herknet° to me, godemen,°	*listen/good men*
Wiues, maydnes, and alle men,	
Of° a tale þat ich° you wile° telle,	*to/I/will*
Wo-so° it wile here° and þer-to duelle.°	*whoso/hear/remain*
⁵ Þe tale is of Hauelok imaked;°	*made*
Wil° he was litel, he yede ful° naked.	*when/walked completely*
Hauelok was a ful god gome.°	*very good man*
He was ful god in eueri trome,°	*group*
He was þe wicteste° man at nede°	*bravest/in necessity*
¹⁰ Þat þurte riden° on ani stede.°	*could ride/steed*
Þat ye mowen° nou yhere,°	*may/hear*
And þe tale ye mowen ylere,°	*learn*
At þe biginning of vre° tale,	*our*
Fil me a cuppe of ful god ale;	
¹⁵ And wile y drinken, her° y spelle,°	*while I drink, here/recite*
Þat Crist vs shilde° alle fro° helle!	*shield/from*
Krist late° vs heuere° so for to do	*let/ever*
Þat we moten comen° him to;	*might come*
And, witþat° it mote ben° so,	*so that/be*
²⁰ *Benedicamus Domino!*	
Here y schal biginnen° a rym;°	*begin/rhyme*
Krist us yeue wel° god fyn!°	*give very/ending*
The rym is maked of Hauelok,	
A stalworþi° man in a flok;°	*stalwart/group*
²⁵ He was þe wihtest° man at nede	*bravest*
Þat may riden on ani stede.	
It° was a king bi are dawes,°	*there/in former days*
Þat in his° time were gode° lawes:	*in whose/good*
He dede maken° an° ful wel holden;°	*caused to be made/and/obeyed*
³⁰ Hym louede yung, him louede holde,°	*old*

Heading: "Here begins the life of Havelok, formerly king of England and Denmark."

1–26. The prologue has all the elements of the typical minstrel opening as outlined in the General Introduction.

20. "May God bless us!"

25–26. Such romance clichés can easily be spotted throughout the work (cf. ll. 9–10). They were tags, used as mnemonic devices by the minstrel.

Erl and barun, dreng° and tayn,°　　　　　　　　*vassal/thane*
Knict, bondeman,° and swain,°　　　　　　　　*knight, serf/peasant*
Wydues,° maydnes, prestes° and clerkes,　　　*widows/priests*
And al for hise° gode werkes.　　　　　　　　*his*
35　He louede God with al his micth,°　　　　　*might*
And holi kirke° and soth ant ricth;°　　　　　*church/truth and right*
Ricth-wise° men he louede alle,　　　　　　　*righteous*
And oueral° made hem° forto calle;°　　　　　*from everywhere/had them/called*
Wreieres° and wrobberes made he falle,　　　*traitors*
40　And hated hem so° man doth galle,　　　　*as*
Vtlawes° and theues° made he bynde,°　　　　*outlaws/thieves/bound*
Alle that he micthe° fynde,　　　　　　　　　*might*
And heye hengen° on galwe-tre;°　　　　　　　*high hanged/gallows*
For hem ne yede° gold ne fe.°　　　　　　　　*not helped/nor fee*
45　In þat time a man þat bore
Wel° fifty pund,° y wot,° or more,　　　　　*fully/pounds/guess*
Of red gold upon hiis bac,
In a male hwit° or blac,　　　　　　　　　　　*bag white*
Ne funde° he non° þat him misseyde,°　　　　*found/none/insulted*
50　Ne with iuele on hond leyde.°　　　　　　*evil a hand laid (on him)*
Þanne° micthe chapmen° fare　　　　　　　　　*then/merchants*
Þuruth° Englond wit here° ware,　　　　　　　*throughout/with their*
And baldelike beye° and sellen,°　　　　　　　*boldly buy/sell*
Oueral þer° he wilen° dwellen,°　　　　　　　*everywhere/they wanted to/stay*
55　In gode burwes,° and þer-fram°　　　　　　*towns/outside*
Ne funden° he non þat dede° hem sham,°　　　*found/caused/shame*
Þat he ne weren sone° to sorwe brouth,°　　　*were soon/sorrow brought*
An pouere° maked, and browt° to nouth.°　　　*poor/brought/naught*
Þanne was Engelond at hayse;°　　　　　　　　*ease*
60　Michel° was svich° a king to preyse,°　　　*much/such/be praised*
Þat held so England in grith!°　　　　　　　　*peace*
Krist of heuene° was him with.　　　　　　　　*heaven*
He was Engelondes blome;°　　　　　　　　　　*flower*
Was non so bold louerd° to° Rome　　　　　　　*lord/as far as*
65　Þat durste° upon his bringhe°　　　　　　*dared/his (subjects) bring*
Hunger, ne othere wicke þinghe.°　　　　　　　*wicked thing*
Hwan° he felede° hise foos,°　　　　　　　　　*when/made flee/foes*
He made hem lurken,° and crepen° in wros:°　*lurk/creep/corners*
Þei hidden hem° alle, and helden° hem stille,　*hid themselves/held*
70　And diden° al his herte° wille.　　　　　　*did/heart's*
Ricth he louede of° alle þinge,　　　　　　　　*above*
To wronge micth him no man bringe,

---

31. A dreng was a vassal with military obligations to his lord. A thane was any free, land-holding vassal.

47. Gold had a reddish cast from being alloyed with copper; indeed, copper was often passed for gold.

Ne for siluer, ne for gold:—
So was he his soule hold.° — *concerned for*
⁷⁵ To þe faderles° was he rath,° — *fatherless/(a) help*
Wo-so dede° hem wrong or lath,° — *whoso did/ill*
Were it clerc, or were it knicth,° — *knight*
He dede hem° sone to hauen ricth;° — *them/receive justice*
And wo dide widuen° wrong, — *who did widows*
⁸⁰ Were he neure° knicth so strong — *never*
Þat he ne made° him sone kesten° — *had/cast*
In feteres,° and ful° faste festen;° — *fetters/very/bound*
And wo-so dide maydne shame
Of hire° bodi, or brouth in blame, — *her*
⁸⁵ Bute° it were bi hire wille, . — *unless*
He made him sone of limes spille.° — *limbs lose*
He was þe beste knith at nede° — *knight in need*
Þat heuere micthe° riden on stede,° — *ever might/steed*
Or wepne wagge,° or folc vt lede;° — *weapon wield/out lead*
⁹⁰ Of knith ne hauede° he neuere drede,° — *not had/never fear*
Þat he ne sprong° forth so° sparke of glede,° — *sprang/like a/fire*
And lete° him knawe° of hise hand-dede,° — *let/feel/deeds of his hand*
Hw° he couþe° with wepne spede;° — *how/could/prevail*
And oþer° he refte him° hors or wede,° — *either/captured his/armor*
⁹⁵ Or made him sone handes sprede,° — *spread*
And "Louerd, merci!" loude grede.° — *cry*
He was large,° and no wicth° gnede;° — *generous/not at all/niggardly*
Hauede he non° so god brede,° — *none/good roast*
Ne on his bord° non so god shrede,° — *table/morsel*
¹⁰⁰ Þat he ne wolde° þorwit° fede° — *would/with it/feed*
Poure° þat on fote yede;° — *poor folk/foot went*
Forto° hauen° of Him þe mede° — *in order to/have/reward*
Þat for vs wolde on rode blede,° — *cross bleed*
Crist, that al kan wisse° and rede° — *teach/advise*
¹⁰⁵ Þat euere woneth° in ani þede.° — *ever live/country*

Þe king was hoten° Aþelwold, — *called*
Of word, of wepne he was bold;
In Engeland was neure knicth
Þat betere° held þe lond° to ricth.° — *better/land/right*

---

86. Mutilation of various kinds, most often severing an ear or hand or splitting the nose, was a common punishment.

87–105. A torrent of nineteen lines rhyming on the same sound seems to be a show of the poet's artistry.

94. Booty was an essential and legal aspect of war. Troops were allowed to loot captured towns as payment for their service; expensive horses and armor went to the victor knights; and prisoners were held for ransom, from squires (Geoffrey Chaucer at the siege of Reims, 1360) to kings (Richard Coeur de Lion). Legal difficulties occurred if prisoners were transferred from one captor to another, as seen during the Spanish campaign of the Black Prince, 1366. On the other hand, the commanding officers and overlords might receive certain prearranged shares of ransom and booty.

110 Of his bodi ne hauede he eyr°   heir
Bute° a mayden, swiþe° fayr,   except for/very
Þat was so yung þat sho° ne couþe   she
Gon° on fote, ne speke wit° mouþe.   go/speak with
Þan° him tok° an iuel° strong,   then/seized/sickness
115 Þat° he wel wiste° and underfong,°   so that/knew/understood
Þat his deth° was comen° him on,   death/come
And seyde,° "Crist, wat° shal y don?°   said/what/I do
Louerd,° wat shal me to rede?°   Lord/counsel
I woth° ful wel ich° haue mi mede: know/I
120 Hw shal nou mi douhter° fare?   daughter
Of hire haue ich michel° kare;   much
Sho is mikel° in mi þouth:°   much/thought
Of me self° is me rith nowt.°   myself/I don't care
No selcouth is þou° me be wo:°   wonder (it) is that/me is woe
125 Sho ne kan speke, ne sho kan go.°   walk
Yif scho couþe on horse ride,
And a thousande men bi hire° syde,   her
And sho were comen intil helde,°   of age
And Engelond sho couþe welde,°   govern
130 And don of° hem þat hire° were queme,°   have to do with/to her/pleasing
An° hire bodi° couþe yeme,°   and/person/guard
Ne wolde° me neuere iuele like,°   not would (it)/never ill please
Ne þou° ich were in heuene-riche!"°   though/heaven

Quanne° he hauede° þis pleinte maked,°   when/had/lament made
135 Þerafter stronglike° he quaked.   strongly
He sende writes° sone onon°   sent letters/quickly
After his erles euereich on;°   every one
And after hise° baruns, riche and poure,°   his/poor
Fro Rokesburw° al° into° Douere,   Roxburgh/all the way/to
140 Þat he shulden° comen swiþe°   they should/quickly
Til° him, þat was ful vnbliþe,°   to/very unhappy
To þat stede þer° he lay   place where
In harde bondes,° nicth° and day.   (i.e., sickness)/night
He was so faste wit yuel fest°   illness bound
145 Þat he ne mouthe hauen° no rest;   might have
He ne mouthe no mete hete,°   food eat
Ne° he ne mouchte° no lyþe gete,°   nor/might/comfort get
Ne non of° his iuel þat couþe red;°   none concerning/could advise (him)
Of° him ne was nouth buten ded.°   to/remained nothing but death

139. From this line scholars have attempted to date the romance to the time (1296) when Roxburgh was the northernmost English fortress on the Scottish border. But the town changed hands so frequently that any evidence from this source is tenuous.

150 Alle þat þe writes herden°	read
Sorful an° sori til him ferden;°	sorrowful and/fared
He wrungen hondes,° and wepen sore,°	wrung hands/wept greatly
And yerne preyden° Cristes hore,°	earnestly prayed/mercy
Þat he wolde turnen° him	turn
155 Vt° of þat yuel þat was so grim!	out
Þanne° he weren comen° alle	when/were come
Bifor þe king into the halle,	
At Winchestre þer he lay:	
"Welcome," he seyde,° be ye ay!°	said/ever
160 Ful michel þank° kan y yow°	much thanks/give I you
That ye aren° comen to me now!"	are
Quanne he weren alle set,°	seated
And þe king aueden igret,°	had greeted
He greten,° and gouleden,° and gouen hem° ille,°	wept/lamented/grieved/bitterly
165 And he bad° hem alle ben° stille,	bade/be
And seyde þat greting° helpeth nouth,	mourning
"For al to dede° am ich brouth.°	death/I brought
Bute nov° ye sen° þat i shal deye,°	but now/see/die
Nou ich wille you alle preye°	ask
170 Of mi douther° þat shal be	daughter
Yure leuedi° after me,	your lady
Wo° may yemen° hire° so longe,	who/care for/her
Boþen° hire and Engelonde,	both
Til þat she wman° be of helde,°	woman/age
175 And þat she mowe hit yemen° and welde?"°	may it govern/rule
He ansuereden,° and seyden anon,°	answered/said immediately
Bi Crist and bi seint Ion,°	Saint John
That þ'erl Godrigh of Cornwayle°	Cornwall
Was trewe° man, wituten° faile;	(a) true/without
180 Wis° man of red,° wis man of dede,°	wise/in counsel/deeds
And men haueden° of him mikel drede:°	had/great fear (i.e., respect)
"He may hire alþer best° yeme,	best of all
Til þat she mowe wel ben quene."	
Þe king was payed of° that rede;°	pleased with/counsel
185 A wel° fair cloth bringen° he dede,°	very/to be brought/caused
And þeron leyde° þe messebok,°	laid/missal
Þe caliz,° and þe pateyn ok,°	chalice/paten also
Þe corporaus,° þe messe-gere;°	corporal/mass implements

---

158. Winchester was the legal capital of England and the seat
of the royal court from before the reign of Alfred the Great.

Þer-on he garte° þe erl suere,°   made/swear
190 Þat he sholde° yemen hire wel,   should
Withuten lac,° wituten tel,°   without fault/reproach
Til þat she were tuelf winter hold,°   twelve winters old
And of speche° were bold;   speech
And þat she covþe° of curteysye°   could/courteous behavior
195 Don,° and speken° of luue-drurye;°   do (i.e., know)/speak/lovemaking
And til þat she louen mouhte°   love might
Wom so° hire to gode þoucte;°   whoever/good seemed
And þat he shulde° hire yeue°   should/give
Þe hexte° man þat micthe° liue,   highest/might
200 Þe beste, fayreste, the strangest° ok;   strongest
Þat dede° he him sweren° on þe bok.°   made/swear/book
And þanne° shulde he Engelond   then
Al bitechen° into hire hond.°   commit/hand

Quanne° þat was sworn on° þis wise,°   when/in/fashion
205 Þe king dede þe mayden arise,
And þe° erl hire bitaucte,°   (to) the/committed
And al the lond° he euere awcte°—   land/ever owned
Engelonde, eueri del°—   part
And preide,° he shulde yeme hire wel.   asked

210 Þe king ne mowcte° don no more,   not might
But ycrne preycde° Godes orc,°   earnestly prayed/mercy
And dede him° hoslen° wel and shriue°   had himself/given the sacrament/
                                                                         confessed
I woth fif° hundred siþes° and fiue;   believe five/times
An° ofte dede him sore swinge,°   and/severely scourged
215 And wit° hondes smerte dinge,°   with/smartly struck
So þat þe blod° ran of° his fleys,°   blood/from/flesh
Þat tendre was and swiþe neys.°   very soft
He made his quiste° swiþe wel   will
And sone gaf° it euereilk del.°   soon executed/every bit
220 Wan° it was gouen,° ne micte° men finde   when/executed/might
So mikel° men micte him in winde,   much (as a sheet)
Of his° in arke, ne° in chiste,°   his (own)/trunk, nor/chest
In Engelond, þat noman° wiste:°   anyone/knew of

---

189. Swearing on holy objects made the oath more solemn. Harold, when captured by William the Conqueror, then duke of Normandy, was made to swear not to oppose William's candidacy to the English crown on a box holding, unbeknownst to him, the bones of saints. Harold thus broke a solemn oath when he allowed himself to be chosen king, and William was able to invade England with the blessing of the Holy See.

201. *bok*: i.e., "prayer book" or "Bible".

214. Flagellation was a harsh penance, and the confessor of the three anchorites in the *Ancrene Riwle* forbids it to his charges. But the penitential orders of Flagellants were popular in Europe, especially during times of pestilence.

For al was youen,° faire and wel,   *given*
225 Þat° him° was leued° no catel.°   *so that/to him/left/possession*

Þanne° he hauede ben° ofte swngen,°   *when/had been/scourged*
Ofte shriuen, and ofte dungen,°   *beaten*
"In manus tuas, louerde,"° he seyde,°   *into thy hands, Lord/said*
Her þat° he þe speche leyde;°   *before/lost (control of)*
230 To Iesu° Crist bigan to calle,   *Jesus*
And deyede° biforn° his heymen° alle.   *died/in front of/nobles*
Þan° he was ded,° þere micte men se°   *when/dead/see*
Þe meste sorwe° that micte be: *greatest sorrow*
Þer was sobbing, siking,° and sor,°   *sighing/sorrow*
235 Handes wringing and drawing bi hor.°   *tearing of hair*
Alle greten° swiþe sore,°   *wept/greatly*
Riche and poure° þat þere wore;°   *poor/were*
An mikel sorwe haueden° alle,   *had*
Leuedyes° in boure, knictes° in halle.   *ladies/bower, knights*
240   Quan þat sorwe was somdel laten°   *somewhat abated*
And he° haueden longe graten,°   *they/lamented*
Belles deden° he sone ringen,°   *did/ring*
Monkes and prestes messe singen;°   *priests mass sing*
And sauteres° deden he manie reden,°   *psalms/read*
245 Þat God self shulde° his soule leden°   *himself should/lead*
Into heuene, biforn° his Sone,°   *heaven, before/Son*
And þer wituten hende wone.°   *without end live*
Þan he was to þe erþe brouth,°   *brought*
Þe riche° erl ne foryat nouth°   *powerful/neglected nothing*
250 Þat he ne dede al Engelond
Sone sayse intil° his hond;°   *seize in/hand*
And in þe castels let° he do°   *had/put*
Þe knictes he micte tristen to;°   *trust in*
And alle þe Englis dede° he swere,°   *English made/swear*
255 Þat he shulden° him ghod fey beren;°   *should/good faith bear*
He yaf° alle men þat god° him þoucte,°   *gave/whatever good/seemed*
Liuen and deyen til þat he moucte,°   *until their death*
Til þat þe kinges dowter° wore   *daughter*
Tuenti winter hold,° and more.   *winters old*

260 Þanne he hauede taken þis oth°   *oath*
Of erles, baruns, lef° and loth,°   *friendly/hostile*
Of knictes, cherles, fre° and þewe,°   *serfs, free/bound*

---

228. Cf. Luke 23:46.

252–53. The Normans built many castles in England, placing   them in strategic locations in order to tighten their rule.

Iustises° dede he maken° newe, *judges|make*
Al Engelond to faren þorw,° *travel through*
265 Fro° Douere into Rokesborw.° *from|to Roxburgh*
Schireues° he sette, bedels,° and greyues,° *sheriffs|appointed, beadles|graves*
Grith-sergeans, wit° longe gleyues,° *peace-sergeants, with|spears*
To yemen° wilde wodes° and paþes° *guard|forests|roads*
Fro wicke° men, that wolde don scaþes,° *wicked|would do harm*
270 And forto° hauen° alle at his cri,° *in order to|have|call*
At his wille, at hise° merci, *his*
Þat° non durste ben° him ageyn,° *so that|none dared be|against*
Erl ne° barun, knict ne sweyn.° *nor|peasant*
Wislike,° for soth,° was him wel° *certainly|in truth|he had plenty*
275 Of folc, of wepne,° of catel.° *weapons|goods*
Soþlike,° in a lite þrawe,° *truly|little while*
Al Engelond of him stod° awe; *stood (in)*
Al Engelond was of him adrad° *afraid*
So his° þe beste° fro þe gad.° *as is|beast|goad*

280 Þe kinges douther° bigan þriue,° *daughter|to thrive*
And wex° þe fayrest wman° on liue.° *grew (to be)|woman|alive*
Of° alle þewes° was she wis° *in|manners|wise*
Þat gode weren° and of pris.° *good were|praiseworthy*
Þe mayden Goldeboru was hoten;° *called*
285 For hire° was mani a ter igroten.° *her|tear wept*

Quanne° þe Erl Godrich him herde° *when|himself heard*
Of þat mayden, hw° wel she ferde°— *how|fared*
Hw wis sho° was, hw chaste, hw fayr, *she*
And þat sho was þe rithe eyr° *true heir*
290 Of Engelond, of al þe rike°— *realm*
Þo° bigan Godrich to sike,° *then|sigh*
And seyde,° "Weþer° she sholde° be *said|whether|should*
Quen° and leuedi° ouer me? *queen|lady*
Hweþer sho sholde al Engelond,
295 And me, and mine, hauen in hire hond?° *hand*
Daþeit hwo° it hire° thaue!° *cursed (be he) who|of her|endures*
Shal sho it neuere° more haue. *never*

263–64. The tradition of circuit justices stems from Anglo-Saxon times, when they represented the crown in outlying districts.

266–67. Sheriffs (shire reeves) were the police officers in the counties, whereas graves kept the peace in town. Beadles were minor parish officers entrusted with various duties of maintaining ecclesiastical order. Peace-sergeants were the burly men involved in the physical activity of maintaining law and order.

Gleives were sometimes long poled knives, like spears, sometimes swords.

285. I.e., for love longing, also for coming hardship.

292. *Weþer she sholde*: i.e., "should she."

296. *dapeit*: supposedly a corrupted contraction of *odium Dei habet*, "may he have the hate of God."

	Sholde ic yeue° a fol,° a þerne,°	*I give/fool/servant girl*
	Engelond, þou° sho it yerne?°	*though/desires*
300	Daþeit hwo it hire yeue°	*gives*
	Euere-more hwil° i liue!	*evermore while*
	Sho is waxen° al to prud,°	*grown to be/too proud*
	For gode metes,° and noble shrud,°	*food/clothing*
	Þat hic° haue youen° hire to offte;°	*I/given/often*
305	Hic haue yemed° hire to softe.°	*cared for/leniently*
	Shal it nouth° ben als° sho þenkes:°	*not/as/thinks*
	Hope maketh fol° man ofte blenkes.°	*foolish/blind*
	Ich° haue a sone,° a ful° fayr knaue:°	*I/son/very/boy*
	He shal Engelond al haue!	
310	He shal king, he shal ben sire,	
	So brouke° i euere° mi blake swire!"°	*may enjoy/ever/white neck*
	Hwan° þis trayson° was al þouth,°	*when/treason/thought (up)*
	Of his oth° ne was him nouth.°	*oath/he did not care*
	He let his oth al ouerga:°	*be forgotten*
315	Þerof ne yaf° he nouth a stra;°	*not gave/straw*
	But sone dede° hire fete,°	*did/fetch*
	Er° he wolde heten° ani mete,°	*before/would eat/food*
	Fro° Winchestre, þer° sho was,	*from/where*
	Also° a wicke° traytur Iudas,°	*like/wicked/Judas*
320	And dede leden° hire to Doure,°	*lead/Dover*
	Þat standeth on þe seis-oure;°	*seashore*
	And þerhinne° dede hire fede°	*therein/feed (i.e., keep)*
	Pourelike° in feble wede.°	*in poverty/humble garment*
	Þe castel dede he yemen° so	*guard*
325	Þat non° ne micte° comen hire° to	*none/might/come her*
	Of hire frend,° with hir to speken,°	*friends/speak*
	Þat heuere° micte hire bale wreken.°	*ever/misfortune avenge*
	Of Goldeboru shul° we nou laten,°	*shall/stop telling*
	Þat nouth ne blinneth° forto graten°	*ceases/weep*
330	Þer sho liggeth° in prisoun:	*she lies*
	Iesu° Crist, that Lazarun°	*Jesus/Lazarus*
	To liue broucte° fro dede° bondes,	*life brought/death's*
	He lese° hire wit hise° hondes!	*loose/with his*
	And leue° sho mote° him yse°	*grant (that)/might/see*
335	Heye hangen° on galwe-tre,°	*high hang/gallows*
	Þat hire haued in sorwe brouth°	*had to sorrow brought*

---

311. I.e., "as I live" (*blake:* from OE *blac, blæc,* "white," "pale"; cf. English *bleach,* German *bleich*).

320. Goldeboro is imprisoned in Dover Castle, where, according to Caxton, was found the cleft skull of Gawain.

331. *Lazarun:* Cf. John 11:1–44.

So as° sho ne misdede nouth!°   *although/did nothing wrong*

Say° we nou forth in hure spelle!°   *proceed/our story*
In þat time, so° it bifelle,   *as*
340 Was in þe lond° of Denemark   *land*
A riche king, and swyþe stark.°   *very strong*
Þe name of him was Birkabeyn,
He hauede mani knict° and sueyn,°   *knights/peasants*
He was fayr man, and wicth,°   *bold*
345 Of° bodi he was þe beste knicth°   *in/knight*
Þat euere micte leden uth here°   *out army*
Or stede° onne° ride, or handlen spere.°   *steed/on/handle spear*
Þre° children he hauede bi his wif;°   *three/wife*
He hem louede° so his lif.°   *them loved/life*
350 He hauede a sone° and douhtres° two,   *son/daughters*
Swiþe fayre, as fel° it so.   *befell*
He þat wile° non forbere,°   *will/spare*
Riche ne poure,° king ne kaysere,°   *nor poor/emperor*
Deth° him tok þan° he best° wolde   *death/took when/most/wanted to*
355 Liuen,°—but hyse dayes were fulde°—   *live/completed*
Þat he ne moucte° no more liue,   *might*
For gold ne siluer, ne for no gyue.°   *gift*

Hwan° he þat wiste,° raþe° he sende°   *when/knew/quickly/sent*
After prestes fer an hende,°   *for priests far and near*
360 Chanounes gode,° and monkes boþe,   *canons good*
Him for to wisse,° and to rede;°   *counsel/advise*
Him for to hoslen,° an forto shriue,°   *give sacrament/confess*
Hwil° his bodi were on liue.°   *while/alive*

Hwan he was hosled and shriuen,
365 His quiste maked,° and for him gyuen, °   *will made/executed*
His knictes dede° he alle site;°   *made/sit (down)*
For þorw° hem he wolde wite°   *through/know*
Hwo micte° yeme° hise children yunge,   *who might/care for*
Til þat he kouþen speken° wit tunge,   *they could speak*
370 Speken and gangen,° on horse riden,°   *go/ride*
Knictes an sweynes° bi here siden.°   *servants/their side*
He spoken þer-offe° and chosen sone°   *spoke thereof/chose soon*

338–446. The romance is organized in parallel parts: two kingdoms, two kings, two traitors, a daughter and a son. Thus the introductions parallel each other, though the second goes on to intensify the horror.

346. *here:* Old English, "army" (cf. German *Heer*). In the *Anglo-Saxon Chronicle* the term always refers to the foreign Danish forces (cf. l. 2205n).

353. *kaysere;* from Latin *Caesar* (cf. German *Kaiser*).

A riche° man þat, under mone,°   *powerful/moon*

Was þe trewest,° as he wende,°   *truest/believed*

375 Godard, þe kinges oune° frende;   *own*

And seyden,° he moucthe° hem best loke,° *said/might/care for*

Yif þat° he hem vndertoke,°   *if/took under his care*

Til hise° sone mouthe bere°   *his/might bear*

Helm° on heued,° and leden vt° here, *helmet/head/lead out*

380 In his hand a spere stark,°   *strong*

And king ben° maked of Denemark.   *be*

He wel trowede þat° he seyde,   *believed what*

And on Godard handes leyde,°   *laid*

And seyde, "Here biteche° i þe°   *commit/to you*

385 Mine children alle þre,

Al Denemark, and al mi fe,°   *property*

Til þat mi sone of helde° be;   *age*

But° þat ich wille° þat þou suere° *except/wish/swear*

On auter° and on messe-gere,°   *altar/mass implements*

390 On þe belles þat men ringes,

On messe-bok° þe prest on° singes,   *missal/from*

Þat þou mine children shalt wel yeme,

Þat hire° kin be ful° wel queme,°   *their/very/pleased*

Til mi sone mowe° ben knicth;°   *son may/knight*

395 Þanne biteche° him þo° his ricth:° *then give/then/due rights*

Denemark, and þat þertil longes,°   *thereto belongs*

Casteles and tunes, wodes° and wonges."° *towns, forests/fields*

Godard stirt° up, an° swor al þat   *rose/and*

Þe king him bad,° and siþen° sat   *asked/then*

400 Bi þe knictes,° þat þer ware,°   *knights/were*

Þat wepen° alle swiþe sare°   *wept/very greatly*

For þe king, þat deide° sone.—   *died*

Iesu° Crist, that makede mone   *Jesus*

On þe mirke nith° to shine,   *dark night*

405 Wite° his soule from helle pine;° *guard/from hell's pain*

And leue° þat it mote wone°   *grant/might live*

In heuene-riche° with Godes sone!   *heaven*

Hwan° Birkabeyn was leyd in graue,   *when*

Þe erl dede° sone take þe knaue,°   *did/boy*

410 Hauelok, þat was þe broþer,

---

373. *under Mone:* i.e., "on earth."

Swanborow, his sister, Helfled, þe toþer,°

And in þe castel dede he hem do,°

Þer non ne micte° hem comen° to

Of here° kyn, þer þei sperd° were;

415 Þer he greten° ofte sore,°

Boþe for hunger and for kold,

Or° he weren þre winter hold.°

Feblelike° he gaf° hem cloþes,

He ne yaf° a note of hise oþes;°

420 He hem cloþede rith ne° fedde,

Ne hem dede richelike° bedde.

Þanne Godard was sikerlike°

Vnder God þe moste swike,°

Þat eure° in erþe shaped° was,

425 Withuten on,° þe wike Iudas.°

Haue he° þe malisun° to-day

Of alle þat cure speken° may!

Of patriark, and of pope,

And of prest° with loken kope,°

430 Of monekes° and hermites boþe,

And of þe leue° holi rode°

Þat° God himselue° ran on blode!°

Crist warie° him with his mouth!

Waried wrþe° he of° norþ and suth!°

435 Offe° alle men þat speken kunne,°

Of Crist, þat made mone° and sunne!

Þanne° he hauede° of al þe lond°

Al þe folk tilled intil° his hond,°

And alle haueden sworen° him oth,

440 Riche and poure, lef° and loth,°

Þat he sholden° hise wille freme,°

And þat he shulden° him nouth greme,°

He þouthe° a ful strong° trechery,

A trayson° and a felony,

445 Of° þe children forto make:

Þe deuel° ol helle him sone° take!

Hwan þat was þouth, onon° he ferde°

To þe tour° þer he woren° sperde,

Þer he greten for hunger and cold.

---

	that other
	them put
	where none not might/come
	their/imprisoned
	they wept/greatly
	before/were three winters old
	sparingly/gave
	gave/nut for his oaths
	(neither) clothed right nor
	richly
	surely
	greatest traitor
	ever/created
	except one/wicked Judas
	may he have/curse
	speak
	priest/fastened cloak
	monks
	dear/cross
	on which/himself/blood
	curse
	be/by/south
	by/can
	moon
	when/had/land
	drawn into/hand
	had sworn
	poor, friendly/hostile
	should/perform
	should/not antagonize
	thought (up)/very great
	treason
	against
	Devil/soon
	quickly/fared
	tower/were

---

411. *þe toþer;* an example of false division or metanalysis, as in *an umpire* for *a nompaire*, or *an apron* for *a napron.*

450 Þe knaue,° þat was sumdel° bold,	boy/somewhat
Kam° him ageyn,° on knes him° sette,	came/to/knees himself
And Godard ful feyre° he þer grette.°	courteously/greeted
And Godard seyde,° "Wat° is yw?°	said/what/wrong
Hwi° grete ye and goulen° nou?"	why/cry
455 For us hungreth swiþe sore,"°	because we hunger very greatly
Seyden° he, "We wolden° more:	said/want
We ne° haue to hete, ne° we ne haue	not/eat, nor
Herinne neyther knith° ne knaue	knight
Þat yeueth° us drinke, ne no mete°—	gives/food
460 Haluendel° þat° we moun ete!°	half of/what/might eat
Wo° is us þat we weren° born!	woe/were
Weilawei!° nis it° no korn°	alas/is there not/grain
Þat men micte maken° of bred?°	might make/bread
Us hungreth: we aren ney ded!"°	are almost dead
465 Godard herde here wa,°	heard their woe
Þeroffe yaf° he nouth a stra,°	thereof gave/straw
But tok° þe maydnes boþe samen,°	took/together
Also° it were up-on hiis gamen°—	as if/in sport
Also he wolde° with hem leyke,°	would/them play
470 Þat weren for hunger grene° and bleike.°	wan/white
Of boþen° he karf on° two here þrotes,	both/cut in
And siþen,° hem al to grotes.°	then/bits
Þer was sorwe, wo-so° it sawe	sorrow, whoso
Hwan° þe children bi þe wawe°	when/wall
475 Leyen° and sprauleden° in þe blod:°	lay/sprawled/blood
Hauelok it saw, and þer bi stod.°	stood
Ful sori was þat seli° knaue;	innocent
Mikel dred° he mouthe° haue,	much fear/might
For at hise° herte he saw a knif°	his/knife
480 For to reuen° him hise lyf.°	rob/of his life
But þe knaue, þat litel was,	
He knelede° bifor þat Iudas,°	knelt/Judas
And seyde, "Louerd,° merci nov!°	lord/now
Manrede,° louerd, biddi° you!	homage/I offer
485 Al Denemark i wile° you yeue,°	will/give
To þat forward þu late° me liue;	if you promise to let
Here hi° wile on boke swere,°	I/book swear
Þat neure° more ne shal i bere°	never/bear
Ayen þe,° louerd, sheld° ne spere,°	against you/shield/spear
490 Ne oþer wepne° that may you dere.°	weapon/hurt
Louerd, haue merci of° me!	on
To-day i wile fro° Denemark fle,°	from/flee
Ne neuere° more comen ageyn:°	never/come again
Sweren° y wole,° þat Bircabein	swear/I will

495 Neuere yete° me ne gat!"°   *yet/begot*
    Hwan þe deuel° herde þat,   *devils*
    Sumdel° bigan him° forto rewe;°   *somewhat/he/pity*
    Withdrow° þe knif, þat was lewe°   *withdrew/warm*
    Of° þe seli children° blod.   *with/children's*
500 Þer was miracle fair and god,°   *good*
    Þat he þe knaue nouth° ne slou,°   *not/not slew*
    But for rewnesse him witdrow.°   *pity himself withdrew*
    Of° Auelok rewede him ful sore,°   *for/he felt great remorse*
    And þoucte° he wolde° þat he ded wore,°   *thought/wished/dead were*
505 But-on° þat he nouth wit his hend°   *except/not with his (own) hand*
    Ne drepe° him nouth, þat fule fend!°   *would kill/foul fiend*
    Þoucte he, als° he him bistod,°   *as/stood over*
    Starinde° als° he were wod:°   *staring/as if/mad*
    "Yif° y late° him liues° go,   *if/let/alive*
510 He micte me wirchen michel wo.°   *cause much woe*
    Grith° ne get y neucre mo,°   *peace/more*
    He may me waiten° for to slo;°   *lie in wait/slay*
    And yf he were brouct of liue,°   *killed*
    And mine children wolden° þriue,   *would*
515 Louerdinges° after me   *lords*
    Of al Denemark micten he° be.   *might they*
    God it wite,° he shal ben° ded,—   *may know/be*
    Wile i taken non° oþer red!°   *take no/counsel*
    I shal do casten him° in þe se,°   *have him cast/sea*
520 Þer° i wile° þat he drenched° be;   *where/command/drowned*
    Abouten° his hals° an anker° god,   *about/neck/anchor*
    Þat° he ne flete° in the flod."°   *so that/float/sea*
    Þer anon° he dede° sende   *immediately/did*
    After a fishere, þat he wende°   *believed*
525 Wolde al his wille do,
    And sone anon° he seyde° him to: *quickly/said*
    "Grim, þou wost þu° art mi þral;°   *know you/thrall*
    Wilte° don° mi wille al   *if you will/do*
    Þat i wile bidden þe,°   *will ask you*
530 To-morwen° shal i maken° þe fre.°   *tomorrow/make/free*
    And aucte° þe yeuen° and riche make,   *property/give*
    Withþan° þu wilt° þis child take,   *provided/will*
    And leden° him with þe to-nicht,°   *lead/tonight*
    Þan° þou sest° þe mone-lith,°   *when/see/moonlight*
535 Into° þe se, and don° him þerinne;   *to/put*

519–22. Casting a prisoner into the sea or putting him adrift in a boat removes the onus from the murderer and puts the blame on fate. A similar situation occurs in *King Horn*, (cf. this volume, p. 145, ll. 105–14), and in classical mythology in the story of Danae and Perseus). Godard, of course, wants to give fate a heavy helping hand.

Al° wile i taken on me þe sinne."   *entirely*
Grim tok° þe child and bond° him faste,   *took/bound*
Hwil° þe bondes micte laste,°   *while/last*
Þat weren° of ful° strong line.   *were/very*
540 Þo° was Hauelok in ful strong pine!°   *then/pain*
Wiste° he neuere her wat° was wo.   *knew/never before what*
Iseu° Crist, þat makede go°   *Jesus/made walk*
Þe halte° and þe doumbe speke,°   *lame/dumb speak*
Hauelok, þe of° Godard wreke!°   *on/avenge*
545   Hwan° Grim him hauede° faste bounden,°   *when/had/bound*
And siþen° in an eld° cloth wnden,°   *then/old/wound*
He þriste° in his muth wel° faste   *thrust/mouth very*
A keuel° of clutes, ful unwraste,°   *gag/clothes, very filthy*
Þat he mouhte speke ne fnaste,°   *might (neither) speak nor breathe*
550 Hwere° he wolde him bere° or lede.   *where/carry*
Hwan he hauede don þat dede,°   *deed*
Hwan þe swike° him bad,° he yede°   *villain/commanded/went*
Þat he shulde° him forth lede   *should*
And him drinchen° in þe se—   *drown*
555 Þat forwarde makeden° he.   *promise made*
In a poke ful° and blac,   *bag foul*
Sone° he caste him on his bac,   *quickly*
Ant bar° him hom° to hise cleue,°   *and carried/home/his hut*
And bitaucte him° dame Leue,   *committed him (to)*
560 And seyde, "Wite° þou þis knaue,°   *guard/boy*
Also thou with me lif haue:°   *on your life*
I shal dreinchen° him in þe se;°   *drown/sea*
For° him shole° we ben° maked fre,   *through/shall/be*
Gold hauen ynou,° and oþer fe:°   *have enough/goods*
565 Þat hauet° mi louerd bihoten° me."   *has/lord promised*

Hwan dame Leue herde þat,
Vp she stirte,° and nouth° ne° sat,   *jumped/not/not*
And caste þe knaue so harde adoune,°   *down*
Þat he crakede° þer his croune°   *cracked/head*
570 Ageyn° a gret ston, þer° it lay: *against/great stone, where*
Þo Hauelok micte sei,° "Weilawei°   *might say/alas*
Þat euere° was i kinges bern!°   *ever/son*
Þat him° ne hauede grip° or ern,°   *(i.e., Godard)/vulture/eagle*
Leoun° or wlf, wluine° or bere,°   *lion/wolf, she-wolf/bear*
575 Or oþer best,° þat wolde° him dere!"°   *beast/would/harm*

537–38. *faste . . . laste:* i.e., "so that he would be secure until
the bonds rotted."

So lay þat child to° middel nicth,°   *until/midnight*
Þat° Grim bad° Leue bringen lict,°   *when/bade/bring light*
For to don° on his cloþes: *put*
"Ne thenkeste nowht of° mine oþes°   *don't you remember/oaths*
580 Þat ich° haue mi louerd sworen?°   *I/sworn*
Ne wile° i nouth be forloren.°   *will/lost (i.e., punished by him)*
I shal beren° him to þe se—   *carry*
Þou wost° þat so houes me°—   *know/I must do*
And i shal drenchen° him þer-inne;   *drown*
585 Ris° up swiþe, an° go þu binne,°   *rise/quickly, and/you within*
And blou° þe fir,° and lith° a kandel."   *blow/fire/light*
Als° she shulde° hise cloþes handel   *as/was about to*
On forto don, and blawe° þe fir,   *blow*
She saw þerinne a lith ful shir,°   *very bright*
590 Also brith° so° it were day,   *as bright/as if*
Aboute þe knaue þer he lay.
Of° hise mouth it stod° a stem°   *from/there came/ray*
Als° it were a sunnebem:°   *as if/sunbeam*
Also lith was it þer-inne
595 So þer brenden cerges inne.°   *burned candles there*
"Iesu° Crist!" wat° dame Leue,   *Jesus/said*
"Hwat° is þat lith in vre cleue?°   *what/our hut*
Ris up, Grim, and loke wat° it menes:°   *see what/means*
Hwat is þe lith, as þou wenes?"°   *think*
600 He stirten° boþe up to the knaue°   *they rushed/boy*
(For man shal god wille haue),°   *normally is kindhearted*
Vnkeueleden˘ him, and swiþe unbounden,˘   *ungagged/unbound*
And sone anon° upon him funden,°   *quickly/found*
Als he tirueden of° his serk,°   *pulled off/shirt*
605 On his rith shuldre° a kyne-merk,°   *right shoulder/royal (birth)mark*
A swiþe brith, a swiþe fair.°   *very fair (one)*
"Goddot!"° quath° Grim, "þis ure eir,°   *by God/said/this (is) our heir*
Þat shal° louerd° of Denemark: *shall be/lord*
He shal ben° king, strong and stark;°   *be/powerful*
610 He shal hauen° in his hand   *have*
Al Denemark and Engeland;
He shal do° Godard ful wo,°   *cause/great woe*
He shal him hangen,° or quik flo;°   *harg/alive flay*
Or he shal him al quic graue:°   *bury*

---

592. Beams of light issuing from parts of the hero's body, usually his head, are typical folkloric signs of royalty. The incident is repeated later during Havelok's wedding night (cf. ll. 1252–58) and in the home of Ubbe (cf. ll. 1931–47). **605.** The "king-mark" is usually a shining birthmark, here probably a cross (cf. ll. 1263–64 and ll. 1960–64). Kings and queens are easily recognized because of their obvious "noble" qualities, in the folktale usually blond hair, white skin, and so on. Goldeboro is the woman peerless in courtesy in all the world, and thus her true nobility is seen (ll. 2609–28).

⁶¹⁵ Of° him shal he no merci haue."   *on*
    Þus seide° Grim, and sore gret,°   *said/greatly wept*
    And sone° fel him° to° þe° fet,°   *quickly/fell/at/(i.e., Havelok's)/feet*
    And seide, "Louerd, haue merci
    Of me, and Leue, þat is me bi!
⁶²⁰ Louerd, we aren° boþe þine,   *are*
    Þine cherles,° þine hine.°   *serfs/thralls*
    Lowerd,° we sholen þe° wel fede°   *lord/shall you/nurture*
    Til þat þu cone riden° on stede,°   *can ride/steed*
    Til þat þu cone ful wel bere°   *bear*
⁶²⁵ Helm° on heued, sheld° and spere.°   *helmet/head, shield/spear*
    He ne° shal neuere, sikerlike,°   *not/never, certainly*
    Wite,° Godard, þat fule swike.°   *know/foul traitor*
    Þoru oþer° man, louerd, þan þoru þe   *through another*
    Sal° i neuere freman° be.   *shall/free man*
⁶³⁰ Þou shalt me, louerd, fre maken,°   *free make*
    For i shal yemen° þe and waken;°   *guard/watch over*
    Þoru þe wile° i fredom haue."   *while*
    Þo° was Haueloc a bliþe° knaue;   *then/happy*
    He sat him° up and crauede° bred,°   *sat/asked for/bread*
⁶³⁵ And seide, "Ich° am ney ded,°   *I/almost dead*
    Hwat° for hunger, wat for bondes   *what*
    Þat þu leidest° on min hondes,°   *you laid/my hands*
    And for þe keuel° at þe laste,   *gag*
    Þat in mi mouth was þrist° faste: *thrust*
⁶⁴⁰ Y° was þer-with so harde prangled°   *I/fully stuffed*
    Þat i was þer-with ney strangled."
    "Wel is me° þat þu mayth hete!°   *I am glad/may eat*
    Goddoth!"° quath Leue, "y shal þe fete°   *by God/fetch*
    Bred an chese, butere° and milk   *and cheese, butter*
⁶⁴⁵ Pastees° and flaunes; al with suilk°   *pasties/such things*
    Shole we sone þe wel fede,°   *feed*
    Louerd,° in þis mikel nede;°   *lord/great need*
    Soth° it is, þat men seyt° and suereth:°   *truth/say/swear*
    Þer° God wile helpen, nouth° ne dereth."°   *where/will help, nothing/injures*

⁶⁵⁰ Þanne sho hauede brouth° þe mete,°   *when she had brought/food*
    Haueloc anon° bigan to ete°   *immediately/eat*
    Grundlike,° and was ful° bliþe;   *heartily/very*

619–32. Kings were divine, ruling by divine right, and their bodies were sacred and anointed; to harm the body of a king was sacrilege. Grim is playing it safe.

645. Pasties were pies filled with meat beaten to a pulp; flaunes were cakes of custard or cheese. Most medieval food, especially meat, was heavily ground, often mushy, and highly seasoned, thus aiding toothless eaters and covering the taste of rot. The greatest art of the cook lay in disguising the original food.

Couþe° he nouth° his hunger miþe.°   *could/not/hide*
A lof° he het,° y woth° and more,   *loaf/ate/guess*
655 For him hungrede swiþe sore.°   *he hungered very greatly*
Þre dayes þer-biforn,° i wene,°   *(for) three days before/guess*
Et° he no mete, þat was wel sene.°   *ate/seen*
Hwan° he hauede eten and was fed,   *when*
Grim dede maken° a ful fayr bed,   *did make*
660 Vncloþede him, and dede° him þer-inne,   *put*
And seyde,° "Slep, sone,° with michel winne!°   *said/sleep, son/much joy*
Slep wel° faste, and dred þe nouth:°   *very/be not afraid*
Fro sorwe° to ioie° art þu brouth."   *from sorrow/joy*
Sone° so° it was lith° of day,   *as soon/as/light*
665 Grim it undertok,° þe wey°   *undertook/way*
To þe wicke° traitour Godard,   *wicked*
Þat was in Denemark a stiward,°   *steward*
And seyde, "Louerd, don ich haue
Þat° þou me bede of° þe knaue;   *what/commanded concerning*
670 He is drenched° in þe flod,°   *drowned/sea*
Abouten° his hals° an anker god;°   *about/neck/anchor good*
He is witerlike° ded: *surely*
Eteth° he neure° more bred.   *will eat/never*
He liþ° drenched in þe se:°—   *lies/sea*
675 Yif° me gold and oþer fe,°   *give/goods*
Þat° y mowe° riche be;   *so that/may*
And with þi chartre make fre,°   *free*
For þu° ful wel bihetet° me   *you/promised*
Þanne i last spak° with þe."°   *spoke/you*
680 Godard stod° and lokede on° him   *stood/looked at*
Þoruthlike,° with cync° grim,   *searchingly/eyes*
And seyde, "Wiltu° ben° erl?   *do you wish/to be (an)*
Go hom swiþe, fule drit-cherl;°   *home quickly, foul dirt-serf*
Go heþen,° and be eueremore°   *hence/evermore*
685 Þral° and cherl, als° þou er wore.°   *thrall/as/before were*
Shaltu° haue non° oþer mede;°   *you shall/no/reward*
For litel° shal i do° þe lede°   *(i.e., on a whim)/have/led*
To þe galues," so God me rede!°   *gallows/as God is my guide*
For þou haues° don a wicke dede.°   *have/deed*
690 Þou mait stonden° her to° longe,   *may be standing/here too*
Bute° þou swiþe heþen gonge!"°   *unless/go*

Grim þoucte° to late þat he ran   *thought*

---

677. Serfs or villeins were bought or sold with the land but could be manumitted by charter.   **692.** *to late:* i.e., "none too soon."

Fro þat traytour, þat wicke man;
And þoucte, "Wat shal° me to rede?° *what shall|I do*
695 Wite he° him onliue,° he wile° us beþe° *if he knows|alive|will|both*
Heye hangen° on galwe-tre:° *high hang|gallows*
Betere° us° is of londe° to fle,° *better|for us (it)|from land|flee*
And berwen boþen ure° liues, *save both our*
And mine children,° and mine wiues."° *children's| wife's*
700 Grim solde sone° al his corn,° *quickly|grain*
Shep wit wolle, neth° wit horn, *sheep with wool, cattle*
Hors, and swin,° and geet° with berd,° *swine|goats|beards*
Þe gees,° þe hennes of þe yerd;° *geese|yard*
Al he solde, þat outh° douthe,° *anything|was worth*
705 Þat he eure° selle moucte,° *ever|might*
And al he to þe peni° drou.° *penny|put into cash*
Hise° ship he greyþede° wel inow:° *his|equipped|enough*
He dede° it tere,° an ful° wel pike,° *did|tar|and very|pitch*
Þat it ne doutede sond ne krike;° *not feared sound nor creek*
710 Þer-inne dide° a ful god° mast, *put|good*
Stronge kables, and ful fast,
Ores gode,° an ful god seyl;° *good|sail*
Þerinne wantede nouth° a nayl, *(it) lacked not*
Þat euere° he sholde° þerinne do.° *ever|should|put*
715 Hwan° he hauedet greyþed° so, *when|had equipped (it)*
Hauelok þe yunge he dede° þerinne, *put*
Him and his wif,° hise sones þrinne,° *wife|sons three*
And hise two doutres,° þat faire wore; *daughters*
And sone dede he leyn° in an ore, *put*
720 And drou him° to þe heye se,° *rowed out|sea*
Þere° he mith° alþerbest° fle. *where|might|best of all*
Fro° londe woren he bote° a mile— *from|were they but*
Ne were it neuere° but ane° hwile°— *never|a|short time*
Þat° it ne bigan a wind to rise *when*
725 Out of þe north—men calleth "bise"—
And drof hem intil° Engelond, *drove them to*
Þat al was siþen° in his hond°— *afterwards|hand*
His, þat Hauelok was þe name°— *whose name was Havelok*
But or,° he hauede michel° shame, *first|had much*
730 Michel sorwe,° and michel tene,° *sorrow|grief*
And yete° he gat° it° al bidene;° *yet|got|(i.e., England)|completely*
Als° ye shulen° nou forthward lere,° *as|shall|presently learn*
Yf that° ye wilen° þerto here.° *if|will|listen*

---

725. The bise is the north wind (Boreas in Greek mythology), thus called in France, Switzerland, and Italy. Other such winds typical of certain geographic areas are the mistral, a constant dry wind in the Provence; the Foehn, a warm, dry wind coming from the Alps and causing all manner of human ills (cf. our Rocky Mountain chinook); and the African sirocco.

In Humber Grim bigan to lende,° — *land*
735 In Lindeseye, rith° at þe north ende. — *Lindsay, right*
Þer sat is° ship upon þe sond,° — *his/sand*
But Grim it drou° up to þe lond;° — *drew/land*
And þere he made a litel cote° — *cottage*
To° him and to hise flote.° — *for/company*
740 Bigan he þere for to erde,° — *dwell*
A litel hus° to maken of erþe, — *house*
So þat he° wel þore° were — *they/there*
Of here herboru herborwed° þere; — *in their shelter harbored*
And for þat° Grim þat place aute,° — *because/owned*
745 Þe stede of° Grim þe name laute,° — *place from/took*
So þat Grimesbi° calleth alle — *Grimsby*
Þat þeroffe speken° alle; — *thereof speak*
And so shulen men callen° it ay,° — *call/ever*
Bituene° þis and domesday. — *between*

750 Grim was fishere swiþe god,° — *very good*
And mikel couþe on° the flod;° — *much knew about/sea*
Mani god fish þerinne he tok,° — *took*
Boþe with neth,° and with hok.° — *net/hook*
He tok þe sturgiun and þe qual° — *whale*
755 And þe turbut and lax° withal,° — *salmon/as well*
He tok þe sele° and þe hwel;° — *seal/eel*
He spedde° ofte swiþe wel. — *prospered*
Keling° he tok, and tumberel,° — *cod/porpoise*
Hering and þe makerel,
760 Þe butte,° þe schulle,° þe þornebake.° — *flounder/plaice/skate*
Gode paniers dede° he make, — *good baskets did*
On til° him, and oþer þrinne° — *one for/three*
Til hise sones,° to beren° fish inne — *his sons/carry*
Vp o-londe,° to selle and fonge;° — *on land/receive (money)*
765 Forbar° he neyþer tun ne gronge° — *neglected/town nor farm*
Þat he ne° to yede° with his ware; — *not/went*
Kam° he neuere hom° hand-bare° — *came/never home/empty-handed*
Þat he ne broucte bred° and sowel° — *brought bread/relish*
In his shirte, or in his couel;° — *cloak*

---

735. Lindsay is on the coast of Lincolnshire.

746. Grimsby is today a fairly large town at the mouth of the Humber. Tradition has it that the town was settled by a fisherman named Grim who rescued a castaway. A 12th-century seal contains the names Grym, Habloc, and Goldenburgh; and other souvenirs of Havelok are pointed out by the townspeople. The romance is thus part of the Lincolnshire heritage.

750–85. The popular qualities of this romance are manifest in such details as Grim's fishing (cf. Havelok's dish washing and so forth, ll. 913–21). The work stands in stark contrast to the courtly *King Horn*. The fish diet in the Middle Ages was varied and extensive. Not only could fish be eaten on meatless Fridays and the numerous fast days occurring during the successive Church seasons throughout the year, but in addition it could be dried and salted away for the winter.

770 In his poke benes° and korn;°   bag beans/grain
    Hise swink° ne hauede° he nowt forlorn.°   work/had/not lost
    And hwan° he tok þe grete laumprei,°   when/great lamprey
    Ful wel he couþe þe rithe wei°   way
    To Lincolne, þe gode boru;°   town
775 Ofte he yede° it þoru and þoru,   crossed/through
    Til he hauede al wel° sold,   completely
    And þerfore° þe penies told.°   for it/pennies counted
    Þanne° he com þenne,° he° were bliþe,°   when/came thence/they/happy
    For hom he brouthe fele siþe°   brought many times
780 Wastels,° simenels with þe horn,°   cakes/horn-shaped bread
    Hise pokes fulle of mele an° korn,   flour and
    Netes° flesh, shepes,° and swines;   cattle/sheep
    And hemp to maken° of gode lines,   make
    And stronge ropes to° hise netes,°   for/nets
785 Þat in þe se° he ofte setes.°   sea/sets

    Þusgate° Grim him fayre ledde:°   in this way/led a good life
    Him and his genge° wel he fedde   household
    Wel twelf winter oþer° more: fully twelve winters or
    Hauelok was war° þat Grim swank sore°   aware/worked hard
790 For his mete,° and he lay at hom: food
    He thouthe,° "Ich° am nou no grom;°   thought/I/boy
    Ich am wel waxen,° and wel may eten°   grown/eat
    More þan euere° Grim may geten.°   ever/get
    Ich ete more, bi God on liue,°   alive
795 Þan Grim an hise children fiue!
    It ne may nouth ben° þus longe: not be
    Goddot!° y wile° with hem gange,°   By God/I will/them go
    For to leren° sum god° to gete;   learn how/good
    Swinken° ich wolde° for mi mete.   work/would
800 It is no shame forto swinken;
    Þe man þat may wel eten and drinken°   drink
    Þat nouth ne haue,° but-on° swink long;   ought not to have/except in
    To liggen° at hom it is full strong.°   lie/shameful
    God yelde° him, þer° i ne may,   requite/where
805 Þat haueth° me fed to þis day!   has
    Gladlike° i wile þe paniers bere;°   gladly/baskets carry

---

772. The great lamprey was for Grim relatively as great a catch as that of Hemingway's Old Man, though with a happier ending. It could weigh as much as five pounds and sold for the then enormous sum of three shillings, not because of its bulk but because it was regarded as a delicacy.

773–74. A distance of about thirty miles.

780. Wastel was a fine white cake-flour bread, which Chaucer's Prioress fed her little dogs. Marie Antoinette's remark "Let them eat cake," when she was told that the people had no bread, probably refers to a type of wastel bread, which was meant for the nobility.

Ich woth, ne° shal it me nouth dere,° *know, not/harm*
Þey° þer be inne° a birþene gret° *though/inside/burden great*
Al so° heui als° a neth.° *as/heavy as/ox*
810 Shal ich neuere lengere dwelle;° *never longer wait*
To-morwen° shal ich forth pelle."° *tomorrow/hasten*

On° þe morwen, hwan° it was day, *in/morning, when*
He stirt° up sone,° and nouth ne lay; *jumped/quickly*
And cast a panier on his bac,° *back*
815 With fish giueled° las° a stac;° *heaped up/in/stack*
Also michel° he bar° him one° *much/carried/alone*
So he foure,° bi° mine mone!° *as they four/on/word*
Wel he it bar, and solde it wel;
Þe siluer he brouthe hom ilk del,° *brought home every bit*
820 Al þat he þer-fore° tok:° *for it/took*
Withheld he nouth a ferþinges nok.° *farthing's bit*
So yede° he forth ilke° day, *went/each*
Þat° he neuere at home lay. *so that*
So wolde he his mester lere.°— *trade learn*
825 Bifel° it so, a strong dere° *befell/severe famine*
Bigan to rise of korn° of bred,° *grain/bread*
Þat Grim ne couþe° no god red,° *knew/counsel*
Hw° he sholde° his meine fede;° *how/should/household feed*
Of Hauelok hauede° he michel drede:° *had/worry*
830 For he was strong, and wel mouthe° ete *might*
More þanne heuere° mouthe he gete;° *ever/get*
Ne° he ne mouthe on þe se° take *nor/sea*
Neyþer lenge,° ne þornbake,° *ling/skate*
Ne non° oþer fish þat douthe° *no/was fit (that)*
835 His meyne feden° with he mouthe. *feed*
Of Hauelok he hauede kare,
Hwilkgat° þat he micthe° fare.— *in what manner/might*
Of his children was him nouth.° *he did not think*
On Hauelok was al hise þouth,° *his thought*
840 And seyde,° "Hauelok, dere sone,° *said/dear son*
I wene° that we deye mone° *think/die must*
For hunger, þis dere is so strong,
And hure mete° is uten° long. *our food/gone*
Betere is° þat þu henne gonge° *better (it) is/you hence go*
845 Þan þu here dwelle° longe; *stay*
Heþen þow mayt gangen° to° late; *hence you might go/too*

---

821. *nok:* "nook," "corner." Silver pennies were cut in half (ha'pennies) and quarters (farthings).

824. *mester:* lit., "mystery," i.e., "guild, craft," altered from Latin *ministerium*, "service" (cf. above, p. 19).

Þou canst ful° wel þe ricthe gate°   *know very/right road*
To Lincolne, þe gode borw°—   *good town*
Þou hauest it gon ful ofte þoru;°   *through*
850 Of° me, ne° is me° nouth° a slo.°   *as for/not/to me/not/sloe berry*
Betere is þat þu þider° go,   *there*
For þer is mani god° man inne:°   *many (a) good/there*
Þer þou mayt þi mete winne.
But wo° is me! þou art so naked,   *woe*
855 Of mi seyl° y wolde þe° were maked°   *sail/you/made*
A cloth, þou mighest inne gongen,°   *go*
Sone, no cold þat þu ne fonge."°   *take*

He tok þe sheres of° þe nayl,   *shears off*
And made him a couel° of þe sayl,   *cloak*
860 And Hauelok dide° it sone° on.   *put/quickly*
Hauede he neyþer hosen° ne shon,°   *hose/shoes*
Ne none kines° oþer wede;°   *no kind (of)/clothes*
To Lincolne barfot° he yede.°   *barefoot/went*
Hwan° he kam° þer, he was ful wil:°   *when/came/puzzled*
865 Ne hauede he no frend to gangen til;°   *to*
Two dayes þer fastinde° he yede,°   *fasting/walked*
Þat non° for his werk wolde° him fede;°   *because none/would/feed*
Þe þridde° day herde° he calle:°   *third/heard/called*
"Berman,° bermen, hider° forth alle!"   *porters/hither*
870 Poure° þat on fote° yede   *poor (men)/foot*
Sprongen° forth so° sparke of glede.°   *sprang/like (a)/fire*
Hauelok shof dune° nyne or ten   *shoved down*
Rith° amidewarde° þe fen,°   *right/in the middle of/mud*
And stirte° forth to þe kok,°   *rushed/cook*
875 Þer° the erles mete he tok°   *where/took*
Þat he bouthe° at þe brigge:°   *bought/bridge*
Þe bermen let he alle ligge,°   *lie*
And bar° þe mete° to þe castel,   *carried/food*
And gat him° þere a ferþing° wastel.°   *got himself/farthing's worth of/cake*
880   Þet oþer° day kepte° he ok°   *the next/watched for/also*
Swiþe yerne° þe erles kok,   *very carefully*
Til þat he say° him on þe brigge,   *saw*
And bi him mani fishes ligge.°   *lying*
Þe herles° mete hauede he bouth   *earl's*
885 Of Cornwaile,° and kalde° oft: *Cornwall/called*

---

850. I.e., "I can do no more."
876. This bridge crossed the Witham, flowing through Lincoln. The castle lies a half mile up a hill.
872–73. Havelok's actions here and in ll. 889–93 are more like the adventures of the folk hero Robin Hood in Nottingham than those of a courtly prince of chivalric romance.
884–85. *herles ... of Cornwaile:* "earl of Cornwall's."

"Bermen, bermen, hider swiþe!"°   *quickly*
Hauelok it herde, and was ful bliþe°   *happy*
Þat he herde "bermen" calle:°   *called*
Alle made he hem dun° falle   *them down*
890 Þat in his gate yeden° and stode,°   *way went/stood*
Wel° sixtene laddes gode.°   *fully/lads good*
Als° he lep° þe kok til,°   *as/leaped/toward*
He shof hem alle upon° an hyl;°   *into/pile*
Astirte° til him with his rippe,°   *hurried/basket*
895 And bigan þe fish to kippe.°   *gather up*
He bar up wel a carte-lode°   *cartload*
Of segges, laxes,° of playces brode,°   *cuttlefish, salmon/plaice broad*
Of grete laumprees,° and of eles;°   *great lampreys/eels*
Sparede he neyþer tos ne heles°   *toes nor heels (in his hurry)*
900 Til þat he to þe castel cam,
Þat° men fro° him his birþene nam.°   *when/from/burden took*
Þan° men haueden holpen° him doun   *when/had helped*
With þe birþene of° his croun,°   *from/head*
Þe kok stod, and on him low,°   *smiled*
905 And þoute° him stalworþe° man ynow,°   *thought/stalwart/enough*
And seyde,° "Wiltu° ben wit° me?   *said/will you/stay with*
Gladlike wile ich feden þe;°   *gladly will I feed you*
Wel is set° þe mete þu etes,°   *earned/you eat*
And þe hire° þat þu getes."°   *pay/get*
910 "Goddot!"° quoth° he, "leue° sire,   *by God/said/dear*
Bidde° ich you° non° oþer hire: *ask/of you/no/*
But yeueþ° me inow° to ete,   *(if you) give/enough*
Fir° and water y wile° you fete,°   *firewood/I will/fetch*
Þe fir° blowe, an ful wele maken;°   *fire/and very well make*
915 Stickes kan ich breken° and kraken,°   *break/crack*
And kindlen° ful wel a fyr,   *kindle*
And maken it to brennen shir;°   *burn brightly*
Ful wel kan ich cleuen shides,°   *split kindling*
Eles to-turuen° of here° hides;   *skin/their*
920 Ful wel kan ich dishes swilen,°   *wash*
And don° al þat ye euere wilen."°   *do/ever want*
Quoth þe kok,° "Wile i no more;   *cook*
Go þu yunder,° and sit þore,°   *yonder/there*
And y shal yeue þe ful fair bred,°   *bread*
925 And make þe broys° in þe led.°   *broth/kettle*
Sit now doun and et° ful yerne:°   *eat/heartily*
Daþeit hwo° þe mete werne!"°   *cursed (be he) who/food refuses*

913–21. This section (and also ll. 932–45), extremely unusual in a romance, points up the bourgeois sympathies, if not temperament, of the author and appeals to the interests of his intended audience.

Hauelok sette him dun anon°   *himself down immediately*
Also° stille als a ston,°   *as/stone*

930 Til he hauede ful wel eten;
Þo° hauede Hauelok fayre geten.°   *then/made out well*
Hwan° he hauede eten inow,   *when*
He kam° to þe welle, water updrow,°   *came/drew up*
And filde° þer a michel so;°   *filled/ great tub*
935 Bad° he non° ageyn him go;°   *asked/none/for help*
But bitwen° his hondes° he bar° it in,   *between/hands/carried*
Al him one,° to þe kichin.°   *alone/kitchen*
Bad he non him water to fete,
Ne° fro brigge° to bere° þe mete.   *nor/(the) bridge/carry*
940 He bar þe turues,° he bar þe star,°   *peat/star-grass (for kindling)*
Þe wode° fro the brigge he bar;   *wood*
Al þat euere shulden he nytte,°   *should they use*
Al he drow,° and al he citte;°   *drew/cut*
Wolde° he neuere hauen° rest,   *would/never have*
945 More þan° he were a best.°   *than (if)/beast*
Of alle men was he mest meke,°   *most gentle*
Lauhwinde ay,° and bliþe° of speke;° *laughing ever/happy/speech*
Euere he was glad and bliþe:
His sorwe° he couþe° ful wel miþe.°   *sorrow/could/hide*
950 It ne° was non so litel knaue,°   *there not/boy*
For to leyken,° ne forto plawe,°   *sport/play*
Þat he ne wolde with him pleye:°   *play*
Þe children that yeden° in þe weie°   *ran/way*
Of him, he deden° al here wille,   *did*
955 And with him leykeden° here fille.   *them played*
Him loueden° alle, stille° and bolde,   *loved/shy*
Knictes,° children, yunge and holde;°   *knights/old*
Alle him loueden þat him sowen,°   *saw*
Boþen heye° men and lowe.   *both high*
960 Of him ful wide þe word sprong,°   *sprang*
Hw° he was mikel,° hw he was strong,   *how/big*
Hw fayr man° God him hauede maked,° *(a) man/had made*
But-on° þat he was almest° naked: *except/almost*
For he ne hauede nouth° to shride°   *nothing/wear*
965 But a kouel ful unride,°   *cloak very coarse*
Þat was ful,° and swiþe wicke,°   *foul/very wretched*
Was it nouth° worth a fir-sticke.° *not/piece of firewood*
Þe cok° bigan of° him to rewe,°   *cook/on/take pity*
And bouthe° him cloþes, al spannewe;° *bought/brand new*
970 He bouthe him boþe hosen° and shon,°   *hose/shoes*
And sone dide° him dones° on.   *soon made/put (them)*

Hwan° he was cloþed, hosed, and shod,	*when*
Was non° so fayr under God,	*(there) was none*
Þat euere yete in° erþe were,	*ever yet on*
975 Non þat euere moder bere;°	*mother bore*
It was neuere man þat yemede°	*ruled*
In kinneriche,° þat so wel semede°	*(a) kingdom/fit seemed*
King or cayser° forto be	*emperor*
Þan° he was shrid, so° semede he;	*when/clothed, as*
980 For þanne° he weren° alle samen°	*when/were/together*
At Lincolne, at þe gamen,°	*games*
And þe erles men woren° al þore,°	*were/there*
Þan° was Hauelok bi þe shuldren more°	*then/shoulders taller*
Þan þe meste° þat þer kam:°	*biggest/came*
985 In armes him noman nam°	*took (in wrestling)*
Þat he doune° sone ne caste.°	*down/did throw*
Hauelok stod° ouer hem als° a mast;	*stood/them like*
Als° he was heie,° als he was long,°	*as/high/tall*
He was boþe stark° and strong;	*powerful*
990 In Engelond was non hise per°	*his peer*
Of° strengþe þat euere kam him ner.°	*in/near*
Als he was strong, so was he softe:°	*gentle*
Þey° a man him misdede° ofte,	*though/mistreated*
Neuere° more he him misseyde,°	*never/answered angrily*
995 Ne hond° on him with yuele° leyde.°	*nor hand/ill intent/laid*
Of bodi was he mayden clene;°	*maiden-pure*
Neuere yete in game,° ne in grene,°	*sport/passion*
With horc ne wolde° he leyke° ne lye,°	*whore not would/play/lie*
No more þan it° were a strie.°	*if she/hag*
1000 In þat time al Hengelond°	*England*
Þerl° Godrich hauede° in his hond,	*the earl/had*
And he gart komen° into þe tun°	*made come/town*
Mani° erl and mani barun;	*many (an)*
And alle þat liues° were	*alive*
1005 In Englond þanne° wer þere	*then*
Þat þey haueden after° sent	*had for*
To ben° þer at þe parlement.	*be*
With hem com mani° champioun,	*came many (a)*

985–86. This type of wrestling, called officially Greco-Roman, is still popular in Grasmere, as well as all over Switzerland, where it is known as *Schwingen*. The contestants hold each other by loose burlap towels around the waist or shoulders or lock arms around each other and try to produce a fall.

1007. The parliament referred to here may be the one held at Lincoln in 1300–1, and scholars have attempted to date the poem from this reference. But many parliaments were held at Lincoln before this, the first recorded being in 1213; and much earlier the *Lai d'Havelok* also mentions Havelok's athletic prowess, thus making the reference here less likely to be to a historical parliament.

1008. *Champion:* Cf. l. 1037n.

Mani with° ladde, blac and brown;	*athletic*
1010 An fel° it so þat yunge men,	*and befell*
Wel abouten° nine or ten,	*fully about*
Bigunnen° þere for to layke:°	*began/wrestle*
Þider komen° boþe stronge and wayke:°	*there came/weak*
Þider komen lesse° and more°	*low/high*
1015 Þat in þe borw° þanne weren þore;	*town*
Chaunpiouns° and starke° laddes,	*champions/strong*
Bondemen° with here gaddes,°	*serfs/their goads*
Als he comen fro° þe plow;	*(just) as they came from*
Þere was sembling inow!°	*assembly enough*
1020 For it° ne was non° horse-knaue,°	*there/no/stable boy*
Þouh° þei sholden° in honde haue,°	*though/should/be at work*
Þat he ne kam þider, þe leyk° to se:°	*sport/see*
Biforn° here fet° þanne lay a tre,°	*in front of/feet/beam (as foul line)*
And putten° with a mikel ston°	*put/great stone*
1025 Þe starke laddes, ful god won.°	*with vigor*
Þe ston was mikel° and ek greth,°	*big/also great*
And al so heui so° a neth;°	*as heavy as/ox*
Grund-stalwrþe° man he sholde be	*very strong*
Þat mouthe liften° it to his kne;°	*might lift/knee*
1030 Was þer neyþer clerc ne prest,°	*priest*
Þat mithe° liften it to his brest.	*might*
Þerwit° putten the chaunpiouns	*therewith*
Þat þider comen with þe barouns;	
Hwo-so° mithe putten þore°	*whoso/there*
1035 Biforn anoþer an inch or more,	
Wore° he yung, wore he hold,°	*were/old*
He was for a kempe told.°	*champion held*
Al-so° þei stoden° an ofte stareden,°	*so/stood/stared*
Þe chaunpiouns and ek the ladden;°	*lads*
1040 And he maden° mikel strout°	*made/competition*
Abouten þe alþerbeste but,°	*best effort*
Hauelok stod and loked þer-til;°	*looked on*
And of puttingge he was ful wil,°	*quite ignorant*
For neuere yete ne° saw he or°	*never yet not/before*
1045 Putten the ston, or þanne þor.°	*that time*
Hise mayster bad° him gon° þer-to,	*his master commanded/to go*
Als° he couþe° þer-with do.°	*as (best)/could/to do*

1009. *blac and brown:* The phrase is most probably used as an all-inclusive tag meaning "light [OE *blaec*, "pale"; cf. l. 311*n*] and dark" (i.e., "everyone"; cf. ll. 1729–30, 2001–6, 2068–70, 2515–16, 2667–69). It could, however, refer to black and brown as typical colors of the peasantry, red and white usually being those of the nobles.

1037. *kempe:* usually "fighter" (cf. Middle High German *Kempe*, "knight"), but here seems to have the value of Mod. Eng. "champion," while ME *champioun* refers to a merely average athlete. Both words derive from Latin *campus*, the "field" where action (generally military) takes place (cf. p. 73, l. 608*n*).

Þo° hise mayster it him bad, — *when*
He was of him sore adrad;° — *greatly afraid*
1050 Þerto he stirte° sone anon,° — *hurried/quickly*
And kipte° up þat heui ston — *picked*
Þat he sholde puten wiþe;° — *put with*
He putte, at þe firste siþe,° — *time*
Ouer alle þat þer wore
1055 Twelue fote° and sumdel° more. — *feet/somewhat*
Þe chaunpiouns° þat put sowen;° — *champions/saw*
Shuldreden he ilc° oþer and lowen:° — *shouldered (i.e., nudged) they each/
laughed*

Wolden° he no more to putting gange,° — *would/go*
But seyde,° "We dwellen her to° longe!" — *said/stay here too*
1060 Þis selkouth° mithe nouth ben hyd;° — *marvel/not be hidden*
Ful sone° it was ful loude° kid° — *very soon/loudly/made known*
Of Hauelok, hw° he warp° þe ston — *how/threw*
Ouer þe laddes euerilkon;° — *every one*
Hw he was fayr, hw he was long,° — *tall*
1065 Hw he was with,° hw he was strong; — *bold*
Þoruth° England yede° þe speche,° — *through/went/tale*
Hw he was strong and ek meke;° — *also gentle*
In the castel, up in þe halle,
Þe knithes speken° þerof alle, — *knights spoke*
1070 So that Godrich it herde° wel: — *heard*
Þei spcken of Hauelok, eueri del,° — *in every particular*
Hw he was strong man and hey,° — *tall*
Hw he was strong, and ek fri,° — *generous*
And þouthte° Godrich, "Þoru° þis knaue° — *thought/through/boy*
1075 Shal ich° Engelond al haue, — *I*
And mi sone° after me; — *son*
For so i wile° þat it be. — *will*
The king Aþelwald me dide swere° — *made swear*
Vpon al þe messe-gere° — *mass implements*
1080 Þat y shulde° his douther yeue° — *I should/daughter give*
Þe hexte° man þat mithe° liue. — *highest/might*
Þe beste, þe fairest, þe strangest ok;° — *strongest also*
Þat gart° he me sweren° on þe bok.° — *made/swear/book*
Hwere° mithe i finden° ani so hey° — *where/find/high*
1085 So° Hauelok is, or so sley?° — *as/skillful*
Þou° y southe° heþen° into Ynde,° — *though/sought/from here/to India*
So fayr, so strong, ne° mithe y finde. — *not*

1050–55. Robert Mannyng of Brunne, writing in 1338, mentions that the stone thrown by Havelok was still preserved in Lincoln Castle.

1078–85. Godrich rationalizes that he is not breaking his oath to King Athelwald: he is giving the "highest" (i.e., tallest—but not, in his opinion, noblest) man to Goldeboro as husband

Hauelok is þat ilke° knaue   *the very*
Þat shal Goldeborw haue!"
1090 Þis þouthe° he with trechery,   *thought*
Wit traysoun,° and wit felony;   *with treason*
For he wende° þat Hauelok wore° *thought/were*
Sum cherles° sone, and no more; *some serf's*
Ne shulde he hauen° of Engellond *have*
1095 Onlepi° forw° in his hond°   *a single/furrow/hand*
With hire° þat was þerof eyr, °   *her/heir*
Þat boþe was god° and swiþe° fair. *good/very*
He wende þat Hauelok wer a þral;° *thrall*
Þerþoru° he wende hauen° al   *in this way/to have*
1100 In Engelond, þat hire rith° was— *right*
He was werse þan Sathanas°   *Satan*
Þat Iesu° Crist in erþe stoc!°   *Jesus/shut up*
Hanged worþe° he on an hok!°   *ought to be/oak*

After° Goldeborw sone° he sende,° *for/soon/sent*
1105 Þat was boþe fayr and hende,° *gracious*
And dide° hire to Lincolne bringe; *did*
Belles dede° he ageyn hire° ringen,° *had/for her arrival/rung*
And ioie° he made hire swiþe mikel;° *joy/great*
But neþeles° he was ful swikel.° *nevertheless/very treacherous*
1110 He seyde° þat he sholde° hire yeue *said/should*
Þe fayreste man þat mithe liue.
She answerede and seyde anon,° *immediately*
Bi Crist and bi seint Iohan,°   *Saint John*
Þat hire sholde noman wedde
1115 Ne noman bringen° hire to bedde, *bring*
But° he were king or kinges eyr, *unless*
Were he neuere° man so fayr.   *never*

Godrich þe erl was swiþe wroth° *angry*
Þat she swor swilk° an oth,°   *such/oath*
1120 And seyde, "Hwor° þou wilt be *whether*
Quen° and leuedi° ouer me?   *queen/lady*
Þou shalt hauen a gadeling°   *rogue*
Ne° shalt þou hauen non° oþer þing! *nor/no*
Þe° shal spusen° mi cokes knaue:° *you/marry/cook's boy*
1125 Shalt þou non oþer louerd° haue! *lord*
Daþeit° þat þe oþer yeue°   *cursed (be he)/another gives*
Eueremore hwil° i liue!   *evermore while*
To-morwe sholen° ye ben weddeth,° *tomorrow shall/be wedded*
And, maugre þin° togidere beddeth.° *in spite of you/together bedded*
1130 Goldeborw gret° and yaf hire ille;° *lamented/was sad*

She wolde° ben ded bi hire wille.	*would*
On° þe morwen hwan° day was sprungen,°	*in/morning when/sprung*
And day-belle° at kirke rungen,°	*morning bells/church rung*
And Hauelok sente þat Iudas	
1135 Þat werse was þanne Sathanas,	
And seyde, "Mayster,° wilte° wif?"°	*master/do you want/(a) wife*
"Nay," quoth° Hauelok, "bi my lif!°	*said/life*
Hwat° sholde ich° with wif do?	*what/I*
I ne° may hire fede° ne cloþe ne sho.°	*not/her feed/shoe*
1140 Wider° sholde ich wimman° bringe?	*whither/woman*
I ne haue none kines þinge.°	*nothing of any kind*
I ne haue hws, y° ne haue cote,°	*house, I/cottage*
I ne haue stikke, y ne haue sprote,°	*twig (for firewood)*
I ne haue neyþer bred° ne sowel°	*bread/relish*
1145 Ne cloth,° but of° an hold with couel.°	*clothes/only/old white cloak*
Þis° cloþes þat ich onne haue	*these*
Aren° þe kokes,° and ich his knaue."°	*are/cook's/boy*
Godrich stirt° up and on him dong°	*jumped/struck*
With dintes swiþe° hard and strong,	*blows very*
1150 And seyde,° "But° þou hire take	*said/unless*
Þat y wole yeuen° þe to make,°	*will give/for mate*
I shal hangen° þe ful heye,°	*hang/very high*
Or y shal þristen uth þin heie."°	*put out your eyes*
Hauelok was one° and was adrad,°	*alone/afraid*
1155 And grauntede him° al þat he bad.°	*agreed to/commanded*
Þo sende° he after° hire sone,°	*then sent/for/soon*
Þe fayrest wymman under monc;°	*(the) moon*
And seyde til° hire, fals and slike,°	*to/treacherous*
Þat wicke þral,° þat foule swike:°	*wicked thrall/traitor*
1160 "But þu° þis man understonde,°	*you/accept*
I shal flemen° þe of londe;°	*exile/from (the) land*
Or þou shalt to þe galwes renne,°	*gallows run*
And þer þou shalt in a fir brenne."°	*fire burn*
Sho° was adrad for he so þrette,°	*she/threatened*
1165 And durste nouth° þe spusing lette;°	*dared not/marriage stop*
But þey° hire likede° swiþe ille,	*though/(it) pleased*
Sho þouthe° it was Godes wille:	*thought*
God, þat makes to growen° þe korn,°	*grow/grain*
Formede hire wimman to be born.	
1170 Hwan he° hauede don° him,° for drede,°	*he (i.e., Godrich)/had made/ (i.e., Havelok)/fear*

1131. I.e., "she would have liked to be dead."
1133. Cf. p. 167, l. 1024n.

1162. The pronoun *þou* refers to Havelok, who will be hanged; in the next line it is Goldeboro who will be burned.

Þat he sholde° hire spusen° and fede,° *should/marry/keep*
And þat she sholde til him holde,
Þer weren penies þicke tolde,° *were pennies many counted*
Mikel plente° upon þe bok:° *(a) great amount/book*
1175 He ys° hire yaf,° and she is tok.° *his/gave/his took*
He° weren spused fayre° and wel, *they/properly*
Þe messe° he dede°—eueridel° *mass/read/every part*
Þat fel to° spusing—a god° clerk, *concerned/good*
Þe erchebishop° uth of Yerk,° *archbishop/York*
1180 Þat kam° to þe parlement, *came*
Als° God him hauede þider° sent. *as/there*

Hwan° he weren togydere° in Godes lawe *when/together*
Þat° þe folc ful wel it sawe, *so that*
He ne wisten hwat° he mouthen,° *not knew what/might (do)*
1185 Ne° he ne wisten wat° hem° douthe,° *nor/what/for them/was best*
Þer to dwellen,° or þenne° to gonge.° *stay/away/go*
Þer ne wolden° he dwellen longe, *would*
For he wisten and ful wel sawe
Þat Godrich hem° hatede, þe deuel° him hawe!° *them/Devil/take*
1190 And yf he dwelleden° þer outh,° *stayed/at all*
Þat fel° Hauelok ful wel on° þouth *it occurred to/in*
Men sholde don° his leman° shame, *do/loved one*
Or elles bringen° in wicke blame,° *else bring/ill repute*
Þat were him leuere to° ben ded.° *than which he would rather/be dead*
1195 Forþi° he token° anoþer red:° *therefore/took/counsel*
Þat þei sholden° þenne fle° *should/flee*
Til° Grim, and til hise sones þre;° *to/his sons three*
Þer wenden° he alþerbest° to spede,° *thought/best/succeed*
Hem° forto cloþe and for to fede.° *themselves/feed*
1200 Þe lond he token under fote°— *foot*
Ne wisten° he non° oþer bote°— *knew/no/remedy*
And helden ay° the rithe sti° *held always/right way*
Til he komen° to Grimesby. *came*
Þanne° he komen þere, þanne° was Grim ded: *when/then*

1173–74. Money paid out "upon the book," as the Salisbury Missal prescribed, may have been the clerk's payment, or a symbol that husband and wife were one body and that they shared property. It may also have been a survival of the Anglo-Saxon *morgengifu*, the present which the husband made to the wife on the morning after the wedding night. Occasionally the gift was made ahead of time, perhaps as a sign of trust and confidence (cf. the Old English *Apollonius of Tyre*). The custom is still found in Germanic countries.

1179. For a long time the archbishops of York and of Canterbury were in competition for the primacy of the English church.

1192. The *jus primae noctis*, "right of the first night," was in many countries equivalent with the *droit du seigneur*, "right of the lord": that is, the legal right of a lord to spend the wedding night with a vassal's bride. (This, of course, is a theme in the Mozart-Beaumarchais opera *The Marriage of Figaro*.) Havelok is obviously afraid that the *jus primae noctis* may be applied to his wife.

1200. I.e., "they started walking."

1205 Of° him ne haueden° he no red; *from/had*
But hise children, alle fyue,
Alle weren yet on liue,° *alive*
Þat ful fayre ayen° hem neme° *very pleasantly toward/went*
Hwan he wisten þat he keme,° *came*
1210 And maden ioie swiþe° mikel, *made joy very*
Ne weren he neuere° ayen hem fikel.° *never/disloyal*
On knes° ful fayre° he hem setten *knees/courteously*
And Hauelok swiþe fayre gretten,° *greeted*
And seyden,° "Welkome, louerd dere!° *said/lord dear*
1215 And welkome be þi fayre fere!° *companion*
Blessed be þat ilke þrawe° *the very time*
Þat þou hire toke in Godes lawe!
Wel is hus° we sen þe° on lyue. *we are glad/see you*
Þou mithe° us boþe selle and yeue,° *might/give (away)*
1220 Þou mayt° us boþe yeue and selle, *might*
Withþat° þou wilt° here dwelle. *if/will*
We hauen,° louerd, alle gode,° *have/good (things)*
Hors and neth° and ship on flode,° *cattle/sea*
Gold and siluer and michel auchte,° *much property*
1225 Þat Grim ure fader° us° bitawchte.° *our father/to us/committed*
Gold and siluer and oþer fe° *goods*
Bad° he us bitaken° þe.° *asked/to commit/to you*
We hauen shep,° we hauen swin;° *sheep/swine*
Bileue her,° louerd, and al be° þin!° *stay here/shall be/yours*
1230 Þou shalt ben° louerd, þou shalt ben syre, *be*
And we sholen seruen° þe and hire; *shall serve*
And hure° sistres sholen do *our*
Al that euere biddes sho:° *ever asks she*
He° sholen hire cloþes washen° and wringen,° *they/wash/wring*
1235 And to hondes° water bringen;° *for (her) hands/bring*
He sholen bedden° hire and þe, *bed*
For leuedi wile° we þat she be." *lady (i.e., our mistress) want*
Hwan° he þis ioie haueden maked,° *when/made*
Sithen stikes broken° and kraked,° *afterwards sticks (they) broke/*
  cracked

1240 And þe fir° brouth on brenne;° *fire/made burn*
Ne° was þer spared gos ne° henne, *not/goose nor*
Ne þe hende° ne þe drake: *duck*
Mete° he deden plente° make; *food/did plenty*
Ne wantede° þere no god° mete, *lacked/good*
1245 Wyn° and ale deden he fete,° *wine/fetch*
And hem made glade and bliþe:° *happy*
Wesseyl ledden° he fele siþe.° *healths drank/many to*
  On° þe nith, als° Goldeborw lay, *in/night, as*

Sory and sorwful° was she ay,°　　　　　　　　　*sorrowful/ever*
1250 For she wende° she were biswike°　　　　　*thought/betrayed*
Þat she were yeuen un-kyndelike.°　　　　　*married unnaturally (i.e., below*
　　　　　　　　　　　　　　　　　　　　　　　her rank)

O° nith saw she þer-inne a lith,°　　　　　　*at/light*
A swiþe° fayr, a swiþe bryth,°　　　　　　　　*very/bright*
Al so° brith, al so shir°　　　　　　　　　　　*as/shining*
1255 So° it were a blase° of fir.　　　　　　　　*as if/blaze*
She lokede° norþ, and ek° south,　　　　　　*looked/also*
And saw it comen ut° of his mouth　　　　　　*coming out*
Þat lay bi hire° in þe bed:　　　　　　　　　*her*
No ferlike þou° she were adred!°　　　　　　*wonder if/afraid*
1260 Þouthe° she, "Wat° may this bimene?°　　　*thought/what/mean*
He beth° heyman° yet, als y wene:°　　　　　*will be/(a)/nobleman/I guess*
He beth heyman er° he be ded!"°　　　　　　*before/is dead*
On hise shuldre,° of gold red　　　　　　　　*his shoulder*
She saw a swiþe noble croiz;°　　　　　　　　*cross*
1265 Of an angel she herde° a uoyz:°　　　　　*heard/voice*

"Goldeborw, lat° þi sorwe° be;　　　　　　　*let/sorrow*
For Hauelok, þat haueþ spuset þe,°　　　　　*has married you*
He° kinges sone° and kinges eyr;°　　　　　　*he (is)/son/heir*
Þat bikenneth° þat croiz so fayr.　　　　　　*indicates*
1270 It bikenneth more: þat he shal
Denemark hauen,° and Englond al;　　　　　　*have*
He shal ben° king, strong and stark,°　　　　*be/powerful*
Of Engelond and Denemark:
Þat shal þu with þen eyne sen,°　　　　　　　*you with your eyes see*
1275 And þou shalt quen° and leuedi ben!"　　*queen*

Þanne° she hauede° herd þe steuene°　　　　*when/had/voice*
Of þe angel uth° of heuene,°　　　　　　　　*out/heaven*
She was so fele siþes° bliþe　　　　　　　　　*very greatly*
Þat she ne mithe° hire ioie mythe;°　　　　　*not might/joy hide*
1280 But Hauelok sone anon° she kiste,°　　　*quickly/kissed*
And he slep° and nouth° ne wiste.°　　　　　*slept/nothing (of it)/knew*
Hwan° þat aungel hauede seyd,°　　　　　　　*when/spoken*
Of° his slep anon° he brayd,°　　　　　　　　*from/sleep immediately/woke*
And seide, "Lemman, slepes° þou?　　　　　　*darling, sleep*
1285 A selkuth drem° dremede me nou:°　　　　*strange dream/I (just) now*

Herkne° nou hwat° me° haueth met!°　　　　*listen/to what/I/dreamed*

_____

1263. *gold red:* Cf. l. 47*n.*

Me þouthe° y was in Denemark set,   *it seemed*
But on on þe moste hil°   *one (of) the highest hills*
Þat euere yete kam° i til.°   *ever yet came/to*
1290 It was so hey,° þat y wel mouthe°   *high/might*
Al þe werd se, als° me þouthe.   *world see, as*
Als i sat upon þat lowe,°   *hill*
I bigan Denemark for to awe,°   *possess*
Þe borwes° and þe castles stronge;   *towns*
1295 And mine armes weren° so longe   *were*
Þat i fadmede,° al at ones,°   *embraced/once*
Denemark, with mine longe bones;
And þanne y wolde° mine armes drawe   *would*
Til me, and hem° for to haue,   *them*
1300 Al that euere in Denemark liueden°   *lived*
On mine armes faste clyueden;°   *clung*
And þe stronge castles alle
On knes bigunnen° for to falle;   *knees began*
Þe keyes fellen° at mine fet.°
1305 Anoþer drem dremede me ek:°   *also*
Þat ich fley° ouer þe salte se°   *I flew/sea*
Til Engeland, and al with me   *fell/feet*
Þat euere was in Denemark lyues°   *alive*
But bondemen° and here° wiues;   *except serfs/their*
1310 And þat ich kom° til Engelond,   *came*
Al closede° it intil min hond,°   *enclosed/in my hand*
And, Goldeborw, y gaf° it þe:°   *I gave/to you*
Deus!° lemman, hwat may þis be?"   *God*
Sho° answerede and seyde sone:°   *she/said quickly*
1315 "Iesu° Crist, þat made mone,°   *Jesus/(the) moon*
Þine dremes turne to ioye, . . .

. . . . . .

Þat wite þw° that sittes in trone!°   *know you/on throne*
Ne non° strong, king ne caysere,°   *none (so)/nor emperor*
So° þou shalt be, for þou shalt bere°   *as/wear*
1320 In Engelond corune° yet.   *crown*
Denemark shal knele° to þi fet: *kneel*
Alle þe castles þat aren° þer-inne   *are*
Shaltow,° lemman, ful° wel winne.   *shall you/very*
I woth° so wel so° ich it sowe,°   *know/as if/saw*
1325 To þe shole comen° heye and lowe,   *you shall come*
And alle þat in Denemark wone,°   *live*

1316. Several lines have been lost following this one.

Em° and broþer, fader° and sone,°   *uncle/father/son*
Erl and baroun, dreng an þayn,°   *vassal and thane*
Knithes° and burgeys° and sweyn,°   *knights/citizens/peasants*
1330 And mad° king heyelike° and wel.   *(you shall be) made/solemnly*
Denemark shal be þin° euere-ilc del:°   *yours/every bit*
Haue þou nouth þeroffe douthe,°   *not thereof doubt*
Nouth þe worth of one nouthe,°   *nut*
Þeroffe withinne þe firste yer°   *year*
1335 Shalt þou ben° king, withouten were.°   *be/without doubt*
But do nou als° y wile rathe:°   *as/wish quickly*
Nimen we° to Denemark baþe,°   *let us go/both*
And do þou nouth on frest° þis fare;°   *delay/journey*
Lith° and selthe felawes° are.   *lightness* (i.e., *initiative*)/
                 prosperity companions

1340 For shal ich neuere bliþe° be   *never happy*
Til i with eyen Denemark se;°   *see*
For ich woth þat al þe lond°   *land*
Shalt þou hauen° in þin° hond.   *have/your*
Prey° Grimes sones, alle þre,°   *ask/three*
1345 Þat he wenden° forþ with þe;   *they go*
I wot° he wilen° þe nouth werne:°   *know/will/refuse*
With þe wende shulen° he yerne,°   *shall/eagerly*
For he louen° þe hertelike.°   *love/heartily*
Þou maght° telle he aren quike,°   *might/ready*
1350 Hwore-so° he o worde° aren;   *wherever/in (the) world*
Þere° ship þou do hem **swithe**° yaren,°   *their/have them quickly/make ready*
And loke° þat þou dwelle° nouth: *see/hesitate*
Dwelling haueth° ofte scaþe wrouth.''°   *has/harm caused*

Hwan° Hauelok herde þat° she radde,°   *when/heard what/advised*
1355 Sone° it was day, sone° he him° cladde,   *as soon as/quickly/himself*
And sone° to þe kirke yede°   *immediately/church went*
Or° he dide° ani oþer dede;°   *before/did/deed*
And bifor þe rode° bigan° falle,   *cross/did*
Croiz° and Crist bigan to kalle,°   *cross/invoke*
1360 And seyde, "Louerd,° þat al weldes,°   *Lord/controls*
Wind and water, wodes° and feldes,°   *forests/fields*
For þe holi milce° of you,   *mercy*
Haue merci of° me, louerd, nou,   *on*
And wreke° me yet on mi fo,°   *avenge/foe*
1365 Þat ich saw biforn min eyne slo°   *before my eyes slay*

1365–75. Summaries and recapitulations like this passage and ll. 1401–35 (cf. ll. 2025–60) were meant for latecomers; or they initiated a new period of storytelling, since the romances were hardly ever told in one sitting. Usually the telling of the tales spanned several days. If the poems were sung or chanted to musical accompaniment, they could be drawn out to great lengths.

Mine sistres with a knif,°   *knife*
And siþen wolde° me mi lyf°   *afterwards would/of my life*
Haue reft,° for in þe se°   *deprived/sea*
Bad° he Grim **haue**° **drenched**° me.   *commanded/to have/drowned*
1370 He hath mi lond with mikel vnrith,°   *great injustice*
With michel wrong, with mikel plith,°   *harm*
For i **ne misdede**° him **neuere**° nouth,°   *not injured/never/not at all*
And haueth me to sorwe brouth.°   *sorrow brought*
He haueth me do° mi mete° to þigge,°   *caused/food/beg*
1375 And ofte in sorwe and pine ligge.°   *pain lie*
Louerd, haue merci of me,
And late° me wel passe° þe se—   *let/safely cross*
Þouh ich° haue þeroffe douthe° and kare°—   *though I/thereof fear/anxiety*
With-uten° stormes ouerfare,°   *without/cross*
1380 Þat° y ne drenched be þerine,°   *so that/therein*
Ne° forfaren° for no sinne;   *nor/be lost*
And bringge me wel to þe lond°   *land*
Þat Godard haldes° in his hond,°   *holds/hand*
Þat is mi rith,° eueri del:°   *right/every bit*
1385 Iesu° Crist, þou wost° it wel!"   *Jesus/know*

Þanne° he hauede° his bede seyd,°   *when/had/prayer said*
His offrende° on þe auter leyd,°   *offering/altar laid*
His leue at° Iesu Crist he tok,°   *leave of/took*
And at his suete moder ok,°   *sweet mother (Mary) also*
1390 And at þe croiz þat he biforn lay;
Siþen° yede sore grotinde awey.°   *then/greatly weeping away*

Hwan he com hom,° he wore yare,°   *came home/they were ready*
Grimes sones,° forto fare   *sons*
Into þe se, fishes to gete,°   *catch*
1395 Þat Hauelok mithe° wel of ete.   *might*
But Auelok þouthe al anoþer.°   *intended quite otherwise*
First he kalde° þe heldeste° broþer,   *called/eldest*
Roberd° þe Rede,° bi his name,   *Robert/Red*
Wiliam Wenduth and Huwe° Rauen,   *Hugh*
1400 Grimes sones alle þre,°   *three*
And seyde, "Liþes° nou alle to me;   *listen*
Louerdinges,° ich wile° you sheue°   *lords/will/show*
A þing of me þat ye wel knewe.
Mi fader° was king of Denshe° lond: *father/Danish*
1405 Denemark was al in his hond
Þe day þat he was quik° and ded;°   *alive/dead*

1406. I.e., "all his life."

But þanne° hauede he wicke red,°	*then/wicked counsel*
Þat he me and Denemark al	
And mine sistres bitawte° a þral:°	*committed to/thrall*
1410 A deueles lime° he hus° bitawte,	*devil's limb/us*
And al his lond and al hise authe,°	*his possessions*
For y° saw þat fule fend°	*I/foul fiend*
Mine sistres slo° with hise hend;°	*slay/hand*
First he shar° a-two° here° þrotes,	*cut/in two/their*
1415 And siþen hem° al to grotes,°	*then them/bits*
And siþen bad° he in þe se°	*commanded/sea*
Grim, youre fader, drenchen° me.	*to drown*
Deplike dede° he him swere°	*solemnly made/swear*
On bok,° þat he sholde° me bere°	*book/should/carry*
1420 Vnto þe se, an° drenchen ine,°	*and/therein*
And he wolde taken° on him þe sinne.	*would take*
But Grim was wis° and swiþe hende;°	*wise/very kind*
Wolde he nouth° his soule shende;°	*not/harm*
Leuere was him to° be forsworen	*he would rather*
1425 Þan drenchen me, and ben forlorn;°	*be lost*
But sone° bigan he forto fle°	*quickly/flee*
Fro° Denemark, forto° berwen° me.	*from/in order to/protect*
For yif ich hauede° þer ben funden,°	*if I had/been found*
Hauede° he ben slayn or harde bunden,°	*would have/bound*
1430 And heye° ben henged° on a tre:°	*high/hanged/tree*
Hauede gon for° him gold ne fe.°	*availed/(neither) gold nor money*
For-þi° fro Denemark hider° he fledde,	*therefore/hither*
And me ful fayre° and ful wel fedde,°	*very kindly/nurtured*
So þat vn-to þis day	
1435 Haue ich ben fed and fostred ay.°	*always*
But nou° ich am up to þat helde°	*now (that)/age*
Cumen,° that ich may wepne welde,°	*come/weapon carry*
And y may grete dintes yeue,°	*great blows give*
Shal i neuere hwil° ich lyue°	*never while/live*
1440 Ben glad, til that ich Denemark se;°	*see*
I preie° you þat ye wende° with me,	*pray/go*
And ich may mak you riche men;	
Ilk° of you shal haue castles ten,	*each*
And þe lond° þat þortil longes,°	*land/thereto belongs*
1445 Borwes, tunes, wodes,° and wonges.° . . .	*cities, towns, forests/fields*

· · · · ·

1410. *deueles lime:* i.e., "rascal."

1445. Following this line a long passage, one leaf, has been lost from the MS; Madden counted it as 180 lines. Perhaps the section contained the information that Grim's sons go with Havelok, sell their property in exchange for peddler's goods and a ring, and sail to Denmark. As they land on the beach, Ubbe, an important Danish noble, rides up, and Havelok asks permission to sell his goods in town.

With swilk als° ich byen° shal: *such as/buy*
Þerof biseche° ich you nou leue;°   *ask/leave*
Wile° ich speke with non° oþer reue,°   *will/no/official*
But with þe,° þat iustise° are,   *you/judge*
1450 Þat y mithe° seken° mi ware   *might/? seek*
In gode borwes° up and doun,   *good towns*
And faren° ich wile fro tun° to tun.''   *travel/from town*
A gold ring drow° he forth anon°   *drew/immediately*
An hundred pund° was worth þe ston°   *pounds/stone*
1455 And yaf° it Ubbe° for to spede.°   *gave/to Ubbe/hoping for success*
He was ful wis þat first yaf mede;°   *reward (also bribe)*
And so was Hauelok ful wis here:
He solde his gold ring ful dere:°   *dearly*
Was neuere non° so dere sold   *none*
1460 Fro chapmen,° neyþer yung ne old: *by merchants*
Þat sholen° ye forthward° ful wel heren,°   *shall/now/hear*
Yif þat° ye wile þe storie heren.   *if*

Hwan° Ubbe hauede þe gold ring,   *when*
Hauede he youenet° for no þing,   *given it up*
1465 Nouth° for þe borw euereilk del.°   *not even/every bit*
Hauelok biheld° he swiþe° wel,   *examined/very*
Hw° he was wel of bones maked,°   *how/limbs made*
Brod° in þe sholdres,° ful wel schaped,   *broad/shoulders*
Þicke in þe brest, of bodi long;
1470 He semede° wel to ben wel° strong.   *seemed/very*
"Deus!"° hwat° Ubbe, "qui ne were° he knith?°   *God/said/why not is/(a) knight*
I woth° þat he is swiþe with!°   *know/bold*
Betere semede him° to bere°   *it would be more fitting (for) him/ bear*

Helm° on heued, sheld° and spere,°   *helmet/head, shield/spear*
1475 Þanne to beye° and selle ware.   *buy*
Allas, þat he shal þerwith fare!°   *have that occupation*
Goddot!° wile he° trowe° me,   *by God/if he will/listen to*
Chaffare° shal he late° be.''   *trading/let*
Neþeles° he seyde sone:°   *nevertheless/said soon*
1480 "Hauelok, haue þi bone,°   *wish*
And y ful° wel rede° þe   *I very/advise*
Þat þou come and ete° with me   *eat*
To-day, þou and þi fayre wif,°   *wife*

1448. *non oþer reue*: i.e., "with lesser men."

1450. *seken mi ware*: referring perhaps to the search for his lost heritage. The paradox of the riddling speech (a merchant would sell, not seek) is a key to the riddle of his disguise.

1455. Ubbe is a name often found in Danish and Low German records. The *Anglo-Saxon Chronicle* mentions Æbbe, a Frisian.

Þat þou louest also° þi lif.°   *as/life*
1485 And haue þou of hire° no drede:°   *for her/fear*
Shal hire no man shame bede.°   *offer*
Bi þe fey° that y owe to þe,   *faith*
Þerof shal i meself borw° be."   *myself surety*

Hauelok herde þat° he bad,°   *heard what/asked*
1490 And thow° was he ful sore adrad°   *yet/greatly afraid*
With him to ete, for° hise° wif;   *because of/his*
For him wore leuere° þat his° lif   *he had rather/of his*
Him wore reft, þan° she in blame   *he were deprived, than (that)*
Felle, or lauthe° ani shame.   *suffered*
1495 Hwanne he hauede° his wille yat,°   *had/assented to*
Þe stede° þat he onne° sat   *steed/on*
Smot° Ubbe with spures° faste,   *pricked/spurs*
And forth awey,° but at þe laste,   *away*
Or° he fro° him ferde,°   *before/from/parted*
1500 Seyde he, þat his folk herde: *see/come both*
"Loke° þat ye comen beþe,°
For ich° it wile,° and ich it rede."   *I/want*

Hauelok ne durste, þey° he were adrad   *dared, though*
Nouth withsitten° þat Ubbe bad: *not oppose*
1505 His wif he dide° with him lede;°   *did/lead*
Vn-to þe heye curt° he yede.°   *high court/went*
Roberd hire ledde, þat was red,
Þat hauede° þoled° for hire þe ded°   *would have/suffered/death*
Or° ani hauede hire misseyd,°   *before/insulted*
1510 Or hand with iuele onne leyd.°   *evil (intent) on (her) laid*
Willam Wendut was þat oþer
Þat hire ledde, Roberdes broþer,
Þat was with° at alle nedes:°   *brave/in necessity*
Wel is him° þat god man fedes!°   *glad is he/(a) good retainer main-*
                                                          tains

1515 Þan he weren° comen to þe halle   *when they were*
Biforen° Ubbe and hise men alle,   *before*
Vbbe stirte hem ageyn,°   *went them toward*
And mani a knith° and mani a sweyn,°   *knight/peasant*
Hem for to se° and forto shewe.°   *see/look at*
1520 Þo stod° Hauelok als° a lowe°   *then stood/like/hill*
Aboven þo° þat þerinne wore,°   *above them/were*
Rith al bi þe heued° more°   *fully a head/taller*

1507. *Robert . . . þat was red:* i.e., "Robert the Red."

Þanne ani þat þerinne stod:
Þo was Ubbe bliþe° of mod° *happy/mind*
1525 Þat he saw him so fayr and hende;° *handsome*
Fro him ne mithe° his herte wende°— *not might/heart turn*
Ne fro him, ne° fro his wif; *nor*
He louede° hem sone so° his lif. *loved/immediately as*
Weren non° in Denemark þat him þouthe° *(there) were none/it seemed*
1530 Þat he so mikel° loue mouthe;° *much/might*
More he louede Hauelok one° *alone*
Þan al Denemark, bi° mine wone!° *on/word*
Loke° nou hw° God helpen° kan *see/how/help*
O° mani wise° wif and man! *in/ways*

1535 Hwan° it was comen time to ete,° *when/eat*
Hise° wif dede° Ubbe sone° in fete,° *his/did/soon/fetch*
And til hire seyde,° al on gamen:° *to her said/in sport*
"Dame, þou and Hauelok shulen° ete samen,° *shall/together*
And Goldeboru shal ete wit° me, *with*
1540 Þat is so fayr so flour° on tre;° *blossom/tree*
In al Denemark nis° wimman° *(there) is not/woman*
So fayr so sche,° bi seint Iohan!"° *she/Saint John*
Þanne he were set,° and bord leyd,° *seated/table set*
And þe beneysun° was seyd, *blessing*
1545 Biforn° hem com° þe beste mete° *before/came/food*
Þat king or cayser° wolde° ete: *emperor/would*
Kranes, swannes, uencysun,° *venison*
Lax,° lampreys, and god sturgun,° *salmon/sturgeon*
Pyment to drinke, and god clare,
1550 Win hwit° and red, ful° god plente.° *wine white/very/plenty*
Was° þerinne no page so lite° *(there) was/ small (or low)*
Þat euere° wolde ale bite.° *ever/drink*
Of þe mete° forto telle, *meal*
Ne of° þe metes bidde° i nout° dwelle; *on/food need/not*
1555 Þat is þe storie for to lenge,° *prolong*
It wolde anuye° þis fayre genge.° *annoy/company*
But hwan he haueden ilk° þing deled,° *they had each/shared*
And fele siþes° haueden wosseyled,° *many times/drunk healths*
And with gode° drinkes seten° longe, *good/sat*
1560 And it was time for to gonge,° *go*
Ilk man to þer° he cam fro,° *where/came from*

1549. Pyment was a spiced wine and claré a mixture of wine and honey, also spiced. As previously mentioned (cf. l. 645*n*), spices and condiments were an important part of medieval fare, both to augment the taste of food and to help preserve it.

1551–52. Ale was everyman's drink, too unrefined for this feast.

Þouthe° Ubbe, "Yf i late hem° go, *thought/let them*
Þus one foure,° withuten mo,° *four alone/without more*
So mote ich brouke° finger or to,° *may I enjoy/toe*
1565 For þis wimman bes° mikel wo!° *(there) will be/woe*
For hire shal men hire louerd slo."° *lord slay*
He tok° sone knithes° ten *took/knights*
And wel° sixti oþer men *fully*
Wit gode bowes and with gleiues,° *spears*
1570 And sende him° unto þe greyues,° *sent them/grave's*
Þe beste man of al þe toun,
Þat was named Bernard Brun;° *Brown*
And bad° him, als° he louede° his lif,° *asked/as/loved/life*
Hauelok wel yemen,° and his wif,° *to guard/wife*
1575 And wel do wayten° al þe nith,° *keep watch/night*
Til þe oþer° day, þat° it were lith.° *next/when/light*
Bernard was trewe° and swiþe with,° *true/very bold*
In al þe borw° ne° was no knith *town/not*
Þat betere couþe° on stede riden,° *could/steed ride*
1580 Helm° on heued, ne swerd° bi side. *helmet/head, and sword*
Hauelok he gladlike understod° *gladly received*
With mikel° loue and herte god,° *much/heart good*
And dide greyþe° a super° riche, *did prepare/supper*
Also° he was no with chinche,° *as/man stingy*
1585 To his bihoue euerilk del,° *need every bit*
Þat he mithe supe° swiþe wel. *might sup*

Also he seten, and sholde soupe,° *should sup*
So comes° a ladde in a ioupe,° *(there) comes/ jacket*
And with him sixti oþer stronge,° *strong (men)*
1590 With swerdes drawen and kniues longe,
Ilkan° in hande a ful° god gleiue, *each/very*
And seyde,° "Undo,° Bernard þe greyue! *said/open*
Vndo swiþe° and lat° us in, *quickly/let*
Or þu° art ded,° bi seint Austin!"° *you/dead/Saint Augustine*
1595 Bernard stirt° up, þat was ful big, *jumped*
And caste a brinie° upon his rig,° *coat of mail/back*
And grop° an ax þat was ful god, *grabbed*
Lep° to þe dore so° he wore wod,° *leaped/as if/were mad*

1564. I.e., "as I live (cf. l. 311n).
1569. *gleiues:* Cf. ll. 266–67n.
1570. *greyues:* Cf. l. 266n.
1588–94. It was hazardous in the Middle Ages to travel on the highroads, especially at night; bands of ragamuffins, outlaws, and thieves often disturbed the peace (see J. J. Jusserand,

English Wayfaring Life in the Middle Ages, 3d ed. [London, 1925]). The work of the town grave was not easy, although the disturbance here—right in the lion's den, so to speak— seems to have been unusual. The motive is supposedly robbery, though in other versions it is the attempted rape of Goldeboro.

And seyde, "Hwat° are ye, þat are þeroute,   *what*
1600 Þat þus biginnen° forto stroute?   *begin/cause a disturbance*
Goth henne° swiþe, fule þeues,°   *go hence/foul thieves*
For bi þe Louerd þat man on leues,°   *in believes*
Shol ich casten° þe dore open,   *if I cast*
Summe° of you shal ich drepen,°   *some/kill*
1605 And þe oþre° shal ich kesten°   *others/cast*
In feteres,° and ful faste festen!"°   *fetters/bind*
"Hwat haue ye seid?" quoth° a ladde,   *said*
"Wenestu° þat we ben adradde?°   *do you think/are afraid*
We sholen° at þis dore gonge,°   *shall/go*
1610 Maugre þin,° carl, or outh longe."°   *in spite of you/fellow, before any*
    long (time)

He gripen sone° a bulder-ston,°   *grabbed quickly/boulder*
And let it fleye,° ful god won,°   *fly/very hard*
Agen° þe dore, þat° it to-rof:°   *against/so that/burst*
Auelok it saw and þider drof,°   *there ran*
1615 And þe barre° sone vt-drow,°   *bolt/drew out*
Þat was unride° and gret ynow,°   *cumbersome/great enough*
And caste þe dore open wide
And seide, "Her° shal y° now abide: *here/I*
Comes° swiþe vnto me;   *come*
1620 Daþeyt° hwo you° henne fle!"°   *cursed (be)/any of you who/flees*
"No," quodh on,° "þat shaltou° coupe,"°   *said one/shall you/pay for*
And bigan til° him to loupe,°   *to/run*
In his hond° his swerd° ut-drawe;°   *hand/sword/drawn out*
Hauelok he wende þore° haue° slawe.°   *thought there/to have/slain*
1625 And with him comen oþer° two,   *came another*
Þat him wolde° of liue haue do.°   *wanted/to kill*
Hauelok lifte° up þe dore-tre,°   *lifted/door beam*
And at a dint° he slow° hem þre;°   *one blow/slew/the three of them*
Was non° of hem° þat his° hernes°   *(there) was none/them/whose/brains*
1630 Ne° lay þerute ageyn° þe sternes.°   *not/open to/stars*
Þe ferþe° þat he siþen° mette,   *fourth/then*
Wit° þe barre so he him grette°   *with/greeted*
Bifor° þe heued° þat þe rith° eye   *on/head/right*
Vt° of þe hole° made he fleye,   *out/socket*
1635 And siþe clapte° him on þe crune°   *then struck/crown*
So þat he stan-ded° fel þor dune.°   *stone-dead/there down*
Þe fifte° þat he ouertok°   *fifth/overtook*

1627–1740. The description of the fight here, with its bloody detail, has unusual similarities to combats in the epic *Beowulf*, especially those between Beowulf and Grendel. In many ways, the romance of *Havelok* stands closer to the stark, realistic epic genre than to the courtly type, with its magic and chivalric characteristics. The Anglo-Danish background also recalls the *Beowulf*, which was set in Denmark but composed in the north of England.

Gaf° he a ful sor° dint ok°   *gave/very great/also*
Bitwen þe sholdres, þer° he stod,°   *shoulders, where/stood*
1640 Þat he spende° his herte blod.°   *spent/heart's blood*
Þe sixte° wende for to fle,   *sixth*
And he clapte him with þe tre°   *beam*
Rith in þe fule° necke so   *foul*
Þat he smot hise° necke on to.°   *smote his/in two*
1645 Þanne° þe sixe weren° doun feld,°   *when/were/struck*
Þe seuenþe brayd° ut his swerd,   *pulled*
And wolde° Hauelok riht in þe eye;   *wanted (to poke)*
And Hauelok let þe barre fleye,
And smot him sone ageyn° þe brest,   *in*
1650 Þat hauede° he neuere schrifte of prest;°   *had/never absolution from priest*
For he was ded° on lesse hwile°   *dead/time*
Þan men mouthe renne° a mile.   *might run*
Alle þe oþere° weren ful kene:°   *others/tough*
A red° þei taken° hem bitwene   *plan/made*
1655 Þat he sholden° him bihalue,°   *they should/surround*
And brisen° so þat wit no salue°   *lay on/ointment*
Ne sholde him helen leche° non.°   *heal physician/no*
Þey drowen° ut swerdes, ful god won,°   *drew/with vigor*
And shoten° on him so don on bere°   *rushed as do on (the) bear*
1660 Dogges þat wolden° him to-tere°   *would/tear apart*
Þanne men doth þe bere beyte.°   *bait*
Þe laddes were kaske° and teyte,°   *energetic/quick*
And vmbiyeden° him ilkon.°   *surrounded/each one*
Sum° smot with tre,° and sum wit ston;°   *some/wood/stone*
1665 Summe putten° with gleyue° in bac° and side   *thrust/spear/back*
And yeuen wundes° longe and wide   *gave wounds*
In twenti stedes° and wel mo,°   *places/many more*
Fro° þe croune til° þe to.°   *from/head to/toe*
Hwan° he saw þat, he was wod,°   *when/mad*
1670 And was it ferlik hw° he stod,   *(a) wonder how*
For þe blod ran of his sides
So° water þat fro þe welle glides;   *like*
But þanne° bigan he for to mowe   *then*
With þe barre,° and let hem shewe°   *bolt/them see*
1675 Hw he cowþe sore° smite;   *could hard*
For was þer non, long ne lite,°   *none, tall nor short*
Þat he mouthe ouertake,
Þat he ne garte° his croune krake,°   *not made/crack*

1659–61. In bearbaiting, on which bets were taken, dogs   usually mauled before the bear succumbed.
attacked a bear chained by a leg to a stake. The dogs were

So þat on a litel stund°	*while*
1680 Felde° he twenti to þe grund.°	*felled/ground*
Þo° bigan gret dine° to rise,	*then/great din*
For þe laddes on ilke wise°	*in every way*
Him asayleden wit grete dintes.°	*assailed with great blows*
Ful° fer° he stoden,° and with flintes°	*very/far off/they stood/stones*
1685 And gleyues schoten° him fro ferne,°	*threw at/afar*
For drepen° him he wolden yerne;°	*kill/eagerly*
But dursten° he newhen° him no more	*dared/approach*
Þanne° he bor° or leun wore.°	*than if/boar/lion were*
Huwe° Rauen þat dine herde,°	*Hugh/heard*
1690 And þowthe wel° þat men misferde°	*thought truly/did wrong*
With his louerd,° for° his wif;°	*lord/because of/wife*
And grop° an ore and a long knif,°	*seized/knife*
And þider drof also° an hert,°	*there ran like/deer*
And cam° þer on a litel stert,°	*came/time*
1695 And saw how þe laddes wode°	*crazed*
Hauelok his louerd umbistode,°	*surrounded*
And beten° on him so doth þe smith	*beat*
With þe hamer° on þe stith.°	*hammer/anvil*
Alas!'' hwat Hwe,° ''þat y° was boren°	*said Hugh/I/born*
1700 Þat euere et ich bred° of korcn,°	*ever ate I bread/grain*
Þat ich here þis sorwe se!°	*sorrow see*
Roberd!° William! hware° are ye?	*Robert/where*
Gripeth eþer° unker° a god tre,°	*grab both/of you two/good club*
And late° we nouth þise doges fle°	*let/not these wretches flee*
1705 Til ure° louerd wreke° be;	*our/avenged*
Cometh swiþe° and folwes° me!	*quickly/follow*
Ich haue in honde° a ful god ore:	*hand*
Daþeit wo° ne smite sore!''	*cursed (be he) who*
''Ya!° leue,° ya!'' quod° Roberd sone,°	*yes/comrade/said/quickly*
1710 ''We hauen° ful god lith° of þe mone.''°	*have/light/moon*
Roberd a staf grop, strong and gret,	
Þat mouth° ful wel bere° a net,°	*might/carry/ox*
And Willam Wendut grop a tre	
Mikel grettere° þan his þe,°	*much greater/thigh*
1715 And Bernard held his ax ful faste—	

1684–88. There is an interesting parallel here to the final Saracen attack on Roland in the *Chanson de Roland:* missiles are thrown at the epic hero because the enemy dares not approach him.

1703. *unker;* OE *uncer,* normally first person dual genitive, ''of us two'' (cf. above, p. 80), l. 844).

I seye,° was he nouth þe laste—	say
And lopen° forth so° he weren wode°	leaped/as if/they were mad
To þe laddes, þer° he stode,°	where/stood
And yaf hem wundes swiþe° grete;	gave them wounds very
1720 Þer mithe° men wel se boyes bete,°	might/beaten
And ribbes in here° sides breke,°	their/broken
And Hauelok on hem wel wreke.	
He broken° armes, he broken knes,°	broke/knees
He broken shankes, he broken thes.°	thighs
1725 He dide° þe blod° þere renne dune°	made/blood/run down
To þe fet rith fro° the crune,°	feet right from/crown
For was þer spared heued non.°	head none
He leyden° on heuedes, ful god won,°	beat/vigorously
And made crounes breke° and crake°	crowns break/crack
1730 Of þe broune and of þe blake;°	fair
He maden° here backes also bloute°	made/as soft
Als° here wombes,° and made hem rowte°	as/stomachs/roar
Als° he weren kradelbarnes,°	as if/babies in cradle
So dos° þe child þat moder þarnes.°	as does/mother loses
1735 Daþeit hwo recke!° for he it seruede,°	who cares/deserved
Hwat dide° he þore!° weren he werewed!°	what did/there/mauled
So longe haueden° he but° and bet°	had/butted/beaten
With neues° under hernes set,°	fists/brains struck
Þat of þo° sixti men and on°	those/one
1740 Ne wente awey° þer liues° non.	away/alive
On° þe morwen, hwan° it was day,	in/morning, when
Ilc° on other wirwed° lay	each/mangled
Als it were dogges° þat weren henged;°	as if/wretches/hanged
And summe leye° in dikes slenget,°	some lay/ditches slung
1745 And summe in gripes° bi þe her°	trenches/hair
Drawen ware,° and laten° ther.	pulled were/left
Sket cam tiding intil° Ubbe	quickly came news to
Þat Hauelok hauede with a clubbe	
Of hise slawen° sixti and on	his slain
1750 Sergaunz,° þe beste þat mithen gon.°	armed men/might go
"Deus!"° quoth° Ubbe, "hwat may þis be?	God/said

1738. A questionable line. Possibly *under her neses* ("noses") or *nekkes* ("necks") *set* ("with fists striking on their noses or necks").

1739. The number of intruders, which seems to increase as the story continues, is rather typical of epic exaggeration. In the *chansons de geste* the hero is capable of killing hundreds by

himself; Roland, Oliver, and Turpin stand off a whole Saracen army.

1741–42. Possibly a reference to the fact that occasionally, it seems, criminal law took vengeance on animals by hanging them.

Betere is° i nime° miself and se   *better (it) is/go*
Wat° þis baret oweth° on wold,°   *what/tumult means/here*
Þanne° i sende yunge° or old.   *than (that)/young (man)*
1755 For yif° i sende him° unto   *if/(i.e., Havelok)*
I wene° men sholde° him shame do,   *think/should*
And þat ne wolde ich° for no þing: *would I*
I loue him wel, bi Heuene° King!   *heaven's*
Me wore leuere° i wore° lame   *I would rather/were*

1760 Þanne men dide him ani shame,
Or tok,° or onne° handes leyde°   *seized (him)/on (him)/laid*
Vnornelike,° or shame seyde."°   *rudely/said (to him)*
He lep° up on a stede lith,°   *leaped/steed lightly*
And with him mani a noble knith,°   *knight*
1765 And ferde° forth unto þe tun,°   *fared/town*
And dide calle Bernard Brun°   *Brown*
Vt° of his hus, wan° he þer cam;   *out/house, when*
And Bernard sone ageyn° him nam,°   *soon toward/came*
Al to-tused° and al to-torn,°   *cut up/wounded*
1770 Ner also° naked so he was born,   *almost as*
And al to-brised, bac° and þe.°   *bruised, back/thigh*
Quoth Ubbe, "Bernard, hwat is þe?°   *what happened to you*
Hwo haues þe° þus ille maked,°   *has you/treated*
Þus to-riuen,° and al mad° naked?"   *cut up/made*
1775   "Louerd,° merci," quot° he sone,°   *lord/said/quickly*
"To-nicht,° also ros° þe monc,°   *tonight/rose/moon*
Comen her mo° þan sixti þeues,°   *came here more/thieves*
With lokene copes° and wide sleues,°   *fastened cloakes/sleeves*
Me forto robben° and to pine,°   *rob/hurt*
1780 And for to drepe° me and mine.   *kill*
Mi dorc he broken° up ful° sket,   *they broke/very*
And wolde me binden, hond° and fet.°   *bind, hands/feet*
Wan þe godemen° þat sawe,   *good men*
Hauelok, and he þat bi þe wowe°   *wall*
1785 Leye,° he stirten° up sone onon,°   *lay/jumped/immediately*
And summe grop tre° and sum grop ston,°   *some grabbed club/stone*
And driue hem° ut, þei° he weren crus,°   *drove them/though/were fierce*
So° dogges ut of milne-hous.°   *as/mill*
Hauelok grop þe dore-tre,°   *door beam*
1790 And at a dint° he slow° hem þre.°   *one blow/slew/three of them*
He is þe beste man at nede°   *when necessary*

1778. The dress of the intruders is obviously meant to be sinister. Were they disguised as clerics (cf. l. 429)?
1784–85. Havelok's comrades slept on benches by the wall, like Beowulf's comitatus in Heorot, Hrothgar's hall, while the hero himself had a separate chamber or a bed niche.

Þat eueremar° shal ride on stede!°   *evermore/steed*
Als helpe° God, bi° mine wone,°   *so help (me)/in/opinion*
A þhousend of men his° he worth one!°   *is/alone*
1795 Yif° he ne were,° ich were° nou ded,°   *if/it were not for him/would be/dead*
So haue ich don° mi soule red!°   *as sure as I follow/soul's counsel*
But it° is of° him mikel sinne:°   *there/to/much harm (done)*
He maden° him swilke° woundes þrinne°   *made/such/three*
Þat of þe alþerleste° wounde   *least*
1800 Were a stede brouht° to grunde.°   *(be) brought/ground*
He haues a wunde° in þe side,   *wound*
With a gleyue,° ful unride;°   *spear/ugly*
And he haues on þoru° his arum°—   *one through/arm*
Þerof° is ful mikel harum!°   *therefrom/harm*
1805 And he haues on þoru his þhe,°   *thigh*
Þe vnrideste þat men may se;°   *see*
And oþere wundes haues he stronge,°   *severe*
Mo than twenti, swiþe longe.°   *very large*
But siþen° he hauede lauth° þe sor°   *after/had suffered/hurt*
1810 Of þe wundes, was neuere bor°   *(there) was never boar*
Þat so fauth° so he fauth þanne;°   *fought/then*
Was non° þat hauede þe hern-panne°   *none/skull*
So hard þat he ne dede° alto-crusshe°   *not did/completely crush*
And alto-shiuere° and alto-frusshe.°   *shatter/smash*
1815 He folwede° hem so hund dos° hare: *followed/as hound does*
Daþeyt on° he wolde° spare,   *cursed (be) anyone/would*
Þat he ne made hem euerilk° on   *every*
Ligge° stille so doth þe ston: *lie*
And þer his° he nouth° to frie,°   *is not/not/blame*
1820 For oþer sholde° he make hem lye°   *either should/lie*
Ded, or þei him hauede° slawen,°   *would have/slain*
Or alto-hewen,° or alto-drawen.°   *cut up/drawn apart*

Louerd,° haui° no more plith°   *lord/I have/harm*
Of° þat ich was þus greyued to-nith.°   *than/mistreated tonight*
1825 Þus wolde þe þeues° me haue reft:°   *thieves/robbed*
But God þank, he° hauenet° sure° keft.°   *they/have it/surely/paid for*
But it is of° him mikel scaþe:°   *for/pity*
I woth° þat he bes° ded ful raþe."°   *believe/will be/very soon*

Quoth° Ubbe, "Bernard, seyst° þou soth?"°   *said/tell/truth*
1830 "Ya,° sire, that i ne leye° o toth.°   *yes/lie/in my teeth*
Yif y,° louerd, a word leye,   *I*

1816. I.e., "he would not spare anyone."

To-morwen do° me hengen heye."° *tomorrow have/hanged high*
Þe burgeys° þat þerbi stode þore° *citizens/stood there*
Grundlike° and grete oþes° swore, *solemn/great oaths*
1835 Litle° and mikle,° yunge and holde,° *small/large/old*
Þat was soth þat Bernard tolde:
Soth was þat he wolden° him bynde, *would*
And trusse° al þat he mithen° fynde *pack/might*
Of hise,° in arke° or in kiste,° *his/trunk/chest*
1840 Þat he mouthe° in seckes þriste.° *might/sacks thrust*
"Louerd, awey° he haueden° al born° *away/would have/carried*
His þing,° and himself al to-torn,° *things/wounded*
But als° God self barw° him wel, *except that/himself preserved*
Þat° he ne tinte° no catel.° *so that/lost/property*
1845 Hwo° mithe so mani stonde ageyn° *who/stand against*
Bi nither-tale,° knith° or swein?° *nighttime/knight/peasant*
He weren° bi tale° sixti and ten, *were/count*
Starke° laddes, stalworþi° men, *strong/stalwart*
And on,° þe mayster° of hem° alle, *one/master/them*
1850 Þat was þe name° Griffin Galle. *whose name was*
Hwo mouthe ageyn so mani stonde,
But als° þis man of ferne londe° *unless/distant land*
Haueth° hem slawen with a tre?° *has/club*
Mikel ioie° haue he!° *much joy/may he have*
1855 God yeue° him mikel god° to welde,° *give/wealth/control*
Boþe in tun,° and ek° in felde!° *town/also/field*
Wel is set° þe mete° he etes."° *earned/food/eats*
Quoth Ubbe, "Gos,° him swiþe fetes,° *go/quickly fetch*
Þat y mouthe his woundes se,° *see*
1860 Yf that he mouthen holed° be. *might healed*
For yf he mouthe couere° yet *recover*
And gangen° wel up-on hise fet,° *go/feet*
Miself shal dubbe him to° knith, *as*
Forþi þat° he is so with.° *because/brave*
1865 And yif he° liuede, þo° foule theues,° *if they/those/thieves*
Þat weren of Kaym° kin and Eues, *Cain's*
He sholden° hange bi þe necke· *should*
Of here ded daþeit wo recke,° *their death cursed (be he) who cares*
Hwan° he yeden° þus on nithes° *when/went/at night*
1870 To binde boþe burgmen° and knithes! *townsmen*

1866. Eve caused the Fall of Man and was regarded in the Middle Ages with opprobrium. In the prevalent medieval antifeminist tracts, most of man's sins were traced to her. If Cain's ancestry was devilish, as was frequently believed, Eve's reputation was further tarnished (although in talmudic and apocryphal lore it was Adam's first wife, Lilith, who was the devil-woman).

For bynderes° loue ich° neuere mo:°   outlaws/I/not at all
Of° hem ne° yeue ich nouht° a slo."°   for/not/not/sloeberry

Hauelok was bifore Ubbe browth,°   brought
Þat hauede° for him ful° mikel þouth,°   had/very/worry
1875 And mikel sorwe° in his herte°   sorrow/heart
For hise wundes,° þat were so smerte.°   wounds/painful

But hwan his wundes weren shewed°   looked at
And a leche° hauede knawed°   physician/found
Þat he hem mouthe ful wel hele,°   heal
1880 Wel make him gange,° and ful wel mele,°   walk/talk
And wel a palefrey° bistride,°   saddle horse/ride on
And wel upon a stede° ride,   steed
Þo° let Ubbe al his care   then
And al his sorwe ouerfare,°   pass
1885 And seyde,° "Cum° now forth with me,   said/come
And Goldeboru þi wif° with þe,°   wife/you
And þine seriaunz° alle þre,°   armed men/three
For nou wile y° youre warant° be;   will I/surety
Wile° y non° of here frend°   desire/(that) none/friends
1890 Þat þu slowe° with þin hend°   you slew/your hand
Moucte° wayte° þe to slo,°   might/lie in wait/slay
Also° þou gange to and fro.   as
I shal lene° þe a bowr°   lend/bower
Þat is up in þe heye tour,°   high tower
1895 Til þou mowe° ful wel go,   may
And wel ben hol° of al þi wo.°   be healed/woe
It° ne shal no þing ben bitwene°   there/between
Þi bour° and min,° also y wene,°   bower/mine/think
But a fayr firrene° wowe;°   fir-wood/wall
1900 Speke° y loude or spek° y lowe,   speak/speak
Þou shalt ful wel heren° me   hear
And þan° þu wilt,° þou shalt me se.°   when/will/see
A rof° shal hile° us boþe o nith,°   one roof/cover/at night
Þat° none of mine, clerk ne knith,°   so that/nor knight
1905 Ne sholen° þi wif no shame bede,°   shall/offer
No more þan min, so God me rede!"°   as God is my guide

He dide° unto þe borw° bringe   did/town
Sone anon,° al with ioynge,°   immediately/joy
His wif, and his serganz° þre,°   armed men/three
1910 Þe beste men þat mouthe° be.   might
Þe firste nith he lay þerinne,
Hise° wif, and his serganz þrinne,°   his/three

Aboute þe middel of þe nith
Wok° Ubbe, and saw a mikel lith°   *woke/great light*
1915 In þe bour þer° Hauelok lay,   *where*
Also brith° so° it were day.   *as bright/as if*

"Deus!"° quoth° Ubbe, "hwat° may þis be?   *God/said/what*
Betere is° i go miself and se: *better (it) is*
Hweþer he sitten° nou and wesseylen,°   *whether they sit/drink healths*
1920 Or ani sotshipe° to-deyle,°   *foolishness/carry on*
Þis tid° nithes,° also foles;°   *time/of night/like fools*
Þan birþe° men casten hem° in poles,°   *then ought/to cast them/pools*
Or in a grip,° or in þe fen:°   *ditch/mud*
Nou ne° sitten° none but wicke° men,   *not/sit up/wicked*
1925 Glotuns, reures,° or wicke þeues,°   *gluttons, robbers/thieves*
Bi Crist, þat alle folk onne leues!"°   *in believe*

He stod° and totede° in at a bord°   *stood/peered/board*
Her° he spak° anilepi° word,   *before/spoke/a single*
And saw hem slepen° faste ilkon,°   *sleeping/each one*
1930 And lye° stille so° þe ston;°   *lying/as/stone*
And saw al þat mikel lith
Fro° Hauelok cam,° þat was so brith: *from/came*
Of° his mouth it com° ilk del°—   *from/came/every bit*
Þat was he war° ful swiþe wel.°   *aware of/certainly*
1935 "Deus!" quoth he, "hwat may þis mene?"°   *mean*
He calde° boþe arwe° men and kene,°   *called/timid/bold*
Knithes and serganz swiþe sleie,°   *very nimble*
Mo° þan an hundred, withuten leye,°   *more/without lie*
And bad° hem alle comen° and se   *bade/come*
1940 Hwat þat selcuth mithe° be.   *marvel might*
Als° þe knithes were comen alle   *as*
Þer Hauelok lay, ut° of þe halle,   *out*
So stod° ut of his mouth a glem°   *came/gleam*
Rith al° swilk so° þe sunne-bem,°   *just/like/sunbeam*
1945 Þat al so lith was þare,° bi heuene,°   *so that/there/heaven*
So þer brenden serges° seuene   *burned candles*
And an hundred serges ok:°   *also*
Þat durste hi sweren° on a bok.°   *dared they swear/book*
He slepen° faste, alle fiue,   *slept*
1950 So he weren° brouth of liue;°   *were/dead*
And Hauelok lay on his lift° side,   *left*
In his armes his brithe bride
Bi° þe pappes° he leyen° naked: *down to/breast/lay*
So faire two weren neuere maked°   *never made*
1955 In a bed to lyen samen.°   *lie together*

Þe knithes þouth° of hem god gamen,° *knights had/good sport*
Hem forto shewe° and loken to.° *look at/examine*
Rith also he stoden° alle so *just as they stood*
And his bac° was toward hem wend,° *back/turned*
1960 So weren he war° of a croiz ful gent° *aware/cross very fair*
On his rith shuldre,° swiþe brith,° *right shoulder/bright*
Brithter þan gold ageyn° þe lith,° *in/light*
So þat he wiste, heye° and lowe, *knew, high*
Þat it was kunmerk° þat he sawe. *(a) royal (birth)mark*
1965 It sparkede° and ful brith shon° *sparkled/shone*
So doth þe gode° charbucle-ston,° *good/carbuncle*
Þat men mouthe se° by þe lith, *might see*
A peni chesen,° so was it brith. *penny found*
Þanne bihelden° he him faste,° *then beheld/closely*
1970 So þat he knewen° at þe laste *knew*
Þat he was Birkabeynes sone,° *son*
Þat was here° king, þat was hem wone° *their/them accustomed*
Wel to yeme° and wel were° *rule/defend*
Ageynes utenladdes here.° *against foreign armies*
1975 "For it° was neuere yet a broþer *there*
In al Denmark so lich° anoþer *like*
So° þis man, þat is so fayr, *as (is)*
Als° Birkabeyn: he is hise eyr."° *like/his heir*

He fellen sone° at hise fet;° *fell quickly/feet*
1980 Was non° of hem þat he ne gret:° *(there) was none/not wept*
Of ioie° he weren alle so fawen° *with joy/glad*
So° he him haueden of erþe drawen:° *as if/had from (the) grave recovered*
Hise fet he kisten° an hundred syþes,° *kissed/times*
Þe tos,° þe nayles, and þe lithes,° *toes/tips*
1985 So þat he bigan to wakne° *waken*
And wit hem° ful sore° to blakne,° *at their presence/greatly/pale*
For he wende° he wolden° him slo,° *thought/would/slay*
Or elles° binde him and do wo.° *else/cause woe*

Quoth° Ubbe, "Louerd,° ne dred þe nowth;° *said/lord/fear not*
1990 Me þinkes° that i se þi þouth:° *I think/thought*
Dere° sone, wel is me° *dear/I am glad*
Þat y þe° with eyn° se! *I you/eyes*
Manred,° louerd, bede° y þe: *homage/offer*
Þi man auht° i ful wel to be, *ought*

1966. In the Middle Ages, stones were considered to have many properties, magic and medicinal. Precious stones gave off their own light.

1995 For þu° art comen° of Birkabeyn,   *you/born*
    Þat hauede mani knith° and sweyn,°   *knights/peasants*
    And so shalt þou, louerd, haue!
    Þou° þu be yet a ful yung knaue,°   *though/boy*
    Þou shalt be king of al Denemark:—
2000 Was þerinne neuere° non so stark.°   *never/strong*
    To-morwen° shaltu° manrede take   *tomorrow/shall you*
    Of þe brune° and of þe blake°—   *brown/fair*
    Of alle þat aren° in þis tun,°   *are/town*
    Boþe of erl and of barun
2005 And of dreng° and of thayn°   *vassal/thane*
    And of knith° and of sweyn.°   *knight/peasant*
    And so shaltu ben mad° knith   *be made*
    Wit° blisse, for þou art so with."°   *with/brave*

    Þo° was Hauelok swiþe bliþe,°   *then/very happy*
2010 And þankede God ful fele siþe.°   *very many times*
    On° þe morwen, wan° it was lith,°   *in/morning, when/light*
    And gon° was þisternesse° of þe nith,°   *gone/darkness/night*
    Vbbe dide° upon a stede°   *made/steed*
    A ladde lepe,° and þider bede°   *leap/thither command*
2015 Erles, barouns, drenges, theynes,
    Klerkes, knithes, burgeys,° sweynes,   *citizens*
    Þat he sholden comen° anon°   *they should come/at once*
    Biforen° him sone° euerilkon,°   *before/immediately/every one*
    "Also° he louen here° liues   *as/love their*
2020 And here children and here wiues."

    Hise bode ne durste° he non at-sitte°   *his command not dared/none resist*
    Þat he ne neme,° for to wite°   *went/know*
    Sone hwat wolde° þe iustise;°   *what wanted/judge*
    And he bigan anon to rise,
2025 And seyde sone,° "Liþes° me,   *said quickly/listen to*
    Alle samen,° þeu° and fre.°   *together/bound/free*
    A þing ich wile° you here shauwe°   *I will/show*
    Þat ye alle ful wel knawe:°   *know*
    Ye witen° wel þat al þis lond°   *know/land*
2030 Was in Birkabeynes hond°   *hand*
    Þe day þat he was quic° and ded,°   *alive/dead*
    And how þat he, bi youre red,°   *advice*
    Bitauhte° hise children þre°   *committed/three*

2025–60. The recapitulation here undoubtedly also served as a   **2031.** Cf. l. 1406*n*.
mental resting place for the minstrel (cf. ll. 1365–75*n*).

Godard° to yeme,° and al his fe.°
2035 Hauelok his sone° he him° tauhte,°
And hise two douhtres,° and al his auhte.°
Alle herden° ye him swere°
On bok° and on messe-gere°
Þat he shulde° yeme hem° wel,
2040 Withuten lac,° withuten tel.°

He let his oth° al ouergo°
(Euere wurþe° him yuel° and wo!),°
For þe maydnes here° lif°
Refte° he boþen° with a knif,°
2045 And him shulde ok° haue slawen:°
Þe knif was at his herte drawen!°
But God him wolde° wel haue saue;°
He hauede reunesse of° þe knaue,°
So þat he with his hend°
2050 Ne drop° him nouth,° þat sori fend!°
But sone dide° he a fishere
Swiþe grete oþes° swere
Þat he sholde drenchen° him
In þe se,° þat was ful brim.°
2055   Hwan° Grim saw þat he was so fayr,
And wiste° he was þe rith eir,°
Fro° Denemark ful sone he fledde
Intil° Englond, and þer him fedde°
Mani winter;° þat° til þis day
2060 Haues° he ben° fed and fostred ay.°
Lokes hware° he stondes her!°
In al þis werd ne° haues he þer°—
Non° so fayr, ne° non so long,°
Ne non so mikel,° ne non so strong.
2065 In þis middelerd° nis° no knith°
Half so strong, ne half so with.°
Bes° of him ful glad and bliþe,°
And cometh alle hider swiþe,°
Manrede° youre louerd° forto make,°
2070 Boþe brune° and þe blake!°
I shal miself do° first þe gamen,°
And ye siþen° alle samen."°

	(to) Godard/guard/possessions
	son/(to) him/committed
	daughters/wealth
	heard/swear
	book/mass implements
	should/them
	without fault/blame
	oath/be forgotten
	ever befall/evil/woe
	of their/life
	deprived/both/knife
	also/slain
	heart drawn
	would/saved
	had pity on/boy
	hand
	killed/not/awful fiend
	soon made
	very great oaths
	drown
	sea/very wild
	when
	knew/true heir
	from
	to/nurtured
	winters/so that
	has/been/always
	see where/stands here
	world not/peer
	none/nor/tall
	big
	earth/is not/knight
	brave
	be/happy
	hither quickly
	homage/lord/pledge
	brown/fair
	perform/pleasant ceremony
	after/together

2065. In Norse mythology, Asgard, the center of the universe, was the home of the gods; Midgard (ME Middelerd), the earth encircled by the sea, was the home of mortals; and Niflheim was the foggy, cold underworld of the dead.

O knes° ful fayre° he him° sette   *on knees/courteously/himself*
(Mouthe° noþing him þerfro° lette),°   *might/from it/hinder*
2075 And bicam° his man rith þare,°   *became/right there*
Þat alle sawen° þat þere ware.°   *saw/were*

After him stirt° up laddes ten   *jumped*
And bicomen hise° men;   *became his*
And siþen° euerilk a° baroun   *then/every*
2080 Þat euere weren° in al that toun;   *were*
And siþen drenges,° and siþen thaynes,°   *vassals/thanes*
And siþen knithes, and siþen sweynes;°   *peasants*
So þat or° þat day was gon,°   *before/gone*
In al þe tun° ne was nouth on°   *town/one*
2085 Þat he ne was his man bicomen:°   *become*
Manrede of alle hauede he nomen.°   *taken*

Hwan he hauede of hem° alle   *them*
Manrede taken in the halle,
Grundlike dide° he hem swere°   *solemnly did/swear*
2090 Þat he sholden° him god feyth bere°   *should/good faith bear*
Ageynes° alle þat woren° on liue;°   *against/were/alive*
Þer-yen° ne wolde° neuer on° striue   *against that/would/no one*
Þat he° ne maden sone° þat oth,°   *they/made quickly/oath*
Riche and poure, lef° and loth,°   *poor, friendly/hostile*
2095 Hwan° þat was maked, sone° he sende,°   *when/done, soon/sent*
Vbbes, writes fer° and hende,°   *letters far/near*
After° alle þat castel yemede,°   *to/ruled*
Burwes,° tunes, sibbe and fremde,°   *cities/towns, relatives and strangers*
Þat þider° sholden he comen° swiþe   *thither/come*
2100 Til° him and heren tiþandes bliþe°   *to/hear tidings happy*
Þat he hem alle shulde° telle.   *should*
Of hem ne° wolde neuere on dwelle°   *not/hesitate*
Þat he ne come° sone plattinde;°   *came/hurrying*
Hwo° hors ne hauede,° com gangande;°   *(he) who/had/walking*
2105 So þat withinne a fourtenith,°   *fortnight*
In al Denemark ne was no knith°   *knight*
Ne conestable° ne shireue°   *nor constable/sheriff*
Þat com of Adam and of Eue
Þat he ne com biforn° sire Ubbe: *before*

2073–76. Homage was sworn by the vassal on his knees before his lord, his hands and sometimes his head placed on the lord's knees. The custom is described in the Old English elegiac poem *Wanderer.* The law of fealty rested in reciprocal protection of lord and "man."

2110 He dredden° him so þhef° doth clubbe.	feared/as thief
Hwan he haueden° alle þe king gret°	had/greeted
And he weren alle dun set,°	down seated
Þo seyde° Ubbe, "Lokes° here	then said/see
Vre louerd, swiþe dere,°	our lord, very dear
2115 Þat shal ben° king of al þe lond,°	be/land
And haue us alle under hond!°	hand
For he is Birkabeynes sone,°	son
Þe king þat was vmbe-stonde wone°	formerly accustomed
Men for to yeme, and wel were°	guard
2120 Wit° sharp swerd° and longe spere.°	with/sword/spear
Lokes nou hw° he is fayr!	how
Sikerlike° he is hise eyr.°	surely/his heir
Falles° alle to hise fet:°	fall/feet
Bicomes° hise men ful sket."°	become/immediately
2125 He weren for° Ubbe swiþe adrad,°	were of/afraid
And dide sone al þat he bad,°	commanded
And yet deden° he sumdel° more:	did/somewhat
O bok ful grundlike° he swore	on book very solemnly
Þat he sholde with him halde°	hold
2130 Boþe ageynes stille° and bolde,	timid
Þat euere° wolde his bodi dere:°	ever/harm
Þat dide° he hem° o boke swere.°	made/them/swear
Hwan he hauede manrede° and oth°	homage/oath
Taken of lef° and of loth,°	friendly/hostile
2135 Vbbe dubbede him to° knith	as
With a swerd ful swiþe° brith;°	exceedingly/bright
And þe folk of al þe lond	
Bitauhte° him° al in his hond,	committed/to him
Þe cunnriche euerilk del,°	kingdom every bit
2140 And made him king heylike° and wel.	solemnly
Hwan° he was king, þer mouthe° men se°	when/might/see
Þe moste ioie° þat mouhte° be:	joy/might
Buttinge° with sharpe speres,	thrusting (i.e., jousting)
Skirming° with taleuaces° þat men beres,°	fencing/shields/carry
2145 Wrastling with laddes, putting of ston,°	stone
Harping and piping, ful god won,°	in great quantity
Leyk° of mine,° of hasard ok,°	game/backgammon/dice also

2135–36. The ceremony of knightly dubbing was normally long and arduous, consisting of a nightlong vigil in church, a ritual bath, and the fastening on of spurs. The "combat commission," in which a knight won his spurs during battle, was, of course, simpler and faster.

2143–44. Jousting, sword-and-buckler engagements, and tilting at the quintain (a pole with crossbar which unhorsed the rider if he missed the target) were favorite amusements, not without danger.

Romanz-reding° on° þe bok;   *romance reading/in*
Þer mouthe men here° þe gestes° singe,°   *hear/heroic tales/sung*
2150 Þe glevmen° on þe tabour dinge;°   *gleemen (i.e., musicians)/drum*
                                                        strike

Þer mouhte men se þe boles beyte,°   *bulls baited*
And þe bores,° with hundes teyte;°   *boars/hounds lively*
Þo° mouthe men se euerilk gleu.°   *then/sport*
Þer mouthe men se hw grim greu;°   *excitement increased*
2155 Was neuere yete° ioie more   *(there) was never yet*
In al þis werd° þan þo was þore.°   *world/there*
Þer was so mikel yeft° of cloþes,   *great gift*
Þat, þou° i swore you grete° othes,   *though/great*
I ne° wore° nouth° þer-offe troud.°   *not/would be/not at all/thereof*
                                                        believed

2160 Þat may i ful wel swere, bi God!
Þere was swiþe gode metes;°   *very good food*
And of wyn° þat men fer° fetes,°   *wine/from afar/fetched*
Rith al° so mikel° and gret plente°   *just/as much/great amount*
So° it were water of þe se.°   *as if/sea*
2165 Þe feste fourti dawes sat;°   *festival forty days lasted*
So riche° was neuere non so° þat.   *noble/none as*
Þe king made Roberd° þere knith,°   *Robert/knight*
Þat was ful° strong and ful with,°   *very/brave*
And Willam Wendut hec,° his broþer,   *also*
2170 And Huwe° Rauen, þat was þat oþer,   *Hugh*
And made hem° barouns alle þre,°   *them/three*
And yaf° hem lond° and oþer feˇ   *gave/land/goods*
So mikel þat ilker° twenti knihtes°   *each/knights*
Hauede° of genge,° dayes and nithes.°   *had/in his retinue/nights*
2175   Hwan þat feste was al don,
A thousand° knihtes ful wel o bon°   *thousand/equipped*
Withheld° þe king, with him to lede,°   *held/lead*
Þat° ilkan° hauede ful god stede,°   *so that/each/good steed*
Helm° and sheld° and brinie° brith,°   *helmet/shield/coat of mail/bright*
2180 And al þe wepne° þat fel° to kniht.   *weapons/belong*
With hem fiue thusand gode
Sergaunz,° þat weren° to fyht wode,°   *armed men/were/fight eager*

2149–50. Here the gestes (stories of the martial deeds of heroes) are sung, whereas the romances are read. The professional entertainers were strictly classified according to rank and type: the minstrels were of higher professional rank, whereas the gleemen were the entertainers of common folk.

2151. A bull was baited differently from a bear: dogs attempted to bite the bull's muzzle shut until he was subdued.

2157–59. Gifts of clothing were common in noble and royal households during Christmas and New Year's. The distribution to many members of the retinue included rolls of expensive cloth as well as silver cups and rings. Geoffrey Chaucer and his wife Philippa received many such donations, which were duly entered in the account books of the duchess of Ulster, Chaucer's first sovereign lady, and later of the kings Edward III and Richard II.

With-held he, al of his genge.
Wile° i namore° þe storie lenge:° *will/no more/prolong*
2185 Yet hwan° he hauede of al þe lond *when*
Þe casteles alle in his hond,° *hand*
And conestables don° þer-inne, *constables placed*
He swor he ne sholde neuer blinne° *cease*
Til þat° he were of° Godard wreken,° *until/on/avenged*
2190 Þat ich° haue of ofte speken.° *I/spoken*
Half hundred knithes dede° he calle, *did*
And hise fif° thusand sergaunz alle, *his five*
And dide sweren° on the bok° *made swear/book*
Sone,° and on þe auter ok,° *soon/altar also*
2195 Þat he° ne sholde neuere° blinne, *they/should never*
Ne for loue ne° for sinne,° *nor/harm*
Til þat he haueden° Godard funde° *had/found*
And brouth biforn° him faste bunde.° *brought before/bound*

Þanne° he haueden sworn þis oth,° *when/oath*
2200 Ne lenten° he nouth,° for lef° ne loth,° *not delayed/not/friendly/hostile*
Þat he ne foren swiþe rathe° *went very quickly*
Þer° he was, unto þe paþe° *where/path*
Þer he yet on hunting° for° *a-hunting/went*
With mikel genge,° and swiþe stor.° *great retinue/proud*
2205 Robert, þat was of al þe ferd° *army*
Mayster, girt° was wit° a swerd,° *master, girded/with/sword*
And sat upon a ful god stede,
Þat vnder him rith wolde wede;° *strongly would gallop*
He was þe firste þat with Godard
2210 Spak,° and seyde,° "Hede, cauenard!° *spoke/said/heed, rogue*
Wat dos þu° here at þis paþe? *what do you*
Cum° to þe king, swiþe° and raþe:° *come/quickly/instantly*
Þat sendes he þe° word, and bedes° *you/commands*
Þat þu þenke hwat° þu him° dedes° *think what/to him/did*
2215 Hwan þu reftes° with a knif° *deprived/knife*
Hise sistres here lif,° *(of) their life*
An siþen bede° þu in þe se° *and then commanded/sea*
Drenchen° him; þat herde° he! *to drown/heard*
He is to° þe swiþe grim.° *with/angry*
2220 Cum nu° swiþe unto him *now*
Þat king is of þis kuneriche,° *kingdom*

2205. *ferd:* the OE *fyrd* was the militia or home guard, made up from the general population. Its members often returned home, sometimes in the midst of a campaign, when their term of service had run out. The *here*, on the other hand, was the standing or regular army (cf. l. 2401). According to the *Anglo-Saxon Chronicle* Alfred fights the Danish *here* with the English *fyrd*.

Þu fule° man! þu wicke swike!°   *foul/wicked traitor*
And he shal yelde° þe þi mede,°   *give/reward*
Bi Crist, þat wolde° on rode° blede!"° *was willing/cross/to bleed*

2225 Hwan Godard herde þat° he þer þrette,°   *what/threatened*
With þe neue° he Robert sette°   *fist/struck*
Biforn° þe teth° a dint ful° strong;   *on/teeth/blow very*
And Robert kipt ut° a knif long   *pulled out*
And smot° him þoru° þe rith arum:°   *smote/through/right arm*
2230 Þerof° was ful litel harum!°   *in that/harm*

Hwan° his folk þat sau° and herde,   *when/saw*
Hou Robert with here louerd ferde,°   *lord behaved*
He haueden° him wel ner° browt of liue,° *would have/almost/killed*
Ne weren° his two breþren and oþre° fiue, *were it not for/others*
2235 Slowen° of here laddes ten   *(who) slew*
Of Godardes alþerbeste° men.   *best*
Hwan þe oþre sawen° þat, he° fledden,°   *others saw/they/fled*
And Godard swiþe loude gredde:°   *shouted*
"Mine knithes,° hwat do ye?   *knights*
2240 Sulc° ye þusgate° fro° me fle?°   *shall/in this way/from/flee*
Ich° haue you fed,° and yet shal fede: *I/kept*
Helpe me nu in þis nede,°   *need*
And late° ye nouth° mi bodi spille,°   *let/not/be killed*
Ne° Hauelok don of° me hise° wille.   *nor/have with/his*
2245 Yif° ye it do, ye do you° shame,   *if/yourselves*
And bringeth youself in mikel° blame."   *much*
Hwan he þat herden,° he wenten ageyn°   *heard/went again*
And slowen a kniht° and a sweyn°   *knight/peasant*
Of þe kinges oune° men,   *own*
2250 And woundeden abuten° ten.   *wounded about*
Þe kinges men, hwan he þat sawe,
Scuten° on hem, heye° and lowe,   *rushed/them, high*
And euerilk fot° of hem slowe   *every foot (i.e., person)*
But° Godard one,° þat he flowe°   *except/alone/flayed*
2255 So° þe þef° men dos henge,°   *like/thief/do hang*
Or hund° men shole° in dike slenge.°   *dog/shall/ditch sling*
He bunden° him ful swiþe° faste   *bound/exceedingly*
Hwil° þe bondes wolden° laste,   *while/would*
Þat° he rorede als° a bole°   *so that/roared like/bull*
2260 Þat wore parred° in an hole   *were imprisoned*
With dogges forto bite° and beite:°   *to be bitten/baited*

2257–58. *faste ... laste:* Cf. ll. 537–38n.

Were þe bondes nouth to leite.°   seek
He bounden° him so fele sore°   bound/very hard
Þat he gan° crien° Godes ore°   began to/cry/mercy
2265 Þat he sholde° his hend of plette.°   should (not)/hands off cut
Wolden he nouht° þerfore° lette°   not/for that/stop
Þat° he ne° bounden hond° and fet°   until/not/hands/feet
(Daþeit° þat on° þat þerfore let!),   cursed (be)/one
But dunten° him so° man doth bere,°   beat/as/bear
2270 And keste° him on a scabbed mere.°   threw/mangy mare
Hise nese° went unto þe crice.°   nose/hole
So ledden° he þat fule swike°   led/foul traitor
Til he biforn° Hauelok was brouth,°   before/brought
Þat he hauede ful wo wrowht°   had great woe caused
2275 Boþe with hungre and with cold
Or° he were twelue winter° old,   before/winters
And with mani heui swink,°   heavy tasks
With poure mete° and feble° drink   poor food/little
And swiþe wikke° cloþes,   very rude
2280 For al hise manie grete othes.°   great oaths
Nu beyes° he his holde blame:°   now pays for/old sins
Old sinne makes newe shame.
Wan° he was brouht° so shamelike°   when/brought/shamefully
Biforn þe king, þe fule swike,
2285 Þe king dede° Ubbe swiþe° calle   made/quickly
Hise° erles and hise barouns alle,   his
Dreng° and thein, burgeis° and knith,°   vassal/thane, citizen/knight
And bad he° sholden demen° him rith,°   commanded they/should judge/right
For he kneu° þe swike dam;°   knew/treacherous scoundrel
2290 Euerilk del,° God was him° gram.°   way/with him/angry
He setten hem° dun° bi þe wawe,°   sat/down/wall
Riche and pouere, heye° and lowe,   poor, high
Þe helde° men, and ek° þe grom,°   old/also/young
And made þer þe rithe dom,°   judgment
2295 And seyden° unto þe king anon,°   said/at once
Þat stille sat al-so° þe ston:°   as/stone
"We deme þat he be al quic flawen,°   alive flayed
And siþen° to þe galwes drawe°   then/gallows drawn

2262. I.e., "the bonds were apparent."
2269. Whipping a blind bear and nimbly avoiding the claws was a sport similar in nature to that of the modern picador.
2271. I.e., "he was facing backward" (cf. ll. 2298–99).
2285–88. The judgment according to the peers of the accused, in which the king has no part but must abide by the verdict, is a procedure common in French romance.

2298–99. It was an added humiliation, especially for a knight, to ride (usually backwards) on a mare or ass (see the fear of a similar punishment by Dame Siriþ, in the fabliau of that name, this volume, p. 449, ll. 246–48). Lancelot, in Chrétien de Troyes's romance, is humiliated by riding in a cart, but does so for the love of Guinevere.

At þis foule mere° tayl—   *mare's*
2300 Þoru° his fet° a ful° strong nayl—   *through|feet|very*
And þore ben henged wit° two feteres;°   *there be hanged with|chains*
And þare° be writen þise° leteres:°   *there|these|letters*
'Þis is þe swike þat wende wel°   *thought fully*
Þe king haue reft° þe lond ilk del,°   *(to) have deprived of|land every bit*
2305 And hise sistres with a knif°   *knife*
Boþe refte here° lif.'°   *their|life*
Þis writ shal henge° bi him þare;   *hang*
Þe dom is demd:° seye we na° more."   *made|no*
    Hwan° þe dom was demd and giue,°   *when|given*
2310 And he was wit° þe prestes shriue,°   *by|priests confessed*
And it ne mouhte° ben non oþer,°   *not might|not otherwise*
Ne for fader ne° for broþer,   *father nor*
But þat he sholde þarne° lif,—   *lose*
Sket cam° a ladde with a knif,   *quickly came*
2315 And bigan rith at þe to°   *toe*
For to ritte,° and for to flo,°   *cut|flay*
So° it were goun° or gore,°   *as if|gown|dress*
And he bigan for to rore°   *roar*
Þat° men mithe þeþen° a mile   *so that|might thence*
2320 Here° him rore, þat fule file.°   *hear|foul wretch*
Þe ladde ne let° no with° forþi,°   *stopped|not at all|for that*
Þey° he criede 'merci! merci!'—   *though*
Þat he ne flow° him euerilk del°   *flayed|every bit*
With knif mad° of grunden stel.°   *made|ground steel*
2325 Þei garte° bringe° þe mere sone,°   *caused|to be brought|mare soon*
Skabbed° and ful iuele o bone,°   *mangy|infirm*
And bunden° him rith at hire° tayl   *bound|her*
With a rop° of an old seyl,°   *rope|sail*
And drowen° him un-to þe galwes,   *drew*
2330 Nouth° bi þe gate,° but ouer þe falwes,°   *not|road|fields*
And henge° him þore bi þe hals:°   *hanged|neck*
Daþeit hwo recke!° he was fals.°   *cursed (be he) who cares|false*

Þanne° he was ded,° þat Sathanas,°   *when|dead|Satan*
Sket was seysed° al þat his was   *seized*

2301. Since criminals were left hanging on the gallows as a warning to others, chains were more functional than ropes, which would deteriorate under weather conditions.

2314–24. The man who killed Richard I (under battle conditions) was supposedly flayed alive.

2333–40. The king, as chief feudal lord, owned all of England, and the great barons held their lands in fief. Thus all property confiscated from traitors went automatically to the crown. Lands held by minors were assigned by the king to "guardians," who received all the income from such "wardships" for themselves until the heirs came of age. Royal favorites, like Geoffrey Chaucer, received several such highly remunerative grants. The staff which Havelok gives Ubbe (l. 2338) symbolizes the granting of land, not as a gift, but to be held as a vassalage.

²³³⁵ In þe kinges hand ilk del—
Lond and lith° and oþer catel°   *folk/property*
And þe king ful sone it yaf°   *gave*
Vbbe in þe hond,° wit a fayr staf,   *hand*
And seyde,° "Her ich sayse þe°   *said/here I grant you*
²³⁴⁰ In° al þe lond, in al þe fe.° ..."   *with/possessions*

. . . . .

Þo° swor Hauelok he sholde° make,   *then/should*
Al for Grim, of monekes blake°   *monks black*
A priorie to seruen° inne ay°   *serve/always*
Iseu° Crist, til domesday,°   *Jesus/Judgment Day*
²³⁴⁵ For þe god° he haueden° him don   *good/had*
Hwil° he was pouere° and iuel o bon.°   *while/poor/miserable*
And þerof held° he wel his oth,°   *kept/oath*
For he it made (God it woth!)°   *knows*
In þe tun þer° Grim was grauen,°   *town where/buried*
²³⁵⁰ Þat of Grim yet haues° þe name.   *has*
Of Grim bidde° ich na° more spelle.°—   *offer/no/story*
But wan° Godrich herde telle,   *when*
Of Cornwayle° þat was erl,   *Cornwall*
Þat fule traytour, that mixed cherl,°   *filthy churl*
²³⁵⁵ Þat Hauelok, was° king of Denemark,   *(who) was*
And ferde° with him, strong and stark,°   *army/powerful*
Comen° Engelond withinne,   *(had) come*
Engelond al for to winne,
And þat she þat was so fayr,
²³⁶⁰ Þat was of Engelond rith eir,°   *true heir*
Was comen up at Grimesbi,
He was ful sorful° and sori,   *very sorrowful*
And seyde, "Hwat shal me to raþe?°   *what shall I do?*
Goddoth!° i shal do slon hem° baþe!°   *by God/have them slain/both*
²³⁶⁵ I shal don hengen hem° ful heye,°   *have them hanged/high*
So mote° ich brouke° mi rith eie,°   *may/enjoy/right eye*
But-yif° he of° mi lond fle!°   *unless/they from/land flee*
Hwat wenden he° to desherite° me?"   *do they think/dispossess*
He dide sone° ferd ut bidde,°   *did soon/out order*
²³⁷⁰ Þat al þat euere mouhte o stede°   *ever might on steed*
Ride, or helm° on heued bere,°   *helmet/head bear*
Brini° on bac,° and sheld° and spere,°   *coat of mail/back/shield/spear*

2340. Following this line, about twenty lines were omitted by the scribe; they probably described the voyage to England.
2341–50. Grimsby (Wellow) Abbey, settled by Augustinian monks, was founded by Henry I in 1110.

2366. I.e., "as I live" (cf. l. 311*n*).

Or ani oþer wepne° bere, *weapon*
Hand-ax, syþe, gisarm,° or spere, *scythe, halberd*
2375 Or aunlaz,° and god long knif,° *dagger/knife*
Þat als° he louede leme° or lif,° *as/loved limb/life*
Þat þey sholden° comen him to, *should*
With ful god wepne yboren° so, *carried*
To Lincolne, þer he lay,
2380 Of Marz° þe seuentenþe° day, *March/seventeenth*
So þat he couþe° hem god° þank, *could/well*
And yif þat° ani were so rank° *if/presumptuous*
Þat he þanne ne come° anon,° *then not came/right away*
He swor bi Crist and Seint Iohan° *Saint John*
2385 Þat he sholde maken° him þral,° *make/thrall*
And al his ofspring forth withal.° *likewise*

Þe Englishe men þat herde þat,
Was non° þat euere his bode atsat,° *none/command resisted*
For he him dredde swiþe sore,° *feared very greatly*
2390 So runci spore,° and mikle° more. *as nag (the) spur/much*
At° þe day he come sone *on*
Þat he hem sette, ful wel o bone,° *equipped*
To Lincolne, with gode° stedes, *good*
And al þe wepne þat knith ledes.° *knight carries*
2395 Hwan° he wore° come, sket° was þe erl yare° *when/were/quickly/eager*
Ageynes Denshe° men to fare,° *against Danish/set out*
And seyde,° "Lyþes nu,° alle samen:° *said/listen now/together*
Haue ich gadred° you for no gamen,° *I assembled/sport*
But ich wile seyen° you forwi:° *will tell/why*
2400 Lokes hware° here at Grimesbi *see where*
Is uten-laddes° here comen,° *foreign/army come*
And haues° nu þe priorie numen;° *has/taken*
Al þat euere mithen he° finde *might they*
He brenne kirkes,° and prestes° binde; *burn churches/priests*
2405 He strangleth monkes and nunnes boþe!
Wat° wile ye, frendes, heroffe rede?° *what/hereof advise*
Yif° he regne° þusgate° longe, *if/continues/this way*
He moun° us alle ouergange:° *might/overcome*
He moun vs alle quic henge° or slo,° *alive hang/slay*
2410 Or þral maken and do ful wo,° *cause great woe*
Or elles reue° us ure° liues, *else deprive/(of) our*

2381. I.e., "in such a manner that he would be grateful to them."

2400–5. The Danish raiders often destroyed monasteries and burned churches; Godrich recalls these ravages and uses past incidents to incite the defenders against Havelok's Danish army. The poet may have identified the Danes with their actions during Alfred's reign, without worrying about the discrepancy here.

And ure children and ure wiues.
But dos° nu als ich wile you lere,°   *do/teach*
Als° ye wile be with° me dere:°   *if/to/dear*
2415 Nimes° nu swiþe° forth and raþe,°   *go/quickly/readily*
And helpes° me and yuself baþe,°   *help/yourselves both*
And slos° upon þe dogges swiþe!   *strike out*
For shal i neuere° more be bliþe,°   *never/happy*
Ne° hoseled ben,° ne of° prest shriuen,°   *nor/receive the sacrament/by/*
                          (be) confessed

2420 Til þat° he ben of londe° driuen.   *until/be from land*
Nime we° swiþe, and do hem fle,°   *let us set out/make them flee*
And folwes° alle faste° me;   *follow/closely*
For ich am he, of al þe ferd,°   *army*
Þat first shal slo° with drawen swerd.°   *strike/sword*
2425 Daþeyt hwo° ne stonde° faste   *cursed (be he) who/not stands*
Bi me, hwil hise° armes laste!"   *while his*
"Ye!° lef,° ye!" quoth° þe erl Gunter;   *yes/dear friend/said*
"Ya!"° quoth þe erl of Cestre,° Reyner.   *yes/Chester*
And so dide° alle þat þer stode,°   *did/stood*
2430 And stirte° forth so° he were wode.°   *rushed/ as if/mad*
Þo mouthe° men se° þe brinies° brihte°   *then might/see/coats of mail/bright*
On backes keste,° and late rithe,°   *thrown/fitted straight*
Þe helmes heye° on heued° sette;   *helmets high/heads*
To armes al so swiþe plette,°   *hastened*
2435 Þat þei wore on° a litel stunde°   *were in/while*
Greyþet,° als men mithe° telle° a pund;°   *ready/might/count out/pound*
And lopen° on stedes° sone anon,°   *leaped/steeds/quickly*
And toward Grimesbi, ful god won,°   *a great number*
He foren softe bi° þe sti,°   *rode quietly on/road*
2440 Til he come ney at° Grimesbi.   *came near to*

Hauelok, þat hauede spired° wel   *had inquired*
Of here fare, euerilk del,°   *their actions, every bit*
With al his ferd cam° hem ageyn.°   *came/against*
Forbar° he noþer knith° ne sweyn:°   *spared/neither knight/peasant*
2445 Þe firste knith þat he þer mette
With þe swerd so he him grette!°   *greeted*
For his heued of° he plette:°   *off/cut*
Wolde° he nouth° for sinne lette.°   *would/not/harm hesitate*
Roberd° saw þat dint° so hende,°   *Robert/blow/worthy*
2450 Wolde he neuere þeþen wende°   *thence turn*

2437. Here the English use the Norman cavalry tactics, first employed during the battle of Hastings. The Saxon comitatus, or troops of the king's household, and the *fyrd* were normally foot soldiers, employing the defensive measure of the shield wall. According to some contemporary documents, fighting on horseback was considered un-English.

Til þat he hauede anoþer slawen°   slain
With þe swerd he held utdrawen.°   drawn out
Willam Wendut his swerd vtdrow,°   drew out
And þe þredde° so sore° he slow,°   third|hard|struck
2455 Þat he made upon þe feld°   field
His lift° arm fleye,° with the swerd.   left|fly

Huwe° Rauen ne forgat° nouth   Hugh|forgot
Þe swerd he hauede þider brouth:°   there brought
He kipte° it up and smot° ful sore   raised|smote
2460 An erl þat he saw priken þore°   riding there
Ful noblelike° upon a stede,   nobly
Þat with° him wolde al quic wede.°   to|vigorously gallop
He smot him on þe heued so
Þat he þe heued clef° a-two,°   split|in two
2465 And þat bi þe shuldre-blade°   shoulder blade
Þe sharpe swerd° let wade°   sword|pass
Þorw° the brest° unto þe herte.°   through|breast|heart
Þe dint bigan ful sore° to smerte,°   greatly|smart
Þat° þe erl fel dun anon°   so that|down immediately
2470 Al so° ded so° ani ston.°   as|dead as|stone
Quoth° Ubbe, "Nu dwelle ich to° longe!"   said|now wait I too
And let his stede sone gonge°   quickly go
To Godrich, with a god° spere   good
Þat he saw anoþer bere,°   carrying another
2475 And smoth° Godrich, and Godrich him,   smote
Hetelike° with herte grim,   furiously
So þat he° boþe felle dune,°   they|down
To þe erþe, first þe croune.°   headfirst
Þanne° he woren° fallen dun boþen,°   when|were|both
2480 Grundlike° here swerdes° utdrowen,°   eagerly|swords|(they) drew out
Þat weren swiþe° sharp and gode,°   were very|good
And fouhten° so° þei woren wode,°   fought|as if|mad
Þat þe swot° ran fro° þe crune°   sweat|from|head
To the fet° riht þere adune.°   feet|down
2485 Þer mouthe° men se° two knithes bete°   might|see|knights strike
Ayþer° on oþer dintes grete,°   either|great
So þat with alþerlest° dint   (the) least
Were al to-shiuered° a flint.°   shattered|stone
So was bitwenen hem° a fiht°   between them|fight
2490 Fro þe morwen ner° to þe niht,°   morning almost|night

2456. *lift arm:* i.e., his shield arm.   used so in several Old English poems.

2483. *swot* (or *swat*) may also be a euphemism for blood, and is

So þat þei nouth° ne blunne,°   not/not stopped
Til þat° to sette bigan þe sunne.   until
Þo yaf° Godrich þorw þe side   then gave
Vbbe a wunde° ful unride,°   wound/ugly
2495 So þat þorw þat ilke° wounde   the very
Hauede he ben° brouth to þe grunde°   would he have been/ground
And his heued° al ofslawen,°   head/struck off
Yif God ne were,° and Huwe° Rauen,   had it not been for God/Hugh
Þat drow° him fro Godrich awey°   pulled/away
2500 And barw° him so þat ilke day.   rescued
But er° he were fro Godrich drawen,°   before/pulled
Þer were a þousind knihtes slawen°   knights slain
Bi° boþe halue,° and mo ynowe°   on/ sides/more aplenty
Þer° þe ferdes togidere slowe.°   where/armies together fought
2505 Þer was swilk dreping° of þe folk,   such slaughter
Þat on þe feld° was neuere° a polk°   field/never/pool
Þat it ne stod° of blod° so ful   stood/blood
Þat þe strem° ran intil° þe hul.°   stream/into/hollow
Þo tarst° bigan Godrich to go   with vigor
2510 Vpon þe Danshe,° and faste to slo,°   Danes/strike
And forth rith,° also leuin° fares,   forthright (i.e., at once)/as lightning
Þat neuere kines best° ne spares,   no kind (of) beast
Þanne his gon;° for he garte° alle   then is gone/made
Þe Denshe men biforn° him falle.   before
2515 He felde° browne, he felde blake,°   felled/fair
Þat he mouthe ouertake.
Was° neuere non° þat mouhte þaue°   (there) was/none/might endure
Hise dintes, noyþer° knith ne knaue,°   his blows neither/boy
Þat he felden° so dos° þe gres°   cut down/as is/grass
2520 Biforn þe syþe° þat ful° sharp is.   scythe/very
Hwan° Hauelok saw his folk so brittene,°   when/broken
And his ferd so swiþe littene,°   very diminished
He cam driuende° upon a stede,°   came galloping/steed
And bigan til° him to grede,°   to/cry
2525 And seyde,° "Godrich, wat is þe,°   said/what is it with you
Þat þou fare° þus with me   behave
And mine gode° knihtes slos?°   good/slay
Sikerlike° þou misgos.°   surely/do wrong
Þou wost° ful wel, yif þu° wilt wite,°   know/if you/know
2530 Þat Aþelwold þe° dide site°   you/made sit
On knes,° and sweren° on messe-bok,°   knees/swear/missal
On caliz,° and on pateyn hok,°   chalice/paten also

2508. *intil þe hul:* i.e., "downhill."

Þat þou hise douhter sholdest yelde,°   *daughter should give*
Þan° she were wimman° of elde,°   *when|woman|age*
2535 Engelond euerilk del:°   *every bit*
Godrich þe erl, þou wost it wel!
Do nu° wel, withuten fiht,°   *now|without fight*
Yeld hire° þe lond,° for þat is rith.°   *her|land|right*
Wile ich° forgiue þe þe lathe,°   *will I|enmity*
2540 Al þi dede° and al mi wrathe,   *deeds*
For y se° þu art so with,°   *I see|courageous*
And of° þi bodi so god knith."°   *in|good knight*
"Þat ne° wile ich neuere mo,"°   *not|more*
Quoth° erl Godrich, "for ich shal slo°   *said|slay*
2545 Þe, and hire forhenge heye.°   *hang high*
I shal þrist ut° þi rith eye   *thrust out*
Þat þou lokes° with on° me,   *look|at*
But° þu swiþe heþen fle."°   *unless|quickly hence flee*
He grop° þe swerd° ut sone anon°   *pulled|sword|quickly*
2550 And hew° on Hauelok ful god won,°   *hewed|vigorously*
So þat he clef° his sheld on° two.   *split|shield in*
Hwan Hauelok saw þat shame do°   *done*
His bodi° þer bi-forn his ferd,°   *person|army*
He drow° ut sone° his gode swerd   *drew|quickly*
2555 And smot° him so upon þe crune°   *smote|head*
Þat Godrich fel to þe erþe adune.°   *down*
But Godrich stirt° up swiþe sket°—   *jumped|quickly*
Lay he nowth° longe at hise fet°—   *not|his feet*
And smot him on þe sholdre° so   *shoulder*
2560 Þat he dide þare° undo   *did there*
Of his brinie° ringes mo   *coat-of-mail*
Þan þat° ich kan tellen fro;°   *than|tell about*
And woundede him rith in þe flesh,
Þat tendre was and swiþe nesh,°   *very soft*
2565 So þat þe blod° ran til° his to:°   *blood|to|toe*
Þo° was Hauelok swiþe wo°   *then|very distressed*
Þat he hauede of° him drawen   *had from*
Blod, and so sore° him slawen.°   *severely|wounded*
Hertelike° til him he wente,   *heatedly*
2570 And Godrich þer fulike shente:°   *foully hurt*
For his swerd he hof° up heye,   *raised*
And þe hand he dide° offleye°   *made|fly off*
Þat he smot him with so sore:°   *hard*
Hw mithe° he don° him shame more?   *how might|do*

2575 Hwan he hauede him so shamed,
His hand ofplat° and yuele° lamed,   *cut off|badly*

He tok° him sone bi þe necke   *seized*
Als° a traytour (daþeyt wo recke!),°   *like/cursed (be he) who cares*
And dide him binde and fetere° wel   *fetter*
2580 With gode° feteres al of stel;°   *good/steel*
And to þe quen° he sende° him,   *queen/sent*
Þat birde° wel to° him ben grim,°   *ought/with/be angry*
And bad° she sholde don° him gete°   *commanded/should have/guarded*
And þat non ne° sholde him bete°   *none not/beat*
2585 Ne° shame do, for he was knith,°   *nor/knight*
Til knithes° haueden demd° him rith.°   *(i.e., his peers)/had judged/right*
Þan° þe Englishe men þat sawe,   *when*
Þat° þei wisten,° heye° and lawe,°   *so that/knew/high/low*
Þat Goldeboru, þat was so fayr,
2590 Was of Engeland rith eyr,°   *true heir*
And þat þe king hire hauede wedded
And haueden ben samen° bedded,   *been together*
He comen° alle to crie merci   *they came*
Vnto þe king at° one cri,°   *with/voice*
2595 And beden° him sone manrede° and oth°   *offered/quickly homage/oath*
Þat he ne sholden,° for lef ne loth,°   *should/better or worse*
Neuere° more ageyn° him go°   *never/against/march*
Ne ride, for wel° ne for wo.°   *good/ill*

Þe king ne wolde° nouth° forsake°   *would/not at all/neglect*
2600 Þat he ne shulde of hem° take   *should from them*
Manrede þat he beden, and ok°   *also*
Hold-oþes° sweren° on þe bok;°   *oaths of loyalty/sworn/book*
But or bad° he þat þider° were brouth°   *first asked/thither/brought*
Þe quen, for hem—swilk° was his þouth°—   *such/purpose*
2605 For to se° and forto shawe°   *see/observe*
Yif þat° he hire wolde knawe.°   *if/know*
Þoru° hem witen° wolde he   *through/know*
Yif þat she aucte° quen to be.   *ought*

Sixe erles weren sone yare°   *were quickly ready*
2610 After hire for to fare;
He nomen° onon° and comen sone,   *set out/quickly*
And brouthen° hire þat under mone°   *brought/(the) moon*
In al þe werd° ne hauede per°   *world/peer*
Of hendeleik, fer° ne ner.°   *in courtesy, far/near*

2598. *for wel ne for wo*: i.e., "for any reason."

2603–8. There seems to be an inconsistency here: Havelok knows that Goldeboro is the princess; on the other hand, she is practically unknown by her people. Probably the poet wants, once again, to prove that truly royal blood will be recognized under whatever conditions. The idea is that of Hans Christian Andersen's story *The Princess and the Pea.*

2615 Hwan° she was come þider, alle — *when*
　　　þe Englishe men bigunne° to falle — *began*
　　　O knes,° and greten swiþe sore,° — *on knees/wept very bitterly*
　　　And seyden,° "Leuedi,° Kristes ore° — *said/lady/mercy*
　　　And youres! we hauen° misdo mikel,° — *have/done much ill*
2620 Þat we ayen° you haue be fikel,° — *toward/been disloyal*
　　　For Englond auhte° forto ben° — *ought/be*
　　　Youres, and we youre men.
　　　Is non° of us, yung ne old, — *(there) is none*
　　　Þat he ne wot° þat Aþelwold — *not knows*
2625 Was king of þis kunerike,° — *kingdom*
　　　And ye his eyr, and þat þe swike° — *traitor*
　　　Haues° it halden° with mikel° wronge, — *has/held/great*
　　　God leue° him sone to honge!"° — *grant/hang*

　　　Quot° Hauelok, "Hwan° þat ye it wite,° — *said/now/know*
2630 Nu wile ich° þat ye doun site,° — *now desire I/sit*
　　　And after° Godrich haues wrouht,° — *according to how/acted*
　　　Þat haues him-self in sorwe° brouth, — *to sorrow*
　　　Lokes° þat ye demen° him rith,° — *see/judge/right*
　　　For dom° ne spareth clerk ne knith;° — *judgment/nor knight*
2635 And siþen° shal ich understonde° — *afterwards/receive*
　　　Of you, after lawe of londe,° — *land*
　　　Manrede° and holde-oþes boþe, — *homage*
　　　Yif° ye it wilen° and ek rothe."° — *if/desire/also counsel*
　　　Anon° þer dune he° hem sette,° — *immediately/down they/sat*
2640 For non þe dom ne durste lette,° — *dared hinder*
　　　And demden° him to binden° faste — *condemned/be bound*
　　　Vpon an asse swiþe unwraste,° — *dirty*
　　　Andelong, nouht ouerþwert,° — *lengthwise, not athwart*
　　　His nose went unto° þe stert,° — *toward/tail*
2645 And so to Lincolne lede° — *led*
　　　Shamelike,° in wicke wede;° — *shamefully/miserable clothes*
　　　And hwan he cam° unto þe borw,° — *came/town*
　　　Shamelike ben led þerþoru,° — *through it*
　　　Bisouþe° þe borw, unto a grene° — *south of/meadow*
2650 Þat þare° is yet, als y wene,° — *there/as I believe*
　　　And þere be bunden til° a stake, — *bound to*
　　　Abouten° him ful grete° fir make,° — *about/very great/fire made*
　　　And al to dust° be brend° rith þere; — *ashes/burned*
　　　And yet demden° he þer more, — *decreed*
2655 Oþer swikes for to warne:
　　　Þat hise° children sulde þarne° — *his/should lose*
　　　Euere-more° þat eritage° — *evermore/heritage*
　　　Þat his was, for hise utrage.° — *outrage*

Hwan° þe dom was demd° and seyd,°   *when/made/spoken*
2660 Sket° was þe swike on þe asse leyd,°   *quickly/laid*
And led° him til þat ilke° grene,   *(they) led/same*
And brend til asken° al bidene.°   *ashes/immediately*
Þo was Goldeboru ful bliþe;°   *happy*
She þanked God fele syþe°   *many times*
2665 Þat þe fule° swike was brend   *foul*
Þat wende wel hire° bodi haue shend,°   *thought fully her/(to) have harmed*
And seyde,° "Nu° is time to take   *said/now*
Manrede of brune° and of blake,°   *brown/fair*
Þat ich se° ride and go:°   *I see/walk*
2670 Nu ich am wreken of° mi fo."°   *avenged on/foe*

Hauelok anon manrede tok°   *took*
Of alle Englishe, on þe bok,°   *book*
And dide hem° grete oþes swere°   *made them/oaths swear*
Þat he sholden° him god feyth bere°   *should/good faith bear*
2675 Ageyn° alle þat woren liues°   *against/were alive*
And þat sholde ben° born of wiues.°   *be/women*

Þanne° he hauede sikernesse°   *when/had surety*
Taken of more° and of lesse°   *from high/low*
Al at hise wille, so dide° he calle   *did*
2680 Þe erl of Cestre,° and hise men alle,   *Chester*
Þat was yung knith wituten wif,°   *knight without wife*
And seyde, "Sire erl, bi mi lif,°   *life*
And° þou wile° mi conseyl tro,°   *if/will/advice trust*
Ful wel shal ich with þe° do: *by you*
2685 For ich shal yeue° þe to wiue°   *give/wife*
Þe fairest þing þat is oliue:°   *alive*
Þat is Gunnild of Grimesby,
Grimes douther,° bi seint Dauy,°   *daughter/Saint David*
Þat me forth broute° and wel fedde°   *brought/nurtured*
2690 And ut° of Denemark with me fledde,   *out*
Me for to berwen fro° mi ded:°   *rescue from/death*
Sikerlike þoru° his red°   *surely through/counsel*
Haue ich liued into° þis day,   *until*
Blissed worþe° his soule ay!°   *blessed be/always*
2695 I rede° þat þu° hire take   *advise/you*
And spuse° and curteyse make,°   *marry/honor do*
For she is fayr and she is fre°   *noble*
And al so° hende so° she may be.   *as/gracious as*
Þertekene° she is wel° with me,   *moreover/in favor*
2700 Þat shal ich ful° wel shewe° þe;   *very/show*
For ich giue° þe a giue°   *make/promise*

Þat eueremore hwil° ich liue   *evermore while*
For hire° shaltu° be with° me dere;°   *her (sake)|you shall|to|dear*
Þat wile° ich þat þis fole al here."°   *want|here*
2705 Þe erl ne wolde° nouth° ageyn   *not would|not at all*
Þe king be, for nith ne sweyn,°   *nor peasant*
Ne of þe spusing seyen° nay,   *marriage say*
But spusede hire° þat ilke° day.   *her|very*
Þat spusinge was in god time maked,°   *made*
2710 For it° ne were neuere° clad ne naked   *there|never (any)*
In a þede samened° two   *land united*
Þat cam togidere, liuede° so,   *came together, (that) lived*
So þey diden° al here liue.°   *did|their life*
He geten samen sones° fiue,   *they begot together sons*
2715 Þat were þe beste men at nede°   *when necessary*
Þat mouthe riden° on ani stede.°   *might ride|steed*
Hwan° Gunnild was to Cestre brouth,°   *when|brought*
Hauelok þe gode° ne forgat° nouth   *good|forgot*
Bertram, þat was þe erles kok,°   *cook*
2720 Þat he ne dide him callen ok°   *call also*
And seyde,° "Frend, so God me rede,°   *said|as God is my guide*
Nu° shaltu haue riche mede°   *now|reward*
For wissing° and þi gode dede°   *guidance|deeds*
Þat tu° me dides° in ful gret nede;°   *you|did|great need*
2725 For þanne y yede° in mi cuuel,°   *when I went|cloak*
And ich° ne hauede bred° ne sowel,°   *I|had bread|relish*
Ne y ne hauede no catel,°   *possessions*
Þou feddes° and claddes° me ful wel.   *fed|clad*
Haue nu forþi° of Cornwayle°   *therefore|Cornwall*
2730 Þe erldom ilk del, withuten° fayle,   *every bit, without*
And al þe lond° þat Godrich held,   *land*
Boþe in towne and ek° in feld;°   *also|field*
And þerto° wile° ich þat þu spuse   *in addition|desire*
And fayre° bring hire un-til huse°   *courteously|to your home*
2735 Grimes douther,° Leuiue þe hende,°   *daughter|gracious*
For þider° shal she with þe wende.°   *thither|you go*
Hire semes° curteys° forto be,   *it suits her|noble*
For she is fayr so flour° on tre;°   *blossom|tree*
Þe heu° is swilk° in hire ler°   *color|such|face*
2740 So° þe rose in roser°   *as that of|on rosebush*
Hwan it is fayr sprad ut° newe   *spread out*
Ageyn þe sunne brith° and lewe."°   *against|bright|warm*
And girde° him sone° with þe swerd°   *girded|soon|sword*

2709. *in . . . maked:* i.e., "a fortunate act."

Of þe erldom, biforn° his ferd,° · *before/army*
2745 And with his hond° he made him knith,° · *hand/knight*
And yaf° him armes, for þat was rith,° · *gave/right*
And dide° him þere sone wedde · *had*
Hire° þat was ful swete° in bedde. · *her/very sweet*

After þat° he spused wore,° · *after/married were*
2750 Wolde° þe erl nouth dwelle þore,° · *would/not stay there*
But sone nam until° his lond, · *went to*
And seysed° it al in his hond, · *took possession of*
And liuede þerinne, he and his wif,° · *wife*
An hundred winter° in god lif,° · *winters/good life*
2755 And gaten° mani children samen,° · *begot/together*
And liueden ay° in blisse and gamen.°— · *lived always/pleasure*
Hwan° þe maydens were spused boþe, · *when*
Hauelok anon° bigan ful rathe° · *right away/quickly*
His Denshe° men to feste° wel · *Danish/endow*
2760 Wit° riche landes and catel,° · *with/goods*
So þat he weren° alle riche: · *they were*
For he was large° and nouth chinche.° · *generous/stingy*

Þer-after sone, with his here,° · *army*
For° he to Lundone,° forto° bere° · *went/London/in order to/be*
2765 Corune,° so þat it sawe · *crowned*
Henglishe ant° Denshe, heye° and lowe, · *English and/high*
Hou he it bar° with mikel° pride, · *wore/much*
For° his barnage° þat was unride.° · *before/nobles/were many*

Þe feste° of his coruning° · *celebration/coronation*
2770 Lastede with gret ioying° · *great joy*
Fourti dawes° and sumdel mo;° · *forty days/somewhat more*
Þo bigunnen° þe Denshe to go · *then began*
Vnto þe king to aske leue,° · *permission (to go)*
And he ne wolde hem nouth° greue;° · *not wanted them not/to offend*
2775 For he saw þat he woren yare° · *were eager*
Into° Denmark for to fare; · *to*
But gaf° hem leue sone anon° · *gave/quickly*
And bitauhte° hem seint Iohan,° · *committed/(to) Saint John*
And bad° Ubbe, his iustise,° · *commanded/justice*
2780 Þat he sholde on ilke wise° · *should in every way*
Denmark yeme° and gete° so · *govern/guard*
Þat no pleynte° come him to. · *complaint*

Hwan he wore parted° alle samen, · *departed*
Hauelok bilefte° wit ioie° and gamen · *remained/joy*

2785 In Engelond, and was þerinne
　　　Sixti winter king with winne,° *joy*
　　　And Goldeboru quen,° þat° i wene° *queen/so that/believe*
　　　So mikel loue was hem bitwene° *between*
　　　Þat al þe werd spak° of hem two. *world spoke*
2790 He louede hire° and she him so, *loved her*
　　　Þat neyþer ower mithe° be *anywhere might*
　　　Fro° oþer, ne° no ioie se° *from/nor/see*
　　　But-yf° he were togidere° boþe; *unless/together*
　　　Neuere yete° ne weren he wroþe,° *never yet/angry*
2795 For here° loue was ay° newe; *their/always*
　　　Neuere yete wordes ne grewe
　　　Bitwene hem, hwarof° ne lathe° *from which/enmity*
　　　Mithe rise, ne no wrathe.

　　　He geten° children hem bitwene *begot*
2800 Sones° and douthres° rith fiuetene,° *sons/daughters/fully fifteen*
　　　Hwarof° þe sones were kinges alle— *of whom*
　　　So wolde° God it sholde bifalle,°— *would/happen*
　　　And þe douhtres alle quenes:
　　　Him° stondes° wel þat god° child strenes.° *for him/(it) is/(a) good/begets*
2805 Nu° haue ye herd° þe gest° al þoru° *now/heard/story/through*
　　　Of Hauelok and of Goldeborw:
　　　Hw he weren° born and hw fedde,° *how they were/raised*
　　　And hou he woren° with wronge ledde° *were/handled*
　　　In here youþe, with trecherie,
2810 With tresoun,° and with felounye;° *treason/felony*
　　　And hou þe swikes haueden tiht° *traitors had intended*
　　　Reuen° hem þat° was here rith,° *to deprive/of what/right*
　　　And hou he weren wreken° wel, *avenged*
　　　Haue ich seyd° you euerilk del;° *I told/every bit*
2815 And forþi° ich wolde biseken° you *therefore/beseech*
　　　Þat hauen° herd þe rim° nu, *have/rhyme*
　　　Þat ilke° of you, with gode° wille, *each/good*
　　　Seye° a pater-noster stille° *say/quietly*
　　　For him þat haueth° þe rym maked,° *has/made*
2820 And þerfore fele nihtes° waked,° *many nights/stayed awake*
　　　Þat Iesu° Crist his soule bringe *Jesus*
　　　Biforn° his fader° at his endinge. Amen. *before/father*

2818. *pater-noster:* Latin, "our father," i.e., the Lord's Prayer.

SIR GAWAIN AND THE GREEN KNIGHT

DATE: c. 1390. ✦ MANUSCRIPT: British Library Cotton Nero A. x (which contains also *Pearl*, *Purity*, and *Patience*). The dialect is that of the Northwest Midlands, probably southern Lancashire. ✦ EDITIONS: Sir Israel Gollancz, Early English Text Society, ES 210 (Oxford, 1940); J. R. R. Tolkien and E. V. Gordon (Oxford, 1925; 2d ed., Norman Davis, 1968). The new emendations and occasional changes in glossarial interpretation of the present text are according to the Davis edition.

The lexical complexities of this poem have necessitated an unusually full gloss, which in turn should remove any translation difficulties for the student. However, certain aspects of the Northwest Midland dialect might bear comment. Typically Northern forms may be seen in (1) the present participle ending *-and(e)*: *farand*, *laȝand*; (2) the *-es/-tz/-ez* ending for the second and third person singular of verbs: (*strokes*, *cnokez*); (3) the interchange of *qu* and *wh*: *quil = while*, *quit = white*, *quat = what*, *whene = queen*; (4) the plural pronouns *þai*, *þay*, *þayres*, and the apocopated imperative *ta* for *take*; (5) the *-ez* ending for noun plurals. On the other hand, *o* before a nasal is typical of West Midland forms: *stonde*, *fong*.

Pronouns should be carefully watched: *ho*, "she" (the Northwest Midland form), *her*, *hir*, *hyr*, "her", *hor*, *her*, "their", and *hi(y)m*, *hom*, *hem*, "them" may cause the greatest confusion.

The scribe, borrowing from the French style, uses *z* and *tz* for final *s/es*: *hatz = has*, *watz = was*, *gotz = goes*, *lykez = likes*; and he often adds the auxiliary *con* to verbs: *con speke*. "does speak" ("speaks") or "did speak" ("spoke"), *con hym bite*, "does him bite" ("bites him"), or "did him bite" ("bit him"). In other words, *con* plus infinitive is used for the present or preterite tense.

Finally, the constant interchange of *u* and *v* must be pointed out: *heuen = heaven*, *euel = evil*, *vnder*, *vnclose*. In names we find an interchange of *g* and *w*: *Gawain = Wawan*, *Guenore = Wenore*.

Sir Gawain and the Green Knight, often considered to be the outstanding Arthurian romance in Middle English—if not the finest example of the whole genre—is a composite of motifs found in Celtic and in Old French romances. The Beheading of The Challenger motif occurs in an 11th-century Irish romance called *Bricriu's Feast*, from which it went into four separate Old French stories (*Le Livre de Caradoc* and others); the Temptation motif is found in French sources and the English *Carl of Carlisle*. G. L. Kittredge theorized that the source of our romance was a French version which already contained the combined motifs, but most recent critics feel that the combining was done by the English author (known as the Pearl Poet, from one of the other works in the MS). It should be noted that Larry Benson in his book *Art and Tradition in*

Sir Gawain and the Green Knight (New Brunswick, N. J., 1965) has shown that the longer version of *Caradoc* may possibly be the direct source for the first scene of the romance.

Sir Gawain is unusual for its plotted action. Whereas in general the incidents of the romances are run together episodically, here the initial New Year's challenge of the Green Knight, a set scene, leads into the description of Gawain's wanderings, which in turn leads to scenes in Bertilak's castle, alternating between temptation and hunting episodes. All are combined in the final meeting with the Green Knight on the barrow. The Pearl Poet shows an unusual tectonic ability, combined with obvious poetic gifts as evidenced in the description of winter scenes and nature in general. In addition, certain of the hunting sequences are of such realistic tenor that they seem to be based on firsthand experience. The author is versed in the customs of court as well as in men's behavior under the courtly veneer. Gawain's actions in bed, and his later sour temper when he discovers the intrigue, are atypical of romance style in their amusing humanity. The demands of alliteration cause problems in reading, and the verbal riches at times tend to embarrass. Yet by these means, in these several thousand words, the poet has presented a picture which is one of the high-water marks of English medieval literature.

FYTTE THE FIRST

I

Siþen° þe sege° and þe assaut° watz sesed° at Troye,	*when/siege/assault/ceased*
þe borȝ brittened° and brent° to brondez° and askez,°	*city destroyed/burned/brands/ashes*
þe tulk° þat þe trammes° of tresoun° þer wroȝt,°	*man/stratagems/treason/wrought*
Watz tried for his tricherie,° þe trewest° on erthe;	*treachery/most patent*
5 Hit° watz Ennias° þe athel,° and his highe kynde,°	*it/Aeneas/noble/noble kindred*
Þat siþen depreced° prouinces, and patrounes bicome°	*afterward conquered/lords became*
Welneȝe° of al þe wele° in þe west iles,	*well-nigh/wealth*
Fro riche° Romulus to Rome ricchis hym° swyþe,°	*when noble/takes his way/quickly*
With gret bobbaunce° þat burȝe° he biges vpon° fyrst,	*great pomp/city/founds at*
10 And neuenes° hit his aune nome,° as hit now hat;°	*names/own name/is called*
Ticius to° Tuskan° and teldes° bigynnes;	*(goes) to/Tuscany/dwellings*
Langaberde° in Lumbardie lyftes° vp homes;	*Langobard/Lombardy raises*

---

5. Aeneas was associated by Guido delle Colonne (*Historia Destructionis Troiae*) with the plot of Antenor, described by Dares Phrygius and Dictys Cretensis, the fraudulent "historians" of the Trojan War, to betray Troy to the Greeks by surrendering to them the Palladium, the sacred statue of Athena preserved in that city. Both were therefore guilty of treason. In addition, Aeneas was later tried and exiled by the Greeks for having concealed Polyxena. Priam's daughter and the beloved of Achilles. That Greek hero was wooing her when Paris gave him his death wound. Aeneas's exile started his wanderings, which led eventually to the founding of Rome by Aeneas and of Britain by his great-grandson Brutus.

7. *west iles;* perhaps the western world, or the British Isles.

11. Ticius has not been identified. He may be Titus Tatius, king of the Sabines, who shared sovereignty over Rome with Romulus after the Sabine women had joined the Roman men.

12. Langobard ("Longbeard"), according to Nennius, the early historian of Britain (*Historia Brittonum*, c. 800), was the eponymous ancestor of the Langobards or Lombards and nephew of Felix Brutus, founder of Britain.

And fer° ouer þe French flod° Felix Brutus   *far/sea*
On mony bonkkes ful brodde° Bretayn° he settez,°   *many slopes very wide/Britain/*
                                                        founds

15   wyth wynne;°   *joy*
     Where werre,° and wrake,° and wonder,°   *war/vengeance/marvel*
     Bi syþez° hatz wont° þer-inne,   *at times/existed*
     And oft boþe blysse and blunder
     Ful skete° hatz skyfted synne.°   *quickly/alternated since*

II

20 Ande quen° þis Bretayn watz bigged° bi þis burn° rych,   *when/founded/knight*
     Bolde° bredden° þer-inne, baret° þat lofden,°   *bold (men)/were bred/fighting/loved*
     In mony turned° tyme tene° þat wroʒten;°   *many (a) difficult/trouble/wrought*
     Mo ferlyes° on þis folde han fallen° here oft   *more marvels/land have happened*
     Þen° in any oþer þat I wot,° syn þat ilk° tyme.   *than/know/same*
25 Bot° of alle þat here bult° of Bretaygne° kynges   *but/dwelt/British*
     Ay° watz Arthur þe hendest,° as I haf herde° telle; *ever/noblest/have heard*
     For-þi° an aunter° in erde° I attle° to schawe,°   *therefore/adventure/land/intend/*
                                                          show

     Þat a selly° in siʒt summe° men hit holden,°   *marvel/sight some/consider*
     And an outtrage° awenture° of Arthurez wonderez;   *very strange/adventure*
30 If ʒe° wyl lysten° þis laye bot on° littel quile,°   *you/listen (to)/a/while*
     I schal telle hit, as-tit,° as I in toun herde,   *right away*
            with tonge;°   *tongue*
        As hit is stad° and stoken,°   *put down/set*
        In stori stif° and stronge,   *firm*
35   With lel° letteres loken,°   *true/fastened*
        In londe so° hatz ben° longe.°   *land as/been/of long usage*

III

Þis kyng lay at Camylot vpon kryst-masse,°   *Christmas*
With mony luflych° lorde, ledez° of þe best,   *worthy/men*

---

13. *French flod:* i.e., English Channel. *Felix Brutus:* the only mention of the first name of the legendary founder of Britain, great-grandson of Aeneas (cf. Geoffrey of Monmouth). Nennius calls him Bryto, i.e., "a Briton."

26. Arthur, according to Nennius a *dux bellorum*, probably a Romanized Celt who successfully stood off the Saxon invaders, may have been the Aurelius Ambrosius mentioned by Gildas as the victor at the battle of Mount Badon in 496. In Geoffrey of Monmouth and other sources Aurelius Ambrosius is often confused with Arthur, perhaps because the two were really identical.

35. The *lel* ("exact") letters which fasten or lock the story characterize the alliterative style of poetry, the *Gawain* poet being part of the great Alliterative Revival of the Northwest. Cf. the Prologue to Chaucer's *Parson's Tale:* "I am a Southren man,/I kan nat geeste 'rum, ram, ruf,' by lettre."

37–43. Malory mentions that Camelot was at Winchester, though there was a Camelot in Somersetshire. Generally the city is also identified with Caerleon-upon-Usk, where Arthur was crowned. Arthur held a full court and wore a crown five times a year: Easter, Ascension Day, Pentecost, All Saints' Day, and Christmas. On these occasions the knights had to wait for an adventure to occur before they could start their evening meal. Christmas, of course, was an especially festive occasion, with feasting, jousting, and *caroles* (ring dances; cf. l. 1026n).

Rekenly° of þe rounde table alle þo° rich breþer,°	*courteous/those/brethren*
40 With rych reuel oryȝt,° and rechles merþes;°	*right well/carefree mirth*
Þer tournayed tulkes° bi-tymez° ful mony,	*jousted knights/at times*
Justed° ful iolilé þise gentyle kniȝtes,°	*jousted/merrily these noble knights*
Syþen kayred° to þe court, caroles to make.	*then returned*
For þer þe fest° watz ilyche° ful fiften° dayes,	*festival/the same/fully fifteen*
45 With alle þe mete° and þe mirþe þat men couþe a-vyse;°	*food/could devise*
Such glaum° ande gle° glorious to here,°	*noise/merrymaking/hear*
Dere dyn vp-on° day, daunsyng on nyȝtes,°	*pleasant noise in/at night*
Al watz hap° vpon heȝe° in hallez and chambrez,	*happiness/high (degree)*
With lordez and ladies, as leuest° him° þoȝt;°	*most pleasant/to them/seemed*
50 With all þe wele of° worlde þay woned° þer samen,°	*joy in/lived/together*
Þe most kyd° knyȝtez vnder kryste seluen,°	*famous/himself*
And þe louelokkest° ladies þat euer lif haden,°	*loveliest/life had*
And he þe comlokest° kyng þat þe court haldes;°	*handsomest/rules*
For al watz þis fayre folk in her° first age,°	*their/(i.e., prime)*
55 on sille;°	*in (the) hall*
Þe hapnest° vnder heuen,	*most fortunate*
Kyng hyȝest mon° of wylle,°	*noblest man/mind*
Hit° were now gret nye° to neuen°	*it/very hard/name*
So hardy a here° on hille.	*host*

IV

60 Wyle nw ȝer° watz so ȝep° þat hit watz nwe cummen,°	*while New Year/fresh/newly come (in)*
Þat day doubble on þe dece° watz þe douth° serued,	*dais/company*
Fro° þe kyng watz cummen with knyȝtes in to þe halle,	*after*
Þe chauntre° of þe chapel cheued° to an ende;	*singing of mass/came*
Loude crye watz þer kest of° clerkez and oþer,	*raised by*
65 Nowel nayted o-newe,° neuened ful° ofte;	*Noel celebrated anew/very*
And syþen riche° forth runnen° to reche honde-selle,°	*noble (men)/run/present gifts*
Ȝeȝed ȝeres ȝiftes° on hiȝ,° ȝelde hem° bi hond,°	*announced (New) Year's gifts/ aloud/offered them/hand*
Debated busyly aboute þo giftes;	

---

44. The fifteen days were from Christmas until the Octave of the Circumcision, January 8.

54. *in her first age:* This may refer to the Golden Age of mankind and society in general; cf. Chaucer's poem *The Former Age*, with the postscript "Finit Etas Prima. Chaucers." The concept of happiness in the First, Former, or Golden Age was common in the Middle Ages; it was discussed by Boethius in *Consolation of Philosophy*, II,m. 5.

65. "Noel" was shouted in celebration all through the Christmas season.

66–68. At every court in medieval England the king dispensed New Year's gifts to his retainers, and the nobility in turn gave gifts to their servants, all of which were duly noted in account books and court rolls. We know that at the New Year Geoffrey Chaucer often received gifts of silver or cloth, as did his wife. This custom went back to a prefeudal heroic society: Hrothgar dispenses gifts in the hall in *Beowulf*, as a good chieftain should. The gifts were evidently proclaimed and contended for in some unknown manner.

Ladies la3ed° ful loude, þo3° þay lost haden,   *laughed/though*
70 And he þat wan° watz not wrothe, þat may 3e° wel trawe.°   *won/you/believe*
Alle þis mirþe þay maden to° þe mete tyme;°   *made at/(i.e., dinner)*
When þay had waschen,° worþyly þay wenten° to sete,°   *washed/went/seats*
Þe best burne ay° abof,° as hit best semed;°   *man ever/above (i.e., in the higher seat)/seemed*

Whene Guenore° ful gay, grayþed° in þe myddes,°   *Guinevere/placed/midst*
75 Dressed° on þe dere des, dubbed° al aboute,   *seated/noble dais, adorned*
Smal sendal bisides,° a selure hir° ouer   *fine silk beside (her)/canopy her*
Of tryed° Tolouse, of Tars tapites in-noghe,°   *excellent-quality/Tharsia carpets many*

Þat were enbrawded° and beten° wyth þe best gemmes,   *embroidered/set*
Þat my3t° be preued° of prys° wyth penyes° to bye,°   *might/proved/worth/pennies (i.e., money/buy*

80   in daye;°   *ever*
      Þe comlokest° to discrye,°   *fairest/behold*
      Þer glent° with y3en° gray,   *glanced/eyes*
      A semloker° þat euer he sy3e,°   *lovelier/saw*
      Soth° mo3t° no mon say.   *in truth/might*

V

85 Bot° Arthure wolde° not ete° til al were serued,   *but/would/eat*
He watz so ioly° of his ioyfnes,° and sum-quat childgered,°   *gay/youthful spirit/somewhat boyish*
His lif liked hym ly3t,° he louied° þe lasse°   *he gay/loved/less*
Auþer° to lenge lye,° or to longe sitte,   *either/long lie*
So bi-sied° him his 3onge blod° and his brayn wylde;°   *stirred/young blood/active*
90 And also anoþer maner meued° him eke,°   *custom moved/also*
Þat he þur3° nobelay° had nomen,° he wolde neuer ete   *through/noble spirit/adopted*
Vpon such a dere° day, er° hym deuised° were   *important/before/told*
Of sum auenturus° þyng an vncouþe° tale,   *some adventurous/strange*
Of sum mayn meruayle,° þat he my3t trawe,   *great marvel*
95 Of alderes,° of armes, of oþer auenturus,   *ancestors*
Oþer° sum segg° hym bi-so3t of° sum siker kny3t,°   *or/man/asked for/trusty knight*
To ioyne° wyth hym in iustyng° in iopardé° to lay,°   *join/jousting/hazard/put (his life)*
Lede lif° for lyf, leue° vchon° oþer,°   *set life/allow/each one/(to the) other*
As fortune wolde fulsun hom° þe fayrer° to haue.   *help him/advantage*

69–70. Davis mentions O. F. Emerson's suggestion (*Journal of English and Germanic Philology*, 21 [1922], 365) that a kiss was the forfeit over which the ladies laughed though they had lost, and concerning which the winners were not "wroth."

73. Evidently the Round Table, built to avoid the distinction of rank (cf. Layamon's *Brut*), is not used here.

77. Both tuly, a red silk from Toulouse, and silk cloth from Tharsia (the kingdom of Tarse, described by Mandeville as bordering on Turkestan) were exceedingly rich and fine materials.

90–99. Other romances, e.g., *Le Livre de Caradoc*, *Le Queste del Saint Graal*, the *Roman de Perceval*, and the Vulgate *Merlin* also mention this custom.

100 Þis watz þe kynges countenaunce° where he in court were, *custom*
    At vch farand fest° among his fre meny,° *each splendid festival/noble company*
                in halle;
        Þer-fore of face so fere° *proud*
        He stiȝtlez stif° in stalle,° *stands fearless/place*
105   Ful ȝep° in þat nw ȝere,° *very valiant/New Year*
        Much mirthe he mas° with alle. *makes*

VI

    Thus þer stondes° in stale° þe stif° kyng his-seluen,° *stands/place/bold/himself*
    Talkkande bifore þe hyȝe° table of trifles ful hende;° *high/graciously*
    There gode° Gawan watȝ grayþed,° Gwenore bisyde, *good/seated*
110 And Agrauayn a la dure mayn on þat oþer syde sittes,
    Boþe þe kynges sister sunes,° and ful siker kniȝtes; *sister's sons*
    Bischop Bawdewyn abof° bi-ginez þe table, *above (i.e., at the head)*
    And Ywan, Vryn son, ette wit hym-seluen;° *ate with him*
    Þise° were diȝt° on þe des,° and derworþly° serued, *these/seated/dais/honorably*
115 And siþen mony siker° segge at þe sidbordez.° *then many (a) good/side tables*
    Þen þe first cors come° with crakkyng° of trumpes,° *course came/flourish/trumpets*
    Wyth mony baner° ful bryȝt,° þat þer-bi henged,° *banner/bright/hung*
    Nwe nakryn° noyse with þe noble pipes, *kettledrum*
    Wylde werbles° and wyȝt wakned lote,° *warblings/loud wakening sound*
120 Þat mony hert° ful hiȝe° hef° at her towches;° *heart/high/was uplifted/their sounds*
    Dayntes dryuen° þer-wyth of ful derc metes,° *delicacies brought/costly foods*
    Foysoun° of þe fresche,° and on so fele° disches, *abundance/fresh (meats)/many*
    Þat pine° to fynde þe place þe peple bi-forne° *it was difficult/people before*
    For to sette þe sylueren,° þat sere sewes halden,° *silver (dishes)/various stews contained*
125   on clothe;
        Iche lede° as he loued hym-selue° *each man/liked himself*
        Þer laght with-outen° loþe,° *took without/being begrudged*
        Ay° two had disches twelue, *each*
        Good ber,° and bryȝt wyn° boþe. *beer/wine*

109–11. Gawain and Agravain were brothers, nephews of Arthur, sons of King Loth of Lodonesia (Orkney) and Arthur's sister Anna. The uncle-nephew relationship in the romances and chansons de geste is an especially close one (cf. above, p. 77, ll. 728–29n); thus Gawain and Agravain are here seated at the high table. Gawain is the chief and most courteous knight of the Round Table, though his fame suffers in later romances. In Malory, Agravain joins with Modred in trapping Lancelot and Guinevere. *a la dure mayn:* "of the hard hand."

112–13. Bishop Baldwin is the Bedwini, bishop to Arthur, in the Mabinogian stories of *Kilhwch and Olwen* and *The Dream of Rhonabwy*, and in one of the Welsh Triads he is named as the chief of bishops in Cornwall. Ywain was another nephew of Arthur, son of Urin and Brimesent, Arthur's half sister. According to l. 128, two people are served from the same dish. Thus Ywain eats with the bishop, Arthur with Guinevere, and Gawain, sitting next to the queen, with Agravain.

115. The high table was situated on a dais at one end of the hall; the *sidbordez* were rows of tables near and parallel to the long sides of the hall. The arrangement is used today in the eating halls of Oxford and Cambridge colleges.

116–20. The laying of the tablecloth was usually accompanied by prayers and trumpets. The ceremony of bringing in the food was quite ritualistic and solemn.

VII

¹³⁰ Now wyl I of hor seruise° say yow° no more,   *their service/to you*
   For vch wyȝe° may wel wit° no wont° þat þer were;   *person/know (of)/lack*
   An oþer noyse ful newe neȝed° biliue,°   *drew near/quickly*
   Þat þe lude myȝt haf leue° lif-lode° to cach.°   *king might have permission/food/ take*

   For vneþe° watz þe noyce° not a whyle sesed,°   *scarcely/noise (of music)/ceased*
¹³⁵ And þe fyrst cource° in þe court kyndely° serued,   *course/duly*
   Þer hales° in at þe halle dor an aghlich mayster,°   *rushes/terrible knight*
   On° þe most on° þe molde° on mesure hyghe;   *one/biggest in/earth*
   Fro° þe swyre° to þe swange° so sware° and so þik,°   *from/neck/waist/square/stout*
   And his lyndes° and his lymes° so longe and so grete,°   *loins/limbs/great*
¹⁴⁰ Half etayn° in erde° I hope° þat he were.   *giant/earth/think*
   Bot mon° most I algate° mynn° hym to bene,°   *but man/at any rate/declare/be*
   And þat þe myriest° in his muckel° þat myȝt ride;   *merriest/size*
   For of bak° and of brest al° were his bodi sturne,°   *in back/although/forbidding*
   Bot his wombe° and his wast° were worthily smale,°   *belly/waist/suitably small*
¹⁴⁵ And alle his fetures° folȝande,° in forme þat he hade,°   *features/in similar manner/had*
         ful clene;°   *very fair*
      For wonder of° his hwe° men hade,   *at/color*
      Set in his semblaunt sene;°   *looks (plain to be) seen*
      He ferde° as freke were fade,°   *fared/man (that) were fey*
¹⁵⁰   And ouer-al enker° grene.   *bright*

VIII

   Ande al grayþed° in grene þis gome° and his wedes,°   *arrayed/man/clothes*
   A strayt cote° ful streȝt,° þat stek° on his sides,   *tight coat/straight/fitted close*
   A mere mantile abof, mensked° with-inne,   *gay mantle above, adorned*
   With pelure pured apert° þe pane° ful clene,   *fur trimmed plainly/fur lining*
¹⁵⁵ With blyþe blaunner° ful bryȝt,° and his hod° boþe,   *splendid ermine/bright/hood*
   Þat watz laȝt° fro his lokkez,° and layde on his schulderes;°   *caught back/locks/shoulders*
   Heme,° wel haled° hose of þat same grene,   *neat/fitted*
   Þat spenet° on his sparlyr,° and clene spures vnder,   *clung/calves*
   Of bryȝt golde, vpon silk bordes,° barred ful ryche,°   *embroidered strips/richly*
¹⁶⁰ And scholes° vnder schankes, þere þe schalk° rides;   *shoeless/man*
   And alle his vesture uerayly° watz clene verdure,°   *clothing truly/pure green*
   Boþe þe barres of his belt and oþer blyþe° stones,   *bright*
   Þat were richely rayled° in his aray clene,   *set*

---

150. Green was the proverbial color of beings from another world—fairies, even devils (cf. Chaucer's *Friar's Tale,* where the Devil's messenger is dressed as a yeoman in Lincoln green).
160. *scholes vnder schankes:* i.e., "without shoes on his feet."

Davis mentions that medieval French and Spanish texts and illustrations show knights on peaceful missions wearing hose without shoes.

Aboutte hym-self and his sadel, vpon silk werkez,°   *embroidery*
165 Þat were to tor° for to telle of tryfles° þe halue,°   *too difficult/details/half*
Þat were enbrauded° abof, wyth bryddes° and flyʒes,°   *embroidered/birds/butterflies*
With gay gaudi° of grene, þe golde ay° in myddes;°   *beads/ever/(the) midst*
Þe pendauntes of his payttrure,° þe proude cropure,°   *breast trappings/splendid crupper*
His molaynes,° and alle þe metail anamayld° was þenne,   *bridle bits/enameled*
170 Þe steropes° þat he stod° on, stayned° of þe same,   *stirrups/stood/colored*
And his arsounz° al after,° and his aþel° skyrtes,°   *saddlebows/behind/noble/saddle skirts*

Þat euer glemered° and glent° al of grene stones.   *glimmered/glinted*
Þe fole° þat he ferkkes° on, fyn° of þat ilke,°   *horse/rides/completely/same (color)*
     sertayn;°   *certainly*
175   A grene hors gret and þikke,°   *sturdy*
   A stede° ful stif° to strayne,°   *steed/strong/manage*
   In brawden° brydel quik,°   *embroidered/restive*
   To þe gome° he watz ful gayn.°   *knight/fully suited*

IX

Wel° gay watz þis gome gered° in grene,   *very/attired*
180 And þe here° of his hed of° his hors swete;°   *hair/head (that) of/matched*
Fayre fannand fax vmbe-foldes° his schulderes;   *waving hair enfolds*
A much berd° as a busk° ouer his brest henges,°   *great beard/bush/hangs*
Þat wyth his hiʒlich° here, þat of° his hed reches,°   *splendid/from/hangs*
Watz euesed° al vmbe-torne,° a-bof his elbowes,   *clipped/around*
185 Þat° half his armes þer vnder were halched° in þe wyse°   *so that/enclosed/manner*
Of a kyngez capados,° þat closes° his swyre.°   *cape/encloses/neck*
Þe mane of þat mayn° hors much to hit° lyke,   *great/it*
Wel cresped° and cemmed° wyth knottes ful mony,°   *curled/combed/very many*
Folden° in wyth fildore° aboute þe fayre grene,   *plaited/gold thread*
190 Ay a herle° of þe here, an oþer of golde;   *strand*
Þe tayl and his toppyng twynnen° of a sute,°   *forelock plaited/to match*
And bounden° boþe wyth a bande of a bryʒt° grene,   *bound/bright*
Dubbed° wyth ful dere° stonez, as þe dok lasted,°   *adorned/precious/tail extended*
Syþen þrawen° wyth a þwong a þwarle° knot alofte,   *then bound/thong/intricate*
195 Þer mony bellez ful bryʒt of brende° golde rungen.°   *burnished/rang*
Such a fole vpon folde, ne freke° þat hym rydes,   *earth, nor man*
Watz neuer sene° in þat sale° wyth syʒt er° þat tyme,   *seen/hall/sight before*
     with yʒe;°   *eye*
   He loked° as layt° so lyʒt,°   *looked/lightning/bright*
200   So sayd al þat hym syʒe,°   *saw*
   Hit semed° as° no mon myʒt,°   *seemed/as if/man might*
   Vnder his dynttez dryʒe.°   *blows survive*

X

Wheþer hade° he no helme° ne hawbergh nauþer,°   *however had/helmet/hauberk neither*
Ne no pysan,° ne no plate þat pented° to armes,   *breast-neck armor/pertained*
205 Ne no schafte° ne no schelde,° to schwue° ne to smyte,   *spear/shield/thrust*
Bot° in his on honde° he hade a holyn bobbe,°   *but/one hand/holly branch*
Þat is grattest° in grene, when greuez° ar bare,   *greatest/groves*
And an ax in his oþer, a hoge° and vn-mete,°   *huge/monstrous*
A spetos sparþe° to expoun° in spelle° quo-so° myȝt;   *cruel ax/describe/words/whoso*
210 Þe lenkþe° of an elnȝerde° þe large hede° hade,   *length/ell yard/head*
Þe grayn° al of grene stele° and of golde hewen,°   *blade/steel/shaped*
Þe bit burnyst bryzt,° with a brod egge,°   *bright/broad edge*
As wel schapen° to schere° as scharp rasores;   *made/cut*
Þe stele° of a stif° staf þe sturne° hit bi-grypte,°   *shaft/stout/grim (knight)/gripped by*

215 Þat watz wounden° wyth yrn° to þe wandez° ende,   *wound/iron/shaft's*
And al bigrauen° with grene, in gracios werkes;°   *engraved/designs*
A lace° lapped aboute, þat louked° at þe hede,   *thong/fastened*
And so after° þe halme halched° ful ofte,   *around/shaft looped*
Wyth tryed° tasselez þerto tacched in-noghe,°   *fine/attached many*
220 On botounz° of þe bryȝt grene brayden° ful ryche.   *buttons/embroidered*
Þis haþel° heldez hym° in, and þe halle entres,   *knight/goes*
Driuande° to þe heȝe dece, dut° he no woþe,°   *going/high dais, feared/danger*
Haylsed° he neuer one, bot heȝe he ouer° loked.   *greeted/over (them)*
Þe fyrst word þat he warp,° "Wher is," he sayd,   *uttered*
225 "Þe gouernour of þis gyng?° Gladly I wolde°   *company/would*
Se° þat segg° in syȝt, and with hym self speke°   *see/man/speak*
    raysoun."°   *words*
    To knyȝtez° he kest° his yȝe,   *knights/cast*
    And reled hym° vp and doun,   *rolled them*
230   He stemmed° and con° studie,   *stopped/did*
    Quo walt° þer most renoun.   *who possessed*

XI

Ther watz lokyng on lenþe,° þe lude° to be-holde,   *for a long time/man*
For vch° mon had meruayle quat hit mene° myȝt,   *each/wonder what it mean*
Þat a haþel and a horse myȝt such a hwe° lach,°   *color/take on*
235 As growe° grene as þe gres° and grener hit semed,°   *(to) grow/grass/seemed*
Þen° grene aumayl° on golde glowande bryȝter;°   *than/enamel/brighter*
Al studied þat þer stod,° and stalked° hym nerre,°   *stood/approached/nearer*
Wyth al þe wonder of° þe worlde, what he worch schulde.°   *in/do should*

---

203. The hauberk was a long tunic of chain mail.
237. *þat þer stod:* This must refer to the servants who were moving about; the nobility would have been sitting at the tables in polite and frozen silence.

For fele sellyez° had þay sen,° bot such neuer are,° *many marvels/seen/before*
240 For-þi° for fantoum° and fayryȝe° þe folk þere hit demed;° *therefore/illusion/magic/judged*
Þer-fore to answare° watz arȝe° mony aþel freke,° *answer/afraid/many (a) noble knight*
And al stouned° at his steuen,° and stonstil° seten,° *were amazed/voice/stone-still/sat*
In a swoghe° sylence þurȝ° þe sale riche° *dead/throughout/hall noble*
As° al were slypped vpon° slepe° so slaked hor lotez° *as if/fallen/asleep/stopped their speech*

245   in hyȝe;° *suddenly*
      I deme° hit not al for doute,° *think/fear*
      Bot sum° for cortaysye,° *but some/courtesy*
      Bot let hym þat al schulde loute,° *reverence*
      Cast° vnto þat wyȝe.° *speak/man*

XII

250 Þenn Arþour bifore þe hiȝ° dece þat auenture° byholdez, *high/adventure*
And rekenly° hym reuerenced,° for rad° was he neuer, *courteously/saluted/afraid*
And sayde, "Wyȝe, welcum iwys° to þis place, *sir, welcome indeed*
Þe hede° of þis ostel° Arthour I hat;° *head/house/am called*
Liȝt luflych° adoun, and lenge,° I þe° praye, *dismount graciously/stay/you*
255 And quat so° þy wylle is, we schal wyt° after." *whatever/learn*
"Nay, as° help me," quod° þe haþel, "he þat on hyȝe syttes,° *so/said/high dwells*
To wone° any quyle° in þis won,° hit watz not myn ernde;° *remain/while/abode/my purpose*
Bot for° þe los° of þe, lede,° is lyft° vp so hyȝe, *because/praise/lord/raised*
And þy burȝ° and þy burnes° best ar holden,° *city/knights/considered*
260 Stifest° vnder stel-gere° on stedes° to ryde, *strongest/steel armor/steeds*
Þe wyȝtest° and þe worþyest of þe worldes kynde,° *boldest/(i.e., among men)*
Preue° for to play° wyth in oþer pure laykez:° *valiant/contend/noble sports*
And here is kydde° cortaysye, as I haf herd carp,° *shown/have heard tell*
And þat hatz wayned° me hider, i-wyis,° at þis tyme. *brought/hither, indeed*
265 Ȝe° may be seker° bi þis braunch° þat I bere° here, *you/sure/branch/bear*
Þat I passe as in pes,° and no plyȝt seche;° *peace/hostility seek*
For had I founded° in fere,° in feȝtyng wyse,° *come/company/fighting manner*
I haue a hauberghe° at home and a helme° boþe, *hauberk/helmet*
A schelde,° and a scharp spere,° schinande bryȝt, *shield/spear*
270 Ande oþer weppenes° to welde,° I wene° wel als,° *weapons/wield/know (how to)/also*
Bot for I wolde° no were,° my wedez° ar softer. *wish/war/clothes*
Bot if þou be so bold as alle burnez tellen,° *men tell*
Þou wyl grant me godly° þe gomen° þat I ask, *graciously/game*
      bi ryȝt."° *right*

---

248. *hym . . . loute:* i.e., Arthur.

265. The holly branch was carried as a sign of peace and the Christmas spirit. The popularity of Holly-versus-Ivy Christmas games, in which men took one part, women another, is evidenced by the numerous holly-and-ivy songs among the Middle English lyrics.

275   Arthour con onsware,°   *did answer*
       And sayd, "Sir cortays kny3t,°   *courteous knight*
       If þou craue batayl bare,°   *battle actual*
       Here faylez þou not to fy3t."°   *fight*

XIII

       "Nay, frayst° I no fy3t, in fayth I þe telle,   *seek*
280   Hit arn° aboute on þis bench bot berdlez chylder;°   *there are/only beardless children*
       If I were hasped° in armes on a he3e° stede,   *fastened/high*
       Here is no mon° me to mach,° for my3tez° so wayke.°   *man/match/(his) might (is)/weak*
       For-þy° I craue in þis court a crystemas gomen,   *therefore*
       For hit° is 3ol° and nwe 3er,° and here ar 3ep mony;°   *it/Yule/New Year/valiant (men)*
                                                                   many

285   If any so hardy in þis hous holdez hym-seluen,°   *himself*
       Be so bolde in his blod, brayn° in hys hede,°   *blood, reckless/head*
       Þat dar stifly° strike a strok° for an oþer,   *boldly/stroke*
       I schal gif° hym of° my gyft þys giserne ryche,°   *give/as/battle-ax noble*
       Þis ax, þat is heué in-nogh,° to hondele° as hym lykes,° *heavy enough/use/he wishes*
290   And I shal bide° þe fyrst bur,° as bare° as I sitte.   *await/blow/unarmed*
       If any freke° be so felle° to fonde þat° I telle,°   *man/fierce/try what/say*
       Lepe ly3tly° me to, and lach° þis weppen,   *leap quickly/take*
       I quit clayme° hit for euer, kepe° hit as his auen,°   *renounce/keep/own*
       And I schal stonde° hym a strok, stif on° þis flet,°   *take from/in/hall*
295   Ellez° þou wyl di3t° me þe dom° to dele° hym an oþer, *provided/grant/right/deal*
                          barlay;°   *when I claim it*
                   And 3et gif° hym respite,   *(I) give*
                   A twelmonyth° and a day;   *year*
                   Now hy3e,° and let se tite°   *hurry/let (us) see quickly*
300   Dar any° her-inne o3t° say."   *if any dare/anything*

XIV

       If he hem stowned vpon° fyrst, stiller were þanne°   *them astonished at/then*
       Alle þe hered-men° in halle, þe hy3° and þe lo3e;°   *courtiers/high/low*
       Þe renk° on his rounce° hym ruched° in his sadel   *man/horse/turned*
       And runisch-ly° his rede y3en° he reled° aboute,   *fiercely/red eyes/rolled*
305   Bende° his bresed bro3ez, bly-cande° grene,   *knitted/bristling brows, shining*
       Wayued his berde° for to wayte quo-so wolde° ryse.   *beard/await whoso would*
       When non wolde° kepe hym with carp° he co3ed ful hy3e,° *none would/talk with him/shouted*
                                                                   very loud

---

288. *giserne:* The gisarm was a halberd, a long-handled ax with a spike or knife at the tip. It is used here loosely to mean "ax," since it does not fit the illustration of Cotton Nero A. x.

296. *barlay;* According to Tolkien and Gordon, this term is used in modern English dialects as a cry for a truce in games, though Davis mentions that the sense of "truce" does not fit the situation here. He glosses it: "(when I claim) my turn."

Ande rimed hym° ful richley,° and ry3t hym° to speke:°   *drew himself up/lordly/proceeded/ speak*

"What, is þis Arþures hous," quod° þe haþel° þenne,   *said/man*

310 "Þat al þe rous rennes° of, þur3 ryalmes° so mony?   *fame runs/through realms*

Where is now your sourquydrye° and your conquestes,   *pride*

Your gryndel-layk,° and your greme,° and your grete° wordes?   *fierceness/anger/great*

Now is þe reuel and þe renoun of þe rounde table

Ouer-walt° wyth a worde of on wy3es speche;°   *overturned/one man's speech*

315 For al dares° for drede,° with-oute dynt schewed!"°   *cowers/fear/blow shown*

Wyth þis he la3es° so loude, þat þe lorde greued;°   *laughs/took offense*

Þe blod schot for scham° in-to his schyre° face   *shame/fair*

       And lere;°   *cheek*

     He wex° as wroth as wynde,°   *grew/(a turbulent) wind*

320   So did alle þat þer were,

     Þe kyng as kene° bi kynde,°   *so bold/nature*

     Þen stod° þat stif mon nere.°   *stood/man near*

XV

Ande sayde, "Haþel,° by hauen þyn° askyng is nys,°   *knight/heaven your/foolish*

And as þou foly° hatz frayst, fynde þe be-houes;°   *folly/sought, (to) find (it) you behooves*

325 I know no gome° þat is gast° of þy grete wordes.   *man/afraid*

Gif me now þy geserne, vpon° Godez halue,°   *ax, for/sake*

And I schal bayþen° þy bone,° þat þou boden habbes."°   *grant/demand/requested have*

Ly3tly lepez he hym to, and la3t° at° his honde;°   *caught hold/of/hand*

Þen feersly° þat oþer freke vpon fote ly3tis.°   *fiercely/feet dismounts*

330 Now hatz Arthure his axe, and þe halme grypez,°   *shaft grips*

And sturnely sturez hit° aboute, þat stryke° wyth hit þo3t.°   *grimly brandishes it/(to) strike/ intended*

Þe stif° mon hym bifore stod vpon hy3t,°   *bold/towering*

Herre þen° ani in þe hous by þe hede° and more;   *taller than/head*

Wyth sturne schere þer° he stod, he stroked his berde,   *face where*

335 And wyth a countenaunce dry3e° he dro3° doun his cote,   *countenance unmoved/drew*

No more mate ne° dismayd for hys mayn dintez,°   *daunted nor/strong blows*

Þen° any burne° vpon bench hade bro3t° hym to drynk   *than (if)/knight/had brought*

       of wyne,

     Gawan, þat sate° bi þe quene,   *sat*

340   To þe kyng he can° enclyne,°   *did/bow his head*

     "I be-seche° now with sa3ez sene,°   *beseech/words plain*

     Þis melly mot° be myne."   *contest might*

XVI

"Wolde 3e, worþilych° lorde," quod Gawan to þe kyng,   *would you, honored*

"Bid me bo3e fro° þis benche, and stonde° by yow° þere,   *go from/stand/you*

³⁴⁵ Þat I wyth-oute vylanye my3t voyde° þis table,   *discourtesy might leave*
And þat my legge° lady lyked not ille,°   *liege/(it) did not displease*
I wolde com to your counseyl,° bifore your cort ryche.°   *counsel/noble*
For me° þink hit° not semly,° as hit is soþ knawen,°   *I/it/right/truly known*
Þer° such an askyng° is heuened° so hy3e° in your sale,°   *when/request/raised/arrogantly/hall*
³⁵⁰ Þa33e° 30ur-self be talenttyf° to take hit to your-seluen,°   *though/desirous/yourself*
Whil mony° so bolde yow aboute vpon bench sytten,°   *many/sit*
Þat vnder heuen, I hope, non° ha3er° er° of wylle,°   *think, none/more warlike/are/mind*
Ne better bodyes° on bent, þer baret° is rered;°   *(i.e., men)/battlefield, where fighting/raised*

I am þe wakkest,° I wot,° and of wyt feblest,   *weakest/know*
³⁵⁵ And lest lur of° my lyf, quo laytes° þe soþe,°   *least loss is/life, who seeks/truth*
Bot° for as much° as 3e ar myn em,° I am only to prayse,°   *only/inasmuch/my uncle/be praised*
No bounté bot° your blod° I in my bodé° knowe;   *virtue but/blood/person*
And syþen° þis note° is so nys,° þat no3t° hit yow falles,°   *since/business/foolish/not at all/ befits*

And I haue frayned° hit at yow fyrst, foldez° hit to me,   *asked/grant*
³⁶⁰ And if I carp° not comlyly,° let alle þis cort ryche   *speak/fittingly*
            bout° blame."   *be without*
      Ryche to-geder con roun,°   *nobles together did whisper*
      And syþen° þay redden° alle same,°   *then/advised/together*
      To ryd° þe kyng wyth croun,   *relieve (of combat)*
³⁶⁵   And gif° Gawan þe game.   *give*

XVII

Þen comaunded° þe kyng þe kny3t° for to ryse;   *commanded/knight*
And he ful radly° vp ros,° and ruchched hym fayre,°   *very promptly/rose/prepared himself well*

Kneled° doun bifore þe kyng, and cachez° þat weppen;°   *knelt/seizes/weapon*
And he luflyly° hit hym laft,° and lyfte vp his honde,°   *graciously/gave/hand*
³⁷⁰ And gef° hym Goddez blessyng, and gladly hum biddes   *gave*
Þat his hert° and his honde schulde° hardi be boþe.   *heart/should*
"Kepe þe° cosyn,"° quod° þe kyng, "þat þou on kyrf sette,°   *take care/cousin/said/to cutting apply (yourself)*

And if þou redez° hym ry3t, redly° I trowe,°   *deal with/right, fully/believe*
Þat þou schal byden° þe bur° þat he schal bede° after."   *survive/blow/offer*
³⁷⁵ Gawan gotz° to þe gome,° with giserne° in honde,   *goes/man/ax*
And he baldly° hym bydez,° he bayst° neuer þe helder.°   *boldly/awaits/was dismayed/more*
Þen carppez to sir Gawan þe kny3t in þe grene,
"Refourme we° oure for-wardes, er° we fyrre passe.°   *let us restate/agreement, before/ further proceed*

358–65. Gawain feels this "game" is beneath the honor of the king. It is not a true adventure which would test Arthur's courage, but rather a facetious jest.

374. Macabre humor on Arthur's part.

Fyrst I eþe þe, haþel,° how þat þou hattes,°   *entreat you, knight/are called*
380 Þat þou me telle truly, as I tryst° may?"   *believe*
"In god° fayth," quod þe goode knyȝt, "Gawan I hatte,°   *good/am called*
Þat bede þe þis buffet, quat-so° bi-fallez after,   *blow, whatever*
And at þis tyme twelmonyth° take at° þe anoþer,   *(in a) year/from*
Wyth what weppen so° þou wylt, and wyth° no wyȝ ellez,°   *whatever weapon/from/man else*
385   on lyue."°   *alive*
    Þat oþer on-swarez° agayn,   *answers*
    "Sir Gawan, so mot° I þryue,   *may*
    As I am ferly fayn,°   *exceedingly glad*
    Þis dint° þat þou schal dryue."°   *blow/strike*

XVIII

390 "Bigog,"° quod þe grene knyȝt, "sir Gawan, me lykes,°   *by God/I am pleased*
Þat I schal fange° at þy fust þat° I haf frayst° here;   *receive/hand what/have sought*
And þou hatz redily rehersed,° bi resoun° ful trwe,°   *rightly repeated/words/true*
Clanly° al þe couenaunt° þat I þe kynge asked,   *exactly/compact*
Saf° þat þou schal siker° me, segge, bi° þi trawþe,°   *except/pledge/knight, on/honor*
395 Þat þou schal seche° me þi-self, where-so° þou hopes°   *seek/wherever/think*
I may be funde° vpon folde,° and foch þe° such wages   *found/earth/take for yourself*
As þou deles° me to day, bifore þis douþe ryche."°   *give/company noble*
"Where schulde I wale° þe," quod Gauan, "where is þy place?   *find*
I wot° neuer where þou wonyes,° bi hym þat me wroȝt,°   *know/dwell/made*
400 Ne° I know not þe, knyȝt, þy cort, nc þi name.   *nor*
Bot teche° me truly þer-to,° and telle me howe þou hattes,   *but inform/thereof*
And I schal ware° alle my wyt to wynne me° þeder,°   *employ/find my way/there*
And þat I swere° þe for soþe,° and by my seker traweþ."°   *swear/truth/plighted word*
"Þat is in-nogh° in nwe ȝer,° hit nedes° no more,"   *enough/New Year/it needs*
405 Quod þe gome in þe grene to Gawan þe hende,°   *gracious*
"Ȝif° I þe telle trwly, quen° I þe tape haue,°   *if/truly, when/blow have (received)*
And þou me smoþely° hatz smyten, smartly° I þe teche   *neatly/smitten, promptly*
Of my hous, and my home, and myn owen nome,°   *my own name*
Þen may þou frayst my fare,° and forwardez holde,°   *see what I will do/keep*
410 And if I spende° no speche,° þenne spedez° þou þe better,   *utter/speech/fare*
For þou may leng° in þy londe,° and layt° no fyrre,   *stay/land/seek*
    bot slokes!°   *enough*
    Ta° now þy grymme tole° to þe,   *take/weapon*
    And let° se how þou cnokez."°   *let (us)/strike*
415   "Gladly sir, for° soþe,"   *in*
    Quod° Gawan; his ax he strokes.   *said*

XIX

The grene knyȝt° vpon grounde grayþely° hym dresses,°   *knight/at once/takes his stand*
A little lut° with þe hede,° þe lere° he discourerez,°   *bent/head/flesh/uncovers*

His longe louelych lokkez° he layd ouer his croun,   *lovely locks*
420 Let þe naked nec° to þe note° schewe.°   *neck/in readiness/show*
Gauan gripped to his ax, and gederes° hit on hyȝt,°   *gathers/high*
Þe kay fot° on þe folde° he be-fore sette,   *left foot/ground*
Let hit doun lyȝtly lyȝt° on þe naked,°   *swiftly land/bare (flesh)*
Þat° þe scharp° of þe schalk schyndered° þe bones,   *so that/sharp (blade)/man cleft*
425 And schrank þurȝ° þe schyire grece,° and scade° hit in twynne,°   *sank through/fair flesh/severed/two*
Þat þe bit° of þe broun stel bot° on þe grounde.   *blade/shining steel bit*
Þe fayre hede fro° þe halce° hit to þe erþe,   *from/neck*
Þat fele° hit foyned° wyth her fete, þere° hit forth roled;   *many/kicked/their feet, where*
Þe blod brayd° fro þe body, þat blykked° on þe grene;   *blood spurted/shone*
430 And nawþer° faltered ne fel þe freke° neuer þe helder,°   *neither/man/more*
Bot styþly° he start° forth vpon styf schonkes,°   *undismayed/sprang/unweakened legs*

And runyschly° he raȝt° out, þere as° renkkez stoden,°   *fiercely/reached/where/knights stood*
Laȝt to° his lufly hed,° and lyft° hit vp sone;°   *seized/fair head/raised/quickly*
And syþen boȝez° to his blonk,° þe brydel he cachchez,°   *then goes/horse/seizes*
435 Steppez in to stel-bawe° and strydez° alofte,   *stirrups/mounts*
And his hede by þe here° in his honde haldez;°   *hair/hand holds*
And as sadly° þe segge hym° in his sadel° sette,   *firmly/knight himself/saddle*
As° non vnhap° had hym ayled, þaȝ hedlez° he were,   *as if/no mishap/though headless*
    in stedde;°   *there*
440   He brayde° his bulk° aboute,   *twisted/trunk*
   Þat vgly bodi þat bledde,
   Moni on° of hym had doute,°   *many (a) one/fear*
   Bi þat° his resounz° were redde.°   *by the time/words/spoken*

XX

For þe hede in his honde he haldez vp euen,°   *straight*
445 To-ward þe derrest° on þe dece° he dressez° þe face,   *noblest/dais/turns*
And hit lyfte° vp þe yȝe-lyddez,° and loked° ful brode,°   *it raised/eyelids/looked/with a broad stare*

And meled° þus much with his muthe,° as ȝe° may now here.°   *said/mouth/you/hear*
"Loke,° Gawan, þou° be grayþe° to go as þou hettez,°   *see/(that) you/ready/promised*
And layte° as lelly° til þou me, lude,° fynde,   *seek/faithfully/knight*
450 As þou hatz hette in þis halle, herande° þise° knyȝtes;   *in the hearing of/these*
To þe grene chapel þou chose,° I charge þe,° to fotte°   *go/you/receive*
Such a dunt° as þou hatz dalt, disserued° þou habbez°   *blow/dealt, deserved/have*
To be ȝederly ȝolden° on nw ȝeres° morn;   *promptly repaid/New Year's*

---

426. The term "brown" applied to metal is already seen in OE *brūnecg* (*Beowulf*: "brown sword") and OF *brunir* (cf. Mod. Eng. *burnish*). It is normally used in the sense of "shining," but may have originally referred to the process of "browning" or tempering steel.

427–39. Originally the Green Knight was under an enchant-ment, and his beheading broke the spell. Of course the story is greatly altered here, but the original motif can be seen in the romance parody *Sir Gawain and the Carl of Carlyle*.

445. *þe derrest*: A. C. Cawley in his edition (New York, Everyman's Library, 1962) feels this probably refers to Guinevere (cf. ll. 2459–62).

Þe knyȝt of þe grene chapel men knowen° me mony;°	*know/many*
455 For-þi° me for to fynde if þou fraystez,° faylez° þou neuer,	*therefore/seek/will fail*
Þer-fore com, oþer recreaunt° be calde° þe be-houeus.''°	*or coward/called/must*
With a runisch rout° þe raynez° he tornez,°	*violent jerk/reins/turns*
Halled° out at þe hal-dor, his hed in his hande,	*passed*
Þat þe fyr° of þe flynt flaȝe° fro fole houes.°	*fire/flew/horse's hooves*
460 To quat kyth° he be-com, knwe non° þere,	*what land/returned, knew none*
Neuermore þen þay wyste fram queþen° he watz wonnen;°	*knew from where/come*
what þenne?	
Þe kyng and Gawen þare,°	*there*
At þat grene þay laȝe° and grenne,°	*green (man) they laugh/grin*
465 Ȝet breued° watz hit ful bare,°	*spoke/quite openly*
A meruayl° among þo° menne.	*marvel/those*

XXI

Þaȝ Arþer þe hende° kyng at hert hade° wonder,	*gracious/heart had*
He let no semblaunt° be sene, bot° sayde ful hyȝe°	*sign/seen, but/very loudly*
To þe comlych° quene, wyth cortays speche,°	*comely/courteous speech*
470 "Dere° dame, to day demay° yow neuer;	*dear/dismayed (be)*
Wel by-commes° such craft vpon° cristmasse,	*is fitting/affairs at*
Laykyng° of enterludez, to laȝe and to syng,	*playing*
Among þise, kynde° caroles of knyȝtez° and ladyez;	*courtly/knights*
Neuer-þe-lece° to my mete° I may me wel dres,°	*nevertheless/meal/turn*
475 For I haf sen° a selly,° I may not for-sake.''°	*have seen/marvel/deny*
He glent° vpon sir Gawen, and gaynly° he sayde,	*looked/pertinently*
"Now sir, heng° vp þyn° ax, þat hatz in-nogh hewen.''°	*hang/your/enough hewn*
And hit watz don abof° þe dece, on doser° to henge,	*put above/tapestry*
Þer° alle men for° meruayl myȝt° on hit loke,	*where/as a/might*
480 And bi trwe tytel° þer-of to telle þe wonder.	*genuine authority*
Þenne þay boȝed° to a borde° þise burnes to-geder,	*turned/table/knights together*
Þe kyng and þe gode° knyȝt, and kene° men hem° serued	*good/bold/them*
Of° alle dayntyez° double, as derrest myȝt falle,°	*with/delicacies/(the) noblest (it) might befit*
Wyth alle maner° of mete° and mynstralcie° boþe;	*manner/food/minstrelsy*
485 Wyth wele walt° þay þat day, til worþed° an ende,	*joy spent/(it) drew to*
in londe.°	*land*
Now þenk° wel, sir Gawan,	*think*
For woþe° þat þou ne wonde,°	*danger/not hesitate*
Þis auenture° forto frayn,°	*adventure/make trial of*
490 Þat þou hatz tan on honde.°	*taken in hand*

---

472. Interludes were short dramatic or musical entertainments presented between the parts of a longer play (in *Hamlet* the "play within the play") or between the courses of a feast.

477. *heng vp þyn ax:* Aside from its literal meaning, this clause is also used in the sense of "Enough of this business!" The expression also occurs in *The Owl and the Nightingale*, where of course neither bird wields axes or hatchets, except verbal ones.

FYTTE THE SECOND

I

This hanselle° hatz Arthur of auenturus° on fyrst,°   *gift/adventures/first of all*

In ȝonge ȝer,° for he ȝerned° ȝelpyng° to here,°   *(the) young year/desired/words of challenge/hear*

Thaȝ hym° wordez were wane,° when þay to sete wenten;°   *though/to them/lacking/they/ seats went*

Now ar þay stoken of sturne werk staf-ful her hond.°   *provided with serious work cram-full (in) their hand*

495   Gawan watz glad to be-gynne þose gomnez° in halle,   *games*

Bot þaȝ þe ende be heuy, haf ȝe no wonder;   *but though/grievous, have you*

For þaȝ men ben mery° in mynde, quen° þay han mayn° drynk,   *be merry/when/have strong*

A ȝere ȝernes ful ȝerne,° and ȝeldez° neuer lyke,°   *passes very swiftly/brings back/ (the) same*

Þe forme° to þe fynisment foldez° ful selden.°   *beginning/end matches/seldom*

500   For-þi þis ȝol ouer-ȝede,° and þe ȝere after,   *therefore/Yule passed*

And vche sesoun° serlepes° sued° after oþer;   *each season/in turn/followed*

After crysten-masse com þe crabbed lentoun,°   *Christmas came/Lent*

Þat fraystez° flesch wyth þe fysche and fode° more symple;   *tests/food*

Bot þenne þe weder° of þe worlde wyth wynter hit þrepez,°   *weather/it contends*

505   Colde clengez adoun,° cloudez vp-lyften,°   *shrinks down/uplift*

Schyre schedez° þe rayn in schowrez ful warme,   *brightly falls*

Fallez vpon fayre flat,° flowrez þere schewen,°   *meadows/appear*

Boþe groundez° and þe greuez° grene ar her wedez.°   *fields/groves/raiment*

Bryddez busken° to bylde, and bremlych syngen,   *birds hasten/gloriously sing*

510   For solace° of þe softe somer° þat sues þer-after   *joy/summer*

        bi bonk;°   *on (the) slopes*

        And blossumez bolne° to blowe,°   *swell/bloom*

        Bi rawez° rych and ronk,°   *hedgerows/luxuriant*

        Þen notez noble in-noȝe.°   *many*

515   Ar herde° in wod° so wlonk.°   *heard/wood/lovely*

---

492. *ȝelpyng:* In Old English heroic poetry, such as *Beowulf* and the *Battle of Maldon,* the *gilp* was the battle boast, pronounced in the mead hall, often by "beer-bold" warriors the night before combat, or in the face of the enemy, as a pledge of vigor in combat. There are many native Old English heroic survivals in the tone and vocabulary of the *Gawain* poet (cf. the emphasis on *wyrd,* the Old English fate, in the latter parts of the poem).

496. *haf ȝe no wonder:* i.e., "don't be surprised."

504. The stormy weather of the spring equinox contends with winter in the Germanic tradition of the strife of Winter versus Summer, a common motif in medieval literature.

506–20. This pleasant description of the coming of spring and summer is the stock *reverdie* of Middle English lyric. One might compare it to the opening lines of the General Prologue in Chaucer's *Canterbury Tales* and to some of the lyrics, e.g., *Alysoun* and *Lenten Is Come with Love to Town.* For a parallel to the mention of Zephrus, l. 517, see *Canterbury Tales,* General Prologue, ll. 5–7: "Whan Zephirus eek with his sweete breeth/Inspired hath in every holt and heeth/The tendre croppes. . . ."

II

After° þe sesoun of somer wyth þe soft wyndez,　*afterward*
Quen Zeferus° syflez° hym-self on sedez° and erbez,°　*when Zephyrus/blows gently/seeds/
　　plants*

Wela-wynne° is þe wort° þat woxes° þer-oute,　*very lovely/plant/grows*
When þe donkande° dewe dropez of° þe leuez,°　*moistening/off/leaves*
520 To bide° a blysful blusch° of þe bryȝt° sunne.　*await/delightful gleam/bright*
Bot þen hyȝes heruest,° and hardenes hym sone,°　*hastens autumn/encourages it
　　quickly*

Warnez hym for° þe wynter to wax ful rype;　*because of*
He dryues wyth droȝt° þe dust for to ryse,　*drought*
Fro° þe face of þe folde° to flyȝe° ful hyȝe;°　*from/earth/fly/high*
525 Wroþe° wynde of þe welkyn wrastelez° with þe sunne,　*angry/heavens wrestles*
Þe leuez lancen° fro þe lynde,° and lyȝten° on þe grounde,　*fly/linden tree/land*
And al grayes° þe gres,° þat grene watz ere;°　*turns gray/grass/before*
Þenne al rypez° and rotez° þat ros vpon fyrst,°　*ripens/decays/rose at first*
And þus ȝirnez° þe ȝere in ȝisterdaycz mony,°　*passes/yesterdays many*
530 And wynter wyndez aȝayn,° as þe worlde askez°　*returns again/requires*
　　　　no fage.°　*in truth*
　　Til meȝel-mas mone,°　*Michaelmas moon*
　　Watz cumen° wyth wynter wage;°　*come/winter's promise*
　　Þen þenkkez° Gawan ful sone,　*thinks*
535　　Of his anious uyage.°　*troublesome journey*

III

Ȝet quyl° al-hal-day° with Arþer he lenges,°　*until/All Saints' Day/stays*
And he made a fare° on þat fest,° for þe frekez° sake,　*feast/festival/knight's*
With much reuel and ryche° of þe rounde table;　*nobles*
Knyȝtez ful cortays° and comlych° ladies,　*knights very courteous/fair*
540 Al for luf° of þat lede° in longynge þay° were,　*love/knight/grief they*
Bot° neuer-þe-lece° ne° þe later° þay neuened° bot merþe,°　*but/nevertheless/not/less readily/
　　talked of/only pleasure*

Mony ioylez° for þat ientyle iapez° þer maden.°　*joyless/noble (knight) jokes/made*
For aftter mete,° with mournyng he melez° to his eme,°　*dinner/speaks/uncle*
And spekez° of his passage, and pertly° he sayde,　*speaks/openly*
545 "Now, lege° lorde of my lyf,° leue I yow° ask;　*liege/life/you*
Ȝe° knowe þe cost° of þis cace, kepe° I no more　*you/terms/affair, care*
To telle yow tenez° þer-of-neuer bot trifel;°　*difficulties/(a) trifle*
Bot I am boun° to þe bur° barely° to morne,°　*bound/blow/without fail/tomorrow*
To sech° þe gome° of þe grene, as God wyl me wysse."°　*seek/man/guide*

---

532. *meȝel-mas mone:* i.e., "harvest moon"; Michaelmas Day is September 29.

536. Allhallows, or All Saints' Day, November 1, was the last of the five feasts that Arthur held before Christmas and the last one that Gawain could attend that year.

550 Þenne þe best of þe burȝ boȝed to-geder,° — *castle came together*
Aywan,° and Errik, and oþer° ful mony, — *Ywain/others*
Sir Doddinaual° de Sauage, þe duk° of Clarence, — *Dodinal/duke*
Launcelot, and Lyonel, and Lucan þe gode,° — *good*
Sir Boos,° and sir Byduer,° big men boþe, — *Bors/Bedevere*
555 And mony oþer menskful,° with Mador de la Port. — *noble (knights)*
Alle þis compayny of court com° þe kyng nerre,° — *came/near*
For to counseyl° þe knyȝt, with care at her hert;° — *counsel/their heart*
Þere watz much derue doel driuen° in þe sale,° — *painful grief suffered/hall*
Þat so worthe° as Wawan schulde wende° on þat ernde,° — *worthy (a one)/Gawain should go/ mission*

560 To dryȝe° a delful dynt,° and dele° no more — *endure/grievous blow/strike*
    wyth bronde.° — *sword*
    Þe knyȝt mad ay god chere,° — *made ever good cheer*
    And sayde, "Quat° schuld I wonde,° — *what/fear*
    Of destines derf° and dere,° — *destinies harsh/pleasant*
565   What may mon° do bot fonde?"° — *man/face (them)*

IV

He dowellez° þer al þat day, and dressez on þe morn, — *remains*
Askez° erly hys armez, and alle were þay broȝt° — *asks for/brought*
Fyrst a tule tapit, tyȝt° ouer þe flet,° — *Toulouse carpet, spread/floor*
And miche° watz þe gyld gere° þat glent° þer alofte; — *much/gold armor/gleamed*
570 Þe stif° mon steppez þeron, and þe stel° hondelez,° — *strong/steel/takes hold of*
Dubbed° in a dublet of a dere tars,° — *clad/precious Tharsia (silk)*
And syþen° a crafty° capados,° closed aloft,° — *then/skilfully made/cape/at the neck*
Þat wyth a bryȝt blaunner° was bounden° with-inne; — *bright ermine/bound*
Þenne set þay þe sabatounz° vpon þe segge fotez,° — *steel shoes/knight's feet*
575 His legez lapped° in stel with luflych greuez,° — *legs enclosed/handsome greaves*
With polaynez° piched° þer-to, policed° ful clene,° — *knee armor/attached/polished/bright*

551–55. Erec is known from Chrétien de Troyes's romance *Erec et Enide* (cf. above, p. 117, ll. 838–39*n*). Sir Dodinal was usually called *le Sauvage*, "the wild," because he enjoyed hunting in wild forests. However, since *sauvage* derives from Latin *silva*, "forest," the name here, *de Sauage*," of the forest," may be just as accurate. The duke of Clarence was Galescin, son of Arthur's half sister Blasine and the king of Nantres, thus Gawain's cousin. He was, according to different sources, the brother or cousin of Sir Dodinal. Lancelot du Lac, the son of King Ban of Benwick, is first mentioned by Chrétien in *Erec et Enide* as the third worthiest knight in Arthur's court, after Gawain and Erec. Later, of course, he becomes Arthur's chief knight. Lionel was the son of King Bohors, brother of King Ban, and therefore Lancelot's cousin. Lucan in the Vulgate *Mort Artu* is Butler ("bottler," i.e., cupbearer) to Arthur; he and Gifflet survive with Arthur the last battle in Salisbury Plain. Sir Bors, brother of Lionel, was also cousin to Lancelot. Sir Bedevere, the Constable, is in Malory the last survivor with Arthur. After some hesitation he casts Excalibur into the lake. In Geoffrey of Monmouth and Layamon, Bedevere and Kay accompany Arthur on the adventure with the giant of Mont-Saint-Michel in Brittany. Mador was Arthur's chief porter.

568. *tule*: i.e., deep red (cf. l. 77*n*).

571. *tars*: Cf. l. 77*n*.

574. *sabatounz*: steel foot armor consisting of toe pieces, which were often long spikes as seen on the effigy of the Black Prince in Canterbury Cathedral, and steel plates. The Black Prince died in 1376; he would therefore be roughly contemporary with the *Gawain* poet.

Aboute his knez knaged° wyth knotez of golde;	*knees fastened*
Queme quyssewes° þen, þat coyntlych closed°	*fine cuisses/elegantly enclosed*
His thik þrawen þyȝez,° with þwonges to-tachched;°	*stout, muscular thighs/ thongs attached*
580 And syþen þe brawden° bryne° of bryȝt stel ryngez	*linked/coat of mail*
Vmbe-weued° þat wyȝ,° vpon wlonk stuffe;°	*covered/man/over splendid cloth*
And wel bornyst° brace° vpon his boþe armes,	*burnished/arm pieces*
With gode cowters° and gay,° and glouez of plate,°	*elbow pieces/fair/(steel) plate*
And alle þe godlych gere° þat hym gayn° schulde	*goodly gear/benefit*
585 þat tyde;°	*time*
Wyth ryche cote armure,°	*splendid coat armor*
His gold sporez spend° with pryde,	*spurs fastened*
Gurde° wyth a bront ful° sure,	*girt/sword very*
With silk sayn vmbe° his syde.	*sash around*

V

590 When he watz hasped° in armes, his harnays° watz ryche,	*buckled/armor*
Þe lest lachet ouþer loupe lemed of° golde;	*least latchet or loop gleamed with*
So harnayst° as he watz he herknez° his masse,	*armed/hears*
Offred and honoured° at þe heȝe auter;°	*celebrated/high altar*
Syþen he comez to þe kyng and to his cort ferez,°	*companions*
595 Lachez lufly° his leue at° lordez and ladyez;	*takes graciously/leave of*
And þay° hym kyst° and conueyed, bikende° hym to kryst.°	*they/kissed/escorted, commending/ Christ*
Bi þat° watz Gryngolet grayth,° and gurde° with a sadel,°	*that (time)/made ready/girt/saddle*
Þat glemed° ful gayly with mony° golde frenges,°	*gleamed/many/fringes*
Ay quere° naylet° ful nwe° for þat note ryched;°	*everywhere/studded with nails/new/ purpose prepared*
600 Þe brydel barred° aboute, with bryȝt golde bounden;	*with bars*
Þe apparayl of þe payttrure,° and of þe proude° skyrtez,°	*breast trappings/splendid/saddle skirts*

---

578. The cuisses were plate armor to protect the thighs. Sir Philip Sidney, who had removed his cuisses in an engagement near Zutphen in September, 1586, because a friend went similarly unprotected, was hit in the thigh and died twenty-six days later. Much medieval armor survived well into the age of firearms.

586. Coat armor was the outermost costly vestment, worn over the hauberk and embroidered with the same heraldic devices borne on the knight's shield. Under the hauberk would be worn the gypon, a tunic of less expensive material. (Chaucer says of the Knight among the Canterbury pilgrims: "Of fustian he wered a gypon/Al bismotered with his habergeon.")

597. Gringolet is Gawain's horse. Gollancz in his edition of this poem mentions Speght's note (1598) to Chaucer, *Canterbury*

Tales, E 1424: "Concerning Wade and his bote called Guinge-lot, as also his strange exploits in the same, because the matter is long and fabulous, I passe it over." Although Wade's boat does seem to bear the same name as Gawain's horse in this reference (sometimes called the most frustrating comment in Chaucer scholarship), the name Gringolet has been attached to Gawain ever since Chrétien, and is probably of Celtic origin.

600–18. The description of Gawain's saddle, bridle, and helmet is a tapestry design directed especially at the ladies of the castle, who were constantly employed in embroidery. In all such passages the author is speaking to an audience of experts. The helmet was carefully joined in all its parts and padded within to avoid shock, similar to our modern helmets.

Þe cropore,° and þe couertor,° acorded° wyth þe arsounez;°   *crupper/horse cloth/matched/*
                                                              saddlebows

And al watz rayled° on red° ryche golde naylez,   *set/red (cloth)*

Þat al glytered and glent° as glem° of þe sunne.   *glinted/gleam*

605 Þenne hentes° he þe helme,° and hastily hit° kysses,   *takes/helmet/it*

Þat watz stapled stifly, and stoffed° wyth-inne;   *padded*

Hit watz hyȝe° on his hede, hasped° bihynde,   *high/head, fastened*

Wyth a lyȝtli° vrysoun° ouer þe auentayle,°   *light/silk band/mail neck guard*

Enbrawden° and bounden wyth þe best gemmez,   *embroidered*

610 On brode° sylkyn borde,° and bryddez° on semez,°   *wide/hem/birds/seams*

As papiayez° paynted peruyng° bitwene,   *parrots/periwinkles*

Tortors° and trulofez° entayled° so þyk,°   *turtledoves/herb Paris/depicted/thick*

As° mony burde° þer-aboute° had ben° seuen wynter°   *as if/ladies/about it/been/winters*
        in toune;

615   Þe cercle° watz more o prys,°   *circlet/of value*

        Þat vmbe-clypped° hys croun,°   *surrounded/(i.e., head)*

        Of diamauntez° a deuys,°   *diamonds/device*

        Þat boþe were bryȝt° and broun.°   *bright/dark*

VI

Then þay schewed° hym þe schelde,° þat was of schyr goulez,°   *showed/shield/bright gules*

620 Wyth þe pentangel de-paynt° of pure golde hwez;°   *painted/hues*

He braydez° hit by þe bauderyk,° aboute þe hals kestes,°   *takes/baldric/neck throws*

Þat bisemed° þe segge semlyly fayre.°   *suited/knight becomingly well*

And quy° þe pentangel apendez° to þat prynce noble,   *why/pertains*

I am in tent° yow° to telle, þof tary° hyt me schulde;°   *intent/you/though delay/should*

625 Hit is a syngne° þat Salamon° set sum-quyle,°   *symbol/Solomon/once*

In bytoknyng° of trawþe,° bi tytle° þat hit habbez,°   *token/fidelity/justly/has*

For hit is a figure þat haldez fyue° poyntez,   *holds five*

And vche° lyne vmbe-lappez° and loukez° in oþer,   *each/overlaps/locks*

And ay quere hit is endelez,° and Englych hit callen°   *endless/call*

---

602. *couertor:* a most ornate and quite large horse covering, reaching almost to the ground. It was embellished with heraldic devices. Contemporary illustrations can be seen in the *Livre du Roi René* and the famous depictions of the German minnesingers in the Heidelberg MS.

610–12. Motifs of birds intertwined with flowers were common both in medieval embroidery and in the illustrations of manuscript borders. Davis specifically mentions periwinkles, with their trailing stems, as being suitable for such purposes. *trulofez:* herb Paris, *Paris quadrifolia,* a plant of the lily type, formerly used in medicine.

615. The circlet was a kind of coronet around the top of the helmet. In the case of kings it was a crown, but in general it was a twined fillet.

618. *broun:* may mean only "shining," (cf. *broun stel,* l. 426),

but medieval lapidaries mention that brown and violet diamonds come out of India. It is possible, therefore, that an especially deep-colored ruby is meant, as these are found in Ceylon, Burma, and Thailand.

619–20. Gawain's shield is the pentangle (also called pentacle or pentagram), or five-pointed star formed of five interlacing lines, in the Middle Ages a mystical symbol of perfection. In other works his arms were a lion, eagle, or griffin, but in this romance the pentangle best suits his character as the ideal knight. It is of gold on a field of red (gules).

625–26. When set in a circle, the pentangle was called Solomon's seal. Like the circle, it had no beginning or end, being made with a single unbroken stroke, and thus was also a sign of eternity.

630 Ouer-al,° as I here,° þe endeles knot. — *everywhere/hear*
 For-þy° hit acordez to° þis knyȝt,° and to his cler° armez, — *therefore/befits/knight/bright*
 For ay° faythful in fyue° and sere° fyue syþez,° — *ever/five (ways)/each way/times*
 Gawan watz for gode knawen,° and as golde pured,° — *good (knight) known/refined*
 Voyded° of vche° vylany, wyth vertuez ennourned° — *free/every/adorned*
635   in mote;° — *castle*
  For-þy þe pen-tangel nwe° — *newly (painted)*
  He ber° in schelde and cote,° — *bore/coat*
  As tulk° of tale° most trwe,° — *man/word/true*
  And gentylest° knyȝt of lote.° — *noblest/speech*

VII

640 Fyrst he watz funden fautlez° in his fyue wyttez,° — *found faultless/senses*
 And efte° fayled neuer þe freke° in his fyue fyngres, — *second/knight*
 And alle his afyaynce° vpon folde° watz in þe fyue woundez — *trust/earth*
 Þat Cryst kaȝt° on þe croys,° as þe crede° tellez; — *received/cross/creed*
 And quere-so-euer° þys mon° in melly° watz stad,° — *wheresoever/man/battle/present*
645 His þro þoȝt° watz in þat, þurȝ alle oþer þyngez, — *steadfast thought/above*
 Þat alle his forsnes° he feng at° þe fyue ioyez, — *fortitude/received from/joys*
 Þat þe hende heuen° quene had of hir° chylde; — *gracious heaven's/her*
 At° þis cause° þe knyȝt comlyche hade° — *for/reason/fittingly had*
 In þe inore° half of his schelde hir ymage depaynted, — *inner*
650 Þat quen° he blusched° þerto, his belde° neuer payred.° — *when/looked/courage/failed*
 Þe fyft° fyue þat I finde þat þe frek vsed, — *fifth (set of)*
 Watz fraunchyse,° and felaȝschyp for-be° al þyng; — *generosity/fellowship above*
 His clannes° and his cortaysye croked° were neuer, — *purity/courtesy crooked*
 And pite,° þat passez° alle poyntez, þyse° pure fyue — *pity/surpasses/qualities, these*
655 Were harder° happed° on þat haþel þen° on any oþer. — *more firmly/fastened/knight than*
 Now alle þese fyue syþez,° forsoþe,° were fetled° on þis knyȝt, — *groups/in truth/fixed*
 And vchone° halched° in oþer, þat non° ende hade, — *each one/joined/no*
 And fyched° vpon fyue poyntez, þat fayld neuer, — *fixed*
 Ne° samned° neuer in° no syde, ne sundred° nouþer,° — *nor/came together/on/came apart/neither*

660 With-outen° ende at any noke° I oquere° fynde, — *without/corner/anywhere*
 Wher-euer þe gomen° bygan, or glod° to an ende, — *device/came*
 Þer-fore on his schene schelde schapen° watz þe knot, — *bright shield shaped*
 Ryalle° wyth red golde vpon rede gowlez,° — *royally/red gules*

---

632. Gawain is perfect in five categories, each representing one side of the pentangle and each having five elements.

642–43. The five wounds, often mentioned in Middle English religious lyrics, were those in the feet, hands, and side.

646–47. The five joys of Mary were those of the Annunciation, Nativity, Resurrection, Ascension, and Assumption.

649. The image of Mary is painted on the inside of Gawain's shield, on the part opposite his eyes and above the arm clasp. The Virgin Mary was also on Arthur's shield and standard, which he carried through many battles. The role of Mary is an important one in this poem: when all help fails, she is invoked by Gawain, and she alone comes to his aid. She is the *dea ex machina* in medieval literature.

663. *red golde:* See above, p. 183, l. 47n.

Þat is þe pure pentaungel wyth° þe peple° called,   *by/people*
665   with lore.°   *learning*
    Now grayþed° is Gawan gay,°   *prepared/fair*
    And laȝt° his launce ryȝt þore,°   *took/lance right there*
    And gef hem° alle goud° day,   *gave them/good*
    He wende° for euer more.   *thought*

VIII

670 He sperred° þe sted° with þe spurez, and sprong° on his way,   *spurred/steed/sprang*
So stif° þat þe ston° fyr stoke° out þer-after;   *vigorously/stone sparks struck*
Al þat seȝ° þat semly syked° in hert,°   *saw/noble (knight) sighed/heart*
And sayde soþly° al same segges til oþer,°   *truly/together knights to (each)*
Carande° for þat comly, "Bi Kryst, hit° is scaþe,°   *grieving/fair (man)/it/pity*
675 Þat þou, leude,° schal be lost, þat art of lyf° noble!   *sir/life*
To fynde hys fere° vpon folde, in fayth is not eþe;°   *equal/easy*
Warloker° to haf wroȝt° had more wyt bene,°   *more carefully/have acted/sense been*
And haf dyȝt° ȝonder dere° a duk° to haue worþed;°   *appointed/noble (man)/duke/become*
A lowande leder° of ledez° in londe° hym wel semez,°   *brilliant leader/people/land/suits*
680 And so had better haf ben° þen britned° to noȝt,°   *been/destroyed/naught*
Hadet wyth° an aluisch mon,° for angardez° pryde.   *beheaded by/elvish man/excessive*
Who knew euer any kyng such counsel to take,
As knyȝtez° in cauelaciounz° on cryst-masse gomnez!"°   *knights/trifling disputes (give)/ games*

Wel° much watz þe warme water þat waltered of yȝen,°   *very/flowed from eyes*
685 When þat semly syre soȝt fro þo wonez°   *lord went from that dwelling*
        þad° daye;   *that*
    He made non abode,°   *stop*
    Bot wyȝtly° went hys way,   *but resolutely*
    Mony wylsum° way he rode,   *many (a) bewildering*
690   Þe bok° as I herde° say.   *book/heard*

IX

Now ridez þis renk þurȝ° þe ryalme° of Logres,   *knight through/realm*
Sir Gauan on° Godez halue, þaȝ hym° no gomen þoȝt;°   *for/sake, though he/game (it) thought*

Oft, leudlez° alone, he lengez on nyȝtez,°   *companionless/stays at night*
Þer° he fonde noȝt° hym byfore þe fare þat he lyked;   *where/found not*
695 Hade° he no fere° bot his fole,° bi frythez° and dounez,°   *had/companion/horse/woods/hills*
Ne no gome° bot God, bi gate° wyth to karp,°   *one/on the road/talk*
Til þat he neȝed° ful neghe° in to þe Norþe Walez;   *approached/near*

---

691. *Logres:* Arthur's kingdom, so named from the legendary British king Locrinus, according to Geoffrey of Monmouth. Gawain's journey is into North Wales.

Alle þe iles of Anglesay on lyft half° he haldez,°   *left side/keeps*
And farez ouer þe fordez by þe for-londez,°   *promontories*
700 Ouer at þe Holy-Hede,° til he hade eft° bonk°   *Holy Head/again/reached shore*
In þe wyldrenesse of Wyrale; wonde° þer bot lyte°   *lived/few*
Þat auþer° God oþer gome° wyth goud hert louied.°   *either/or man/loved*
And ay° he frayned,° as he ferde, at frekez° þat he met,   *ever/inquired/traveled, of people*
If þay° hade herde any karp of a knyȝt grene,   *they*
705 In any grounde þer-aboute, of þe grene chapel;
And al nykked hym wyth nay,° þat neuer in her lyue°   *said no to him/their life*
Þay seȝe neuer no segge þat watz of suche hwez°   *colors*
     of grene.
     Þe knyȝt tok gates straunge,°   *took ways strange*
710   In mony° a bonk vnbene,°   *many/hillside dreary*
     His cher ful° oft con chaunge,°   *mood very/did change*
     Þat chapel er° he myȝt sene.°   *before/might see*

X

Mony klyf he ouer-clambe° in contrayez straunge,   *climbed over*
Fer floten° fro his frendez fremedly° he rydez;   *far removed/as a stranger*
715 At vche warþe° oþer water þer þe wyȝe° passed,   *each ford/man*
He fonde a foo° hym byfore, bot ferly hit° were,   *foe/unless unusual it*
And þat so foule and so felle,° þat feȝt hym° by-hode;°   *fierce/fight he/had to*
So mony meruayl° bi mount° þer þe mon° fyndez,   *marvels/in the hills/man*
Hit were to tore° for to telle of þe tenþe dole.°   *too difficult/part*
720 Sumwhyle° wyth wormez° he werrez,° and with wolues als,°   *sometimes/dragons/fights/also*
Sumwhyle wyth wodwos,° þat woned° in þe knarrez,°   *forest trolls/lived/crags*
Boþe wyth bullez and berez,° and borez° oþer-quyle,°   *bears/boars/at other times*
And etaynez,° þat hym a-nelede,° of þe heȝe felle;°   *giants/pursued/high rock*
Nade° he ben duȝty° and dryȝe,° and dryȝtyn,° had serued,   *had not/been doughty/enduring/God*
725 Douteles° he hade ben ded,° and dreped° ful ofte.   *doubtless/dead/slain*
For werre wrathed° hym not so much, þat wynter nas° wors,   *bothered/was not*
When þe colde cler° water fro° þe cloudez schadden,°   *clear/from/was shed*
And fres° er hit falle myȝt to þe fale° erþe: *froze/pale*
Ner° slayn wyth° þe slete° he sleped° in his yrnes,°   *nearly/by/sleet/slept/armor*
730 Mo nyȝtez þen in-noghe in° naked rokkez,°   *more nights than enough on/rocks*

---

698. *þe iles of Anglesay :* Anglesey, Holyhead, Puffin Island, and various smaller islands off Menai Bridge. He evidently rode through Caernarvonshire, Denbighshire, and Flintshire along the coast of the Irish Sea.

700. *Holy-Hede:* There is some confusion about Gawain's itinerary. This Holy Head cannot be the island of Anglesey mentioned in l. 698*n.* Tolkien and Gordon feel that it must be on the river Dee between Chester and the estuary, since this is the point where Gawain enters the Wirral.

701. The Wirral was made into a forest by the famous Randolf (Randle Meschines), earl of Chester, whose name is mentioned with Robin Hood in *Piers Plowman* as being a figure of legend and song. The section was the home of outlaws and marauders and extremely unsafe for travelers, and armed bands continually terrorized the citizenry. The citizens of Chester begged that the region be disafforested, and in July, 1376, Edward III granted that this be done.

Þer as° claterande° fro þe crest þe colde borne rennez,°   *where/splashing/stream runs*
And henged° heȝe ouer his hede in hard iisse-ikkles.°   *hung/icicles*
Þus in peryl, and payne, and plytes° ful harde,   *plights*
Bi contray° caryez° þis knyȝt,° tyl kryst-masse euen,°   *over the land/rides/knight/Christmas eve*

735   al one;°   *alone*
        Þe knyȝt wel þat tyde,°   *time*
        To Mary made his mone,°   *complaint*
        Þat ho° hym red° to ryde,   *she/show where*
        And wysse° hym to sum wone.°   *guide/some dwelling*

XI

740 Bi a mounte on þe morne meryly he rydes,
    Into a forest ful dep,° þat ferly° watz wylde,   *deep/wondrously*
    Hiȝe° hillez on vche a° halue,° and holtwodez vnder,°   *high/each/side/woods below*
    Of hore okez° ful hoge° a hundreth to-geder;°   *gray oaks/huge/hundred together*
    Þe hasel and þe haȝ-þorne° were harled° al samen,°   *hawthorne/tangled/together*
745 With roȝe raged° mosse rayled ay-where,°   *rough ragged/arrayed everywhere*
    With mony bryddez vnblyþe° vpon bare twyges,   *birds unhappy*
    Þat pitosly° þer piped for pyne° of þe colde.   *piteously/pain*
    Þe gome° vpon Gryngolet glydez hem° vnder,   *man/hastens them*
    Þurȝ mony misy° and myre, mon° al hym one,°   *through many (a) swamp/man/alone*
750 Carande° for his costes,° lest he ne keuer schulde,°   *concerned/(religious) observances/ not manage should*

    To se° þe seruyse° of þat syre,° þat on þat self° nyȝt   *see/service/lord/same*
    Of a burde° watz borne, oure baret° to quelle;°   *maiden/sorrow/end*
    And þerfore sykyng° he sayde, "I be-seche þe,° lorde,   *sighing/beseech thee*
    And Mary, þat is myldest moder° so dere,°   *mother/dear*
755 Of° sum herber, þer heȝly° I myȝt here° masse,   *for/haven, where devoutly/might hear*

    Ande þy matynez to-morne, mekely° I ask,   *matins tomorrow, meekly*
    And þer-to prestly° I pray my pater° and aue,°   *promptly/Paternoster/Ave (Maria)*
        and crede."°   *Creed*
        He rode in his prayere,
760   And cryed for his mysdede,°   *sin*
        He sayned hym in syþes sere,°   *crossed himself at times several*
        And sayde "Cros Kryst° me spede!"°   *of Christ/help*

741–47. Madden identifies the wood as Inglewood Forest in Cumberland: Gawain and Arthur have other adventures there (cf. *The Wedding of Sir Gawain and Dame Ragnell*); and the section is mountainous, as described below.

750–52. Gawain fears he will not be able to reach a chapel in time to hear the Christmas mass.

756. Matins is the first of the seven canonical hours; its service begins between midnight and daybreak.

757. The Paternoster (Latin, "our father") is the Lord's Prayer; the Ave Maria is the Hail Mary.

XII

Nade° he sayned hym-self, segge, bot þrye,°   *had not/knight, but thrice*
Er° he watz war° in þe wod° of a won° in a mote.°   *before/aware/wood/dwelling/moat*
765 Abof° a launde,° on a lawe, loken° vnder boȝez,°   *above/open space/mound, shut/ branches*

Of mony borelych bole,° aboute bi þe diches;°   *massive tree/moat*
A castel þe comlokest° þat euer knyȝt aȝte,°   *handsomest/owned*
Pyched° on a prayere,° a park al aboute,   *erected/meadow*
With a pyked palays, pyned ful þik,°   *spiked palisade, enclosed very closely*
770 Þat vmbe-teȝe° mony tre mo þen° two myle.   *surrounded/tree more than*
Þat holde° on þat on° syde þe haþel° auysed,°   *stronghold/one/knight/looked at*
As hit schemered° and schon° þurȝ þe schyre° okez;   *it shimmered/shone/bright*
Þenne hatz° he hendly of° his helme,° and heȝly he þonkez°   *takes/reverently off/helmet/thanks*
Jesus and saynt Gilyan,° þat gentyle° ar boþe,   *Julian/gentle*
775 Þat cortaysly hade hym kydde,° and his cry herkened.°   *had shown him courtesy/heard*
"Now bone hostel,"° coþe° þe burne,° "I be-seche yow ȝette!"°   *good lodging/said/knight/you grant*
Þenne gerdez he to° Gryngolet with þe gilt helez,°   *he spurs/heels*
And he ful° chauncely° hatz chosen to þe chef gate,°   *quite/by chance/main road*
Þat broȝt bremly° þe burne to þe bryge° ende,   *brought quickly/bridge's*
780   in haste;

Þe bryge watz breme° vp-braydc,°   *stoutly/pulled up*
Þe ȝatez° wer stoken° faste,   *gates/shut*
Þe wallez were wel arayed,°   *constructed*
Hit dut° no wyndez blaste.   *feared*

XIII

785 Þe burne bode° on blonk,° þat on bonk houed,°   *remained/horse/bank halted*
Of þe depe° double dich þat drof to° þe place,   *deep/enclosed*
Þe walle wod° in þe water wonderly° depe,   *stood/wonderously*
Ande eft° a ful huge heȝt° hit haled° vpon lofte,°   *then/height/rose/above*
Of harde hewen ston° vp to þe tablez,°   *hewn stone/cornice moldings*
790 Enbaned° vnder þe abataylment,° in þe best lawe;°   *provided with bantels/battlement/ style*

And syþen garytez° ful gaye gered° bi-twene,°   *then turrets/ fair built/at intervals*
Wyth mony luflych loupe,° þat louked° ful clene;°   *many (a) goodly loophole/fastened/ neatly*

A better barbican þat burne blusched° vpon neuer;   *looked*

---

774. Saint Julian was the patron saint of hospitality. Chaucer says of his food-conscious Franklin, "Seint Julian he was in his contree."

790–802. The castle described here is unusually elaborate. Tolkien and Gordon mention that the last half of the 14th century began to see such buildings and that the poet is there-fore describing the latest architectural development. Bantels (*enbaned*, l. 790) were long horizontal juttings of stone, set under the battlements as protection against attack by ladders. The barbican (l. 793) was the outer defense work of a castle, i.e., the turrets and gates of the outer wall.

And innermore° he be-helde þat halle ful hyȝe,°   *further in/high*
795 Towre telded° bytwene trochet° ful þik,°   *set up/with ornamental pinnacles/*
                                                              *   many*

Fayre fylyolez° þat fyȝed,° and ferlyly long,°   *pinnacles/fitted/exceedingly tall*
With coruon coprounes, craftyly sleȝe;°   *carved tops, cunningly made*
Chalk whyt° chymnees þer ches° he in-noȝe,°   *chalk-white/perceived/many*
Vpon bastel rouez,° þat blenked° ful quyte;°   *tower roofs/gleamed/white*
800 So mony pynakle° payntet watz poudred° ay quere,°   *many pinnacles/scattered/everywhere*
Among þe castel carnelez, clambred° so þik,°   *embrasures clustered/thick*
Þat pared° out of papure purely° hit semed.°   *cut/paper certainly/seemed*
Þe fre freke° on þe fole° hit fayr in-noghe þoȝt,°   *good knight/horse/enough thought*
If he myȝt keuer° to com þe cloyster° wyth-inne,   *might manage/enclosure*
805 To herber° in þat hostel,° whyl halyday lested°   *lodge/dwelling/holiday lasted*
            auinant;°   *pleasantly*
        He calde,° and sone° þer com°   *called/immediately/came*
        A porter pure plesaunt,°   *certainly pleasant*
        On þe wal his ernd° he nome,°   *message/received*
810   And haylsed° þe knyȝt erraunt.°   *greeted/knight wandering*

XIV

"Gode° sir," quod° Gawan, "woldez° þou go myn° ernde,   *good/said/would/go (with) my*
To þe heȝ° lorde of þis hous, herber° to craue?"   *noble/lodging*
"Ȝe, Peter,"° quod þe porter, "and purely I trowee°   *yea, (by Saint) Peter/think*
Þat ȝe° be, wyȝe, welcum° to won quyle yow° lykez."   *you/sir, welcome/stay while you*
815 Þen ȝede° þat wyȝe ȝerne° and com aȝayn swyþe,°   *went/man eagerly/again quickly*
And folke frely° hym wyth, to fonge° þe knyȝt;   *readily/receive*
Þay° let doun þe grete draȝt,° and derely° out ȝeden,°   *they/great drawbridge/courteously/*
                                                            *   went*

And kneled° doun on her knes° vpon þe colde erþe,   *knelt/their knees*
To welcum þis ilk° wyȝ, as worþy hom° þoȝt;   *same/suitable they*
820 Þay ȝolden hym° þe brode° ȝate, ȝarked° vp wyde,°   *allowed him (to pass)/wide/opened*
And he hem° raysed° rekenly,° and rod° ouer þe brygge;°   *them/bade rise/graciously/rode/*
                                                            *   bridge*

Sere seggez° hym sesed° by sadel, quel° he lyȝt,°   *several men/held/saddle, while/*
                                                            *   dismounted*

And syþen stabeled his stede stif° men in-noȝe.   *steed good*
Knyȝtez and swyerez comen° doun þenne,°   *squires came*
825 For to bryng þis buurne° wyth blys° in-to halle;°   *knight/joy*
Quen he hef° vp his helme,° þer hiȝed° in-noghe   *lifted/helmet/hastened*
For to hent hit at° his honde,° þe hende° to seruen,°   *take it from/hand/noble (man)/serve*
His bronde° and his blasoun° boþe þay token.°   *sword/shield/took*
Þen haylsed he ful hendly þo haþelez vch° one,°   *very courteously the knights each*
830 And mony proud mon° þer presed,° þat prynce to honour;   *man/pressed (forward)*
Alle hasped° in his heȝ wede° to halle þay hym wonnen,°   *buckled/armor/brought*

Þer° fayre fyre vpon flet fersly brenned.° *where/in (the) hall fiercely burned*
Þenne þe lorde of þe lede loutez fro° his chambre, *company comes from*
For to mete° wyth menske° þe mon on þe flor; *meet/honor*
835 He sayde, "ȝe ar welcum to welde° as yow lykez, *use*
Þat° here is, al is yowre awen,° to haue at yowre wylle° *what/your own/pleasure*
        and welde."° *control*
   "Graunt mercy,"° quod Gawayn, *thank you*
   "Þer Kryst hit° yow for-ȝelde,"° *for it/reward*
840 As frekez° þat semed fayn,° *men/glad*
Ayþer oþer° in armez con felde.° *each (the) other/did embrace*

XV

Gawayn glyȝt on° þe gome° þat godly° hym gret,° *looked at/man/graciously/greeted*
And þuȝt° hit a bolde burne° þat þe burȝ aȝte,° *thought/worthy man/castle owned*
A hoge° haþel for þe nonez,° and of hyghe eldee;° *huge/indeed/in his prime*
845 Brode bryȝt° watz his berde,° and al beuer hwed,° *broad, bright/beard/beaver colored*
Sturne, stif on° þe stryþþe° on stal-worth schonkez,° *stern, strong in/stride/stalwart legs*
Felle° face as þe fyre, and fre° of hys speche;° *fierce/noble/speech*
And wel hym semed° for soþe,° as þe segge° þuȝt, *it suited/in truth/knight*
To lede a lortschyp° in lee° of leudez° ful gode. *have lordship/protection/company*
850 Þe lorde hym charred° to a chambre, and chefly cumaundez° *took/particularly orders*
To delyuer° hym a leude,° hym loȝly° to serue; *assign/man/humbly*
And þere were boun° at his bode° burnez in-noȝe,° *ready/command/many*
Þat broȝt hym to a bryȝt boure,° þer bcddyng watz noble, *brought/chamber*
Of cortynes° of clene° sylk, wyth cler° golde hemmez,° *curtains/pure/bright/borders*
855 And couertorez° ful curious,° with comlych panez,° *coverlets/skillfully made/fair panels*
Of bryȝt blaunnier° a-boue enbrawded° bisydez,° *ermine/embroidered/at the sides*
Rudelez rennande° on ropez, red golde ryngez, *curtains running*
Tapytez tyȝt° to þe woȝe,° of tuly° and tars,° *hangings attached/walls/Toulouse/*
                          Tharsia (silk)

And vnder fete,° on þe flet,° of folȝande sute.° *feet/floor/similar sort*
860 Þer he watz dispoyled,° wyth spechez of myerþe,° *relieved/pleasure*
Þe burn° of his bruny,° and of his bryȝt wedez;° *knight/coat of mail/clothes*
Ryche robes ful rad renkkez° hym broȝten,° *promptly knights/brought*
For to charge,° and to chaunge,° and chose° of þe best. *put on/change/choose*
Sone° as he on hent,° and happed° þcr-inne, *as soon/one took/was clothed*
865 Þat sete on° hym semly,° wyth saylande° skyrtez, *fitted/well/flowing*
Þe ver° by his uisage verayly hit semed° *springtime/appearance truly it seemed*
Wel neȝ° to vche haþel° alle on hwes,° *almost/man/colors*
Lowande° and lufly,° alle his lymmez vnder,° *glowing/lovely/limbs beneath*

---

858. *tuly and tars:* Cf. l. 77n.

Þat a comloker° knyȝt neuer Kryst made,   *handsomer*
870 hem þoȝt;°   *they thought*
Wheþen° in worlde he were,   *from wherever*
Hit semed as° he myȝt   *as if/might*
Be prynce with-outen pere,°   *without peer*
In felde þer° felle men foȝt.°   *battle where/fought*

XVI

875 A cheyer° by-fore þe chemne,° þer charcole brenned,°   *chair/fireplace/charcoal burned*
Watz brayþed° for sir Gawan, grayþely° with cloþez,°   *prepared/promptly/coverings*
Whyssynes° vpon queldepoyntes,° þat koynt° wer boþe;   *cushions/quilted coverings/*
    beautiful

And þenne a mere° mantyle watz on þat mon° cast,   *gay/man*
Of a broun bleeaunt,° enbrauded ful° ryche,   *rich fabric/embroidered very*
880 And fayre° furred wyth-inne with fellez° of þe best,   *well/skins*
Alle of ermyn in erde,° his hode° of þe same;   *actually/hood*
And he sete° in þat settle semlych° ryche,°   *sat/seat becomingly/splendid*
And achaufed hym chefly,° and þenne his cher mended.°   *warmed himself quickly/spirits*
    improved

Sone° watz telded° vp a tabil on trestez° ful fayre,   *quickly/set/trestles*
885 Clad° wyth a clene° cloþe, þat cler quyt schewed,°   *covered/clean/pure white appeared*
Sanap,° and salure,° and syluerin sponez;°   *overcloth/saltcellar/silver spoons*
Þe wyȝe wesche° at his wylle,° and went to his mete.°   *man washed/pleasure/dinner*
Seggez° hym serued semly in-noȝe.°   *men/fittingly enough*
Wyth sere sewes° and sete, sesounde of° þe best,   *various soups/excellent, seasoned*
890 Double felde,° as hit fallez,° and fele kyn° fischez;   *quantity/is fitting/many kinds (of)*
Summe baken° in bred,° summe brad° on þe gledez,°   *some baked/bread/grilled/coals*
Summe soþen,° summe in sewe,° sauered° with spyces,   *boiled/stew/flavored*
And ay sawes° so sleȝe,° þat þe segge lyked.   *ever sauces/delicate*
Þe freke calde° hit a fest° ful frely° and ofte,   *knight called/feast/readily*
895 Ful hendely, quen° alle þe haþeles re-hayted° hym at onez°   *politely, when/men encouraged/once*
    as hende;°   *courteously*
"Þis penaunce° now ȝe° take,   *penance/you*
And eft° hit schal amende";°   *afterwards/improve*
Þat mon much merþe con° make,   *merriment did*
900 For wyn in° his hed° þat wende.°   *wine to/head/went*

---

874. *felde:* Cf. above, p. 73, l. 608n.

884. The tables on trestles were not permanent but were removed when the meal was over. Rarely was there a permanent "table dormant" like that of Chaucer's Franklin.

897–98. Since Christmas Eve is a fast day, Gawain's "feast" of fish is in reality a penance, and a real banquet will be served later.

XVII

Þenne watz spyed° and spured vpon spare wyse,° — *inquired/asked in tactful way*
Bi preue poyntez° of þat prynce, put to hym-seluen,° — *discreet questions/him*
Þat° he be-knew cortaysly° of þe court þat he were, — *until/acknowledged courteously*
Þat aþel° Arthure þe hende haldez° hym one,° — *noble/gracious rules/alone*
905 Þat is þe ryche ryal° kyng of þe rounde table; — *great royal*
And hit° watz Wawen° hym-self þat in þat won° syttes, — *it/Gawain/dwelling*
Comen° to þat krystmasse,° as case° hym þen lymped.° — *come/Christmas/chance/befell*
When þe lorde hade° lerned þat he þe leude° hade, — *had/knight*
Loude laȝed° he þerat, so lef° hit hym þoȝt,° — *laughed/delightful/he thought*
910 And alle þe men in þat mote maden° much joye, — *castle made*
To apere° in his presence prestly° þat tyme, — *appear/promptly*
Þat alle prys,° and prowes,° and pured þewes° — *excellence/prowess/refined manners*
Appendes° to hys persoun, and praysed is euer, — *belongs*
By-fore alle men vpon molde,° his mensk° is þe most.° — *earth/fame/greatest*
915 Vch segge° ful softly sayde to his fere,° — *each knight/companion*
"Now schal we semlych se° sleȝtez° of þewez, — *pleasantly see/skillful display*
And þe teccheles° termes of talkyng noble, — *faultless*
Wich spede° is in speche, vnspurd° may we lerne, — *what success/speech, unasked*
Syn° we haf fonged° þat fyne fader° of nurture; — *since/have received/perfect father/ good breeding*

920 God hatz geuen vus° his grace godly for soþe,° — *granted us/graciously in truth*
Þat such a gest° as Gawan grauntez° vus to haue, — *guest/grants*
When burnez blyþe° of his burþe° schal sitte — *men happily/(i.e., Christ's) birth*
                and synge.
      In menyng° of manerez mere,° — *understanding/manners noble*
925   Þis burne° now schal vus bryng, — *knight*
      I hope° þat may° hym here,° — *believe/(they who) may/hear*
      Schal lerne of luf-talkyng."° — *lovers' conversation*

XVIII

Bi þat° þe diner° watz done, and þe dere° vp,° — *(the time) that/dinner/noble company/risen*

Hit watz neȝ at° þe niyȝt neȝed° þe tyme; — *close to/night neared*
930 Chaplaynez to þe chapeles chosen þe gate,° — *took their way*
Rungen ful rychely, ryȝt° as þay schulden,° — *rang very festively, just/they should*
To þe hersum° euensong of þe hyȝe tyde.° — *devout/high festival*
Þe lorde loutes° þerto, and þe lady als,° — *goes/also*
In-to a comly° closet° coyntly ho° entrez; — *fair/private pew/gracefully she*

912–27. Gawain is the first knight of the Round Table in courtesy and "cheer of court." Chaucer in the *Squire's Tale* mentions "Gawayn with his olde curteisye." *haf fonged* (l. 919): i.e., "entertain."

935 Gawan glydez° ful gay,° and gos þeder sone;° — *hastens/cheerful/goes there immediately*

Þe lorde laches° hym by þe lappe,° and ledez° hym to sytte, — *takes/fold (of his gown)/leads*
And couþly° hym knowez,° and callez hym his nome,° — *familiarly/greets/(by) his name*
And sayde he watz þe welcomest wyȝe° of þe worlde; — *person*
And he hym þonkked þroly,° and ayþer halched° oþer, — *thanked heartily/each embraced*
940 And seten soberly samen° þe seruise-quyle;° — *sat quietly together/(during) the service time*

Þenne lyst° þe lady to loke° on þe knyȝt.° — *desired/look/knight*
Þenne com° ho of hir° closet, with mony cler burdez,° — *came/from her/many fair maidens*
Ho watz þe fayrest in felle,° of flesche and of lyre,° — *skin/face*
And of compas,° and colour, and costes of° alle oþer,° — *form/qualities over/others*
945 And wener þen Wenore,° as þe wyȝe° þoȝt. — *fairer than Guinevere/man*
Ho ches þurȝ° þe chaunsel,° to cheryche° þat hende;° — *came through/chancel/salute/gracious (man)*

An oþer lady hir lad° bi þe lyft honde,° — *led/left hand*
Þat watz alder° þen ho, an auncian hit semed,° — *older/aged (one) it seemed*
And heȝly° honowred with haþelez° aboute. — *highly/knights*
950 Bot° vn-lyke on to loke þo° ladyes were, — *but/those*
For if þe ȝonge° watz ȝep, ȝolȝe° watz þat oþer; — *young (one)/fresh, yellow (i.e., withered)*

Riche red on þat on rayled° ay quere,° — *one appeared/everywhere*
Rugh ronkled chekez° þat oþer on rolled; — *rough wrinkled cheeks*
Kerchofes° of þat on wyth mony cler° perlez — *kerchiefs/shining*
955 Hir brest and hir bryȝt þrote bar° displayed, — *white throat bare*
Schon schyrer° þen snawe,° þat schedez° on hillez; — *shone whiter/snow/falls*
Þat oþer wyth a gorger° watz gered° ouer þe swyre,° — *gorget/clothed/neck*
Chymbled° ouer hir blake° chyn with chalk-quyte° vayles, — *wrapped up/black/chalk-white*
Hir frount folden° in sylk, enfoubled° ay quere, — *forehead folded/muffled*
960 Toreted° and treleted° with tryflez° aboute, — *with embroidered edges/meshed/details*

Þat° noȝt° watz bare of þat burde° bot þe blake broȝes,° — *so that/naught/lady/brows*
Þe tweyne yȝen,° and þe nase,° þe naked lyppez, — *two eyes/nose*
And þose were soure to se,° and sellyly blered;° — *see/marvelously bleared*
A mensk° lady on molde mon° may hir calle, — *honorable/earth men*
965   for° Gode! — *before*
    Hir body watz schort and þik,° — *thick*
    Hir buttokez blaȝ° and brode,° — *swollen/broad*
    More lykker-wys° on to lyk,° — *sweet/taste*
    Watz þat scho hade on lode.° — *that (one) she had in tow*

947–48. The second woman is Morgan la Fay, who, as we shall see, has initiated the whole "game" in order to frighten Guinevere. Her description is similar to that of the loathly hag in the burlesque *Wedding of Sir Gawain and Dame Ragnell*.

957. *gorger:* A gorget was a kind of wimple fastened around the neck and head.

XIX

970 When Gawayn gly3t° on þat gay,° þat graciously loked,°   *looked/gay (lady)/gazed*
Wyth leue la3t° of þe lorde he lent hem a3aynes;°   *permission taken/went them towards*
Þe alder he haylses, heldande ful° lowe,   *greets, bowing very*
Þe loueloker° he lappez° a lyttel in armez,   *lovelier/embraces*
He kysses hir comlyly,° and kny3tly° he melez;°   *courteously/chivalrously/speaks*
975 Þay° kallen hym of° aquoyntaunce,° and he hit quyk askez   *they/beg for his/acquaintance*
To be her seruaunt sothly,° if hem-self° lyked.°   *servant truly/them/it pleased*
Þay tan° hym bytwene hem, wyth talkyng hym leden°   *take/lead*
To chambre, to chemné,° and chefly° þay asken°   *fireplace/particularly/ask (for)*
Spycez, þat vn-sparely° men speded hom° to bryng,   *unsparingly/hastened them*
980 And þe wynne-lych° wyne þer-with vche° tyme.   *cheerful/each*
Þe lorde luflych° aloft lepez° ful ofte,   *courteously/leaps*
Mynned merthe° to be made vpon mony sy þez,°   *urged mirth/at many times*
Hent he3ly of° his hode,° and on a spere henged,°   *took gaily off/hood/spear hung*
And wayned° hym to wynne þe worchip° þer-of,   *urged/honor*
985 Þat most myrþe my3t meue° þat crystenmas whyle;°   *mirth might devise/Christmastime*
"And I shal fonde,° bi my fayth, to fylter° wyth þe best,   *try/contend*
Er me wont° þe wede,° with help of my frendez."   *before I lose/garment*
Þus wyth la3ande lotez° þe lorde hit tayt° makez,   *laughing words/it merry*
For to glade° sir Gawayn with gommez° in halle   *gladden/games*
990   þat ny3t;°   *night*
        Til þat° watz tyme,   *until*
        Þe lord comaundet ly3t,°   *ordered lights*
        Sir Gawen his leue con nyme,°   *leave did take*
        And to his bed hym di3t.°   *he went*

XX

995 On þe morne, as vch mon mynez° þat tyme,   *man remembers*
Þat dry3tyn° for oure destyné° to de3e° watz borne,   *(the) Lord/destiny/die*
Wele° waxez in vche a° won° in worlde, for his sake;   *joy/each/dwelling*
So did hit þere on þat day, þur3 dayntes° mony;   *through delicacies*
Boþe at mes° and at mele, messes° ful quaynt°   *buffet/mealtime, dishes/well prepared*

1000 Derf° men vpon dece drest° of þe best.   *doughty/dais prepared*
Þe olde auncian wyf he3est ho° syttez;   *aged woman highest she*
Þe lorde lufly° her by lent,° as I trowe;°   *courteously/sat/believe*
Gawan and þe gay burde° to-geder° þay seten,°   *lady/together/sat*

---

979. The spices were for wine, such as the *piment* and *hippocras* served at the banquet for the Roman envoys in the Alliterative *Morte Arthure.*

983–87. There were many Christmas games played at court, usually with men and women taking opposite sides, such as the popular Holly-versus-Ivy games (cf. l. 265n). The exact nature of the hood game here is unknown, except that the garment is offered as a prize.

Euen° in-myddez,° as° þe messe metely come;°

exactly/in the middle/where/food
fittingly came

1005 And syþen° þurȝ al þe sale,° as hem best semed,°   *then/hall/it suited*
Bi vche grome° at his degre grayþely° watz serued.   *man/rank promptly*
Þer watz mete,° þer watz myrþe, þer watz much ioye,°   *food/joy*
Þat for to telle þerof hit me tene° were,   *trouble*
And° to poynte hit ȝet° I pyned me° parauenture;°   *even if/to describe it/took pains/*

perhaps

1010 Bot° ȝet I wot° þat Wawen° and þe wale° burde   *but/know/Gawain/fair*
Such comfort of her° compaynye caȝten° to-geder,   *their/got*
Þurȝ her dere dalyaunce° of her derne° wordez,   *pleasant conversation/private*
Wyth clene cortays carp, closed fro fylþe,°   *pure courteous talk, free from sin*
Þat hor° play watz passande° vche prynce gomen,°   *their/surpassing/princely game*
1015   in vayres;°   *truth*
      Trumpez° and nakerys,°   *trumpets/kettledrums*
      Much pypyng þer repayres,°   *is present*
      Vche mon tented hys,°   *minded his (business)*
      And þay two tented þayres.°   *theirs*

XXI

1020 Much dut° watz þer dryuen° þat day and þat oþer,°   *joy/made/next*
And þe þryd° as þro° þronge° in þerafter;   *third/intensely pleasurable/pressed*
Þe ioye of sayn Jonez° day watz gentyle° to here,°   *Saint John's/pleasant/hear*
And watz þe last of þe layk, leudez° þer þoȝten.°   *entertainment, people/thought*
Þer wer gestes° to go vpon þe gray morne,   *guests*
1025 For-þy° wonderly° þay woke,° and þe wyn dronken,°   *therefore/in wonderful manner/*

stayed up/wine drank

Daunsed ful dreȝly° wyth dere° carolez;   *danced quite continuously/merry*
At þe last, when hit watz late, þay lachen° her leue,   *took*
Vchon° to wende° on his way, þat watz wyȝe stronge.°   *each one/go/ person strange*
Gawan gef hym god-day,° þe god mon° hym lachchez,°   *gave them good-day/good man/takes*
1030 Ledes° hym to his awen° chambre, þe chymné bysyde,   *leads/own/fireplace*
And þere he draȝez° hym on-dryȝe,° and derely° hym þonkkez,°   *holds/back/courteously/thanks*
Of° þe wynne worschip° þat he hym wayued hade,°   *for/delightful honor/shown had*

1020–23. Christmas Day was followed by Saint Stephen's Day, Saint John's Day, and Childermas Day. Saint John's Day was the occasion for all-night festivity and drinking (Saint John's Blessing or Draught). However, there seems to be some confusion in the time sequence here, as Childermas Day (December 28) is omitted. The guests leave the castle on the morning of the lord's first hunt (cf. ll. 1126ff.); Gawain says (l. 1066) he has only three days left, coinciding with the three days of the hunt, before his appointment with the Green Knight on New Year's Day. Since the *Gawain* poet is usually most accurate with elements of time, Gollancz believes a line has been left out after 1022.

1026. Carols were originally ring dances accompanied by songs before they were connected with Christmas in the 15th century (cf. Robert Mannyng of Brunne's exemplum of the carolers of Colbek [see above, p. 15]).

1028. *wyȝe stronge:* i.e., "a stranger."

1029. *god mon:* i.e., "lord."

As to honour his hous on þat hyȝe tyde,° — *high time*

And enbelyse° his burȝ° with his bele chere.° — *adorn/castle/gracious company*

1035 "I-wysse° sir, quyl° I leue,° me worþez° þe better,° — *indeed/while/live/I shall be/the better (for it)*

Þat Gawayn hatz ben° my gest, at Goddez awen fest."° — *been/festival*

"Grant merci° sir." quod° Gawayn, "in god fayth hit° is yowrez,° — *thank you/said/it/yours*

Al þe honour is your awen, þe heȝe kyng yow ȝelde;° — *you reward*

And I am, wyȝe,° at your wylle, to worch° youre hest,° — *sir/do/bidding*

1040 As I am halden° þer-to, in hyȝe° and in loȝe,° — *bound/great (things)/small*

     bi riȝt."° — *right*

     Þe lorde fast can° hym payne,° — *earnestly did/take pains*

     To holde lenger° þe knyȝt,° — *longer/knight*

     To hym answrez Gawayn,

1045 Bi non° way þat he myȝt.° — *in no/might*

XXII

Then frayned° þe freke ful fayre at him-seluen,° — *asked/knight very courteously of him*

Quat derue dede° had hym dryuen, at þat dere° tyme, — *what grievous occurrence/festive*

So kenly° fro þe kyngez kourt to kayre° al his one,° — *boldly/ride/alone*

Er° þe halidayez holly° were halet° out of toun? — *before/holidays completely/past*

1050 "For soþe° sir," quod þe segge,° "ȝe sayn bot° þe trawþe;° — *in truth/knight/you say but/truth*

A heȝe ernde° and a hasty° me hade° fro þo wonez,° — *important mission/urgent/took/that dwelling*

For I am sumned° my selfe to sech° to a place, — *summoned/go*

I ne wot° in worlde whederwarde° to wende, hit to fynde; — *don't know/where*

I nolde, bot if I hit negh myȝt° on nwȝeres° morne, — *wouldn't care not to reach it/.New Year's*

1055 For alle þe londe in-wyth° Logres, so me oure lorde help! — *land in*

For-þy, sir, þis enquest° I require° yow here, — *inquiry/ask*

Þat ȝe me telle with trawþe, if euer ȝe tale herde° — *heard*

Of þe grene chapel, quere° hit on grounde stondez,° — *where/stands*

And of þe knyȝt þat hit kepes,° of colour of grene? — *guards*

1060 Þer watz stabled° bi statut° a steuen vus° by-twene, — *established/agreement/appointment us*

To mete° þat mon° at þat mere,° ȝif° I myȝt last;° — *meet/mun/appointed place/if/live*

And of þat ilk° nwȝere° bot neked° now wontez,° — *same/New Year's (Day)/little/ lacks*

And I wolde loke° on þat lede,° if God me let wolde, — *would look/man*

Gladloker,° bi Goddez sun, þen° any god welde!° — *more gladly/Son, than/good (thing) have*

1065 For-þi, i-wysse, bi ȝowre wylle,° wende me bi-houes,° — *your leave/I must*

1033. *hyȝe tyde:* i.e., "festival."   **1038.** *heȝe kyng:* i.e., God.

Naf° I now to busy° bot bare þre° dayez, *not have/(be) busy/barely three*
And me als fayn° to falle feye as fayly° of myyn° ernde." *I would rather/dead than fail/my*
Þenne laȝande° quod þe lorde, "Now leng þe by-houes,° *laughing/stay you must*
For I schal teche° yow to þat terme° bi þe tymez ende, *take/appointed place*
1070 Þe grene chapayle° vpon grounde, greue° yow no more; *chapel/may it trouble*
Bot ȝe schal be in yowre bed, burne,° at þyn ese,° *knight/your ease*
Quyle forth dayez,° and ferk° on þe fyrst of þe ȝere,° *until late in the day/travel/year*
And cum° to þat merk° at mydmorn, to make° quat yow likez *come/appointed place/do*
        in spenne;° *there*
1075   Dowellez whyle° new ȝeres daye, *remain until*
        And rys,° and raykez° þenne, *rise/depart*
        Mon° schal yow sette in° waye, *we/put on (the)*
        Hit° is not two myle henne."° *it/miles hence*

XXIII

Þenne watz Gawan ful glad, and gomenly° he laȝed, *merrily*
1080 "Now I þonk yow þryuandely þurȝ° alle oþer þynge,° *thank you heartily beyond/things*
Now acheued° is my chaunce,° I schal at your wylle° *achieved/adventure/pleasure*
Dowelle, and ellez° do quat ȝe demen."° *else/determine*
Þenne sesed° hym þe syre,° and set hym bysyde, *took hold of/lord*
Let þe ladiez be fette,° to lyke hem° þe better; *brought/please them*
1085 Þer watz seme solace° by hem-self stille;° *excellent pleasure/themselves*
                                                privately

Þe lorde let° for luf lotez° so myry,° *uttered/joy sounds/merry*
As wyȝ° þat wolde of° his wyte, ne wyst quat° he myȝt.° *man/about to take leave of/senses,*
                                                nor knew what/did

Þenne he carped° to þe knyȝt, criande° loude, *said/knight, crying*
"ȝe han demed° to do þe dede° þat I bidde; *you have decided/deed*
1090 Wyl ȝe halde° þis hes° here at þys onez?"° *keep/promise/very moment*
"ȝe° sir, for-soþe,"° sayd þe segge trwe,° *yes/in truth/knight true*
"Whyl I byde° in yowre borȝe,° be bayn° to ȝowre hest."° *remain/your castle/obedient/bidding*
"For° ȝe haf trauayled,"° quod þe tulk,° towen fro ferre,° *since/have traveled/man/journeyed*
                                                from afar

And syþen waked° me wyth, ȝe arn° not wel waryst,° *then stayed up/are/recovered*
1095 Nauþer° of sostnaunce ne° of slepe, soþly° I knowe; *neither/food nor/sleep, truly*
ȝe schal lenge° in your lofte,° and lyȝe in° your ese, *remain/room/lie at*
To morn° quyle° þe messe-quyle,° and to mete wende,° *tomorrow/until/mass time/meal go*
When ȝe wyl, wyth my wyf,° þat wyth yow schal sitte, *wife*

1067. *feye*: from OE *fæge*, "doomed to die," "dead" (cf. above,
p. 65, ll. 379–429*n*; p. 71, l. 555*n*).

And comfort yow with compayny, til I to cort **torne**;°   *court return*
1100   ʒe lende,°   *stay*
     and I schal erly ryse,
     On huntyng wyl I wende."
     Gauayn grantez alle þyse,°   *this*
     Hym heldande,° as þe hende.°   *bowing/courteously*

XXIV

1105 "ʒet firre,"° quod þe freke,° "a forwarde° we make;   *further/man/agreement*
Quat-so-euer I wynne in þe wod,° hit worþez to° yourez,   *wood/becomes*
And quat chek so° ʒe acheue, chaunge° me þer-forne;°   *whatever fortune/exchange (with)/ for it*

Swete,° swap we so, sware° with trawþe,°   *good sir/swear/on your honor*
Queþer, leude,° so lymp lere oþer° better."   *whether, sir/befall worthless or good/it*
1110 "Bi God," quod Gawayn þe gode,° "I grant þer-tylle,°   *good/it*
And þat yow lyst° forto layke, lef° hit me° þynkes.°   *it pleases/to play, delightful/to me/ seems*

"Who bryngez° vus° þis beuerage, þis bargayn is maked";°   *if someone will bring/us/made*
So sayde þe lorde of þat lede;° þay laʒed° vchone,°   *company/they laughed/each one*
Þay dronken,° and daylyeden,° and dalten vntyʒtel,°   *drank/chatted/reveled*
1115 Þise° lordez and ladyez, quyle þat° hem lyked;°   *these/while/it pleased*
And syþen with frenkysch fare° and fele° fayre lotez°   *polite observance/many/words*
Þay stoden,° and stemed,° and stylly speken,°   *stood/stopped/softly spoke*
Kysten ful comlyly,° and kaʒten her leue.°   *kissed very courteously/took their leave*

With mony leude° ful lyʒt,° and lemande° torches,   *many (a) servant/eager/shining*
1120 Vche burne° to his bed watz broʒt° at þe laste,   *each man/brought*
     ful softe;°   *comfortably*
     To bed ʒet er° þay ʒede,°   *before/went*
     Recorded couenauntez° ofte;   *recalled compacts*
     Þe olde lorde of þat leude°   *company*
1125   Cowþe° wel halde layk a-lofte.°   *could/keep a game going*

FYTTE THE THIRD

I

Ful° erly bifore þe day þe folk vp-rysen,°   *very/arose*
Gestes° þat go wolde, hor gromez þay calden,°   *guests/would, their grooms they called*

1112. The drink must be brought in order to seal the bargain.

And þay busken° vp bilyue, blonkkez° to sadel,　　　　*hasten/quickly, horses*

Tyffen her takles, trussen° her males,°　　　　*prepare their gear, pack/bags*

1130　Richen hem° þe rychest,° to ryde alle arayde,　　　　*dress themselves/noblest (men)*

Lepen° vp lyȝtly, lachen° her brydeles,　　　　*leap/eagerly, take*

Vche wyȝe° on his way, þer° hym wel lyked.°　　　　*each man/where/it pleased*

Þe leue° lorde of þe londe° watz not þe last,　　　　*dear/land*

A-rayed for þe rydyng, with renkkez° ful mony;°　　　　*men/many*

1135　Ete° a sop° hastyly, when he hade herde° masse,　　　　*ate/light meal/had heard*

With bugle to bent felde° he buskez by-lyue;　　　　*hunting field*

By þat° any day-lyȝt lemed° vpon erþe,　　　　*(the time) that/daylight shone*

He with his haþeles° on hyȝe° horsses weren.°　　　　*men/tall/were*

Þenne þise cacheres° þat couþe,° cowpled° hor houndez,　　　　*the huntsmen/knew how/coupled*

1140　Vnclosed þe kenel dore, and calde hem° þer-oute,　　　　*them*

Blwe bygly in° buglez þre bare mote;°　　　　*blew strongly on/three single notes*

Braches° bayed þerfore, and breme° noyse maked,°　　　　*hounds/fierce/made*

And þay chastysed,° and charred,° on chasyng þat° went;　　　　*whipped/turned back/chasing (off hounds) that*

A hundreth of° hunteres, as I haf° herde telle,　　　　*hundred/have*

1145　　　　of þe best;

To trystors° vewters° ȝod,°　　　　*hunting stations/deerhound keepers/went*

Couples huntes of kest,°　　　　*leashes hunters off cast*

Þer ros° for° blastez gode°　　　　*rose/because of/good*

Gret rurd° in þat forest.　　　　*great noise*

II

1150　At þe fyrst quethe° of þe quest° quaked þe wylde;°　　　　*utterance/baying of hounds/wild (creatures)*

Der drof° in þe dale, doted° for drede,°　　　　*deer fled/dazed/fear*

Hiȝed° to þe hyȝe, bot heterly° þay were　　　　*rushed/high (ground) but vigorously*

Restayed° with° þe stablye,° þat stoutly ascryed;°　　　　*turned back/by/beaters/shouted*

Þay let þe herttez° haf þe gate,° with þe hyȝe hedes,°　　　　*harts/pass by/heads*

1139–49. The dogs, which were kept all together in one kennel, were coupled before being let out. At their release, three long notes were played on the horn; when they had caught the scent, they were uncoupled and more blasts were sounded. Since the 14th-century horn had only one note, the variation was accomplished by blasts of different lengths (Tolkien and Gordon). Braches were small beaglelike hounds used for their keen scent.

1150ff. The hunt here follows a standard formula. Around the area of the hunt were men and hounds at several stations (cf. *trystors*, l. 1146). Light greyhounds pursued the game, and the beaters at the stations directed the flow of wild traffic toward the lord and his hunting party. If the deer approached the special stations where they were to be killed or "received" (cf. *resayt*, l. 1168), the beaters attempted to kill them, using the larger greyhounds to pull down the game (cf. *The Master of Game* written by Edward, second duke of York, in 1406–13, ed. W. A. and E. Baillie-Grohman [Edinburgh, 1904; modernized ed. London, 1909]). In this case the resayts were located near the river (cf. l. 1169).

1154–57. Harts (stags) and bucks were the male deer of the red and the fallow species respectively. For them the close season was September 14–June 24. Hinds and does, the females of the same species respectively, were hunted September 14–February 2.

1155 Þe breme bukkez° also, with hor brode paumez;°   *bucks/wide antlers*
For þe fre° lorde hade de-fende° in fermysoun° tyme,   *noble/forbidden/close-season*
Þat þer schulde° no mon meue to° þe male dere.   *should/man interfere with*
Þe hindez were halden° in, with hay° and war,°   *held/(cries of) "Hey!"/"Ware!"*
Þe does dryuen with gret dyn° to þe depe sladez;°   *noise/deep valleys*
1160 Þer myȝt mon se,° as þay slypte,° slentyng° of arwes,°   *might one see/were loosed/flight/
    arrows*

At vche wende vnder wande wapped° a flone,°   *turn in (the) wood flew/arrow*
Þat bigly bote° on þe broun,° with ful brode hedez,   *bit/brown (hide)*
What!° þay brayen,° and bleden, bi bonkkez° þay deȝen.°   *lo/cry out/bleed, on hills/die*
And ay rachches° in a res radly° hem folȝes,°   *ever hounds/rush swiftly/follows*
1165 Hunterez wyth hyȝe° horne hasted hem after,   *loud*
Wyth such a crakkande° kry, as° klyffes haden brusten;°   *ringing/as (if)/had broken*
What wylde so° at-waped° wyȝes þat schotten,°   *whatever deer/escaped/shot*
Watz al to-raced° and rent,° at þe resayt.°   *pulled down/torn apart/receiving
    station*

Bi þay° were tened at° þe hyȝe, and taysed° to þe wattres°   *after they/harassed from/driven/
    waters*

1170 Þe ledez° were so lerned° at þe loȝe trysteres,°   *men/expert/low stations*
And þe gre-houndez° so grete, þat geten° hem bylyue,°   *greyhounds/large, that (they) caught/
    quickly*

And hem tofylched,° as fast as frekez° myȝt loke,°   *pulled down/men/look*
        þer ryȝt.°   *right there*
    Þe lorde for blys° abloy°   *joy/was carried away*
1175   Ful° oft con launce° and lyȝt,°   *very/did gallop/dismount*
    And drof° þat day wyth joy,°   *passed/joy*
    Thus to þe derk nyȝt.°   *dark night*

III

Þus laykez° þis lorde by lunde wodez° euez,°   *sports/linden-wood/borders*
And Gawayn þe god° mon, in gay° bed lygez,°   *good/fair/lies*
1180 Lurkkez° quyl° þe day-lyȝt lemed° on þe wowes,°   *lies snug/until/daylight shone/walls*
Vnder couertour° ful clere, cortyned° aboute;   *coverlet/bright, curtained*
And as in slomberyng° he slode,° slcȝly° he herde°   *slumbering/slept softly/made wary/
    heard*

A littel dyn at his dor, and dernly vpon;°   *stealthily open*
And he heuez° vp his hed out of þe cloþes,°   *lifts/coverings*
1185 A corner of þe cortyn he caȝt° vp a lyttel,   *raised*
And waytez warly° þider-warde,° quat hit° be myȝt.   *looks (to see) warily/in that
    direction/what it*

Hit watz þe ladi, loflyest° to be-holde,   *loveliest*
Þat droȝ° þe dor after hir° ful dernly and stylle,°   *drew/her/softly*
And boȝed° to-warde þe bed; and þe burne° schamed,°   *moved/knight/was embarrassed*
1190 And layde hym° doun lystyly,° and let as° he slepte.   *himself/craftily/pretended that*

And ho° stepped stilly,° and stel° to his bedde,   *she/softly/stole*
Kest° vp þe cortyn, and creped° with-inne,   *drew/crept*
And set hir° ful softly on þe bed-syde,   *herself*
And lenged° þere selly° longe, to loke quen° he wakened.   *remained/very/see when*
1195 Þe lede lay lurked° a ful longe quyle,°   *lurking/while*
Compast° in his concience to° quat þat cace° myȝt   *pondered/mind (as) to/affair*
Mene oþer° amount,° to meruayle° hym° þoȝt;°   *mean or/come to/like (a) marvel/to him/it seemed*

Bot° ȝet he sayde in° hym-self, "More semly° hit were   *but/to/suitable*
To aspye° wyth my spelle° in space° quat ho wolde."°   *find out/speech/soon/wanted*
1200 Þen he wakenede, and wroth,° and to hir warde° torned,°   *stretched/toward her/turned*
And vn-louked° his yȝe-lyddez,° and let as hym° wondered,°   *opened/eyelids/he/was astonished*
And sayned° hym, as° bi his saȝe° þe sauer° to worthe,°   *crossed/as if/prayer/safer/be*
    with hande;
    Wyth chynne and cheke° ful swete,°   *cheek/sweet*
1205   Boþe quit° and red in-blande,°   *white/together*
    Ful lufly° con ho lete,°   *pleasantly/behave*
    Wyth lyppez smal laȝande.°   *laughing*

IV

"God moroun,° sir Gawayn," sayde þat fayr lady,   *morning*
"Ȝe° ar a sleper vn-slyȝe,° þat mon° may slyde hider;°   *you/sleeper unwary/one/steal hither*
1210 Now ar ȝe tan° astyt,° bot true vus° may schape,°   *taken/in a moment/unless (a) truce ourselves (we)/arrange*

I schal bynde yow° in your bedde, þat° be ȝe trayst";°   *you/of it/sure*
Al laȝande þe lady lanced þo bourdez.°   *uttered those jests*
"Goud° moroun gay,"° quod° Gawayn þe blyþe,°   *good/gay (lady)/said/cheerful*
"Me schal worþe° at your wille,° and þat me wel lykez,°   *I am/command/pleases*
1215 For I ȝelde me ȝederly,° and ȝeȝe after grace,°   *yield myself quickly/cry for mercy*
And þat is þe best, be° my dome,° for me by-houez° nede";°   *by/judgment/I must/of necessity*
And þus he bourded° a-ȝayn° with mony° a blyþe laȝter.°   *jested/in return/many/laugh*
"Bot wolde ȝe,° lady louely, þen leue° me grante,   *if you would/permission*
And de-prece° your prysoun,° and pray hym to ryse,   *release/prisoner*
1220 I wolde boȝe° of þis bed, and busk° me better,   *would get out/dress*
I schulde keuer° þe more comfort° to karp° yow wyth."   *should get/pleasure/talk*
"Nay, for soþe, beau° sir," sayd þat swete,°   *in truth, fair/sweet (one)*
"Ȝe schal not rise of° your bedde, I rych yow° better,   *from/intend (for) you*
I schal happe° yow here þat oþer half als,°   *tuck in/side also*

1191–94. In the first temptation scene, the lord's wife pulls aside the curtains surrounding Gawain's bed. It must not be supposed that she crept into the bed itself.

1218–21. There is a certain burlesque quality to this scene of the most courteous knight of Arthur's court caught in bed in his underwear, in a paradox of *courtoisie* and gaucheness. The tone may have been borrowed from humorous romances concerning Gawain and his various encounters with seductive beauties and hags.

1225 And syþen° karp wyth my knyȝt° þat I kaȝt° haue;　　*then/knight/caught*
　　　For I wene° wel, iwysse,° sir Wawen° ȝe are,　　*believe/indeed/Gawain*
　　　Þat alle þe worlde worchipez, quere-so° ȝe ride;　　*honors, wherever*
　　　Your honour, your hendelayk° is hendely° praysed　　*courtliness/graciously*
　　　With° lordez, wyth ladyes, with alle þat lyf bere.°　　*by/life bear*
1230 And now ȝe ar here, iwysse, and we bot oure one;°　　*alone by ourselves*
　　　My lorde and his ledez° ar on lenþe° faren,°　　*men/afar/gone away*
　　　Oþer burnez° in her bedde,° and my burdez° als,　　*men/their beds/maids*
　　　Þe dor drawen,° and dit° with a derf° haspe;°　　*closed/locked/strong/door pin*
　　　And syþen° I haue in þis hous hym þat al lykez,°　　*since/love*
1235 I schal ware° my whyle° wel, quyl hit° lastez,　　*spend/time/while it*
　　　　　　with tale;°　　*in conversation*
　　　　ȝe ar welcum° to my cors,°　　*welcome/person*
　　　　Yowre awen won° to wale,°　　*your own pleasure/take*
　　　　Me be-houez° of fyne force,°　　*(it) behooves/sheer necessity*
1240　　Your seruaunt be° and schale."°　　*servant (that I) be/shall*

　　　　　　　　　V

　　　"In god° fayth," quod Gawayn, "gayn° hit me° þynkkez,°　　*good/a good thing/to me/seems*
　　　Þaȝ° I be not now he þat° ȝe of speken;　　*though/such a man as*
　　　To reche to° such reuerence° as ȝe reherce° herc　　*merit/honor/describe*
　　　I am wyȝe° vn-worþy, I wot° wel my-seluen;°　　*person/know/myself*
1245 Bi God, I were° glad, and° yow god þoȝt,°　　*would be/if/fit thought*
　　　At saȝe oþer° at seruyce° þat I sette myȝt°　　*in word or/service/devote (myself) might*

　　　To þe plesaunce° of your prys,° hit were a pure ioye."°　　*pleasure/you/joy*
　　　"In god fayth, sir Gawayn," quod þe gay lady,
　　　"Þe prys° and þe prowes° þat plesez° al oþer,°　　*excellence/prowess/pleases/others*
1250 If I hit lakked,° oþer set at lyȝt,° hit were littel daynté;°　　*disparaged/thought light of/courtesy*

　　　Bot hit° ar ladyes in-noȝe,° þat leuer wer° nowþe°　　*but there/many/would rather/now*
　　　Haf þe, hende,° in hor holde,° as I þe habbe° here,　　*have you, gracious (man)/their power/have*

　　　To daly° with derely° your daynté wordez,　　*trifle/pleasantly/delightful*
　　　Keuer hem° comfort, and colen° her carez,　　*obtain themselves/relieve*
1255 Þen° much of þe garysoun° oþer golde þat þay hauen.°　　*than/possessions/they have*

1229. *lyf bere:* i.e., "are alive."

1237. I.e., "you are welcome to me." *Cors* has in the past been given here its literal translation of "body," which has given rise to some wanton critical interpretation and prudish astonishment. But Davis seems to be right in pointing out that it is too early in the lady's "game" for such a direct attack, that her advances increase in intensity each time around. Thus *cors* is used in the sense of "person," as it is often in French, and Gawain answers the lady in similar courteous fashion; one

would expect that a "proposition" would have elicited a more marked response. (It has been suggested that the nature of the animals successively hunted by the lord [timid deer, forthright boar, sly fox] is paralleled by Gawain's actions when "hunted" by the lady.)

1238. I.e., "to do as you like."

1247. *þe plesaunce of your prys:* i.e., "your pleasure."

Bot I louue° þat ilk° lorde þat þe lyfte haldez,° — *praise/same/heavens rules*
I haf hit holly° in my honde° þat al desyres, — *wholly/hand*
        þur3e grace."° — *through (His) mercy*
Scho° made hym so gret chere,° — *she/behaved so graciously to him*
1260 Þat watz so fayr of face,
Þe kny3t with speches skere,° — *speeches pure*
Answared° to vche a cace.° — *answered/everything*

VI

"Madame," quod° þe myry mon,° "Mary yow 3elde° — *said/merry man/you reward*
For I haf founden,° in god fayth, yowre fraunchis nobele° — *found/generosity noble*
1265 And oþer ful much° of oþer folk fongen° bi hor dedez;° — *much else/received/deeds*
Bot þe daynté° þat þay delen, for° my disert° nys° even,° — *honor/give (me), since/merit/is not/ equal (to it)*

Hit is þe worchyp° of your-self, þat no3t bot° wel connez."° — *honor/only/behaves*
"Bi Mary," quod þe menskful,° "me þynk° hit anoþer° — *noble (lady) I believe/otherwise*
For were I worth al þe wone° of wymmen° alyue, — *host/women*
1270 And al þe wele° of þe worlde were in my honde, — *wealth*
And I schulde chepen° and chose,° to cheue me° a lorde° — *should bargain/choose/acquire myself/husband*

For þe costes° þat I haf knowen vpon° þe kny3t° here, — *qualities/discovered in/knight*
Of bewté,° and debonerté,° and blyþe semblaunt,° — *beauty/courtesy/cheerful manner*
And þat I haf er herkkened,° and halde° hit here trwee,° — *before heard/maintain/true*
1275 Þer schulde no freke° vpon folde° bifore yow be chosen." — *man/earth*
"I-wysse, worþy,"° quod þe wy3e,° "3e° haf waled wel° better, — *indeed, noble (lady)/man/you/ chosen much*

Bot I am proude of þe prys° þat 3e put on me, — *value*
And, soberly° your seruaunt, my souerayn° I holde yow, — *seriously/(as)my liege lady*
And yowre° kny3t I be-com, and Kryst° yow for-3elde."° — *your/Christ/reward*
1280 Þus þay meled° of much-quat,° til myd-morn paste,° — *talked/many things/passed*
And ay° þe lady let lyk, as° hym loued mych;° — *ever/behaved as if she/much*
Þe freke° ferde with defence,° and feted ful fayre.° — *knight/was on his guard/behaved very courteously*

"Þa3° I were burde bry3test,"° þe burde in mynde hade,° — *though/lady (the) fairest/reflected*
"Þe lasse luf° in his lode,° for lur° þat he so3t,° — *less love (would he bring)/ journey/sorrow/sought*
1285   boute hone";° — *without delay*
Þe dunte° þat schulde hym deue,° — *blow/strike down*
And nedez° hit most° be done; — *of necessity/it must*
Þe lady þenn spek° of leue,° — *spoke/leaving*
He granted hir° ful sone.° — *granted (it) her/immediately*

1264–67. The passage seems corrupt: "For I have found in you, in good faith, a noble generosity, and received much else from other people by their actions; but the honour that they assign to me, since my desert is not equal to it, is to the honour of yourself, who can behave no otherwise than well" (Davis).

VII

1290 Þenne ho gef° hym god-day,° and wyth a glent la3ed,°	*she gave/good-day/glance laughed*
And as ho stod,° ho stonyed° hym wyth ful stor° wordez:	*stood/astonished/severe*
"Now he þat spedez vche spech,° þis disport 3elde° yow!	*blesses each speech/entertainment repay*
Bot° þat 3e be Gawan, hit gotz in mynde."°	*but/is a matter of doubt*
"Quer-fore?"° quod þe freke, and freschly° he askez,	*why/quickly*
1295 Ferde° lest he hade° fayled in fourme° of his castes;°	*afraid/had/manner/speech*
Bot þe burde hym blessed, and bi þis skyl° sayde,	*as follows*
"So god° as Gawayn gaynly° is halden,°	*good/rightly/accounted*
And cortaysye° is closed° so clene° in hym-seluen,°	*courtesy/contained/completely/him*
Couth° not ly3tly haf lenged° so long wyth a lady,	*could/easily have remained*
1300 Bot he had craued a cosse,° bi his courtaysye,	*kiss*
Bi sum towch° of summe tryfle, at sum talez° ende."	*some hint/talk's*
Þen quod Wowen,° "I-wysse, worþe° as yow lykez,°	*said Gawain/let it be/you wish*
I schal kysse at your comaundement,° as a kny3t fallez,°	*bidding/it befits*
And fire° lest he displese° yow, so plede° hit no more."	*(go) further/displease/plead*
1305 Ho comes nerre° with þat, and cachez° hym in armez,	*nearer/takes*
Loutez luflych adoun,° and þe leude° kyssez;	*bends lovingly down/knight*
Þay comly bykennen° to Kryst ayþer° oþer;	*they fittingly commend/each*
Ho dos hir° forth at þe dore, with-outen dyn° more.	*goes/without ado*
And he ryches hym° to ryse, and rapes hym° sone,°	*prepares/hurries/quickly*
1310 Clepes° to his chamberlayn, choses his wede,°	*calls/garment*
Bo3ez° forth, quen° he watz boun,° blyþely to masse,	*goes/when/ready*
And þenne he meued° to his mete,° þat menskly° hym keped,°	*went/meal/suitably/awaited*
And made myry° al day til þe mone rysed,°	*merry/moon rose*
with game;	
1315 Watz neuer freke° fayrer fonge,°	*man/entertained*
Bitwene two so dyngne dame,°	*worthy ladies*
Þe alder° and þe 3onge,°	*older/young*
Much solace set° þay same.°	*pleasure had/together*

VIII

And ay þe lorde of þe londe° is lent° on his gammez,°	*land/gone/games*
1320 To hunt in holtez° and heþe,° at hyndez barayne,°	*woods/heath/hinds barren*
Such a sowme° he þer slowe° bi þat° þe sunne heldet,°	*number/slew/(the time) that/set*
Of dos° and of oþer dere,° to deme° were° wonder.°	*does/deer/judge/would be/marvelous*
Þenne fersly þay flokked° in folk° at þe laste,°	*eagerly they flocked/(a) throng/at last*
And quykly of þe quelled° dere a querré° þay maked;°	*killed/quarry/made*

1292. *he þat spedez vche spech:* i.e., "God."
1324. *Querré:* used here for the collection of slain deer. The word was originally *cuirée,* "leather," on which the offal was served to the hounds.

¹³²⁵ Þe best boȝed° þerto, with burnez in-noghe,°   *gentry came/men many*
   Gedered° þe grattest of gres° þat þer were,   *collected/greatest in fat*
   And didden hem derely° vndo,° as þe dede askez:°   *did them neatly/cut open/task*
                                                            requires

   Serched° hem at þe asay,° summe þat þer were,   *examined/assay*
   Two fyngeres° þay fonde° of þe fowlest° of alle;   *fingerbreadths (of fat)/found/*
                                                            poorest

¹³³⁰ Syþen° þay slyt þe slot, sesed° þe erber,°   *then/took/gullet*
   Schaued° wyth a scharp knyf,° and þe schyre knitten;°   *scraped (it)/knife/white (flesh) tied*
   Syþen rytte° þay þe foure lymmes,° and rent of° þe hyde,   *cut off/legs/tore off*
   Þen brek° þay þe bale,° þe balez° out token,°   *cut open/belly/bowels/took*
   Lystily° for laucyng° þe lere° of þe knot;   *deftly/not to loosen/ligature*
¹³³⁵ Þay gryped to° þe gargulun,° and grayþely departed°   *laid hold of/throat/quickly*
                                                            separated

   Þe wesaunt fro° þe wynt-hole,° and walt° out þe guttez;   *esophagus from/windpipe/tossed*
   Þen scher° þay out þe schulderez° with her° scharp knyuez,   *cut/shoulders/their*
   Haled° hem by a lyttel hole, to haue hole° sydes;   *drew/whole (i.e., intact)*
   Siþen° britned° þay þe brest, and brayden hit° in twynne,°   *then/cut up/pulled it/two*
¹³⁴⁰ And eft° at þe gargulun bigynez on° þenne,   *again/start*
   Ryuez° hit vp radly, ryȝt° to þe byȝt,°   *cut/promptly, right/fork of the legs*
   Voydez° out þe avanters,° and verayly° þerafter   *clear/numbles/truly*
   Alle þe rymez° by þe rybbez° radly þay lance;°   *membranes/ribs/loosen*
   So ryde° þay of by resoun° bi þe rygge° bonez,   *cleared/correctly/back*
¹³⁴⁵ Euenden° to þe haunche, þat henged° alle samen,°   *trimmed/hung/together*
   And heuen° hit vp al hole, and hwen° hit of þere,   *lifted/cut*
   And þat þay neme for° þe noumbles,° bi nome° as I trowe,°   *name as/numbles/name/believe*
                   bi kynde;°   *properly*
       Bi þe byȝt al° of þe þyȝes,°   *fork moreover/thighs*
¹³⁵⁰   Þe lappez° þay lance bi-hynde,   *skin folds*
       To hewe hit° in two þay hyȝes,°   *(i.e., the carcass)/hurry*
       Bi þe bak-bon° to vnbynde.°   *backbone/undo*

1325. It was the sign of the gentleman that he knew how to break up a deer in the proper fashion. As Andersen's Princess on the Pea proved her aristocracy through the sensitivity of her skin, so unrecognized princes in medieval romances gave evidence of nobility when they prepared the deer correctly (*Tristram, Ipomadon*).

1328. The spot of assay is found by the chief huntsman, who holds the deer by the forefoot, and the chief hunter. The latter cuts from the breast to the belly to check the goodness and thickness of the meat.

1330–34. The *slot* started at the hollow at the base of the throat and ran down the middle of the breast. The *erber* was the gullet, which was scraped free of flesh and then tied in a knot so as to keep the stomach contents from escaping.

1337–38. Special shoulder knives were used to cut a small hole between the leg and the breast. The shoulder was then carefully loosened from the hide through the hole, leaving the skin almost intact.

1342. *avanters;* heart, liver, lungs, etc., also called *numbles* (cf. l. 1347) and used for food. A dish made of these numbles came through false division to be called *an umble pie,* hence Mod. Eng. *humble pie.* The numbles were not among the delicacies of the deer, and today a humble apology or humiliation is called "eating humble pie."

IX

Boþe þe hede° and þe hals° þay hwen of þenne,	head/neck
And syþen sunder° þay þe sydez swyft fro þe chyne,°	separate/backbone
1355 And corbeles fee° þay kest° in a greue;°	ravens' portion/threw/thicket
Þenne þurled° þay ayþer þik° side þurȝ,° bi þe rybbe,	pierced/both thick/flanks through
And henged þenne ayþer bi hoȝes° of þe fourchez,°	hocks/legs
Vche freke° for his fee, as fallez° forto° haue.	each hunter/he was due/to
Vpon a felle° of þe fayre best, fede þay þayr° houndes,	skin/beast, feed they their
1360 Wyth þe lyuer and þe lyȝtez,° þe leþer° of þe paunchez,°	lungs/skin/stomachs (i.e., tripe)
And bred baþed° in blod, blende° þer amongez;°	steeped/blood, mixed/amongst
Baldely° þay blw prys,° bayed þayr rachchez,°	vigorously/blew (the) capture/ hounds
Syþen fonge° þay her flesche, folden° to home,	took/turned
Strakande ful stoutly mony stif motez.°	sounding very strongly many loud notes
1365 Bi þat° þe daylyȝt° watz done, þe douthe° watz al wonen°	(the time) that/daylight/company/ come
In-to þe comly° castel, þer° þe knyȝt bidez°	fair/where/knight stays
ful stille;°	quietly
Wyth blys° and bryȝt fyr bette,°	joy/bright fire kindled
Þe lord is comen° þer-tylle,°	come/to it
1370 When Gawayn wyth hym mette,	
Þer watz bot wele° at wylle.°	only delight/(his) pleasure

X

Thenne comaunded° þe lorde in þat sale° to samen° all þe meny,°	commanded/hall/gather/company
Boþe þe ladyes on loghe° to lyȝt° with her burdes,°	down/descend/maids
Bi-fore alle þe fold on° þe flette, frekez° he beddez°	in/hall, men/asks
1375 Veraly his venysoun to fech° hym byforne;°	fetch/before
And al godly° in gomen° Gawayn he called,	courteously/merrily
Techez hym° to þe tayles of ful tayt° bestes,	directs his attention/nimble
Schewez° hym þe schyree grece schorne° vpon rybbes.	shows/white flesh cut

---

1355. The "corbies' fee" was the gristle at the end of the breastbone thrown into the trees to feed the gathering ravens and crows. The animals were rewarded in the hunt, and serving them became as much a ritual as the breaking up of the deer.

1358. Tolkien and Gordon mention that each man received part of the deer as fee: the man who killed it claimed the hide; the forester, the right shoulder; the lord, the numbles and sides; etc.

1362. The *prys* (OF *prise*, "capture") was a blast proving the capture of the quarry: four notes, a pause, then four longer notes. The rest of the hunt blew two shorts and two longs and then continued this on the way home.

1377. According to the hunting expertise of the *Boke of St. Albans*, the tails remained on the carcasses.

"How payez yow° þis play?° haf° I prys wonnen?°   *pleases you/sport/have/praise won*
1380 Haue I þryaundely þonk° þurȝ my craft serued?"°   *thoroughly thanks/skill deserved*
"Ȝe i-wysse,"° quod° þat oþer wyȝe,° "here is wayth° fayrest   *yes indeed/said/man/meat*
Þat I seȝ þis° seuen ȝere° in sesoun° of wynter."   *saw these/years/season*
"And al I gif° yow, Gawayn," quod þe gome° þenne,   *give/man*
"For by a-corde of couenaunt ȝe° craue° hit° as your awen."°   *compact you/may claim/it/own*
1385 "Þis is soth,"° quod þe segge,° "I say yow° þat ilke,°   *true/knight/to you/the same*
Þat I haf worthyly° wommen þis wonez° wyth-inne,   *what/honorably/house*
I-wysse with as god° wylle hit worþez to° ȝourez."°   *good/shall become/yours*
He hasppez° his fayre hals his armez wyth-inne,   *clasps*
And kysses hym as comlyly° as he couþe awyse:°   *graciously/could manage*
1390 "Tas° yow þere my cheuicaunce,° I cheued° no more,   *take/winnings/gained*
I wowche hit saf° fynly, þaȝ feler° hit were."   *freely grant it/completely, though more*

"Hit is god," quod þe god mon,° "grant mercy° þerfore,   *man/thank you*
Hit may be such, hit is þe better, and° ȝe me breue wolde°   *better (gain), if/tell would*
Where ȝe wan° þis ilk wele,° bi wytte° of yorseluen?"°   *won/same wealth/cleverness/your own*
1395 "Þat watz not forward,"° quod he, "frayst° me no more,   *(the) agreement/ask*
For° ȝe haf tan° þat yow tydez,° trawe non° oþer   *since/taken/is due/expect no*
ȝe mowe."°   *may*
Þay laȝed,° and made hem blyþe,°   *laughed/merry*
Wyth lotez° þat were to lowe,°   *words/praiseworthy*
1400 To soper þay ȝede asswyþe,°   *supper they went straightway*
Wyth dayntes nwe° in-nowe.°   *delicacies new/in plenty*

XI

And syþen° by þe chymné° in chamber þay seten,°   *then/fireplace/sat*
Wyȝez þe walle wyn weȝed° to hem° oft,   *choice wine brought/them*
And efte° in her bourdyng° þay bayþen° in þe morn,   *again/their jesting/agreed*
1405 To fylle° þe same forwardez þat þay by-fore maden,°   *carry out/made*
Wat chaunce so° bytydez hor cheuysaunce° to chaunge,°   *whatever chance/befalls their winnings/exchange*

What nwez° so þay nome,° at naȝt quen° þay metten°   *new (things)/took/night when/met*
Þat acorded of° þe couenauntez byfore þe court alle;   *agreed to*
Þe beuerage watz broȝt° forth in bourde at þat tyme;   *brought*
1410 Þenne þay louelych leȝten leue° at þe last,°   *courteously took leave/at last*
Vche burne° to his bedde busked bylyue.°   *each man/hastened quickly*
Bi þat° þe coke hade crowen° and cakled bot þryse,°   *(the time) that/cock had crowed/cackled but thrice*

Þe lorde watz lopen of° his bedde, þe leudez° vch one,   *had leaped from/(and) the men*
So þat þe mete° and þe masse watz metely delyuered;°   *meal/duly over*
1415 Þe douthe dressed° to þe wod, er° any day sprenged,°   *company went/wood, before/broke*
to chace;°   *(the) hunt*

He3° with hunte° and hornez,	*eagerly/huntsman*
Þur3 playnez° þay passe in space,°	*through plains/soon after*
Vn-coupled among þo° þornez,	*the*
1420 Rachez° þat ran on race.°	*hounds/track*

XII

Sone° þay calle of° a quest° in a ker° syde,	*quickly/for/search/marsh*
Þe hunt re-hayted° þe houndez, þat hit° fyrst mynged,°	*encouraged/it/scented*
Wylde wordez° hym° warp° wyth a wrast noyce;°	*cries/to them/uttered/loud noise*
Þe howndez þat hit herde, hastid þider swyþe,°	*heard, hastened there quickly*
1425 And fellen° as fast to þe fuyt,° fourty at ones;°	*fell/trail/once*
Þenne such a glauer° ande glam° of gedered° rachchez	*babble/clamor/assembled*
Ros,° þat þe rocherez° rungen° aboute;	*rose/rocky banks/rang*
Hunterez hem hardened° with horne and wyth muthe.°	*encouraged/mouth*
Þen al in a semblé sweyed to-geder,°	*company rushed together*
1430 Bitwene a flosche° in þat fryth,° and a foo° cragge;	*pool/wood/forbidding*
In° a knot,° bi a clyffe, at þe kerre syde,	*on/rocky hill*
Þer as° þe rogh° rocher vn-rydely° watz fallen,	*where/rough/in confusion*
Þay ferden° to þe fyndyng, and frekez° hem after;	*rushed/men*
Þay vmbe-kesten° þe knarre° and þe knot boþe,	*surrounded/crag*
1435 Wy3ez° whyl° þay wysten° wel wythinne hem hit were,	*men/until/knew*
Þe best° þat þer breued° watz wyth° þe blod° houndez.	*beast/announced/by/blood*
Þenne þay beten° on þe buskez° and bede° hym vp ryse,	*beat/bushes/bade*
And he vnsoundyly° out so3t° seggez ouer-þwert,°	*disastrously/(a way) out sought/(a line of) men through*
On° þe sellokest° swyn swenged° out þere,	*one (of)/most marvelous/boars rushed*
1440 Long sythen fro° þe sounder° þat si3ed° for° olde,°	*since from/herd/was gone/because of /old age*
For he watz breme bor° alþer° grattest,°	*fierce boar/of all/(the) greatest*
Ful° grymme quen he gronyed,° þenne greued° mony,°	*very/grunted/were dismayed/many*
For þre at þe fyrst þrast° he þry3t° to þe erþe,	*rush/thrust*
And sparred° forth good sped, boute spyt° more,	*sprang/(at) great speed, without harm*
1445 Þise oþer halowed° "hyghe!°" ful hy3e° and "hay!° hay!" cryed,	*these others shouted/ "Hi!"/ loudly/"Hey!"*
Haden° hornez to mouþe, heterly° rechated;°	*put/vigorously/blew the recall*
Mony watz þe myry mouthe° of men and of houndez,	*merry cries*

1419. The lairs of boars were in the thickest thorn bushes.

1422. The hounds that first caught the scent and gave tongue at it were called by name, and the hunters encouraged the rest to come up.

1436. The *blod houndez* were also called *limers* since they were led on a *liam* ("leash") to the hunting place. They were of black and tan coloring, built like modern bloodhounds

Þat buskkez° after þis bor, with bost° and wyth noyse,　　*hastens/clamor*
　　To quelle;°　　*kill*
1450　Ful oft he bydez þe baye,°　　*stands at bay*
　And maymez þe mute inn melle,°　　*pack in (the) midst*
　He hurtez of° þe houndez, and þay°　　*(some) of/they*
　Ful ȝomerly ȝaule° and ȝelle.　　*piteously yowl*

XIII

Schalkez° to schote° at hym schowen to° þenne,　　*men/shoot/pressed forward*
1455　Haled to° hym of her arewez, hitten° hym oft;　　*loosed at/their arrows, hit*
　Bot° þe poyntez payred° at þe pyth° þat pyȝt° in his scheldez,°　　*but/failed/toughness/struck/ shoulder skin*

　And þe barbez of° his browe bite non wolde,°　　*(of the) barbs into/none would*
　Þaȝ° þe schauen° schaft schyndered° in pecez,°　　*though/smooth/shattered/pieces*
　Þe hede hypped aȝayn, were-so-euer° hit hitte;　　*head rebounded again, wherever*
1460　Bot quen° þe dyntez° hym dered of her dryȝe° strokez,　　*when/blows/hurt by their incessant*
　Þen, brayn-wod° for bate,° on burnez° he rasez,°　　*frenzied/fighting/men/rushes*
　Hurtez hem° ful heterly þer° he forth hyȝez,°　　*them/savagely where/rushes*
　And mony arȝed° þerat, and on-lyte droȝen.°　　*feared/back drew*
　Bot þe lorde on a lyȝt horce launces° hym after,　　*active horse gallops*
1465　As burne bolde vpon bent° his bugle he blowez,　　*battlefield*
　He rechated, and rode þurȝ ronez° ful þyk,°　　*through bushes/thick*
　Suande° þis wylde swyn til þe sunne schafted.°　　*pursuing/set*
　Þis day wyth þis ilk dede° þay dryuen on° þis wyse,°　　*same activity/pass in/manner*
　Whyle oure luflych lede lys° in his bedde,　　*good knight lies*
1470　Gawayn grayþely° at home, in gerez° ful ryche　　*pleasantly/bedclothes*
　　of hewe;°　　*in color*
　　Þe lady noȝt forȝate,°　　*not forgot*
　　Com° to hym to salue,°　　*came/greet*
　　Ful erly ho° watz hym ate,°　　*she/at*
1475　　His mode forto remwe.°　　*mood to alter*

XIV

Ho commes to þe cortyn,° and at þe knyȝt totes,°　　*curtain/knight peeps*
　Sir Wawen° her welcumed worþy° on fyrst,°　　*Gawain/welcomed courteously/first*
　And ho hym ȝeldez° aȝayn, ful ȝerne° of hir° wordez,　　*answers/eagerly/her*
　Settez hir° softly by his syde, and swyþely° ho laȝez,°　　*herself/very much/laughs*
1480　And wyth a luflych loke° ho layde° hym þyse° wordez:　　*loving look/delivered/these*
　"Sir, ȝif ȝe° be Wawen, wonder° me° þynkkez,°　　*if you/strange/to me/it seems*

1451. *mute:* the group name for a pack of hounds, as cited in the *Boke of St. Albans,* which distinguishes it from a "kenell of Rachis." The list of terms, including "a worship of writeris," "an vncredibilite of Cocoldis," and "a Gagle of women," may be considered partly facetious, not necessarily to be strictly respected, as Davis points out (a *Gaggle,* for instance, normally referring to a flock of geese).

Wyʒe° þat is so wel wrast° alway to god,°
And connez° not of compaynye° þe costez vnder-take,°
And if mon kennes yow hom° to knowe, ʒe kest° hom of your
   mynde;
¹⁴⁸⁵ Þou hatz for-ʒeten ʒederly þat ʒisterday° I taʒtte°

Bi alder-truest token° of talk þat I cowþe."°
"What is þat?" quod° þe wyghe,° "I-wysse° I wot° neuer,
If hit° be sothe° þat ʒe breue,° þe blame is myn awen."°
"ʒet I kende° yow of kyssyng," quod þe clere° þenne,
¹⁴⁹⁰ "Quere-so countenaunce° is couþe, quikly° to clayme,
Þat bicumes° vche° knyʒt, þat cortaysy vses."°
"Do way,"° quod þat derf mon, "my dere, þat speche,°

For þat durst° I not do, lest I deuayed° were,
If I were werned,° I were° wrang° i-wysse, ʒif I profered."
¹⁴⁹⁵ "Ma fay,"° quod þe mere wyf,° "ʒe may not be werned,
ʒe ar stif in-noghe° to constrayne wyth strenkþe,° ʒif yow lykez,
ʒif any were so vilanous° þat yow deuaye wolde."°
"ʒe,° be° God," quod Gawayn, "good is your speche,
Bot þrete° is vn-þryuande° in þede° þer I lende,°

¹⁵⁰⁰ And vche° gift þat is geuen° not with goud° wylle;
I am at your comaundement,° to kysse quen° yow lykez,
ʒe may lach° quen yow lyst,° leue° quen yow° þynkkez,°

      in space."°
   Þe lady loutez a-doun,°
¹⁵⁰⁵   And comlyly° kysses his face,
   Much speche þay° þer expoun,°
   Of druryes greme° and grace.°

(a) man/disposed/goodness
can/polite society/manners perceive
someone teaches you them/cast out

forgotten quickly what yesterday/
   taught
truest teaching/knew
said/man/indeed/know
it/true/say/my own
taught/fair (lady)
wherever favor/evident, quickly
befits/each/courtesy practices
enough/brave man/dear, (of) that
   speech
dared/refused
refused/would be/wrong/offered
in faith/merry lady
strong enough/strength
ill bred/(he) would
yea/by
but force/unworthy/(the) country/
   dwell
each/given/good
command/when
take one/like/abstain/to you/it
   seems good
straightway
bends down
graciously
talk they/have
love's grief/happiness

XV

"I woled° wyt° at° yow, wyʒe,"° þat worþy° þer sayde,

"And° yow wrathed° not þer-wyth, what were þe skylle,°
¹⁵¹⁰ Þat so ʒong° and so ʒepe,° as ʒe at þis tyme,
So cortayse,° so knyʒtyly, as ʒe ar knowen oute°—
And of alle cheualry° to chose,° þe chef þyng a-losed,°

would like/to learn/from/sir/noble
   (lady)
if/be angry/reason
young/bold
courteous/known widely
knightly conduct/choose/chief/to be
   praised

1499. I.e., force may be the custom in the "provinces," but the manners of Camelot, at least, are courteous and gentle.
1511. There is a break in the lady's speech at the end of this line, and a long digression follows on knightly service in love. The interruption ends with l. 1519.

Is þe lel layk° of luf,° þe lettrure° of armes;   *true observance|love|lore*
For to telle of þis teuelyng° of þis trwe knyȝtez,°   *these deeds|true knights*
1515 Hit is þe tytelet token,° and tyxt° of her werkkez,°   *inscribed title|text|their works*
How ledes° for her lele luf hor° lyuez han auntered,°   *men|their|have ventured*
Endured for her drury dulful stoundez,°   *love grievous times*
And after wenged° with her walour° and voyded° her care,   *avenged|valor|got rid of*
And broȝt° blysse in-to boure,° with bountees° hor awen°—   *brought|(lady's) bower|virtues|own*
1520 And ȝe ar knyȝt comlokest kyd° of your elde,°   *noblest known|age*
Your worde° and your worchip° walkez° ay quere,°   *fame|honor|are spread|everywhere*
And I haf seten° by your-self° here sere twyes,°   *have sat|you|on two occasions*
Ȝet herde I neuer of° your hed° helde° no wordez   *from|(i.e., mouth)|come*
Þat euer longed° to luf, lasse ne° more;   *pertained|less nor*
1525 And ȝe,° þat ar so cortays and coynt° of your hetes,°   *you|polite|vows*
Oghe° to a ȝonke þynk° ȝern° to schewe,°   *ought|young person|be eager|show*
And teche sum° tokenez of trweluf° craftes.°   *teach some|true love's|skills*
Why! ar ȝe lewed,° þat alle þe los weldez,°   *ignorant|renown has*
Oþer elles° ȝe demen° me to dille,° your dalyaunce° to   *or else|consider|too stupid|*
        herken?°   *conversation|hear*
1530   for schame!
        I com hider sengel,° and sitte,   *hither alone*
        To lerne at yow° sum game,   *you*
        Dos,° techez me of your wytte,°   *do|cleverness*
        Whil my lorde is fro hame."°   *(away) from home*

XVI

1535 "In goud fayþe," quod° Gawayn, "God yow for-ȝelde,°   *said|reward*
Gret° is þe gode gle,° and gomen° to me huge,   *great|good gladness|pleasure*
Þat so worþy as ȝe wolde wynne° hidere,   *would come*
And pyne yow° with so pouer° a mon, as° play wyth your knyȝt,   *trouble yourself|poor|man, as (to)*
With anyskynnez countenaunce,° hit keuerez° me ese;°   *any kind of favor|it gives|*
                                                                   pleasure
1540 Bot to take þe toruayle° to my-self, to trwluf° expoun,   *hard task|true love*
And towche° þe temez° of tyxt,° and talez of armez,   *treat|themes|story*
To yow þat, I wot° wel, weldez more slyȝt°   *know|skill*
Of þat art, bi þe half, or a hundreth° of seche°   *hundred|such*
As I am, oþer euer schal,° in erde þer° I leue,°   *shall (be)|earth while|live*
1545 Hit were° a fole fele-folde,° my fre, by° my trawþe.°   *would be|folly manifold|noble*
                                                                   (lady), on|word

I wolde yowre wylnyng worche at° my myȝt,°   *your will do within|power*
As I am hyȝly bihalden,° and euer-more wylle   *deeply beholden*

1515. *Hit;* i.e., the service of courtly love in which the knights   poems of romance and adventure.
participate and which forms the subject matter of the long

Be seruaunt to your-seluen,° so saue me dry3tyn!"° *you/God*
Þus hym frayned° þat fre, and fondet° hym ofte, *tested/tempted*
1550 Forto° haf wonnen° hym to wo3e, what-so scho° þo3t° ellez, *to/brought/woo, whatever she/had in mind*

Bot° he defended hym° so fayr,° þat no faut° semed,° *but/himself/politely/fault/was seen*
Ne non euel° on nawþer halue, nawþer þay wysten,° *no evil/neither side, nothing they knew*
          bot blysse;
Þay la3ed° and layked° longe, *laughed/amused themselves*
1555   At þe last scho con° hym kysse, *did*
Hir leue° fayre con° scho fonge,° *her leave/did/take*
And went hir waye iwysse.° *indeed*

XVII

Then ruþes° hym þe renk,° and ryses to þe masse, *bestirs/knight*
And siþen hor diner° watz dy3t° and derely° serued. *then their dinner/prepared/splendidly*
1560 Þe lede° with þe ladyez layked alle day, *knight*
Bot þe lorde ouer þe londez launced ful° ofte, *countryside galloped very*
Swe3° his vncely swyn,° þat swyngez° bi þe bonkkez,° *pursues/disastrous boar/rushes/slopes*

And bote° þe best of his brachez° þe bakkez° in sunder;° *bit/hounds/backs/asunder*
Þer he bode in his° bay, tcl bawe-men° hit breken,° *stood at/until bowmen/broke*
1565 And madee° hym, maw-gref° his hed,° forto mwe° vtter;° *made/in spite of/resistance/move/into the open*

So felle flonez° þer flete,° when þe folk gedered;° *many arrows/flew/gathered*
Bot 3et þe styffest° to start° bi stoundez° he made, *bravest/flinch/at times*
Til at þe last he watz so mat,° he my3t° no more renne,° *exhausted/might/run*
Bot in þe hast þat he my3t,° he to a hole wynnez,° *as fast as he could/comes*
1570 Of a rasse,° bi a rokk, þer° rennez þe boerne,° *bank/rock, where/stream*
He gete° þe bonk° at his bak, bigynez° to scrape,° *got/bank/back, begins/paw the ground*

Þe froþe femed° at his mouth vnfayre° bi þe wykez,° *foamed/hideous/corners*
Whettez his whyte tuschez;° with° hym þen irked° *tusks/of/were wearied*
Alle þe burnez° so bolde, þat hym by stoden,° *men/about stood*
1575 To nye° hym on-ferum,° bot ne3e° hym non durst,° *harass/from afar/approach/none dared*

          for woþe;° *danger*
He hade° hurt so mony byforne,° *had/before*
Þat al þu3t° þenne ful loþe,° *seemed/loath*
Be° more wyth his tuschez torne, *(to) be*
1580   Þat breme° watz and brayn-wod° bothe. *fierce/frenzied*

1564. *hit:* i.e., the bay.

XVIII

Til þe knyȝt com° hym-self, kachande° his blonk,°   *knight came/urging on/horse*
Syȝ° hym byde at þe° bay, his burnez bysyde,°   *saw/stand at/beside (him)*
He lyȝtes luflych adoun,° leuez his corsour,°   *dismounts graciously down/courser*
Braydez° out a bryȝt bront,° and bigly° forth strydez,   *pulls/bright sword/mightily*
1585 Foundez° fast þurȝ° þe forth,° þer þe felle bydez,°   *hastens/through/ford/fierce (beast) waits*

Þe wylde° watz war° of þe wyȝe° with weppen° in honde,°   *wild (beast)/aware/man/weapon/hand*

Hef hyȝly° þe here,° so hetterly° he fnast,°   *raised high/bristles/fiercely/snorted*
Þat fele ferde° for þe freke,° lest felle° hym þe worre;°   *many feared/knight/befall/worst*
Þe swyn° settez hym° out on þe segge euen,°   *boar/rushes/man straight*
1590 Þat° þe burne° and þe bor° were boþe vpon hepez,°   *so that/man/boar/in a heap*
In þe wyȝt-est° of þe water, þe worre hade þat oþer;   *wildest*
For þe mon merkkez° hym wel, as þay° mette fyrst,   *man aims at/they*
Set sadly° þe scharp° in þe slot° euen,   *firmly/sharp (blade)/breast hollow*
Hit hym vp to þe hult,° þat þe hert schyndered,°   *hilt/heart burst*
1595 And he ȝarrande° hym ȝelde,° and ȝedoun° þe water,   *snarlingly/surrendered/went down in*
   ful tyt;°   *quickly*
   A hundreth° houndez hym hent,°   *hundred/caught*
   Þat bremely con° hym bite   *did*
   Burnez him broȝt° to bent,°   *brought/bank*
1600   And doggez to dethe endite.°   *death do (him)*

XIX

There watz blawyng° of prys in mony breme° horne,   *blowing/(the) capture on many (a) loud*

Heȝe halowing° on hiȝe,° with haþelez° þat myȝt;°   *high shouting/aloud/by men/were able*

Brachetes° bayed þat best,° as bidden° þe maysterez,°   *hounds/(at) that beast/commanded/men*

Of þat chargeaunt chace° þat were chef huntes.°   *hard chase/chief huntsmen*
1605 Þenne a wyȝe þat watz wys° vpon wod° craftez,   *wise/in wood*
To vnlace° þis bor lufly° bigynnez;   *cut up/gladly*
Fyrst he hewes of° his hed,° and on hiȝe° settez,   *off/head/high*
And syþen° rendez him al roghe bi° þe rygge after,°   *then/roughly along/backbone afterward*

1591. *þat oþer:* i.e., the boar.
1592–94. It was considered more noble to kill a free boar with the sword than to pierce it with a spear while it was worried by the hounds. *slot:* Cf. ll. 1330–34n.
1601. *prys:* Cf. l. 1362n.

1605. The *Master of Game* mentions that the undoing of a deer or the unlacing of a boar is more appropriate to a woodman's skill than a hunter's, even though it is fitting for hunters also to be adept in the art.

Braydez out þe boweles, brennez hom° on glede,°　　*burns them/hot coals*
1610　With bred blent° þer-with his braches° rewardez;　　*bread mixed/hounds*
Syþen he britnez° out þe brawen° in bryȝt brode cheldez°　　*cuts/flesh/white broad slabs*
And hatz° out þe hastlettez,° as hiȝtly bisemez;°　　*takes/entrails/fitly beseems*
And ȝet hem halchez° al hole° þe haluez to-geder,°　　*them fastens/whole/halves (of the*
　　　　　　carcass) together

And syþen on a stif stange stoutly° hem henges.°　　*strong pole vigorously/hangs*
1615　Now with þis ilk° swyn þay swengen° to home;　　*same/hasten*
Þe bores hed watz borne bifore þe burnes seluen,°　　*knight himself*
Þat him for-ferde° in þe forþe,° þurȝ forse° of his honde,　　*had killed/stream/force*
　　　　so stronge;
　　　Til he seȝ° sir Gawayne,　　*saw*
1620　　In halle hym° þoȝt° ful° longe,　　*to him/it seemed/very*
　　　He calde,° and he com gayn,°　　*called/came immediately*
　　　His feez° þer for to fonge.°　　*payment/receive*

XX

Þe lorde ful lowde° with lote,° and laȝter myry,°　　*loud/speech/laughter merry*
When he seȝe° sir Gawayn with solace° he spekez;°　　*saw/joy/speaks*
1625　Þe goude° ladyez were geten,° and gedered° þe meyny,°　　*good/fetched/gathered/household*
He schewez° hem þe scheldez,° and schapes° hem þe tale,　　*shows/slabs/tells*
Of þe largesse,° and þe lenþe,° þe liþernez also,°　　*great size/length/ferocity also*
Of þe were° of þe wylde swyn, in wod þer° he fled.　　*fighting power/woods where*
Þat oþer knyȝt° ful comly° commended his dedez,°　　*knight/graciously/deeds*
1630　And praysed hit° as gret prys,° þat he proued° hade;°　　*it/great excellence/given proof of/had*
　　　　　　flesh
For suche a brawne° of a best, þe bolde burne sayde,　　
Ne° such sydes of a swyn, segh° he neuer are.°　　*nor/boar, saw/before*
Þenne hondeled° þay þe hoge° hed, þe hende mon° hit praysed,　　*handled/huge/courteous man*
And let lodly° þerat þe lorde forto° here:°　　*expressed horror/in order to/praise*
1635　"Now Gawayn," quod° þe god° mon, "þis gomen° is your　　*said/good/game/own*
　　　　awen,°
Bi fyn for-warde° and faste, faythely ȝe° knowe."　　*ratified agreement/binding, truly you*
"Hit is sothe,"° quod þe segge,° "and as siker trwe;°　　*true/knight/surely true*
Alle my get° I schal yow gif agayn, bi° my trawþe."°　　*gains/you give again, on/word*
He hent° þe haþel° aboute þe halse,° and hendely° hym kysses,　　*clasped/lord/neck/courteously*
1640　And etter-sones° of þe same he serued hym þere.　　*again immediately*
"Now ar we euen," quod þe haþel, "in þis euen-tide,°　　*evening*
Of alle þe couenauntes° þat we knyt, syþen° I com hider,°　　*compacts/made, since/came hither*
　　　　bi lawe;"°　　*duly*

1610. *rewardez:* technically the correct word here. The bowels are not served on a hide; they are not, therefore, *cuirée,* "quarry" (cf. l. 1324n).

1633. *hoge hed:* The boar's head was a traditional Christmas feast, and the boar was usually hunted from Christmas to Candlemas.

Þe lorde sayde, "Bi saynt Gile,
1645   Ȝe ar þe best þat I knowe,
Ȝe ben° ryche in a whyle,°   *will be/presently*
Such chaffer and° Ȝe drowe."°   *trade if/carry on*

XXI

Þenne þay teldet° tablez trestes alofte,°   *set up/trestles on*
Kesten cloþez° vpon, clere lyȝt° þenne   *put coverings/bright lights*
1650   Waknedˊ bi woȝez,° waxen torches   *kindled/walls*
Seggez° sette, and serued in sale° al aboute;   *men/hall*
Much glam° and gle glent° vp þer-inne,   *merrymaking/gladness sprang*
Aboute þe fyre vpon flet,° and on fele wyse,°   *in (the) hall/in many ways*
At þe soper° and after, mony aþel° songez,   *supper/many noble*
1655   As coundutes° of kryst-masse,° and carolez newe, *part-songs/Christmas*
With alle þe manerly merþe° þat mon° may of telle. *seemly mirth/men*
And euer oure luflych° knyȝt þe lady bi-syde;   *gracious*
Such semblaunt° to þat segge semly ho° made,   *demeanor/sweetly she*
Wyth stille stollen countenaunce,° þat stalworth° to plese,° *secret, stealthy looks/stalwart (man)/please*

1660   Þat al for-wondered° watz þe wyȝe,° and wroth with hym-   *astonished/man/within himself*
seluen,°
Bot° he nolde° not for° his nurture° nurne hir a-ȝaynez,° *but/would not/because of/good breeding/repel her in return*

Bot dalt° with hir al in daynte, how-se-euer° þe dede° turned *behaved/courtesy, however/affair*
towrast;°   *amiss*
Quen þay° hade played in halle,   *when they*
1665   As longe as hor wylle hom last,°   *they wished*
To chambre he° con hym° calle,   *(i.e., the lord)/did them*
And to þe chemne° þay past.°   *fireplace/passed*

XXII

Ande þer þay dronken,° and dalten,° demed eft nwe,° *drank/talked/decided again anew*
To norne° on þe same note,° on nweȝerez° euen;°   *bargain/terms/New Year's/Eve*
1670   Bot þe knyȝt craued leue° to kayre° on þe morn, *knight asked permission/depart*
For hit° watz neȝ at° þe terme,° þat he to° schulde.° *it/near to/appointed time/go/had to*
Þe lorde hym letted° of þat, to lenge° hym° resteyed,° *dissuaded/to stay/on him/prevailed*
And sayde, "As I am trwe segge, I siker° my trawþe, *pledge*
Þou schal cheue° to þe grene chapel, þy charres° to make,° *get/business/do*
1675   Leude,° on nwȝerez lyȝt,° longe before pryme; *knight/dawn*

1644. Saint Giles was a 7th-century hermit famous for his sanctity. In order to seek greater seclusion he lived in a forest near Nîmes, with a hind. When she was being hunted by the king, the hind led him to the hermitage of Saint Giles, on the site of which a Benedictine monastery was later built. As the patron saint of the woodland, St. Giles, who is always pictured with the hind, is especially venerated in England.

1675. Prime was the second of the seven canonical hours; its service started at 6 A.M., the period then lasting till 9 A.M.

For-þy þow lye° in þy loft,° and lach þyn ese,°   *therefore you lie/chamber/take your ease*

And I shal hunt in þis holt,° and halde° þe towchez,°   *forest/hold (to)/agreement*
Chaunge° wyth þe cheuisaunce,° bi þat° I charre° hider;   *exchange/you winnings/(the time) that/return*

For I haf fraysted° þe twys,° and faythful I fynde þe,   *have tested/twice*
1680 Now "Þrid° tyme þrowe° best" þenk° on þe morne,   *third/turns out/remember*
Make we mery quyl° we may, and mynne° vpon joye,°   *merry while/think/joy*
For þe lur° may mon lach,° when so mon lykez."   *sorrow/one find*
Þis watz grayþely graunted,° and Gawayn is lenged,°   *promptly granted/made to stay*
Bliþe broȝt° watz hym drynk, and þay to bedde ȝeden,°   *cheerfully brought/went*
1685   with liȝt;°   *lights*
     Sir Gawayn lis° and slepes,°   *lies/sleeps*
     Ful° stille and softe al niȝt;°   *very/night*
     Þe lorde þat his craftez° kepes,°   *affairs/attends to*
     Ful erly he watz diȝt.°   *dressed*

XXIII

1690 After messe° a morsel° he and his men token,°   *mass/bite/took*
Miry° watz þe mornyng, his mounture° he askes;°   *pleasant/mount/asks (for)*
Alle þe haþeles° þat on horse schulde° helden° hym after,   *men/were to/follow*
Were boun busked° on hor blonkkez,° bi-fore þe halle ȝatez;°   *ready prepared/their horses/gates*
Ferly° fayre watz þe folde,° for þe forst clenged,°   *wondrously/earth/frost clung*
1695 In rede° rudede° vpon rak° rises þe sunne,   *red/fiery/drifting clouds*
And ful clere° costez° þe clowdes of þe welkyn.°   *bright/coasts by/sky*
Hunteres vnhardeled° bi a holt syde,   *unleashed (the hounds)*
Rocheres° roungen bi rys,° for rurde° of her° hornes;   *rocky banks/rang in (the) woods/noise/their*

Summe fel in° þe fute, þer° þe fox bade,°   *some hit on/trail, where/lurked*
1700 Traylez ofte a traueres,° bi traunt° of her wyles;   *from side to side/cunning*
A kenet° kryes° þerof, þe hunt° on hym calles,   *small hound/gives tongue/hunter*
His felaȝes fallen° hym to, þat fnasted° ful þike,°   *fellows fall/panted/hard*
Runnen° forth in a rabel,° in his ryȝt fare;°   *run/rabble/very track*
And he fyskez hem° by-fore, þay founden° hym sone,°   *scampers them/they found/right away*

1705 And quen° þay seghe° hym with syȝt,° þay sued° hym fast,   *when/saw/sight/pursued*
Wrȝande° hym ful weterly° with a wroth° noyse;   *denouncing/clearly/loud*
And he trantes° and tornayeez° þurȝ mony tene greue;°   *dodges/doubles back/through many (a) rough thicket*

1699ff. The comparison in Layamon's *Brut* of Arthur's pursuit of Childric to a fox hunt, a section in *The Owl and the Nightingale*, and the description here are rare instances of the appearance of the sport in medieval English literature.

1700. The fox has a habit of looping and doubling back on its own tracks; thus the hounds often move from side to side to find the scent for a clear trail.

1701. A *kenet* (also called *harrier*) was a small, very fast running hound, useful for all manner of game.

Hamlounez° and herkenez,° bi heggez° ful ofte;   *doubles/listens/hedges*

At þe last° bi a littel dich° he lepez° ouer a spenné,°   *at last/ditch/leaps/thorny hedge*

1710 Stelez° out ful stilly° bi a strothe rande,°   *steals/secretly/thicket edge*

Went haf° wylt of° þe wode,° with wylez fro° þe houndes,   *hoped (to) have/escaped from/ wood/from*

Þenne watz he went, er° he wyst,° to a wale° tryster,°   *come, before/knew/fair/hunting station*

Þer þre þro° at a þrich þrat° hym at ones,°   *three fierce (ones)/rush attacked/once*

     al graye;°   *greyhounds*

1715 He blenched aȝayn bilyue,°   *swerved again quickly*

And stifly start onstray,°   *bold started astray*

With alle þe wo° on lyue,°   *woe/earth*

To þe wod he went away.

XXIV

Thenne watz hit list vpon lif° to lyþen° þe houndez,   *it joy in life/listen to*

1720 When alle þe mute hade° hym met, menged to-geder,°   *pack had/mingled together*

Suche a sorȝe° at þat syȝt þay sette on his hede,°   *curse/head*

As° alle þe clamberande° clyffes hade clatered on hepes;°   *as if/clustering/clattered in heaps*

Here he watz halawed,° when haþelez hym metten,°   *hallooed/met*

Loude he watz ȝayned,° with ȝarande speche;°   *greeted/chiding speech*

1725 þer he watz þreted,° and ofte þef° called,   *reviled/thief*

And ay° þe titleres° at his tayl, þat° tary° he ne myȝt;°   *ever/relay hounds/so that/delay/ not might*

Ofte he watz runnen at, when he out rayked,°   *made for the open*

And ofte reled° in aȝayn, so reniarde° watȝ wylé.°   *turned/Reynard/wily*

And ȝe° he lad° hem bi lagmon,° þe lorde and his meyny,°   *indeed/led/at his heels/company*

1730 On þis maner° bi þe mountes, quyle myd-ouer-vnder,°   *manner/hills, until afternoon*

Whyle þe hende knyȝt° at home holsumly slepez,°   *gracious knight/soundly sleeps*

With-inne þe comly cortynes,° on þe colde morne.   *fair curtains*

Bot° þe lady for luf° let not° to slepe,   *but/love/did not allow herself*

Ne° þe purpose to payre,° þat pyȝt° in hir hert,°   *nor/weaken/was fixed/her heart*

1735 Bot ros hir° vp radly,° rayked hir° þeder,°   *rose/quickly/went/there*

In a mery° mantyle, mete° to þe erþe,   *gay/reaching*

Þat watz furred° ful° fyne with fellez,° wel pured,°   *fur-lined/very/skins/trimmed*

No hwez goud° on hir hede, bot° þe haȝer° stones   *colors good/except/well-wrought*

Trased° aboute hir tressour, be° twenty in clusters;   *entwined/hairnet, by*

1740 Hir þryuen° face and hir þrote þrowen° al naked,   *fair/throat exposed*

1726. *titleres*: hounds kept at the relay stations placed throughout the forest. As the fox or deer ran past, the dogs were loosed in pursuit.

1728. *reniarde*: In the medieval beast epic Reynard is the standard name for the fox; his opponent is always the wolf Ysigrim or Ysengrim (cf. *The Fox and the Wolf*, this volume, pp. 545–53).

Hir brest bare bifore,° and bihinde° eke.°	*in front/(i.e., her back)/also*
Ho° comez with-inne þe chambre dore, and closes hit hir after,	*she*
Wayuez° vp a wyndow, and on þe wyȝe° callez,	*swings/man*
And radly þus re-hayted° hym, with hir riche° wordez,	*rebuked/noble*
1745 with chere;°	*gaily*
"A!° mon,° how may þou slepe,	*ah/man*
Þis morning is so clere?"°	*beautiful*
He watz in drowping° depe,°	*troubled sleep/deep*
Bot þenne he con° hir here.°	*did/hear*

XXV

1750 In dreȝ° droupyng of dreme draueled° þat noble,	*heavy/dreams muttered*
As mon þat watz in mornyng° of mony þro þoȝtes,°	*troubled/by many oppressive thoughts*
How þat destiné schulde° þat day dele° hym his wyrde,°	*destiny should/deal/fate*
At þe grene chapel, when he þe gome° metes,°	*man/meets*
And bi-houes° his buffet abide,° with-oute debate° more;	*must/endure/resistance*
1755 Bot quen þat° comly° he keuered° his wyttes,°	*when/properly/recovered/conscious-ness*
Swenges° out of þe sweuenes,° and swarez° with hast.°	*(he) comes suddenly/dreams/answers/haste*
Þe lady luflych com laȝande swete,°	*lovely came laughing sweetly*
Felle° ouer his fayre face, and fetly° hym kyssed;	*bent/daintily*
He welcumez hir worþily,° with a wale chere;°	*courteously/fair manner*
1760 He seȝ° hir so glorious, and gayly atyred,	*saw*
So fautles of° hir fetures,° and of so fyne hewes,°	*faultless in/all parts of her body/perfect colors*
Wiȝt wallande joye° warmed his hert;	*ardently welling joy*
With smoþe° smylyng and smolt þay smeten° in-to merþe,°	*courteous/gentle they fell/merry speech*
Þat° al watz blis° and bonchef,° þat breke° hem° bi-twene,	*so that/joy/happiness/was uttered/them*
1765 And wynne;°	*joy*
Þay lanced° wordes gode,°	*spoke/good*
Much wele° þen watz þer-inne,	*delight*
Gret° perile bi-twene hem stod,°	*great/was*
Nif° Maré° of hir knyȝt mynne.°	*if not/Mary/should take care*

XXVI

1770 For þat prynces° of pris depresed° hym so þikke,°	*princess/worth pressed/hard*
Nurned° hym so neȝe° þe þred,° þat nede hym bi-houed°	*urged/near/limit/he had to*
Oþer lach° þer hir luf, oþer lodly° refuse;	*either accept/or offensively*
He cared° for his cortaysye,° lest craþayn° he were	*was concerned/courtesy/boor*
And more for his meschef, ȝif° he schulde make° synne,	*his (own) disaster, if/commit*

¹⁷⁷⁵ And be traytor to þat tolke,° þat þat telde aȝt.°	*man/dwelling owned*
"God schylde,"° quod þe schalk,° "þat schal not be-falle!"	*forbid/knight*
With luf-laȝyng a lyt,° he layd° hym by-syde°	*playful, light laugh/put/aside*
Alle þe spechez° of specialté° þat sprange of° her mouthe.	*speeches/fondness/from*
Quod° þat burde° to þe burne,° "Blame ȝe disserue,°	*said/lady/knight/you deserve*
¹⁷⁸⁰ Ȝif ȝe luf° not þat lyf° þat ȝe lye nexte,°	*love/person/lie next (to)*
Bifore° alle þe wyȝez° in þe worlde, wounded in hert,°	*more than/women/heart*
Bot if° ȝe haf° a lemman,° a leuer,° þat yow° lykez better,	*unless/have/mistress/dearer/you*
And folden° fayth to þat fre, festned° so harde,°	*plighted/noble (lady), pledged/ firmly*
Þat yow lausen° ne lyst,° and þat I leue nouþe;°	*(to) break troth/not desire/believe now*
¹⁷⁸⁵ And þat ȝe telle me þat, now trwly° I pray yow,	*truly*
For alle þe lufez vpon lyue,° layne° not þe soþe,°	*on earth/hide/truth*
for gile."°	*guile*
Þe knyȝt° sayde, "Be sayn Ion,"°	*knight/by Saint John*
And smeþely con° he smyle,	*gently did*
¹⁷⁹⁰ "In fayth I welde° riȝt non,°	*have/none at all*
Ne non° wil welde þe quile."°	*none/for a while*

XXVII

"Þat is a worde," quod þat wyȝt,° "þat worst is of alle,	*person*
Bot° I am swared for soþe,° þat sore° me° þinkkez;°	*but/truly/painful/to me/seems*
Kysse me now comly,° and I schal cach heþen,°	*graciously/go hence*
¹⁷⁹⁵ I may bot mourne vpon molde,° as may° þat much louyes."°	*earth/woman/loves*
Sykande ho sweȝe° doun, and semly° hym kyssed,	*sighing she stooped/pleasantly*
And siþen° ho seueres° hym fro,° and says as ho stondes,°	*then/departs/from/stands*
"Now, dere,° at þis de-partyng,° do° me þis ese,°	*dear/parting/give/consolation*
Gif° me sumquat of° þy gifte, þi gloue if hit° were,	*give/something as/it*
¹⁸⁰⁰ Þat I may mynne° on þe,° mon,° my mournyng to lassen."°	*be reminded/of you/man/lessen*
"Now iwysse,"° quod þat wyȝe,° "I wolde° I hade° here	*indeed/man/wish/had*
Þe leuest þing for þy luf, þat I in londe° welde,	*land*
For ȝe haf deserued, forsoþe, sellyly° ofte	*truly, exceedingly*
More rewarde bi resoun, þen° I reche myȝt,°	*rights, than/give might*
¹⁸⁰⁵ Bot to dele° yow for drurye,° þat dawed° bot neked;°	*give/love token/would profit/little*
Hit is not your honour to haf at þis tyme	
A gloue for a garysoun,° of Gawaynez giftez,	*keepsake*
And I am here an erande° in erdez vncouþe,°	*on (a) mission/regions strange*
And haue no men wyth no malez,° with menskful þingez;°	*bags/things of worth*

1782. *lemman*: "lover," "mistress." Davis mentions that the word was at this time already derogatory, and cites Chaucer's *Manciple's Tale* (ll. 217–20): "the gentile, in estaat above,/She shal be cleped his lady, as in love;/And for that oother is a povre womman,/She shal be cleped his wenche or his lemman."

1786. *For alle þe lufez upon lyue*: "by all the loves there are." In this omnibus oath are combined many: "By the love of God," "... of Christ," "... of Mary," and so forth.

1810 Þat mislykez° me, ladé,° for luf° at þis tyme, *displeases/lady/your sake*
Iche° tolke mon° do as he is tan, tas° to non ille,° *each/must/granted, take (it)/not amiss*

   ne pine."° *grieve*
"Nay, hende° of hyȝe° honours," *worthy (man)/great*
Quod þat lufsum° vnder lyne,° *lovely (one)/linen*
1815 "Þaȝ° I hade noȝt° of yourez, *though/nothing*
Ȝet schulde° ȝe haue of° myne." *should/(something) of*

XXVIII

Ho raȝt° hym a riche rynk° of red golde werkez,° *offered/ring/workmanship*
Wyth a starande ston, stondande° alofte,° *blazing stone, set/on top*
Þat bere blusschande bemez° as þe bryȝt° sunne; *cast shining beams/bright*
1820 Wyt ȝe wel,° hit watz worth wele ful hoge.° *be assured/fortune very huge*
Bot þe renk° hit renayed,° and redyly° he sayde, *knight/refused/promptly*
"I wil° no giftez for Gode,° my gay,° at þis tyme; *wish/by God/gay (lady)*
I haf° none yow° to norne,° ne noȝt wyl I take." *have/you/offer*
Ho bede° hit hym ful bysily,° and he hir bode wernes,° *offered/earnestly/her offer refuses*
1825 And swere° swyfte by his sothe,° þat he hit sese° nolde;° *swore/honor/take/would not*
And ho sore° þat he forsoke,° and sayde þer-after, *was grieved/refused*
"If ȝe° renay my rynk, to ryche for° hit semez,° *you/too costly because/seems*
Ȝe wolde° not so hyȝly halden° be to me, *(if) you would/deeply obliged*
I schal gif yow my girdel, þat gaynes° yow lasse."° *profits/less*
1830 Ho laȝt° a lace lyȝtly,° þat leke vmbe° hir sydez,° *took/belt quickly/fastened around/waist*

Knit° vpon hir kyrtel,° vnder þe clere° mantyle, *tied/gown/bright*
Gered° hit watz with grene sylke, and with golde schaped,° *fashioned/trimmed*
Noȝt bot° arounde° brayden, beten° with fyngrez; *only/at the edges/embroidered, set (with stones)*

And þat ho bede to þe burne,° and blyþely bi-soȝt° *knight/gaily implored*
1835 Þaȝ° hit vn-worþi were, þat he hit take wolde. *though*
And he nay° þat he nolde neghe° in no wyse,° *denied/touch/manner*
Nauþer° golde ne garysoun, er° God hym grace sende,° *neither/nor treasure, before/sent*
To acheue to° þe chaunce° þat he hade chosen° þere. *accomplish/adventure/undertaken*
"And þerfore, I pray yow, displese° yow noȝt,° *(let it) displease/not at all*
1840 And lettez be° your bisinesse,° for I bayþe hit° yow neuer *cease from/importunity/consent it*
   to graunte;° *grant*
I am derely° to yow biholde,° *deeply/obliged*
Bi-cause of your sembelaunt,° *behavior*
And euer in hot and colde° *(i.e., for better or worse)*
1845 To be your trwe seruaunt."° *true servant*

1814. *lufsum vnder lyne:* "loveliest on earth." "Under linen," like "under gore" (i.e., "cloth"), was a catch-all phrase used very often in Middle English lyric and romance and equated with "on earth" or "alive." Normally the phrases were alliterative: *lufsum vnder lyne, geynest vnder gore, worthy vnder wede,* and so forth.

XXIX

"Now forsake° ȝe þis silke," sayde þe burde° þenne,   *refuse/lady*
"For hit is symple in hit-self? And so hit wel° semez!   *indeed*
Lo! so hit is littel, and lasse hit is worþy;°   *of value*
Bot° who-so knew þe costes° þat knit ar þer-inne,   *but/properties*
1850 He wolde hit prayse° at more prys, parauenture;°   *esteem/value, perhaps*
For quat gome so° is gorde° with þis grene lace,   *whatever man/girt*
While he hit hade hemely halched° aboute,   *had neatly fastened*
Þer is no haþel° vnder heuen to-hewe° hym þat myȝt;°   *man/heaven slay/might*
For he myȝt not be slayn, for slyȝt vpon erþe."°   *any means*
1855 Þen kest° þe knyȝt,° and hit come° to his hert,°   *pondered/knight/came/heart (i.e., mind*

Hit were° a juel° for þe jopardé,° þat hym iugged° were,   *would be/talisman/peril/assigned*
When he acheued° to þe chapel, his chek forto fech;°   *came/fortune to obtain*
Myȝt he haf slypped° to be vn-slayn, þe sleȝt° were noble.   *escaped/device*
Þenne he þulged° with hir þrepe,° and þoled° hir to speke,°   *was patient/importunity/allowed/speak*
1860 And ho bere° on hym þe belt, and bede hit hym swyþe,°   *she pressed/earnestly*
And he granted,° and hym gafe° with a goud° wylle,   *consented/surrendered/good*
And bisoȝt° hym, for hir sake, disceuer° hit neuer,   *(she) implored/(to) reveal*
Bot to lelly layne fro° hir lorde; þe leude° hym acordez,°   *loyally conceal (it) from/knight/agrees*

Þat neuer wyȝe schulde° hit wyt, iwysse,° but þay twayne,°   *man should/know, indeed/they two*
1865   for noȝte;°   *on any account*
He þonkked hir° oft ful° swyþe,   *thanked her/very*
Ful þro° with hert and þoȝt.°   *earnestly/thought*
Bi þat° on þrynne syþe,°   *that (time)/three times*
Ho hatz kyst° þe knyȝt so toȝt.°   *kissed/brave*

XXX

1870 Thenne lachchez° ho hir leue,° and leuez hym þere,   *takes/leave*
For more myrþe° of þat mon moȝt° ho not gete;°   *pleasure/man might/get*
When ho watz gon, sir Gawayn gerez hym sone,°   *dresses himself immediately*
Rises, and riches° hym in araye noble,   *clothes*
Lays vp° þe luf-lace,° þe lady hym raȝt,°   *puts away safely/love-belt/had given*
1875 Hid hit ful holdely, þer° he hit eft° fonde;°   *carefully, where/again/might find*
Syþen cheuely° to þe chapel choses° he þe waye,   *then quickly/takes*
Preuely aproched° to a prest,° and prayed° hym þere   *privately approached/priest/begged*
Þat he wolde lyste° his lyf,° and lern° hym better,   *would hear/confession/teach*

1862–63. The promise of secrecy is exacted of Gawain only after he has, in fact, accepted a love token and is therefore already in error. Of course he could not in any case, out of courtesy, have refused the lady's request for secrecy, even had he known of it before she offered the gift; but then his fault would have been a lesser one in respect to the compact he had sworn with the lord.

1874. *luf-lace:* i.e., "love token."

How his sawle° schulde be saued, when he schuld seye heþen.° *soul/go hence*
1880 Þere he schrof hym° schyrly,° and schewed° his mysdedez,° *confessed/fully/revealed/sins*
Of þe more° and þe mynne,° and merci besechez,° *greater/smaller/beseeches*
And of° absolucioun he on° þe segge calles;° *for/of/man begs*
And he asoyled° hym surely, and sette° hym so clene,° *absolved/made/as pure*
As° domez-day° schulde haf ben di3t° on þe morn.° *as if/Judgment Day/have been appointed/(next) morning*

1885 And syþen he mace° hym as mery° among þe fre° ladyes, *makes/merry/noble*
With comlych° caroles, and alle kynnes ioye,° *pleasant/kinds (of) joy*
As neuer he did bot° þat daye, to° þe derk ny3t,° *except/till/dark night*
with blys;° *happiness*
Vche° mon hade daynte° þare,° *each/courteous treatment/there*
1890 Of° hym, and sayde, "Iwysse, *from*
Þus myry° he watz neuer are,° *merry/before*
Syn° he com hider, er° þis." *since/hither, before*

XXXI

Now hym lenge° in þat lee,° þer luf hym bi-tyde;° *(let) him stay/comfortable place/befall*

3et is þe lorde on þe launde, ledande° his gomnes,° *field, leading/games*
1895 He hatz forfaren° þis fox, þat he fol3ed° longe; *killed/followed*
As he sprent° ouer a spenné,° to spye þe schrewe,° *leaped/thorny hedge/villain*
Þer as° he herd° þe howndes, þat hasted° hym swyþe,° *where/heard/pressed after/eagerly*
Renaud com° richchande° þur3 a ro3e greue,° *Reynard came/making his way/through/rough thicket*

And alle þe rabel° in a res, ry3t° at his helez.° *rabble/rush, right/heels*
1900 Þe wy3e watz war° of þe wylde,° and warly abidcs,° *aware/wild (animal)/carefully waits*

And braydez° out þe bry3t bronde,° and at þe best castez;° *pulls/bright sword/beast strikes*
And he schunt° for° þe scharp,° and schulde° haf arered;° *swerved/because of/sharp (blade)/would/retreated*

A rach rapes° hym to, ry3t° er he my3t,° *hound rushes/just/might*
And ry3t bifore þe hors fete þay° fel on hym alle, *horse's feet they*
1905 And woried me þis wyly° wyth a wroth° noyse. *wily (beast)/fierce*
Þe lorde ly3tez bilyue,° and lachez° hym sone, *dismounts quickly/takes*
Rased° hym ful radly° out of þe rach° mouþcs, *snatched/very quickly/dogs'*
Haldez he3e° ouer his hede, halowez faste,° *holds (him) high/head, halloos loudly*

And þer bayen° hym mony braþ° houndez; *bay (at)/many fierce*
1910 Huntes° hy3ed hem° þeder,° with hornez ful mony, *hunters/hurried/there*
Ay° re-chatande° ary3t° til þay þe renk se3en;° *ever/blowing recall/correctly/lord saw*

Bi þat° watz comen° his compeyny° noble, *that (time)/come/company*
Alle þat eucr ber° bugle blowed at ones,° *carried/once*

And alle þise oþer° halowed, þat hade° no hornes,   *those others|had*
1915 Hit° watz þe myriest mute° þat euer men herde,   *it|merriest baying of hounds*
Þe rich rurd° þat þer watz raysed for renaude saule,°   *great uproar|Reynard's soul*
    with lote;°   *clamor*
    Hor° houndez þay þer rewarde,   *their*
    Her° hedez þay fawne° and frote,°   *their|stroke|rub*
1920   And syþen° þay tan° reynarde,   *then|take*
    And tyruen of° his cote.   *strip off*

XXXII

And þenne þay helden° to home, for hit watz neȝ° nyȝt,   *turned|nearly*
Strakande° ful stoutly in° hor store° hornez;   *sounding|strongly on|mighty*
Þe lorde is lyȝt° at þe laste at hys lef° home,   *arrived|beloved*
1925 Fyndez fire vpon flet,° þe freke° þer by-side,   *in (the) hall|knight*
Sir Gawayn þe gode,° þat glad watz with alle,   *good*
Among þe ladies for luf° he ladde° much ioye,°   *friendship|had|joy*
He were° a bleaunt° of blwe,° þat bradde° to þe erþe,   *wore|rich mantle|blue|reached*
His surkot semed° hym wel, þat softe watz forred,°   *surcoat suited|furred*
1930 And his hode° of þat ilke henged° on his schulder,°   *hood|same (material) hung| shoulder*

Blande° al of blaunner° were boþe al aboute.   *adorned|with ermine*
He metez° me þis god mon° in myddez° þe flore,   *meets|man|(the) middle (of)*
And al° with gomen° he hym gret,° and goudly° he sayde,   *entirely|joy|greeted|courteously*
"I schal fylle° vpon fyrst° oure forwardez nouþe,°   *carry out|first of all|agreement now*
1935 Þat we spedly° han° spoken, þer° spared watz no drynk";   *in good fortune|have|when*
Þen acoles° he þe knyȝt,° and kysses hym þryes,°   *embraces|knight|thrice*
As sauerly° and sadly° as he hem sette couþe.°   *with as much relish|firmly|them plant could*

"Bi Kryst,"° quod° þat oþer knyȝt, "ȝe cach° much sele,°   *Christ|said|you get|good fortune*
In cheuisaunce° of þis chaffer, ȝif° ȝe hade goud chepez."°   *obtaining|merchandise, if|good bargain*

1940 "Ȝe, of° þe chepe no charg,"° quod chefly° þat oþer,   *yea, about|it doesn't matter| quickly*

"As is pertly° payed þe chepez° þat I aȝte."°   *openly|goods|received*
"Mary," quod þat oþer mon, "myn° is bi-hynde,°   *mine|inferior*
For I haf° hunted al þis day, and noȝt° haf I geten,°   *have|nothing|got*
Bot þis foule fox felle,° þe fende haf° þe godez,   *skin|Fiend take*
1945 And þat is ful pore,° for to pay for suche prys° þinges,   *poor|valuable*
As ȝe haf þryȝt° me here þro,° suche þre cosses,°   *pressed on|warmly|three kisses*
    so gode."

1944. *fende:* i.e., "Devil."

"I-no3,"° quod sir Gawayn, — *enough*
"I þonk yow,° bi þe rode;"° — *thank you/cross*
1950 And how þe fox watz slayn,
He tolde hym, as þay stode.° — *they stood*

XXXIII

With merþe° and mynstralsye, wyth metez° at hor wylle,° — *mirth/all the foods/pleasure*
Þay maden° as mery° as any men mo3ten,° — *made/merry/might*
With la3yng° of ladies, with lotez° of bordes,° — *laughing/words/jest*
1955 Gawayn and þe gode mon so glad were þay boþe,
Bot if° þe douthe° had doted,° oþer dronken ben oþer.° — *unless/company/lost their wits/ or drunk been else*

Boþe þe mon° and þe meyny° maden mony iapez,° — *men/retinue/many jests*
Til þe sesoun° watz se3en,° þat þay seuer moste;° — *time/come/part must*
Burnez° to hor° bedde be-houed° at þe laste. — *men/their/had to go*
1960 Þenne lo3ly° his leue at° þe lorde fyrst — *humbly/leave of*
Fochchez° þis fre° mon, and fayre° he hym þonkkez; — *takes/noble/courteously*
"Of° such a selly soiorne,° as I haf hade° here, — *for/excellent stay/had*
Your honour, at þis hy3e fest,° þe hy3e kyng yow 3elde!° — *high festival/reward*
I 3ef° yow me° for on° of yourez, if yowre-self° lykez, — *give/myself/one/your (men)/you*
1965 For I mot° nedes,° as 3e wot, meue° to morne;° — *must/of necessity/know, leave/ tomorrow*

And° 3e me take sum tolke,° to teche,° as 3e hy3t, — *if/assign some man/direct/promised*
Þe gate° to þe grene chapel, as God wyl me suffer° — *way/allow*
To dele,° on nw3erez° day, þe dome° of my wyrdes."° — *receive/New Year's/judgment/fate*
"In god° fayþe," quod þe god mon, "wyth a goud wylle; — *good*
1970 Al þat euer I yow hy3t, halde° schal I rede."° — *hold to/readily*
Þer asyngnes° he a seruaunt,° to sett hym in° þe waye, — *assigns/servant/on*
And coundue° hym by° þe downez,° þat° he no drechch° had, — *guide/over/hills/so that/delay*
For to ferk þur3° þe fryth,° and fare at° þe gaynest,° — *travel through/wood/proceed by/ shortest way*

    bi greue.° — *in (the) thicket*
1975 Þe lorde Gawayn con° þonk, — *did*
Such worchip° he wolde° hym weue;° — *honor/would/show*
Þen at þo° ladyez wlonk,° — *the/noble*
Þe kny3t° hatz tan° his leue.° — *knight/taken/leave*

XXXIV

With care° and wyth kyssyng he carppez hem tille,° — *sorrow/talks them to*
1980 And fele þryuande° þonkkez he þrat hom° to haue, — *many hearty/pressed them*
And þay 3elden° hym a3ayn 3eply þat ilk;° — *returned/again promptly the same*

Þay bikende° hym to Kryst,° with ful colde sykyngez.° — commended/Christ/very grievous sighs

Syþen fro° þe meyny° he menskly° de-partes; — then from/company/courteously
Vche mon° þat he mette, he made° hem a þonke, — each man/gave
1985 For his seruyse,° and his solace, and his sere pyne,° — kindness/special trouble
Þat þay wyth busynes° had ben aboute hym to serue; — solicitude
And vche segge as sore,° to seuer with hym þere, — man (was) as grieved
As° þay hade wonde worþyly° with þat wlonk euer.° — as if/lived honorably/noble (man) always

Þen with ledes° and ly3t° he watz ladde° to his chambre, — servants/lights/led
1990 And blyþely bro3t° to his bedde, to be at his rest; — joyfully brought
3if° he ne slepe° soundyly, say ne dar° I, — if/not slept/dare
For he hade muche on þe morn to mynne,° 3if he wolde, in þo3t;° — think about / thought
    Let hym ly3e° þere stille, — lie
1995   He hatz nere° þat° he so3t;° — close at hand/what/sought
    And 3e° wyl a whyle be stylle, — if you
    I schal telle yow° how þay wro3t.° — you/they acted

FYTTE THE FOURTH

I

Now ne3ez° þe nw3ere,° and þe ny3t° passez, — draws near/New Year/night
Þe day dryuez to° þe derk,° as dry3tyn biddez;° — comes up on/dark/Lord commands
2000 Bot wylde wederez of° þe worlde wakned° þeroute, — storms in/arose
Clowdes kesten kenly° þe colde to þe erþe, — cast sharply
Wyth ny3e in-noghe of° þe norþe, þe naked° to tene;° — bitterness enough from/ill-clad/ torment

Þe snawe° snitered° ful snart,° þat snayped° þe wylde;° — snow/came shivering/very bitterly/ nipped/wild (beasts)

Þe werbelande° wynde wrapped fro° þe hy3e,° — shrill-blowing/rushed from/heights
2005 And drof vche° dale ful of dryftes ful grete.° — drove each/great
Þe leude° lystened ful wel, þat le3° in his bedde, — knight/lay
Þa3° he lowkez° his liddez, ful lyttel he slepes;° — though/shuts/sleeps
Bi vch kok° þat crue,° he knwe° wel þe steuen.° — cock/crowed/was reminded of/ appointed time

Deliuerly° he dressed° vp, er° þe day sprenged,° — quickly/got/before/broke
2010 For þere watz ly3t° of a laumpe,° þat lemed° in his chambre; — light/lamp/shone
He called to his chamberlayn, þat cofly° hym swared,° — promptly/answered
And bede° hym bryng hym his bruny,° and his blonk sadel;° — bade/coat of mail/horse (to) saddle

---

2000–5. Cf. the lyric *Mirie It Is While Sumer Ilast*, this volume, p. 634. The relationship of "outer" to "inner weather" (cf. Robert Frost, *Tree at My Window*) was a common poetic device in the Middle Ages.

Þat oþer ferkez hym° vp, and fechez hym his wedez,° — gets/clothes
And grayþez° me sir Gawayn vpon° a grett wyse.° — dresses/in/splendid manner
2015 Fyrst he clad hym in his cloþez, þe colde for to were;° — ward off
And syþen° his oþer harnays,° þat holdely° watz keped,° — then/armor/carefully/kept
Boþe his paunce,° and his platez, piked° ful clene,° — stomach armor/(steel) plates, polished/bright

Þe ryngez rokked° of þe roust,° of his riche° bruny; — rolled (free)/rust/noble
And al watz fresch° as vpon fyrst,° and he watz fayn° þenne — (as) clean/in the beginning/glad
2020   to þonk;° — give thanks
    He hade vpon° vche pece,° — put on/piece
    Wypped° ful wel and wlonk;° — wiped/lovely
    Þe gayest° in° to Grece, — handsomest/from here
    Þe burne° bede bryng° his blonk. — knight/ordered brought

II

2025 Whyle þe wlonkest° wedes he warp° on hym-seluen°— — noblest/put/himself
His cote,° wyth þe conysaunce° of þe clere werkez,° — coat armor/badge/fair workmanship
Ennurned° vpon veluet vertuus° stonez, — set/potent
Aboute beten,° and bounden, enbrauded semez,° — set/adorned, embroidered seams
And fayre° furred with-inne wyth fayre pelures°— — well/furs
2030 Ȝet laft° he not þe lace,° þe ladiez° gifte, — left/belt/lady's
Þat for-gat° not Gawayn, for gode° of hym-seluen;° — forgot/good/his own
Bi° he hade° belted þe bronde° vpon his balȝe haunchez,° — when/had/sword/smooth hips
Þenn dressed° his drurye° double hym° aboute; — bound/love token/himself
Swyþe sweþled vmbe° his swange swetely,° þat knyȝt,° — quickly wound around/waist happily/knight

2035 Þe gordel° of þe grene silke, þat gay° wel bisemed,° — belt/(the) good (knight)/suited
Vpon þat ryol° red cloþe, þat ryche watz to schewe.° — splendid/show
Bot wered° not þis ilk wyȝe for wele° þis gordel, — but wore/same man/(its) richness
For pryde of þe pendauntez,° þaȝ polyst þay° were, — pendants/polished they
And þaȝ þe glyterande° golde glent vpon° endez, — glittering/gleamed at (the)
2040 Bot forto° sauen° hym-self, when suffer° hym by-houed,° — in order to/save/submit/he had to
To byde bale° with-oute dabate, of° bronde hym to were,° — await death/resistance, with/defend
    oþer knyffe;° — or knife
    Bi þat° þe bolde mon° boun,° — when/man/was ready
    Wynnez° þeroute bilyue,° — (he) goes/quickly
2045   Alle þe meyny° of renoun — company
    He þonkkez° ofte ful ryue.° — thanks/very much

2018. *rokked:* Armor was burnished by placing it in barrels of sand and rolling it about.

2026. *conysaunce:* i.e., the pentangle (cf. above, ll. 619–20n).

2027. *vertuus stonez:* In the Middle Ages many stones were considered to have special powers of protection. Their magic was fully described in medieval lapidaries.

III

Thenne watz Gryngolet grayþe,° þat gret° watz and huge,   *ready/great*
And hade ben soiourned° sauerly,° and in a siker wyse,°   *been lodged/to his liking/secure way*
Hym lyst° prik° for° poynt,° þat proude hors þenne;   *he was eager/(to) gallop/because of/ (his) good condition*

2050 Þe wyȝe wynnez hym to, and wytez on° his lyre,°   *looks at/coat*
And sayde soberly hym-self,° and by his soth swerez,°   *earnestly (to) himself/word swears*
"Here is a meyny in þis mote,° þat on menske þenkkez,°   *castle/courtesy thinks*
Þe mon hem maynteines, ioy mot° þay haue;   *(and) the man (that) them maintains, joy may*

Þe leue° lady, on lyue° luf hir bityde;°   *dear/all her life/regard her befall*
2055 Ȝif° þay for charyté cherysen° a gest,°   *if/charity entertain/guest*
And halden° honour in her honde,° þe haþel° hem ȝelde,°   *hold/their hand/Lord/reward*
Þat haldez° þe heuen° vpon hyȝe,° and also yow° alle!   *rules/heaven/high/you*
And ȝif I myȝt lyf° vpon londe lede° any quyle,°   *might life/earth lead/length of time*
I schuld rech° yow sum° rewarde redyly,° if I myȝt."   *should give/some/willingly*
2060 Þenn steppez he in-to stirop,° and strydez° alofte;   *stirrup/mounts*
His schalk schewed° hym his schelde,° on schulder° he hit laȝt,°   *man gave/shield/shoulder/it took*
Gordez to° Gryngolet, with his gilt helez,°   *spurs/heels*
And he startez° on þe ston, stod° he no lenger,°   *springs forward/stone, waited/ longer*

        to praunce;°   *prance*
2065   His haþel° on hors watz þenne,   *man*
    Þat bere° his spere° and launce.°   *bore/spear/lance*
    "Þis kastel to Kryst° I kenne,°   *Christ/commend*
    He gef° hit ay° god chaunce!"°   *give/ever/fortune*

IV

The brygge° watz brayde° doun, and þe brode ȝatez°   *bridge/pulled/wide gates*
2070 Vnbarred, and born° open, vpon boþe halue;°   *laid/sides*
Þe burne blessed° hym bilyue, and þe bredez passed;°   *knight crossed/planks passed (over)*
Prayses þe porter,° bifore þe prynce kneled,°   *porter, (who)/knelt*
Gef° hym God and goud° day, þat Gawayn he saue;°   *wished/good/keep safe*
And went on his way, with his wyȝe one,°   *attendant only*
2075 Þat schulde teche° hym to tourne° to þat tene° place,   *direct/go/perilous*
Þer° þe ruful race° he schulde resayue.°   *where/grievous stroke/receive*
Þay boȝen° bi bonkkez,° þer boȝez° ar bare   *they traveled/banks/branches*
Þay clomben° bi clyffez, þer clengez° þe colde;   *climbed/clings*

2073. Davis reads this line as: "Gave him a God-save-you and a good-day" (i.e., "good-bye" ["God be with you"]).

2077–83. Cf. this picture of the landscape with the description in *Beowulf* of the land of Grendel (ll. 1347–80) and the path to the mere (ll. 1399–1424). The depiction of nature is in the gothic tradition of the epic and Old English poetry in general— more native English than the motifs of the *reverdie*, influenced by French poetry.

Þe heuen° watz vp halt,° bot vgly° þer vnder,° — *clouds/high/but threatening/below*
2080 Mist muged° on þe mor, malt° on þe mountez, — *drizzled/moor, melted*
Vch° hille hade° a hatte, a myst-hakel° huge; — *each/had/cloak of mist*
Brokez byled,° and breke,° bi bonkkez aboute, — *streams boiled/foamed*
Schyre schaterande on schorez,° þer þay doun schowued.° — *brightly dashing/banks/pressed*
Wela wylle° watz þe way, þer þay bi wod schulden,° — *very wandering/through (the) forest must (go)*

2085 Til hit watz sone sesoun° þat þe sunne ryses, — *soon time*
þat tyde;° — *time*
Þay were on a hille ful° hyʒe, — *very*
Þe quyte snaw° lay bisyde;° — *white snow/about*
Þe burne° þat rod° hym by,° — *man/rode/with*
2090 Bede° his mayster abide.° — *asked/master (to) wait*

V

"For I haf wonnen° yow hider, wyʒe,° at þis tyme, — *have brought/hither, sir*
And now nar° ʒe° not fer fro° þat note° place, — *are not/you/far from/noted*
Þat ʒe han spied° and spuryed° so specially after; — *have sought/asked*
Bot I schal say yow° for soþe, syþen° I yow knowe, — *to you/in truth, since*
2095 And ʒe ar a lede vpon lyue° þat I wel louy,° — *man on earth/love*
Wolde ʒe° worch° bi my wytte,° ʒe worþed° þe better. — *if you would/act/advice/would fare*
Þe place þat ʒe prece° to, ful perelous° is halden;° — *hasten/perilous/considered*
Þer wonez° a wyʒe° in þat waste, þe worst vpon erþe; — *dwells/man*
For he is stiffe,° and sturne,° and to strike louies,° — *strong/grim/loves*
2100 And more° he is þen° any mon° vpon myddelerde,° — *greater/than/man/earth*
And his body bigger þen þe best fowre° — *four*
Þat ar in Arþurez hous, Hestor oþer° oþer. — *Hector or*
He cheuez þat chaunce° at þe chapel grene — *brings it to pass*
Þer passes non bi þat place, so proude in his armes,
2105 Þat he ne dynnez° hym to deþe,° with dynt° of his honde;° — *not strikes/death/blow/hand*
For he is a mon methles,° and mercy non vses,° — *violent/none shows*
For be hit chorle,° oþer chaplayn, þat bi þe chapel rydes, — *it churl*
Monk, oþer masse-prest,° oþer any mon elles,° — *mass priest/else*
Hym þynk° as queme° hym to quelle,° as quyk go° hym seluen.° — *he thinks (it)/pleasant/kill/alive (to) be/himself*

2110 For-þy° I say þe° as soþe° as ʒe in sadel° sitte, — *therefore/you/true/saddle*
Com ʒe° þere, ʒe be° kylled, may° þe knyʒt° rede,° — *if you come/will be/if/knight/has his way*

2100. *myddelerde:* "middle-earth," the *Midgard* of Norse cosmography.

2102. *Hestor:* a common variant of *Hector*, found in French romances (cf. the Vulgate *Merlin*).

2107. *chorle:* A churl was a man of low birth.

Trawe° ȝe me þat trwely, þaȝ° ȝe had twenty lyues° *believe/truly, though/lives*
        to spende;
He hatz wonyd° here ful ȝore,° *lived/for a long time*
2115 On bent° much baret° bende,° *field/strife/brought about*
Aȝayn° his dyntez sore *against*
Ȝe may not yow° defende." *yourself*

VI

"For-þy, goude° sir Gawayn, let þe gome one,° *good/man alone*
And gotz° a-way sum° oþer gate,° vpon° Goddez halue;° *go/some/way/for/sake*
2120 Cayrez° bi sum oþer kyth, þer Kryst mot yow spede;° *ride/land, where Christ may you help*
And I schal hyȝ me° hom aȝayn,° and hete° yow fyrre,° *hurry/again/promise/further*
Þat I schal swere° bi God, and alle his gode halȝez,° *swear/good saints*
As° help me God and þe halydam,° and oþez in-noghe,° *so/holy relics/oaths many*
Þat I schal lelly° yow layne,° and lance° neuer tale, *faithfully/keep your secret/tell*
2125 Þat euer ȝe fondet° to fle,° for° freke° þat I wyst."° *hastened/flee/because of/(any) man/ knew*

"Grant merci,"° quod° Gawayn, and gruchyng° he sayde, *thank you/said/reluctantly*
"Wel worth þe,° wyȝe, þat woldez° my gode, *good luck to you/wishes*
And þat lelly me layne, I leue° wel þou woldez!° *believe/would*
Bot° helde þou° hit neuer so holde,° and I here passed,° *but/if you kept/loyally/proceeded*
2130 Founded° for ferde° for to fle, in fourme° þat þou tellez,° *hastened/fear/manner/advise*
I were° a knyȝt kowarde, I myȝt° not be excused. *would be/might*
Bot I wyl° to þe chapel, for chaunce° þat may falle,° *will (go)/whatever fate/befall*
And talk wyth þat ilk tulk° þe tale þat me lyste,° *same man/I wish*
Worþe hit wele,° oþer wo,° as þe wyrde lykez° *come joy/woe/fate will*
2135   hit hafe;° *have*
Þaȝe he be a sturn knape,° *fellow*
To stiȝtel,° and stad° with staue,° *deal with/stand/club*
Ful° wel con dryȝtyn° schape,° *very/can (the) Lord/bring about*
His seruauntez forto saud."° *servants to save*

VII

2140 "Mary!" quod þat oþer mon,° "now þou so much spellez,° *man/go so far as to say*
Þat þou wylt þyn awen nye nyme° to þy-seluen, *your own harm take*
And° þe lyst lese° þy lyf,° þe lette° I ne kepe;° *if/(to) lose/life/hinder/care to*
Haf° here þi helme° on þy hede,° þi spere° in þi honde, *take/helmet/head/spear*
And ryde me doun þis ilk rake,° bi ȝon rokke° syde, *path/that rock*
2145 Til þou be broȝt° to þe boþem° of þe brem valay;° *brought/bottom/wild valley*
Þenne loke° a littel on þe launde,° on þi lyfte honde,° *look/glade/left hand*
And þou schal se° in þat slade° þe self° chapel, *see/valley/very*

2133. *talk wyth:* i.e., "say to."

And þe borelych burne° on bent, þat hit kepez.° *strong man/it guards*
Now farez° wel on° Godez half,° Gawayn þe noble, *fare/for/sake*
2150 For alle þe golde vpon grounde° I nolde° go wyth þe,° *on earth/would not/you*
Ne bere° þe felaȝschip þurȝ° þis fryth on fote° fyrre." *nor keep/company through/wood one foot*

Bi° þat þe wyȝe° in þe wod wendez° his brydel, *with/man/wood turns*
Hit þe hors with þe helez,° as harde as he myȝt, *heels*
Lepez hym° ouer þe launde,° and leuez° þe knyȝt þere, *leaps/field/leaves/knight*
2155   al one.
"Bi Goddez self," quod Gawayn,
"I wyl nauþer grete° ne grone, *neither weep*
To Goddez wylle I am ful bayn,° *completely obedient*
And to hym I haf me tone."° *myself committed*

VIII

2160 Thenne gyrdez he to° Gryngolet, and gederez° þe rake, *he spurs/picks up*
Schowuez° in bi a schore,° at a schaȝe° syde, *makes his way/hillside/small wood*
Ridez þurȝ° þe roȝe bonk, ryȝt° to þe dale; *over/rough slope, right*
And þenne he wayted° hym aboute, and wylde hit hym þoȝt,° *looked/to him seemed*
And seȝe° no syngne° of resette,° bisydez° nowhere, *saw/sign/shelter/round about*
2165 Bot hyȝe° bonkkez and brent,° vpon boþe halue,° *high/steep/sides*
And ruȝe knokled knarrez,° with knorned° stonez; *rough, rugged crags/gnarled*
Þe skwez of° þe scowtes° skayned° hym þoȝt.° *clouds by/rocks/were grazed/(it) seemed*

Þenne he houed,° and wythhylde° his hors at þat tyde,° *halted/checked/time*
And ofte chaunged his cher,° þe chapel to seche;° *looked here and there/seek*
2170 He seȝ non° suche in° no syde, and selly° hym þoȝt, *no/on/strange*
Saue° a lyttel° on a launde, a lawe° as hit were; *except/little (way off)/mound*
A balȝ berȝ,° bi a bonke, þe brymme° by-syde, *smoothly rounded/barrow/water's edge*

Bi a forȝ° of a flode,° þat ferked þare;° *watercourse/stream/ran there*
Þe borne blubred° þer-inne, as° hit boyled hade.° *stream bubbled/as if/had*
2175 Þe knyȝt kachez° his caple,° and com° to þe lawe, *urges on/horse/comes*
Liȝtez° doun luflyly,° and at a lynde tachez° *dismounts/quickly/tree fastens*
Þe rayne,° and his riche,° with° a roȝe braunche;° *reins/noble (steed)/to/branch*
Þenne he boȝez° to þe berȝe, aboute hit he walkez, *goes*
Debatande with hym-self, quat° hit be myȝt.° *what/might*
2180 Hit hade a hole on þe ende, and on ayþer° syde, *either*
And ouer-growen with gresse° in glodes° ay where,° *grass/patches/everywhere*
And al watz holȝ in-with,° nobot° an olde caue, *hollow within/nothing but*

2180. The barrow is undoubtedly an old burial mound which had been broken into. Barrows, especially those of slain Vikings, were often placed near water so that the soul could escape to the sea.

Or a creuisse° of an olde cragge, he couþe° hit noȝt deme°   *fissure/could/not judge*
    with spelle,°   *words*
2185   "We, lorde,"° quod° þe gentyle° knyȝt,   *alas, Lord/said/noble*
    "Wheþer° þis be þe grene chapelle?   *might*
    Here myȝt aboute myd-nyȝt°   *midnight*
    Þe dele° his matynnes telle!"°   *Devil/matins say*

IX

"Now i-wysse,"° quod Wowayn,° "wysty is° here;   *indeed/Gawain/desolate (it) is*
2190 Þis oritore° is vgly, with erbez ouer-growen;°   *chapel/weeds overgrown*
Wel bisemez° þe wyȝe wruxled° in grene   *it suits/man clad*
Dele° here his deuocioun, on° þe deuelez wyse;°   *(to) perform/in/Devil's manner*
Now I fele qit° is þe fende,° in my fyue wyttez,°   *feel it/Fiend/five senses*
Þat hatz stoken° me þis steuen,° to strye° me here;   *imposed on/appointment/destroy*
2195 Þis is a chapel of meschaunce,° þat° chekke° hit by-tyde,°   *disaster/may/ill luck/befall*
Hit is þe corsedest° kyrk° þat euer I com° inne!"   *most accursed/church/came*
With heȝe helme° on his hede,° his launce° in his honde,°   *high helmet/head/lance/hand*
He romez° vp to þe roffe° of þe roȝ wonez;°   *makes his way/roof/dwelling*
Þene herde° he of° þat hil, in a harde roche,°   *heard/from/rock*
2200 Biȝonde° þe broke,° in a bonk, a wonder breme° noyse,   *beyond/stream/wondrously loud*
Quat!° hit clatered° in þe clyff, as hit cleue schulde,°   *lo/clattered/split would*
As one vpon a gryndelston° hade grounden° a syþe;°   *grindstone/ground/scythe*
What!° hit wharred,° and whette,° as water at a mulne,°   *lo/whirred/made a grinding noise/ mill*

What! hit rusched, and ronge, rawþe° to here.°   *rang, horrible/hear*
2205 Þenne "Bi Godde," quod Gawayn, "þat gere as° I trowe°   *contrivance so/believe*
Is ryched° at þe reuerence,° me, renk,° to mete,°   *prepared/out of respect/knight/ receive*

    bi rote;°   *duly*
    Let God worche,° "we loo,"°   *act/(to say) "alas"*
    Hit helppez me not a mote;°   *bit*
2210   My lif þaȝ° I for-goo,°   *life though/lose*
    Drede dotz° me no lote."°   *afraid makes/noise*

X

Thenne þe knyȝt con° calle ful hyȝe,°   *knight did/very loudly*
"Who stiȝtlez° in þis sted,° me° steuen to holde?°   *rules/here/my/keep*
For now is gode° Gawayn goande ryȝt° here,   *good/walking right*
2215 If any wyȝe oȝt wyl° wynne° hider° fast,   *anything wishes/let him come/hither*
Oþer° now, oþer° neuer, his nedez° to spede."°   *either/or/business/get done*
"Abyde,"° quod on° on þe bonke, abouen° ouer his hede,   *wait/one/slope, above*

2183–84. *deme with spelle:* i.e., "presume to say."

"And þou schal haf° al in hast° þat° I þe hyȝt ones."° *have/a hurry/what/you promised once*

Ȝet° he rusched on° þat rurde,° rapely° a þrowe,° *still/continued in/rushing noise/quickly/time*

2220 And wyth quettyng° a-wharf,° er° he wolde° lyȝt;° *whetting/turned aside/before/would/come down*

And syþen° he keuerez° bi a cragge, and comez of° a hole, *then/makes his way/(out) of*
Whyrlande° out of a wro,° wyth a felle weppen,° *whirling/nook/fierce weapon*
A denez° ax nwe dyȝt,° þe dynt° with to ȝelde° *Danish/newly made/blow/return*
With a borelych bytte, bende by° þe halme,° *massive blade, curved to/shaft*
2225 Fyled in° a fylor, fowre fote large,° *sharpened on/grindstone, four feet long*

Hit watz no lasse, bi° þat lace° þat lemed° ful bryȝt.° *less, (measured) by/thong/shone bright*

And þe gome° in þe grene gered° as fyrst,° *man/dressed/at first*
Boþe þe lyre° and þe leggez, lokkez,° and berde,° *face/locks/beard*
Saue° þat fayre° on his fote he foundez° on þe erþe, *except/firmly/moves*
2230 Sette þe stele° to þe stone,° and stalked bysyde.° *handle/ground/round about*
When he wan° to þe watter, þer he wade nolde,° *came/would not*
He hypped° ouer on hys ax, and orpedly° strydez, *vaulted/boldly*
Bremly broþe° on a bent,° þat brode° watz a-boute, *fiercely grim/field/wide*
    on snawe.° *snow*
2235   Sir Gawayn þe knyȝt con mete,° *meet*
    He ne° lutte hym° no þyng° lowe; *not/bowed/not at all*
    Þat oþer sayde, "Now, sir swete,° *good*
    Of° steuen mon° may þe trowe."° *as to/(an) appointment one/you trust*

XI

"Gawayn," quod° þat grene gome, "God þe mot loke!° *said/may guard*
2240 I-wysse° þou art welcom, wyȝe,° to my place, *indeed/sir*
And þou hatz tymed þi trauayl° as truee mon schulde;° *journey/true man should*
And þou knowez þe couenauntez kest vus° by-twene, *compacts made us*
At þis tyme twelmonyth° þou toke° þat þe falled,° *a year ago/took/befell*
And I schulde at þis nwe ȝere ȝeply° þe quyte.° *New Year promptly/repay*
2245 And we ar in þis valay, verayly° oure one,° *valley, truly/by ourselves*
Here ar no renkes° vs to rydde,° rele° as vus° likez; *men/separate/we can fight/we*
Haf° þy helme of° þy hede,° and haf here þy pay; *take/helmet off/head*
Busk° no more debate þen° I þe bede° þenne, *make/resistance than/offered*
When þou wypped° of my hede at a wap one."° *slashed/blow single*

2223. The Danish ax (so called because it was a common weapon of the Viking raiders in England and France) was a curved battle-ax with a long blade and no spike.

2226. *lace:* This may refer to the thong tied around the handle, and already mentioned (l. 217) as being on the Green Knight's ax.

2230. *Sette þe stele to þe stone:* He used the ax handle as support for walking and later (l. 2232) for jumping, in a rudimentary form of pole vault.

²²⁵⁰ "Nay, bi God," quod Gawayn, "þat me gost lante,°	*soul gave*
I schal gruch þe° no grwe,° for grem° þat fallez;°	*bear you/grudge/harm/happens*
Bot° styȝtel þe vpon on strok,° and I schal stonde° stylle,	*but/limit yourself to one stroke/ stand*
And warp° þe no wernyng,° to worch° as þe lykez,	*offer/resistance/do*
no whare."°	*in no case*
²²⁵⁵ He lened° with þe nek,° and lutte,°	*leaned over/neck/bent down*
And schewed° þat schyre° al bare,	*showed/white flesh*
And lette° as° he noȝt dutte,°	*acted/as if/nothing feared*
For drede° he wolde not dare.°	*fear/recoil*

XII

Then þe gome in þe grene grayþed hym swyþe,°	*prepared himself quickly*
²²⁶⁰ Gederez° vp hys grymme tole,° Gawayn to smyte;	*takes/weapon*
With alle þe bur° in his body he ber hit° on lofte,	*strength/lifted it/aloft*
Munt° as maȝtyly,° as marre° hym he wolde;°	*aimed/mightily/destroy/would*
Hade° hit dryuen adoun,° as dreȝ° as he atled,°	*had/down/fiercely/intended*
Þer hade ben ded of his dynt,° þat doȝty° watz euer.	*blow/(he) that doughty*
²²⁶⁵ Bot Gawayn on þat giserne glyfte° hym bysyde,°	*battle-ax glanced/sideways*
As hit com° glydande adoun, on glode° hym to schende,°	*came/ground/destroy*
And schranke° a lytel with þe schulderes,° for° þe scharp yrne.°	*shrank/shoulders/for (fear of)/iron*
Þat oþer schalk° wyth a schunt° þe schene° wythhaldez,°	*man/jerk/bright (blade)/checks*
And þenne repreued° he þe prynce with mony° prowde wordez:	*reproved/many*
²²⁷⁰ "Þou art not Gawayn," quod þe gome,° "þat is so goud halden,°	*man/good considered*
Þat neuer arȝed° for no here,° by hylle ne be° vale,	*feared/army/nor by*
And now þou fles° for ferde, er° þou fele° harmez;	*flinch/fear, before/feel*
Such cowardise of þat knyȝt cowþe° I neuer here.°	*did/hear*
Nawþer fyked° I, ne flaȝe, freke, quen° þou myntest,°	*neither flinched/fled, knight, when/ struck*
²²⁷⁵ Ne kest no kauelacion,° in kyngez hous Arthor,°	*objection/King Arthur's house*
My hede flaȝ° to my fote,° and ȝet flaȝ° I neuer;	*flew/feet/fled*
And þou, er any harme hent,° arȝez in hert,°	*received/heart*
Wherfore þe better burne me° burde° be called	*man I/ought to*
þer-fore."	
²²⁸⁰ Quod° Gawayn, "I schunt onez,°	*said/flinched once*
And so wyl I no more,	
Bot þaȝ° my hede falle on þe stonez,	*though*
I con° not hit restore.	*can*

XIII

Bot busk,° burne, bi þi fayth, and bryng me° to þe poynt,	*hurry/come*
²²⁸⁵ Dele° to me my destiné,° and do hit out of honde,°	*give/destiny/right away*
For I schal stonde° þe° a strok, and start° no more,	*take from/you/cringe*
Til þyn° ax haue me hitte, haf° here my trawþe."°	*your/take/word*

"Haf° at þe þenne," quod þat oþer, and heuez° hit alofte,   *let me get/raises*
And waytez° as wroþely,° as he wode° were;   *looks/fiercely/mad*
2290 He myntez° at hym maȝtyly, bot not þe mon rynez,°   *feints/man touches*
Withhelde heterly° his honde,° er hit hurt myȝt.°   *suddenly/hand/might*
Gawayn grayþely° hit bydez,° and glent° with no membre,   *duly/awaits/flinched/limb*
Bot stode° stylle as þe ston, oþer° a stubbe auþer,°   *but stood/stone, or/stump either*
Þat raþeled° is in roche° grounde, with rotez° a hundreth.°   *entwined/rocky/roots/hundred*
2295 Þen muryly efte con° he mele,° þe mon in þe grene,   *merrily again did/speak*
"So now° þou hatz þi hert holle,° hitte° me bihous;°   *now (that)/intact/strike/I must*
Halde° þe now þe hyȝe hode,° þat Arþur þe raȝt,°   *may protect/high order (of knight-hood)/gave*

And kepe° þy kanel at° þis kest, ȝif° hit keuer° may."   *guard/neck from/blow, if/manage*
Gawayn ful gryndelly° with greme° þenne sayde,   *very fiercely/anger*
2300 "Wy!° þresch° on, þou þro° mon, þou þretez to° longe,   *ah!/strike/fierce/threaten too*
I hope° þat þi hert arȝe° wyth° þyn awen seluen."°   *believe/is afraid/of/own self*
"For soþe,"° quod þat oþer freke,° "so felly° þou spekez,°   *in truth/man/fiercely/speak*
I wyl no lenger on lyte lette° þin ernde,°   *longer in delay hinder/mission*
       riȝt° nowe."   *right*
2305 Þenne tas° he hym° stryþe° to stryke,   *takes/for himself/stance*
       And frounses° boþe lyppe and browe,   *puckers*
       No meruayle° þaȝ hym myslyke,°   *wonder/he is unhappy*
       Þat hoped of° no rescowe.°   *for/rescue*

XIV

He lyftes lyȝtly° his lome,° and let hit° doun fayre,°   *quickly/weapon/it/straight*
2310 With þe barbe° of þe bitte bi° þe bare nek;   *edge/blade toward*
Þaȝ he homered heterly,° hurt hym no more,   *struck/fiercely*
Bot snyrt° hym on þat on° syde, þat° seuered° þe hyde;°   *nicked/one/cut/so that/was cut/skin*
Þe scharp schrank° to þe flesche þurȝ° þe schyre grece,°   *sharp (blade) cut/through/fair tissue*
Þat þe schene blod° ouer his schulderes schot° to þe erþe.   *bright blood/shoulders shot*
2315 And quen° þe burne seȝ° þe blode blenk° on þe snawe,°   *when/knight saw/gleam/snow*
He sprit° forth spenne fote° more þen° a spere lenþe,°   *leaped/feet together/than/spear length*

Hent heterly° his helme,° and on his hed° cast,   *seized quickly/helmet/head*
Schot° with his schulderez his fayre schelde° vnder,°   *tossed/shield/in front of him*
Braydez° out a bryȝt° sworde, and bremely° he spekez;   *pulls/bright/fiercely*
2320 Neuer syn þat° he watz burne borne° of his moder,   *since/man born/mother*
Watz he neuer in þis worlde wyȝe° half so blyþe:°   *man/happy*
"Blynne,° burne, of° þy bur, bede° me no mo;°   *cease/from/blows, offer/more*
I haf° a stroke in þis sted° with-oute stryf hent,°   *have/here/resistance received*
And if þow rechez° me any mo, I redyly° schal quyte,°   *give/promptly/repay*

2318. The description here is of a knight well trained to put on his armor in a hurry. The shield when not in use hangs on Gawain's back; with a twist of his shoulders it swings in front of him, ready for protection.

2325 And ȝelde ȝederly aȝayn,° and þer to° ȝe° tryst,°   *reply promptly again|that|you|can believe*

        and foo;°   *fiercely*
Bot on° stroke here me fallez,°   *only one|befalls*
Þe couenaunt schop ryȝt° so,   *compact directed just*
Fermed° in Arþurez hallez,   *confirmed*
2330 And þer-fore, hende,° now hoo!"°   *good (sir)|stop*

XV

The haþel heldet° hym fro,° and on his ax rested,   *man turned|from*
Sette þe schaft vpon schore,° and to° þe scharp lened,°   *on (the) ground|on|leaned*
And loked to° þe leude,° þat on þe launde ȝede,°   *looked at|knight|field stood*
How þat doȝty dredles deruely° þer stondez,°   *doughty (man) fearless boldly| stands*

2335 Armed ful aȝlez;° in hert° hit hym lykez.°   *completely undaunted|heart|pleases*
Þenn he meleȝ muryly,° wyth a much steuen,°   *speaks merrily|loud voice*
And wyth a rynkande rurde° he to þe renk° sayde,   *ringing voice|knight*
"Bolde burne, on þis bent° be not so gryndel;°   *field|fierce*
No mon° here vn-manerly þe mys-boden habbe,°   *man|unmannerly you ill-used has*
2340 Ne kyd,° bot as° couenaunde,° at kyngez kort schaped;°   *nor behaved|according to|compact| court made*

I hyȝt° þe a strok,° and þou hit hatz, halde þe° wel payed,   *promised|stroke|consider yourself*
I relece° þe of þe remnaunt,° of ryȝtes° alle oþer;   *release|rest|claims*
Ȝif° I deliuer° had bene,° a boffet, paraunter,°   *if|nimble|been|blow, perhaps*
I couþe° wroþeloker° haf waret,° to þe haf wroȝt anger.°   *could|more harshly|dealt|done harm*
2345 Fyrst I mansed° þe muryly,° with a mynt one.°   *threatened|in fun|feint single*
And roue° þe wyth no rof-sore° with ryȝt° I þe profered,   *rent|wound (which)|right|offered*
For° þe forwarde° þat we fest in° þe fyrst nyȝt,°   *by|agreement|made on|night*
And þou trystyly° þe trawþe° and trwly° me haldez,°   *faithfully|compact|truly|have kept with me*

Al þe gayne° þow me gef,° as god° mon schulde;°   *winnings|gave|good|should*
2350 Þat oþer munt° for þe morne,° mon, I þe profered,   *feint|morning*
Þou kyssedes° my clere wyf,° þe cossez° me raȝtez,°   *kissed|fair wife|kisses|gave*
For boþe two here I þe bede bot° two bare° myntes,°   *offered only|mere|feints*
        boute scaþe;°   *without harm*
Trwe mon trwe° restore,   *must honestly*
2355 Þenne þar mon drede° no waþe;°   *need one fear|danger*
At þe þrid° þou fayled þore,°   *third|there*
And þer-for þat tappe ta° þe.   *tap take*

2346. I.e., "and I did not rend you with a wound although I was justified in offering it."

XVI

For hit° is my wede° þat þou werez,° þat ilke° wouen girdel,   *it/garment/wear/same*
Myn owen° wyf hit þe weued,° I wot° wel for soþe;°   *my own/gave/know/truly*
2360 Now know I wel þy cosses, and þy costes als,°   *behavior also*
And þe wowyng° of my wyf, I wroȝt° hit myseluen;°   *wooing/contrived/myself*
I sende hir° to asay° þe, and sothly me þynkkez,°   *sent her/test/truly I believe*
On° þe fautlest° freke,° þat euer on fote ȝede;°   *one of/most faultless/men/walked*
As perle bi° þe quite pese° is of prys° more,   *pearl than/white pea/worth*
2365 So is Gawayn, in god fayth, bi oþer gay knyȝtez.°   *good knights*
Bot° here yow lakked° a lyttel, sir, and lewte° yow wonted,°   *only/you lacked/loyalty/lacked*
Bot° þat watz for no wylyde werke,° ne wowyng nauþer,°   *but/skillful work/love-making*
                                                             neither

Bot for ȝe lufed° your lyf,° þe lasse° I yow blame."   *because you loved/life/less*
Þat oþer stif° mon in study stod° a gret° whyle;   *sturdy/stood/great*
2370 So agreued° for greme° he gryed° with-inne,   *overcome/grief/shuddered*
Alle þe blode of° his brest blende in° his face,   *blood from/heart rushed to*
Þat al° he schrank for schome,° þat° þe schalk° talked.   *entirely/shame/at what/man said*
Þe forme° worde vpon folde° þat þe freke meled:°   *first/on earth/knight spoke*
"Corsed worth° cowarddyse and couetyse° boþe!   *cursed be/covetousness*
2375 In yow is vylany° and vyse,° þat vertue disstryez."°   *villainy/vice/destroys*
Þenne he kaȝt to° þe knot, and þe kest lawsez,°   *caught hold of/fastening loosens*
Brayde broþely° þe belt to þe burne seluen:°   *flung angrily/man himself*
"Lo! þer þe falssyng,° foule mot hit falle!°   *breaking of faith/ill luck to it*
For care° of þy knokke° cowardyse me taȝt°   *fear/blow/taught*
2380 To acorde me° with couetyse, my kynde° to for-sake,   *come to terms/true nature*
Þat is larges° and lewte, þat longez to° knyȝtez,   *generosity/befits*
Now am I fawty,° and falce,° and ferde haf ben° euer   *faulty/untrue/afraid have been*
Of trecherye and vn-trawþe:° boþe bityde° sorȝe°   *dishonesty/may befall/sorrow*
                                    and care!
2385   I biknowe° yow,° knyȝt, here stylle,°   *confess/to you/privately*
         Al fawty is my fare,°   *conduct*
         Letez me ouer-take° your wylle,   *do*
         And efte° I schal be ware."°   *afterwards/on my guard*

XVII

Thenn loȝe° þat oþer leude,° and luflyly° sayde,   *laughed/man/pleasantly*
2390 "I halde° hit hardily° hole,° þe harme þat I hade;°   *consider/certainly/made whole/had*
Þou art confessed so clene, beknowen° of þy mysses,°   *clean, absolved/faults*
And hatz þe penaunce apert° of þe poynt of myn egge,°   *penance open/my sword*
I halde þe polysed° of þat plyȝt,° and pured° as clene,   *you cleansed/offense/purified*
As° þou hadez neuer forfeted, syþen° þou watz fyrst borne.°   *as if/sinned, since/born*
2395 And I gif° þe, sir, þe gurdel° þat is golde hemmed;   *give/belt*
For° hit is grene as my goune, sir Gawayn, ȝe maye   *because*

Þenk° vpon þis ilke þrepe,° þer° þou forth þryngez°   *think|same contest|where|ride*
Among prynces of prys, and þis a pure° token   *excellent*
Of þe chaunce° of þe grene chapel, at chevalrous° knyʒtez;   *adventure|with chivalrous*
2400 And ʒe schal in þis nwe ʒer° aʒayn° to my wonez,°   *New Year|(come) again|dwelling*
And we schyn° reuel þe remnaunt° of þis ryche fest,°   *shall|rest|noble festival*
    ful bene."°   *very pleasantly*
    Þer laþed° hym fast° þe lorde,   *invited|earnestly*
    And sayde, "With my wyf,° I wene,°   *wife|believe*
2405   We shal yow wel acorde,°   *reconcile*
    Þat watz your enmy kene."°   *enemy keen*

XVIII

"Nay, for soþe,"° quod° þe segge,° and sesed° hys helme,°   *truly|said|knight|seized|helmet*
And hatʒ hit of hendely,° and þe haþel þonkkez,°   *takes it off courteously|man thanks*
"I haf soiorned° sadly,° sele yow bytyde,°   *stayed|long enough|(may) joy you befall*

2410 And he ʒelde° hit° yow ʒare,° þat ʒarkkez° al menskes!°   *(may) he reward|for it|fully|grants| honors*

And comaundez° me to þat cortays,° your comlych fere,°   *commend|courteous (lady)|fair wife*
Boþe þat on° and þat oþer, myn honoured ladyez,   *one*
Þat þus hor knyʒt° wyth hor kest han koyntly bigyled.°   *their knight|trickery have cunningly deceived*

Bot° hit is no ferly þaʒ° a fole° madde,°   *but|wonder though|fool|behaves madly*

2415 And þurʒ wyles° of wymmen° be wonen° to sorze;°   *through cunning|women|brought| sorrow*

For so watz Adam in erde with° one bygyled,   *on earth by*
And Salamon° with fele sere,° and Samson eft sonez,°   *Solomon|many various (ones)|also*
Dalyda dalt° hym hys wyrde,° and Dauyth° þer-after   *Delilah dealt|fate|David*
Watz blended° with Barsabe, þat° much bale þoled.°   *deluded|Bathsheba, (he) that| misery suffered*

2420 Now° þese were wrathed° wyth her. wyles, hit were° a wynne° huge,   *since|brought to grief|their|would be| gain*
To luf hom° wel, and leue hem° not, a° leude þat couþe.°   *love them|believe them|(if) a|could*
For þes° wer forne° þe freest° þat folʒed° alle þe sele,°   *these|of old|noblest|achieved| prosperity*

2416–19. This list is in the tradition of antifeminist sentiment in medieval literature: Eve caused the fall of man, and all women are infected by her sin: Mary alone redeems womankind.

2420–21. *hit . . . coupe:* "it would be fortunate if one could love, but not believe them."

Excellently of° alle þyse oþer,° vnder heuen-ryche,°
     þat mused;°
2425 And° alle þay° were bi-wyled,°
With wymmen þat þay vsed,°
Þaȝ I be now bigyled,
Me° þink me burde° be excused."

over|the others|heaven
thought (i.e., lived)
if|they|beguiled
had dealings with

I|I ought to

XIX

"Bot your gordel,"° quod Gawayn, "God yow for-ȝelde!°
2430 Þat wyl I welde° wyth guod° wylle, not for þe wynne° golde,
Ne° þe saynt,° ne þe sylk, ne þe syde pendaundes,°
For wele,° ne for worchyp,° ne for þe wlonk werkkez,°
Bot in syngne° of my surfet° I schal se° hit ofte;
When I ride in renoun, remorde° to myseluen°
2435 Þe faut° and þe fayntyse° of þe flesche crabbed,°
How tender° hit is to entyse teches° of fylþe;°
And þus, quen° pryde schal mc pryk,° for prowes° of armes,
Þe loke to° þis luf-lace° schal leþe° my hert.°
Bot on° I wolde° yow pray, displeses° yow neuer;

(for) your belt|reward
wear|good|delightful
nor|belt|long pendants
wealth|honor|lovely workmanship
token|misdeed|see
remember with remorse|myself
fault|frailty|perverse
easy|catch spots|sin
when|stir|prowess
glance at|love-belt|humble|heart
one (thing)|would|ask, (may it)
    displease

2440 Syn ȝe° be lorde of þe ȝonder londe, þer° I haf lent° inne,
Wyth yow wyth worschyp°—þe wyȝe° hit yow ȝelde
Þat vp-haldez° þe heuen,° and on hyȝ° sittez—
How norne° ȝe yowre ryȝt nome,° and þenne no more?"
"Þat schal I telle þe trwly,"° quod þat oþer þenne,
2445 "Bertilak de Hautdesert I hat° in þis londe,
Þurȝ myȝt° of Morgne° la Faye, þat in my hous lenges,°
And koyntyse° of clergye,° bi craftes° wel lerned,
Þe maystres° of Merlyn, mony° hatz taken;
For ho° hatz dalt drwry° ful dere° sum tyme,°

since you|land, where|have stayed
honor|One
rules|heaven|high
call|your right name
you truly
am called
magic power|Morgan|dwells
skill|magical knowledge|arts
arts|many
she|had a love-affair|very passion-
    ate|once

2445. The name *Bertilak* is according to Gollancz, and is the same in the Middle English prose Merlin romance (*Bertelak*) and in the Old French Vulgate cycle (*Bertolais*); all are of Celtic origin. Previous editors translated *Hautdesert* as "High Hermitage," from the Celtic *disert*, "hermitage." But Davis correctly points out that the valley barrow of the Green Knight is neither high nor a hermitage. The lord would take his name from his castle, to which *Hautdesert* undoubtedly refers (the compound *haut-desert*, and especially *desert*, "deserted place" or "solitary place," being common in French place-names) rather than from the neglected "chapel" which he frequented in his "Mr. Hyde" nature as the Green Knight.

2446. Morgan la Fay was the daughter of Ygerne, wife of Gorlois, duke of Cornwall (cf. ll. 2464–66n), and also of Avallach, ruler of Avalon.

2448–51. Merlin was the famous magician at Arthur's court, who became infatuated with Vivien (also spelled *Nimue* through scribal errors and confused with Morgan la Fay). Merlin taught her all his magical powers, whereupon she enslaved him in a kind of love bondage and finally enclosed him in a hole under a rock. Vivien, or Nimue, is often equated with the Lady of the Lake and with Morgan la Fay herself. In Malory, both appear to take Arthur to Avalon, Morgan's original home.

2450 With þat conable klerk,° þat knowes alle your kny3tez   excellent wizard
            at hame;°   home
        Morgne þe goddes,°   goddess
        Þer-fore hit° is hir° name;   it/her
        Weldez° non° so hy3e hawtesse,°   possesses/no one/pride
2455   Þat ho ne con° make ful tame.   not can

XX

        Ho wayned° me vpon° þis wyse° to your wynne° halle,   sent/in/manner/splendid
        For to assay° þe surquidre, 3if° hit soth° were,   test/pride, if/truth
        Þat rennes° of þe grete° renoun of þe Rounde Table;   is current/great
        Ho wayned me þis wonder, your wyttez to reue,°   deprive (you) of
2460   For to haf greued Gaynour,° and gart° hir to dy3e,°   distressed Guinevere/made/die
        With glopnyng° of þat ilke gomen,° þat gostlych° speked,° fright/same man/like an apparition/
                                                                    spoke

        With his hede° in his honde,° bifore þe hy3e table.   head/hand
        Þat is ho þat is at home, þe auncian° lady;   aged
        Ho is euen þyn° aunt, Arþurez half suster,°   actually your/sister
2465   Þe duches do3ter° of Tyntagelle, þat dere Vter after° daughter of the duchess/noble Uther
                                                                    afterward

        Hade° Arþur vpon, þat aþel° is nowþe.°   begot/glorious/now
        Þerfore I eþe° þe, haþel,° to com to þyn aunt,   entreat/knight
        Make myry° in my hous, my meny° þe louies,°   merry/household/loves
        And I wol° þe as wel, wy3e,° bi my faythe,   desire/sir
2470   As any gome vnder God, for þy grete trauþe."°   faithfulness
        And he nikked hym naye,° he nolde° bi° no wayes;   said no to him/would not/in
        Þay acolen° and kyssen,° and kennen ayþer° oþer   they embrace/kiss/commend each

---

2452. Morgan is called a goddess by Giraldus Cambrensis (c. 1216). Geoffrey of Monmouth in the *Vita Merlini* names Morgan chief of the nine sisters who rule over the "insula pomorum que fortunata vocatur" (the "isle of apples," whence the erroneous etymology of *Avalon*; cf. above, p. 91, ll. 1184–85n). Some scholars have identified Morgan with the Celtic goddess Morrigu or Morrigain, but this has recently been questioned (J. Vendryes, rev. of *La Légende arthurienne et la Graal* by Jean Marx [Paris, 1952], *Études Celtiques*, 6 [1953–54], 356–66; cf. specifically p. 365).

2459–62. The reason for Morgan's hatred of Guinevere is given in the Prose *Lancelot*: Morgan has a love affair with a knight called Guiomar at Arthur's court; when the intrigue is discovered by Guinevere, she sends the lovers away. In revenge, Morgan builds a chapel from which no one faithless in love can escape. Lancelot releases several of Arthur's knights who fail the test, but Gawain proves himself pure. In fact, Morgan is the "heavy" of the Arthurian legends, continually annoying the knights of the Round Table with her magic devices (as the Celtic goddess Morrigain pursues Cuchulainn). According to

one source it is she who sends the magic horn to Arthur in order to test the loyalty of the court ladies and expose Guinevere's liaison with Lancelot (cf. *The Lay of the Horn* by Robert Biket). Morgan's character alternates between a kindly healer, Arthur's sister with whom he takes his final refuge, and an evil witch, often involved in seductive machinations. There is a hint here (l. 2446) that Bertilak and his wife are in Morgan's power, and that the curse of his transformation into the Green Knight can only be broken by Gawain's honesty.

2463. *auncian:* Morgan was beautiful, and as young as Arthur, until she started to devote herself to magic and the Devil. Thereupon she lost her beauty and became ugly and old (cf. *Le Roman de Merlin*, ed. G. Paris and J. Ulrich [Paris, 1886], p. 166).

2464–66. With the help of Merlin, Uther Pendragon gained entrance to Tintagel, the castle of Gorlois, and slept with Ygerne. Arthur was born of this union (cf. Layamon's *Brut*, pp. 57–62).

To þe prynce of paradise, and parten° ryȝt þere,   *part*
        on coolde;°   *cold (ground)*
2475   Gawayn on blonk° ful bene,°   *steed/fine*
    To þe kyngez burȝ buskez° bolde,   *city hastens*
    And þe knyȝt° in þe enker° grene   *knight/bright*
    Whider-warde so euer° he wolde.   *wherever*

XXI

Wylde wayez in þe worlde Wowen° now rydez,   *Gawain*
2480 On Gryngolet, þat þe grace hade geten° of his lyue;°   *mercy had obtained/life*
Ofte he herbered° in house, and ofte al þeroute,°   *lodged/completely outdoors*
And mony a-venture° in vale,° and venquyst° ofte,   *(had) many adventures/dales/won*
                                           victories

Þat I ne tyȝt,° at þis tyme, in tale to remene.°   *intend/recount*
Þe hurt watz hole,° þat he hade hent° in his nek,°   *healed/received/neck*
2485 And þe blykkande° belt he bere þeraboute,°   *shining/wore around (him)*
Abelef° as a bauderyk, bounden° bi his syde,   *across/baldric, fastened*
Loken° vnder his lyfte° arme, þe lace,° with a knot,   *secured/left/belt*
In tokenyng° he watz tane° in tech° of a faute;°   *as a sign/found/guilty/fault*
And þus he commes to þe court, knyȝt al in sounde.°   *safety*
2490 Þer wakned wele° in þat wone,° when wyst° þe grete,°   *arose joy/castle/learned/great (king)*
Þat gode° Gawayn watz commen,° gayn° hit hym° þoȝt;°   *good/come/a good thing/to him/*
                                           seemed

Þe kyng kyssez þe knyȝt, and þe whcnc alce,°   *queen also*
And syþen mony syker° knyȝt, þat soȝt° hym to haylce,°   *afterward many (a) trusty/sought/*
                                           greet

Of his fare° þat hym frayned,° and ferlyly° he telles;   *journey/asked/of the marvels*
2495 Biknowez° alle þe costes of care° þat he hade—   *confesses/hardships*
Þe chaunce° of þe chapel, þe chere° of þe knyȝt,   *adventure/behavior*
Þe luf° of þe ladi, þe lace at þe last.°   *love/finally*
Þe nirt° in þe nek he naked hem schewed,°   *nick/them showed*
Þat he laȝt° for his vnleute° at þe leudes° hondes,   *received/disloyalty/man's*
2500   for blame;
He tened° quen° he schulde° telle,   *was grieved/when/had to*
He groned for gref° and grame;°   *grief/mortification*
Þe blod° in his face con melle,°   *blood/did rush*
When he hit° schulde schewe, for schame.   *it*

XXII

2505 "Lo! lorde," quod° þe leude,° and þe lace hondeled,°   *said/knight/touched*
"Þis is þe bende° of þis blame I bere in° my nek,   *band/on*
Þis is þe laþe° and þe losse, þat I laȝt haue,   *injury*
Of couardise° and couetyse,° þat I haf caȝt þare,°   *for cowardice/covetousness/have*
                                           acquired there

Þis is þe token of vntrawþe,° þat I am tan° inne, *unfaithfulness/taken*
2510 And I mot° nedez° hit were, wyle° I may last;° *must/of necessity/wear, while/live*
For mon° may hyden° his harme, bot vnhap ne° may hit, *man/hide/(spiritual) harm, but loosen (i.e., get rid of) not*

For þer° hit onez° is tachched, twynne° wil hit neuer." *where/once/attached, leave*
Þe kyng comfortez þe knyȝt, and alle þe court als,° *also*
Laȝen° loude þer-at, and luflyly acorden,° *laugh/graciously agree*
2515 Þat lordes and ladis þat longed° to þe Table, *belonged*
Vche burne° of þe broþer-hede° a bauderyk schulde° haue, *each man/brotherhood/should*
A bende, abelef° hym aboute, of a bryȝt° grene, *obliquely/bright*
And þat, for sake of þat segge,° in swete° to were. *knight/following suit*
For þat watz acorded° þe renoun of þe Rounde Table, *granted for*
2520 And he honoured þat hit hade,° euer-more after, *had*
As hit is breued° in þe best boke° of romaunce.° *told/book/romance*
Þus in Arthurus° day þis aunter bitidde,° *Arthur's/adventure befell*
Þe Brutus bokez þer-of beres wyttenesse;° *bears witness*
Syþen° Brutus, þe bolde burne, boȝed hider° fyrst, *since/warrior, came hither*
2525 After þe segge° and þe asaute° watz sesed° at Troye, *siege/assault/ceased*
I-wysse;° *indeed*
Mony° aunterez° here bi-forne,° *many/strange events/before*
Haf fallen° suche er þis:° *happened/before now*
Now þat bere° þe croun of þorne, *(he) that wore*
2530 He° bryng vus° to his blysse!   AMEN. *(may) he/us*

HONY SOYT QUI MAL PENCE

2523. *Brutus bokez:* "books of Brutus" probably refers to any chronicles of Britain.

2531. "Honi soit qui mal y pense" ("Shamed be the one who thinks evil of it") is the motto of the Order of the Garter, founded c. 1350 by Edward III. During a royal dance the garter of a lady (perhaps the countess of Salisbury) snapped off; and, whereas the court stood around snickering, the king stooped, put the garter around his own thigh, and shamed the scoffers with these famous words. It has been supposed that the decision in the present poem of the knights of the court to wear baldrics over their shoulders is meant to commemorate or represent an order of knighthood—that in fact, the poem was written for a celebration of the Order of the Garter. But the Garter is blue and is worn around the thigh. A later ballad, *The Green Knight*, treats a white lace, perhaps the origin of the insigne of the Order of the Bath.

The phrase "Honi soit qui . . ." is however, found in French literature long before the time of Edward II. Since it is here in the same scribal hand as the rest of Cotton Nero A x, it could possibly be an editorial (or authorial?) comment on the whole of the poem, in the manner of minstrel endings as an address (see, e.g., *Havelok the Dane* and *Sir Launfal*), or, specifically, on Gawain's own plight and shame. In either case it would be very apropos, and couched in elegant language compatible with the theme and style of the poem.

THE BRETON LAI

The concise Anglo-Norman poetic romances composed by Marie de France in the twelfth century were called Breton lais, to designate the source of their inspiration. In contrast to the usual chivalric poems, the lais could be recited at one sitting, but they treat the same themes of courtly love, adventure, and supernatural exploits as do the longer works. Many contain remnants of Celtic and Arthurian folk motifs. In the fourteenth century the lais of Marie were translated and imitated in English, and the genre became traditional (cf. Chaucer's *Franklin's Tale*).

A Breton lai can be identified by its setting in Brittany, or by the author's remark that the story originated in Brittany. Often, too, there is a plain statement at the beginning: "This is a Breton lai." In later times this identification proved a selling point for the poem even though it no longer had any factual basis. The lai became a literary genre which profited from the fame of the old Breton poets and the spell of bygone days. Matthew Arnold's phrase "Celtic magic" fittingly describes the lais of Marie de France.

REFERENCES

Mason, Eugene, trans. *The Lays of Marie de France and Other French Legends*. London, 1954.
Rickert, Edith, trans. *Marie de France: Seven of Her Lais*. New York, 1901.
Rumble, Thomas, ed. *The Breton Lays in Middle English*. Detroit, 1965.
Sands, Donald, ed. *Middle English Verse Romances*. New York, 1966.

The Breton lai is treated in the General Introduction of this volume, pp. 5–6.

THE LAY OF THE HORN

Robert Biket

DATE: c. 1150. ✦ MANUSCRIPT: Bodleian Library, Oxford, Digby 86. The dialect shows that the writer was composing in Anglo-Norman. ✦ EDITIONS: F. Wulff, ed., *Robert Biket, "Le Lai du Cor"* (Lund, 1888); H. Dörner, ed., *Robert Biket, "Le Lai du Cor"* (Strasbourg, 1907). See also the article by Ernest Hoepffner, "The Breton Lais," in *Arthurian Literature in the Middle Ages,* ed. R. S. Loomis (Oxford, 1959). The translation used here is by Isabel Butler, *Tales from the Old French* (Boston, 1910). A highly detailed and lengthy account of all the stories relating to the horn-mantle Chastity Test can be found in F. J. Child, *English and Scottish Popular Ballads,* introduction to *The Boy and the Mantle* (Child 29).

Robert Biket's *Lai du Cor* (*Lay of the Horn*) is a Breton lai only through its reference to Brittany in the introduction, but as such it is the earliest of its type. Written in six-syllable instead of the normal eight-syllable verses, it lacks some of the romantic gentility of the lais of Marie de France; but there is enough of the courtly tradition in its description of Caradoc and his wife to counter its being defined as a fabliau, which has been suggested in the past. In fact, it is the traditional courtly-heroic matter of Caradoc and Arthur's court and the example of the ever-recurrent Chastity Test which puts this lai in the romance genre. It is important also because of its position in the evolutionary flow of oral transmission of folk themes. The ballad *The Boy and the Mantle* (this volume, p. 497) has the same motifs in a slightly different version, and the courtly lyric *Annot and Johon* (this volume, p. 642) refers to the feats of Caradoc and the fidelity of his wife Tegau. Although Caradoc is a Welsh hero, Biket, the otherwise unknown author of the lai, probably derived his material not from Welsh but rather from Breton or French sources. At any rate, whenever the Chastity Test motif, whatever its form (a horn or a mantle) appears in this group of stories, it always has the same hero, Caradoc, and the same setting, Arthur's hall. An interesting chain of folk motifs can here be traced through lai, lyric, and ballad.

Once upon a time, King Arthur held a mighty feast at Carlion.[1] Our tale saith that the king hath sent through all his realm; and from Esparlot in Bretagne[2] into Alemaigne,[3] from the city of Boillande[4] down even into Ireland, the king, for fellowship, hath summoned his barons, that they

---

1. Caerleon-upon-Usk in Monmouthshire, the traditional site of Camelot.
2. St. Malo in Brittany?
3. Germany.
4. Boulogne sur Mer.

be at Carlion at Ascension tide. On this day all came, both high and low; twenty thousand knights sat at the board, and thereto twenty thousand damoiselles, maidens and dames. It was of great mark that each man had his mate, for he who had no wife yet sat with a woman, whether sister or friend: and herein lay great courtesy. But before they may eat[5] one and all shall be sore angered; for now, lo you, a youth, fair and pleasing and mounted upon a swift horse, who cometh riding into the palace.

In his hand he held a horn banded about four times with gold. Of ivory was that horn, and wrought with inlay wherein amid the gold were set stones of beryl and sardonyx and rich chalcedony; of elephant's ivory was it made, and its like for size and beauty and strength was never seen. Upon it was a ring inlaid with silver, and it had a hundred little bells of pure gold—a fairy, wise and skilful, wrought them in the time of Constantine,[6] and laid such a spell upon the horn as ye shall now hear: whoever struck it lightly with his finger, the hundred bells rang out so sweetly that neither harp nor viol, nor mirth of maidens, nor siren of the sea were so joyous to hear. Rather would a man travel a league on foot than lose that sound, and whoso hearkeneth thereto straightway forgetteth all things.

So the messenger came into the palace and looked upon that great and valiant company of barons. He was clad in a bliaut,[7] and the horn was hung about his neck, and he took it in his hand and raised it on high, and struck upon it that all the palace resounded. The bells rang out in so sweet accord that all the knights left eating. Not a damsel looked down at her plate; and of the ready varlets[8] who were serving drink, and bore about cups of maplewood and beakers of fine gold filled with mulled wine and hippocrass,[9] with drinks spiced and aromatic, not one of these but stopped where he was, and he who held aught scattered it abroad. Nor was there any seneschal so strong or so skilful but if he carried a plate, let it tremble or fall. He who would cut the bread cut his own hand. All were astounded by the horn and fell into forgetfulness; all ceased from speech to hearken to it; Arthur the great king grew silent, and by reason of the horn both king and barons became so still that no word was spoken.

The messenger goeth straightway to the king, bearing in his hand the ivory horn; well knew he the ten kings[10] by their rich array; and still because of the horn's music all were silent about King Arthur. The comely youth addressed him, greeted him fairly, and laughing, bespoke him: "King Arthur, may God who dwells above save you and all your baronage I see here assembled." And Arthur answered him: "May he give you joy likewise." Saith the messenger: "Lord, now give heed to me for a little space. The king of Moraine,[11] the brave and courteous, sendeth you this horn from out his treasure, on such a covenant—hearken to his desire herein—that you give neither love nor hate therefor." "Friend," then saith the king, "courteous is thy lord, and I will take the horn with its four bands of gold, but will return him neither love nor hate therefor." So King Arthur took the horn which the varlet

---

5. As in many Arthurian stories, the adventure takes place at mealtime (cf. *Sir Gawain and the Green Knight*); and often, especially the five times a year when Arthur holds a full court, the assembled lords cannot eat until an adventure has occurred. The wait is never longer than the introductory paragraph, however.

6. Constantine II, according to Geoffrey of Monmouth a brother of the king of Brittany, invaded Britain with two thousand men, was chosen king, and crowned at Silchester. He had three sons, Constans, Aurelius Ambrosius (often confused with Arthur), and Uther Pendragon, father of Arthur (cf.

Layamon's *Brut*, this volume, pp. 56–62). He was murdered by a Pict.

7. A rich garment.

8. Attendants.

9. Hippocras was a wine mixed with many spices.

10. See below, p. 338.

11. Arthur made Urian king of Moray (Moraine) after fighting a battle there in which the Picts and Scots were slaughtered. The horn is sent by his sorcerer son, King Mangoun of Moraine.

proffered him; and he let fill with wine his cup of pure gold, and then bespoke the youth: "Take this beaker, sit you down before me, and eat and drink; and when we have eaten I will make you a knight, and on the morrow I will give you a hundred *livres*[12] of pure gold." But laughing the youth maketh answer: "It is not meet that the squire sit at table with the knight, rather will I go to the inn and repose me; and then when I am clothed and equipped and adorned I will come again to you, and claim my promise." Thereupon the messenger goeth his way; and forthright he issueth out of the city, for he feareth lest he be followed.

The king was in his palace, and his barons were gathered about him: never before was he in so deep a study. He still held the horn by its ring, never had he seen one so fair; and he showeth it to Gawain and Iwain and Giflet;[13] the eighty brethren looked at it, and so likewise did all the barons there gathered. Again the king took the horn, and on it he saw letters in the gold, enameled with silver, and saith to his chamberlain: "Take this horn, and show it to my chaplain, that he may read this writing, for I would know what it saith." The chamberlain taketh it, and gave it to the chaplain who read the writing. When he saw it he laughed, and saith to the king: "Sir, give heed, and anon I will tell you privately such a marvel that its like was never heard in England or any other realm; but here now it may not be spoken." None the less the king will not so suffer it, rather he swore and declared that the chaplain should speak out before them all, and that his barons should hear it. "Nor shall a thing so desired be kept from the dames and demoiselles and gentle maidens here assembled from many a far land," so saith the king.

One and all rejoiced when they heard from the king that they should know what the writing said; but many a one made merry who thereafter repented him, many a one was glad who thereafter was sorry. Now the chaplain, who was neither fool nor churl, saith: "If I had been heeded what is here written would not be read out in this place; but since it is your will, hear it now openly: 'Thus saith to you Mangon of Moraine, the Fair: this horn was wrought by an evil fay and a spiteful, who laid such a spell upon it that no man, howsoever wise and valiant, shall drink therefrom if he be either jealous or deceived, or if he hath a wife who has ever in folly turned her thoughts towards any man save him only; never will the horn suffer such a one to drink from it, rather will it spill out upon him what it may contain; howsoever valiant he be, and howsoever high, yet will it bespatter him and his garments, though they be worth a thousand marks. For whoso would drink from this horn must have a wife who has never thought, whether from disloyalty, or love of power, or desire of fortune, that she would fain have another, better than her lord; if his wife be wholly true, then only may he drink from it.' But I do not believe that any knight from here to Montpelier[14] who hath taken to him a wife will ever drink any whit therefrom, if it so be that the writing speaketh truth."

God! then was many a happy dame made sorrowful. Not one was there so true but she bowed her head; even the queen sat with bent brow, and so did all the barons around and about who had wives that they doubted. The maidens talked and jested among themselves, and looked at their lovers, and smiled courteously, saying: "Now will we see the jealous brought to the test; now will we learn who is shamed and deceived."

---

12. Pounds of sterling gold (0.995 pure).

13. Gawain, Iwain (Ywain), and Giflet were all knights of the Round Table. In the Vulgate *Mort Artu*, it is Giflet who takes Arthur's sword Excalibur when the king is dying and at first refuses to cast it into the lake; in Malory, Sir Bedevere takes his place in the episode.

14. Montpellier in southern France on the Mediterranean coast was famous in the Middle Ages for its university and medical school.

Arthur was in great wrath, but made semblance of gladness, and he calleth to Kay:[15] "Now fill for me this rich horn, for I would make assay, and know if I may drink therefrom." And Kay the seneschal straightway filled it with a spiced wine, and offered it to the emperor. King Arthur took it and set his lips to it, for he thought to drink, but the wine poured out upon him, down even to his feet.[16] Then was the king in sore wrath. "This is the worst," crieth he, and he seized a knife, and would have struck the queen in the heart below the breast, had not Gawain and Iwain and Cadain[17] wrung it from him; they three and Giflet between them took the knife from his hand, and bitterly blamed him. "Lord," then saith Iwain, "be not so churlish, for there is no woman born who, if she be brought to the test, hath not sometime thought folly. No marvel is it that the horn spilled its wine. All here that have wives shall try it, to know if they can drink from it— thereafter may ye blame the queen of the fair face. Ye are of great valiance, and my lady is true; none ever spoke blame of her." "Iwain," saith the queen, "now may my lord let kindle a fire of thorns, and cast me into it, and if one hair of my head burneth, or any of my garments, then may he let me be dragged to death by horses.[18] No man have I loved, and none will I ever love, save my lord only. This horn is too veracious, it has attacked me for a small cause. In years past I gave a ring to

a damoiseau,[19] a young boy who had slain a giant, a hateful felon who here in the court accused Gawain of sore treason. The boy, Gawain's cousin germain,[20] gave him the lie, and did battle with him, and cut off his head with his sword: and as soon as the giant was slain the boy asked leave of us.[21] I granted him my favour, and gave him a ring, for I hoped to retain him to strengthen the court, but even had he remained here, he had never been loved by me. Certes,"[22] saith the queen, "since I was a maid and was given to thee—blessed was that hour—no other evil have I done on any day of my life. On all the earth is no man so mighty—no, not though he were king of Rome—that I would love him, even for all the gold of Pavia, no, nor any count or amiral.[23] Great shame hath he done me who sent this horn; never did he love lady. And until I be revenged, I shall never know gladness."

Then said Arthur, "Speak no more of this. Were any mighty neighbor, or cousin or kinsman, to make war upon Mangon, never more would my heart love him; for I made the king a covenant before all my folk, and by all that is true, that I would hate him no hate for his gift. It is not meet to gainsay my word—that were great villainy; I like not the king who swiftly belies himself." "Lord," saith the queen, "blessed was I when as a maiden I was given to you. When a lady of high parentry who hath a good lord seeketh another

---

15. In all the legends Kay is Arthur's Seneschal (a steward in a princely household) and general overseer of his domestic establishment.

16. It may be that Biket knew the romance *Lancelot* by Chrétien de Troyes, wherein the adulterous love between Guinevere and Lancelot is first mentioned, since the authors were contemporaries.

17. See n. 26.

18. Guinevere asks to be judged by trial through ordeal, in the Middle Ages a common method of testing the guilt or innocence of the accused. For example, if the accused dipped a hand into boiling water without resulting redness or pain, or if he sank when bound and tossed into water over his head, he was considered to be innocent. Anything which went against the laws of nature was considered a miraculous intervention of God. Depending on the ordeal, it seems, the outcome could be predicted: in some cases the accused would always be found

guilty; in others he would always be found innocent but dead or severely hurt. God's intervention is seen in the romance *Athelston*, where the accused earl of Stane and his family prove their innocence by walking over red-hot stones (cf. the legend of Queen Emma and the plowshares).

19. Page.

20. First cousin.

21. In the ballad *The Boy and the Mantle* (see this volume, p. 503), the boy (Caradoc) takes out his knife and cuts off a boar's head. The story of the mantle, the horn, and the courageous boy who ventures a task avoided by all the knights of the court is a linking of motifs which evolved from the fabliau to the ballad.

22. Certainly.

23. A Saracen ruler of great power and wealth, from Arabic *amir al*, "commander of"(cf. Mod. Eng. *Admiral*).

friend, she doth great wrong. He who seeketh a better wine than that of the grape, or better bread than that of the wheat, such a one should be hung and his ashes given to the winds. I have the best one of the three who were ever king under God, why then should I go seeking a fairer or a braver? I promise you, lord, that wrongfully are you angry with me. Never should a noble knight be offered this horn to the shaming of his lady." But the king saith, "Let them do it. All shall try it, kings and counts and dukes; I alone will not have shame herein."

So Arthur giveth it to the king of Sinadone,[24] but so soon as he took it, the wine spilled out upon him; then King Nuz[25] taketh it, and it spilled out upon him; and Angus of Scotland would fain drink from it by force, but the wine all poured out upon him, at which he was sore angered. The king of Cornwall thought certes to drink from it, but it splashed all over him that he was in great wrath; and the horn splashed over King Gahor, and spilled great plenty upon King Glovien, and it spilled out upon King Cadain as soon as he took it in his hands. Then King Lot taketh it, and looketh on himself as a fool; and it splashed the beard of Caraton;[26] and of the two kings of Ireland there was not one it did not bespatter; and it splashed all the thirty counts, who had great shame thereof; nor of all the barons present who tried the horn was there one who might take a drop therefrom. It poured out over each king, and each was in great wrath; they passed it on and were in great sorrow by reason of it; and they all said, may the horn, and he who brought it and he who sent it, be given over to the devils, for whoso believeth this horn shameth his wife.

Now when King Arthur saw it spilled out upon all, he forgot his sorrow and wrath, and began to laugh and made great joy. "Lords," he saith to his barons, "now hear me. I am not the only one bemocked. He who sent me this horn gave me a good gift: by the faith I owe all those here gathered, I will never part with it for all the gold of Pavia; no man shall have it save he who shall drink from it." The queen grew bright red because of the marvel whereof she dared not speak; fairer than the rose was she. The king looked on her and found her most fair; he drew her to him and three times he kissed her: "Gladly, dame, I forget my ill will." "Lord, gramercy,"[27] saith she.

Then all, high and low, tried the ivory horn. A knight took it and laughed across at his wife; he was the most joyous of all the court, and the most courteous; none boasted less, yet when he was armed none was more feared; for in Arthur's court there was no better warrior, none mightier of his hands, save only my lord Gawain. Fair was his hair, his beard russet, his eyes gray-blue and laughing, his body comely, his feet straight and well arched; Caradoc[28] was his name, a well skilled knight, and of full good renown. His wife

---

24. The king of the Snowdon section of North Wales is called by his Anglo-Norman title. Sinadone is also a ruined castle or ghost city which Breton storytellers derived from the deserted Roman fort of Segontium near Caernarvon in Wales. The enchanted city plays a part in the romance of *Guinglain* (Gawain's son), also called *Le Bel Inconnu*.

25. In the Welsh *Mabinogion*, Nudd is father of Gwyn, both mythological characters. In a 16th-century story Nudd is called king of Annwfn and the fairies.

26. Gahor, Glovien, Cadain, Caraton, and Galahal (see below), according to Ernest Hoepffner's essay in Loomis, *Arthurian Literature*, cannot be recognized in the Welsh; their origin is uncertain. King Loth of Lodonesia (Orkney) and Norway is Arthur's brother-in-law, husband of Anna, Arthur's sister, and father of Gawain and Modred, among others (cf. above, p. 77, ll. 728–29*n*).

27. Thank you.

28. This is the great hero called Karadues Briebraz ("Short-Arm") by Chrétien de Troyes, Karadoc Brech Bras ("Arm-strong") by the Bretons, and Caradawc Vreichvras by the Welsh. Caradoc is the central figure in many romances and legends, specifically in Welsh folklore. In later tales and ballads the mantle, which fits only women who are chaste and loyal to their husbands, is substituted for the horn, and such a garment is assigned to Tegau Eurvron, the wife of Caradawc in Welsh texts. Both characters appear in the lyric *Annot and Johon*: "Trewe ase Tegeu in tour" and "Cud ase Cradoc in court carf þe brede" (here the reference is to the boy and his knife). In the Welsh Triads Caradoc's wife is one of the three chaste and three fair ladies at Arthur's court. In the Alliterative *Morte Arthure*, Sir Craddock, dressed as a pilgrim, meets Arthur on the Continent with news of Modred's treason (cf. this volume, pp. 109–110).

sat at his left; she was sister to King Galahal and was born at Cirencester.[29] Full true was she, and thereto comely and gracious, featly fashioned and like unto a fay; her hair was long and golden; fairer woman was there none, save the queen only. She looked upon Caradoc, nor changed colour, but bespoke him, saying: "Fair friend, fear not to drink from the horn at this high feast; lift up your head and do me honour. I would not take any man for lord however mighty; no, though he were amiral, I would not have him for my husband and leave you, friend; rather would I become a nun and wear the veil. For every woman should be as the turtle dove, who after she has had one mate will never take another: thus should a lady do if she be of good lineage."

Full glad was Caradoc, and he sprang to his feet; fair he was, a well skilled and a courteous knight. When they had filled the horn it held a *lot*[30] and a half; full to the brim it was of red wine; "Wassail," he saith to the king. He was tall and strong, and he set the horn to his lips, and I tell you truly that he tasted the wine and drank it all down. Right glad was he thereof, but all the table started in wonder. Straightway he goeth

before Arthur, and as he goeth he saith to him, nor did he speak low-voiced: "Lord, I have emptied the horn, be ye certain thereof." "Caradoc," saith the king, "brave and courteous are you; of a sooth[31] ye have drunk it, as was seen of more than a hundred. Keep you Cirencester; two years is it since I gave it in charge to you, and never will I take it from you, I give it to you for life and to your children; and for your wife—who is of great worth—I will give you this horn which is prized at a hundred pounds of gold." "Lord, I give you good thanks," Caradoc made answer, and sat down again at the board beside his wife of the fair face. Now when they had eaten, each man took leave and went back to his own domain whence he had come, taking with him the woman he best loved.

Lords, this lay was first sung by Caradoc, who wrought its adventure. And whoso goeth to a high feast at Cirencester, will, of a sooth, see there the horn: so say I, Robert Biquet,[32] who have learned much concerning the matter from an abbot, and do now, by his bidding, tell the tale—how in this wise the horn was tested at Carlion.[33]

---

29. Near the Cotswold Hills of Gloucestershire.

30. French, "portion."

31. Truly.

32. *Biquet* seems to be the Anglo-Norman (French) form of the author's name, *Biket* (or *Bicket*) the anglicized form; most authorities use the latter.

33. The reference to an authority, preferably a clerical one,

was an important aspect of medieval storytelling. Creative genius was suspect; plagiarism from impeccable sources (as Fielding points out in the preface to Book XII of *Tom Jones*) was considered a virtue. Also, like Caxton's reference (in the preface to Malory's *Morte Darthur*) to Gawain's skull in Dover Castle, Biket's mention of the horn to be seen at Cirencester is "proof" that the story related is true. And there is no reason to doubt that a horn, or a skull, was actually seen.

LANVAL

Marie de France

DATE: C. 1175. ⚔ MANUSCRIPTS: Bibliothéque Nationale (Paris) and elsewhere. The language is Anglo-Norman. ⚔ EDITIONS: Jean Rychner has the four main manuscripts of *Lanval* in a diplomatic edition, *Marie de France, "Le Lai de Lanval"* (Geneva, Paris, 1958). All the lais have been edited by Ernest Hoepffner, *Les Lais de Marie de France* (Paris, 1955), and K. Warnke, *Die Lais der Marie de France*, 3d ed. (Halle, 1925). The translation used here is by Eugene Mason, *Lays of Marie de France* (London, 1911; rpt. ed., 1954).

As noted in the General Introduction, the author of the twelve Breton lais called herself Marie of France (i.e., the section generally known today as Île-de-France). She wrote in England and dedicated her work to a king usually identified as Henry II. Since her work shows the influence of Wace, the lais must have been composed between 1155 and the date of Henry's death, 1189. Perhaps she was Henry's half sister, Marie, abbess of Shaftesbury, who died in 1216. Certainly the poet was well read and moved in the court circles frequented by Breton singers. Artistically *Lanval*, one of her few Arthurian stories, is among the finest of her productions. There is much of "Celtic magic" in the development of suspense, the richness of imagery, and the ardent power of language. It may be that Marie used the plot of the anonymous lai of *Graelent* as the basis of *Lanval* and added the Arthurian material from Wace's *Brut*. Thomas of Chestre's *Sir Launfal* seems to have been influenced by *Graelent* as much as by a translation of *Lanval*. It is of interest to compare the versions of Chestre and Marie. Both authors use the same motifs; but one writes a chivalric romance, and the other creates a fairy legend suffused with the twilight of otherworldliness.

I will tell you the story of another Lay. It relates the adventures of a rich and mighty baron, and the Breton[1] calls it, the Lay of Sir Lanval.

King Arthur—that fearless knight and courteous lord—removed to Wales, and lodged at Caerleon-on-Usk,[2] since the Picts and Scots did much mischief in the land. For it was the wont of the wild people of the north to enter in the realm of Logres,[3] and burn and damage at their will. At the time of Pentecost, the King cried a great

---

1. *Lanval* is the title used in the Anglo-Norman of Marie de France. The mention of a Breton source marks the poem as a Breton lai.
2. Caerleon-upon-Usk was the site of Camelot, situated in Gloucestershire.

3. Logres is usually identified with Arthur's realm in England. Geoffrey of Monmouth mentions that Loegria was assigned to King Locrinus of England, the oldest son of Brutus (cf. above, p. 125, n. 12).

feast.[4] Thereat he gave many rich gifts to his counts and barons,[5] and to the Knights of the Round Table. Never were such worship and bounty shown before at any feast, for Arthur bestowed honours and lands on all his servants—save only on one. This lord, who was forgotten and misliked of the King, was named Lanval. He was beloved by many of the Court, because of his beauty and prowess, for he was a worthy knight, open of heart and heavy of hand. These lords, to whom their comrade was dear, felt little joy to see so stout a knight misprized. Sir Lanval was son to a King of high descent, though his heritage was in a distant land. He was of the King's household, but since Arthur gave him naught, and he was of too proud a mind to pray for his due, he had spent all that he had. Right heavy was Sir Lanval, when he considered these things, for he knew himself taken in the toils. Gentles,[6] marvel not overmuch hereat. Ever must the pilgrim go heavily in a strange land, where there is none to counsel and direct him in the path.

Now, on a day, Sir Lanval got him on his horse, that he might take his pleasure for a little. He came forth from the city, alone, attended by neither servant nor squire. He went his way through a green mead, till he stood by a river of clear running water. Sir Lanval would have crossed this stream, without thought of pass or ford, but he might not do so, for reason that his horse was all fearful and trembling. Seeing that he was hindered in this fashion, Lanval unbitted his steed, and let him pasture in that fair meadow, where they had come. Then he folded his cloak to serve him as a pillow, and lay upon the ground. Lanval lay in great misease, because of his heavy thoughts, and the discomfort of his bed. He turned from side to side, and might not sleep. Now as the knight looked towards the river he saw two damsels coming towards him; fairer maidens Lanval had never seen. These two maidens were richly dressed in kirtles closely laced and shapen to their persons and wore mantles of a goodly purple hue. Sweet and dainty were the damsels, alike in raiment and in face. The elder of these ladies carried in her hands a basin of pure gold, cunningly wrought by some crafty smith—very fair and precious was the cup; and the younger bore a towel of soft white linen.[7] These maidens turned neither to the right hand nor to the left, but went directly to the place where Lanval lay. When Lanval saw that their business was with him, he stood upon his feet, like a discreet and courteous gentleman. After they had greeted the knight, one of the maidens delivered the message with which she was charged.

"Sir Lanval, my demoiselle, as gracious as she is fair, prays that you will follow us, her messengers, as she has a certain word to speak with you. We will lead you swiftly to her pavilion, for our lady is very near at hand. If you but lift your eyes you may see where her tent is spread."

Right glad was the knight to do the bidding of the maidens. He gave no heed to his horse, but left him at his provand[8] in the meadow. All his desire was to go with the damsels, to that pavilion of silk and divers colours, pitched in so fair a place.

---

4. Arthur held a full court and wore his crown five times each year, at Easter, Ascension Day, Pentecost, All Saints' Day, and Christmas. Normally these were the days at which an adventure had to occur before the feast (cf. Biket's *Lay of the Horn*, *Sir Gawain and the Green Knight*). In the *Roman de Merlin*, it is stated that "King Arthur, after his first dinner at Logres when he brought home his bride, made a vow that while he wore a crown he would never seat himself at table till some adventure had occurred." In Malory, Kay reminds Arthur that this was the custom of the court at Pentecost.

5. Generosity or "largesse" was one of the qualities of a good feudal lord and part of the chivalric code (cf. Chaucer's Knight, who "loved chivalrie,/Trouthe and honour, fredom and curteisie"). But especially at banquets the lord had to dispense gifts. In *Beowulf*, ll. 1719–20, Heremōd is a bad king because he did not distribute gifts to his people as Hrothgar had done: "nallas bēagas geaf/Denum æfter dōme."

6. The minstrel is here addressing his audience, in a fashion similar to the beginning of romances. It seems certain that the Breton lais were sung in court.

7. The cup and towel may have been part of a ritual cleansing, or a preparation for the ensuing feast with the fairy lady.

8. Pasture.

Certainly neither Semiramis[9] in the days of her most wanton power, nor Octavian,[10] the Emperor of all the West, had so gracious a covering from sun and rain. Above the tent was set an eagle of gold, so rich and precious, that none might count the cost. The cords and fringes thereof were of silken thread, and the lances which bore aloft the pavilion were of refined gold. No King on earth might have so sweet a shelter, not though he gave in fee the value of his realm. Within this pavilion Lanval came upon the Maiden. Whiter she was than any altar lily, and more sweetly flushed than the new born rose in time of summer heat. She lay upon a bed with napery and coverlet of richer worth than could be furnished by a castle's spoil. Very fresh and slender showed the lady in her vesture of spotless linen. About her person she had drawn a mantle of ermine, edged with purple dye from the vats of Alexandria. By reason of the heat her raiment was unfastened for a little, and her throat and the rondure of her bosom showed whiter and more untouched than hawthorn in May. The knight came before the bed, and stood gazing on so sweet a sight. The Maiden beckoned him to draw near, and when he had seated himself at the foot of her couch, spoke her mind.

"Lanval," she said, "fair friend, it is for you that I have come from my own far land. I bring you my love. If you are prudent and discreet, as you are goodly to the view, there is no emperor nor count, nor king, whose day shall be so filled with riches and with mirth as yours."

When Lanval heard these words he rejoiced greatly, for his heart was litten by another's torch.

"Fair lady," he answered, "since it pleases you to be so gracious, and to dower so graceless a knight with your love, there is naught that you may bid me do—right or wrong, evil or good— that I will not do to the utmost of my power. I will observe your commandment, and serve in your quarrels. For you I renounce my father and my father's house. This only I pray, that I may dwell with you in your lodging, and that you will never send me from your side."

When the Maiden heard the words of him whom so fondly she desired to love, she was altogether moved, and granted him forthwith her heart and her tenderness. To her bounty she added another gift besides. Never might Lanval be desirous of aught, but he would have according to his wish. He might waste and spend at will and pleasure, but in his purse[11] ever there was to spare. No more was Lanval sad. Right merry was the pilgrim, since one had set him on the way, with such a gift, that the more pennies he bestowed, the more silver and gold were in his pouch.

But the Maiden had yet a word to say.

"Friend," she said, "hearken to my counsel. I lay this charge upon you, and pray you urgently, that you tell not to any man the secret of our love.[12] If you show this matter, you will lose your friend, for ever and a day. Never again may you see my face. Never again will you have seisin[13] of that body, which is now so tender in your eyes."

Lanval plighted faith, that right strictly he would observe this commandment. So the Maiden granted him her kiss and her embrace, and very sweetly in that fair lodging passed the day till evensong was come.

Right loath was Lanval to depart from the

---

9. A mythical queen of Assyria who married Ninus, the builder of Nineveh, and succeeded him as ruler. She founded many cities of fabulous wealth and may have originated one of the Seven Wonders of the World, the Hanging Gardens of Babylon, though this has been disputed.

10. Gaius Julius Caesar Octavianus Augustus, first Roman emperor (27 B.C.–A.D. 14).

11. This is the purse of Fortunatus which is never empty (cf. below, p. 375, ll. 319–24n).

12. In Fairy Love stories, the secrecy of the love affair is one of the *geis*, taboos, or requirements exacted of the lover. These *geis*, as well as the fairy gifts, are standard in Celtic legend. In countless folktales, discovery of the secret leads to misfortune and to abandonment by the mistress.

13. I.e., "possession," a feudal term usually referring to property, specifically land.

pavilion at the vesper hour, and gladly would he have stayed, had he been able, and his lady wished.

"Fair friend," said she, "rise up, for no longer may you tarry. The hour is come that we must part. But one thing I have to say before you go. When you would speak with me I shall hasten to come before your wish. Well I deem that you will only call your friend where she may be found without reproach or shame of men. You may see me at your pleasure; my voice shall speak softly in your ear at will; but I must never be known of your comrades, nor must they ever learn my speech."

Right joyous was Lanval to hear this thing. He sealed the covenant with a kiss, and stood upon his feet. Then there entered the two maidens who had led him to the pavilion, bringing with them rich raiment, fitting for a knight's apparel. When Lanval had clothed himself therewith, there seemed no goodlier varlet[14] under heaven, for certainly he was fair and true. After these maidens had refreshed him with clear water, and dried his hands upon the napkin, Lanval went to meat. His friend sat at table with him, and small will had he to refuse her courtesy. Very serviceably the damsels bore the meats, and Lanval and the Maiden ate and drank with mirth and content. But one dish was more to the knight's relish than any other. Sweeter than the dainties within his mouth, was the lady's kiss upon his lips.

When supper was ended, Lanval rose from table, for his horse stood waiting without the pavilion. The destrier[15] was newly saddled and bridled, and showed proudly in his rich gay trappings. So Lanval kissed, and bade farewell, and went his way. He rode back towards the city at a slow pace. Often he checked his steed, and looked behind him, for he was filled with amazement, and all bemused concerning this adventure. In his heart he doubted that it was but a dream.

He was altogether astonished, and knew not what to do. He feared that pavilion and Maiden alike were from the realm of faery.

Lanval returned to his lodging, and was greeted by servitors, clad no longer in ragged raiment. He fared richly, lay softly, and spent largely, but never knew how his purse was filled. There was no lord who had need of a lodging in the town, but Lanval brought him to his hall, for refreshment and delight. Lanval bestowed rich gifts. Lanval redeemed the poor captive. Lanval clothed in scarlet the minstrel. Lanval gave honour where honour was due. Stranger and friend alike he comforted at need. So, whether by night or by day, Lanval lived greatly at his ease. His lady, she came at will and pleasure, and, for the rest, all was added unto him.

Now it chanced, the same year, about the feast of St. John,[16] a company of knights came, for their solace, to an orchard, beneath that tower where dwelt the Queen. Together with these lords went Gawain and his cousin, Yvain the fair.[17] Then said Gawain, that goodly knight, beloved and dear to all:

"Lords, we do wrong to disport ourselves in this pleasaunce without our comrade Lanval. It is not well to slight a prince as brave as he is courteous, and of a lineage prouder than our own."

Then certain of the lords returned to the city, and finding Lanval within his hostel, entreated him to take his pastime with them in that fair meadow. The Queen looked out from a window in her tower, she and three ladies of her fellowship. They saw the lords at their pleasure, and Lanval also, whom well they knew. So the Queen chose of her Court thirty damsels—the sweetest of face and most dainty of fashion—and commanded that they should descend with her to take their delight in the garden. When the knights beheld this gay company of ladies come down the steps

---

14. A young man of gentility.

15. War-horse.

16. June 24, the birthday of Saint John the Baptist.

17. Gawain, nephew of Arthur, and Yvain (Ywain) were both Knights of the Round Table.

of the perron,[18] they rejoiced beyond measure. They hastened before to lead them by the hand, and said such words in their ear as were seemly and pleasant to be spoken. Amongst these merry and courteous lords hasted not Sir Lanval. He drew apart from the throng, for with him time went heavily, till he might have clasp and greeting of his friend. The ladies of the Queen's fellowship seemed but kitchen wenches to his sight, in comparison with the loveliness of the Maiden. When the Queen marked Lanval go aside, she went his way, and seating herself upon the herb,[19] called the knight before her. Then she opened out her heart.

"Lanval, I have honoured you for long as a worthy knight, and have praised and cherished you very dearly. You may receive a queen's whole love, if such be your care. Be content: he to whom my heart is given, has small reason to complain him of the alms."[20]

"Lady," answered the knight, "grant me leave to go, for this grace is not for me. I am the King's man, and dare not break my troth. Not for the highest lady in the world, not even for her love, will I set this reproach upon my lord."

When the Queen heard this, she was full of wrath, and spoke many hot and bitter words.

"Lanval," she cried, "well I know that you think little of woman and her love. There are sins more black that a man may have upon his soul.[21] Traitor you are, and false. Right evil counsel gave they to my lord, who prayed him to suffer you about his person. You remain only for his harm and loss."

Lanval was very dolent[22] to hear this thing. He was not slow to take up the Queen's glove,[23] and

in his haste spake words that he repented long, and with tears.

" Lady," said he, "I am not of that guild of which you speak. Neither am I a despiser of woman, since I love, and am loved of, one who would bear the prize from all the ladies in the land. Dame, know now and be persuaded, that she, whom I serve, is so rich in state, that the very meanest of her maidens excels you, Lady Queen, as much in clerkly skill and goodness, as in sweetness of body and face, and in every virtue."

The Queen rose straightway to her feet, and fled to her chamber, weeping. Right wrathful and heavy was she, because of the words that had besmirched her. She lay sick upon her bed, from which, she said, she would never rise, till the King had done her justice, and righted this bitter wrong. Now the King that day had taken his pleasure within the woods. He returned from the chase towards evening, and sought the chamber of the Queen. When the lady saw him, she sprang from her bed, and kneeling at his feet, pleaded for grace and pity. Lanval—she said—had shamed her, since he required her love. When she had put him by, very foully had he reviled her, boasting that his love was already set on a lady, so proud and noble, that her meanest wench went more richly, and smiled more sweetly, than the Queen. Thereat the King waxed marvellously wrathful, and swore a great oath that he would set Lanval within a fire, or hang him from a tree, if he could not deny this thing, before his peers.

Arthur came forth from the Queen's chamber, and called to him three of his lords. These he sent to seek the knight who so evilly had entreated

---

18. Usually the stone staircase leading from an upper terrace to the garden.

19. Meadow.

20. This is the motif of the Wooing Lady, better known as Potiphar's Wife, K 2111 in Stith Thompson's *Motif-Index* (from the wife of Potiphar, who wooed Joseph and when he refused her accused him to her husband of attempted rape [Genesis 39: 7–20]).

21. The queen accuses Lanval of misogyny, if not more. This

was a serious matter in a courtly, chivalric society based on the *code d'amour*, but evidently especially repugnant to a woman of her passionate temperament. The accusation is poignant enough for Lanval to break his vow of silence.

22. Sorrowful.

23. To take up her challenge, to defend himself forcefully. The challenger threw down his glove or gauntlet; if the challenge was accepted, the glove was taken up. In this case the sense is figurative.

the Queen. Lanval, for his part, had returned to his lodging, in a sad and sorrowful case. He saw very clearly that he had lost his friend, since he had declared their love to men. Lanval sat within his chamber, sick and heavy of thought. Often he called upon his friend, but the lady would not hear his voice. He bewailed his evil lot, with tears; for grief he came nigh to swoon; a hundred times he implored the Maiden that she would deign to speak with her knight. Then, since the lady yet refrained from speech, Lanval cursed his hot and unruly tongue. Very near he came to ending all this trouble with his knife. Naught he found to do but to wring his hands, and call upon the Maiden, begging her to forgive his trespass, and to talk with him again, as friend to friend.

But little peace is there for him who is harassed by a King. There came presently to Lanval's hostel those three barons from the Court. These bade the knight forthwith to go with them to Arthur's presence, to acquit him of this wrong against the Queen. Lanval went forth, to his own deep sorrow. Had any man slain him on the road, he would have counted him his friend. He stood before the King, downcast and speechless, being dumb by reason of that great grief, of which he showed the picture and image.

Arthur looked upon his captive very evilly.

"Vassal," said he, harshly, "you have done me a bitter wrong. It was a foul deed to seek to shame me in this ugly fashion, and to smirch the honour of the Queen. Is it folly or lightness which leads you to boast of that lady, the least of whose maidens is fairer, and goes more richly, than the Queen?"

Lanval protested that never had he set such shame upon his lord. Word by word he told the tale of how he denied the Queen, within the orchard. But concerning that which he had spoken of the lady, he owned the truth, and his folly. The love of which he bragged was now lost to him, by his own exceeding fault. He cared little for his life, and was content to obey the judgment of the Court.

Right wrathful was the King at Lanval's words.

He conjured his barons to give him such wise counsel herein, that wrong might be done to none. The lords did the King's bidding, whether good came of the matter, or evil. They gathered themselves together, and appointed a certain day that Lanval should abide the judgment of his peers. For his part Lanval must give pledge and surety to his lord, that he would come before this judgment in his own body. If he might not give such surety then he should be held captive till the appointed day. When the lords of the King's household returned to tell him of their counsel, Arthur demanded that Lanval should put such pledge in his hand, as they had said. Lanval was altogether mazed and bewildered at this judgment, for he had neither friend nor kindred in the land. He would have been set in prison, but Gawain came first to offer himself as his surety, and with him, all the knights of his fellowship. These gave into the King's hand as pledge, the fiefs and lands that they held of his Crown. The King having taken pledges from the sureties, Lanval returned to his lodging, and with him certain knights of his company. They blamed him greatly because of his foolish love, and chastened him grievously by reason of the sorrow he made before men. Every day they came to his chamber, to know of his meat and drink, for much they feared that presently he would become mad.

The lords of the household came together on the day appointed for this judgment. The King was on his chair, with the Queen sitting at his side. The sureties brought Lanval within the hall, and rendered him into the hands of his peers. Right sorrowful were they because of his plight. A great company of his fellowship did all that they were able to acquit him of this charge. When all was set out, the King demanded the judgment of the Court, according to the accusation and the answer. The barons went forth in much trouble and thought to consider this matter. Many amongst them grieved for the peril of a good knight in a strange land; others held that it were well for Lanval to suffer, because of the wish and malice of their lord. Whilst they were thus perplexed, the Duke of Cornwall[24] rose in the council, and said,

"Lords, the King pursues Lanval as a traitor, and would slay him with the sword, by reason that he bragged of the beauty of his maiden, and roused the jealousy of the Queen. By the faith that I owe this company, none complains of Lanval, save only the King. For our part we would know the truth of this business,[25] and do justice between the King and his man. We would also show proper reverence to our own liege lord. Now, if it be according to Arthur's will, let us take oath of Lanval, that he seek this lady, who has put such strife between him and the Queen. If her beauty be such as he has told us, the Queen will have no cause for wrath. She must pardon Lanval for his rudeness, since it will be plain that he did not speak out of a malicious heart. Should Lanval fail his word, and not return with the lady, or should her fairness fall beneath his boast, then let him be cast off from our fellowship, and be sent forth from the service of the King."

This counsel seemed good to the lords of the household. They sent certain of his friends to Lanval, to acquaint him with their judgment, bidding him to pray his damsel to the Court, that he might be acquitted of this blame. The knight made answer that in no wise could he do this thing. So the sureties returned before the judges, saying that Lanval hoped neither for refuge nor for succour from the lady, and Arthur urged them to a speedy ending, because of the prompting of the Queen.

The judges were about to give sentence upon Lanval, when they saw two maidens come riding towards the palace, upon two white ambling palfreys.[26] Very sweet and dainty were these maidens, and richly clothed in garments of crimson sendal,[27] closely girt and fashioned to their bodies. All men, old and young, looked willingly upon them, for fair they were to see. Gawain, and three knights of his company, went straight to Lanval, and showed him these maidens, praying him to say which of them was his friend. But he answered never a word. The maidens dismounted from their palfreys, and coming before the daïs where the King was seated, spake him fairly, as they were fair.

"Sire, prepare now a chamber, hung with silken cloths, where it is seemly for my lady to dwell; for she would lodge with you awhile."

This gift the King granted gladly. He called to him two knights of his household, and bade them bestow the maidens in such chambers as were fitting to their degree. The maidens being gone, the King required of his barons to proceed with their judgment, saying that he had sore displeasure at the slowness of the cause.[28]

"Sire," replied the barons, "we rose from Council, because of the damsels who entered in the hall. We will at once resume the sitting, and give our judgment without more delay."

The barons again were gathered together, in much thought and trouble, to consider this matter. There was great strife and dissension amongst them, for they knew not what to do. In the midst of all this noise and tumult, there came two other damsels riding to the hall on two Spanish mules. Very richly arrayed were these damsels in raiment of fine needlework, and their kirtles were

---

24. Cador, one of Arthur's chief and most courageous advisers. In Geoffrey of Monmouth he defeats the Saxon Baldulf at York and pursues his army after the famous battle of Bath (cf. this volume, p. 127); he later distinguishes himself at the battle of Saussy against the legions of the Roman emperor Lucius Hiberius (cf. this volume, pp. 135–36).

25. There is a hint that the barons know of Guinevere's reputation for amorous affairs and vindictiveness. Her unpleasant characteristics may be traced to a Celtic legend of her otherworldly origin, perhaps originally as a kind of succubus. Marie de France, however, never mentions the queen by name.

26. Gentle saddle horses suited for women. The ambling gait (pace), in which the feet on the same side are lifted and put down together, was favored by female riders (cf. Chaucer's Wife of Bath: "Upon an amblere esily she sat").

27. Silk.

28. Arthur either stupidly does not see the relationship between the coming of the damsels and Lanval's cause, as the barons do, or he does not wish to see it. Neither Arthur nor his queen is presented to best advantage in this lai.

covered by fresh fair mantles, embroidered with gold. Great joy had Lanval's comrades when they marked these ladies. They said between themselves that doubtless they came for the succour of the good knight. Gawain, and certain of his company, made haste to Lanval, and said,

"Sir, be not cast down. Two ladies are near at hand, right dainty of dress, and gracious of person. Tell us truly, for the love of God, is one of these your friend?"

But Lanval answered very simply that never before had he seen these damsels with his eyes, nor known and loved them in his heart.

The maidens dismounted from their mules, and stood before Arthur, in the sight of all. Greatly were they praised of many, because of their beauty, and of the colour of their face and hair. Some there were who deemed already that the Queen was overborne.

The elder of the damsels carried herself modestly and well, and sweetly told over the message wherewith she was charged.

"Sire, make ready for us chambers, where we may abide with our lady, for even now she comes to speak with thee."

The King commanded that the ladies should be led to their companions, and bestowed in the same honourable fashion as they. Then he bade the lords of his household to consider their judgment, since he would endure no further respite. The Court already had given too much time to the business, and the Queen was growing wrathful, because of the blame that was hers. Now the judges were about to proclaim their sentence, when, amidst the tumult of the town, there came riding to the palace the flower of all the ladies of the world. She came mounted upon a palfrey, white as snow, which carried her softly, as though she loved her burthen. Beneath the sky was no goodlier steed, nor one more gentle to the hand. The harness of the palfrey was so rich, that no king on earth might hope to buy trappings so precious,

unless he sold or set his realm in pledge. The Maiden herself showed such as I will tell you. Passing slim was the lady, sweet of bodice and slender of girdle. Her throat was whiter than snow on branch, and her eyes were like flowers in the pallor of her face. She had a witching[29] mouth, a dainty nose, and an open brow. Her eyebrows were brown, and her golden hair parted in two soft waves upon her head. She was clad in a shift of spotless linen, and above her snowy kirtle was set a mantle of royal purple, clasped upon her breast. She carried a hooded falcon upon her glove, and a greyhound followed closely after. As the Maiden rode at a slow pace through the streets of the city, there was none, neither great nor small, youth nor sergeant,[30] but ran forth from his house, that he might content his heart with so great beauty. Every man that saw her with his eyes marvelled at a fairness beyond that of any earthly woman. Little he cared for any mortal maiden, after he had seen this sight. The friends of Sir Lanval hastened to the knight, to tell him of his lady's succour, if so it were according to God's will.

"Sir comrade, truly is not this your friend? This lady is neither black nor golden, mean nor tall. She is only the most lovely thing in all the world."

When Lanval heard this, he sighed, for by their words he knew again his friend. He raised his head, and as the blood rushed to his face, speech flowed from his lips.

"By my faith," cried he, "yes, she is indeed my friend. It is a small matter now whether men slay me, or set me free; for I am made whole of my hurt just by looking on her face."

The Maiden entered in the palace—where none so fair had come before—and stood before the King, in the presence of his household. She loosed the clasp of her mantle, so that men might the more easily perceive the grace of her person. The courteous King advanced to meet her, and all the Court got them on their feet, and pained them-

---

29. Bewitching.

30. In Anglo-Norman, a servant or footman.

selves in her service. When the lords had gazed upon her for a space, and praised the sum of her beauty, the lady spake to Arthur in this fashion, for she was anxious to be gone.

"Sire, I have loved one of thy vassals—the knight who stands in bonds, Sir Lanval. He was always misprized in thy Court, and his every action turned to blame. What he said, that thou knowest; for over hasty was his tongue before the Queen. But he never craved her in love, however loud his boasting. I cannot choose that he should come to hurt or harm by me. In the hope of freeing Lanval from his bonds, I have obeyed thy summons. Let now thy barons look boldly upon my face, and deal justly in this quarrel between the Queen and me."

The King commanded that this should be done, and looking upon her eyes, not one of the judges but was persuaded that her favour exceeded that of the Queen.

Since then Lanval had not spoken in malice against his lady, the lords of the household gave him again his sword. When the trial had come thus to an end the Maiden took her leave of the King, and made her ready to depart. Gladly would Arthur have had her lodge with him for a little, and many a lord would have rejoiced in her service, but she might not tarry. Now without the hall stood a great stone of dull marble, where it was the wont of lords, departing from the Court, to climb into the saddle, and Lanval by the stone.[31] The Maiden came forth from the doors of the palace, and mounting on the stone, seated herself on the palfrey, behind her friend. Then they rode across the plain together, and were no more seen.

The Bretons tell that the knight was ravished by his lady to an island, very dim and very fair, known as Avalon. But none has had speech with Lanval and his faery love since then, and for my part I can tell you no more of the matter.[32]

---

31. I.e., mounted by the stone.
32. Cf. the ballad *Thomas Rymer*, or a similar motif in Keats's *La Belle Dame Sans Merci*. Lanval is said to have become a ruler of Avalon (cf. above, p. 91, ll. 1184–85*n*); Thomas of Chestre's romance *Sir Launfal* is somewhat more detailed on this point.

SIR ORFEO

DATE: c. 1325. ✦ MANUSCRIPTS: Auchinleck, Advocates' Library, Edinburgh, c. 1330 (given to the library by Boswell's father, Alexander Boswell, Lord Auchinleck, a Scottish judge); British Library Harleian 3810, 15th century; Bodleian Library, Oxford, Ashmole 61, 15th century. The dialect is Southeast Midland. ✦ EDITIONS: A. J. Bliss, *Sir Orfeo* (Oxford, 1954), which prints three manuscripts; Donald Sands, *Middle English Verse Romances* (New York, 1966); W. H. French and C. B. Hale, *Middle English Metrical Romances* (New York, 1964). J. Burke Severs contributed an article, "The Antecedents of Sir Orfeo," to *Studies in Medieval Literature in Honor of Professor Albert Cross Baugh*, ed. MacEdward Leach (Philadelphia, 1961), which analyzes the sources of the romance and examines critically the Middle English contributions.

The dialect, having the general aspects of the Southeast, is fairly regular and close to Chaucer's London English. It should cause no trouble in translation, though several variations might be noted: (1) *sche, he, hye,* and *hie* are used for "she"; *ich* and *y* are often used for "I"; *þai, þey, he,* and *hye* often appear for "they"; *her* is used for "their"; *hem* is used for "them." (2) Past participles of verbs normally have the prefix *y-* (*ynome, ycome*). (3) Present and preterite plural of verbs end in *-yn* (*redyn, heryn, weryn*), *-en* (*maden*), and *-e* (*dede*). (4) The present participle has the regular *-ing* ending, but sometimes through a Northern copyist the Northern *-and* (*liggeand*). Noun plurals occasionally end in *-en* (*honden*).

Sir Orfeo has been justly cited as the most outstanding of the Breton lais in English, always excepting Chaucer's contributions in the *Wife of Bath's Tale* and the *Franklin's Tale*. Probably taken from an unknown French source and from Celtic legends, the story was known in the Middle Ages through Ovid (*Metamorphoses*, X) and Virgil (*Georgics*, IV), where Eurydice, bitten by a snake, is taken to Hades. Orpheus, son of Calliope, the Muse of epic poetry, leads her out, looks back, and loses her. King Alfred, in his translation of Boethius, brings the story into English as a didactic exemplum: Orpheus cannot refrain from looking back at his old "sins" and thus is punished. "Celtic magic" transforms the plot into a fairy tale with a happy ending. The lai is a repertoire of folk motifs (the ballad *King Orfeo* has Orfeo play "da göd gabber reel")[1] and an interesting combination of Celtic and classical themes. The skill of the author has transfigured this raw material into a small gem of conscious art.

---

1. According to Francis Child, the editor of *English and Scottish Popular Ballads*, "the good gabber reel" was "evidently a sprightly air." The *Scottish National Dictionary* glosses *gabber reel* as a corruption of *Gramarie*, "boisterous merriment."

We redyn° ofte and fynde ywryte,° — *read/written*
As clerkes don° us to wyte,° — *give/know*
Þe layes þat ben° of harpyng — *are*
Ben yfounde° of frely þing.° — *composed/pleasant things*
5 Sum° ben of wele° and sum of wo,° — *some/happiness/woe*
And sum of ioy° and merþe° also, — *joy/mirth*
Sum of trechery and sum of gyle,° — *guile*
And sum of happes° þat fallen° by whyle,° — *events/befall/now and then*
Sum of bourdys° and sum of rybaudry,° — *jests/ribaldry*
10 And sum þer ben of þe feyré.° — *fairies*
Off° alle þing° þat men may se,° — *of/things/see*
Moost° to lowe forsoþe° þey be. — *most/praise truly*
In Brytayn þis° layes arne° ywryte, — *Brittany these/are*
Furst° yfounde and forþe° ygete°— — *first/from there/gotten*
15 Of aventures° þat fillen° by° dayes, — *adventures/befell/in bygone*
Wherof Brytouns made her° layes; — *their*
When þey myght owher heryn° — *anywhere hear*
Of aventures þat þer weryn,° — *were*
Þey toke° her harpys° wiþ game,° — *took/harps/pleasure*
20 Maden° layes and ȝaf° it name. — *made/gave*
Of aventures þat han° befalle, — *have*
Y° can sum telle, but nouȝt° all. — *I/not*
Herken, lordyngys° þat ben trewe,° — *listen, lords/true*
And y wol° ȝou telle of Sir Orphewe. — *will*
25 Orfeo was a king,
In Inglond° an heiȝe° lording, — *England/high*
A stalworþ° man and hardi bo,° — *stalwart/both*
Large,° and curteys° he was also. — *generous/courteous*
His fader° was comen° of King Pluto — *father/come*
30 And his moder° of King Iuno,° — *mother/Juno*
Þat sum time were as godes yhold° — *gods regarded*
For auentours° þat þai dede° and told. — *adventures/they did*
Orpheo most of ony° þing — *any*
Louede þe gle° of harpyng; — *joy*
35 Syker° was euery gode harpoure° — *surely/good harper*
Of hym to haue moche° honoure. — *much*
Hymself° loued for to harpe — *he*
And layde þeron° his wittes scharpe; — *applied thereto*

1–25. These lines, missing in the Auchinleck MS, are taken from Harleian 3810.

13. The standard beginning that mentions the Breton source of the lai.

23. The normal opening for romances is an appeal to the listeners (cf. above, General Introduction, p. 38).

29–30. This confusing mythical genealogy is a remnant of the classical source of the Orpheus and Eurydice story, but has no authority whatsoever. It may be remembered that in English folklore Pluto became the king of fairyland (Chaucer's *Merchant's Tale*) and that in the classical story Eurydice remains with Pluto in the underworld.

He lernyd° so, þer noþing° was	*learned/by no means*
40 A better harper in no plas.°	*place*
In þe world was neuer man born	
Þat euer Orpheo sat byforn,°	*before*
And° he myȝt° of his harpyng here,°	*and (if)/might/hear*
He schulde° þinke þat he were	*should*
45 In one of þe ioys° of paradys,	*joys*
Suche ioy and melody in his harpyng is.	
Þis king soiourned° in Traciens,°	*dwelt/Thrace*
Þat was a cité° of noble defens;°	*city/fortifications*
For Winchester was cleped þo°	*called then*
50 Traciens wiþouten no.°	*without doubt*
Þe King hadde a Quen° of priis,°	*queen/excellence*
Þat was ycleped° Dame Herodis,	*called*
Þe fairest leuedi° for þe nones°	*lady/certainly*
Þat miȝt gon° on bodi and bones,	*go*
55 Ful of love and godenisse,°	*goodness*
Ac° no man may telle hir fairnise.°	*but/describe her fairness*
Bifel° so in þe comessing° of May,	*it happened/beginning*
When miri° and hot is þe day,	*pleasant*
And oway beþ° winterschours,°	*gone are/winter showers*
60 And eueri feld° is ful of flours,°	*field/flowers*
And blosme breme° on eueri bouȝ°	*blossoms fresh/bough*
Oueral wexeþ miri anouȝ,°	*everywhere grow merry enough*
Þis ich° Quen, Dame Heurodis,	*same*
Tok to° maidens of priis	*took two*
65 And went in an vndrentide°	*morning*
To play bi an orchardside,	
To se° þe floures sprede° and spring	*see/spread*
And to here þe foules° sing.	*birds*
Þai sett hem° doun al þre°	*sat themselves/three*
70 Vnder a fair ympe-tre,°	*grafted tree*
And wel sone° þis fair Quene	*very soon*
Fel on slepe° opon° þe grene.°	*asleep/upon/grass*
Þe maidens durst° hir nouȝt° awake,	*dared/not*
Bot lete° hir ligge° and rest take.	*but let/lie*
75 So sche slepe° til afternone,°	*slept/afternoon*

49–50. Winchester was for a time capital of England and is mentioned as one of the chief cities of King Arthur's realm (cf. Layamon's *Brut*). But obviously it cannot be identified with Thrace (which is, of course, a region—not a city—in Greece). The English author, instead of changing the locale, simply annexed and anglicized it.

52. *Herodis;* i.e., Eurydice.

69–72. Sleeping under a tree (especially one whose nature has been changed) in the morning was most foolhardy since it openly invited the intervention of fairies and placed one in their power (cf. *Sir Launfal* and the ballad *Thomas Rymer*). The *ympe-tre* may have been an apple tree (see Alice E. Lasater, "Under the Ympe-Tre or: Where the Action Is in *Sir Orfeo*," *The Southern Quarterly*, Vol. XII, No. 4, July 1974, pp. 353–363, for a full discussion of this topic).

Þat vndertide° was al ydone.°   morning/passed
Ac as sone as sche gan° awake,   did
Sche crid° and loþli bere° gan make,   cried/terrible cry
Sche froted° hir honden° and hir fet,°   rubbed/hands/feet
80 And crached° hir visage;° it bled wete.°   scratched/face/wet
Hir riche° robe hye al torett°   precious/she completely tore
And was reueysed° out of hir witt.°   ravished/senses
Þe tvo° maidens hir biside   two
No° durst wiþ hir no leng° abide,   not/longer
85 Bot ourn° to þe palays° ful riȝt,°   ran/palace/directly
And told boþe squier° and kniȝt°   squire/knight
Þat her° Quen awede° wold,°   their/go mad/would
And bad hem° go and hir at-hold.°   bade them/seize
Kniȝtes vrn° and leuedis also,   ran
90 Damisels sexti° and mo.°   sixty/more
In þe orchard to þe Quen hye come°   they came
And her vp in her armes nome°   took
And brouȝt° hir to bed atte last   brought
And held hir þere fine° fast.   very
95 Ac euer sche held in° o cri°   continued/her crying
And wold° vp and owy.°   would (be)/away
When Orfeo herd° þat tiding,°   heard/news
Neuer him° nas° wers° for no þing.   he/felt not/worse
He come° wiþ kniȝtes tene°   came/ten
100 To chaumber riȝt° bifor þe Quene   chamber right
And biheld, and seyd° wiþ grete pité:°   said/great pity
"O lef liif,° what is te°   dear life/wrong with you
Þat euer ȝete° hast ben° so stille,   yet/been
And now gredest° wonder° schille!°   cries/so very/loud
105 Þi bodi, þat was so white ycore,°   choicely
Wiþ þine nailes is al totore!°   torn
Alas, þi rode,° þat was so red,   complexion
Is al wan as° þou were ded!°   as if/dead
And also þine fingers smale°   small
110 Beþ° al blodi° and al pale!   are/bloody
Allas! þi louesum eyȝen to°   lovely eyes two
Lokeþ so° man doþ on his fo!°   look as/foe
A° dame, ich biseche,° merci!°   ah/I beg/mercy
Lete ben° al þis reweful° cri,   let be/pitiful
115 And tel me what þe is° and hou,   (with) you (it) is
And what þing may þe help now!"
Þo° lay sche stille atte last   then
And gan° to wepe swiþe° fast   began/weep very
And seyd þus þe King to:
120 "Allas, mi lord, Sir Orfeo!

Seþþen° we first togider° were, *since/together*
Ones wroþ° neuer we nere;° *once angry/ were not*
Bot° euer ich haue yloued° þe *but/loved*
As mi liif, and so þou me.
125 Ac° now we mot° delen ato,° *but/must/part*
Do þi best, for y° mot go!" *I*
"Allas," quaþ° he, "forlorn icham!° *said/I am*
Whider° wiltow° go, and to wham?° *where/will you/whom*
Whider þou gost,° ichil° wiþ þe, *go/I will (go)*
130 And whider y go, þou schalt wiþ me."
"Nay, nay, sir, þat nouȝt° nis,° *of no avail/is not*
Ichil þe telle al hou it is:
As ich lay þis vndertide° *morning*
And slepe vnder° our orchardside, *slept by*
135 Þer come to me to fair kniȝtes° *knights*
Wele yarmed al° to riȝtes° *well armed quite/properly*
And bad° me comen an heiȝing° *commanded/(to) come in haste*
And speke° wiþ her° lord þe King. *speak/their*
And ich answerd at° wordes bold, *to*
140 Y durst nouȝt no° y nold.° *dared not nor/would not*
Þai° priked° oȝain,° as° þai miȝt° driue; *they/rode off/again/as (quickly as)/ might*

Þo com° her King al° so bliue° *then came/just/fast*
Wiþ an hundred kniȝtes and mo,° *more*
And damisels an hundred also,
145 Al on snowewhite stedes:° *steeds*
As white as milke were her wedes.° *clothes*
Y no sciȝe° neuer ȝete° bifore *not saw/yet*
So fair creatours ycore:° *creatures choice*
Þe King hadde a croun on hed:° *head*
150 It nas° of siluer no of gold red, *was not*
Ac it was of a precious ston:° *stone*
As briȝt° as þe sonne° it schon. *bright/sun*
And as son° as he to me cam,° *soon/came*
Wold ich, nold ich,° he me nam° *willy-nilly/took*
155 And made me wiþ him ride
Opon° a palfray° bi his side *upon/riding horse*
And brouȝt° me to his palays,° *brought/palace*
Wele atird° in ich ways,° *ordered/every way*
And schewed° me castels and tours,° *showed/towers*
160 Riuers, forestes, friþ° wiþ flours,° *woods/flowers*
And his riche° stedes ichon,° *proud/each one*

---

150. *gold red:* Cf. above, p. 183, l. 47n. **156.** *palfray:* Cf. above, p. 346, n. 26.

And seþþen° me brouȝt oȝain hom°	then/home
Into our owhen° orchard	own
And said to me þus afterward:	
165 'Loke,° dame, to morwe° þatow° be	look/tomorrow/that you
Riȝt° here vnder þis ympe-tre,°	right/grafted tree
And þan° þou schalt wiþ ous° go	then/us
And liue wiþ ous euer-mo.°	evermore
And ȝif° þou makest ous ylet,°	if/delay
170 Whar° þou be, þou worst° yfet,°	wherever/will be/fetched
And totore° þine limes° al	torn/limbs
Þat° noþing help þe° no schal;	so that/you
And þei° þou best° so totorn,	although/are
Ȝete þou worst wiþ ous yborn.'"°	carried
175 When King Orfeo herd° þis cas,°	heard/happening
"O we,"° quaþ° he, "allas, allas!	woe/said
Leuer me were to° lete° mi liif°	I would rather/lose/life
Þan þus to lese° þe Quen° mi wiif!"°	lose/queen/wife
He asked conseyl at ich° man,	counsel from each
180 Ac° no man him help no can.	but
Amorwe° þe vndertide° is come,	the next day/morning
And Orfeo haþ his armes ynome,°	weapons taken
And wele° ten hundred kniȝtes° wiþ him,	fully/knights
Ich yarmed° stout and grim;	armed
185 And wiþ þe Quen wenten° he	went
Riȝt vnto þat ympe-tre.	
Þai° made scheltrom° in° ich a° side	they/wall of shielded men/on/each
And sayd þai wold° þere abide,	would
And dye° þer euerichon,°	die/every one
190 Er° þe Quen schuld fram hem gon.°	before/should from them go
Ac ȝete° amiddes hem° ful riȝt°	yet/from their midst/directly
Þe Quen was oway ytuiȝt,°	away snatched
Wiþ fairi° forþ ynome,	by magic
Men wist° neuer wher sche was bicome.°	knew/gone
195 Þo° was þer criing, wepe,° and wo!°	then/weeping/woe
Þe King into his chaumber° is go°	chamber/gone
And oft swoned opon° þe ston°	swooned upon/stone (floor)
And made swiche diol° and swiche mon,°	such lament/moan
Þat neiȝe° his liif was yspent.°	almost/destroyed
200 Þer was non amendement;°	no remedy
He cleped togider° his barouns,	called together
Erls, lordes of renouns.°	renown

---

187. *scheltrom*: the famous "shield wall," the defensive strategy of the Saxon armies used to great advantage (though not ultimate success) at Hastings.

191–94. The Fairy Love–Seduction motif (cf. Stith Thompson, *Motif-Index*, F 302ff., F 320ff.).

And when þai al ycomen° were,   *come*
"Lordinges,"° he said, "bifor ʒou here   *lords*
205 Ich ordainy min heiʒe° steward   *I appoint my high*
To wite° mi kingdom afterward;   *guard*
In mi stede ben° he schal,   *stead be*
To kepe° mi londes° oueral.   *rule/lands*
For now° ichaue° mi quen ylore,°   *now (that)/I have/lost*
210 Þe fairest leuedi° þat euer was bore,°   *lady/born*
Neuer eft y° nil° no woman se:°   *again I/will not/see*
Into wildernes° ichil° te°   *wilderness/I will/go*
And liue þer euer-more
Wiþ wilde bestes° in holtes hore.°   *beasts/forests ancient*
215 And when ʒe vnderstond° þat y be spent,°   *you believe/dead*
Make ʒou þan° a parlement   *then*
And chese° ʒou° a newe king.   *choose/for yourselves*
Now doþ° ʒour best wiþ al mi þing!"°   *do/affairs*
Þo was þer wepeing in þe halle
220 And grete cri° among hem alle.   *great crying*
Vnneþe miʒt° old or ʒong°   *scarcely might/young*
For wepeing speke° a word wiþ tong.°   *speak/tongue*
Þai kneled adoun° al yfere°   *knelt down/in a group*
And praid° him, ʒif° his wille were,°   *begged/if/(it) were*
225 Þat he no° schuld nouʒt° fram hem go   *not/not*
"Do way,"° quaþ° he, "it schal be so."   *enough/said*
Al his kingdom he forsoke;°   *forsook*
Bot° a sclauin° on him he toke:°   *only/pilgrim's gown/took*
He no hadde kirtel no hode,°   *tunic nor hood*
230 Schert ne° no noþer gode.°   *shirt nor/other possession*
Bot° his harp he tok algate°   *but/at least*
And dede him° barfot° out atte° ʒate:°   *walked/barefoot/at the/gate*
No man most° wiþ him go.   *might*
O way,° what þer was wepe° and wo,   *alas/weeping*
235 When he þat hadde ben° king wiþ croun   *been*
Went so pouerlich° out of toun!   *poorly*
Þurch wode° and ouer heþ°   *through wood/heath*
Into þe wildernes he geþ.°   *goes*
Noþing he fint° þat him° is ays,°   *finds/to him/comforting*
240 Bot euer he liueþ in gret malais.°   *distress*

204–8. In *King Horn* and *Havelok the Dane* we have the False Steward motif; although the reader expects the same here, the author uses instead the motif of the Faithful Retainer Rewarded (or Loyal Steward). All of these folkloric "seeds" can be found in the fairy tales of the Grimm brothers (cf. above, p. 31).

237–66. The theme of the "wild man" or rustic exile, developed in Shakespeare's *As You Like It* (cf. R. Bernheimer, *Wild Men in the Middle Ages* [Cambridge, Mass., 1952]). The winter adventures of Sir Orfeo closely parallel the description of the winter journey in *Sir Gawain and the Green Knight* (this volume, pp. 277–78).

He þat hadde ywerd° þe fowe° and griis°   worn/variegated fur/gray fur
And on bed þe purper biis°   purple linen
Now on hard heþe he liþ,°   lies
Wiþ leues° and gresse° he him wriþ.°   leaves/grass/himself covers
245 He þat hadde had castels and tours,°   towers
Riuer, forest, friþ° wiþ flours,°   woods/flowers
Now, þei° it comenci° to snewe° and frese,°   when/starts/snow/freeze
Þis King mote° make his bed in mese.°   must/moss
He þat had yhad kniʒtes° of priis°   had knights/worth
250 Bifor him kneland° and leuedis,°   kneeling/ladies
Now seþ° he noþing þat him likeþ,°   sees/pleases
Bot wilde wormes° bi him strikeþ.°   serpents/glide
He þat had yhad plenté°   plenty
Of mete° and drink, of ich deynté,°   food/every luxury
255 Now may he al day digge and wrote,°   grub
Er° he finde his fille of rote.°   before/root
In somer° he liueþ bi° wild frut°   summer/on/fruit
And berien° bot gode lite;°   berries/worth little
In winter may he noþing finde
260 Bot rote, grases,° and þe rinde.°   grass/bark of trees
Al his bodi was oway duine°   away wasted
For° missays,° and al to-chine.°   because of/misfortune/chapped
Lord! who may telle þe sore°   grief
Þis King sufferd ten ʒere° and more!   years
265 His here° of his berd, blac° and rowe,°   hair/beard, black/rough
To his girdel-stede° was growe.°   waist/grown
His harp, whereon was al his gle,°   joy
He hidde in an holwe tre;°   hollow tree
And when þe weder° was clere° and briʒt,°   weather/clear/bright
270 He toke° his harp to him wel riʒt°   took/straightway
And harped at his owhen° wille;°   own
Into alle þe wode° þe soun gan schille,°   forest/sound did ring
Þat° alle þe wilde bestes° þat þer beþ,°   so that/beasts/are
For ioie abouten° him þai teþ.°   joy about/they throng
275 And alle þe foules° þat þer were   birds
Come and sete° on ich a° brere,°   sit/each/briar
To here° his harping afine,°   hear/to the end
So miche° melody was þerin.   much
And when he his harping lete wold,°   stop would
280 No best bi him abide nold.°   would not
He miʒt se° him° bisides°   might see/for himself/near
Oft in hot vndertides,°   mornings

281–313. The fairy hunt is similar to the *Wilde Jagd* in German folktales.

Þe King o fairy° wiþ his rout°	*of fairyland/company*
Com to hunt him al about	
285 Wiþ dim° cri, and bloweing,	*faint*
And houndes also wiþ him berking.°	*barking*
Ac° no best þai no nome,°	*but/never took*
No° neuer he nist° whider° þai bicome.°	*nor/knew not/where/went*
And oþerwhile° he miȝt him se	*at other times*
290 As a gret ost° bi him te,°	*great host/passed*
Wele atourned° ten hundred kniȝtes,°	*well attired/knights*
Ich yarmed° to his riȝtes,°	*each armed/properly*
Of cuntenaunce° stout and fers,°	*countenance/fierce*
Wiþ mani desplaid baners,°	*displayed banners*
295 And ich his swerd ydrawe hold,°	*sword drawn held*
Ac neuer he nist whider þai wold.°	*wanted (to go)*
And oþerwhile he seiȝe° oþer þing:°	*saw/things*
Kniȝtes and leuedis com daunceing°	*ladies came dancing*
In queynt° atire, gisely,°	*strange/skillfully*
300 Queynt pas° and softly;	*step*
Tabours and trunpes ȝede hem bi°	*trumpets went them with*
And al maner menstraci.°	*manner (of) minstrelsy*
And on a° day he seiȝe him biside	*one*
Sexti° leuedis on hors ride,	*sixty*
305 Gentil° and iolif° as brid° on ris,°	*fair/pleasant/bird/branch*
Nouȝt o° man amonges hem þer nis.°	*not one/is not*
And ich a faucoun° on hond berc°	*falcon/hand bore*
And riden° on haukin° bi o riuere;°	*rode/a-hawking/a river*
Of game þai founde wel gode haunt:°	*very good resort*
310 Maulardes, hayroun,° and cormeraunt.	*mallards, heron/cormorant*
Þe foules of þe water ariseþ,	
Þe faucouns hem wele deviseþ:°	*spy*
Ich faucoun his pray slouȝ.°	*prey killed*
Þat seiȝe Orfeo and louȝ.°	*laughed*
315 "Parfay,"° quaþ he, "þer is fair game;	*in faith/said*
Þider° ichil,° bi Godes name;	*there/I will (go)*
Ich° was ywon swiche werk° to se."	*I/wont such work*
He aros° and þider gan te.°	*arose/did go*
To a leuedi he was ycome,°	*come*
320 Biheld and haþ wele vndernome°	*perceived*
And seþ° bi al þing° þat it is	*sees/signs*
His owhen quen, Dam° Heurodis.	*own queen, Dame*
Ȝern° he biheld hir,° and sche him eke,°	*eagerly/her/also*
Ac noiþer° to oþer a word no° speke.°	*neither/not/did speak*

---

321. There is perhaps a hint of the original Orpheus-Eurydice story here in this magic communication ban. Still, in folklore one could not bluntly address fairies for fear they might disappear.

325 For messais° þat sche on him seiȝe,	misfortune
Þat had ben° so riche and so heiȝe,°	been/powerful
Þe teres° fel out of her eiȝe.°	tears/eyes
Þe oþer leuedis þis yseiȝe°	saw
And maked° hir oway° to ride;	made/away
330 Sche most° wiþ him no lenger° abide.	might/longer
"Alas," quaþ he, "now me is wo!°	woe
Whi nil° deþ° now me slo!°	will not/death/slay
Allas wreche,° þat y° no miȝt°	wretch/I/might
Dye° now after þis siȝt!°	die/sight
335 Allas! to° long last mi liif,°	too/life
When y no dar° nouȝt wiþ mi wiif,°	dare/wife
No hye° to me, o word speke.°	nor she/speak
Allas, whi nil min hert breke!°	my heart break
Parfay," quaþ he, "tide wat bitide,°	happen what may
340 Whider-so þis leuedis° ride,	wherever these ladies
Þe selue° way ichil° streche:°	same/I will/go
Of liif no deþ y me° no reche!"°	myself/care
His sclauain° he dede° on al so° spac°	pilgrim's gown/put/very/quickly
And henge° his harp opon° his bac°	hung/upon/back
345 And had wel gode wil° to gon°—	intent/go
He no spard° noiþer stub° no ston.°	spared/stump/stone
In at a roche° þe leuedis rideþ,	rock (i.e., cave)
And he after and nouȝt abideþ.°	not waits
When he was in þe roche ygo,°	gone
350 Wele þre mile oþer mo,°	fully three miles or more
He com° into a fair cuntray,°	came/country
As briȝt so sonne° on somers° day,	bright as sun/summer's
Smoþe° and plain° and al° grene,	smooth/flat/completely
Hille no dale was þer non ysene.°	none seen
355 Amidde þe lond° a castel he siȝe,°	land/saw
Riche and real° and wonder heiȝe;°	regal/wondrously high
Al þe vtmast° wal	outer
Was clere° and schine° as cristal.	clear/shining
An hundred tours° þer were about	towers
360 Degiselich° and bataild stout;°	wonderfully/crenellated stoutly
Þe butras° com out of þe diche,°	buttress/moat
Of rede° gold yarched riche;°	red/arched nobly
Þe vousour° was anowrned° al	vaulting/adorned
Of ich maner diuers° animal.	every manner (of) diverse

---

346. *Spard ... ston:* i.e., "hastened."

347. Caves, in Celtic legends, were the usual entrances to the fairy world.

360. I.e., "wonderfully and stoutly crenellated."

³⁶⁵ Wiþin þer wer wide wones°	*roomy chambers*
Al of precious stones.	
Þe werst piler° on to biholde°	*worst pillar/look*
Was al of burnist° gold	*burnished*
Al þat lond was euer liȝt,°	*lighted*
³⁷⁰ For when it schuld° be þerk° and niȝt,°	*should/dark/night*
Þe riche stones liȝt gonne,°	*(to) shine began*
As briȝt as doþ° at none° þe sonne.	*does/noon*
No man may telle no þenche° in þouȝt°	*think/thought*
Þe riche werk° þat þer was wrouȝt.°	*work/fashioned*
³⁷⁵ Bi al þing,° him° þink° þat it is	*signs/to him/(it) seems*
Þe proude° court of paradis.	*splendid*
In þis castel þe leuedis aliȝt;°	*dismounted*
He wold° in after, ȝif° he miȝt.°	*wanted (to go)/if/might*
Orfeo knokkeþ° atte° gate;	*knocks/at the*
³⁸⁰ Þe porter was redi þerate°	*ready there*
And asked what he wold° haue ydo:°	*would/done*
"Parfay,"° quaþ° he, "icham° a minstrel, lo!	*in faith/said/I am*
To solas° þi lord wiþ mi gle,°	*entertain/music*
Ȝif his swete° wille be."°	*sweet/(it) be*
³⁸⁵ Þe porter vndede° þe ȝate anon°	*unlocked/gate immediately*
And lete° him into þe castel gon.°	*let/go*
Þan° he gan° bihold about al	*then/did*
And seiȝe liggeand° wiþin þe wal	*saw lying*
Of folk þat were þider ybrouȝt	*there brought*
³⁹⁰ And þouȝt dede° and nare° nouȝt:°	*seemed dead/are not/not*
Sum stode wiþouten hade,°	*some stood without head*
And sum non° armes nade,°	*no/had not*
And sum þurch° þe bodi hadde wounde,	*through*
And sum lay wode, ybounde,°	*crazed, bound*
³⁹⁵ And sum armed on hors sete,°	*sat*
And sum astrangled° as þai ete,°	*choked/they ate*
And sum were in water adreynt,°	*drowned*
And sum wiþ fire al forschreynt:°	*shriveled*
Wiues þer lay on child-bedde,	
⁴⁰⁰ Sum ded,° and sum awedde;°	*dead/crazed*
And wonder fele° þer lay bisides,	*wondrous many*
Riȝt° as þai slepe her° vndertides;°	*just/slept here/in the morning*
Eche° was þus in þis warld ynome,°	*each/world taken*
Wiþ fairi° þider ycome.°	*by magic/come*
⁴⁰⁵ Þer he seiȝe his owhen wiif,°	*own wife*

382–4. Minstrels in Ireland and Wales were feared for the sharp lampoons and satirical verses which they wrote against inhospitable hosts. Doors were usually open to them, but not always with a welcome mat.

Dame Heurodis, his liif liif,°   *dear life*
Slepe° vnder an ympe-tre;°   *asleep/grafted tree*
Bi her cloþes he knewe þat it was he.°   *she*
And when he hadde bihold þis meruails° alle,   *beheld these marvels*
410 He went into þe Kinges halle.
Þan seiȝe he þer a semly siȝt:°   *seemly sight*
A tabernacle blisseful° and briȝt,°   *canopy splendid/bright*
Þerin her maister° King sete   *there their master*
And her Quen° fair and swete.   *queen*
415 Her crounes, her cloþes schine° so briȝt,   *shone*
Þat vnneþe° bihold° he hem° miȝt.   *scarcely/look at/them*
When he hadde biholden° al þat þing,   *beheld*
He kneled adoun° bifor þe King.   *knelt down*
"O lord," he seyd,° "ȝif° it þi wille were,   *said/if*
420 Mi menstraci° þou schust yhere."°   *minstrelsy/should hear*
Þe King answerd, "What man artow,°   *are you*
Þat art hider ycomen° now?   *here come*
Ich, no° non þat is wiþ me,   *I, nor*
No° sent neuer after þe.°   *not/you*
425 Seþþen þat° ich here regni gan,°   *since/(to) reign began*
Y° no fond° neuer so folehardi° man,   *I/found/foolhardy*
Þat hider to ous durst wende,°   *us dared come*
Bot þat° ichim° wald° ofsende."°   *unless/I him/would/send for*
"Lord," quaþ° he, "trowe ful wel,°   *said/believe me*
430 Y nam bot° a pouer° menstrel,   *am only/poor*
And, sir, it is þe maner° of ous   *custom*
To seche° mani a lordes hous;   *seek*
Þei° we nouȝt° welcom no be,   *though/not*
Ȝete° we mot proferi° forþ our gle."°   *yet/must offer/song*
435 Bifor þe King he sat adoun
And tok° his harp so miri° of soun°   *took/merry/sound*
And tempreþ° his harp, as he wele° can,   *tunes/well*
And blisseful notes he þer gan,
Þat° al þat in þe palays° were   *so that/palace*
440 Com° to him forto here,°   *came/to hear*
And liggeþ° adoun to° his fete,°   *lie/at/feet*
Hem þenkeþ° his melody so swete.°   *they think/sweet*
Þe King herkneþ° and sitt ful° stille;   *listens/very*
To here his gle he haþ gode wille:°   *great pleasure*
445 Gode bourde° he hadde of° his gle;   *enjoyment/from*
Þe riche° Quen al so° hadde he.   *noble/also*
When he hadde stint° his harping,   *stopped*

---

431. *þe maner of ous:* i.e., "our custom."

Þan° seyd to him þe King,　　　　　　　　　　*then*

"Menstrel, me° likeþ wele þi gle;　　　　　　*I*

450　Now aske of me what° it be,　　　　　　　*whatever*

Largelich° ichil° þe pay.　　　　　　　*generously/I will*

Now speke,° and tow miȝt° asay."°　　*speak/you may/find out*

Sir," he seyd, "ich biseche° þe　　　　　　*beg*

Þatow° woldest ȝiue° me　　　　*that you/will give*

455　Þat ich leuedi, briȝt on ble,°　　*same lady, bright in complexion*

Þat slepeþ° vnder þe ympe-tre."°　　*sleeps/grafted tree*

"Nay" quaþ þe King, "þat nouȝt nere!°　　*would not be right*

A sori° couple of ȝou it were,°　　　　*sorry/would be*

For þou art lene, rowe,° and blac,°　　*lean, rough/black*

460　And sche is louesum wiþouten lac.°　*lovely without lack (i.e., fault)*

A loþlich° þing it were forþi°　　　　*loathly/therfore*

To sen hir° in þi compayni."°　　　　*see her/company*

"O sir," he seyd,° "gentil° King,　　*said/gracious*

Ȝete were it a wele fouler° þing　　　　*much worse*

465　To here a lesing° of þi mouþe;　　　　*lie*

So, sir, as ȝe° seyd nouþe,°　　　　　*you/now*

What i wold aski,° haue y schold,°　　*would ask/I should*

And nedes° þou most° þi word hold."°　*of necessity/must/keep*

Þe King seyd, "Seþþen° it is so,　　　*since*

470　Take hir bi þe hond° and go.　　　　*hand*

Of° hir ichil° þatow be bliþe."°　　*with/I wish/happy*

He kneled adoun° and þonked° him swiþe;°　*knelt down/thanked/quickly*

His wiif° he tok bi þe hond　　　　　*wife*

And dede him° swiþe out of þat lond,°　*went/land*

475　And went him out of þat þede:°　　*country*

Riȝt° as he come, þe way he ȝede.°　　*just/went*

So long he haþ þe way ynome,°　　　*taken*

To Winchester he is ycome,°　　　　*come*

Þat was his owhen cité;°　　　　　　*own city*

480　Ac° no man knew þat it was he.　　*but*

No forþer° þan þe tounes ende　　　*farther*

For knoweleche° he durst wende;°　*to escape recognition/dared go*

Bot° wiþ a begger ybilt ful narwe°　*but/lodged very poorly*

Þer he tok° his herbarwe,°　　　　*made/dwelling*

485　To° him and to his owhen wiif,　　*for*

As a minstrel of pouer liif,°　　　*poor life*

And asked tidings° of þat lond,　　*news*

And who þe kingdom held in hond.

Þe pouer begger in his cote°　　　　*hut*

450–51. The motif of the Rash Promise and Boon.

490 Told him euerich a° grot:°	*every/bit*
How her Quen° was stole owy,°	*their queen/away*
Ten ȝer gon, wiþ fairy,°	*years ago, by magic*
And hou her King en° exile ȝede,	*into*
Bot no man nist° in wiche° þede,	*knew not/which*
495 And hou þe steward þe lond gan° hold,	*did*
And oþer mani þinges him told.	
Amorwe,° oȝain° none tide,°	*the next day/toward/noon*
He maked° his wiif þer abide;°	*made/wait*
Þe beggers cloþes he borwed anon°	*borrowed then*
500 And heng° his harp his rigge opon,°	*hung/back upon*
And went him into þat cité,	
Þat° men miȝt° him bihold and se:°	*so that/might/see*
Erls and barouns bold,	
Buriays° and leuedis° him gun° bihold.	*burgesses/ladies/did*
505 "Lo," þai seyd,° "swiche° a man!	*they said/such*
Hou long þe here hongeþ° him opan!°	*hair hangs/upon*
Lo, hou his berd° hongeþ to his kne!°	*beard/knee*
He is yclongen also° a tre!"°	*withered as/tree*
And as he ȝede in þe strete,°	*street*
510 Wiþ his steward he gan mete,°	*meet*
And loude° he sett on him a crie:°	*loudly/called on him*
"Sir steward," he seyd, "merci!°	*mercy*
Icham° an harpour° of heþenisse;°	*I am/harper/heathendom*
Help me now in þis destresse!"	
515 Þe steward seyd, "Hom° wiþ me come:	*home*
Of þat° ichaue,° þou schalt haue some.	*what/I have*
Euerich gode° harpour is welcom me to	*good*
For mi lordes loue, Sir Orfeo."	
In þe castel þe steward sat atte mete,°	*meal*
520 And mani lording° was bi him sete.°	*many (a) noble/placed*
Þer were trompours° and tabourers,	*trumpeters*
Harpours fele° and crouders.°	*many/fiddlers*
Miche° melody þai maked alle,	*much*
And Orfeo sat stille in þe halle	
525 And herkneþ.° When þai ben° al stille,	*listens/were*
He toke° his harp and tempred schille.°	*took/tuned tightly*
Þe blissefulest notes he harped þere,	
Þat euer ani man yherd° wiþ ere;°	*heard/ear*
Ich° man liked wele° his gle.°	*every/well/song*
530 Þe steward biheld and gan yse°	*did see*

493–94. The motif of the Exile and Return (cf. *King Horn*, *Havelok the Dane*).

513. Sir Orfeo, without telling a falsehood, may hope that he will be regarded as a minstrel returned from the Holy Land (controlled by Saracens). As such, he is sure to be invited to a meal (cf. above p. 178, l. 1483).

And knewe þe harp als bliue:°   *as quickly*
"Menstrel," he seyd, "so mot° þou þriue,°   *as may/prosper*
Where hadestow° þis harp and hou?   *did you get*
Y° pray þat þou me telle now."   *I*

535 "Lord," quaþ° he, "in vncouþe þede°   *said/foreign land*
    Þurch° a wildernes° as y ȝede,°   *through/wilderness/went*
    Þer y founde in a dale
    Wiþ lyouns° a man totorn° smale,°   *by lions/torn/to bits*
    And wolues him frete° wiþ teþ° so scharp.   *ate/teeth*

540 Bi him y fond° þis ich° harp;   *found/same*
    Wele° ten ȝere° it is ygo."°   *fully/years/ago*
    "O," quaþ þe steward, "now me is wo!°   *woe*
    Þat was mi lord, Sir Orfeo.
    Allas wreche,° what schal y do,   *wretch*

545 Þat haue swiche° a lord ylore!°   *such/lost*
    A way,° þat ich° was ybore!°   *alas/I/born*
    Þat him° was so hard grace yȝarked°   *to him/fate appointed*
    And so vile deþ ymarked!"°   *death ordained*
    Adoun° he fel aswon° to grounde;   *down/swooning*

550 His barouns him toke vp in þat stounde°   *moment*
    And telleþ him hou it geþ:°   *goes*
    It° nis° no bot of manes° deþ!   *there/is not/remedy for man's*
    King Orfeo knewe wele bi þan°   *this*
    His steward was a trewe° man,   *true*

555 And loued him as he auȝt° to do,   *ought*
    And stont° vp and seyt° þus, "Lo,   *stood/said*
    Steward, herkne° now þis þing: *listen (to)*
    Ȝif° ich were Orfeo þe King,   *if*
    And hadde ysuffred ful° ȝore°   *suffered very/long ago*

560 In wildernisse miche sore,°   *grief*
    And hadde ywon° mi quen owy°   *won/queen away*
    Out of þe lond° of fairy,   *land*
    And hadde ybrouȝt° þe leuedi hende°   *brought/lady gracious*
    Riȝt° here to þe tounes ende,   *right*

565 And wiþ a begger° her in ynome,°   *to the home of a beggar/had taken*
    And were miself hider ycome°   *hither come*
    Pouerlich° to þe,° þus stille,°   *poorly/you/secretly*
    For to asay° þi gode° wille;   *test/good*
    And ich founde þe þus trewe,

570 Þou no° schust° it neuer rewe:°   *not/should/regret*
    Sikerlich° for loue or ay°   *surely/fear*

---

531. *als bliue:* i.e., "immediately."
562. *lond of fairy:* i.e., "fairyland."

567. *Pouerlich:* i.e., "in the guise of a poor man."

Þou schust be king after mi day.
And ȝif þou of mi deþ hadest ben bliþe,°   *been glad*
Þou schust haue voided also swiþe."°   *left very quickly*
575 Þo° al þo° þat þerin sete°   *when/those/there sat*
Þat it was King Orfeo vnderȝete,°   *recognized*
And þe steward him wele° knewe,   *well*
Ouer and ouer þe bord° he þrewe°   *table/turned*
And fel adoun to his fet;°   *feet*
580 So dede euerich° lord þat þer sete,   *did every*
And al þai seyd at o criing:°   *they said in one shout*
"Ȝe beþ° our lord, sir, and our king!"   *you are*
Glad þai were of his liue.°   *life*
To chaumber° þai ladde° him als biliue,°   *chamber/led/very quickly*
585 And baþed him and schaued° his berd°   *shaved (off)/beard*
And tired° him as a king apert.°   *dressed/manifest*
And seþþen° wiþ gret° processioun   *then/great*
Þai brouȝt° þe Quen into þe toun,   **brought**
Wiþ al maner menstraci.°   *kinds (of) minstrelsy*
590 Lord, þer was grete melody!
For ioie° þai wepe° wiþ her eiȝe,°   *joy/wept/their eyes*
Þat hem° so sounde ycomen seiȝe.°   *them/safely coming saw*
Now King Orfeo newe coround° is   *newly crowned*
And his quen, Dame Heurodis,
595 And liued long afterward,
And seþþen° was king þe steward.   *afterward*
Harpours° in Bretaine° after þan°   *harpers/Brittany/this*
Herd hou° þis meruaile° bigan,   *heard how/marvel*
And made herof° a lay of gode likeing°   *thereof/much charm*
600 And nempned° it after þe King.   *named*
Þat lay "Orfeo" is yhote;°   *called*
Gode° is þe lay, swete° is þe note.   *good/sweet*
Þus com° Sir Orfeo out of his care.°   *came/sorrow*
God graunt ous° alle wele to fare!   *grant us*

---

574. I.e., "you would have had to leave immediately."
578. Medieval delight was boisterous; turning over the table trestles in joy was a frequent occurrence.

SIR LAUNFAL

Thomas Chestre

DATE: a. 1400. ✦ MANUSCRIPT: British Library. Cotton Caligula A. ii, early 15th century. The dialect is Southeastern (Kentish) and similar to Chaucer's. ✦ EDITIONS: A. J. Bliss, *Sir Launfal* (London, 1960), which has a full bibliography and prints the analogues *Lanval* and *Sir Landevale;* a concise study by Donald Sands in *Middle English Verse Romances* (New York, 1966); W. H. French and C. B. Hale, *Middle English Metrical Romances* (New York, 1964).

The Southeastern (Kentish) dialect of *Sir Launfal* is in many ways close to the language of Chaucer, although certain local sound changes are in operation. (1) Most important is the orthographical interchange of *þ* and *d* (*cloþing = clothing; þepartyng = departing*). According to A. J. Bliss ("The Spelling of Sir Launfal," *Anglia*, 75 [1957], 275–89), in an area confined to Kent and East Sussex (from the evidence of the modern pronunciation) *þ* (representing the voiced spirant [ð]) was actually pronounced [d] in all positions. Thus the scribe could use either *þ* or *d* when writing the [d] sound. The orthographical interchange of *þ* and *d* really represented a local sound change of [ð] to [d] in all positions. Normally, though not always, when the voiceless spirant was intended, *th* was used instead of *þ*. (2) Southern change of *f* to *v* can also be seen, resulting in spellings like *fyle = vile, feluet = velvet*. (3) The Southern infinitive ending in *-y* also occurs: *changy*. (4) The usual *i* (for OE *y*) is here *e: keste = kissed*. (5) Late Middle English loss of *ȝ* may be seen: *knytes = knights*. (6) The past participle usually has a *y-* prefix (*yfounde, ynome*), cognate of the German *ge-* (*gefunden, genommen*). (7) Pronouns are varied, e.g., *sche, hi* for "she"; *hem, ham, hym* for "them"; *har(e), here* for "their"; *here, har, hyr(e)* for "her"; *y* for "I."

Nothing is known of Thomas Chestre, author of *Sir Launfal*, a Breton lai whose original source is the story of *Lanval* by the Anglo-Norman Marie de France. Between these two works is a shorter version of Marie's poem, *Sir Landevale*, which directly influenced Chestre. But the author drew on other Old French romances, such as *Graelent*, and his own invention to rework a tale of fairy lore which has certain similarities to the ballad *Thomas Rymer*. The folk motif of the Wooing Lady or Potiphar's Wife is woven into a tightly plotted structure. The feminine characters are well drawn, especially the portrait of the promiscuous Guinevere, and in general the lai provides interesting views of all-too-human nature. *Sir Launfal* is written in the popular tail-rhyme stanza, which usually comprises four sections of three lines each, twelve lines in all. A rhymed four-beat couplet is followed by a three-beat line having a different rhyme. This tail line carries the same rhyme throughout the stanza, which in *Sir Launfal* is divided in half. Chaucer parodies this verse form in *Sir Thopas* (cf. Urs Dürmüller, *Narrative Possibilities of the Tail-Rime Romance* [Bern, 1975], which thoroughly explores the tail rhyme in every respect).

Be douȝty Artours dawes°   *in doughty Arthur's days*
Þat helde° Engelond yn° good lawes,   *ruled/under*
   Þere fell° a wondyre cas°   *happened/wondrous event*
Of a ley þat° was ysette,°   *of which a lay/composed*
5 Þat hyȝt° Launual,° and hatte° ȝette;° *was called/Launfal/is called/still*
   Now herkeneþ° how hyt° was: *hear/it*

Douȝty Artoure som whyle°   *at one time*
Soiournede° yn Kardeuyle,°   *lodged/Carlisle*
   Wythe ioye° and greet solas;°   *joy/great pleasure*
10 And knyȝtes° þat were profitable°   *knights/worthy*
With Artour of þe Rounde Table,
   Neuere noon° bettere þer nas:°   *never none/was not*

Sere Perseuall° and Sere Gawayn,   *Sir Percival*
Syr Gyheryes° and Syr Agrafrayn°   *Gaheres/Agravain*
15   And Launcelet du Lake;
Syr Kay and Syr Ewayn,°   *Ywain*
Þat well couþe fyȝte° yn playn,   *could fight*
   Bateles° for to take;°   *battles/undertake*

Kyng Banbooȝt and Kyng Bos—
20 Of ham° þer was a greet° los:°   *them/much/praise*
   Men sawe þo° nowhere here make°— *then/their equal*
Syre Galafre and Syr Launfale,
Whereof a noble tale
   Among vs schall awake.°   *arise*

25 With Artoure þer was a bachelere,°   *bachelor*
And hadde ybe well° many a ȝere:°   *been fully/year*
   Launfal for soþ° he hyȝt;   *in truth*
He gaf gyftys largelyche°—   *gave gifts generously*
Golde and syluere° and clodes° ryche, *silver/clothes*

---

8. *Kardeuyle*: Carlisle in Cumberland; it is in many Arthurian stories confused with Karlyoun (Caerleon-upon-Usk in Monmouthshire), the supposed site of Camelot.

13. *Perseuall*: the hero of *Parzival* by Wolfram von Eschenbach. He becomes guardian of the Holy Grail, the cup Christ used at the Last Supper, which was the object of a long quest by knights of the Round Table.

14. The brothers of Gawain, Gaheres and Agravain, were later involved in the betrayal of Lancelot during his tryst with Guinevere.

16. Kay was Arthur's Seneschal or steward; Ywain was Arthur's cousin and the hero of a romance by Chrétien de Troyes.

19. *Banbooȝt*: probably King Ban of Benwick in France; *Bos*: his brother, King Bors of Gaul.

22. *Galafre*: in Old French poetry a Saracen name, not mentioned elsewhere in Middle English literature.

25. A bachelor was a young man who had not completed military or academic training. In this instance it is a young knight who was not yet prepared to lead a company but served in the retinue of others.

28. Generosity is the outstanding trait of Launfal (cf. above, p. 341, n. 5).

³⁰ To squyer° and to kny3t.   *squire*

For hys largesse° and hys bounté,°   *liberality|bounty*
Þe kynges stuward° made was he   *steward*
  Ten yere, y° you ply3t;°   *years, I|assure*
Of alle þe kny3tes of þe Table Rounde,
³⁵ So large° þer nas noone yfounde,°   *generous|found*
  Be° dayes ne° be ny3t.°   *by|nor|night*

So hyt befyll° yn þe tenþe 3ere,   *happened*
Marlyn° was Artours counsalere;°   *Merlin|counselor*
  He radde° hym for to wende°   *advised|go*
⁴⁰ To Kyng Ryon° of Irlond° ry3t,°   *Ryence|Ireland|right away*
And fette° hym° þer a lady bry3t,°   *fetch|for himself|bright*
  Gwennere° hys dou3tyr hende.°   ***Guinevere|daughter gracious***

So he dede,° and hom° her brou3t;°   *did|home|brought*
But Syr Launfal lykede° her no3t,°   *liked|not*
⁴⁵   Ne oþer kny3tes þat were hende;°   *gracious*
For þe lady bar los° of swych word°   *bore (a) reputation|such report*
Þat sche hadde lemannys vnþer here° lord,   *lovers under her*
  So fele° þere nas noon ende.   *many*

Þey were ywedded,° as y you say,°   ***wedded|tell***
⁵⁰ Vpon a Wytsonday,°   *Whitsunday*
  Before princes of moch pryde;°   *much honor*
No man ne° may telle yn tale°   *not|the count*
What folk þer was at þat bredale,°   *bridal*
  Of countreys fere° and wyde!   *far*

⁵⁵ No noþer° man was yn halle ysette°   *nor any|seated*
But° he were prelat oþer° baronette   *unless|or*
  (In herte° ys no3t° to hyde°);   *heart|no reason|hide (it)*
Yf° þey satte no3t alle ylyke,°   *(but even) if|alike*
Hare seruyse° was good and ryche,   *their service*
⁶⁰   Certeyn yn° ech a° syde;   *certainly on|every*

And whan° þe lordes hadde ete° yn þe halle   *when|eaten*

39–42. In other Arthurian versions, Arthur helps Leodegen, king of Camelide, father of Guinevere and enemy of Ryence.
47. *vnþer:* i.e., "in the retinue of." The promiscuity of Guinevere and her generally unpleasant characteristics seem to be survivals of Celtic otherworld motifs, in which Guinevere is a supernatural creature married to a mortal and is claimed by her fairy husband.

53. A bridal was originally a prewedding ceremony in which the bride brewed ale and served it to guests for payment.
57. I.e., "there is no need to deny it."
59. I. e., "they were well attended."

And þe cloþes° were drawen° alle,   *tablecloths/removed*
  As ye mowe her° and lyþe,°   *may hear/listen*
The botelers sentyn wyn°   *cupbearers served **wine***
65 To alle þe lordes þat were þeryn,°   *therein*
  With chere° boþe glad and blyþe.°   *spirit/happy*

Þe Quene yaf° gyftes for þe nones,°   *gave/at that time*
Gold and seluere° and precyous stonys,°   *silver/stones*
  Here curtasye° to kyþe;°   *kindness/show*
70 Euerych knyʒt° sche ʒaf broche° oþer ryng,   *every knight/gave brooch*
But Syr Launfal sche yaf no þyng—
  Þat greuede° hym many a syde.°   *grieved/time*

And whan þe bredale was at ende,
Launfal tok° hys leue° to wende   *took/leave*
75   At Artoure° þe kyng,   *from Arthur*
And seyde° a lettere was to hym come   *said*
Þat deþ° hadde hys fadyr ynome:°   *death/father taken*
  He most° to hys beryynge.°   *must (go)/burial*
Þo° seyde Kyng Artour, þat was hende,   *then*
80 "Launfal, yf þou wylt fro° me wende,°   *from/go*
  Tak° with þe greet spendyng,°   *take/you much money*
And my sustere sones° two: *sister's sons*
Boþe þey schull° with þe go,   *shall*
  At hom° þe for to bryng."   *home*

85 Launfal tok leue, withoute fable,°   *lie*
With knyʒtes of þe Rounde Table,
  And wente forþ yn hys iourné°   *journey*
Tyl he com° to Karlyoun,°   *came/Caerleon*
To þe Meyrys° hous of þe toune,   *mayor's*
90   Hys seruaunt° þat hadde ybe.°   *servant/been*

The Meyr stod,° as ye may here,°   *stood/**hear***
And sawe hym come ryde° vp anblere,°   *riding/ambling*
  With two knyʒtes and oþer mayné;°   *retinue*
Agayns° hym he haþ wey° ynome,   *toward/(his) way*
95 And seyde, "Syre, þou art wellcome;
  How faryþ° oure Kyng, tel me."   *fares*

---

64. *botelers:* The "bottlers," or wine stewards, enlarged their functions as "butlers."

82. The uncle-nephew relationship is peculiarly close (more so than that of father-son) in the romances. Charlemagne-Roland, Mark-Tristram, and Arthur-Gawain are other examples of a bond which may be traced back to a primitive matrilineal society. Thus, when Arthur sends his "sister's sons," Hugh and John, with Launfal, he is doing the knight a great honor.

88. *Karlyoun;* Cf. l. 8*n.*

Launfal answerede and seyde þan,°   *then*
"He faryþ as well as any man,
  And elles greet ruþe hyt° wore;°   *otherwise great pity it/would be*
100 But, Syr Meyr, without lesyng,°   *lie*
I am þepartyþ fram° þe Kyng,   *departed from*
  And þat rewythe me° sore;°   *I rue/greatly*

Neþer þare° no man, beneþe ne° aboue,   *nor need/beneath nor*
For þe Kyng Artours loue
105   Onowre° me neuer-more;   *honor*
But, Syr Meyr, y pray° þe, par amoure,°   *I beg/for love*
May y take with þe soioure?°   *lodging*
  Som° tyme we knewe vs° yore."°   *at one/each other/long ago*

Þe Meyr stod and beþoȝte hym° þere   *reflected*
110 What myȝt° be hys answere,   *(on) what might*
  And to hym þan gan° he sayn:°   *did/say*
"Syr, vii knyȝtes han° here hare in° ynome,   *knights have/their lodging*
And euer y wayte whan° þey wyl come,   *await when*
  Þat arn° of Lytyll Bretayne."°   *are/Little Britain (i.e., Brittany)*

115 Launfal turnede hym self and lowȝ:°   *laughed*
Þerof he hadde scorn inowȝ;°   *much*
  And seyde to hys knyȝtes tweyne,°   *two*
"Now may ye se, swych° ys seruice   *see, such*
Vnþer° a lord of lytyll pryse°—   *under/worth*
120   How he may þerof be fayn!"°   *glad*

Launfal awayward gan° to ryde;   *away began*
Þe Meyr bad° he schuld abyde,°   *asked (that)/should wait*
  And seyde yn þys manere:°   *manner*
"Syr, yn a chamber by my orchard syde,
125 Þer may ye dwelle, with ioye° and pryde,°   *joy/honor*
  Ȝyf° hyt your wyll were."   *if*

Launfal anoon ryȝtes,°   *then directly*
He and hys two kyntes,°   *knights*
  Soiournede° þer yn fere.°   *lodged/together*
130 So sauagelych° hys good° he besette°   *wildly/possessions/spent*

112–14. The mayor tries to find an excuse for not lodging Launfal. He takes rather too seriously the knight's statement that no man need honor him. *Lytyll Bretayne:* i.e., "Brittany." **118–20.** The lines are difficult. Probably the essence is: "Now you can see what it means to serve under a lord who is valued lightly by others [has small power]. What a pleasure [meant, of course, ironically] this is for him [either any servant of his, or Launfal himself]!" This reaction would be in line with Launfal's bitter laughter, l. 115.

Þat he ward yn° greet dette°   *fell into/debt*
   Ryȝt° yn þe ferst yere.°   *right away/first year*

So hyt befell at Pentecost,
Swych tyme as þe Holy Gost
135   Among mankend° gan lyȝt,°   *mankind/descend*
Þat Syr Huwe° and Syr Ion°   *Hugh/John*
Tok here leue° for to gon°   *took their leave/go*
   At° Syr Launfal þe knyȝt;   *from*

Þey seyd, "Sir, our robes beþ torent,°   *are torn*
140 And your tresoure° ys all yspent,°   *treasure/spent*
   And we goþ ewyll ydyȝt."°   *go poorly clothed*
Þanne° seyde Sir Launfal to þe knyȝtes fre,°   *then/good*
Tellyd° no man of my pouerté,°   *tell/poverty*
   For þe loue of God Almyȝt."

145 Þe knyȝtes answerede and seyde þo°   *then*
Þat þey nolde° hym wreye neuir-mo,°   *would not/betray never*
   All þys world to wynne;°   *gain*
With þat word þey wente hym fro°   *from*
To Glastyngbery,° boþe two,   *Glastonbury*
150   Þer° Kyng Artoure° was inne.   *where/Arthur*

Þe Kyng sawe þe knyȝtes hende,°   *gracious*
And aȝens ham° he gan wende,°   *toward them/go*
   For þey were of hys kenne;°   *kindred*
Noon° oþer robes þey ne° hadde   *no/not*
155 Þan þey owt° with ham ladde,°   *away/(had) carried*
   And þo° were totore° and thynne.°   *they/all torn/threadbare*

Þan seyde° Quene Gwenore,° þat was fel,°   *said/Guinevere/malicious*
"How faryþ° þe prowde knyȝt° Launfal?   *fares/knight*
   May he hys armes welde?"°   *weapons (still) wield*
160 "Ȝe,° madame," sayde þe knytes þan,   *yes*
"He faryþ as well as any man,
   And ellys,° God hyt schelde!"°   *otherwise/it forbid*

Moche worchyp° and greet° honour   *much respect/great*
To Gonnore° þe Quene and Kyng Artoure   *Guinevere*
165   Of Syr Launfal þey telde,°   *told*

---

133. Pentecost (Whitsunday) marks one year of Launfal's absence.

149. *Glastyngbery:* Glastonbury is often identified with the Isle of Avalon. It is the supposed site of the grave of Arthur, but here it is just one of his cities.

And seyde, "He louede° vs so   *loved*
Þat he wold° vs euir-mo°   *would/evermore*
  At wyll haue yhelde.°   *retained*

But vpon a rayny day hyt befel
170 An-huntynge° wente Syr Launfel,   *a-hunting*
  To chasy° yn holtes hore;°   *hunt/woods ancient*
In oure old robes we yede° þat day,   *went*
And þus we beþ ywent° away,   *gone*
  As we before hym wore."

175 Glad was Artoure þe Kyng
Þat Launfal was yn good lykyng;°   *state*
  Þe Quene hyt rew well sore,°   *regretted very greatly*
For sche wold,° with all here myȝt,°   *wished/her might*
Þat he hadde be,° boþe day and nyȝt,°   *been/night*
180   In paynys° more and more.   *pains*

Vpon a day of þe Trinité,°   *Trinity*
A feste° of greet solempnité°   *feast/solemnity*
  In Carlyoun° was holde;°   *Caerleon/held*
Erles and barones of þat countré,°   *country*
185 Ladyes and borieics° of þat cité,°   *burgesses/city*
  Þyder come,° boþe yongh° and olde;   *there came/young*

But Launfal, for° hys pouerté,°   *because of/poverty*
Was not bede° to þat semblé:°   *invited/assembly*
  Lyte° men of hym tolde.°   *little/thought*
190 Þe Meyr° to þe feste was ofsent;°   *mayor/summoned*
Þe Meyrys douȝter° to Launfal went,   *mayor's daughter*
  And axede° yf he wolde   *asked*

In halle dyne with here þat day.
"Damesele," he sayde, "nay:
195   To dyne haue i no herte;°   *heart*
Þre° dayes þer ben agon,°   *three/are passed*
Mete ne° drynke eet y noon,°   *food nor/ate I none*
  And all was fore° pouert.°   *because of/poverty*

To-day to cherche° y wolde haue gon,   *church*
200 But me fawtede hosyn° and schon,°   *I lacked stockings/shoes*

---

174. I.e., "as at that time we were dressed."
181. *a day of þe Trinité:* the Sunday after Pentecost, eight weeks after Easter.

Clenly brech° and scherte;°   *clean breeches/shirt*
And fore defawte° of clodynge,°   *for lack/clothing*
Ne° myȝte y yn° with þe peple þrynge;°   *not/inside/people press*
No wonþer douȝ° me smerte!°   *wonder that/smart*

205 But o° þyng, damesele, y pray þe:°   *one/beg you*
Sadel° and brydel lene° þou me   *saddle/lend*
    A whyle for to ryde,
Þat y myȝte confortede° be   *comforted*
By° a launde vnþer° þys cyté,°   *on/meadow near/city*
210   Al° yn þys vndern-tyde."°   *quite/morning time*

Launfal dyȝte° hys courser°   *prepared/horse*
Withoute knaue° oþer squyer;°   *servant boy/or squire*
    He rood° with lytyll pryde;°   *rode/little honor*
Hys hors slod° and fel yn þe fen,°   *slipped/mud*
215 Wherefore hym scornede many men
    Abowte hym fere° and wyde.   *far*

Pouerly° þe knyȝte° to hors gan° sprynge;   *humbly/knight/did*
For to dryue° away lokynge,°   *drive/attention*
    He rood toward þe west.
220 Þe weþer° was hot þe° vndern-tyde;   *weather/(in) the*
He lyȝte adoun° and gan abyde°   *alighted down/remain*
    Vnder a fayr forest;

And for hete° of þe wedere,°   *heat/weather*
Hys mantell he felde togydere,°   *folded together*
225   And sette hym° doun to reste;   *sat*
Þus sat þe knyȝt yn symplyté,°   *humility*
In þe shadwe, vnþer° a tre,°   *shadow, under/tree*
    Þer þat° hym lykede° best.   *where/(it) pleased*

As he sat, yn sorow and sore,°   *grief*
230 He sawe come out of holtes hore°   *woods ancient*
    Gentyll° maydenes two;   *noble*
Har kerteles° were of Inde-sandel°   *their gowns/Indian silk*
Ilased smalle, iolyf,° and well: *laced tightly, attractively*
    Þer myȝt° noon gayere go.   *might*

235 Hare manteles were of grene felwet,°   *velvet*

223–28. Mortals resting under a tree in the heat of the day were common prey for seductive fairies; cf. the lai of *Sir Orfeo*, and the ballad *Thomas Rymer*, the story of Thomas of Erceldoune.

Ybordured° with gold, ry3t° well ysette,°   *bordered/very/arranged*
    Ipelured° with grys° and gro.°   *trimmed/gray/white (fur)*
Hare heddys° were dy3t° well withalle:°   *heads/adorned/also*
Euerych° hadde oon° a iolyf coronall°   *each/on/handsome diadem*
240   With syxty gemmys° and mo.°   *gems/more*

Hare faces were whyt° as snow on downe;°   *white/hill*
Har rode° was red, here eyn° were browne   *complexion/their eyes*
    I sawe neuir non swyche!°   *never none such*
Þat oon bare° of gold a basyn,   *one bore*
245 Þat oþer a towayle,° whyt and fyn,°   *towel/fine*
    Of selk° þat was good and ryche.   *silk*

Hare kercheues° were well schyre,°   *kerchiefs/very bright*
Arayd° with ryche golde wyre;°   *decorated/thread*
    Launfal began to syche.°   *sigh*
250 Þey com° to hym ouir° þe heth:°   *came/over/heath*
He was curteys,° and a3ens hem geth,°   *courteous/toward them goes*
    And greette° hem myldelyche:°   *greeted/gently*

"Damesels," he seyde,° "God yow se!"°   *said/you watch (over)*
"Sir kny3t," þey seyde, "well þe° be!   *you*
255   Oure lady, Dame Tryamour,
Bad° þou schuldest° com speke° with here,°   *asked (that)/should/speak/her*
3yf hyt° wcre þy wylle, sere,°   *if it/sir*
    Withoute more soiour."°   *delay*

Launfal hcm grauntede curteyslyche,°   *granted (it) courteously*
260 And wente with hem myldelyche;
    Þey wheryn° whyt as floure.   *were*
And when þey comc° in þe forest an hy3,°   *came/on high*
A pauyloun yteld° he sy3,°   *pavilion pitched/saw*
    With merthe° and mochell° honoure.   *joy/much*

265 Þe pauyloun was wrouth, fore soþe° ywys,°   *wrought, in truth/indeed*
All of werk° of Sarsynys:°   *work/Saracens*
    Þe pomclles° of crystall;   *pole knobs*
Vpon þe toppe an ern° þer stod°   *eagle/stood*
Of bournede° golde, ryche and goode,   *burnished*
270   Iflorysched° with ryche amall;°   *decorated/enamel*

244–46. These items are to be used prior to the meal of which Launfal partakes.

249. Launfal sighs in ecstasy at their beauty.

255. *Tryamour:* from OF *trier,* "to choose," and *amour,* "love."

266. Saracen work was considered cunning and expert.

Hys eyn were carbonkeles bryȝt°—   carbuncles bright
As þe mone° þey schon° a-nyȝt,°   moon/shone/at night
    Þat spreteþ° out ouyr° all;   spreads/over
Alysaundre° þe conqueroure   Alexander (the Great)
275 Ne° Kyng Artoure° yn hys most honour°   nor/Arthur/greatest pride
    Ne° hadde noon scwych iuell!°   not/none such jewel

He fond° yn þe pauyloun   found
Þe Kynges douȝter° of Olyroun,   daughter
    Dame Tryamoure þat hyȝte;°   was called
280 Here fadyr° was kyng of fayrye°   father/fairyland
Of Occient, fere° and nyȝe,°   far/near
    A man of mochell myȝte.°   great might

In þe pauyloun he fond a bed of prys°   worth
Iheled° with purpur bys,°   covered/purple linen
285   Þat semyle° was of syȝte.°   seemly/in sight
Þerinne lay þat lady gent°   noble
Þat aftere° Sir Launfal hedde ysent;°   for/had sent
    Þat lefsom lemede° bryȝt.   lovely (one) shone

For° hete° her cloþes down sche dede°   because of/heat/slipped
290 Almest° to here gerdylstede;°   almost/waist
    Þan° lay sche vncouert;°   then/uncovered
Sche was as whyt° as lylye yn May   white
Or snow þat sneweþ yn wynterys° day: snows on winter's
    He seygh neuere non° so pert.°   saw never none/attractive

295 Þe rede° rose, whan° sche ys newe,   red/when
Aȝens here rode° nes° nauȝt° of hewe,°   against her complexion/was not/
                                                       nothing/hue
    I dar° well say yn sert;°   dare/certainty
Here here° schon as gold wyre;°   hair/thread
May no man rede° here atyre,°   read (of)/attire
300   Ne nauȝt° well þenke° yn hert.°   not/think/heart

Sche seyde,° "Launfal, my lemman swete,°   said/beloved sweet
Al my ioye° for þe y lete,°   joy/you I lose

---

278. *Kynges douȝter of:* "daughter of the king of." *Olyroun:* perhaps the fairy Isle of Avalon, confused here with the Breton Île d'Oléron (cf. above, p. 91, ll. 1184–85n).

281. *Occient:* in Old French poetry a land of the Saracens, but it may just mean "west," as the "Western Isles" are sometimes identified with the "Blessed Isles" (cf. Tennyson's *Ulysses*).

285. *of syȝte:* i.e., "to see."

296. *Aȝens:* i.e., "next to."

301–6. This is the Fairy Love–Seduction motif of folklore (cf. Stith Thompson, *Motif-Index*, F 302ff., F 320ff.).

Swetyng paramour:°   *sweetheart lover*
Þer nys° no man yn Cristenté°   *is not/Christendom*
305 Þat y loue so moche° as þe,   *much*
    Kyng neyþer° emperoure!"   *nor*

Launfal beheld þat swete wyȝth°—   *person*
All hys loue yn her was lyȝth°—   *set*
    And keste° þat swete flour,°   *kissed/flower*
310 And sat adoun° her bysyde,°   *down/beside*
And seyde, "Swetyng, what so° betyde,°   *whatever/happens*
    I am to þyn honoure."°   *at your service*

She seyde, "Sir Knyȝt, gentyl° and hende,° *knight, noble/gracious*
I wot° þy stat, ord° ane ende;   *know/state, beginning*
315   Be nauȝt aschamed of° me.   *before*
Yf þou wylt truly to me take,°   *come*
And alle wemen° for me forsake,   *women*
    Ryche i wyll make þe.

I wyll þe ȝeue° an alner°   *give/purse*
320 Imad° of sylk and of gold cler,°   *made/pure*
    With fayre ymages þre;°   *three*
As oft° þou puttest° þe hond° þerinne,   *often (as)/put/hand*
A mark of gold þou schalt wynne,°   *gain*
    In wat° place þat þou be."   *whatever*

325 Also sche seyde, "Syr Launfal,
I ȝeue þe Blaunchard, my stede lel,°   *steed true*
    And Gyfre, my owen° knaue;°   *own/servant boy*
And of my armes oo pensel,°   *(coat of) arms a banner*
With þre ermyns ypeynted° well,   *ermines depicted*
330   Also þou schalt haue.

In werre ne° yn turnement,°   *war nor/tournament*
Ne° schall þe greue° no knyȝtes dent,°   *not/hurt/blow*
    So well y schall þe saue."°   *protect*
Þan° answerede þe gantyl° knyȝt,   *then/noble*
335 And seyde, "Gramarcy,° my swete wyȝt:° *much thanks/one*
    No bettere chepe° y haue."   *bargain*

319–24. The Fortunatus motif of the purse that is never empty is known in folklore. (Fortunatus of Famagusta, the hero of an anonymous German prose novel written around 1440 and first edited in Augsburg in 1509, is given such a purse by the goddess Fortuna. The story, a very old one, was dramatized by Hans Sachs [1553] and Thomas Dekker [1660].) Peter Schlemihl, the hero of Adelbert von Chamisso's tale *Peter Schlemihls wundersame Geschichte* (1814), sells his shadow to the Devil in return for the never-empty purse. mark (l. 323): the equivalent value of eight ounces of gold.

Þe damesell gan° here vp sette,°   did/sit
And bad here° maydenes here fette°   bade her/fetch
    To hyr hondys° watyr clere;°   for her hands/clear
340 Hyt° was ydo° without lette.°   it/done/delay
Þe cloþ was spred,° þe bord° was sette,   spread/table
    Þey wente to hare sopere.°   their supper

Mete° and drynk þey hadde afyn,°   food/the best
Pyement,° claré,° and Reynysch wyn,°   spiced wine/claret/Rhenish wine
345   And elles, greet° wondyr hyt were.° otherwise, great/had been
Whan° þey had sowpeþ° and þe day was gon,   when/supped
Þey wente to bedde, and þat anoon,°   directly
    Launfal and sche yn fere.°   together

For° play lytyll° þey sclepte° þat ny3t,°   because of/little/slept/night
350 Tyll on morn° hyt was day ly3t;°   in (the)morning/light
    Sche badde° hym aryse anoon.   bade
He seyde° to hym, "Syr gantyl Kny3t,   she said
And° þou wylt speke° with me any wy3t,°   if/speak/at all
    To a derne stede° þou gon:°   secret place/(must) go

355 Well priuyly° i woll° come to þe°—   very secretly/will/you
No man alyue ne schall me se°—   see
    As stylle° as any ston."°   quiet/stone
Þo° was Launfal glad and blyþe°—   then/happy
He cowde no° man hys ioye° kyþe°—   could (to) no/joy/make known
360   And keste° here well good won.°   kissed/many times

"But of o° þyng, Sir Kny3t,° i warne þe: one/knight
Þat þou make no bost° of me   boast
    For no kennes mede;°   kind (of) recompense
And yf þou doost,° y warny° þe before,   do/I warn
365 All my loue þou hast forlore!"°   lost
    And þus to hym sche seyde.

Launfal tok° hys leue° to wende;°   took/leave/go
Gyfre kedde° þat he was hende,°   showed/handy
    And brou3t° Launfal hys stede.°   brought/steed
370 Launfal lepte° yn to þe arsoun°   leaped/saddle
And rood hom° to Karlyoun°   rode home/Caerleon
    In hys pouere wede.°   poor clothes

353–57. Fairy wives avoided public appearances and were inclined to private tête-à-têtes with their husbands (cf. above, p. 342, n. 12).

359. I.e., because it was so great.

Þo was þe knyȝt yn herte° at wylle:° *heart/pleased*
In hys chaunber° he hyld hym° stylle *chamber/kept himself*
375   All þat vndern-tyde.° *morning time*
Þan come° þer þorwgh° þe cyté° ten *then came/through/city*
Well yharneysyth° men, *equipped*
   Vpon ten somers ryde,° *packhorses riding*

Some with syluer,° some with golde; *silver*
380 All to Syr Launfal hyt scholde;° *it should (go)*
   To presente hym wythe pryde° *with honor*
With ryche cloþes and armure bryȝt,° *armor bright*
Þey axede aftyr° Launfal, þe knyȝt, *asked for*
   Whare° he gan abyde.° *where/did lodge*

385 Þe yong° men wer clodeþ° yn ynde;° *young/clothed/Indian (silk)*
Gyfre he rood all behynde
   Vp° Blaunchard, whyt° as flour. *upon/white*
Þo seyde a boy þat yn þe market stod,° *stood*
   "How fere° schall all þys good?° *far/wealth (go)*
390   Tell vs, par amour."° *for love*

Þo seyde° Gyfre, "Hyt ys ysent° *said/sent*
To Syr Launfal yn° present, *as a*
   Þat haþ leued° yn greet doloure."° *lived/great sorrow*
Þan seyde þe boy, "Nys° he but° a wrecche!° *is not/(nothing) but/wretch*
395 What þar° any man of° hym recche?° *need/for/care*
   At þe Meyrys° hous he takeþ soioure."° *mayor's/lodging*

At þe Merys hous þey gon alyȝte,° *did alight*
And presented þe noble Knyȝte
   With swych° good as hym° was sent; *such/he*
400 And whan° þe Meyr seyȝ þat rychesse° *when/saw those riches*
And Syr Launfales noblenesse,
   He held hymself foule yschent.° *foully shamed*

Þo° seyde þe Meyr, "Syr, par charyté,° *then/charity*
In halle to-day þat° þou wylt ete° with me; *(would) that/eat*
405   Ȝesterday y° hadde yment° *I/hoped*
At þe feste° we wold han be° yn same,° *feast/would have been/together*
And yhadde solas° and game,° *had pleasure/amusement*
   And erst° þou were ywent."° *but already/gone*

"Syr Meyr, God forȝelde þe:° *reward you*
410 Whyles° y was yn my pouerté,° *while/poverty*
   Þou bede° me neuer dyne;° *invited/(to) dine*

Now y haue more gold and fe°	*possessions*
Þat myne° frendes han sent me,	*my*
Þan þou and alle dyne!"°	*thine*

415 Þe Meyr for schame away ȝede;°	*went*
Launfal yn purpure° gan hym schrede,°	*purple (cloth)/himself dress*
Ipelured° with whyt ermyne.	*trimmed*
All þat Launfal hadde borwyþ° before,	*borrowed*
Gyfre, be tayle° and be score,	*by tally*
420 ȝald hyt° well and fyne.°	*repaid it/properly*

Launfal helde ryche festes,	
Fyfty fedde pouere gestes,°	*poor guests*
Þat yn myschef° were;	*misfortune*
Fyfty bouȝte° stronge stedes;°	*bought/steeds*
425 Fyfty yaf° ryche wedes°	*gave/clothes*
To knyȝtes° and squyere;°	*knights/squires*

Fyfty rewardede relygyons;°	*clerics*
Fyfty delyuerede° pouere prysouns,°	*freed/prisoners*
And made ham quyt° and schere;°	*them quit/clear (of debt)*
430 Fyfty clodede gestours°—	*clothed minstrels*
To many men he dede honours,°	*performed services*
In countreys fere° and nere.°	*far/near*

Alle þe lordes of Karlyoun°	*Caerleon*
Lette crye° a turnement° yn þe toun,	*had proclaimed/tournament*
435 For loue of Syr Launfel	
And for Blaunchard hys good stede,	
To wyte° how hym° wold spede,°	*know/he/succeed*
Þat was ymade° so well.	*endowed*

And whan þe day was ycome°	*come*
440 Þat þe iustes° were yn ynome,°	*jousts/(to be) held*
Þey ryde out also snell;°	*as quickly (as possible)*
Trompours gon hare bemes° blowe,	*trumpeters did their horns*
Þe lordes ryden° out arowe°	*ride/in order*
Þat were yn þat castell;	

445 There began þe turnement,	
And ech° knyȝt leyd on° oþer° good dent°	*every/struck/another (a)/blow*

---

419. *tayle:* a "tally stick" which was "scored" or notched and then split, creditor and debtor each receiving half.

422. *Fyfty:* Repeated in this stanza and the next as a rhetorical device, the number refers not to *festes,* l. 421, but to the nouns that follow: "Fifty (he) fed (of) poor guests," etc.

With mases° and with swerdes° boþe. *maces/swords*
Me myȝte yse° some þerfore° *one might see/as a result*
Stedes ywonne,° and some ylore,° *won/lost*
450   And knyȝtes wonþer wroȝth.° *wondrously enraged*

Sythe° þe Rounde Table was,° *since/was (founded)*
A bettere turnement þer nas,° *was not*
I dare well say for soþe;° *in truth*
Many a lord of Karlyoun
455 Þat day were ybore adoun,° *was thrown down*
Certayn, withouten oþe.° *certainly, without oath*

Of Karlyoun þe ryche° constable *powerful*
Rod to° Launfal, without fable:° *rode at/lie*
He nolde° no lengere abyde;° *would not/longer wait*
460 He smot° to Launfal, and he to hym; *struck*
Well sterne° strokes and well grym *very hard*
Þer were, yn° eche a° syde. *on/every*

Launfal was of hym yware:° *aware*
Out of hys sadell he hym bare° *threw*
465   To grounde þat ylke tyde;° *same moment*
And whan° þe constable was bore° adoun, *when/thrown*
Gyfre lepte° ynto þe arsoun,° *leaped/saddle*
And awey° he gan° to ryde. *away/began*

Þe Erl of Chestere þerof segh;° *it saw*
470   For° wreþþe° yn herte° he was wod negh,° *because of/anger/heart/mad nearly*
And rood° to Syr Launfale, *rode*
And smot hym yn þe helm° on hegh,° *helmet/top*
Þat° þe crest adoun flegh:° *so that/flew*
Þus seyd° þe Frenssche° tale. *said/French*

475 Launfal was mochel of° myȝt: *great in*
Of° hys stede° he dede° hym lyȝt° *from/steed/made/fall*
And bare° hym doun yn þe dale.° *bore/ground*
Þan come° þer Syr Launfal abowte° *then came/around*
Of Walssche knyȝtes° a greet rowte,° *Welsh knights/great company*
480   Þe numbre y° not° how fale.° *I/know not/many*

---

456. *withouten oþe:* i.e., "without doubt" ("no need to swear an oath on it").

469. The earl of Chester was a common figure in folktale and legend. He may be the "Randolph, Earl of Chester" whose songs are mentioned in *Piers Plowman* in connection with Robin Hood.

474. The "French tale" may really be two works: the Old French romance of *Graelent* and another, lost, source of the present work.

Þan my3te me se scheldes ryue,°   *see shields broken*
Speres tobreste° and todryue,°   *spears splintered/split*
    Behynde and ek° before;   *also*
Þoru3° Launfal and hys stedes° dent,   *through/steed's*
485 Many a kny3t, verement,°   *truly*
    To ground was ibore.°   *thrown*

So þe prys° of þat turnay°   *prize/tournament*
Was delyuered° to Launfal þat day,   *delivered*
    Without oþ° y swore.°   *oath/swear*
490 Launfal rod to Karlyoun,°   *Caerleon*
    To þe Meyrys° hous of þe toun,   *mayor's*
    And many a lord hym before;

And þan þe noble kny3t Launfal
Held a feste,° ryche and ryall,°   *feast/royal*
495   Þat leste fourteny3t;°   *lasted (a) fortnight*
Erles and barouns fale
Semely° were sette° yn sale,°   *properly/seated/hall*
    And ryaly were ady3t;°   *arrayed*

And euery day Dame Triamour,
500 Sche com to Syr Launfal boure,°   *chamber*
    A-day° whan hyt° was ny3t;°   *daily/it/night*
Of all þat euer were þer þo,°   *then*
Segh her non° but þey° two,   *none/these*
    Gyfre and Launfal þe kny3t.

505 A kny3t þer was yn Lumbardye;°   *Lombardy*
To° Syr Launfal hadde he greet enuye:°   *of/envy*
    Syr Valentyne he hy3te.°   *was called*
He herde speke° of Syr Launfal,   *heard spoken*
How þat he couþ iusty° well,   *could joust*
510   And was a man of mochel my3te.°   *might*

Syr Valentyne was wonþere° strong;   *wondrously*
Fyftene feet he was longe:°   *tall*
    Hym þo3te° he brente bry3t°   *to him (it) seemed/burned bright*
But° he my3te with Launfal pleye,°   *unless/joust*
515 In þe feld,° betwene ham tweye°   *field/them two*
    To iusty oþer° to fy3te.°   *or/fight*

---

484. The aggressiveness of the war-horse greatly aided the knight in tournament and battle.

513. *he brente bry3t:* i.e., "he would be consumed with desire."

515. *feld:* Cf. above, p. 73, l. 608*n.*

Syr Valentyne sat yn hys halle;
Hys massengere° he let ycalle,°   *messenger/ordered called*
And seyde° he moste wende°   *said/must go*
520 To Syr Launfal, þe noble knyȝt,°   *knight*
Þat was yholde° so mychel° of myȝt: *considered/great*
To Bretayne° he wolde° hym sende;   *Britain/would*

"And sey° hym, fore° loue of hys lemman,°   *tell/for/beloved*
Yf sche be any gantyle° woman,   *noble*
525 Courteys, fre,° oþer hende,°   *courteous, generous/gracious*
Þat he come with me to iuste,°   *joust*
To kepe° hys harneys° from þe ruste,   *keep/armor*
And elles° hys manhod schende."°   *or else/manhood disgrace*

Þe messengere ys forþ ywent;°   *gone*
530 To þo° hys lordys commaundement,°   *do/lord's command*
He hadde wynde at wylle.°   *favorable*
Whan° he was ouer þe water ycome,°   *when/come*
Þe way to Syr Launfal he haþ ynome,°   *taken*
And grette° hym with wordes stylle,°   *greeted/quiet*

535 And seyd, "Syr, my lord, Syr Valentyne,
A noble werrour° and queynte° of gynne,°   *warrior/skillful/strategy*
Haþ me sent þe tylle,°   *you to*
And praythe° þe, for þy lemmanes sake,   *begs*
Þou schuldest° with hym iustes take."°   *should/undertake*
540 Þo louȝ° Launfal full stylle,°   *laughed/very quietly*

And seyde, as he was gentyl° knyȝt,   *noble*
Þylke° day a fourtenyȝt°   *(from) that/fortnight*
He wold with hym play.°   *joust*
He yaf° þe messengere, for þat tydyng,°   *gave/news*
545 A noble courser° and a ryng,   *horse*
And a robe of ray.°   *striped cloth*

Launfal tok leue at° Triamoure,   *took leave of*
Þat was þe bryȝt berde° yn boure,°   *fair lady/chamber*
And keste° þat swete may;°   *kissed/sweet maid*
550 Þanne° seyde þat swete wyȝt,°   *then/person*
"Dreed° þe no þyng, syr gentyl Knyȝt: *fear*
Þou schalt hym sle° þat day."   *slay*

Launfal nolde° noþyng with hym haue   *would not*
But Blaunchard hys stede° and Gyfre hys knaue,°   *steed/servant boy*
555 Of all hys fayre mayné.°   *retinue*

He schypede,° and hadde wynd well° good,   *boarded ship/very*
And wente ouer þe salte flod°   *sea*
   Into Lumbardye.°   *Lombardy*

Whan he was ouir° þe watir° ycome   *over/water*
560 Þer° þe iustes schulde be nome°   *where/held*
   In þe cyte° of Atalye,   *city*
Syr Valentyn hadde a greet ost,°   *great host*
And Syr Launfal abatede here bost°   *lessened their boasting*
   Wythe lytyll° companye.   *with little*

565 And whan Syre Launfal was ydyȝt°   *prepared*
Vpon Blaunchard, hys stede lyȝt,°   *agile*
   With helm° and spere° and schelde,° *helmet/spear/shield*
All þat sawe hym yn armes bryȝt°   *bright*
Seyde° þey sawe neuir swych° a knyȝt,°   *said/never such/knight*
570   Þat hym wythe eyen° behelde. *eyes*

Þo° ryde togydere þes° knyȝtes two,   *then/together these*
Þat° hare° schaftes tobroste bo°   *so that/their/splintered both*
   And toscyuerede° yn þe felde;°   *broke/field*
Anoþer cours togedere° þey rod,°   *together/rode*
575 Þat Syre Launfal helm of glod,°   *off fell*
   In tale as hyt° ys telde.°   *it/told*

Syr Valentyn logh° and hadde good game:°   *laughed/fun*
Hadde Launfal neuer so moche° schame   *much*
   Beforhond° yn no fyȝt!°   *before/fight*
580 Gyfre kedde° he was good at nede,°   *showed/need*
And lepte° vpon hys maystrys° stede: *leaped/master's*
   No man ne segh° with syȝt.°   *not saw/sight*

And er þan° þay togedere mette,°   *before/clashed*
Hys lordes helm he on sette,°   *put*
585   Fayre and well adyȝt.°   *arrayed*
Þo was Launfal glad and blyþe,°   *happy*
And donkede° Gyfre many syde°   *thanked/times*
   For hys dede° so mochel° of myȝt.° *deed/great/might*

---

561. *Atalye:* a city in Lombardy, supposedly built by Saracens. In the Old French romance of *Otinel*, Charlemagne captures the city and grants it to Otinel as his capital.

574. *cours:* The attempt to unhorse the opponent with a lance while passing him was called "riding a course." A railing separated the riders, as cars in opposing traffic lanes today are separated by the line on a divided highway. Once down, the knight could be raised only with the help of his squires.

582. As a fairy, Gyfre was invisible at will.

Syr Valentyne smot° Launfal soo°   *struck/so*
590 Þat hys scheld fel hym fro,°   *from*
    Anoon ryȝt yn° þat stounde;°   *directly right at/time*
And Gyfre þe scheld vp hente°   *took*
And broȝte° hyt hys lord to presente   *brought*
    Ere hyt cam þoune° to grounde.   *fell down*

595 Þo was Launfal glad and blyþe,
And rode ayen° þe þrydde syde,°   *again/third time*
    As a knyȝt of mochell mounde;°   *power*
Syr Valentyne he smot so þere°   *vigorously*
Þat hors and man boþe deed° were,   *dead*
600   Gronyng° with grysly wounde.   *groaning*

Alle þe lordes of Atalye
To° Syr Launfal hadde greet envye°   *of/great enmity*
    Þat Valentyne was yslawe,°   *slain*
And swore þat he schold dye°   *should die*
605 Er he wente out of Lumbardye,°   *Lombardy*
    And be hongede° and todrawe.°   *hanged/drawn apart*

Syr Launfal brayde° out hys fachon,°   *pulled/sword*
And as lyȝt as° dew he leyde hem° doune,   *lightly as (falls)/struck them*
    In a lytyll drawe,°   *little space*
610 And whan° he hadde þe lordes sclayn,°   *when/slain*
He wente ayen yn to Bretayn,°   *Britain*
    Withe solas° and wyth plawe.°   *with joy/merriment*

Þe tydyng com° to Artoure° þe Kyng,   *news came/Arthur*
Anoon, without lesyng,°   *lie*
615   Of Syr Launfales noblesse;°   *noble conduct*
Anoon he let° to hym sende°   *ordered/sent*
Þat Launfall schuld° to hym wende°   *should/go*
    At Seynt Ionnys° Masse,   *Saint John's*

For Kyng Artoure wold° a feste° holde   *would/feast*
620 Of erles and of barouns bolde,
    Of lordynges more° and lesse.   *lord's greater*
Syr Launfal schud° be stward° of halle,   *should/steward*

---

606. To be drawn or pulled apart was a punishment mentioned in *Havelok the Dane* and *The Cuckoo and the Nightingale*.

616. *let . . . sende:* i.e., "ordered word sent to him."

618. Saint John's Day was June 24.

For° to agye° hys gestes° alle,   *in order/manage/guests*
  For he cowþe of largesse.°   *knew about liberality*

625 Launfal toke leue at° Triamoure   *took leave of*
For to wende to Kyng Artoure,
  Hys feste for to agye;
Þer he fond merthe° and moch° honour,   *found joy/much*
Ladyes þat wer well bryȝt° yn boure,°   *very fair/chamber*
630   Of knyȝtes° greet companye.   *knights*

Fourty dayes leste° þe feste,   *lasted*
Ryche, ryall,° and honeste:°   *royal/worthy*
  What help hyt° for to lye?°   *it/deny*
And at þe fourty dayes ende,
635 Þe lordes toke har° leue to wende,   *their*
  Euerych° yn hys partye;°   *each/his (own) direction*

And aftyr mete° Syr Gaweyn,   *dinner*
Syr Gyeryes° and Agrafayn,°   *Gaheres/Agravain*
  And Syr Launfal also
640 Wente to daunce° vpon þe grene,   *dance*
Vnþer° þe toure þer lay° þe Quene,   *under/tower where rested*
  With syxty ladyes and mo.°   *more*

To lede° þe daunce Launfal was set:°   *lead/appointed*
For hys largesse he was louede° þe bet,°   *loved/better*
645   Sertayn, of° alle þo.°   *certainly, by/those*
Þe Quene lay° out and beheld hem alle;   *leaned*
"I se,"° sche seyde,° "daunce large° Launfalle: *see/said/dancing generous*
  To hym þan° wyll y° go.   *then/I*

Of alle þe knyȝtes þat y se þere,
650 He ys þe fayreste bachelere:°   *bachelor*
  He ne° hadde neuer no wyf.°   *not/woman*
Tyde° me good oþer° ylle,   *betide/or*
I wyll go and wyte° hys wylle;°   *know/desire*
  Y loue hym as my lyf!"°   *life*

655 Sche tok° with here° a companye,   *took/her*
Þe fayrest þat sche myȝte aspye°—   *might see*
  Syxty ladyes and fyf°—   *five*
And wente hem° doun anoon ryȝtes,°   *took themselves/then directly*
Ham° to pley° among þe knyȝtes   *themselves/disport*
660 Well stylle, withouten stryf.°   *quietly, without ado*

Þe Quene yede° to Þe formeste° ende,   *went/top*
Betwene Launfal and Gauweyn Þe hende;°   *gracious*
   And after, here ladyes bryȝt,
To daunce Þey wente alle yn same:°   *together*
665 To se hem play°, hyt was fayr game,°   *them sport/amusement*
   A lady and a knyȝt.

Þey hadde menstrales° of moch honours°—   *minstrels/excellence*
Fydelers,° sytolyrs,° and trompours°   *fiddlers/citole players/trumpeters*
   And elles° hyt were° vnryȝt.°   *otherwise/would have been/not right*
670 Þere Þey playde, for soÞe° to say,   *in truth*
After mete Þe somerys° day   *summer's*
   All-what° hyt was neyȝ nyȝt.°   *until/nearly night*

And whanne° Þe daunce began to slake,°   *when/slacken*
Þe Quene gan° Launfal to counsell° take,   *did/in (her) confidence*
675   And seyde yn Þys mainere:°   *manner*
"Sertaynlyche,° Syre Knyȝt,°   *certainly/knight*
I haue Þe louyd° with all my myȝt   *you loved*
   More Þan Þys° seuen ȝere;°   *these/years*

But-Þat° Þou louye me,   *unless*
680 Sertes° y dye fore° loue of Þe,   *certainly/die for*
   Launfal, my lemman dere!"°   *beloved dear*
Þannc° answerede Þe gentyll° Knyȝt,   *then/noble*
"I nell° be traytoure, day ne° nyȝt,   *will not/traitor, day nor*
   Be° God, Þat all may stere!"°   *by/guide*

685 Sche seyde, "Fy° on Þe, Þou coward!   *fie*
An-hongeÞ° worÞ° Þou hye° and hard!   *hanged/(will) be/high*
   Þat Þou euir° were ybore°—   *ever/born*
Þat Þou lyuest, hyt° ys pyte;°   *live, it/pity*
Þou louyst° no woman, ne no woman Þe;   *love*
690   Þow° were worÞy° forelore!"°   *you/deserving (to be)/destroyed*

Þe Knyȝt was sore° aschamed Þo:°   *greatly/then*
To speke ne° myȝte he forgo,°   *speak not/refrain*
   And seyde° Þe Quene before,   *said*
"I haue loued a fayryr° woman   *fairer*

---

668. *sytolyrs:* The citole was a stringed instrument similar to the zither.

685–90. Guinevere's savage reaction to Launfal's supposed chastity may be a reflection of contemporary social mores, or perhaps her own lecherous nature.

⁶⁹⁵ Þan þou euir leydest þyn ey° vpon,   *laid your eye*
    Þys seuen yere° and more!   *years*

    Hyre loþlokste° mayde, withoute wene,°   *her ugliest/doubt*
    Myȝte bet° be a quene   *might better*
    Þan þou, yn all þy lyue!'"°   *life*
⁷⁰⁰ Þerfore° þe Quene was swyþe wroȝt;°   *at that/very angry*
    Sche takeþ hyre maydenes, and forþ hy goþ°   *she goes*
    Into here tour also blyue;°   *her tower as fast (as possible)*

    And anon° sche ley° doun yn her bedde;   *directly/lay*
    For° wrethe, syk° sche hyre bredde,°   *because of/anger, sick/herself made*
⁷⁰⁵ And swore, so moste° sche thryue,°   *as might/prosper*
    Sche wold of° Launfal be so awreke°   *would on/avenged*
    Þat all þe lond schuld° of hym speke   *land should*
    Withinne þe dayes fyfe.°   *five*

    Kyng Artour com fro° huntynge,   *Arthur came from*
⁷¹⁰ Blyþe° and glad yn all þyng;°   *happy/things*
    To hys chambere þan° wente he.   *then*
    Anoon° þe Quene on° hym gan° crye,   *directly/to/did*
    "But y° be awreke, y schall dye!   *unless I*
    Myn herte° wyll breke° a-þre!°   *my heart/break/in three (pieces)*

⁷¹⁵ I spak° to Launfal yn my game,°   *spoke/play*
    And he besofte° me of° schame—   *besought/of me*
    My lemman° fore° to be!   *lover/in order*
    And of a lemman hys yelp° he made,   *boast*
    Þat þe lodlokest° mayde þat sche hadde   *ugliest*
⁷²⁰ Myȝt be a quene aboue me."

    Kyng Artour was well wroþ,°   *very angry*
    And be God he swor hys oþ°   *oath*
    Þat Launfal schuld be sclawe.°   *slain*
    He wente aftyr doȝty knyȝtes°   *for doughty knights*
⁷²⁵ To brynge Launfal anoon ryȝtes°   *then directly*
    To be hongeþ° and todrawe.°   *hanged/drawn apart*

    Þe knyȝtes softe° hym anoon,   *sought*
    But Launfal was to hys chaumber° gon,   *chamber*
    To han° hadde solas° and plawe;°   *have/joy/merriment*

712–20. This is the Potiphar's Wife motif (Stith Thompson, *Motif-Index*) of folklore, from the biblical incident concerning Joseph and the amorous wife of Potiphar in Egypt.

beloved/lost

then/unhappy

looked/purse
provided/money altogether plentiful
when/need
was not/none, in truth
ridden
upon/steed

gained
it melted/before
romance/read
armor/white
turned/black
said

darling
(away) from you
sweetheart
joy/lost
for me is the worst
lady/chamber

beat/head also
spoke
grief/great sorrow
hour
directly/fainting
came

bound/led
double woe
Arthur
then
vile tainted traitor
such (a) boast

lover's ugliest
wife

730 He softe hys leef,° but sche was lore,°
   As sche hadde warnede hym before;
     Þo° was Launfal vnfawe.°

He lokede° yn hys alnere,°
Þat fond° hym spendyng all plenere°
735   Whan þat° he hadde nede;°
And þer nas° noon, for soþ° to say;
And Gyfre was yryde° away
     Vp° Blaunchard, hys stede.°

All þat he hadde before ywonne,°
740 Hyt malt° as snow aȝens° þe sunne,
   In romaunce° as we rede;°
Hys armur,° þat was whyt° as floure,
Hyt becom° of blak° coloure,
     And þus þan Launfal seyde:°

745 "Alas!" he seyde, "my creature,°
How schall i from þe° endure,
   Swetyng° Tryamoure?
All my ioye° i have forelore,°
And þc: þat me ys worst fore,°
750   Þou blyssfull berde° yn boure!"°

He bet° hys body and hys hedde ek,°
And cursede þe mouþ þat he with spek,°
   With care° and grect doloure,°
And for sorow yn þat stounde°
755 Anoon° he fell aswowe° to grounde;
   With þat come° knyȝtes foure,

And bond° hym, and ladde° hym þo—
Þo was þe Knyȝte yn doble wo!°—
   Before Artoure° þe Kyng.
760 Þan° seyde Kyng Artoure,
   "Fyle ataynte traytoure,°
     Why madest þou swyche yelpyng?°

Þat þy lemmannes lodlokest° mayde
Was fayrer þan my wyf,° þou seyde:

742–43. The Love Token motif in romances usually concerns a change in color or state of the love gift exchanged, if one of the lovers proves to be unfaithful.

749. *þat . . . fore:* i.e., "that is the worst for me."

765	Þat was a fowll lesynge!°	*foul lie*
	And þou besoftest here° before þan	*besought her*
	Þat sche schold° be þy lemman:	*should*
	Þat was mysprowd lykynge!"°	*arrogant desire*

	Þe Knyȝt° answerede with egre mode,°	*knight/in excited mood*
770	Before þe Kyng þer° he stode,°	*where/stood*
	Þe° Quene on° hym gan lye:°	*(that) the/about/did lie*
	"Sethe þat° y euere° was yborn,°	*since/I ever/born*
	I besofte her here beforn°	*before*
	Neuir° of no folye!°	*never/folly*

775	But sche seyde y nas no man,	
	Ne° þat me louede° no woman,	*nor/I loved*
	Ne no womannes companye;	
	And i answerede her, and sayde	
	Þat my lemmannes lodelkest° mayde	*ugliest*
780	To be a quene was bettere wordye.°	*worthy*

	Certes, lordynges, hyt° ys so;	*certainly, lords, it*
	I am aredy° for to þo°	*ready/do*
	All þat þe court wyll loke!"°	*ordain*
	To say þe soþ,° without les,°	*truth/lie*
785	All togedere° how hyt was,	*altogether*
	xii knyȝtis° were dryue to boke;°	*knights/made to (consult law) books*

	All þey° seyde, ham betwene,°	*all of them/said, themselves among*
	Þat knewe þe maners° of þe Quene	*custom*
	And þe queste toke,°	*inquiry undertook*
790	Þe Quene bar los° of swych a word°	*bore (a) reputation/report*
	Þat sche louede lemmannes without° her lord;	*besides*
	'Har° neuir on° hyt foresoke;°	*(of) her/one/denied*

	Þerfor þey seyden° alle	*said*
	Hyt was long on° þe Quene, and not on° Launfal;	*the fault of/of*
795	Þereof þey gonne° hym skere;°	*did/acquit*
	And yf he myȝte° hys lemman brynge,	*might*
	Þat he made of swych ȝelpynge,°	*boast*
	Oþere° þe maydenes were°	*or/(who) were*

	Bryȝtere° þan þe Quene of hewe,°	*fairer/countenance*
800	Launfal schuld° be holde trewe°	*should/held honest*

---

795. *Þereof:* i.e., "of the charge of attempted seduction."

Of° þat, yn all manere;°   *in/ways*
And yf he myȝte not brynge hys lef,°   *beloved*
He schud° be hongede° as a þef:°   *should/hanged/thief*
 Þey seyden all yn fere.°   *together*

805 All yn fere þey made proferynge°   *proposal*
 Þat Launfal schuld hys lemman° brynge: *beloved*
  Hys heed° he gan to° laye.°   *head/did/pledge*
 Þan° seyde þe Quene, without lesynge,° *then/lie*
 "ȝyf° he bryngeþ a fayrere þynge,°   *if/one*
810 Put out my eeyn° gray!"   *eyes*

 Whan° þat waiowr° was take on honde,° *when/wager/agreed on*
 Launfal þerto two borwes fonde,°   *sureties provided*
  Noble knyȝtes twayn:°   *knights two*
 Syre Perceuall° and Syr Gawayn,   *Percival*
815 Þey were hys borwes, soþ to sayn,° *say*
  Tyll a certayn° day.   *appointed*

 Þe certayn day, i ȝow plyȝt,°   *you assure*
 Was xii moneþ° and fourtenyȝt,°   *months/fortnight (hence)*
  Þat he schuld hys lemman brynge.
820 Syr Launfal, þat noble knyȝt,
 Greet° sorow and care yn hym was lyȝt:° *great/arisen*
  Hys hondys° he gan° wrynge.   *hands/did*

 So greet sorowe hym was vpan,°   *upon*
 Gladlyche° hys lyf° he wold forgon,° *gladly/life/would lose*
825 In care and in marnynge;°   *mourning*
 Gladlyche he wold hys hed forego:° *head lose*
 Euerych° man þerfore was wo,°   *every/sorrowful*
  Þat wyste° of þat tydynde.°   *knew/happening*

 Þe certayn day was nyȝyng:°   *drawing close*
830 Hys borowes° hym broȝt° befor þe Kyng; *sureties/brought*
  Þe Kyng recordede þo,°   *reconvened (the trial) then*
 And bad° hym bryng hys lef yn syȝt;° *bade/sight*
 Syr Launfal seyde° þat he ne° myȝt— *said/not*
  Þerfore hym° was well° wo.   *he/very*

835 Þe Kyng commaundede° þe barouns alle *commanded*
 To yeue iugement° on Launfal,   *give judgment*

---

810. A foreshadowing of l. 1008.

And dampny° hym to sclo.°	*condemn/be slain*
Þan sayde þe Erl of Cornewayle,°	*Cornwall*
Þat was with ham° at þat counceyle,°	*them/council*
840 "We wyllyd naȝt° do so.	*will not*

Greet schame hyt° wer° vs alle vpon	*it/would be*
For to dampny þat gantylman,°	*gentleman*
Þat haþ be hende° and fre:°	*been gracious/generous*
Þerfore, lordynges, doþ° be° my reed:°	*lords, do/according to/advice*
845 Oure Kyng we wyllyþ anoþer wey lede;°	*way lead*
Out of lond° Launfal schall fle."°	*land/flee*

And as þey stod° þus spekynge,°	*stood/speaking*
Þe barouns sawe come rydynge	
Ten maydenes bryȝt° of ble:°	*fair/face*
850 Ham° þoȝte° þey were so bryȝt and schene°	*to them/(it) seemed/shining*
Þat þe lodlokest,° without wene,°	*ugliest/doubt*
Hare° quene þan myȝte° be.	*their/then might*

Þo seyde Gawayn, þat corteys knyȝt:°	*courteous knight*
"Launfal, brodyr, drede þe° no wyȝt:°	*brother, fear you/not at all*
855 Here comeþ þy lemman° hende."	*beloved*
Launfal answerede and seyde ywys,°	*indeed*
"Non° of ham my lemman nys,°	*none/is not*
Gawayn, my lefly° frende!"	*dear*

To þat castell þey wente ryȝt;°	*right away*
860 At þe gate þey gonne alyȝt;°	*did alight*
Before Kyng Artoure° gonne þey wende,°	*Arthur/go*
And bede° hym make aredy° hastyly	*bade/ready*
A fayre chambere, for here° lady,	*their*
Þat was come of° kynges kende.°	*descended from/blood*

865 "Ho° ys your lady?" Artoure seyde;	*who*
"Ye schull ywyte,"° seyde þe mayde,	*shall know*
"For sche comeþ ryde."°	*riding*
Þe Kyng commaundede, for here° sake,	*her*
Þe fayryst chaunber° for to take	*fairest chamber*
870 In hys palys° þat tyde;°	*palace/moment*

And anon° to hys barouns he sente	*directly*
For to yeue iugemente	

---

838. *Erl of Cornewayle:* The earl (in *Lanval* duke) of Cornwall was Cador, one of Arthur's chief and most famous counselors (cf. above, p. 346), n. 24).

Vpon þat traytour,° full of pryde.   *traitor*
Þe barouns answerede anoon ryȝt,°   *then directly*
875 "Haue we seyn° þe madenes° bryȝt,   *seen/maidens*
    Whe° schull not longe abyde."°   *we/wait*

A newe tale° þey gonne þo,°   *discussion/began then*
Some of wele° and some of wo,°   *happiness/woe*
    Har lord þe Kyng to queme;°   *please*
880 Some dampnede° Launfal þere,   *condemned*
    And some made hym quyt° and skere:°   *quit/clear*
        Hare tales were well breme.°   *very fierce*

Þo saw þey oþer ten maydenes bryȝt,
Fayryre° þan þe oþer ten of syȝt,°   *fairer/in appearance*
885   As þey gone hym deme;°   *did them judge*
    Þey ryd° upon ioly moyles° of Spayne,   *rode/fine mules*
    With sadell° and brydell of Champayne;   *saddle*
        Hare lorayns lyȝt° gonne leme.°   *harness brightly/shine*

Þey were yclodeþ° yn samyt tyre,°   *clothed/satin attire*
890 Ech° man hadde greet° desyre   *every/great*
    To se° hare clodynge.°   *see/clothing*
    Þo seyde° Gaweyn, þat curtayse° knyȝt,   *said/courteous*
    "Launfal, here comeþ þy swete wyȝt,°   *sweet one*
        Þat may þy hote° brynge."   *salvation*

895 Launfal answerede with drery doȝt,°   *dreary thought*
    And seyde, "Alas, y° knowe hem noȝt,°   *I/them not*
        Ne non° of all þe of sprynge!"°   *nor none/they from come*
    Forþ þey wente to þat palys
    And lyȝte° at þe hye deys,°   *alighted/high dais*
900   Before Artoure° þe Kynge,   *Arthur*

And grette° þe Kyng and Quene ek,°   *greeted/also*
And oo° mayde þys° wordes spak°   *one/these/spoke*
    To þe Kyng Artoure:
    "Þyn° halle agrayde,° and hele° þe walles   *your/prepare/decorate*
905 With clodes° and with ryche palles°   *cloths/coverings*
        Aȝens° my lady Tryamoure."   *for (the arrival of)*

Þe Kyng answerede bedene,°   *at once*
    "Well come, ye maydenes schene,°   *shining*

---

875. *Haue we seyn:* i.e., "once we have seen."
889. *samyt:* Samite was a heavy silk cloth, sometimes interwoven with gold thread.

Be° oure lord þe Sauyoure!"°   *by/Savior*
910 He commaundede Launcelet° du Lake to brynge hem yn fere°   *commanded Lancelot/together*
In þe chamber þere hare felawes° were,   *where their companions*
   With merthe° and moche° honoure.   *joy/much*

Anoon° þe Quene supposed gyle:°   *directly/suspected (a) trick*
Þat Launfal schuld° yn a whyle   *should*
915   Be ymade° quyt and skere   *made*
Þoruȝ° hys lemman,° þat was commynge.°   *through/beloved/coming*
Anon° sche seyde to Artoure þe Kyng,   *then*
   "Syre, curtays yf þou were,

Or yf þou louedest° þyn honoure,   *loved*
920 I schuld be awreke of° þat traytoure°   *avenged on/traitor*
   Þat doþ° me changy chere!°   *makes/change (my good) cheer*
To Launfal þou schuldest not spare;°   *be lenient*
Þy barouns dryueþ þe° to bysmare;°   *drive you/mockery*
   He ys hem° lef° and dere!"°   *to them/beloved/dear*

925 And as þe Quene spak to þe Kyng,
Þe barouns seyȝ° come rydynge   *saw*
   A damesele alone,
Vpoon° a whyt° comely palfrey;°   *upon/white/riding horse*
Þey saw neuere° non so gay°   *never/brilliant*
930   Vpon þe grounde gone:°   *go*

Gentyll, iolyf° as bryd° on bowe,°   *noble, pretty/bird/bough*
In all manere° fayre inowe°   *ways/enough*
   To wonye° yn wordly wone.°   *live/worldly state*
Þe lady was bryȝt° as blosme° on brere,°   *fair/blossom/briar*
935 With eyen° gray, with louelych chere;°   *eyes/lovely countenance*
   Her leyre lyȝt schoone.°   *face brightly shone*

As rose on rys here rode° was red;   *branch her complexion*
Þe here schon° vpon here hed°   *hair shone/head*
   As gold wyre° þat schynyth° bryȝt.°   *thread/shines/bright*
940 Sche hadde a crounne° vpon here molde°   *crown/head*
Of ryche stones and of golde,
   Þat lofsom lemede° lyȝt.   *lovely shone*

---

910. *Launcelot du Lake:* Lancelot du Lac was Arthur's foremost knight, in later romances the lover of Guinevere (cf. Malory, *Morte Darthur*) and by Elaine, Tennyson's "lily maid of Astolat," the father of the pure Sir Galahad. Lancelot was raised by the Lady of the Lake, a water fairy.

928. *Palfrey:* Cf. above, p. 346, n. 26.

Þe lady was clad yn purpere palle,°   *purple cloth*
With gentyll° body and myddyll° small,   *dainty/waist*
945   Þat semely° was of syȝt.°   *seemly/to see*
Her mantyll was furryþ° with whyt ermyn,°   *furred/ermine*
Ireuersyd iolyf° and fyn;°   *trimmed delicately/fine*
    No rychere be ne myȝt.°   *not might*

Her sadell° was semyly set:°   *saddle/fittingly decorated*
950 Þe sambus° were grene feluet,°   *saddlecloths/velvet*
    Ipaynted° with ymagerye;°   *painted/pictures*
Þe bordure° was of belles   *border*
Of ryche gold, and noþyng elles,°   *else*
    Þat any man myȝte aspye.°   *see*

955 In þe arsouns,° before and behynde,   *saddlebows*
Were twey° stones of Ynde,°   *two/India*
    Gay° for þe maystrye;°   *brilliant/exceedingly*
Þe paytrelle° of her palfraye   *breast trappings*
Was worþ an erldome stoute° and gay,   *stately*
960   Þe best yn Lumbardye.°   *Lombardy*

A gerfawcon° sche bar° on here hond;°   *hawk/bore/hand*
A softe pas° here palfray fond,°   *easy pace/trod*
    Þat° men here schuld° beholde.   *so that/should*
Þoruȝ° Karlyon rood° þat lady;   *through/rode*
965 Twey whyte grehoundys ronne hyre by;°   *greyhounds ran her beside*
    Hare colers° were of golde.   *their collars*

And whan° Launfal sawe þat lady,   *when*
To alle þe folk he gon° crye an hy,°   *did/aloud*
    Boþe to yonge° and olde,   *young*
970 "Here," he seyde,° "comyþ my lemman swete!°   *said/beloved sweet*
Sche myȝte me of my balys bete,°   *sorrows heal*
    Ȝef° þat lady wolde."°   *if/would*

Forþ sche wente ynto þe halle,
Þer° was þe Quene and þe ladyes alle,   *where*
975   And also Kyng Artoure;°   *Arthur*
Here° maydenes come ayens° here ryȝt,°   *her/came toward/right away*
To take here styrop° whan sche lyȝt°—   *stirrup/alighted*
    Of þe lady Dame Tryamoure.

---

964. *Karlyon:* Kardevyle (Carlisle) is probably meant here; cf. above, l. 8*n*, and below, l. 1021.

Sche dede of° here mantyll on þe flet,°   *slipped off | floor*
980 Þat men schuld here beholde þe bet,°   *better*
 Withoute a more soiour.°   *greater delay*
Kyng Artoure gan° here fayre grete,°   *did | pleasantly-greet*
And sche hym agayn,° with wordes swete,   *in return*
 Þat were of greet valoure.°   *great (good) breeding*

985 Vp stod° þe Quene and ladyes stoute,   *stood*
Her for° to beholde all aboute,   *in order*
 How euene° sche stod vpryȝt; °   *gracefully | erect*
Þan° were þey with° here also donne°   *then | against | as dun*
As ys þe mone ayen° þe sonne,°   *moon against | sun*
990 A-day° whan hyt° ys lyȝt.°   *in daytime | it | light*

Þan seyde sche to Artour þe Kyng,
"Syr, hydyr° i com for swych° a þyng: *hither | such*
 To skere° Launfal þe knyȝt:°   *clear | knight*
Þat he neuer, yn no folye,°   *folly*
995 Besofte° þe Quene of° no drurye,°   *besought | of the queen | lovemaking*
 By dayes ne be nyȝt.°   *nor by night*

Þerfor, Syr Kyng, good kepe° þou myne:°   *well mark | my (words)*
He bad naȝt° here, but sche bad hym   *asked not*
 Here lemman° for to be;   *lover*
1000 And he answerede here, and seyde
Þat hys lemmannes loþlokest° mayde   *beloved's ugliest*
 Was fayryre° þan was sche."   *fairer*

Kyng Artoure seyde, withouten oþe,°   *without oath*
"Ech° man may yse° þat ys soþe,°   *every | see | truth*
1005 Bryȝtere° þat ye be."   *fairer*
With þat, Dame Tryamour to þe Quene geþ,°   *goes*
And blew on here swych a breþ°   *breath*
 Þat neuer eft myȝt° sche se.°   *again might | see*

Þe lady lep an hyre° palfray°   *leaped on her | riding horse*
1010 And bad hem° alle haue good day: *bade them*
 Sche nolde° no lengere abyde.°   *would not | longer remain*
With þat com° Gyfre, all so prest,°   *came | in a hurry*
With Launfalys stede° out of þe forest,   *Launfal's steed*
 And stod Launfal besyde.

988–89. *with, ayen:* i.e., "next to."

¹⁰¹⁵ Þe knyȝt to horse began to sprynge,
   Anoon,° without any lettynge,°   *directly/delay*
      With hys lemman away to ryde;
   Þe lady tok here maydenys° achon,°   *took her maidens/every one*
   And wente þe way þat sche hadde er° gon,   *before*
¹⁰²⁰   With solas° and wyth pryde.   *joy*

   Þe lady rod dorþ Cardeuyle,°   *rode through Carlisle*
   Fere° yn to a iolyf ile,°   *far/pleasant isle*
      Olyroun þat hyȝte;°   *was called*
   Euery yere,° vpon a certayn day,   *year*
¹⁰²⁵ Me° may here° Launfales stede nay,°   *one/hear/neigh*
      And hym se with syȝt.°   *sight*

   Ho þat° wyll þer axsy° iustus°   *whoever/ask for/joust*
   To kepe° hys armes fro° þe rustus,°   *keep/weapons from/rust*
      In turnement oþer fyȝt,°   *tournament or fight*
¹⁰³⁰ Dare° hc neuer forþer gon:°   *need/further go*
   Þer he may fynde iustes anoon,
      With Syr Launfal þe knyȝt.°   *knight*

   Þus Launfal, withouten fable,°   *lie*
   Þat noble knyȝt of þe Rounde Table,
¹⁰³⁵   Was take° yn to fayrye:°   *taken/fairyland*
   Seþþe° saw hym yn þis lond° no man,   *since (then)/land*
   Ne° no more of hym telle y ne° can,   *nor/I not*
      For° soþe, without lye.°   *in/lie*

   Thomas Chestre made þys tale
¹⁰⁴⁰ Of þe noble knyȝt Syr Launfale,
      Good° of chyualrye;°   *good (man)/chivalry*
   Ihesus,° þat ys Heuene-kyng,°   *Jesus/heaven's king*
   Ȝeue° vs alle Hys blessyng,   *give*
      And Hys Modyr° Marye!   AMEN   *mother*

      EXPLICIT LAUNFAL

THE PARODY-BURLESQUE

Whenever a certain type of literature has run its course, has passed the peak of its popular appeal, or represents a social system no longer au courant with the times, parody and burlesque of it will appear, often symbolic of new trends or an end to old ways. The medieval romance was of course peculiarly vulnerable to satire, and the fabliaux mocked many of the courtly ways. Chaucer's *Sir Thopas* is a brilliant example of how romance style, characterization, and plot can be made absolutely ridiculous. It is an obvious parody, mocking established style and technique, but it is also a burlesque romance of which there appeared several in later times: *The Tournament of Tottenham, The Wedding of Sir Gawain and Dame Ragnall*, and *Sir Gawain and the Carl of Carlyle* combine aristocratic backgrounds with popular and low-class elements. The anti-romance hero makes his appearance in the Scottish poem of *Rauf Coilyear*, the collier who stands up to Charlemagne. In most of these burlesques we find rowdy peasant humor and depictions of town life, as in the Tottenham tournament (which may be a sophisticated satire of low-class pretensions); and there are examples of the folkloric process of the "decline of the hero," as when Gawain is placed into ludicrous situations while the collier is honored above his position.

REFERENCES

Dürmüller, Urs. *Narrative Possibilities of the Tail-Rime Romance*. Bern, 1975.

Herrtage, S. J., ed. *Rauf Coilyear*. Early English Test Society, ES 39. Oxford, 1882.

Jones, G. F. "The Tournaments of Tottenham and Lappenhausen." *PMLA*, 66 (December, 1951), 1123–40.

Sands, Donald, ed. *Middle English Verse Romances*. New York, 1966.

The parody-burlesque is treated in the General Introduction of this volume, p. 29.

SIR THOPAS

Geoffrey Chaucer

DATE: C. 1390. ❖ MANUSCRIPTS: *Sir Thopas* is one of the *Canterbury Tales* by Geoffrey Chaucer; the great popularity of this work in the Middle Ages is attested by the eighty-three MSS. which are extant. The dialect is that of 14th century London. ❖ EDITIONS: A. C. Baugh, *Chaucer's Major Poetry* (New York, 1963); F. N. Robinson, *The Complete Works of Geoffrey Chaucer,* rev. ed. (Boston, 1957); Walter W. Skeat, *The Complete Works of Geoffrey Chaucer,* 7 vols. (Oxford, 1894–97), known as the *Oxford Chaucer;* Robert Pratt, *The Tales of Canterbury* (Boston, 1966); John H. Fisher, *The Complete Poetry and Prose of Geoffrey Chaucer* (New York, 1977). Robinson's text is at present the fullest work for graduate study; and the notes in the edition of Skeat are of lasting value.

Chaucer wrote in the London English of his day. Because of the power of the capital, arising from its increasing population and economic growth, its language, like Parisian or Central French, became a kind of standard Middle English from which Modern English developed. Chaucer's English, therefore, should pose few difficulties for modern readers.

Sir Thopas is one of the first satires in English literature, and a brilliant one. It is a parody, in plot, meter, and vocabulary, of the long chivalric romances so popular in the Middle Ages. At the same time, it is a social satire on certain *nouveaux riches* Flemish merchants who were commonly seen in London and the Low Countries; the Flemish bourgeoisie and their aspirations to knighthood were ridiculed by the nobility of England and France.

Sir Thopas is one of the most amusing pieces in the *Canterbury Tales;* and the fact that it is the pilgrim "Geoffrey," and not one of the others, who tells this story compounds the joke. For this gem of wit is deemed by Harry Bailey, the Host and master of ceremonies, to be worth not a "tord." Geoffrey Chaucer, the genius of Middle English literature, is the worst storyteller of the whole Canterbury pilgrimage! And thereby hangs another tale of Chaucer's sense of humor.

PROLOGUE TO SIR THOPAS.

BIHOLD THE MURYE WORDES OF THE HOST TO CHAUCER.

Whan seyd° was al this miracle, every man	*told*
As sobre° was, that wonder was to se,°	*so silent/see*

Heading. *murye:* "merry."

1–4. In the sequence of the *Canterbury Tales,* the Prioress has just finished her somber story: a tale of the Miracle of the Virgin genre, in which a little boy whose throat had been cut and who had been thrown into a privy continued to sing a holy song, and so was discovered. The Host, Harry Bailey, a big, rather blunt-humored man and self-appointed moderator, now approaches "Geoffrey" and hopes to hear a merry tale from him.

Til that° our hoste japen tho° bigan,   *until/(to) joke then*
And than° at erst° he loked° up-on me,   *then/first/looked*
5 And seyde° thus, "What man artow?"° quod° he;   *said/are you/said*
"Thou lokest as° thou woldest° finde an hare,   *as if/wanted to*
For ever up-on the ground I see thee stare.

Approche neer,° and loke up merily.°   *approach nearer/merrily*
Now war° yow,° sirs, and lat° this man have place;   *take care/you/let*
10 He in the waast° is shape° as wel as I;   *waist/shaped*
This were° a popet° in an arm tenbrace°   *would be/pet/to embrace*
For any womman, smal and fair of face.
He semeth° elvish by his contenaunce,°   *seems/look*
For un-to no wight dooth° he daliaunce.°   *man makes/chatter*

15 Sey now somwhat, sin° other folk han° sayd;   *something, since/have*
Tel us a tale of mirthe, and that anoon."°   *quickly*
"Hoste," quod I, "ne° beth nat yvel apayd,°   *not/be not ill pleased*
For other tale certes can° I noon,°   *certainly know/none*
But of a ryme I lerned longe agoon."°   *ago*
20 "Ye,° that is good," quod he; "now shul"° we here°   *yea/shall/hear*
Som deyntee° thing, me° thinketh by his chere."°   *pleasant/I/look*

EXPLICIT

SIR THOPAS

HERE BIGINNETH CHAUCERS TALE OF THOPAS.

THE FIRST FIT

Listeth,° lordes, in good entent,   *listen*
And I wol° telle verrayment°   *will/truly*
Of mirthe and of solas;°   *entertainment*
25 Al of a knyght was° fair and gent°   *(that) was/noble*
In bataille° and in tourneyment,   *battle*
    His name was sir Thopas.

Y-born° he was in fer contree,°   *born/far country*
In Flaundres, al° biyonde the see,°   *Flanders, quite/sea*

---

10. One of Geoffrey Chaucer's most endearing traits is his capacity for poking fun at himself. In the *Canterbury Tales*, the pilgrim "Geoffrey" is an affable dullard (or one who appears so and plays the king's fool in order to point out the foibles of others). He is a rather stout man (the Host compares his own waist with Chaucer's, the latter's corpulence being confirmed in l. 31 of *Lenvoy a Scogan*).

13. *elvish*: i.e., "aloof," perhaps "thoughtful."

22. This is a typical minstrel beginning for romances (cf. *King Horn, Havelok the Dane,* and the General Introduction, p. 38).

27. *Thopas*: i.e., the gem topaz. The name is interpreted in various ways: for instance, as a sign of purity or of effeminacy. At any rate it is a far cry from the martial-sounding names of Guy of Warwick, Bevis of Hampton, King Horn, or Havelok the Dane.

30 At Popering,° in the place;	*Poperinghe*
His fader° was a man ful free,°	*father/very noble*
And lord he was of that contree,	
As it was Goddes grace.	
Sir Thopas wex° a doghty swayn,°	*grew (to be)/doughty youth*
35 Whyt° was his face as payndemayn,°	*white/fine white bread*
His lippes rede° as rose;	*red*
His rode° is lyk scarlet° in grayn,	*complexion/like scarlet (cloth dyed)*
And I yow telle in good certayn,°	*certainty*
He hadde a semely° nose.	*handsome*
40 His heer,° his berd° was lyk saffroun,°	*hair/beard/saffron*
That to his girdel raughte adoun;°	*belt reached down*
His shoon° of Cordewane.°	*shoes/cordovan (leather)*
Of Brugges° were his hosen° broun,	*Bruges/hose*
His robe was of ciclatoun,	
45 That coste many a Jane.	
He coude° hunte at wilde deer,	*could*
And ryde an hauking° for riveer,°	*a-hawking/river fowl*
With grey goshauk° on honde;°	*goshawk/hand*
Ther-to° he was a good archeer,	*also*
50 Of wrastling° was there noon his peer,	*wrestling*
Ther° any ram shal stonde.°	*where/stand*
Ful many a mayde, bright in bour,°	*bower*
They moorne° for him, paramour,°	*mourn/passionately*
Whan hem° were° bet° to slepe;°	*when for them/(it) would be/better/ sleep*
55 But he was chast° and no lechour,	*chaste*
And sweet as is the bremble-flour°	*bramble flower*
That bereth° the rede hepe.°	*bears/hip*

---

30. *Popering:* There was a tradition, according to John M. Manly, that the men of Poperinghe, a Belgian town near the French border in West Flanders, were regarded as stupid.

31. *free:* also here in the sense of "generous," "gracious."

35. *payndemayn:* bread made of especially finely ground flour. The comparison is a mercantile one, rather unknightly.

36. The rose-red lips were typical of romance heroines.

37. *scarlet in grayn:* a reference to the Flemish weaving and cloth trade.

40. The long, antiquated beard of Sir Thopas is compared to the saffron powder used in cooking.

42. *Cordewane:* A shoemaker was usually called a cordwainer.

43. *Brugges:* Bruges was a center of the Flemish cloth trade.

44. *ciclatoun:* a costly cloth.

45. *Jane:* A jane was a small coin from Genoa.

49–51. Though some scholars have mentioned that archery and wrestling were middle-class accomplishments, Chaucer may have wanted to point out the universal attributes of his hero. Havelok the Dane wrestles, albeit as a commoner, but the inference in that romance is that all classes engaged in this sport. The *ram* was a wrestling prize.

56–57. *bremble-flour:* i.e., the dog rose. *hepe:* i.e., the fruit of the rosebush.

And so bifel° up-on a day, (*it*) *happened*
For sothe,° as I yow° telle may, *in truth/you*
60 Sir Thopas wolde° out ryde; *wanted to*
He worth° upon his stede° gray, *got/steed*
And in his honde a launcegay,° *lance*
A long swerd° by his syde. *sword*

He priketh thurgh° a fair forest, *rides through*
65 Ther-inne is many a wilde best,° *beast*
Ye,° bothe bukke° and hare; *yea/buck*
And, as he priketh north and est,° *east*
I telle it yow, him° hadde almest° *to him/almost*
Bitid° a sory care.° *happened/unfortunate event*

70 Ther springen° herbes grete° and smale,° *grow/large/small*
The lycorys° and cetewale,° *licorice/zedoary* (i.e., *ginger*)
And many a clowe-gilofre;° *clove gillyflower*
And notemuge° to putte in ale, *nutmeg*
Whether it be moyste° or stale, (i.e., *new*)
75 Or for to leye° in cofre.° *lay/chest*

The briddes° singe, it is no nay,° *birds/denial*
The sparhauk° and the papeiay,° *sparrowhawk/parrot*
That° joye° it was to here;° *so that/joy/hear*
The thrustelcok° made eek° his lay,° *thrush/also/song*
80 The wodedowve° upon the spray° *wood pigeon/branch*
She sang ful° loude and clere.° *very/clear*

Sir Thopas fil° in love-longinge *fell*
Al° whan he herde° the thrustel° singe, *just/heard/thrush*
And priked as° he were wood:° *as if/mad*
85 His faire stede in his prikinge° *spurring*
So swatte° that men mighte him wringe, *sweated* (i.e., *bled*)
His sydes were al blood.

Sir Thopas eek so wery° was *weary*
For° prikinge on the softe gras, *from*
90 So fiers° was his corage,° *fierce/ardor*
That doun he leyde him° in that plas° *laid himself/place*

---

62. The launcegay (Spanish *azagaya*) was a thin, lightweight weapon, somewhat different from the heavy jousting lance.

64. *priketh:* To "prick" meant to spur or follow the pricks (tracks) of animals. The word also had other meanings, and Chaucer was not the man to avoid *double entendre.*

70–75. The plants are herbs such as might be grown in a cook's spice garden or kept in a herbarium. Such lists of flowers, birds, etc., were common to medieval romance.

To make his stede som solas,°   *comfort*
And yaf° him good forage.   *gave*

"O seinte° Marie, *benedicite!*   *Saint*
95 What eyleth° this love at° me   *ails/in*
To binde me so sore?°   *greatly*
Me dremed° al this night, pardee,°   *I dreamed/by God* (i.e., *verily*)
An elf-queen shal my lemman° be,   *lover*
And slepe° under my gore.°   *sleep/garment*

100 An elf-queen wol° I love, y-wis,°   *will/indeed*
For in this world no womman is
Worthy to be my make°   *mate*
       In toune;
Alle othere wommen I forsake,
105 And to an elf-queen I me° take   *myself*
By dale and eek by doune!"°   *hill*

In-to his sadel° he clamb anoon,°   *saddle/climbed quickly*
And priketh° over style° and stoon°   *rides/stile/stone*
An elf-queen for tespye,°   *to seek*
110 Til he so longe had riden° and goon°   *ridden/gone*
That he fond,° in a privee woon,°   *found/secret abode*
The contree° of Fairye°   *country/fairyland*
       So wilde;
For in that contree was ther noon°   *none*
115 That to him dorste° ryde or goon,°   *it dared/go*
Neither wyf ne° childe.   *woman nor*

Til that° ther cam° a greet geaunt,°   *until/came/great giant*
His name was sir Olifaunt,°   *Elephant*
A perilous man of dede;°   *deeds*
120 He seyde,° "Child,° by Termagaunt,   *said/knight*
But-if° thou prike out of myn haunt,°   *unless/my realm*
Anon° I slee° thy stede°   *quickly/will slay/steed*
       With mace.
Heer° is the queen of Fayërye,   *here*
125 With harpe and pype and simphonye°   *tabor*
Dwelling in this place."

---

94. *benedicite:* "bless ye (the Lord)."

97–106. Knights were often loved by fairy women (cf. the lai of *Lanval*), and to love an unknown lady through hearsay was the fate of some of the Provençal troubadours. Such passionate love visions at a distance were among the sentimental features of courtly love.

117. Giants and other horrible wights usually guarded the otherworld.

120. *Child:* here, "knight," as in Byron's *Childe Harold's Pilgrimage* (cf. above, p. 143, ll. 27–28n). *Termagaunt:* Termagant was considered a Mohammedan idol or god in the Middle Ages. All evil beings swore by non-Christian symbols.

The child seyde, "Al-so mote° I thee,°   *as may/prosper*
Tomorwe° wol I mete° thee   *tomorrow/meet*
 Whan° I have myn armoure;   *when*
130 And yet I hope, *par ma fay,*
That thou shalt with this launcegay° *lance*
 Abyen° it ful soure;°   *pay for/very sorely*
      Thy mawe°   *stomach*
Shal I percen,° if I may,   *pierce*
135 Er° it be fully pryme of day,   *before*
 For heer thou shalt be slawe."° *slain*

Sir Thopas drow abak° ful faste; *drew back*
This geaunt at him stones caste
 Out of a fel staf-slinge;°   *terrible slingshot*
140 But faire° escapeth child Thopas, *well*
And al it was thurgh° Goddes gras,° *through/grace*
 And thurgh his fair beringe.° *bearing*

Yet listeth,° lordes, to my tale   *listen*
Merier° than the nightingale,   *merrier*
145 For now I wol° yow° roune° *will/to you/whisper*
How sir Thopas with sydes smale,° *slender*
Priking over hil and dale,
 Is come agayn to toune.

His merie men comanded he
150 To make him bothe game° and glee,° *amusement/entertainment*
 For nedes° moste° he fighte *of necessity/must*
With a geaunt with hevedes° three, *heads*
For paramour° and jolitee°   *love/passion*
 Of oon° that shoon° ful brighte. *for one/shone*

155 "Do come," he seyde, "my minstrales,
And gestours,° for to tellen° tales *storytellers/tell*
 Anon in myn arminge;
Of romances that been royales,° *are royal*
Of popes and of cardinales,
160 And eek° of love-lykinge."° *also/loving*

They fette° him first the swete wyn,° *fetched/sweet wine*
And mede° eek in a maselyn,° *mead/maple-wood bowl*

---

130. *par ma fay:* "by my faith."

133–34. Only a middle-class, citizen's army thinks of or travels on its stomach. Knightly thrusts were aimed at heart or throat or head.

135. *pryme:* the canonical hours beginning at 6 A.M.

156. *gestours:* originally tellers of tales of adventure (*geste,* from Latin *gesta,* "deeds").

And royal spicerye;°   *spices*
Of gingebreed° that was ful fyn,°   *some gingerbread/excellent*
165 And lycorys,° and eek comyn,°   *licorice/cumin*
With sugre° that is so trye.°   *sugar/good*

He dide next° his whyte lere°   *put next (to)/flesh*
Of clooth° of lake fyn and clere°   *cloth/bright*
A breech° and eek a sherte;°   *(i.e., pair of breeches)/shirt*
170 And next his sherte an aketoun,
And over that an habergeoun
For° percinge of his herte;°   *against/heart*

And over that a fyn hauberk,
Was al y-wroght° of Jewes werk,°   *made/Jews' work*
175 Ful° strong it was of plate;   *very*
And over that his cote-armour°   *coat of arms*
As whyt° as is a lily-flour,°   *white/lily flower*
In which he wol debate.°   *fight*

His sheeld was al of gold so reed,°   *red*
180 And ther-in was a bores heed,°   *boar's head*
A charbocle bisyde;°   *carbuncle beside (it)*
And there he swoor,° on ale and breed,°   *swore/bread*
How that "the geaunt° shal be deed,°   *giant/dead*
Bityde° what bityde!"°   *happen/(may) happen*

185 His jambeux° were of quirboilly,°   *leg armor/leather*
His swerdes shethe° of yvory,   *sword's sheath*

167–93. The arming of Sir Thopas is here made ludicrous in its tediousness and pomposity. Such rituals were commonly described in romances (similar accounts of armor, clothing, etc., may be found in *Sir Gawain and the Green Knight*). Sir Thopas's arming is thorough but by no means exceptional. Over his hauberk (plate armor), for instance, he might put a jupon (a tight tunic, often emblazoned). Possibly such a jupon might also be worn between haubergeon (coat of mail) and hauberk. The *cote-armour* (1.176) might be the emblazoned jupon; if so, then Sir Thopas is indeed properly dressed. From evidence of existing armor, the average medieval knight was relatively short but very strongly built. Sir Thopas's physical description, however, leads one to question whether he would have even been able to lift his right arm when he was fully clothed. His white skin (1.167), like his slender sides (1.146), is a further sign of his delicacy.

168. *lake:* delicate linen.

170. *aketoun:* The aketon was a quilted or leather jacket worn under the armor.

171. *habergeoun:* The haubergeon was a coat of mail worn under plate armor.

173. *hauberk:* Originally denoting neck and shoulder protection, this term was later applied to the outer coat of mail. Here it seems to refer to the breast and back plates.

174. Jewish armorers, like those of Toledo, were famous throughout Europe.

176–77. His coat of arms was pure, chaste white, like that of Sir Galahad. Normally the coat of arms and the shield bear the same heraldic device.

179. *gold so reed:* Cf. above, p. 183, l. 47*n.*

182. The oaths of Sir Thopas might have been those of a well-fed Flemish burgher.

185. *quirboilly:* (French *cuir bouilli*) leather boiled in hot water for softening.

186–88. The sword's sheath is of unusually precious material, whereas the helmet of latten (a mixture of copper and zinc) is quite shabby; neither is made to withstand the dints of battle. The saddle is of narwhal bone (ivory), which in the Middle Ages was often taken to be the tusk of the unicorn, an animal that could only be captured by virgins.

His helm° of laton° bright;   *helmet/latten*
His sadel° was of rewel-boon,°   *saddle/whale ivory*
His brydel as the sonne° shoon,   *sun*
190   Or as the mone° light.   *moon*

His spere° was of fyn ciprees,°   *spear/cypress*
That bodeth werre,° and no-thing° pees,°   *forebodes war/not at all/peace*
    The heed ful sharpe y-grounde;°   *ground*
His stede° was al dappel-gray,   *steed*
195 It gooth° an ambel° in the way   *goes/ambling*
    Ful softely and rounde°   *easily*
                        In londe.°   *land*
Lo, lordes myne, heer° is a fit!°   *here/song*
If ye wol° any more of it,   *want*
200   To telle it wol° I fonde.°   *will/try*

THE SECOND FIT

Now hold your mouth, *par charitee*,
Bothe knight and lady free,°   *noble*
    And herkneth° to my spelle;°   *listen/tale*
Of bataille° and of chivalry,   *battle*
205 And of ladyes love-drury°   *ladies' affection*
    Anon° I wol yow° telle.   *directly/will you*

Men speke° of romances of prys,°   *speak/excellence*
Of Horn child° and of Ypotys,   *knight*
    Of Bevis and sir Gy,
210 Of sir Libeux and Pleyn-damour;
But sir Thopas, he bereth° the flour°   *bears/flower*
    Of royal chivalry.

His gode stede° al he bistrood,°   *good steed/bestrode*
And forth upon his wey° he glood°   *way/passed*
215   As sparkle out of the bronde;°   *firebrand*

---

191. Spears were normally of stiff ash, not pliant cypress.

194–97. The Wife of Bath, in Chaucer's General Prologue to the *Canterbury Tales*, rides on an ambler, whose easy pace is more suited to women than knights. The gait, in which the legs of either side are lifted together, looks somewhat ridiculous in a war-horse.

201. Normally the romances were quite long and therefore interrupted by the murmurings of the audience. The minstrels frequently had to beg, or command, attention. *par charitee:* "for charity."

207–10. The list is of known romances: *King Horn*; *Ypotys*, a shorter tale; *Bevis of Hampton* and *Guy of Warwick*, the most popular Middle English romances, always mentioned together; and *Libeaus Desconus* (*The Fair Unknown*), in which the hero is Gawain's son. *Pleyn-damour* has not been identified.

Up-on his crest he bar° a tour,°   *bore/tower*
And ther-in stiked° a lily-flour,°   *was stuck/lily flower*
   God shilde° his cors fro shonde!°   *shield/body from harm*

And for° he was a knight auntrous,°   *because/adventurous*
220 He nolde° slepen° in non°hous,   *would not/sleep/no*
   But liggen° in his hode;°   *lie/hood*
His brighte helm° was his wonger,°   *helmet/pillow*
And by him baiteth° his dextrer°   *feeds/war-horse*
   Of° herbes fyne and gode.   *on*

225 Him-self° drank water of the wel,   *he*
As did the knight sir Percivel,
   So worthy under wede,°   *garment*
Til on a day—

HERE THE HOST STINTETH CHAUCER
OF HIS TALE OF THOPAS.

PROLOGUE TO MELIBEUS

"No more of this, for Goddes dignitee,"
230 Quod° oure hoste, "for thou makest me   *said*
So wery° of thy verray lewednesse°   *weary/real ignorance*
That, also wisly° God my soule blesse,   *as surely (may)*
Myn eres aken° of thy drasty speche;°   *my ears ache/worthless speech*
Now swiche° a rym° the devel I biteche!°   *such/rhyme/give to*
235 This may wel be rym dogerel," quod he.
   "Why so?" quod I, "why wiltow° lette° me   *will you/hinder*
More of my tale than another man,
Sin° that it is the beste rym I can?"°   *since/know*
   "By God," quod he, "for pleynly,° at a word,   *plainly*
240 Thy drasty ryming is nat° worth a tord;°   *not/turd*
Thou doost° nought elles° but despendest° tyme,   *do/nothing else/waste*

216–17. This is the second mention of the lily in connection with Sir Thopas. Although a "sunflower or a lily" was also carried by a later romantic aesthete, Oscar Wilde, it must be remembered that in the Middle Ages, from 1179 on, the fleur-de-lis was an honored symbol, appearing in the coat of arms of the Bourbons and later of cities like Florence, Lille, and Wiesbaden. The crest was the heraldic bearing worn on top of the helmet.

225–26. Percival, it may be remembered, was also a nature boy in his youth, naïve in the ways of the world, rustic as the forest.

227. *worthy under wede:* Cf. above, p. 311, l. 1814n.

Heading. *stinteth:* "restrains." *of:* "from."

229–52. The so-called persona, or mask, of Chaucer as the ignorant poet is again presented here. The Host does not understand the joke of *Sir Thopas*, takes it seriously, and deems it worthless. Chaucer answers that he will tell "a little thing" in prose, which turns out to be an extremely long and dull (at least for modern audiences) moral tale. *geste* (l. 243): This may mean "poetry"—i.e., the meter in which the *chansons de geste*, or romances of adventure, were written—as contrasted to *prose* in the next line.

Sir, at o° word, thou shalt no lenger° ryme.   *one/longer*
Lat° see wher° thou canst tellen aught° in geste,°   *let (us)/whether/tell anything/*
                                                                    romance style

Or telle in prose somwhat° at the leste°   *something/least*
245 In which ther be som mirthe or some doctryne."
        "Gladly," quod I, "by Goddes swete pyne,°   *sweet suffering*
     I wol yow° telle a litel° thing in prose,   *will you/little*
     That oghte lyken° yow, as I suppose,   *ought (to) please*
     Or elles, certes,° ye been to° daungerous.°   *certainly/are too/hard to please*
250 It is a moral tale vertuous,
     Al° be it told som-tyme° in sondry wyse°   *although/sometimes/various ways*
     Of sondry folk, as I shal yow devyse."°   *tell*

                    .   .   .   .   .

COMPLAINT TO HIS PURSE

Geoffrey Chaucer

DATE: C. 1400. ✦ MANUSCRIPTS: The poem is found in eleven MSS in the British Library (Additional 22139; Harley 7333; Harley 2251; Cotton Otho A. xviii; etc.) and elsewhere (Bodleian Library, Oxford; Cambridge University Library; etc.). ✦ EDITIONS: W. W. Skeat, *The Complete Works of Geoffrey Chaucer*, 6 vols. and Supplement (Oxford, 1894–97); F. N. Robinson, *The Works of Geoffrey Chaucer*, 2d ed. (Boston, 1957); George B. Pace, Alfred David, *The Minor Poems*, Part 1, in Paul G. Ruggiers, editor, *A Variorum Edition of the Works of Geoffrey Chaucer*, Vol. V (Norman, Oklahoma, 1982).

Chaucer's dialect is that of the London English of his time, from which standard Modern English developed. As late Middle English of the Southeast Midland, it is probably the easiest dialect for modern readers to understand.

The Envoy of this poem was written between September 30, 1399, when Parliament agreed to the accession of Henry IV, and February, 1400, when Chaucer received a grant (antedated to October 13, 1399, Henry's coronation date) of forty marks for life; it is possible but not probable that the poem proper was composed earlier. It is a brilliant satire, and one of the finest parodies ever written of the complaint, a specific genre of poems addressed by lovers to their mistresses. The "sovereign lady" is normally accused of cruelty and scorn (*daunger*), and her physical attributes are described in hyperbolic Petrarchan terms: her hair is gold, her voice is music, etc.

To you, my purse, and to noon° other wyght°	*none/person*
Compleyne° I, for ye be my lady dere!°	*complain/dear*
I am so sory,° now that ye ben° light;	*sorry/are*
For certes, but° ye make me hevy chere,°	*certainly, unless/heavy aspect*
5 Me were as leef° be leyd° upon my bere;°	*I had rather/laid/bier*
For whiche unto your mercy thus I crye	
"Beth° hevy ageyn,° or elles mot° I dye!"°	*be/again/else must/die*

3–4. Here Chaucer works with paradox and pun. *hevy chere:* lit., "sorrowful spirit."

6. The ritualistic vocabulary of the cult of courtly love imitated that of Christian dogma: the lover begs for "grace" and "mercy" from his mistress; he confesses his sins in love and prays to Venus, mother of the love god Cupid, to intercede for him. The lady is thus equated with Venus and ultimately with the Virgin Mary. Chaucer plays on this progression in his three stanzas.

Now voucheth sauf° this day, or hit° be nyght, *grant/before it*
That I of you the blisful soun° may here,° *sound/hear*
10 Or see your colour lyk° the sonne° bright, *like/sun*
That of yelownesse hadde never pere.° *peer*
Ye be my lyf,° ye be myn hertes stere,° *life/my heart's rudder*
Quene of comfort and of good companye;
Beth hevy ageyn, or elles mot I dye!

15 Now purse, that be to me my lyves° light *life's*
And saveour, as doun in this worlde here,
Out of this toun° help me throgh° your myght, *town/through*
Syn that° ye wole° not been° my tresorere;° *since/will/be/treasurer*
For I am shave as nye° as any frere.° *closely/friar*
20 But yet I pray unto your curtesye,° *courtesy*
Beth hevy ageyn, or elles mot I dye!

Envoy of Chaucer

O conquerour of Brutes Albioun,
Which that by lyne and free eleccioun
Ben verray° king, this song to you I sende; *be true*
25 And ye, that mowen° al oure harm amende, *may*
Have mynde upon my supplicacioun!

     GEOFFREY CHAUCER

---

12. Such formulas were often used in the religious lyrics addressed to **Mary** (cf. *Edi Beo Thu, Heuene Quene*, this volume, p. 636) as well as in secular love songs.

13. The word *Quene* leads directly into the religious aspect of courtly love found in stanza 3. However, though *comfort* has spiritual connotations, *companye* has more physical ones, and it must be remembered that in Chaucer's time the word *quene* was also used for *quean*, "wench." The purse, the lady, is therefore given a mercenary and meretricious aspect here, is thus both debased and elevated in a brilliant play on words and parody of the courtly-love literary tradition.

16–17. The religious parody and progression, purse→lady→ Mary, comes to a point here and in line 20.

17. *toun:* The town may be the area of Westminster or even the Westminster Abbey enclosure where Chaucer had rented a house, possibly as sanctuary to escape suits for debt.

20. The "conqueror" of Albion (England), founded by the mythical Brutus (cf. Geoffrey of Monmouth) is in l. 24 called "true" king, i.e., elected by Parliament and in the royal line. Henry IV, who had deposed Richard II, was the son of Geoffrey Chaucer's lifelong patron, John of Gaunt, duke of Lancaster and Richard's uncle. The Envoy seems a compromise, on Chaucer's part, of truth for the sake of need. An Agnes Chaucer, perhaps the poet's daughter or sister, was *domicella* (lady-in-waiting) at the coronation of Henry IV in 1399.

THE TOURNAMENT OF TOTTENHAM

DATE: 1400–40. ✦ MANUSCRIPTS: British Library, Harleian 5306 (H), 1456; Cambridge University Library Ff. II 38 (C), 1431. The dialect is Northern. ✦ EDITIONS: W. H. French and C. B. Hale, *Middle English Metrical Romances* (New York, 1964); Donald Sands, *Middle English Verse Romances* (New York, 1966). George F. Jones, "The Tournaments of Tottenham and Lappenhausen," *PMLA*, 66 (December, 1951), 1123–40, gives an interesting discussion of rustic tournaments and speculates on the direction of the satire.

The Northern dialect is seen specifically in the retention of the OE *ā* where other dialects would have *o*: *baldely* = *boldly*, *amang* = *among*, *lang* = *long*, *sa* = *so*. Verb and noun forms also show special characteristics of the North. (1) The present participle ends in *-and* (*rydand*). (2) Noun and verb plurals and the third person singular of verbs end in *-ys*, *-is* (*bonys*, *stonys* = *bones*, *stones*; *getis* = *gets*.) Other Northern characteristics, such as *quh* for *wh* and *till* in the infinitive, are lacking.

Although the dialect of *The Tournament of Tottenham* is Northern, the events take place close to London. That is the first mystery concerning this raucous peasant combat. The second problem is the nature of the satire, the object of the wit. Knightly rituals of tournaments—the vows, the coats of arms, the banners, and the inspiration of love and honor—are obviously being burlesqued. But whether the tournaments of gentry are being satirized, or the rustics themselves, is open to question. There are certain similarities to the bourgeois comedy in Beaumont and Fletcher's *Knight of the Burning Pestle*. Perhaps the poet is commemorating a real peasant brawl of "trewe drynkers," such as happened occasionally during Shrovetide festivals, and giving it a country-courtly flavor as a quasi-ennobling reductio ad absurdum. Perhaps, too, a mundane agricultural or trade dispute, (like the one between Greeks and Trojans that led to the Trojan War) has been transfigured here, if not to Homeric seriousness, still into a mock-heroic country free-for-all to gain the favor and possession of Tyb, the Tottenham Helen of Troy.

Of all þes kene° conquerours to carpe° it were° kynde:°   *these bold/talk/would be/natural*
Of fele° fe3tyng-folk° ferly° we fynde;   *many/fighting folk/strange things*
The Turnament of Totenham haue we in mynde:

It were harme sych hardynes° were holden byhynde,°   *evil (if) such bravery/held back*
5   In story as we rede°—   *read*
Of Hawkyn, of Herry,
Of Tomkyn, of Terry,
Of þem þat were dughty°   *doughty*
And stalworth° in dede.°   *stalwart/deed*

10 It befel in Totenham, on a dere° day,   *memorable*
Þer was mad° a schurtyng be° þe hyway.   *made/festival by*
Þeder com° al þe men of þe contray°—   *there came/country*
Of Hyssyltoun,° of Hygate,° and of Hakenay,°   *Islington/Highgate/Hackney*
And all þe swete swynkers.°   *good workers*
15   Þer hopped Hawkyn,
Þer davnsed° Dawkyn,   *danced*
Þer trumped° Tomkyn;   *trumpeted*
And all were trewe° drynkers,   *true*

Tyl þe day was gon, and euyn-song° past,   *evensong*
20 Þat þay schuld rekyn þer scot° and þer contes° cast,   *they should reckon their bill/ accounts*

Perkyn þe potter in to þe press past,°   *group pushed*
And sayd, "Rondol þe refe,° a doȝter° þou hast,   *reeve/daughter*
Tyb, þe dere:°   *dear*
Þer-for wyt wold° i   *know would*
25   Whych of all þys bachelery°   *company*
Were best worthy
To wed hur to° hys fere."°   *her as/mate*

Vp styrt þes gadelyngys° with þer long staues,   *started those fellows*
And sayd, "Randal þe refe, lo! þis lad raues!
30 Baldely amang° us þy duȝter° he craues,   *boldly among/daughter*
And we er° rycher men þen° he, and more god haues,°   *are/than/possessions have*
Of catell° and corn."   *cattle*
Þen sayd Perkyn, "To Tybbe i haue hyȝt°   *promised*
Þat i schal be alway redy° in° my ryȝt,°   *ready/to defend/right*
35   If þat it schuld be þys day seuenyȝt,°   *a week from today*
Or ellis° ȝet to-morn."°   *else/tomorrow*

4. *holden byhynde:* i.e., "concealed."

10–14. Tottenham, Islington, Highgate, and Hackney were then parishes north of London. Today Tottenham, six miles north of the City, is part of Greater London. All the men are involved in rural occupations and fight with country tools.

22. The reeve is either the sheriff (the bailiff of the shire), or the steward or overseer in charge of a specific estate. In either case he is a person of prestige.

Þen sayd Randolfe þe refe, "Euer be he waryed°   *cursed*
Þat about þys carpyng lenger wold° be taryed!°   *talk longer would/delayed*
I wold not þat my doȝter þat scho° were myscaryed,°   *she/did poorly*
40 But at° hur most worschyp° i wold scho were maryed.° *to/greatest honor/married*
  Þer-for a turnament schal begin
  Þys day seuenyȝt,
  With a flayl for to fyȝt,°   *fight*
  And he þat ys of most myght
45   Schal brouke° hur with wynne.°   *enjoy/pleasure*

"Whoso berys hym° best in þe turnament,   *bears himself*
Hym schall be granted þe gre,° be þe comon° assent,   *prize/common*
For to wynne my doȝter with dughtynes° of dent,°   *strength/blows*
And Coppeld, my brode-henne, was broȝt° out of Kent,   *brood-hen, (that) was brought*
50   And my donnyd kowe.°   *brown cow*
  For no spens° wyl i spare,   *expense*
  For no catell° wyl i care: *possession*
  He schal haue my gray mare,
  And my spottyd° sowe!"   *spotted*

55 Þer was many° bold lad þer bodyes° to bede;°   *many (a)/bodies/venture*
Þan° þay toke þayr leue,° and homward þay ȝede,°   *then/took their leave/went*
And all þe woke° afterward þay grayþed° þer wede,°   *week/prepared/clothes*
Tyll it come° to þe day þat þay suld° do þer dede.°   *came/should/deed*
  Þay° armed ham° in mattis:°   *they/themselves/mattings*
60   Þay set on þer nollys,°   *heads*
  For to kepe° þer pollys,°   *guard/crowns*
  Gode blake bollys,°   *good black bowls*
  For batryng° of battis.°   *against battering/bats*

Þay sowed þam° in schepe-skynnes,° for° þay suld not brest;°   *sewed them/sheepskins/so that/burst*
65 Ilkon° toke a blak° hat insted of a crest,   *each one/black*
A harow brod° as a fanne aboune° on þer brest,   *arrow broad/above*
And a flayle in þer hande, for to fyght prest.°   *ready*
  Furth don° þay fare!   *forth did*
  Þer was kyd mekyl fors°   *shown much might*
70   Who schuld° best fend° his cors,°   *should/defend/body*
  He þat had no gode hors,
  He gat° hym a mare.   *got*

Sych° anoþer gadryng° haue i not sene° oft!   *such/assembly/seen*
When all þe gret° cumpany com rydand° to þe croft,°   *great/riding/field*

---

65. The knight's crest was the armorial device on his helmet, for identification: a plume, the figure of a bird, etc.

72. A mare was a ludicrous and ignominious substitute for the powerful war-horse of the tournaments.

⁷⁵ Tyb on a gray mare was set upon loft,°   *on high*
On a sek° ful of sedys,° for scho schuld syt soft,   *sack/seeds*
    And led hur° to þe gap.°   *(they) led her/hedge opening*
    For cryeng° of al þe men,   *shouting*
    Forþer wold° not Tyb þen   *would (go)*
⁸⁰   Tyl sche had hur gode brode-hen
      Set in hur lap.

A gay gyrdyl° Tyb had on, borwed° for þe nonys,°   *belt/borrowed/occasion*
And a garland on hur hed,° ful of rounde bonys.°   *head/bones*
And a broche° on hur brest, ful of safer stonys°—   *brooch/sapphire stones*
⁸⁵ With þe holy rode° tokenyng° was wrethyn° for þe nonys:°   *cross/as a symbol (it)/worked/also*
    No catel was þer spared!
    When ioly° Gyb saw hure þare,°   *gay/her there*
    He gyrd° so hys gray mere°   *struck/mare*
    Þat sche lete a faucon-fare°   *broke wind*
⁹⁰   At þe rereward.°   *rear*

"I wow° to God," quod° Herry, "i schal not lefe behende!°   *vow/said/remain behind*
May i mete° with Bernard, on Bayard þe blynde,   *meet*
Ich° man kepe hym° out of my wynde;°   *every/keep himself/rush*
For whatsoeuer þat he be befor° me i fynde,   *(whom) before*
⁹⁵   I wot° i schal hym greue!"°   *think/hurt*
    "Wele° sayd!" quod Hawkyn;   *well*
    "And i avow,"° quod Dawkyn,   *declare*
    "May i mete with Tomkyn,
      His flayl hym refe."°   *(to) deprive of*

¹⁰⁰ "I vow to God," quod Hud, "Tyb, sone° schal þou sc°   *soon/see*
Whych of all þis bachelery grant° is þe grc!°   *company granted/prize*
I schal scomfet þaym° all, for þe loue of þi;°   *discomfit them/you*
In what place so° i come, þay° schal haue dout° of me,   *whatever place/they/fear*
    Myn° armes ar so clere:°   *my/bright*
¹⁰⁵   I bere° a reddyl° and a rake,   *carry/sieve*
    Poudred° with a brenand drake,°   *decorated/burning dragon*
    And iii cantell° of a cake   *slices*
      In ycha cornare."°   *each corner*

91–144. There is a satire here of the series of knightly vows usually found in romances. *The Avowis of Alexander*, a Scottish poem, has a similar group of pledges.

92. Bayard, the famous steed in the romance *Les Quatre Fils d'Aymon* (the English *Foure Sonnes of Aymon*) of the Charlemagne cycle, is supposedly fierce and blind. What Bernard's horse lacks in fierceness he probably makes up for in blindness.

105–8. A burlesque of the coat of arms. Cf. Beaumont and Fletcher's *Knight of the Burning Pestle*.

"I vow to God," quod Hawkyn, "yf° i haue þe gowt,°	*(even) if/gout*
110 Al þat i fynde in þe felde presand° here aboute,	*field/thronging*
Haue i° twyes° or thryes redyn þurgh° þe route,°	*when I have/twice/thrice ridden through/throng*
In ycha stede þer° þay me se, of me þay schal haue doute	*every place where*
When i begyn to play.	
I make a vow þat i ne° schall,	*not*
115 But-yf° Tybbe wyl me call,	*unless*
Or i be thryes doun fall,°	*fallen*
Ry3t onys com° away."	*even once run*
Þen sayd Terry, and swore, be° hys crede,°	*by/creed*
"Saw þou neuer 3ong° boy forþi° hys body bede,°	*young/so/venture*
120 For when þay fy3t fastest,° and most are in drede,°	*fight hardest/fear*
I schal take Tyb by þe hand and hur° away lede.°	*her/lead*
I am armed at þe full:°	*fully*
In° myn armys° i bere wele	*on/coat of arms*
A do3 trogh° and a pele,°	*dough trough/baker's shovel*
125 A sadyll withouten° a panell,°	*saddle without/saddlecloth*
With a fles° of woll."°	*fleece/wool*
"I vow to God," quod Dudman, "and swor° be þe stra,°	*swear/straw*
Whyls° me° ys left my mere,° þou getis° hur not swa;°	*while/to me/mare/will get/so*
For scho° ys wele schapen,° and ly3t° as þe ro:°	*she/shaped/light/roe*
130 Þer ys no capul° in þys myle° befor hur schal ga;°	*horse/a mile/shall excel her*
Sche wil me no3t begyle.°	*not beguile*
She wyl me bere, i dar° wele say,	*dare*
On a lang somerys° day,	*long summer's*
Fro Hyssyltoun° to Hakenay,°	*from Islington/Hackney*
135 No3t oþer° half myle!"	*another*
"I vow to God," quod° Perkyn, "þou spekis° of cold rost!°	*said/speak/roast*
I schal wyrch° wyselyer,° withouten any bost:°	*act/more wisely/boast*
V of þe best capullys° þat ar in þys ost,°	*horses/host*
I wot° i schal þaym wynne, and bryng þaym to my cost;°	*know/side*
140 And here i graunt þam° Tybbe.°	*grant them/to Tyb*
Wele,° boyes, here ys he	*well*
Þat wyl fy3t and not fle,°	*flee*
For i am in my iolyté,°	*best of spirits*
With io forth, Gybbe!"°	*(a) 'let's go, Gib!'*

130–35. Either Dudman does not understand that Terry is referring to the reeve's daughter Tyb, or he unconsciously shifts the praise from Tyb to his own mare. In either case, Tyb cannot have been flattered.

134. The distance is about three miles.

135. I.e., "and not a half mile more."

136. *cold rost:* i.e., something not worthwhile, perhaps nonsense.

145 When þay° had þer° vowes made, furth gan° þey hye,°   *they/their/forth did/hasten*
     With flayles and hornes and trumpes mad° of tre.°   *trumpets made/wood*
     Þer were all þe bachelerys° of þat contré:°   *young men/countryside*
     Þay were dyȝt° in aray° as þamselfe° wold° be.   *dressed/attire/they/wanted (to)*
       Þayr baners° were ful bryȝt,°   *their banners/very bright*
150   Of an old roten fell;°   *rotten hide*
       Þe cheuerone,° of a plow-mell°   *chevron/plow mallet*
       And þe schadow° of a bell,   *silhouette*
       Poudred° with mone-lyȝt.°   *sprinkled/moonbeams*

     I wot it ys no chylder-game° whan° þay togedyr° met!   *children's game/when/together*
155 When icha freke° in þa feld° on hys felay bet,°   *each man/that field/fellow beat*
     And layd on styfly;° for noþyng wold° þay let!°   *vigorously/would/stop*
     And faght ferly fast,° tyll þer horses swet,°   *fought wondrously hard/sweated*
       And fewe wordys° spoken.   *words*
       Þer were flayles al to-slatred,°   *split*
160   Þer were scheldys° al to-clatred,°   *shields/smashed*
       Bollys° and dysches° al to-schatred,°   *bowls/dishes/shattered*
       And many hedys brokyn.°   *heads broken*

     Þer was clynkyng of cart-sadellys° and clattiryng of cannes;°   *cart saddles/cans*
     Of fele frekis° in þe feld, brokyn were þer fannes;°   *many men/wicker shields*
165 Of sum° were þe hedys brokyn, of sum þe brayn-panes;°   *some/skulls*
     And yll ware° it be° sum or° þay went þens,°   *went/with/before/thence*
       With swyppyng° of swepyllys.°   *swiping/flail heads*
       Þe boyes were so wery° for-fught°   *wearily/fought out*
       Þat þay myȝt° not fyȝt mare° oloft,°   *might/fight more/on horse*
170   But creped° þen about in þe croft°   *crept/field*
       As° þey were croked crepyls.°   *as if/crooked cripples*

     Perkyn was so wery° þat he began to loute;°   *weary/sink*
     "Help, Hud! i am ded° in þys ylk rowte!°   *dead/very crowd*
     A hors for xl pens,° a gode° and a stoute,   *pence/good (one)*
175 Þat i may lyȝtly° come of my noye° out!   *easily/distress*
       For no cost wyl i spare."
       He styrt° up as a snayle   *jumped*
       And hent° a capul be° þe tayle,   *grabbed/horse by*
       And raȝt° Dawkyn hys flayle,   *took from*
180   And wan° þer a mare.   *won*

     Perkyn wan v and Hud wan twa;°   *two*
     Glad and blyþe° þay ware° þat þay had don sa:°   *happy/were/so*

---

174. Cf. Shakespeare's *Richard III*, V. iv. 7: "A horse! a horse! my kingdom for a horse!" The value of a horse is directly proportional to the status of the owner and the urgency of the need.

Þay wold haue þam° to Tyb and present hur° with þa.° — *bring them/her/them*

Þe capull° were so wery þat þay° my3t not ga,° — *horses/they/go*

185   But styl gon° þay stand. — *still did*

"Allas!" quod° Hudde, "my ioye° i lese!° — *said/joy/lose*

Me° had leuer þen° a ston° of chese° — *I/rather than/stone/cheese*

Þat dere° Tyb had al þese, — *dear*

And wyst° it were my sand."° — *knew/present*

190 Perkyn turnyd hym° about in þat ych thrange;° — *himself/very throng*

Among þes° wery boyes he wrest° and he wrang:° — *those/wrestled/fought*

He threw þam doun to þe erth, and þrast þaim amang,° — *thrust them among*

When he saw Tyrry away with Tyb fang,° — *start*

And after hym ran.

195   Of° hys hors he hym drogh,° — *from/pulled*

And gaf° hym of hys flayl inogh.° — *gave/enough*

"We,° te-he!" quod Tyb, and lugh,° — *oh my!/laughed*

"3e er° a dughty° man." — *you are/doughty*

Þus þay tugged and rugged° tyl yt was nere ny3t.° — *pulled/near night*

200 All þe wyues° of Totenham come° to se° þat sy3t,° — *women/came/see/sight*

With wyspes° and kexis° and ryschys° þer ly3t,° — *straw/flax/rushes/lighted*

To fech hom þer° husbandes, þat were þam° trouth-ply3t;° — *fetch home their/to them/married*

And sum bro3t gret harwes,° — *some brought great sledges*

Þer husbandes hom for to fech;

205   Sum on dores and sum on hech,° — *gratings*

Sum on hyrdyllys° and sum on crech,° — *hurdles/lattices*

And sum on welebaraws.° — *wheelbarrows*

Þay gaderyd° Perkyn about, euerych° syde, — *gathered/(on) every*

And graunt° hym þer þe gre;° þe more was hys pride. — *granted/prize*

210 Tyb and he, with gret merthe° homward con° þay ryde, — *mirth/did*

And were al ny3t togedyr,° tyl þe morn-tude;° — *together/morning*

And þay in fere° assent:° — *together/were of one mind*

So wele° hys nedys° he has sped° — *well/desires/achieved*

Þat dere Tyb he has wed;

215   Þe pryse° folk þat hur led — *noble*

Were of þe turnament.

To þat ylk fest° com many, for þe nones:° — *same feast/occasion*

Some come hyp-halt,° and sum tryppand° on þe stonys;° — *limping/stumbling/stones*

Sum a staf in hys hand, and sum two at onys:° — *once*

---

187. *ston:* fourteen pounds.

202. It seems that married men also engaged in this violent flirtation—not an uncommon occurrence by any means. However, in this case "husband" may simply mean "betrothed."

220 Of sum were þe hedys° to-broken,° and sum þe schulder-bonys:° *heads/broken up/shoulder bones*
  With sorow com þay þedyr!° *there*
  Wo° was Hawkyn, wo was Herry; *woe*
  Wo was Tomkyn, wo was Terry;
  And so was al þe bachelary,° *company*
225 When þay° met togedyr. *they*

 At þat fest þay were seruyd° with a ryche aray: *served*
 Euery v and v had a cokenay;° *?cook ?rotten egg*
 And so þay sat in iolyté° al þe lang° day, *merriment/long*
 And at þe last þay went to bed, with ful° gret deray.° *very/disarray*
230 Mekyl° myrth was þem amang: *much*
  In euery corner of þe hous
  Was melody delycyous,
  For to here precyus,° *hear precious*
  Of vi menys° sang.° *six-part/song*

EXPLICIT

---

227. French and Hale gloss *cokenay* as "cook" (the line meaning that every fifth guest has his own). The *OED* gives "small egg," and the *MED* suggests "bad egg." None of these meanings seems entirely satisfactory. Could it possibly have been a cooked egg?

THE WEDDING OF SIR GAWAIN AND DAME RAGNELL

DATE: C. 1450. ✦ MANUSCRIPT: Bodleian Library, Oxford, Rawlinson C 86, c. 1500. The dialect is East Midland. ✦ EDITIONS: Laura Sumner, *The Weddynge of Sir Gawen and Dame Ragnell*, Smith College Studies in Modern Languages, Vol. 5, No. 4 (Northampton, Mass., 1924); B. J. Whiting, "The Wife of Bath's Table," in *Sources and Analogues of Chaucer's Canterbury Tales*, ed. W. F. Bryan and Germaine Dempster (New York, 1958) pp. 242–64, which compares the Sumner edition with the MS. The poem has also been edited by Donald Sands, *Middle English Verse Romances* (New York, 1966), pp. 323–47.

The 15th-century East Midland dialect of the poem is very easy to read: only the interchange of *y* and *i* (*lyf, fyrst*) and especially *y* and *e* (*sholdyst, woldyst, armyd, opynyd*) may at first seem strange. It might also be noted that, as elsewhere, the word *gan* indicates the auxiliary verb "did," and that the scribe has a habit of doubling final *t*.

The humorous romance of Gawain's wedding with the Loathly Lady is one of several analogues—like Gower's *Tale of Florent* and the ballad of *The Marriage of Sir Gawain*—to Geoffrey Chaucer's *The Wife of Bath's Tale*, all of which have the motifs of the Loathly Lady, the Wooing Lady, and the Riddle Asked and Answered. Yet *The Wedding of Sir Gawain and Dame Ragnell* is quite different in tone from Chaucer's story, which is less direct because of a didactic purpose and psychological development. Here we have a burlesque, not so much of chivalric attitudes, as of the character of Arthur, Gawain, and Ragnell. The king's predicament, his "passing the buck" to Gawain, and his collecting answers to the question, What is it that women most desire? and carefully noting them in a book, make Arthur a much more ludicrous figure than the ineffective cuckold of other versions. The plot is simple, but the incongruity of character and action throughout is funny in the extreme. The poem can be viewed as a prime example of the folkloric process of the decline of the hero.

> Lythe° and listenythe° the lif° of a lord riche,   *harken/listen (to)/life*
> The while that he lyvid° was none hym liche,°   *lived/like*
> Nether° in bowre ne° in halle;   *neither/chamber nor*
> In the tyme of Arthoure thys adventure betyd,°   *happened*
> ⁵ And of the greatt adventure that he hym-self dyd,

That kyng curteys° and royalle.   *courteous*
Of alle kynges Arture berythe° the flowyr,   *bears*
And of alle knyghtod° he bare° away the honour,   *knighthood/bore*
Where-so-euere° he wentt.   *wherever*
10 In his contrey° was nothyng butt chyvalry,   *country*
And knyghtes were belovid by that doughty,°   *brave (man)*
For cowardes were eueremore shent.°   *evermore disgraced*
Nowe wylle ye lyst° a whyle to my talkyng,   *if you will listen*
I shalle you telle of Arthowre the kyng,
15 Howe ones° hym befelle.°   *once/(it) befell*
On huntyng° he was in Ingleswod,°   *a-hunting/Inglewood*
Withe alle his bold knyghtes good,
Nowe herken° to my spelle.°   *listen/tale*
The kyng was sett att his trestylle-tree,°   *hunting station*
20 Withe hys bowe to sle° the wylde venere,°   *slay/deer*
And hys lordes were sett hym besyde;
As the kyng stode,° then was he ware,°   *stood/aware*
Where a greatt hartt was and a fayre,
And forthe fast dyd he glyde.
25 The hartt was in a braken ferne,°   *fern thicket*
And hard° the groundes, and stode fulle derne,°   *heard/very still*
Alle that sawe the kyng.
"Hold you stylle, euery man,
And I wolle goo° my-self, yf I can   *will go*
30 Withe crafte° of stalkyng."   *skill*
The kyng in hys hand toke° a bowe,   *took*
And wodmanly° he stowpyd° lowe,   *woodsmanlike/stooped*
To stalk vnto that dere;°   *deer*
When that he cam° the dere fulle nere.°   *came/near*
35 The dere lept forthe into a brere,°   *briar patch*
And euere° the kyng went nere° and nere,   *ever/nearer*
So kyng Arthure went a whyle,
After the dere, I trowe,° half a myle,   *believe*
And no man withe hym went;
40 And att the last to the dere he lett flye,°   *fly (arrows)*
And smote hym sore° and sewerly°   *mightily/unerringly*
Suche grace God hym sent.
Doun the dere tumblyd so deron,°   *wounded*
And felle into a greatt brake° of fferon;°   *thicket/fern*
45 The kyng folowyd fulle fast.

---

26. *hard the groundes:* The hart undoubtedly sensed the vibrations of the earth to perceive distant pursuers; but perhaps *groundes* is an error for *houndes.*

32. *wodmanly:* Donald Sands suggests that this word might go back to OE *wāth,* "hunting," the meaning being therefore "like a hunter."

Anon° the kyng bothe ferce° and felle°   *then/fierce/savage*
Was withe the dere and dyd hym serve welle.
And after the grasse he taste.°   *tasted*
As the kyng was withe the dere alone,
⁵⁰ Streyghte° ther cam to hym a quaynt grome,°   *straightway/strange fellow*
Armyd welle and sure;
A knyghte fulle strong and of greatt myghte,
And grymly wordes to the kyng he sayd:
"Well i-mett,° kyng Arthour!   *met*
⁵⁵ Thou hast me done wrong many a yere,°   *year*
And wofully° I shalle quytte the° here;   *woefully/repay you*
I hold thy lyfe days nyghe° done;   *almost*
Thou hast gevyn° my landes in certayn,°   *given/indeed*
Withe greatt wrong vnto Sir Gawen.
⁶⁰ Whate sayest thou, kyng alone?"
"Syr knyghte, whate is thy name withe honour?"°   *honored*
"Syr kyng," he sayd, "Gromer Somer Joure,
I telle the nowe withe ryghte."°   *truth*
"A,° Sir Gromer Somer, bethynk the° welle,   *ah/reflect*
⁶⁵ To sle° me here honour getyst° thou no delle,°   *slay/get/not a bit of*
Be-thynk the thou artt a knyghte,
Yf thou sle me nowe in thys case,
Alle knyghtes wolle refuse the in euery place.
That shame shalle neuere° the froo;°   *never/(go) from*
⁷⁰ Lett be thy wylle° and folowe wytt,°   *anger/reason*
And that° is amys° I shalle amend itt,   *what/amiss*
And° thou wolt,° or that° I goo."°   *if/will/before/go*
"Nay," sayd Sir Gromer Somer, "by hevyn° kyng!   *heaven's*
So shalt thou nott skape° withoute lesyng,°   *escape/lie*
⁷⁵ I haue the nowe att avaylle;°   *advantage*
Yf I shold° lett the thus goo withe mokery,°   *should/mockery*
Anoder° tyme thou wolt me defye;   *another*
Of that I shalle nott faylle."
Now sayd the kyng, "So God me saue,
⁸⁰ Save my lyfe, and whate thou wolt crave,
I shalle now graunt° itt the;   *grant*
Shame thou shalt haue to sle me in venere,°   *hunting*
Thou armyd and I clothyd butt in grene, perde."°   *indeed*

---

47. *dyd ... welle:* i.e., "killed him."

48. *the grasse he taste:* Cf. "He bit the dust."

62. *Gromer Somer Joure:* literally, "man" (ME), "summer" (ME), "day" (Fr.); i.e., "Summertime Man"—perhaps originally a symbolic figure.

74. *withoute lesyng:* i.e., "truly."

76. *mokery:* i.e., "only threats."

78. *that:* i.e., "my advantage."

83. *clothyd butt in grene:* Arthur is clothed in the green camouflage of foresters and hunters; cf. the "Lincoln green" of Robin Hood.

"Alle thys shalle nott help the, sekyrly,°   *surely*

85 For I wolle nother lond ne° gold truly;   *want neither land nor*

Butt yf° thou graunt me att a certayn day,   *unless*

Suche as I shalle sett,° and in thys same araye."°   *demand/attire*

"Yes," sayd the kyng, "lo, here my hand."

"Ye,° butt abyde,° kyng, and here° me a stound;°   *yea/wait/hear/while*

90 Fyrst thow shalt swere° vpon my sword broun,°   *swear/burnished*

To shewe° me att thy comyng whate wemen° love best in feld°   *tell/women/field*
    and town;

And thou shalt mete° me here witheouten send,°   *meet/without sending*

Evyn° att this day xij monethes° end;   *even/months'*

And thou shalt swere vpon my swerd° good,   *sword*

95 That of thy knyghtes shalle none com with the, by the rood,° *cross*

Nowther fremde° ne freynd.°   *neither stranger/friend*

And yf thou bryng nott answere withe-oute faylle;

Thyne hed° thou shalt lose for thy traveylle°—   *head/trouble*

Thys shalle nowe be thyne othe.°   *oath*

100 Whate sayst thou, kyng, lett se,° haue done."   *let's*

"Syr, I graunt° to thys, now lett me gone;°   *agree/(be) gone*

Thoughe itt be to me fulle lothe,°   *very unpleasant*

I ensure the,° as I am true kyng,   *you*

To com agayn att thys xij monethes end,

105 And bryng the thyne answere."

"Now go thy way, kyng Arthure,

Thy lyfe is in my hand, I am fulle sure,

Of thy sorowe thow artt nott ware.°   *aware*

Abyde, kyng Arthure, a lytelle° whyle,   *little*

110 Loke° nott to-day thou me begyle,°   *see to it (that)/deceive*

And kepe° alle thyng in close;°   *keep/secret*

For and° I wyst,° by Mary mylde,   *if/knew*

Thou woldyst° betray me in the feld,°   *would/anywhere*

Thy lyf° fyrst sholdyst° thou lose."   *life/should*

115 "Nay," sayd kyng Arthure, "that may nott be,

Vntrewe° knyghte shalt thou neuere° fynde me;   *(an) unfaithful/never*

To dye° yett were me lever.°   *die/I had rather*

Farwelle, Sir knyghte and evylle° mett,   *ill*

I wolle° com, and I be on lyve° att the day sett,   *will/alive*

120 Thoughe I shold scape° neuere."   *escape*

The kyng his bugle gan° blowe,   *did*

That° hard° euery knyghte and itt gan knowe,°   *so that/heard/recognize*

Vnto hym can° they rake;°   *did/hasten*

Ther they fond° the kyng and the dere,°   *found/deer*

---

92. *send:* i.e., "my having to send for you."   **100.** *have done:* i.e., "make up your mind."

125 Withe sembland° sad and hevy chere,°	*countenance/sorrowful spirit*
That had no lust° to layk.°	*desire/sport*
"Go we home nowe to Carlylle,°	*Carlisle*
Thys hyntyng lykys° me nott welle"—	*hunting pleases*
So sayd kyng Arthure.	
130 Alle the lordes knewe by his countenaunce	
That the kyng had mett withe sume° dysturbaunce.	*some*
Vnto Carlylle then the kyng cam,°	*came*
Butt of his hevynesse° knewe no man,	*sorrow*
Hys hartt° was wonder hevy;°	*heart/very heavy*
135 In this hevynesse he dyd a-byde,	
That many of his knyghtes mervelyd that tyde,°	*wondered (in) that time*
Tylle att the last Sir Gawen	
To the kyng he sayd than,°	*then*
"Syr, me marvaylythe ryghte sore,°	*I wonder very much*
140 Whate thyng that thou sorowyst fore."°	*for*
Then **answeryd** the kyng as tyghte,°	*immediately*
"I shalle the telle, gentylle° Gawen knyghte.	*noble*
In the fforest as I was this daye,	
Ther I mett withe a knyghte in his araye,°	*array*
145 And serteyn° wordes to me he gan sayn,°	*certain/say*
And chargyd me I shold hym nott bewrayne;°	*betray*
Hys councelle° must I kepe therfore,	*secret*
Or els° I am forswore."°	*else/forsworn*
"Nay, drede° you nott, lord, by Mary flower,	*fear*
150 I am nott that man that wold you dishonour,	
Nother° by euyn ne° by moron."°	*neither/evening nor/morning*
"Forsothe° I was on huntyng° in Ingleswod,°	*truly/a-hunting/Inglewood*
Thowe knowest well I slewe an hartt by the rode,°	*cross*
Alle my-self alon;	
155 Ther mett I withe a knyghte armyd sure,°	*well*
His name he told me was Sir Gromer Somer Joure,	
Therfor° I make my mone.°	*for that/lament*
Ther that knyghte fast° dyd me threte,°	*much/threaten*
And wold° haue slayn me withe greatt heatt,°	*would/anger*
160 But° I spak° fayre agayn;°	*except that/spoke/in turn*
Wepyns° withe me ther had I none,	*weapons*
Alas! my worshypp° therfor is nowe gone."	*honor*
"What therof?" sayd Gawen;	

---

127. *Carlylle:* Carlisle in Cumberland is often confused in the romances with Caerleon-upon-Usk in Monmouthshire, the supposed site of the legendary Camelot (cf. *Sir Launfal*, l. 1021*n*).

149. *by Mary flower:* He swears by Mary the flower. In medieval verse the Virgin is often represented as a flower, usually the lily (cf. *I Sing of a Maiden*, this volume, p. 661).

163. *"What therof?"* i.e., "Why?"

"Whatt nedys more° I shalle nott lye,° *what there is more to say/lie*
165 He wold haue slayn me ther withe-oute mercy,
And that me° was fulle lothe;° *to me/very hateful*
He made me to swere° that att the xij monethes° end, *swear/month's*
That I shold mete° hym ther in the same kynde,° *should meet/manner*
To that I plyghte° my trowithe.° *pledged/faith*
170 And also I shold tell hym att the same day,
What wemen desyren° moste in good faye,° *women desire/faith*
My lyf els° shold I lese.° *life otherwise/lose*
This othe° I made vnto that knyghte, *oath*
And that I shold neuere° telle itt to no wighte,° *never/person*
175 Of thys I myghte nott chese.° *choose*
And also I shold com in none oder araye,° *no other attire*
Butt euyn° as I was the same daye; *just*
And yf I faylyd of myne answere,
I wott° I shal be slayn ryghte there. *know*
180 Blame me nott thoughe° I be a wofulle° man; *if/woeful*
Alle thys is my drede° and fere."° *dread/fear*
"Ye,° Sir, make° good chere° *yea/be of/cheer*
Lett make° your hors redy,° *be made/ready*
To ryde into straunge contrey;° *foreign country*
185 And euere wher-as° ye mete owther° man or woman, in faye° *ever where/either/indeed*
Ask of theym° whate thay° therto saye. *them/they*
And I shalle also ryde a-noder° waye, *another*
And enquere° of euery man and woman, and gett whatt I may *inquire*
Of euery man and womans answere,
190 And in a boke° I shalle theym wryte." *book*
"I graunt,"° sayd the kyng as tyte,° *agree/quickly*
"Ytt is welle advysed, Gawen the good,
Evyn° by the holy rood."° *even/cross*
Sone° were they bothe redy, *soon*
195 Gawen and the kyng, wytterly.° *certainly*
The kyng rode on° way, and Gawen a-noder, *one*
And euere enquyred of man, woman, and other,
Whate wemen desyred moste dere.° *dearly*
Somme sayd they lovyd to be welle arayd,
200 Somme sayd they lovyd to be fayre prayed;° *gallantly courted*
Somme sayd they lovyd a lusty man,
That in theyr armys can clypp° them and kysse them than;° *did embrace/then*
Somme sayd one;° somme sayd other; *one (thing)*
And so had Gawen getyn° many an answere. *gotten*
205 By° that Gawen had geten° whate he maye, *by (the time)/gotten*
And come agayn by a certeyn° daye, *certain*
Syr Gawen had goten° answerys so many, *gotten*
That had made a boke greatt, wytterly;

To the courte he cam° agayn.   came
210 By that° was the kyng comyn° withe hys boke,   that (time)/come
And eyther° on others pamplett° dyd loke.°   either/pamphlet/look
"Thys may nott ffaylle," sayd Gawen.
"By God," sayd the kyng, "I dred me° sore,°   fear/much
I cast me° to seke° a lytelle° more   intend/seek/little
215 In Yngleswod° Fforest;   Inglewood
I haue butt a monethe to° my day sett,°   month till/appointed
I may hapen° on somme good tydynges° to hytt—   happen/information
Thys thynkythe° me° nowe best."   seems/to me
"Do as ye lyst,"° then Gawen sayd,   please
220 "What-so-euere° ye do I hold me° payd,   whatever/account myself
Hytt° is good to be spyrryng;°   it/inquiring
Doute° you nott, lord, ye shalle welle spede;°   doubt/succeed
Sume° of your sawes° shalle help att nede,°   some/answers/need
Els° itt were° ylle lykyng."°   otherwise/would be/luck
225 Kyng Arthoure rode forthe on the other° day,   next
In-to Yngleswod as° hys gate° laye,   where/road
And ther he mett withe a lady;
She was as vngoodly° a creature   ugly
As euere° man sawe witheoute mesure.°   ever/measure
230 Kyng Arthure mervaylyd securly.°   marveled surely
Her face was red, her nose snotyd withalle,°   runny also
Her mowithe° wyde, her tethe yalowe° ouere alle,°   mouth/teeth yellow/everywhere
Withe bleryd eyen gretter then° a balle,   bleary eyes greater than
Her mowithe was nott to lak;°   lacked nothing
235 Her tethe hyng ouer° her lyppes;   hung over
Her chekys syde° as wemens° hyppes;   cheeks broad/women's
A lute she bare° vpon her bak.°   bore/back
Her nek° long and therto° greatt,   neck/also
Her here cloteryd on° an hepe,°   hair clotted in/heap
240 In the sholders she was a yard brode,°   broad
Hangyng pappys to° be an hors lode;°   paps (enough) to/load
And lyke a barelle° she was made;   barrel
And to reherse° the fowlnesse° of that lady,   recite/foulness
Ther is no tung° may telle, securly   tongue
245 Of lothynesse inowghe° she had.   ugliness enough
She satt on a palfray° was gay begon,°   riding horse/(which) was gaily
                                                                        decorated

Withe gold besett and many a precious stone,
Ther was an vnsemely° syghte;   unseemly

---

229. *witheoute mesure*: i.e., "exceedingly."   **241.** *to . . . lode*: i.e., "heavy enough to be a full load for a horse."
234. *was nott to lak*: i.e., "was ugly."   **246.** *palfray*: Cf. above, p. 346, n. 26.

So fowlle a creature withe-oute mesure,

250 To ryde so gayly, I you ensure,°   *assure*

Ytt was no° reason ne° ryghte.   *neither/nor*

She rode to Arthoure, and thus she sayd:

"God spede,° Sir kyng, I am welle payd,°   *prosper (you)/pleased*

That I haue withe the° mett;   *you*

255 Speke° withe me, I rede, or° thou goo,°   *speak/advise, before/go*

For thy lyfe is in my hand, I warn the soo,°   *so*

That shalt thou fynde, and° I itt° nott lett."°   *if/(i.e., your death)/prevent*

"Why, whatt wold° ye, lady, nowe withe me?"   *want*

"Syr, I wold fayn° nowe speke withe the,   *would gladly*

260 And telle the tydynges° good;   *information*

For alle the answerys that thou canst yelpe,°   *boast of*

None of theym° alle shalle the helpe,   *them*

That shalt thou knowe, by the rood,°   *cross*

Thou wenyst° I knowe nott thy councelle,°   *think/secret*

265 Butt I warn the I knowe itt euery dealle,°   *bit*

Yf I help the nott, thou art butt° dead.   *as good as*

Graunt° me, Sir kyng, butt one thyng,   *grant*

And for thy lyfe, I make warrauntyng,°   *give guarantee*

Or elles° thou shalt lose thy hed."°   *else/head*

270 "Whate mean you, lady, telle me tyghte,°   *quickly*

For of thy wordes I haue great dispyte,°   *contempt*

To° you I haue no nede.°   *of/need*

Whate is your desyre, fayre lady,

Lett me wete° shortly;°   *know/in short*

275 Whate is your meanyng,

And why my lyfe is in your hand,

Telle me, and I shalle you warraunt,°   *guarantee*

Alle your oun° askyng."   *own*

"For-sothe,"° sayd the lady, I am no qued,°   *truly/bad person*

280 Thou must graunt me a knyghte to wed,

His name is Sir Gawen;

And suche covenaunt° I wolle° make the,   *agreement/will*

Butt thorowe° myne answere thy lyf sauyd° be,   *unless through/life saved*

Elles° lett my desyre be in vayne.   *then*

285 And yf myne answere sauc thy lyf,

Graunt me to be Gawens wyf,°   *wife*

Advyse the° nowe, Sir kyng;   *consider*

For itt must be so, or thou artt butt dead,

Chose° nowe, for thou mayste sone° lose thyne hed.   *choose/may soon*

290 Telle me nowe in hying."°   *haste*

---

278. I.e., "everything you ask."

"Mary,"° sayd the kyng, "I maye nott graunt the,   *marry*
To make warraunt Sir Gawen to wed the;
Alle lyethe in° hym alon.   *depends on*
Butt and itt be so, I wolle do my labour,
295 In savyng of my lyfe to make itt° secour,°   *(i.e., the wedding)/sure*
To Gawen wolle I make my mone."°   *lament*
"Welle," sayd she, "nowe go home agayn,
And fayre wordes speke° to Sir Gawen,   *speak*
For thy lyf I may saue;
300 Thoughe I be foulle, yett am I gaye,°   *lusty*
Thourghe° me thy lyfe saue he maye,   *through*
Or sewer° thy dethe° to haue."   *allow/death*
"Alas!" he sayd, "nowe woo° is me,   *woe*
That I shold° cause Gawen to wed the,°   *should/you*
305 For he wol° be lothe° to saye naye.   *will/unwilling*
So foulle a lady as ye ar nowe one
Sawe I neuere° in my lyfe on ground gone,°   *never/earth walk*
I nott° whate I do may."   *know not*
"No force,° Sir kyng, thoughe I be foulle,   *matter*
310 Choyse° for a make hathe an° owlle,   *choice/mate has (even) an*
Thou getest of me no more;
When thou comyst agayn to° thyne answere,   *for*
Ryghte in this place I shalle mete° the here,   *meet*
Or elles° I wott° thou artt lore."°   *else/know/lost*
315 "Now farewelle," sayd the kyng, "lady."
"Ye,° Sir," she sayd, "ther is a byrd men calle an owlle,   *yea*
And yett a lady I am."
"Whate is your name, I pray you telle me?"
"Syr kyng, I highte° Dame Ragnelle, truly,   *am called*
320 That neuere yett begylyd° man."   *deceived*
"Dame Ragnelle, now haue good daye."
"Syr kyng, God spede° the on thy way,   *prosper*
Ryghte here I shalle the mete."
Thus they departyd fayre and welle,
325 The kyng fulle° sone com° to Carlylle,°   *very/came/Carlisle*
And his hartt hevy° and greatt.°   *heart heavy/sad*
The fyrst man he mett was Sir Gawen,
That vnto the kyng thus gan sayn,°   *did say*
"Syr, howe haue ye sped?"°   *succeeded*
330 "Forsothe,"° sayd the kyng, "neuere so ylle.   *truly*
Alas! I am in° poynt my-self to spylle,°   *at (the)/kill*

---

291. *Mary:* i.e., "by Mary [the Virgin]," an exclamation of
surprise.

294. *wolle . . . labour;* i.e., "make an effort."

316–17. Dame Ragnell implies that if the ugly owl can choose
a mate, she as a lady should certainly be allowed to do likewise.

For nedely° I most° be ded.'"°   *of necessity/must/dead*
"Nay," sayd Gawen, "that may nott be,
I had lever° my-self be dead, so mott° I the,°   *rather/may/thrive*
335 Thys is ille tydand."°   *news*
"Gawen, I mett to-day withe the fowlyst° lady,   *foulest*
That euere° I sawe sertenly;°   *ever/certainly*
She sayd to me my lyfe she wold° saue,   *would*
Butt fyrst she wold° the to husbond haue,°   *wants/husband (to) have*
340 Wherfor I am wo begon,°   *woebegone*
Thus in my hartt I make my mone."°   *lament*
"Ys this alle?" then sayd Gawen,
"I shalle wed her and wed her agayn,
Thowghe° she were a fend,°   *though/fiend*
345 Thowghe she were as foulle as Belsabub,°   *Beelzebub*
Her shalle I wed, by the rood;°   *cross*
Or elles were nott I your frende,
For ye ar my kyng withe honour,
And haue worshypt° me in many a stowre,°   *honored/time*
350 Therfor shalle I nott lett;°   *hesitate*
To saue your lyfe, lorde, itt were° my parte,°   *would be/duty*
Or were I false and a greatt coward,
And my worshypp is the bett."°   *better*
"I-wys,° Gawen, I mett her in Inglyswod,°   *indeed/Inglewood*
355 She told me her name, by the rode,°   *cross*
That itt was Dame Ragnelle;
She told me butt° I had of° her answere,   *unless/from*
Elles° alle my laboure is neuere° the nere,°   *then/never/nearer (a solution)*
Thus she gan me telle.
360 And butt yf° her answere help me welle,   *unless*
Elles lett her haue her desyre no dele,°   *not a bit of*
This was her covenaunt;°   *agreement*
And yf her answere help me, and none other,
Then wold she haue you, here is alle to-geder,°   *that's the gist of it*
365 That made° she warraunt."°   *gave/guarantee*
"As for this," sayd Gawen, "it shalle nott lett,°   *stop (me)*
I wolle° wed her att whate tyme ye wolle sett,°   *will/appoint*
I pray you make no care;°   *don't worry*
For and° she were the moste fowlyst wyghte,°   *if/person*
370 That euere men myghte se° withe syghte,   *see*
For your love I wolle nott spare."
"Garamercy,° Gawen," then sayd kyng Arthor,   *thank you*
"Of alle knyghtes thou berest° the flowre,°   *bear/prize*
That euere yett I fond;°   *found*
375 My worshypp and my lyf° thou savyst for-euere,   *life*
Therefore my loue shalle nott frome the° dyssevyr,°   *you/be severed*

As I am kyng in lond."°   *land*

Then within v or vj days,

The kyng must nedys° goo° his ways,   *of necessity/go*

380   To bere his answere.

The kyng and Sir Gawen rode oute of toun,

No man withe them, butt they alone,

Neder ferre ne nere.°   *neither far nor near*

When the kyng was withe-in the fforest,

385   "Syr Gawen, farewell, I must go west,

Thou shalt no furder° goo."   *further*

"My lord, God spede° you on your jorney,°   *prosper/journey*

I wold° I shold° nowe ryde your way,   *wish/should (i.e., could)*

For to departe I am ryghte wo."°   *very sorry*

390   The kyng had rydden butt a while,

Lytelle° more then° the space of a myle,   *little/than*

Or° he mett Dame Ragnelle.   *before*

"A,° Sir kyng, ye arre nowe welcum° here,   *ah/welcome*

I wott° ye ryde to bere your answere,   *know*

395   That wolle avaylle° you no dele."°   *help/bit*

"Nowe," sayd the kyng, "sithe° itt wolle none other be,   *since*

Telle me your answere nowe, and my lyfe saue me,

Gawen shalle you wed;

So he hathe promysed me my lyf to saue,

400   And your desyre nowe shalle ye haue,

Bothe in bowre° and in bed.   *chamber*

Therfor telle me nowe alle in hast,°   *haste*

Whate wolle help now att last—.

Haue done, I may nott tary."°   *tarry*

405   Syr," quod° Dame Ragnelle, "nowe shalt thou knowe   *said*

Whate wemen desyren° moste of highe° and lowe,   *women desire/from high (men)*

From this I wolle° nott varaye.°   *will/deviate*

Summe° men sayn° we desyre to be fayre,   *some/say*

Also we desyre to haue repayre,°   *intercourse*

410   Of diuerse straunge° men;   *with various strange*

Also we loue to haue lust° in bed,   *pleasure*

And often we desyre to wed,

Thus ye men nott ken.°   *understand*

Yett we desyre a-noder° maner° thyng,   *another/kind (of)*

415   To be holden° nott old, butt fresshe and yong,°   *regarded as/young*

Withe flatryng° and glosyng° and quaynt gyn,°   *flattering/complimenting/clever device*

So ye men may vs wemen euere° wyn,   *ever*

---

404. *Haue done:* i.e., "get it over with."

Of whate ye wolle crave.

Ye goo fulle nyse,° I wolle nott lye,°   *go (about it) very foolishly/lie*

420 Butt there is one thyng is alle oure fantasye,°   *wish*

And that nowe shalle ye knowe:

We desyren of men aboue alle maner thyng,

To haue the souereynte,° withoute lesyng,°   *sovereignty/lie*

Of alle, bothe hyghe and lowe.

425 For where we haue souereynte alle is ourys,°   *ours*

Thoughe a knyghte be neuere° so ferys,°   *never/fierce*

And euere the mastry wynne;°   *mastery gain*

Of the moste manlyest is oure desyre,

To haue the souereynte of° suche a syre,   *over*

430 Suche is oure crafte° and gynne.°   *skill/purpose*

Therfore wend,° Sir kyng, on thy way,   *go*

And telle that knyghte, as I the° saye,   *to you*

That° itt is as° we desyren moste;   *what/that*

He wol° be wrothe° and vnsoughte,°   *will/angry/harsh*

435 And curse her fast° that itt the° taughte,   *much/you*

For his laboure is lost.

Go forthe, Sir kyng, and hold° promyse   *keep*

For thy lyfe is sure nowe in alle wyse,°   *ways*

That dare I well vndertake."°   *vouch for*

440 The kyng rode forthe a greatt shake,°   *distance*

As fast as he myghte gate,°   *go*

Thorowe myre, more,° and fenne,°   *through mire, moor/bog*

Where-as° the place was sygnyd° and sett then,   *where/appointed*

Evyn° there withe Sir Gromer he mett.   *right*

445 And stern wordes to the kyng he spak° withe that,°   *spoke/then*

"Com of,° Sir kyng, nowe lett se,°   *on/let's see*

Of thyne answere whate itt shal be,

For I am redy grathyd."°   *prepared*

The kyng pullyd oute bokes twayne;°   *books two*

450 "Syr, ther is myne answer, I dare sayn°   *say*

For somme wolle° help att nede."°   *will/need*

Syr Gromer lokyd° on theym° euerychon;°   *looked/them/every one*

"Nay, nay, Sir kyng, thou artt butt a dead man,

Therfor nowe shalt thou blede."°   *bleed*

455 "Abyde,° Sir Gromer," sayd kyng Arthoure,   *wait*

"I haue one answere shalle° make alle sure."   *(that) shall*

"Lett se," then sayd Sir Gromer,

"Or els° so God me help as I the say,   *else*

Thy dethe° thou shalt haue with large paye,°   *death/forcefully*

---

425. *ourys:* i.e., "in our control."

460 I telle the nowe ensure."° — *for sure*
   "Now," sayd the kyng, "I se as I gesse,° — *guess*
   In the is butt a lytelle gentilnesse,° — *little kindness*
   By God that ay° is helpand.° — *ever/helping*
   Here is oure answere and that is alle,
465 That wemen desyren° moste specialle,° — *women desire/specially*
   Bothe of fre° and bond.° — *from free (men)/bound*
   I saye no more, butt aboue al thyng,
   Wemen desyre souereynte,° for that is theyr lykyng, — *sovereignty*
   And that is ther moste° desyre; — *greatest*
470 To haue the rewlle of° the manlyest men, — *rule over*
   And then ar they welle,° thus they me dyd ken,° — *happy/teach*
   To rule the, Gromer syre."
   "And she that told the nowe, Sir Arthoure,
   I pray to God, I maye se her bren° on a fyre, — *burn*
475 For that was my suster,° Dame Ragnelle; — *sister*
   That old scott,° God geve° her shame, — *hag/give*
   Elles° had I° made the fulle° tame; — *otherwise/I would have/you very*
   Nowe haue I lost moche travaylle.° — *much effort*
   Go where thou wolt,° kyng Arthoure, — *will*
480 For of me thou maiste° be euere° sure; — *may/ever*
   Alas! that I euere se° this day; — *saw*
   Nowe, welle I wott,° myne enime° thou wolt be, — *know/enemy*
   And att° suche a pryk° shalle I neuere° gett the, — *on/note/never*
   My song may be welle-away!"° — *alas*
485 "No," sayd the kyng, "that make° I warraunt,° — *give/guarantee*
   Some harnys° I wolle haue to make me defendaunt,° — *armor/defensible*
   That make I God avowe,° — *I swear to God*
   In suche a plyghte shalt thou neuere me fynde,
   And yf thou do, lett me bete° and bynde,° — *be beaten/bound*
490 As is for thy best prouf."° — *advantage*
   "Nowe haue good day," sayd Sir Gromer,
   "Farewell," sayd Sir Arthoure, "so mott° I the,° — *may/thrive*
   I am glad I haue so sped."° — *succeeded*
   Kyng Arthoure turnyd hys hors into the playn,
495 And sone° he mett withe Dame Ragnelle agayn, — *soon*
   In the same place and stede.° — *spot*
   "Syr kyng, I am glad ye haue sped welle,
   I told howe itt wold° be euery delle;° — *would/bit*
   Nowe hold that° ye haue hyghte.° — *keep what/promised*
500 Syn° I haue sauyd° your lyf,° and none other, — *since/saved/life*

---

466. *bond:* i.e., "serfs."
483. *att . . . pryk:* i.e., "in such an awkward situation," or "in such a critical moment." Sands suggests that "prick" refers to the medieval musical note, and is linked to the *song* of l. 484.

Gawen must me wed, Sir Arthoure,

That is a fulle gentille° knyghte."   *very noble*

"No, lady, that I you hyghte I shalle nott faylle,

So° ye wol° be rulyd by my councelle,°   *if/will/advice*

505 Your wille then shalle ye haue."

"Nay, Sir kyng, nowe wolle° I nott soo,°   *will/so*

Openly I wol be weddyd, or° I parte the froo,°   *before/from*

Elles shame wolle I haue.

Ryde before, and I wolle com after,

510 Vnto thy courte, Syr kyng Arthoure;

Of° no man I wolle° shame;   *from/desire*

Be-thynk you° howe I haue sauyd your lyf.   *consider*

Therfor withe me nowe shalle ye nott stryfe,°   *quarrel*

For and° ye do, ye be° to blame."   *if/are*

515 The kyng of° her had greatt shame;   *because of*

Butt forthe she rood,° thoughe he were grevyd,°   *rode/grieved*

Tylle they cam° to Karlyle forthe they mevyd.°   *came/moved*

In-to the courte she rode hym by,°   *by his side*

For no man wold she spare, securly°—   *surely*

520 Itt likyd° the kyng fulle° ylle.   *pleased/very*

Alle the contraye° had wonder greatt,   *people*

Fro whens° she com,° that foule vnswete,°   *from whence/came/ugly thing*

They sawe neuere° of so fowlle° a thyng;   *never/foul*

In-to the halle she went, in certen:°   *indeed*

525 "Arthoure, kyng, lett fetche° me Sir Gaweyn,   *be fetched*

Before the knyghtes, alle in hying,°   *haste*

That I may nowe be made sekyr,°   *certain*

In welle° and wo trowithe° plyghte vs togeder,°   *happiness/woe troth/together*

Before alle thy chyvalry.°   *knights*

530 This is your graunt, lett se,° haue done;°   *promise, let's see/do it*

Sett° forthe Sir Gawen, my love, anon,°   *bring/quickly*

For lenger tarying kepe° nott I."   *longer delay care*

Then cam forthe Sir Gawen the knyghte,

"Syr, I am redy° of that I you hyghte,°   *ready/promised*

535 Alle forwardes° to fulfylle";   *promises*

"Godhauemercy," sayd Dame Ragnelle then,

"For thy sake I wold° I were a fayre woman,   *wish*

For thou art of so good wylle."

Then Sir Gawen to her his trowthe° plyghte,   *troth*

540 In welle and in woo,° as he was a true knyghte,   *woe*

---

504. *councelle:* Arthur's "advice" is probably similar to Guinevere's in ll. 570–71, i.e., a secret wedding; but throughout Dame Ragnell insists on a proper ceremony with all the trimmings.

511. The irony is that Dame Ragnell wishes not to be shamed by a secret wedding and thereby dishonors Gawain the more in public.

Then was Dame Ragnelle fayn.°   *happy*
"Alas!" then sayd Dame Gaynour;°   *Guinevere*
So sayd alle the ladyes in her bower,°   *chamber*
And wept for Sir Gawen.
545 "Alas!" then sayd bothe kyng and knyghte,
That euere° he shold° wed such a wyghte,°   *ever/should/person*
She was so fowlle and horyble.°   *horrible*
She had two tethe° on euery° syde,   *teeth/each*
As borys° tuskes, I wolle° nott hyde,°   *boar's/will/deny*
550 Of lengthe a large handfulle;
The one tusk went vp, and the other doun;
A mowthe° fulle wyde, and fowlle igrown°   *mouth/foully grown*
With grey herys° many on;°   *hairs/(a) one*
Her lyppes laye lumpryd° on her chyn;   *lumped*
555 Nek forsothe° on her was none i-seen°—   *neck truly/seen*
She was a lothly on!°   *loathly one*
She wold° nott be weddyd in no maner,°   *would/manner*
Butt° there were made a krye° in all the shyre,   *unless/proclamation*
Bothe in town and in borowe.°   *borough*
560 Alle the ladyes nowe of the lond,°   *land*
She lett kry° to com to hand,°   *had called/there*
To kepe° that brydalle thorowe.°   *make/proper*
So itt befylle° after on a daye,   *befell*
That maryed shold° be that fowlle° lady,   *married must/foul*
565 Vnto Sir Gawen.
The daye was comyn° the daye shold be,   *come (that)*
Therof the ladyes had greatt pitey;°   *pity*
"Alas!" then gan° they sayn.°   *did/say*
The queen prayd Dame Ragnelle sekerly°   *earnestly*
570 To be maryed in the mornyng erly,
"As pryvaly° as we may."   *secretly*
"Nay," she sayd, "by hevyn° kyng,   *heaven's*
That wolle I neuere° for no-thyng,   *never*
For oughte° that ye can saye;   *anything*
575 I wol° be weddyd alle openly,   *will*
For with the kyng suche covenaunt° made I;   *agreement*
I putt you oute of dowte,°   *doubt*
I wolle nott to° churche tylle highe masse tyme,   *(go) to*
And in the open halle I wolle dyne,
580 In myddys° of alle the rowte."°   *midst/company*
"I am greed,"° sayd Dame Gaynour,°   *agreed/Guinevere*
"Butt me° wold thynk° more honour,°   *I/think (it)/honorable*

---

582. I.e., "but I would think a secret wedding more honorable."

And your worshypp° moste."   *(to) your benefit*
"Ye,"° as for that, lady, God you saue,   *yea*
585 This daye my worshypp° wolle I haue,   *advantage*
I telle you withoute boste."°   *boast*
She made her redy° to churche to fare,   *herself ready*
And alle the states° that there ware,°   *ranking people/were*
Syrs, withoute lesyng.°   *lie*
590 She was arrayd° in the richest maner,   *attired*
More fressher than Dame Gaynour,
Her arayment° was worthe iij mlle. mark,   *raiment/thousand marks*
Of good red nobles styff° and stark,°   *gold coins sturdy/strong*
So rychely she was begon.°   *dressed*
595 For° alle her rayment she bare° the belle   *despite/bore*
Of° fowlnesse that euere° I hard° telle,   *for/ever/heard*
So fowlle a sowe° sawe neuere man,   *sow*
For to make a shortt conclusion.
When she was weddyd, they hyed theym° home,   *hurried*
600 To metc° alle they went.   *dinner*
This fowlle lady bygan° the highe dese,°   *sat at the head of/dais*
She was fulle° foulle and nott curteys,°   *very/well behaved*
So sayd they all verament.°   *truly*
When the seruyce cam° her before,   *servings came*
605 She etc° as moche° as vj that ther wore,°   *ate/much/were*
That° mervaylyd° many a man;   *so that/marveled*
Her nayles were long ynchys iij^e,
Therwithe she breke° her mete vngoodly,°   *cut/food uncouthly*
Therfore she ete alone.
610 She ette° iij^e capons and also curlues° iij^e,   *ate/curlews*
And greatt bake metes° she ete vp, perde,°   *meat pies/indeed*
All men therof had mervaylle;°   *wonder*
Ther was no mete cam her before,
Butt she ete itt vp lesse and more,
615 That praty fowlle° dameselle.   *odious, foul*
Alle men then that euere her sawe,
Bad° the deville her bonys° gnawe,   *prayed/bones*
Bothe knyghte and squyre;
So she ete tylle mete was done,
620 Tylle they drewe clothes° and had wasshen,°   *took towels/washed*

---

592. Three thousand marks is an outrageous sum, literally a king's ransom.

593. *red:* Cf. above, p. 183, l. 47n.

595. *bare the belle:* i.e., "took the prize."

608. It may be that she actually cut her meat with her long nails.

620. The normal cloths were already on the table. Those which were drawn for washing must have been special napkins or towels.

As is the gyse° and maner.°   *custom/fashion*
Meny° men wold speke° of diuerse seruice,°   *many/would speak/various foods*
I trowe° ye may wete inowghe° ther was,   *believe/know enough*
Bothe of tame° and wylde;   *tame (meat)*
625 In king Arthours courte ther was no wontt,°   *lack*
That° myghte be gotten withe mannys hond,°   *of what/man's hand*
Noder° in fforest ne° in feld.°   *neither/nor/field*
There were mynstralles of diuerse contrey.°   *lands*

· · · · ·

"A,° Sir Gawen, syn° I haue you wed,   *ah/since*
630 Shewe° me your cortesy° in bed,   *show/courtesy*
Withe° ryghte itt may nott be denyed.   *by*
I-wyse,° Sir Gawen," that lady sayd,   *indeed*
"And° I were fayre ye wold do a-noder brayd,°   *if/act differently*
Butt of wedlok° ye take no hed;°   *marriage/heed*
635 Yett for Arthours sake kysse me att the leste,°   *least*
I pray you do this att my request,
Lett se° howe ye can spede."°   *let's see/manage*
Sir Gawen sayd, "I wolle° do more   *will*
Then° for to kysse, and God before!"   *than*
640 He turnyd hym° her vntille;°   *himself/to*
He sawe her the fayrest creature
That euere° he sawe withoute mesure.°   *ever/measure*
She sayd, "Whatt is your wylle?"
"A, Ihesu!"° he sayd, "whate ar ye?"   *Jesus*
645 "Sir, I am your wyf, securly;°   *wife, certainly*
Why ar ye so vnkynde?"
"A, lady, I am to blame;
I cry you mercy, my fayre madame—
Itt was nott in my mynde.
650 A lady ye are fayre in my syghte,
And to-day ye were the foulyst wyghte°   *being*
That euere I sawe withe myne ie.°   *eye*
Wele is me,° my lady, I haue you thus";   *happy am I*
And brasyd° her in his armys,° and gan° her kysse,   *embraced/arms/did*
655 And made greatt joye, sycurly.°   *certainly*
"Syr," she sayd, "thus shalle ye me haue,
Chese of° the one, so God me saue,   *choose*
My beawty° wolle nott hold;°   *beauty/remain*
Wheder° ye wolle haue me fayre on° nyghtes,   *whether/in*

---

628. A missing leaf following this line must have consisted of about seventy lines in which the married couple left the feast and went to bed.

649. I.e., "I did not mean to be."

660 And as foulle on days to alle men° sightes,   *men's*
     Or els° to haue me fayre on days,   *else*
     And on nyghtes on° the fowlyst wyfe,°   *one of/foulest women*
     The one ye must nedes° haue;   *of necessity*
     Chese° the one or the oder,°   *choose/other*
665 Chese on,° Sir knyghte, whiche you° is leuere,°   *one/to you/dearer*
     Your worshypp° for to saue."   *honor*
     "Alas!" sayd Gawen, "the choyse° is hard;   *choice*
     To chese the best itt is froward;°   *difficult*
     Wheder° choyse that I chese,   *whichever*
670 To haue you fayre on nyghtes and no more,
     That wold greve° my hartt ryghte sore,°   *would grieve/heart very greatly*
     And my worshypp **shold°** I **lese.°**   *should/lose*
     And yf I desyre on days to haue you fayre,
     Then on nyghtes I shold haue a symple repayre.°   *lean **time***
675 Now fayn° wold I chose° the best,   *gladly/choose*
     I ne° wott° in this world whatt I shalle saye,   *not/know*
     Butt do as ye lyst° nowe, my lady gaye,   *please*
     The choyse I putt in your fyst.°   *hand*
     Euyn° as ye wolle° I putt itt in your hand,   *just/want*
680 Lose° me when ye lyst, for I am bond;°   *relieve/bound*
     I putt the choyse in you;
     Bothe body and goodes, hartt, and euery dele,°   *part*
     Ys alle your oun,° for to by° and selle—   *own/buy*
     That make I God avowe!"°   *swear to God*
685 "Garamercy,° corteys° knyghte," sayd the lady,   *thank you/courteous*
     "Of alle erthly knyghtes blyssyd mott° thou be,   *blessed may*
     For now am I worshyppyd;
     Thou shalle haue me fayre bothe day and nyghte,
     And euere° whyle I lyve as fayre and bryghte;   *ever*
690 Therfore be nott greuyd.°   *grieved*
     For I was shapen° by nygramancy,°   *transformed/magic*
     Withe° my stepdame,° God haue on her mercy,   *by/stepmother*
     And by enchauntement,°   *enchantment*
     And shold haue bene oderwyse vnderstond,°   *been (as) different (from my true self) taken*

695 Euyn° tylle the best of Englond   *even*
     Had wedyd° me verament.°   *wedded/truly*
     And also he shold geve° me the souereynte°   *give/sovereignty*
     Of alle his body and goodes, sycurly,°   *certainly*
     Thus was I disformyd;°   *misshapen*
700 And thou, Sir knyghte, curteys° Gawen,   *courteous*
     Has gevyn° me the souereynte serteyn,°   *given/indeed*
     That wolle° nott wrothe the° erly ne° late.   *will/anger you/nor*
     Kysse me, Sir knyghte, euyn now here,

I pray the, be glad, and make good chere,°   *be happy*
705 For welle is° me° begon.”°   *has (it)|for me|turned out*
Ther they made joye oute of mynde,°   *exceedingly*
So was itt reason and cours° of kynde,°   *way|nature*
They two theym-self° alone.   *themselves*
She thankyd God and Mary mylde,
710 She was recouered of° that that° she was defoylyd,°   *from|by which|defiled*
So dyd Sir Gawen;
He made myrthe alle in her boure,°   *chamber*
And thankyd of° alle oure Sauyoure,°   *for|Savior*
I telle you, in certeyn.°   *indeed*
715 Withe joye and myrthe they wakyd tylle daye,
And than wold° ryse that fayre maye.°   *would|maid*
“Ye shalle nott,” Sir Gawen sayd,
“We wolle lye° and slepe° tylle pryme,   *lie|sleep*
And then lett the kyng calle vs to dyne.”
720 “I am greed,”° then sayd the mayd.   *agreed*
Thus itt passyd forth tylle mid-daye.
“Syrs,” quod° the kyng, “lett vs go and asaye,°   *said|find out*
Yf Sir Gawen be on lyve;°   *alive*
I am fulle ferd of° Sir Gawen,   *very afraid for*
725 Nowe lest the fende° haue hym slayn,   *fiend*
Nowe wold I fayn° preve.°   *gladly|find out*
Go we nowe,” sayd Arthoure the kyng.
“We wolle go se° theyr vprysyng,   *see*
Howe welle that he hathe sped.”°   *succeeded*
730 They cam° to the chambre, alle in certeyn.   *came*
“Aryse,” sayd the kyng to Sir Gawen,
“Why slepyst thou so long in bed?”
“Mary,”° quod Gawen, “Sir kyng, sicurly,°   *marry|surely*
I wold be glad and° ye wold lett me be,°   *if|alone*
735 For I am fulle welle° att eas;°   *much|ease*
Abyde,° ye shalle se the dore vndone,°   *wait|unlocked*
I trowe° that ye wolle say I am welle goon,°   *believe|settled*
I am fulle lothe° to ryse.”   *reluctant*
Syr Gawen rose, and in his hand he toke°   *took*
740 His fayr lady, and to the dore he shoke,°   *hurried*
And opynyd° the dore fulle fayre;   *opened*
She stod° in her smok alle° by that fyre,   *stood|smock right*
Her her° was to her knees as red as gold wyre,   *hair*
“Lo! this is my repayre,°   *pleasure*

---

718. Prime is normally the time between 6 and 9 A.M., but here
the implication is that the couple “slept in,” perhaps until noon.

⁷⁴⁵ Lo!" sayd Gawen Arthoure vntille,°   *to*
"Syr, this is my wyfe, Dame Ragnelle,
That sauyd onys° your lyfe."   *saved once*
He told the kyng and the queen hem beforn,°   *them before*
Howe sodenly° from her shap° she dyd torne,°   *suddenly/shape/turn*
⁷⁵⁰ "My lord, nowe be° your leve."°   *by/leave*
And whate was the cause she forshapen° was,   *transformed*
Syr Gawen told the kyng both more and lesse.
"I thank God," sayd the queen,
"I wenyd,° Sir Gawen, she wold the° haue myscaryed;°   *thought/you/harmed*
⁷⁵⁵ Therfore in my hartt° I was sore agrevyd;°   *heart/much grieved*
Butt the contrary is here seen."
Ther was game, revelle,° and playe,   *revelry*
And euery man to other gan° saye: *did*
"She is a fayre wyghte."°   *person*
⁷⁶⁰ Than° the kyng them alle gan telle,   *then*
How did held° hym att nede° Dame Ragnelle,   *preserve/need*
"Or my dethe° had bene dyghte."°   *death/been prepared*
Ther the kyng told the queen, by the rood,°   *cross*
Howe he was bestad° in Ingleswod,°   *beset/Inglewood*
⁷⁶⁵ Withe° Sir Gromer Somer Joure;   *by*
And whate othe° the knyghte made hym swere,°   *oath/swear*
"Or elles° he had slayn me ryghte there,   *else*
Withoute mercy or mesure.°   *measure*
This same lady, Dame Ragnelle,
⁷⁷⁰ From my dethe she dyd help° me rygyte° welle,   *save/very*
Alle for the love of Gawen."
Then Gawen told the kyng alle togeder,°   *together*
Howe forshapen she was withe her stepmoder,°   *stepmother*
Tylle a knyghte had holpen° her agayn;   *helped*
⁷⁷⁵ Ther she told the kyng fayre and welle,
Howe Gawen gave her the souereynte° euery delle,°   *sovereignty/bit*
And whate choyse° she gave to hym;   *choice*
"God thank hym of° his curtesye,°   *for/courtesy*
He savid° me from chaunce° and vilony,°   *saved/fate/villainy*
⁷⁸⁰ That was fulle° foulle and grym.   *very*
Therfore, curteys° knyghte and hend° Gawen,   *courteous/gracious*
Shalle I neuere wrathe° the serteyn,°   *never anger/certainly*
That promyse nowe here I make—
Whilles that° I lyve I shal be obaysaunt,°   *while/obedient*
⁷⁸⁵ To God aboue I shalle itt warraunt,°   *guarantee*
And neuere withe you to debate."°   *quarrel*

---

752. *both . . . lesse:* i.e., "all of it."

"Garamercy,° lady," then sayd Gawen,   *thank you*
"With you I hold me° fulle welle content,   *feel*
And that I trust to fynde."
790 He sayd, "My loue shalle she haue,
Therafter° nede° she neuere more craue,   *for it/need*
For she hathe bene to me so kynde."
The queen sayd, and the ladyes alle,
"She is the fayrest nowe in this halle,
795 I swere by Seynt° John!   *Saint*
My loue, lady, ye shalle haue euere,°   *ever*
For that° ye savid my lord Arthoure,   *because*
As I am a gentilwoman."
Syr Gawen gatt° on her Gyngolyn,   *begot*
800 That was a good knyghte of strengthe and kynn,°   *quality*
And of the Table Round.
Att euery greatt fest° that lady shold° be,   *festival (where)/should*
Of° fayrnesse she bare° away the bewtye,°   *in/bore/(prize for) beauty*
Wher she yed° on the ground.   *walked*
805 Gawen louyd° that lady Dame Ragnelle,   *loved*
In alle his lyfe he louyd none so welle,
I telle you withoute lesyng;°   *lie*
As a coward he lay by her bothe day and nyghte,
Neuere wold° he haunt° justyng° aryghte,   *would/engage in/jousting*
810 Ther-att mervayled° Arthoure the kyng.   *wondered*
She prayd the kyng for his gentilnes,°   *kindness*
"To be good lord to Sir Gromer, i-wysse,°   *indeed*
Of that to you° he hathe offendyd";   *that (matter) in which you*
"Yes, lady, that shalle I nowe for your sake,
815 For I wott° welle he may nott amendes make,   *know*
He dyd° to me fulle vnhend."°   *acted/ungraciously*
Now for to make you a short conclusyon,
I cast me° for to make an end fulle sone,°   *intend/soon*
Of this gentylle° lady.   *noble*
820 She lyvyd° with Sir Gawen butt yerys° v,   *lived/only years*
That grevyd° Gawen alle his lyfe,   *grieved*
I telle you, securly,°   *surely*

---

799. Gyngolyn (Guinglein, Gingelein), Gawain's son, is the hero of the romance *Libeaus Desconus* (*The Fair Unknown*). He is not to be confused with Gringolet, Gawain's horse.

808. A similar occurrence of "cowardliness" or apathy caused by love's bliss is seen in Chrétien de Troyes's romance *Erec et Enide*. After his marriage Erec forgets all knightly activities until the whispers and taunts of his court rouse him to action.

820ff. The pathetic ending of the poem is starker, in contrast to the humorous content, than the conclusion of Malory's *Morte Darthur*, where, too, the author asks the reader to pray for the "knight prisoner." One may wonder whether the account of Gawain's short, five-year happiness with this best-loved wife may not contain an autobiographical hint on the part of the poet, especially since the last lines are intensely personal and poignant.

In her lyfe she grevyd hym neuere,°   *never*
Therfor was neuere woman to hym lever,°   *dearer*
825 Thus leves° my talkyng;°   *ends/story*
She was the ffayrest lady of alle Englond,
When she was on lyve,° I vnderstand,   *alive*
So sayd Arthoure the kyng.
Thus endythe the aduenture of kyng Arthoure,
830 That oft in his days was grevyd sore,°   *troubled greatly*
And of the weddyng of Gawen.
Gawen was weddyd oft in his days,
Butt so welle he neuere lovyd woman always,
As I haue hard° men sayn.°   *heard/say*
835 This aduenture befelle in Ingleswod,
As good kyng Arthoure on huntyng yod,°   *went*
Thus haue I hard men telle.
Nowe God as thou were in Bethleme born,
Suffer neuere her° soules be forlorne,°   *their/(to) be lost*
840 In the brynnyng° fyre of helle!   *burning*
And, Ihesu,° as thou were borne of a virgyn,   *Jesus*
Help hym oute of sorowe that this tale dyd devyne,°   *compose*
And that nowe in alle hast,°   *haste*
For he is be-sett withe gaylours° many,   *jailers*
845 That kepen° hym fulle sewerly,°   *keep/very securely*
Withe wyles wrong and wraste.°   *hard*
Nowe God as thou art veray° kyng royalle,   *true*
Help hym oute of daunger° that made this tale,   *danger*
For therin he hathe bene° long;   *been*
850 And of greatt pety° help thy seruaunt,°   *pity/servant*
For body and soulle I yeld° into thyne hand,   *yield*
For paynes he hathe strong.

Here endythe the weddyng of
Syr Gawen and Dame Ragnelle
For helpyng of kyng Arthoure.

THE FABLIAU

Fabliaux are short, humerous, and often very bawdy narrative poems found mainly in France in the Middle Ages. Originally, perhaps, some were composed in Latin, though many of their motifs come from the Orient. Their content normally turns on the jokes of domestic comedy. The most brilliant fabliaux in English are those by Chaucer, whereas Boccaccio's *Decameron* best represents the type in prose.

The theory of Bédier that the fabliaux were middle- and lower-class entertainment has been countered strongly by Nykrog, who argues that the fabliaux, though treating of bourgeois themes and having a popular content, were created for an aristocratic audience and were written from a courtly point of view. Their inherent courtly burlesque could only be understood by a group intimate with the ideas of *l'amour courtois*, since the humor of these bawdy tales rests in the constant reversal of courtly motifs.

REFERENCES

Bédier, Joseph. *Les Fabliaux*. 4th ed. Paris, 1925.

McKnight, George H. *Middle English Humorous Tales in Verse*. Boston, 1913.

Nykrog, Per. *Les Fabliaux: Étude d'histoire littéraire et de stylistique médiévale*. Copenhagen, 1957.

Rychner, Jean. *Contributions à l'étude des fabliaux: Variantes, remaniements, dégradations*. 2 vols. Geneva, 1960.

The fabliau is treated in the General Introduction of this volume, pp. 28–29.

DAME SIRIÞ

DATE: a. 1300. ✚ MANUSCRIPT: Bodleian Library, Oxford, Digby 86. The dialect is Southern, mixed. The MS. was written at the prior of Worcester. ✚ EDITION: George H. McKnight, *Middle English Humorous Tales in Verse* (*Boston*, 1913).

Translation is simplified if the following Southern dialectal peculiarities are kept in mind, (aside from the usual interchange of *u* and *v*): (1) the Southern *i* preceding a past participle; (2) the survival of the OE *heo* in the third personal pronoun feminine, *hoe*, "she"; (3) the constant misplacement of *h* before initial vowels, a trait of London Cockney dialect today. ("Ampstead Eath!" called the conductor. "Should it not be Hampstead Heath?" inquired the passenger. "Sorry, guvnor, hi dropped the haitch at Hoxford Circus.")

The origin of the tale seems to be Oriental. The story is found in Indian folklore and was widely circulated in western Europe.

As I com° bi an waie,°	*came/way*
Hof on ich herde saie,°	*of one I heard tell*
Ful modi mon° and proud;	*very courageous man*
Wis° he wes° of lore,°	*wise/was/learning*
5 And gouþlich° vnder gore,°	*handsome/clothes*
And cloþed in fair sroud.°	*garment*
To louien° he bigon°	*love/began*
On wedded wimmon,°	*woman*
Þer-of he heuede° wrong;	*had*
10 His herte hire° wes alon,°	*heart hers/alone*
Þat reste neuede° he non,°	*not had/none*
Þe loue wes so strong.	
Wel ȝerne° he him biþoute°	*very earnestly/considered*
How he hire gete moute°	*her get might*

---

1. There is no direct address to the audience, as in the romances. The beginning is similar to the first line of several ballads, e.g., *The Twa Corbies, The Wee Man, Christopher White, King James and Brown, Archie O Cawfield.*

5. *vnder gore:* The usual meaning, as also in the Harley Lyrics, is "on earth" (cf. above, p. 311, l. 1814*n*).

15	In ani cunnes wise.°	*kind (of) way*
	Þat° befel on an day	*it*
	Þe louerd wend° away	*lord went*
	Hon° his marchaundise.°	*on/business*

	He wente him° to þen inne°	*went/the house*
20	Þer hoe wonede° inne,	*where she lived*
	Þat wes riche won;°	*dwelling*
	And com in to þen halle,	
	Þer hoe wes srud° wiþ palle,°	*dressed/elegant garment*
	And þus he bigon:	

25	"God almiʒtten° be her-inne!"°	*almighty/herein*
	"Welcome, so° ich euer bide wenne,"°	*as/await joy*
	Quod° þis wif.°	*said/wife*
	"His hit° þi wille, com and site,°	*if it is/sit*
	And wat° is þi wille let me wite,°	*what/know*
30	Mi leuelif.°	*sweetheart*

	Bi houre° louerd, heuene-king,°	*our/heaven's king*
	If I mai don° ani þing	*do*
	Þat þe° is lef,°	*to you/dear*
	Þou miʒtt finden° me ful fre.°	*might find/very liberal*
35	Fol bleþeli° willi° don for þe,°	*very happily/will I/you*
	Wiþ-houten gref."°	*without reluctance*

	"Dame, God þe forʒelde,°	*repay*
	Bote° on þat þou me nout bimelde,°	*if/(do) not betray*
	Ne° make þe wroþ,°	*nor/get angry*
40	Min hernde° willi to þe bede;°	*my errand/tell*
	Bote° wraþþen° þe for ani dede°	*but/to anger/deed*
	Were° me° loþ."°	*would be/to me/hateful*

	Nai I-wis,° wilekin,°	*indeed/Wilkin*
	For no-þing þat euer is min,°	*mine*
45	Þau° þou hit ʒirne,°	*though/it desire*
	Houncurteis ne° willi be;	*discourteous not*
	Ne con° I nout on° vilte,°	*know/of/ill manners*
	Ne nout I nelle° lerne.°	*will not/learn*

---

17. *louerd:* i.e., "husband."

25. A clerical greeting.

37. The clerk keeps a sanctimonious manner; cf. ll. 112, 146, 161.

43. *wilekin:* diminutive form of *Will* (surviving in the surname *Wilkin*) deriving from Low German.

þou mait saien° al þine wille,   *may say*
50 And I shal herknen° and sitten° stille,   *listen/sit*
        þat° þou haue told.   *to what*
  And if þat þou me tellest skil,°   *right*
  I shal don after þi wil,
        þat be þou bold.°   *you may be sure of*

55 And þau þou saie me ani same,°   *shame*
  Ne shal I þe noui&yogh;t° blame   *not*
        For þi sawe."°   *words*
  "Nou ich° haue wonne leue,°   *I/gained permission*
  &yogh;if þat° I me shulde greue,°   *if/myself should grieve*
60   Hit were hounlawe.°   *wrong*

  Certes,° dame, þou seist° as hende,°   *certainly/say/pleasantly*
  And I shal setten spel on ende,°   *start at the beginning*
        And tellen° þe al,   *tell*
  Wat ich wolde,° and wi° ich com;°   *want/why/came*
65 Ne con° ich saien non falsdom,°   *can/no falsehood*
        Ne non° I ne shal.   *none*

  Ich habbe I-loued° þe moni &yogh;er,°   *have loved/many (a) year*
  þau ich nabbe° nout ben her°   *have not/been here*
        Mi loue to schowe.
70 Wile° þi louerd° is in toune,   *while/lord*
  Ne mai no mon° wiþ þe holden roune°   *man/hold speech*
        Wiþ no þewe.°   *propriety*

  &yogh;urstendai° ich herde saie,°   *yesterday/heard tell*
  As ich wende° bi þe waie,°   *went/way*
75   Of oure sire;
  Me° tolde me þat he was gon   *they*
  To þe feire° of botolfston°   *fair/Boston*
        In lincolne-schire.

  And for° ich weste° þat he ves houte,°   *because/knew/was out*
80 þarfore° ich am I-gon° aboute   *therefore/come*
        To speken° wiþ þe.°   *speak/you*
  Him burþ° to liken° wel his lif,°   *he has good reason/enjoy/life*
  þat mi&yogh;tte welde secc° a vif°   *might govern such/wife*
        In priuite.°   *privately*

---

77. *feire of botolfson:* Boston, a seaport important after the Conquest, was named after Saint Botolph, patron saint of sailors. After 1204 an annual fair was held there.

82–83. Cf. *Interludium,* this volume, p. 475, ll. 6–7.

⁸⁵ Dame, if hit° is þi wille,   *it*
    Boþ dernelike° and stille,°   *secretly/quietly*
        Ich wille þe loue."
    "Þat woldi° don° for non þing,   *I would/do*
    Bi houre° louerd, heuene-king,°   *our/heaven's king*
⁹⁰   Þat ous° is boue!°   *us/above*

    Ich habe° mi louerd þat is mi spouse,   *have*
    Þat maiden broute° me to house   *virginal brought*
        Mid menske I-nou;°   *with honor enough*
    He loueþ me and ich him wel,
⁹⁵ Oure loue is also trewe° as stel,°   *true/steel*
        Wiþ-houten wou.°   *without woe*

    Þau° he be from hom° on his hernde,°   *though/home/errand*
    Ich° were° ounseli,° if ich lernede°   *I/would be/unhappy/learned*
        To ben on hore.°   *be a whore*
¹⁰⁰ Þat ne° shal neuere° be,   *not/never*
    Þat I shal don selk falsete,°   *such deceit*
        On bedde ne° on flore.   *nor*

    Neuer more his lif-wile,°   *all his life*
    Thau he were on hondred° mile   *hundred*
¹⁰⁵   Bi-ȝende° rome,   *beyond*
    For no þing ne shuldi° take   *should I*
    Mon on erþe to ben mi make,°   *mate*
        Ar° his hom come."°   *before/homecoming*

    "Dame, dame, torn° þi mod;°   *change/mind*
¹¹⁰ Þi curteisi° was euer god,°   *courtesy/good*
        And ȝet shal be;
    For þe louerd° þat ous haueþ wrout,°   *Lord/has created*
    Amend þi mod, and torn þi þout,°   *mind*
        And rew° on me."   *pity*

¹¹⁵ "We,° we! oldest° þou me a fol?°   *alas/hold/fool*
    So° ich euer mote biden ȝol,°   *as/may expect Yule*
        Þou art ounwis.°   *unwise*
    Mi þout ne shalt þou newer wende;°   *never change*
    Mi louerd is curteis mon° and hende,°   *man/gracious*
¹²⁰   And mon of pris;°   *worth*

---

102. Cf. *Interludium*, this volume, p. 476, l. 10.   **116.** I.e., "as sure as Christmas."

And ich am wif° boþe god and trewe;	*wife*
Trewer womon° ne mai no mon cnowe°	*woman/know*
Þen° ich am.	*than*
Þilke° time ne shal neuer bitide°	*that/happen*
125 Þat mon for wouing° ne þoru prude°	*wooing/through pride*
Shal do me scham.''°	*shame*
	but secret
''Swete leumon,° merci!°	*sweet lover/mercy*
Same° ne vilani°	*shame/baseness*
Ne bede° I þe non;°	*ask/you none*
130 Bote derne° loue I þe bede,	*but secret*
As mon þat wolde° of loue spede,°	*would/succeed*
And finde won.''°	*happiness*
''So bide Ich euere mete oþer° drinke,	*ever food or*
Her° þou lesest° al þi swinke;°	*here/lose/effort*
135 Þou miȝt gon° hom, leue° broþer,	*might go/dear*
For ne wille ich þe loue, ne non oþer,	
Bote mi wedde houssebonde;°	*wedded husband*
To tellen hit° þe ne wille ich wonde.''°	*tell it/hesitate*
''Certes,° dame, þat me° forþinkeþ;°	*certainly/I/repent of*
140 And wo° is þe mon þat muchel swinkeþ,°	*woe/much works*
And at þe laste leseþ his sped!°	*reward*
To maken menis his him ned.°	*make lament is his need*
Bi me° I saie ful I-wis,°	*(i.e., my example)/say very certainly*
Þat loue þe loue þat I shal mis.	
145 And, dame, haue nou godnedai!°	*good-day*
And þilke louerd, þat al welde mai,°	*govern does*
Leue° þat þi þout so tourne,°	*grant/change*
Þat ihc° for þe no leng ne° mourne.''	*I/longer not*
Dreri-mod° he wente awai,	*sadly*
150 And þoute° boþe niȝt° and dai	*thought/night*
Hire al° for to wende.	*her completely*
A frend him radde° for to fare,°	*advised/go*
And leuen° al his muchele kare,°	*leave/great care*
To dame siriz þe hende.	
155 Þider° he wente him° anon,°	*there/went/quickly*

133. I.e., ''as sure as I eat and drink.''

149–60. The quick transition from the first dialogue to the second hints at an originally dramatic form. Wilekin is not the typical languishing romance hero, like Chaucer's Troilus, but more like Pamphilus, the hero of the Latin fabliau *Pamphilus de Amore*, who acts forthrightly in his own interests. The similarities between *Dame Siriþ* and that work are many.

154. *siriz:* This is the common spelling, but the rhyme shows the *z* to have been originally a thorn. The name occurs only in this piece.

So suiþe° so he miȝtte gon,	*as quickly*
No mon he ni° mette.	*not*
Ful he wes° of tene° and treie;°	*was/grief/woe*
Mid° wordes milde and eke sleie°	*with/also sly*
160 Faire he hire grette.°	*greeted*
"God þe I-blessi,° dame siriz!	*bless*
Ich am I-com° to speken° þe wiz,°	*come/speak/with*
For° ful muchele nede.°	*because of/need*
And° ich mai haue help of þe	*if*
165 Þou shalt haue, þat þou shalt se,°	*see*
Ful riche mede."°	*reward*
"Welcomen° art þou, leue sone;°	*welcome/son*
And if ich mai oþer cone°	*can*
In eni wise° for þe° do,	*any way/you*
170 I shal strengþen me° þer-to.	*myself*
For-þi,° leue sone, tel þou me	*therefore*
Wat° þou woldest° I dude° for þe."	*what/would/did*
"Bote,° leue nelde,° ful euele° I fare;	*but/old one/evil*
I lede° mi lif° wiþ tene and kare;	*lead/life*
175 Wiþ muchel hounsele ich° lede mi lif,	*misery I*
And þat is for on suete wif°	*a sweet woman*
Þat hciȝtte° margeri.	*is called*
Ich haue I-loued° hire moni° dai,	*loved/many (a)*
And of hire loue hoe seiz° me nai;	*she says*
180 Hider° ich com for-þi.	*here*
Bote if° hoe wende° hire mod,°	*unless/changes/mind*
For serewe mon° ich wakese wod,°	*sorrow must/go mad*
Oþer° mi selue quelle.°	*or/self kill*
Ich heuede I-þout° miself to slo;°	*had thought/slay*
185 For-þen° radde a frend me go	*therefore*
To þe mi sereue° telle.	*sorrow*
He saide° me, wiþ-houten° faille,	*told/without*
Þat þou me couþest° helpe and uaile,°	*could/avail*
And bringen° me of wo°	*bring/from woe*
190 Þoru° þine crafftes° and þine dedes;°	*through/skill/deeds*

173–84. The love complaints are stock phrases in Middle English lyrics. *nelde* (l. 173): an example of the wrong split between the indefinite article *an* and a noun with initial vowel; cf. *apron-napkin, umpire-non peer* (OF *nompaire*), etc.

179. *seiȝ me nai:* i.e., "denies me."

And ich wile ʒeue° þe riche mede,   *will give*
Wiþ þat° hit° be so."   *if/it*

"Benedicite be herinne!°   *herein*
Her° hauest þou, sone, mikel senne.°   *here/much sin*
195 Louerd,° for his suete nome,°   *Lord/name*
Lete° þe þerfore hauen° no shome!°   *let/have/shame*
Þou seruest affter° Godes grome,°   *deserve/anger*
Wen° þou seist on° me silk° blame.   *when/say to/such*
For ich am old, and sek° and lame;   *sick*
200 Seknesse haueþ maked° me ful° tame.   *has made/very*
Blesse þe, blesse þe, leue° knaue!°   *dear/young man*
Leste þou mes-auenter° haue,   *misfortune*
For þis lesing° þat is founden°   *falsehood/found*
Opp-on° me, þat am harde I-bonden.°   *about/bound*
205 Ich am on holi wimon,°   *woman*
On wicchecrafft nout° I ne con,°   *of witchcraft nothing/not know*
Bote wiþ gode men almesdede°   *good men's almsgiving*
Ilke° dai mi lif I fede,°   *each/sustain*
And bidde° mi pater noster and mi crede,°   *pray/Creed*
210 Þat Goed hem° helpe at hore nede,°   *God them/their need*
Þat helpen° me mi lif to lede,   *help*
And leue° þat hem mote° wel spede.°   *grant/may/prosper*
His lif and his soule worþe I-shend,°   *be destroyed*
Þat þe° to me þis hernde° haueþ send;°   *you/(on) this errand/sent*
215 And leue me to ben I-wreken°   *be avenged*
On him þis° shome me° haueþ speken."°   *(who) this/of me/spoken*

"Leue nelde,° bilef° al þis;   *old one/leave*
Me° þinkeþ þat þou art onwis.°   *I/unwise*
Þe mon° þat me to þe taute,°   *man/directed*
220 He weste° þat þou hous° couþest saute.°   *knew/us/reconcile*
Help, dame siriþ, if þou maut,°   *may*
To make me wiþ þe sueting° saut,   *sweetheart*
And ich wille geue° þe gift ful stark,°   *give/large*
Moni° a pound and moni a marke,   *many*
225 Warme pilche° and warme shon,°   *fur/shoes*
Wiþ° þat min° hernde be wel don.   *provided/my*

---

193. *Benedicite be herinne!* : "Bless us here?"
204. *harde I-bonden:* i.e., "in difficulty."
205. Typical hypocritical protestation of the old bawds in literature.
207. *wiþ ... almesdede:* i.e., "by giving alms to good men."
209. *pater noster:* Latin, "our father," i.e., the Lord's Prayer.

225. The gifts to the go-between are also typical: furs, garments, and shoes are very common (cf. *Pamphilus de Amore,* l. 303; see also T. J. Garbáty, "Chaucer's Weaving Wife," *Journal of American Folklore,* 81 (1968) 322, where the links to Chaucer's Wife of Bath are traced).

Of muchel godlec miȝt° þou ȝelpe,° *great benefit might/boast*
If hit° be so þat þou me helpe." *it*
"Liȝ° me° nout, wilekin,° bi þi leute° *lie/to me/not, Wilkin/faith*
230 Is hit þin° hernest þou tekest° me? *your/tell*
Louest þou wel dame margeri?"
"Ȝe,° nelde, witerli;° *yea/surely*
Ich hire° loue, hit mot° me spille,° *I her/may/kill*
Bote° ich gete° hire to mi wille." *unless/get*
235 "Wat, god° wilekin, me reweþ° þi scaþe,° *lo, good/pity/trouble*
Houre louerd° sende þe help raþe!° *our Lord/quickly*

Weste hic° hit miȝtte ben forholen,° *if I knew/concealed*
Me wolde þunche wel solen° *would think quite alone*
  þi wille for to fullen.° *fulfill*
240 Make me siker° wiþ word on honde,° *sure/in hand*
þat þou wolt helen,° and I wile fonde° *will hide/will try*
  If ich mai hire tellen.° *tell*

For al þe world ne woldi° nout *would I*
þat ich were to chapitre I-brout° *account brought*
245   For none selke werkes.° *no such actions*
Mi iugement° were° sone I-giuen° *judgment/would be/quickly given*
To ben wiþ shome° somer° driuen *shame/(on a) mule*
  Wiþ prestes° and with clarkes."° *by priests/clerks*

"I-wis,° nelde, ne° woldi *indeed/not*
250 þat þou heuedest uilani° *had humiliation*
  Ne° shame for mi goed.° *nor/benefit*
Her° I þe mi trouþe pliȝtte,° *here/troth plight*
Ich shal helen bi mi miȝtte,
  Bi þe holi roed!"° *cross*

255 "Welcome, wilekin, hiderward;° *here*
Her hauest I-maked° a foreward° *(you) have made/promise*
  þat þe° mai ful° wel like. *you/very*
þou maiȝt° blesse þilke siþ,° *may/this time*
For þou maiȝt make þe° ful bliþ;° *yourself/happy*
260   Dar° þou namore° sike.° *need/no more/sigh*

To goder-hele° euer come þou hider,° *good fortune/here*

---

233. Cf. *Interludium*, this volume, p. 476, l. 23.
235. *Wat:* Cf. the first word of *Beowulf*, the interjection *hwæt*.
240. *word on honde:* i.e., "certain promise."

244. *to chapitre:* i.e., "before a court."
247. A bawdy woman was customarily driven on a sumpter (a mule or an ass), facing its rump.

For sone willi° gange þider,°   *will I/go there*
   And maken° hire hounderstonde.°   *make/understand*
I shal kenne° hire sulke a lore,°   *teach/in such manner*
265 Þat hoe° shal louien° þe mikel° more   *she/love/much*
   Þen° ani mon° in londe."°   *than/man/land*

"Al so° haui° Godes griþ,°   *as/may I have/peace*
Wel hauest þou said, dame siriþ,
   And goder-hele shal ben þin.°   *be yours*
270 Haue her twenti shiling,°   *shillings*
   Þis ich ʒeue° þe to meding,°   *give/as payment*
   To buggen° þe sep° and swin."°   *buy/sheep/swine*

"So ich euere brouke° hous oþer flet,°   *as (sure as) I ever use/or floor*
Neren° neuer penes beter biset°   *were not/pennies better invested*
275 Þen þes shulen° ben.   *these shall*
For I shal don° a iuperti,°   *perform/venture*
And a ferli maistri,°   *wonderful trick*
   Þat þou shalt ful wel sen.°   *see*

Pepir° nou shalt þou eten,°   *pepper/eat*
280 Þis mustart° shal ben þi mete,°   *mustard/food*
   And gar þin eien° to rene;°   *make your eyes/run*
I shal make° a lesing°   *tell/lie*
Of þin heie-renning,°   *weeping*
   Ich wot° wel wer° and wenne."°   *know/where/when*

285 "Wat!° nou const° þou no god?°   *what/know/good*
Me° þinkeþ þat þou art wod:°   *I/mad*
ʒeuest þo° þe welpe° mustard?"   *you/whelp*
"Be stille, boinard!°   *fool*
I shal mit° þis ilke gin°   *with/same trap*
290 Gar hire loue to ben al þin.
Ne° shal ich neuer haue reste ne ro°   *not/peace*
Til ich haue told hou þou shalt do.
Abide° me her° til min hom-come."°   *wait for/here/my homecoming*
"ʒus,° bi þe somer blome,°   *yes/summer bloom*
295 Heþen° nulli° ben binomen,°   *hence/will I not/taken away*
Til þou be aʒein comen."°   *again come*
Dame siriþ bigone° to go,   *began*
As a wrecche° þat is wo,°   *wretch/woeful*

---

276. *iuperti:* "jeopardy" (OF *jeu parti,* "equal game").
279. At this point Dame Siriþ addresses her dog.

285. *const . . . god:* i.e., "aren't you in your right mind?"

Þat° hoe come hire° to þen inne°   *until/came/the house*
300 Þer° þis gode wif wes° inne.   *where/good wife was*
Þo° hoe to þe dore com,°   *when/came*
Swiþe reuliche° hoe bigon: *very pitiful*
"Louerd,"° hoe seiþ,° wo° is holde° wiues, *Lord/says/woe/old*
Þat in pouerte ledeþ ay liues;°   *poverty lead ever (their) lives*
305 Not° no mon° so muchel° of pine°   *knows not/man/much/pain*
As poure° wif þat falleþ in ansine.°   *poor/want*
Þat mai ilke° mon bi me wite°   *every/know*
For mai I nouþer gange ne site.°   *neither walk nor sit*
Ded° woldi° ben ful fain.°   *dead/would I/be very gladly*
310 Hounger° and þurst° me haueþ nei° slain; *hunger/thirst/almost*
Ich ne mai mine limes on-wold,°   *limbs control*
For mikel° hounger and þurst and cold.   *much*
War-to° liueth selke° a wrecche?   *why/such*
Wi° nul° Goed° mi soule fecche?"°   *why/will not/God/fetch*

315 "Seli° wif, God þe hounbinde!°   *good/help*
To dai wille I þe mete° finde   *you food*
    For loue of Goed.
Ich° haue reuþe° of þi wo,   *I/pity*
For euele I-cloþed° I se° þe go,   *ill clothed/see*
320   And euele I-shoed.°   *shod*

Com her-in, ich wile° þe fede,°   *will/feed*
Goed almiȝtten do° þe mede,°   *almighty give/reward*
And þe louerd þat wes on rode I-don,°   *cross put*
And faste° fourti daus° to non,°   *fasted/days/noon*
325 And heuene° and erþe haueþ to welde.°   *heaven/has/govern*
As þilke° louerd þe forȝelde.°   *so (may) that same/repay*
Haue her fles° and eke bred,°   *flesh/also bread*
And make þe° glad, hit° is mi red;°   *yourself/it/advice*
And haue her þe coppe° wiþ þe drinke;   *cup*
330 Goed do þe mede for þi swinke."°   *trouble*
Þenne spac° þat holde wif,   *spoke*
Crist awarie hire lif!°   *curse her life*
"Alas! Alas! þat euer I liue!
Al þe sunne° ich wolde° forgiue   *sin/would*
335 Þe mon þat smite of min heued!°   *smote off my head*
Ich wolde mi lif me° were bireued!"°   *from me/taken away*
"Seli wif, what eilleþ° þe?"   *ails*
"Bote eþe° mai I sori be: *but easily/sorrowful*
Ich heuede° a douter feir° and fre,°   *had/daughter fair/noble*
340 Feiror ne miȝtte° no mon se.   *fairer not might*
Hoe° heuede a curteis hossebonde;°   *she/courteous husband*

    Freour° mon miȝtte no mon fonde.° — *nobler/find*
    Mi douter louede° him al to° wel; — *loved/too*
    For þi° maki° sori del.° — *therefore/I make/lament*
345 Oppon° a dai he was out wend,° — *upon/gone*
    And þar-þoru wes° mi douter shend.° — *thereby was/hurt*
    He hede on ernde° out of toune; — *had an errand*
    And com° a modi clarc° wiþ croune,° — *came/lusty clerk/tonsure*
    To mi douter his loue beed,° — *offered*
350 And hoe nolde° nout folewe° his red.° — *would not/not follow/counsel*
    He ne miȝtte his wille haue,
    For no þing he miȝtte craue.
    Þenne bigon° þe clerc to wiche,° — *began/engage in witchcraft*
    And shop° mi douter til° a biche.° — *transformed/into/bitch*
355 Þis is mi douter þat ich of speke;° — *speak*
    For del of° hire min herte breke.° — *grief for/heart breaks*
    Loke° hou hire heien greten,° — *look/eyes weep*
    On hire cheken° þe teres meten.° — *cheeks/tears meet*
    For þi, dame, were° hit no wonder, — *would be*
360 Þau° min herte burste assunder. — *though*
    And wose° euer is ȝong houssewif,° — *whoso/young housewife*
    Ha° loueþ ful luitel° hire lif, — *she/very little*
    And eni° clerc of loue hire bede,° — *if any/ask*
    Bote° hoe grante and lete° him spede."° — *unless/let/succeed*
365 "A!° louerd° crist, wat° mai° þenne do! — *ah/Lord/what/may I*
    Þis enderdai° com a clarc me to, — *other day*
    And bed° me loue on° his manere,° — *bade/in/manner*
    And ich° him nolde nout I-here.° — *I/listen to*
    Ich trouue° he wolle° me forsape.° — *believe/will/transform*
370 Hou troustu,° nelde,° ich moue ascape?"° — *do you think/old one/might escape*
    "God almiȝtten° be þin° help — *almighty/your*
    Þat þou ne be nouþer° bicche ne welp!° — *neither/nor whelp*
    Leue° dame, if eni clerc — *dear*
    Bedeþ þe° þat loue-werc,° — *you/lovemaking*
375 Ich rede° þat þou grante his bone,° — *advise/wish*
    And bicom his lefmon sone.° — *lover soon*
    And if þat þou so ne dost,
    A worse red þou ounderfost."° — *receive*

    "Louerd crist, þat me is wo,° — *grieves*
380 Þat þe clarc me hede fro,° — *went from*
      Ar° he me heuede biwonne.° — *before/had won*
    Me were leuere þen° ani fe° — *I had rather than/money*

---

353. Clerks were known to be adept in both white and black magic; Roger Bacon had this reputation. Cf. also Chaucer's Canon and his Yeoman, who were alchemists.

That he heuede enes leien bi° me,   *once slept with*
 And efft-sones bigunne.°   *again begun*

385 Euer-more, nelde, ich wille be þin,°   *yours*
 Wiþ þat° þou feche° me willekin,°   *if|fetch|Wilkin*
  Þe clarc of wam° I telle,   *whom*
 Giftes willi° geue° þe   *will I|give*
 Þat° þou maizt° euer þe betere° be,   *so that|might|better*
390 Bi Godes houne° belle!"   *own*

 "Soþliche,° mi swete° dame,   *truly|sweet*
 And if I mai wiþ-houte° blame,   *without*
  Fain° ich wille ffonde;°   *gladly|try*
 And if ich mai wiþ him mete,
395 Bi eni wei oþer° bi strete,°   *path or|street*
  Nout ne° willi wonde.°   *not at all|hesitate*

 Haue goddai,° dame! forþ willi go."   *good-day*
 "Allegate° loke° þat þou do so   *in every way|look*
  As ich þe bad;°   *asked*
400 Bote þat° þou me wilekin bringe,   *unless*
 Ne° mai neuer lawe° ne singe,   *not|laugh*
  Ne be glad."

 "I wis,° dame, if I mai,   *indeed*
 Ich wille bringen° him zet to-dai,   *bring*
405 Bi mine miztte."°   *my effort*
 Hoe° wente hire° to hire inne,°   *she|went|her house*
 Her° hoe founde wilekinne,   *there*
  Bi houre driztte!°   *our Lord*

 "Swete wilekin, be þou nout dred,°   *not afraid*
410 For of° þin hernde ich° haue wel sped.°   *on|errand I|succeeded*
 Swiþe° com for þider° wiþ me,   *quickly|there*
 For hoe haueþ send° affter þe.°   *has sent|you*
 I-wis nou maizt þou ben° aboue,°   *be|on top*
 For þou hauest grantise° of hire loue."   *granting*
415 "God þe for-zelde, leue° nelde,°   *requite, dear|old one*
 Þat heuene° and erþe haueþ to welde!"°   *heaven|govern*

 Þis modi mon bigon° to gon°   *lusty man began|go*

---

390. *belle:* perhaps "belly," the line thus being an oath on a part of Christ's body, like those on his bones and blood (cf. below, p. 472, l. 596*n*). More probably *belle* refers to the chapel bell, as in bell, book, and candle, or the bell in the Mass (cf. l. 421).

Wiþ Siriz to his leuemon°   lover
   In þilke stounde.°   that hour
420 Dame Siriz bigon to telle,
And swor bi Godes ouene° belle,   own
   Hoe heuede° him founde.   had

"Dame, so haue ich wilekin sout,°   Wilkin/sought
For nou haue ich him I-brout."°   brought
425 "Welcome, wilekin, swete þing,
Þou art welcomore° þen° þe king.   more welcome/than

Wilekin þe swete,
Mi loue I þe bihete,°   promise
   To don° al þine wille.   do
430 Turnd° ich haue mi þout,°   changed/mind
For I ne wolde° nout   would
   Þat þou þe shuldest spille."°   yourself should kill

"Dame, so° ich euere bide noen,°   as (sure as)/ever expect noon
And ich am redi° and I-boen°   ready/prepared
435   To don al þat þou saie.°   say
Nelde, par ma fai!
Þou most gange° awai,   must go
   Wile° ich and hoe shulen plaie."°   while/shall play

"Goddot° so I wille: God knows
440 And loke° þat þou hire tille,   look
And strek° out hire þes.°   stretch/thighs
God ȝeue° þe muchel kare,°   give/much care
Ȝeif þat° þou hire spare,   if
   Þe wile þou mid° hire bes.°   with/are

445 And wose° is onwis,°   whoso/unwise
And for non pris°   in no manner
   Ne con geten° his leuemon,   not can get
I shal, for mi mede,°   reward
Garen° him to spede,°   cause/succeed
450   For ful° wel I con."   very

---

436. *par ma fai:* "by my faith" (French *par ma foi*).

439. *Goddot:* exclamatory contraction of *God wot.*

THE MILLER'S TALE
Geoffrey Chaucer

DATE: c. 1390. ✒ MANUSCRIPTS: There are eighty-three MSS (eighty-four if we include the Morgan Fragment of the *Pardoner's Tale*) of the *Canterbury Tales* known to be in existence. They have all been studied and classified by J. M. Manly and Edith Rickert, *The Text of the Canterbury Tales* (Chicago, 1940). Perhaps the best and most famous MS, noted for its fine illustrations, is the Ellesmere 26 c. 12, now in the Huntingdon Library, San Marino, California. The dialect is London English. ✒ EDITIONS: W. W. Skeat, *The Complete Works of Geoffrey Chaucer*, 6 vols. and Supplement (Oxford, 1894–97); F. N. Robinson, *The Works of Geoffrey Chaucer*, 2d ed. (Boston, 1957); A. C. Baugh, *Chaucer's Major Poetry* (New York, 1963); R. A. Pratt, *The Tales of Canterbury* (Atlanta, 1974); J. Fisher, *The Complete Poetry and Prose of Geoffrey Chaucer* (New York, 1977).

Chaucer's dialect is the London English out of which developed standard Modern English. His language, therefore, approaches our own, and his are among the easiest Middle English texts to translate. The third personal pronouns alone, perhaps, may cause confusion. *Him* is often used in the reflexive, i.e., as "himself" (*he sat him down*). *Hem* is used for "them" or for the reflexive "themselves."

The Miller's Tale is undoubtedly the most brilliant fabliau in the English language, written by Britain's greatest poet of the Middle Ages. It is the second tale in the *Canterbury Tales* sequence, and starts the quarrel between the Miller and the Reeve, a former carpenter, whose own story follows in revenge. The Miller is a huge, coarse, loud-mouthed fellow, and his narrative fits his personality. Two folk motifs, the Misdirected Kiss and the Fear of a Second Flood, form the core of the story, which is No. 1361 in A. Aarne's collection *Types of the Folk-Tale*, trans. Stith Thompson (Helsinki, 1928).

HERE BIGINNETH THE MILLERE HIS TALE.

Whylom° ther was dwellinge at Oxenford°	*some time ago/Oxford*
A riche gnof,° that gestes° heeld to bord,°	*lout/guests/boarded*
And of his craft he was a Carpenter.	
With him ther was dwellinge a povre scoler,°	*poor student*
⁵ Had lerned art, but al his fantasye°	*imagination*
Was turned for to lerne astrologye,°	*astronomy*

---

3. This story is the beginning of a feud between the Miller and the Reeve, who was formerly a carpenter.

And coude° a certeyn° of conclusiouns° — *knew how/certain (number)/ problems*

To demen° by interrogaciouns, — *solve*
If that men axed° him in certein houres, — *asked*
10 Whan° that men sholde° have droghte° or elles shoures,° — *when/should/drought/else showers*
Or if men axed him what sholde bifalle
Of every thing, I may nat rekene hem° alle. — *not reckon them*

This clerk was cleped hende° Nicholas; — *called gentle*
Of derne° love he coude° and of solas;° — *secret/knew/pleasure*
15 And ther-to° he was sleigh° and ful privee,° — *also/subtle/very secret*
And lyk° a mayden meke° for to see. — *like/meek*
A chambre hadde he in that hostelrye
Allone, with-outen° any companye, — *alone, without*
Ful fetisly y-dight° with herbes swote;° — *handsomely supplied/sweet*
20 And he him-self as swete° as is the rote° — *sweet/root*
Of licorys,° or any cetewale.° — *licorice/zedoary (i.e., ginger)*
His Almageste and bokes grete° and smale,° — *books large/small*
His astrelabie,° longinge for° his art, — *astrolabe/belonging to*
His augrim-stones° layen° faire a-part — *algorism stones/lay*
25 On shelves couched° at his beddes heed:° — *resting/head*
His presse y-covered° with a falding° reed.° — *clothespress covered/wool cloth/red*
And al above ther lay a gay sautrye,° — *psaltery (i.e., zither)*
On which he made a nightes° melodye — *at night*
So swetely, that al the chambre rong;° — *rang*
30 And *Angelus ad virginem* he song;° — *sang*
And after that he song the kinges note;
For often blessed was his mery throte.
And thus this swete clerk° his tyme spente — *student*
After° his freendes finding° and his rente.° — *by means of/friends' provisions/his (own) income*

35 This Carpenter had wedded newe° a wyf° — *recently/wife*
Which that he lovede more than his lyf;° — *life*
Of eightetene yeer° she was of age. — *years*

---

10. The showers foreshadow the prophecy of Noah's Flood.

13. *hende:* As E. Talbot Donaldson has pointed out (*Speaking of Chaucer* [London, 1970], p. 17), the pun on *hende* is played progressively with "gentle," "handy" or "clever," and "at hand."

22. *Almageste:* ("Greatest Composition," from Arabic *al majisti*) Ptolemy's astronomical work; later, any work connected with astrology.

23. *astrelabie:* An astrolabe was an instrument, now superseded by the sextant, for observing the position of heavenly

bodies. Chaucer wrote a treatise on the astrolabe for his son *Lyte Lowys* ("little Lewis"), undoubtedly a most precocious child.

24. *augrim-stones:* These were marked with numerals of algorism (i.e., numbers from 1 to 9 and 0, from the Arab mathematician al-Khuwarizmi) and used in calculating.

30. *Angelus ad virginem:* Latin, "The angel to the Virgin," the first words of a hymn on the Annunciation.

31. *kinges note:* This has been identified with various Scottish and Welsh songs of similar title.

Jalous° he was, and heeld hir narwe° in cage,	*jealous/held her closely*
For she was wilde and yong,° and he was old	*young*
40 And demed° him-self ben° lyk a cokewold.°	*supposed/to be/cuckold*
He knew nat Catoun,° for his wit° was rude,°	*Cato/knowledge/rough*
That bad° man sholde wedde his similitude.	*bade*
Men sholde wedden° after° hir estaat,°	*wed/according to/their condition*
For youthe and elde° is often at debaat.°	*age/strife*
45 But sith° that he was fallen in the snare,	*since*
He moste° endure, as other folk, his care.	*must*
Fair was this yonge wyf, and ther-with-al°	*also*
As any wesele° hir body gent° and smal.	*weasel/graceful*
A ceynt° she werede° barred° al of silk,	*belt/wore/with bars*
50 A barmclooth eek° as whyt° as morne° milk	*apron also/white/morning*
Up-on hir lendes,° ful of many a gore.°	*loins/piece of cloth*
Whyt was hir smok,° and brouded° al bifore	*smock/embroidered*
And eek bihinde, on hir coler° aboute,	*collar*
Of col-blak° silk, with-inne and eek with-oute.	*coal-black*
55 The tapes° of hir whyte voluper°	*ribbons/cap*
Were of the same suyte of° hir coler;	*set as*
Hir filet brood° of silk, and set ful hye:°	*headband broad/very high*
And sikerly° she hadde a likerous yë.°	*surely/amorous eye*
Ful smale y-pulled° were hir browes two,	*daintily plucked*
60 And tho° were bent, and blake° as any sloo.°	*those/black/sloe*
She was ful° more blisful on to see°	*much/look*
Than is the newe pere-jonette° tree;	*early-ripe pear*
And softer than the wolle° is of a wether.	*wool*
And by hir girdel heeng° a purs° of lether°	*belt hung/purse/leather*
65 Tasseld with silk, and perled with° latoun.°	*studded with drops of/latten*
In al this world, to seken° up and doun,	*seek*
There nis° no man so wys,° that coude thenche°	*is not/wise/could imagine*
So gay a popelote,° or swich° a wenche.	*darling/such*
Ful brighter was the shyning of hir hewe°	*complexion*
70 Than in the tour° the noble y-forged° newe.	*Tower/minted*
But of hir song, it was as loude and yerne°	*lively*
As any swalwe° sittinge on a berne.°	*swallow/barn*
Ther-to° she coude skippe and make game,	*also*
As any kide or calf folwinge° his dame.°	*following/dam*
75 Hir mouth was swete° as bragot° or the meeth,°	*sweet/bragget/mead*

---

41. Dionysius Cato supposedly wrote the *Disticha de Moribus ad Filium* (*Sayings Concerning Manners to His Son*), a collection of maxims from the 3d and 4th centuries. The work was exceedingly popular in the Middle Ages and is quoted also in *Piers Plowman*.

62. The pere-jonette, according to Skeat, ripened on Saint John's Day, and is called in French *pomme de Saint Jean*.

65. *latoun:* Latten is a mixture of copper and zinc.

70. The noble, a gold coin of 6s. 8d., was minted in the Tower of London.

75. Bragget and mead were honeyed drinks.

Or hord of apples leyd° in hey° or heeth.°   laid/hay/heath
Winsinge° she was, as is a joly° colt,   skittish/jolly
Long as a mast, and upright as a bolt.
A brooch she baar° up-on hir° lowe coler,   wore/her
80   As brood as is the bos° of a bocler.°   boss/buckler
Hir shoes were laced on hir legges hye;
She was a prymerole,° a pigges-nye°   primrose/? trillium
For any lord to leggen° in his bedde,   lay
Or yet for any good yeman° to wedde.   yeoman

85   Now sire, and eft° sire, so bifel° the cas,°   again/happened/case
That on a day this hende° Nicholas   gentle
Fil° with this yonge wyf° to rage° and pleye,°   started/young wife/flirt/play
Whyl° that hir housbond° was at Oseneye,   while/husband
As clerkes ben° ful subtile and ful queynte;°   students are/sly
90   And prively° he caughte hir by the queynte,°   intimately/pudendum
And seyde,° "Y-wis,° but if° ich have my wille,   said/surely/unless
For derne° love of thee, lemman,° I spille."°   secret/lover/die
And heeld° hir harde by the haunche-bones,°   held/thighs
And seyde, "Lemman, love me al at-ones,°   at once
95   Or I wol dyen, also° God me save!"°   will die, so/help
And she sprong° as a colt doth in the trave,   sprang
And with hir heed° she wryed° faste awey,°   head/turned/away
And seyde, "I wol nat° kisse thee, by my fey,°   not/faith
Why, lat° be," quod° she, "lat be, Nicholas,   let/said
100 Or I wol crye out harrow and allas.°   alas
Do wey° your handes for your curteisye!"°   put away/courtesy

This Nicholas gan° mercy for to crye,   began
And spak° so faire, and profred° hir so faste,°   spoke/pressed/strongly
That she hir love him graunted° atte laste,   granted
105 And swoor° hir ooth,° by seint° Thomas of Kent,   swore/oath/Saint
That she wol been° at his comandement,   be
Whan° that she may hir leyser° wel espye.°   when/opportunity/see
"Myn° housbond is so ful of jalousye,°   my/jealousy
That but° ye wayte° wel and been privee,°   unless/watch/secret
110 I woot° right wel I nam° but deed,"° quod she.   know/am not/dead
"Ye moste° been ful° derne, as in this cas."   must/very

"Nay ther-of care thee noght,"° quod Nicholas,   naught

---

82. *pigges-nye:* "pig's eye," a term of endearment.
88. At Oseney, near Oxford was an abbey of the Augustinian order.
96. *trave:* a frame to hold horses.
100. *harrow:* a cry for help.

105. *Seint Thomas of Kent:* Saint Thomas à Becket, whose shrine the pilgrims of the *Canterbury Tales* were seeking.
110. *nam but:* "am surely."
112. *ther-of . . . noght:* i.e., "don't worry."

"A clerk had° litherly biset° his whyle,°   *would have/poorly used/time*
But-if he coude° a Carpenter bigyle."°   *could/beguile*
115 And thus they been° acorded° and y-sworn°   *were/in accord/sworn*
To wayte° a tyme,° as I have told biforn.°   *watch for/(proper) time/before*
Whan Nicholas had doon° thus everydeel,°   *done/every bit*
And thakked hir° aboute the lendes weel,°   *stroked her/loins well*
He kist° hir swete,° and taketh his sautrye,°   *kissed/sweetly/psaltery*
120 And pleyeth faste, and maketh melodye.

Than fil° it thus, that to the parish-chirche,°   *then happened/parish church*
Cristes owne werkes° for to wirche,°   *works/do*
This gode° wyf wente on an haliday;°   *good/holiday*
Hir forheed shoon° as bright as any day,   *forehead shone*
125 So was it wasshen° whan she leet° hir werk.   *washed/stopped*

Now was ther of that chirche a parish-clerk,
The which that was y-cleped° Absolon.   *called*
Crul° was his heer,° and as the gold it shoon,   *curled/hair*
And strouted° as a fanne large and brode;°   *spread out/broad*
130 Ful streight° and even lay his joly shode.°   *straight/pleasant part (in his hair)*
His rode° was reed,° his eyen° greye as goos;°   *complexion/red/eyes/goose*
With Powles° window corven° on his shoos,°   *(Saint) Paul's/carved (in leather) shoes*

In hoses rede° he wente fetisly.°   *stockings red/handsomely*
Y-clad° he was ful smal° and proprely,   *dressed/daintily*
135 Al in a kirtel° of a light wachet;°   *tunic/blue*
Ful faire and thikke° been the poyntes° set.   *thick/tagged laces*
And ther-up-on he hadde a gay surplys°   *surplice*
As whyt° as is the blosme° up-on the rys.°   *white/blossom/branch*
A mery° child he was, so God me save,°   *merry/help*
140 Wel coude he laten° blood and clippe and shave,   *let*
And make a chartre of lond° or acquitaunce.°   *land/deed of release*
In twenty manere° coude he trippe and daunce°   *ways/dance*
After the scole° of Oxenforde tho,°   *school/Oxford then*
And with his legges casten° to and fro,   *kick*
145 And pleyen° songes on a small rubible;°   *play/rebec*
Ther-to° he song° som-tyme° a° loud quinible;°   *also/sang/at times/(in) a/high voice*
And as wel coude he pleye on his giterne.°   *guitar*
In al the toun nas° brewhous ne° taverne   *was not/nor*

---

132. Fancy shoes with the design of the windows of Saint Paul's cathedral cut in their leather were called "calcei fenestrati."

140. Absolon, a scholar, was skilled in such minor medical matters as letting blood, which was the regular duty of barbers. He had the universal attributes of the courtly lover.

143. Oxford, with its large numbers of students, may have been noted as a center for dancing and other kinds of social pleasures.

145. *rubible:* The rebeck was an instrument similar to the lute.

146. *quinible:* an octave above the treble.

That he ne° visited with his solas,°   *not/entertainment*
150 Ther° any gaylard tappestere° was.   *where/gay barmaid*
But sooth° to seyn,° he was somdel squaymous°   *truth/say/somewhat squeamish*
Of farting, and of speche daungerous.°   *speech fastidious*

This Absolon, that jolif° was and gay,   *jolly*
Gooth° with a sencer° on the haliday,   *goes/censer*
155 Sensinge° the wyves of the parish faste;°   *censing/eagerly*
And many a lovely° look on hem° he caste,   *loving/them*
And namely on this carpenteres wyf.°   *wife*
To loke° on hir° him° thoughte° a mery lyf,°   *look/her/to him/seemed/life*
She was so propre° and swete° and likerous.°   *comely/sweet/amorous*
160 I dar° wel seyn, if she had been a mous,   *dare*
And he a cat, he wolde° hir hente anon.°   *would have/caught quickly*

This parish-clerk, this joly° Absolon,   *jolly*
Hath in his herte swich° a love-longinge,   *heart such*
That of° no wyf ne took he noon offringe;°   *from/no offering*
165 For curteisye,° he seyde,° he wolde noon.°   *courtesy/said/wanted none*
The mone, whan° it was night, ful° brighte shoon,°   *moon, when/very/shone*
And Absolon his giterne hath y-take,°   *taken*
For paramours,° he thoghte° for to wake.   *lovemaking/meant*
And forth he gooth, jolif and amorous,
170 Til he cam° to the carpenteres hous   *came*
A litel° after cokkes° hadde y-crowe;°   *little/cocks/crowed*
And dressed him° up by a shot-windowe°   *stationed himself/hinged window*
That was up-on the carpenteres wal.
He singeth in his vois gentil° and smal,°   *gentle/high*
175 "Now, dere° lady, if thy wille be,   *dear*
I preye yow° that ye wol° rewe° on me,"   *pray you/will/have mercy*
Ful wel acordaunt° to° his giterninge.°   *in harmony/with/guitar playing*
This carpenter awook,° and herde° him singe,   *awoke/heard*
And spak° un-to his wyf, and seyde anon,   *spoke*
180 "What!° Alison! herestow° nat° Absolon   *lo/hear you/not*
That chaunteth° thus under our boures° wal?"   *sings/chamber's*
And she answerde hir housbond ther-with-al,°   *husband thereupon*
"Yis,° God wot,° Iohn,° I here° it every-del.°   *yes/knows, John/hear/every bit*

This passeth forth;° what wol ye bet° than wel?°   *goes on/more/this*
185 Fro° day to day this joly Absolon,   *from*
So woweth° hir, that him° is wo bigon.°   *woos/he/woebegone*
He waketh al the night and al the day;
He kempte hise lokkes brode,° and made him gay;   *combed his locks broad*
He woweth hir by menes° and brocage,°   *go-betweens/mediation*
190 And swoor° he wolde been° hir owne page;   *swore/would be*

He singeth, brokkinge° as a nightingale;   *quavering*
He sente hir piment,° meeth,° and spyced ale,   *spiced wine/mead*
And wafres,° pyping hote° out of the glede;°   *wafer cakes/hot/fire*
And for° she was of° toune, he profred mede.°   *because/from/offered bribe*
195 For som folk wol ben wonnen° for richesse,°   *be won/riches*
And som for strokes, and som for gentillesse.°   *courtesy*

Somtyme,° to shewe° his lightnesse° and maistrye,° *once/show/agility/skill*
He pleyeth° Herodes on a scaffold hye.°   *plays/high*
But what availleth him as in this cas?°   *matter*
200 She loveth so this hende° Nicholas,   *gentle*
That Absolon may blowe the bukkes° horn;   *buck's*
He ne° hadde for his labour but a scorn;   *not*
And thus she maketh Absolon hir° ape,   *her*
And al his ernest turneth til° a jape.°   *into/joke*
205 Ful sooth° is this proverbe, it is no lye,°   *true/lie*
Men seyn° right thus, "Alwey° the nye slye°   *say/always/near/sly (one)*
Maketh the ferre° leve° to be looth."°   *distant/loved one/disliked*
For though that Absolon be wood° or wrooth,°   *mad/angry*
By-cause° that he fer° was from hir sighte,   *because/far*
210 This nye Nicholas stood in his lighte.

Now bere thee° wel, thou hende Nicholas!   *bear yourself*
For Absolon may waille° and singe "allas."°   *wail/alas*
And so bifel° it on a Saterday,°   *happened/Saturday*
This carpenter was goon til° Osenay;   *gone to*
215 And hende Nicholas and Alisoun
Acorded been° to this conclusioun,   *agreed were*
That Nicholas shal shapen him a wyle°   *arrange a trick*
This sely jalous° housbond to bigyle;°   *hapless jealous/beguile*
And if so be the game wente aright,
220 She sholde slepen° in his arm al night,   *should sleep*
For this was his desyr and hir° also.   *hers*
And right anon, with-outen° wordes mo,°   *then, without/more*
This Nicholas no lenger° wolde tarie,°   *longer/delay*
But doth ful° softe un-to his chambre carie°   *very/carry*
225 Bothe mete° and drinke for a day or tweye,°   *food/two*
And to hir housbonde bad° hir for to seye,°   *husband bade/say*
If that he axed° after Nicholas,   *asked*
She sholde seye she niste° where he was,   *knew not*

---

194. A reflection on the mercenary characteristics of town girls.
198. Absolon acted the part of Herod in a miracle play, put on by the guilds. Herod usually blustered and ranted loudly (an actor in a violent rage might be said to "out-Herod Herod" [*Hamlet*, III,ii]), and such a part would show much variety of voice for a man who could sing in "quinible."
206–7. We would say, "Out of sight, out of mind."

Of al that day she saugh° him nat with yë;°   *saw/eye*
230 She trowed° that he was in maladye,°   *believed/illness*
For, for no cry, hir mayde coude° him calle;   *could*
He nolde° answere, for no-thing that mighte falle.°   *would not/happen*

This passeth forth° al thilke° Saterday,   *goes on/that*
That Nicholas stille in his chambre lay,
235 And eet° and sleep,° or dide° what him leste,°   *ate/slept/did/he wanted*
Til Sonday, that° the sonne gooth° to reste.   *Sunday, when/sun goes*

This sely carpenter hath greet merveyle°   *great wonder*
Of Nicholas, or what thing mighte him eyle,°   *ail*
And seyde,° "I am adrad,° by seint° Thomas,   *said/afraid/Saint*
240 It stondeth nat aright° with Nicholas.   *stands not right*
God shilde° that he deyde sodeynly!°   *forbid/died suddenly*
This world is now ful tikel, sikerly;°   *unstable, surely*
I saugh to-day a cors y-born° to chirche°   *corpse carried/church*
That now, on Monday last, I saugh him wirche.°   *working*

245 Go up," quod° he un-to his knave anoon,°   *said/boy then*
"Clepe° at his dore, or knokke° with a stoon,°   *call/knock/stone*
Loke° how it is, and tel me boldely."   *see*

This knave gooth him° up ful sturdily,   *goes*
And at the chambre-dore, whyl° that he stood,   *while*
250 He cryde and knokked as that° he were wood:°   *if/crazy*
"What! how! what do ye, maister° Nicholay?   *master*
How may ye slepen al the longe day?"

But al for noght,° he herde° nat a word;   *naught/heard*
An hole he fond,° ful lowe up-on a bord,°   *found/board*
255 Ther as° the cat was wont in for to crepe;°   *where/creep*
And at that hole he looked in ful depe,°   *far*
And at the laste he hadde of him a sighte.
This Nicholas sat gaping ever up-righte,
As° he had kyked° on the newe mone.°   *as if/gazed/moon*
260 Adoun° he gooth, and tolde his maister sone°   *down/immediately*
In what array° he saugh this ilke° man.   *state/same*

This carpenter to blessen him° bigan,   *bless himself*
And seyde, "Help us, seinte Frideswyde!

_____

263. *seinte Frideswyde:* The priory of Saint Frideswide was
near Oxford.

A man woot litel° what him° shal bityde.°   *knows little/to him/happen*
265 This man is falle,° with his astromye,°   *fallen/astronomy*
In som woodnesse° or in som agonye;   *madness*
I thoghte ay° wel how **that it sholde**° be!   *knew ever/should*
Men sholde nat knowe of Goddes privetee,°   *secrets*
Ye,° blessed be alwey° a lewed° man,   *yea/always/ignorant*
270 That noght but oonly° his bileve can!°   *only/Creed knows*
So ferde° another **clerk with astromye**;   *fared*
He walked in the feeldes° for to prye   *fields*
Up-on the sterres,° what ther sholde bifalle,°   *stars/occur*
Til he was in a marle-pit y-falle;°   *fallen*
275 He saugh° nat that. But yet, by seint Thomas,   *saw*
Me° reweth sore of° hende° Nicholas.   *I/pity greatly/gentle*
He shal be rated of° his studying,   *scolded for*
If that I may, by Iesus, hevene° king!   *Jesus, heaven's*

Get me a staf, that I may underspore,°   *pry under (it)*
280 Whyl that thou, Robin, hevest° up the dore.   *heave*
He shal out° of his studying, as I gesse"°   *(come) out/guess*
And to the chambre-dore he gan° him dresse.°   *did/prepare to turn*
His knave was a strong carl° for the nones,°   *fellow/occasion*
And by the haspe he haf° it up atones;°   *heaved/at once*
285 In-to° the floor the dore fil anon.°   *onto/fell directly*
This Nicholas sat ay as stille as stoon,°   *stone*
And ever gaped upward in-to the eir.°   *air*
This carpenter wende° he were in despeir,°   *thought/despair*
And hente° him by the sholdres° mightily,   *grabbed/shoulders*
290 And shook him harde, and cryde spitously,°   *angrily*
"What! Nicholay! what, how! what! loke° adoun!   *look*
Awake, and thenk° on Cristes passioun;   *think*
I crouche° thee from elves and fro wightes!"°   *sign with a cross/from creatures*
Ther-with the night-spel seyde° he anon-rightes°   *said/quickly*
295 On foure halves° of the hous aboute,   *sides*
And on the threshfold° of the dore with-oute:°   *threshold/outside*
"Iesu Crist, and seynt Benedight,°   *Saint Benedict*
Blesse this hous from every wikked° wight,   *wicked*

271–75. The fable of Thales is well known from Plato, *Theaetetus*, 174 A.

272–73. *prye Up-on:* i.e., "examine."

274. *marle-pit:* a hole used for storing a type of clay fertilizer.

283. *for the nones:* Found numerous times in Chaucer, this phrase is a tag like the Mod. Eng. *now* used for emphasis

294. *night-spel:* The "night spell" was a prayer of pre-Christian origin to protect the sleeper from harm, such as the one said to guard man from "all things that go bump in the night." The one quoted here came from a popular charm.

For nightes verye,° the white *pater-noster!*   *evil spirits*
300 Where wentestow,° seynt Petres soster?"°   *go you/Peter's sister*

And atte laste this hende Nicholas
Gan° for to syke sore,° and seyde, "Allas!°   *began/sigh greatly/alas*
Shal al the world be lost eftsones° now?"   *hereafter*

This carpenter answerde, "What seystow?°   *say you*
305 What! thenk on God, as we don,° men that swinke."°   *do/work*

This Nicholas answerde, "Fecche° me drinke;   *fetch*
And after wol° I speke° in privetee   *will/speak*
Of certeyn° thing that toucheth° me and thee;   *certain/pertains to*
I wol telle it non° other man, certeyn."°   *no/certainly*

310 This carpenter goth° doun, and comth ageyn,°   *goes/comes again*
And broghte° of mighty ale a large quart;   *brought*
And whan° that ech° of hem° had dronke° his part,   *when/each/them/drunk*
This Nicholas his dore faste shette,°   *shut*
And doun the carpenter by him he sette.

315 He seyde, "Iohn, myn° hoste lief° and dere,°   *John, my/beloved/dear*
Thou shalt up-on thy trouthe swere° me here,   *honor swear*
That to no wight° thou shalt this conseil wreye;°   *man/counsel betray*
For it is Cristes conseil that I seye,°   *say*
And if thou telle it man,° thou are forlore;°   *(to any) man/lost*
320 For this vengaunce° thou shalt han° therfore,   *vengeance/have*
That if thou wreye me, thou shalt be wood!"°   *mad*
"Nay, Crist forbede° it, for his holy blood!"   *forbid*
Quod tho° this sely° man, "I nam° no labbe,°   *said then/good/am not/telltale*
Ne,° though I seye, I nam nat lief° to gabbe.   *nor/not eager*
325 Sey what thou wolt,° I shal it never telle   *will*
To child ne wyf,° by him that harwed° helle!"°   *woman/harrowed*

"Now John," quod Nicholas, "I wol nat lye;°   *lie*
I have y-founde° in myn astrologye,°   *found/astronomy*

299–300. *pater-noster*: Latin, "our father," i.e., the Lord's Prayer. The "White Paternoster" was a night spell which is here personified as protecting the house. W. W. Skeat cites various charms, among them one connected with Saint Peter's brother. However, Robinson believes the White Paternoster is itself identified with Saint Peter's sister, as having the key to the gates of heaven. In the central Catholic cantons of Switzerland, whole alpine valleys are protected by a night spell, the so-called *Betruf* ("prayer call"), which invokes a list of saints for pro-

tection of men and cattle during the night. A mountaineer chants the call from an elevated spot through a milking funnel, and it resounds and echoes through the valley for great distances.

326. The "Harrowing of Hell," in which Christ descends into hell to save those whose only sin was to be born before his Coming, is a medieval legend from the apocryphal Gospel of Nicodemus, and a subject of miracle plays.

As I have loked in° the mone° bright,   *at/moon*
330 That now, a° Monday next, at quarter-night,   *on*
Shal falle a reyn° and that so wilde and wood,°   *rain/fierce*
That half so greet° was never Noës° flood.   *great/Noah's*
This world," he seyde, "in lasse° than in an hour   *less*
Shal al be dreynt,° so hidous° is the shour;°   *drowned/hideous/shower*
335 Thus shal mankynde drenche° and lese hir lyf."°   *drown/lose/their life*

This carpenter answerde, "Allas, my wyf!°   *wife*
And shal she drenche? allas! myn Alisoun!"
For sorwe° of this he fil° almost adoun,°   *sorrow/fell/down*
And seyde,° "Is ther no remedie in this cas?"°   *said/matter*

340 "Why, yis, for° Gode," quod hende° Nicholas,   *yes, by/gentle*
"If thou wolt werken° after lore° and reed;°   *act/wisdom/counsel*
Thou mayst nat werken after thyn owene heed.°   *your own head*
For thus seith Salomon,° that was ful trewe,°   *says Solomon/very wise.*
"Werk al by conseil, and thou shalt nat rewe."°   *regret*
345 And if thou werken wolt by good conseil,
I undertake, with-outen° mast and seyl,°   *declare, without/sail*
Yet shal I saven hir° and thee and me.   *save her*
Hastow° nat herd° how saved was Noë,   *have you/heard*
Whan that our lord had warned him biforn°   *before*
350 That al the world with water sholde° be lorn?"°   *should/lost*

"Yis," quod this carpenter, "ful yore° ago."   *long*

"Hastow nat herd," quod Nicholas, "also
The sorwe of Noë with his felawshipe,°   *family*
Er° that he mighte gete° his wyf to° shipe?   *before/get/into (the)*
355 Him had be lever,° I dar° wel undertake,   *he would rather/dare*
At thilke° tyme, than alle hise° wetheres blake,°   *that/his/black*
That she hadde had a ship hir-self allone.°   *alone*
And ther-fore, wostou° what is best to done?°   *know you/do*
This asketh° haste, and of an hastif° thing   *demands/hasty*
360 Men may nat preche° or maken tarying.°   *preach/make delay*

Anon go° gete us faste in-to this in°   *now (let us) go/lodging*
A kneding-trogh,° or elles° a kimelin,°   *kneading trough/else/shallow tub*
For ech° of us, but loke° that they be large,   *each/see*

---

330. *quarter-night:* 9 P.M., when a quarter of the night was passed.

353–57. Cf. the York-cycle play of the fishers and mariners, *Noah and His Wife,* this volume, pp. 863–72. Mrs. Noah was always obstreperous and refused to enter the ark.

In whiche we mowe° swimme as in a barge,   *may*
365 And han° ther-inne vitaille suffisant°   *have/food sufficient*
But for a day; fy° on the remenant!°   *fie/rest*
The water shall aslake° and goon° away   *abate/go*
Aboute pryme up-on the nexte day.
But Robin may nat wite° of this, thy knave,°   *not know/boy*
370 Ne eek° thy mayde Gille I may nat save;   *nor also*
Axe° nat why, for though thou aske me,   *ask*
I wol° nat tellen° Goddes privetee.°   *will/tell/secret*
Suffiseth° thee, but if° thy wittes madde,°   *(let it) suffice/unless/go mad*
To han as greet° a grace as Noë hadde.   *great/Noah*
375 Thy wyf° shal I wel saven, out of doute,   *wife*
Go now thy wey,° and speed thee° heer-aboute.°   *way/hurry/about it*

But whan° thou hast, for hir and thee and me,   *when*
Y-geten° us thise° kneding-tubbes three,   *gotten/these*
Than° shaltow° hange hem° in the roof ful hye,°   *then/shall you/them/high*
380 That° no man of our purveyaunce spye.°   *so that/equipment discover*
And whan thou thus hast doon° as I have seyd,°   *done/said*
And hast our vitaille faire° in hem y-leyd,°   *well/laid*
And eek an ax, to smyte the corde atwo°   *in two*
When that the water comth,° that we may go,   *comes*
385 And broke° an hole an heigh,° up-on the gable,   *break/on high*
Unto° the gardin-ward,° over the stable,   *into/garden gate*
That we may frely passen° forth our way   *freely pass*
Whan that the grete shour° is goon° away—   *great shower/gone*
Than shaltow swimme as myrie,° I undertake,°   *merry/declare*
390 As doth the whyte doke° after hir° drake.   *duck/her*
Than wol I clepe,° "How! Alison! how! John!   *call*
Be myrie, for the flood wol passe anon."
And thou wolt seyn,° "Hayl, maister° Nicholay!   *will say/master*
Good morwe,° I se° thee wel, for it is day."   *morning/see*
395 And than shul° we be lordes al our lyf°   *shall/life*
Of al the world, as Noë and his wyf.

But of o° thyng I warne thee ful° right,   *one/very*
Be wel avysed,° on that ilke° night   *forewarned/same*
That we ben° entred in-to shippes bord,°   *are/board*
400 That noon° of us ne speke° nat a word,   *none/not speak*
Ne clepe, ne crye, but been° in his preyere;°   *remain/prayers*
For it is Goddes owne heste dere.°   *command dear*

---

366. *fy on the remenant:* i.e., "let the rest go!"   **399.** *in-to shippes bord:* "on board ship."
368. *pryme:* Prime was 9 A.M.

Thy wyf and thou mote° hange fer a-twinne,°   *must/far apart*
For° that bitwixe yow° shal be no sinne   *so/between you*
405 No more in looking than ther shall in dede;°   *deed*
This ordinance° is seyd, go, God thee spede!°   *command/prosper*
Tomorwe° at night, when men ben alle aslepe,°   *tomorrow/asleep*
In-to our kneding-tubbes° wol we crepe,°   *kneading tubs/creep*
And sitten° ther, abyding Goddes grace.   *sit*
410 Go now thy wey, I have no lenger space°   *longer time*
To make of this no lenger sermoning.
Men seyn thus, 'Send the wyse, and sey no-thing;'
Thou art so wys,° it nedeth° thee nat teche;°   *wise/is necessary/not (to) teach*
Go, save our lyf, and that I thee biseche."°   *beseech*

415 This sely° carpenter goth° forth his wey.   *innocent/goes*
Ful ofte he seith° "allas"° and "weylawey,"°   *says/alas/woe*
And to his wyf° he tolde his privetee;°   *wife/secret*
And she was war,° and knew it bet° than he,   *aware/better*
What al this queynte cast° was for to seye.°   *odd affair/meant*
420 But nathelees° she ferde° as° she wolde deye,°   *nevertheless/acted/as if/would die*
And seyde,° "Allas! go forth thy wey anon,°   *said/way quickly*
Help us to scape,° or we ben lost echon;°   *escape/every one*
I am thy trewe verray° wedded wyf;   *honest true*
Go, dere spouse, and help to save our lyf."

425 Lo! which° a greet° thyng is affeccioun!°   *what/great/emotion*
Men may dye° of imaginacioun,   *die*
So depe° may impressioun be take.°   *deeply/taken*
This sely carpenter biginneth° quake;   *begins to*
Him° thinketh verraily° that he may see   *he/truly*
430 Noës° flood come walwing° as the see°   *Noah's/rolling/sea*
To drenchen° Alisoun, his hony dere.   *drown*
He wepeth, weyleth,° maketh sory chere,°   *weeps, wails/sorrowful lamentation*
He syketh° with ful many a sory swogh.°   *sighs/groan*
He gooth° and geteth him° a kneding-trogh,°   *goes/gets himself/kneading trough*
435 And after that a tubbe and a kimelin,°   *shallow tub*
And prively° he sente hem° to his in,°   *secretly/them/lodging*
And heng° hem in the roof in privetee.   *hung*
His° owne hand he made laddres three,   *(with) his*
To climben° by the ronges° and the stalkes°   *climb/rungs/steps*
440 Un-to the tubbes hanginge in the balkes,°   *beams*
And hem vitailled,° bothe trogh and tubbe,   *provided with food*
With breed° and chese,° and good ale in a jubbe,°   *bread/cheese/container*
Suffysinge right y-nogh° as for a day.   *sufficing just enough*
But er° that he had maad° al this array,°   *before/made/arrangement*
445 He sente his knave,° and eek° his wenche also,   *boy/likewise*

Up-on his nede° to London for to go.   *business*
And on the Monday, whan° it drow° to night,   *when/turned*
He shette° his dore with-oute candel-light,   *shut*
And dressed° al thing as it sholde° be.   *prepared/should*
450 And shortly,° up they clomben° alle three;   *in short/climbed*
They sitten° stille wel° a furlong-way.   *sit/fully*

"Now, *Pater-noster*, clom!"° seyde Nicholay,   *(and then) quiet*
And "clom,"° quod° John, and "clom," seyde Alisoun.   *mum/said*
This carpenter seyde his devocioun,
455 And stille he sit, and biddeth° his preyere,°   *says/prayers*
Awaytinge on the reyn,° if he it here.°   *rain/hear*
The dede° sleep, for wery bisinesse,°   *dead/weariness of attention*
Fil° on this carpenter right, as I gesse,°   *fell/guess*
Aboute corfew-tyme,° or litel° more;   *curfew time/(a) little*
460 For travail° of his goost° he groneth sore,°   *anxiety/spirit/groans greatly*
And eft° he routeth,° for his heed° mislay.°   *again/snores/head/lay wrong*
Doun of° the laddre stalketh° Nicholay,   *off/tiptoes*
And Alisoun, ful° softe adoun° she spedde;   *very/down*
With-outen° wordes mo,° they goon° to bedde   *without/more/go*
465 Ther-as° the carpenter is wont to lye.°   *where/lie*
Ther was the revel and the melodye;
And thus lyth° Alison and Nicholas,   *lie*
In bisinesse° of mirthe and of solas,°   *occupation/pleasure*
Til that the belle of laudes gan° to ringe,   *began*
470 And freres° in the chauncel° gonne° singe.   *friars/chancel/began (to)*

This parish-clerk, this amorous Absolon,
That is for love alwey° so wo bigon,°   *always/woebegone*
Up-on the Monday was at Oseneye
With companye, him° to disporte and pleye,°   *himself/play*
475 And axed° up-on cas° a cloisterer°   *asked/by chance/cloister resident*
Ful prively° after Iohn° the carpenter;   *secretly/John*
And he drough° him a-part° out of the chirche,°   *drew/aside/church*
And seyde,° "I noot,° I saugh° him here nat wirche°   *said/know not/saw/not work*
Sin Saterday;° I trow° that he be went°   *since Saturday/believe/is gone*
480 For timber, ther° our abbot hath him sent;   *where*
For he is wont for timber for to go,

---

451. *a furlong-way:* i.e., "the time it takes to travel a furlong." Medieval time is often measured by the time it takes to travel a certain distance. Thus in romances we have the phrase "They clipped and kissed a mile," meaning the lovers embraced for the time it took to travel one mile.

452. *Pater-noster:* i.e., "say a Paternoster."

459. *corfew-tyme:* 8 P.M.

469. *laudes:* Lauds follows nocturns in the canonical hours and is usually sung at dawn; but the night is still dark according to the events of the story.

And dwellen° at the grange° a day or two;   *dwell/barn*
Or elles° he is at his hous, certeyn;°   *else/certainly*
Wher that he be, I can nat sothly seyn."°   *truly say*

485 This Absolon ful joly° was and light,°   *jolly/lighthearted*
And thoghte,° "Now is tyme wake° al night;   *thought/(to) wake*
For sikirly° I saugh him nat stiringe°   *surely/stirring*
Aboute his dore sin day bigan to springe.°   *dawn*
So moot° I thryve,° I shal, at cokkes° crowe,   *may/prosper/cocks'*
490 Ful prively knokken° at his windowe   *knock*
That stant° ful lowe up-on his boures° wal.   *stands/chamber's*
To Alison now wol° I tellen° al   *will/tell*
My love-longing, for yet I shal nat misse
That at the leste wey° I shal hir° kisse.   *at least/her*
495 Som maner° confort° shal I have, parfay,°   *kind (of)/comfort/in faith*
My mouth hath icched° al this longe day;   *itched*
That is a signe of kissing atte leste.
Al night me mette eek,° I was at a feste.°   *I dreamed also/festival*
Therfor I wol gon slepe° an houre or tweye,°   *go sleep/two*
500 And al the night than° wol I wake and pleye."   *then*

Whan° that the firste cok hath crowe, anon°   *when/crowed, directly*
Up rist° this joly lover Absolon,   *rose*
And him arrayeth gay, at point-devys.°   *to perfection*
But first he cheweth greyn° and lycorys,°   *grain/licorice*
505 To smellen swete, er° he had kembd° his heer.°   *smell sweet, before/combed/hair*
Under his tonge° a trewe love° he beer,°   *tongue/leaves of herb Paris/bore*
For ther-by wende° he to ben° gracious.   *thought/be*
He rometh° to the carpenteres hous,   *wanders*
And stille he stant under the shot-windowe;°   *hinged window*
510 Un-to his brest it raughte,° it was so lowe;   *reached*
And softe he cogheth° with a semi-soun°—   *coughs/half voice*
"What do ye, hony-comb, swete Alisoun?
My faire brid,° my swete cinamome,°   *bird/cinnamon*
Awaketh, lemman myn,° and speketh° to me!   *beloved mine/speak*
515 Wel litel thenken° ye up-on my wo,°   *very little think/woe*
That for your love I swete° ther I go.   *sweat*
No wonder is thogh° that I swelte° and swete;   *(it) is though/faint*

---

494. *leste wey:* i.e., "very least."

496. Itching mouths and hands usually foretold events; Desdemona's "mine eyes do itch" prophesied weeping and sorrow.

504. *greyn:* here perhaps the "grain of paradise" or cardamom, an aromatic herb.

506. *trewe love:* The herb-Paris leaves grew, like a four-leaf clover, in the form of a truelove knot. Since, however, it is reputed to be poisonous, it is questionable whether just this herb was meant by Chaucer.

I moorne° as doth a lamb after the tete.°   *yearn/teat*
Y-wis,° lemman, I have swich° love-longinge,   *indeed/such*
520 That lyk° a turtel trewe° is my moorninge;   *like/turtledove true*
I may nat ete na° more than a mayde."   *not eat no*

"Go fro° the window, Iakke° fool," she sayde,   *from/Jack*
"As° help me God, it wol nat be 'com ba me.'°   *so/"come-kiss-me"*
I love another, and elles° I were° to blame,   *else/would be*
525 Wel bet° than thee, by Iesu,° Absolon!   *much better/Jesus*
Go forth thy wey, or I wol caste a ston,°   *stone*
And lat° me slepe, a twenty devel wey!"°   *let/in the Devil's name*

"Allas,"° quod° Absolon, "and weylawey!°   *alas/said/woe*
That trewe love was ever so yvel biset!°   *ill used*
530 Than kisse me, sin° it may be no bet,   *since*
For Iesus° love and for the love of me."   *Jesus'*

"Wiltow° than go thy wey ther-with?" quod she.   *will you*

"Ye, certes,° lemman," quod this Absolon.   *yea, certainly*

"Thanne° make thee redy,"° quod she, "I come anon";   *then/yourself ready*
535 And un-to Nicholas she seyde stille,°   *said quietly*
"Now hust,° and thou shalt laughen° al thy fille."   *hush/laugh*
This Absolon doun sette him° on his knees,   *himself*
And seyde, "I am a lord at° alle degrees;°   *of/ranks*
For after this I hope ther cometh more!
540 Lemman, thy grace, and swete brid, thyn ore!"°   *your favor*

The window she undoth,° and that in haste,   *opens*
"Have do,"° quod she, "com of,° and speed thee° faste,   *done/along/hurry*
Lest that our neighebores thee espye."°   *discover*

This Absolon gan° wype his mouth ful° drye;   *did/very*
545 Derk° was the night as pich, or as the cole,°   *dark/coal*
And at the window out she putte hir° hole,   *her*
And Absolon, him fil° no bet ne wers,°   *befell/nor worse*
But with his mouth he kiste° hir naked ers°   *kissed/ass*
Ful savoury,° er° he was war° of this.   *with gusto/before/aware*

550 Abak° he sterte,° and thoghte° it was amis,°   *back/jumped/thought/amiss*

---

522. *Iakke:* (in contempt).
527. *twenty devel wey:* formerly just an emphatic form for "away."

For wel he wiste° a womman hath no berd;°	knew/beard
He felte a thing al rough and long y-herd,°	haired
And seyde, "Fy!° allas! what have I do?"	fie
"Tehee!" quod she, and clapte° the window to;	clapped
555 And Absolon goth° forth a sory pas.°	goes/sorrowful way
"A berd, a berd!" quod hende° Nicholas,	gentle
"By Goddes *corpus*, this goth faire and weel!"°	well
This sely° Absolon herde° every deel,°	wretched/heard/bit
And on his lippe he gan for anger byte;	
560 And to him-self he seyde, "I shal thee quyte!"°	repay
Who rubbeth now, who froteth° now his lippes	scrubs
With dust, with sond,° with straw, with clooth,° with chippes,	sand/cloth
But Absolon, that seith° ful ofte, "Allas!	says
My soule bitake° I un-to Sathanas,	commit/Satan
565 But me wer lever° than al this toun," quod he,	I would rather
"Of this despyt awroken° for to be!	shame avenged
Allas!" quod he, "allas! I ne° hadde y-bleynt°!"	(that) I not/turned aside
His hote° love was cold and al y-queynt;°	hot/quenched
For fro° that tyme that he had kiste hir ers,	from
570 Of paramours° he sette nat° a kers,°	for lovemaking/gave not/cress
For he was heled° of his maladye;°	healed/illness
Ful ofte paramours he gan deffye,°	denounce
And weep as dooth° a child that is y-bete.°	does/beaten
A softe paas° he wente over the strete°	step/street
575 Un-til° a smith men cleped daun° Gerveys,	to/called master
That in his forge smithed plough-harneys;°	plow fittings
He sharpeth shaar° and culter bisily.°	sharpens share/coulter busily
This Absolon knokketh° al esily,°	knocks/softly
And seyde,° "Undo,° Gerveys, and that anon."°	said/open/quickly
580 "What, who artow?"° "It am I, Absolon."	are you
"What, Absolon! for Cristes swete° tree,°	sweet/(i.e., cross)
Why ryse ye so rathe,° ey,° *benedicite!*	early, eh
What eyleth you?° Som gay gerl,° God it woot,°	ails you/girl/knows
Hath broght° yow thus up-on the viritoot;°	brought/astir
585 By sëynt Note,° ye woot wel what I mene."°	Saint Neot/mean

---

557. *corpus*: Latin, "body."

570. *kers*: i.e., a worthless object. It is used in *Piers Plowman* and elsewhere.

582. *benedicite*: Latin, "bless you."

585. Saint Neot lived in the 9th century.

This Absolon ne roghte° nat a bene°   cared/bean
Of al his pley,° no word agayn he yaf;°   joke/gave
He hadde more tow on his distaf
Than Gerveys knew, and seyde, "Freend° so dere,°   friend/dear
590 That hote culter in the chimenee° here,   chimney
As lene° it me, I have ther-with to done,°   do lend/(something) to do
And I wol° bringe it thee agayn ful sone."°   will/very soon

Gerveys answerde, "Certes,° were it gold,   certainly
Or in a poke° nobles° alle untold,°   bag/(i.e., coins)/uncounted
595 Thou sholdest have,° as I am trewe° smith;   should have (them)/true
Ey, Cristes foo!° what wol ye do ther-with?"   foot

"Ther-of," quod° Absolon, "be as be may;°   said/be it as it may
I shal wel telle it thee to-morwe° day"—   tomorrow
And caughte the culter by the colde stele.°   handle
600 Ful softe out at the dore he gan° to stele,°   began/steal
And wente un-to the carpenteres wal.
He cogheth° first, and knokketh ther-with-al°   coughs/then
Upon the windowe, right° as he dide er.°   just/did before

This Alison answerde, "Who is ther
605 That knokketh so? I warante it° a theef."   believe it (is)

"Why, nay," quod he, "God woot, my swete leef,°   beloved
I am thyn° Absolon, my dereling!°   your/darling
Of gold," quod he, "I have thee broght a ring;
My moder° yaf it me, so God me save,   mother
610 Ful fyn° it is, and ther-to° wel y-grave;°   delicate/also/engraved
This wol I yeve° thee, if thou me kisse!"   give

This Nicholas was risen for to pisse,
And thoghte° he wolde amenden° al the jape,°   thought/would surpass/joke
He sholde kisse his ers° er that he scape.°   ass/escaped
615 And up the windowe dide° he hastily,   put
And out his ers he putteth prively°   secretly
Over the buttok, to the haunche-bon;°   thigh

---

588. I.e., "he had more in mind."

596. *Cristes foo:* Oaths on parts of Christ's body were frequent, but the language was usually disguised or corrupted: *cokkes bones* ("God's bones"), *gadzooks* ("God's hooks," i.e., "nails"), *zounds* ("God's wounds"), etc.

599–600. "Identical rhyme" was fashionable in French and English poetry and often affected by Chaucer.

And ther-with spak° this clerk, this Absolon, *thereupon spoke*
"Spek,° swete brid,° I noot° nat° wher thou art." *speak/bird/know not/not*

620 This Nicholas anon leet flee° a fart, *directly let fly*
As greet° as° it had been a thonder-dent,° *great/as if/thunderclap*
That with the strook° he was almost y-blent;° *stroke/blinded*
And he was redy° with his iren hoot,° *ready/iron hot*
And Nicholas amidde the ers he smoot.° *smote*

625 Of gooth° the skin an hande-brede° aboute, *off goes/hand's breadth*
The hote culter brende° so his toute,° *hot coulter burned/rump*
And for the smert° he wende° for to dye.° *smart/thought/die*
As he were wood,° for wo° he gan to crye— *crazy/woe*
"Help! water! water! help, for Goddes herte!"° *heart*

630 This carpenter out of his slomber sterte,° *slumber started*
And herde oon cryen° "water" as he were wood, *heard someone cry*
And thoghte, "Allas!° now comth Nowelis° flood!" *alas/comes Noel's*
He sit him° up with-outen° wordes mo,° *sits/without/more*
And with his ax he smoot the corde a-two,° *in two*
635 And doun goth° al; he fond° neither to selle, *goes/tried*
Ne breed ne° ale, til he came to the celle° *neither bread nor/sill*
Up-on the floor; and ther aswowne° he lay. *in a swoon*

Up sterte hir° Alison, and Nicholay, *jumped*
And cryden° "out" and "harrow" in the strete.° *cried/street*
640 The neighebores, bothe smale° and grete,° *low/high*
In ronnen,° for to gauren° on this man, *ran/stare*
That yet aswowne he lay, bothe pale and wan;
For with the fal he brosten° hadde his arm; *broken*
But stonde° he moste un-to° his owne harm. *stand/must to*
645 For whan° he spak, he was anon bore doun° *when/overcome*
With hende° Nicholas and Alisoun. *by gentle*
They tolden° every man that he was wood, *told*
He was agast° so of "Nowelis flood" *afraid*
Thurgh fantasye,° that of his vanitee *through imagination*
650 He hadde y-boght him° kneding-tubbes° three, *bought himself/kneading tubs*
And hadde hem° hanged in the roof above; *them*

---

632. The carpenter, the proverbial *senex amans* ("old man in love") whose wisdom is praised by Nicholas, is in reality quite stupid and ignorant. His confusion of "Noah" with "Nowel" ("Noel," i.e., Christmas) is evidence of his unlearned state.

635. *fond neither to selle:* i.e., "didn't stop to sell."

And that he preyed° hem, for Goddes love,   *begged*
To sitten° in the roof, *par companye.*   *sit*

The folk gan laughen° at his fantasye;   *did laugh*
655 In-to the roof they kyken° and they gape,   *peep*
And turned al his harm un-to° a jape.°   *into/joke*
For what so that° this carpenter answerde,   *whatever*
It was for noght,° no man his reson° herde;   *naught/argument*
With othes grete° he was so sworn adoun,°   *oaths great/down*
660 That he was holden° wood in al the toun;   *considered*
For every clerk anon-right heeld° with other.   *scholar immediately agreed*
They seyde,° "The man is wood, my leve° brother";   *said/dear*
And every wight° gan laughen of° this stryf.°   *man/at/quarrel*

Thus swyved° was the carpenteres wyf,°   *laid/wife*
665 For al his keping° and his jalousye;°   *guarding/jealousy*
And Absolon hath kist hir nether yë;°   *kissed her lower eye*
And Nicholas is scalded in the toute.°   *rump*
This tale is doon,° and God save al the route!°   *done/company*

HERE ENDETH THE MILLERE HIS TALE.

---

653. *par companye:* "for company."

INTERLUDIUM DE CLERICO ET PUELLA

DATE: Early 14th century. ◆ MANUSCRIPT: British Library Additional 23986. The dialect is Northern (North Lincoln or South York). The MS. was probably written in Lincolnshire. ◆ EDITIONS: George H. McKnight, *Middle English Humorous Tales in Verse* (Boston, 1913); E. K. Chambers, *The Medieval Stage* (London, 1903).

The corruption of *þ* (thorn) to *y* in many words here (either through scribal carelessness or by error in transcription) is an example of the evolution of *þe* to *ye*, as in Elizabethan or antiquated *ye olde taverne*, etc. This also sometimes came about because the early printers, not having in their fonts the character *þ*, often substituted a *y*. The following points should also be noted: (1) Often *th* occurs for *ht*; with the loss of the spirant we get the use of *th* for *t*, hence *þ* for *t*, as in *bether* = *better*, *losye* = *lost* (presumably *loste*, copied as *losthe*, copied as *losþe*, copied as *losye*). (2) The interchange of *w* and *v* is frequent: *hawy* = *have I*, *vat* = *what*. (3) Another change is *t* for *þ* after *d* or *t*: *canstu* = *canst thou*, *God te blis* = *God thee bless*. (4) The first person *I*, spelled *i*, *y*, is usually attached to the end of the verb; *kepi* = *I keep*. (5) The pronoun *she* is *yo* (for *heo*). (6) The letter *h* often precedes initial vowels or is dropped when it should be present (cf. *Dame Siriþ*).

The exact parallels in phrasing, theme, and plot between this interlude and *Dame Siriþ* have long been recognized. Both works must go back to a common original. The *Interludium* is the only surviving example of drama among the wares of the medieval minstrel. Appearing several centuries before the interlude became popular in England, it is a very important literary specimen.

Hic Incipit Interludium
De Clerico Et Puella

	Clericus ait,		
	CLERICUS.	Damishel,° reste wel!	*damsel*
	PUELLA.	Sir, welcum,° by saynt michel!°	*welcome/Michael*
	CLERICUS.	Wer° esty° sire, wer esty damc?°	*where/is your/mother*
5	PUELLA.	By Gode, es noyer her° at hame.°	*is neither here/home*
	CLERICUS.	Wel wor suilc° a man to life°	*were such/live*
		Yat° suilc a may mithe° haue to wyfe.	*that/maid might*
	PUELLA.	Do way,° by crist and leonard,	*go on!*
		No° wily° lufe na° clerc fayllard,°	*not/will I/love no/beggarly*

---

1. *ait* · "speaks."

10 Na kepi° herbherg,° clerc, in huse,° no y° flore   *keep I/lodging/house/on*
  Bot° his hers ly° wit uten° dore.   *unless/ass lie/outside*
  Go forth yi° way, god° sire,   *your/good*
  For her hastu° losye° al yi wile.°   *have you/lost/time*
  CLERICUS.   Nu,° nu, by crist and by sant ihon;°   *now/Saint John*
15 In al yis° land ne wis hi° none,   *this/not know I*
  Mayden, yat hi luf° mor yan° ye,   *love/than*
  Hif° me° micht° euer ye bether° be.   *if/I/might/better*
  For ye hy sory nicht° and day,   *I sorrow night*
  Y° may say, hay wayleuay!°   *I/alas*
20 Y luf ye mar° yan mi lif,°   *more/life*
  Yu° hates me mar yayt dos chnief.°   *you/cattle does knife*
  Yat es nouct° for mys-gilt,°   *not at all/having sinned*
  Certhes,° for yi luf ham° hi spilt.°   *certainly/am/killed*
  A, suythe° mayden, reu of° me,   *oh, sweet/(have) pity on*
25 Yat es ty° luf hand ay° salbe,°   *your/and ever/shall be*
  For ye° luf of ye moder° of efne,°   *the/mother/heaven*
  Yu mend° yi mode° and her° my steuene!°   *change/mind/hear/words*
  PUELLA.   By crist of heuene° and sant ione,°   *heaven/John*
  Clerc of scole° ne kepi non,°   *school/none*
30 For many god wymman haf yai don scam°—   *women have they done shame*
  By crist, yu michtis° haf ben° at hame!   *might/(i.e., stayed)*
  CLERICUS.   Synt° it noyir gat° may be   *since/neither way*
  Ihesu° crist by-techy° ye,   *Jesus/deliver*
  And send neulic bot yar° inne,   *soon remedy there*
35 Yat yi° be lesit° of al my pyne.°   *I/delivered/pain*
  PUELLA.   Go nu, truan,° go nu, go,   *truant (? from school)*
  For mikel° yu canstu° of sory and wo!°   *much/do you know/woe*

  CLERICUS.   God te blis,° mome helwis!   *you bless*
  MOME ELWIS.   Son, welcum, by san dinis!°   *Saint Denis*
40 CLERICUS.   Hic° am comin° to ye, mome,   *I/come*
  Yu hel° me noth,° yu say° me sone.°   *(if) you heal/not/tell/at once*
  Hic am a clerc yat hauntes° scole,   *goes to*
  Y lydy° my lif wyt° mikel dole.°   *lead/with/grief*
  Me wor leuer° to be dedh,°   *I would rather/dead*
45 Yan led° ye lif yat hyc ledh°   *lead/I (have) led*
  For ay mayden with° and schen,°   *white/bright*
  Fayrer ho lond° hawy° non syen.°   *in land/have I/seen*
  Yo hat° mayden Malkyn, y wene.°   *she is called/believe*
  Nu yu wost quam° y mene.°   *know whom/mean*
50 Yo wonys° at the tounes ende,   *lives*
  Yat suyt° lif so fayr and hende.°   *that sweet/gracious*
  Bot if° yo wil hir° mod amende,°   *unless/her/change*
  Neuly° crist my ded° me send!   *soon/death*

Men send° me hyder, vyt-vten° fayle,   *sent|hither, without*
55 To haf yi° help anty° cunsayle;°   *your|and your|counsel*
   Yar for° amy° cummen° here,   *therefore|am I|come*
   Yat° yu salt° be my herand-bere,°   *that|shall|errand bearer* (i.e., *go-between*)

   To mac° me and yat mayden sayct,°   *make|reconciled*
   And hi sal gef° ye of my nayct,°   *I shall give|possessions*
60 So yat heuer° al yy lyf°   *ever|your life*
   Saltu° be ye better wyf.°   *shall you|woman*
   So help me crist, and hy° may spede,°   *if I|succeed*
   Riche° saltu haf yi mede.°   *richly|reward*
   MOME ELWIS.   A,° son, vat° saystu?° Benedicite!   *oh|what|do you say*
65 Lift hup° yi hand and blis ye!   *up*
   For it es boyt° syn and scam,°   *is only|shame*
   Yat yu° on me hafs layt° thys blam.°   *you|have laid|blame*
   For hic am anald° quyne° and a lam,°   *an old|bawd,* i.e., *woman|lame*
   Y° led my lyf wit Godis° loue,   *I|with God's*
70 Wit my roc° y me fede,°   *distaff|myself feed*
   Cani° do non oyir dede,°   *can I|no other deed*
   Bot° my pater noster and my crede,°   *but|Creed*
   To say crist° for missedede,°   *to Christ|misdeeds*
   And myn auy mary° —   *my Ave Maria*
75 For my scynnes° hic am sory° —   *sins|sorry*
   And my deprofundis
   For al yat y sin lys;°   *all (those) that in sin lie*
   For cani me° non oyir yink° —   *I know|thing*
   Yat wot° crist, of heuene kync.°   *knows|heaven king*
80 Ihesu° crist of heuene hey,°   *Jesus|high*
   Gef° yat hay may heng° hey,   *grant|ever may (they) hang*
   And gef yat hy may se°   *see*
   Yat yay° be heng° on a tre,°   *they|hanged|tree*
   Yat yis ley as leyit° onne me.   *this lie have put*
85 For aly wymam° ami° on.°   *holy woman|am I|one*

· · ·

---

59. *my nayct:* an example of false division of article and noun (from OE *æht*).

64. *Benedicite:* Latin, "bless you."

70. *roc:* The old bawds were always spinning, sewing, or weaving women (cf. the Anus in *Pamphilus de Amore*, the Spanish Celestina, Frau Holle, the Wife of Bath, and many others).

Originally these women can probably all be traced to the Parcae (Three Fates) motif (cf. T. J. Garbáty, "Chaucer's Weaving Wife," *Journal of American Folklore*, 81 [1968] 322).

72. *pater noster:* Latin, "our father." i.e., the Lord's Prayer.

76. *deprofundis:* Latin, "out of the depths" (a cry of misery).

THE BALLAD

The ballad is a specific type of narrative song showing definite folk characteristics in style, content, and development. The story, shortened over the years by the folk process, usually starts near the climax (or with Act V of a drama) and develops by "leaping" over details, "lingering" on the plotted action. Secondary characteristics are the objective impersonality of the singer, who relates the most horrifying incidents without any show of emotion or sympathy, and the concentration on a single incident. Many ballads also have refrains, and most build up suspense from an unstable situation to the solution through a series of questions and answers and a linking style between stanzas called "incremental repetition," in which a phrase is repeated but with new information added. Ballads treat many themes: fairy elements, outlaw tradition, courtly and chivalric episodes, domestic tragedies, comic situations, national and historical incidents.

The traditional English and Scottish songs are known as "Child ballads" after the Harvard professor, Francis Child, who first collected and classified them. (They are usually referred to by their numbers in his edition of *The English and Scottish Popular Ballads;* these Child numbers for the ballads included in the present volume will be found in the headnotes preceding each.) Although many ballads seem to originate early in the Middle Ages, most of the manuscripts which we have today date from the sixteenth century on. Interest in their recovery was first stimulated in the eighteenth century through the antiquarian Bishop Thomas Percy.

The text for all of the ballads included in the present volume is that of the Sargent-Kittredge edition (see below). Detailed information on sources, analogues, and variations will be found in the edition of Francis Child.

REFERENCES

Bronson, Bertrand. *The Traditional Tunes of the Child Ballads.* Princeton, 1959.

Child, F. J. *The English and Scottish Popular Ballads.* 5 vols. Boston, 1882–98.

Coffin, Tristram P. *The British Traditional Ballad in North America.* Philadelphia, 1950.

Fowler, David C. *A Literary History of the Popular Ballad.* Durham, N.C., 1968.

Gerould, Gordon H. *The Ballad of Tradition.* Oxford, 1932.

Laws, G. Malcolm, Jr. *Native American Balladry,* Philadelphia, 1950.

Leach, MacEdward. *The Ballad Book.* New York, 1955.

Percy, Thomas. *Reliques of Ancient English Poetry.* 4th ed. London, 1794.

Pound, Louise. *Poetic Origins and the Ballad.* New York, 1921.

Sargent, Helen G., and Kittredge, G. L. *English and Scottish Popular Ballads.* Boston, 1904. (1-vol. abridgement of the Child collection.)

Scott, Sir Walter. *Minstrelsy of the Scottish Border*, Ed. T. F. Henderson. 4 vols., New York, 1902.

The ballad is treated in the General Introduction of this volume, pp. 31–32, 36–39.

JUDAS

Child 20. This ballad is the earliest one that is extant (from a 13th-century MS), written originally in couplets of fourteen syllables each, the famous ballad "Fourteener." It is unknown whether the poem was ever sung or passed into oral tradition; however, it has the dramatic movement and vigor of the ballad type in addition to being in the ballad stanza. It is one of the few ballads with religious themes and may go back to a passage in John 12, where Mary Magdalene perfumes the feet of Christ with an ointment. Judas angrily asks why it was not sold for three hundred pence and given to the poor. But the Evangelist explains that Judas did not care for the poor but "had the bag, and bare what was put therein." The legend thus developed which makes Judas the collector and stealer of tithes. He regains the three hundred pence which he lost through the unsold ointment by selling Christ for thirty pieces of silver. In a Wendish ballad Judas is sent out to buy bread but loses his money in gambling. The present version is unique in giving Judas a sister who is as wicked as he seems stupid.

I

Hit wes° upon a Screþorsday° þat vre louerd arose;°   *it was/Maundy Thursday/our Lord arose*

Ful° milde were þe wordes he spec° to Iudas.°   *very/spoke/Judas*

II

"Iudas, þou most° to Iurselem,° oure mete° for to bugge;°   *must (go)/Jerusalem/food/buy*

Þritti platen° of seluer° þou bere° up oþi° rugge.°   *thirty pieces/silver/bear/on your/back*

III

5 "Þou comest fer° iþe° brode stret,° fer iþe brode strete;   *far/on the/high road*

Summe° of þine tunesmen° þer þou meist i-mete."°   *some/townsmen/might meet*

IV

Imette° wid is soster,° þe swikele wimon°   *he met/with his sister/wicked woman*

"Iudas, þou were wrþe me stende þe° wid ston;°   *worthy (that) men stone you/stone*

V

"Iudas, þou were wrþe me stende þe wid ston,

10 For þe false prophete þat tou bileuest° upon."   *you believe*

VI

"Be stille, leue° soster, þin herte þe to-breke!°   *dear/your heart (may) you break*
Wiste min° louerd Crist, ful wel he wolde° be wreke."°   *(if it) knew my/would/avenged*

VII

"Iudas, go þou on þe roc, heie° up-on þe ston;   *rock, high*
Lei° þin heued i° my barm,° slep þou þe° anon."°   *lay/head in/lap/sleep/now*

VIII

¹⁵ Sone so° Iudas of slepe° was awake,   *(as) soon as/from sleep*
Þritti platen of seluer from hym weren itake.°   *were taken*

IX

He drou° hym selue bi° þe cop,° þat° al it lauede° ablode;°   *struck/self on/head/so that/swam/ in blood*

Þe Iewes° our of Iurslem awenden° he were wode.°   *Jews/thought/mad*

X

Foret° hym com° þe riche Ieu° þat heiste° Pilatus: *forward/came/Jew/was called*
²⁰ "Wolte° sulle° þi louerd, þat hette° Iesus?"   *will you/sell/is called*

XI

"I nul° sulle my louerd for nones cunnes eiste,°   *will not/no kind (of) goods*
Bote° hit be for þe þritti platen þat he me° bi-taiste."°   *except/to me/entrusted*

XII

"Wolte sulle þi lord Crist for enes° cunnes golde?"   *any*
"Nay, bote hit be for þe platen þat he habben° wolde."   *have*

XIII

²⁵ In him com ur° lord gon,° as is postles seten° at mete:° *our/walking/his apostles sit/supper*
"Wou° sitte ye, postles, ant wi° nule° ye ete?°   *why/and why/will not/eat*

XIV

"Wou sitte ye, postles, ant wi nule ye ete?
Ic° am iboust° ant isold° to day for oure mete."   *I/bought/sold*

XV

Vp stod him° Iudas: "Lord, am I þat° . . . ?   *stood/(i.e., the one)*
³⁰ I nas° neuer oþe° stude þer° me þe euel spec."°   *was not/in the/place where/you were slandered*

---

19. Pilate is here equated with the Jews. This is consistent with medieval as well as ballad tradition: the former concentrated the blame for the Crucifixion specifically on the Jews, and the latter generally simplified motives and causes.

XVI

Vp him stod Peter, ant spec wid al is miste,°   *might*
"Þau° Pilatus him come wid ten hundred cnistes,°   *though/knights*

XVII

"Þau Pilatus him com wid ten hundred cnistes,
Yet ic wolde, louerd, for þi loue fiste."°   *fight*

XVIII

35 "Still þou be, Peter, wel I þe i-cnowe;°   *know*
Þou wolt fur-sake° me þrien ar° þe coc° him crowe."°   *will forsake/thrice before/cock/crows*

LORD RANDAL

Child 12. A true international ballad, *Lord Randal* is found from Italy to Iceland. Although the knight's name has undergone a variety of changes, he is usually poisoned by his sweetheart with fish of some kind.

I

"O where ha° you been, Lord Randal, my son?   *have*
And where ha you been, my handsome young man?"
"I ha been at the greenwood; mother, mak° my bed soon,   *make*
For I'm wearied wi° hunting, and fain wad° lie down."   *with/gladly would*

II

5 "An wha° met ye there, Lord Randal, my son?   *and who*
An wha met you there, my handsome young man?"
"O I met wi my true-love; mother, mak my bed soon,
For I'm wearied wi huntin, and fain wad lie down."

III

"And what did she give you, Lord Randal, my son?
10 And what did she give you, my handsome young man?"
"Eels fried in a pan; mother, mak my bed soon,
For I'm wearied wi huntin, and fain wad lie down."

IV

"And wha gat° your leavins,° Lord Randal, my son?   *got/leftovers*
And wha gat your leavins, my handsom young man?"
15 "My hawks and my hounds; mother, mak my bed soon,
For I'm wearied wi hunting, and fain wad lie down."

V

"And what becam° of them, Lord Randal, my son?   *became*
And what became of them, my handsome young man?"
"They stretched their legs out an died; mother, mak my bed soon,
20 For I'm wearied wi huntin, and fain wad lie down."

VI

"O I fear you are poisoned, Lord Randal, my son!
I fear you are poisoned, my handsome young man!"
"O yes, I am poisoned; mother, mak my bed soon,
For I'm sick at the heart, and I fain wad lie down."

VII

25 "What d' ye leave to your mother, Lord Randal, my son?
What d' ye leave to your mother, my handsome young man?"
"Four and twenty milk kye;° mother, mak my bed soon,   *cows*
For I'm sick at the heart, and I fain wad lie down."

VIII

"What d' ye leave to your sister, Lord Randal, my son?
30 What d' ye leave to your sister, my handsome young man?"
"My gold and my silver; mother, mak my bed soon,
For I'm sick at the heart, an I fain wad lie down."

IX

"What d' ye leave to your brother, Lord Randal, my son?
What d' ye leave to your brother, my handsome young man?"
35 "My houses and my lands; mother, mak my bed soon,
For I'm sick at the heart, and I fain wad lie down."

X

"What d' ye leave to your true-love, Lord Randal, my son?
What d' ye leave to your true-love, my handsome young man?"
"I leave her hell and fire; mother, mak my bed soon,
40 For I'm sick at the heart, and I fain wad lie down."

EDWARD

Child 13. This ballad is found in Finland and Germanic countries, but the crime is usually fratricide and the mother is not implicated. It is a "ballad's ballad," as typical as we can get: (1) The stanzas alternate iambic tetrameter and iambic trimeter lines, the ballad fourteener or septenary. (2) There is a refrain, "Edward, Edward," "Mither, Mither" (a characteristic not always present). (3) There is "incremental repetition": the stanzas' last lines add new matter to the repetition. (4) The ballad shows "leaping and lingering": the story lingers on facts but leaps over motivation, description, setting, etc., all of which are extraneous to ballad development. (5) The climax is reached in the last line. The ballad starts with Act V of the drama and concentrates on the moment of truth. (6) The structure is in the usual dialogue-testament form.

I

"Why dois° your brand sae drap wi bluid,°	*does/sword so drip with blood*
Edward, Edward,	
Why dois your brand sae drap wi bluid,	
And why sae sad gang° yee O?"	*go*
5 "O I hae° killed my hauke° sae guid,°	*have/hawk/good*
Mither,° mither,	*mother*
O I hae killed my hauke sae guid,	
And I had nae mair bot hee° O."	*no more but he*

II

"Your haukis° bluid was nevir sae reid,°	*hawk's/red*
10 Edward, Edward,	
Your haukis bluid was nevir sae reid,	
My deir° son I tell thee O."	*dear*
"O I hae killed my reid-roan steid,°	*steed*
Mither, mither,	
15 O I hae killed my reid-roan steid,	
That erst° was sae fair and frie° O."	*once/free*

---

13. *reid-roan steid:* typical ballad cliché, like *wan water, lily-white hand, sewing a silken seam.* Many of these seem to have been taken from romance tradition.

III

"Your steid was auld,° and ye hae gat mair,°   *old/have got more*
        Edward, Edward,
Your steid was auld, and ye hae gat mair,
20   Sum° other dule° ye drie° O."   *some/grief/suffer*
"O I hae killed my fadir° deir,   *father*
        Mither, mither,
O I hae killed my fadir deir,
    Alas, and wae° is mee O!"   *woe*

IV

25 "And whatten° penance wul° ye drie for that,   *what/will*
        Edward, Edward?
And whatten penance will ye drie for that?
    My deir son, now tell me O."
"Ile° set my feit° in yonder boat,   *I'll/feet*
30   Mither, mither,
Ile set my feit in yonder boat,
    And Ile fare ovir the sea O."

V

"And what wul ye doe° wi your towirs and your ha,°   *do/hall*
        Edward, Edward?
35 And what wul ye doe wi your towirs and your ha,
    That were sae fair to see O?"
Ile let thame° stand tul° they doun fa,°   *them/till/fall*
        Mither, mither,
Ile let thame stand tul they doun fa,
40   For here nevir mair maun° I bee° O."   *may/be*

VI

"And what wul ye leive° to your bairns° and your wife,   *leave/children*
        Edward, Edward?
And what wul ye leive to your bairns and your wife,
    Whan° ye gang° ovir the sea O?"   *when/go*
45 "The warldis° room, late° them beg thrae° life,   *world's/let/through*
        Mither,° mither,   *mother*
The warldis room, late them beg thrae life,
    For thame nevir mair° wul I see O."   *more*

VII

"And what wul ye leive to your ain° mither deir,°   *own/dear*
50   Edward, Edward?

And what wul ye leive to your ain mither deir?°   *dear*
    My deir son, now tell me O."
"The curse of hell frae° me sall° ye beir,°   *from/shall/bear*
    Mither, mither,
55 The curse of hell frae me sall ye beir,
    Sic counseils° ye gave to me O."   *such counsels*

HIND HORN

Child 17. The story of Horn and Rymenhild was developed in England and France from the 13th through the 15th century. The ballad, which concentrates again on the climax of the Exile and Return motif and the recognition of Horn, should be compared to the romance of *King Horn*, this volume, pp. 142–180.

I

In Scotland there was a babie born,
  Lill lal, etc.
And his name it was called young Hind° Horn.   *Courteous*
  With a fal lal, etc.

II

⁵ He sent a letter to our king
That he was in love with his daughter Jean.

III

He's gien° to her a silver wand,   *given*
With seven living lavrocks° sitting thereon.   *larks*

IV

She's gien to him a diamond ring,
¹⁰ With seven bright diamonds set therein.

V

"When this ring grows pale and wan,
You may know by it my love is gane."°   *gone*

VI

One day as he looked his ring upon,
He saw the diamonds pale and wan.

---

6. *his daughter Jean:* Rymenhild in the romance.

9–12. In the romance Rymenhild gives Horn the ring to protect him as long as he is faithful. The token is a common element in the Recognition motif. Sometimes only half a ring is given (the Broken Token), or rings begin to pinch when the partner is unfaithful. Our wedding rings are in this Love Token tradition.

VII

¹⁵ He left the sea and came to land,
And the first that he met was an old beggar man.

VIII

"What news, what news?" said young Hind Horn;
"No news, no news," said the old beggar man.

IX

"No news," said the beggar, "no news at a',°   *all*
²⁰ But there is a wedding in the king's ha.°   *hall*

X

"But there is a wedding in the king's ha,
That has halden° these forty days and twa."°   *been held/two*

XI

"Will ye lend me your begging coat?
And I'll lend you my scarlet cloak.

XII

²⁵ "Will you lend me your beggar's rung?°   *staff*
And I'll gie° you my steed to ride upon.   *give*

XIII

"Will you lend me your wig o° hair,   *of*
To cover mine, because it is fair?"

XIV

The auld° beggar man was bound for the mill,   *old*
³⁰ But young Hind Horn for the king's hall.

XV

The auld beggar man was bound for to ride,
But young Hind Horn was bound for the bride.

XVI

When he came to the king's gate,
He sought a drink for Hind Horn's sake.

23–28. In the romance, Horn takes the disguise of a palmer, and later as a minstrel, and gains entrance to the castle, but in the *Geste of King Horn* (c. 1275–1300) the beggar costume is retained. *fair* (l. 28); i.e., "blond," typical of the romance hero. These ideals of beauty held from the troubadours and courtly romance into the Petrarchan sonnet tradition.

XVII

³⁵ The bride came down with a glass of wine,
When he drank out the glass, and dropt° in the ring.   *dropped*

XVIII

"O got ye this by sea or land?
Or got ye it off a dead man's hand?"

XIX

"I got not it by sea, I got it by land,
⁴⁰ And I got it, madam, out of your own hand."

XX

"O I'll cast off my gowns of brown,
And beg wi° you frae° town to town.   *with|from*

XXI

"O I'll cast off my gowns of red,
And I'll beg wi you to win my bread."

XXII

⁴⁵ "Ye needna° cast off your gowns of brown,
For I'll make you lady o many a town.   *need not*

XXIII

"Ye needna cast off your gowns of red,
It's only a sham, the begging o my bread."

XXIV

The bridegroom he had wedded the bride,
⁵⁰ But young Hind Horn he took her to bed.

---

35. During the bridal feast it was the custom of the bride personally to serve beggars, palmers, minstrels, and all others seeking entrance.

49–50. The idea of an abduction seems implied here; i.e., Horn is not the husband, but he gets the bride. This is not the case in the romance.

SAINT STEPHEN AND HEROD

Child 22. This ballad, which is from a 15th-century MS, is another of the rare religious types. The legend occurs also in Scandinavian songs, and it is found in two late MSS. of the apocryphal Gospel of Nicodemus. The original story has the three Wise Men proclaim the birth of Christ to Herod, who answers that this is as much an impossibility as that the roast capon in his dish could crow. The bird however rises, flaps its wings, and crows "Christus natus est." Folklore is full of miraculous answers to doubting Thomases, from Aaron's rod to the Pope's flowering dead stick in the Tannhäuser legend.

I

Seynt Steuene° was a clerk in kyng Herowdes halle, *Saint Stephen*
And seruyd° him of bred° and cloþ,° as euery kyng befalle.° *served (at dinner)/bread/table linen/ is used to*

II

Steuyn° out of kechone cam,° wyth boris hed on honde;° *Stephen/kitchen came/boar's head in hand*

He saw a sterre was° fayr and bryȝt° ouer Bedlem stonde.° *star (that) was/bright/Bethlehem stand*

III

⁵ He kyst adoun° þe boris hed and went in to þe halle: *threw down*
"I forsak þe,° kyng Herowdes,° and þi werkes° alle. *forsake you/Herod/works*

IV

"I forsak þe, kyng Herowdes, and þi werkes alle;
Þer is a chyld in Bedlem born is beter° þan we alle." *(that) is better*

V

"Quat eylyt° þe, Steuene? quat is þe° befalle?° *what ails/to you/happened*
¹⁰ Lakkyt þe° eyþer mete° or drynk in kyng Herowdes halle?" *do you lack/either food*

---

1. Stephen is a courtier or page in the household of Herod and serves him like Horn, who also carves and presents the cup for Aylmar the king. Young men of gentle birth were trained as pages in court.

VI

"Lakit me° neyþer° mete ne° drynk in kyng Herowdes halle;   *I lack/neither/nor*
Þer is a chyld in Bedlem born is beter þan we alle."

VII

"Quat eylyt þe, Steuyn? art þu wod,° or þu gynnyst° to brede?°°   *you mad/do you begin/be crazy*
Lakkyt þe eyþer gold or fe,° or ony° ryche wede?"°   *goods/any/clothes*

VIII

¹⁵ "Lakyt me neyþer gold ne fe, ne non° ryche wede;   *no*
Þer is a chyld in Bedlem born xal helpyn° vs at our nede."°   *(that) shall help/need*

IX

"Þat is al so soþ,° Steuyn, al so soþ, iwys,°   *just as true/indeed*
As° þis capoun° crowe xal þat lyþ° here in myn° dysh."   *as (that)/capon/lies/my*

X

Þat word was not so sone seyd,° þat word in þat halle,   *soon said*
²⁰ Þe° capoun crew° "Cristus natus est!" among þe lordes alle.   *(as) the/crowed*

XI

"Rysyt° vp, myn turmentowres,° be to° and al be on,°   *rise/torturers/by twos/ones*
And ledyt° Steuyn out of þis town, and stonyt° hym wyth ston!"° *lead/stone/stone*

XII

Tokyn he° Steuene, and stonyd hym in the way,°   *took they/road*
And þerfore is his euyn° on Crystes owyn° day.   *eve/own*

---

13. *brede:* The *MED* defines *breiden* v. (1) as "to rave," "to turn
mad" (*breiden out of wit*).

19. *not so sone:* i.e., "no sooner."

20. *þe:* i.e., "than the"; *Cristus natus est:* Latin, "Christ is
born."

21. *be . . . on:* i.e., "all together."

24. *euyn:* December 26.

THE THREE RAVENS

Child 26. This English ballad and the Scottish version, *The Twa Corbies*, that follows are two of the finest, most lyrical and poignant examples of the form in our tradition. The so-called "sea change," the variations which ballads pass through as they are adapted to different geographical surroundings and ethnic environments, can be seen here clearly defined. The English ballad is one of hope, of loyalty, of a death remembered and mourned; the Scottish version is stark, cold, bitter in its picture of futility. The American version, *Billy McGee, McGaw*, makes an incident of grief and tragedy into a macabre, mocking nonsense song.

I

There were three rauens sat on a tree,
   Downe a downe, hay down, hay downe.
There were three rauens sat on a tree,
   With a downe.
5 There were three rauens sat on a tree,
They were as blacke as they might be.
   With a downe derrie, derrie, derrie, downe, downe.

II

The one of them said to his mate,
"Where shall we our breakefast take?"

III

10 "Downe in yonder greene field,
There lies a knight slain vnder his shield.

IV

"His hounds they lie downe at his feete,
So well they can their master keepe.°   *guard*

V

"His haukes° they flie so eagerly,   *hawks*
15 There's no fowle dare him come nie."°   *near*

VI

Downe there comes a fallow doe,
As great with yong° as she might goe.   *young*

VII

She lift° vp his bloudy hed,°   *lifted/bloody head*
And kist° his wounds that were so red.   *kissed*

VIII

20 She got him vp vpon her backe,
And carried him to earthen lake.

IX

She buried him before the prime,
She was dead herselfe ere euen-song time.

X

God send euery gentleman
25 Such haukes, such hounds, and such a leman.°   *lover*

---

16. *fallow doe:* the knight's wife, of course; but the ballad concentration is on animals, and through oral transmission and confusion a complete shift into the animal kingdom seems to have taken place.

21. *earthen lake:* i.e., "grave."

22–23. *prime:* the first daytime canonical hour, or 6–9 A.M.; *euen-song;* vespers, the time of evening service.

THE TWA CORBIES

I

As I was walking all alane,°   *alone*
I heard twa corbies° making a mane;°   *two crows/moan*
The tane° unto the t'other say,   *one*
"Where sall° we gang° and dine to-day?"   *shall/go*

II

5 "In behint° yon auld fail dyke,°   *behind/old foul ditch*
I wot° there lies a new° slain knight;   *know/newly*
And naebody kens° that he lies there,   *nobody knows*
But his hawk, his hound, and lady fair.

III

"His hound is to the hunting gane,°   *gone*
10 His hawk to fetch the wild-fowl hame,°   *home*
His lady's ta'en° another mate,   *taken*
So we may mak° our dinner sweet.   *make*

IV

"Ye'll sit on his white hause-bane,°   *neck bone*
And I'll pike° out his bonny blue een;°   *pick/eyes*
15 Wi ae° lock o° his gowden° hair   *with a/of/golden*
We'll theek° our nest when it grows bare.   *thatch*

V

"Mony° a one for him makes mane,   *many*
But nane° sall ken where he is gane;   *none*
Oer his white banes, when they are bare,
20 The wind sall blaw° for evermair."°   *blow/evermore*

5–6. The difference in tone between this ballad and *The Three Ravens* can be seen here: in the English version the dead knight lies in a green field.

13. *hause-bane:* The Old English tradition is strong throughout, with the epic "beasts of battle," the birds of death hovering over the corpse (cf. *The Battle of Brunanburg*, this volume, p. 49). The survival of the old tradition was strongest in the North.

17–20. This stanza has been considered the high-water mark of ballad lyricism. The idea of emptiness and loneliness in the face of eternity is nowhere else projected so poignantly.

THE BOY AND THE MANTLE

Child 29. Rather from minstrel composition and romance tradition than from the middle-class origin of many other ballads, this song has its source in the Anglo-Norman Breton lai of Robert Biket (1150), the *Lay of the Horn* (*Lay du Cor;* cf. this volume, pp. 334–339) and the 13th-century French fabliau *Le Mantel Mautaillié* (also called *Cort Mantel*). In several of the versions the Chastity Test employs different instruments: the horn which spills over cuckolded husbands, the coat which does not fit adulterous wives. Biket's version uses the first, *Cort Mantel* the second. Both of these and a third, the knife, are combined in this ballad, which also has Caradoc Briebras as its hero. Some critics have felt that Biket's version should not be called a Breton lai because of its ready humor, but that seems tame compared to the tone of stag-party ribaldry in the ballad.

I

In the third day of May
    to Carleile° did come   *Carlisle*
A kind curteous° child,   *courteous*
    that cold° much of wisdome.   *knew*

II

⁵ A kirtle° and a mantle   *tunic*
    this child had vppon,°   *on*
With brauches° and ringes   *brooches*
    full° richelye bedone.°   *very/ornamented*

III

He had a sute° of silke,   *suit* (i.e., ? *band*)
¹⁰   about his middle drawne;
Without° he cold ol curtesye,°   *unless/acted in courtesy*
    he thought itt much shame.

IV

"God speed° thee, King Arthur,   *prosper*
    sitting att thy meate!

---

2. *Carleile:* Carlisle in Cumberland, often confused with Caerleon-upon-Usk in Monmouthshire.   **3.** *child:* i.e., "boy" (cf. above, p. 143, ll. 27–28n).

¹⁵ And the goodly Queene Gueneuer!°   *Guinevere*
  I canott° her fforgett.   *cannot*

V

"I tell you lords in this hall,
  I hett° you all heede,°   *ask/to listen*
Except you be the more surer,
²⁰ is you for° to dread."   *you ought*

VI

He plucked out of his potewer,°   *pouch*
  and longer wold° not dwell,°   *would/stay*
He pulled forth a pretty mantle,
  betweene two nut-shells.

VII

²⁵ "Haue thou here, King Arthure,
  haue thou heere of° mee;   *(something) from*
Giue itt to thy comely queene,
  shapen° as itt is alreadye.   *shaped*

VII

"Itt shall neuer become that wiffe°   *wife*
³⁰ that hath once done amisse";
Then euery knight in the kings court
  began to care for° his.   *worry about*

IX

Forth came dame Gueneuer,
  to the mantle shee her bed;°   *herself offered*
³⁵ The ladye shee was new-fangle,°   *fickle*
  but yett she was affrayd.

X

When shee had taken the mantle,
  shee stoode as she had beene madd;°   *born*
It was from the top to the toe
⁴⁰ as° sheeres° had itt shread.°   *as if/shears/shredded*

33–60. Guinevere is here portrayed in a most unfavorable light, similar to her characterization in Thomas Chestre's romance *Sir Launfal.* In Biket's *Lay of the Horn* she offers a halfway convincing excuse.

XI

One while was itt gaule,°   *red*
  another while was itt greene;
Another while was itt wadded;°   *woad color* (i.e., *blue*)
  ill itt did her beseeme.°   *become*

XII

⁴⁵ Another while was it blacke,
  and bore the worst hue;
"By my troth,"° quod° King Arthur,   *faith/said*
  "I thinke thou be not true."

XIII

Shee threw downe the mantle,
⁵⁰   that bright was of blee,°   *hue*
Fast with a rudd° redd   *blush*
  to her chamber can° shee flee.   *did*

XIV

Shee curst the weauer and the walker°   *fuller*
  that clothe° that had wrought,   *cloth*
⁵⁵ And bade° a vengeance on his crowne   *swore*
  that hither hath itt brought.

XV

"I had rather be in a wood,
  vnder a greene tree,
Then° in King Arthurs court   *than*
⁶⁰   shamed for to bee."

XVI

Kay called forth his ladye,
  and bade her come neere;
Saies,° "Madam, and° thou be guiltye,   *says/if*
  I pray thee hold thee° there."   *yourself*

XVII

⁶⁵ Forth came his ladye
  shortlye and anon,°   *at once*

---

61. Kay, the Seneschal, is usually an object of humor for his morose and surly manner.

Boldlye to the mantle
    then is shee gone.

XVIII

When she had tane° the mantle,   *taken*
70   and cast it her about,
Then was shee bare
    all aboue the buttocckes.

XIX

Then euery knight
    that was in the kings court
75 Talked, laughed, and showted,°   *shouted*
    full° oft att that sport.   *very*

XX

Shee threw downe the mantle,
    that bright was of blee,
Fast with a red rudd
80   to her chamber can shee flee.

XXI

Forth came an old knight,
    pattering ore a creede,°   *mumbling over his prayers*
And he proferred to this little boy
    twenty markes to° his meede,°   *as/reward*

XXII

85 And all the time of the Christmasse
    willinglye to ffeede;°   *to eat all he wanted*
For why,° this mantle might   *because*
    doe° his wiffe° some need.°   *do/wife/good*

XXIII

When shee had tane the mantle,
90   of cloth that was made,
Shee had no more left on her
    but a tassell and a threed:°   *thread*
Then euery knight in the kings court
    bade euill might shee speed.°   *wished her ill luck*

---

82. The knight is so old that he is mumbling over his beads. The pious old man, *senex religiosus*, is a stereotyped concept in literature. Chaucer's January in *The Merchant's Tale* is a caricature of this figure.

87–88. I.e., he hoped the mantle would teach his wife a lesson.

XXIV

95 Shee threw downe the mantle,
    that bright was of blee,°   *hue*
And fast with a redd rudd
    to her chamber can° shee flee.   *did*

XXV

Craddocke called forth his ladye,
100   and bade her come in;
Saith, "Winne this mantle, ladye,
    with a litle dinne.°   *little trouble*

XXVI

"Winne this mantle, ladye,
    and it shalbe thine
105 If thou neuer did amisse
    since thou wast mine."

XXVII

Forth came Craddockes ladye
    shortlye and anon,°   *at once*
But boldlye to the mantle
110   then is shee gone.

XXVIII

When shee had tane° the mantle,   *taken*
    and cast itt her about,
Vpp att her great toe
    itt began to crinkle and crowt;°   *draw together*
115 Shee said, "Bowe downe, mantle,
    and shame me not for nought.°   *naught*

XXIX

"Once I did amisse,
    I tell you certainlye,
When I kist° Craddockes mouth   *kissed*
120   vnder a greene tree,
When I kist Craddockes mouth
    before he marryed mee."

---

99. The famous Welsh hero Caradoc Briebras (cf. above, p. 338, n. 28).

107. Caradoc's wife was Tegau Eurvron, according to the Welsh Triads one of the three chaste and three fair ladies at Arthur's Court.

XXX

When shee had her shreeuen,°   *herself confessed*
  and her sines° shee had tolde,   *sins*
125 The mantle stoode about her
  right° as shee wold;°   *just/wanted*

XXXI

Seemelye° of coulour,°   *pleasant/color*
  glittering like gold;
Then euery knight in Arthurs court
130 did her behold.

XXXII

Then spake° dame Gueneuer°   *spoke/Guinevere*
  to Arthur our king:
"She hath tane yonder mantle,
  not with wright° but with wronge!   *right*

XXXIII

135 "See you not yonder woman
  that maketh her selfe° soe clene?°   *acts/so pure*
I haue seene tane out of her bedd
  of men fiueteene;°   *fifteen*

XXXIV

"Preists, clarkes,° and wedded men,   *priests, clerks*
140 from her by-deene;°   *one after another*
Yett shee taketh the mantle,
  and maketh her-selfe cleane!"

XXXV

Then spake the litle° boy   *little*
  that kept the mantle in hold;°   *(his) grasp*
145 Sayes "King, chasten thy wiffe;°   *wife*
  of her words shee is to° bold.   *too*

XXXVI

"Shee is a bitch and a witch,
  and a whore bold;
King, in thine owne hall
150 thou art a cuchold."°   *cuckold*

XXXVII

The litle boy stoode
  looking ouer a dore;

He was ware° of a wyld bore,°   *aware/boar*
   wold° haue werryed° a man.   *(that) would/harmed*

XXXVIII

155 He pulled forth a wood kniffe,°   *knife*
   fast thither that he ran;
He brought in the bores head,
   and quitted him° like a man.   *acquitted himself*

XXXIX

He brought in the bores head,
160   and was wonderous bold;
He said there was neuer a cucholds kniffe
   carue itt that cold.°   *could*

XL

Some rubbed their kniues
   vppon a whetstone;
165 Some threw them vnder the table,
   and said they had none.

XLI

King Arthur and the child
   stood looking them vpon;
All thcir kniues edges
170   turned backe againe.

XLII

Craddoccke had a litle kniue°   *knife*
   of iron and of steele;
He birtled° the bores head   *cut up*
   wonderous weele,°   *well*
175 That° euery knight in the kings court   *so that*
   had a morssell.

XLIII

Thc litle boy had a horne,
   of red gold that ronge;°   *rang*
He said, "There was noe cuckolde
180   shall° drinke of my horne,   *(that) shall*
But he shold° itt sheede,°   *should/spill*
   either behind or beforne."°   *before*

161–62. The test of the knife is not found in *The Lay of the Horn*   **178.** *red gold:* Cf. above, p. 183, l. 47*n.*
or *Cort Mantel.*

XLIV

Some shedd° on their shoulder,   *spilled*
   and some on their knee;
185 He that cold not hitt his mouth
    put it in his eye;
And he that was a cuckold,
    euery man might him see.

XLV

Craddoccke wan° the horne   *won*
190   and the bores head;
His ladye wan the mantle
   vnto° her meede;°   *for/reward*
Euerye such a louely ladye,
    God send° her well to speede!°   *grant/succeed*

THE MARRIAGE OF SIR GAWAIN

Child 31. The analogues to the story of the Loathly Lady and the question What is it that women most desire? can be seen in Chaucer's *Wife of Bath's Tale* and John Gower's *Tale of Florent* as well as the burlesque romance *The Wedding of Sir Gawain and Dame Ragnell* (the latter two in this volume). In addition, the ballad *The Knight and Shepherd's Daughter* treats the theme of False Appearance. The sources for the story seem to lie in Irish tales, specifically in the 12th-century MS. of the Book of Leinster, in which a hero gains sovereignty over Ireland by meeting the amorous demands of a loathly hag. The Gawain cycle early incorporated the motifs.

I

Kinge Arthur liues in merry Carleile,°   *Carlisle*
 And seemely is to see,
And there he hath with him Queene Genever,°   *Guinevere*
 That bride soe bright of blee.°   *hue*

II

5 And there he hath with him Queene Genever,
 That bride soe bright in bower,°   *chamber*
And all his barons about him stoode,
 That were both stiffe° and stowre.°   *brave/strong*

III

The king kept a royall Christmasse,
10 Of mirth and great honor,
And when. . . .

     .   .   .   .   .

IV

"And bring me word what thing it is
 That a woman will most desire;

---

1. *Carleile:* Carlisle in Cumberland, often confused with Caerleon-upon-Usk in Monmouthshire.

11. The lost passage tells how, when hunting in Inglewood Forest in Cumberland, Arthur meets a knight called Sir Gromer Somer Jour at Tarn Wadling. Arthur is challenged to fight but refuses, and Sir Gromer releases him on condition that he return in a year with the answer to the question that follows in the next surviving stanza. In the romance Sir Gromer is upset because Arthur had given his lands to Gawain.

This shalbe thy ransome, Arthur," he says,

15   "For Ile° haue noe other hier."°   *I'll/payment*

V

King Arthur then held vp his hand,
    According thene° as was the law;   *then*
He tooke his leaue of the baron there,
    And homward can° he draw.°   *homeward did/travel*

VI

20   And when he came to merry Carlile,
    To his chamber he is gone,
And ther came to him his cozen° Sir Gawaine,   *cousin*
    As he did make his mone.°   *lament*

VII

And there came to him his cozen Sir Gawaine,
25   That was a curteous° knight;   *courteous*
    "Why sigh you soe sore, vnckle° Arthur," he said,   *uncle*
    "Or who hath done thee vnright?"°   *wrong*

VIII

"O peace, O peace, thou gentle° Gawaine,   *noble*
    That faire may thee beffall!°   *may you have success*
30   For if thou knew my sighing soe deepe,
    Thou wold° not meruaile° att all.   *would/wonder*

IX

"For when I came to Tearne Wadling,
    A bold barron there I fand,°   *found*
With a great club vpon his backe,
35   Standing stiffe° and strong.   *stout*

X

"And he asked me wether° I wold fight   *whether*
    Or° from him I shold° begone,   *before/should*
Or else I must him a ransome pay,
    And soe depart him from.

XI

40   "To fight with him I saw noe cause;
    Methought° it was not meet;°   *it seemed to me/right*

---

22. *cozen:* Gawain is really Arthur's nephew.   **32.** *Tearne Wadling:* Tarn Wadling in Inglewood Forest.

For he was stiffe and strong with-all,°   *also*
    His strokes were nothing sweete.

XII

"Therefor this is my ransome, Gawaine,
45   I ought to him to pay;
I must come againe, as I am sworne,
    Vpon the New Yeers day;

XIII

"And I must bring him word what thing it is

. . . . .

XIV

Then king Arthur drest him° for to ryde,   *got ready*
50   In one soe° rich array,   *a very*
Toward the fore-said Tearne Wadling,
    That he might keepe his day.°   (i.e., *appointment*)

XV

And as he rode over a more,°   *moor*
    Hee see° a lady where shee sate°   *he saw/sat*
55 Betwixt an oke° and a greene hollen;°   *oak/holly*
    She was cladd in red scarlett.

XVI

Then there as° shold haue stood her mouth,   *where*
    Then there was sett her eye;
The other was in her forhead fast,
60   The way that she might see.

XVII

Her nose was crooked and turnd outward,
    Her mouth stood foule a-wry;
A worse formed lady than shee was,
    Neuer man saw with his eye.

XVIII

65 To halch vpon° him, King Arthur,   *greet*
    This lady was full faine,°   *very eager*

---

48. Several following stanzas are lost, describing how Arthur went out and assembled from various sources a book of answers to the question, What is it that women most desire?

57–64. The description of the hag's ugliness is intensified in the romance.

But King Arthur had forgott his lesson,
    What he shold say againe.

XIX

"What knight art thou," the lady sayd,
70   "That will not speak to me?
Of° me be thou nothing dismayd,   *by*
    Tho I be vgly to see.

XX

"For I haue halched° you curteouslye,°   *greeted/courteously*
    And you will not me againe;
75 Yett I may happen Sir Knight," shee said,
    "To ease thee of thy paine."

XXI

"Giue° thou ease me, lady," he said,   *if*
    "Or helpe me any thing,°   *(in) any way*
Thou shalt have gentle° Gawain, my cozen,°   *noble/cousin*
80   And marry him with a ring."

XXII

"Why, if I help thee not, thou noble King Arthur,
    Of thy owne hearts desiringe,
Of gentle Gawaine. . . .

.   .   .   .   .

XXIII

And when he came to the Tearne Wadling,
85   The baron there cold° he finde,   *did*
With a great weapon on his backe,
    Standing stiffe° and stronge.   *stout*

XXIV

And then he tooke King Arthurs letters in his hands,
    And away he cold them fling,
90 And then he puld° out a good browne sword,   *pulled*
    And cryd° himselfe a king.   *proclaimed*

77–80. Although both ballad and romance are examples of "degeneration of the hero" in that Arthur is seen as a ridiculous figure, in the romance he at least asks Gawain's consent, although of course, as Gawain's feudal lord, he did not have to do so. The point is that in the ballad the lady has not even asked for Gawain's hand.

83. In the missing passage the answer to the question is given.

88. The letters are the sheaf of answers that Arthur had painstakingly collected.

XXV

And he sayd, "I have thee and thy land, Arthur,
    To doe° as it pleaseth me,   *do (with)*
For this is not thy ransome sure,
95   Therfore yeeld thee° to me."   *yourself*

XXVI

And then bespoke him° noble Arthur,   *spoke up*
    And bad° him hold his hand: *bade*
"And giue me leaue to speake my mind
    In defence of all my land."

XXVII

100 He said, "As I came over a more,°   *moor*
    I see° a lady where shee sate°   *saw/sat*
Betweene an oke° and a green hollen;°   *oak/holly*
    Shee was clad in red scarlett.

XXVIII

"And she says a woman will haue her will,
105   And this is all her cheef desire:
Doe me right, as thou art a baron of sckill,°   *good judgment*
    This is thy ransome and all thy hyer."   *payment*

XXIX

He sayes, "An early vengeance light on her!
    She walkes on yonder more;
110 It was my sister that told thee this,
    And she is a misshappen hore.°   *misshapen whore*

XXX

"But heer Ile° make mine avow° to God   *here I'll/vow*
    To doe her an euill turne,
For an° euer I may thate fowle° theefe get,   *if/foul*
115   In a fyer° I will her burne."   *fire*

.   .   .   .   .

XXXI

Sir Lancelott and Sir Steven bold,
    They rode with them that day,

116–19. Lancelot du Lac was Arthur's chief knight and in several romances the lover of Guinevere. Sir Kay the Seneschal figures prominently in Arthurian literature, often as a gruff, spiteful, though courageous individual. Of Sir Stephen there is no further record.

And the formost of the company
There rode the steward Kay.

XXXII

120 Soe did Sir Banier and Sir Bore,
Sir Garrett with them soe gay,
Soe did Sir Tristeram that gentle° knight,   *noble*
To the forrest fresh and gay.

XXXIII

And when he came to the greene forrest,
125   Vnderneath a greene holly tree,
Their° sate that lady in red scarlet   *there*
That vnseemly was to see.

XXXIV

Sir Kay beheld this ladys face,
And looked vppon her swire;°   *neck*
130 "Whosoeuer kisses this lady," he sayes,
"Of his kisse he stands in feare."

XXXV

Sir Kay beheld the lady againe,
And looked vpon her snout;
"Whosoeuer kisses this lady," he saies,°   *says*
135   "Of his kisse he stands in doubt."

XXXVI

"Peace, cozen° Kay," then said Sir Gawaine,   *cousin*
"Amend thee of thy life;
For there is a knight amongst vs all
That must marry her to his wife."

XXXVII

140 "What! wedd her to wiffe!"° then said Sir Kay,   *wife*
"In the diuells° name anon!°   *Devil's/then*
Gett me a wiffe where-ere° I may,   *wherever*
For I had rather be slaine!"

XXXVIII

Then some tooke vp their hawkes in hast,°   *haste*
145   And some tooke vp their hounds,

120–22. Sir Banier is perhaps King Ban of Benwick, Lancelot's father. Sir Bore is probably King Bors, or Bohort of Gannes, Ban's brother. The others are Sir Gareth and Tristram.

And some sware° they wold° not marry her   *swore/would*
  For citty nor for towne.

XXXIX

And then be-spake him° noble King Arthur,   *spoke up*
  And sware there by this day,
150 For a litle foule sight and misliking

      .   .   .   .

XL

Then shee said, "Choose thee, gentle Gawaine,
  Truth as I doe° say,   *do*
Wether° thou wilt haue me in this likenesse   *whether*
  In the night or else in the day."

XLI

155 And then bespake him gentle Gawaine,
  Was° one soe mild of moode,   *(who) was*
Sayes, "Well I know what I wold say,
  God grant it may be good!

XLII

"To haue thee fowle° in the night   *foul*
160   When I with thee shold° play—   *should*
Yet I had rather, if I might
  Haue thee fowle in the day."

XLIII

"What! when lords goe with ther fcires," shee said,   *their mates*
  "Both to the ale and wine,
165 Alas! then I must hyde my selfe,
  I must not goe withinne."

XLIV

And then bespake him gentle° Gawaine,   *noble*
  Said, "Lady, that's but skill;°   *only reasonable*
And because thou art my owne lady,
170   Thou shalt haue all thy will."

---

150. In the lost stanzas that follow are described the wedding and Gawain's repugnance to make love to his wife on the wedding night. Gawain finally does kiss her, and she is transformed into a beautiful woman.

151–54. In Chaucer the choice is between having the wife fair and fickle or foul and faithful. When she has her will, the outcome is happy in all instances.

XLV

Then she said, "Blesed° be thou, gentle Gawain,   *blessed*
    This day that I thee see,
For as thou seest me att this time,
    From hencforth I wilbe.

XLVI

175 "My father was an old knight,
    And yett it chanced soe
That he marryed a younge lady
    That brought me to this woe.

XLVII

"Shee witched° me, being a faire young lady,   *bewitched*
180   To the greene forrest to dwell,
And there I must walke in womans liknesse,°   *likeness*
    Most like a feend of hell.

XLVIII

"She witched my brother to a carlish° b. . . .   *churlish*

. . . . .

"That looked soe foule, and that was wont
185   On the wild more° to goe."   *moor*

XLIX

"Come kisse her, brother Kay," then said Sir Gawaine,
    "And amend the of thy liffe;°   *life*
I sweare this is the same lady
    That I marryed to my wiffe."°   *wife*

L

190 Sir Kay kissed that lady bright,
    Standing vpon his ffecte;
He swore, as he was trew° knight,   *true*
    The spice was neuer soe sweete.

LI

"Well, cozer° Gawaine," sayes Sir Kay,   *cousin*
195   "Thy chance is fallen arright,
For thou hast gotten one of the fairest maids
    I euer saw with my sight."

LII

"It is my fortune," said Sir Gawaine;
  "For my vnckle° Arthurs sake   *uncle*
200 I am glad as grasse wold° be of raine,   *would*
  Great ioy° that I may take."   *joy*

LIII

Sir Gawaine tooke the lady by the one arme,
  Sir Kay tooke her by the tother,°   *other*
They led her straight to King Arthur,
205 As° they were brother and brother.   *as if*

LIV

King Arthur welcomed them there all,
  And soe did Lady Geneuer° his queene,   *Guinevere*
With all the knights of the Round Table,
  Most seemly to be seene.

LV

210 King Arthur beheld that lady faire
  That was soe faire and bright,
He thanked Christ in Trinity
  For Sir Gawaine that gentle° knight.   *noble*

LVI

Soe did the knights, both more° and lesse,° *high/low*
215 Reioyced° all that day   *rejoiced*
For the good chance that hapened was° *happened*
  To Sir Gawaine and his lady gay.

THOMAS RYMER

Child 37. Thomas the Rhymer, also called Thomas of Erceldoune or Learmont, was a historical figure who lived in Erceldoune, now Earlstoun in Berwickshire, Scotland, c. 1210–96. He was very early regarded as a seer and poet, and a MS. of 1320 records some of his predictions. He is said to have written a story about Tristram, and he is the author of a romance called *True Thomas*, in which he tells how he received his magical prophetic gifts from the fairies. In Scotland he is still revered for his oracles.

The ballad, which was probably composed before the middle of the 15th century, is analogous to the story of Ogier le Danois, who was seduced by Morgan la Fay. Thomas Chestre's romance *Sir Launfal* and Marie de France's lai *Lanval* have similar themes of Fairy Seduction, as does Keats's poem *La Belle Dame Sans Merci*. Of all these lovers, only Ogier has the chance to return, after staying two hundred years in Avalon, to fight the enemies of Christianity. After this he too retires for the rest of his transfigured life. The Return of the Hero motif is also seen in the legends of Arthur, Barbarossa (waiting for his cue in the Kyffhäuser Mountains), and Siegfried.

I

True Thomas lay oer yond grassy bank,
 And he beheld a ladie gay,
A ladie that was brisk and bold,
 Come riding oer the fernie brae.°   *ferny hill*

II

5 Her skirt was of the grass-green silk,
 Her mantel of the velvet fine,
At ilka tett° of her horse's mane   *each lock*
 Hung fifty silver bells and nine.

III

True Thomas he took off his hat,
10 And bowed him low down till° his knee: *to*

---

1. In another version Thomas sleeps on "Huntlie Bank" near the river Leader at Erceldoune. The site is still today regarded as a gathering place for fairies. The appearance of the fairy usually occurs as the mortal is resting or asleep, as in the lai of *Sir Orfeo*, where the queen sleeps under an "ympe-tree."

5–8. In folklore fairies as well as demons (*Sir Gawain and the Green Knight* or the hellish yeoman in Chaucer's *Friar's Tale*) are usually dressed in green. The little silver bells on the horses' manes are also fairy signs.

"All hail, thou mighty Queen of Heaven!
 For your peer on earth I never did see."

IV

"O no, O no, True Thomas," she says,
 "That name does not belong to me;
¹⁵ I am but the queen of fair Elfland,
 And I'm come here for to visit thee."

V

"Harp and carp,° Thomas," she said,   *sing (to the harp)*
 "Harp and carp along wi° me,   *with*
And if ye dare to kiss my lips,
²⁰ Sure of your bodie I will be."

VI

"Betide me weal, betide me woe,
 That weird° shall never daunton° me."   *fate/daunt*
Syne° he has kissed her rosy lips,   *then*
 All underneath the Eildon trae.°   *elderberry tree*

VII

²⁵ "But ye maun° go wi me now, Thomas,   *must*
 True Thomas, ye maun go wi me,
For ye maun serve me seven years,
 Thro weel° or wae° as may chance to be."   *through weal/woe*

VIII

She turned about her milk-white steed,
³⁰ And took True Thomas up behind,
And aye° wheneer her bridle rang,   *always*
 The steed flew swifter than the wind.

IX

For forty days and forty nights
 He wade° thro red blude° to the knee,   *waded/blood*
³⁵ And he saw neither sun nor moon,
 But heard the roaring of the sea.

---

11. Ogier also mistakes the fairy queen for the Virgin Mary.
33–34. A river of blood here separates earth from underground fairyland (cf. Norse mythology, in which the blood of slain heroes flows around Valhalla), although normally the fairy river is of water.

X

O they rade° on, and further on,   *rode*
   Until they came to a garden green:
"Light down, light down, ye ladie free,
40   Some of that fruit let me pull to thee."

XI

"O no, O no, True Thomas," she says,
   "That fruit maun not be touched by thee,
For a'° the plagues that are in hell   *all*
   Light on the fruit of this countrie.

XII

45 "But I have a loaf here in my lap,
   Likewise a bottle of claret wine,
And now ere we go farther on,
   We'll rest a while, and ye may dine."

XIII

When he had eaten and drunk his fill,
50   "Lay down your head upon my knee,"
The lady sayd, "ere we climb yon hill,
   And I will show you fairlies° three.   *wonders*

XIV

"O see not ye yon narrow road,
   So thick beset wi thorns and briers?
55 That is the path of righteousness,
   Tho° after it but few enquires.   *though*

XV

"And see not ye that braid° braid road,   *broad*
   That lies across yon lillie leven?°   *lily* (or *lovely*) *glade*
That is the path of wickedness,
60   Tho some call it the road to heaven.

XVI

"And see not ye that bonny road,
   Which winds about the fernie brae?°   *ferny hill*
That is the road to fair Elfland,
   Where you and I this night maun gae.°   *must go*

---

42. The mortal must not eat in fairyland; if he partakes of anything (often an apple), he can never return.

53–60. These stanzas seem Christian intrusions in the fairy element.

XVII

65 "But Thomas, ye maun hold your tongue,
   Whatever you may hear or see,
For gin ae° word you should chance to speak,   *if one*
   You will neer get back to your ain° countrie."   *own*

XVIII

He has gotten a coat of the even° cloth,   *smooth*
70   And a pair of shoes of velvet green,
And till seven years were past and gone
   True Thomas on earth was never seen.

SIR PATRICK SPENS

Child 58. There may be a historical incident connected with this ballad. In 1281 when Margaret, daughter of King Alexander III of Scotland, was married to Eric, king of Norway, many knights and nobles who took her to Norway were drowned on the return trip. And in fact a fuller version of *Sir Patrick Spens* shows the knight taking a princess (daughter of the king of Scotland or of Norway) to Norway, or bringing her home. However, no Patrick Spens has been found in historical records.

I

The king sits in Dumferling toune,
    Drinking the blude-reid° wine: *blood-red*
"O whar° will I get guid° sailor,   *where/good*
    To sail this schip of mine?"

II

⁵ Up and spak° an eldern knicht,°   *spoke/old knight*
    Sat at the kings richt kne:°   *right knee*
"Sir Patrick Spens is the best sailor
    That sails upon the se."°   *sea*

III

The king has written a braid° letter,   *long*
¹⁰   And signd it wi° his hand,   *with*
And sent it to Sir Patrick Spence,
    Was° walking on the sand.   *(who) was*

IV

The first line that Sir Patrick red,°   *read*
    A loud lauch° lauched he;   *laugh*
¹⁵ The next line that Sir Patrick red,
    The teir° blinded his ee.°   *tear/eye*

---

1. Dumferling, now Dunfermline, the old capital of Scotland.
5–6. There seems a hint here that political jealousy was a motivation. In the Old English romance *Apollonius of Tyre*, the reception of Apollonius by Arcestrates the king is disturbed by "sum eald ond sum æfestig ealdormann" ("an old and envious retainer"). In folklore, age is often linked to a malevolent disposition, especially if the old man is also a right-hand man whose position of power or as favorite may be challenged.

V

"O wha° is this has don° this deid,°
  This ill deid don to me,
To send me out this time o' the yeir,°
20 To sail upon the se!

who/done/deed

year

VI

"Mak° hast, mak haste, my mirry° men all,
  Our guid schip sails the morne:"
"O say na sae,° my master deir,°
  For I feir° a deadlie storme.

make/merry

not so/dear

fear

VII

25 "Late late yestreen° I saw the new moone,
  Wi the auld° moone in hir° arme,
And I feir, I feir, my deir master,
  That we will cum° to harme."

last night

old/her

come

VIII

O our Scots nobles wer richt laith°
30 To weet° their cork-heild schoone;°
Bot lang owre a'° the play wer playd,
  Thair° hats they swam aboone.°

very loath

wet/cork-heeled shoes

but long before all

their/above (them)

IX

O lang, lang may their ladies sit,
  Wi thair fans into° their hand,
35 Or eir° they se° Sir Patrick Spence
  Cum sailing to the land.

in

before ever/see

X

O lang, lang may the ladies stand,
  Wi thair gold kems° in their hair,
Waiting for thair ain° deir lords,
40 For they'll se thame na mair.°

combs

own

them no more

XI

Haf owre,° haf owre to Aberdour,
  It's fiftie fadom deip,°
And thair° lies guid° Sir Patrick Spence,
  Wi the Scots lords at his feit.°

half over

fathoms deep

there/good

feet

---

41. The ship is lost off Aberdeenshire in one version. Aberdour is near Dunfermline, on the Firth of Forth.

43–44. There is a Germanic epic quality in these lines. The faithful retainers lie at the feet of their leader in death the way the Viking warriors were buried with their most faithful companions, their dogs. The end of the ballad is in the spirit of the *comitatus* (cf. above, p. 2).

THE UNQUIET GRAVE

Child 78. MacEdward Leach pointed out that the end of a stylistic evolution in ballads is often the lyric form. *The Twa Corbies* approaches this, and *The Unquiet Grave* is an example of a pure lyric having developed out of a narrative, within the context of the ballad.

The folklore theme here is that too much mourning disturbs the dead. The tears of the mourner wet the shroud, drown the corpse, or make heavy work for dead children who must carry the water away in buckets. Thus the dead lover returns as a "revenant" to plead for the cessation of lamenting.

I

"The wind doth blow today, my love,
    And a few small drops of rain;
I never had but one true-love,
    In cold grave she was lain.

II

5 "I'll do as much for my true-love
    As any young man may;
I'll sit and mourn all at her grave
    For a twelvemonth and a day."

III

The twelvemonth and a day being up,
10   The dead began to speak:
"Oh who sits weeping on my grave,
    And will not let me sleep?"

IV

"'T is I, my love, sits on your grave,
    And will not let you sleep;
15 For I crave one kiss of your clay-cold lips,
    And that is all I seek."

---

8. The normal period of mourning.

V

"You crave one kiss of my clay-cold lips;
  But my breath smells earthy strong;
If you have one kiss of my clay-cold lips,
20   Your time will not be long.

VI

"'T is down in yonder garden green,
  Love, where we used to walk,
The finest flower that ere was seen
  Is withered to a stalk.

VII

25 "The stalk is withered dry, my love,
  So will our hearts decay;
So make yourself content, my love,
  Till God calls you away."

THE KNIGHT AND SHEPHERD'S DAUGHTER

Child 110. Old French lyric poetry, specifically the *pastourelle*, has several such stories of a knight forcing a peasant girl, or attempting to, with the wench holding out for marriage or maidenhood in a clever manner of quick repartee. The best example in English is this ballad and the beginning of Chaucer's *Wife of Bath's Tale*. Other analogies are the Loathly Lady-False Appearance stories of the Gawain legend. There is also a Scottish version of this poem, and the ballad *Child Waters* (63) shows many similarities in the early stanzas.

I

There was a shepherd's daughter
  Came triping° on the way,   *tripping*
And there she met a courteous knight,
  Which caused her to stay.
5 *Sing trang dil do lee.*

II

"Good morow to you, beautious maid,"
  These words pronounced he;
"O I shall dye° this day," he said,   *die*
  "If I have not my will of thee."

III

10 "The Lord forbid," the maid reply'd,
  "That such a thing should be,
That ever such a courteous yong° knight   *young*
  Should dye for love of me."

IV

He took her by the middle so small,
15 And laid her down on the plain,
And after he had had his will,
  He took her up again.

V

"Now you have had your wil, good sir,
  And put my body thus to shame,

²⁰ Even as you are a courteous knight,
    Tel me what is your name."

VI

"Some men do call me Jack, sweet heart,
    And some do call me John,
But when I come to the king's fair court,
²⁵   They call me Sweet William."

VII

He set his foot in the stirrop,
    And away then did he ride;
She tuckt° her kirtle° about her middle,   *tucked/tunic*
    And run° close by his side.   *ran*

VIII

³⁰ But when she came to the broad water,
    She set her brest and swom,°   *swam*
And when she was got out again,
    She took° her heels and run.   *took (to)*

IX

He never was the courteous knight
³⁵   To say, "Fair maid, will you ride?"
Nor she never was so loving a maid
    To say, "Sir Knight, abide."

X

But when she came to the king's fair court,
    She knocked at° the ring;   *with*
⁴⁰ So ready was the king himself
    To let this fair maid in.

XI

"O Christ you save, my gracious liege
    Your body Christ save and see!
You have got a knight within your court
⁴⁵   This day hath robbed me."

XII

"What hath he robbed thee of, fair maid?
    Of purple or of pall?

---

39. *ring:* hammer of a door knocker.

Or hath he took thy gay gold ring,
  From off thy finger small?"

XIII

⁵⁰ "He hath not robbed me, my liege,
  Of purple nor of pall;
But he hath got my maidenhead,
  Which grieves me worst of all."

XIV

"Now if he be a batchelor,
⁵⁵   His body I'le° give to thee;   *I'll*
But if he be a married man,
  High hanged shall he be."

XV

He called down his merry men all,
  By one, by two, and by three;
⁶⁰ Sweet William was us'd to be the first,
  But now the last comes hee.°   *he*

XVI

He brought her down full° forty pound,   *fully*
  Ty'd up within a glove:
"Fair maid, I give the same to the,°   *you*
⁶⁵   And seek another love."

XVII

"O I'le have none of your gold," she said,
  "Nor I'le have none of your fee;°   *wealth*
But I must have your fair body
  The king hath given me."

XVIII

⁷⁰ Sweet William ran and fetcht° her then   *fetched*
  Five hundred pound in gold,
Saying, "Fair maid, take this unto thee.
  Thy fault will never be told."

XIX

"'T is not your gold that shall me tempt,"
⁷⁵   These words then answered she,

"But I must have your own body;
 So the king hath granted me."

XX

"Would I had drank the fair water
 When I did drink the wine,
80 That ever any shepherd's daughter
 Should be a fair lady of mine!

XXI

"Would I had drunk the puddle-water
 When I did drink the ale,
That ever any shepherd's daughter
85 Should have told me such a tale!"

XXII

"A shepheard's daughter as I was,
 You might have let me be;
I'd never come to the king's fair court
 To have craved any love of thee."

XXIII

90 He set her on a milk-white steed,
 And himselfe upon a gray;
He hung a bugle about his neck,
 And so they rode away.

XXIV

But when they came unto the place
95 Where marriage rites were done,
She provd her self a duke's daughter,
 And he but a squire's son.

XXV

"Now you have married me, sir knight,
 Your pleasures may be free;
100 If you make me lady of one good town
 I'le° make you lord of three."   *I'll*

XXVI

"Accursed be the gold," he said,
 "If thou hadst not bin° true,   *been*

That should have parted thee from me
105   To have chang'd thee for a new."

XXVII

Their hearts being then so linked fast
   And joyning hand in hand,
He had both purse and person too,
   And all at his command.

JOHNIE COCK

Child 114. The outlaw tradition and the tales of Border raids in which Scottish clans rustled cattle at night in the "Debatable Land" between England and Scotland produced many fine ballads, of which this (found in the Percy papers) is one. The whole group is known as the Border Ballads; and the villain was as often the Scottish king (*Johnie Armstrong* [169]) as the English, for the Border lords acted independently of any crown, and the kings had difficulty in mastering them. The Scottish outlaw Johnie Cock may be compared to the English Robin Hood. As always the tone of the Northern ballad is much more somber.

I

Johnie he has risen up i° the morn,   *in*
    Calls for water to wash his hands;
But little knew he that his bloody° hounds   *blood*
    Were bound in iron bands.
5   Were bound in iron bands.

II

Johnie's mother has gotten word o° that,   *of*
    And care-bed° she has taen:°   *bed of sorrow/taken*
"O Johnie, for my benison,°   *blessing*
    I beg you'l stay at hame;°   *home*
10 For the wine so red, and the well baken° bread,   *baked*
    My Johnie shall want nane.°   *none*

III

"There are seven forsters° at Pickeram Side,   *foresters*
    At Pickeram where they dwell,
And for a drop of thy heart's bluid°   *blood*
15   They wad° ride the fords of hell."   *would*

3–6. Johnie's dogs were probably bewitched. They did not wake to warn him of the foresters, and his mother had a premonition of this.

12. These are king's men. Percy mentions that Pickeram Side is in Northumbria.

15. A river of blood supposedly separates earth from the underworld, Valhalla, or hell (cf. *Thomas Rymer*).

IV

Johnie he's gotten word of that,
 And he's turned wondrous keen;
He's put off the red scarlett,
 And he's put on the Lincoln green.

V

20 With a sheaf of arrows by his side,
 And a bent bow in his hand,
He's mounted on a prancing steed,
 And he has ridden fast oer the strand.

VI

He's up i Braidhouplee, and down i Bradyslee,
25 And under a buss° o broom,   *clump*
And there he found a good dun° deer,   *dark brown*
 Feeding in a buss of ling.°   *tall grass*

VII

Johnie shot, and the dun deer lap,°   *leaped*
 And she lap wondrous wide,
30 Until they came to the wan° water,   *dark*
 And he stemd° her of° her pride.   *stopped/in*

VIII

He 'as° taen out the little pen-knife,   *has*
 'T was full three quarters long,
And he has taen out of that dun deer
35 The liver bot and° the tongue.   *and also*

IX

They eat° of the flesh, and they drank of the blood,   *ate*
 And the blood it was so sweet,
Which caused Johnie and his bloody hounds
 To fall in a deep sleep.

18–19. Here Johnie puts on the Lincoln green of outlaws in place of the king's scarlet.

24. The names are undoubtedly of the North Country, but have not been identified.

25. *broom:* the famous *Planta Genista* (*Plantagenet* of English history) is a shrub with a yellow flower.

32. *little pen-knife:* In many versions it is a "wee pen knife" (perhaps a corruption of "weapon knife"), and the three-quarter-yard length, l. 33, is specific ballad convention.

35. In folklore, the liver was regarded as the center of life. Eating it and drinking the blood of the slain victim (man or animal) was regarded in primitive society as transferring the virtues (bravery, cunning, loyalty) of the dead to the living.

X

⁴⁰ By then came an old palmer,
     And an ill death may he die!
For he's away to Pickram Side,
     As fast as he can drie°   *is able*

XI

"What news, what news?" says the Seven Forsters,
⁴⁵   "What news have ye brought to me?"
"I have noe news," the palmer said,
     "But what I saw with my eye.

XII

"High up i° Bradyslee, low down i Bradisslee,   *in*
     And under a buss of scroggs,°   *underbrush*
⁵⁰ O there I spied a well-wight° man,   *strong*
     Sleeping among his dogs.

XIII

"His coat it was of light Lincoln,
     And his breeches of the same,
His shoes of the American leather,
⁵⁵   And gold buckles tying them."

XIV

Up bespake° the Seven Forsters,°   *spoke/Foresters*
     Up bespake they ane° and a':°   *one/all*
O that is Johnie o° Cockleys Well,   *of*
     And near him we will draw.

XV

⁶⁰ O the first y° stroke that they gae° him;   *one/gave*
     They struck him off by the knee;
Then up bespake his sister's son:
     "O the next'll gar° him die!"   *make*

---

40. *palmer:* a pilgrim who has returned from the Holy Land, carrying a palm leaf as a symbol of his pilgrimage. In medieval literature palmers were often used as sources of information because of their easy access to houses and gatherings; they were welcome for the news they brought and for their stories of adventure.

54. In colonial times American leather was imported to England, and the activities of the Hudson Bay Company lent to American pelts an aura of luxury. This is probably a very late intrusion in the ballad.

62. The treachery against Johnie is the greater because one of the foresters is "his sister's son," i.e., his nephew. In romance tradition there is no closer kinship than that of uncle to nephew. Modred's treason against his uncle Arthur has a similar effect. It is interesting to note that such romance motifs (Arthur/ Gawain, Modred; Charlemagne/Roland; Mark/Tristram; etc.) have been incorporated even in the outlaw ballad tradition, proof certainly that the ballad is a link in the evolution of oral traditional literature.

XVI

"O some they count ye well-wight° men,   *brave*
65   But I do count ye nane;°   *none*
For you might well ha° wakend me,   *have*
   And askd gin° I wad° be taen.°   *if/would/taken*

XVII

"The wildest wolf in aw° this wood   *all*
   Wad not ha done so by me;
70   She'd ha wet her foot ith° wan° water,   *in the/dark*
   And sprinkled it oer my brae,°   *brow*
And if that wad not ha wakend me,
   She wad ha gone and let me be.

XVIII

"O bows of yew, if ye be true,
75   In London, where ye were bought,
Fingers five, get up belive,°   *quickly*
   Manhuid° shall fail me nought."°   *manhood/not*

XIX

He has killd the Seven Forsters,
   He has killd them all but ane,°   *one*
80   And that° wan scarce° to Pickeram Side,   *that (one)/reached scarcely*
   To carry the bode-words° hame.°   *message/home*

XX

"Is there never a boy in a' this wood
   That will tell what I can say;
That will go to Cockleys Well
85   Tell my mither° to fetch me away?"   *mother*

XI

There was a boy into° that wood,   *in*
   That carried the tidings away,
And many ae° was the well-wight man   *(a) one*
   At the fetching o Johnie away.

68–73. MacEdward Leach notes that this belief, held also of bears, is common in Scotland.

74–76. Yews grow in southern England, as in the gardens of Hampton Court near London. The address to weapons and hands is an epic device. (Hemingway echoes this tradition in his account of the futile, heroic battle of *The Old Man and the Sea*).

ROBIN HOOD AND THE BUTCHER

Child 122. In *Piers Plowman*, B text (dated c. 1377) Passus V, 1. 401, we find the earliest reference to Robin Hood, when Sloth remarks, "But I can rymes of Robyn Hood and Randolf, erle of Chestre." Robin Hood is also mentioned in some 15th-century chronicles, and he is the hero of a long poetic sequence, *The Geste of Robin Hood*, from the same period. It is not known whether a Robin Hood ever lived. He seems rather to be part of the ever-popular outlaw tradition in ballads. The *Geste*, which linked many of his adventures into a unified whole, contributed to his survival, and he is as much an English folk hero today as his more courtly counterparts, Arthur and Richard the Lion-hearted. The Robin Hood ballads are, however, dead in oral tradition. They are no longer sung by the folk, although Benjamin Franklin remarked testily that he sold Robin Hood ballads much faster than the books of Psalms which he had in stock—and what was this generation coming to!

The Robin Hood narratives are examples of late ballads which show definite signs of the degeneration of the hero. Robin Hood challenges and is beaten by tinkers, potters, and butchers but usually shows himself a good loser and invites the victor to join his band. A corrupted and fragmentary version of *Robin Hood and the Butcher* recounts the fight, which is left out here; in a variant called *Robin Hood and the Potter*, the hero is bested at quarterstaves.

I

Come, all you brave gallants, and listen a while,
   With hey down, down, an a down,
  That are in the bowers within;
For of Robin Hood, that archer good,
⁵ A song I intend for to sing.

II

Upon a time it chanced so
  Bold Robin in forrest did spy
A jolly butcher, with a bonny fine mare,
  With° his flesh to the market did hye.°   *(that) with/hasten*

III

¹⁰ "Good morrow, good fellow," said jolly Robin,
  "What food hast?° tell unto me;   *do you have*

And thy trade to me tell, and where thou dost dwell,
    For I like well thy company."

IV

The butcher he answered jolly Robin:
15 "No matter where I dwell;
For a butcher I am, and to Notingham
    I am going, my flesh to sell."

V

"What is the price of thy flesh?" said jolly Robin,
    "Come, tell it soon unto me;
20 And the price of thy mare, be she never so dear,
    For a butcher fain° would I be."   *gladly*

VI

"The price of my flesh," the butcher repli'd,
    "I soon will tell unto thee;
With my bonny mare, and they are not dear,
25   Four mark thou must give unto me."

VII

"Four mark I will give thee," saith jolly Robin,
    "Four mark it shall be thy fee;
Thy mony° come count, and let me mount,   *money*
    For a butcher I fain would be."

VIII

30 Now Robin he is to Notingham gone,
    His butcher's trade for to begin;
With good intent, to the sheriff he went,
    And there he took up his inn.°   *lodging*

IX

When other butchers they opened their meat,
35   Bold Robin he then begun;
But how for to sell he knew not well,
    For a butcher he was but young.

X

When other butchers no meat could sell,
    Robin got both gold and fee;

40 For he sold more meat for one peny°   *penny*
    Than others could do for three.

XI

But when he sold his meat so fast,
    No butcher by him could thrive;
For he sold more meat for one peny
45   Than others could do for five.

XII

Which made the butchers of Notingham
    To study as they did stand,
Saying, surely he was some prodigal,
    That had sold his father's land.

XIII

50 The butchers they stepped to jolly Robin,
    Acquainted with him for to be;
"Come, brother," one said, "we be all of one trade,
    Come, will you go dine with me?"

XIV

"Accurst of his heart," said jolly Robin,
55   "That a butcher doth deny;
I will go with you, my brethren true,
    And as fast as I can hie."°   *hasten*

XV

But when to the sheriff's house they came,
    To dinner they hied apace,
60 And Robin he the man must be
    Before them all to say grace.

XVI

"Pray God bless us all," said jolly Robin,
    "And our meat within this place,
A cup of sack so good will nourish our blood,
65   And so I do end my grace.

XVII

"Come fill us more wine," said jolly Robin,
    "Let us merry be while we do stay;

For wine and good cheer, be it never so dear,
    I vow I the reckning will pay.

XVIII

70 "Come, brothers, be merry," said jolly Robin,
    "Let us drink, and never give ore;°   *stop*
For the shot° I will pay, ere I go my way,   *reckoning*
    If it cost me five pounds and more."

XIX

"This is a mad blade," the butchers then said;
75 Saies° the sheriff, "He is some prodigal,   *says*
That some land has sold, for silver and gold,
    And now he doth mean to spend all.

XX

"Hast thou any horn-beasts," the sheriff repli'd,
    "Good fellow, to sell unto me?"
80 "Yes, that I have, good Master Sheriff,
    I have hundreds two or three.

XXI

"And a hundred aker° of good free land,   *acres*
    If you please it to see;
And I'le° make you as good assurance of it   *I'll*
85   As ever my father made me."

XXII

The sheriff he saddled a good palfrey,°   *riding horse*
    With three hundred pound in gold,
And away he went with bold Robin Hood,
    His horned beasts to behold.

XXIII

90 Away then the sheriff and Robin did ride,
    To the forrest of merry Sherwood;
Then the sheriff did say, "God bless us this day
    From a man they call Robin Hood!"

XXIV

But when that a little further they came,
95   Bold Robin he chanced to spy

78–81. The sheriff refers to cattle, of course; Robin means the
deer of Sherwood Forest.

A hundred head of good red deer,
    Come tripping the sheriff full nigh.

XXV

"How like you my hornd beasts, good Master Sheriff?
    They be fat and fair for to see";
100 "I tell thee, good fellow, I would I were gone,
    For I like not thy company."

XXVI

Then Robin he set his horn to his mouth
    And blew but blasts three;
Then quickly anon° there came Little John,   *at once*
105   And all his company.

XXVII

"What is your will?" then said Little John,
    "Good master come tell it to me";
"I have brought hither the sheriff of Notingham,
    This day to dine with thee."

XXVIII

110 "He is welcome to me," then said Little John,
    "I hope he will honestly pay;
I know he has gold, if it be but well told,°   *counted*
    Will serve us to drink a whole day."

XXIX

Then Robin took his mantle from his back,
115   And laid it upon the ground,
And out of the sheriffe's portmantle
    He told three hundred pound.

XXX

Then Robin he brought him thorow° the wood,   *through*
    And set him on his dapple gray:
120 "O have me commended to your wife at home";
    So Robin went laughing away.

---

116. *portmantle:* a traveling case carried behind the saddle.

THE BEAST FABLE

Allegorical stories in which animals talk and take on human personality are as old as Aesop and can be found all over Europe. Often the animals become symbols of moral attributes, like the panther and the whale in the Middle English *Bestiary*. By far the most popular and widespread episodes, however, concern the characters in the beast epic: Reynard the fox and Isengrim the wolf. The cunning of one is set against the stupidity of the other. The French *Roman de Renart* deals with this theme extensively, though the long *Ysengrimus*, written by Master Nivardus of Ghent c. 1150, is usually considered the prototype of the beast epics. In later times mock-heroic elements were attached to this genre through bombastic speeches, the heroic stance of Chauntecleer, and the chivalric adventures in the chicken yard. Chaucer and Caxton (*Reynard the Fox*, 1481) represent the type in English, and the allegorical fables have been continued by La Fontaine, Goethe, and George Orwell. The talking animal, the trickster, and the dullard can be found in the *Gesta Romanorum*. The motif is a universal one.

REFERENCES

Lenaghan, R. T., ed. *Caxton's Aesop*. Cambridge, Mass., 1967.

McKnight, George H. *Middle English Humorous Tales in Verse*. Boston, 1913.

Sands, Donald, ed. *The History of Reynard the Fox; Translated and Printed by William Caxton in 1481*. Cambridge, Mass., 1960.

The beast fable is treated in the General Introduction of this volume, p. 29.

from THE BESTIARY

DATE: c. 1250. ✦ MANUSCRIPT: British Library Arundel 292. The dialect is East Midland. ✦ EDITIONS: Richard Morris, *An Old English Miscellany*, Early English Text Society, ES 49 (London, 1872); Joseph Hall, *Selections from Early Middle English* (Oxford, 1920).

The early East Midland dialect of the *Bestiary* has certain characteristics which should be noted as they may cause difficulty. (1) Single *s* replaces *sh* (*fis* = *fish*, *fles* = *flesh*, *sipes* = *ships*). (2) Single *t* replaces *þ* or *ð* after a *d* or a *t* (*ðat tu*). (3) The present participle is formed by adding *-and* to the root (*sakand*, "shaking"). (4) Pronoun forms are *he*, "they," "he"; *here*, "their," "her"; *him*, "himself"; *ge*, "they," "she"; *gu*, "you". (5) The interchange of *u* and *v* is regular (*euer* = *ever*, *ovr* = *our*).

The *Bestiary* is a poem of about eight hundred lines, treating thirteen animals, fantastic and real: lion, eagle, serpent, ant, hart, fox, spider, whale, mermaid, elephant, turtle-dove, panther, and dove. A *significacio* translating the description into Christian allegorical terms follows each animal section. The original *Bestiary* was a Greek text of the 4th century, written perhaps in Alexandria or in Palestinean Caesarea but now lost. The Middle English *Bestiary*, as well as the Old English *Physiologus* (treating the panther, the whale, and a bird, perhaps a partridge) from the *Exeter Book*, follows in a free fashion the Latin *Physiologus* composed by the 11th-century monk Theobaldus of Monte Cassino. An interest in natural history alone incited the composition of the Greek original and kept up the popularity of the work in the Middle Ages. The Christian significance was added later, as was true of the exempla of the *Gesta Romanorum*. It can be said that in its influence on medieval art and on later literature and in its pervasiveness and general application, the *Bestiary* is one of the most important works to come out of the repository of legend and learned tradition from the Middle Ages.

The Whale's Nature

Cethegrande° is a fis° *the whale/fish*
ðe moste° ðat in water is; *largest*
ðat tu wuldes seien get,° *you would say indeed*
gef ðu° it soge wan° it flet,° *if you/saw when/floated*
⁵ ðat it were a neilond° *an island*

---

5. *a neilond*: false division for *an island*. Normally the reverse process holds true; *an adder* for *a nadder* (OE *nædre*).

ðat sete one° ðe se sond.°	*sits on/sea sand*
Ðis fis ðat is vnride,°	*huge*
ðanne him° hungreð he gapeð wide,	*when he*
vt° of his ðrote° it smit° an onde,°	*out/throat/emits/breath*
¹⁰ ðe swetteste° ðing ðat is o londe;°	*sweetest/on earth*
ðer-fore oðre fisses to him dragen,°	*draw*
wan he° it felen° he aren fagen,°	*they/feel/are glad*
he cumen° and houen° in his muð,°	*come/hover/mouth*
of his swike° he arn uncuð;°	*treachery/are ignorant*
¹⁵ ðis cete ðanne hise chaueles lukeð,°	*whale then his jaws locks*
ðise° fisses alle in sukeð,°	*these/sucks*
ðe smale° he wile° ðus biswiken,°	*small/will/betray*
ðe grete maig° he nogt bigripen.°	*great/may/not grasp*
Ðis fis wuneð° wið° ðe se grund,°	*dwells/on/bottom*
²⁰ and liued ðer eure heil° and sund,°	*ever hale/sound*
til it cumeð ðe time	
ðat storm stireð° al ðe se,	*stirs*
ðanne sumer° and winter winnen;°	*summer/battle*
ne° mai it wunnen° ðer-inne,	*not/dwell*
²⁵ So droui° is te° sees grund,	*turbulent/the*
nc mai hc wunen ðer ðat stund,°	*time*
oc stireð° up and houeð° stille;	*but starts/floats*
wiles ðat weder° is so ille,	*while the weather*
ðe sipes° ðat arn on se fordriuen,°	*ships/driven about*
³⁰ loð° hem° is ded,° and lef° to liuen,°	*hateful/to them/death/dear/live*
biloken hem° and sen° ðis fis,	*they look about/see*
an eilond° he wenen° it is,	*island/think*
ðer-of he aren swiðe° fagen,	*very*
and mid hcrc migt ðar-to° he dragen,°	*with (all) their might thereto/pull*
³⁵ sipes on festen,°	*to anchor*
and alle up gangen;°	*climb*
Of ston mid stel° in ðe tunder°	*stone/steel/tinder*
wel to brennen° one ðis wunder,°	*burn/strange being*
warmen hem° wel and heten° and drinken;°	*warm themselves/eat/drink*
⁴⁰ ðe fir° he feleð° and doð hem sinken,°	*fire/feels/makes them sink*
for sone° he diueð dun° to grunde,	*at once/down*
he drepeð° hem alle wið-uten wunde.°	*kills/without wound*

9–10. The whale's sweet breath, likened to the enticement of the Devil, may be compared with that of the panther, who is likened to Christ. When the Savior rose from the grave there was "a sweet smell, fair and pleasing, in the whole world"; this odor issued from the panther after he had slept three days.

16–17. Cf. Shakespeare, *All's Well That Ends Well*, IV. iii: "Who is a whale to virginity and devours up all the fry it finds."

32–36. Milton (*Paradise Lost*, I, 200–8) compares Satan to

". . . that sea beast/Leviathan, which God of all his works/ Created hugest that swim th' ocean-stream./Him, haply, slumbering on the Norway foam,/The pilot of some small night-foundered skiff,/Deeming some island, oft, as seamen tell,/With fixéd anchor in his scaly rind,/Moors by his side under the lee, while night/Invests the sea, and wishéd morn delays."

Significacio

    Ðis deuel° is mikel wið° wil and magt,°   *Devil/great in/might*
    So wicches hauen° in here° craft,   *as witches are/their*
45 he doð men hungren° and hauen ðrist,°   *hunger/have thirst*
    and mani oðer° sinful list,°   *another/lust*
    tolleð° men to him wið his onde,°   *draws/scent*
    wo so° him folegeð° he findeð sonde;°   *whoso/follows/shame*
    ðo° arn ðe little in leue lage,°   *they/faith's law*
50 ðe mikle ne maig he to him dragen:°   *draw*
    ðe mikle, i mene° ðe stedefast°   *mean/steadfast*
    in rigte leue° mid fles° and gast.°   *righteous faith/flesh/spirit*
    Wo so listneð° deueles lore,   *listens to*
    on lengðe° it sal° him rewen° sore;   *at length/shall/make rue*
55 wo so festeð° hope on him,   *fastens*
    he sal him folgen° to helle dim.   *follow*

The Nature of the Siren

    In ðe se° senden°   *sea/are found*
    selcuðes° manie;°   *strange things/many*
    ðe mereman° is   *mermaid*
60 a meiden ilike°   *maiden like*
    on° brest and on bodi,   *in*
    oc° al ðus ge° is bunden:°   *but/she/joined together*
    fro° ðe noule niðerward°   *from/navel downward*
    ne° is ge no man like,   *not*
65 oc fis° to fuliwis°   *fish/completely*
    mid° finnes waxen.°   *with/grown*
    Ðis wunder wuneð°   *marvel lives*
    in wankel stede,°   *treacherous places*
    ðer° ðe water sinkeð,°   *where/is deep*
70 sipes° ge sinkeð,   *ships*
    and scaðe° ðus werkeð.˘   *evil/works*
    Mirie° ge singeð ðis mere,°   *merry/monster*

---

59. *mereman:* the classical Siren of the *Odyssey*. Odysseus heard and escaped the Sirens only by having his sailors tie him to the mast and plug their own ears with wax as they rowed. Hypnotized by the song of the Sirens, he commanded his men to loosen him, but they only bound him tighter until the danger was past. Near the right bank of the Rhine river, by Saint Goar, is a rock on which sits the Lorelei, combing her golden hair; the effect on sailors is the same as that of the song of the Sirens. **72.** Cf. Chaucer, *Nun's Priest's Tale*, ll. 4459–62: "... Chauntecleer so free/Soong murier than the mermayde in the see;/For Phisiologus seith sikerly/How that they syngen wel and myrily."

and haueð manie stefnes,°	has many voices
manie and sille,°	shrill
75 oc it ben wel° ille;	they are very
sipmen here steringe forgeten°	sailors their steering forget
for° hire stefninge,°	because of/her singing
slumeren° and slepen,°	slumber/sleep
and to° late waken;	too
80 ðe sipes sinken mitte suk,°	sink in suction
ne cumen he° nummor° up.	nor come they/no more
Oc wise men and warre°	wary
agen cunen chare,°	again can turn
ofte arn atbrosten,°	have escaped
85 mid here brest ouel;°	from her intention evil
he hauen herd° told of ðis mere	have heard
ðat tus unie-mete,°	thus unnatural
half man and half fis,	
sum° ðing tokneð° bi ðis.	some/betokens

Significacio

90 Fele° men hauen° ðe tokning°	many/(i.e., are like)/what is betokened
of° ðis forbisnede° ðing,	by/(here) exemplified
wiðuten weren sepes fel,°	outside wear sheep's skin
wiðinnen arn° he wulucs° al;	inside are/wolves
he speken° godcundhede,°	speak/of divine things
95 and wikke° is here dede;°	wicked/deeds
here dede is al vncuð°	foreign
wið ðat° spekeð here muð;°	to what/mouth
twifold arn° on mode,°	twofold (i.e., equivocal) are (they)/ mind
he sweren° bi ðe rode,°	swear/cross
100 bi ðe sunne and bi ðe mone,°	moon
and he ðe legen sone,°	then lie quickly
mid here sage° and mid here song	word
he ðe swiken° ðer imong,°	betray/among
ðin agte° wið swiking,°	your possessions/treachery
105 ði soule wið lesing.°	falsehood

The Nature of the Elephant

Elpes arn° in Inde riche,	elephants are
on° bodi borlic berges ilike;°	in/burly mountains like

he to-gaddre gon o wolde,°   *they together (to) go always desire*
so sep° ðat cumen ut° of folde,   *like sheep/come out*
110 and behinden° he hem° sampnen°   *behind/themselves/join together*
ðanne° he sulen° oðre strenen;°   *when/shall others beget*
Oc° he arn so kolde of kinde°   *but/nature*
ðat no golsipe° is hem minde,°   *lasciviousness/do they feel*
til he noten° of a gres,°   *eat/herb*
115 ðe name is mandragores.°   *mandrake*
Siðen° he bigeten on,°   *then/ beget one*
and two ger° he ðer-mide° gon.   *years/therewith*
Ðog° he ðre hundred ger   *though*
on werlde° more wuneden her,°   *world/lived here*
120 bigeten he neuermor non,°   *none*
so kold is hem° siðen blod° and bon;°   *in them/blood/bone*
ðanne ge sal hire kindles beren,°   *she shall her young bear*
In water ge sal stonden,°   *stand*
In water to mid side,°   *middle*
125 ðat° wanne° hire harde tide,°   *so that/when/labor starts*
ðat ge ne° falle niðer nogt,°   *not/down not*
ðat is most in hire ðogt,°   *thought*
For he ne hauen° no lið°   *have/limb*
ðat he mugen risen° wið.   *may rise*
130 Hu° he resteð him° ðis der,°   *how/himself/animal*
ðanne he walkeð wide,°   *widely*
herkne wu° it telleð her,   *listen (to) who*
for he is al unride.°   *very enormous*
A tre° he sekeð to fuligewis,°   *tree/seeks in certainly*
135 ðat is strong and stedefast° is;   *steadfast*
and leneð° him trostlike° ðer-bi,   *leans/trustingly*
ðanne he is of walke weri.°   *weary*
Ðe hunte haueð biholden° ðis,   *hunter has seen*
ðe° him wille swiken,°   *who/trick*
140 wor° his beste wune° is,   *where/opportunity*
to don° his willen;°   *do/will*
Sageð° ðis tre and under-set,°   *saws/props (it) up*
o° ðe wise° ðat he mai bet,°   *in/way/best*
and hileð° it wel ðat he it nes° war°   *conceals/is not/aware (of)*
145 ðanne he makeð ðer-to char,°   *resort*
him seluen° sit olon, bihalt,°   *he/alone, looks*

---

115. *mandragores:* The mandrake (*Mandragora officinarum*), found in Southern Europe and Africa, has a forked root, making it resemble a human being. Its shape undoubtedly fostered the belief that the plant had unusual powers, specifically that eating it was an aid to conception (cf. John Donne, *Song:* "Go and catch a falling star,/Get with child a mandrake root").

weðer° his gin° him out biwalt.°　　*whether/trap/deceives*
Ðanne cumeð° ðis elp° unride,　　*then comes/elephant*
and leneð him up on his side,
slepeð° bi ðe tre in ðe sadue,°　　*sleeps/shadow*
and fallen boden° so to-gaddre;°　　*fall both/together*
gef° ðer is noman° ðanne° he falleð,　　*if/no one/when*
he remeð° and helpe calleð,　　*cries out*
remeð reufulike on° his wise,°　　*pitifully in/manner*
155　hopeð he sal ðurg° helpe risen;°　　*through/rise*
ðanne cumeð ðer on gangande,°　　*one going*
hopeð he sal him don ut standen,°　　*make up stand*
Fikeð° and fondeð al° his migt,°　　*is busy/tries (with) all/might*
ne mai he it forðen° no wigt;°　　*accomplish/way*
160　Ne canne ðan non oðer,°　　*can (he do) then no other (thing)*
oc° remeð mid° his broðer,　　*but/with*
manie° and mikle° cume ðer sacande,°　　*many/great/shaking*
wenen° him on stalle° maken,°　　*hope/(back) in place/to put*
oc for ðe helpe of hem° alle　　*them*
165　ne mai he cumen° so on stalle;　　*come*
ðanne remen he° alle a rem,°　　*cry they/cry*
so° hornes blast oðer° belles drem,°　　*as/or/sound*
For here° mikle reming°　　*their/crying*
rennande° cumeð a gungling,°　　*running/youngling*
170　raðe° to him luteð,°　　*quickly/approaches*
his snute° him under puteð,°　　*snout/puts*
and mitte° helpe of hem alle　　*with*
ðis elp he reisen° on stalle;　　*raises*
and tus atbrested° ðis huntes breid,°　　*thus escaped/hunter's trap*
175　oðe° wise ðat ic° haue gu° seid.°　　*in the/I/to you/said*

Significacio

Ðus fel adam ðurg° a tre,°　　*because of/tree*
vre° firste fader,° ðat fele° we:　　*our/father/feel*
Moses wulde° him reisen,°　　*Moses wanted/to raise*
migte° it no wigt forðen;°　　*might/accomplish*
180　After him prophetes alle
migte her non° him maken on stalle,　　*here none*
on stalle, i seie, ðer° he er stod,°　　*say, where/formerly stood*
to hauen heuenriche god.°　　*have heavenly wealth*
He suggeden° and sorgeden° and weren° in ðogt,°　　*sighed/sorrowed/were/thought*
185　wu° he migten° him helpen° ovt;　　*how/might/help*
ðo remeden° he alle onder° steuene°　　*then cried/in one/voice*
alle hege° up to ðe heuene,°　　*high/heaven*
for here care and here calling

hem cam to° crist heuen° king;   *to them came/heaven's*
¹⁹⁰ he ðe° is ai° in heuene mikel,   *that/is ever*
wurð° her man, and tus was litel,°   *became/small*
drowing ðolede° in ure manhede,°   *suffering endured/manhood*
and tus adam he under-gede,°   *supported*
reisede° him up, and al mankin,°   *raised/mankind*
¹⁹⁵ ðat was fallen to helle dim.

---

192. *in ure manhede:* i.e., "as a man like us."

THE FOX AND THE WOLF

DATE: ? a. 1300. ✤ MANUSCRIPT: Bodleian Library, Oxford, Digby 86. The dialect is mainly Southern, with West Midland scribal intrusions. The MS. was written at the priory of Worcestershire; it also contains the fabliau *Dame Siriþ*. ✤ EDITION: George H. McKnight, *Middle English Humorous Tales in Verse* (Boston, 1913).

An understanding of the dialect and spelling peculiarities will aid in translation: (1) *i-* is a prefix in the past participle but also elsewhere, as in *I-siist* "do you see"; (2) *u* remains from OE *y* and is interchanged with *i* (*putte = pit*, *kunne = kin*); (3) *f* is often voiced to *v* (*vox = fox*); also *w* is sometimes used for *v* (*wous = vous = fus*, "eager," *wox = fox, wroggen*, "frogs"); (4) *h* often appears before initial vowels; (5) *o* is exchanged with *a* before nasals (*lond, honde, shome*); negative contractions are very frequent (*nis*, "is not," *not*, "know not").

This episode of the beast epic follows Branch IV of the French *Roman de Renart*. In that version Reynard, seeing his own reflection in the well, thinks it is his wife Hermeline and calls to her. An echo answers. After a second call, he jumps into a bucket and descends too rapidly for his own peace of mind. Ysengrim comes along and, seeing his own reflection in the water next to Reynard, thinks it is his wife Hersent and abuses Reynard. The fox then paints the joys of paradise and, after having the wolf confess his sins, allows him to descend as he rises. The next morning the monks beat the wolf. German and Flemish versions of the tale are also found, with variations; Goethe refers to the episode in his *Reineke Fuchs*; Caxton's *Reynard the Fox* is a translation from the Flemish. But the motif of the reflection in the well, the search for paradise under water, is a universal one found in Oriental and European folktale.

A vox gon° out of þe wode° go,	*fox did/woods*
Afingret° so, þat him wes wo;°	*hungry/was woe*
He nes° neuere° in none wise°	*was not/never/no way*
Afingret erour° half so swiþe.°	*before/much*
5 He ne° hoeld° nouþer wey ne strete,°	*not/went by/neither path nor street*
For him° wes loþ° men to mete;°	*he/loath/meet*
Him were leuere meten° one hen,	*would rather meet*
Þen° haf anoundred° wimmen.°	*than/a hundred/women*
He strok° swiþe ouer-al,°	*struck out/widely everywhere*
10 So þat° he ofsei ane° wal;	*until/observed a*
Wiþinne þe walle wes on° hous,	*a*
The wox° wes þider swiþe wous;°	*fox/there very eager*

For he þohute° his hounger aquenche,°	*thought/hunger (to) quench*
Oþer mid mete, oþer° mid drunche.°	*either with food, or/drink*
15 Abouten° he biheld wel ȝerne;°	*around/looked very eagerly*
Þo eroust bigon° þe vox to erne.°	*then first began/run*
Al fort° he come° to one° walle,	*until/came/a*
And som þer-of wes afalle,°	*fallen down*
And wes þe wal ouer-al to-broke,°	*broken*
20 And on ȝat° þer wes I-loke;°	*gate/locked*
At þe furmeste bruche° þat he fond,°	*first break/found*
He lep° in, and ouer he wond.°	*leaped/went*
Þo° he wes inne, smere° he lou,°	*when/scornfully/laughed*
And þer-of he hadde gome I-nou;°	*game enough*
25 For he com in wiþ-outen leue°	*without leave*
Boþen° of haiward° and of reue.°	*both/hayward/reeve*
On hous þer wes, þe dore wes ope,°	*open*
Hennen weren° þerinne I-crope,°	*hens were/crept*
Fiue, þat makeþ anne flok,°	*a flock*
30 And mid hem° sat on kok.°	*them/cock*
Þe kok him wes flowen° on hey,°	*flown/high*
And two hennen him seten ney.°	*sat near*
"Wox," quod° þe kok, "wat dest° þou þare?°	*said/do/there*
Go hom,° crist þe ȝeue kare!°	*home/you give care*
35 Houre° hennen þou dest ofte shome."°	*our/shame*
"Be stille, ich hote, a° Godes nome!"°	*I command, in/name*
Quaþ° þe wox, "Sire chauntecler,	*said*
Þou fle adoun,° and com me ner.°	*fly down/near*
I nabbe° don her nout bote goed,°	*have not/ done here nothing but good*
40 I have leten° þine hennen blod;°	*let/hens' blood*
Hy weren seke ounder° þe ribe,°	*they were sick under/rib*
Þat° hy ne miȝtte non lengour libe°	*so that/might no longer live*
Bote here heddre° were I-take;°	*unless their veins/opened*
Þat I do for almes° sake.	*charity's*
45 Ich haue hem° letten eddre° blod,	*for them/veins'*
And þe, chauntecler, hit wolde don° goed.	*it would do*

---

16. *erne:* = *run.* An example of the common metathesis of *r* (English *burn* = German *brennen*).

26. *haiward:* The hayward was a hedge ward, or guardian of enclosed fields. He is mentioned in the Middle English lyric *The Man in the Moon* as a minor police official and is found occasionally in some New England states today. *reue:* The shire reeve was the sheriff (cf. Chaucer's Reeve in the General Prologue of the *Canterbury Tales*).

31. There must be some lines omitted before this one, since the fox seems to have eaten some of the hens (cf. also ll. 40, 54–55, etc.).

37. *chauntecler:* the name of the cock in Chaucer's *Nun's Priest's Tale.*

40. The fox refers of course to medical bloodletting, an example of his wit compared to the wolf's later stupidity.

Þou hauest þat ilke° ounder þe splen,°   *same (problem)/spleen*
Þou nestes° neuere daies° ten;   *will nest/never days*
For þine lif-dayes° beþ° al ago,°   *life days/are/gone*
50 Bote þou bi mine rede° do;   *advice*
I do þe lete° blod ounder þe brest,   *for you let*
Oþer sone axe° after þe prest."°   *soon ask/priest*
"Go wei,"° quod þe kok, "wo° þe bi-go!°   *away/woe/take*
Þou hauest don oure kunne° wo.   *kin*
55 Go mid þan þat° þou hauest nouþe;°   *with that which/now*
Acoursed° be þou of° Godes mouþe!   *cursed/by*
For were I adoun bi Godes nome
Ich miȝte ben siker° of oþre shome!   *be sure*
Ac° weste° hit houre cellerer,°   *but if/knew/cellarer*
60 Þat þou were I-comen° her,   *come*
He wolde sone° after þe ȝonge,°   *at once/go*
Mid pikes and stones and staues stronge;
Alle þine bones he wolde to-breke;°   *break*
Þene° we weren° wel awreke."°   *then/would be/avenged*

65 He wes° stille, ne spak° namore,°   *was/nor spoke/no more*
Ac° he werþ aþurst° wel sore;°   *but/became thirsty/very greatly*
Þe þurst him dede° more wo,   *did*
Þen heuede raþer° his hounger do.°   *than had before/hunger done*
Ouer-al° he ede° and sohvte;°   *everywhere/went/searched*
70 On auenture° his wiit° him brohute,°   *by chance/wits/brought*
To one putte wes° water inne   *a well (where) was*
Þat wes I-maked° mid grete ginne.°   *made/great contrivance*
Tuo boketes° þer he founde,   *two buckets*
Þat oþer wende° to þe grounde,°   *both went/bottom*
75 Þat wen me shulde þat on° opwinde,°   *when one should the one/wind up*
Þat oþer wolde adoun winde.
He ne hounderstod° nout of þe ginne,   *not understood*
He nom° þat boket, and lep° þerinne;   *took/leaped*
For he hopede I-nou° to drinke.   *enough*
80 Þis boket biginneþ to sinke;
To° late þe vox° wes biþout,°   *too/fox/reflecting*
Þo° he wes in þe ginne I-brout.°   *when/brought*
I-nou° he gon° him bi-þenche,°   *(i.e., much)/did/think*

---

47. According to medieval medical theory, the spleen was the seat of negative passions: anger and spite. The fox not only shows off his knowledge but uses it for an ironic thrust.

56. *of Godes mouþe:* a typical oath on part of Christ's body (cf.

above, p. 472, l. 596*n*).

73–76. The contrivance seems to have interested all medieval writers of this tale, perhaps because of its novelty.

Ac hit ne halp° mid none wrenche;°   *helped/no trick*
85 Adoun° he moste,° he wes þerinne;   *down/must (go)*
    I-kaut° he wes mid swikele ginne.°   *caught/deceitful trap*
    Hit miȝte han iben° wel his wille   *it might have been*
    To lete þat boket hongi° stille.   *hang*
    Wat° mid serewe° and mid drede,°   *what/sorrow/fear*
90 Al his þurst him ouer-hede.°   *passed by*
    Al þus he com° to þe grounde,   *came*
    And water I-nou þer he founde.
    Þo he fond° water, ȝerne° he dronk,°   *found/eagerly/drank*
    Him þoute° þat water þere stonk,°   *he thought/stank*
95 For hit wes to-ȝeines° his wille.   *against*
    "Wo° worþe,"° quaþ° þe vox, "lust° and wille,°   *woe/(let) become/said/pleasure/*
                                                         desire

    Þat° ne can meþ to° his mete!°   *(for him) that/knows moderation*
                                                         in/food

    Ȝef ich° neuede° to muchel I-ete,°   *if I/had not/much eaten*
    Þis ilke shome° neddi° nouþe;°   *same shame/I would not have had/*
                                                         now

100 Nedde lust I-ben° of mine mouþe.   *had I not had a craving*
    Him is wo in euche londe,°   *every land*
    Þat is þef mid° his honde.°   *thief with/hand*
    Ich am I-kaut mid swikele ginne,
    Oþer soum deuel° me broute her-inne.°   *or some devil/brought herein*
105 I was woned° to ben wiis,°   *wont/be wise*
    Ac nou° of me I-don hit hiis."°   *but now/I am done for*

    Þe vox wep,° and reuliche° bigan.   *wept/piteously*
    Þer com a wolf gon° after þan°   *walking by/that*
    Out of þe depe wode bliue,°   *deep woods quickly*
110 For he wes afingret° swiþe.°   *was hungry/very*
    Noþing he ne founde in al þe niȝte,°   *night*
    Wer-mide° his honger aquenche miȝtte.°   *wherewith/hunger quench (he)*
                                                         might

    He com to þe putte, þene° vox I-herde;°   *well, the/heard*
    He him kneu° wel bi his rerde,°   *knew/speech*
115 For hit wes his neiȝebore,°   *neighbor*
    And his gossip,° of children bore.°   *chum/from childhood*
    A-doun bi þe putte he sat.

---

93. *ȝerne he dronk:* Was a negative left out here?

96–97. "Let pleasure and desire be turned to woe for the man who cannot moderate his desire for food." Such moralistic or gnomic expressions are frequently found in folk and popular literature (cf. also ll. 101–2).

116. *gossip:* The original meaning of this word was one who sponsored another at baptism, a godparent. It soon took on connotations of friendship, as well as of motherly old women and thence of their common occupation.

Quod° þe wolf, "Wat may ben þat   *said*
Þat ich in þe putte I-here?°   *hear*
¹²⁰ Hertou° cristine,° oþer mi fere?°   *are you|(a) Christian (i.e., man)|*
                                        companion

Say° me soþ, ne gabbe° þou me° nout,°   *tell|truth, nor lie|to me|not*
Wo° haueþ þe° in þe putte I-brout?"°   *who|you|put*
Þe vox hine I-kneu° wel for his kun,°   *fox him knew|kin*
And þo eroust kom wiit° to him;   *then first came (his) wits*
¹²⁵ For he þoute mid soumme ginne,°   *(a) certain trick*
Him-self houpbringe,° þene° wolf þerinne.   *(to) bring up|(and) the*
Quod þe vox, "Wo is nou þere?
Ich wene hit° is sigrim° þat ich here."°   *believe it|Ysengrim|hear*
"Þat is soþ," þe wolf sede,°   *said*
¹³⁰ "Ac wat° art þou, so God þe rede?"°   *what|counsel*

"A"° quod þe vox, "ich wille þe telle;   *ah*
On alpi° word ich lie nelle.°   *one single|will not*
Ich am reneuard,° þi frend,   *Reynard*
And ȝif° ich þine come heuede I-wend,°   *if|coming had known*
¹³⁵ Ich hedde° so I-bede for° þe,   *would have|asked of*
Þat þou sholdest comen° to me."   *should come*
"Mid þe?" quod þe wolf, "War° to?   *where*
Wat shulde ich ine° þe putte do?"   *should I in*
Quod þe vox, "Þou art ounwiis,°   *unwise*
¹⁴⁰ Her° is þe blisse of paradiis;   *here*
Her ich mai euere° wel fare,   *ever*
Wiþ-outen pine,° wiþouten kare;°   *without pain|care*
Her is mete,° her is drinke,   *food*
Her is blisse wiþouten swinke;°   *work*
¹⁴⁵ Her nis° hounger neuermo,°   *is not|hunger nevermore*
Ne non° oþer kunnes wo;°   *no|kind (of) woe*
Of alle gode° her is I-nou."°   *good|enough*
Mid þilke° wordes þe volf lou.°   *with these|wolf laughed*

"Art þou ded,° so God þe rede,   *dead*
¹⁵⁰ Oþer° of þe worldc?" þc wolf sede.   *or*
Quod þe wolf, "Wenne storue° þou,   *when died*

---

123. *hine:* the Old English. third personal pronoun, masculine accusative form. Old English inflections survived in the 13th century more prominently in the South than elsewhere.

128. *sigrim:* The shortened, colloquial English form of the name Ysengrim is evidence that the story circulated in popular literature (cf. *reneuard,* l. 133).

140–47. The description of paradise is shorter here than in other versions, but it is pictured as the typical land of milk and honey

150. Some lines of the fox's answer must have been lost at this point.

151. *storue:* In Old English the word *starve* meant "die" (cf. German *sterben*).

And wat dest° þou þere nou?   *do*
Ne beþ° nout ʒet þre daies ago,°   *not are/three days gone*
Þat þou and þi wif° also,   *wife*
155 And þine children, smale° and grete,°   *small/large*
Alle to-gedere° mid me hete."°   *together/ate*
"Þat is soþ," quod þe vox,
"Gode° þonk,° nou hit is þus,   *God/thank*
Þat ihc° am to criste vend.°   *I/gone*
160 Not° hit non° of mine frend.°   *know not/none/friends*
I nolde,° for al þe worldes goed,°   *would not/goods*
Ben° ine þe worlde, þer° ich hem fond.°   *be/where/them found*
Wat° shuldich° ine þe worlde go,   *why/should I*
Þer nis bote° kare and wo,   *(anything) but*
165 And liuie° in fulþe° and in sunne?°   *live/filth/sin*
Ac° her beþ ioies° fele cunne;°   *but/joys/of many kinds*
Her beþ boþe shep° and get."°   *sheep/goats*
Þe wolf haueþ° hounger swiþe gret,°   *has/very great*
For he nedde° ʒare° I-ete;°   *had not/for a long time/eaten*
170 And þo° he herde speken° of mete,   *when/heard spoken*
He wolde° bleþeliche° ben þare.°   *would/with pleasure/there*
"A!"° quod þe wolf, "gode I-fere,°   *ah/said/friend*
Moni goed mel° þou hauest me° binome;°   *many good meals/from me/taken*
Let me adoun° to þe kome.°   *down/you come*
175 And al ich wole° þe for-ʒeue."°   *will/forgive*
"ʒe,"° quod þe vox,° "were þou I-sriue,°   *yea/fox/shriven*
And sunnen heuedest° al forsake,°   *sin had/forsaken*
And to klene lif I-take,°   *clean life taken*
Ich° wolde so bidde° for þe,   *I/pray*
180 Þat þou sholdest comen° to me."   *should come*

"To wom° shuldich,"° þe wolfe seide,°   *whom/should I/said*
Ben I-knowe° of mine misdede?°   *confessed/misdeeds*
Her° nis noþing aliue,   *here*
Þat me kouþe° her nou sriue.°   *could/shrive*
185 Þou hauest ben° ofte min° I-fere,   *been/my*
Woltou° nou mi srift I-here,°   *will you/confession hear*
And al mi liif° I shal þe telle?"   *life*
"Nay," quod þe vox, "I nelle."°   *will not*
"Neltou,"° quod þe wolf, "þin ore,°   *will you not/(i.e., please) your mercy*
190 Ich am afingret° swiþe sore;°   *hungry/greatly*
Ich wot° to niʒt° ich worþe° ded,°   *think/tonight/will be/dead*
Bote° þou do° me somne reed.°   *unless/give/some advice*
For cristes loue be mi prest."°   *priest*
Þe wolf bey° adoun his brest,   *bowed*

¹⁹⁵ And gon° to siken° harde and stronge.   *began/sigh*
    "Woltou,"° quod þe vox, "srift ounderfonge,°   *(if) you will/receive*
    Tel þine sunnen on° and on,   *one*
    Þat° þer bileue° neuer on."   *so that/remains*

    "Sone,"° quod þe wolf, "wel I-faie,°   *at once/very gladly*
²⁰⁰ Ich habbe° ben qued° al mi lifdaie;°   *have/evil/the days of my life*
    Ich habbe widewene kors,°   *widows' curse*
    Þerfore ich fare þe wors.
    A þousent° shep ich habbe abiten,°   *thousand/bitten*
    And mo, ȝef hy weren I-writen.°   *more, if they were written (down)*
²⁰⁵ Ac hit° me of-þinkeþ° sore.   *of it/I repent*
    Maister,° shal I tellen° more?"   *master/say*
    "Ȝe," quod þe vox, "al þou most sugge,°   *must tell*
    Oþer elles-wer° þou most abugge."°   *or elsewhere/atone (for it)*
    "Gossip,"° quod þe wolf, "forȝef° hit me,   *chum/forgive*
²¹⁰ Ich habbe ofte sehid° qued bi° þe,   *said/of*
    Men seide þat þou on° þine liue°   *in/life*
    Misferdest mid° mine wiue;°   *sinned with/wife*
    Ich þe aperseiuede° one stounde,°   *observed/time*
    And in bedde togedere ou° founde.   *together you*
²¹⁵ Ich wes° ofte ou ful ney,°   *was/very near*
    And in bedde, to-gedere ou sey.°   *saw*
    Ich wende, al-so oþre doþ,°   *believe/as others do*
    Þat° ich I-seie° were soþ,°   *that what/saw/true*
    And þerfore þou were me° loþ;°   *to me/hateful*
²²⁰ Gode° gossip, ne° be þou nohut wroþ."°   *good/not/not angry*

    "Vuolf,"° quod° þe vox° him° þo,°   *wolf/said/fox/to him/then*
    "Al þat þou hauest her bifore I-do,°   *done*
    In þohut,° in speche,° and in dede,°   *thought/speech/deed*
    In euche oþeres kunnes quede,°   *every other kind (of) evil*
²²⁵ Ich þe forȝeue° at þisse nede."°   *I you forgive/need*
    "Crist þe forȝelde!"° þe wolf seide.°   *requite/said*
    "Nou ich am in clene° liue,   *clean*
    Ne recche° ich of° childe ne° of wiue.   *care/about/nor*
    Ac sei° me wat° I shal do,   *but tell/what*
²³⁰ And ou° ich may comen° þe to."   *how/come*

---

197. *on and on:* i.e., "every one."

198. At this point in the French version Ysengrim tells Reynard that he has already confessed to a rabbit and a goat (and eaten them after?). The wolf then turns his rear to the orient and produces musical sounds from one end and howls from the other. Thus he purges himself, asking remission of his sins.

201. *widewene kors:* i.e., for having eaten their husbands.

220. The wolf is rather cautious in confessing that he suspected his confessor of adultery. With paradise at stake, his prudence is justified.

"Do?" quod þe vox. "Ich wille þe lere.°   teach
I-siist° þou a boket hongi° þere?   see/bucket hanging
Þere is a bruche of heuene° blisse,   way to heaven's
Lep° þerinne, mid I-wisse,°   leap/certainly
235 And þou shalt comen to me sone."
Quod the wolf, "Þat is liȝt° to done."°   easy/do
He lep° in, and way sumdel;°   leaped/weighed somewhat
Þat weste° þe vox ful wel.   knew
Þe wolf gon° sinke, þe vox arise;   did
240 Þo gon° þe wolf sore° agrise.°   did/greatly/become alarmed
Þo° he com° amidde° þe putte,°   when/came/in the middle of/well
Þe wolfe þene° vox opward° mette.   the/upward
"Gossip," quod þe wolf, "Wat nou?
Wat hauest þou I-munt?° weder° wolt° þou?"   in mind/whither/want (to go)
245 "Weder Ich wille?"° þe vox sede.°   want (to go)/said
"Ich wille oup,° so God me rede!°   up/counsel
And nou go doun, wiþ° þi meel,°   to/meal
Þi biȝete° worþ° wel° smal.   spoils/will be/very
Ac ich am þerof glad and bliþe,°   happy
250 Þat þou art nomen° in clene liue.   taken
Þi soule-cnul° ich wille do ringe,°   soul knell/have rung
And masse for þine soule singe."°   sung
Þe wrecche bineþe° noþing ne vind,°   wretch beneath/found
Bote° cold water, and hounger° him bind;°   but/hunger/bound
255 To colde gistninge° he wes I-bede,°   feast/was bidden
Wroggen° haueþ his dou I-knede.°   frogs/dough kneaded

Þe wolf in þe putte stod,°   stayed
Afingret° so þat he ves wod.°   hungry/was mad
Inou° he cursede þat þider° him broute;°   much/him (that) there/had brought
260 Þe vox þer of luitel route.°   little cared
Þe put him° wes þe house ney,°   pit it/near
Þer freren woneden swiþe sley.°   where friars lived very quietly
Þo° þat hit° com to þe time,   when/it
Þat hoe shulden arisen Ine,°   they should arise inside
265 For to suggen here houssong,°   say their matins
O° frere þere wes among,   one
Of° here slep hem° shulde awecche,°   from/sleep them/awake
Wen° hoe shulden þidere recche.°   when/come
He seide,° "Ariseþ on° and on,   said/one

---

233. *bruche:* lit., "break," "opening."
237. *way sumdel:* ironic understatement.
242. *opward:* i.e., "on the way up."

246. *"Ich wille oup:* Cf. Mod. Eng. "I want out."
265. *houssong:* (OE *uhtsang,* "out song") matins or morning prayers, with lauds the first of the canonical hours.

²⁷⁰ And komeþ to houssong heuereuchon."°   *everyone*
Þis ilke° frere heyte° Ailmer;   *same/was called*
He wes hoere maister curtiler.°   *their master gardener*
He wes hofþurst° swiþe stronge;°   *athirst/greatly*
Riȝt° amidward° here houssonge   *right/in the midst of*
²⁷⁵ Al-hone° to þe putte he hede;°   *alone/went*
For he wende bete° his nede.°   *thought (to) remedy/need*
He com to þe putte, and drou,°   *drew*
And þe wolf wes heui° I-nou.°   *heavy/very*
Þe frere mid° al his maine tey°   *with/strength pulled*
²⁸⁰ So longe þat he þene wolf I-sey!°   *saw*
For he sei° þene wolf þer sitte,   *saw*
He gradde,° "Þe deuel° is in þe putte!"°   *cried/Devil/well*

To þe putte hy gounnen° gon,°   *began/to go*
Alle mid pikes and staues and ston,°   *stones*
²⁸⁵ Euch mon° mid þat° he hedde;°   *each man/what/had*
Wo° wes him þat wepne° nedde.°   *woe/weapons/had not*
Hy comen° to þe putte, þene° wolf opdrowe;°   *they came/the/drew up*
Þo hede° þe wreche fomen I-nowe,°   *then had/wretch foemen enough*
Þat weren egre° him to slete°   *were eager/bait*
²⁹⁰ Mid grete° houndes, and to bete.°   *great/beat*
Wel and wroþe° he wes I-swonge,°   *angrily/beaten*
Mid staues and speres° he wes I-stounge.°   *spears/pierced*
Þe wox bicharde° him, mid Iwisse,°   *fox beguiled/certainly*
For he ne fond nones kunnes° blisse,   *not found no kind (of)*
²⁹⁵ Ne hof duntes forȝeuenesse. explicit.   *nor of blows forgiveness*

---

272. *curtiler*: Robin Hood's Friar Tuck was a curtil friar. The *OED* defines this under *curtal* as "a friar with a short coat," but Francis Child (in *English and Scottish Popular Ballads*) took him to be the gardener of his house. The peaceful occupation seems to have hidden aggressive traits among these religious men (cf. Wrath in *Piers Plowman*, a former gardener in a convent).

295. *explicit*: Latin, short for *Explicitus est liber*, "The book is unrolled," or, as a verb in the 3d person sing., "here ends." The word is usually used to signal the end of a literary work.

THE DEBATE

Literary argument is a medieval phenomenon, though its origins may lie in the *Eclogues* of Virgil with the verbal repartee between shepherds. The debate is a game of wit, and the subject is less important than the manner in which it is discussed. In the eighth century Alcuin composed his *Conflictus Veris et Hiemis* (*The Strife between Spring and Winter*), but one of the most widespread themes concerned the dialogue between Body and Soul. At first only the Soul spoke, as in the Old English version, with the Body keeping silent. In the Middle English *Disputisoun between the Body and the Soul* (c. 1400), the Body replies, rationalizing its sins and blaming the Soul. The most famous of the secular debates is, of course, *The Owl and the Nightingale*, which influenced the less important *Thrush and Nightingale* (c. 1300).

The *tensouns* of the twelfth-century Provençal troubadours initiated the caustic, satiric tensions which are the inherent quality of many debates. Everything was ground for argument: hand versus eye, heart versus mind, true love versus fickleness. The style ranged from high and solemn to low and cantankerous. Judgments were sometimes rendered, but the main pleasure lay in portraying a vigorous intellectual strife. The quarrel between Owl and Nightingale seriously questions the thesis about sticks and stones and that "names will never hurt you."

REFERENCES

Baugh, Nita Scudder, ed. *A Worcestershire Miscellany, compiled by John Northwood, c. 1400, from B.M.MS. Add. 37, 787*. Philadelphia, 1956. (Prints the text of *The Debate of the Body and Soul*).

Dudley, Louise. *The Egyptian Elements in the Legend of the Body and Soul*. Baltimore, 1911.

Grattan, J. H. G., and Sykes, G. F. H., eds. *The Owl and the Nightingale*. Early English Text Society, ES 119. London, 1935.

Hanford, J. H. "Classical Eclogue and Mediaeval Debate." *Romanic Review*, 2 (1911), 16–31, 129–143.

Huganir, K. *The Owl and the Nightingale: Sources, date, author*. Philadelphia, 1931.

Walther, Hans. *Das Streitgedicht in der lateinischen Literatur des Mittelalters*. Munich, 1926.

The debate is treated in the General Introduction of this volume, pp. 9–10.

THE OWL AND THE NIGHTINGALE

DATE: a. 1200. ✦ MANUSCRIPT: British Library Cotton Caligula A. ix (c. 1250); Jesus College, Oxford, E 29. The dialect of the Caligula MS. is Southwest, although the original language is believed to be Southeast, perhaps that of Guildford itself. ✦ EDITIONS: J. W. Atkins, *The Owl and the Nightingale* (Cambridge, 1922); W. Gadow, *Das mittelenglische Streitgedicht Eule und Nachtigall* (Berlin, 1909); J. H. G. Grattan and G. F. H. Sykes, *The Owl and the Nightingale*, Early English Text Society, ES 119 (London, 1935); Eric Gerald Stanley, *The Owl and the Nightingale*, Nelson's Medieval and Renaissance Library (London, 1960). Valuable also is Bertil Sundby, *The Dialect and the Provenance of the Middle English Poem "The Owl and the Nightingale": A Linguistic Study*, Lund Studies in English, 18 (Lund, Sweden, 1950).

Specific characteristics of the Southern dialect should be noted: (1) *v* is very often exchanged with *f* (*vor = for, vrom = from*); (2) *h* often appears before vowels (*hule*, "owl"); (3) *t* and *d* often replace each other; (4) inflectional *þ, ð* also appear frequently as *t, d* (*quad, segget, haved*); (5) metathesis of *r* is common (*wercche = wrecche, worþ = wroþ*); (6) paragogic (inorganically added) *e* occurs between certain consonants (*narewe = narwe, harem = harm*). A knowledge of pronoun forms will greatly facilitate translation: e.g., *ich*, "I"; *hine*, "him"; *heo, ho,* "she"; *unker,* "our"; *hi, heo,* "they"; *hore, here,* "their"; *hom, heom,* "them." In syntax the verb often precedes the subject.

The Owl and the Nightingale, composed some time after the death of Henry II (1189), was probably written by a judge, Nicholas of Guildford, in parody of his more serious daily work. The French octosyllabic couplet (iambic tetrameter, also known as romance meter) is here used for the first time. As the first and most amusing example of the debate poem in English, it mixes the legal procedure of medieval pleading with the colloquial style of Chaucer. The poem presents a veritable casebook of medieval legal procedure. Today lawsuits may be won or lost through mistakes in pleading, and the situation was no different in the common law of 13th-century England—in fact, it was more complex. Mistakes in pleading are mentioned in ll. 675 and 677. One of the legal tricks or *plaites wrenche* (l. 472) was to anger the opponent into making a mistake (stultiloquium). The Owl tries this (l. 933), but the Nightingale is not caught (l. 951) and controls herself (l. 952). The Nightingale feels that the Owl commits a stultiloquium at the end, when she seems to brag about her own disgrace (ll. 640–52). This argument of cantankerous birds marks one of the high points of wit, dialogue, and slander in Middle English literature.

Ich° was in one sumere° dale, — *I/a summer*
in one suþe diȝele hale;° — *very hidden corner*
iherde° ich holde grete tale° — *heard/great argument*
an hule° and one niȝtingale.° — *owl/nightingale*
5 Þat plait° was stif° and starc° and strong, — *strife/vigorous/hard*
sum wile° softe and lud among;° — *sometimes/loud occasionally*
and eiþer aȝen oþer sval° — *toward (the) other swelled*
and let þat uvole mod ut° al; — *evil mood out*
and eiþer seide° of oþeres custe° — *said/nature (i.e., character)*
10 Þat alre° worste þat hi wuste° — *the/of all/they knew*
and hure and hure° of oþeres songe. — *especially*
Hi holde plaiding° suþe stronge. — *held strife*

Þe niȝtingale bigon° þe speche° — *began/speech*
in one hurne° of one breche,° — *corner/fallow field*
15 and sat up one vaire boȝe,° — *upon a fair bough*
þar° were abute blosme inoȝe,° — *where/(all) about blossoms many*
in ore waste° þicke hegge° — *on a lonely/hedge*
imeind mid spire° and grene segge.° — *mingled with shoots/sedge*
Ho° was þe gladur° vor° þe rise° — *she/gladder/because of/bough*
20 and song a vele cunne wise.° — *sang in many kinds (of) ways*
Bet þuȝte° þe drem° þat he° were — *better seemed/sound/it*
of harpe and pipe, þan he nere;° — *were not*
bet þuȝte þat he were ishote° — *issued*
of° harpe and pipe þan of þrote.° — *from/throat*
25 Þo stod on° old stoc þar° bi side,° — *there stood an/stump there/beside*
þar þo ule° song hire tide,° — *the owl/her hours*
and was mid ivi al bigrowe,° — *overgrown*
hit° was þare hule° eardingstowe.° — *it/the owl's/dwelling*
  Þe niȝtingale hi iseȝ° — *her saw*
30 and hi bihold° and overseȝ,° — *beheld/despised*
and þuȝte wel vul° of þare hule, — *thought very badly*
for me° hi halt lodlich° and fule.° — *men/considered loathly/foul*
"Unwiȝt,"° ho sede,° "awei þu flo!"° — *monster/said/away you fly*
Me is° þe wurs° þat ich þe so.° — *I am/worse/you see*
35 Iwis° for þine vule lete° — *indeed/foul voice*
wel oft ich mine song forlete.° — *interrupted*
Min horte atfliþ° and falt° mi tonge,° — *my heart sinks/falters/tongue*

1–28. The beginning shows a typical example of Middle English reverdie, the traditional return-of-spring theme found in the Prologue to Chaucer's *Canterbury Tales* and many English lyrics.

wonne° þu art to me iþrunge.°   *when/approached*
Me luste bet° speten þane° singe   *I would rather/spit than*
40 of þine fule ȝoȝelinge."°   *howling*

Þos° hule abod fort° hit was eve,   *this/waited until*
ho ne miȝte° no leng bileve:°   *not might/longer stop*
vor° hire horte was so gret°   *for/full*
þat° wel neȝ° hire fnast° atschet,°   *that (it)/nigh/breath/shot out*
45 and warp° a word þarafter° longe: *uttered/thereafter*
"Hu° þincþe° nu bi° mine songe?   *how/think you/now of*
Wenst° þu þat ich° ne cunne° singe,   *think/I/know how to*
þeȝ° ich ne cunne° of writelinge?°   *though/nothing know/trilling*
Ilome° þu dest° me grame°   *often/do/wrong*
50 and seist° me° boþe tone° and schame.   *say/to me/insult*
Ȝif° ich þe holde on° mine vote°—   *if/held in/foot (i.e., claw)*
so hit bitide° þat ich mote!°—   *happen/might*
and þu were ut° of þine rise,   *out*
þu sholdest° singe an oþer wise."°   *should/way*

55   Þe niȝtingale ȝaf answare:°   *nightingale gave answer*
"Ȝif ich me loki wit° þe bare°   *myself guard against/exposure*
and me schilde° wit þe blete,°   *shield/bareness*
ne reche° ich noȝt of° þine þrete;°   *care/nothing for/threats*
ȝif ich me holde° in mine hegge,°   *keep/hedge*
60 ne recche° ich never what þu segge.°   *care/say*
Ich wot° þat þu art unmilde°   *know/cruel*
wiþ hom° þat ne muȝe° from þe schilde;°   *them/may not/shield (themselves)*
and þu tukest wroþe° and uvele,°   *torture cruelly/evilly*
whar° þu miȝt over smale fuȝele.°   *where (i.e., when)/small birds*
65 Vorþi° þu art loþ° al fuelkunne,°   *therefore/hated by/birdkind*
and alle ho° þe driveþ honne°   *they/hence*
and þe bischricheþ° and bigredet°   *screech at/chide*
and wel narewe° þe biledet;°   *closely/pursue*
and ek forþe° þe sulve mose°   *also therefore/titmouse itself*
70 hire þonkes wolde° þe totose.°   *willingly would/tear apart*
Þu° art lodlich to biholde   *you*
and þu art loþ° in monie volde;°   *horrible/many ways*
þi bodi is short, þi swore° is smal,   *neck*
grettere° is þin heved° þan þu al;°   *greater/your head/the rest of you*
75 þin eȝen° boþ colblake° and brode,°   *eyes/coal black/big*
riȝt° swo° ho weren ipeint mid wode;°   *just/as if/were painted with woad*

---

41. Since both birds are nocturnal creatures, the dispute takes place at night.

56. *ȝif:* i.e., "as long as."

76. *wode:* a plant of the mustard family, the leaves of which were used for blue dye.

þu starest so° þu wille abiten°   *as if/bite*
al þat þu miȝt mid clivre smiten.°   *talons strike*
Þi bile° is stif° and scharp and hoked,°   *beak/strong/hooked*
80 riȝt so° an owel° þat is croked;°   *like/awl/crooked*
þarmid° þu clackest oft and longe,   *therewith*
and þat is on° of þine songe.°   *one/songs*
Ac° þu þretest to° mine fleshe,   *but/threaten*
mid þine clivres woldest me meshe;°   *mash*
85 þe were icundur to° one° frogge,   *for you (it) would be more natural*
                                                           (to eat)/a

þat sit at mulne° under cogge;°   *mill/cogwheel*
snailes, mus,° and fule wiȝte°   *mice/foul animals*
boþ° þine cunde° and þine riȝte.°   *are/nature/right*
Þu sittest adai° and fliȝst aniȝt,°   *by day/fly/by night*
90 þu cuþest° þat þu art in unwiȝt.°   *show/a monster*
Þu art lodlich° and unclene,°   *loathly/unclean*
bi° þine neste ich hit mene°   *concerning/I it mean*
and ek bi þine fule brode,°   *brood*
þu fedest on° hom a wel ful fode.°   *feed/very foul food*
95 Vel° wostu° þat hi doþ þarinne,°   *well/you know/what they do therein*
hi fuleþ° hit up to þe chinne,   *befoul*
ho sitteþ þar,° so hi bo bisne;°   *there/be blind*
þarbi° men segget° a vorbisne:°   *by that/say/proverb*
'Dahet habbe° þat ilke best°   *cursed be/same beast*
100 þat fuleþ his owe° nest.'   *own*
Þat oþer ȝer° a faukun° bredde,   *the past year/falcon*
his nest noȝt° wel he ne bihedde;°   *not/not guarded*
þarto° þu stelc in o° dai   *to it/stole on a*
and leidest þaron° þi fole ey.°   *laid therein/foul egg*
105 Þo° hit bicom° þat he haȝte°   *then/happened/hatched*
and of his eyre briddes° wraȝte,°   *eggs nestlings/brought forth*
he broȝte° his briddes mete,°   *brought/food*
bihold° his nest, iseȝ hi ete;°   *beheld/saw them eat*
he iseȝ bi° one halve°   *on/side*
110 his nest ifuled uthalve.°   *befouled outside*
Þe faucun was wroþ° wit his bridde°   *angry/nestlings*
and lude ȝal° and sterne chidde:°   *loudly screamed/sternly chided*
'Segget° me, wo havet° þis ido,°   *tell/who has/done*
ou nas never icunde þarto;°   *it was never natural for you*
115 hit was idon° ou° a loþe custe,°   *done/to you/(in) a loathly manner*
segge° me ȝif ȝe° hit wiste!'°   *tell/if you/know*

101–38. The fables of Marie de France contain a parallel to   the moral being the same as in this poem.
this story. owl and hawk breed their young ones in common,

þo quaþ° þat on and quad° þat oþer: *said/said*
'Iwis° hit was ure oȝe° broþer,   *indeed/our own*
þe ȝond° þat haved° þat grete heved;°   *that one/has/great head*
120 wai° þat he nis° þarof° bireved!°   *woe/is not/of it/deprived*
Worp° hit ut mid° þe alre° worste,   *throw/out with/of all*
þat° his necke him toberste.'°   *so that/he breaks*
Þe faucun ilefde° his bridde   *believed*
and nom° þat fule brid° amidde°   *took/bird/from their midst*
125 and warp° hit of þan° wilde bowe,°   *threw/from the/branch*
þar pie° and crowe hit todrowe.°   *where magpie/pulled apart*
Herbi° men segget a bispel,°   *hereby/example*
þeȝ° hit ne bo fuliche spel:°   *though/complete tale*
Also° hit is bi þan ungode,°   *just so/low-class creature*
130 þat is icumen° of fule° brode   *come/foul*
and is meind wit fro monne,°   *mingled with noble men*
ever he cuþ° he com þonne,°   *makes known/comes thence*
þat he com of þan adeleye,°   *addled egg*
þeȝ he a° fro neste leie.°   *in a/was laid*
135 Þeȝ appel trendli° from þon trowe,°   *falls/the tree*
þar he and oþer mide growe,°   *others together grew*
þeȝ he bo þarfrom bicume,°   *be therefrom taken*
he cuþ wel whonene° he is icume.'   *whence*

Þos° word aȝaf° þe niȝtingale,°   *this/gave/nightingale*
140 and after þare° longe tale   *the*
heo song° so lude and so scharpe,°   *she sang/sharply*
riȝt so me° grulde° schille° harpe.   *just as men/let sound/shrill*
Þos hule luste° þiderward°   *owl listened/to this*
and hold hire eȝe noþerward,°   *held her eyes down*
145 and sat tosvolle° and ibolwe°   *swollen/blown up*
also° ho° hadde one° frogge isvolȝe.°   *as if/she/a/swallowed*
For ho wel wiste and was iwar°   *aware*
þat ho song hire a bisemar;°   *mocking song*
and noþeles° ho ȝaf andsvare:°   *nevertheless/gave answer*
150 "Whi neltu° flon° into þe bare°   *will you not/fly/open*
and sewi hweþer° unker° bo   *show which/of us two*
of briȝter howe,° of vairur blo?"°   *brighter hue/fairer color*
"No! þu° havest wel° scharpe clawe;   *you/very*
ne° kepe ich noȝt° þat þu me clawe.   *not/care I not*

---

131. *fro:* perhaps used here as "generous" or "liberal," normally in medieval literature a sign of gentility and nobility.

132. *þonne:* i.e., from a different background.

135–38. Many of the proverbs mentioned in the poem are biblical; for this one, cf. Luke 6:44, Matt. 7:16.

155 Þu havest clivers suþe° stronge,   talons very
    þu tvengst þarmid° so doþ° a tonge.   pinch therewith/does
    Þu þo3test,° so doþ þine ilike,°   thought/like
    mid faire worde me biswike.°   to deceive
    Ich nolde° don þat° þu me raddest,°   would not/do what/advised
160 ich wiste° wel þat þu me misraddest.   know
    Schamie þe° for þin° unrede!°   shame (on) you/your/bad advice
    Unwro3en° is þi svikelhede.°   revealed/deception
    Schild° þine svikeldom vram° þe li3te°   guard/treachery from/light
    and hud° þat wo3e° among þe ri3te!°   hide/evil/righteous
165 Wane° þu wilt þin unri3t spene,°   when/evil do
    loke° þat hit° ne bo isene;°   look/it/seen
    vor svikedom haved schome° and hete,°   for wickedness has shame/hate
    3if° hit is ope° and under3ete.°   if/open/noticed
    Ne speddestu° no3t mid° þine unwrenche,°   you will succeed/with/sins
170 for ich am war° and can wel blenche.°   cautious/avoid (you)
    Ne helpþ° no3t þat þu bo to þriste,°   (it) helps/too bold
    Ich wolde vi3te bet° mid liste°   would fight better/trick
    þan þu mid al þine strengþe.
    Ich habbe on brede° and ek° on lengþe   have in breadth/also
175 castel god° on mine rise:°   good/branches
    Wel fi3t° þat wel fli3t,° sciþ° þc wisc.   fights/escapes/say
    Ac lete° we awei° þos cheste,°   but put/away/quarrel
    vor sviche° wordes boþ unwerste,°   such/are bad
    and fo we on° mid ri3te dome,°   let us start/right judgment
180 mid faire worde and mid ysome.°   friendly
    Þe3° we ne bo° at one acorde,   though/be
    we mu3e° bet mid fayre worde,   might
    witute° cheste and bute° fi3te,   without/without
    plaidi° mid fo3e° and mid ri3te;   plead/moderation
185 and mai ure eiþer, wat° he wile,°   we either (one), what/will
    mid ri3te segge° and mid sckile.""°   say/reason

        Þo quaþ° þe hule:° "Wu° schal us seme,°   then said/owl/who/reconcile
        þat kunne° and wille ri3t us deme?""°   can/judge
        "Ich wot° wel," quaþ þe ni3tingale,°   know/nightingale
190   "ne þarf þarof° bo no tale:°   need thereof/argument
        Maister Nichole° of Guldeforde,°   Master Nicholas/Guildford
        he is wis° and war of worde,   wise
        he is of dome suþe gleu,°   intelligent

---

191. Nicholas of Guildford, exceedingly praised, was very
possibly the author of the poem (cf. below, ll. 1751–78).

and him° is loþ evrich unþeu.°	*to him/hateful every vice*
195 He wot insiȝt in eche° songe,	*has understanding of each*
wo singet° wel, wo singet wronge,	*who sings*
and he can schede vrom° þe riȝte	*distinguish from*
þat° woȝe, þat þuster° from þe liȝte."	*the/darkness*
Þo° hule one wile° hi biþoȝte°	*the/some while/considered*
200 and after þan° þis word up broȝte:°	*that/brought*
"Ich granti° wel þat he us deme;	*I agree*
vor þeȝ he were wile° breme,°	*in the past/wild*
and lof° him were niȝtingale	*dear*
and oþer wiȝte gente° and smale,°	*creatures delicate/small*
205 ich wot, he is nu suþe acoled;°	*now very cooled*
nis° he vor þe° noȝt afoled,°	*is not/therefore/not fooled*
þat he for þine olde love	
me adun legge° and þe buve;°	*down put/you above*
ne° schaltu° nevre° so him queme,°	*not/shall you/never/please*
210 þat he for þe fals dom deme.°	*false judgment gives*
He is nu ripe° and fastrede,°	*mature/wise in counsel*
ne lust him° nu to none unrede;°	*desires he/no foolishness*
nu him ne lust namore° pleie,°	*no more/play*
he wile gon° a riȝte weie."°	*go/way*
215 Þe niȝtingale was al ȝare,°	*prepared*
ho° hadde ilorned wel aiware:°	*she/learned much everywhere*
"Hule," ho sede,° "seie° me soþ!°	*said/tell/truth*
Wi° dostu° þat unwiȝtis doþ?°	*why/do you/what monsters do*
Þu° singist aniȝt° and noȝt adai,°	*you/by night/by day*
220 and al þi song is wai la wai.°	*alas*
Þu miȝt mid° þine songe afere°	*might with/frighten*
alle þat ihereþ° þine ibere.°	*hear/cry*
Þu schirchest° and ȝollest° to þine fere,°	*screech/yell/mate*
þat° hit° is grislich° to ihere;	*so that/it/grisly*
225 hit þincheþ° boþe wise and snepe,°	*think/stupid*
noȝt þat þu singe, ac° þat þu wepe.°	*but/weep*
Þu fliȝst° aniȝt and noȝt adai,	*fly*
þarof° ich wundri,° and wel mai;	*at that/wonder*
vor° evrich þing þat schuniet riȝt,°	*for/shuns right*
230 hit luveþ° þuster and hatiet liȝt,°	*loves/hates light*
and evrich þing þat is lof° misdede,°	*loves/misdeeds*
hit luveþ þuster to° his dede.°	*for/deeds*
A wis° word, þeȝ° hit bo unclene,°	*wise/though/be unclean*
is fele manne a muþe imene,°	*(to) many men in mouth common*

235 for Alvred° king hit seide° and wrot:°
'He schunet° þat hine vul wot.'°

Ich wene° þat þu dost also,°
vor þu fliȝst niȝtes° ever mo.°
An oþer þing me° is a wene:°
240 Þu havest aniȝt wel briȝte sene.°
Bi daie° þu art stareblind,°
þat þu ne sichst ne boȝ ne strind;°
adai þu art blind oþer bisne,°
þarbi° men segget° a vorbisne:°
245 Riȝt° so hit farþ bi þan° ungode,°
þat noȝt° ne suþ° to none gode°
and is so ful of uvele wrenche,°
þat him ne mai no man atprenche,°
and can° wel þane þurste° wai
250 and þane briȝte lat awai.°
So doþ þat boþ° of þine cunde,°
of liȝte nabbeþ° hi° none imunde.''°

Þos hule luste suþe° longe
and was oftoned° suþe stronge;
255 ho quaþ:° ''Þu hattest° niȝtingale,°
þu miȝtest bet° hoten° galegale,°
vor þu havest to monie tale.°
Lat° þine tunge habbe spale!°
Þu⁰ wenest þat þes⁰ dai bo þin oȝe,⁰
260 lat me nu° habbe mine þroȝe!°
Bo nu stille and lat me speke,°
ich° wille bon° of þe awreke,°
and lust° hu° ich con me bitelle°
mid riȝte soþe, witute spelle.°

265 Þu seist þat ich me hude° adai;°
þarto ne segge° ich ne nai;
and lust, ich telle þe warevore,°
al wi hit° is and warevore.

alfred/said/wrote
shrinks (from others)/himself (to be) foul knows
believe/do likewise
by night/more
to me/in thought
very bright sight
day/stone-blind
see neither bough nor stream
or dim
by that/say/example
just/goes with the/bad one
nothing/sees/no good
evil trick
overcome
knows/the dark
lets go
(they) that are/kind
have not/they/mind

this owl listened very
enraged
said/are called/nightingale
might better/be called/chatterer
too many arguments
let/tongue have rest
you/this/is your own
now/turn
speak
I/be/you avenged
listen (to)/how/can myself defend
with straight truth, without digression

hide/by day
thereto not say
wherefore
why it

---

235. Only three of the many proverbs ascribed by the poet to Alfred are actually found in the *Proverbs of Alfred*. This work seems to have been originally assembled in Sussex in the 12th century, and Alfred's reputation for wisdom fostered it, although he himself was certainly not responsible for its contents. Written in Old English alliterative verse, the *Proverbs* offer advice on public and personal conduct and give parental counsel. The various traditional sayings, of which there are 35 in the fullest form of the work, were widely disseminated, passed on in oral tradition.

	Ich habbe bile stif° and stronge	beak hard
270	and gode clivers° scharp and longe,	talons
	so° hit bicumeþ to° havekes cunne;°	as/befits/hawks' nature
	hit is min hiȝte,° hit is mi wune;°	my pleasure/joy
	þat ich me draȝe° to mine cunde,	draw
	ne mai no man þarevore schende.°	therefore scold (me)
275	On° me hit is wel isene,°	in/seen
	vor° riȝte cunde° ich am so kene.°	because of/true nature/bold
	Vorþi° ich am loþ smale foȝele,°	therefore/hateful (to) small birds
	þat floþ bi grunde° and bi þuvele;°	fly near (the) ground/bush
	hi me° bichermet° and bigredeþ°	at me/screech/cry
280	and hore° flockes to° me ledeþ.°	their/at/rush
	Me is lof° to habbe reste	I would rather
	and sitte stille in mine neste;	
	vor° nere° ich never no° þe betere,°	for/would not be/none/better
	ȝif° ich mid chavling° and mid chatere°	if/chiding/chatter
285	hom° schende and mid fule° worde,	them/foul
	so herdes doþ, oþer° mid schitworde.°	shepherds do, or/dirty language
	Ne lust me wit° þe screwen chide;°	desire I with/shrews (to) chide
	forþi° ich wende° from hom wide.°	therefore/go/far
	Hit is a wise monne dome,°	man's judgment
290	and hi hit segget wel ilome,°	say very often
	þat me ne° chide wit þe gidie,°	one (should) not/stupid
	ne wit þan ofne° me ne ȝonie.°	nor against the oven/yawn
	At sume° siþe herde° i telle,	a certain/time heard
	hu Alvred sede° on his spelle:°	Alfred said/speech
295	'Loke þat þu ne bo þare,°	look/be there
	þar° chavling boþ° and cheste ȝare,°	where/is/strife eager
	lat sottes° chide and vorþ° þu go;	fools/forth
	and ich am wis° and do also.'	wise
	And ȝet Alvred seide° an oþer side°	said/time
300	a word þat is isprunge° wide:	traveled
	'þat° wiþ þe fule haveþ imene,°	(he) that/keeps company
	ne cumeþ° he never from him clene.'°	comes/clean
	Wenestu° þat haveck bo° þe worse,	think you/hawk is
	þoȝ° crowe bigrede° him bi° þe mershe,°	though/scolds/in/marsh
305	and goþ° to him mid hore chirme,°	goes/her noise
	riȝt° so° hi° wille wit him schirme?°	just/as if/she/fight
	þe havec folȝeþ gode rede°	follows good counsel
	and fliȝt his wei° and lat° hi grede.°	flies (on) his way/lets/her cry
	Ȝet þu° me seist° of oþer þinge,	you/tell
310	and telst þat ich ne° can noȝt° singe,	I not/not

---

271. The Owl compliments herself by comparing herself to a hawk.

ac° al mi rorde° is woning° *but/voice/lamenting*
and to ihire grislich° þing. *hear (a) horrible*
Þat nis° noȝt soþ;° ich singe efne° *is not/true/even*
mid° fulle dreme° and lude stefne.° *with/sound/loud voice*
315 Þu wenist° þat ech° song bo grislich, *think/every*
þat þine pipinge nis ilich.° *like*
Mi stefne is bold and noȝt unorne,° *weak*
ho° is ilich one grete° horne, *it/a great*
and þin° is ilich one pipe *yours*
320 of one smale wode° unripe. *small (piece of) wood*
Ich singe bet° þan þu dest;° *better/do*
þu chaterest so doþ on° irish prost.° *chatter as does an/priest*
Ich singe an eve a riȝte° time, *in evening at right*
and soþþe won hit° is bedtime, *then when it*
325 þe þridde° siþe ad middelniȝte;° *third/at midnight*
and so ich mine song adiȝte,° *make ready*
wone° ich iso° arise vorre° *when/see/from afar*
oþer dairim oþer° daisterre.° *either dawn or/morning star*
Ich do god° mid mine þrote° *good/throat*
330 and warni° men to hore note.° *warn/their needs*
Ac þu singest alle longe niȝt,° *night*
from eve fort° hit is dailiȝt,° *until/daylight*
and evre lesteþ þin o° song *ever lasts your one*
so longe so þe niȝt is long,
335 and evre croweþ þi wrecche crei,° *wretched crying*
þat° he° ne swikeþ° niȝt ne° dai. *so that/it/ceases/nor*
Mid þine pipinge þu adunest° *deafen*
þas monnes earen, þar° wunest,° *the man's ears, where/live*
and makest þine song so unwurþ,° *worthless*
340 þat me° ne telþ of þar° noȝt wurþ.° *people/count it of/no worth*
Evrich murȝþe° mai so longe ileste,° *every mirth/last*
þat° ho shal liki wel unwreste;° *until/please very ill*
vor° harpe and pipe and fuȝeles° song *for/birds'*
mislikeþ, ȝif° hit is to° long. *displeases, if/too*
345 Ne bo° þe song never so murie,° *be/merry*
þat he ne shal þinche° wel unmurie,° *seem/unpleasant*
ȝef° he ilesteþ over unwille;° *if/until disgust*
so þu miȝt° þine song aspille.° *might/waste*
Vor hit is soþ, Alvred° hit seide° *Alfred/said*

---

322. Two reasons may be given for this sarcastic remark. (1) The Church of Ireland was for centuries a major proselyting force in Europe, and its clergy supplied the early monastic learning in England and Scotland. A certain religious zeal on the part of the Irish may have caused a reaction in England. (2) From 1171 the English campaigned in Ireland and attempted to subject the land (Henry II [d. 1189] was called Lord of Ireland). This poem, therefore, falls into the period of the Irish wars, the beginning of antipathy between the two countries.

350 and me° hit mai ine boke rede:° — *one/in book read*
'Evrich þing mai losen his godhede° — *lose its goodness*
mid unmeþe° and mid overdede.'° — *excess/overdoing*
Mid este þu þe° miȝt overquatie,° — *pleasure you yourself/satiate*
and overfulle° makeþ wlatie;° — *surfeit/(one) feel disgust*
355 and evrich mureȝþe° mai agon,° — *mirth/pass*
ȝif me hit° halt° evre forþ in on,° — *to it/hold/the same*
bute° one, þat is Godes riche,° — *except/realm*
þat evre is svete° and evre iliche;° — *sweet/the same*
þeȝ° þu nime° evere of þan lepe,° — *though/take/from the basket*
360 hit is evre ful bi hepe.° — *heaped up*
Wunder° hit is of Godes riche, — *wonderful*
þat evre spenþ° and ever is iliche. — *spends*

    Ȝut° þu me° seist on° oþer shome,° — *yet/of me/an/shame*
þat ich° am on° mine eȝen lome,° — *I/in/eyes lame*
365 and seist, for þat° ich flo° bi niȝte, — *because/fly*
þat ich ne° mai iso bi liȝte.° — *not/light*
Þu liest! On me hit° is isene° — *it/seen*
þat ich habbe gode sene;° — *have good sight*
vor nis° non° so dim þusternesse,° — *is not/none/darkness*
370 þat ich ever iso° þe lasse.° — *see/less*
Þu wenest° þat ich ne miȝte iso, — *think*
vor° ich bi daie° noȝt° ne flo. — *because/day/not at all*
Þe hare luteþ° alle dai, — *hides*
ac noþeles° iso he mai. — *but nevertheless*
375 Ȝif hundes urneþ° to him ward,° — *hounds run/toward him*
he gengþ° wel sviþe° awai wart° — *goes/quickly/up and away*
and hokeþ° paþes sviþe narewe° — *runs through/paths very narrow*
and haveþ mid° him his blenches ȝarewe° — *has with/tricks prepared*
and huppþ° and stard suþe cove° — *hops/jumps very fast*
380 and secheþ° paþes to þe grove. — *seeks*
Ne sholde° he vor boþe his eȝe° — *should/eyes*
so don,° ȝif he þe bet° niseȝe.° — *do/better/not saw*
Ich mai ison so° wel so on° harc, — *see as/a*
þeȝ ich bi daie sitte and dare.° — *hide*
385 Þar aȝte° men boþ° in worre° — *where brave/are/war*
and fareþ boþe ner° and forre° — *near/far*
and overvareþ° fele þode° — *pass through/many lands*
and doþ° bi niȝte gode node,° — *do/night good service*
ich folȝi° þan aȝte manne° — *follow/men*
390 and flo bi niȝte in hore banne."° — *their troop*

    Þe niȝtingale° in hire þoȝte° — *nightingale/her thought*
athold° al þis and longe þoȝte, — *considered*

wat ho þarafter miȝte segge;°   *what she thereafter might say*
vor° ho ne miȝte noȝt alegge°   *for/not rebut*
395 þat° þe hule° hadde hire° ised,°   *what/owl/to her/said*
vor ho spac° boþe riȝt° and red.°   *spoke/right/wisdom*
And hire ofþuȝte° þat ho hadde   *she was grieved*
þe speche° so for vorþ iladde,°   *speech/far on carried*
and was oferd° þat hire answare°   *afraid/answer*
400 ne wurþe° noȝt ariȝt ifare.°   *would/right come*
Ac° noþeles he° spac boldeliche,°   *but/she/boldly*
vor he is wis° þat hardeliche°   *wise/bravely*
wiþ° his vo berþ grete ilete,°   *against/foe bears firm countenance*
þat° he vor areȝþe° hit ne forlete;°   *so that/fear/give up*
405 vor svich worþ° bold, ȝif þu fliȝst,°   *such (men) grow/if you flee*
þat wile flo,° ȝif þu vicst;°   *will fly/fight*
ȝif he isiþ° þat þu nart° areȝ,°   *sees/are not/afraid*
he wile of bore wurchen° bareȝ.°   *from boar make (himself)/*
                                     castrated hog

And forþi, þeȝ° þe niȝtingale   *therefore, though*
410 were aferd,° ho spac bolde tale.   *afraid*

    "Hule," ho seide,° "wi° dostu° so?   *said/why/do you*
Þu singest a° winter wo la wo;°   *in/alas*
Þu singest so doþ° hen a snowe,   *does*
al þat ho singcþ, hit° is for wowe.°   *it/woe*
415 A wintere þu singest wroþe° and ȝomere°   *angry/sad*
and evre° þu art dumb a sumere.°   *ever/summer*
Hit is for þine fule niþe,°   *foul envy*
þat þu ne° miȝt mid°'us bo bliþe;°   *not/with/be happy*
vor þu forbernest° wel neȝ° for onde,°   *burn up/nigh/hate*
420 wane ure° blisse cumeþ° to londe.°   *when our/comes/land*
Þu farest° so doþ þe ille,°   *behave/sick (man) (or evil [man])*
evrich° blisse him° is unwille;°   *every/to him/disgust*
grucching° and luring° him boþ rade,°   *grumbling/lowering/ready*
ȝif he isoþ° þat men boþ glade;°   *sees/glad*
425 he wolde° þat he iseȝe°   *would/saw*
tercs° in evrich monncs cȝc;°   *tears/man's eye*
ne roȝte° he, þeȝ flockes were   *cares*
imeind bi toppes° and bi here.°   *mixed with threads/hair*
Also° þu dost° on þire° side;   *so/do/your*
430 vor wanne snov liþ° þicke and wide,°   *when snow lies/far*

427–28. "Nor would he care if flocks [i.e., coarse stuff made of
refuse of wool] were mixed up with fine carded wool or hair."

and alle wiȝtes habbeþ sorȝe,°   creatures have sorrow
þu singest from eve fort a° morȝe.°   until/morning
Ac ich° alle blisse mid me bringe,   I
ech° wiȝt is glad for° mine þinge°   every/on/account
435 and blisseþ hit,° wanne ich cume,   rejoices
and hiȝteþ aȝen° mine cume.°   looks forward to/coming
þe blostme° ginneþ° springe and sprede°   blossoms/begin to/spread
boþe ine tro° and ek° on mede,°   in tree/also/meadow
þe lilie mid hire° faire wlite°   her/aspect
440 wolcumeþ° me, þat þu hit wite,°   welcomes/know
bid° me mid hire faire blo°   asks/hue
þat ich shulle° to hire flo.   shall
þe rose also mid hire rude,°   ruddy color
þat cumeþ ut° of þe þorne wode,°   out/wood
445 bit° me þat ich shulle singe   begs
vor° hire luve one° skentinge.°   for/love a/song of joy
And ich so do þurȝ niȝt° and dai,   through night
þe more ich singe, þe more i mai,
and skente hi° mid mine songe,   please them
450 ac noþeles noȝt° overlonge;   but nevertheless not
wane ich iso° þat men boþ° glade,   see/are
ich nelle° þat hi bon to sade;°   will not/they be too surfeited
wan° is ido° vor wan° ich com,   when/done/what
ich fare aȝen° and do wisdom.   go again
455 Wane mon hoȝeþ of° his sheve,°   man worries about/sheaves
and falewi° cumeþ on grene leve,°   yellow/leaves
ich fare hom° and nime leve,°   home/take leave
ne recche° ich noȝt of° winteres reve.°   nor care/about/destruction
Wan ich iso þat cumeþ þat harde,°   hardship
460 ich fare hom to mine erde°   dwelling
and habbe boþe luve and þonc,°   thanks
þat ich her com° and hider swonk.°   here came/here endeavored
Wan min erende° is ido,   my mission
sholde° ich bileve?° Nai, warto?°   should/remain/for what
465 Vor he nis° noþer ȝeþ° ne wis,°   is not/neither clever/wise
þat longe abid, þar° him° nod° nis."   remains, where/for him/need

  Þos hule luste° and leide an hord°   this owl listened/stored up
al þis mot,° word after word,   speech
and after þoȝte, hu° he miȝte°   thought, how/might
470 ansvere vinde° best mid riȝte;°   answer find/with right
vor he mot hine ful° wel biþenche,°   must himself very/bethink
þat is aferd° of plaites wrenche.°   afraid/dispute's tricks

     "Þu aishest° me," þe hule sede,°   *you ask/said*
     "wi ich a° winter singe and grede.°   *why I in/cry*
475 Hit° is gode monne iwone°   *it/good man's custom*
     and was from þe worlde frome,°   *world's beginning*
     þat ech god° man his frond icnowe°   *each good/friend know*
     and blisse° mid hom sume þrowe°   *rejoice/them some time*
     in his huse,° at his borde,°   *house/table*
480 mid faire speche° and faire worde.   *speech*
     And hure and hure° to° cristes masse,°   *especially/at/Christmas*
     wane° riche and povre,° more and lasse,°   *when/poor/less*
     singeþ cundut° niȝt and dai,   *carols*
     ich hom helpe what° ich mai.   *as*
485 And ek° ich þenche° of oþer þinge°   *also/think/things*
     þane° to pleien oþer° to singe.   *than/play or*
     Ich habbe° herto° gode ansvare°   *have/for this/answer*
     anon iredi° and al ȝare;°   *quickly ready/prepared*
     vor sumeres tidc° is al to wlonc°   *for summer's time/too splendid*
490 and doþ misreken° monnes þonk;°   *does mislead/thought*
     vor he ne recþ noȝt of clennesse,°   *not cares nothing for purity*
     al his þoȝt is of golnesse;°   *lustfulness*
     vor none dor° no leng° nabideþ,°   *no animal/longer/waits not*
     ac evrich° upon oþer rideþ.   *but each*
495 Þe sulve stottes ine° þe stode°   *very steeds in/stud*
     boþ° boþe wilde and merewode;°   *are/mare-mad*
     and þu sulf° art þaramong,°   *yourself/among them*
     for of golnesse is al þi song;
     and aȝen þet° þu wilt teme,°   *at that (time)/breed*
500 þu art wel modi° and wel breme.°   *very brave/wild*
     Sone° so° þu havest itrede,°   *as soon/as/generated*
     ne miȝtu° leng a word iqueþe,°   *might you/speak*
     ac pipest, also° doþ a mose,°   *as/mouse*
     mid chokeringe,° mid stevne hose.°   *quavering/voice hoarse*
505 Ȝet þu singst worse þon° þe heisugge,° *than/hedge sparrow*
     þat fliȝþ bi grundc° among þc stubbc;° *flies near (the) ground/stumps*
     wane þi lust° is ago,°   *desire/past*

473–542. The Owl often seems to be driven into a corner. Her arguments are more tendentious than those of the Nightingale. Others, however, disagree with this, e.g., Douglas L. Peterson ("The *Owl and Nightingale* and Christian Dialectic" [*JEGP*, 55 (1956), 13–26]), who argues that the Owl is on very sound ground throughout and that the Nightingale's arguments are sophistical.

482. *more and lasse:* i.e., "high and low."

504. There is an interesting analogy to this hoarse voice of the Nightingale during the mating season in the Old English elegiac poem the *Seafarer;* "Swylce geac monaþ geomran reorde,/singeþ sumeres weard, sorge beodeþ" ("Also the cuckoo calls with a sad voice,/the guardian of summer sings, announces sorrow"). Evidently many birds were thought to lose their voice in passion when breeding in the spring.

þanne° is þi song ago also.	then
A sumere chorles° awedeþ°	in summer rustics/go mad
510 and vorcrempeþ° and vorbredeþ;°	writhe/are transformed
hit nis° for luve noþeles,°	is not/love nonetheless
ac is þe chorles wode res;°	mad desire
vor wane he haveþ ido° his dede,°	has done/deed
ifallen° is al his boldhede;°	fallen off/boldness
515 habbe he° istunge° under gore,°	if he has/stung/skirt
ne last° his luve no leng more.	lasts
Also° hit° is on° þine mode;°	just so/it/in/temperament
so sone° so þu° sittest a brode,°	soon/you/on brood
þu forlost° al þine wise.°	lose/melody
520 Also þu farest° on þine rise;°	behave/branch
wane þu havest ido þi gome,°	same
þi stevne goþ° anon to shome.°	goes/shame
Ac wane niȝtes cumeþ° longe	nights come
and bringeþ forstes starke° and stronge,	frosts fierce
525 þanne erest° hit is isene,°	only/seen
war° is þe snelle,° war is þe kene:°	where/bold/keen
at þan harde me° mai avinde,°	in that hardship one/find
wo geþ° forþ, wo liþ° bihinde.	who goes/lies
Me° mai ison° at þare° node,°	men/see/the/time of need
530 wan° me shal harde wike bode,°	when/duties command
þanne ich° am snel and pleie° and singe	I/play
and hiȝte° me mid° mi skentinge.°	delight/with/entertainment
Of none° wintere ich ne recche,°	about no/not worry
vor° ich nam° aswunde wrecche.°	for/am not/no faint wretch
535 And ek° ich frovri vele wiȝte,°	also/console many people
þat mid hom° nabbeþ° none miȝtte;°	amongst themselves/have not/power
hi boþ° hoȝfule° and vel arme°	they are/care ridden/very wretched
and secheþ ȝorne° to þe warme;°	seek eagerly/warmth
oft ich singe vor hom° þe more,	them
540 for lutli sum° of hore sore.°	to lessen somewhat/their sorrow
Hu þincþ þe,° artu° ȝut inume?°	how think you/are you/yet caught
	(i.e., refuted)
Artu mid riȝte overcume?"°	overcome
"Nay, nay," sede° þe niȝtingale,°	said/nightingale
"þu shalt ihere° an oþer tale.	hear
545 Ȝet nis þos speche ibroȝte° to dome;°	this speech brought/judgment
ac bo wel° stille and lust nu° to me!	but be very/listen now
Ich shal mid one bare worde	
do þat° þi speche wurþ° forworþe."°	so that/will be made/worthless
"Þat nere° noht riȝt,"° þe hule° sede,	would not be/not right/owl

⁵⁵⁰ "þu havest bicloped, also° þu bede,°   accused, as/asked
    and ich þe habbe iȝive ansvare.°   have given answer
    Ac ar° we to unker° dome fare,°   before/our/go
    ich wille speke toward° þe,   speak against
    also þu° speke toward me;   you
⁵⁵⁵ and þu me ansvare, ȝif° þu miȝt!°   if/might
    Seie° me nu, þu wrecche wiȝt,°   tell/wretched creature
    is in þe eni° oþer note,°   any/use
    bute° þu havest schille þrote?°   except/shrill throat
    Þu° nart noȝt to° non oþer þinge,   you/are not/not (of use) for
⁵⁶⁰ bute þu canst° of chateringe;°   know/chattering
    vor þu art lutel° and unstrong,°   little/weak
    and nis° þi reȝel° noþing° long.   is not/dress/not at all
    Wat° dostu° godes° among monne?°   what/do you/good/men
    Namo° þe deþ° a wercche wranne.°   no more/than does/wretched wren
⁵⁶⁵ Of° þe ne cumeþ° non oþer god,°   from/comes/good
    bute þu gredest,° svich° þu bo wod;°   cry/as if/are crazy
    and bo þi piping° overgo,°   if your piping is/passed over
    ne boþ on° þe craftes° namo.   is in/ability
    Alvred° sede, þat was wis,°   Alfred/wise
⁵⁷⁰ he miȝte wel, for soþ hit° is: truth it
    'Nis no man for his bare° songe   mere
    lof ne wurþ° noȝt suþe° longe,   dear nor worthwhile/very
    vor þat is a forworþe man,
    þat bute singe noȝt ne° can.'   nothing not
⁵⁷⁵ Þu nart bute on° forworþe þing,   but a
    on þe nis° bute chatering.   is not (anything)
    Þu art dim° and of fule howe°   dark/foul hue
    and þinchest° a lutel soti clowe.°   seem/sooty ball
    Þu nart fair, no° þu nart strong,   nor
⁵⁸⁰ ne þu nart þicke, ne þu nart long;
    þu havest imist° al of fairhede,°   missed/beauty
    and lutel is al þi godhede.°   goodness
    An oþer þing of þe ich mene,°   you I mean
    þu nart vair° ne þu nart clene.°   fair/clean
⁵⁸⁵ Wane° þu comest to manne haȝe,°   when/men's enclosures

550–51. According to Gadow, the Nightingale has finished her accusation (ll. 215–52, 411–66), and the Owl has answered (ll. 255–390, 473–542). By the rules, the action is now complete and judgment could be rendered. But the use of the *exceptio* ("objection") allowed the Nightingale to continue. The Owl, too, makes use of the exceptio and attacks (ll. 556–668, 837–932), forcing the Nightingale onto the defensive (ll. 707–836, 955–1042). The exceptio demanded loose arguments ad hominem, in which all stops were pulled and anything was used. These are the most amusing parts of the poem, of course. The Owl starts (ll. 1045–66), is thrown back by the Nightingale (ll. 1075–1174), and replies (ll. 1177–1290). The Nightingale rebuts an Owlish statement (ll. 1039–54) with a retort (ll. 1298–1510) on illicit love which is answered by the Owl (ll. 1515–1602). A mistake in pleading (cf. above, p. 556) causes the Nightingale to claim victory (ll. 1640–52).

585. *haȝe:* lit., "hedges."

þar° þornes boþ° and ris° idraȝe,° *where/are/twigs/drawn together*
bi hegge° and bi þicke wode,°   *in hedges/wood*
þar men goþ° oft to hore node,°   *go/to (do) their business*
þarto° þu draȝst,° þarto þu wunest,°   *there/are drawn/dwell*
590 and oþer clene stede° þu schunest.°   *place/shun*
Wan° ich flo° niȝtes° after muse,°   *when/fly/by night/mice*
i mai þe vinde° ate° rumhus;°   *find/at the/latrine*
among þe wode, among þe netle,°   *nettles*
þu° sittest and singst bihinde þe setle;°   *you/toilet seat*
595 þar me° mai þe ilomest° finde,   *there men/most often*
þar men worpeþ° hore bihinde.   *thrust out*
Ȝet þu atvitest° me mine mete°   *blame/(for) my food*
and seist° þat ich fule wiȝtes ete;°   *say/creatures eat*
ac° wat etestu,° þat° þu ne liȝe,°   *but/eat you/if/lie*
600 bute attercoppe° and fule vliȝe,°   *spiders/flies*
and wormes, ȝif° þu miȝte° finde   *if/might*
among þe volde° of harde rinde?   *cracks*
Ȝet ich can do wel gode wike,°   *very good service*
vor° ich can loki° manne wike;°   *for/guard/dwellings*
605 and mine wike boþ wel gode,
for ich helpe to° manne vode.°   *with/food*
Ich can nimen° mus at berne°   *capture/in barn*
and ek° at chirche ine° þe derne:°   *also/church in/dark*
vor me is lof to° Cristes huse,°   *to me is dear/house*
610 to clansi hit wiþ° fule muse: *cleanse it of*
ne schal þar nevre° come to   *never*
ful° wiȝt, ȝif ich hit mai ivo.°   *foul/capture*
And ȝif me lust one° mi skentinge°   *I wish in/pleasure*
to wernen° oþer wunienge,°   *avoid/dwelling*
615 ich habbe at wude tron° wel grete,°   *have in (the) forest (a) tree/great*
mit° þicke boȝe noþing blete,°   *with/boughs not bare*
mid° ivi grene al bigrowe,°   *with/overgrown*
þat evre stont° iliche° iblowe,°   *ever stands/the same/in bloom*
and his hou° never ne vorlost,°   *its color/not lost*
620 wan hit snivþ ne° wan hit frost.   *snows nor*
Þarin° ich habbe god ihold,°   *therein/good refuge*
a° winter warm, a sumere° cold;   *in/summer*
wane min° hus stont briȝt° and grene,   *my/bright*
of þine nis° noþing isene.°   *is not/seen*
625 Ȝet þu me telst of oþer þinge,
of mine briddes° seist gabbinge,°   *nestlings/lies*
þat hore nest nis noȝt clene.°   *not clean*

---

592. *rumhouse:* lit., "room house," a privy.

Hit is fale° oþer wiȝte imene;° *(to) many/common*
vor hors a stable and oxe a stalle
630 doþ al° þat hom° wule° þar falle;° *do all (their business)/from them/ will/drop*

and lutle° children in þe cradele,° *little/cradle*
boþe chorles° and ek aþele,° *common people/nobles*
doþ al þat in hore ȝoeþe,° *their youth*
þat hi vorleteþ° in hore duȝeþe.° *they stop/adulthood*
635 Wat!° can þat ȝongling° hit bihede?° *what/youngster/prevent*
Ȝif hit misdeþ,° hit mod° nede.° *does wrong/must/of necessity*
A vorbisne° is of olde ivurne,° *proverb/times past*
þat node° makeþ old wif urne.° *need/woman run*
And ȝet ich° habbe an oþer andsware:° *I/answer*
640 wiltu° to mine neste vare° *will you/go*
and loki, hu° hit is idiȝt?° *look, how/arranged*
Ȝif þu° art wis, lorni° þu miȝt.° *if you/wise, learn/might*
Mi nest is holȝ° and rum° amidde,° *hollow/room/in the middle*
so hit is softest mine° bridde; *(for) my*
645 hit is broiden° al abute,° *braided/about*
vrom° þe neste° vor wiþute;° *from/nearest (i.e., innermost)/ to the outside*

þarto° hi god° to hore node, *thereto/go*
ac þat° þu menest° ich hom forbode.° *but what/complain (of)/them forbid*
We nimeþ ȝeme° of manne bure° *take note/men's chamber*
650 and after þan° we makeþ ure;° *it/our (own)*
men habbet° among oþer iwende° *have/inventions*
a rumhus° at hore bures ende, *latrine*
vor þat° hi nelleþ° to vor go;° *because/want not/too far (to) go*
and mine briddes doþ also.° *just so*
655 Site nu° stille, chaterestre,° *sit now/chatterer*
nere° þu never ibunde° vastre;° *were not/bound/more tightly*
herto° ne vindestu° never andsware. *for this/you will find*
Hong° up þin° ax, nu þu miȝt° fare!°'' *hang/your/may/go away*

Þe niȝtingale° at þisse worde *nightingale*
660 was wel neȝ ut^ of rede iworþe,^ *nigh out/counsel made*
and þoȝte ȝorne on hire mode,° *thought earnestly in her mind*
ȝif ho oȝt elles understode,° *she anything else understood*
ȝif ho kuþe° oȝt bute° singe, *could (do)/but*
þat miȝte helpe to° oþer þinge.° *for/anything else*

---

638. An old French proverb, "Besoing fait vieille troter," may be interpreted in several ways, depending on the definition of *need*.

647. The Owl means that her nestlings excrete not in the nest but on the twig wall surrounding the hollow middle.

660. *ut . . . iworþe:* i.e., "stumped."

⁶⁶⁵ Herto ho moste° andswere vinde°   *had to/answer find*
oþer mid° alle bon° bihinde;   *or with/be*
and hit° is suþe strong° to fiȝte°   *it/very hard/fight*
aȝen soþ° and aȝen riȝte.°   *against truth/right*
He mot gon° to al° mid ginne,°   *must go/ahead/trickery*
⁶⁷⁰ wan° þe horte boþ° on winne;°   *when/heart (i.e., mind) is/strife*
and þe man mot on oþer° segge,°   *differently/speak*
he mot bihemmen° and bilegge,°   *(it) trim up/gloss over*
ȝif muþ wiþute° mai biwro,°   *mouth outside/hide*
þat° me° þe horte noȝt° niso.°   *so that/men/not/see not*
⁶⁷⁵ And sone° mai a word misreke,°   *quickly/go wrong*
þar° muþ shal aȝen horte speke;°   *where/speak*
and sone mai a word misstorte,°   *start wrong*
þar muþ shal speken° aȝen horte.   *speak*
Ac noþeles ȝut upe þon!°   *nonetheless yet up then*
⁶⁸⁰ Her° is to red, wo hine kon;°   *here/counsel, who it knows*
vor° never nis° wit so kene,°   *for/is not/sharp*
so wane° red him° is a wene;°   *as when/to him/in doubt*
þanne erest kumed° his ȝephede,°   *then only comes/cleverness*
wone° hit is alre° mest° on drede.°   *when/of all/most/doubt*
⁶⁸⁵ For Alvered° seide of old quide,°   *Alfred/proverb*
and ȝut hit nis of° horte islide:°   *from/slipped*
'Wone þe bale° is alre hecst,°   *calamity/greatest*
þone° is þe bote° alre necst.'°   *then/remedy/nearest*
Vor wit west° among his sore°   *grows/its worries*
⁶⁹⁰ and for his sore hit is þe more;°   *greater*
vorþi° nis nevere mon° redles,°   *therefore/never man/lacking in counsel*

ar° his horte bo° witles.°   *before/is/without sense*
Ac ȝif° þat he forlost° his wit,   *but if/lost*
þonne° is his redpurs° al toslit;°   *then/purse of wisdom/cut to pieces*
⁶⁹⁵ ȝif he ne kon° his wit atholde,°   *not can/hold together*
ne vint° he red in one volde.°   *finds/a crack*
Vor Alvred seide, þat wel kuþe,°   *knew*
evre° he spac° mid soþe muþe:°   *ever/spoke/true mouth*
'Wone þe bale is alre hecst,
⁷⁰⁰ þanne is þe bote alre nest.'°   *nearest*

Þe niȝtingale° al hire hoȝe°   *nightingale/her care*
mid rede° hadde wel bitoȝe,°   *counsel/employed*
among þe harde, among þe toȝte,°   *tough (thoughts)*
ful° wel mid rede hire biþoȝte,°   *very/she reflected*
⁷⁰⁵ and hadde andsvere gode ifunde°   *answer good found*
among al hire harde stunde.°   *time*

"Hule, þu axest° me," ho° seide,   *owl, you ask/she*
"ʒif ich kon eni° oþer dede,°   *I can (do) any/deed*
bute singen° in sume tide°   *but sing/summer time*
710 and bringe blisse for° and wide.   *far*
Wi° axestu° of craftes° mine?   *why/ask you/skill*
Betere° is min on° þan alle þine,   *better/my (single) one*
betere is o° song of mine muþe,   *one*
þan al þat evre þi kun° kuþe.   *kin*
715 And lust!° ich telle þe warevore.°   *listen/you wherefore*
Wostu° to wan° man was ibore?°   *know you/what end/born*
To þare° blisse of hoveneriche,°   *the/heaven*
þar° ever is song and murʒþe° iliche;°   *where/joy/without change*
þider fundeþ evrich° man   *(to go) there strives every*
720 þat eni þing of gode kan.°   *knows*
Vorþi me singþ° in holi chirche,°   *men sing/church*
and clerkes ginneþ° songes wirche,°   *do/compose*
þat° man iþenche° bi þe songe,   *so that/thinks*
wider° he shal,° and þar bon° longe;   *whither/shall (go)/there be*
725 þat he þe murʒþe ne vorʒete,°   *forget*
ac þarof þenche° and biʒete,°   *thereof think/attain*
and nime ʒeme of° chirche stevene,°   *take note from/voice*
hu murie° is þe blisse of hovene.°   *how joyful/heaven*
Clerkes, munekes,° and kanunes,°   *monks/canons*
730 þar boþ þos° gode wicketunes,°   *are these/dwellings*
ariseþ up to midelniʒte˘   *at midnight*
and singeþ of þe hoveneliʒte;°   *heaven's light*
and prostes° upe londe° singeþ,   *priests/in the country*
wane° þe liʒt° of daie° springeþ.   *when/light/day*
735 And ich hom° helpe wat° i mai,   *them/as*
ich singe mid° hom niʒt° and dai,   *with/night*
and ho° boþ alle for me þe gladdere°   *they/happier*
and to þe songe boþ þe raddere.°   *more ready*
Ich warni° men to here° gode,   *remind/their*
740 þat hi° bon bliþe on hore mode,°   *they/happy in their spirit*
and bidde° þat hi moten iseche°   *ask/must seek*
þat ilke° song þat ever is eche.˘   *that same/eternal*
Nu° þu miʒt,° hule, sitte and clinge,°   *now/may/wither*
heramong° nis° no chateringe;°   *herein/is not/chattering*
745 ich graunti° þat we go to dome°   *consent/judgment*
tofore° þe sulfe° þe pope of Rome.   *before/himself*

---

733. *prostes upe londe:* The priests in the country were the secular clergy, the parish priests, as distinct from the regular clergy, who were bound by monastic vows.

746. After 1216, clergy were frequently called to Rome for the election of bishops.

Ac abid ȝete noþeles,°   *but wait yet nonetheless*
þu° shalt ihere° an oþer° þes;° *you/hear/another (thing about)/this*
ne° shaltu° for Engelonde° *not/shall you/(all of) England*
750 at° þisse worde me atstonde.° *in/oppose*
Wi° atvitestu° me mine unstrengþe,° *why/blame you/(for) my weakness*
and mine ungrete° and mine unlengþe,° *smallness/shortness*
and seist° þat ich° nam° noȝt° strong, *say/I/am not/not*
vor° ich nam noþer gret ne° long? *for/neither large nor*
755 Ac þu nost° never wat° þu menst,° *know not/what/mean*
bute lese° wordes þu me lenst;° *only useless/give*
for ich kan craft° and ich kan liste,° *skill/trick*
and þarevore° ich am þus þriste.° *therefore/bold*
Ich kan wit and song manieine,° *many a one*
760 ne triste° ich to non° oþer maine;° *trust/in no/strength*
vor soþ hit° is þat° seide Alvred:° *true it/what/Alfred*
'Ne mai° no strengþe aȝen red.'° *may (assert itself)/against wisdom*
Oft spet° wel a litte° liste, *succeeds/little*
þar° muche strengþe solde miste;° *where/must fail*
765 mid lutle° strengþe, þurȝ ginne,° *little/through trickery*
castel and burȝ me° mai iwinne;° *town one/conquer*
mid liste me mai walles felle° *tear down*
and worpe of° horsse kniȝtes snelle.° *throw off/knights bold*
Uvel° strengþe is lutel wurþ,° *evil/little worth*
770 ac wisdom ne wurþ° never unwurþ;° *becomes/worthless*
þu myht iseo þurh° alle þing,° *might see through/things*
þat wisdom naveþ° non evening.° *has not/equal*
An hors is strengur° þan a mon;° *stronger/man*
ac for° hit non iwit° ne kon,° *because/wisdom/has*
775 hit berþ° on rugge grete semes° *bears/back great loads*
and draȝþ° bivore° grete temes° *pulls/in front of/teams*
and þoleþ° boþe ȝerd° and spure° *suffers/stick/spur*
and stont iteid° at mulne dure,° *stands tied/mill door*
and hit deþ° þat mon hit hot:° *does/commands*
780 and for þan° þat hit no wit° not,° *because/intelligence/knows not*
ne mai his strenþe° hit ishilde° *strength/prevent*
þat hit nabuȝþ° þe lutle childe. *humbles not*
Mon deþ mid° strengþe and mid witte, *with*
þat° oþer þing° nis° non° his fitte.° *so that/creature/is not/none/equal*
785 Þeȝ alle strengþe at one° were, *though/together*
monnes° wit ȝet more° were,° *men's/greater/would be*
vor þe mon mid his crafte

---

776. Teams of horses were hitched one before the other; the reference here is to the lead horse.

overkumeþ° al orþliche shafte.° — *overcomes/earthly creatures*
Also° ich do mid mine one songe — *just so*
790 bet° þan þu° al þe зer° longe. — *better/you/year*
Vor mine crafte men me luvieþ,° — *love*
vor þine strengþe men þe shunieþ.° — *you shun*
Telstu° bi° me þe wurs° for þan — *say you/of/worse*
þat ich° bute anne° crafte ne kan?° — *I/one/not know*
795 Зif tveie° men goþ° to wraslinge° — *if two/go/wrestling*
and eiþer oþer faste þringe,° — *(the) other closely presses*
and þe on can swenges suþe fele° — *one knows holds very many*
and kan his wrenches° wel forhele,° — *tricks/disguise*
and þe oþer ne can sweng but anne,
800 and þe° is god wiþ eche° manne, — *that/good against every*
and mid þon° one leiþ° to grunde° — *that/throws/ground*
anne after oþer a° lutle stunde,° — *in a/time*
wat þarf° he recche of° a mo° swenge, — *what need/care about/greater*
wone° þe on him° is swo genge?° — *when/for him/so handy*
805 Þu seist° þat þu canst° fele wike,° — *say/can (do)/services*
ac° ever ich am þin° unilike.° — *but/to you/unlike*
Do° þine craftes° alle togadere,° — *put/skills/together*
зet is min° on horte° betere.° — *mine/radically/better*
Oft wan hundes° foxes driveþ, — *when hounds*
810 þe kat ful° wel him sulve° liveþ,° — *very/(in) himself/trusts*
þeз he ne kunne° wrench butc° anne; — *knows/but*
þe fox so godne° ne can nanne,° — *good/none*
þeз he kunne so vele° wrenche, — *many*
þat he wenþ° eche hunde atprenche.° — *thinks/to trick*
815 Vor° he can paþes riзte° and woзe,° — *for/paths straight/crooked*
and he kan hongi° bi þe boзe,° — *hang/branch*
and so forlost° þe hund his fore° — *loses/trail*
and turnþ aзen eft° to° þan more.° — *turns again/toward/the moor*
Þe vox° kan crope° bi þe heie° — *fox/creep/hedge*
820 and turne ut° from his forme weie° — *out/former way*
and eft sone° kume þarto;° — *quickly/come thereto*
þonne° is þe hundes smel fordo;° — *then/scent lost*
he not° þurз° þe imeinde smak,° — *knows not/by/mixed scent*
weþer° he shal avorþ þe abak.° — *whether/shall (go) forward or back*

795–804. Wrestling was a favorite sport during the country fairs in England and is mentioned in *Havelok the Dane* and by Chaucer in the General Prologue to the *Canterbury Tales*. The Greco-Roman style is in Switzerland today called *Schwingen* (cf. *swenges*, l. 797).

809–34. We have here one of the earliest descriptions of the fox hunt (cf. also *Sir Gawain and the Green Knight*, ll. 1690–1730, 1894–1921) Marie de France's fable of the fox and the cat relates how the fox boasted to the cat of his hundred tricks and a bag of others to use when those failed. The cat answered that she had only one trick. When two hounds ran after them, the fox asked the cat for help. The cat jumped on a thorn bush and was safe. "Help yourself," he said to the fox. "I have only one trick, and this is it." When he saw the hounds pulling the fox about, he said, "Why don't you open your bag of tricks?" The fox would gladly have exchanged his bag of tricks for the cat's one.

825 Ȝif þe vox mist of° al þis dwole,°   escapes by/deception
at þan ende he cropþ° to hole;   creeps
ac naþeles mid° alle his wrenche   nevertheless with
ne kan he° hine° so biþenche,°   it/for himself/contrive
þeȝ° he bo ȝep° and suþe snel,°   though/be clever/agile
830 þat he ne lost° his rede vel.°   loses/red pelt
Þe cat ne kan wrench bute anne,
noþer° bi dune ne° bi venne,°   neither/hill nor/swamp
bute he kan climbe suþe wel,
þarmid° he wereþ° his greie° vel.   whereby/guards/gray
835 Also° ich segge bi° me solve,°   just so/I say concerning/myself
betere is min on þan þine twelve."

    "Abid,° abid!" þe ule° seide,   wait/owl
"Þu gest° al to° mid swikelhede;°   you go/about/falsehood
alle þine wordes þu bileist,°   wrap up
840 þat° hit þincþ soþ° al þat þu seist;   so that/it seems truth
alle þine wordes boþ isliked°   are polished
and so bisemed° and biliked,°   seemly/pleasant
þat alle þo° þat hi avoþ,°   they/them hear
hi weneþ° þat þu segge soþ.   they think
845 Abid, abid! me° shal þe° ȝene.°   one/to you/reply
Nu° hit shal wurþe° wel isene°   now/be/seen
þat þu havest muchel iloȝe,°   much lied
wone° þi lesing boþ unwroȝe.°   when/falsehood is discovered
Þu seist° þat þu singist mankunne,°   say/for mankind
850 and techest hom° þat hi fundieþ honne°   teach them/strive hence
up to þe songe þat evre ilest;°   ever lasts
ac° hit is alre° wunder mest,°   but/of all/marvels greatest
þat þu darst liȝe° so opeliche.°   dare lie/openly
Wenest° þu hi bringe so liȝtliche°   think/lightly
855 to Godes riche° al singinde?°   God's kingdom/singing
Nai, nai! hi shulle° wel avinde°   shall/find out
þat hi mid longe wope mote°   lamentation must
of hore sunne bidde bote,°   for their sin beg mercy
ar° hi mote° ever kume þare.°   before/might/there
860 Ich rede þi° þat men bo ȝare°   advise therefore/ready
and more wepe þane° singe,   weep than
þat fundeþ° to þan° hovenkinge.°   aspire/the/heavenly king
Vor° nis° no man witute° sunne;   for/is not/without
vorþi° he mot,° ar he wende° honne,   therefore/must/goes
865 mid teres° and mid wope bete,°   tears/expatiate
þat him bo sur° þat er° was swete.°   sour/before/sweet

Þarto° ich helpe, God hit wot,°   *to that end/knows*
ne° singe ich hom no foliot;°   *not/foolishness*
for al mi song is of longinge
870 and imend° sum del° mid woninge,°   *mixed/a bit/with weeping*
    þat mon° bi me hine biþenche,°   *man/reflect*
    þat he groni° for his unwrenche;°   *groans/sins*
    mid mine songe ich hine pulte,°   *him impel*
    þat he groni for his gulte.°   *guilt*
875 Ȝif° þu gest° herof° to disputinge,   *if/enter/about this*
    ich° wepe bet° þane þu singe;   *I/better*
    ȝif riȝt goþ forþ° and abak° wrong,   *right goes forward/back*
    betere° is mi wop° þane þi song.   *better/lamentation*
    Þeȝ sume° men bo þurȝut gode°   *though some/be entirely good*
880 and þurȝut clene on° hore mode,°   *pure in/mind*
    hom longeþ° honne noþeles,°   *they long (to go)/nonetheless*
    þat boþ her, wo° is hom þes.°   *(they) that are here, woe/for it*
    Vor þeȝ hi bon° hom solve° iborȝe,°   *be/themselves/protected*
    hi° ne soþ° her nowiȝt bote sorwe;°   *they/see/nothing but sorrow*
885 vor oþer men hi wepeþ sore
    and for hom biddeþ° Cristes ore.°   *ask/favor*
    Ich helpe monne° on eiþer halve,°   *man/both sides*
    mi muþ haveþ tweire kunne° salve: *mouth has two kinds (of)*
    þan gode ich fulste° to longinge,   *encourage*
890 vor wan him° longeþ, ich him° singe;   *when he/to him*
    and þan sunfulle° ich helpe alswo,°   *sinful/also*
    vor ich him teche ware° is wo.   *teach where*
    Ȝet ich þe ȝene° in oþer wise;°   *you counter/way*
    vor wane þu° sittest on þine rise,°   *when you/branch*
895 þu draȝst° men to fleses luste,°   *draw/fleshly pleasure*
    þat willeþ þine songes luste.°   *listen to*
    Al þu forlost° þe murȝþe° of hovene,°   *lose/joy/heaven*
    for þarto° nevestu° none stevene;°   *for that/have you not/no voice*
    al þat þu singst is of golnesse,°   *wantonness*
900 for nis on þe non° holincsse;   *no*
    ne wened na° man for þi pipinge,   *believes no*
    þat eni preost° in chirche° singe.   *any priest/church (will)*
    Ȝet i þe wulle° an oder° segge,°   *will/another (thing)/say*
    ȝif þu hit const ariht bilegge.°   *it can aright explain*
905 Wi° nultu° singe an oder þeode,°   *why/will you not/in other lands*

---

868. *foliot:* an allusion to Bishop Foliot of London (1163–87), adversary of Thomas à Becket?

þar° hit is muchele° more neode?°	*where/much/need*
Þu neaver ne° singst in Irlonde,°	*never not/Ireland*
ne° þu ne cumest noȝt° in Scotlonde;	*nor/come not*
hwi° nultu fare to Noreweie,°	*why/Norway*
910 and singin° men° of Galeweie?°	*sing/to men/Galloway*
Þar beoð° men þat lutel kunne°	*there are/little know*
of songe þat is bineoðe° þe sunne.	*beneath*
Wi nultu þare preoste° singe	*there (to) priest*
and teche° of þire writelinge,°	*teach/your warbling*
915 and wisi hom mid° þire stevene	*show them with*
hu engeles° singeð ine° heovene?	*how angels/in*
Þu farest so doð° an ydel° wel,	*behave as does/useless*
þat springeþ bi burne° þat is snel,°	*rivulet/fast*
and let fordrue° þe dune	*dry up/hill*
920 and floþ° on idel° þar adune.°	*flows/needlessly/down*
Ac ich° fare boþe norþ and soþ,°	*but I/south*
in eavereuch londe° ich am cuuþ;°	*every land/known*
east and west, feor° and neor,°	*far/near*
i do wel° faire mi meoster,°	*ply very/trade*
925 and warni° men mid mine bere,°	*warn/cry*
þat þi dweolesong° heo° ne forlere.°	*deceitful song/them/seduce*
Ich wisse° men mid mine songe,	*guide*
þat hi° ne sunegi° nowiht° longe;	*they/sin/in no way*
i bidde hom þat heo iswike,°	*they stop*
930 þat heom seolve° ne biswike;°	*(they) themselves/deceive*
for betere is° þat heo wepen° here,	*better (it) is/weep*
þan elles hwar° to beon deovlene fere."°	*elsewhere/be Devil's companion*
Þe niȝtingale° was agromed,°	*nightingale/angry*
and ek heo° was sum del° ofschamed,°	*also she/a bit/ashamed*
935 for þe hule hire atwiten° hadde	*owl her reproached*
in° hwucche° stude he° sat and gradde,°	*with/what sort of/place she/cried*
bihinde þe bure° among þe wede,°	*chamber/weeds*
þar men goð to here° neode;	*go to (do) their*
and sat sum del and heo biþohte,°	*reflected*
940 and wiste° wel on° hire þohte,°	*knew/in/thought*
þe°wraþþe binimeþ° monnes° red;°	*that/takes away/man's/common sense*
for hit seide° þe king Alfred:	*said*
'Selde° endeð wel þe loþe°	*seldom/hateful*

907–8. These are again satirical references to Ireland (cf. above, l. 322n) and Scotland, although Neckham in *De Naturis Rerum* states that the nightingale loses its voice in cold countries.

910. Galloway, a kingdom in southwest Scotland, remained independent throughout the reign of Henry II. It was, therefore, as foreign and truculent as Ireland, from the viewpoint of the poet.

912. *songe:* i.e., "church song."

and selde plaideð° wel þe wroþe.'° *argue/angry*
945 For wraþþe meinþ° þe horte blod,° *agitates/heart's blood*
þat° hit° floweþ so wilde flod° *so that/it/flood*
and al þe heorte overgeþ,° *heart dominates*
þat heo naveþ° noþing bute breþ,° *has not/except passion*
and so forleost° al hire liht,° *loses/light*
950 þat heo ne siþ soð ne riht.° *not sees truth nor right*
Þe niȝtingale hi understod° *herself understood*
and overgan° lette hire mod;° *pass away/anger*
he mihte bet speken a° sele,° *might better speak/in/happy mood*
þan mid wraþþe wordes deale.° *exchange*

955   "Hule," heo seide, "lust nu hider!° *listen now here*
Þu° schalt falle, þe wei° is slider.° *you/path/slippery*
Þu seist ich fleo° bihinde bure; *fly*
hit is riht, þe bur° is ure,° *chamber/ours*
þar laverd liggeþ° and lavedi,° *where lord lies/lady*
960 ich schal heom° singe and sitte bi. *to them*
Wenstu° þat vise° men forlete° *think you/wise/leave*
for° fule venne° ðe riȝtte strete?° *because of/foul ditch/right road*
Ne sunne þe later shine,
þeȝ° hit beo ful ine° neste þine? *though/be foul in*
965 Sholde ich° for one° hole brede° *should I/a/board with a hole in it*
forlete mine riȝte stede,° *rightful place*
þat ich ne singe bi þe bedde,
þar loverd haveþ° his love ibedde?° *lord has/bedfellow*
Hit is mi riȝt, hit is mi laȝe,° *custom*
970 þat to þe hexste° ich me draȝe.° *highest/myself draw*
Ac° ȝet þu ȝelpst° of þine songe, *but/boast*
þat þu canst ȝolle wroþe° and stronge, *yell angrily*
and seist þu visest mankunne,° *guide mankind*
þat hi° biwepen° hore sunne.° *they/weep for/their sin*
975 Solde euch mon wonie° and grede,° *should every man lament/cry out*
riȝt° svich° hi weren unlede,° *just/as if/were unhappy*
solde hi ȝollen also° þu dest,° *yell as/do*
hi miȝte oferen here prost.° *might frighten their priest*
Man schal bo° stille and noȝt° grede; *be/not*
980 he mot° biwepe his misdede,° *must/misdeeds*
ac þar is Cristes heriinge,° *praise*
þar me° shal grede and lude° singe; *there men/loudly*
nis° noþer to° lud ne to long *is not/neither too*
at riȝte time chirchesong.° *church song*

---

965. *hole brede:* i.e., the seat in an outhouse.

⁹⁸⁵ Þu 3olst° and wonest,° and ich singe;   *yell/lament*
    Þi stevene° is wop° and min skentinge.°   *voice/weeping/mine delight*
    Ever mote° þu 3olle and wepen°   *may/weep*
    þat þu þi lif mote° forleten,°   *life must/give up*
    and 3ollen mote þu so he3e,°   *loudly*
⁹⁹⁰ þat ut berste bo þin e3e.°   *out burst both your eyes*
    Weþer° is betere° of twere twom,°   *which/better/two choices*
    þat mon bo bliþe oþer grom?°   *happy or sad*
    So bo hit° ever in unker siþe,°   *it/our time*
    þat þu bo sori° and ich bliþe.   *sorry*
⁹⁹⁵ 3ut° þu aishest, wi° ich ne° fare   *yet/ask, why/not*
    into oþer londe° and singe þare.°   *land/there*
    No! wat° sholde ich among hom° do,   *what/them*
    þar never blisse ne com° to?   *came*
    Þat lond nis god, ne° hit nis este,°   *good, nor/pleasant*
¹⁰⁰⁰ ac wildernisse hit is and weste;°   *waste*
    knarres° and cludes hoventinge,°   *stones/rocks sky-high*
    snou° and ha3el° hom° is genge.°   *snow/hail/to them/common*
    Þat lond is grislich° and unvele,°   *horrible/disgusting*
    þe men boþ° wilde and unisele;°   *are/miserable*
¹⁰⁰⁵ hi° nabbeþ° noþer griþ° ne sibbe,°   *they/have not/peace/quiet*
    hi ne reccheþ hu° hi libbe;°   *care how/live*
    hi eteþ fihs° and flehs unsode,°   *eat fish/meat uncooked*
    svich wulves° hit hadde tobrode;°   *wolves/pulled apart*
    hi drinkeþ milc° and wei þarto,°   *milk/whey besides*
¹⁰¹⁰ hi nute° elles° wat hi do;   *know not/else*
    hi nabbeþ noþer win° ne bor,°   *wine/beer*
    ac° libbeþ also° wilde dor;°   *but/as/animals*
    hi goþ biti3t mid ru3e velle,°   *go covered with rough skins*
    ri3t svich hi comen° ut of helle.   *come*
¹⁰¹⁵ Þe3 eni° god man to hom° come,   *though any/them*
    so wile dude° sum° from Rome,   *as recently did/some*
    for hom to lere gode þewes°   *teach good manners*
    and for to leten hore° unþewes,°   *stop their/wicked ways*
    he mi3te bet° sitte stille,   *might better*

999–1014. This description is very similar to that of Norway by Ohthere (Ottar) of Helgoland: Norway is rocky, waste, and not peaceful. An account of Ohthere's voyage was appended by King Alfred to his translation of Orosius's *Compendious History of the World* (893–99).

1001. *cludes:* Cf. Mod. Eng. *clod*, German *Klotz*. Our word *cloud* has the same origin.

1009. *wei:* Whey was the food of the lower classes, shepherds and goatherds.

1016. The mission from Rome was perhaps (according to Atkins) the embassy of Cardinal Vivian in 1176 to Scotland, Ireland, and Norway.

1018. *hore unþewes:* If the visit from Rome was indeed a clerical one, then these may very well have included the corrupt behavior of certain churchmen. The "wicked ways" of the Church were such things as wooden altars, watered communion wine, a dirty Host, the baptism of noble children with milk—all of which occurred in Ireland, perhaps because of the "chattering Irish priests" (J. Lanigan, *Ecclesiastical History of Ireland* [Dublin, 1829]).

¹⁰²⁰ vor° al his wile° he sholde spille;°   for/time/should waste
he miȝte bet teche ane bore°   a boar
to weȝe° boþe sheld° and spere,°   bear/shield/spear
þan me þat° wilde folc ibringe,°   (to) that/folk bring
þat hi me wolde ihere° singe.   would hear
¹⁰²⁵ Wat sol ich þar° mid mine songe?   should I there
Ne sunge ich° hom never so longe,   (though) I sang
mi song were° ispild° ech del;°   would be/wasted/every bit
for hom ne mai halter ne bridel
bringe vrom° hore wude wise,°   from/mad customs
¹⁰³⁰ ne mon° mid stele° ne mid ire.°   man/steel/iron
Ac war° lond is boþe este and god,   where
and þar° men habbeþ° milde mod,°   where/have/manner
ich noti° mid hom mine þrote,°   use/throat
vor ich mai do þar gode note,°   service
¹⁰³⁵ and bringe hom love tiþinge,°   tidings
vor ich of chirchesonge° singe.   church song
Hit° was iseid° in olde laȝe,°   it/said/law
and ȝet ilast þilke° soþsaȝe,°   still endures this/true saying
þat man shal erien° and sowe,   plow
¹⁰⁴⁰ þar hc wenþ after° sum god mowe;°   thinks afterward/good (to) reap
for he is wod° þat soweþ his sed,°   mad/seed
þar never gras ne sprinþ ne bled."°   not grows nor flowers

Þe hule° was wroþ,° to cheste rad,°   owl/angry/dispute ready
mid þisse worde hire eȝen° abrad:°   these words her eyes/opened wide
¹⁰⁴⁵ "Þu seist° þu witest manne bures,°   you say/guard men's chambers
þar leves boþ° and faire flores,°   leaves are/flowers
þar two ilove° in one bedde,   love
liggeþ biclupt° and wel bihedde.°   lie embraced/guarded
Enes° þu sunge,° ic wod° wel ware,°   once/sang/I know/where
¹⁰⁵⁰ bi one° bure, and woldest lere°   a/wanted (to) instruct
þe lefdi to° an uvel luve,°   lady in/evil love
and sunge boþe loȝe° and buve,°   low/high
and lerdest hi° to done shome°   taught her/do shame
and unriȝt of° hire licome.°   wrong with/body
¹⁰⁵⁵ Þe loverd° þat sone underȝat,°   lord/quickly noticed
lim° and grine,° wel eiwat,°   birdlime/snare/everything proper
sette and ledde þe° for to lacche;°   laid you/catch
þu come° sone to þan hacche,°   came/the trap
þu were inume° in one grine,   caught

^{1049ff.} The story is found in Alexander Neckham (1157–
1217), *De Naturis Rerum*

1060 al hit aboʒte° þine shine.°   *paid for/shins*
    Þu naddest° non° oþer dom° ne laʒe,°   *had not/no/judgment/sentence*
    bute mid° wilde horse were° todraʒe.°   *but with/to be/pulled apart*
    Vonde ʒif° þu miʒt eft misrede,°   *try if/might again miscounsel*
    waþer° þu wult wif þe° maide;   *whether/will wife or*
1065 þi song mai bo° so longe genge,°   *be/lasting*
    þat þu shalt wippen on° a sprenge.''°   *dangle in/snare*

    Þe niʒtingale° at þisse worde   *nightingale*
    mid sworde and mid speres orde,°   *spear's point*
    ʒif ho° mon were, wolde fiʒte;°   *she/fight*
1070 ac þo° ho bet° do ne miʒte,   *but since/better*
    ho vaʒt° mid hire wise tunge.°   *fought/tongue*
    Wel fiʒt þat wel specþ, seiþ° in þe songe.   *speaks, (it) says*
    Of° hire tunge ho nom red.°   *from/took advice*
    'Wel fiʒt þat wel specþ,' seide Alvred.°   *Alfred*

1075   "Wat!° seistu° þis for mine shome?   *what/say you*
    Þe loverd hadde herof° grame.°   *because of this/blame*
    He was so gelus° of his wive,°   *jealous/wife*
    þat he ne miʒte for his live°   *life*
    iso° þat man wiþ hire speke,°   *see/speak*
1080 þat his horte° nolde° breke.°   *heart/would not/break*
    He hire bileck° in one bure,   *locked*
    þat hire° was boþe stronge and sure;   *for her*
    ich° hadde of hire milse° and ore,°   *I/for her pity/compassion*
    and sori° was for hire sore,°   *sorry/grief*
1085 and skente° hi mid mine songe   *cheered*
    al þat ich miʒte raþe° and longe.   *early*
    Vor þan° þe kniʒt° was wiþ me wroþ,°   *for this/knight/angry*
    vor riʒte niþe° ich was him° loþ;°   *very malice/to him/hateful*
    he dude° me his oʒene° shome,   *put on/own*
1090 ac al him° turnde it to grome.°   *for him/harm*
    Þat underwat° þe king Henri—   *noticed*
    Jesus his soule do° merci!   *grant*
    He let forbonne þene° kniʒt,   *had banished the*
    þat hadde idon° so muchel unriʒt°   *done/much wrong*
1095 ine° so gode° kinges londe,°   *in/good (a)/land*
    vor riʒte niþe and for fule onde°   *foul hate*
    let þane lutle fuʒel nime°   *the little bird taken*
    and him fordeme lif° and lime.°   *condemned (to lose) life/limb*

1062. Death through being pulled apart by horses was a common medieval punishment. It was the fate of the traitor Ganelon in the *Chanson de Roland.*

1091. *king Henri:* Henry II (d. 1189).

Hit° was wurþsipe° al mine kunne;°	it/honor (to)/kin
1100 forþon° þe kniʒt forles° his wunne,°	because/lost/joy
and ʒaf° for me an hundred punde;°	gave/pounds
and mine briddes seten° isunde°	nestlings sat/in health
and hadde soþþe° blisse and hiʒte°	true/pleasure
and were bliþe and wel miʒte.°	might (be)
1105 Vorþon° ich was so wel awreke,°	because/avenged
ever eft° ich darr° þe bet speke;	after/dare
for° hit bitidde ene swo,°	because/happened once so
ich am þe bliþur° ever mo.°	happier/more
Nu° ich mai singe war° ich wulle,°	now/where/will
1110 ne° dar me never eft mon agrulle;°	nor/man disturb
ac þu° ereming,° þu wrecche gost,°	but you/poor thing/wretched spirit
þu ne° canst finde, ne° þu nost,°	not/nor/know not
an holʒ stok þar° þu þe° miʒt hude,°	hollow stump where/yourself/hide
þat° me° ne twengeþ° þine hude.	so that/men/twinge
1115 For children, gromes, heme° and hine,°	boys, villagers/monastics
hi þencheþ° alle of þire pine;°	they think/your torment
ʒif° hi muʒe° iso þe° sitte,	if/may/you
stones hi doþ° in hore slitte°	put/their pockets
and þe totorveþ° and tohcncþ°	smash completely/stone to bits
1120 and þine fule bon° tosheneþ.°	ugly bones/break to pieces
Ʒif þu art iworpe oþer° ishote,°	hit or/shot down
þanne° þu miʒt crcst° to note;°	then/first/he of use
vor me þe hoþ in one rodde,°	hang on a stick
and þu, mid° þine fule codde°	with/belly
1125 and mid þine ateliche swore,°	ugly neck
biwerest manne° corn vrom dore.°	guard man's/from animals
Nis° noþer noʒt° þi lif nc þi blod,°	is not/neither nothing (of use)/blood
ac þu art shueles suþe god;°	scarecrow very good
þar nowe sedes boþ isowe,°	where newly seeds are sown
1130 pinnuc,° golfinc, rok° ne crowe	hedge sparrow/goldfinch, rook
ne dar þar never cumen ihende,°	come near
ʒif þi buc hongeþ° at þan° ende.	carcass hangs/the
Þar tron shulle a ʒere blowe°	tree shall every year bloom
and ʒunge° sedes springe and growe,	young
1135 ne dar no fuʒel þarto vonge,°	thereto reach
ʒif þu art þarover° ihonge.°	there above/hung
Þi lif is evre luþer° and qued,°	ever evil/bad
þu nard° noʒt bute ded.°	are not/except (when) dead

1101. A bit of hyperbole here: £ 100 is an exaggeration as a *wergild* (according to Germanic and Anglo-Saxon law, a specified sum of money paid by the kindred of a slayer to the kindred of the slain in order to avoid an endless blood feud) given for a bird. Though this price is high, we might compare it to the king's ransom, the exorbitant amount of £ 100,000 set for Richard I, which bled England for years.

Nu þu miȝt wite sikerliche°   *know truly*
1140 þat þine leches° boþ grisliche°   *looks/grisly*
þe wile° þu art on lifdaȝe;°   *while/alive*
vor wane° þu hongest islaȝe,°   *for when/slain*
ȝut° hi boþ of þe ofdradde,°   *still/afraid*
þe fuȝeles° þat þe er bigradde.°   *birds/formerly blamed*
1145 Mid riȝte° men boþ wiþ þe wroþe,°   *right/angry*
for þu singist ever of hore loþe;°   *harm*
al þat þu singst raþe° oþer late,   *early*
hit° is ever of manne unwate;°   *it/misfortune*
wane þu havest aniȝt° igrad,°   *at night/cried out*
1150 men boþ of þe wel° sore ofdrad.   *very*
Þu° singst þar sum° man shal be ded;   *you/some*
ever þu bodest sumne qued.°   *foretell some misfortune*
Þu singst aȝen eiȝte lure,°   *before property loss*
oþer of summe frondes rure;°   *friend's ruin*
1155 oþer þu bodest huses brune,°   *houses' burning*
oþer ferde° of manne, oþer þoves° rune;°   *wars/thief's/hue and cry*
oþer þu bodest cvalm° of oreve,°   *pestilence/cattle*
oþer þat londfolc° wurþ° idorve,°   *farmers/will be/plagued*
oþer þat wif° lost° hire make;°   *wife/will lose/her husband*
1160 oþer þu bodest cheste° and sake.°   *strife/quarrel*
Ever þu singist of manne hareme,°   *harm*
þurȝ þe hi° boþ sori° and areme;°   *through you they/sorry/wretched*
þu ne° singst never one siþe,°   *not/time*
þat hit nis for sum unsiþe.°   *misfortune*
1165 Hervore° hit is þat me° þe shuneþ,°   *therefore/men/shun*
and þe totorveþ° and tobuneþ°   *smash completely/beat to pieces*
mid stave° and stoone° and turf and clute,°   *with sticks/stones/clods*
þat° þu ne miȝt nowar atrute.°   *so that/might nowhere escape*
Dahet° ever svich° budel in tune,°   *cursed/such/town crier*
1170 þat ever bodeþ unwreste rune°   *bad news*
and ever bringeþ uvele tiþinge,°   *evil tidings*
and þat ever specþ° of uvele þinge.   *speaks*
God almiȝti wurþe° him wroþ,   *almighty be (with)*
and al þat werieþ linnene° cloþ."   *wear/linen*

1175   Þe hule° ne abot noȝt swiþe° longe,   *owl/waited not very*
ah ȝef ondsware starke° and stronge: *but gave answer fierce*

1151–60. The forebodings of the Owl belong to medieval folklore and can be found in Elizabethan literature. Since they belong to "standard procedure," the Nightingale can use them as "precedent" in common-law pleading.

1156. *þoves:* i.e., "after a thief." *rune:* Cf. l. 1215n.

1174. *linnene cloþ:* All respectable people wore linen, but not the poor, the peasants, and the monks.

"Wat!" quaþ ho,° "artu° ihoded,°   *what/said she/are you/ordained*
oþer° þu kursest° al unihoded?   *or/curse*
For prestes wike, ich wat,° þu dest;°   *priest's work, I know/do*
1180 ich not° ȝef° þu were ȝavre° prest,   *know not/if/ever*
ich not ȝef þu canst masse singe,
inoh° þu canst° of mansinge.°   *enough/know/cursing*
Ah hit is for þine alde niþe,°   *old malice*
þat þu me akursedest oðer siðe;°   *curse once more*
1185 ah þarto° is lihtlich° ondsware;   *thereto/easy*
Drah° to þe! cwað° þe cartare.°   *draw/said/carter*
Wi° attwitestu° me mine insihte°   *why/reproach you/insight*
and min iwit° and mine miȝte?   *my knowledge*
For ich am witi ful iwis°   *wise enough indeed*
1190 and wod° al þat to kumen° is;   *know/come*
ich wot° of hunger, of hergonge,°   *know/military campaign*
ich wot ȝef men schule libbe° longe,   *shall live*
ich wat ȝef wif lust° hire make,   *will lose*
ich wat war° schal beo° niþ and wrake.°   *where/be/vengeance*
1195 ich wot hwo° schal beon anhonge°   *who/be hanged*
oþer elles fulne deþ afonge;°   *else foul death receive*
ȝef men habbeþ bataile inume;°   *have battle undertaken*
ich wat hwaþer° schal beon overkumc;°   *who/overcome*
ich wat ȝif cwalm° scal comen° on orfe,°   *if pestilence/shall come/cattle*
1200 and ȝif dor° schule ligge astorve,°   *animals/lie dead*
ich wot ȝef treon schule blowe,°   *trees/blossom*
ich wat ȝef cornes schule growe,
ich wot ȝef huses° schule berne,°   *houses/burn*
ich wot ȝef men schule eorne° oþer erne,°   *run/ride*
1205 ich wot ȝcf sea schal schipes drenche,°   *sink*
ich wot ȝef smiþes schule uvele clenche.°   *badly rivet*
And ȝet ich con muchel° more;   *know much*
ich con inoh in bokes° lore,   *books'*
and eke° ich can of þe goddspelle°   *also/gospel*
1210 more þan ich nule° þe° telle;   *will not/you*
for ich at chirche° come ilome°   *church/often*
and muche leorni° of wisdome.   *learn*
Ich wat al of þe tacninge°   *signification*
and of oþer feole þinge.°   *many things*

1186. *Drah to þe:* i.e., "Pull your horses over to your side," or "Pull over!" as the policeman shouts to the speeding driver.

1204. *eorne oþer erne:* Gadow interprets this phrase as a legal formula for seeking asylum in church, quoting from the Laws of Alfred: "Ȝif hie fahmon *geierne oþþe geærne* þæt hine seofan nihtum nan mon ut ne teo" ("If they reach church asylum by running or riding, no man may pull him out for seven nights"). The Owl can foretell when a man must flee from the law.

1213. *tacninge:* the interpretation of church symbolism.

1215 ʒef eni mon° schal rem° abide,°   any man|hue and cry|endure
al ich hit° wot, ear° hit itide.°   it|before|happens
Ofte for mine muchele iwitte°   great knowledge
wel sorimod° and worþ ich° sitte;   very sad|angry I
wan° ich iseo° þat sum wrechede°   when|see|some misery
1220 is manne° neh, innoh° ich grede.°   to man|near, much|cry
Ich bidde° þat men beon iwarre°   ask|aware
and habbe gode reades ʒarre;°   have good advice ready
for Alfred seide° a wis° word,   said|wise
euch° mon hit schulde legge on hord:°   every|should lay in store
1225 'ʒef þu isihst, er he beo icume,°   if you see (woe), before it is come
his strencþe° is him° wel neh° binume';°   its strength|from it|nigh|taken away
and grete duntes beoþ° þe lasse,°   great blows are|less
ʒif me ikepþ mid iwarnesse;°   one guards with care
and flo° schal toward° misgenge,°   arrow|in direction|miss
1230 ʒef þu isihst, hu fleo of strenge,°   how (it) flies from string
for þu miʒt blenche° wel and fleo,°   might dodge|flee
ʒif þu isihst heo° to þe teo.°   it|go
Þat eni man beo falle° in odwite,°   fallen|disgrace
wi° schal he me his sor atwite?°   why|(for) his grief blame
1235 Þah° ich iseo his harm bivore,°   though|before
ne° comeþ hit noʒt° of me þarvore.°   not|not|therefore
Þah þu iseo þat sum blind mon,
þat nanne° rihtne wei° ne con,   not any|right way
to þare diche his dweole fulied°   the ditch (in) his error goes
1240 and falleþ and þarone° sulied,°   therein|is soiled
wenest° þu, þah ich al iseo,   think
þat hit for° me þe raþere° beo?   because of|sooner
Alswo° hit fareþ bi° mine witte;°   so|goes with|knowledge
hwanne° ich on mine bowe° sitte,   when|bough
1245 ich wot° and iseo swiþe brihte,°   know|very clearly
an° summe men kumed° harm þar rihte.°   on|comes|there|right
Schal he, þat þerof noþing not,°   knows not
hit wite me, for° ich hit wot?   reproach me (for), because
Schal he his mishap wite me,
1250 for ich am wisure þane° he?   wiser than
Hwanne ich iseo þat sum wrechede
is manne neh, inoh° ich grede,   much
and bidde inoh þat hi heom schilde,°   they themselves shield
for toward heom° is harm unmilde;°   to them|merciless
1255 ah° þah ich grede lude° and stille,°   but|loud|soft

1215. *rem:* Raising the hue and cry was the medieval method of gathering a posse. At the cry of "Stop thief!" for instance, everyone was legally committed to join in and pursue the culprit with weapons. The cry naturally traveled faster than the thief, though he often called with the others and added to the confusion.

al hit itid þurh° Godes wille.   *it happens through*
Hwi wulleþ° men of me hi mene,°   *why will/complain*
þah ich mid soþe hi awene?°   *truth them disturb*
Þah ich° hi warni° al þat ʒer,°   *I/warn/year*
1260 nis° heom þerfore harem no° þe ner.°   *is not/harm none/nearer*
Ah ich heom° singe, for ich wolde°   *to them/would*
þat hi wel understonde° schulde,   *understand*
þat sum unselþe° heom is ihende,°   *some misfortune/near*
hwan° ich min huing° to heom sende. *when/my hooting*
1265 Naveþ° no man none sikerhede,°   *has not/no certainty*
þat he ne mai wene° and adrede,°   *expect/fear*
þat sum unhwate neh° him beo,°   *misfortune near/is*
þah he ne conne° hit iseo.°   *can/see*
Forþi seide° Alfred swiþe wel,   *therefore said*
1270 and his word was goddspel,°   *gospel*
þat evereuch° man, þe bet him° beo, *every/better he*
eaver° þe bet he hine beseo;°   *ever/himself guards*
ne truste no mon° to his weole°   *man/prosperity*
to swiþe,° þah he habbe veole.°   *too strongly/have much*
1275 Nis non° so hot þat hit nacoleþ,°   *none/not cools*
ne noʒt° so hwit° þat hit ne soleþ,° *nor not/white/not soils*
ne noʒt so leof° þat hit ne aloþeþ,° *dear/turns hateful*
ne noʒt so glad þat hit ne awroþeþ;° *becomes angry*
ah eavereuch° þing þat eche° nis,   *every/eternal*
1280 agon° schal and al þis worldes blis. *pass*
Nu þu miʒt wite readliche,°   *now you might know readily*
þat eavere þu spekest gideliche;°   *speak foolishly*
for al þat þu me° seist for schame,   *to me*
ever þe seolve° hit turneþ to grome.° *for yourself/harm*
1285 Go so° hit go,° at eche fenge°   *as/(may) go/each turn*
þu fallest mid° þine ahene swenge.° *with/own stroke*
Al þat þu seist for me to schende,° *shame*
hit is mi wurschipe° at þan° ende.   *honor/the*
Bute° þu wille bet aginne,°   *unless/begin*
1290 ne schaltu° bute° schame iwinne."° *shall you/(anything) but/win*

    Þe niʒtingale° sat and siʒte°   *nightingale/sighed*
and hohful° was and ful° wel miʒte;° *worried/very/might (be)*
for þe hule swo ispeke° hadde   *owl so spoken*
and hire speche° swo iladde.°   *her speech/carried on*
1295 Heo° was hohful and erede,°   *she/at a loss*
hwat° heo þarafter° hire° sede;°   *(as to) what/thereafter/to her/*
                                  would say

ah neoþeles° heo hire understod.°   *but nevertheless/reflected*
"Wat!"° heo seide, "hule, artu° wod?° *what/are you/mad*

Þu ȝeolpest° of seolliche° wisdome,   *boast/wonderful*
1300 Þu nustest° wanene he° Þe° come,°   *knew not/whence it/to you/came*
bute hit° of wicchecrefte° were;   *it/witchcraft*
Þarof° Þu, wrecche, moste Þe skere,°   *thereof/wretch, must yourself clear*
ȝif° Þu wult° among manne boe,°   *if/will/men be*
oÞer° Þu most of londe fleo.°   *or/from land flee*
1305 For alle Þeo° Þat Þerof cuÞe,°   *those/know*
heo vere° ifurn° of prestes muÞe°   *they were/long ago/by priests'*
                                                                           mouth

amanset;° swuch° Þu art ȝette,   *cursed/such*
Þu wicchecrafte neaver° ne lete.°   *never/will leave off*
Ich° Þe seide° nu lutel ere,°   *I/said/(a) little before*
1310 and Þu askedest ȝef° ich were,   *if*
a bisemere, to preost ihoded;°   *in mockery, as (a) priest ordained*
ah Þe mansing° is so ibroded,°   *cursing/widespread*
Þah° no preost a londe nere,°   *though/were not*
a wrecche neoÞeles Þu were;°   *would be*
1315 for eavereuch child Þe cleopeÞ fule,°   *you/calls foul*
and evereuch° man a wrecche° hule.   *every/wretched*
Ich habbe iherd,° and soÞ° hit is,   *have heard/true*
Þe mon mot beo wel storrewis°   *must be very star-wise*
Þat wite° innoÞ° of wuche° Þinge kume,°   *knows/(the) inner source/whatever/*
                                                                           (may) come

1320 so Þu seist, Þe° is iwune.°   *for you/usual*
Hwat canstu,° wrecche Þing, of storre,°   *know you/stars*
bute Þat Þu bihaltest hi feorre?°   *you behold them afar*
Alswo° deÞ° mani dor° and man,   *just so/do/animals*
Þeo° of swucche nawiht ne con.°   *that/such nothing not knows*
1325 On° ape mai a boc bihalde°   *an/book behold*
and leves wenden° and eft° folde,   *leaves turn/again*
ah he ne con Þe bet Þarvore°   *better therefore*
of clerkes lore top ne more.°   *learning head nor root*
Þah Þu iseo° Þe steorre alswa,°   *see/stars so*
1330 nartu° Þe wisure° neaver Þe mo.˘   *you are not/wiser/more*
Ah ȝet Þu fule Þing me chist°   *chide*
and wel grimliche° me atwist,°   *grimly/blame*
Þat ich singe bi manne huse°   *men's houses*
and teache wif° breke spuse.°   *wife/to commit adultery*
1335 Þu liest iwis,° Þu fule Þing,   *lie indeed*
Þurh° me nas° neaver ischend spusing.°   *through/was not/harmed marriage*
Ah° soÞ hit is, ich singe and grede°   *but/cry*
Þar lavedies beoÞ° and faire maide;°   *where ladies are/maids*
and soÞ hit is, of luve° ich singe;   *love*
1340 for god° wif mai i° spusinge   *good/in*
bet luvien hire oȝene were°   *love her own man*

þane° awer° hire copenere;° — *than/in any way/lover*
and maide mai luve cheose° — *lover choose*
þat° hire wurþschipe° ne forleose,° — *so that/honor/(she) lose*
1345 and luvie mid rihte° luve — *with true*
þane° þe schal beon° hire buve.° — *him/be/above (as husband)*
Swiche° luve ich itache° and lere,° — *such/show/teach*
þerof beoþ al mine ibere.° — *cries*
Þah sum° wif beo of nesche mode,° — *some/tender heart*
1350 for wummon° beoþ of softe blode,° — *women/blood*
þat heo,° þurh sume sottes lore° — *she/some fool's teaching*
þe ȝeorne bit° and sikeþ° sore, — *eagerly desires/sighs*
misrempe° and misdo° summe stunde,° — *goes wrong/does wrong/times*
schal ich° þarvore beon ibunde?° — *I/responsible*
1355 Ȝif wimmen° luvieþ unrede,° — *if women/folly*
witistu° me hore misdede?° — *blame you/(for) their misdeeds*
Ȝef wimmon þencheþ° luvie derne,° — *if women want (to)/secretly*
ne mai ich mine songes werne.° — *deny*
Wummon mai pleie° under cloþe,° — *play/cloth*
1360 weþer° heo wile° wel þe wroþe,° — *whether/will/or wickedly*
and heo mai do bi° mine songe, — *according to*
hwaþer° heo wule wel° þe wronge. — *whether/will (love) honestly*
For nis° a° worlde þing so god, — *is not/in*
þat ne° mai do sum ungod,° — *not/wrong*
1365 ȝif me hit° wule turne amis. — *men it*
Vor° gold and seolver, god hit is, — *for/silver*
and noþeles þarmid þu miȝt° — *nonetheless therewith you might*
spusbruche buggen° and unriȝt.° — *adultery buy/wrong*
Wepne° beoþ gode griþ° to halde, — *weapons/good peace/keep*
1370 ah ȝet þarmide beoþ men acwalde° — *killed*
aȝeines° riht an fale londe,° — *contrary to/right in many lands*
þar þeoves hi bereð° an honde.° — *thieves them carry/hand*
Alswa° hit is bi° mine songe, — *just so/with*
þah he beo° god, me hine° mai misfonge,° — *though it be/it/misinterpret*
1375 and drahe° hine to sothede° — *convert/folly*
and to oþre uvele dede.° — *other evil deeds*
Ah° schaltu,° wrecche,° luve tele?° — *but/shall you/wretch/reproach*
Bo wuch ho° bo, vich° luve is fele° — *be however it/each/good*
bitweone wepmon° and wimmane;° — *between men/women*
1380 ah ȝef heo° is atbroide,° þenne — *it/stolen*
he is unfele° and forbrode.° — *wrong/corrupted*
Wroþ° wurþe° heom° þe holi rode,° — *angry/may become/with them/cross*
þe° rihte ikunde swo forbreideþ;° — *that/nature so perverts*
wunder° hit is þat heo° nawedeþ;° — *amazing/they/don't go mad*
1385 and swo heo doþ,° for heo beoþ wode° — *do/are mad*
þe bute° neste goþ° to brode.° — *outside/go/breed*

Wummon° is of nesche° flesche,   woman/frail
and flesches° lustes is strong° to cwesse;°   fleshly/hard/subdue
nis° wunder nan° þah he abide.°   (it) is not/wonder none/remains
1390 For flesches lustes hi makeþ slide,°   slip
ne beoþ heo nowt° alle forlore°   not/lost
þat stumpeþ° at þe flesches more,°   stumble/flesh's root
for moni wummon° haveþ misdo°   many women/done wrong
þat arist op of° þe slo.°   rose up from/mire
1395 Ne° beoþ nowt ones° alle sunne,°   nor/the same/sins
forþan hi° beoþ tweire kunne;°   because they/two kinds
sum° arist of þe flesches luste   some
and sum of þe gostes custe.°   spirit's nature
Þar° flesch draheþ° men to druncnesse°   where/draws/drunkenness
1400 and to wrouehede° and to golnesse,°   anger/lust
þe gost misdeþ þurh niþe° and onde°   corrupts through envy/hate
and seoþþe mid murhþe of monne shonde,°   then with joy at men's shame
and ȝeorneþ° after more and more,   yearns
and lutel rehþ of milce° and ore,°   little cares about pity/mercy
1405 and stiȝþ° on heh° þurh modinesse°   climbs/high/pride
and overhoheð þanne lasse.°   despises the lowly
Sei° me sooþ, ȝef þu hit wost,°   tell/truly, if you it know
hweþer deþ wurse,° flesch þe° gost?   which does worse/or
Þu miȝt segge,° ȝef þu wult,°   might say/will
1410 þat lasse° is þe flesches gult;°   less/guilt
moni° man is of his flesche clene,°   many (a)/pure
þat is mid mode deovel imene.°   in pride Devil's companion
Ne° schal non mon wimman bigrede°   not/no man woman reproach
and flesches° lustes hire upbreide;°   (for) fleshly/her blame
1415 swuch° he may tellen of° golnesse,   such (a one)/reproach for
þat sunegeþ° wurse i° modinesse.   sins/in
Ȝet, ȝif ich schulde a luve° bringe   yet if I should to love
wif oþer° maide hwanne° ich singe,   wife or/when
ich wolde° wiþ þe maide holde,°   would/agree
1420 ȝif þu hit const ariht atholde.°   can aright understand
Lust nu,° ich segge þe hwarvore,°   listen now/tell you why
up to þe toppe° from þe more.°   end/beginning
Ȝef maide luveþ dernliche,°   loves secretly
heo° stumpeþ and falþ icundeliche;°   she/falls naturally
1425 for þah° heo sum hwile pleie,°   though/a while play
heo nis° nout feor ut° of þe weie;°   is not/not far out/way
heo mai hire gult atwende°   turn away
a rihte° weie þurh chirche bende,°   in right/church bonds
and mai eft habbe to make°   again have as husband
1430 hire leofmon wiþute sake,°   lover without blame

and go to him bi daies lihte,°   *day's light*
þat er stal° to bi þeostre nihte.°   *before stole/dark night*
An ȝungling° not° hwat swuch þing is,   *youngster/knows not*
his ȝunge blod hit draȝeþ amis,°   *her young blood leads her amiss*
1435 and sum sot° mon hit tihþ þarto°   *foolish/entices thereto*
mid alle þan þat° he mai do.   *that which*
He comeþ and fareþ,° and beod° and bid,°   *goes/commands/asks*
and heo° bistant° and oversid,°   *her/takes pains (with)/neglects*
and bisehþ ilome° and longe;   *begs often*
1440 hwat mai þat child þah° hit misfonge?°   *but/misunderstand*
Hit° nuste° neaver° hwat hit was,   *she/knew not/never*
forþi° hit þohte fondi þas,°   *therefore/thought (to) try it*
and wite iwis hwuch beo° þe gome°   *know indeed what is/game*
þat of so wilde° makeþ tome.°   *wild (a one)/tame*
1445 Ne mai ich for reowe lete,°   *pity stop*
wanne° ich iseo° þe tohte ilete°   *when/see/strained face*
þe° luve bringþ on þe ȝunglinge,   *that*
þat ich of murȝþe° him° ne singe.   *joy/to her*
Ich teache him bi mine songe
1450 þat swucch luve ne lest noȝt° longe;   *lasts not*
for mi song lutle° hwile ileste,°   *little/lasts*
and luve ne deþ noȝt bute° reste   *does nothing but*
on swuch childre,° and sone ageþ,°   *children/quickly passes*
and falþ adun° þe hote breþ.°   *away/hot passion*
1455 Ich singe mid heom one þroȝe,°   *with them a while*
biginne on heh° and endi laȝe,°   *high/end low*
and lete° mine songes falle   *let*
an° lutle wile adun mid alle.°   *a/while/altogether*
þat maide wot,° hwanne ich swike,°   *knows/when I stop*
1460 þat luve° is mine songes iliche;°   *love/like*
for hit° nis bute a lutel° breþ,   *it/little*
þat sone kumeþ° and sone geþ.°   *comes/goes*
Þat child bi me hit understond,°   *understands*
and his unred° to rede wend,°   *foolishness/wisdom turns*
1465 and iseȝþ° wel bi mine songe,   *sees*
þat dusi° luve ne° last noȝt longe.   *foolish/not*
Ah° wel ich wule° þat þu° hit wite,   *but/wish/you*
loþ° me° beoþ wives utschute;°   *hateful/to me/are wife's excesses*
ah wif° mai of me nime ȝeme,°   *wife/take note*
1470 ich ne singe nawt hwan° ich teme.°   *nothing when/breed*
And wif ah° lete sottes lore,°   *ought to/leave fool's teaching*

1470. Cf. above, p. 569, l. 504*n.*

þah spusingbendes þuncheþ sore.°   *though (they) wedlock think (a) sad (affair)*

Wunder° me þungþ wel starc° and stor,°   *(a) wonder/(it) seems very great/ exceeding*

hu eni mon° so eavar for,°   *how any man/whatever*
1475 þat he his heorte miȝte° drive   *heart might*
to do hit to oþers mannes wive.°   *other men's wives*
For oþer° hit is of twam þinge,°   *either/two things*
ne° mai þat þridde° no man bringe: *nor/third*
oþar° þe laverd° is wel aht,°   *either/lord/worthy*
1480 oþer aswunde° and nis° naht.°   *or feeble/is not/(good for) nothing*
Ȝef° he is wurþful° and aht man,   *if/honorable*
nele° no man þat wisdom can°   *will not/knows*
hure° of° his wive° do him schame;   *least of all/with/wife*
for he mai him adrede grame,°   *himself fear harm*
1485 and þat he forleose þat° þer hongeþ,°   *lose what/hangs*
þat° him eft° þarto° noȝt ne longeþ;   *so that/he again/for it*
and þah he þat noȝt ne adrede,
hit is unriȝt° and gret sothede°   *wrong/great stupidity*
to misdon° one gode° manne   *do amiss (to)/good*
1490 and his ibedde° from him spanne.°   *bedfellow/seduce*
Ȝef hire° laverd is forwurde°   *her/enfeebled*
and unorne at° bedde and at borde,°   *mean in/table*
hu° miȝte þar beo° eni luve,   *how/there be*
wanne° a swuch° cheorles buc° hire ley buve?°   *when/such a/boor's body/lay above*
1495 Hu mai þar eni luve beo,
war° swuch man gropeþ hire þeo?°   *where/thigh*
Herbi° þu miȝt wel understonde,   *by this*
þat on° is a reu,° þat oþer schonde,°   *one/sorrow/shame*
to stele° to oþres° mannes bedde.   *steal/another*
1500 For ȝif° aht man is hire bedde,°   *if/bedfellow*
þu miȝt wene° þat þe° mistide,°   *believe/with you/it will go ill*
wanne þu list° bi hire side;   *lie*
and ȝef þe laverd is a wercche,°   *wretch*
hwuch este° miȝtistu° þar vecche?°   *what pleasure/might you/get*
1505 Ȝif þu biþenchest hwo° hire ofligge,°   *reflect who/lies with*
þu miȝt mid wlate° þe este bugge.°   *with disgust/buy*
Ich° not° hu mai eni freo° man   *I/know not/upstanding*
for hire sechen° after þan;°   *seek/that*

1485. Castration was a punishment for adulterers and rapists (cf. *Havelok the Dane*, l. 86). Mutilation was practiced into the 17th century.

1492. *at . . . borde:* a legal phrase (Latin *a mensa et thoro*) meaning "full marital relations." It was part of the bride's response during the marriage service.

ȝef he biþencþ° bi hwan he° lai,　　　　　　　　　reflects/whom she
1510　al mai þe luve gan° awai.''　　　　　　　　　　love go

　　　Þe hule° was glad of swuche tale.　　　　　owl
　　Heo þoȝte° þat te nihtegale,°　　　　　　　she thought/the nightingale
　　þah° heo wel speke° atte° frume,°　　　　　though/spoke/at the/beginning
　　hadde at þen° ende misnume,°　　　　　　　the/erred
1515　and seide:° "Nu° ich habbe ifunde°　　　　said/now/have found
　　þat maidenes beoþ of° þine imunde:°　　　　are in/mind
　　mid heom þu holdest° and heom biwerest,°　them you agree/defend
　　and overswiþe° þu hi herest.°　　　　　　　immoderately/them praise
　　Þe lavedies° beoþ to me iwended,°　　　　　ladies/turned
1520　to me heo hire mode° sendeþ.　　　　　　they their thoughts
　　For hit itit° ofte and ilome,°　　　　　　　it happens/frequently
　　þat wif° and were° beoþ unisome;°　　　　wife/husband/at odds
　　and þerfore þe were gulte,°　　　　　　　offends
　　þat leof is° oþer wummon° to pulte°　　　　likes/woman/assail
1525　and speneþ° on þare° al þat he haveþ,°　　spends/her/has
　　and siveþ° þare þat no riht° naveþ;°　　　follows/right/has not
　　and haveþ attom° his riȝte spuse,°　　　　at home/rightful spouse
　　wowes weste° and lere huse,°　　　　　　walls desolate/empty house
　　wel þunne ischrud° and ived wroþe,°　　very thinly dressed/fed ill
1530　and let heo bute mete° and cloþe.°　　leaves her without food/clothes
　　Wan° he comeþ ham eft° to his wive,°　　when/home again/wife
　　ne dar° heo noȝt° a word ischire;°　　　not dare/not/speak
　　he chid° and gred° swuch° he beo wod,°　chides/shouts/as if/be mad
　　and ne bringþ hom non° oþer god;°　　　brings home no/good
1535　al þat heo deþ° him° is unwille,°　　　does/to him/repugnant
　　al þat heo spekeþ° hit is him ille,　　　speaks
　　and oft hwan° heo noȝt° ne misdeþ,°　when/nothing/does wrong
　　heo haveþ þe fust° in hire teþ.°　　　fist/her teeth
　　Nis° nan mon° þat ne mai ibringe°　　(there is) not/no man/bring
1540　his wif amis° mid swucche° þinge;　　astray/such
　　me° hire mai so ofte misbeode,°　　　one/mistreat
　　þat heo do wule° hire ahene neode.°　satisfy will/own needs
　　La,° Godd hit wot!° heo nah iweld,°　ah/knows/cannot help it
　　þah heo hine makie kukeweld.°　　　him make cuckold
1545　For hit itit lome° and ofte,　　　　frequently
　　þat his wif is wel nesche° and softe,　frail
　　of faire bleo° and wel idiht;°　　　face/proportioned
　　þi° hit is þe more unriht°　　　　　then/wrong
　　þat he his luve spene° on þare　　waste
1550　þat nis wurþ° one of hire heare.°　worth/hairs

And swucche men beoþ wel manifolde,° numerous
þat wif ne kunne nowt° arizt holde;° cannot/aright keep
ne mot° non mon wiþ hire speke, may
he veneð heo° wule anon tobreke° thinks she/quickly break
1555 hire spusing, zef° heo lokeþ° wedlock, if/looks
oþer° wiþ manne faire spekeþ; or
he hire biluþ° mid keie° and loke,° locks up/with key/lock
þarþurh° is spusing ofte tobroke.° through this/broken
For zef heo is þarto ibroht,° thereto brought
1560 he° deþ þat° heo nadde° ear iþoht.° she/what/had not/before thought
Dahet° þat to swuþe hit° bispeke,° cursed (be they)/too quickly it/ talk of

þah° swucche wives heom awreke.° though/themselves avenge
Herof° þe lavedies° to me meneþ,° of this/ladies/complain
and wel sore me ahweneþ;° sadden
1565 wel neh min heorte° wule tochine,° nigh my heart/break
hwon ich° biholde hire pine;° when I/their suffering
mid heom° ich wepe swiþe° sore them/weep very
and for heom bidde Cristis ore,° ask Christ's mercy
þat° þe lavedi sone° aredde° that (he)/quickly/set free
1570 and hire sende betere ibedde.° better bedfellow
An oþer þing ich mai þe° telle, you
þat þu ne schald° for þine felle° you not shall/skin
ondswere° none þarto finde, answer
al þi sputing° shal aswinde.° argument/disappear
1575 Moni chapmon° and moni cniht° many (a) merchant/knight
luveþ° and hald° his wif ariht,° loves/keeps/wife aright
and swa deþ° moni bondeman;° so does/peasant
þat gode° wif deþ after þan,° good/like to this
and serveþ him to° bedde and to borde° in/at table
1580 mid faire dede° and faire worde,° deeds/words
and zeorne fondeþ hu° heo muhe° eagerly tries how/might
do þing þat him° beo iduze.° to him/is pleasing
Þe laverd° into þare þeode° lord/the land
fareþ ut on° þare beire nede,° travels out for/the necessity of them both

1585 and is þat gode wif unbliþe° unhappy
for° hire° laverdes oudsiþe,° because of/her/departure
and sit° and sihð° wel° sore oflonged,° sits/sighs/very/in longing
and hire° sore on horte ongred,° herself/in heart afflicted
al for hire loverdes° sake lord's

1554–55. *tobreke hire spusing:* i.e., "commit adultery."   **1572.** *for þine felle:* i.e., "to save your life."

1590 haveþ° daies° kare° and niȝtes° wake,° — *has/by day/care/by night/wakefulness*

and swuþe° longe hire° is þe hwile,° — *very/to her/time*
and ech steape° hire þunþ° a mile. — *each step/seems*
Hwanne oþre slepeþ° hire abute,° — *when others sleep/around*
ich one luste þar wiðþute,° — *alone listen there outside*
1595 and wot° of hire sore mode,° — *know/sad spirit*
and singe aniȝt° for hire gode; — *at night*
and mine gode song for° hire þinge — *in/case*
ich turne sum del° to murninge.° — *a little/mourning*
Of hure seorhe° ich bere sume,° — *her sorrow/bear some*
1600 forþan° ich am hire wel welcume;° — *therefore/welcome*
ich hire helpe hwat° i mai, — *as*
for ho geþ þane rehte° wai. — *she goes the right*
Ah° þu me havest sore igramed,° — *but/angered*
þat° min heorte is wel neh alamed,° — *so that/lamed*
1605 þat ich mai unneaþe speke,° — *scarcely speak*
ah ȝet ich wule forþure reke.° — *I will further talk*
Þu seist° þat ich am manne lað,° — *say/(to) men hateful*
and evereuch° man is wið me wroð° — *every/angry*
and me mid° stone and lugge þreteþ° — *with/stick threatens*
1610 and me tobusteþ° and tobeteþ,° — *smashes to bits/beats to pieces*
and hwanne heo habeþ° me ofslahe,° — *they have/slain*
heo hongeþ° me on heore hahe,° — *hang/their enclosures*
þar° ich aschewele° pie° and crowe — *where/scare off/magpie*
from þan þe° þar is isowe.° — *that which/sown*
1615 Þah hit beo soþ,° ich do heom god,° — *though it be true/them good*
and for heom ich schadde° mi blod.° — *shed/blood*
Ich do heom god mid mine deaþe,
warvore° þe° is° wel unneaþe.° — *wherefore/for you/(it) is/hard*
For þah þu ligge° dead and clinge,° — *you lie/wither*
1620 þi deþ° nis° nawt° to none° þinge. — *death/is not/no good/no*
Ich not° neaver° to hwan° þu miȝt,° — *know not/never/what end/might (be of use)*

for þu nart° bute° a wrecche wiȝt.° — *are not/(nothing) but/wretched thing*

Ah þah mi lif° me° beo atschote,° — *life/from me/shot away*
þe ȝet° ich mai do gode note;° — *even then/good service*
1625 me° mai up one smale° sticke — *men/upon a small*
me sette a wude ine° þe þicke, — *(of) a forest in*
and swa° mai mon tolli° him to — *so/man entice*
lutle briddes° and ivo,° — *little birds/capture (them)*
and swa me mai mid me biȝete° — *obtain*
1630 wel° gode brede° to° his mete.° — *very/roast meat/for/food*

Ah þu nevre mon to° gode   *never men for*
lives ne deaþes° stal ne stode;°   *alive nor dead|were of no use*
ich not to hwan þu bretst° þi brod,°   *breed|brood*
lives ne draþes ne deþ° hit god.°   *does*

1635   Þe nihtegale iherde° þis,   *nightingale heard*
and hupte° uppon on blowe ris,°   *hopped|a blooming branch*
and herre° sat þan heo dude ear:°   *higher|she did before*
"Hule,"° heo seide, "beo nu wear!°   *owl|beware now*
Nulle° ich wiþ þe plaidi° namore,°   *will not|you dispute|no more*
1640   for her° þe mist° þi rihte lore.°   *here|missed|right learning*
Þu ʒulpest° þat þu art manne loþ,°   *boast|hateful*
and evereuch wiht° is wið þe worþ;°   *creature|angry*
and mid ʒulinge° and mid igrede°   *yelling|cry*
þu wanst wel° þat þu art unlede.°   *lament greatly|wretched*
1645   Þu seist þat gromes° þe ifoð,°   *boys|capture*
and heie° on rodde° þe anhoð,°   *high|stick|hang*
and þe totwichet° and toschakeð,°   *pluck to pieces|shake to bits*
and summe° of þe schawles° makeð;°   *some|scarecrow*
me° þuncþ° þat þu forleost° þat game.°   *to me|(it) seems|lose*
1650   Þu ʒulpest of þire oʒe° schame;°   *your own*
me þuncþ þat þu me gest an honde,°   *are submitting*
þu ʒulpest of þire oʒene schonde."°   *own disgrace*
Þo° heo hadde þeos word icwede,°   *when|these words spoken*
heo sat in one° faire stude,°   *a|place*
1655   and þarafter hire stevene dihte,°   *thereafter her voice employed*
and song° so schille° and so brihte,°   *sang|shrilly|brightly*
þat feor° and ner° me hit° iherde.   *far|near|it*
Þarvore anan° to hire cherde°   *therefore quickly|came*
þrusche and þrostle and wudewale°   *woodpecker*
1660   and fuheles° boþe grete° and smale.   *birds|large*
Forþan° heom° þuhte þat heo hadde   *because|to them|(it) seemed*
þe houle° overcome; vor þan° heo gradde°   *owl|therefore|they cried*
and sungen alswa valc wisc,°   *sang likewise many tunes*
and blisse was among þe rise;°   *branches*
1665   riʒt° swa me gred° þe manne a schame, *just|men cry (to)*
þat taveleþ° and forleost þat gome.°   *dices|game*

Þeos° hule, þo heo þis iherde,   *this*

1631–32. *mon . . . stode:* i.e., "stood men in good stead in life nor death." Stanley suggests that there is a pun here on *stal,* "decoy bird": i.e., "you were never of use to mankind as a decoy bird, alive or dead."

1666. *taveleþ:* Tavel was any game played with movable pieces: backgammon, dice, etc.

"Havestu,"° heo seide,° "ibanned ferde,°   *have you|said|mustered (an) army*
and wultu° wreche° wið me fiȝte?°   *will you|wretch|fight*
1670 Na,° nai, navestu° no miȝte.°   *no|you have not|strength*
Hwat° gredeþ þeo° þat hider° come?   *what|they|here*
Me þuncþ þu ledest° ferde to me.   *you lead*
Ȝe schule wite, ar° ȝe fleo heonne,°   *you shall know, before|fly hence*
hwuch° is þe strenþe° of mine kunne.°   *what|strength|tribe*
1675 For þeo þe° haveþ bile ihoked°   *that|beaks hooked*
and clivres° scharpe and wel icroked,°   *talons|very crooked*
alle heo beoþ° of mine kunrede,°   *are|kindred*
and walde° come ȝif ich bede.°   *would|if I ask*
Þe seolfe coc,° þat wel can fiȝte,   *cock himself*
1680 he mot mid° me holde° mid riȝte;°   *must with|side|right*
for boþe we habbeþ° stevene briȝte°   *have|bright*
and sitteþ under weolcne° bi niȝte.°   *sky|night*
Schulle ich° an utest° uppen ow grede,°   *if I shall|hue and cry|against you raise*

ich schal swo° stronge ferde lede,   *so*
1685 þat ower proude° schal avalle;°   *your pride|fall*
an tort ne ȝive° ich for ow alle.   *turd not give*
Ne schal, ar hit beo fulliche eve,°   *is fully evening*
a wreche feþer° on ow bileave.°   *wretched feather|remain*
Ah° hit was unker voreward,°   *but|our agreement*
1690 þo we come hiderward,°   *came here*
þat we þarto° holde scholde°   *by him|abide should*
þar riht dom° us ȝive wolde.°   *that right judgment|would*
Wultu nu breke foreward?°   *now break agreement*
Ich wene,° dom þe° þingþ to° hard;   *I believe|to you|seems too*
1695 for þu ne darst domes° abide,°   *dare judgment|wait for*
þu wult° nu, wreche, fiȝt and chide.   *will*
Ȝot° ich ow alle wolde rede,°   *yet|advise*
ar ich uthest° uppon ow grede,   *hue and cry*
þat ower fihtlac leteþ beo°   *fight (you) let be*
1700 and ginneþ raþe awei fleo.°   *start quickly away (to) fly*
For bi þe clivres þat ich bere,°   *bear*
ȝef° ȝe abideþ mine here,°   *if|army*
ȝe schule on oþer° wise° singe   *another|tune*
and acursi° alle fiȝtinge.   *curse*
1705 Vor° nis° of ow non° so kene,°   *for|is not|none|bold*
þat durre abide° mine onsene."°   *dare endure|countenance*

1679. Cockfighting can be traced back to the 12th century and in Chaucer's time was regarded as a fashionable amusement. It was forbidden in England from 1849, though it is un- doubtedly still practiced secretly there today, as in the United States.

Þeos hule spac° wel baldeliche;°   *this owl spoke/boldly*
for þah heo° nadde° swo hwatliche°   *though she/had not/quickly*
ifare after hire° here,   *gone for her*
¹⁷¹⁰ heo walde neoþeles ȝefe answere°   *wanted nevertheless (to) give answer*
                                                        (to)

Þe nihtegale° mid swucche worde.°   *nightingale/such words*
For moni° man mid speres orde°   *many (a)/spear's point*
haveþ lutle strencþe° and mid his schelde;°   *has little strength/shield*
ah neoþeles in one felde,°   *on the battlefield*
¹⁷¹⁵ þurh belde° worde and mid ilete,°   *through bold/(fierce) uproar*
deþ° his ivo° for arehþe swete.°   *makes/foe/fear sweat*
Þe wranne, for° heo cuþe° singe,   *wren, because/could*
þar com° in þare moreȝeninge°   *there came/the morning*
to helpe þare niȝtegale;
¹⁷²⁰ for þah heo hadde stevene smale,°   *voice small*
heo hadde gode þorte° and schille,°   *good throat/shrill*
and fale manne° song a wille.°   *(for) many men/sang to (their)*
                                                       delight

Þe wranne was wel wis iholde,°   *very wise considered*
vor þeg° heo nere° ibred a wolde,°   *though/was not/bred in forest*
¹⁷²⁵ ho° was itoȝen° among mannenne°   *she/raised/men*
and hire wisdom brohte° þenne;°   *brought/from them*
heo miȝte speke hwar° heo walde,   *might speak where*
tovore° þe kinge þah° heo scholde.°   *before/if/had to*
"Lusteþ,"° heo cwaþ,° "lateþ° me speke!   *listen/said/let*
¹⁷³⁰ Hwat!° wulle ȝe° þis pes tobreke°   *what/will you/peace break*
and do þan° kinge swuch° schame?   *the/such*
Ȝet nis he nouþer ded ne° lame;   *neither dead nor*
unk° schal itide° harm and schonde,°   *to us/happen/shame*
ȝef ȝe doþ° griþbruche° on° his londe.°   *make/breach of peace/in/land*
¹⁷³⁵ Lateþ beo and beoþ isome,°   *be united*
and fareþ riht° to ower dome,°   *go straight/your judgment*
and lateþ dom° þis plait° tobreke,°   *judgment/pleading/(i.e., settle)*
alswo hit° was erur bispeke."   *as it/before agreed*

    "Ich an° wel," cwað þe niȝtegale,   *I agree*
¹⁷⁴⁰ "ah,° wranne, nawt° for° þire tale,°   *but/not/because of/your speech*
ah do° for mire° lahfulnesse;°   *(I) do (so)/my/respect for law*
ich nolde° þat unrihtfulnesse°   *would not/lawlessness*

1712–16. The "battle boast" or "yelp," either before or during the engagement, was a common element in Teutonic military society (cf. *Beowulf* and *The Battle of Maldon*).

1714. *felde:* Cf. above, p. 73, l. 608n.

1730–31. King's Peace was proclaimed in 1195 by the Justiciar Hubert Walter during the absence of Richard I from England (1194–98). Men above the age of fifteen were required on oath not to breach it.

me at þen° ende overkome;°   *the/(should) overcome*
ich nam° ofdrad° of none° dome.   *am not/afraid/no*
1745 Bihote° ich habbe, soþ° hit is,   *promised/have, true*
þat Maister Nichole, þat is wis,
bituxen° us deme schule,°   *between/judge shall*
and ȝet° ich wene° þat he wule;°   *still/believe/will*
ah war mihte° we hine° finde?"   *where might/him*
1750 Þe wranne sat in ore° linde:°   *a/linden tree*
"Hwat! nuste° ȝe," cwaþ heo,° "his hom?°   *know not/she/home*
He wuneþ° at Porteshom,   *lives*
at one tune ine° Dorsete,   *in a town in*
bi þare see° in ore utlete.°   *the sea/an outlet*
1755 Þar° he demeþ manie riȝte° dom,   *there/gives **many** (a) right*
and diht° and writ mani° wisdom,   *sets down/writes much*
and þurh° his muþe° and þurh his honde°   *through/mouth/hand*
hit is° þe betere° into° Scotlonde.   *(i.e., things are) better/as far as*
To seche° hine is lihtlich° þing,   *find/easy*
1760 he naveþ° bute° one woning,°   *has not/but/dwelling*
þat is bischopen° muchel° schame,   *for the bishops/much*
and alle þan° þat of his nome°   *those/name*
habbeþ ihert° and of his dede.°   *heard/deeds*
Hwi° nulleþ° hi° nimen heom to rede,°   *why/will not/they/adopt as their decision*

1765 þat he were mid heom ilome,°   *be with them often*
for teche° heom of his wisdome,   *to teach*
and ȝive° him rente a vale stude,°   *give/income in many places*
þat° he miȝte° heom ilome be mide?"°   *so that/might/with*

"Certes,"° cwaþ° þe hule,° "þat is soð,   *certainly/said/owl*
1770 þeos° riche men wel° muche misdoð,°   *these/very/do wrong*
þat leteþ þane gode mon,°   *neglect that good man*
þat of so feole þinge con,°   *many things knows*
and ȝiveþ rente wel misliche,°   *indiscriminately*
and of him leteþ wel lihtliche.°   *think little*
1775 Wið heore cunne heo beoþ mildre,°   *their kin they are kinder*
and ȝeveþ° rente litle childre;°   *grant/little children*
swo° heore wit hi demþ a dwole,°   *thus/them condemns into error*
þat ever abid° Maistre Nichole.   *waits*

1752–54. The outlet mentioned here is probably the one called East and West Fleet, formed by the Chesil Bank near Portisham, in Dorsetshire.

1761–76. Nicholas of Guildford, a cleric, complains that he has had no preference from the bishops, who could have given him a *rente*, a benefice or living. Such a vicarage, perhaps several, meant security for life. But it is precisely this accusation (that the bishops practiced nepotism in advancing their own relatives over the more worthy Nicholas) that casts some doubt on his authorship. He would surely have realized that one does not gain advancement by insulting one's potential patrons.

Ah ute we þah° to him fare,°   *let us however|go*
1780 for þar is unker dom° al ʒare."°   *our judgment|ready*

"Do we,"° þe niʒtegale seide,°   *let us do so|nightingale said*
"ah wa° schal unker speche° rede°   *but who|pleas|bring forward*
and telle tovore° unker deme?"°   *before|judge*

"Þarof° ich° schal þe° wel icweme,"°   *concerning that|I|you|please*
1785 cwaþ þe houle,° "for al, ende of orde,°   *owl|beginning to end*
telle ich con° word after worde;   *can*
and ʒef° þe° þincþ° þat ich misrempe,°   *if|to you|(it) seems|err*
þu° stond aʒein° and do me crempe."°   *you|contradict|constrain*
Mid þisse worde° forþ hi ferden°   *these words|went*
1790 al bute here° and bute verde,°   *without army|martial host*
to Portesham þat° heo bicome.   *until|came*
Ah hu° heo spedde of° heore dome,°   *how|succeeded in|judgment*
ne° can ich eu° namore° telle;   *not|you|no more*
her° nis° namore of þis spelle.°   *here|is not|tale*

THE DEBATE OF THE BODY AND SOUL

DATE: c. 1400. ⚹ MANUSCRIPTS: Bodleian Library, Oxford, Laud 108 (Summary Cat., No. 1486), the end of the 13th century; Edinburgh University Auchinleck, c. 1330–40; Bodleian Library, Oxford, Vernon (Summary Cat., No. 3938), the end of the 14th century; British Library Simeon (Additional 22,283), the end of the 14th century; British Library Additional 37,787, c. 1400; British Library Royal 18 A. x, 1350–1400; Bodleian Library, Oxford, Digby 102 (Summary Cat., No. 1703), c. 1400. The dialect is West Midland, though it is impure. ⚹ EDITIONS: Wilhelm Linow, *The Desputisoun bitwen the Body and the Soule* (Erlangen, 1889), containing Laud, Auchinleck, Vernon, Simeon, and Digby; Nita Scudder Baugh, *A Worcestershire Miscellany, compiled by John Northwood, c. 1400* (Philadelphia, 1956), which is the edition used here. The MS. was written at the Cistercian Abbey of Saint Mary's Bordesley, fourteen miles northeast of the city of Worcester, sometime after 1388.

The West Midland nature of the dialect will cause the student little trouble. A few points in connection with the text might be mentioned: (1) *a* before nasals is normally *o* (*mon*); (2) *u* will be exchanged for *v* (*lyues* = *lives*); (3) OE *y* (*i*) will be written *u* (*mysdude* = *misdid*, *sunne* [*synne*] = *sin*); (4) the 3d person present singular of verbs and noun plurals occasionally end in *-ys/-is*. The order of the stanzas in this text is not that of British Library MS. Additional 37,787 (the Worcestershire Miscellany compiled by John Northwood), but is the one proposed by Nita Scudder Baugh in her edition. The Latin rubrics of the MS. have been deleted.

As can be seen from the dates of the various MSS listed above, the Debate of the Body and Soul kept its popularity for centuries, beginning with an Address of the Soul in the Old English Exeter and Vercelli books. Sermons and homilies continued the theme. At first only the Soul spoke, but in the *Conflictus Corporis et Animae*, perhaps by Bishop Grosseteste in the 13th century, a true debate, angry and to the point, between Body and Soul came into being. This poem and the *Noctis sub Silentio* (Thomas Wright, *The Latin Poems Commonly Attributed to Walter Mapes* [London, 1841]) are the main sources of the Middle English version here printed.

I

As I lay in a wynteres nyʒt,°   *night*
In a droupnyng° to-fore° þe day,   *drowsy sleep/before*

1–3. The poem begins with the traditional dream-vision device, very common in medieval literature (specifically in Chaucer) and seen to perfection in the Old English poem the *Dream of the Rood*.

603

Me° þou3t° I seye° a sely sy3t,°   *to me/(it) seemed/saw/marvelous*
                                                                          sight

A body þere hit° on bere° lay,   *where it/bier*
5 Þat had ben° a cumly kny3t,°   *been/handsome knight*
   And lytel seruyd° God to pay.°   *little served/his liking*
   Lorne° he hadde hys lyues ly3t.°   *lost/life's light*
   Þe goste° was owte and wolde° away.   *soul/would (be)*

II

   And when þe goste hym scholde° go,   *it should*
10 Hit turned a3en° and so hit stode,°   *again/stood*
   Be-helde þe fleche° þer hit come fro,°   *flesh/came from*
   So sorfullyche° wiþ drery mode,°   *sorrowful/dreary heart*
   And seyde,° "Allas° and welowo.°   *said/alas/woe*
   Þu fekul° fleche, þu false blode,°   *you treacherous/blood*
15 Why lyest° þu now stynkyng so,   *lie*
   Þat sum tyme° were so wyle° and wode?°   *formerly/wily/mad (? crafty)*

III

   Þu þat were I-wonte° to ryde,   *wont*
   So hye° on horse in and owte,   *high*
   So worþi a kny3te and kyd° so wyde,   *known*
20 As a lyon ferse° and prowde,   *fierce*
   Where ys now alle þi grete° pryde,   *great*
   And alle þi nete° þat was so lowde?   *cattle*
   Why lyste° þu þere so bare by syde,°   *lie/beside (me)*
   Pryckyd° in so pore° a schroude?   *dressed/poor*

IV

25 "Where ben° now alle þi worþi wedis,°   *are/clothes*
   þo somurse° wiþ þe ryche beddys,°   *the packhorses/trappings*
   þe palfreys° and þe hye stedis,°   *riding horses/tall steeds*
   Þat þu abowte in þe strete ledys,°   *road led*
   Þo fawkunse° þat were wonte° to grede,°   *falcons/used/cry*
30 Ande þe grehoundus° þat þu feddys?°   *greyhounds/fed*
   Me þinkyth° þi goode° ys þe° ful gnede,°   *(it) seems/property/for you/very*
                                                                          scanty

   Now alle þine frendys ben from þe° fledde.   *you*

V

   "Where ben þi castelse° and þyne tourus,°   *castles/towers*
   Þi chamburs and þi hye hallus,°   *halls*

---

27. *palfreys:* Cf. above, p. 346, n. 26.

³⁵ Þat payntyd were wiþ fayre flowrus,°   *flowers*
   And þe ryche robus° alle,   *robes*
   Þe quyltus° and þe couertourus,°   *quilts/covers*
   Þat cendal° and þat purpul palle?°   *silken/cloth*
   Lo, wreche,° where is now þi bowre?°   *wretch/chamber*
⁴⁰ To morwe° schal þu þer-in falle.   *tomorrow*

VI

   "Where ben now alle þese kokys snelle,°   *those cooks quick*
   Þat scholde so greyþe° þi mete,°   *prepare/food*
   Wiþ ryche spyseryes° for to smel,   *spices*
   Þat þu were gredy° for to frete,°   *greedy/devour*
⁴⁵ To done° þat fowle° fleche to swelle,   *cause/foul*
   Þat now wole° wylde wormys ete?°   *will/eat*
   And me þe pytte and pyne° of helle   *pain*
   Wiþ þi glotenye° hast þu geten.°   *gluttony/gotten*

VII

   "Where be þes glemen° þe to gleon,°   *are those gleemen/entertain*
⁵⁰ Harpe and fedel° and tabur bete,°   *fiddle/tabor beat*
   Þe pypurs° þat þes baggus blewen,°   *pipers/bags* (i.e., *bagpipes*) *blew*
   And hem° þu gafe° gyftys grete,   *them/gave*
   Þe ryche robys olde and new,
   To ȝelpen° of þe þere° þey seton?°   *boast/where/sat*
⁵⁵ Soche trowlors° were not trew.°   *such singers/true*
   Þey had of° þe þat° þey myȝt geton.°   *took from/what/might get*

VIII

   "For to bere° þi worde so wyde,   *bear*
   And maken° of þe rym° and raffe,°   *make/rhyme/scurrilous verses*
   Sowche guylors° for pompe and pryde,   *such deceivers*
⁶⁰ Largelyche of° hem þu ȝaffe,°   *generously to/you gave*
   And þe pore ȝedun° alle be-syde.°   *left/aside*
   For euer hem þu ouer-haf,°   *passed over*
   And ȝyf° þey come° in eny° vnryde,°   *if/came/any/? disorder*
   Sone° were þey strekun° wiþ a staf.   *soon/struck*

IX

⁶⁵ "Of sowche pore° þu hit name,°   *poor/it took*
   Þat° mony° a glotun ete° and dranke,   *so that/many/glutton ate*
   Ne° neuer þu rowste° of whom,   *nor/cared*
   Ne ho° þer-for harduste swanke.°   *who/hardest worked*

49–72. Cf. above, p. 341, n. 5.

Þe ryche was welcom when he came,
70 Þe pore was betun° þat he stanke.°   *beaten/(i.e., farted)*
Now is alle gone wiþ Godys grame,°   *wrath*
And now haste° þu wreche lytel þonke.°   *have/little thanks*

X

"Of alle þat þu to-gedur drowhe,°   *together drew*
And were° harder þan þe flynte,   *(to whom you) were*
75 Sowche schal make hit° large I-nowhe,°   *of it/free enough*
Þat° þu neuer hadduste° hit mynte.°   *as/had intended*
And þu þat madeste hit so towhe,°   *difficult*
Alle þi boste° is sone astynte.°   *boasting/ended*
As° I may wepe° þat þu be lowhe,°   *so/weep/low*
80 For alle my blysse is for° þe tynte.°   *because of/you lost*

XI

"Þu wreche° þat in alle þat sythe°   *wretch/time*
Nere° neuer of° worldes wynne sade,°   *were not/with/joy satisfied*
Now haste þu neyþer londe° ne lythe,°   *neither land/subjects*
But VII fote° and vnneþe° þat.   *feet/scarcely*
85 Now seste° þu and þe sothe° hit kythe,°   *see/truth/is known*
Alle is lorne° þat þu here gatte,°   *lost/got*
And þu ne° schalte neuer efte° be blyþe.°   *not/again/happy*
Of° þat oþer wol° maken hem° glad.   *over/others/will/themselves*

XII

"As to-morue° as sone° hit is day,   *tomorrow/soon as*
60 Owte from þe kyþe° and þi kynne,   *your kith*
Bare schalte þu wende° þat way,   *go*
And leuen° alle þi worldes wynne.   *leave*
A° pore paleyse syth° þu here lay°   *(in) a/palace since/lie*
Wiþ wormys now schal be þine Ine.°   *lodging*
95 Þi bowre° is bylde° so colde in clay,   *chamber/built*
Þe rofe° to restun° vpon þi chynne.   *roof/rest*

XIII

"And þi false ere° is now fayne°   *heir/glad*
Þi fayre feo° for to vndur fo.°   *goods/receive*
Wel ys° hym° þis day isein,°   *fair is/to him/seen*

---

70. The image of men beaten until they lost control of their bodily functions, i.e., farted or made water, was a common medieval idea, and undoubtedly a realistic one (cf. Noe in the Towneley Plays).

75–76. "People that you did not want to get your money will inherit it, rather than the heirs you intended."

97. A false heir here may mean anyone who betrays, in any way, the intentions of his father.

¹⁰⁰ Þat lytel good schal for þe do.	
Nolde° he nouȝt° now ȝeuen aȝen,°	would not/not/give again
To bryngun° vs in reste and ro,°	bring/peace
Of alle þat londe a fote or tweyne,°	two
Þat þu° so synfullyche cum° to.	you/sinfully came

XIV

¹⁰⁵ "And þine seketourus° wol now seke°	executors/seek
Þyne oþer þyng° now þu arte dede.°	things/dead
Alle schal gaynelyche° go to wreke.°	completely/ruin
Haue þey delyd° a lytel brede,°	divided/bread
Vche° to pyke þat° he can kache,	each/pick what/catch
¹¹⁰ Schepe° or swyne or horse or nete.°	sheep/cattle
As lytel þer-fore° we ne recke,°	about it/care
Siþen° we ben° boþe betawht° þe qwed."°	since/are/delivered to/Devil

XV

And when þe goste° wiþ gryslyche chere°	soul/grisly countenance
Had þus made his mekyl mone,°	great complaint
¹¹⁵ Þe body þer hit° lay on bere,°	where it/bier
An vngliche° þyng as hit was one,	ugly
Þe hede hefe° vp on þe swyre.°	head raised/neck
As a þyng al seke° hit gafe° a grone,°	sick/gave/groan
And seyde,° "Whyder° þowhtestu° ficrc,°	said/whither thought you (to go)/ companion
¹²⁰ Þat were þus freshliche° from me gone?	freshly

XVI

"What eylyth þe,° þu grymlyche° gostc,	ails you/grim
Þat me þus breydest of° myne vn-hap,°	upbraids for/misfortune
So broþlyche° as myne herte braste,°	violently/heart burst
Þe dethe° so delfully° me drap?°	that death/dolefully/struck
¹²⁵ I ne am fyrste ne° laste	nor
Þat schal drynken° of þat nap.°	drink/cup
Nis° non° so kene° þat he nys caste,°	(there) is not/none/good/thrown
Þe pruddeste° may arstc kepe° hys clap.°	proudest/first hold/tongue

XVII

"What° braydest° þu me þat I schal rote,°	why/upbraids/rot
¹³⁰ For so dude° Samson and Sesar,°	did/Caesar
Þat° no man can now fynde one mote°	so that/particle
Of hem° ne of moder° þat hem bare.°	them/mother/bore

---

130. *Samson and Sesar.* These names of famous men vary in all the French, English, and Latin versions.

Wormys hath her þrote eten,°   *throat eaten*
So schal þey myne I am wel war.°   *aware*
135 Þer dethe fynde° þe dore opun,°   *finds|open*
Þer is no helpe agayne° to char.°   *toward|turn*

XVIII

"And when I syhe° boþe clerke and knyȝt,°   *saw|knight*
And oþer men by þe way go,
And I was man of mekyl myȝt,°   *might*
140 And euer wende° haue duryd° so,   *thought (to)|remained*
Hye hallys and bowrys bryȝt°   *high|chambers bright*
Had I made wiþ murþis mo,°   *mirth great*
My dwellyng here so fayre dyȝt,°   *established*
Þat dethe hath me þus demyd fro.°   *doomed (to go) from*

XIX

145 "My wonyng° here so mury° I wroht,°   *dwelling|pleasant|made*
And wend had leuyd ȝyt ȝeris fele,°   *(to have) lived yet years many*
Wyde wonys° and byldes boht,°   *dwellings|buildings bought*
Wiþ alle þat euer I myȝt spele.°   *mention*
Now wente° þe worlde a-ȝen° my þoht,°   *turned|against|thought*
150 And dethe þat can so stylle stele°   *quietly steal*
Hath me demde a-way° wiþ noht,°   *doomed away (to go)|nothing*
And oþer° to weldun° alle þis wele.°   *others|wield|wealth*

XX

"And ȝyf þu° wylt me þer-of° quite°   *if you|for that|repay*
Þat boþe schul° we ben I-spylte,°   *shall|be destroyed*
155 Wiþ þi-selfe þu scholdest flyte,°   *should contend*
For alle was hit° þine owne gylte.   *it*
Þat schewde° I þe wiþ wordis lyte,°   *would show|few*
And wiþ ryȝt reson° if þu wylte.   *right reason*
Þu arte to blame and I alle quite,°   *acquitted*
160 For boþen schuldest° þu fro schame haue schylte.° *both should|shielded*

XXI

"For God þe schope° aftur hys schafte°   *you created|kind*
And ȝaf° þe boþe wyt and skylle,   *gave*
And in þi lokyng° alle was I lafte,°   *care|left*
To wysen° alle aftur þyne owne wylle.   *manage*
165 Ne kowþe° I neuer of wycked crafte,   *not knew*
Ne wyste° what was goode ne ille,   *nor knew*

But as a beste dombe° and dafte.°   *beast dumb/stupid*
And as þu tauhtest° me þer-tylle.°   *taught/of it*

XXII

"For I was betakyn° þe° to ȝeme,°   *committed/to you/control*
170 A wytlese° þyng as I was borne,°   *mindless/born*
And set to seruen° þe to qwem,°   *serve/for pleasure*
Boþe at euen° and at morne.   *evening*
As° þu þat dedys° cowþest° deme°   *so/deeds/knew how to/judge*
Scholdest haue be war be-forne°   *been aware beforehand*
175 Of my foly° as hit now seme,°   *folly/seems*
And þus arte þu þi-selfe I-lorne."°   *lost*

XXIII

The soule seyde,° "Body, be stylle.   *said*
Ho° hath lerned° þe þis wyt,   *who/taught*
To ȝeuen° me þes° wordis grylle,°   *give/these/harsh*
180 Þer° þu lyste bolned° as a byt?°   *where/lie swollen/leather bottle*
Weneste° þu, wrech,° seþen° þu fylle   *think/wretch/when*
Wyth þat fowle fleche° a pit,   *foul flesh*
Of alle þat euer þu hastc° done ille   *have*
Þat þu so lyȝtlyche° schalt be quyt?°   *lightly/acquitted*

XXIV

185 "Wenest þu þus to getun gryþ,°   *think/get peace*
Þouȝ° þu lye rotun° in þat clay?   *though/lie rotten*
Nay þouȝ þu rote pyle° and pyþe,°   *rot hair/pith*
And blowen° wyth þe wynde a-way,   *blow*
Ȝet schalte þu comc wiþ lym° and lyþe°   *limb/joint*
190 A-ȝen° to me at domis day,°   *again/Judgment Day*
Ande come to courte and i þe wyth,
For to kepe owre° ryȝt pay.°   *receive our/recompense*

XXV

"To loke, seyst þu, where° þu me° tauht.°   *guard, say you, were/to me/entrusted*
As sone° þu knowest eny quede,°   *soon as/knew any evil*
195 Wiþ þi tethe° þe brydul° þu lawht°   *teeth/bridle/seized*
And deduste° alle þat I þe forbede.°   *did/forbade*
To synne and sorw° was þi drawht,°   *sorrow/inclination*
To sorwe and wyckyd-hede.°   *wickedness*
Sor° I chydde aȝen° and faute,°   *sorely/chided against/fought*
200 And euer þu nome° þyne owne rede.°   *took/counsel*

XXVI

"For when I spake° of soule nedys,°
Mas, matynse° or euensong,
þu moste arste done° oþer dedys,
And toldest hit° alle ydul° songe.

²⁰⁵ To reuer° or to chase° þu ȝede,°
Or to courte to deme wronge,
But for pryde or muchel mede,°
Lytel° good þu dedust a-monge.°

spoke/soul's needs
mass, matins
must first do
counted it/idle
river/hunt/went

great reward
little/in the meantime

XXVII

"So ofte hath be tolde þe° þat
²¹⁰ What° þu, wreche, scholdeste° haue,
And litel þu ȝafe alle-way of° þat.
Ȝyt° þu sye° alle þi kyn in graue,
Þu dyst alle° as þe worlde þe bad,°
And as þi fowle flesche wolde° craue.

²¹⁵ I suffurde° þe and dude° as mad.
Þow° were mayster° and I þi knaue."°

you
which/should
bothered ever with
though/saw
did always/bade
would

endured/acted
you/master/servant

XXVIII

Þe bodi grunte° and gan° to sey,
"Goste,° þu haste° wrong, I-wyse,°
Alle þe gylte on me to leye,°
²²⁰ Þat þu haste þus I-lore° þi blysse.
Where was I by wode° or by way
Sat° or stode° or dyd owht misse,°
Þat I was° euer vndur þine eye?
Wele° þu woste° þat soþe hit is.

groaned/began
soul/are/indeed
lay
lost
forest
(when) sat (I)/stood/anything amiss
was (not)
well/know/truth

XXIX

²²⁵ "And þu þat were so worþi I-wroht,°
Þu seyste I made þe my þralle,
As þouhe° I nere° of þe rouht.°
Þu hit dyste and I wiþ-alle.°
Ne mysdude° I neuer nowth,°
²³⁰ Ne° I ne rafte° ne I ne stale,°

created

though/never/cared
together
not misdid/not at all
nor/took/stole

---

202. *matynse:* the service for the first of the seven canonical hours; *euensong:* the service of vespers, the sixth of the canonical hours, held in late afternoon or evening.

205. *To reuer:* i.e., to hunt for river fowl (cf. above, p. 148, l. 234*n*).

Þat arst of þe come° þe þouht,° came (not)/thought
A-bye° who a-bye schal. account (for it)

XXX

"What wyste° I what was wrong or ryȝt,° knew/right
What to take or what to schone,° shun
235 But as þu° puttyst in my syȝte° you/sight
Þat alle þe wysdome scholdest hafe cunne?° have known
When I dude° an vnryȝt° did/misdeed
Þat þu schuste° of me haue mone,° should/reminded
Þen wolde I wiþ alle my myȝt° might
240 A-noþer tyme to haue þat wone.° (good) custom

XXXI

"Wele owhtest° þu to wete° what was my kynde,° ought/know/nature
As owre eldrun werun or þo,° our ancestors were before then
To haue þis wrechyd° worlde so in mynde, wretched
And euer coueten mo° and mo. covet more
245 Allas° why noldeste° þu me bynde, alas/would not
When I wolde to synne haue to?° gone
For þer° þe blynde ledyth° þe blynde, where/lead
In þe dyche° þey fallyth boþe to. ditch

XXXII

"I ne scholde haue ben° but as a schepe,° been/sheep
250 Or as an oxe or as a swyne,
Þat etyth° and drynke, lye° and slepe,° eats/lies/sleeps
Slayne and passed alle his pyne.° pain
Ne of° no catel° men toke° no kepe,° to/cattle/paid/attention
Þey chesun° þe watur fro° þe wyne. chose/instead of
255 Ne þu scholdest° not into hel depe,° should (go)/deep
Nere þe wytte° þat alle was þyne." were it not for reason

XXXIII

"Carone° vnkynde, what haste° þu sayde? body/have
For euer ȝyt° were þu leþur° and lese,° yet/evil/untrue
For to brew me byttur breid,° affliction
260 And me to pylton° out of pes.° push/peace
Wiþ lyme I-wroht,° wiþ tongge I-seyde,° by limbs done/tongue said
To harme was þi rapelych res.° hasty course

---

248. *In þe dyche ... to:* i.e., "in the ditch."

Wyth schame is now þi lyfe I-leyde,°   *done*
Wyth sorw mynewith me° þat mes.°   *sorrow remember I/food*

XXXIV

265 "A° who may more treson° do,   *oh/treason*
Or hys louer bettur begyle,
Þan he þat alle hys truste is to.°   *in*
Now may I say allas þe whyle,
Euer seþen° þat þu couste° go.   *since/could*
270 Stynte° nolste° þu neuer ne lyne°   *stop/would not/nor incline*
Þiselfe to dyhten° rest and ro,°   *prepare/peace*
And me° to purchacen° pyt and pyne.   *for me/purchasing*

XXXV

"And now may þese bestis renne,°   *beasts run*
And lye undur lynde° and lefe,°   *linden tree/leaf*
275 And foulus fleyth° by felde° and fenne,   *birds fly/field*
Seþen þi false herte to-clefe.°   *heart broke*
Þi ey is blynde and can not kenne,°   *perceive*
Þi mowthe is dome,° þine ere° is defe,°   *dumb/ear/deaf*
And þu° begynnest þus to grenne.°   *you/grin*
280 From þe° comyth a wyckyd wefe.°   *you/evil odor*

XXXVI

"Nis° no leuedy° so bryht° of ble,°   *(there) is not/lady/bright/hue*
Þat of þe were wel wone° to lete,°   *wont/esteem*
Þat one day wolde° now wiþ þe be,   *would*
For alle þe golde þu euer gete.°   *got*
285 Vnsemelyche° ar-tow° now to se,°   *ugly/are you/see*
Vnkumlyche° for to kys swete.°   *unpleasant/kiss sweet*
Now hast þu no frende but he wolde fle,°   *flee*
And° þu come stertyng° forþe in þe strete."°   *if/came advancing/street*

XXXVII

"Nay, grymlyche gost° alle þis is noht°   *grim soul/naught*
290 Wiþ me to holden° chyde° and cheste,°   *engage in/chiding/strife*
For cliuen° I moste° to þi þoht,°   *adhere/had to/thought*
And bowen° as a bounden beste,°   *bend/bound beast*
To done° alle þat þe of roht.°   *do/wanted*
I was euer at þi hest.°   *command*

270–72. "You never would stop or incline to prepare yourself for rest and peace, while for me you purchased the pit and pain."

295 Wythstonde° þe durste° I noht,°   *withstand/dared/not*
    For wiþ þe weren° þe myӡtis moste.°   *were/powers greatest*

XXXVIII

    "For alle° I was unto þe ӡeuen,°   *completely/given*
    And as þine ase° I þe bare,°   *ass/bore*
    And mayster° ouer me to leuen,°   *master/live*
300 Þat was wel of myne wrenches ware,°   *tricks aware*
    And when þu haddeste me fordreuen,°   *driven about*
    And I-put til eny char,°   *put to any task*
    Alle to þi counsayle° moste I cleuen,°   *counsel/adhere*
    As he dothe þat none oþer dar.°   *nothing else dares*

XXXIX

305 "And haddest þu,° so° Criste hit ouþe,°   *if you had/as/it willed*
    Ӡeuen me boþe hongur° and colde,   *hunger*
    And I-tauht° me þat noht ne kouþe°   *taught/not knew*
    But lye° in bysmere° so bolde,   *(to) lie/shame*
    Þat° I vsed° in my ӡouþe°   *that which/practiced/youth*
310 Had° I-holden° when I was olde.   *would have/held*
    As° þu me lete rayken° norþe and sowþe   *but/let wander*
    And hauen° alle my wylle as I wolde."   *have*

XL

    "Haa,° þu foulc flesche vnsyete,°   *ha/unseemly*
    Ful of falsenes° and fallaz,°   *falseness/lies*
315 Þat I sye° þe euer ӡytte,°   *see/yet*
    For alle my loue on þe I las.°   *wasted*
    Þat þu louest me þu lyet,°   *lied*
    And madist° me an houue° of glasse.   *made/cap*
    I dude° alle þat þe þouӡt° swete,   *did/thought*
320 And þu traytur° euer wasse.°   *you (a) traitor/were*

XLI

    "For when I bade þe schryfte° take,   *you confession*
    And leuc° þi synnus° euer and o,°   *leave/sins/all*
    Done penance and faste and wake,
    Þe fende° sayde, 'Schalte þu not so,   *Devil*
325 Þus ӡonge° þi ryote° forsake,   *so young/rioting*
    To leuyn° longe in sorwe° and wo.°   *live/sorrow/woe*

---

318. *house of glasse:* i.e., "fool's cap." To make a cap of glass meant to mock
or ridicule (cf. Chaucer, *Troilus and Criseyde*, II, l. 987; V, l. 469).

Ioy° and myrthe I rede° þu make,   *joy/advise*
And þenke° to leue° ȝytte ȝerys mo.'°   *think/live/years more*

XLII

"And when I bad° þe leue pryde,   *bade*
330 Þine mony° messe,° þi semelyche schrowde,° *many/food courses/handsome dress*
Þis wrechyd° worlde þe stode bysyde,°   *wretched/stood beside*
And bad þe be ful qweynte° and proude, *very elegant*
Þi flesche wiþ ryche robys schryde,°   *robes (to) clothe*
Noht as a begger in a cloute,°   *rag*
335 And on hye° horse for to ryde,   *tall*
Wiþ mekul meyny° in and owte.   *large retinue*

XLIII

"And when I bad þe erly to ryse,
And of me take goode kepe,°   *care*
Þu seydest° þu myȝtyst° in no wyse,°   *said/might/way*
340 For° þe mery° morne-slepe.°   *because of/pleasant/morning sleep*
And when ȝe haddun° set ȝowre assise,° *you had/your trial*
Ȝe iij trayters,° sore I wepe.°   *traitors/wept*
Ȝe ladden° me wiþ oure empryse,°   *led/your enterprise*
As þe boþelere° doþ þe shep."°   *butcher/sheep*

XLIV

345 And þo° þe body seyh° þe gast°   *when/saw/soul*
Swych dole° and swych mone° make,   *such woe/moan*
Hyt° sayde, "Allas° my lyues laste,°   *it/alas/life's burden*
Þat euer I leuyd° for þyne sake.   *lived*
Þat° my herte a-non° had berste,°   *(would) that/heart quickly/burst*
350 As sone° hit° was fro° my modur take,° *soon as/it/from/mother taken*
Or ben° in to a pyt I-caste,°   *been/thrown*
Wyth a tode° or wyth a snake.   *toad*

XLV

"For þen had I neuer I-lerned°   *learned*
What was euel ne° what was goode,   *nor*
355 Ne no þyng wiþ wrong ȝerned,°   *yearned*
Ne payne suffurde° and now I mote,°   *suffered/must*

---

342. *iij trayters:* Stanzas concerning the "fend of helle" and "þe world" are inserted in the Digby MS. as companions of the body (perhaps with a reference to Saint Bernard's treatise *De Tribus Inimicis Hominis, Carne, Mundo, et Diabolo* [*On the Three Foes of Man: The Flesh, the World, and the Devil*] The three traitors are, therefore, the world, the flesh, and the Devil.

344. A passage on the assize, found at this point in other MSS, is lacking here.

Wheþer no seynt° may byd owre ernde,°   *any saint/make our petition*
To hym þat bou3t° vs wiþ hys blode,°   *bought/blood*
Þat we ne bene° in þis fyre forbrende,°   *not be/burned up*
360 Þrow° hys mercy to done° vs bote."°   *through/do/good*

XLVI

"Nay, wrech,° nay, now ys to° late   *wretch/(it) is too*
For to pray or for to preche.°   *preach*
Now is ry3t° at þe 3ate,°   *righteousness/gate*
And þi tongge° hath leyde þe speche.°   *tongue/lost the (faculty of) speech*
365 A-pon° erþe peyne° to a-bate   *upon/pain*
In alle þis londe° is now no leche,°   *land/physician*
But boþe we schul gon o gate.°   *shall go one way*
Suche ys Godes wrathe and wreche.°   *vengeance*

XLVII

"I ne may no lenger° dwel   *longer*
370 Ne stonden° here to speke° wiþ þe,°   *stand/speak/you*
For helle-houndes here° I 3elle,°   *hear/yelling*
And fendys mo° þan I may se,°   *devils more/see*
Þat comyth to feche° me to helle.   *fetch*
I may no way fle°   *flee*
375 And þu° schalt come in fleche° and felle°   *you/flesh/skin*
At domys-day° to wone° wiþ me."   *Judgment Day/live*

XLVIII

And as hit had þus I-sayde,°   *said*
Nyst° hit whider° hit schulde° go,   *knew not/where/should*
And þo° hit had a heuy brayde.°   *then/heavy blow*
380 Comyn° a þowsande fendus° or mo.   *came/devils*
And sone° þey hadden° on hym leyde°   *soon/had/laid*
Her° scharpe clawes alle þo.°   *their/then*
Hit was in a pore pleyte,°   *poor plight*
Rufullych þolyd° to and fro.   *lamentably tormented*

XLIX

385 For sum weren° ragged and tayled,   *some were*
Wiþ brode bunches° on her backe,   *broad swellings*
Scharpe clawes and longe nayles.
Nos° none of hem wiþ-owten lacke.°   *(there) was not/them without
                                         deformity*

On alle halwe° hit was asayled   *sides*
390 Of mony° a deuel blo° and black.   *by many/devil blue*
Mercy crying lytel° hym avayled,   *little*
Seþen° God hit wolde° so harde hym wrakc.°   *since/willed/(to) punish*

L

Sum hys chaules° alle to-wraste,°   *jowls/tore away*
And ȝoten° in lede° alle hote.°   *poured/lead/hot*
395 Þey bade he scholde° drynke faste,   *should*
And shenche° aboute hym a brode.°   *pour out/ ? far and wide*
A fowle fende come° þere at þe laste,   *foul devil came*
Þat was mayster° þer wel I wote.°   *master/believe*
A cultur° glowyng on hym he caste,°   *plowshare/threw*
400 Þat° hit þrow° hys herte° smote.   *so that/through/heart*

LI

Gleyuys° glowyng sum setten°   *swords/put*
To° backe, to brest, to vche a° syde.   *on/each*
Þat at hys herte þe poyntis met
And maden° hym woundys wyde.   *made*
405 Þey askyd hym how wel hit lette°   *left*
Þe herte þat was so fulle of pride,
Yf he had ȝet þat° men hym het°   *what/promised*
For more hym° moste° sone betyde.°   *to him/must/happen*

LII

Worþelyche wedis° for to were,°   *costly clothes/wear*
410 Seyden° þey þat he louyd° beste.   *said/loved*
An heuy borþen° for to beren°   *burden/bear*
Alle brennyng° on hym was kaste,°   *burning/thrown*
Wiþ strayte° haspis for to sperren,°   *tight/fasten*
Þat faste to backe and breste.
415 An helm° þat lytel was to heren°   *helmet/praise*
Come him, and an horse ful prest.°   *very ready*

LIII

He was þere in a sadel slunggun,°   *saddle slung*
And scholde° to þe turnement.°   *had to (go)/tournament*
An hundurde° deueles on hym dunggun.°   *hundred/struck*
420 Here and þere he was I-hente°   *seized*
And vche a° dynt° þe sparkys sprongun,°   *(at) each/blow/sprang*
As a bronde° þat were forbrent.°   *brand/burned*
Wiþ hote speris° was he stonggun,°   *spears/stung*
Wiþ scharpe swerdis° alle to-rent.°   *swords/torn apart*

---

418. Tournaments were often criticized by clerics in the Middle Ages. Robert Mannyng of Brunne in *Handlyng Synne* (1303) has a section condemning them.

LIV

425 Þey byddun° hym for to hunten° and blow,°   *commanded/hunt/blow (the horn)*
And clepen° bautȝan and beau fyȝ,   *call*
Þe racchys° þat hym scholde know,   *hunting dogs*
For sone mosten° þey blowen prys.°   *soon must/blow "Prize!"*
An hondurde° racchys in a row   *hundred*
430 Dryuen° hym alle vnþankys,°   *drove/unwillingly*
Tyl he come at° a lodlyche lowe.°   *to/hideous hole*
Helle hit° was I wote to-wys.°   *it/indeed*

LV

And þo° þey come at þat wyckyd wone,°   *when/evil place*
Þe fendis kestun° vp a ȝelle.°   *devils threw/yell*
435 Þe erþe opunde° vp a-non.°   *opened/at once*
Smoke and smolder° vp þer welle,°   *smoldering/rose*
Of° þe pych° and þe brymstone,   *from/pitch*
Men myȝt mony° a mylc haue smelle.°   *(that) men might many/smelled*
Loud wo° hym bydon,°   *grievous woe/be*
440 Þat þere schal haue þe haluendele.°   *half part*

LVI

And þo þe goste° þe sothe seih,°   *soul/truth saw*
Whyder° hit scholde° hit kest° a crye,   *whither/should/uttered*
And seyde, "God þat syttest an hyeh,°   *on high*
On me þu° haue mynde° and mercye.   *thou/remembrance*
445 Ne schope° þu me þat arte so slye?°   *not created/wise*
And þi creature was I,
As mony° one þat now settyþ þc nye,°   *many (a)/sits you near*
And þat þu hast so wel done bye.°   *by*

LVII

"Þu God þat wystest° alle to-forne,°   *knows/before*
450 Why schope þu me to wroþer-hele,°   *destruction*
To ben° þus toggcd° or to-torne,°   *be/pulled/torn to pieces*
Or for to welden eny wele?°   *enjoy any prosperity*
Þo° þat scholden° haue ben I-lorne,°   *they/should/been lost*
Wel myȝtyst° þu suche wrecches° spele.°   *might/wretches/? warn*

425–43. We have here a travesty of the fox hunt, a theme used several times in Middle English literature, e.g., in *The Owl and the Nightingale* and Layamon's *Brut*. The hunting dogs of the Devil are mentioned in *Gesta Romanorum* and by Nicolas Bozon (cf. *Histoire Littéraire de la France*, XXXVI, 405). The latter gives eight, including Bauwiz, who chases all men inclined to lechery, and Baudewyn, who pursues men of law.

426. *bautȝan and beau fyȝ*: dogs' names; in some MSS Bauson and Beaufils, the French forms.

428. *prys*: i.e., the tune signaling the capture.

⁴⁵⁵ Allas,° why letyste° þu us be borne,°   alas/let/born
To ȝeuen° þe foule fende° so felle?"°   be given/Devil/fierce

LVIII

Þe fendys began a-ȝen° to crye,   again
"Caytyfe, helpyth° þe now no more,   rascal, (it) helps
To clepen on ihesu ne° on marye,°   Jesus nor/Mary
⁴⁶⁰ Ne for to craue Crystis ore.°   grace
Lorne° hast þu° þat cumpanye,°   lost/you/company
For seruyd° hast þu vs so ȝore,°   served/long
Þe bulted brede° þu moste° aby,°   white bread/must/pay for
As oþer° þat leuyth° on owre lore."°   others/believe/our faith

LIX

⁴⁶⁵ Þe fendis þat of° hym weren ful fayne,°   for/were very eager
By top and tayle þey hentun hyt,°   seized it
And slonggun° hit wiþ a mody mayne°   threw/mighty strength
In-to þe aller° deppyst° pyt,   very/deepest
Þere° neuer sunne ne° schal schyne.   where/not
⁴⁷⁰ Hem-selfe° þer sonkun° in þayre° myȝt,   themselves/sank/their
Þe erþe lockud° hit-selfe a-ȝen,   locked (i.e., shut)
Anon þe dungun° was fordyȝt.°   dungeon/closed up

LX

And þen° þe sowle° was forþe I-lad,°   when/soul/led
Faste° can hit nyȝhe° þe day.   at once/appeared
⁴⁷⁵ On euery here° a drope stode,°   hair/drop stood
For sore aferde° þer I lay.   afraid
To ihesu cryste wiþ° mylde mode°   of/heart
Ȝorne° I clepe° and cryde ay.°   earnestly/called/ever
So was I ferde° I was ny wode,°   afraid/nearly mad
⁴⁸⁰ Lesten° I scholde be borne away.   lest

LXI

I þanke hym þat suffurde dethe,°   suffered death
Hys mekyl° mercy and hys ore,°   great/grace
Þat schylded° me from so mony° a quede,°   shielded/many/evil
A sinful wreche° as I lay þere.   wretch
⁴⁸⁵ Alle sinful° I rede hym rede°   sinful (ones)/give them counsel
Her° synnes for to rewen° sore,   their/repent

---

463. *bulted brede:* lit., "bolted bread," made from sifted or bolted flour and representing gluttony and luxury; cf. the similar wastel bread which Chaucer's Prioress feeds to her dogs. (The **MS.** has *bulgebrede*, probably a scribal error.)
468. *aller deppyst pyt:* i.e., "deepest pit of all."

For nys° no synne in worlde so grete,°   (there) is not/great
Þat Crystys mercy nis° wel more.°   is not/much greater

LXII

And ihesu þat us alle hat wroht,°   has made
490 And formyd vs aftur þi fayre face,
And wyth þi precyous blode° vs boht,°   blood/redeemed
Of amendement ȝyf° vs space,°   amends give/opportunity
So þat þyne hondewarke lese noht°   handiwork lose not
In so blesful stede° a place,   blissful spot
495 And þe ioy þu haste° vs wroht   joy thou hast
Graunt° vs, God, for þine holy grace.   grant

AMEN

THE CUCKOO AND THE NIGHTINGALE
or The Book of Cupid, God of Love

Thomas Clanvowe

DATE: ? c. 1403 ✦ MANUSCRIPTS: Cambridge University Library Ff. 1.6; Bodleian Library, Oxford, Tanner 346; et al. ✦ EDITION: W. W. Skeat, *Chaucerian and Other Pieces*, Supplement to *The Complete Works of Geoffrey Chaucer*, 6 vols. (Oxford, 1894–97), pp. 347–358.

The dialect of the poem is similar to Chaucer's Kentish and London forms. Since by this time the language of the capital had come close to a standard Middle English, there are few orthographic irregularities to speak of in the poem. Translation, therefore, should cause little difficulty.

The Cuckoo and the Nightingale is the title given by Thynne, an early Chaucer editor (1532), to a debate poem which is called in the MS. *The Book of Cupid, God of Love*. It is written in the tradition of the "English Chaucerians," those men who honored and imitated their greater predecessor. Skeat identified the author as Sir Thomas Clanvowe of a Herefordshire family and a friend of Lewis Clifford, who was closely connected with Chaucer. This lighthearted and pleasant debate poem moved Milton to write his sonnet *To the Nightingale*, and Wordsworth has given us a modernization. It is composed in the manner of a spring dream vision, which Chaucer used in the *Book of the Duchess*, the *Parliament of Fowls*, the *House of Fame*, and the *Legend of Good Women*.

The god of love, a!° *benedicite!*	*ah*
How mighty and how greet° a lord is he!	*great*
For he can make of lowe hertes hye,°	*hearts high*
And of hye lowe, and lyke° for to dye,°	*ready/die*
⁵ And harde hertes he can maken free.°	*make generous*
And he can make, within a litel stounde,°	*little while*
Of seke° folk ful hole,° fresshe and sounde,	*sick/very healthy*
And of the hole, he can make seke;	
And he can binden° and unbinden eke°	*bind/also*
¹⁰ What he wol° have bounden° or unbounde.	*will/bound*

1–2. Cf. Chaucer, *Knight's Tale*, A ll. 1785–86. *benedicite:* Latin, "bless you."

To telle his might my wit may not suffyse;°   *suffice*
For he may do al that he wol devyse.°   *plan*
For he can make of wyse folk ful nyce,°   *foolish*
And eke in lyther° folk distroyen° vyce;   *vicious/destroy*
¹⁵ And proude hertes he can make agryse.°   *feel terror*

Shortly,° al that ever he wol° he may;   *in short/wishes (to do)*
Ageines° him ther dar° no wight sey° nay.   *against/dare/man say*
For he can gladde° and greve° whom him lyketh;°   *gladden/grieve/he likes (to do so)*
And, who that he wol, he laugheth° or he syketh;°   *makes laugh/makes sigh*
²⁰ And most his might he sheweth° ever in May.   *shows*

For every trewe gentil° herte free   *true noble*
That with him is, or thinketh for to be,
Ageines° May now shal have som steringe°   *during/stirring*
Other° to joye, or elles° to morninge,°   *either/else/mourning*
²⁵ In no sesoun° so greet, as thinketh me.°   *season/believe I*

For whan° they mowe here° the briddes° singe,   *when/may hear/birds*
And see the floures° and the leves° springe,   *flowers/leaves*
That bringeth into hertes remembraunce
A maner ese, medled° with grevaunce,°   *kind (of) pleasure, mingled/sorrow*
³⁰ And lusty thoughtes fulle of greet longinge.

And of that longing cometh hevinesse,°   *sorrow*
And therof groweth ofte greet seknesse,°   *sickness*
And al for lak° of that that they desyre;   *lack*
And thus in May ben° hertes sette on fyre,   *are*
³⁵ So that they brennen° forth in greet distresse.   *burn*

I speke° this of feling,° trewely;   *speak/from experience*
For, althogh° I be old and unlusty,°   *although/infirm*
Yet have I felt of that seknesse, in May,
Bothe hoot° and cold, an access° every day,   *hot/feverish attack*
⁴⁰ How sore, y-wis,° ther wot° no wight but I.   *indeed/knows*

I am so shaken with the fevers whyte,
Of° al this May yet slepte I but a lyte;°   *during/little*
And also it naught° lyketh° unto me,   *not/seems right*
That any herte shulde slepy° be   *heart should sleepy*
⁴⁵ In whom that Love his fyry° dart wol smyte.   *fiery*

---

39. *hoot:* i.e., "eager," "hopeful in love"; *cold:* i.e., "in dull despair."   **41.** *whyte:* i.e., causing paleness.

But as I lay this° other night wakinge, *the*
I thoghte° how lovers had a tokeninge,° *thought/sign*
And among hem° it was a comune tale,° *them/common saying*
That it were° good to here the nightingale *would be*
50 Rather than the lewde cukkow° singe. *ignorant cuckoo*

And then I thoghte, anon° as it was day, *as soon*
I wolde° go som whider° to assay° *would/where/try*
If that I might a nightingale here;
For yet had I non herd° of al this yere,° *none heard/year*
55 And hit° was tho° the thridde° night of May. *it/then/third*

And than,° anon as I the day espyde,° *then/saw*
No lenger° wolde I in my bedde abyde,° *longer/rest*
But unto a wode,° that was faste° by, *wood/close*
I wente forth alone, boldely,
60 And held my way doun by a broke-syde,° *brookside*

Til I com° to a launde° of whyte and grene; *came/meadow*
So fair oon° had I never inne° been; *(a) one/in*
The ground was grene, y-poudred° with daisye,° *powdered/daisies*
The floures and the gras y-lyke hye,° *alike high*
65 Al grene and whyte; was nothing elles sene.° *else seen*

Ther sat I doun among the faire floures;
And saw the briddes° trippe out of her boures° *birds/their bowers*
Ther-as° they had hem° rested al the night. *where/themselves*
They were so joyful of° the dayes light *for*
70 That they begonne° of° May to don hir° houres! *began/because of/sing their*

They coude° that servyce al by rote;° *knew/heart*
Ther was many a lovely straunge° note; *strange*
Some songe° loude, as° they hadde pleyned,° *sang/as if/were complaining*

48–50. According to Skeat, the cuckoo reaches England first at the end of March or beginning of April from its African winter quarters, announcing the arrival of spring. The nightingale is heard from about April 3 to June 3. But since they both come at about the same time, their song was considered a love omen, good or bad depending on whether the nightingale or the cuckoo was heard first.

55. May 3 occurs several times in Chaucer: on this day in *Troilus and Criseyde*, II, l. 55, Pandarus feels a love pain; in *The Knight's Tale*, A l. 1462, Palamon escapes prison (eventually to marry Emily); in *The Nun's Priest's Tale*, B², ll. 3187ff.,

Chauntecleer is captured by the fox. Evidently May 3 was a traditionally unlucky day, or it was connected with misfortune in love. The author of the present poem may have simply followed Chaucer.

63. The daisy is Chaucer's flower. He meditates on it and dreams in the *Legend of Good Women*, ll. 182–87, 201–2, 211.

70. The canonical church hours referred to are probably lauds (sometimes sung in the evening but normally before daybreak), with matins the first, or prime, the second.

And some in other maner vois y-feyned,°	*kind (of) voice imitated*
⁷⁵ And some al out, with al the fulle throte.°	*throat*
They proyned° hem, and maden° hem right° gay,	*preened/made/very*
And daunseden,° and lepten° on the spray,°	*danced/leaped/branch*
And evermore two and two in-fere;°	*together*
Right° so as they had chosen hem to-yere°	*just/this year*
⁸⁰ In Feverere,° on seint° Valentynes day.	*February/Saint*
And eke° the river, that I sat upon,°	*also/by*
It made suche a noise, as it ron,°	*ran*
Accordaunt° with the briddes armonye,°	*agreeing/harmony*
Me° thoughte, it was the beste melodye	*I*
⁸⁵ That mighte been y-herd of° any mon.°	*heard by/man*
And for delyt° ther-of, I wot° never how,	*delight/know*
I fel in suche a slomber° and a swow,°	*slumber/swoon*
Not al a-slepe, ne° fully wakinge;	*asleep, nor*
And in that swow me thoughte I herde singe	
⁹⁰ That sory° brid, the lewede cukkow.°	*unpleasant/ignorant cuckoo*
And that was on a tree right faste by;	
But who was than evel apayd° but I?	*ill repaid*
"Now God," quod° I, "that dyed° on the crois°	*said/died/cross*
Yeve sorow° on thee, and on thy lewde vois!	*give sorrow*
⁹⁵ For litel° joye have I now of thy cry."	*little*
And as I with the cukkow thus gan° chyde,	*did*
I herde,° in the nexte bush besyde,	*heard*
A Nightingale so lustily singe	
That with her clere° vois she made ringe	*clear*
¹⁰⁰ Through-out al the grene wode° wyde.	*wood*
"A!° goode Nightingale!" quod° I thenne,	*ah/said*
"A litel hast thou been to° longe henne;°	*too/away*
For here hath been the lewede Cukkow,	

---

80. Saint Valentine's Day in February was the occasion when all men and birds chose their mates. The action of Chaucer's poem the *Parliament of Fowls* occurs on this day.

93–95. The cuckoo in spring was said to have a mournful, dreary voice, a phenomenon already mentioned in the Old English elegiac poem the *Seafarer;* and in the debate poem *The Owl and the Nightingale*, the nightingale is mentioned as having a harsh note in the spring. It may be that this change of voice is connected with the mating call of the birds. It is only in German folksong and Middle English lyric, e.g., *Sumer Is Icumen In,* that the cuckoo's song is loud and cheerful.

And songen° songes rather° than hast thou;   *sung/sooner*
105 I pray to God that evel fyr° him brenne!"°   *evil fire/burn*

But now I wol° you telle a wonder° thing: *will/wondrous*
As longe as I lay in that swowning,°   *swooning*
Me thoughte I wiste° what the briddes ment,°   *knew/birds meant*
And what they seyde,° and what was her entent,°   *said/their intent*
110 And of her speche° I hadde good knowing.°   *speech/knowledge*

And than° herde I the Nightingale say,   *then*
"Now, gode° Cukkow! go som-where away,   *good*
And let us that can singen dwellen° here;   *sing remain*
For every wight escheweth° thee to here,°   *man avoids/hearing*
115 Thy songes be so elenge,° in good fay!"°   *mournful/faith*

"What?" quod he, "what may thee eylen° now?   *ail*
It thinketh° me,° I singe as wel as thou,   *seems/to me*
For my song is bothe trewe° and playn;°   *true/simple*
Al-though I can not crakel° so in vayn   *cackle*
120 As thou dost in thy throte,° I wot never how.   *throat*

"And every wight may understande me;
But, Nightingale, so may they not do thee;
For thou hast many a nyce queinte° cry.   *foolish strange*
I have herd thee seyn,° *ocy! ocy!*   *say*
125 How mighte I knowe what that shulde° be?"   *should*

"A fole!"° quod she, "wost° thou not what it is?   *fool/know*
Whan° that I say *ocy! ocy!* y-wis,°   *when/indeed*
That mene° I that I wolde, wonder fayn,°   *means/would, very eagerly*
That alle they were shamfully y-slayn°   *shamefully slain*
130 That menen aught ayeines° love amis.°   *intend anything against/amiss*

"And also I wolde° alle tho° were dede°   *would (that)/they/dead*
That thenke° not in love hir lyf° to lede;°   *think/their life/lead*
For who that wol the god of love not serve,
I dar° wel say, is worthy for to sterve;°   *dare/die*
135 And for that skil° *ocy! ocy!* I grede."°   *reason/cry*

"Ey!"° quod° the Cukkow,° "this is a queint lawe,   *alas/said/Cuckoo*
That every wight shal love or be to-drawe!"°   *drawn asunder*

124–35. Skeat mentions that in Old French literature *oci* was the cry of the nightingale, yet *ocire* was the Old French verb "to kill." The poet here puns on the word.

137. *to-drawe:* To be drawn apart by horses was a common punishment. It is mentioned in *Havelok the Dane*, l. 1822.

But I forsake° al suche companye.   *avoid*
For myn° entent is neither for to dye,°   *my/die*
¹⁴⁰ Ne, whyl° I live, in loves yok° to drawe.°   *nor, while/yoke/pull*

"For lovers ben° the folk that been on-lyve°   *are/are in life*
That most disese han,° and most unthryve,°   *sickness have/unhappiness*
And most enduren sorow, wo,° and care;   *endure sorrow, woe*
And, at the laste, failen of welfare;°   *fail in prosperity*
¹⁴⁵ What nedeth hit° ayeines trouth° to stryve?"   *why is it necessary/truth*

"What?" quod she, "thou art out of thy minde!
How might thou in thy cherles herte finde°   *churl's heart attempt*
To speke° of loves servaunts° in this wyse?°   *speak/servants/manner*
For in this worlde is noon° so good servyse°   *none/service*
¹⁵⁰ To every wight that gentil° is of kinde.°   *noble/by nature*

"For ther-of, trewly,° cometh al goodnesse,   *truly*
Al honour, and eke° al gentilnesse,°   *also/nobility*
Worship, ese,° and al hertes lust,°   *praise, ease/pleasure*
Parfit° joye, and ful° assured trust,   *perfect/fully*
¹⁵⁵ Jolitee, plesaunce,° and freshnesse,   *happiness, pleasure*

"Lowliheed,° and trewe companye,°   *humility/companionship*
Seemliheed, largesse,° and curtesye,°   *seemliness, generosity/courtesy*
Drede° of shame for to doon° amis;   *fear/do*
For he that trewly Loves servaunt is
¹⁶⁰ Were° lother° to be shamed than to dye.   *would be/more loath*

"And that this is sooth,° al that I seye,°   *truth/say*
In that beleve° I wol° bothe live and deye,°   *belief/will/die*
And Cukkow, so rede° I thou do, y-wis."   *advise*
"Ye, than,"° quod he, "God let me never have blis°   *yea, then/joy*
¹⁶⁵ If ever I to that counseyl° obeye!   *counsel*

"Nightingale, thou spekest wonder° fayre,   *wondrous*
But, for al that, the sooth is the contrayre;°   *contrary*
For loving is, in yonge° folk, but rage,°   *young/passion*
And in olde folk hit° is a greet° dotage;   *it/great*
¹⁷⁰ Who most hit useth,° most he shal apeyre.°   *practices/be harmed*

---

151. That love was the source of all good was a basic tenet in *l'amour courtois*, the rules of courtly love as explained by Andreas Capellanus, chaplain to Marie of Champagne, and exhibited in the poems of the troubadours who flourished in southern France under the patronage of Marie and Eleanor of Aquitaine.

"For therof comth° disese and hevinesse,°   *comes/heaviness (of heart)*
Sorowe and care, and mony° a greet seknesse,°   *many/sickness*
Dispyt, debat,° and anger, and envye,   *spite, quarrel*
Repreef° and shame, untrust° and jelousye,°   *reproof/distrust/jealousy*
175 Pryde and mischeef,° povertee, and woodnesse.° *mischief/madness*

"What! Loving is an office° of dispayr,°   *work/despair*
And oo° thing is ther-in that is not fayr;°   *one/pleasant*
For who that° geteth° of love a litel° blis,   *whoever/receives/little*
But-if° he be alway therwith, y-wis,°   *unless/always there, indeed*
180 He may ful sone of age° have his heyr.°   *very soon in time/heir*

"And, Nightingale, therfor hold thee ny;°   *restrain yourself*
For, leve° me wel, for al thy queynte° cry,   *believe/pretty*
If thou be fer° or longe fro° thy make,°   *far/from/mate*
Thou shalt be as other that been forsake,°   *are forsaken*
185 And thanne° thou shalt hoten° as do° I!"   *then/be called/am*

"Fy!" quod° she, "on thy name and on thee!   *fie, said*
The god of love ne° let thee never y-thee!°   *not/prosper*
For thou art wors° a thousand-fold than wood.°   *worse/mad*
For many on° is ful worthy and ful good,   *(a) one*
190 That had° be° naught, ne hadde love y-be!°   *would have/been/been*

"For Love his servaunts° ever-more amendeth,°   *servants/helps*
And from al evel taches hem° defendeth,   *evil defects them*
And maketh hem to brenne right° as fyr°   *burn just/fire*
In trouthe° and in worshipful desyr,°   *truth/desire*
195 And, whom him° liketh, joye y-nough° hem sendeth." *he/enough*

"Thou Nightingale," he seyde,° "hold thee° stille; *said/yourself*
For Love hath no resoun° but his wille;   *reason*
For ofte sithe untrewe° folk he eseth,°   *times untrue/gives comfort*
And trewe folk so bitterly displeseth°   *displeases*
200 That, for defaute° of grace,° he let° hem spille.° *lack/mercy/lets/die*

"With such a lorde wol I never be;
For he is blind alwey,° and may not see;   *always*
And whom he hit° he not,° or whom he fayleth;°   *hits/knows not/misses*
And in his court ful selden° trouthe avayleth;°   *seldom/prevails*
205 So dyvers° and so wilful is he."   *variable*

179–80. I.e., his heir or successor will soon come into his own, unless the lover is continually on guard; therefore the lover is always insecure.

185. *hoten . . . I:* i.e., be called by the cuckoo's name, a cuckold.
202. Cupid is proverbially blind.

Than° took I of the Nightingale kepe,°   *then/heed*
She caste a sigh out of her herte depe,°   *heart deep*
And seyde, "Alas! that ever I was bore!°   *born*
I can, for tene,° say not oon° word more";   *grief/one*
210 And right with that she brast° out for to wepe.°   *burst/weeping*

"Alas!" quod she, "my herte wol° to-breke°   *will/break asunder*
To heren° thus this false brid° to speke°   *hear/bird/speak*
Of love, and of his worshipful servyse;°   *service*
Now, god of love, thou help me in som wyse°   *way*
215 That I may on this Cukkow been awreke!"°   **Cuckoo be avenged**

Me° thoughte than, that I sterte° up anon,°   *I/jumped/quickly*
And to the broke° I ran, and gat° a stoon,°   *brook/got/stone*
And at the Cukkow hertely° I caste;°   *hard/threw*
And he, for drede, fley° away ful faste;   *fear, flew*
220 And glad was I when that he was a-goon.°   *gone*

And evermore the Cukkow, as he fley,
He seyde, "Farewel! farewel, papinjay!"°   *parrot*
As though he hadde scorned, thoughte me;
But ay° I hunted him fro° tree to tree   *ever/from*
225 'Til he was fer° al out of sighte awey.°   *far/away*

And thanne com° the Nightingale to me,   *then came*
And seyde, "Frend, forsothe° I thanke thee   *truly*
That thou hast lyked° me thus to rescowe,°   *it has pleased you/rescue*
And oon avow° to Love I wol avowe,°   *vow/pledge*
230 That al this May I wol thy singer be."

I thanked her, and was right wel apayed;°   *pleased*
"Ye,"° quod° she, "and be thou not amayed,°   *yea/said/upset*
Though thou have herd° the Cukkow er° than me.   *heard/earlier*
For, if I live, it shal amended be
235 The nexte May, if I be not affrayed.°   *frightened*

"And oon thing I wol rede° thee also;   *counsel*
Ne leve° thou not the Cukkow, loves fo;°   *not believe/foe*
For al that he hath seyd° is strong lesinge."°   *said/outright lies*
"Nay," quod I, "therto° shal no thing me bringe   *to that point*
240 Fro love; and yet he doth me mochel wo."°   *much woe*

232–35. The poet unfortunately heard the cuckoo first, but the nightingale will remedy the situation the next May 3.

"Ye, use thou," quod she, "this medicyne;
Every day this May, or° that thou dyne,   *before*
Go loke° upon the fresshe dayesye.°   *look/daisy*
And though thou be for wo in poynt° to dye,°   *about/die*
245 That shal ful gretly lissen° thee of thy pyne.°   *very greatly relieve/pain*

"And loke alwey° that thou be good and trewe,°   *see always/true*
And I wol singe oon of my songes newe,
For love of thee, as loude as I may crye";
And thanne she began this song full hye°—   *loud*
250 "I shrewe° al hem° that been of° love untrewe!"   *curse/them/are in*

And whan° she hadde songe hit° to the ende,   *when/sung it*
"Now farewel," quod she, "for I mot wende;°   *must go*
And god of love, that can° right wel and may,   *can (work)*
As mochel joye sende thee this day
255 As ever yet he any lover sende!"°   *sent*

Thus took the Nightingale her leve° of me.   *leave*
I pray to God, he alway° with her be,   *always*
And joye of love he sende her evermore;
And shilde° us fro the Cukkow° and his lore;°   *shield/Cuckoo/teaching*
260 For ther is noon° so fals° a brid° as he.   *none/false/bird*

Forth she fley,° the gentil° Nightingale,   *flew/gentle*
To al the briddes that were in that dale,
And gat° hem alle into a place in-fere,°   *got/together*
And hem besoughte° that they wolde here°   *asked/would hear*
265 Her disese;° and thus began her tale: *trouble*

"Ye witen° wel, it is not fro yow° hid   *know/from you*
How the Cukkow and I faste° have chid°   *seriously/argued*
Ever sithen° it was dayes light;   *since*
I pray yow alle, that ye do me right
270 Of° that foule, false, unkinde° brid."   *regarding/unnatural*

Than spak oo° brid for alle, by oon° assent,   *then spoke one/one*
"This mater asketh° good avysement;°   *matter demands/counsel*
For we ben° fewe briddes here in-fere.   *are*
And sooth° it is, the Cukkow is not here;   *true*
275 And therefor we wol° have a parlement.°   *will/parliament*

---

243. Cf. l. 63*n*.
275–76. This is a reference to Chaucer's *Parliament of Fowls*, where the royal eagle is the first to speak.

And therat shal the Egle° be our lord,   *Eagle*
And other peres° that ben of record,   *peers*
And the Cukkow shal be after sent.
And ther shal be yeven° the jugement,°   *given/judgment*
280 Or elles° we shal make som accord.   *else*

And this shal be, withouten° any nay,°   *without/contrary argument*
The morow° of seynt° Valentynes day,   *morning/Saint*
Under a maple that is fayr and grene,
Before the chambre-window of the quene
285 At Wodestok, upon the grene lay."°   *lea*

She thanked hem, and than her leve took,
And fley into an hawthorn by the brook,
And ther she sat, and song° upon that tree,   *sang*
"Terme° of my lyf,° Love hath with-holde° me,"   *during all/life/sustained*
290 So loude, that I with that song awook.°   *awoke*

EXPLICIT CLANVOWE

284–85. The queen was undoubtedly Joan of Navarre, second wife of Henry IV, who received the estate of Woodstock as dower. Chaucer, too, spent some time at Woodstock. Moreover, in the *Legend of Good Women* he states that the poem is to be presented to the queen at Shene, the favorite residence of Anne of Bohemia, and the author of *The Cuckoo and the Nightingale* follows Chaucer closely in investing his poem with the prestige of a gift to royalty.

THE LYRIC

The vast majority of Middle English lyric poems (short, emotional expressions of personal feeling) are religious verses sung in praise of the Virgin or of Christ. Many are also moral and didactic in tone. The secular poems are mainly love songs, comic accounts of seduction, verses in praise of spring (the reverdie theme), and satires against friars, women, and fashions.

The native popular English lyrics are so different in tone from the aristocratic Provençal songs of the troubadours and those of the German Minnesänger that, aside from the influence of motifs of *courtoisie* and the language of the courtly-love cult, the source of English song must be found elsewhere, either in native secular or religious tradition or among the Continental Latin love lyrics. Undoubtedly the enthusiastic verse of the goliards, the wandering scholars, also played its part in the English lyrics' realistic portrayal of emotion and desire. Whereas the troubadour hopelessly worshiped an ideal, a cold, distant goddess whose real name he dared not mention, the author of the Harley Lyrics seems more familiar with his *burd* ("girl") or his *make* ("intimate friend"). He knew her well—Alysoun, the fair-haired, brown-eyed, laughing maiden—and no doubt his hope was the better repaid.

REFERENCES

Brook, G. L., ed. *The Harley Lyrics*. Manchester, 1948.

Brown, Carleton, ed. *English Lyrics of the XIIIth Century*. Oxford, 1932.

———, ed. *Religious Lyrics of the XVth Century*. Oxford, 1939.

———, ed. *Religious Lyrics of the XIVth Century*. Oxford, 1924.

Brown, Carleton, and Robbins, R. H. *The Index of Middle English Verse*. New York, 1943.

Davies, R. T. *Medieval English Lyrics, A Critical Anthology*. London, 1963.

Dronke, Peter. *Medieval Latin and the Rise of European Love-Lyric*. 2d ed. 2 vols. Oxford, 1968.

———. *Medieval Lyric*, London, 1968.

Greene, R. L., ed. *The Early English Carols*. Oxford, 1935.

Luria, Maxwell S., and Hoffman, Richard L., eds. *Middle English Lyrics*. New York, 1974.

Moore, A. K. *The Secular Lyric in Middle English*. Lexington, Ky., 1951.

Robbins, R. H., ed. *Historical Poems of the XIVth and XVth Centuries*, New York, 1959.

———, ed. *Secular Lyrics of the XIVth and XVth Centuries*. Oxford, 1955.

Stone, Brian, trans. *Medieval English Verse*. Baltimore, 1964.

Wadell, Helen. *Mediaeval Latin Lyrics*. London, 1944.

The lyric is treated in the General Introduction of this volume, pp. 15–17, 30–31.

SUMER IS ICUMEN IN

DATE: The words c. 1240 or earlier. According to the study by M. F. Bukofzer (*Sumer is icumen in: A Revision,* Univ. of California Publications in Music, Vol. II, No. 2 [Berkeley and Los Angeles, 1944]) the date of the MS. must be put at 1310–25. ◆ MANUSCRIPT: British Library Harley 978, f. 11 b. This MS. is a monk's commonplace book from Reading Abbey. The dialect is Southern.

This song is the only secular lyric in a MS. containing mainly Latin and French religious music. It is a *rota* or round, a double canon for six voices and thus a musical phenomenon, since no other canon for more than four voices is known this early in history. The poem is in the French tradition of the reverdie, the celebration of the rebirth of spring, which Chaucer uses in the General Prologue to the *Canterbury Tales* and the Prologue to the *Legend of Good Women.*

Svmer° is icumen° in!	summer/coming
Lhude° sing, cuccu!°	loud/cuckoo
Growcþ sed° and bloweþ med,°	seed/flowers meadow
And springþ° þe wude nu.°	revives/wood now
5 Sing, cuccu!	
Awe bleteþ° after lomb,°	ewe bleats/lamb
Lhouþ° after calue cu.°	lows/calf cow
Bulluc sterteþ,° bucke uerteþ.°	bullock jumps/breaks wind
Murie° sing, cuccu!	merrily
10 Cuccu! cuccu!	
Wel singes þu,° cuccu.	sing you
Ne° swik þu° nauer° nu.	not/may you stop/never

PES°   *burden*

Sing cuccu nu! Sing cuccu!
Hoc repetit unus quociens opus est, faciens pausacionem in fine.
Sing cuccu nu! Sing cuccu!
Hoc dicit alius, pausans im medio et non in fine, set immediate repetens principium.

---

1. *Svmer:* i.e., "spring."
13. *Hoc...fine:* "One repeats this as many times as necessary, making a pause at the end."

14. *Hoc ... principium:* "Another says this, pausing in the middle and not at the end but immediately repeating the beginning."

MIRIE IT IS WHILE SUMER ILAST

DATE: c. 1225. ❧ MANUSCRIPT: Bodleian Library, Oxford, Rawlinson G. 22 f. 1 b.

"Inner" and "outer weather" (as Robert Frost uses the terms) correspond here in the poet's mood.

Mirie° it is while sumer ilast,°	*merry/summer lasts*
Wið fugheles° song.	*birds'*
Oc nu necheð° windes blast,	*but now approaches*
And weder strong.°	*weather fierce*
⁵ Ej!° ej! what° þis nicht° is long!	*alas/how/night*
And ich° wið wel michel wrong°	*I/very much grief*
Soregh° and murne° and fast.	*sorrow/mourn*

FOWELES IN THE FRITH

DATE: c. 1270. ✦ MANUSCRIPT: Bodleian Library, Oxford, Douce 139, f. 5 a.

The survival of Anglo-Saxon alliteration in this two-part song should be noted.

> Foweles° in þe frith,°   *birds/forest*
>   Þe fisses° in þe flod,°   *fishes/water*
> And i mon waxe wod!°   *must go mad*
>   Mulch sorw° I walke with   *much sorrow*
> ⁵ For° beste° of bon° and blod.°   *because of/best (maiden)/bone/blood*

---

3. *i mon:* Although *mon* is usually translated "must," it has been suggested by Sister Mary Jeremy ("'Mon' in 'Foweles in the Frith,'" *English Language Notes*, V [1967], 80–81) that the word is "man," in apposition to *i*, and thus in progression with birds and fishes—the last, man, being the only one out of his element.

5. *of bon and blod:* i.e., "alive."

EDI BEO THU, HEUENE QUENE

DATE: 13th century. ◢ MANUSCRIPT: Corpus Christi College, Oxford, 59.

This two-part song, a quite typical religious lyric to the Virgin Mary, parallels in many phrases the courtly language of the secular love poems, and it is interesting to note here the influence of expressions of spiritualized, metaphysical love on songs dedicated to divine worship. The poet is in the bonds of love for the Virgin; he is "her man." He is the completely spiritualized courtly lover. It is important also to compare the religious imagery here with that in *I Sing of a Maiden* (this volume, p. 661).

Edi beo þu, heuene° quene,	*blessed be you, heaven's*
Folkes froure° and engles blis,°	*men's comfort/ angels' joy*
Moder unwemmed° and maiden clene,°	*mother unspotted/pure*
Swich° in world non° oþer nis.°	*such/no/is not*
5 On þe hit° is wel sene,°	*you it/seen*
Of alle wimmen° þu hauest þet pris,°	*women/are the prize*
Mi suete leuedi, her° mi bene,°	*sweet lady, hear/prayer*
And reu of° me, yif° þi wille is.°	*(take) pity on/if/(it) be*
Thu asteye so° þe dais-rewe,°	*you ascended as/day's first streak*
10 The deleth° from þe deorke nicht,°	*that separates/dark night*
Of° þe sprong° a leome° newe	*from/sprang/light*
That al þis world haueth ilight.°	*has lit*
Nis° non maide of þine heowe,°	*(there) is not/appearance*
Swa° fair, so schene,° so rudi,° swa bright,	*so/beautiful/fresh*
15 Swete° leuedi, of me þu reowe,°	*sweet/(take) pity*
And haue merci of þin knicht.°	*your knight*
Sprenge blostme° of one rote,°	*sprung blossom/root*
The holi gost° þe reste° upon,	*Ghost/rested*
That wes° for monkunnes bote°	*was/mankind's salvation*
20 And heore° soule to alesen° for on.°	*their/ ? free/ forever*

---

6. *hauest þet pris:* i.e., "are the best."

7–8. The request is often seen in secular lyrics, where the lady is asked to have pity on the lover.

13–16. Mary is described in courtly, Petrarchan terms of physical beauty by the supplicant, who is her "knight."

(However, the word *knicht* could also mean "servant" still at this date.)

17. The blossom (Mary the flower) is sprung from the branch, the Tree of Jesse and David (cf. *I Sing of a Maiden*).

Leuedi milde, softe and swote,°   *sweet*
Ic° crie þe merci, ic am þi mon,°   *I/man*
Boþe to honde° and to fote,°   *in hand/foot*
On alle wise° þat ic kon.°   *in every way/am able*

25 Thu art eorþe° to gode sede,°   *earth (i.e., soil)/good seed*
On þe lighte þe heouene deus,°   *heavenly dew*
Of þe sprong þe edi blede,°   *fruit*
The holi gost hire° on þe sews.°   *it/sows*
Thu bring us ut° of kare° of drede,°   *out/misery/fear*
30 That Eve bitterliche° us brews,   *bitterly*
Thu shalt us into heouene lede,°   *heaven lead*
Welle° swete is þe ilke dews.°   *very/that same dew*

Moder, ful of þewes hende,°   *virtues gracious*
Maide dreigh° and wel itaught,°   *patient/taught*
35 Ic em° in þine loue bende,°   *am/bond*
And to þe is al mi draucht.°   *inclination*
Thu me shilde° from þe feonde,°   *shield/Fiend (i.e., Devil)*
Ase° þu ert freo,° and wilt,° and maucht;°   *as/are generous/will/are able*
Help me to mc liues° ende,   *my life's*
40 And make me wiþ þin sone isaught.°   *son reconciled*

Thu ert icumen° of heghe kunne,°   *come/high (i.e., noble) family*
Of Dauid þe riche° king,   *powerful*
Nis non maiden under sunne,
The mei beo° þin euening;°   *may be/equal*
45 Ne° þat swo derne louiye kunne,°   *nor/so deeply love can*
Ne non° swo treowe of° alle þing;°   *none/true in/things*
Thi loue us brouchte eche wunne,°   *brought eternal joys*
Ihered ibeo þu,° swete þing.   *praised be you*

Selcudliche ure louerd hit dighte,°   *marvelously our Lord it prepared*
50 That þu, maide, wiþute were,°   *without (knowing) man*

22–24. The feudal image of the "liege man" who pledges his vassalage, both "hand and foot," to his "sovereign lady" is an interesting example of the social-political tradition taken over by the cult of courtly love and transferred ultimately to the Marian lyrics. Courtly love may be termed a feudalization and spiritualization of love, with all forces—social, political, religious, and amatory—working interchangeably.

26. *heouene deus:* The "heavenly dew" in medieval Christian symbolism is equated with Christ, who came in April (the first month of Mary's pregnancy) to give new life to the earth, as do the spring rains (cf. *I Sing of a Maiden*). A 16th-century song

follows the tradition of linking Christ and the "small rain":

Western Wind, when wilt thou blow,
The small rain down can rain?
Christ, that my love were in my arms
And I in my bed again!

29–30. Medieval antifeminism was based on the sin of Eve, who caused the Fall, but all medieval women participated in the honor given to Mary.

45. It may be that the line reads: "Nor that so passionately (deeply, secretly) love I can."

That° al þis worlde bicluppe ne° mighte,   *(he) that|encompass not*
Thu sholdest° of þin boseme bere.°   *you should|bosom bear*
The ne stighte, ne þe ne prighte,°   *you felt no stabbing, nor no prick*
In side, in lende,° ne elleswhere;°   *loins|elsewhere*
55 That wes wiþ ful muchel° righte,   *most*
For þu bere° þine helere.°   *bore|Savior*

Tho° Godes sune° alighte° wolde,°   *when|son|to come|wished*
On eorþe al for ure sake,
Herre teyen° he him° nolde°   *(a) nobler servant|himself|*
                                                              wished not
60 Thene° þat maide to beon° his make;°   *than|be|mate*
Betere ne° mighte he, þaigh° he wolde,   *better not|though*
Ne swetture° þing, on eorþe take.   *sweeter*
Leuedi,° bring us to þine bolde,°   *lady|abode*
And shild us from helle wrake.°   *hell's vengeance*

                    AMEN

55–56. The word *helere* is cognate to *hale, healer* (the German   of him who would "heal" her.
Heiland); thus it is right that Mary felt no pain at the conception

NOU SKRINKETH ROSE

DATE: c. 1314–25. ◆ MANUSCRIPT: British Library Harley 2253.

This Marian lyric shows the native tradition in its alliteration and formulaic structure. One can note several parallels to secular love songs of the Harley Lyrics. The opening of the second stanza is a French motif (*chanson d'aventure*) often found in English songs.

Nou skrinketh° rose and lylie flour,°	*wither/lily flower*
That whilen ber° that suete savour°	*formerly bore/sweet scent*
In somer,° that suete tyde;°	*summer/time*
Ne is° no quene so stark ne stour,°	*(there) is not/strong nor stalwart*
5 Ne no levedy° so bryht° in bour,°	*lady/bright/chamber*
That ded ne° shal by glyde.°	*death not/creep up to*
Whose wol° fleyshlust° forgon,°	*whoever wishes/fleshly lust/(to) forgo*
And hevene blis abyde,°	*heavenly joy attain*
On Jesu be is thoht anon,°	*his thought straightway*
10 That therled° was ys° side.	*pierced/his*
From Petresbourh in o morewenyng,°	*Peterborough on one morning*
As I me wende° omy° pleyghyng,°	*traveled/on my/pleasure*
On mi folie° I thohte.°	*folly/thought*
Menen° I gon° my mournyng°	*(to) communicate/began/lament*
15 To hire° that ber the hevene kyng;	*her*
Of° merci hire bysohte,°	*for/asked*
"Ledy, preye thi sone° for ous,°	*lady, pray (to) your son/us*
That us duere bohte,°	*dearly bought (i.e., redeemed)*
Ant shild° us from the lothe° hous	*and shield/loathly*
20 That to° the fend° is wrohte!"°	*for/Fiend (i.e., Devil)/made*
Myn herte° of dedes wes fordred,°	*my heart/(my) deeds was frightened*
Of synne that I have my fleish° fed,	*flesh*
Ant folewed° al my tyme,	*followed*

11–12. Peterborough is in central England. These lines normally end in an *aventure d'amour*, the seduction of a peasant girl (cf. the ballad *The Knight and Shepherd's Daughter*, this volume, p. 522). G. L. Brook remarks that *folie* in Old French normally referred to illicit love.

That° I not° whider° I shal be led,
25 When I lygge° on dethes° bed,
   In ioie ore° in to pyne.°
On° a ledy myn hope is,
   Moder° and virgyne;
We shulen in° to hevene blis
30   Thurh° hire medicine.

so that/know not/where
lie/death's
joy or/suffering
in
mother
shall attain
through

Betere° is hire medycyn
Then eny mede° or eny wyn;°
   Hire erbes smulleth° suete.
From Catenas° in to Dyvelyn°
35 Nis° ther no leche° so fyn°
   Oure serewes° to bete.°
Mon° that feleth° eni sor,°
   Ant his folie wol lete,°
Withoute gold other° eny tresor,°
40 He may be sound ant sete.°

better
than any mead/wine
herbs smell
Caithness/Dublin
is not/physician/fine
sorrows/relieve
(the) man/feels/grief
(to) leave
or/treasure
content

Of penaunce° is hire plastre al,°
Ant ever serven° hire I shal,
   Nou ant al my lyve.°
Nou is fre° that er° wes thral,°
45 Al thourh° that levedy gent° ant smal.°
   Heried° be hyre ioies fyve!
Wher so° eny sek° ys,
   Thider° hye blyve;°
Thurh hire beoth ybroht° to blis°
50   Bo° maiden ant wyve.°

penance/completely
serve
life
free/before/slave
through/lady noble/slender
praised
wherever/anyone sick
there/let him hurry
are brought/joy
both/wife

For he° that dude° his body on tre,°
Of° oure sunnes° have piete,°
   That weldes heouene boures!°
Wymmon, with° thi iolyfte,°
55   Thou thench° on Godes shoures;°

him/put/tree
on/sins/pity
(you) that rule heaven's chambers
women, in/happiness
think/pains

---

34. G. L. Brook states that Caithness (in northern Scotland) and Dublin were the boundaries of the areas occupied by the Western Vikings and that the phrase is therefore of Scandinavian origin.

41. *plastre:* used here to follow the metaphor of Mary as physician.

42. The lover-supplicant will "serve" Mary as a secular lover would his lady.

46. The five joys of Mary were the Annunciation, the Nativity, the Epiphany and visit of the Magi, the Resurrection on Easter Day, and the Assumption. At times the Ascension is substituted for the Epiphany.

51. *tre:* i.e., the cross.

Thah° thou be whyt° and bryht on ble,°   *though/fair/bright of complexion*
   Falewen shule° thy floures.°   *fade shall/flowers*
Jesu, have merci of me,
   That al this world honoures.
        AMEN

ANNOT AND IOHON

DATE: c. 1314–25. ✏ MANUSCRIPT: British Library Harley 2253, f. 63a–63b. The emendations of Brook have been followed.

Though occasionally, perhaps, the comparisons in this poem may seem farfetched, the type often appears in Middle English literature. A list of stones similar to the one here, with their miraculous powers and beauties, may be found in the *Pearl* (cf. this volume, p. 748, ll. 997–1020); the Middle English lapidaries contain much useful information, raw material for the poetic imagination. The sequence is from gems to flowers to birds to medications and spices and finally to romance heroes and heroines. Many of these last, sharing the fate of lesser mortals, have lapsed into obscurity, though Carlton Brown (*English Lyrics of the XIIIth Century*) has attempted to identify some of them.

Ichot° a burde° in a bour ase° beryl so bryht,°

Ase saphyr° in selver semly on syht,°
Ase iaspe° þe gentil° þat lemeþ° wiþ lyht,°
Ase gernet° in golde ant° ruby wel ryht.°
5 Ase onycle he° ys on yholden on hyht,°
Ase diamaund° þe dere° in day when he is dyht.°
He is coral ycud° wiþ cayser° ant knyht,°
Ase emeraude° amorewen° þis may haveþ myht.°

Þe myht of þe margarite° haveþ þis mai mere.°
10 For charbocle ich hire ches° bi chyn° ant by chere.°

Hire rode° is ase rose þat red is on rys,°
Wiþ lilye white leres lossum° he is.
Þe primerole° he passeþ,° þe pervenke° of pris,°

Wiþ alisaundre° þareto, ache° ant anys.°
15 Coynte° ase columbine such hire cunde° ys,
Glad° vnder gore° in gro ant in grys.

I know/maiden/chamber as/as bright
sapphire/silver pleasant in sight
jasper/fair/shines/light
garnet/and/very true
onyx she/regarded highly
diamond/precious/placed
famous/emperor/knight
emerald/in the morning/ maid has power
pearl/maiden excellent
carbuncle I her took/chin/ expression

color/branch
complexion lovely
primrose/surpasses/periwinkle/ value
horse parsley/also, celery/anise
pretty/her nature
beautiful/garment

16–17. *Glad vnder gore:* "beautiful among women"; *brihtest vnder bis:* "brightest on earth." These are tag phrases (cf. above, p. 311, l. 1814n). *gro, grys:* Both are terms for gray fur.

642

He is blosme opon bleo,° brihtest vnder bis,°   *flower in face/linen*
Wiþ celydoyne° ant sauge,° ase þou þiself sys.°   *celandine/sage/sees*
   Þat syht° vpon þat semly° to blis° he is broht;°   *whoever looks/beauty/bliss/brought*
20   He is solsecle,° to sauue° ys forsoht.°   *marigold/(that) for healing/*
                                                  sought out

He is papeiai° in pyn° þat beteþ° me my bale,°   *popinjay/(my) pain/cures/(of)*
                                          my sorrow

To trewe tortle° in a tour y° telle þe° mi tale.   *true turtledove/tower I/you*
He is þrustle þryuen° in þro° þat singeþ in sale,°   *thrush successful/debate/hall*
Þe wilde laueroc° ant wolc° ant þe wodewale.°   *lark/hawk/golden oriole*
25 He is faucoun° in friht,° dernest° in dale,   *falcon/wood/most hidden*
Ant wiþ eueruch a° gome° gladest° in gale.°   *every/person/gladdest/gaiety*
From Weye° he is wisist into Wyrhale;   *Wye/wisest unto Wirral*
Hire nome° is in a note of þe nyhtegale.°   *name/nightingale*
   In Annote° is hire nome; nempneþ° hit° nom?°   *Annie/(can) guess/it/no one*
30   Whose ryht redeþ roune° to Iohon.°   *whoever right reads (it) whisper/*
                                       John

Muge° he is ant mondrake þourh° miht of þe mone,°   *nutmeg/mandrake by/moon*
Trewe triacle ytold wiþ tonges° in trone.°   *remedy told by tongues/heaven*
Such licoris° mai leche° from Lyne° to Lone,°   *licorice/heal/Lyn/Lune*
Such sucre mon secheþ° þat saneþ° men sone.°   *sugar man seeks/heals/quickly*
35 Bliþe yblessed of° Crist, þat bayþeþ° me mi bone,°   *happy (one) blessed by/grants/prayer*
When derne dedis° in day derne° are done.   *discreet deeds/secretly*
Ase gromyl° in greue° grene is þe grone,°   *gromwell/thicket/seed*
Ase quibibe° ant comyn cud° is in crone,°   *cubeb/cumin known/by its head*
   Cud° comyn in court, canel° in cofre,°   *famous/cinnamon/chest*
40   Wiþ gyngyure° ant sedewale° ant þe gylofre.°   *ginger/valerian/clove*

He is medicine of miht,° mercie of mede,°   *strength/reward*
Rekene ase Regnas resoun° to rede,°   *ready as Ragna reason/counsel*

---

21. The chatter of the popinjay (parrot) cheers the poet.

22. The turtledove, because it stays with the same mate for its lifetime, is the symbol of fidelity.

23. The thrush (as in the debate *The Thrush and the Nightingale* and the lyric *Lenten Is Come with Love to Town* [this volume, pp. 649–50]) had a reputation for quarrel and debate.

27. *From . . . into Wyrhale:* This shows the provenance of the poem to be the Welsh border, which is further attested by the references to Celtic heroes and legends in the last stanza.

28–30. Secrecy is also a characteristic of Provençal troubadour poetry, where the poets, as here, hide the name of the lover in puns or pseudonyms.

31. Mandrake, the root in the shape of a man, was supposed to have the power to cause conception under certain conditions, e.g., the light of the full moon (cf. John Donne's *Song:* "Get with child a mandrake root").

33. *Lyne, Lone:* the rivers Lyn in Devonshire and Lune in Lancashire.

38. Cumin has a very conspicuous flower.

42. The wise Ragna (fl. c. 1128) is found in the *Orkneyingers Saga* of Iceland, where she persuades a man not to seek vengeance for a slaying.

Trewe ase Tegeu in tour, ase Wyrwein in wede,°   *garments*
Baldore þen° Byrne þat oft þe bor bede.°   *bolder than/boar challenged*
45 Ase Wylcadoun he° is wys, dohty° of dede,   *she/wise, doughty*
Feyrore° þen Floyres folkes° to fede;°   *fairer/people/please*
Cud ase Cradoc in court carf° þe brede,°   *carved/roast*
Hendore° þen Hilde, þat haueþ° me to hede.°   *more gracious/has/care for*
He haueþ me to hede, þis hendy anon,°   *gracious/(one) now*
50 Gentil° ase Ionas, heo ioyeþ° wiþ Ion.°   *fair/Jonas, she rejoices/ John*

---

43. *Tegeu, Wyrwein:* Tegau Eurvron, the wife of Caradoc (Cradoc; cf. l. 47*n*), was one of the three fair and chaste ladies at Arthur's court, and is mentioned in the Welsh Triads. She alone proves her chastity and loyalty to her husband by being able to wear the magic mantle. Wyrwein (Gyrwein) may be Eurvron, Tegau's other name, and here mentioned in apposition to Tegau, with *wede* being the magic mantle. Or perhaps, according to Brown, she is Garwen, one of the three mistresses of Arthur.

44. *Byrne:* perhaps Bjorn from the *Orkneyingers Saga*, whose brother shoots a nut from the top of his head.

45. *Wylcadoun:* not identified.

46. *Floyres:* Flores the lover of Blancheflur, the Christian princess, in the Middle English romance who is abducted by Saracens and raised together with him. They fall in love, are separated, and meet again in Egypt where Blancheflur is kept in a harem. A token ring brings Flores to her. The emir forgives them and they are united.

47. *Cradoc:* Caradoc Briebras (Karadawc Vreichvras in Welsh), one of the foremost heroes in Arthurian legend, who alone can carve the boar's head because his is the only knife not dulled by his wife's disloyalty (cf. the *Lay of the Horn*, this volume, pp. 334–339, and the ballad *The Boy and the Mantle*, this volume, pp. 497–504).

48. *Hilde:* Gudrun, in the *þiþriks Saga* the daughter of King Artus of Bretangenland.

50. *Ionas:* perhaps the Hebrew prophet.

ALYSOUN

DATE: c. 1314–25. ✣ MANUSCRIPT: British Library Harley 2253, f. 63b.

This is undoubtedly one of the finest and most refreshing of the noted Harley Lyrics. Though there is much of the courtly flavor in lines 8 and 13 ff., the music and popular spirit is seen in the refrain, especially the justly famous lines 11–12.

Bytuene Mersh ant Aueril,°	*between March and April*
When spray° biginneþ to springe,°	*branches/blossom*
Þe lutel foul° haþ hire wyl°	*little bird/her wish*
On° hyre lud° to synge.	*in/warbling*
5 Ich libbe° in loue longinge,	*I live*
For semlokest° of alle þynge.°	*(the) most beautiful/things*
He° may me blisse bringe:	*she*
Ich'am° in hire baundoun.°	*I am/power*
An hendy hap° ichabbe° yhent.°	*fair fortune/I have/received*
10 Ichot° from heuene° it is me sent;	*I know/heaven*
From alle wymmen° mi loue is lent,°	*women/taken away*
Ant lyht° on Alysoun.	*alights*
On heu° hire her° is fayr ynoh,°	*color/hair/enough*
Hire browe brounc, hirc cʒe blake.°	*eye black*
15 Wiþ lossum chere° he on me loh,°	*pleasant look/laughed*
Wiþ middel smal ant wel ymake.°	*formed*
Bote° he me wolle° to hire take,	*unless/will*
Forte° buen° hire owen make,°	*in order to/be/own mate*
Longe to lyuen° ichulle° forsake,	*live/I shall*
20 Ant feye fallen adoun.°	*doomed fall down*
An hendy hap, &c.	
Nihtes° when y wende° ant wake,	*at night/I turn*
Forþi myn wonges waxeþ won;°	*therefore my cheeks grow pale*
Leuedi,° al for þine sake	*lady*
25 Longinge is ylent° me on.	*settled*
In world nis° non° so wyter mon°	*(there) is not/none/wise (a) man*
Þat al hire bounte° telle con.°	*bounty (i.e., goodness)/can*

Hire swyre° is whittore þen° þe swon,°   *neck/whiter than/swan*
    Ant feyrest may° in toune.   *(she is) fairest maiden*
30   An hendi, &c.

Icham for wowyng° al forwake,°   *wooing* (i.e., *longing*)/*sleepless*
    Wery so° water in wore,°   *weary as/pool*
Lest eny reue° me my make,°   *anyone deprive/(of) my companion*
    Ychabbe° yȝyrned ȝore.°   *(for whom) I have/yearned ever*
35 Betere° is þolien whyle° sore,   *better/(to) suffer (a) while*
    Þen mournen euermore.   *(to) mourn*
Geynest° vnder gore,°   *kindest/garment*
    Herkne° to my roun.°   *listen/song*
        An hendi, &c.

---

37. *Geynest vnder gore:* a tag phrase meaning "alive" or "on earth" (cf. above, p. 311, l. 1814*n*).

A WAYLE WHYT

DATE: c. 1314–25. ◆ MANUSCRIPT: British Library Harley 2253, f. 67a. In its refer-ence to the "other man," husband or lover, one might compare this lyric to some of the Minnesänger poems. Although, in the context of the Minnesänger tradition, these seem occasionally artificial in their high courtly-love ideals and code, the English poet does not seem to be hampered by the ritual of love. In many aspects, especially the last stanza, his song shows an honesty and originality of feeling.

A wayle,° whyt ase° whalles bon,°	*beautiful woman/white as/ whalebone*
A grein° in golde þat godly shon,°	*pearl/gracious (one) shone*
A tortle° þat min herte° is on,°	*turtledove/my heart/in*
In tounes° trewe.°	*this place/truly*
⁵ Hire gladshipeᵘ nes° neuer gon°	*her joy/is not/passed*
Whil y° may glewe.°	*while I/make songs*
When heo° is glad	*she*
Of al þis world namore° y bad,°	*no more/ask*
Þen beo° wiþ hire myn one° bistad,°	*than be/alone/placed*
¹⁰ Wiþoute strif;°	*strife*
Þe care þat icham° yn ybrad°	*I am/put*
Y wyte° a wyf.°	*blame on/woman*
A wyf nis° non° so worly wroht°	*(there) is not/none/beautifully made*
When° heo ys blyþe° to bedde ybroht.°	*(as) when/happily/brought*
¹⁵ Wel° were° him° þat wiste° hire þoht,°	*fortunate/would be/he/knew/ thought*
Þat þryuen ant þro.°	*virtuous and excellent (person)*
Wel y wot° heo nul° me noht;°	*know/wants not/not*
Myn herte is wo.°	*woe*
Hou shal þat lefly° syng,	*can that (man) well*
²⁰ Þat þus is marred in mournyng?	
Heo me wol° to deþe° bryng—	*will/death*
Longe er° my day.	*before*
Gret° hire wel, þat swete° þing	*greet/sweet*
Wiþ eȝen° gray.	*eyes*

²⁵ Hyre he3e° haueþ wounded me ywisse,°	*eyes/indeed*
Hire bende browen° þat bringeþ blisse.	*arched eyebrows*
Hire comely mouth, þat mihte cusse,°	*whoever might kiss (it)*
In muche murþe° he were;	*happiness*
Y wolde chaunge myn° for his	*would change my (lot)*
³⁰ Þat is here fere.°	*her companion*
Wolde hyre fere° beo so freo°	*if her companion would/generous*
Ant wurþes° were° þat so myhte beo,°	*(equivalent things of) worth (there) were/be (to trade)*
Al for on° y wolde 3eue þreo,°	*one/give three*
Wiþoute chep.°	*bargaining*
³⁵ From helle to heuene° ant sonne° to see,°	*heaven/sun/sea*
Nys non se 3eep,°	*so wise*
Ne° half so freo.°	*nor/noble*
Whose wole of° loue be trewe,° do lystne° me.	*whoso will in/true/listen (to)*
Herkneþ° me, y ou° telle:	*hearken (to)/you*
⁴⁰ In such wondryng° for wo y welle.°	*distress/suffer*
Nys no fur° so hot in helle	*fire*
Al to mon°	*(as that) all for (the) man*
Þat loueþ derne° ant dar nout° telle	*secretly/dares not*
Whet him° ys on.°	*what (with) him/the matter*
⁴⁵ Ich vnne hire° wel ant heo me wo;	*I wish her*
(Ycham° hire frend ant heo my fo).	*I am/enemy*
Me° þuncheþ min herte° wol brek a° two,	*to me/(it) seems my heart/ break in*
For sorewe° ant syke.°	*sorrow/sighing*
In Godes greting mote heo° go,	*welcome may she*
⁵⁰ Þat wayle° whyte.	*beautiful woman*
Ich wolde° ich were a þrestelcok,°	*would/song thrush*
A bountyng oþer° a lauercok,°	*bunting or/lark*
Swete bryd!°	*bird*
Bituene° hire curtel° ant hire smok°	*between/gown/smok*
⁵⁵ Y° wolde ben° hyd.	*I/be*

---

29. *myn*: Some critics have the interpreted this as "my (love),"
seeing the line as a reference to the poet's own wife or mistress, a
cynical comment on his boredom with the old.

51–55. The intimacy of the last stanza reminds one of Edmund
Waller's poem *On a Girdle*:

> That which her slender waist confined,
> Shall now my joyful temples bind;
> No monarch but would give his crown,
> His arms might do what this has done.

LENTEN IS COME WITH LOVE TO TOWN

DATE: c. 1314–25. ✧ MANUSCRIPT: British Library Harley 2253, f. 71 b.

The reverdie, or celebration of the revival of spring, is a common introduction to German and Provençal love poems. Rarely, however, is the theme continued throughout the whole song, as here. The feeling here echoes that of *Sumer Is Icumen In* and *Foweles in the Frith*, especially in the correspondence of "outer" to "inner weather."

Lenten° ys come wiþ loue to toune,	spring
Wiþ blosmen ant° wiþ briddes roune,°	blossoms and/birds' song
Þat al þis blisse bryngeþ.	
Dayeseȝes° in þis° dales,	daisies/these
5 Notes suete° of nyhtegales,°	sweet/nightingales
Vch foul° song singeþ.	each bird
Þe þrestelcoc° him þreteþ oo.°	song thrush/he quarrels ever
Away is here° wynter wo°	their/woe
When woderoue springeþ.°	woodruff grows
10 Þis foules singeþ ferly fele,°	very many
Ant wlyteþ on huere wynne wele,°	warble in their joy happy
Þat° al þe wode rungeþ.	so that
Þe rose rayleþ hire rode,°	adorns her countenance
Þe leues° on þe lyhte wode°	leaves/bright wood
15 Waxen° al wiþ wille.	grow
Þe mone° mandeþ° hire bleo.°	moon/sends out/light
Þe lilie is lossom° to seo,°	fair/see
Þe fenyl° ant þe fille.°	fennel/wild thyme
Wowes° þis wilde drakes.	woo
20 Miles murgeþ° hucre makes,°	animals gladden/mates
Ase strem° þat strikeþ° stille.	as stream/flows
Mody° meneþ,° so doþ mo;°	a man in love/complains/do more
Ichot° ycham° on° of þo,°	I know/I am/one/them
For° loue þat likes° ille.	because of/pleases

---

1. *to toune:* The phrase can be translated as "to our place" or "spot."

13–24. This stanza shows interesting parallels to the second stanza of Wordsworth's *Ode on Intimations of Immortality from Recollections of Early Childhood.*

²⁵ Þe mone mandeþ hire lyht;
    So doþ þe semly sonne bryht°   *fair sun bright*
       When briddes singeþ breme.°   *tunefully*
    Deawes donkeþ° þe dounes;   *dews wet*
    Deores° wiþ huere derne rounes,°   *animals/secret cries*
³⁰   Domes° forte° deme.°   *tales/in order to/tell*
    Wormes woweþ vnder cloude;°   *clod* (i.e., *earth*)
    Wymmen° waxeþ wounder° proude, *women/exceedingly*
       So wel hit wol hem seme.°   *it will them suit*
    Ʒef me° shal wonte wille° of on,   *if I/lack possession*
³⁵ Þis wunne weole y wole forgon,°   *happy joy I will forgo*
       Ant wyht° in wode be fleme.°   *quickly/(an) outcast*

---

29. *derne:* i.e., "not understood."

WHEN THE NIGHTINGALE SINGS

DATE: C. 1314–25. ✒ MANUSCRIPT: British Library Harley 2253, f. 80 b–81 a.

In the MS. the poem is written in four-line stanzas of seven stresses, the septenary or fourteener, which, broken into alternate lines of four and three stresses, is the old ballad stanza. There is, however, much evidence of internal rhyme.

When þe nyhtegale° singes	*nightingale*
Þe wodes waxen° grene;	*woods grow*
Lef ant° gras ant blosme springes,°	*leaf and/blossom blooms*
In Aueryl, y wene.°	*April, I know*
5 Ant loue is to myn herte gon°	*my heart gone*
Wiþ one spere° so kene,°	*spear/sharp*
Nyht° ant day my blod hit° drynkes;	*night/blood it*
Myn herte deþ° me tene.°	*does/sorrow*
Ich° hauc loued al þis ȝer,°	*I/year*
10 Þat y may loue namore;°	*no more*
Ich haue siked moni syk,°	*sighed many (a) sigh*
Lemmon,° for þin ore.°	*lover/your favor*
Me° nis° loue neuer þe ner,°	*to me/is not/nearer*
Ant þat mc rcweþ° sore.	*troubles*
15 Suete° lemmon, þench° on me—	*sweet/think*
Ich haue loued þe ȝore.°	*you earnestly*
Suete lemmon, y preye° þe	*pray*
Of loue one speche;°	*word*
Whil° y lyue° in world so wyde	*while/live*
20 Oþer° nulle° y seche.°	*another/will not/seek*
Wiþ þy loue, my suete leof,°	*dear one*
Mi blis° þou mihtes eche.°	*bliss/might increase*
A suete cos° of þy mouþ	*kiss*
Mihte be my leche.°	*physician*

---

12. This is the phrase that the priest heard all night and inadvertently substituted for the Dominus Vobiscum in the mass the next day, according to the story of Giraldus Cambrensis (*Gemma Ecclesiastica* [*Opera*, Rolls Series II, 120]; cf. above, p. 15).

²⁵ Suete lemmon, y preȝe° þe   *pray*
    Of° a loue-bene:°   *for/love boon*
    Ȝef° þou me louest ase° men says,   *if/as*
    Lemmon, as y wene,°   *trust*
    Ant ȝef hit þi wille be,
³⁰ Þou loke° þat hit be sene.°   *make sure/seen*
    So muchel° y þenke° vpon þe   *much/think*
    Þat al y waxe grene.

    Bituene Lyncolne° ant Lyndeseye,°   *between Lincoln/Lindsey*
    Norhamptoun° ant Lounde,°   *Northampton/Lound*
³⁵ Ne wot° y non° so fayr a may°   *not know/none/maiden*
    As y go fore ybounde.°   *bound by love for*
    Suete lemmon, y preȝe þe
    Þou louie° me a stounde.°   *(that) you love/while*
      Y wole° mone° my song   *will/sorrowfully sing*
⁴⁰   On wham° þat hit ys on ylong.°   *about her/to due*

33–34. The places, undoubtedly chosen for their alliteration,   **40.** *ys on ylong:* "concerns."
are all in the English Midlands.

THE MAN IN THE MOON

DATE: c. 1314–25. ✦ MANUSCRIPT: British Library Harley 2253, f. 114 b–115 a.

The poem must be viewed as an unusual example of verse in the native folk tradition. Not only is the Old English alliterative line used, but the picture we get has less to do with the moon than with the hedges and fields of an English farm community, and a roaring fire and good stout ale when the day's chores are done. In its themes of country folk, as also in its rough and ready speech, the author of *The Man in the Moon* shows a peculiar kinship to the plowboy poet Robert Burns.

Mon° in þe mone stond ant strit,° *man/moon stands and strides*
On is° bot-forke° is burþen° he bereþ;° *his/forked stick/bundle/bears*
Hit° is muche wonder þat he na° doun slyt,° *it/not/slips*
For doute° leste he valle° he shoddreþ° ant shereþ.° *fear/fall/trembles/veers*
⁵ When þe forst freseþ° muche chele° he byd;° *frost freezes/chill/endures*
Þe þornes beþ kene,° is hattren° to-tereþ.° *are/sharp/clothes/tear apart*
Nis° no wyht° in þe world þat wot° when he syt,° *(there) is not/man/knows/sits*
Ne, bote° hit bue° þe hegge,° whet wedes° he wereþ.° *nor, unless/be/hedge/what clothes/ wears*

Whider° trowe° þis mon ha þe wey take?° *where/do you think/has his way taken*

¹⁰ He haþ set is o fot° is oþer toforen.° *one foot/before*
For non hihte° þat he haþ ne syht° me hym° ner shake;° *no effort/sight/is he/never moved*
He is þe sloweste mon þat euer wes yboren.° *was born*
Wher° he were o° þe feld pycchynde° stake, *whether/on/field pitching*
For hope of ys° þornes to dutten° is doren,° *by his/close/holes*
¹⁵ He mot myd° is twybyl° oþer trous° make, *must with/two-edged ax/bundles*
Oþer° is dayes werk° þer were° yloren.° *or/work/would be/lost*

---

2. The man in the moon is usually represented as carrying a bundle of sticks (cf. the Pyramus-and-Thisbe episode in *A Midsummer Night's Dream*) which he is supposed to have stolen. In Robert Henryson's *Testament of Cresseid* (this volume, p. 950, ll. 261–63) the moon is described as having painted on her breast a churl, bearing on his back a bush of thorns which he had stolen.

8. I.e. the hedge, which has torn his clothes, is the only thing "acquainted" with them.

13–14. *o þe feld . . . doren:* i.e., driving stakes to shut the gaps in the hedge with his thorns. According to one story, he was condemned to the moon for gathering sticks on the Sabbath.

Þis ilke° mon vpon heh whener° he were,   *same/on high whether (or not)*
　　Wher he were y° þe mone boren° ant yfed,°   *in/born/nourished*
He leneþ° on is forke ase° a grey frere.°   *leans/as/friar*
20　Þis crokede caynard sore° he is adred.°   *crooked idler much/afraid*
Hit is mony° day go° þat he was here;   *many (a)/ago*
　　Ichot° of° is ernde° he naþ° nout° ysped.°   *I know/in/errand/has not/not/been*
　　　　　　　　　　　　　　　　　　　　successful

He haþ hewe sumwher° a burþen of brere;°   *cut somewhere/briars*
　　Þarefore sum° hayward° haþ taken ys wed.°   *therefore some/hedge guardian/*
　　　　　　　　　　　　　　　　　　　　pledge

25　ȝef° þy wed ys ytake,° bring hom° þe trous,   *if/taken/home*
　　Sete° forþ þyn° oþer fot, stryd° ouer sty.°   *set/your/step/(the) path*
We shule preȝe° þe haywart hom to vr° hous   *shall invite/our*
　　Ant maken° hym at heyse° for þe maystry,°   *put/ease/best*
Drynke to hym deorly° of fol god bous,°   *affectionately/very good booze*
30　Ant our dame douse° shal sitten° hym by.   *sweet/sit*
When þat he is dronke° ase a dreynt° mous,   *drunk/drowned*
　　Þenne we schule borewe° þe wed ate° bayly.°   *obtain/from the/bailiff*

Þis mon hereþ° me nout þah ich° to hym crye;   *hears/though I*
　　Ichot þe cherl° is def,° þe Del° hym to-drawe!°   *fellow/deaf/Devil/tear apart*
35　Þah ich ȝeȝe° vpon heh° nulle° nout hye,°   *shout/loudly/he will not/hurry*
　　Þe lostlase° ladde con° nout o° lawe.   *listless/knows/of*
Hupe forþ,° Hubert, hosede pye!°   *go on/trousered magpie*
　　Ichot þart° amarscled into° þe mawe!°   *you are/ ? stuffed in/stomach*
Þah me teone° wiþ hym þat° myn teþ mye,°   *I am angry/so that/my teeth grate*
40　Þe cherl nul nout adoun er° þe day dawe.°   *(come) down before/dawns*

---

19. *grey frere:* i.e., "Franciscan." In the 14th century friars were regarded as lazy and in ill repute (cf. Chaucer's Friar Hubert in the *Canterbury Tales*), and satirical songs were written against them.

24. The hayward was a municipal officer who policed the private land to see that cattle from the village commons did not break through the enclosures and that hedges were kept intact. The man in the moon has been caught and has had to give a pledge as security for a later fine to be levied against him.

28. *for þe maystry:* "extremely."

32. The meaning is obscure here. If the bailiff and hayward are the same man, then perhaps the point is that he will return the pledge after a night of good fellowship and drink, or, if they are two men, the hayward is so drunk that they can steal the money from him to redeem the pledge already given to the bailiff (as R. T. Davies suggested).

36. *lawe:* i.e., "correct behavior."

37. *hosede pye:* The magpie is a thieving bird, here in trousers.

THE IRISH DANCER

DATE: Early 14th century. ✒ MANUSCRIPT: Bodleian Library, Oxford, Rawlinson D.913, Item I, g.

This poem and the following two are written on a narrow strip of parchment heavily covered with paste which obscures many of the lines. The poems are genuinely in the folk tradition and may ultimately go back to the earliest lyric charms and songs in our language. These are the Rawlinson Fragments, songs completely divorced from the courtly flavor with which even the best of the Harley Lyrics are imbued. *The Irish Dancer* is one of the most haunting and mysterious of the Rawlinson Fragments. Is the dancer inviting us to join a ritual? Or does the little song hark back to the distant past when the Church of Ireland stoutly defended its dominance against the Church of Rome? Ireland is the holy land of saints, and the dance may have had a religious significance. Whatever its history and purpose, however, the lines move us today in a manner hypnotic and somewhat seductive.

Ich° am of Irlaunde,°   *I/Ireland*
Ant° of the holy londe°   *and/land*
   Of Irlande.

Gode sire,° pray ich þe,°   *good sir/you*
5 For of Saynte Charite,°   *(the sake) of holy charity*
Come ant daunce wyt° me—   *dance with*
   In Irlaunde.

ALL NIGHT BY THE ROSE

DATE: Early 14th century. ✦ MANUSCRIPT: Bodleian Library, Oxford, Rawlinson D.913, Item I, j.

As in *Annot and Iohon*, the maiden's name is cleverly worked into the theme of the song.

Al nist° by þe rose, rose,   *night*
Al nist bi the rose i lay.
Darf ich noust° þe rose stele°—   *dared I not/steal*
    Ant° ʒet ich bar° þe flour° away.   *and/bore/flower*

MAIDEN IN THE MOOR LAY

DATE: Early 14th century. ✦ MANUSCRIPT: Bodleian Library, Oxford, Rawlinson D.913, Item I, h.

Between 1317 and 1360, Richard de Ledrede, the Franciscan bishop of Ossory, composed for the spiritual enlightenment of his clergy (who, he felt, were benighted by popular songs) religious words to be sung to the profane tunes. The first lines of the English lyrics often precede the Latin to indicate the music, and one of them is the beginning of *Maiden in the Moor Lay*. The fact that the bishop had to resort to such a practice gives evidence that his clergy were all too well acquainted with these "devilish" songs. It has been suggested that there is Christian allegory in *Maiden in the Moor Lay*, with the moor as the wilderness before the coming of Christ, the well as the fount of grace, and the maiden as Mary. The poem may even have a religious connotation of another kind, possibly that of a fertility ritual, the pun on the word *well* referring to the rite of "welling," or sleeping beside a well as an aid to conception (cf. *Sir John Doth Play*, this volume, p. 669). On the other hand, perhaps it is just a pleasant folk song of a maiden in the moor, possibly a kind of water sprite known in German folklore as a *Moorjungfer*.

Maiden in the mor° lay,	moor (i.e., *wilderness*)
In the mor lay—	
Seuenyst° fulle, seuenist fulle.	*seven nights*
Maiden in the mor lay,	
5 In the mor lay—	
Seuenistes fulle ant° a day.	*and*
Welle° was hire mete.°	*good/her food*
Wat° was hire mete?	*what*
Þe primerole° ant the	*primrose*
10 Þe primerole ant the—	
Welle was hire mete.	
Wat was hire mete?	
Þe primerole ant the violet.	
Welle was hire dryng.°	*drink*
15 Wat was hire dryng?	
Þe chelde° water of þe	*chill*
Þe chelde water of þe—	

Well was hire dryng.
Wat was hire dryng?
20   Þe chelde water of þe welle-spring.

Welle was hire bour.°   *chamber*
Wat was hire bour?
   Þe rede° rose an te°—   *red/and the*
   Þe rede rose an te—
25 Welle was hire bour.
Wat was hire bour?
   Þe rede rose an te lilie flour.°   *flower*

COMPLAINT TO A PITILESS MISTRESS

DATE: 15th century. ✦ MANUSCRIPT: British Library Sloane 1212.

The poem is a typical courtly complaint, a genre of verse which was usually addressed to a fickle mistress, the poet's lover, or the variable Dame Fortune. Chaucer's parody, the *Complaint to His Purse* (cf. this volume, pp. 408–09), might be read as an antidote to this.

Mercy me graunt° of þat° I me compleyne,°   *grant/what/complain (of)*
To yow° my lyfes soueraigne plesauns°   *you/chief pleasure*
And ese° your seruaunt° of the importabel peyne,°   *ease/servant/unbearable pain*
That I suffre in your obeysauns;°   *worship*
5 And lete° your femenygne° natur dissolue þe cheyne,°   *let/feminine/chain*
That me bonde thorgh oo° look of your eyen tweyne,°   *bound through one/eyes two*
A, þan° **to this fyne**° entende° shall my compleynt.   *ah, then/purpose/be directed*

Syth° yow like noght° my peynes to remedy,   *since/not*
Nor at my request to graunte me mercy,
10 In your seruyse° to deye° and þat I neuer repent.   *service/die (I intend)*
For yow to obeye and serue entendeth° my best cure,°   *is directed/care*
Tyl my lyfe relese° his ryght withouten forfeture.°   *release/without liability*
A, lady nature, what meved the°   *prompted you*
Orpassand beaute° in hir° face to steyne,°   *surpassing beauty/her/paint*
15 Whose herte, deuoyde° of mercy and pite,°   *heart, devoid/pity*
On me to rewe° euer hath disdeyne?°   *pity/disdain*

But sith° hope hath given me herdinesse°   *since/courage*
To love yow best and neuer to repent,
Whiles° þat I lyfe° with al faythfulnesse   *while/live*
20 To drede° and serue, þough daunger° neuer assent,   *worship/scorn*
And her upon° knoweth wele myn° entent,   *herein/well my*
How I haue vowed fully in my mynde
To be your man þough I no mercy fynde.

17–35. These lines are taken almost literally from John Lydgate's *Temple of Glas*, ll. 736–54.

For in myn herte enprented° is so sore°   *imprinted|deeply*
25 Your shappe,° your forme, and eek° your gentilnes,°   *shape|also|gentleness*
Your port,° your chere,° your goodness mor° and mor,   *bearing|manner|more*
Your womanhode,° and eek your semelynes;°   *femininity|beauty*
Your trouthe,° your faith, and eek your kendeness,°   *fidelity|kindness*
With alle vertewes eche° sette in his degre°—   *virtues each|degree*
30 There is no lack, but onely° of pite.   *only*

Your sad demenyng,° of wil° noght variabel,°   *serious behavior|whim|changeable*
Of look benygne, and rote° of al plesauns,   *root*
And exemplary° to alle þat ben stabyl,°   *example|are constant*
Discrete, prudent, of wisdom suffisauns,°   *sufficient*
35 Mirour° of witte, ground of gouernauns,°   *mirror|self-control*
So þat I, shortly,° shal noght fayne,°   *in short|lie*
Saue upon° mercy, I can noght complayne!   *except for*

I SING OF A MAIDEN

DATE: Early 15th century. ◆ MANUSCRIPT: British Library Sloane 2593, f. 10 b.

This is one of the finest of medieval religious lyrics. Much of its power is associated with the balladlike incremental repetition of folk motifs from nature (dew, grass, flower, spray) seen in other poems celebrating reverdie, the rebirth and coming of spring. Similar to *Maiden in the Moor Lay*, this lyric gives the effect of a charm or incantation. It has been much studied in the light of Christian allegory.

I sing of a maiden	
That is makeles,°	*mateless, matchless, spotless*
King of all kinges	
To° her sone° sche ches.°	*for/son/chose*
5 He cam° also° stille	*came/all so*
There° his moder° was,	*where/mother*
As dew in Aprille	
That falleth on the grass.	
He cam also stille	
10 To his moderes bour,°	*chamber*
As dew in Aprille	
That falleth on the flour.°	*flower*
He cam also stille	
There his moder lay,	
15 As dew in Aprille	
That falleth on the spray.°	*branch*
Moder and maiden	
Was never non° but sche;	*none*
Well may swich° a lady	*such*
20 Godes moder be.	

---

2. *makeles:* The play on the word *make* is also found in the *Pearl*.

5–6. The hushed tone of the whole poem harks back to the stillness of Christmas Eve.

7–8. The fertilizing dew, a symbol of Christ, causes a rebirth in springtime. Also, the Annunciation is celebrated on March 25 (in the Middle Ages, March 25 was celebrated as New Year's Day), and April was the first month of Mary's pregnancy.

12. *flour:* Mary is the flower, the "lily among thorns" of the Song of Songs. Much of Old Testament literature was seen as allegorical in terms of Christianity; and R. T. Davies notes that, according to medieval biblical exegesis, anything happening or mentioned in the Old Testament prefigures the New.

16. *spray:* The branch is the Tree of Jesse and David, and also the flowering rod of Aaron.

JOLLY JANKYN

DATE: c. 1450. ❧ MANUSCRIPT: British Library Sloane 2593, f. 34a–34b.

The song is a carol, or dance song, in which the participants held hands and danced in a circle (ring dance) to the burden or refrain and stood still for the separate stanzas.

The theme of the clerical seducer seems an especially popular one in Middle English lyric; and the parody of the Mass with the prayer Kyrie Eleison ("Lord have mercy upon us") punning on the name Alisoun puts this song into the tradition of religious satire and ribaldry (at the expense of the most sacred) which was found mostly in the Latin lyrics of the *Carmina Burana*. The last verse comes with special force; and in its "leaping and lingering" technique, the skipping of the unimportant details, it reminds us of the ballad style. Jankyn, as far as we are told, had done no more than step on Alisoun's foot.

> *Kyrie, so Kyrie,*
> *Iankyn syngyt merie,°*   *Jankyn sings merrily*
> *With aleyson.*

    As I went on ʒol° Day,   *Yule (i.e., Christmas)*
5   In owr prosessyon,°   *our procession*
    Knew I ioly° Iankyn   *jolly*
      Be° his mery ton:°   *by/merry tone*
      Kyrieleyson!

    Iankyn be-gan þe offys,°   *office*
10   On þe ʒol Day,
    And ʒyt° me° þynkyt° it dos° me good,   *still/to me/it seems/does*
      So merie gan° he say: *did*
      Kyrieleyson!

    Iankyn red° þe Pystyl,°   *read/Epistle*
15   Ful° fayr and ful wel,   *very*

---

1. *Kyrie:* Greek, "Lord."

2. *Iankyn:* Jankyn, John, Johon are all nicknames for clerics (cf. the Nun's Priest in Chaucer's *Canterbury Tales*, B² l. 2810).

3. *aleyson:* i.e., Greek *eleison*, "have mercy."

9. *offys:* i.e., the office of the Mass. The poem works through the Mass from the beginning through the Epistle, the Sanctus, and the Agnus Dei to the final Benedicamus Domino, the dismissal statement from the priest on a feast day instead of the better-known Ite Missa Est, the response to either being the Deo Gratias.

And ȝyt me þinkyt it dos me good—
  As euere haue° I sel.°   *ever (may) have/good fortune*
      Kyrieleyson!

Iankyn at þe Sanctus
20   Crakit° a merie° note;   *sang/merry*
And ȝyt me þinkyt it dos me good—
  I payid° for his cote!°   *paid/coat*
      Kyrieleyson!

Iankyn crakit notes,
25   An hunderid on° a knot,°   *hundred at/time*
And ȝyt he hakkyt hem° smaller   *chopped them*
Þan wortes° to þe pot.   *herbs*
      Kyrieleyson!

Iankyn at þe Angnus°   *Agnus*
30   Beryt° þe pax-brede.   *carried*
He twynkelid,° but sayd nowt,°   *winked/nothing*
And on myn fot° he trede!°   *my foot/stepped*
      Kyrieleyson!

Benedicamus Domino,
35   Cryst fro° schame me schylde°   *from/shield*
Deo gracias þerto,°   *also*
  Alas, I go with schylde!°   *child*
      Kyrieleyson!

---

19. *Sanctus:* Latin, "Holy."

29. *Angnus:* i.e., Latin *Agnus Dei,* "Lamb of God."

30. *pax-brede:* a tablet of gold for people to kiss, instead of each other, during the Mass at the Pax Vobiscum, just before Communion.

34. *Benedicamus Domino:* Latin, "Let us bless the Lord."

36. *Deo gracias:* Latin, "Thanks be to God."

JACK, THE NIMBLE HOLY-WATER CLERK

DATE: Mid 15th century. ❧ MANUSCRIPT: Gonville and Caius College, Cambridge, 383, p. 41.

This carol (cf. introduction to *Jolly Jankyn*, this volume, p. 662) refers specifically to the dance (l. 1) and the ring (l. 12). The connection of carols with the Christmas celebration occurred later in the 15th century.

R. T. Davies feels that such songs as this, the one preceding, and the two following, of a clerical seduction were written by clerics themselves, and the idea is a pleasing one. What the Church prohibited in deed might perhaps be expressed and vicariously enjoyed in song. On the other hand, the colloquialism and realism of the lines, the girl's coy dance steps, Jack's wink and clandestine kiss, the white gloves which lead to bed, not only give evidence of a truly popular origin but also make one suspect that the author was more than an observer. We can believe in the truth of each detail here— except, perhaps, that of the refrain.

Ladd y° þe daunce a Myssomur° Day;	*led I/dance on midsummer*
Y made smale trippus soþ fore° to say.	*small steps truth for*
Iak,° oure haly° watur clerk, com be° þe way,	*Jack/holy/came by*
And he lokede° me vpon—he þout° þat y was gay!°	*looked/thought/attractive*
5 Þout yc° on no gyle.°	*I/guile*

Alas, ales° þe wyle°	*alas/time*
Þout y on no gyle,	
So haue° y god chaunce.°	*(may) have/good fortune*
Alas, ales þe wyle	
10 Þat euer y cowde° daunce.	*could*

Iak, oure haly watur clerk, þe ȝonge strippelyng,°	*young stripling*
For þe chesone° of me he com to þe ryng,	*reason*
And he trippede° on my to,° and made a twynkelyng.°	*stepped/toe/wink*

---

1. The Feast of Saint John (Johannestag in Wagner's *Meister-singer*) was celebrated on Midsummer Day and Night, an occasion for dancing, drinking, and general amorous play.

12. *For þe chesone:* i.e., "because."

Euer he cam ner;° he sparet° for no þynge.   *came nearer/stopped*
15 Þout y on no gyle!

Iak, ic wot, priyede° in my fayre face;   *know, looked*
He þout me ful worly,° so haue y god grace.° *very attractive/luck*
As we turndun owre° daunce in a narw° place, *turned our/narrow*
Iak bed° me þe mouþ—a cussynge° þer was— *offered/kissing*
20 Þout y on no gyle!

Iak þo° began to rowne° in myn ere:°   *then/whisper/my ear*
"Loke° þat þou be priuey° and grante þat þou þe bere,° *see/discreet/? yourself bear (well)*
A peyre wyth glouus ich ha to þyn were!"° *pair (of) white gloves I have for*
               your wearing

"Gremercy,° Iacke," þat was myn answere— *thank you*
25 Þout yc on no gyle!

Sone° after euensong, Iak me mette;   *soon*
"Com hom aftur° þy glouus, þat ic þe byhette."° *home for/you promised*
Wan° ic to his chambur com, doun he me sette; *when*
From hym mytte° y nat° go wan we were mette— *might/not*
30 Þout y on no gyle!

Schetus° and chalonus° ic wot were yspredde;° *sheets/blankets/spread*
Fore-soþe,° þo Iak and yc wenten° to beddc. *truly/went*
He prikede° and hc pransede,° nolde° he neuer lynne.˘ *pricked/pranced/not would/stop*
Yt was þe murgust nyt° þat euer y cam ynne°— *merriest night/in*
35 Þout y on no gyle!

Wan Iak had don,° þo he rong° þe belle;   *done/rang*
Al nyȝt þer° he made me to dwelle.   *night there*
Oft, y trewe,° we haddun yserued° þe reaggeth deuel° of helle! *believe/had served/ragged Devil*
Of oþur smale burdus kep° y nout° to telle. *games care/not*
40 Þout y on no gyle!

Þe oþur day at prime y com° hom, as ic wene;° *I came/suppose*
Meth° y my dame° cuppud° and kene:°   *met/mother/bad-tempered/sharp*
"Sey,° þou stronge strumpeth, ware° hastu bene?° *say/foul strumpet, where/have*
               you/been

---

26. *euensong:* vespers, a religious service in the evening.

36. *belle:* The *MED* glosses *bell* as "?maidenhead, ?vulva," (short for *bele chose,* as the Wife of Bath uses the term). The citation in the *MED* is to *Sir John Doth Play* (cf. this volume, pp. 669–70), ll. 8–9: "He gafe my mayden-hed a spurne,/And rofe my bell." But the word there seems to be not *bell* but *kell,* a membrane, probably the hymen. Still, the *MED* definition of *bell* seems to fit here.

41. *prime:* 6–9 A.M.

Þy trippyng and þy dauncyng,° wel it wol° be sene!''°   *dancing/will/seen*
45   Þout° y on no gyle!°   *thought/guile*

Euer bi on and by on° my damme° reched° me clot;°   *every so often/(prob. mother)/*
                                                           gave/(a) clout
Euer y ber° it priuey wyle° þat y mouth,°   *bore/secretly while/might*
Tyl my gurdul° a-ros,° my wombe wax° out: *girdle/rose up/grew*
"Euel yspunne ȝern° euer it wole out"°—   *ill spun yarn/unravel*
50   Þout y on no gyle!

THE SERVANT GIRL'S HOLIDAY

DATE: Mid 15th century. ⚓ MANUSCRIPT: Gonville and Caius College, Cambridge, 383, p. 41.

It is hard to escape the surmise that the author of this and the preceding lyric, perhaps a cleric, is involved in an oblique and very gentle satire of women in general. The total naïveté of these beguiled maidens is forcefully pointed up both by the refrain of the first song, which becomes ever more astounding as the poem progresses, and the last stanza of this one—a very climax of innocence! It is this lack of suspicion on the part of the maid that is the cause of Jack's easy success, and of which he takes advantage. Is there just a hint here, perhaps, albeit in a very good-natured and humorous fashion, of the scorn of women, the clerical antifeminism, that was so common in the Middle Ages?

Wybbe ne rele° ne spynne yc ne° may   *weave nor wind/spin I not*
For ioy�ze° þat it ys holyday.   *joy*

Al þis day ic han souꝝt°   *I have sought*
Spyndul° ne werue,° ne wond y nouꝝt;°   *(neither) spindle/reel/wound I nothing*

5 To myche° blisse ic am brout,°   *much/brought*
    Aꝝen° þis hyꝝe° holyday.   *at/high*
    Wybbe & c.

All vnswope° ys owre vleth,°   *unswept/our floor*
And owre fyre ys vnbeth,°   *not built up*
10 Oure rushen ben vnrepe ꝝeth,°   *rushes (for the floor) are uncut yet*
    Aꝝen þis hy halyday.°   *high holiday*

Yc moste feꝝchun worton° in,   *must fetch herbs*
Þredele° my kerchef vndur my khyn.°   *tie/chin*
Leue Iakke,° lend me a pyn,   *dear Jack*
15   To þredele me° þis holiday.   *myself*

Now yt draweþ to° þe none,°   *approaches/noon*
And al my cherrus° ben vndone;   *chores*
Y moste a lyte solas mye schone,°   *little polish my shoes*
    To make hem dowge° þis holiday.   *them useful*

²⁰ Y moste mylkyn° in þis payl.   *milk*
Outh me° bred° al° þis schayl,°   *ought I/(to) spread out (**dough**)/*
                                                            (in) all/bowl

Зut° is þe dow° vndur my nayl,   *yet/dough*
   As ic knad° þis holyday.   *knead*

Iakke wol° brynge me onward in° my wey,°   *will/on/way*
²⁵ Wyþ me desyre for te pleзe.°   *to play*
Of my dame° stant me° non eyзe,°   *mother/I have/no fear*
   An° neuer a god° haliday.   *and/(on) a good*

Iacke wol pay for my scoth,°   *contribution*
A sonday atte° þe ale-schoth.°   *on Sunday at/ale-scot*
³⁰ Iacke wol sowse° wel my þroth°—   *soak/throat*
   Euery god haliday.

Sone° he wolle take me be° þe hand,   *soon/by*
And he wolle legge° me on þe lond,°   *lay/earth*
Þat° al my buttockus ben of sond,°   *so that/sand*
³⁵   Opon° þis hye holyday.   *on*

In he pult° and out he drow,°   *thrust/drew*
And euer yc lay on hym y-low:°   *below him*
"By godus deth,° þou dest° me wow,°   *God's death/do/woo*
   Vpon þis hey° holyday!"   *high*

⁴⁰ Sone my wombe began to swelle
As greth° as a belle.   *great*
Durst° y nat° my dame telle,   *dared/not*
   Wat° me° betydde° þis holyday.   *what/to me/happened*

28–29. Scot and lot (the two usually being mentioned together) were taxes and tributes levied on certain occasions; the ale-scot was a celebration during which contributions were made so that ale might be brewed for the community.

SIR JOHN DOTH PLAY

DATE: Late 15th century. ✦ MANUSCRIPT: Cambridge University Ff. 5. 48, f. 114b.

The clerical seducer again appears as the girl watches beside the well (l. 2; cf. *Maiden in the Moor Lay*, this volume, p. 657). Here is one instance where the beguiled maiden might have been caught napping, but at least awoke to understand the realities of the day. Evidently her "welling" was more successful than she had expected.

I haue for-sworne hit whil° I life°	*it while/live*
To wake the well-ey.	
The last tyme I the wel woke,	
Ser Iohn caght° me with a croke;°	*Sir John caught/crook*
5 He made me to swere be° bel and boke°	*swear by/book*
I shuld° not tell-ey.	*should*
ȝet he did me a wel wors° turne;	*much worse*
He leyde° my hed agayn° the burne°—	*laid/heud against/well*
He gafe° my mayden-hed a spurne,°	*gave/stroke*
10 And rofe° my kell°-ey.	*tore away/maidenhead*
Sir Iohn came to oure hows° to play,	*house*
Froᵘ euensong tyme til light of the day.	*from*
We made as mery° as flowres in May—	*merry*
I was begyled°-ay.	*beguiled*
15 Sir Iohn he came to our hows.	
He made hit wondur copious;°	*very full (with presents)*
He seyd° that I was gracious—	*said*
To beyre° a childe-ey!	*bear*

---

4. *croke:* a crooked staff like a shepherd's.

10. *kell:* probably *calle*, a membrane, the hymen (cf. above, p. 665, l. 36*n*).

12. *euensong:* vespers, a religious service in the evening.

I go with childe, wel I wot;°   *know*
20 I schrew° the fadur° þat hit gate,°   *curse/father/begot*
With-outen° he fynde hit mylk and pap   *unless*
  A long while-ey!

  Bryan hys° my name iet.°   *is/yet*

THE SMITHS

DATE: 15th century. ✦ MANUSCRIPT: British Library Arundel 292, f. 71 b.

The native tradition in this poem is found not only in the alliteration, giving an emphatic onomatopoetic effect, but in the general vigor and realism of the images. The poem harks back to the sturdiness of *The Man in the Moon* and looks forward to the stylistic power of Gerard Manley Hopkins in evoking color and sound. *The Smiths* is a rare item in the generally vapid flow of 15th-century English verse.

Swarte-smeked smeþes, smatered° with smoke,	*black-smoked smiths, begrimed*
Dryve me to deth° wyth din of here dyntes.°	*death/their blows*
Swich noys on nyghtes ne herd° men neuer!	*such noise at night not heard*
What knavene° cry and clateryng° of knockes,°	*workers'/clattering/blows*
5 The cammede kongons cryen° after "Col!° Col!"	*pug-nosed rascals cry/coal*
And blowen° here bellewes° þat° al here brayn brestes!°	*blow/bellows/so that/brains burst*
"Huf, puf," seith° þat one, "Haf, paf," þat oþer,	*says*
Thei spytten° and spraulen° and spellen° many spelles;°	*spit/sprawl/tell/tales*
Thei gnauen° and gnacchen,° þei grones togydere,°	*gnaw/gnash/groan together*
10 And holden hem° hot wyth here hard hamers.	*keep themselves/hammers*
Of a bole° hyde ben° here barm-felles,°	*bull/are/leather aprons*
Here shankes° ben shakeled for° þe fere-flunderes.°	*legs/protected from/fiery sparks*
Heuy° hameres þei han° þat hard ben handled,	*heavy/have*
Stark° strokes þei stryken° on a steled stokke,°	*hard/strike/steel anvil*
15 "Lus, bus; las, das!" rowten be rowe,°	*(they) crash in turn*
Swich dolful° a dreme° þe deuyl° it todryue.°	*so awful/noise/Devil (may)/stop*
The master longeth° a litel° and lascheth° a lesse,°	*lengthens/small (piece)/hammers/ smaller (one)*
Twyneth hem tweyn° and toucheth° a treble.°	*twists the two/hits/treble (note)*
"Tik, tak; hic, hac! tiket, taket; tyk, tak!	
20 Lus, bus; lus, das!" Swich lyf° þei leden!°	*life/lead*
Alle cloþemeres,° Cryst hem gyue sorwe,°	*mare-clothiers/them give sorrow*
May no man for° brenwaters on° nyght han hys rest.	*because of/water-burners at*

---

21. *cloþemeres:* Smiths not only put shoes on horses but provided them with total armor, and this is probably what is referred to.

22. *brenwateres:* The smiths put the hot metal into the cold water to harden it.

THE FOX AND THE GOOSE

DATE: 15th century. ✧ MANUSCRIPT: British Library Royal 19. B. iv.

This song and the following one are in the tradition of the beast fable, examples of late popular verse.

It fell ageyns° the next nyght,	*upon*
The fox yede to° with all his myghte,	*went at (it)*
Withouten cole° or candlelight,	*without coal*
Whan° that he cam° unto the towne.	*when/came*
5 Whan he cam all in the yarde,	
Sore the geys° wer ill aferde;°	*geese/very afraid*
"I shall macke some° of your berde,°	*deprive some (of you)/beards*
Or° that I go from the towne."	*before*
Whan he cam all in the crofte,	
10 There he stalked wunderful softe,	
"For here haue I be frayed full° ofte,	*been afraid very*
When that I haue come to towne."	
He hente° a goose all be the heye,°	*took/in a twinkling*
Faste the goose began to creye!°	*cry*
15 Owte° yede men as° they myght heye,°	*out/as (fast as)/hasten*
And seyde,° "Fals° fox, ley° it down!"	*said/false/lay*
"Nay," he saide, "so mote° I the,°	*may/prosper*
Sche shall go unto the wode° with me,	*wood*
Sche and I unther° a tre,°	*under/tree*
20 Emange° the berys° browne.	*among/berries*
I haue a wyf° and sche lyeth seke,°	*wife/lies sick*
Many smale whelpis° sche haue to eke,°	*small whelps/feed*
Many bonis° they must pike,°	*bones/pick*
Will° they ley adowne."°	*when/lie down*

---

7. I.e., "I'll make fools of some of you."

THE FALSE FOX

DATE: 15th century. ✒ MANUSCRIPT: Cambridge University Ec. 1. 12.

The false fox came unto our croft,
And so our gese ful faste° he sought.   *geese very eagerly*
  With how, fox, how! with hey, fox, hey!
  Come no more unto our house to bere° our gese away!   *bear*

⁵ The false fox came unto our stye,
And toke° our gese ther, by and by.   *took*

The false fox came into our yerde,°   *yard*
And ther he made the gese aferde.°   *afraid*

The false fox came unto our gate,
¹⁰ And toke our gese there where they sat.

The false fox came unto our hall dore,
And shrove° our gese ther in° the flore.   *confessed/on*

The false fox came into our halle,
And assoyled° our gese both grete° and small.   *absolved/great*

¹⁵ The false fox came unto our coope,
And ther he made our gese to stoope.

He toke a gose° fast by the neck,   *goose*
And the gose tho° began to quek.°   *then/quack*

The good wyfe came out in her smock,
²⁰ And at the fox she threw hir° rock.   *her*

The good man came out with his flayle,
And smote the fox upon the tayle.

He threw the gose upon his back,
And forth he went then with his pack.

²⁵ The good man swore if that he myght,°   *might*
He would him slay ere° it wer nyght.   *before*

The false fox went into his denne,
And there was he full merry thenne.

He came ayene° yet the next weke,°   *again/week*
³⁰ And toke awey both hen and cheke.°   *chick*

The good man saide unto his wyfe,
"This false fox liveth a merry lyfe."

The false fox came upon a day,
And with our gese he made affray.

³⁵ He toke a gose fast by the neck,
And made her say "wheccumquek."

"I praye thee, fox," seid° the goose tho,   *said*
"Take of my feders,° but not of my to!"°   *feathers/toe*

ALLEGORICAL AND RELIGIOUS VERSE

The north of England, that great repository of religious allegory and of moral and didactic verse and prose, produced the *Northern Homily Cycle* (c. 1300), a collection of sermons; and the *Cursor Mundi*, a long poem of twenty-nine thousand lines describing the events of both Testaments, was also northern in provenance. The *Pearl* and the allegorical dream vision called *Piers Plowman* belong to the Alliterative Revival of the fourteenth century, a literary phenomenon of strong religious tone occurring in the North and West. Although the long didactic poem *The Prick of Conscience* muddles in an uninteresting fashion through ten thousand lines concerning man's bestial nature, worldly vanity, the inexorability of death, and the joys of the world to come, more than a hundred manuscripts survive, which is proof of its popularity in the fifteenth century. In the hundred years before, there were some more interesting pieces of religious allegory, including *The Bestiary* of c. 1250, a collection of animal descriptions with moral applications, and from the same period *The Harrowing of Hell*, describing Christ's descent to free the worthy souls of men who died before his birth. The *Ormulum* (c. 1200), often called the dullest poem in the English language, attempts to expound the Gospels of the Mass. Its value lies in the new system of spelling devised by the author, Orm, by which philologists can ascertain the quantity of vowels, and in its reflection of the literary pleasures of the poor and the pious.

REFERENCES

Cargill, Oscar and Schlauch, Margaret. "The Pearl and Its Jeweler." *PMLA*, 43 (1928), 105–23.

Cawley, A. C., ed. *Pearl, Gawain and the Green Knight*. London, 1962.

Morris, Richard, ed. *An Old English Miscellany*. London, 1872.

Owst, G. R. *Literature and Pulpit in Medieval England*. Cambridge, 1933.

———. *Preaching in Medieval England*. Cambridge, 1926.

Allegorical and religious verse is treated in the General Introduction to this volume, pp. 13–14.

[Handwritten annotations at top: "DREAM VISION / ALLEGORY" and "HISTORY OF CHRISTIANITY / Describes failures of society / Directed at lower class"]

PIERS PLOWMAN

William Langland

DATE: A text, a. 1376; B text, 1378; C text, c. 1387. ⟡ MANUSCRIPT: About fifty MSS and fragments survive, seventeen of the A text alone (described in the edition by George Kane and W. W. Skeat). These are found in the Huntingdon Library, the British Library, the Bodleian Library, the Cambridge University Library, and elsewhere; most date from the 15th and 16th centuries. The dialect of the poem is of the Southwest Midlands. ⟡ EDITIONS: W. W. Skeat, *The Vision of William concerning Piers the Plowman*, Early English Text Society, OS 28, 38, 54, notes and glossary, 67, 81 (London, 1867–84), which is the edition used here; Thomas A. Knott and David Fowler, eds., *Piers the Plowman, A Critical Text of the A Version* (Baltimore, 1952); George Kane, ed., *Piers Plowman, The A Version* (London, 1960); George Kane and E. Talbot Donaldson, eds., *Piers Plowman, The B Version* (London, 1975). The C version is being edited by the University of London under the supervision of George Kane. Volumes that might also be consulted are: Allan H. Bright, *New Light on "Piers Plowman"* (Oxford, 1928); David Fowler, *Piers the Plowman* (Seattle, 1961); J. J. Jusserand, *Piers Plowman* (London, 1894).

The Southwest Midland dialect of the text, though impure, will give little trouble in reading. (1) The pronouns should be watched: e.g., *hem*, "them" or "themselves"; *here, her*, "their," and in the C text *hure*, "their"; *hue, hu*, "she." (2) OE *y* (pronounced like German *ü*) has been kept and is spelled *u* where we would expect an *i*: *hulle* = *hill*, *culle* = *kill*. (3) OE *a* before a nasal plus consonant is here usually spelled *o*, as was typical of the West Midland dialect (*londe, monie*), though there are exceptions. (4) *Yogh*, *ʒ*, as always represents Mod. Eng. *ch* or *gh*: *syʒt, bryʒt*.

The monumental work of social consciousness of the 14th century, earnest in its satire, realistic in its humor, is found in three different versions. The A text contains 2,569 lines; the B text is three times as long, with 7,241 lines; and the C text contains 7,353 lines. The hypothetical author was a certain William Langland, born in 1332 in Ledbury, Shropshire, illegitimate son of Eustace de la Rokayle. He took minor orders and probably spent some years in a Benedictine or possibly Cistercian monastery. For a time he lived in Cornhill, London, with his wife Kit, serving as a chantry priest. He died in the last years of the 1380s, according to the evidence of John But's addition to the A text (A Passus XII), where he is mentioned as already dead (John But himself was dead by 1387 or 1389).

Piers Plowman supplements Chaucer in that it treats specifically of the poor; it surpasses Chaucer in its earnest involvement with contemporary issues. There is little that can be called light-handed about the work. The author warns like an Old Testament prophet, whose vision is mystical and realistic at the same time yet whose laughter can also be loud and uninhibited.

THE VISION OF WILLIAM CONCERNING PIERS THE PLOWMAN

B PROLOGUS

In a somer seson whan° soft was the sonne,° *summer season when/sun*
I shope me° in shroudes° as° I a shepe° were, *dressed myself/rough clothes/ as if /shepherd*

In habite as an heremite vnholy of° workes, *hermit irreligious in*
Went wyde in þis world wondres to here.° *hear*
5 Ac° on a May mornynge on Maluerne hulles° *but/hills*
Me byfel° a ferly° of fairy° me° thouȝte;° *befell/strange experience/fairy (quality)/to me/(it) seemed*

I was wery° forwandred° and went me to reste *weary/of wandering*
Vnder a brode° banke bi a bornes° side, *broad/brook's*
And as I lay and lened° and loked° in þe waters, *leaned/looked*
10 I slombred° in a slepyng,° it sweyued° so mcryc.° *slumbered/sleeping/flowed/merrily*
   Thanne gan° I to meten° a merueilouse sweuene,° *then began/dream/marvelous dream*
That I was in a wildernesse, wist° I neuer where, *knew*
As I bihelde° in-to þe est an hiegh° to þe sonne, *looked/east on high*
I seigh° a toure° on a toft trielich ymaked;° *saw/tower/hill perfectly made*
15 A depe dale binethe,° a dongeon° þere-Inne, *deep/beneath/dungeon*
With depe dyches° and derke° and dredful of sight. *ditches/dark*
A faire felde° ful of folke fonde° I there bytwene,° *field/found/between*
Of alle maner° of men, þe mene° and þe riche, *manner/poor*
Worchyng° and wandryng as þe worlde asketh. *working*
20 Some putten hem° to þe plow; pleyed ful selde,° *put themselves/played very seldom*
In settyng° and in sowyng swonken° ful harde, *planting/worked*
And wonnen that wastours° with glotonye destruyeth.° *won what wasters/gluttony destroy*
   And some putten° hem to pruyde,° apparailed° hem þere-after, *inclined/pride/dressed*
In contenaunce° of clothyng comen° disgised.° *display/came/dressed up*
25   In prayers and in penance putten hem manye,° *many*
Al for loue of owre° lorde lyueden° ful streyte,° *our/lived/strictly*

---

1. The beginning is typical of the reverdie, the introduction in praise of spring and summer.

3. *vnholy of workes:* The phase is derogatory of false wandering hermits, i.e., beggars.

5. *Maluerne hulles:* Malvern Hills in Worcestershire, near the border of Herefordshire. A 15th-century MS notes that William Langland was born in Shropshire near Malvern. Allan H. Bright, in *New Light on "Piers Plowman,"* has done much to identify the "field full of folk" near Malvern. The dream of the poet is of London, however, as Skeat pointed out.

8. *bornes side:* Bright identified the brook as Primeswell (in Langland's time Promeswelle) near the Herefordshire Beacon. Above this spot in the east on a hill may have been the remains of a Norman tower. Below the dreamer is a dale, and to his left the dungeon of Old Castle. Between Old Castle and the Herefordshire Beacon is the field of working folk which William sees.

14–15. Truth, or God the Father, lives in the tower; Death lives in the dale; and Falsehood, Care, or Lucifer lives in the dungeon.

17. Critics mention that the "fair field full of folk" resembles the scaffolding of old morality plays, representing the world, heaven, and hell.

In hope forto haue heueneriche° blisse;   *heavenly*
As ancres° and heremites that holden hem° in here selles,°   *anchorites/stay/their cells*
And coueiten nought° in contre° to kairen° aboute,   *care not/land/wander*
30 For no likerous liflode her lykam° to plese.°   *luxurious life their body/please*
    And somme chosen° chaffare,° they cheuen° the bettere,   *some chose/commerce/prosper*
As it semeth to° owre syʒt° that suche men thryueth;°   *seems in/ view/thrive*
And somme murthes° to make as mynstralles° conneth,°   *mirth/minstrels/are able*
And geten° gold with here glee synneles,° I leue.°   *get/sinless/believe*
35 Ac iapers° and iangelers, Iudas chylderen,°   *jesters/jugglers, Judas's children*
Feynen° hem fantasies and foles hem° maketh,   *invent/fools (of) themselves*
And han° here witte° at wille to worche ʒif° þei sholde.°   *yet have/wits/if/should*
That Poule precheth° of hem° I nel° nought preue° it here;   *Paul preaches/them/will not/prove*
Qui turpiloquium loquitur is luciferes hyne.°   *Lucifer's servant*
40 Bidders° and beggeres° fast aboute ʒede,°   *mendicants/beggars/went*
With her bely° and her bagges of bred° ful ycrammed;°   *belly/bread/crammed*
Fayteden° for here fode, fouʒten atte ale;°   *shammed/food, fought at alehouse*
In glotonye, God it wote, gon hij° to bedde,   *knows, go they*
And risen° with ribaudye, tho roberdes° knaues;   *rise/ribaldry, those Roberts*
45 Slepe° and sori sleuthe seweth° hem eure.°   *sleep/wretched sloth follows/ever*
    Pilgrymes and palmers pliʒted° hem togidere°   *swore/together*
To seke seynt Iames° and seyntes in rome.   *seek Saint James*
Thei went forth in here wey° with many wise tales,   *way*
And hadden leue° to lye° al here lyf° after.   *had permission/lie/life*
50 I seigh somme that seiden° þei had ysouʒt° seyntes;   *said/sought*
To eche a° tale þat þei tolde here tonge° was tempred° to lye, *each/tongue/fitted*
More þan to sey soth,° it semed bi here speche.°   *say truth/speech*
    Heremites on° an heep,° with hoked° staues,   *hermits in/heap/hooked*
Wenten° to Walsyngham and here wenches after;°   *went/with them*

33–37. Sinless minstrels earn their money with music and song, but jesters and jugglers are liars and cheats and give the whole entertainment profession a bad name.

38–39. *Qui turpiloquium loquitur:* "he who slanders." Paul's sermon is in 2 Thess. 3:10: "if any would not work, neither should he eat." William does not quote this, but implies that he could.

44. *roberdes knaues:* Roberts knaves were vagabonds, marauders, and thieves; they were also called Robartes men or Roberts men. "Divers manslaughters, felonies, and robberies, done by people that be called Roberdesmen, Wastours, and drawlacches" are mentioned in a statute of Edward III (1331); Richard II also inveighed against them. Roberts men entered homes by manipulating the latches and then robbed the owners; in *Havelok the Dane* there is such an occurrence (cf. this volume, p. 222). It should also be noted that after Sloth has finished confessing his sins, Robert the Robber asks to be shriven.

46–47. Palmers were originally pilgrims who had gone to the Holy Land and brought back a palm as a sign of their journey. Later the word *palmer* was used for any pilgrim whose business was to travel continually from shrine to shrine. The pilgrimage shrine of Saint James or Santiago of Compostela in Galicia (Spain) was, outside of Rome, the most famous one in Europe.

48. *wise:* of course meant ironically here.

53–57. In the 14th century a man could become a hermit only with the permission of the bishop. Thereupon, however, he might live in comfort in a small house, near the high road, with a servant and chaplain, although many did seclude themselves away from populated areas.

54. The shrine of Our Lady of Walsingham in Norfolk almost surpassed in fame that of Saint Thomas à Becket at Canterbury.

⁵⁵ Grete lobyes° and longe,° that loth° were to swynke,°
    great lubbers/tall/loath/work

Clotheden° hem in copis° to ben knowen fram othere;°
    clothed/copes/be distinguished from others

And shopen° hem heremites here ese° to haue.
    made/ease

    I fonde° þere Freris,° alle þe foure ordres,
    found/friars

Preched° þe peple° for profit of hem-seluen,°
    preached (to)/people/themselves

⁶⁰ Glosed° þe gospel as hem good lyked,°
    interpreted/(it) pleased

For coueitise° of copis construed it as þei wolde.°
    greed/would

Many of þis maistres° Freris mowe clothen hem° at lykyng,°
    these master/may clothe themselves/as they please

For here money and marchandise marchen togideres.°
    merchandise march together

For sith charite° haþ be chapman° and chief° to shryue° lordes,
    since charity/been (made) peddler/interested/confess

⁶⁵ Many ferlis° han fallen° in a fewe ȝeris.°
    strange events/happened/years

But° holychirche° and hij° holde better togideres,
    unless/Holy Church/(i.e., friars)

The moste° myschief on molde° is mountyng wel° faste.
    greatest/earth/very

    Þere preched a Pardonere as° he a prest° were,
    as if/priest

Brouȝte° forth a bulle with bishopes seles,°
    brought/seals

⁷⁰ And seide þat hym-self myȝte assoilen° hem alle
    might absolve

Of falshed° of fastyng,° of vowes ybroken.°
    breaking/fast/broken

    Lewed° men leued hym wel and lyked his wordes,
    ignorant

Comen° vp knelyngᵘ to kissen° his bulles;
    came/kneeling/kiss

He bonched° hem with his breuet° and blered here° eyes,
    banged/letter of indulgence/blinded their

⁷⁵ And rauȝte° with his ragman° rynges and broches.
    gained/papal charter

Thus þey geuen° here golde glotones to kepe,°
    give/gluttons/support

And leueth° such loseles° þat lecherye haunten.°
    leave (it to)/vagabonds/practice

Were þe bischop yblissed° and worth bothe his eres,°
    holy/ears

His seel shulde nouȝt° be sent to deceyuc° þe peple.
    seal should not/deceive

⁸⁰ Ac° it is nauȝt° by° þe bischop þat þe boy precheth,°
    but/not/the fault of/fellow preaches

---

56. A cope signified a monk or a friar.

58. The four orders of friars were the Carmelites (White Friars), Augustines (Austin Friars), Dominicans or Jacobins (Black Friars), and Franciscans or Minorites (Gray Friars). Wycliffe put the initials of the orders together to form *CAIM,* and called the friars Cain's kin.

63. Reference is to the custom of confessing only nobles, at a high price. The friars who heard confession carried pins, knives, and other trinkets in their bags and literally peddled their wares (cf. Hubert, Chaucer's Friar).

66–67. The friars and secular clergy were severely at odds over the right to hear confession.

68. Pardoners sold certificates of papal "pardons," which here, as usually in Middle English, meant "indulgences."

According to the theology of the time, an indulgence remitted to anyone gaining it an amount of punishment in purgatory equivalent to what would have been remitted to him if he had fasted, prayed, worn a hair shirt, etc., for the amount of time specified in the "pardon": forty days, seven years, or whatever. This was a "partial" indulgence; a "plenary" indulgence would get rid of all punishment in purgatory. Professional pardoners were, of course, quite corrupt, and they were severely satirized; cf. the unpleasant description of Chaucer's Pardoner in the *Canterbury Tales.*

74–75. The *ragman* was the bishop's charter with seals. The *brevet* was the letter of indulgence which the pardoner thrust into the faces of the ignorant folk to "blear" or blind their eyes.

For the parisch prest and þe pardonere parten° þe siluer,   *share*
That þe poraille° of þe parisch sholde° haue ʒif° þei nere.°   *poor/should/if/were not (there)*
   Persones° and parisch prestes pleyned hem° to þe bischop,   *parsons/complained*
Þat here parisshes were pore° sith þe pestilence tyme,   *poor*
85 To haue a lycence and a leue at London to dwelle,
And syngen° þere for symonye,° for siluer is swete.°   *sing/simony/sweet*
   Bischopes and bachelers,° bothe maistres and doctours,   *novices in divinity*
Þat han° cure° vnder criste and crounyng° in tokne°   *have/charge of souls/tonsure/token*
And signe þat þei sholden shryuen° here paroschienes,°   *should confess/parishioners*
90 Prechen° and prey° for hem° and þe pore fede,°   *preach/pray/them/feed*
Liggen° in London in lenten, an° elles.°   *live/Lent, and/other times*
Somme seruen° þe kyng and his siluer tellen,°   *some serve/count*
In cheker° and in chancerye chalengen° his dettes°   *exchequer/claim/debts*
Of wardes° and wardmotes,° weyues° and streyues.°   *from (city) wards/ward meetings/ waifs/strays*

95   And some seruen as seruantz° lordes and ladyes,   *servants*
And in stede° of stuwardes sytten° and demen.°   *place/stewards sit/judge*
Here messe° and here matynes° and many of here oures°   *mass/matins/(canonical) hours*
Arn don vndeuoutlych;° drede° is at þe laste   *are done undevoutly/fear*
Lest crist in consistorie° acorse ful manye.°   *church council/curse very many*
100 I parceyued° of þe power þat Peter had to kepe,°   *perceived/hold*
To bynde and to vnbynde as þe boke° telleth,   *book*
How he it left wiþ loue, as owre° lorde hight,°   *our/commanded*
Amonges° foure vertues,° þe best of alle vertues,   *among/virtues*
Þat cardinales ben° called and closyng ʒatis,°   *cardinal (virtues) are/gates*
105 Þere° crist is in kyngdome to close and to shutte,   *where*
And to opne° it to hem and heuene° blisse shewe.°   *open/heavenly/show*
Ac of þe cardinales atte° Courte þat cauʒt of° þat name,   *at/gained*
And power presumed in hem a Pope to make,
To han þat power þat peter hadde inpugnen° I nelle;°   *impugn/will not*

---

84. Outbreaks of the pestilence, bubonic plague or the so-called Black Death, occurred in 1348–49, 1361–62, July 2–Sept. 29, 1369, and 1375–76. The first was the Great Pestilence, referred to here. These pestilences ravaged all of Europe, carrying off two-thirds of the population.

83–96. Parish priests asked permission to leave home and settle in London, where they became "chantry priests" and sang masses for guilds or wealthy patrons—a more remunerative occupation than dealing only with the serfs in their own parishes. Chaucer's Parson was *not* one of these.

92–94. With the dearth of a literate lay cadre, the clergy supplied the government bureaucracy. Bishops and other clergy sat on the courts of law, the King's Bench, the Common Pleas, and the Exchequer. The last collected the revenue and "challenged" or claimed the taxes from the city wards. There was much criticism of the worldly activities of the clergy. Chaucer asks ironically, "How should the world be served?" when he

notes the lay duties of his Monk. What would happen to the "world" if it were not for the "worldly" clergy?

94. Waifs (property without an owner) and strays (strayed cattle) belonged to the crown.

97. *matynes:* morning prayer service beginning at midnight.

99. By "consistory" is here meant the last council on Judgment Day; it is usually any church council or assembly of prelates.

100–4. The four cardinal virtues to whom Saint Peter deputed the power of the keys are Prudence, Temperance, Fortitude, and Justice. They here lead to discussion of the Roman cardinals—or probably in this case the French cardinals who split off from Rome and elected a French antipope in 1378 (the Babylonian Captivity or Great Schism). This is a clear hint for dating the poem, which Skeat missed when he dated the B text 1377.

107. The court referred to would be Avignon.

¹¹⁰ For in° loue and letterure° þe eleccioun bilongeth,° — *to/learning/election belongs*
For þi° I can and can° nauȝte of courte speke° more. — *therefore/yet will/speak*
Þanne come° þere a kyng, knyȝthod° hym ladde,° — *then came/knighthood/conducted*
Miȝt° of þe comunes° made hym to regne,° — *power/commons/reign*
And þanne cam kynde wytte° and clerkes he made, — *came common sense*
¹¹⁵ For to conseille° þe kyng and þe comune° saue. — *counsel/common people*
   The kyng and knyȝthode and clergye bothe
Casten° þat þe comune shulde hem-self fynde.° — *decided/themselves support*
   Þe comune contreued° of kynde witte craftes,° — *contrived/skill*
And for profit of alle þe poeple° plowmen ordeygned,° — ***people/appointed***
¹²⁰ To tilie° and trauaile° as trewe lyf askeþ.° — *till/work/true life demands*
Þe kynge and þe comune and kynde witte þe thridde° — *third*
Shope° lawe and lewte,° eche° man to knowe his owne. — *made/obedience to law/each*
   Þanne loked° vp a lunatik, a lene° þing with-alle, — *looked/lean*
And knelyng° to þe kyng clergealy° he seyde.° — *kneeling/in a scholarly manner/said*
¹²⁵ "Crist kepe þe,° sire kyng and þi kyngriche,° — *you/kingdom*
And leue° þe lede° þi londe° so° leute° þe louye,° — *allow/(to) rule/land/so that/loyal subjects/love*

And for þi riȝtful rewlyng° be rewarded in heuene!"° — *honest rule/heaven*
   And sithen° in þe eyre an hiegh° an angel of heuene — *then/air on high*
Lowed° to speke in latyn—for lewed° men ne coude° — *condescended/ignorant/not could*
¹³⁰ Iangle ne iugge° þat° iustifie hem shulde,° — *argue nor judge/so that/justify themselves (they) might*

But suffren° and seruen— for-thi seyde þe angel, — *endure*
"*Sum Rex, sum Princeps neutrum fortasse deinceps—*
O qui iura regis Christi specialia regis,
Hoc quod agas melius iustus es, esto pius!
¹³⁵ *Nudum ius a te vestiri vult pietate;*
Qualia vis metere talia grana sere.
Si ius nudatur nudo de iure metatur.
Si seritur pietas de pietate metas!"
   Thanne greued hym° a Goliardeys, a glotoun° of wordes, — *was annoyed/glutton*

---

123. Skeat believes the "lunatic" to be William Langland himself, who takes this guise because (1) a lunatic was thought to speak the truth or allowed to say strange things; (2) it is mad to hope for a king who is loved by his subjects; (3) William was thought to be a fool, as he himself states later in the poem.

128–31. The angel speaks in Latin. The common folk ought not to know how to plead in Latin or French; they only have to be patient and serve!

132–38: Skeat translates the lines as follows:

(You say) "I am a king, I am a prince," (but you will be) neither perhaps hereafter.
O thou who dost administer the special laws of Christ the King

That thou mayst do this the better, as you are just, be merciful!
Naked justice requires to be clothed by thee with mercy;
Whatever crops thou wouldst reap, such be sure to sow.
If justice is stripped bare, let it be meted to thee of naked justice;
If mercy is sown, mayest thou reap of mercy!

139. Goliards were tellers of ribald tales, clerical buffoons, defrocked clerks. They formed a kind of "sect," named after a fictitious Bishop Golias, and they were held in disrepute. Some were minstrels or jongleurs, some wandering scholars (vagantes), some just vagabonds.

¹⁴⁰ And to þe angel an heiȝ° answered after,   *high*

"*Dum rex a regere dicatur nomen habere,*

Nomen habet sine re nisi studet iura tenere."

    And þanne gan° alle þe comune crye° in vers of latin,   *began/(to) cry*

To þe kynges conseille construe ho-so wolde°—   *council interpret whoever would*

¹⁴⁵ "*Precepta Regis sunt nobis vincula legis.*"

    Wiþ þat° ran þere a route° of ratones° at ones,°   *then/troop/rats/once*

And smale mys° with hem mo þen° a þousande,   *small mice/them more than*

And comen° to a conseille for here° comune profit;   *came/their*

For a cat of a courte cam whan hym° lyked,   *when he*

¹⁵⁰ And ouerlepe° hem lyȝtlich° and lauȝte° hem at his wille,   *jumped over/lightly/laughed (at)*

And pleyde° wiþ hem perilouslych° and possed° hem aboute.   *played/dangerously/pushed*

"For doute° of dyuerse dredes° we dar nouȝte° wel loke;°   *fear/various dangers/dare not/*
                                                                                   guard (ourselves)

And ȝif° we grucche° of his gamen° he wil greue° vs alle,   *if/complain/game/harm*

Cracche° vs, or clowe° vs and in his cloches° holde,   *scratch/claw/clutches*

¹⁵⁵ That° vs lotheth° þe lyf or° he lete° vs passe.   *so that/we loathe/before/lets*

Myȝte° we wiþ any witte his wille withstonde,°   *might/withstand*

We myȝte be lordes aloft° and lyuen° at owre ese."°   *on high/live/our ease*

    A raton of renon° most renable° of tonge,°   *renown/eloquent/tongue*

Seide° for a souereygne° help to hym-selue.°   *said/what seemed the best/himself*

¹⁶⁰ "I haue ysein segges,"° quod he "in þe cite° of london   *seen knights/said/city*

Beren biȝes ful briȝte abouten° here nekkes,°   *bear collars very bright **about**/necks*

And some colers° of crafty werk;° vncoupled° þei wenden°   *collars/skillful work/unfastened/go*

Boþe in wareine° and in waste° where hem leue lyketh;°   *hunting preserves/uncultivated land/*
                                                                                    they like

And otherwhile° þei aren elles-where° as I here° telle.   *sometimes/are elsewhere/hear*

¹⁶⁵ Were þere a belle on here beiȝ,° bi Ihesu,° as me° thynketh,° *collar/Jesus/to me/(it) seems*

Men myȝte wite° where þei went and awei renne!°   *know/away run*

And riȝt° so," quod þat ratoun,° "reson° me sheweth,°   *right/rat/reason/tells*

To bugge° a belle of brasse or of briȝte syluer,°   *buy/silver*

And knitten° on a colere for owre comune° profit,   *attach/common*

¹⁷⁰ And hangen° it vp-on þe cattes hals;° þanne° here we mowen° *hang/neck/then/**may***

Where° he ritt° or rest or renneth to playe.   *whether/moves*

And ȝif him list° for to laike° þenne loke° we mowen,   *likes/play/look*

And peren° in his presence þer while hym plaie° liketh,   *appear/(to) play*

141–42. "Though it is said a king receives his name from reigning, he will have the name without the royal quality if he does not attempt to keep the laws."

145. "The commands of the king are our legal cords."

146ff. The story of the belling of the cat is already found in the 13th-century Latin fables of Odo of Cheriton. This version was composed after the deaths of the Black Prince (June, 1376) and Edward III (June, 1377). Skeat felt that the cat is John of Gaunt, who was rumored to have aspired to the kingship but who in October, 1377, denied these accusations before Parliament. The excesses of the court had become too much, and in 1376 Parliament instituted a "vigilance committee" to oversee all the king's activities. John of Gaunt then dissolved Parliament. Whether, as Mossé states, the "rat of renown" is Peter de la Mare, speaker of the house, or whether the cat is truly John of Gaunt is impossible to say today. However, the section is important for its pleasant fable, and for its clue as to the composition of the B text.

And ʒif him wrattheth,° be ywar° and his weye shonye."°   *is angry/wary/path shun*
175   Alle þis route of ratones to þis reson þei assented.
Ac þo° þe belle was ybouʒt° and on þe beiʒe hanged,   *but when/bought*
Þere ne° was ratoun in alle þe route, for alle þe rewme° of   *not/kingdom*
    Fraunce,
Þat dorst° haue ybounden° þe belle aboute þe cattis nekke,   *dared/bound*
Ne° hangen it aboute þe cattes hals al Engelonde to wynne;   *nor*
180 And helden hem vnhardy° and here conseille feble,°   *admitted themselves weak/counsel feeble*

And leten° here laboure lost and alle here longe studye.   *allowed*
    A mous þat moche° good couthe,° as me thouʒte,°   *much/knew/(it) seemed*
Stroke° forth sternly and stode biforn° hem alle,   *came/stood before*
And to þe route of ratones reherced° þese wordes.   *repeated*
185 "Thouʒ° we culled° þe catte ʒut sholde° þer come another,   *though/killed/yet should*
To cracchy° vs and al owre kynde þouʒ we croupe° vnder   *scratch/creep*
    benches.
For-þi° I conseille alle þe comune° to lat° þe catte worthe,°   *therefore/common people/let/be*
And be we neuer so bolde þe belle hym to shewe;°   *show*
For I herde° my sire seyn,° is° seuene ʒere ypassed,°   *heard/say/it was/seven years ago*
190 Þere° þe catte is a kitoun° þe courte is ful elyng;°   *where/kitten/wretched*
Þat witnisseth holiwrite° who-so wil it rede,°   *Holy Writ/read*
    Ve terre vbi puer rex est, &c.
For may no renke° þere rest haue for° ratones° bi nyʒte;°   *man/because of/rats/night*
Þe while he cacchcþ conynges° he coueiteth nouʒt° owre   *catches rabbits/desires not/bodies*
    caroyne,°
195 But fet hym° al with venesoun defame° we hym neuere.°   *feeds himself/venison (if) defame/never*

For better is a litel° losse þan a longe sorwe,°   *little/sorrow*
Þe mase° amonge vs alle þouʒ° we mysse° a schrewe.   *confusion/though/are rid of/tyrant*
For many mannus° malt we mys wolde destruye,°   *many (a) man's/mice would destroy*

And also ʒe route° of ratones rende mennes clothes,   *you troop*
200 Nere° þat cat of þat courte þat can ʒow° ouerlepe;°   *were (it) not (for)/you/jump over*
For had ʒe rattes ʒowre° wille ʒe couthe° nouʒt reule   *your/could/rule yourselves*
    ʒowre-selue.°
I sey° for me," quod° þe mous, "I se° so mykel after,°   *say/said/see/far in the future*
Shal neuer þe cat ne þe kitoun bi my conseille be greued,°   *grieved*
Ne carpyng° of þis coler° þat costed° me neure.°   *(by) talking/collar/cost/nothing*
205 And þouʒ it had coste me catel biknowen° it I nolde,°   *money acknowledge/would not*
But suffre° as hym-self wolde° to do as hym liketh,°   *allow/they want/they please*

---

190. The kitten is perhaps Richard II, 10-year-old heir to the crown on the death of his father, Edward, the Black Prince.

192. "Woe to thee, O land, when thy king is a child" (Eccles. 10:16).

201. In June, 1381, the peasants rose in rebellion under Wat Tyler. The author evidently disapproves as much of violence by the commons as he does of royal injustices.

Coupled° and vncoupled to cacche what thei mowe.° *fastened/may*

For-þi vche a° wise wiȝte° I warne, wite° wel his owne." *each/person/guard*

   What þis meteles bemeneth,° ȝe men þat be merye,° *vision signifies/are merry*

210 Deuine° ȝe, for I ne dar° bi dere° God in heuene!° *guess/dare/dear/heaven*

   Ȝit houed° þere an hondreth° in houues° of selke,° *yet hovered/hundred/hoods/silk*

Seriauntȝ° it semed° þat serueden° atte° barre, *sergeants/seemed/served/at the/bar*

Pleden° for penyes° and poundes þe lawe, *pleaded/pennies*

And nouȝt for loue of owre° lorde vnlese here° lippes onis.° *our/loosen their/once*

215 Þow myȝtest° better mete° þe myste on maluerne hulles,° *you might/measure/hills*

Þan gete° a momme of° here mouthe but° money were shewed. *get/mumble from/unless*

   Barones an burgeis° and bonde-men als° *and burgesses/laborers also*

I seiȝ° in þis assemble° as ȝe shul here° after, *saw/assembly/shall hear*

Baxsteres° and brewesteres° and bocheres manye,° *bakers/alewives/butchers many*

220 Wollewebsteres° and weueres° of lynnen, *wool weavers/weavers*

Taillours° and tynkeres and tolleres° in marketes, *tailors/toll takers*

Masons and mynours° and many other craftes. *miners*

Of alkin° libbyng° laboreres lopen° forth somme,° *all kinds (of)/living/leaped/
       together*

As dykers° and delueres° þat doth here dedes° ille, *diggers/delvers/deeds*

225 And dryuen forth° þe longe day with *"Dieu vous saue, Dame* *spend*
    Emme!"

Cokes° and here knaues° crieden,° "Hote° pies, hote! *cooks/servant boys/cried/hot*

Gode gris° and gees, gowe° dyne, gowe!" *good pigs/geese, go*

   Tauerners vn-til hem tolde° þe same, *toward them called*

"White wyn° of Oseye and red wyn of Gascoigne,° *wine/Gascony*

230 Of þe Ryne° and of þe Rochel,° þe roste° to defye."° *Rhine/Rochelle/roast/digest*

Al þis seiȝ I slepyng° and seuene sythes° more. *sleeping/seven times*

B PASSUS II

The Vision of Lady Meed and Her Disrupted Marriage

Yet I courbed° on my knees and cryed hir of° grace, *knelt/her (i.e., Holy Church) for*

And seide,° "Mercy, Madame, for Marie loue° of heuene,° *said/love of Mary/heaven*

That bar° þat blisful barne° þat bouȝte° vs on þe Rode,° *bore/blessed child/redeemed/cross*

Kenne° me bi somme crafte° to knowe þe fals."° *teach/some skill/Falsehood*

---

211. *houues of selke:* white silk coifs worn for distinction by the sergeants at law, or lawyers, when they sat in court. They were evidently allowed to wear the hoods even in the king's presence.

219. Brewing, a lowly occupation, was mainly done by women. The ending *ster* on a noun (*baxsteres, wollewebsteres*) often signifies, as here, a female worker.

223. *libbyng laboreres:* i.e., "laborers alive."

225. *"Dieu . . . Emme!":* refrain of a popular song: "God save you, Dame Emme!"

226–30. Cooks and tavern keepers urge the people to dine. Tourists will find this custom today in certain countries, as for instance in Greece, where waiters solicit customers from the street.

229. *White . . . Oseye:* a sweet white wine (*Osaye* is probably a corruption of *Alsace*).

5 "Loke° vppon þi left half° and lo where he standeth, *look/side*
Bothe fals and fauel° and here feres manye!"° *Flattery/their companions many*
   I loked on my left half as þe lady me taughte,
And was war° of a womman wortheli yclothed,° *aware/richly clothed*
Purfiled° with pelure° þe finest vpon erthe, *trimmed/fur*
10 Y-crounede° with a corone° þe kyng hath non° better. *crowned/crown/none*
Fetislich° hir fyngres° were fretted° with golde wyre, *handsomely/fingers/adorned*
And þere-on red rubyes as red as any glede,° *fire*
And diamantz° of derrest pris° and double manere safferes,° *diamonds/greatest value/two kinds (of) sapphires*

Orientales° and ewages enuenymes° to destroye. *Oriental (sapphires)/beryls diseases*

15   Hire° robe was ful° riche, of red scarlet engreyned,° *her/very/dyed in grain*
With ribanes° of red golde and of riche stones; *ribbons*
Hire arraye me rauysshed,° suche ricchesse° saw I neuere;° *ravished/richness/never*
I had wondre what she was and whas wyf° she were.° *whose wife/was*
   "What is þis womman," quod° I, "so worthily atired?" *said*
   "That is Mede° þe Mayde," quod she "hath noyed° *Meed/(who) has annoyed*
20   me ful oft,
And ylakked° my lemman° þat lewte° is hoten,° *blamed/sweetheart/Loyalty/called*
And bilowen° hire to lordes þat lawes han° to kepe.° *lied against/have/support*
In þe popis paleys° she is pryue° as my-self, *pope's palace/familiar*
But sothenesse wolde nouȝt° so for she° is a bastarde. *Truth would not (have it)/(i.e., Meed)*

25   "For fals was hire fader° þat hath a fykel tonge,° *father/fickle tongue*
And neuere sothe° seide sithen° he come° to erthe. *truth/since/came*
   And Mede is manered° after hym riȝte° as kynde axeth;° *mannered/just/(her) nature demands*

   Qualis pater, talis filius; bona arbor bonum fructum facit.
I auȝte ben herre° þan she, I cam° of a better. *ought (to) be higher/came*
30   "Mi fader þe grete° God is and grounde of alle graces, *great*
O° God with-oute gynnynge° and I his gode douȝter,° *one/beginning/good daughter*
And hath ȝoue° me mercy to marye° with myself; *given/marry*
And what° man be merciful and lelly° me loue, *whatever/loyally*
Schal be my lorde and I his leef° in þe heiȝe° heuene. *beloved/high*
35   "And what man taketh Mede, myne hed dar° I legge,° *head dare/pledge*
That he shal lese° for hir loue a lappe° of *caritatis*. *lose/share*
How construeth° dauid þe kynge of men þat taketh Mede, *interprets*
And men of þis molde° þat meynteneth treuthe,° *earth/maintain truth*

---

8. *womman:* Lady Meed (in general *meed* signifies "bribery," but it can also mean "reward").

14. Precious stones in the Middle Ages were thought to have a number of properties, many of them medicinal.

15. *red scarlet engreyned:* a red dye made from cochineal, or any fast dye.

16. *red golde:* Cf. above, p. 183, l. 47.

28. "As the father, so the son; a good tree bears good fruit" (Cf. Matt. 7:17.)

36. *caritatis:* Latin, "of charity."

And how ȝe° shal saue ȝow-self° þe Sauter bereth° witnesse,   *you/yourself/Psalter bears*

40   *Domine, quis habitabit in tabernaculo tuo, &c.*

And now worth° þis Mede ymaried° al to a mansed schrewe,°   *will be/married/cursed villain*

To one fals fikel-tonge, a fendes biȝete;°   *fiend's offspring*

Fauel þorw° his faire speche° hath þis folke enchaunted,°   *through/speech/enchanted*

And al is lyeres ledyng° þat she is þus ywedded.°   *Lying's plan/wedded*

45   "To-morwe° worth ymade° þe maydenes bruydale,°   *tomorrow/made/maid's bride-ale*

And þere miȝte þow wite,° if þow wolt, which° þei ben° alle   *might you know/would, who/are*

That longeth° to þat lordeship° þe lasse° and þe more.°   *belong/group/less (i.e., low)/ (i.e., high)*

Knowe hem° þere if þow canst and kepe° þi tonge,   *them/hold*

And lakke° hem nouȝt, but lat° hem worth° til lewte be iustice,°   *blame/let/be/judge*

50   And haue powere to punyschen° hem; þanne° put forth þi resoun.°   *punish/then/argument*

"Now I bikenne þe° criste,"° quod she, "and his clene moder,°   *commend you/to Christ/pure mother*

And lat no conscience acombre° þe for coueitise° of Mede."   *trouble/desire*

Thus left me þat lady liggyng aslepe,°   *lying asleep*

And how Mede was ymaried in meteles° me° þouȝte;°   *dream/to me/(it) seemed*

55   Þat alle þe riche retenauns° þat regneth° with þe false°   *retinue/reigns/**Falsehood***

Were boden° to þe bridale on bothe two sydes,   *asked*

Of alle maner° of men, þe mene° and þe riche.   *manner/poor*

To marie° þis maydene was many man assembled,   *marry*

As of kniȝtes° and of clerkis° and other comune poeple,°   *knights/clerks/common people*

60   As sysours° and sompnours, shireues° and here° clerkes,   *jurors/summoners, sheriffs/their*

Bedelles° and bailliues° and brokoures° of chaffare,°   *beadles/bailiffs/brokers/goods*

Forgoeres° and vitaillers° and vokates° of þe arches;   *lord's harbingers/victuallers/ advocates*

I can nouȝt rekene° þe route° þat ran aboute mede.°   *estimate/troop/**Meed***

Ac° Symonye and cyuile° and sisoures of courtes   *but/Civil (Law)*

65   Were moste pryue° with Mede of any men, me þouȝte.   *intimate*

Ac fauel° was þe first þat fette hire° out of boure,°   *Flattery/fetched her/chamber*

And as a brokour brouȝte hir° to be with fals enioigned.°   *(marriage) broker brought her/ Falsehood joined*

Whan° Symonye and cyuile seiȝ° here beire° wille,°   *saw/both their/intent*

Thei assented for siluer to sei° as bothe wolde.°   *say/would*

70   Thanne lepe° lyer forth, and seide,° "Lo there! a chartre,   *leaped/said*

---

40. "Lord, who shall abide in thy tabernacle?" (Ps. 15:1).

45. *bruydale:* lit., "bride-ale," the feast at which the bride brewed her own ale for the wedding day, which the guests then bought at a high price.

60. *sysours:* or *sisours*, jurors or inquest men at assizes. *sompnours:* minor lay officials of the Church who arraigned persons having broken specific Church laws, especially of a moral nature.

61. *Bedelles:* police officers working on the land and identified with the haywards. They saw that suspicious persons kept out of private property, and generally kept the peace. *brokoures:* men who brought bargaining parties together for a fee.

62. *Forgoeres:* Forgoers preceded the party of a noble household and arranged for appropriate lodging and food. *vokates:* Advocates of the court of the arches were men of distinction who pleaded at the consistory court of the archbishop of Canterbury, held at the Bow Church (Saint Mary de Arcubus, Mary le Bow) in London.

That gyle° with his gret othes gaf° hem togidere,"°   *Guile/great oaths gave/together*
And preide° cyuile to se° and symonye to rede° it.   *asked/see/read*
Thanne Symonye and cyuile stonden° forth bothe,   *stand*
And vnfoldeth þe feffement° þat fals hath ymaked,°   *deed of endowment/made*
75 And þus bigynneth þes gomes° to greden ful heiȝ:°   *men/cry very loudly*
   "*Sciant presentes & futuri, &c.*

   "Witeth and witnesseth þat wonieth° vpon þis erthe,   *(all) that live*
Þat Mede is y-maried more for here goodis,°   *her goods*
Þan for ani vertue or fairenesse or any free kynde.°   *liberal nature*
80 Falsenesse is faine° of hire for he wote hire° riche;   *glad/knows her (to be)*
And fauel with his fikel° speche feffeth° bi þis chartre   *fickle/grants*
To be prynces in pryde and pouerte° to dispise,°   *poverty/despise*
To bakbite,° and to bosten° and bere fals° witnesse,   *defame/boast/bear false*
To scorne and to scolde and sclaundere° to make,   *slander*
85 Vnboxome° and bolde to breke° þe ten hestes;°   *disobedient/break/Commandments*
   "And þe Erldome of enuye° and Wratthe togideres,°   *Envy/together*
With þe chastelet° of chest° and chateryng-oute-of-rcsoun,°   *castle/Strife/Chattering-Out-of-Reason*

Þe counte° of coueitise° and alle þe costes° aboute,   *county/Greed/borders*
That is, vsure° and auarice, alle I hem graunte,°   *Usury/them grant*
90 In bargaines and in brokages° with al þe borghe° of theft;   *brokers' treaties/borough*
   "And al þe lordeship of lecherye in lenthe° and in brede,°   *length/breadth*
As in werkes° and in wordes and waitynges° with eies,°   *works/watching/eyes*
And in wedes° and in wisshynges° and with ydel thouȝtes,°   *clothes/wishes/idle thoughts*
There as wille° wolde and werkmanship° failleth."   *where desire/performance*
95   Glotonye° he gaf hem eke° and grete° othes togydere,   *Gluttony/also/great*
And alday° to drynke at dyuerse° tauernes,   *all day/various*
And there to iangle° and to iape° and iugge° here euene cristene,°   *gossip/mock/judge/fellow-Christians*
And in° fastyng-dayes° to frete ar ful° tyme were.°   *on/fast days/eat before proper/(it) was*

And þanne° to sitten° and soupen° til slepe° hem assaille,   *then/sit/sup/sleep*
100 And breden° as burgh-swyn° and bedden hem esily,°   *breed/town pigs/repose themselves easy*

Tyl sleuth° and slepe slyken° his sides;   *Sloth/make sleek*
And þanne wanhope° to awake hym so with no wille to amende,°   *Despair/make amends*
For he leueth be° lost: þis is here° last ende.   *believes (himself to) be/their*
   "And þei to haue and to holde and here eyres° after,   *heirs*
105 A dwellyng with þe deuel° and dampned° be for eure,°   *Devil/damned/ever*

---

76. "Know ye all present and future!" (the salutation of a charter).

92. *waitynges with eies:* i.e., "wanton looks."

98. *frete:* The Middle English verbs *freten* and *eten* should be distinguished from each other as are the German verbs *fressen* and *essen.* In both cases the first is applied to animals and devouring, animal-like eating.

Wiþ al þe purtenaunces° of purgatorie in-to þe pyne° of helle,　*appurtenances/pain*

зeldyng° for þis þinge at one зeres° ende,　*yielding/year's*

Here soules to Sathan° to suffre with hym peynes,°　*Satan/pains*

And with him to wonye° with wo whil° God is in heuene."°　*dwell/woe while/heaven*

110　In witnesse of which þing wronge was þe first,

And Pieres þe pardonere of paulynes doctrine,°　*Pauline order*

Bette° þe bedel° of Bokyngham-shire,°　*Bat/beadle/Buckinghamshire*

Rainalde þe Reue° of Rotland sokene,°　*reeve/Rutland district*

Munde þe Mellere° and many moo other.°　*miller/more others*

115　"In þe date of þe deuel þis dede° I assele,°　*deed/seal*

Bi siзte° of Sire Symonye and cyuyles° leue."°　*in view/(by) Civil Law's/permission*

　　Þenne tened hym° theologye whan° he þis tale herde,°　*vexed himself/when/heard*

And seide° to cyuile, "Now sorwe mot þow° haue,　*said/sorrow may you*

Such weddynges to worche° to wratthe with treuthe;°　*make/rage against Truth*

120　And ar þis weddyng be wrouзte° wo þe bityde!°　*made/you befall*

　　"For Mede° is moylere° of amendes° engendred,　*Meed/honest woman/Satisfaction*

And God graunteth to gyf° Mede to treuthe,　*give*

And þow hast gyuen hire° to a gyloure,° now God gyf þe sorwe!　*given her/deceiver*

Thi tixt° telleth þe nouзt° so treuthe wote° þe sothe,°　*text/not/knows/truth*

125　For *dignus est operarius* his hyre° to haue,　*wage*

And þow hast fest° hire to fals, fy° on þi lawe!　*joined/Falsehood, fie*

For al by lesynges° þow lyuest° and lecherouse werkes;　*lying/live*

Symonye and þi-self schenden° holicherche;°　*damage/Holy Church*

Þe notaries and зee noyeth° þe peple;°　*you injure/people*

130　зe shul° abiggen° it bothe, bi God þat me made!　*you shall/pay for*

Wel зe witen, wernardes,° but if° зowre° witte faille,　*know, liars/ unless/your*

That fals is faithlees° and fikel° in his werkes,°　*faithless/treacherous/works*

And was a bastarde y-bore° of belsabubbes kynne.°　*born/Beelzebub's kin*

And Mede is moylere, a mayden of gode,°　*good (family)*

135　And myзte° kisse þe kynge for cosyn, an° she wolde.°　*might/as relative, if/would*

　　"For-þi worcheth° bi wisdome and bi witt also,　*therefore work*

And ledeth° hire to londoun þere° lawe is yshewed,°　*lead/where/practiced*

If any lawe wil loke° þei ligge togederes.°　*permit that/lie together*

And þouз Iustices iugge hir° to be ioigned° with fals,　*though judges judge her/joined*

140　зet beth war° of weddyng for witty° is truthe,　*be wary/wise*

And conscience is of his conseille° and knoweth зow° vchone;°　*counsel/you/each one*

And if he fynde зow in defaute° and with þe fals holde,　*at fault*

It shal bisitte° зowre soules ful soure° atte° laste!"　*oppress/very bitterly/at the*

---

111. *of paulynes doctrine:* The friars of the Order of Paulines, also known as the Crutched (Crossed) Friars, came to England in 1244, according to Matthew Paris. They were active in the consistory courts.

112. *Bette:* Bartholomew. *Bokyngham-shire:* Buckinghamshire was notorious for its thieves.

113. *sokene:* the legal term for a district in which the privilege or power of a reeve, who was in charge of the farming and husbandry on an estate, was exercised.

125. *dignus est operarius:* "the labourer is worthy" (Luke 70:7).

Here-to assenteth cyuile ac° symonye ne° wolde,	*but/not*
145 Tyl he had siluer for his seruise° and also þe notaries.	*service*
Thanne fette fauel° forth floreynes ynowe,°	*then fetched Flattery/florins enough*
And bad gyle° to gyue° golde al aboute,	*asked Guile/give*
And namelich° to þe notaries þat hem° none ne faille,	*especially/them*
And feffe° false-witnes with floreines ynowe;	*endow*
150 "For he may mede amaistrye° and maken at° my wille."°	*control/put in/power*
Tho° þis golde was gyue grete° was þe þonkynge°	*when/given great/thanks*
To fals and to fauel for her° faire ʒiftes,°	*their/gifts*
And comen° to conforte fram care° þe fals,	*(they) came/comfort from anxiety*
And seiden,° "Certis,° sire, cesse° shal we neuere°	*said/certainly/cease/never*
155 Til Mede be þi wedded wyf þorw wittis° of vs alle.	*wife through wits*
For we haue Mede amaistried with owre mery speche,°	*our cheerful speech*
That° she graunteth° to gon° with a gode wille,	*so that/grants/go*
To Londoun to loke ʒif° þat þe lawe wolde	*see if*
Iugge ʒow ioyntly° in ioye° for euere."°	*in union/joy/ever*
160 Thanne was falsenesse fayne° and fauel as blithe,	*glad*
And leten sompne° alle segges° in schires aboute,	*had summoned/men*
And bad° hem alle be bown, beggeres° and othere,°	*bade/ready, beggars/others*
To wenden° wyth hem to Westmynstre to witnesse þis dede.°	*go/deed*
Ac þanne cared° þei for caplus° to kairen hem þider,°	*desired/horses/betake themselves there*
165 And fauel fette forth þanne folus° ynowe;	*horses*
And sette Mede° vpon a Schyreue° shodde al newe,	*Meed/sheriff*
And fals° sat on a sisoure° þat softlich° trotted,	*Falsehood/juror/softly*
And fauel on a flaterere fetislich atired.°	*flatterer handsomely dressed*
Tho haued° notaries none annoyed þei were,	*when had*
170 For Symonye and cyuile° shulde° on hire fete gange.	*Civil Law/should/their feet go*
Ac þanne swore Symonye and cyuile bothe,	
That sompnoures° shulde be sadled° and serue hem vchone,	*summoners/saddled*
And lat apparaille þis prouisoures° in palfreis wyse.°	*let dress these provisors/like riding horses*
"Sire Symonye hym-seluen° shal sitte vpon here bakkes.°	*himself/their backs*
175 "Denes° and suddenes° drawe ʒow togideres,	*deans/subdeans*
Erchdekenes° and officiales and alle ʒowre Regystreres,°	*archdeacons/your registrars*
Lat sadel hem° with siluer owre synne to suffre,°	*them be saddled/allow*
As auoutrie° and deuorses° and derne° vsurye,	*adultery/divorces/secret*
To bere° bischopes aboute abrode° in visytynge.	*carry/abroad*
180 "Paulynes pryues° for pleyntes° in þe consistorie,	*Pauline members/pleas*

---

146. *floreynes:* Florins (after the city of Florence) were coined of fine gold by Edward III in 1343 to support his wars in France.

163. Westminster was the center for law courts.

173. *prouisoures:* Provisors sued to the court of Rome for a *provision* (a benefice or living) not yet vacant, before the incumbent had died. Laws were enacted against the abuse of this practice.

179. *visytynge:* i.e., inspecting cloisters. Bishops occasionally went on visitations to monasteries to investigate their activities and control religious laxity.

Shul° serue my-self þat cyuile is nempned;°   *shall/called*
And cartesadel° þe comissarie,° **owre carte shal he lede**,°   *harness/commissary/draw*
And fecchen° vs vytailles at° *fornicatores*.   *fetch/food from*
    "And maketh of lyer° a longe carte to lede alle þese othere,   *Lying*
185 As freres° and faitours° þat on here fete rennen."°   *friars/deceivers/run*
And thus fals and fauel° fareth forth togideres,°   *Flattery/together*
And Mede in þe myddes° and alle þise° men after.   *middle/these*
    I haue no tome° to telle° þe taille° þat hem folweth,°   *leisure/count/train/them follows*
Of many maner° man þat on þis molde libbeth;°   *kinds (of)/earth live*
190 Ac gyle° was forgoer° and gyed° hem alle.   *Guile/harbinger/guided*
    Sothenesse seiȝ° hym wel and seide but a litel,°   *Honesty saw/little*
And priked° his palfrey and passed hem alle,   *spurred*
And come° to þe kynges courte and conscience it tolde,   *came*
And conscience to þe kynge carped° it after.   *told*
195   "Now by cryst," quod° þe kynge, "and° I cacche myȝte°   *said/if/catch might*
Fals or fauel or any of his feres,°   *companions*
I wolde° be wroke of þo wrecches° þat worcheth° so ille,   *would/avenged on these wretches/work*
    And don° hem hange° by þe hals° and alle þat hem   *have/hanged/neck/support*
      meynteneth!°
Shal neure° man of° molde meynprise° þe leste,°   *never/on/furnish bail for/least*
200 But riȝte° as þe lawe wil loke late° falle on° hem alle."   *just/state let/befall*
    And comanded a constable þat come atte furst,°   *immediately*
To "attache° þo tyrauntz° for eny° thynge, I hote,°   *arrest/tyrants/any/command*
And fettereth fast falsenesse for° enykynnes° ȝiftes,°   *in spite of/any kind (of)/gifts*
And gurdeth of° gyles hed° and lat hym go no furthere.   *strike off/head*
205 And ȝif ȝe lacche° lyer late hym nouȝt ascapen°   *if you seize/not escape*
Er° he be put on þe pilorye° for eny preyere,° I hote;   *before/pillory/prayer*
And bryngeth Mede° to me maugre° hem alle."   *Meed/in spite of*
    Drede° atte° dore stode° and þe dome herde,°   *Fear/at the/stood/judgment heard*
And how þe kynge comaunded° constables and seriantz,°   *commanded/sergeants*
210 Falsenesse and his felawschip° to fettren an° to bynden.°   *fellows/fetter and/bind*
Þanne° drede went wiȝtliche° and warned þe fals,°   *then/quickly/Falsehood*
And bad° hym flee for fere° and his felawes° alle.   *bade/fear/fellows*
    Falsenesse for fere þanne fleiȝ° to þe freres,   *fled*
And gyle doþ hym° to go, agast° for to dye.°   *prepared himself/afraid/die*
215 Ac marchantz° mette with hym and made hym abide,°   *merchants/stay*
And bishetten° hym in here shope° to shewen° here ware,   *shut/their shops/show*
And apparailled° hym as a prentice° þe poeple° to serue.   *dressed/apprentice/people*
    Liȝtliche° lyer lepe awey° þanne,   *lightly/leaped away*

---

182. *comissarie:* The commissary represented the bishop's spiritual jurisdiction in places distant from the consistory courts.

183. *fornicatores:* Wealthy sinners were more heavily fined, and such persons were more easily victims of prosecution for offenses of a moral nature.

Lorkynge thorw° lanes to-lugged° of manye.° *lurking through/pulled about/by many*

220 He was nawhere° welcome for his manye tales, *nowhere*
Ouer al° yhowted° and yhote° trusse;° *everywhere/hooted at/told/to be gone*
Tyl pardoneres haued pite° and pulled hym in-to house. *had pity*
They wesshen° hym and wyped hym and wonden° hym
      in cloutes,° *washed/dressed/clothes*
And sente hym with seles° on sondayes° to cherches,° *seals/Sundays/churches*
225 And gaf° pardoun for pens° poundmel aboute.° *gave/pennies/by pounds at a time*
   Thanne loured° leches° and lettres þei sent, *looked sad/physicians*
Þat he sholde wonye° with hem wateres° to loke.° *live/urine/inspect*
Spiceres° spoke with hym to spien° here ware, *grocers/examine*
For he couth of° here craft° and knewe many gommes.° *understood/skill/(kinds of) gum*
230   Ac mynstralles° and messageres° mette with hym ones,° *but minstrels/messengers/once*
And helden° hym an half-ȝere° and elleuene° dayes. *entertained/half year/eleven*
   Freres° with faire speche fetten° hym þennes,° *friars/speech fetched/thence*
And for knowyng of comeres° coped° hym as a frere. *to prevent recognition/dressed*
Ac he hath leue° to lepe° out as oft as hym° liketh, *permission/leap/he*
235 And is welcome whan° he wil and woneth° wyth hem° oft. *when/dwells/them*
   Alle fledden° for fere and flowen° in-to hernes;° *fled/escaped/corners*
Saue° Mede þe Mayde na mo durst° abide. *except/no more dared*
Ac trewli° to telle she trembled for drede,° *truly/fear*
And ek° wept and wronge° whan she was attached.° *also/wrung (her hands)/arrested*

from C PASSUS VI

The Author Describes His Life

Thus ich° a-waked, God wot, whanne° ich wonede on
      cornehulle,° *I/knows, when/ lived in Cornhill*
Kytte and ich in a cote° cloþed as a lollere,° *cottage/vagabond*
And lytel° y-lete by,° leyue° me for soþe,° *little/esteemed/believe/truth*
Among lollares° of london and lewede heremytes;° *idlers/ignorant hermits*
5 For ich made° of þo° men as reson° me tauhte.° *wrote/those/Reason/taught*
For as ich cam° by conscience with reson ich mette *came*
In an hote heruest° whenne ich hadde myn hele,° *hot autumn/my prosperity*
And lymes° to labore with and louede wel fare,° *limbs/loved good living*
And no dede° to do bote° drynke and to slepe.° *deed/but/sleep*

---

1. This autobiographical section is found only in the C text. *cornehulle:* Cornhill is a section of London.

2. *Kytte:* Kit, the author's wife. *lollere:* (from the verb *loll*) a lounger, a vagabond, not to be confused with Wycliffe's Lollards (Latin *lollardus*, "a mumbler of prayers"), although indeed the words were purposely confused at this time to satirize the Wycliffites. Both words were terms of opprobrium.

5. *made:* To *make* is to compose verses; a *poet* (Greek, "creator") was called a *maker*.

10	In hele° and in vnite on° me aposede,°	*health/sanity someone/asked*
	Romynge° in remembraunce thus reson me aratede:°	*wandering/scolded*
	"Canstow° seruen,"° he seide,° "oþer syngen° in a churche,	*can you/serve/said/or sing*
	Oþer coke° for my cokers° oþer to þe cart picche,°	*cock hay/harvesters/pitch*
	Mowe oþer mowen° oþer make bond to sheues,°	*stack hay/binding for sheaves*
15	Repe° oþer be a repereyue° and a-ryse erliche,°	*reap/overseer/early*
	Oþer haue an horne and be haywarde and liggen° oute a nyghtes,°	*lie/at night*
	And kepe° my corn in my croft fro pykers° and þeeues?°	*guard/field from pickers/thieves*
	Oþer shappe shon° oþer cloþes oþer shep° oþer kyn° kepe,	*make shoes/sheep/cows*
	Heggen° oþer harwen° oþer swyn° oþer gees dryue,°	*cut hedges/harrow/swine/geese drive*
20	Oþer eny° oþer kyns° craft þat to þe comune° nedeþ,°	*any/kind (of)/**community**/**is necessary***
	Hem° þat bedreden be° by-lyue° to fynde?"	*them/bedridden are/sustenance*
	"Certes,"° ich seyde,° "and so me God helpe,	*certainly/said*
	Ich am to waik° to worche° with sykel° oþer with sythe,°	*too weak/work/sickle/scythe*
	And to long, leyf° me, lowe for to stoupe,°	*tall, believe/stoop*
25	To worchen° as a workeman eny whyle° to dure."°	*work/time/endure*
	"Thenne hauest þow londes° to lyue° by," quath° reson, "oþer lynage riche°	*you lands/**live**/said/lineage noble*
	That fynden þe° þy fode?° For an ydel° man þow semest,°	*find you/food/idle/seem*
	A spendour° þat spende mot° oþer a spille-tyme,°	*spender/can/waster of time*
	Oþer beggest þy bylyue° a-boute at menne° hacches,°	*livelihood/men's/buttery doors*
30	Oþer faitest° vp-on frydays oþer feste-dayes° in churches,	*deceives/feast days*
	The whiche is lollarene lyf° þat lytel ys preysed,°	*idler's life/praised*
	Þer ryghtfulnesse° rewardeþ ryght° as men deserueþ,	*where righteousness/just*
	Reddit unicuique iuxta opera sua.	
	Oþer þow art broke,° so may be, in body oþer in membre,°	*lame/limb*
35	Oþer ymaymed þorw° som mys-hap wher-by þow myȝt° be excused?"	*maimed through/might*
	"Whanne ich ȝong° was," quath ich, "meny ȝer hennes,°	*young/many years ago*
	My fader° and my frendes founden° me to scole,°	*father/found (means to send)/school*
	Tyl ich wiste wyterliche° what holy wryt menede,°	*knew surely/meant*
	And what is best for þe body as þe bok° telleþ,	*book*
40	And sykerest° for þe soule by° so ich wolle° continue.	*surest/provided/will*
	And ȝut fond° ich neuere° in faith sytthen° my frendes deyden,°	*yet found/never/since/died*
	Lyf þat me° lyked bote° in þes° longe clothes.	*I/except/these*

---

15. *repereyue:* lit., "head reaper."

16. *haywarde:* a hedge warden who saw that the cattle stayed in their prescribed bounds (cf. above, p. 654, l. 24n).

24. Will is too long (i.e., tall; cf. *Langland*) to stoop down. Elsewhere in the poem he is called "Long Will."

33. "He rendereth unto each according to his works" (Vulgate, Ps. 61:13).

42. *þes longe clothes:* i.e., his dress as a member of the secular clergy, or perhaps the clothes which cover "Long Will" (cf. l. 24n).

Yf ich° by laboure sholde° lyue and lyflode deseruen,°   *I/should/livelihood earn*
That labour þat ich lerned best þer-with lyue ich sholde;
45   *In eadem uocatione in qua uocati estis, manete.*
And ich lyue in londone and on londone bothe,
The lomes° þat ich laboure with and lyflode deserue   *tools*
Ys *pater-noster* and my prymer, *placebo* and *dirige*,
And my sauter° som tyme and my seuene° psalmes.   *Psalter/seven*
50 Thus ich synge for hure° soules of suche as me helpen,°   *their/help*
And þo° þat fynden me my fode vouchen saf,° ich trowe,°   *they/vouchsafe/believe*
To° be welcome whanne° ich come oþer-whyle° in a monthe,   *(me) to/when/occasionally*
Now with hym and now with hure,° and þusgate° ich begge,   *her/thus*
Withoute bagge oþer botel° bote my wombe one.°   *bottle/belly alone*

from B PASSUS V

The Confessions of the Seven Sins

The kyng and his knightes to the kirke° wente   *church*
To here matynes° of þe day and þe masse after.   *hear matins*
Þanne° waked I of° my wynkynge° and wo° was with-alle,   *then/from/sleeping/woe*
Þat I ne° hadde sleped° sadder° and yseiʒen° more.   *not/slept/more soundly/seen*
5 Ac er⁰ I hadde faren° a fourlonge feyntise° me hente,°   *but before/gone/furlong weakness/*
     overtook

That° I ne myʒte ferther⁰ a-foot for dcfaute° of slepynge;°   *so that/might (go) further/lack/*
     sleeping

And sat softly adown° and seide° my bileue,°   *down/said/creed*
And so I babeled° on my bedes þei brouʒte° me a-slepe.°   *babbled/beads (that) they put/*
     to sleep

And þanne saw I moche° more þan I before tolde,   *much*
10 For I say° þe felde° ful of folke þat I bifore° of seyde,°   *saw/field/before/spoke*
And how resoun gan arrayen hym° alle þe reume° to preche,°   *Reason did prepare himself/*
     realm/preach (to)

And with a crosse afor° þe kynge comsed° þus to techen.°   *before/began/teach*
He preued° þat þise° pestilences were for pure synne,   *proved/these*
And þe southwest wynde on saterday° at euene°   *Saturday/evening*

---

45. "Let every man abide in the same calling wherein he was called" (1 Cor. 7:20).

46–50. Will sings masses for the souls of wealthy dead patrons, thus living in London "on" London. *prymer*: elementary book of religious instruction; *placebo*: antiphon, "Placebo domino in regione viventium," in the office of the dead at vespers; *dirige*: antiphon, "Dirige, Dominus meum, in conspectu tuo vitam meam," the first nocturn at matins in the office of the dead.

48. *pater-noster*: Latin, "our father," i.e., the Lord's Prayer.

49. The seven penitential psalms, sung on Ash Wednesday, were 6, 32, 38, 51, 102, 130, and 143.

13. Cf. above, p. 680, l. 84n.

14. *þe southwest wynde*: according to Thomas Tyrwhitt, the famous 18th-century editor of Chaucer, the fierce storm on Saturday, Jan. 15, 1362. The tempest, mentioned in many chronicles, started in the evening and lasted five days. This, and the plague which was raging at the same time, were seen as signs of God's wrath.

¹⁵ Was pertliche° for pure pryde and for no poynt elles.° *plainly/reason else*
Piries° and plomtrees° were puffed to þe erthe, *pear trees/plum trees*
In ensample, ȝe segges,° ȝe shulden° do þe bettere. *as example, you men/should*
Beches° and brode okes° were blowen° to þe grounde, *beeches/broad oaks/blown*
Torned° vpward her° tailles in tokenynge° of drede,° *turned/their/as a sign/fear*
²⁰ Þat dedly° synne at domesday° shal fordon hem° alle. *deadly/Judgment Day/destroy them*
Of þis matere° I myȝte mamely ful° longe, *matter/prate very*
Ac I shal seye° as I saw so me God helpe! *say*
How pertly° afor þe poeple° resoun gan° to preche. *plainly/people/Reason began*
He bad wastoure° go worche what° he best couthe,° *bade Waster/work as/could*
²⁵ And wynnen° his wastyng° with somme manere° crafte. *earn/extravagance/kind (of)*
And preyed° peronelle her purfyle° to lete,° *prayed/fur trimming/leave off*
And kepe° it in hir cofre° for catel° at hire nede.° *keep/her chest/wealth/her need*
Thomme stowue° he tauȝte° to take two staues, *Tom Stowe/taught*
And fecche° felice home fro° þe wyuen pyne.° *fetch/from/women's punishment (i.e., cucking stool)*

³⁰   He warned watt° his wyf° was to blame, *Wat/wife*
Þat hire hed° was worth halue° a marke, his hode nouȝte° *headdress/half/hood not/groat*
    worth a grote.°
And bad bette kut° a bow other tweyne,° *Bat cut/bough or two*
And bete betoun° þer-with but if° she wolde° worche. *beat Betty/unless/would*
And þanne he charged chapmen° to chasten her childeren; *tradesmen*
³⁵ **Late° no wynnynge° hem forweny whil° þei be ȝonge,°** *let/extravagance/spoil while/ are young*

Ne° for° no pouste° of pestilence plese° hem nouȝte out of resoun. *nor/because of/virulence/indulge*
"My syre seyde° so to me and so did my dame,° *father said/mother*
Þat þe leuere° childe þe more lore bihoueth,° *dearer (the)/teaching (it) needs*
And Salamon° seide þe same þat Sapience made,° *Solomon/(Book of) Wisdom wrote*
⁴⁰   *Qui parcit virge, odit filium.*
Þe Englich of þis latyn is, who-so wil it knowe,
"Who-so spareth þe sprynge spilleth° his children." *rod spoils*
And sithen° he preyed prelatȝ° and prestes to-gideres,° *then/asked prelates/priests together*
"Þat° ȝe prechen° to þe peple° preue it on ȝowre-seluen,° *what/preach/people/yourselves*
⁴⁵ And doth° it in dede;° it shal drawe ȝow° to good; *do/deed/you*
If ȝe lyuen° as ȝe leren° vs we shal leue° ȝow þe bettere." *live/teach/believe*

---

15. Pride was the primary one of the Seven Deadly Sins.

26. *peronelle:* (also Pernel, Purnel) the traditional name for a bold, gaily dressed woman.

28–29. Tom Stowe is to take two sticks (necessary to beat a path through an unruly mob), and free his wife Felice from the shame of the cucking stool, where, probably, he had sent her in the first place to be punished as a scold.

30–31. Walter allows his wife to be too extravagant in her headdress.

32–33. Bartholomew is to beat lazy Betty.

36. Fear of the plague, which killed many children, ought not to influence parents to spoil them.

39. *made:* Cf. above, p. 691, l. 5*n.*

40. "He that spareth his rod hateth his son" (Prov. 13:24).

And sithen he radde° Religioun° here reule° to holde°—   *advised/religious orders/their rule/ maintain*

"Leste þe kynge and his conseille ȝowre comunes appayre,°   *council your communities harm*
And ben stuwardes° of ȝowre stedes° til ȝe be ruled bettre."   *be stewards/places*
50   And sithen he conseilled° þe kynge þe comune° to louye,°   *counseled/commons/love*
"It is þi tresore,° if tresoun ne were° and triacle° at þi nede."   *treasure/treason (there) not were/ remedy*

And sithen he prayed þe° pope haue pite° on holicherche,°   *(that) the/pity/Holy Church*
And er° he gyue° any grace gouerne firste hym-selue.°   *before/give/himself*
     "And ȝe that han° lawes to kepe° late treuthe° be ȝowre coueytise,°   *have/support/truth/desire*

55 More þan golde or other gyftes if ȝe wil God plese;°   *please*
For who-so contrarieth° treuthe, he telleth in þe gospel,   *opposes*
That God knoweth hym nouȝte ne° no seynte° of heuene,°   *nor/saint/heaven*
     Amen dico vobis, nescio vos.
And ȝe° þat seke° seynte James and seintes of Rome,   *you/seek*
60 Seketh seynt treuthe for he may saue ȝow alle;
     Qui cum patre & filio þat feire hem bifalle°   *fair/befall*
Þat suweth° my sermon"; and þus seyde resoun.   *follow*
Thanne° ran repentance and reherced his teme,°   *then/repeated his (i.e., Reason's) theme*

And gert° wille to wepe° water with his eyen.°   *made/weep/eyes*

Superbia

65 Peronelle proude-herte platte hir° to þe erthe,   *proud-heart threw herself*
And lay longe ar° she loked° and "Lorde, mercy!" cryed,   *before/looked*
And byhiȝte° to hym þat vs alle made,   *promised*
She shulde vnsowen hir serke° and sette þere an heyre°   *should unsew her smock/hair shirt*
To affaiten hire° flesshe þat fierce° was to synne: *tame her/eager*
70 "Shal neuere heiȝe° herte me hente° but holde me° lowe,   *never proud/govern/(I shall) hold myself*

And suffre° to be myssayde°— and so did I neuere.   *allow/slandered*
But now wil I meke me° and mercy biseche,°   *be meek/beseech*
For al þis° I haue hated in myne herte."   *those (that)*

Luxuria

     Þanne lecchoure° seyde "allas!"° and on owre° lady he cryed,   *Lechery/alas/our*
75 To make° mercy for his mis-dedes bitwene God and his soule,   *grant*

---

58. "Verily I say unto you, I know you not" (Matt. 25:12).
59. Cf. above, p. 678, ll. 46–47*n*.
61. *Qui . . . filio:* The normal formula is "qui cum Patre et Spiritu Sancto vivit et regnet per omnia saecula saeculorum" (who with the Father and the Holy Ghost lives and reigns forever and ever). It was the usual ending of a homily.

64. *wille:* Here and elsewhere this stands for the personification of willfulness as well as being a pun on the name of the author, William Langland.
Heading. *Superbia:* Latin, "Pride."
Heading. *Luxuria:* Latin, "Lechery."

With° þat he shulde þe saterday seuene ȝere° þere-after   *promising/on Saturday (for) seven years*

Drynke but myd° þe doke° and dyne but ones.°   *only with/duck/once*

Inuidia

Enuye° with heuy° herte asked after scrifte,°   *Envy/heavy/for confession*

And carefullich° *mea culpa* he comsed° to shewe.°   *full of care/started/declare*

80 He was as pale as a pelet°; in þe palsye° **he semed,**°   *(stone) pellet/(i.e., palsied)/seemed*

And clothed in a caurimaury, I couthe° it nouȝte discreue;°   *could/not describe*

In kirtel° and kourteby° and a knyf° bi his syde,   *underjacket/jacket/knife*

Of a freres frokke° were þe forsleues.°   *friar's habit/foresleeves*

And as a leke° hadde yleye° longe in þe sonne,°   *leek (that)/lain/sun*

85 So loked he with lene chekes **lourynge**° foule.°   *lean cheeks **scowling**/foully*

His body was to-bolle° for wratthe þat° he bote° his lippes,   *swollen/so that/bit*

And wryngynge he ȝede° with þe fiste; to wreke° hymself he þouȝte°   *went/avenge/thought*

With werkes° or with wordes whan° he seighe° his tyme.   *works/when/saw*

Eche a° worde þat he warpe° was of an Addres tonge,°   *each/uttered/adder's tongue*

90 Of chydynge and of chalangynge° was his chief lyflode,°   *accusing/livelihood*

With bakbitynge° and bismer° and beryng° of fals° witnesse;   *detraction/calumny/**bearing**/false*

Þis was al his curteisye° where þat euere° he shewed hym.°   *behavior/ever/showed himself*

"I wolde ben yshryue,"° quod° þis schrewe° "and° I for shame durst;°   *would be shriven/said/villain/if/dared*

I wolde be gladder, bi God þat gybbe° had meschaunce,°   *Gib/misfortune*

95 Than þouze° I had þis woke ywonne° a weye° of essex chese.°   *though/week won/weight/cheese*

"I haue a neighbore neyȝe° me, I haue ennuyed° hym ofte,   *near/annoyed*

And lowen on° hym to lordes to don° hym lese° his siluer,   *lied against/make/lose*

And made his frendes ben his foon thorw° my false tonge;   *foes through*

His grace and his good happes **greueth**° me ful° sore.   *successes grieve/very*

100 Bitwene many and many I make debate° ofte,   *strife*

Þat bothe lyf° and lyme° is lost þorw° **my speche.**°   *life/limb/**through**/speech*

And whan I mete° him in market þat I moste hate,   *meet*

I hailse° hym hendeliche° as° I his frende were;   *greet/courteously/as if*

For he is douȝtier° þan I, I dar° do non° other.   *stronger/dare/no*

105 Ac° hadde I maystrye° and myȝte,° God wote° my wille!   *but/mastery/power/knows*

"And whan I come to þe kirke° and sholde knele° to þe Rode,°   *church/should kneel/cross*

And preye° for þe pople° as þe prest techeth,°   *pray/people/priest teaches*

For pilgrimes and for palmers, for alle þe poeple after,°   *people too*

Þanne° I crye on my knees þat cryste ȝif hem sorwe°   *then/give them sorrow*

110 Þat baren awey° my bolle° and my broke schete.°   *stole away/bowl/torn sheet*

---

76. *seuene ȝere þere-after:* i.e., "for seven years."

Heading. *Invidia:* Latin, "Envy."

79. *mea culpa:* Latin, "my sin."

81. *caurimaury:* some kind of coarse material.

94. *gybbe:* Gilbert.

95. Essex cheese was of heavy weight.

"Awey fro° þe auter° þanne turne I myn eyghen,° *from/altar/my eyes*
And biholde how Eleyne hath a newe cote;° *coat*
I wisshe þanne it were myne and al þe webbe° after, *the whole cloth*
  "And of° mennes lesynge° I laughe, þat liketh° myn herte;° *at/losses/pleases/heart*
115 And for her° wynnynge I wepe° and waille° þe tyme, *their/weep/bewail*
  "And deme° þat hij don° ille þere° I do wel° worse; *judge/they do/where/much*
Who-so vndernymeth° me here-of I hate hym dedly° after. *reproves/deadly*
I wolde þat vche a° wyght° were my knaue,° *each/man/servant*
For who-so hath more þan I þat angreth° me sore. *angers*
120 And þus I lyue louelees° lyke a luther° dogge, *live loveless/wicked*
That° al my body bolneth° for bitter° of my galle. *so that/swells/bitterness*
  "I myȝte nouȝte eet° many ȝeres° as a man ouȝte,° *might not eat/years/ought*
For enuye° and yuel° wille is yuel° to defye;° *envy/ill/difficult/digest*
May no sugre ne swete° þinge asswage° my swellynge, *sugar nor sweet/relieve*
125 Ne no *diapenidion* dryue° it fro myne herte, *drive*
Ne noyther schrifte° ne shame but ho-so schrape° my mawe?"° *neither confession/unless one*
      scrape/stomach

  "Ȝus, redili,"° quod repentaunce and radde° hym to° þe beste, *yes, readily/advised/for*
"Sorwe of° synnes is sauacioun° of soules." *for/salvation*
  "I am sori,"° quod þat segge,° "I am but selde other,° *sorry/fellow/seldom otherwise*
130 And þat maketh me° þus megre° for I ne° may me venge.° *myself/thin/not/avenge*
Amonges Burgeyses° haue I be° dwellynge at Londoun, *among burgesses/been*
And gert bakbitinge° be a brocoure° to blame mennes ware. *made Backbite/broker*
Whan° he solde and I nouȝte þanne was I redy° *when/ready*
To lye° and to loure° on my neighbore and to lakke° his *lie/scowl/find fault with/goods*
  chaffare.°
135 I wil amende þis, ȝif° I may þorw myȝte of God almyȝty."° *if*

Ira

Now awaketh wratthe with two whyte eyen,° *eyes*
And nyuelynge° with þe nose and his nekke° hangynge. *sniveling/neck*
  "I am wrath," quod° he; "I was sum° tyme a frere,° *said/some/friar*
And þe couentes° Gardyner for to graffe ympes;° *convent's/graft shoots*
140 On limitoures° and listres lesynges° I ymped,° *begging friars/lectors lies/grafted*
Tyl þei bere leues° of low speche° lordes to plese,° *bear leaves/servile speech/please*
And sithen° þei blosmed obrode° in houre to here shriftes.° *then/blossomed abroad/(ladies)*
      chambers to hear confessions

And now is fallen þer-of a frute° þat folke han wel leuere° *fruit/would rather*

---

125. *diapenidion:* Greek, "barley sugar."

Heading. *Ira:* Latin, "Wrath."

139. Wrath is the gardener of a convent, i.e., a curtil friar. Cf. *The Fox and the Wolf* p. 553.

140. *limitoures:* friars, members of a convent, who had license to beg within a certain limited area; every household was therefore touched by a friar, but there was no overlapping. Chaucer's Friar was a limitour. *listres:* Lectors were readers who occupied a low place in the hierarchy of the Church, just above the doorkeeper.

142. *in boure:* i.e., in the chambers of noble households.

Schewen her° schriftes to hem° þan shryue hem° to her
        persones.°

tell their°|(i.e., friars)|confess
themselves°|parsons

145   "And now persones han parceyued° þat Freres parte°
        with hem,°

have noticed|share (profits)|them

Þise° possessioneres° preche° and depraue° freres,

these|beneficed clergy|preach|
defame

And freres fyndeth hem in defaute° as folke bereth witnes,

at fault

That whan þei preche° þc poeple° in many place° aboute,

preach (to)|people|places

I, wrath, walke with hem and wisse° hem of° my bokes.°

teach|from|books

150 Þus þei speken° of spiritualte° þat eyther° despiseth other,°

speak|spiritual authority|each|
(the) other

Til þei be bothe beggers and by my spiritualte libben,°

live

Or elles° alle riche and riden° aboute.

else|ride

I, wrath, rest neuere° þat I ne moste folwe°

never|might follow

This wykked° folke for suche is my grace.

wicked

155   "I haue an aunte to° nonne° and an abbesse bothe,

who is a|nun

Hir were leuere swowe° or swelte° þan suffre any peyne.°

she would rather swoon|die|pain

I haue be cook in hir kichyne° and þe couent serued

her kitchen

Many monthes with hem and with monkes bothe.

I was þe priouresses potagere° and other poure° ladyes,

pottage maker|poor

160 And made hem ioutes° of iangelynge° þat dame Iohanne°
        was a bastard,

broths|gossip|Joan

And dame Clarice a kniȝtes douȝter ac° a kokewolde°
        was hire syre,°

knight's daughter but|cuckold|
her father

And dame Peronelle a prestes file;° Priouresse worth°
        she neuere,

priest's mistress|will be

For she had childe in chirityme,° al owre chapitere° it wiste.°

cherry-time (i.e., at the cherry
fair)|our chapter|knew

"Of wykked wordes I, wrath, here wortes° I-made,°

boiled vegetables|made

165 Til 'þow lixte'° and 'þow lixte' lopen° oute at ones,°

you lie|leaped|together

And eyther hitte other vnder þe cheke;°

cheek

Hadde þei had knyues,° bi cryst her eyther° had killed other.

knives|each of them

"Seynt° Gregorie was a gode° pope and had a gode forwit,°

Saint|good|precept

Þat no priouresse were° prest for þat he ordeigned.°

should be|ordained

170 Þei had° þanne ben *infamis* þe firste day þei can so yuel hele
        conseille.°

would have|then been|poorly
prosperity counsel

"Amonge monkes I miȝte° be ac many tyme I shonye;°

might|shun (them)

For þere ben° many felle frekis° my feres° to aspye,°

are|cruel fellows|companions|spy

Bothe Prioure an supprioure° and owre *pater abbas;*

and subprior

145–52. The reference is to the bitter quarrel between bene-
ficed clergy and friars about the right to hear confession.
163. The cherry fairs were the occasion for much pleasant and
unlicensed behavior.
169. *were prest:* i.e., hear confession; Gregory IX had strongly

forbidden abbesses to do this.
170. *infamis:* Latin, "censured."
173. *pater abbas:* Latin, "abbot."

And if I telle any tales þei taken hem togyderes,°   *take counsel*
175 And do° me faste frydayes to bred° and to water,   *make/on bread*
And am chalanged° in þe chapitelhous° as° I a childe were,   *accused/chapter house/as if*
And baleised° on þe bare ers° and no breche **bitwene**;°   *punished (with a rod)/buttocks/*
    *breeches **between***

For-þi° haue I no lykyng with þo leodes° to wonye.°   *therefore/those people/live*
I ete° there vnthende° fisshe and fieble° ale drynke;   *eat/out-of-season/weak*
180 Ac other while,° whan wyn° cometh, whan I drynke   *sometimes/when wine/evening*
    wyn at eue,°
I haue a fluxe of a foule mouthe wel fyue° dayes after.   *fully five*
Al þe wikkednesse þat I wote bi° any of owre bretheren,   *know of*
I couth° it in owre cloistre þat° al owre couent° wote it."   *declare/so that/convent*
    "Now repent þe,"° quod° Repentaunce, "and reherce°   *you/said/repeat/never*
    þow neure°
185 Conseille° þat þow cnowest° bi contenaunce ne° bi riȝte;°   *secret/know/look nor/claim*
And drynke nouȝte ouer° delicatly ne to depe noyther,°   *not overly/too deep neither*
Þat þi wille bi cause° þer-of° to wrath myȝte torne.°   *because/of it/might turn*
Esto sobrius," he seyde° and assoilled° me after,   *said/absolved*
And bad° me wilne° to wepe° my wikkednesse to amende.   *bade/try/weep*

Auaricia

190   And þanne cam coueytise,° can I hym nouȝte descryue,°   *came **Covetousness**/describe*
So hungriliche° and holwe° sire Heruy hym loked.°   *hungrily/hollow/he looked*
He was bitelbrowed° and baberlipped° also,   *beetle browed/thick lipped*
With two blered cyghen° as a blynde hagge;   *bleared eyes*
And as a letheren **purs lolled**° his chekes,   *leather **purs flapped***
195 Wel sydder° þan his chyn þei chiueled for elde;°   *much longer/trembled from age*
And as a bondman of° his bacoun° his berde° was bidraueled.°   *laborer from/bacon/beard/be-*
    slobbered

With an hode° on his hed,° a lousi hatte aboue,°   *hood/head/on top*
And in a tauny tabarde° of twelue wynter° age,   *tawny coat/winters*
Al totorne° and baudy° and ful of lys crepynge;°   *torn/dirty/lice creeping*
200 But if° þat a lous couthe° haue lopen þe bettre,   *unless/could*
She sholde° nouȝte haue walked on þat welche° so was it   *should/? Welsh cloth/threadbare*
    thredebare.°
    "I haue ben coueytouse,"° quod þis caityue,° "I biknowe°   *covetous/rogue/acknowledge*
    it here;
For some tyme I serued Symme atte° Stile,   *at the*
And was his prentis ypliȝte,° his profit to wayte.°   *apprentice pledged/guard*
205 First I lerned to lye° a leef other tweyne,°   *lie/leaf or two*
Wikkedlich° to weye° was my furst° lessoun.   *wickedly/weigh/first*

---

188. *Esto sobrius:* Latin, "Be sober" (1 Pet. 5:8).   **191.** *Heruy:* Harvey, name for a covetous man.
Heading. *Auaricia:* Latin, "Covetousness."   **205.** *leef:* i.e., "small portion."

To Wy° and to Wynchestre I went to þe faire,   *Weyhill*
With many manere marchandise° as my Maistre° me hiȝte;°   *kinds (of) merchandise/master/ ordered*

Ne had° þe grace of gyle ygo° amonge my ware,   *had not/Guile gone*
210 It had be° vnsolde þis seuene ȝere,° so me God helpe!   *been/these seven years*
    "Thanne° drowe I me° amonges° draperes my donet° to lerne,   *then/I went/among/primer*
To drawe þe lyser° alonge þe lenger° it semed;°   *edge of the cloth/(so that) the longer/ seemed*

Among þe riche rayes° I rendred° a lessoun,   *striped cloth/taught*
To broche hem° with a pak-nedle° and plaited° hem togyderes,°   *pierce them/packing needle/fastened/ together*
215 And put hem in a presse and pynned hem þerinne,
Tyl ten ȝerdes° or twelue hadde tolled out threttene.°   *yards/stretched out (to) thirteen*
    "My wyf° was a webbe° and wollen° cloth made;   *wife/weaver/woolen*
She spak° to spynnesteres° to spynnen° it oute.   *spoke/spinners/spin*
Ac° þe pounde þat she payed by poised° a quarteroun° more,   *but/weighed/quarter*
220 Than myne owne auncere° who-so weyȝed treuthe.°   *scales/weighed honestly*
    "I bouȝte hir° barly malte; she brewe° it to selle,   *bought her/brewed*
Peny° ale and podyng° ale she poured togideres   *penny/pudding*
For laboreres and for low folke; þat° lay by hymselue.°   *(i.e., the ale)/itself*
    "The best ale lay in my boure° or in my bedchambre,   *chamber*
225 And who-so bummed° þer-of bouȝte it þer-after,   *tasted*
A galoun° for a grote° God wote,° no lesse;   *gallon/groat/knows*
And ȝit° it cam in cupmel;° þis° crafte my wyf vsed.   *yet/cupfuls/such*
Rose þe regratere° was hir riȝte° name;   *retail dealer/right*
She hath holden° hokkerye° al hire lyf° tyme.   *practiced/retail trade/her life*
230 "Ac I swere° now, so the ik° þat synne wil I lete,°   *swear/(may) thrive I/leave off*
And neuere° wikkedliche weye ne wikke chaffare° vse,   *never/nor false merchandise*
But wenden° to Walsyngham and my wyf als,°   *go/also*
And bidde° þe Rode° of bromeholme brynge° me oute of dette."°   *ask/Cross/(to) bring/debt*
    "Repentedestow° þe euere,"° quod° repentance "ne restitucioun° madest?"   *did you repent/yourself ever/said/ restitution*

---

207. Fairs like the one at Weyhill, near Andover in Hampshire, often lasting several days, were the markets for all kinds of farm produce. The one of Saint Giles's hill, near Winchester, was instituted by William the Conqueror as revenue for the bishop of Winchester.

211. *donet:* The Donet was the primary grammar, named after Aelius Donatus, the Roman grammarian; it preceded the Priscian grammar.

219–20. She paid by the pound, but her "pound" weight was heavier than a pound; thus she cheated her workers out of their just wages.

222–23. Penny ale was the weak, thin ale (the weakest being half-penny ale), whereas pudding ale was of the thickest variety. She mixed the two and asked the highest price (four pence instead of a penny a gallon).

232. Cf. above, p. 678, l. 54*n.*

233. The Cross of Bromholm in Norfolk, said to have been made from part of the True Cross discovered by Saint Helen, mother of Constantine, was brought there from Constantinople by an English priest. The shrine of Walsingham is close to Bromholm.

235 "ȝus, ones° I was herberwed,"° quod he, "with an hep° of   *yes, once/lodged/group/merchants*
      chapmen,°
      I roos whan° þei were arest° and yrifled here males."°   *rose when/at rest/rifled*
                                                                  their bags

      "That was no restitucioun," quod repentance, "but a
        robberes thefte,
      Þow° haddest° be better worthy be° hanged þerfore°   *you/would have/(to) be/for that*
      Þan for al þat þat þow hast here shewed."°   *told*
240   "I wende ryflynge were° restitucioun," quod he, "for I   *thought robbing was/(to) read in*
        lerned neuere rede on boke,°   *book*
      And I can° no frenche in feith° but of þe ferthest° ende of   *know/faith/furthest*
        norfolke."
      "Vsedestow° euere vsurie,"° quod repentaunce, "in alle þi   *did you practice/usury*
        lyf tyme?"
      "Nay, sothly,"° he seyde,° "saue° in my ȝouthe.   *truly/said/except*
      I lerned amonge lumbardes° and iewes° a lessoun,   *Lombards/Jews*
245   To wey pens° with a peys° and pare° þe heuyest,°   *weigh pennies/weight/clip/heaviest*
      And lene° it for loue of þe crosse, to legge° a wedde° and lese° it;   *lend/lay/pledge/lose*
      Suche dedes° I did wryte ȝif° he his day breke.°   *charters/if/day (of payment) missed*
      I haue mo maneres þorw rerages° þan þorw *miseretur &*   *more manors through arrears*
        comodat.
      "I haue lent lordes and ladyes my chaffare,°   *goods*
250   And ben her brocour° after and bouȝte it my-self.   *been their broker*
      Eschaunges° and cheuesances,° with suche chaffare° I dele,°   *exchanges/(loan) agreements/wares/*
                                                                  deal

      And lene folke þat lese wol° a lyppe at° euery noble.°   *want to/part of/(gold coin)*
      And with lumbardes lettres I ladde° golde to Rome,   *carried*
      And toke° it by taille° here and tolde° hem° þere lasse."°   *took/tally/counted out/to them/less*
255   "Lentestow° euere lordes for loue of her mayntenaunce?"°   *did you lend/support*
      "ȝe,° I haue lent lordes loued° me neuere after,   *yea/(who) loved*
      And haue ymade° many a knyȝte° bothe mercere and drapere,   *made/knight*
      Þat payed neuere for his prentishode nouȝte° a peire° gloues."   *apprenticeship not/pair (of)*
      "Hastow° pite° on pore° men þat mote nedes borwe?"°   *have you/pity/poor/must needs*
                                                                  borrow

---

244. Although usury was forbidden by canon law, Italian and Jewish bankers lent money at interest, especially since the latter were forbidden to engage in other trades.

245–46. Avarice clipped coins and lent the light money for a pledge which the borrower often lost when he could not repay in time. The "cross" was the coin itself, from the symbol on the reverse side.

248. *miseretur & comodat:* i.e., "liberality" ("Jucundus homo qui miseretur et commodat, disponet sermones suos in judicio" ["Good is the man who is merciful and generous, who arranges his affairs equitably"], Ps. 112 [Vulgate, Ps. 111]:5).

252. *noble:* a gold coin (6s. 8d.) worth more than a florin (cf. above, p. 689, l. 146*n*).

253. *lumbardes lettres:* i.e., money drafts or checks. The Italian bankers were the first to exchange money without cash, through the use of letters of credit and the like.

257–58. Avarice has lent money to knights who in payment gave him some of their clothes for a cheap price. *mercere:* a dealer in textiles.

260 "I haue as moche° pite of pore men as pedlere° hath of cattes,   *much/peddler*

Þat wolde° kille hem, yf° he cacche° hem myȝte,° for   *would/them, if/catch/might/desire*
   coueitise° of here skynnes."

   "Artow° manlyche° amonge þi neiȝbores of° þi mete° and   *are you/generous/neighbors with/*
   drynke?"   *food*

   "I am holden,"° quod he, "as hende° as hounde is in   *held/courteous*
   kychyne,

Amonges° my neighbores, namelich,° such a name ich° haue."   *among/especially/I*

265   "Now God lene neure,"° quod repentance, "but° þow   *grant never/unless*
   repent þe rather,

Þe° grace on þis grounde° þi good° wel to bisette,°   *you/earth/property/employ*

Ne þine ysue° after þe haue ioye° of þat° þow wynnest,   *issue/joy/what*

Ne þi executours wel bisett þe siluer þat þow hem leuest;°   *leave*

And þat was wonne with wronge with wikked° men be   *wicked/spent*
   despended.°

270 For were I frere° of þat hous þere gode° faith and charite° is,   *friar/where good/charity*

I nolde° cope° vs with þi catel ne owre kyrke amende,°   *would not/dress/goods nor our*
                                              church repair

Ne haue a peny to° my pitaunce° of þyne, bi my soule hele,°   *penny for/share/soul's salvation*

For þe best boke in owre hous þeiȝe brent° golde were þe leues,°   *though bright/leaves*

And° I wyst wytterly° þow were suche as þow tellest,   *if/knew truly*

275 Or elles° þat I kouþe° knowe it by any kynnes wise.°   *else/could/kind (of)* **manner**

Seruus es alterius cum fercula pinguia queris,

Pane tuo pocius vescere, liber eris.

   "Thow art an vnkynde° creature, I can þe nouȝte assoille,°   *uncharitable/absolve*

Til þow make restitucioun° and rekne° with hem alle,   *restitution/reckon (up)*

280 And sithen° þat resoun rolle° it in þe regystre° of heuene,°   *then/Reason enroll/register/heaven*

That þow hast made vche° man good I may þe nouȝte assoille;   *each*

   Non dimittitur peccatum donec restituatur ablatum, &c.

   "For alle þat haue of þi good,° haue God my trouthe!°   *wealth/pledge*

Ben holden° at þe heighe dome° to helpe þe to restitue.°   *are bound/high judgment/make*
                                              restitution

285 And who so° leueth° nouȝte þis be soth loke° in þe sauter   *whoever/believes/(to) be truth look/*
   glose,°   *Psalter gloss*

In *miserere mei deus* where I mene treuthe,°   *tell truth*

   Ecce enim veritatem dilexisti, &c.

   "Shal neuere werkman° in þis worlde þryue° wyth þat þow   *never workman/thrive/gained*
   wynnest;°

Cum sancto sanctus eris, construe me þat on° englische."   *in*

276–77. "You are slave of another when you seek after dainty dishes; feed rather on you own bread, and you will be a free man."

282. "Thy sins will not be remitted until restitution is made."

284. *þe heighe dome:* i.e., "Judgment Day."

285–6. *glose:* i.e., "commentary." *miserere mei deus:* "Have mercy upon me, O God," the first three words of Ps. 51.

287. "Behold, thou desirest truth" (Ps. 51:6 [Vulgate, 8]).

289. *Cum . . . eris:* "With the pure thou wilt show thyself pure (Ps. 18 [Vulgate, Ps. 17]: 26).

290   Thanne wex° þat shrewe° in wanhope° and walde° haue   *then grew/villain/despair/would*
        hanged him-self,
      Ne° hadde repentaunce þe rather° reconforted° hym in þis   *not/quickly/comforted again/*
        manere,°   *manner*
      "Haue mercye in þi mynde and with þi mouth biseche° it,   *pray for*
      For Goddes mercye is more° þan alle hise° other werkes,°   *greater/his/works*
        Misericordia eius super omnia opera eius, &c.
295   "And al þe wikkednesse in þis worlde þat man myȝte worche°   *do*
        or thynke,
      Ne is no more to þe mercye of God þan in þe see° a glede,°   *sea/spark*
        Omnis iniquitas quantum ad misericordiam dei, est quasi
           sintilla in medio maris.
       "For-þi° haue mercy in þi mynde and marchandise,° leue it,   *therefore/merchandise*
      For þow hast no good grounde° to gete° þe with° a wastel,°   *means/get/yourself/wastel bread*
           (i.e., cake)
300 But if° it were with thi tonge° or ellis° with þi two hondes.°   *unless/tongue/else/hands*
      For þe good þat þow hast geten bigan° al with falsehede,°   *gotten began/falsehood*
      And as long as þow lyuest° þer-with þow ȝeldest nouȝte,° but   *live/pay not/borrow*
        borwest.°
       "And if þow wite° neuere to whiche ne whom to restitue,   *know*
      Bere° it to þe bisschop and bidde hym of his grace,   *give*
305 Bisette it hym-selue° as best is for þi soule.   *himself*
      For he shal answere for þe at þe heygh° dome,   *high*
      For þe and for many mo° þat man shal ȝif° a rekenynge,°   *more/give/reckoning*
      What he lerned ȝow° in lente° leue þow none° other,   *taught you/Lent/no*
      And what he lent° ȝow of owre° lordes good° to lette° ȝow fro°   *gave/our/(spiritual) wealth/keep/*
        synne."   *from*

      Gula

310   Now bigynneth glotoun° for to go to schrifte,°   *Glutton/confession*
      And kaires hym° to-kirke-ward° his coupe° to schewe.°   *betakes himself/to church/sin/*
           declare

      Ac Beton° þe brewestere bad° hym good morwe,°   *but Betty/alewife bade/morning*
      And axed° of hym with þat° whiderward° he wolde.°   *asked/then/where/would (go)*
      "To holi cherche,"° quod° he, "forto here° masse,   *church/said/to hear*
315 And sithen I wil be shryuen° and synne namore."°   *shriven/no more*
      "I haue gode° ale, gossib,"° quod she, "glotown,° wiltow°   *good/gossip (i.e., friend)/Glutton/*
        assaye?"°   *will you/try*
      "Hastow° auȝte° in þi purs,° any hote° spices?"   *have you/anything/purse/hot*

---

294. Vulgate, Ps. 144:9.   **299.** *wastel:* Cf. below, p. 716, ll. 180–82.
297. A similar passage appears in Richard Rolle of Hampole's   **Heading.** *Gula:* Latin, "Gluttony."
Prick of Conscience, ll. 6311–19. There is no specific source.
Vulgate, Ps. 143:2 is close in meaning.

"I haue peper° and piones,"° quod she "and a pounde of
    garlike,° *pepper/peonies/garlic*
A ferthyngworth° of fenel-seed° for fastyngdayes."° *farthing's worth/fennel seed/fast days*

320 Þanne goth° glotoun in and grete othes after;° *goes/Great Oaths after (him)*
Cesse° þe souteresse° sat on þe benche, *Cis/cobbler's wife*
Watte° þe warner° and his wyf° bothe, *Wat/warren keeper/wife*
Tymme° þe tynkere and tweyne° of his prentis,° *Tim/two/apprentices*
Hikke° þe hakeneyman° and hughe þe nedeler,° *Hick/horse dealer/needle seller*
325 Clarice of cokkeslane° and þe clerke of þe cherche, *Cock Lane*
Dawe þe dykere° and a dozeine other;° *ditch digger/dozen others*
Sire Piers of Pridie and Peronelle of Flaundres,° *Flanders*
A ribibour,° a ratonere,° a rakyer° of chepe,° *fiddler/rat catcher/street sweeper/Cheapside*

A ropere,° a redyngkyng,° and Rose þe dissheres,° *rope maker/retainer/dish seller*
330 Godfrey of garlekehithe and gryfin° þe walshe,° *Griffin/Welshman*
And vpholderes° an hepe° erly bi° þe morwe *secondhand dealers/crowd/in*
Geuen° glotoun with glad chere° good ale to hansel.° *gave/cheer/quiet him*
    Clement þe cobelere° cast of° his cloke,° *cobbler/off/cloak*
And atte° new faire he nempned° it to selle; *at/named (i.e., put it up)*
335 Hikke þe hakeneyman hitte° his hood after, *cast down*
And badde bette° þe bochere ben° on his side. *bade Bat/butcher be*
Þere were chapmen y-chose þis chaffare° to preise;° *merchants chosen these goods/appraise*

Who-so haueth þe hood shuld° haue amendes of° þe cloke. *should/for (the value of)*
    Two risen° vp in rape° and rouned togideres,° *got/haste/whispered together*
340 And preised° þese penyworthes° apart bi hem-selue;° *appraised/pennyworths/themselves*
Þei couth nouȝte° bi her° conscience acorden° in treuthe,° *could not/their/agree/truth*
Tyl Robyn þe ropere arose bi° þe southe, *on*

---

318. *piones:* Peony seeds were used as spices.

319. *ferthyngworth:* A farthing was a quarter of a penny. *for fastyngdayes:* The occasion is a Friday.

320. Glutton follows Betty into a tavern.

321. *Cesse:* Cicely, Cecelia.

324. *Hikke:* Hick, the hackneyman, was an innkeeper (cf. l. 345) who rented out horses.

325. *cokkeslane:* Cock Lane was the abode of women of ill repute, after they had been punished in the pillory. *cherche:* either that of Bow Lane in Cheapside or Saint Peter's in Cornhill, where Langland lived.

327. *Sire Piers:* most likely a monk, or possibly the local vicar. The title *Sir* was often applied to monks, and Chaucer uses the name Piers in this respect. According to Skeat, *Pridie* may be a pun on *prie-dieu*, a praying chair—obviously not in use here. *Flaundres:* Streetwalkers at this time were identified as "Flemish women," who according to law had to live in the stews of Southwark or Cock Lane. If one was found elsewhere, she forfeited her upper garment and hood.

328. *ribibour:* A ribibe was a three-stringed instrument played with a bow.

330. *garlekehithe:* Garlickhithe, near the Vintry Ward on the banks of the Thames.

334. *new faire:* New Fair was a game in which one man challenges another for an article in exchange for something of his own. An umpire judges the value of the different articles, and the three men put equal forfeit money in a hat. The umpire then declares his award for the inferior article. Both challengers reach into the hat and draw out full hands if they agree to the award, empty hands if they do not want to bargain. If both men agree either way, the umpire gets the money; if they do not, the one who agrees to bargain wins. But the course of New Fair does not run as smoothly here as the rules demanded.

336. *ben . . . side:* i.e., "to take his part."

340. *penyworthes:* i.e., "secondhand goods."

And nempned hym° for a noumpere° þat° no debate nere,°   *was named/umpire/so that/were not*
For to trye° þis chaffare bitwixen hem þre.°   *choose/between them three*

345   Hikke þe hostellere° hadde° þe cloke,   *innkeeper/got*
In couenaunte° þat Clement shulde þe cuppe fille,   *agreement*
And haue Hikkes hode° hostellere and holde hym yserued;°   *hood/satisfied*
And who-so repented rathest° shulde arise after,   *soonest*
And grete° sire glotoun° with a galoun° ale.   *greet/Glutton/gallon (of)*

350   Þere was laughyng and louryng° and "Let go þe cuppe,"   *frowning*
And seten° so til euensonge° and songen vmwhile,°   *(they) sat/evening/sang occasionally*
Tyl glotoun had y-globbed° a galoun an a Iille.°   *gulped down/gill*
His guttis gunne° to gothely° as two gredy° sowes;   *guts began/rumble/greedy*
He pissed a potel° in a pater-noster while,°   *pottle (i.e., two quarts)/time*
355 And blew his rounde ruwet° at his rigge-bon° ende,   *trumpet/backbone's*
That alle þat herde° þat horne held her nose after,   *heard*
And wissheden° it had be° wexed° with a wispe of firses.°   *wished/been/stopped up/furze*
He myȝte° neither steppe ne stonde er° he his staffe hadde;   *might/nor stand before*
And þanne gan° he go liche° a glewmannes bicche,°   *then did/like/(blind) gleeman's bitch*

360 Somme° tyme aside and somme tyme arrere,°   *some/to the rear*
As who-so leyth lynes° forto lacche foules.°   *lays lines/to catch birds*
And whan° he drowgh° to þe dore þanne dymmed his eighen,°   *when/came/eyes*
He stumbled on þe thresshewolde an threwe° to þe erthe.   *threshold and was thrown*
Clement þe cobelere cauȝte° hym bi þe myddel,   *caught*
365 For to lifte hym alofte and leyde° him on his knowes;°   *laid/knees*
Ac glotoun was a gret cherle° and a grym° in þe liftynge,   *great fellow/heavy (one)*
And coughed vp a caudel° in clementis° lappe;   *mess/Clement's*
Is non° so hungri hounde in Hertford schire   *(there) is none*
Durst lape° of þe leuynges° so vnlouely þei smauȝte.°   *dared lap/leavings/tasted*

370 With al þe wo° of þis worlde his wyf° and his wenche°   *woe/wife/daughter*
Baren° hym home to his bedde and brouȝte° hym þerinne.   *bore/brought*
And after al þis excesse he had an accidie,°   *fit of sloth*
Þat he slepe saterday° and sonday° til sonne ȝede° to reste.   *slept Saturday/Sunday/sun went*
Þanne waked he of° his wynkyng° and wiped his eyghen;°   *from/sleeping/eyes*
375 Þe fyrste worde þat he warpe° was, "Where is þe bolle?"°   *uttered/(drinking) bowl*
His wif gan edwite° hym þo° how wikkedlich° he lyued,°   *reprove/then/wickedly/lived*
And repentance riȝte so° rebuked hym þat tyme: *likewise*

---

343. *noumpere:* from OF *nompere, nonpere,* "non peer," a person "not equal" to either party. By the process of shifting the initial letter, we get Mod. Eng. *an umpire.*

347. *Hikkes hode hostellere:* i.e., "Hick the innkeeper's hood."

352. *Iille:* a quarter of a pint.

351. *potel:* a half-gallon, here eliminated in the time it takes to say the Lord's Prayer (*pater-noster:* Latin, "our father").

359. The dog leading a blind minstrel was not a trained seeing-eye dog, but wandered about in a desultory fashion.

367. *caudel:* A caudle was a warm drink of thin gruel, sweetened with spices and mixed with wine or ale, given to the sick (? as a purgative).

"As þow° with wordes and werkes° hast wrouȝte yuel° in þi lyue,°   *you/works/done evil/life*

Shryue þe° and be shamed° þer-of and shewe° it with þi mouth."   *confess yourself/ashamed/declare*

380   "I, glotoun," quod° þe gome,° "gylti me ȝelde,°   *said/ fellow/guilty myself confess*

Þat I haue trespassed with my tonge° I can nouȝte° telle how ofte,   *tongue/not*

Sworen° 'Goddes soule' and 'so God me help and halidom,'°   *sworn/holy relics*

Þere° no nede ne° was nyne hundreth° tymes;   *where/need not/hundred*

"And ouer-seye° me at my sopere° and some tyme at nones,°   *forgot/supper/noon meal*

385   Þat° I glotoun girt° it vp er I hadde gone a myle,   *so that/threw*

And y-spilte þat° myȝte be spared and spended° on somme° hungrie;   *wasted what/spent/someone*

Ouerdelicatly° on fastyng° dayes drunken and eten° bothe,   *too luxuriously/fast/eaten*

And sat some tyme so longe þere þat I slepe and ete° at ones.°   *ate/(both) at once*

For loue of tales in tauernes to drynke þe more, I dyned,

390   And hyed° to þe mete° er none° whan fastyng-dayes were."   *rushed/food/noon*

"This shewyng° shrifte,"° quod repentance, "shal be meryte° to þe."°   *show of/confession/merit/you*

And þanne gan glotoun grete° and gret doel° to make   *began Glutton (to) weep/lamentation*

For his lither lyf° þat he lyued hadde,   *wicked life*

And avowed to fast—"For hunger or for thurst°   *thirst*

395   Shal neuere° fisshe on þe fryday defien° in my wombe,°   *never/digest/stomach*

Tyl abstinence myn° aunte haue ȝiue° me leue;°   *my/has given/permission*

And ȝit° haue I hated hir° al my lyf tyme."

Accidia

Þanne come sleuthe° al bislabered° with two slymy eiȝen,°   *came Sloth/beslobbered/eyes*

"I most° sitte," seyde° þe segge° "or elles shulde° I nappe;   *must/said/man/else should*

400   I may nouȝte stonde ne stoupe° ne with-oute a stole knele.°   *stand nor stoop/stool kneel*

Were I brouȝte abedde,° but if° my taille-end it made,°   *to bed/unless/made (me)*

Sholde° no ryngynge do° me ryse ar° I were rype to dyne."   *should/ringing (of bells) make/ before*

He bygan° *benedicite* with a bolke° and his brest knocked,°   *began/belch/beat*

And roxed° and rored° and rutte atte° laste.   *stretched/roared/snored at*

405   "What! awake, renke!"° quod repentance, "and rape þe° to shrifte."   *man/hasten*

"If I shulde deye bi° þis day me liste° nouȝte to loke;°   *die on/I care/look*

I can° nouȝte perfitly° my pater-noster as þe prest° it syngeth,   *know/perfectly/priest*

But I can rymes of Robyn hood and Randolf erle of Chestre,

---

384. *nones:* originally 3 P.M., later taken as noon. The two chief mealtimes were dinner at 9–10 A.M. and supper at 5–6 P.M. On fast days, when there was only one meal, dinner was at noon.

Heading. *Accidia:* Latin, "Sloth."
403. *benedicite:* "Bless ye (the Lord)," the start of his (? morning) prayers.

Ac° neither of owre° lorde ne of owre lady þe leste° þat euere°   *but/our/least/ever*
   was made.

410   "I haue made vowes fourty and for-ȝete hem° on þe morne;   *forgotten them*
   I parfourned neure penaunce° as þe prest me hiȝte,°   *performed never penance/ordered*
   Ne ryȝte sori° for my synnes ȝet was I neuere.   *right sorry*
   And ȝif° I bidde any bedes,° but if it be in wrath,   *if/beads*
   Þat I telle with my tonge is two myle fro° myne herte.°   *miles from/heart*
415   I am occupied eche° day haliday,° and other,   *each/holiday*
   With ydel° tales atte ale° and otherwhile° in cherches;°   *idle/(a) tavern/sometimes/churches*
   Goddes peyne° and his passioun ful selde° þynke I þere-on.   *pain/very seldom*

    "I visited neuere fieble° men ne fettered folke in puttes,°   *feeble/pits (i.e., dungeons)*
   I haue leuere here° an harlotrie° or a somer° game of   *had rather hear/scurrilous tale/*
     souteres,°   *midsummer/shoemakers*
420 Or lesynges° to laughe at and belye° my neighbore,   *lies/belie*
   Þan al þat euere Marke made,° Mathew, John, and Lucas.°   *wrote/Luke*
   And vigilies° and fastyng dayes alle þise late° I passe,   *vigils/these let*
   And ligge° abedde° in lenten an° my lemman° in myn armes,   *lie/in bed/Lent and/sweetheart*
   Tyl matynes° and masse be do° and þanne° go to þe freres;°   *matins/over/then/friars*
425 Come I to° *ite, missa est* I holde me yserued.°   *if I arrive at/myself satisfied*
   I nam nouȝte shryuen° some tyme, but if sekenesse° it make,°   *am not shriven/sickness/make (me)*
   Nouȝte tweies° in two ȝere° and þanne vp gesse° I schryue me.   *twice/years/by guesswork*

    "I haue be° prest and parsoun passynge° thretti wynter,°   *been/these past/thirty winters*
   Ȝete° can I neither solfe° ne synge ne seyntes lyues rede,°   *yet/(sing) sol-fa/saints' lives read*
430 But I can fynde in a felde° or in a fourlonge° an hare,   *field/furlong*
   Better þan in *beatus vir* or in *beati omnes*
   Construe oon° clause wel and kenne° it to my parochienes.°   *one/teach/parishioners*
   I can holde louedayes° and here a Reues rekenynge,°   *arbitration days/steward's reckoning*
   Ac in canoun° ne in þe decretales° I can nouȝte rede a lyne.   *canon law/popes' edicts*
435   "Ȝif I bigge° and borwe° it but ȝif° it be ytailled,°   *buy/borrow/unless/marked on a*
      tally

   I forȝete° it as ȝerne° and ȝif men me it axe°   *forget/quickly/ask for*
   Sixe sithes° or seuene° I forsake° it with othes,°   *times/seven/deny/oaths*
   And þus tene° I trewe° men ten hundreth° tymes.   *vex/true/hundred*
    "And my seruauntz° some tyme her° salarye is bihynde,°   *servants/their/behind*

---

408. This is the earliest mention of the Robin Hood songs and tradition in literature. No Robin Hood ballads, however, have survived from this time; nor do we know any songs or stories about Randulph, earl of Chester, though Skeat identifies him with the earl who lived 1181–1231 and married Constance, widow of Geoffrey Plantagenet and mother of Prince Arthur.

413. *bidde any bedes:* i.e., "say any prayers."

419. The shoemakers' holidays were celebrated on Midsummer's Day, or Saint John the Baptist's Eve. These were called "summerings," and it may be remembered that in Wagner's opera *Die Meistersinger von Nürnberg* the celebration of Johannestag is connected with the shoemaker Hans Sachs.

425. *ite, missa est:* "Go, you are sent," the last words of the Mass.

429. *solfe:* i.e., a scale of notes.

431. *beatus vir:* "Blessed is the man," the beginning of Pss. 1 and 112; *beati omnes:* "Blessed is every one," the beginning of Ps. 128.

433. *louedayes:* days during which matters in conflict were settled by mutual agreement, with clerics acting as mediators.

434. *decretales:* the edicts of popes or Church councils making up canon law.

440 Reuthe is° to here þe rekenynge whan° we shal rede° acomptes;°   *pity (it) is|when|talk about|accounts*
    So with wikked° wille and wraththe° my werkmen° I paye.   *wicked|wrath|workmen*
      "Ȝif any man doth me a benfait° or helpeth me at nede,°   *kind deed|need*
    I am vnkynde aȝein° his curteisye° and can nouȝte   *toward|courtesy|understand*
      vnderstonde° it;
    For I haue and haue hadde some dele° haukes maneres,°   *somewhat|hawk's manners*
445 I nam nouȝte lured with loue but° þere ligge auȝte° vnder þe   *unless|something|thumb*
      thombe.°
      "The kyndenesse þat myne euene-cristene kidde° me   *fellow-Christians showed| formerly*
      fernyere,°
    Sixty sythes° I, sleuthe,° haue forȝete it sith,°   *times|Sloth|since*
    In speche° and in sparynge of speche yspilte° many a tyme   *speech|wasted*
    Bothe flesche and fissche and many other vitailles;°   *victuals*
450 Bothe bred° and ale, butter, melke,° and chese°   *bread|milk|cheese*
    Forsleuthed° in my seruyse° til it myȝte° serue noman.°   *wasted by carelessness|service|*
        might|no one

      "I ran aboute in ȝouthe and ȝaf° me nouȝte to lerne,°   *gave|learning*
    And euere° sith haue be beggere° for my foule sleuthe;   *ever|(a) beggar*
    Heu michi, quod sterilem vitam duxi Iuuenilem."
455 "Repentestow° þe nauȝte?"° quod° repentance, and riȝte°   *do you repent|yourself not|said|*
      with þat° he swowned,°   *right|then|swooned*
    Til *vigilate*° þe veille fette° water at his eyȝen,°   *Vigilance|watcher dashed|eyes*
    And flatte° it on his face and faste° on hym criede,   *threw|loudly*
    And seide,° "Ware þe° fram wanhope wolde þe° bitraye.   *said|beware|of Despair (which)*
        would you

    'I am sori° for my synnes,' sey° so to þi-selue,°   *sorry|say|yourself*
460 And bete° þi-selue on þe breste and bidde° hym of° grace;   *beat|pray to|for*
    For is° no gult° here so grete° þat his goodnesse nys° more."°   *(there) is|guilt|great|is not|greater*
    Þanne sat sleuthe vp and seyned hym swithe,°   *crossed himself quickly*
    And made avowe° to-fore° God for his foule sleuthe,   *a vow|before*
    "Shal° no sondaye° be þis° seuene ȝere, but sykenesse° it lette,°   *(there) shall|Sunday|these|sickness|*
        prevent
465 Þat I ne° shal do me° er day° to þe dere cherche,°   *not|go|before daybreak|dear church*
    And heren matines° and masse as° I a monke were.   *hear matins|as if*
    Shal none° ale after mete° holde me þennes,°   *no|food|thence*
    Tyl I haue euensonge herde,° I behote to° þe Rode.°   *heard|swear by|cross*
    And ȝete° wil I ȝelde aȝein,° if I so moche° haue,   *yet|yield again|much*
470 Al þat I wikkedly wan sithen° I wytte° hadde.   *gained since|sense*
      "And þough my liflode lakke leten° I nelle,°   *sustenance suffer cease|will not*
    Þat eche° man ne shal haue his ar° I hennes wende:°   *each|before|hence go*

---

454. "Alas, what a sterile life I led in youth." The source is   **458.** Despair was the usual result of sloth.
unknown.

And with þe residue and þe remenaunt,° bi þe Rode of chestre!° *remnant/Chester*
I shal seke treuthe arst° ar I se° Rome!" *seek Truth first/see*

from C PASSUS VIII

The Search for Saint Truth

155 A þousend of men þo þrongen to-gederes,° *then thronged together*
Cryyng vpward to crist and to hus clene moder,° *his pure mother*
To haue grace to go to treuthe° God leyue° þat þei mote!° *Truth/grant/might*
Ac° þer was weye non° so wys° þat þe way þider couthe,° *but/man none/wise/there knew*
Bote blostrede° forth as bestes° ouer baches° and hulles,° *but blundered/beasts/dales/hills*
160 Til late was and longe þat þei a lede° mette, *person*
A-paraild° as a paynym° in pylgrymes wise.° *dressed/Saracen/manner*
He bar° a bordon ybounde° with a brod° lyste,° *carried/staff bound/broad/ strip of cloth*

In a weythwynde° wyse ywryþe° al aboute; *bindweed/wound*
A bolle° and a bagge he bar by hus syde, *bowl*
165 And an hondred hanypeles° on hus hatte seten,° *hundred ampullae/stuck*
Signes of syse° and shilles° of galys,° *Assisi/shells/Galicia*
And meny crouche° on hus cloke° and keyes of rome, *many crosses/cloak*
And þe fernycle° by-fore° for° men sholde° knowe, *vernicle/in front/so that/should*
And se° by hus sygnes wham° he souht° hadde. *see/whom(i.e., whose shrines)/ sought*

170 Thys folke frayned° hym furst fro whennes° he come.° *asked/first from whence/came*
"Fro sinay,"° he sayde, "and fro þe sepulcre. *Sinai*
In bethleem,° in babilonie, ich° haue ybe° bothe, *Bethlehem/Babylon, I/been*
In ermanie,° in alisaundre° and in damascle.° *Armenia/Alexandria/Damascus*
3e° may see by my sygnes þat sitten° on my cappe, *you/sit*
175 Ich haue ysouht° goode seyntes° for my soules helthe,° *sought/saints/health*
And walked ful wide° in wete° and in drye." *very far/wet*
"Knowst þow° ou3t° a cor-seynt,"° quaþ° ich, "þat men *you/at all/saint/said/call*
clepeþ° treuthe?

---

473. In former days a famous cross stood in Chester, at a place called the *Rood eye* (Rood–Island).

161. *paynym:* i.e. "pagan," "Saracen," because of his bronzed features and foreign dress. He was evidently a palmer, or professional pilgrim.

165. *hanypeles:* Ampullae were lead or pewter phials containing holy water or oil from the various shrines visited by the pilgrim.

166–76. The "signs" of palmers were souvenirs of the pilgrimage sites and proof that the men had indeed been there: shells from Saint James of Compostela; palms from Jerusalem;

ampullae from Canterbury; crossed keys, effigies of Saint Peter, and vernicles (the features of Christ on a copy of the towel with which Saint Veronica supposedly wiped the Savior's face) from Rome. Two crossed pieces of colored cloth meant a trip to the Holy Land.

166. *syse:* Assisi in Umbria, the home of Saint Francis; *galys:* Galicia, location of the shrine of Saint James of Compostela.

171. *sinay:* i.e., the convent of Saint Catherine on Mount Sinai.

173. In Armenia could be seen Noah's ark; Alexandria was the port of arrival for pilgrims and the site of Saint Catherine's martyrdom; Damascus was the scene of the Creation.

Couthest° þow wissen ous° þe way whoder out° treuthe   *could/show us/where/dwells*
    wonyeþ?"°
"Nay, so God me helpe," seyde° þe gome° þenne,   *said/man*
180 Ich seyh neuere° palmere with pyk ne° with scrippe°   *saw never/pikestaff nor/bag*
Asken° after hym, er° now in þys ilke° place."   *ask/before/same*

Hic Primo Comparet Petrus Plouhman

"Peter!" quaþ a plouhman,° and putte forth hus hefd,°   *plowman/head*
"Ich knowe hym as kyndeliche° as clerkus don hure bokes.°   *naturally/clerks do their books*
Conscience and kyndewit° kende° me to hus place,   *Common Sense/guided*
185 And maked° me sykeren° hym sitthen° to seruen° hym for   *made/promise/then/serve/ever*
    euere,°
Boþe to sowe° and to setten° þe whyle ich swynke° myghte,   *sow/plant/work*
With-ynne and with-oute to wayten° hus profyt.   *guard*
Ich haue yben° his folwer° al þes° fourty wynter,°   *been/follower/these/winters*
And serued treuthe sothlyche° somdel to paye;°   *truly/to his satisfaction*
190 In alle kynne craftes° þat he couthe deuyse°   *kinds (of) work/devise*
Profitable to þe plouh he putte me to lerne;°   *learning*
And þauh° ich seye hit° my-self ich seruede° hym to paye.°   *though/say it/served/to his*
    satisfaction

Ich haue myn hyre° of hym wel and oþer whyle° more;   *my wages/sometimes*
He ys þe most prest paiere° þat eny poure° man knoweth.   *ready payer/any poor*
195 He with-halt non hewe hus° hyre ouere euen;°   *witholds (from) no servant his/*
    over evening

He ys louh° as a lombe° and leel° of hus tonge,°   *humble/lamb/honest/tongue*
And ho so° wilneþ° to wyte° wher þat treuthe° wonyeþ,   *whoever/wishes/know/Truth*
Ich wol wissen ȝow° wel ryght to hus place."   *will guide you*
"Ȝe, leue peers,"° quaþ þo° pylgrymes, and profrede° peers   *yea, dear Piers/those/offered/*
    mede.°   *reward*
200 "Nay, by þe peril of my soule," peers gan swere,°   *did swear*
"Ich nolde° fonge° a ferthing,° for seynt Thomas shryne!   *would not/receive/farthing*
Were it told to treuthe þat ich toke mede,
He wolde louye° me þe lasse° a longe tyme after.   *would love/less*

Alta Uia ad Fidelitatem Est Observatio X Preceptorum,
Ut Dicit Petrus Plouhman

Ac° who so wol wende° þer as° treuthe dwelleþ,   *but/go/where*
205 This ys þe heye weye° þyderwarde,° wyteþ wel þe soþe.°   *highway/there/truth*
Ȝe most gon þorwe meknesse,° alle men and wommen,   *must go through Meekness*
Tyl ȝe come to conscience, knowen of° God selue,°   *known by/himself*

Heading. *Hic . . . Plouhman:* "Here first appears Peter Plowman.

201. *seynt Thomas shryne:* that of Saint Thomas à Becket at Canterbury.

Heading. *Alta . . . Plouhman:* "'The highway to Truth is to follow the Ten Commandments,' thus says Piers Plowman."

That ȝe loue hym as lord leelliche a-bouen° alle;   *honestly above*
That ys to seye sothliche ȝe sholde° raþer deye°   *should/die*
210 Than eny dedliche° synne do for drede oþer° for preyere.°   *deadly/fear or/prayer*

     .   .   .   .   .

270 Ther ben seuene sustres° that seruen treuthe euere,   *are seven sisters*
And aren° porters at posternes° þat to þe place longen;°   *are/gates/belong*
Þat on° hatte° abstinence and humilite° anoþer,   *one/is called/Humility*
Charite° and chastite° ben hus chef maydenes,°   *Charity/Chastity/chief maidens*
Pacience° and pees° muche puple helpen,°   *Patience/Peace/(the) people help*
275 Largenesse° þat lady lat° yn ful menye;°   *Generosity/lets/very many*
Non° of hem° alle helpe may yn betere,°   *none/them/(more to get) in better*
For hue paieþ° for prisons° in places and in peynes.°   *she pays (ransom)/prisoners/ troubles*

And ho° is sybbe° to þuse° seuene, so me God helpe!   *whoever/akin/these*
He is wondirlich° welcome and fayre vndirfonge.°   *wonderfully/well received*
280 Ho is not sib° to þese seuene, sothly° to telle,   *akin/truly*
Hit is ful hard, by myn heued° eny of ȝou alle   *head*
To geten ingang° at eny gate bote grace° be þe more."°   *get entrance/unless mercy/greater*
"By cryst," quath° a kitte-pors,° "ich° haue no kyn þere."   *said/cutpurse/I*
"Ne° ich," quath an apewarde,° "by ouht þat ich knowe!"   *nor/ape keeper/anything*
285 "Wyte° God," quaþ a wafrestre,° "wist ich° þe soþe,   *defend/wafer maker/if I knew*
Ich wolde no forþer° a fot° for no freres prechinge."°   *would (go) not further/foot/friar's preaching*

"Ȝus,"° quaþ peers plouhman,° and pokede° hem alle to goode;   *yes/Plowman/urged*
"Mercy is a mayde þere hath° myght ouer hem alle;   *(who) has*
And hue is sybbe to alle synful° and hure sone° boþe.   *sinful (people)/her son*
290 And þorwe þe help of hem two, hope þow non° oþer,   *(need) hope you (for) no*
Thow myght gete grace ther so° þow go by° tyme."   *if/in*
"Ȝe, villam emi," quaþ on, "and now most ich þudere,°   *(go) there*
To loke° how me° lykeþ hit"° and tok° hus leue at° peers.   *see/I/it/took/leave of*
Anoþer a-non ryght° nede seyde° he hadde   *immediately/need said*
295 To folwen fif ȝokes;° "For-thy° me by-houeþ°   *follow five yoke (of oxen)/therefore/ need*

To gon with a good wil and greiþliche° hem dryue;°   *quickly/drive*
For-þy ich praye ȝow,° peers, paraunter,° yf ȝe metcþ°   *you/perhaps/you meet*
Treuthe,° telleþ to hym þat ich be excused."   *Truth*
Thenne was þer on heihte actif,° an hosebounde° he semed;°   *called Active/husband/seemed*

---

270. *seuene sustres:* seven Christian Virtues to oppose the Seven Deadly Sins.

277. *paieþ for prisons:* i.e., "ransoms prisoners."

292. *villam emi:* "I have bought a piece of ground" (Luke 14:18).

294–98. Luke 14:19.
299–305. Luke 14:20.

300 "Ich haue ywedded° a wyf,"° quaþ he, "wel wantowen° of   *wedded/wife/very wanton/behavior*
     maners;°
   Were ich seuenyght° fro° hure syghte synnen° hue wolde,   *seven nights/from/sin*
   And loure° on me and lyghtliche° chide and seye° ich loue   *scowl/readily/say*
     anoþere.
   For-þy, peers° plouhman, ich praye þe° telle hit treuthe,   *Piers/you*
   Ich may nat° come for a kytte so hue cleueþ° on me;   *not/clings*
305   *Vxorem duxi, et ideo non possum uenire.*"
   Quaþ contemplacion, "By crist, thauh° ich care suffre,°   *though/sorrow (may) suffer*
   Famyn and defaute,° folwen ich wolle° peers;   *poverty/will*
   Ac° þe wey° ys so wyckede° bote ho so° hadde a gyde°   *but/way/bad/one/guide*
   Þat myght folwen ous ech° fot for drede° of mys-tornynge."°   *accompany us each/fear/wrong*
                                                                    turning

from C PASSUS IX

Piers Guides the People

   Tho seyde perken **plouhman,**° "by seynt° peter of rome,   *then said Peterkin Plowman/Saint*
   Ich° haue an half acre to eren° by þe hye weye.°   *I/plow/high way*
   Hadde ich ered þat half acre and sowen hit° after,   *planted it*
   Ich wolde wende° with ȝow° and þe wey teche."°   *would go/you/teach*
5 "That were a long lettynge,"° quaþ a lady in a skleire,°   *wait/said/veil*
   "What sholde° we wommen worche° þe whiles?"°   *should/do/in the meantime*
   "Ich praye ȝow, for ȝoure profit," quaþ peers° to þe ladyes,   *Piers*
   "Þat somme sewe þe sak° for° shedynge° of þe whete;°   *sack/to prevent/spilling/wheat*
   And þe worþly° wommen with ȝoure longe fyngres,   *you worthy*
10 Þat ȝe on selke° and sendel sewen,° whenne tyme ys,°   *silk/sendal sew/you have*
   Chesybles° for chapelayns,° churches to honoure.   *chasubles/chaplains*
   Wyues° and widowes wolle° and flax spynneþ;   *wives/wool*
   Conscience consaileþ° ȝow cloþ for to make   *advises*
   For profit of þe poure° and plesaunce° of ȝow-selue.°   *poor/pleasure/yourselves*
15 For ich shal lene hem lyflode° bote yf° þe lond° faile,   *give them sustenance/unless/land*
   As longe as ich lyuc° for oure lordes loue in heuene.°   *live/heaven*
   And alle manere° men þat by þis molde buþ susteyned,°   *kinds (of)/earth are supported*
   Helpeþ hem to worche wyghtly° þat wynneþ ȝoure fode."°   *work vigorously/food*
   "By cryst," quaþ a knyȝt þo,° "he kenneþ ous° þe beste;   *knight then/teaches us*
20 Ac° on þe teeme trewely tauht° was ich neuere;°   *but/ team (of oxen) truly taught/*
                                                                    never

---

304. *kytte:* i.e., his wife; Kit happens to be the name of Will's   **10.** *sendel:* Sendal was a thin silken stuff.
wife.   **11.** *Chesybles:* A chasuble was a sleeveless outer vestment worn
305. "I have married a wife, and therefore I cannot come."   by the chaplain when celebrating mass.
(Luke 14:20).

Ich wolde ich couthe,"° quaþ þe knyȝt, "by cryst and hus
    moder;° — *knew/his mother*
Ich wolde a-saye° som tyme for solas,° as hit were." — *try/amusement*
"Sykerliche,° syre knyȝt," seide° peers þenne, — *surely/said*
"Ich shal swynke° and swete° and sowe for us boþe, — *work/sweat*
25 And laboure for þe° while þou lyuest al þy lyf-tyme,° — *you/lifetime*
In couenaunt° þat þou kepe° holy kirke° and my-selue° — *with the agreement/guard/church/ myself*

Fro wastours° and wyckede men þat þis worlde struen.° — *from wasters/destroy*
And go honte hardiliche to° hares and to foxes, — *hunt vigorously for*
To bores° and to bockes° þat brekeþ a-doune menne hegges;° — *boars/bucks/break down men's hedges*

30 And faite° þy faucones° to culle° wylde foules;° — *tame/falcons/kill/birds*
For þei comen° to my croft° my corn to defoule."° — *come/field/despoil*
Corteysliche° þe knyȝt þen comsede° þese wordes: — *courteously/began*
"By my power, peers, ich plyghte° þe my treuthe,° — *pledge/word*
To defende þe in faith fyghte þauh° ich sholde."° — *though/might (have to)*
35 "And ȝut on° poynt," quaþ peers, "ich praye ȝow ouermore;° — *yet one/besides*
Loke° ȝe tene° no tenaunt bote yf treuth wolle° assente. — *see (that)/harm/Truth will*
Whenne ȝe amercyn eny° man let mercy be taxour,° — *fine any/assessor*
And meknesse° þy maister° maugre° mede chekes.° — *Meekness/master/in spite of/Meed's influence*

Þauh poure men profre° ȝou presentes and ȝiftes,° — *offer/gifts*
40 Nym° hit nat,° an aunter° thow mowe° hit nat deserue; — *take/not/perhaps/you may*
For þow shalt ȝulde,° so may° be, and somdel a-bygge.° — *repay/(it) may/somewhat (more) pay*
Mys-beede nouht° þy bondemen,° þe bet° may þou spede;° — *injure not/serfs/better/prosper*
Þauh he be here þyn° vnderling, in heuene, paraunter,° — *your/perhaps*
He worth° raþer receyued° and reuerentloker° sette;° — *will be/sooner accepted/more reverently/placed*

45   *Amice, ascende superius.*
At churche in þe charnel cheorles aren vuel° to knowe,° — *laborers are hard/distinguish*
Oþer a knyght fro a knaue° oþer a queyne° fro a queene. — *or/servant/prostitute*
Hit° by-comeþ° to a knyght to be curteys° and hende,° — *it/is becoming/courteous/gracious*
Trewe° of hys tonge,° tales loth° to huyre,° — *true/tongue/loath/hear*
50 Bote° þei be of bounte,° of batailes° and of treuthe.° — *unless/goodness/battles/truth*
Hald° nat of harlotes,° huyre nat here° tales, — *hold with/ribalds/their*
Nameliche atte mete° suche men eschewe;° — *especially at meals/avoid*
Hit ben° þe deueles disours° to drawe men to synne. — *they are/Devil's storytellers*
Contreplede° nat conscience ne° holy kirke ryghtes." — *oppose/nor*
55 "Ich° assente, by seynt Gyle,"° seyde° þe knyght þenne, — *I/Saint Giles/said*
"For to worche by þy witt,° and my wyf boþe."° — *wisdom/wife also*

---

45. "Friend, go up higher" (Luke 14:10).　　**46.** *charnel:* the bone house, where the dead are kept.

"Ich shal aparaile me," quaþ perkyn,° "in pylgrymes wyse,°   *dress myself|said Peterkin|like a pilgrim*

And wende° with alle þo° þat wolle lyue° in treuthe."   *go|those|live*
He caste on hym hus° cloþes of alle kynne craftes,°   *himself his|manner (of) kinds*
⁶⁰ Hus cokeres° and hus cuffes° as kynde witt° hym tauhte,°   *stockings|mittens|common sense|taught*

And heng° hus hoper° on hus hals° in stede° of a scrippe;°   *hung|seed basket|neck|place|bag*
A boussel° of bred-corn° brouht° was þer-ynne.   *bushel|bread corn|brought*
"For ich wolle sowe° hit my-self and sitthe wol y-wende°   *plant|then will go*
To pylgrimages, as palmers don,° pardon to wynne.   *do*
⁶⁵ My plouh-fot° shal be my pyk-staf° and picche a° two þe rotes,°   *plow foot|pikestaff|cut in|roots*
And help my culter° to kerue° and clanse° þe forwes.°   *plowshare|cut|clear|furrows*
And alle þat helpen° me to erye° oþer elles° to weden,°   *help|plow|else|weed*
Shal haue leue,° by oure lorde to go and glene° after,   *permission|glean*
And make hym murye þer-myd° maugre ho by-grucche.°   *themselves merry therewith|(him) who grumbles*

⁷⁰ And alle kynne° crafty° men þat conne° lyue in treuthe,   *kinds (of)|skillful|can*
Ich shal fynde hem fode° þat feythfullech lybben;°   *them food|faithfully live*
Saf Iack° þe Iogelour° and Ionette° of þe styues,°   *except Jack|juggler|Janet|brothel*
And danyel þe dees-pleyere° and denote° þe baude,°   *dice player|Denot|bawd*
And al-so frere faytour° and folke of þat order,   *Friar Deceiver*
⁷⁵ Þat lollers° and loseles for leel° men halden,°   *vagabonds|profligates as honest|hold*

And Robyn þe rybaudour° for hus rusty° wordes.   *tale teller|obscene*
For treuthe° tolde me ones° and bade me telle hit forthere,°   *Truth|once|further*
Deleantur de libro uiuencium. Ich sholde° nat dele° with hem,   *should|deal*
For holy churche hoteþ° of hem to aske no tythe,   *commands*
⁸⁰   *Quia cum iustis non scribantur.*
Thei ben ascaped good aunter° now **God hem amende!**"   *have escaped (payment by) good luck*

. . . . .

Now perkyn with þe pilgrimes to þe plouh° is faren;°   *plow|gone*
To eryen° hus half aker, holpen° hym menye.°   *plow|acre, helped|many*
Dykers° and deluers diggeden° vp þe balkes;°   *ditchers|diggers dug|unplowed land*
Ther-with was perkyn apayed° and paied wel here hyre.°   *pleased|wages*
¹²⁰ Oþer werkmen° þer were þat wrouhten ful ȝurne;°   *workmen|worked very earnestly*
Eche° man in hus manere° made hym-self to done;°   *each|manner|do*
And somme° to plese° perkyn, pykede° aweye° þe wedes.°   *some|please|picked|away|weeds*

---

60. *cokeres:* Cockers were stockings without feet, or possibly also short boots worn by countrymen.

65–66. The plow foot was a metal stick which raised or lowered the colter or plowshare.

78. *Deleantur . . . uiuencium:* "Let them be blotted out from the book of the living" (Vulgate, Ps. 68:29).

80. "And let them not be inscribed with the just" (ibid.).

Atte hye° pryme peers° let þe plouh stonde,° — *high/Piers/stand*
And ouer-seyh° hem hym-self ho so° best wrouhte; — *looked over/whoever*
125 He sholde be hyred þer-after when heruest-tyme come.° — *harvest time came*
Þenne seten° some and songen atten° ale, — *sat/sang/at*
And holpen to erie° þis half acre with "Hoy! troly! lolly!" — *plow*
Quath peers þe plouhman al in pure tene,° — *vexation*
"Bote 3e° aryse þe raþere° and rape 3ow° to worche,° — *unless you/quicker/hasten/work*
130 Shal no greyn° þat here groweþ gladen 3ow° at neede; — *grain/cheer you*
And þauh° 3e deye° for deul° þe deuel haue þat recche!"° — *though/die/grief/Devil take (him) that cares*

Tho° were faitours aferede° and feynede hem° blynde, — *then/shirkers afraid/feigned themselves*

And leyden here° legges a-lyry° as suche lorelles° conneþ,° — *laid their/across/rascals/know how*
And maden° here mone° to peers how þei mowe nat° worche: — *made/complaint/could not*
135 "Ac° we prayeþ for 3ow, peers, and for 3oure plouh boþe, — *but*
Þat God for hus° grace 3oure grayn multiplie, — *of his*
And 3elde° 3ow of 3oure almesse° þat 3e 3euen° us here. — *repay/alms/give*
We may nayþer swynke ne swete° suche syknesse ous ayleþ;° — *neither work nor sweat/sickness us ails*

We haue none lymes° to laborie° with, lord God we þonkeþ."° — *no limbs/labor/thank*
140 "3oure praiers,"° quath° peers "and° 3e parfit° were, — *prayers/said/if/righteous*
Myght help, as ich° hope; ac hye treuthe wolde° — *I/would*
Þat no faiterye° were founde in° folk þat gon a-begged.° — *deception/among/go begging*
3e ben wastours,° ich wot° wel, þat wasten° and deuouren° — *are wasters/know/waste/devour*
Þat leel land tylynge° men leelliche° byswynken.° — *what honest farming/faithfully/ work for*

145 Ac treuthe shal teche° 3ow hus teeme° for to dryue,° — *teach/team/drive*
Oþer° 3e shulle etc barliche brede° and of þe brok° drynke, — *or/shall eat barley bread/brook*
Bote° 3e be° blynde oþer brokelegged° oþer bolted° with yren.° — *unless/are/broken legged/fettered/ iron (chains)*

Suche poure,"° quaþ peers, "shullen partye° with my goodes, — *poor/shall share*
Boþe of my corn and of my cloþ, to kepe hem fro defaute;° — *guard them from want*
150 Ancres° and heremites° þat eten bote° at nones,° — *anchorites/hermits eat only/noon*
And freres° þat flateren° nat and poure folke syke,° — *friars/flatter/sick*
What!° ich and myne wolleþ° fynde hem þat hem° needeþ." — *lo/will/they*

. . . . . .

"Now, by crist," quaþ peers, "y° shal apeyre° 3ow alle!" — *I/punish*
And hopede° after hunger þat herde° him at þe ferste.° — *called loudly/heard/immediately*

---

123. *Atte hye pryme:* Prime was 6–9 A.M.; high prime was 9 A.M., the traditional hour of the morning snack for farmhands. In Switzerland this repast is called *z'nüni* (German *zum neun*), "for the nine o'clock."

150. Anchorites and hermits fast, eating only once a day (cf. above, p. 706, l. 384n).

152. In the passage that follows, omitted here, Waster and a "Britoner" (cf. below, l. 177n) refuse to work and start a fight; Piers is angered.

"Ich praye þe,"° quath peers þo,° "pur charite,° sire honger,°   *you|then|for charity|Hunger*
Awreke° me of° þese wastours for þe knyght wol° nat."   *avenge|on|will*
175 Honger hente° in haste wastour by þe mawe°   *caught|stomach*
And wrang° hym by þe wombe° þat° al waterede hus eyen.°   *twisted|belly|so that|eyes*
He buffated° þe brutener° a-boute þe chekes,°   *buffeted|Britoner|cheeks*
Þat he loked lyk° a lanterne al hus lyf° after.   *looked like|life*
He bet° hem so boþe he barst neih hure° guttes,   *beat|burst almost their*
180 Ne hadde° peers° with a peese-lof° prayede hym by-leue.°   *had not|Piers|loaf of peas|(to) stop*
"Honger, haue mercy of hem," quath peers, "and let me ȝeue°   *give|beans*
    hem benes;°
And þat was bake° for bayarde° may be here bote."°   *baked|(i.e., the horse)|remedy*
Tho were faitours a-fered° and flowen° to peersses bernes,°   *afraid|flew|Piers's barns*
And flapten° on with flailes fro morwe° til euene,°   *struck|morning|evening*
185 Þat honger was nat hardy° on hem for to loke.   *eager*
For a potful of potage° þat peersses wyf° made,   *soup|wife*
An hep° of eremites henten° hem spades,   *crowd|hermits seized*
Spitten° and spradde donge° in despit of° hunger.   *dug|spread dung|to spite*
Thei coruen° here copes and courtepies° hem made,   *cut|(into) jackets*
190 And wenten° as workmen to weden° and mowen;°   *went|weed|mow*
Al for drede° of here deþ° suche dyntes ȝaf° hunger.   *fear|their death|blows gave*
Blynde and brokeleggede he botnede° a þousande,   *cured*
And lame men he lechede° with longen° of bestes.°   *healed|lungs|beasts*
Preestes and oþer peple° to peers þei drowen,°   *people|came*
195 And freres of alle fyue° orders al for fere° of hunger.   *five|fear*
For þat þat° was bake for bayarde was bote for menye° hungry,   *which|many*
Drosenes° and dregges drynke for menye beggeres.°   *lees|beggars*
Þer was no lad þat lyuede° þat ne lowede hym° to peers,   *lived|not humbled himself*
To be hus hole hewe þauh° he hadde no more   *his complete servant though*
200 Bute lyf-lode° for hus labour and hus loue at nones.   *except food*
Tho was peers ful° proude and putte hem alle to werke,°   *very|work*
In daubyng° and in deluyng, in donge a-feld° berynge,°   *plastering|to the fields|carrying*
In þresshynge, in þecchynge,° in thwytynge° of pynnes,   *thatching|cutting*
And alle kynne trewe° craft þat man couthe deuyse.°   *kinds (of) true|could devise*
205 Was° no beggere so bolde, bote yf° he blynde were,   *(there) was|unless*
Þat dorst with-sitte þat° peeres seyde° for fere of syre hunger.   *dared oppose what|said*
And peers was proud þer-of and putte hem° alle to swynke,°   *them|work*
And ȝaf hem mete° and monye° as þey myght deseruen.°   *food|money|deserve*
Tho hadde peers pite° of alle poure puple,°   *pity|poor people*

---

177. *brutener:* an inhabitant of Brittany, a loud, swaggering fellow, a term of reproach growing out of the French wars.

180–82. Bayarde was a common name for horses, which were fed bread made of beans and peas; poor people sometimes could afford only horse bread. Hound bread was made from the chippings of trencher bread, the thick round bread which served as plates for meat in noble households and which was given to beggars at the end of the meal. The average person ate brown bread. The finest white wheat was used to make the soft *paindemain* or wastel bread which Chaucer's Prioress fed to her dogs.

195. *fyue ordres:* Cf. above, p. 679, l. 58*n*, and p. 688, l. 111*n*.

210 And bad° hunger in haste hyhe° out of contre°　*bade/hurry/country*
 Home in-to his owen erthe° and halde hym° þer euere°—　*own land/stay/ever*
 "For ich° am wel awreke° of wastours þorw° þy myghte.　*I/avenged/wasters through*
 Ac° ich praye þe,"° quaþ° peers, "hunger, er þow wende,°　*but/you/said/before you go*
 Of° beggers and of bydders° what best be° to done?°　*about/mendicants/is/do*
215 For ich wot° wel, be þou° went, worche° þei wolle° ful ylle;°　*know/if you are/gone, work/will/ poorly*

 Meschief hit° makeþ thei ben° so meke nouthe,°　*misfortune it/(that) they are/meek now*

 And for defaute° þis folke folwen° my hestes.°　*out of need/follow/commands*
 Hit is no þyng° for loue thei labour þus faste,　*not at all*
 Bote° for fere of famyn, in faith," seide° peers;　*but/said*
220 "Ys° no final° loue with þis folke for al here faire speche;°　*(there) is/complete/speech*
 And hit° ben my blody broþren° for **God bouhte**° vs alle.　*they/blood brothers/redeemed*
 Treuthe tauhte° me ones° to louye° hem echone,°　*Truth taught/once/love/each one*
 And helpen° hem of° alle þyng ay° as hem nedeþ.°　*help/in/things ever/they need*
 Now wolde° ich wite, or° þow wentest,° what were þe beste,　*would/know, before/go*
225 How ich myghte a-maistren° hem to louye and laboure　*compel*
 For here lyflode;° lere° me, syre hunger."　*sustenance/teach*
 "Now herkne,"° quaþ hunger, "and hold° hit for° a wysdome;°　*listen/regard/as/truth*
 Bolde **beggeres** and bygge° þat mowe° here bred° byswynke,°　*strong/may/bread/work for*
 With houndes° bred and hors-bred helc hem° when þei hungren,°　*hound/heal themselves/hunger*
230 And a-bane° hem with benes° for° bollynge° of here wombe.°　*poison/beans/to prevent/swelling/ stomach*

 And yf þe gromes grucche° bid hem go swynke,　*men grumble*
 And he shal soupe° þe swettere° when he hath deserued.°　*sup/sweeter/deserved (it)*
 And yf þow fynde eny° folke wham° false men han apaired,°　*any/whom/have harmed*
 Comforte hem with þy catel° for so comaundeþ° treuthe;　*goods/commands*
235 Loue hem and lene° hem so° lawe of kynde wolde;°　*give to/as/nature would (have you)*
  Alter alterius onera portate.
 And alle manere° men þat þow myght aspye°　*manner (of)/spy*
 In meschief oþer° in mal-ese and° þow mowe hem helpe,　*or/disease if*
 Loke° by þy lyf° let hem nouht for-fare.°　*see/life/not perish*
240 Yf þow hast wonne ouht wickeliche wisliche dispende° hit;　*anything wickedly wisely spend*
  Facite uobis amicos de mammona iniquitatis."

   .   .   .   .   .

 "By seynt° paul," quath peers þo,° "thou poyntest neih° þe treuthe,　*Saint/Piers then/near*
 And leelly seist,° as ich leue,° lord þe for-ȝelde!°　*honestly speak/believe/repay*

229–30. Cf. ll. 180–82n.
236. "Bear ye one another's burdens" (Gal. 6:2).

241. "Make to yourselves friends of the mammon of unrighteousness" (Luke 16:9).

Wend now whenne þou wolt° and wel be þow euere,   *will*
310 For þow hast wel ywroke° me and also wel ytauht° me."   *avenged/taught*
"Ich by-hote° þe," quaþ hunger, "þat hennes° nel° ich wende   *promise/hence/will not*
Er ich haue y-dyned by° þys day and y-dronke° boþe!"   *dined on/drunk*
"Ich haue no peny,"° quath peers, "polettes° for to bigge,°   *penny/chickens/buy*
Noþer goos noþer grys bote° two grene° cheses,°   *neither geese nor pigs except/(i.e.,*
                                                                       new)/cheeses

315 A fewe croddes° and creyme° and a cake of otes,°   *curds/cream/oats*
And bred for my barnes° of benes and of peses.°   *children/peas*
And ʒut ich sey,° by my saule,° ich haue no salt bacon;   *yet I say/soul*
Nouht a cokeney,° by cryst, colhoppes° to make,   *egg/collops*
Ac° ich haue porett-plontes, perselye° and scalones,°   *but/leeks, parsley/scallions*
320 Chiboles° and chiruylles° and chiries sam-rede,°   *small onions/chervils/cherries half-*
                                                                       ripe

And a cow with a calf and a cart mare,
To drawe a feld° my donge° þe whyle drouth° lasteþ.   *into the field/dung/drought*
By þis lyflode we mote lyue° tyl lammasse tyme;   *must live*
And by þat,° ich hope to haue heruest° in my crofte;°   *that (time)/harvest/field*
325 Thenne may I dyghte° þy dyner° as me° dere lykeþ."°   *prepare/dinner/I/please*
Alle þe poure puple þo peescoddes fetten;°   *poor people then peascods fetched*
Benes° and baken° apples thei brouhte° in here° lappes,   *beans/baked/brought/their*
And profrede° peers this present to plese° þer-with hunger.   *offered/please*
Hunger eet° al in haste and askede after more;   *ate*
330 Poure folke for fere° þo fedde hunger ʒerne°   *fear/eagerly*
With creym and with croddes, with carses° and oþer herbes.   *cresses*
By that yt neihed° heruest and newe corn com° to chepyng,°   *neared/came/market*
Thenne was þis folke feyn° and fedde hunger deynteuosliche,°   *pleased/sumptuously*
And gloton° þo with good ale gerte° hunger to slepe.°   *Glutton/made/sleep*
335 Tho wolde wastour nat worche bote° wandrede aboute,   *would Waster not work but*
Noþer beggere eete bred° þat benes were ynne,°   *beggar eat bread/in*
Bote° clerematyn and Coket and of clene whete;°   *only/pure wheat*
Thei wolde non halpeny° ale in none° wyse drynke,   *no half-penny/no way*
Bote of þe best and brounest° þat brewesters sellen.°   *darkest/alewives sell*
340 Laboreres þat han no londe° to lyuen° on bote here handes   *had/land/live*
Deyned noght° to dyne a day° nyght-olde wortes.°   *deigned not/daily/(on) night-old*
                                                                       vegetables

May no peny ale hem paye ne° a pece° of bacon,   *them please nor/piece*

---

314. *grene cheses:* New cheeses were still moist and cold.

316. Cf. ll. 180–82n. Skeat mentions an interesting list of prices for the year 1363, from Riley's *Memorials of London:* goose, 6d; pig, 8d; capon, 6d; hen, 4d; rabbit, 4d; roast goose, 7d—all of the best variety.

318. *colhoppes:* slices of salted and dried meat which were beaten and cooked.

323. *lammasse tyme:* i.e., August, (Lammas is lit. "Loaf Mass," a festival when bread made from the first harvest was blessed.)

337. Coket (the name refers to the stamp on the bread) was only slightly inferior to wastel bread; clerematyn was also of the finest variety.

338. *halpeny:* i.e., "thin" (cf. above, p. 700, ll. 222–23n.)

Bote hit° be freesch fleesch oþer° fysch fried oþer ybake,°   *unless it/fresh flesh or/baked*
And þat *chaud* and *pluschaud* for° chillyng of here mawe.°   *to prevent/belly*
345 Bote he be heyliche° yhyred elles° wol he chide,   *at high wages/hired else*
That he was a werkman ywroght waryen° þe tyme;   *workman created curse*
Corteis Catones consail comseth° he by-grucche,°   *courteous Cato's advice begins/(to) grumble at*

Paupertatis onus pacienter ferre memento.
And þenne he corseþ° þe kyng and alle þe kynges Iustices,°   *curses/judges*
350 Suche lawes to lere° laborers to greue.°   *make/vex*
Ac while hunger was here mayster° wolde non° chide,   *master/none*
Ne stryue a-ȝens° þe statute, he lokede° so sturne.°   *fight against/looked/stern*
Ac ich warne ȝow° werkmen, wynne° whyle ȝe mowe,°   *you/earn/you may*
For hunger hyderwardes° hyeþ hym° faste;   *hither/hurries*
355 He shal awake þorw° water° wasters to chaste.°   *through/(i.e., floods)/chasten*
Ar° fewe ȝeres° be fulfilled famyne shal aryse,   *before/years*
And so seith° *saturnus* and sent ȝow to warne.   *says*
Þorwe flodes° and foule wederes frutes shullen° faile,   *floods/weather fruits shall*
Pruyde° and pestilences shal muche puple fecche.°   *pride/bear away*
360 Thre shupes° and a shaft,° with an vm. folwyng,°   *three ships/arrow/following*
Shal brynge bane° and bataile° on bothe half þe mone.°   *death/battle/sides (of) the moon*
And þanne° shal deþ° with-drawe and derthe° be Iustice,   *then/(i.e., Black) Death/Famine*
And dawe þe deluere deye° for defaute,°   *ditcher die/hunger*
Bote God of hus° goodnesse graunte ous° a trewe.°   *his/grant us/truce*

from C PASSUS X

Piers Shows His Pardon

"Peers," quaþ° a prest þo,° "þy pardoune most ich rede,°   *Piers, said/priest then/must I read*
Ich can construen ech° worde and kenne hit þe° in englishe."   *decipher each/teach it (to) you*
290 And peers at hus preyere° þe pardon vnfolded,   *his request*
And ich by-hynde hem° boþe by-heeld° al þe bulle.   *behind them/beheld*
In two lynes hit lay and no lettere more,
And was ywryte ryght° þus in witnesse of treuthe.°   *written exactly/truth*
    Qui bona egerunt ibunt in uitam eternam :
295   *Qui uero mala, in ignem eternum.*

---

344. *chaud, pluschaud:* French, "hot," "hotter."

345–46. Edward III issued the Statute of Laborers after the pestilence of 1349, stating that wages were frozen and serfs had to stay on the land. The dearth of laborers had pushed wages sky-high, but the statute was ineffective; laborers took to the road, and the law of supply and demand ran its course.

347–48. Dionysius Cato was the supposed author of a four-volume work of the 4th century, *Disticha de Moribus ad Filium,* found in English, Latin, and French. Vol. 1, Distich 21, is here quoted: "Remember to bear the burden of poverty patiently."

357ff. Saturn's influence brings about disasters and calamity; a saturnine countenance is gloomy, foreboding, dark. William's mysterious riddling prophecy here, as were many in his time, is wrapped in obscurity; it has not been deciphered, though it may have been fulfilled.

362. *deþ:* Cf. above, p. 680, l. 84*n.*

294–95. "And these shall go away into everlasting punishment: but the righteous into life eternal" (Matt. 25:46).

"Peter!"° quaþ þe prest þo, "ich can no pardon fynde,   *by Saint Peter*
Bote° 'Do wel and haue wel and God shal haue þy saule,°   *except/soul*
Do vuel° and haue vuel and hope þow non° oþer   *evil/expect you none*
Bote° he þat vuel lyueþ° vuel shal ende!'"   *but that/lives*
300 The preest þus and perkyn of° þe pardon Iangled.°   *Peterkin about/argued*
Throgh° here° wordes ich awook° and waitede aboute,   *because of/their/awoke*
And seih° þe sonne° in þe south sitte þat° tyme.   *saw/sun/(at) that*
Meteles° and moneyles° on maluerne hulles,°   *without food/without money/hills*
Musynge on þis meteles° a myle-wey° ich ȝeode.°   *dream/mile/walked*
305 And meny° tymes this meteles made me to studie   *many*
Of þat° ich seih slepynge° yf hit so be myghte,   *what/sleeping*
And of peers plouhman ful pensyf° in herte,°   *plowman very pensive/heart*
And which° a pardon peers hadde the puple° to gladen,°   *what/people/cheer*
And how þe preest inpugned° hit thorwe° two propre° wordes.   *impugned/through/distinct*

·   ·   ·   ·   ·

---

309. *two propre wordes:* possibly a reference to "Dowel," the search for which by "Will" constitutes a theme of the "Vita" ("The Life of Dowel, Dobet, Dobest"), a second part of the whole work.

PEARL

DATE: 1380–1400. ◢ MANUSCRIPT: British Library. Cotton Nero A. x. The dialect is of the Northwest Midlands (South Lancashire or northwest of Derby). ◢ EDITIONS: Richard Morris, *Early English Alliterative Poems*, 2d ed., Early English Text Society, 1, (London, 1869); Charles G. Osgood, *The Pearl*, Belles Lettres Series (Boston, 1906); E. V. Gordon, *The Pearl* (Oxford, 1953). There is a translation by John Gardner, *The Complete Works of the Gawain-Poet, in a Modern Version with a Critical Introduction* (Chicago, 1965). Further bibliography of translations and critical studies may be found in A. C. Baugh and Kemp Malone, *The Middle Ages*, Vol. I of *A Literary History of England*, ed. A. C. Baugh, 2d ed., 4 vols. (New York, 1967).

The dialect of the Pearl Poet, that of the Northwest Midlands and of the Alliterative Revival, has Northern as well as Midland features and several peculiar spelling characteristics (1) *Qu* is often written for *wh* (*quo* = *who*, *quen* = *when*, *quyte* = *white*). There should be no confusion with the oft-cited word *quene*, "queen," however. (2) Final *tz* and *z* normally stand for *s* (*watz* = *was*, *dotz* = *does*, *hatz* = *has*, *nedez* = *needs*, *spysez* = *spices*) and medial *ȝ* stands for *gh* (*oȝt* = *ought*, *bryȝt* = *bright*); initial *ȝ* is pronounced like consonantal *y*. (3) The usual interchange of the letters *v* and *w* with *u* is also prevalent here (*fortwne* = *fortune*, *trwe* = *true*). (4) Final *-i/-ie* is often written *e* (*cortayse*). (5) A West Midland characteristic is the final *b, d, g*, often written *p, t, k* (*lamp* = *lamb*, *justyfyet* = *justified*, *nothynk* = *nothing*). (6) The student should recognize the pronouns *ho*, "she," *hem*, "them," "themselves," and *her*, "their," when they occur. (7) The Pearl Poet uses the auxiliary verb *con* for "did" and the adverb *ful* for "very."

The Pearl Poet (whose works, which are found in one MS. by the same hand, include four poems: *Pearl, Purity* or *Cleanness, Patience*, and *Sir Gawain and the Green Knight*) wrote in the style of the northern Alliterative Revival of the late 14th century. The *Pearl* is one of the most technically perfect poems of Middle English literature as regards prosody, rhyme scheme, and the linking of stanzas through rhyming words. An analysis of the plan would prove an interesting exercise in versification for the student. More than this, the *Pearl* shows the most intense poetic confession of grief, of loss, and of final spiritual hope that we find in an age known for its mystical fervor. Thus some readers see the poem as a consolation and the Pearl as representing salvation. According to most accepted interpretations, the narrator has lost a two-year-old daughter, his Pearl. His mood is yearningly sad, though not bitter. His elegy is in the form of a dream vision, an allegory which shows him on the brink of Carlyle's "Everlasting Nay." Through a kind of lyric therapy he brings himself, at the end, toward the "Everlasting Yea." This very personal quality in the poem involves the reader powerfully.

I

Perle plesaunte° to prynces paye,° *pleasing/delight*
To clanly clos° in golde so clere,° *very neatly set/bright*
Oute of oryent I hardyly° saye, *boldly*
Ne proued° I neuer her precios pere,° *not knew/precious peer*
5 So rounde, so reken° in vche araye,° *beautiful/every setting*
So smal, so smoþe° her sydez were. *smooth*
Quere-so-euer° I Iugged° gemmez gaye,° *wherever/judged/bright*
I sette hyr sengeley° in synglure;° *her apart/as unique*
Allas! I leste° hyr in on erbere,° *lost/an arbor*
10 Þurȝ gresse° to grounde hit fro° me yot;° *through grass/it from/went*
I dewyne for-dolked of luf daungere,° *pine grief-stricken (because) of love's power*

Of° þat pryuy° perle with-outen° spot. *for/my own/without*
    Syþen° in þat spote° hit fro me sprange, *since/spot*
Ofte haf° I wayted wyschande° þat wele,° *have/watched longing (for)/good (one)*

15 Þat wont watz° whyle deuoyde° my wrange,° *used to/formerly relieve/sorrow*
And heuen° my happe° and al my hele.° *increase/happiness/welfare*
Þat dotz bot þrych° my hert þrange,° *only oppress/heart grievously*
My breste in bale° bot bolne° and bele.° *sorrow/swell/burn*
Ȝet þoȝt° me° neuer so swete° a sange,° *seemed/to me/sweet/song*
20 As stylle stounde° let to me stele,° *moment/steal*
For-soþe° þer fleten° to me fele,° *truly/floated/many*
To þenke hir° color so clad in clot;° *think her/clod*
O moul° þou marreȝ° a myry iuele.° *earth/mar/goodly jewel*
My priuy perle with-outen spotte
25   Þat spot of spysez myȝt° nedez° sprede,° *with spices must/of necessity/(be) spread*

Þer° such rychez to rot is runnen;° *where/have gone*
Blomez blayke° and blwe° and rede,° *blooms yellow/blue/red*
Þer schynez ful schyr agayn° þe sunne. *very bright under*
Flor° and fryte° may not be fede,° *flower/fruit/faded*
30 Þer hit doun drof° in moldez dunne,° *dropped/earth brown*
For vch gresse mot° grow of° graynez dede,° *must/from/dead*
No whete° were ellez° to wonez wonne;° *wheat/else/barns brought*
Of goud° vche goude is ay by-gonne.° *good/ever begun*
So semly° a sede moȝt fayly° not, *fair/seed may fail*
35 Þat spryngande° spycez vp ne sponne,° *growing/come*
Of þat precios perle wyth-outen spotte.

---

2. The Pearl is evidently set in gold, here literally.

5–6. Lines such as these have led editors to identify the Pearl with a young girl, and later verses strengthen this conclusion.

31. Cf. John 12:24–25: "Except a corn of wheat fall into the ground and die, it abideth alone: but if it die, it bringeth forth much fruit." The grains only seem dead and withered.

To þat spot þat I in speche expoun° — *speech discuss*
I entred in þat erber grene,
In augoste° in a hyȝ seysoun,° — *August/festival*
40 Quen° corne is coruen° wyth crokez kene.° — *when/cut/sickles sharp*
On huyle° þer perle hit trendeled° doun, — *mound/rolled*
Schadowed þis wortez° ful schyre and schene,° — *these plants/shining*
Gilofre, gyngure° and gromylyoun,° — *gillyflower, ginger/gromwell*
And pyonys powdered° ay by-twene.° — *peonies scattered/between*
45 Ȝif° hit watz semly on to sene,° — *as/look*
A fayr reflayr° ȝet fro hit flot,° — *scent/flowed*
Þer wonys° þat worþyly° I wot° and wene.° — *dwells/precious one/know/believe*
My precious perle, wyth-outen spot.
Bifore þat spot my honde° I spenned,° — *hands/clasped*
50 For care ful colde þat to° me caȝte;° — *on/seized*
A deuely dele° in my hert denned,° — *dreary grief/lurked*
Þaȝ resoun° sette my seluen° saȝte.° — *though reason/self/at peace*
I playned° my perle þat þer watz spenned° — *mourned/imprisoned*
Wyth fyrce skyllez° þat faste faȝte,° — *fierce doubts/obstinately struggled*
55 Þaȝ kynde° of kryst° me comfort kenned,° — *nature/Christ/taught*
My wreched° wylle in wo° ay wraȝte.° — *wretched/woe/suffered*
I felle vpon þat floury flaȝte,° — *flowery plot*
Suche odour to my hernez° schot; — *brains*
I slode vpon° a slepyng slaȝte,° — *slipped into/drowsy spell*
60 On° þat precios° perle with-outen° spot. — *on (account of)/precious/without*

II

Fro° spot my spyryt þer sprang in space,° — *from (the)/after a while*
My body on balke° þer bod° in sweuen,° — *earth/abode/sleep*
My goste° is gon in Godez grace, — *spirit*
In auenture° þer meruaylez meuen;° — *adventurous search/**marvels** occur*

65 I ne wyste° in þis worlde quere° þat hit wace,° — *not knew/where/it was*
Bot° I knew me° keste° þer klyfez cleuen;° — *only/myself/set down/cliffs cleave (the heavens)*

Towarde a foreste I bere° þe° face, — *turned/(i.e., my)*
Where rych rokkez° were to dyscreuen;° — *splendid rocks/be seen*
Þe lyȝt° of hem myȝt° no mon leuen,° — *light/them might/man believe*
70 Þe glemande° glory þat of hem glent;° — *gleaming/shone*
For wern° neuer webbez° þat wyȝez weuen° — *were/cloths/men weave*
Of half so dere adubmente.° — *glorious splendor*

39–40. *hyȝ seysoun:* Corn (wheat) was first cut by August 1 (Lammas), and this might be the feast that the poet is talking about. August 1 c. 1400 would correspond to our August 10, so that *hyȝ seysoun* could mean not only a feast day but also "high summer."

42. *Schadowed:* i.e., "cast a shadow."

Dubbed° wern alle þo downez° sydez — *arrayed/those hill*
With crystal klyffez so cler° of kynde, — *bright*
75 Holte-wodez bryȝt° aboute hem bydez° — *forests bright/stand*
Of bollez° as blwe° as ble° of ynde;° — *trunks/blue/hue/indigo*
As bornyst syluer° þe lef on° slydez, — *polished silver/leaves on (them)*
Þat þike con trylle° on vch a° tynde;° — *thick do rustle/every/branch*
Quen glem° of glodez agaynz° hem glydez, — *flash/light toward*
80 Wyth schymeryng schene ful schrylle þay schynde.° — *shimmering fair very bright they gleam*

Þe grauayl° þat on grounde con grynde° — *gravel/did crunch*
Wern precious perlez of oryente; —
Þe sunne bemez bot blo° and blynde,° — *beams (were) but dark/dim*
In respecte of° þat adubbement. — *compared to*
85   The adubbmente of þo downez dere
Garten° my goste al greffe for-ȝete.° — *made/grief forget*
So frech flauorez° of frytez° were, — *fresh fragrance/fruits*
As fode° hit con me fayre refete.° — *food/refresh*
Fowlez° þer flowen° in fryth° in fere,° — *birds/flew/forest/flocks*
90 Of flaumbande hwez,° boþe smale° and grete,° — *flaming colors/small/great*
Bot sytole° stryng and gyternere° — *even citole/gittern player*
Her reken myrþe moȝt° not retrete,° — *their gay song might/reproduce*
For quen° þose bryddez° her wyngez bete° — *when/birds/beat*
Þay songen° wyth a swete asent;° — *sang/sweet harmony*
95 So gracios gle couþe° no mon gete° — *pleasing joy could/get*
As here° and se° her adubbement. — *hear/see*
So al watz dubbet on° dere asyse;° — *in/fashion*
Þat fryth þer fortwne° forth me ferez,° — *fate/carries*
Þe derþe° þer-of for to deuyse° — *value/describe*
100 Nis° no wyȝ worþe° þat tonge berez.° — *(there) is not/man worthy/tongue has*
I welke ay° forth in wely wyse,° — *walk ever/happy manner*
No bonk° so byg þat did° me derez,° — *bank/caused/hindrances*
Þe fyrre° in þe fryth þe feier° con ryse° — *farther/fairer/grow*
Þe playn, þe plonttez,° þe spyse,° þe perez,° — *plants/spices/pear trees*
105 And rawez° and randez° and rych reuerez,° — *hedgerows/banks/river lands*
As fyldor° fyn° her bonkes brent.° — *gold thread/pure/glittered*
I wan° to a water by schore þat scherez,° — *came/meanders*
Lorde! dere watz hit° adubbement! — *its*
The dubbemente° of þo derworth depe° — *splendor/precious depths*
110 Wern° bonkez bene° of beryl bryȝt; — *were/fair*
Swangeande° swete þe water con swepe° — *swirling/sweep (by)*
Wyth a rownande rourde raykande aryȝt;° — *murmuring sound flowing straight*

---

91. The citole was a kind of guitar; the gittern was a wire-strung instrument like a guitar.

In° þe founce° þer stonden° stonez stepe,° *on/bottom/stood/bright*
As glente þur3° glas þat glowed and gly3t,° *as (if they) shone through/glistened*
115 As stremande sternez,° quen stroþe° men slepe,° *glittering stars/earthbound/sleep*
Staren° in welkyn° in wynter ny3t;° *shine/sky/night*
For vche a° pobbel° in pole° þer py3t° *every/pebble/pool/placed*
Watz Emerad, saffer, oþer° gemme gente,° *emerald, sapphire, or/noble*
Þat° alle þe lo3e lemed of ly3t,° *so that/deep shone with light*
120 So dere° watz hit adubbement.° *glorious/splendor*

III

The dubbement dere of doun° and dalez, *hills*
Of wod° and water and wlonk° playnez, *forest/lovely*
Bylde° in me blys,° abated my balez,° *raised/bliss/sorrows*
For-didden° my distresse, dystryed° my paynez. *vanquished/destroyed*
125 Doun after° a strem° þat dry3ly halez° *along/stream/strongly flows*
I bowed° in blys, bredful° my braynez; *turned/brimful*
Þe fyrre I fol3ed° þose floty° valez, *followed/watery*
Þe more strenghþe° of ioye myn herte° straynez, *power/joy my heart*
As fortune fares þer as° ho fraynez,° *wherever/she tests*
130 Wheþer solace ho sende oþer ellez sore,° *else sorrow*
Þe wy3 to wham° her wylle ho waynez° *whom/grants*
Hyttez° to haue ay more and more. *chances*
  More of wele° watz in þat wyse° *joy/guise*
Þen° I cowþe° telle þa3° I tom hade,° *than/could/though/time had*
135 For vrþely° herte my3t° not suffyse° *human/might/suffice*
To þe tenþe dole° of þo gladnez glade;° *part/that gladness joyful*
For-þy° I þo3t° þat paradyse *therefore/thought*
Watz þer ouer gayn þo° bonkez brade;° *opposite those/broad*
I hoped° þe water were a deuyse° *thought/division*
140 By-twene myrþez° by merez° made; *between delights/pools*
By-3onde° þe broke,° by slente° oþer slade,° *beyond/brook/slope/valley*
I hopede þat mote merked wore.° *(a) city situated were*
Bot° þe water watz depe,° I dorst° not wade, *but/deep/dared*
And euer me° longed ay° more and more. *I/always*
145   More and more, and 3et wel mare,° *still more*
Me lyste° to se° þe broke by-3onde, *wished/see*
For if hit° watz fayr þer° I con fare,° *it/where/did walk*
Wel loucloker° watz þe fyrre londe.° *lovelier/farther land*
Abowte me con I stote° and stare; *stand*
150 To fynde a forþe faste° con I fonde,° *ford diligently/try*

139–40. The river is the boundary between worldly, temporal joys and the eternal felicity of the spirit. The dreamer is in a countryside with cliffs of jewels and silver-leaved trees, untouched by seasonal changes. Some kind of earthly paradise may be intended, since the river can only be crossed in death.
142. *mote:* the New Jerusalem, which the dreamer sees later.

Bot woþez mo i-wysse° þer ware,° *perils more indeed/were*
Þe fyrre I stalked° by þe stronde,° *walked/shore*
And euer me þo3t I schulde° not wonde° *should/hesitate*
For wo,° þer welez so wynne° wore. *perils/delightful*

155 Þenne nwe note° me° com on honde° *new matter/to me/became evident*
Þat meued° my mynde ay° more and more. *stirred/ever*
   More meruayle° con my dom adaunt;° *marvels/reason daunt*
I se3° by-3onde þat myry° mere *saw/fair*
A crystal clyffe ful relusaunt;° *very shining*

160 Mony ryal° ray con fro° hit rere;° *many (a) royal/from/rise*
At þe fote° þer-of þer sete° a faunt,° *foot/sat/child*
A mayden of menske,° ful debonere;° *courtesy/gracious*
Blysnande whyt° watz hyr bleaunt,° *glistening white/her robe*
(I knew hyr wel, I hade sen° hyr ere)° *seen/before*

165 As glysnande° golde þat man con schere,° *glistening/one can cut*
So schon° þat schene an-vnder schore;° *shone/fair (one) below (the) shore*
On lenghe° I loked to° hyr þere; *a long time/looked at*
Þe lenger,° I knew hyr more and more. *longer*
   The more I frayste° hyr fayre face, *examined*

170 Her fygure fyn quen° I had fonte,° *delicate when/perceived*
Suche gladande° glory con to me glace,° *gladdening/come*
As lyttel byfore þerto° watz wonte;° *before then/accustomed*
To calle hyr lyste° con me enchace,° *desire/urge*
Bot baysment gef myn hert° a brunt° *amazement gave my heart/blow*

175 I se3 hyr in so strange a place,
Such a burre my3t° make myn herte blunt.° *blow might/dull*
Þenne verez ho° vp her fayre frount,° *lifts she/forehead*
Hyr vysayge° whyt as playn yuore,° *countenance/pure ivory*
Þat stonge° myn hert ful stray atount,° *stung/distractedly astonished*

180 And euer þe lenger, þe more and more.

IV

More þen° me lyste° my drede° aros. *than/desired/fear*
I stod° ful stylle and dorste° not calle. *stood/dared*
Wyth y3en° open and mouth ful clos,ᵛ *eyes/completely closed*
I stod as hende° as hawk in halle. *still*

185 I hoped° þat gostly° watz þat porpose;° *believed/mystical/significance*
I dred onende quat° schulde byfalle,° *feared concerning what/befall*
Lest ho me eschaped° þat I þer chos,° *escaped/sought*
Er I at steuen hir mo3t stalle.° *with voice her might stop*
Þat gracios gay with-outen galle,° *charming fair (one) without spot*

190 So smoþe,° so smal, so seme sly3t,° *smooth/becomingly slender*
Rysez vp in hir araye° ryalle, *robes*
A precios pyece° in perlez py3t.° *precious creature/adorned*
   Perlez py3te° of ryal prys,° *set/value*

Þere moȝt mon° by grace haf sene,° — *one/have seen*
195 Quen þat frech° as flor-de-lys° — *(one) fair/fleur-de-lis*
Doun þe bonke con boȝe by-dene.° — *bank did go quickly*
Al blysnande whyt watz hir beau biys,° — *fair linen*
Vpon° at sydez and bounden bene° — *open/trimmed splendidly*
Wyth þe myryeste margarys at° my deuyse,° — *fairest pearls in/opinion*
200 Þat euer I seȝ° ȝet with myn yȝen; — *saw*
Wyth lappez° large I wot° and I wene,° — *folds/know/believe*
Dubbed° with double perle and dyȝte,° — *arrayed/adorned*
Her cortel° of self sute schene,° — *gown/same material bright*
With precios perlez al vmbe-pyȝte.° — *adorned about*
205   A pyȝt coroune ȝet wer° þat gyrle, — *crown also wore*
Of mariorys° and non° oþer ston,° — *pearls/no/stone*
Hiȝe pynakled° of cler quyt° perle, — *high pinnacled/bright white*
Wyth flurted° flowrez perfet° vpon; — *figured/perfect*
To hed hade° ho non oþer werle.° — *on (her) head had/circlet*
210 Her here leke,° al hyr vmbe-gon,° — *hair enclosed/her encompassing*
Her semblaunt sade, for doc oþer° erle, — *face solemn, like duke or*
Her ble° more blaȝt° þen whallez bon;° — *color/white/whale bone*
As schorne° golde schyr° her fax° þenne schon,° — *cut/bright/hair/shone*
On schylderez° þat leghe vnlapped lyȝte;° — *shoulders/lay unbound lightly*
215 Her depe° colour ȝet wonted non° — *intense/lacked none (of the color)*
Of precios perle in porfyl° pyȝte, — *embroidery*
    Pyȝt watz poyned° and vche a° hemme, — *wristband/each*
At honde,° at sydez, at ouerture,° — *hand/opening*
Wyth whyte perle and non oþer gemme,
220 And bornyste° quyte watz hyr uesture.° — *polished/garment*
Bot° a wonder° perle with-outen wemme° — *but/wondrous/flaw*
In myddez° hyr breste watz sette so sure; — *middle (of)*
A mannez dom° moȝt dryȝly° demme,° — *man's judgment/greatly/be baffled*
Er° mynde moȝt malte in° hit mesure;° — *before/comprehend/its value*
225 I hope° no tong° moȝt endure° — *believe/tongue/suffice*
No sauerly saghe say° of þat syȝt,° — *appropriate word (to) say/sight*
So watz hit clene° and cler and pure, — *it bright*
Þat precios perle þer° hit watz pyȝt. — *where*
    Pyȝt in perle, þat precios pyese° — *creature*
230 On wyþer half° water com° doun þe schore. — *opposite side (of the)/came*
No gladder gome° heþen° in to grece° — *man/from here/Greece*
Þen° I, quen ho on brymme wore.° — *than/when she on (the) brink was*
Ho watz me° nerre° þen aunte or nece;° — *to me/closer/niece*
My Ioy for-þy° watz much þe more. — *joy therefore*

---

212. *whallez bon:* the tusk of the narwhal, identified in the Middle Ages with the horn of the unicorn, a mythical animal that could be captured only by a virgin.

235 Ho profered me speche,° þat special spyce,°   *addressed (to) me words/person*
    Enclynande° lowe in wommon lore,°   *bowing/woman's manner*
    Caȝte of° her coroun of grete tresore,°   *took off/great price*
    And haylsed° me wyth a lote lyȝte.°   *greeted/speech joyful*
    Wel° watz me° þat euer I watz bore,°   *fortunate/I/born*
240 To sware° þat swete° in perlez pyȝte!°   *answer/sweet (one)/adorned*

V

    "O perle," quod° I, "in perlez pyȝt,   *said*
    Art þou my perle þat I haf playned,°   *have mourned*
    Regretted° by myn one, on nyȝte?°   *grieved for/myself alone, at night*
    Much longeyng° haf I for þe layned,°   *longing/you concealed*
245 Syþen° into gresse° þou me° aglyȝte;°   *since/grass/from me/slipped away*
    Pensyf, payred,° I am for-payned,°   *sorrowful, worn/greatly pained*
    And þou in a lyf° of lykyng lyȝte°   *life/joy alighted*
    In paradys erde, of stryf vnstrayned.°   *land, from strife freed*
    What wyrde° hatz hyder° my iuel vayned,°   *fate/hither/jewel brought*
250 And don° me in þys del° and gret daunger?°   *put/grief/distress*
    Fro° we in twynne° wern towen° and twayned,°   *since (the time)/asunder/were severed/parted*

    I haf ben° a ioylez Iuelere."°   *been/joyless jeweler*
      That Iuel þenne in gemmyz gente,°   *gems fair*
    Vered° vp her vyse° with yȝen° graye,   *turned/face/eyes*
255 Set° on hyr coroun° of perle orient,   *put/her crown*
    And soberly° after þenne con° ho say: *gravely/did*
    "Sir, ȝe° haf your tale mysetente,°   *you/words misstated*
    To say your perle is al awaye
    Þat is in cofer° so comly clente°   *chest/fairly enclosed*
260 As in þis gardyn gracios° gaye,   *charmingly*
    Here-inne to lenge° for euer and play,   *dwell*
    Þer mys nee mornyng° com neuer nere.°   *where grief nor mourning/near*
    Her° were° a forser° for þe in faye,°   *here/would be/casket/indeed*
    If þou were a gentyl° Iueler.   *noble*
265   "Bot,° Iueler gente,° if þou schal loȝe   *but/gracious*
    Þy ioy for a gemme þat þe° watz lef,°   *to you/dear*
    Me þynk° þe put° in a mad porpose,°   *believe/(are) set/purpose*
    And busyez þe° aboute a raysoun bref,°   *trouble yourself/cause passing*
    For þat° þou lestez° watz bot a rose,   *what/lost*
270 Þat flowred and fayled as kynde hyt gef;°   *nature it decreed*
    Now þurȝ° kynde of þe kyste° þat hyt con close,°   *through/chest/does enclose*

---

249. *wyrde*: the pre-Christian Old English "fate" found in *Beowulf* (cf. below, p. 954, l. 385*n*). Words like this, and also *dryȝtyn* (OE *Drihten*), l. 324, are evidence of the conservatism in vocabulary and theme, the remnants of native English tradition, typical of the northern Alliterative Revival. Of course, the very nature of such alliterative verse forced the poet to increase his "word hoard."

To° a perle of prys° hit is put° in pref;°   *to (be)|value|proved|fact*
And þou hatz called þy wyrde a þef,°   *thief*
Þat oȝt° of noȝt° hatz mad° þe cler;°   *something|nothing|made|clearly*
275 Þou blamez þe bote° of þy meschef,°   *remedy|misery*
Þou art no kynde° Iueler."   *gentle*
    A Iuel to me þen watz þys geste,°   *visitor*
And iuelez wern hyr gentyl sawez;°   *words*
"I-wyse,"° quod I, "my blysfol beste,°   *indeed|joyous best (one)*
280 My grete° dystresse þou al to-drawez.°   *great|completely dispel*
To be excused I make requeste;
I trawed° my perle don out° of dawez.°   *believed|deprived|of life*
Now haf I° fonde° hyt I schal ma feste,°   *have I| found|make rejoicing*
And wony° with hyt in schyr wod schawez,°   *dwell|bright forest groves*
285 And loue my lorde and al his lawez,
Þat hatz me broȝt° þys blys ner;°   *brought|bliss near*
Now were I at yow by-ȝonde þise wawez,°   *with you beyond these waves*
I were a ioyfol° Iueler."   *joyful*
    "Iueler," sayde þat gemme clcne,°   *bright*
290 "Wy borde° ȝe men, so madde ȝe be?   *why jest*
Þre° wordez hatz° þou spoken at ene,°   *three|have|once*
Vn-avysed,° for soþe,° wern° alle þre.   *ill-advised|truly|were*
Þou ne woste° in worlde° quat on° dotz mene;°   *not know|at all|what one|mean*
Þy worde byfore° þy wytte con fle.°   *before| flee*
295 Þou says þou trawez me in þis dene,°   *vale*
By cawse° þou may with yȝen° me se;°   *because|eyes|see*
Anoþer þou says, in þys countre°   *country*
Þy self schal won° with me ryȝt° here;   *dwell|right*
Þe þrydde,° to passe þys water fre,°   *third|noble*
300 Þat may no ioyfol Iueler.°   *jeweler*

<h2 style="text-align:center">VI</h2>

"I halde° þat iueler lyttel to prayse°   *consider|be praised*
Þat leuez° wel þat he sez° wyth yȝe,°   *believes|sees|eye*
And much to blame and vn-cortoyse°   *discourteous*
Þat leuez oure lorde wolde° make a lyȝe,°   *would|lie*
305 Þat lelly hyȝte° your lyf° to rayse,   *faithfully promised|life*
Þaȝ° fortune dyd° your flesch to dyȝe;°   *though|caused|die*
ȝe setten° hys wordez ful westernays°   *you set|very awry*
Þat leuez no þynk bot° ȝe hit syȝe,°   *thing unless|see*
And þat is a poynt o sorquydryȝe,°   *of presumption*

271–72. The coffer is here the grave, or death, the catalyst which has transfigured the transient body into an essence of permanent value.

273–75. Death has made "something" of what was previously "nothing" or worthless. The Jeweler ought to be happy that his worthless creation is refined by death, which is the "remedy" for his "misfortune."

³¹⁰ Þat vche god mon° may euel byseme,°   *every good man/ill befit*
To leue no tale be true to tryȝe,°   *when tested*
Bot þat° hys one skyl° may deme.°   *except that (which)/judgment alone/*
    consider

    "Deme now þy-self, if þou con dayly°   *did dispute*
As° man to God wordez schulde heue.°   *as (to how)/should address*
³¹⁵ Þou saytz° þou schal won in þis bayly;°   *say/domain*
Me° þynk þe burde° fyrst aske leue,°   *I/you ought/permission*
And ȝet of graunt° þou myȝtez° fayle.   *permission/might*
Þou wylnez° ouer þys water to weue;°   *wish/go*
Er moste° þou ceuer to° oþer counsayl,°   *first must/follow/counsel*
³²⁰ Þy corse° in clot mot calder keue,°   *body/clay must colder sink*
For hit° watz for-garte° at paradys greue;°   *it/lost/grove*
Oure ȝore fader° hit con misseȝeme;°   *forefather/misuse*
Þurȝ drwry deth boȝ° vch man dreue,°   *through cruel death (it) behooves/*
    (to) go

Er° ouer þys dam° hym dryȝtyn deme."°   *before/water/God allow*
³²⁵   "Demez þou° me," quod° I, "my swete,°   *if you condemn/said/sweet (one)*
To dol° agayn, þenne I dowyne;°   *grief/pine away*
Now haf I° fonte þat° I for-lete,°   *have I/ found what/lost*
Schal I efte for-go° hit er euer I fyne?°   *again lose/end (my life)*
Why schal I hit boþe mysse° and mete?°   *lack/meet*
³³⁰ My precios° perle dotz me gret pyne.°   *precious/great distress*
What seruez tresor, bot garez men grete°   *profits treasure, but makes one weep*
When he hit schal efte with tenez tyne?°   *sorrows lose*
Now rech° I neuer forto° declyne,   *care/(i.e., if I)*
Ne° how fer of folde° þat man° me fleme;°   *nor/far from land/men/drive*
³³⁵ When I am partlez° of perle myne,   *deprived*
Bot durande doel° what may men deme?"°   *lasting grief/consider (it)*
    "Thow° demez° noȝt° bot doel° dystresse,"   *you/speak of/nothing/grief's*
Þenne sayde þat wyȝt,° "why dotz° þou so?   *person/do*
For dyne° of doel of lurez lesse,°   *noise/over cares lesser*
³⁴⁰ Ofte mony° mon for-gos° þe mo;°   *many (a)/misses/greater*
Þe oȝte° better þy seluen° blesse,   *ought/self*
And loue ay° God in wele° and wo,°   *ever/happiness/woe*
For anger gaynez þe not a cresse.
Who nedez° schal þole be° not so þro;°   *of necessity/endure (should) be/*
    impatient

³⁴⁵ For þoȝ° þou daunce° as any do,°   *though/dance/doe*
Braundysch° and bray þy braþez breme,°   *struggle/agony fierce*
When þou no fyrre may,° to ne fro,   *farther may (go)*

---

321. *paradys greue:* i.e., the Garden of Eden.
343. *cresse:* In *Piers Plowman* a cress is considered of little worth, and wisdom and wit are not worth even that.

Þou moste abyde þat° he schal deme.°   *what/judge*
  "Deme° dryȝtyn, euer hym adyte,°   *(though you) judge/arraign*
350 Of þe way a fote ne° wyl he wryþe;°   *foot not/turn*
  Þy mendez mountez° not a myte,   *recompense increases*
  Þaȝ° þou for sorȝe° be neuer blyþe°   *though/sorrow/happy*
  Stynt of° þy strot° and fyne to flyte,°   *stop/opposition/chiding*
  And sech° hys blyþe ful swefte° and swyþe.°   *seek/mercy very quickly/swiftly*
355 Þy prayer may hys pyte byte,°   *pity move*
  Þat° mercy shal hyr craftez kyþe;°   *so that/her powers show*
  Hys comforte may þy langour lyþe,°   *anguish lessen*
  And þy lurez of lyȝtly fleme,°   *off lightly cast*
  For marre oþer madde, morne° and myþe,°   *lament or rage, mourn/conceal*
360 Al lys in° hym to dyȝt° and deme."   *lies with/ordain*

VII

  Thenne demed° I to þat damyselle,°   *spoke/damsel*
  "Ne worþe° no wrathþe° vnto my lorde,   *let there be/offense*
  If rapely° I raue spornande° in spelle.°   *hastily/stumbling/words*
  My herte watz° al with mysse remorde,°   *heart was/grief stricken*
365 As wallande° water gotz out of welle;   *gushing*
  I do me° ay in hys myserecorde.°   *put myself/mercy*
  Rebuke me neuer with wordez felle,°   *harsh*
  Þaȝ I forloyne,° my dere endorde,°   *err/dear adored (one)*
  Bot° kyþez me kyndely your coumforde,°   *but/consolation*
370 Pytosly þenkande vpon° þysse: *compassionately mindful of*
  Of° care and me ȝe° made acorde,   *between/you*
  Þat er watz grounde° of alle my blysse.   *(you) that before were foundation*
    "My blysse, my bale,° ȝe han ben° boþe,   *sorrow/have been*
  Bot° much þe bygger ȝet watz my mon;°   *but/grief*
375 Fro° þou watz wroken fro° vch a° woþe,°   *since/removed from/every/danger*
  I wyste° neuer quere° my perle watz gon.   *knew/where*
  Now I hit se,° now leþez° my loþe,°   *it see/softens/sorrow*
  And quen° we departed° we wern° at on;°   *when/were parted/were/one*
  God forbede° we be now wroþe,°   *forbid/angry*
380 We meten° so selden° by stok° oþer ston.°   *meet/seldom/stick/stone*
  Þaȝ cortaysly° ȝe carp con,°   *courteously/speak can*
  I am bot mol° and manerez mysse,°   *dust/manners lack*
  Bot crystes mersy° and mary and Ion,°   *mercy/John*
  Þise arn° þe grounde of alle my blysse.   *these are*
385   "In blysse I se þe° blyþely blent°   *you/immersed*
  And I a man al mornyf mate;°   *mournfully dejected*

---

373. *blysse, bale:* terms of courtly love found in Middle English lyrics: the lover receives joy and sorrow from his beloved. Middle English religious verse borrowed its terminology from secular poetry.

3e take þer-on° ful lyttel tente,°   *thereof/heed*
Þaȝ I hente° ofte harmez hate.°   *receive/cares hot*
Bot now° I am here in your presente,°   *now (that)/presence*
390 I wolde bysech, wythouten debate,°   *would beg, without strife*
3e° wolde me say° in sobre asente   *(that) you/tell/serious speech*
What lyf° ȝe lede,° erly and late,   *life/lead*
For I am ful fayn° þat your astate°   *happy/condition*
Is worþen° to worschyp° and wele Iwysse,°   *turned/honor/happiness indeed*
395 Of alle my Ioy° þe hyȝe gate,°   *joy/high way*
Hit° is in° grounde of alle my blysse."   *it/at (the)*
    "Now blysse, burne, mot° þe bytyde,"°   *sir, may/befall*
Þen sayde þat lufsoum° of lyth° and lere,°   *(one) lovely/limb/countenance*
"And welcum° here to walk and byde,°   *welcome/stay*
400 For now þy speche° is to me dere;   *speech*
Maysterful mod° and hyȝe pryde   *masterful mood*
I hete° þe arn heterly° hated here;   *promise/bitterly*
My lorde ne° louez not forto chyde,   *not*
For meke° arn alle þat wonez° hym nere,°   *meek/dwell/near*
405 And when in hys place þou schal apere,°   *appear*
Be dep deuote° in hol° mekenesse;   *deeply devout/holy*
My lorde þe lamb louez ay° such chere,°   *ever/behavior*
Þat is þe grounde of alle my blysse.
    "A blysful° lyf þou says I lede;   *blissful*
410 Þou woldez knaw° þer-of þe stage.°   *know/degree*
Þow wost° wel when þy perle con schede,°   *know/did fall*
I watz ful ȝong° and tender of age,   *very young*
Bot my lorde þe lombe, þurȝ° hys god-hede,°   *lamb, through/divinity*
He toke° my self to° hys maryage,°   *took/for/spouse*
415 Corounde° me quene in blysse to brede,°   *crowned/flourish*
In lenghe° of dayez þat euer schal wage;°   *length/endure*
And sesed in° alle hys herytage   *endowed with*
Hys lef° is. I am holy hysse:°   *beloved (one)/wholly his*
Hys prese,° hys prys° and hys parage°   *worth/excellence/nobleness*
420 Is rote° and grounde° of alle my blysse."   *root/foundation*

VIII

"Blysful,"° quod° I, "may þys be trwe?°   *blissful (one)/said/true*
Dysplesez° not if I speke° errour.°   *be displeased/speak*
Art þou þe quene of heuenez blwe,°   *heaven blue*
Þat al þys worlde schal do honour?
425 We leuen on marye° þat grace of° grewe,   *believe in Mary/from*
Þat ber° a barne° of vyrgyn flour;°   *bore/child/flower*

---

395. *hyȝe gate:* either "highest state" or "heavenly portals."   **425.** *þat ... grewe:* i.e., "from whom grew grace."

þe croune fro hyr quo moȝt remwe° — *from her who might remove*
Bot ho hir passed° in sum fauour?° — *unless she her surpassed/some grace*
Now for synglerty o° hyr dousour° — *uniqueness of/sweetness*
430 We calle hyr fenyx° of Arraby, — *Phoenix*
þat freles fleȝe° of hyr fasor,° — *flawless flew/Creator*
Lyk° to þe quen° of cortaysye."° — *like/queen/grace*
    "Cortayse° quen," þenne sayde þat gaye,° — *gracious/fair (maiden)*
Knelande° to grounde, folde° vp hyr face, — *kneeling/lifted*
435 "Makelez moder° and myryest may,° — *matchless mother/fairest maid*
Blessed bygyner° of vch a° grace!" — *source/every*
þenne ros° ho vp and con restay,° — *rose/stay*
And speke° me towarde in° þat space:° — *spoke/ to at/time*
"Sir, fele° here porchasez° and fongez pray° — *many/seek/receive prize*
440 Bot supplantorez none° with-inne þys place; — *but defrauders none (are)*
þat emperise° al heuenz hatz — *empress*
And vrþe° and helle in her bayly;° — *earth/domain*
Of erytage° ȝet non° wyl ho chace,° — *heritage/none/drive out*
For ho is quen of cortaysye.
445   "The court of þe kyndom° of God alyue° — *kingdom/living*
Hatz a property in hyt self beyng:° — *its very nature*
Alle þat may þer-inne aryue° — *arrive*
Of alle þe reme° is quen oþer° kyng, — *realm/or*
And neuer oþer° ȝet schal depryue, — *another*
450 Bot vchon° fayn of° oþerez hafyng,° — *each one (is)/happy in/possession*
And wolde° her° corounez wern° worþe þo fyue,° — *wished/their (i.e., others')/were/five times more*

If possyble were her mendyng.° — *improvement*
Bot my lady of quom Iesu con° spryng, — *whom Jesus did*
Ho haldez° þe empyre° ouer vus ful hyȝe,° — *holds/imperial rule/us very high*
455 And þat dysplesez° non of oure gyng,° — *displeases/gathering*
For ho is quene of cortaysye.
    "Of courtaysye, as saytz saynt poule,° — *Paul*
Al arn° we membrez of ihesu kryst,° — *are/Christ*
As heued° and arme and legg and naule,° — *head/navel*
460 Temen° to hys body ful trwe° and tryste;° — *joined/truly/faithfully*
Ryȝt° so is vch a krysten sawle,° — *just/Christian soul*
A longande lym° to þe mayster° of myste;° — *limb belonging/lord/spirit*
þenne loke° what hate oþer any gawle° — *consider/bitterness*
Is tached° oþer tyȝed° þy lymmez by-twyste.° — *fixed/fastened (on)/limbs between*

430–31. Mary, spotless from the time of her conception, is like the mythical phoenix which is reborn in a purifying fire.

432. *cortaysye:* "courtesy" in a courtly sense, "grace" in a spiritual sense. The blurring of distinctions between courtly and religious diction is very evident here. It is also seen in the religious lyrics dedicated to the Virgin Mary.

439. Those who seek spiritual salvation gain it.

457. *as . . . poule:* in I Cor. 12:12–31.

465	Þy heued hatz nauþer greme ne gryste,°	*neither anger nor malice*
	On° arme oþer fynger, þaȝ° þou ber byȝe;°	*toward/though/wear ring*
	So fare we alle wyth luf° and lyste,°	*love/joy*
	To kyng and quene by cortaysye."°	*generosity*
	"Cortayse,"° quod I, "I leue°	*generosity/said/believe*
470	And charyte grete° be yow° among,	*charity great/you*
	Bot my speche° þat yow ne greue,°	*speech/(should) not offend*

. . . .

	Þy self in heuen ouer° hyȝ þou heue,°	*heaven too/raise*
	To make þe quen° þat watz so ȝonge.°	*yourself queen/young*
475	What more honor moȝte° he acheue°	*might/achieve*
	Þat hade° endured in worlde stronge,°	*had/steadfast*
	And lyued° in penaunce° hys lyuez° longe,	*lived/penance/life*
	With bodyly bale hym° blysse to byye?°	*sorrow himself/buy*
	What more worschyp° moȝt he fonge,°	*honor/receive*
480	Þen corounde° be kyng by cortayse?	*than crowned*

IX

	"That cortayse is to fre° of dede,°	*too liberal/action*
	Ȝyf hyt° be soth þat° þou conez° saye.	*if it/true what/did*
	Þou lyfed° not two ȝer° in oure þede;°	*lived/years/land*
	Þou cowþez° neuer God nauþer plese° ne pray,	*could/please*
485	Ne neuer nawþer pater° ne crede,°	*(knew) neither Paternoster/creed*
	And quen mad° on þe fyrst day!	*made*
	I may not traw,° so God me spede,°	*believe/help*
	Þat God wolde wryþe° so wrange away;°	*would turn/unjustly aside*
	Of countes, damysel,° par ma fay,	*as (a) countess, damsel*
490	Wer° fayr° in heuen to halde asstate°	*(it) would be/right/rank*
	Oþer ellez° a lady of lasse aray,°	*or else/lesser degree*
	Bot° a quene, hit° is to dere° a date."°	*but/it/exalted/goal*
	"Þer is no date of° hys god-nesse,"°	*limit to/generosity*
	Þen sayde to me þat worþy wyȝte,°	*creature*
495	"For al is trawþe° þat he con dresse,°	*justice/did ordain*
	And he may do noþynk° bot ryȝt.°	*nothing/right*
	As mathew melez° in your messe,°	*discusses/Mass*
	In sothfol° gospel of God al-myȝt°	*truthful/almighty*
	In sample° he can ful grayþely gesse,°	*parable/very aptly portray*

---

468. *cortaysye:* Cf. l. 432n. Here the word takes on a moral sense of "favor," "generosity," in addition to its other values.
472. The line is missing in the MS.
483–86. The lines reflect true astonishment in quite a humorous way. *pater:* The Paternoster (Latin, "our father") is the Lord's Prayer.

489. *par ma fay:* (French, "by my faith") i.e., "indeed."
492. The word *date* is here used as "time limit" and *dere* as "good." Today we say, "You've arrived in good time," when we mean "early."
497. Matt. 20:1–16.

500 And lyknez° hit to heuen ly3te.°	*likens/bright*
'My regne,'° he saytz, 'is lyk° on hy3t°	*kingdom/like/high*
To a lorde þat hade a uyne,° I wate,°	*vineyard/believe*
Of tyme of 3ere° þe terme° watz ty3t,	*year/period/come*
To labor vyne° watz dere° þe date.'°	*cultivate (the) vineyard/good/time*
505 "Þat date of 3ere wel knawe þys hyne.°	*know the laborers*
Þe lorde ful° erly vp he ros,°	*very/rose*
To hyre werkmen to° hys vyne,	*workmen for*
And fyndez þer summe° to hys porpos.°	*some/purpose*
Into acorde þay° con de-clyne°	*agreement they/come*
510 For a pene on a° day, and forth þay gotz,°	*penny a/go*
Wryþen° and worchen° and don gret pyne,°	*exert themselves/work/perform great toil*
Keruen° and caggen° and man° hit clos.°	*cut/tie/make/secure*
Aboute vnder° þe lorde to marked totz,°	*9 A.M./market goes*
And ydel° men stande° he fyndez þer-ate.°	*idle/standing/there*
515 'Why stande 3e° ydel?' he sayde to þos.°	*you/them*
'Ne° knawe 3e of þis day no date?'°	*not/end*
"'Er date° of daye hider arn° we wonne,'°	*before beginning/here are/come*
So watz al samen her answar so3t;°	*together their answer given*
'We haf standen her syn° ros þe sunne,	*have remained here since*
520 And no mon byddez vus do° ry3t no3t.'°	*one asks us (to) do/anything at all*
'Gos° in-to my vyne, dotz þat° 3e conne.'°	*go/do what/can*
So sayde þe lorde and made hit to3t.°	*binding*
'What resonabele hyre be na3t° be runne,°	*reasonable pay by night/earned*
I yow pay° in dede° and þo3te.'°	*you (will) pay/act/intention*
525 Þay wente in to þe vyne and wro3te,°	*worked*
And al day þe lorde þus 3ede° his gate,°	*went/way*
And nw° men to hys vyne he bro3te°	*new/brought*
Welne3 wyl° day watz passed date.°	*almost until/ended*
"At þe day of date° of euen-songe,	*day's time*
530 On oure byfore° þe sonne° go° doun,	*an hour before/sun/went*
He se3° þer ydel men ful stronge	*saw*
And sayde to hem° with sobre soun,°	*them/serious voice*
'Wy stonde° 3e ydel þise° dayez longe?'°	*why stand/the/whole day*
Þay sayden° her hyre watz nawhere boun.°	*said/nowhere arranged*
535 'Gotz to my vyne, 3emen 3onge,°	*laborers young*
And wyrkez° and dotz þat at° 3e moun.'°	*work/what/can*
Sone° þe worlde by-com wel broun,°	*quickly/became very dark*
Þe sunne watz doun and hit wex° late.	*it grew*
To° take her hyre he mad sumoun;°	*(for them) to/gave summons*
540 Þe day watz al apassed date.°	*ended*

---

513. *vnder:* the canonical hour of tierce.

516. I.e., "Don't you realize this day has an end?"

X

"The date° of þe daye þe lorde con° knaw, *time|did*
Called to þe reue,° 'Lede,° pay þe meyny.° *steward|man|company*
Gyf° hem þe hyre þat I hem owe, *give*
And fyrre,° þat non° me may reprene,° *further|none|find fault with*
545 Set hem alle vpon° a rawe,° *in|row*
And gyf vchon° in-lyche° a peny.° *each one|alike|penny*
Bygyn° at þe laste þat standez lowe, *begin*
Tyl to þe fyrste þat þou atteny.'° *reach*
And þenne þe fyrst by-gonne° to pleny° *began|complain*
550 And sayden þat þay hade trauayled sore.° *they had worked hard*
'Þese bot° an houre hem° con streny;° *but|themselves|exert*
Vus° þynk vus oȝe° to take more. *we|ought*
  "'More haf° we serued, vus þynk so, *have*
Þat suffred han° þe dayez hete,° *have|heat*
555 Þenn þyse° þat wroȝte not hourez two, *than these*
And þou dotz° hem vus to counterfete.'° *make|resemble*
Þenne sayde þe lorde to on° of þo,° *one|them*
'Frende, no waning° I wyl° þe° ȝete;° *curtailment|intend|to you|*
    (to) propose

Take þat is þyn° owne and go. *your*
560 And° I hyred þe° for a peny agrete,° *if|you|all together*
Quy° bygynnez þou now to þrete?° *why|argue*
Watz not a pené° þy couenaunt þore?° *penny|agreement there*
Fyrre þen couenaunde° is noȝt° to plete.° *agreement|not at all|be claimed*
Wy schalte þou þenne ask more?'
565 "'More, weþer louyly° is me° my gyfte, *furthermore, whether lawful|for me*
To do wyth myn° quat so me lykez?° *mine|whatsoever|I please*
Oþer ellez° þyn yȝe° to lyþer° is lyfte,° *or else|eye|evil|turned*
For° I am goude° and non by-swykez.'° *because|good|deceive*
'Þus schal I,' quod kryste,° 'hit skyfte,° *said Christ|arrange*
570 Þe laste schal be þe fyrst þat strykez,° *comes*
And þe fyrst þe laste, be he neuer so swyft,
For mony ben° called þaȝ° fewe be mykez.'° *many are|though|chosen*
Þus pore° men her° part ay pykez,° *poor|their|ever get*
Þaȝ þay com° late and lyttel wore,° *came|unimportant were*
575 And þaȝ her sweng° wyth lyttel° at-slykez.° *labor|small (result)|is spent*
Þe merci of God is much þe more.
  "More haf I of ioye° and blysse here-inne, *joy*
Of ladyschyp° gret° and lyuez blom,° *queenly state|great|life's bloom*
Þen alle þe wyȝez° in þe worlde myȝt° wynne *men|might*

---

565. *Weþer:* In Middle English this word can introduce a direct question, unlike modern usage.

580 By þe way of ryȝt° to aske dome.°   *justice/award*
    Wheþer° welnygh° now I con° bygynne—   *even though/just/did*
    In euentyde° in-to þe vyne° I come°—   *evening/vineyard/came*
    Fyrst of° my hyre° my lorde con mynne:° *about/pay/remember*
    I watz payed anon° of al and sum.°   *immediately/in toto*
585 Ȝet oþer° þer werne° þat toke° more tom,° *others/were/spent/time*
    Þat swange° and swat° for long ȝore,°   *labored/sweated/time*
    Þat ȝet of hyre noþynk° þay nom,°   *nothing/received*
    Paraunter noȝt° schal to ȝere° more."   *perhaps not/for years*
    Then more I meled° and sayde apert,°   *spoke/plainly*
590 "Me þynk þy tale vnresounable.°   *unreasonable*
    Goddez ryȝt is redy° and euer more rert,° *ready/supreme*
    Oþer holy wryt is bot° a fable;   *but*
    In sauter° is sayd a verce ouerte°   *Psalter/verse plain*
    Þat spekez° a poynt determynable;   *speaks*
595 'Þou quytez° vchon° as° hys desserte,°   *repay/each one/according to/desert*
    Þou hyȝe° kyng ay pretermynable.'°   *high/foreordaining*
    Now he þat stod° þe long day stable,°   *stood/steadfast*
    And þou to payment com hym byfore,°   *before*
    Þenne þe lasse° in werke° to take more able,° *less/work/(is) able*
600 And euer þe lenger° þe lasse, þe more." *longer*

XI

    "Of more and lasse in Godez ryche,"°   *kingdom*
    Þat gentyl° sayde, "lys° no Ioparde,°   *gentle (maiden)/exists/uncertainty*
    For þer is vch mon° payed inliche,°   *each man/alike*
    Wheþer lyttel oþer much be hys rewarde,
605 For þe gentyl cheuentayn° is no chyche,° *chieftain (i.e., Lord)/niggard*
    Queþer-so-euer° he dele nesch° oþer harde. *whether/deal gentle*
    He lauez° hys gyftez as water of dyche,° *pours/from drain*
    Oþer gotez° of golf° þat neuer charde.° *or streams/source/have ceased*
    Hys fraunchyse° is large þat euer dard° *privilege/submitted*
610 To hym þat matz in° synne rescoghe;°   *makes from/rescue*
    No blysse betz fro hem reparde,°   *is from them withheld*
    For þe grace of God is gret I-noghe.°   *enough*
        "Bot now þou motez,° me for to mate° *argue/abash*
    Þat I my peny haf wrang tan° here;   *penny have unjustly taken*
615 Þou sayz þat I þat com to° late   *came too*
    Am not worþy so gret fere.°   *company*
    Where wystez° þou euer any bourne abate° *knew/man endure*
    Euer so holy in hys prayere,

599–600. I.e., "then he who works less will receive more; and
ever the longer he does less work, the more will he receive."

Þat he ne° forfeted by sumkyn gate,° — *not/in some way*
620 Þe mede sum-tyme° of heuenez clere?° — *reward sometime/heaven bright*
And ay° þe ofter,° þe alder° þay were, — *ever/more often/older*
Þay laften ry3t° and wro3ten woghe.° — *left righteousness/wrought woe*
Mercy and grace moste° hem þen stere,° — *must/govern*
For þe grace of **God** is gret in-noghe.° — *great enough*
625   "Bot in-noghe of grace hatz innocent.° — *have (the) innocent*
As sone° as þay arn borne,° by lyne° — *soon/are born/in regular succession*
In þe water of babtem° þay dyssente;° — *baptism/descend*
Þen arne þay boro3t° in-to þe vyne.° — *brought/vineyard*
Anon° þe day, with derk endente,° — *at once/darkness suffused*
630 Þe ni3t° of deth° dotz to en-clyne;° — *night/death/toward sink*
Þat wro3t neuer wrang er° þenne° þay wente, — *before/thence*
Þe gentyle lorde þenne payez hys hyne.° — *laborers*
Þay dyden° hys heste,° þay wern þere-ine;° — *performed/commands/were there*
Why schulde° he not her° labour alow,° — *should/their/allow*
635 3ys,° and pay hem at þe fyrst° fyne?° — *yes/immediately/in full*
For þe grace of **God** is gret in-noghe.
    "Ino3e° is knawen° þat man-kyn grete° — *(well) enough/known/mankind great*

Fyrste watz wro3t to blysse parfyt;° — *perfect*
Oure forme-fader° hit con forfete,° — *first father/it did forfeit*
640 Þur3° an apple þat he vpon con byte. — *through*
Al were we dampned° for þat mete,° — *damned/food*
To dy3e° in doel out° of delyt,° — *die/grief away/delight*
And syþen wende° to helle hete,° — *afterwards go/hell's heat*
Þer-inne to won° with-oute respyt. — *dwell*
645 Bot° þeron com° a bote° as-tyt.° — *but/came/remedy/at once*
Ryche blod° ran on rode° so roghe,° — *blood/cross/cruel*
And wynne° water þen at þat plyt:° — *precious/plight*
Þe grace of **God** wex° gret in-noghe. — *became*
    "Innoghe þer wax° out of þat welle, — *flowed*
650 Blod and water of brode° wounde. — *from wide*
Þe blod vus bo3t fro balc° of helle, — *us redeemed from torment*
And delyuered° vus of þe deth secounde;° — *delivered/second*
Þe water is baptem, þe soþe° to telle, — *truth*
Þat fol3ed° þe glayue° so grymly° grounde, — *followed/lance/cruelly*
655 Þat waschez away þe gyltez felle,° — *sins deadly*
Þat adam wyth° inne° deth vus drounde.° — *with which Adam/in/drowned*
Now is þer no3t° in þe worlde rounde — *nothing*

646–56. The lance with which Christ was wounded on the cross drew blood and fluid, which is equated with the water of baptism.

Bytwene° vus and blysse bot þat° he° with-droȝ,°

And þat is restored in sely stounde;°
660 And þe grace of God is gret in-nogh.°

XII

"Grace in-nogh þe mon° may haue,
Þat synnez þenne new, ȝif hym° repente,
Bot with sorȝ° and syt° he mot° hit craue,
And byde° þe payne þer-to is bent,°
665 Bot resoun° of ryȝt° þat con° not raue°
Sauez euer more þe innossent;°
Hit is a dom° þat neuer God gaue,
Þat euer þe gyltlez° schulde be schente.°
Þe gyltyf° may contryssyoun hente°
670 And be þurȝ mercy to grace þryȝt;°
Bot he to gyle° þat neuer glente°
As inoscente° is saf° and ryȝte.°

    "Ryȝt° þus I knaw° wel in þis cas°
Two men to saue is god° by skylle:°
675 Þe ryȝtwys° man schal se° hys face,
Þe harmlez haþel° schal com hym tylle.°
Þe sauter° hyt satz° þus in a pace:°
'Lorde, quo° schal klymbe þy hyȝ° hylle
Oþer° rest with-inne þy holy place?'
680 Hymself to on-sware° he is not dylle,°
'Hondelyngez° harme þat dyt° not ille,°
Þat is of hert° boþe clene° and lyȝt,°
Þer schal hys step stable° stylle,'°
Þe innosent° is ay° saf by ryȝt.°
685   "The ryȝtwys man also sertayn°
Aproche° he schal þat proper pyle,°
Þat takcz° not her lyf° in vayne°
Ne glauerez° her nieȝbor° wyth no gyle.
Of þys ryȝtwys saz salamon playn°

690 How Koyntise onoure con aquyle;°
By wayez ful streȝt ho° con hym strayn,°
And scheued° hym þe rengne° of God a whyle,

between/what/(i.e., Adam)/with-drew	
blessed time	
enough	
man	
anew, if he	
contrition/grief/must	
endure/(that) is attached	
reason/justice/can/deviate	
innocent	
judgment	
guiltless/harmed	
guilty/contrition find	
brought	
guile/deviated	
innocent/redeemed/sanctified (by grace)	
right/know/case	
good/reason	
righteous/see	
innocent man/to	
Psalter/says/passage	
who/high	
or	
answer/slow	
with (his) hands/did/wrongfully	
heart/clean/pure	
remain/at rest	
innocent/ever/justification (by grace)	
certainly	
approach/fair house	
spends/their life/(i.e., foolishly)	
nor deceives/neighbor	
righteous (man)/says Solomon plainly	
Wisdom honor did obtain (for him)	
very straight she/urge	
showed/kingdom	

---

690. This line corresponds to Wisd. 10:10 in the Douay Version of the Bible (Wisd. of Sol. in the Apocrypha of the Authorized Version).

As quo° says 'Lo, ȝon° louely yle,° *(one) who/yonder/domain*
Þou may hit wynne° if þou be wyȝte.'° *it attain/brave*
695 Bot, hardyly,° with-oute peryle,° *assuredly/risk*
Þe innosent is ay saue° by ryȝte! *redeemed*
  "Anende° ryȝtwys men, ȝet saytz a gome,° *concerning/man*
Dauid in sauter, if euer ȝe seȝ° hit, *you saw*
'Lorde, þy seruaunt draȝ° neuer to dome, *servant bring*
700 For non lyuyande° to þe° is Iustyfyet.'° *none alive/you/justified*
For-þy° to corte quen° þou schal com *therefore/court when*
Þer° alle oure causez schal be tryed, *where*
Alegge þe ryȝt° þou may be in-nome,° *(if you) plead your right/refuted*
By þys ilke spech° I haue asspyed;° *same speech/observed*
705 Bot he° on rode° þat blody dyed,° *but (may) he/cross/bloody died*
Delfully þurȝ hondeȝ þryȝt,° *grievously through hands pierced*
Gyue° þe to passe when þou arte tryed *allow*
By innocens° and not by ryȝte. *innocence*
  "Ryȝt-wysly° quo con rede,° *rightly/can read*
710 He loke on bok° and be awayed° *looks at book/is instructed*
How Ihesuc hym welke in are þede,° *Jesus himself walked among former people*

And burnez° her barnez° vnto hym brayde,° *men/children/brought*
For happe° and hele° þat fro° hym ȝede,° *joy/healing/from/came*
To touch her chylder° þay fayr° hym prayed. *children/they courteously*
715 His dessypelez° with blame let° be hym bede,° *disciples/(them to) let/commanded*
And wyth her resounez° ful fele restayed;° *speeches/many restrained*
Ihesuc þenne hem° swetely° sayde, *to them/sweetly*
'Do way,° let chylder vnto me tyȝt.° *stop that/come*
To° suche is heuen-ryche° arayed.'° *for/heavenly kingdom/prepared*
720 Þe innocent is ay saf° by ryȝt.° *redeemed/justification (by grace)*

XIII

"Ihesuc con calle to hym hys mylde° *disciples*
And sayde hys ryche° no wyȝ myȝt° wynne *kingdom/man might*
Bot° he com þyder ryȝt° as a chylde, *unless/came there even*
Oþer ellez° neuer more com þer-inne.° *or else/therein*
725 Harmlez, trwe° and vnde-fylde,° *innocent, faithful/undefiled*
With-outen mote° oþer mascle° of sulpande° synne, *without stain/spot/polluting*
Quen such þer cnoken° on þe bylde,° *knock/building*
Tyt° schal hem° men þe ȝate vnpynne.° *quickly/for them/gate unbolt*
Þer is þe blys° þat con not blynne,° *bliss/cease*

---

703. *in-nome*: here, "trapped" or "refuted" (by one's own plea). It is a legal term (cf. *The Owl and Nightingale*, l. 541). The point is that one cannot gain entrance by arguing one's right; Christ must allow one to *passe* freely (ll. 705–7).

721. Group XIII is the only one the first stanza of which is not linked to the preceding stanzas (although the link word *Iohan*, l. 997, is not in the MS.).

730 Þat þe Iueler soȝte° þurȝ perre pres°   *jeweler sought/jewels (of) value*
    And solde alle hys goud,° boþe wolen° and lynne,°   *goods/woolen/linen*
    To bye° hym a perle þat watz mascellez.°   *buy/spotless*
        "This makellez° perle þat boȝt° is dere,°   *matchless/bought/dearly*
    Þe Ioueler gef fore° alle hys god,°   *(which) the jeweler gave for/wealth*
735 Is lyke þe reme° of heuenesse clere,°   *kingdom/heaven bright*
    So sayde þe Fader° of folde° and flode;°   *Father/earth/sea*
    For hit° is wemlez, clene° and clere,   *it/spotless, pure*
    And endelez° rounde and blyþe of mode,°   *endlessly/glad in character*
    And commune° to alle þat ryȝtwys° were.   *belonging/righteous*
740 Lo! euen in myddez° my breste hit stode.°   *middle (of)/stood*
    My lorde, þe lombe° þat schede° hys blode,°   *lamb/shed/blood*
    He pyȝt° hit þere in token of pes.°   *set/peace*
    I rede þe° forsake þe worlde wode,°   *advise you/mad*
    And porchace° þy perle maskelles."   *seek*
745   "O maskelez perle in perlez pure,
    Þat berez,"° quod° I, "þe perle of prys,°   *wears/said/value*
    Quo° formed þe° þy fayre fygure?   *who/for you*
    Þat wroȝt° þy wede,° he watz ful wys.°   *(he) that made/clothing/very wise*
    Þy beaute° com neuer of° nature;   *beauty/from*
750 Pymalyon° paynted neuer þy vys,°   *Pygmalion/face*
    Ne arystotel nawþer° by hys lettrure°   *nor (did) Aristotle neither/writing*
    Of carpe° þe kynde° þese propertez.°   *speak of/nature (of)/properties*
    Þy colour passez° þe flour-de-lys,°   *surpasses/fleur-de-lis*
    Þyn angel hauyng° so clenc cortez.°   *your angelic manner/purely gracious*
755 Breue° me, bryȝt,° quat-kyn° offys°   *tell/bright (one)/what kind (of)/*
                                      position
    Berez° þe perle so maskellez?"   *has*
        "My makelez lambe þat al may bete,"°   *amend*
    Quod scho,° "my dere destyné°   *she/precious destiny*
    Me ches to° hys make, al-þaȝ vnmete°   *chose for/bride, although unfit*
760 Sum° tyme semed° þat assemble.°   *(at) one/seemed/union*
    When I wente fro yor° worlde wete,°   *from your/dank*
    He calde° me to hys bonerté:°   *called/blessedness*
    'Cum hyder° to me, my lemman swete,°   *come here/beloved sweet*

---

733. *makellez:* The poet is obviously playing on the similarity in sound of this word and *mascellez,* l. 732, to pun on the two qualities of the Pearl. The fact that here, as in ll. 612–13 with *I-noghe/now,* the sound echo rather than the written word is used as an aural linking device suggests that the poem may have been written for oral reading or recitation (See also the religious lyric *I Sing of a Maiden* [this volume, p. 661], where *makeles* is a triple pun: "spotless," "matchless," and "mateless").

750. Pygmalion was the legendary king of Cyprus and a sculptor who in Ovid's *Metamorphoses* becomes enamored of his own creation, a statue called Galatea. Aphrodite brings the statue to life. The passage here, however, is connected with the *Romance of the Rose,* ll. 16013ff.

755. *Breue:* "tell shortly" (cf. the modern verb *brief*). *offys:* The MS. form is either *oftriys* or *ostriys.* C. G. Osgood and E. V. Gordon amend this to *offys,* where Henry Bradley, strongly supported by E. T. Donaldson ("Oysters Forsooth," Studies Presented to Tauno F. Mustanoja on the Occasion of His Sixtieth Birthday, *Neuphilologische Mitteilungen,* 73, Nos. 1–2 [1972], 78, 79), suggests *ostriys* as "oysters."

For mote° ne spot is non° in þe.' *stain/none*
765 He gef me myʒt° and als bewté.° *power/also beauty*
In hys blod he wesch° my wede on dese,° *washed/dais*
And coronde° clene in vergynté,° *crowned (me)/virginity*
And pyʒt° me in perlez maskellez." *adorned*
    "Why, maskellez bryd° þat bryʒt con flambe,° *bride/does shine*
770 Þat reiatez° hatz so ryche° and ryf,° *royal honors/noble/abundant*
Quat-kyn þyng may be þat lambe
Þat þe wolde° wedde vnto° hys vyf?° *would/as/wife*
Ouer alle oþer° so hyʒ° þou clambe,° *others/high/climbed*
To lede° with hym so ladyly lyf.° *lead/queenly life*
775 So mony° a cumly on-vunder cambe° *many/fair (one) under comb*
For kryst han° lyued in much stryf;° *Christ has/strife*
And þou con° alle þo dere° out-dryf,° *can/these worthy (ones)/drive out*
And fro þat maryag° al oþer depres,° *marriage/drive*
Al only° þyself so stout° and styf,° *except/valiant/bold*
780 A makelez may° and maskellez."° *matchless maid/spotless*

XIV

"Maskelles," quod þat myry quene,° *happy queen*
"Vnblemyst° I am, wyth-outen° blot, *unblemished/without*
And þat may I with mensk menteene;° *courtesy maintain*
Bot 'makelez quene' þenne sade° I not. *said*
785 Þe lambes vyuez° in blysse we bene,° *wives/are*
A hondred° and forty þowsande flot° *hundred/host*
As in þe apocalyppez hit° is sene;° *Apocalypse it/seen*
Sant Iohan hem syʒ° al in a knot. *Saint John them saw*
On þe hyl of syon,° þat semly clot,° *Zion/fair ground*
790 Þe apostel hem segh° in gostly drem° *saw/mystical dream*
Arayed° to þe weddyng in° þat hyl coppe,° *prepared/on/top*
Þe nwe cyte o Ierusalem.° *new city of Jerusalem*
    "Of Ierusalem I in speche spelle.° *words tell*
If þou wyl knaw° what kyn° he be,° *know/kind/is*
795 My lombe,° my lorde, my dere Iuelle,° *lamb/jewel*
My ioy,° my blys,° my lemman fre,° *joy/bliss/generous*
Þe profete ysaye° of hym con melle° *prophet Isaiah/speak*
Pitously° of hys debonerté:° *compassionately/humility*
'Þat gloryous gyltlez þat mon con quelle,° *guiltless (one)/men did kill*

---

769. *bryd:* There is a triple pun here. "bride," "bird" (phoenix), and "maiden" (ME *burd*).

775. *cumly on-vunder cambe:* i.e., "on earth" (cf. above, p. 311, l. 1814n).

784. *makelez:* The pun here is on the two meanings "matchless" and "mateless" (i.e., "virgin" or "without companion"). The Pearl is *maskelez* ("spotless"), but not (in two specific senses) *makelez*.

787. Rev. 14:1–5.

800 With-outen any sake° of felonye,°   *charge/crime*
   As a schep° to þe slaȝt° þer lad° watz he;   *sheep/slaughter/led*
   And as lombe þat clypper° in hande nem,°   *shearer/took*
   So closed he hys mouth fro vch query,°   *from every complaint*
   Quen Iuez° hym iugged° in Iherusalem.'   *when Jews/judged*
805   "In Ierusalem watz my lemman° slayn   *beloved*
   And rent on rode with boyez° bolde.   *cross by ruffians*
   Al oure balez° to bere ful bayn,°   *woes/bear very willingly*
   He toke° on hym self oure carez colde.   *took*
   With boffetez° watz hys face flayn°   *buffets/flayed*
810 Þat watz so fayr on to byholde.°   *look*
   For synne he set° hym self in vayn,°   *valued/at naught*
   Þat neuer hade non° hym self to wolde.°   *had none/be responsible for*
   For vus° he lette hym° flyȝe° and folde°   *us/himself/be flayed/bowed*
   And brede° vpon a bostwys bem,°   *stretched/rough beam*
815 As meke° as lomb þat no playnt tolde.°   *meek/complaint uttered*
   For vus he swalt° in Ierusalem.   *died*
      "Ierusalem, Iordan° and galalye,°   *Jordan/Galilee*
   Þer as° baptysed þe goude° saynt Ion,°   *where/good/John*
   His wordez acorded to° ysaye.   *agreed with*
820 When Ihesuc° con to hym warde° gon°   *Jesus/toward him/go*
   He sayde of hym þys professye:°   *prophesy*
   'Lo, Godez lombe as trwe° as ston,°   *firm/stone*
   Þat dotz° away þe synnez dryȝe!'°   *takes/heavy*
   Þat° alle þys worlde hatz wroȝt vpon,°   *(the sins) that/practiced*
825 Hym self ne wroȝt° neuer ȝet non,   *not committed*
   Wheþer° on hym self he con al clem.°   *and yet/claim*
   Hys generacyoun quo recen con,°   *generation who recount can*
   Þat dyȝed° for vus in Ierusalem?   *died*
      "In Ierusalem þus my lemman swete°   *sweet*
830 Twyez for° lombe watz taken þere,   *twice for (a)*
   By trw° recorde of ayþer° prophete,   *true/either*
   For mode° so meke and al hys fare.°   *mood/manner*
   Þe þryde° tyme is þer-to ful mete°   *third/fittingly*
   In apokalypez wryten° ful ȝare.°   *Apocalypse written/plainly*
835 In mydez° þe trone þere° sayntez sete,°   *middle (of)/throne where/sat*
   Þe apostel iohan° hym saȝ° as bare,°   *John/saw/plainly*
   Lesande° þe boke° with leuez sware,°   *opening/book/leaves square*
   Þere seuen syngnettez wern° sette in seme°   *seals were/(the) border*
   And at þat syȝt° vche douth con dare,°   *sight/host does tremble*
840 In helle, in erþe and Ierusalem.°   *Jerusalem*

---

811. The line causes difficulty: it probably means "for the sake of man's sin he set his own life at naught."
819. John 1:28–36.

827. *generacyoun:* i.e., the mystery of the spiritual engendering of Christ.
833–34. Rev. 5:1–14.

XV

"Thys Ierusalem lombe° hade neuer pechche°   *lamb/stain*
Of oþer huee bot quyt Iolyf°   *color but white bright*
Þat mot ne masklle moзt° on streche°   *blot nor spot might/rest*
For wolle° quyte so ronk° and ryf.°   *fleece/thick/abundant*
845 For-þy vche saule° þat hade neuer teche°   *therefore every soul/stain*
Is to þat lombe a worthyly wyf;°   *worthy wife*
And þaз° vch day a store he feche,°   *though/fetch*
Among vus commez noþer strot° ne stryf,°   *arises neither quarrel/strife*
Bot vchon° enle° we wolde° were fyf,°   *each one/singly/wish/five*
850 Þe mo° þe myryer,° so God me blesse.   *more/happier*
In compayny, gret° our luf° con þryf°   *great/love/thrive*
In honour more and neuer þe lesse.

    "Lasse° of blysse may non vus° bryng   *less/none us*
Þat beren° þys perle vpon oure bereste,°   *wear/breast*
855 For þay° of mote couþe° neuer mynge;°   *they/quarrel could/think (of)*
Of spotlez° perlez þay beren þe creste.°   *spotless/crown*
Al-þaз° oure corses° in clottez clynge,°   *although/bodies/earth molder*
And зe remen° for rauþe wyth-outen° reste,   *you lament/sorrow without*
We þurз-outly hauen cnawyng;°   *throughout (i.e., complete) have*
                                                       understanding

860 Of on dethe ful° oure hope is drest.°   *from one death completely/drawn*
Þe loumbe° vus gladez,° oure care is kest;°   *lamb/gladdens/removed*
He myrþez° vus alle at vch a° mes.°   *cheers/every/mass*
Vchonez° blysse is breme° and beste,   *each one's/intense*
And neuer onez honour зet neuer þe les.°   *less*
865   "Lest les þou leue° my tale farande,°   *believe/pleasing*
In appocalyppece° is wryten in wro:°   *Apocalypse/passage*
'I seghe,'° says Iohan, 'þe loumbe hym stande°   *saw/himself standing*
On þe mount of syon ful þryuen° and þro,°   *Zion very fair/noble*
And wyth hym maydennez an hundreþe° þowsande   *hundred*
870 And fowre° and forty þowsande mo.   *four*
On alle her forhedez° wryten I fande°   *their foreheads/found*
Þe lombez nome,° hys faderez° also.   *name/Father's*
A hue fro heuen° I herde þoo,°   *shout from heaven/heard then*
Lyk flodez fele laden,° runnen on resse,°   *like (of) rivers many voice, running*
                                                       in torrent

875 And as þunder þrowez in torrez blo,°   *rolls among cliffs dark*
Þat lote° I leue watz neuer° þe les.   *sound/not*
    "'Nauþeles° þaз hit schowted scharpe.°   *nevertheless/shouted strongly*

---

850. *Þe mo þe myryer:* This is the first recorded instance of the phrase in literature.

860. The "one death" is Christ's, through which comes hope for salvation.

And ledden° loude al-þaȝ hit were,   *voice*
A note ful nwe° I herde hem warpe,°   *new/them utter*
880 To lysten° þat watz ful lufly dere.°   *listen (to)/delightfully pleasing*
As harporez harpen in her° harpe,   *harpers harp on their*
Þat nwe songe þay songen° ful cler,°   *sang/cleanly*
In sounande° notez a gentyl carpe;°   *sonorous/excellent discourse*
Ful fayre° þe modez° þay fonge° in fere.°   *rightly/tunes/took/together*
885 Ryȝt byfore° Godez chayere,°   *right before/throne*
And þe fowre bestez° þat hym obes,°   *beasts/obeys*
And þe alder-men° so sadde of chere,°   *elders/grave in looks*
Her songe þay songen neuer þe les.
  "'Nowþe-lese° non watz neuer so quoynt,°   *nevertheless/skilled*
890 For alle þe craftez° þat euer þay knewe,   *arts*
Þat of þat songe myȝt° synge a poynt,°   *might/phrase*
Bot° þat meyny° þe lombe° þay swe;°   *but/company/lamb/follow*
For þay arn boȝt° fro þe vrþe aloynte°   *are redeemed/earth removed*
As newe fryt° to God ful due,   *first fruit*
895 And to þe gentyl° lombe hit° arn anioynt;°   *gentle/they/united*
As lyk to hym self of lote° and hwe;°   *word/color*
For neuer lesyng ne° tale vn-trwe°   *lie nor/untrue*
Ne towched° her tonge° for° no dysstresse.°   *not touched/tongue/because of/constraint*

Þat moteles° mcyny may neuer remwe°   *stainless/withdraw*
900 Fro þat maskelez mayster° neucr þe less.'"°   *spotless lord/notwithstanding*
  "Neuer° þe les let be my þonc,"°   *not/thanks*
Quod° I, "my perle þaȝ I appose;°   *said/though/question*
I schulde° not tempte° þy wyt° so wlonc,°   *should/test/wisdom/noble*
To krystez° chambre þat art Ichose.°   *for Christ's/chosen*
905 I am bot mokke° and mul among,°   *muck/dust mingled*
And þou so ryche° a reken° rose,   *splendid/fresh*
And bydez° here by þys blysful bonc°   *bide/blissful bank*
Þer lyuez lyste° may neuer lose.°   *where life's joy/fade*
Now, hynde,° þat sympelnesse conez enclose,°   *gracious (one)/simplicity does endue*
910 I wolde þe° aske a þynge expresse,°   *would you/particular*
And þaȝ I be bustwys° as a blose,°   *crude/churl*
Let my bone vayl° neuer þe lese,°   *prayer prevail/less*

XVI

"Neuer þe lese cler I yow by-calle°   *you call (upon)*
If ȝe con se hyt° be to done,°   *you can see it (possible)/do*
915 As þou art gloryous with-outen galle,°   *without impurity*
With-nay° þou neuer my ruful° bone.   *refuse/piteous*
Haf° ȝe no wonez° in castel walle,   *have/dwellings*
Ne maner° þer ȝe may mete° and won?°   *manor/meet/live*

Þou tellez me of Ierusalem þe ryche ryalle,°   *kingdom royal*
920 Þer dauid dere° watz dyȝt° on trone,°   *noble/placed/throne*
Bot by þyse holtez° hit con not hone,°   *in these woods/be situated*
Bot in Iudee° hit is, þat noble note.°   *Judea/structure*
As ȝe ar maskelez vnder mone,°   *moon*
Your wonez schulde be wyth-outen mote.°   *stain*
925   "Þys motelez meyny þou conez° of mele,°   *do/speak*
Of þousandez þryȝt° so gret° a route,°   *thronged/great/crowd*
A gret cete,° for ȝe arn fele,°   *city/many*
You by-hod° haue with-outen doute.°   *ought to/doubt*
So cumly° a pakke° of Ioly Iuele°   *fair/collection/bright jewels*
930 Wer° euel don° schulde lyȝ þer-oute,°   *would be/ill-treated/(they) sleep outdoors*

And by þyse bonkez° þer I con gele°   *banks/do stroll*
And I se no bygyng nawhere° aboute.   *building nowhere*
I trowe al-one° ȝe lenge° and loute,°   *believe alone/linger/go*
To loke° on þe glory of þys gracious gote;°   *look/stream*
935 If þou hatz° oþer lygyngez stoute,°   *have/lodgings stately*
Now tech° me to þat myry mote."°   *guide/fair city*
    "That mote þou menez° in Iudy londe,"°   *mean/Judea land*
Þat specyal spyce° þen to me spakk,°   *person/said*
"Þat is þe cyte° þat þe lombe con fonde°   *city/lamb did visit*
940 To soffer inne sor° for manez sake,   *suffer in pain*
Þe olde Ierusalem,° to vnder-stonde;°   *Jerusalem/that is to say*
For þere þe olde gulte° watz don° to slake.°   *sin/brought/end*
Bot° þe nwe,° þat lyȝt of° Godez sonde,°   *but/new/descended from/sending*
Þe apostel in apocalyppce in° theme con take.   *Apocalypse for (his)*
945 Þe lombe þer, with-outen spottez blake,°   *black*
Hatz feryed þyder° hys fayre flote,°   *brought there/host*
And as hys flok° is with-outen flake,°   *flock/spot*
So is hys mote with-outen moote.°   *stain*
    "Of motes two to carpe clene,°   *speak exactly*
950 And Ierusalem hyȝt° boþe nawþeles°—   *are called/nevertheless*
Þat nys° to yow no more to mene   *is not*
Bot 'cete of God' oþer° 'syȝt° of pes:'°   *or/sight/peace*
In þat on° oure pes watz mad° at ene;°   *one/made/once*
With payne to suffer þe lombe hit chese;°   *it chose*
955 In þat oþer is noȝt° bot pes to glene,°   *nothing/gather*
Þat ay° schal laste with-outen reles,°   *ever/without ceasing*
Þat is þe borȝ° þat we to pres,°   *city/toward hasten*
Fro þat° oure flesch be layd° to rote;°   *ever since/buried/rot*

---

923. *vnder mone:* i.e., "completely."
954. The lamb chose the earthly Jerusalem as the city in which to suffer pain.

Þer glory and blysse schal euer encres°   *increase*
960 To þe meyny° þat is with-outen mote."   *company*
    "Motelez may° so meke° and mylde,"   *spotless maid/meek*
Þen sayde I to þat lufly flor,°   *lovely flower*
"Bryng me to þat bygly bylde,°   *pleasant building*
And let me se° þy blysful bor."°   *see/blissful dwelling*
965 Þat schene° sayde, "Þat God wyl schylde;°   *fair (one)/prevent*
Þou may not enter with-inne hys tor,°   *tower*
Bot of þe lombe I haue þe° aquylde°   *for you/obtained (permission)*
For a syȝt þer-of þurȝ gret° fauor.   *through great*
Vt-wyth° to se þat clene cloystor°   *from outside/pure enclosure*
970 Þou may, bot inwyth° not a fote,°   *inside/ foot*
To strech° in þe strete° þou hatz no vygour,°   *go/street/power*
Bot° þou wer clene with-outen mote.°   *unless/stain*

XVII

"If I þis mote° þe° schal vn-hyde,°   *city/to you/disclose*
Bow° vp to-warde þys bornez heued,°   *turn/stream's source*
975 and I an-endez þe° on þis syde   *opposite you*
Schal sve,° tyl þou to a hil be veued."°   *follow/brought*
Þen wolde° I no lenger byde,°   *would/longer wait*
Bot lurked by launcez° so lufly leued,°   *stole under branches/delightfully
                                                                leaved*

Tyl on a hyl þat I asspycd°   *espied*
980 And blusched° on þe burghe,° as I forth dreued,°   *looked/city/moved*
By-ȝonde° þe brok fro° me warde keued,°   *beyond/brook from/away sunk*
Þat schyrrer þen° sunne with schaftez schon.°   *brighter than/beams shone*
In þe apokalypce° is þe fasoun preued,°   *Apocalypse/manner shown*
As deuysez° hit þe apostel Ihon.ᵁ   *describes/ John*
985   As Iohan þe apostel hit syȝ° with syȝt,   *saw*
I syȝe þat cyty of gret renoun,
Ierusalem so nwe° and ryally dyȝt,°   *new/royally adorned*
As hit watz lyȝt° fro þe heuen adoun.°   *descended/heaven down*
Þe borȝ watz al of brende° golde bryȝt,°   *refined/bright*
990 As glemande° glas burnist broun,°   *gleaming/burnished shiny*
With gentyl° gemmez an-vnder pyȝt,°   *excellent/beneath fixed*
With bantelez twelue on basyng boun,°   *base bound*
Þe foundementez° twelue of riche tenoun;°   *foundations/joining*
Vch tabelment° watz a serlypez ston,°   *each tier/single stone*
995 As derely° deuysez þis ilk° toun   *splendidly/same*
In apocalyppez° þe apostel Iohan.°   *Apocalypse/John*

983–84. The New Jerusalem is described in Rev. 21:10–25   **992.** *bantelez:* tiers, providing a steplike foundation for the city.
and 22:1–2, 23.

As Iohan þise° stonez in writ con nemme,° *these/Scripture did name*
I knew þe name after his tale:° *enumeration*
Iasper° hyȝt° þe fyrst gemme *jasper/was called*
1000 Þat I on þe fyrst basse° con wale;° *base/discern*
He glente° grene in þe lowest hemme.° *it glinted/step*
Saffer° helde þe secounde stale,° *sapphire/second place*
Þe calsydoyne° þenne with-outen wemme° *chalcedony/without flaw*
In þe þryd table° con purly pale;° *tier/show purely pale*
1005 Þe emerade° þe furþe° so grene of scale;° *emerald/fourth/surface*
Þe sardonyse° þe fyfþe ston; *sardonyx*
Þe sexte° þe rybe° he con hit° wale, *sixth/ruby/it*
In þe apocalyppce° þe apostel Iohan. *Apocalypse*
ȝet Ioyned° Iohan þe crysolyt,° *also added/chrysolite*
1010 Þe seuenþe gemme in fundament;° *foundation*
Þe aȝtþe° þe beryl cler° and quyt;° *eighth/clear/white*
Þe topasye twynne-hew° þe nente endent;° *topaz double-colored/ninth set*
Þe crysopase° þe tenþe is tyȝt;° *chrysoprase/set*
Þe Iacyngh° þe enleuenþe gent;° *jacinth/eleventh fair*
1015 Þe twelfþe, þe gentyleste° in vch a° plyt,° *best/every/trouble*
Þe amatyst purpre° with ynde blente;° *amethyst purple/indigo (blue) mixed*
Þe wal abof° þe bantels bent° *above/fastened*
O Iasporye,° as glas þat glysnande° schon, *of jasper/glistening*
I knew hit by his deuysement° *description*
1020 In þe apocalyppez, þe apostel Iohan.
As Iohan deuysed ȝet saȝ° I þare:° *saw/there*
Þise twelue degres wern brode° and stayre;° *tiers were broad/steep*
Þe cyte stod° abof ful sware,° *city stood/quite square*
As longe as brode as hyȝe° ful fayre;° *high/evenly*
1025 Þe stretez° of golde as glasse al bare,° *streets/clear*
Þe wal of Iasper þat glent as glayre;° *egg white*
Þe wonez° with-inne enurned ware° *dwellings/adorned were*
Wyth alle kynnez° perre° þat moȝt° repayre.° *kinds (of)/precious stones/might/ be had*

Þenne helde vch° sware of þis manayre° *contained each/estate*
1030 Twelue forlonge° space er° euer hit fon,° *furlongs'/before/ended*
Of heȝt,° of brede,° of lenþe° to cayre,° *height/breadth/length/traverse*
For meten° hit syȝ° þe apostel Iohan. *measured/saw*

1015–16. The medieval lapidaries mention the amethyst as providing protection against many misfortunes and sorrows. In a French source it is considered a comfort against drunkenness—specifically, one might suppose, the aftereffects of drunkenness.

1023–24. The city is cubic in form (cf. ll. 1029–31).

XVIII

As Iohan hym° wrytez ȝet more I syȝe: — *himself*
Vch pane° of þat place had þre ȝatez,° — *side/three gates*
1035 So twelue in poursent° I con asspye,° — *compass/espy*
Þe portalez pyked of° rych platez — *adorned with*
And vch ȝate of a margyrye,° — *pearl*
A parfyt° perle þat neuer fatez.° — *perfect/fades*
Vchon° in scrypture° a name con plye° — *each one/writing/did express*
1040 Of israel barnez,° folewande° her° datez, — *Israel's children/in order (of)/their*
Þat is to say, as her byrþ-whatez;° — *fortunes of birth*
Þe aldest ay° fyrst þer-on watz done.° — *eldest ever/put*
Such lyȝt° þer lemed° in alle þe stratez° — *light/shone/streets*
Hem nedde nawþer° sunne ne mone.° — *they needed neither/nor moon*
1045   Of sunne ne mone had þay° no nede;° — *they/need*
Þe self° God watz her lompe° lyȝt, — *very/lamp*
Þe lombe° her lantyrne with-outen drede;° — *lamb/lantern without doubt*
Þurȝ° hym blysned° þe borȝ° al bryȝt.° — *through/shone/city/bright*
Þurȝ woȝe° and won° my lokyng ȝede;° — *wall/dwelling/gaze passed*
1050 For° sotyle cler noȝt lette° no lyȝt. — *because of/translucence clear*
                                                    nothing stopped

Þe hyȝe trone° þer moȝt ȝe hede° — *throne/you notice*
With alle þe apparaylmente vmbe-pyȝte,° — *ornaments adorned*
As Iohan° þe appostel in termez° tyȝte;° — *John/formal terms/described*
Þe hyȝe Godez self hit set vpone.° — *God himself it sat upon*
1055 A reuer of° þe trone þer ran out-ryȝte° — *river from/directly*
Watz° bryȝter þen° boþe þe sunne and mone. — *(that) was/than*
    Sunne ne mone schon° neuer so swete° — *shone/pleasantly*
As þat foysoun flode° out of þat flet;° — *abundant river/ground*
Swyþe° hit swange° þurȝ vch a° strete, — *swiftly/flowed/every*
1060 With-outen fylþe oþer galle° oþer glet.° — *or impurity/slime*
Kyrk° þer-inne watz non ȝete,° — *church/none yet*
Chapel ne temple þat euer watz set;° — *established*
Þe almyȝty° watz her mynster mete,° — *Almighty/church excellent*
Þe lombe þe sakerfyse° þer to refet.° — *sacrifice/as refreshment*
1065 Þe ȝates stoken° watz neuer ȝet, — *shut*
Bot° euer more vpen° at vche a lonc;° — *but/open/lane*
Þer entrez non to take reset,° — *refuge*
Þat berez° any spot an-vnder° mone. — *bears/under*

1041. *as her byrþ-whatez:* i.e., "according to the order of their birth."

1060. It must be remembered that in earthly cities the "rivers" that ran through the streets were gutters used as sewers. The poet is careful to point out the cleanliness of the New Jerusalem.

1063. *mynster:* either "minster" (church) or "minister." The word can have both meanings, since the Lord's house, the New Jerusalem, is the Church as well as the body of Christ.
1068. *an-vnder mone:* i.e., "anywhere."

The mone may þer-of acroche° no myȝte;°   acquire/power
1070 To° spotty ho° is, of body to grym,°   too/she/ugly
And al-so° þer ne° is neuer nyȝt.°   moreover/not/night
What schulde° þe mone þer compas clym°   why should/(its) circuit climb
And to euen° wyth þat worþly° lyȝt   compare/glorious
Þat schynez vpon þe brokez° brym?   stream's
1075 Þe planetez arn° in to pouer° a plyȝt,°   are/wretched/state
And þe self sunne ful fer° to dym.   quite far
Aboute þat water arn tres ful schym,°   trees very bright
Þat twelue frytez° of lyf con° bere ful sone;°   fruits/life can/quickly
Twelue syþez on ȝer° þay beren° ful frym°   times each year/bear/abundant
1080 And re-nowlez nwe° in vche a mone.°   renew anew/(i.e., month)
    An-vnder mone so gret merwayle°   great marvel
No fleschly hert° ne myȝt endeure,°   heart/might endure
As quen° I blusched° vpon þat bayle,°   when/looked/wall
So ferly° þer-of watz þe fasure.°   wondrous/appearance
1085 I stod° as stylle as dased° quayle,   stood/dazed
For ferly° of þat frelich fygure,°   wonder/noble appearance
Þat° felde° I nawþer° reste ne trauayle,°   so that/felt/neither/nor toil
So watz I rauyste° wyth glymme° pure;   ravished/brightness
For I dar° say, with conciens° sure,   dare/conscience
1090 Hade bodyly burne abiden° þat bone,°   had mortal man endured/favor
Þaȝ° alle clerkez° hym hade in cure,   though/(i.e., physicians)
His lyf wer° loste an-vnder mone.°   would be/moon

XIX

Ryȝt° as þe maynful° mone con rys,°   just/powerful/does rise
Er þenne° þe day-glem dryue al° doun,   before/daylight sinks completely
1095 So sodanly on° a wonder wyse°   suddenly in/wondrous manner
I watz war° of a prosessyoun.°   aware/procession
Þis noble cite° of ryche enpresse°   city/glorious renown
Watz sodanly ful with-outen sommoun°   without summons
Of such vergynez° in þe same gyse°   virgins/garb
1100 Þat watz my blysful° an-vnder croun,°   blissful (one)/(her) crown
And coronde wern° alle of° þe same fasoun,°   crowned were/in/fashion
Depaynt° in perlez and wedez qwyte;°   adorned/garments white
In vchonez° breste watz bounden boun°   each one's/bound fast
Þe blysful perle with gret delyt.°   delight
1105   With gret delyt þay glod° in fere,°   proceeded/together
On golden gatez° þat glent° as glasse;   streets/shone
Hundreth° þowsandez I wot° þer were,   hundred/believe

1069–70. The poet refers to the common idea of the moon's stealing light from the sun. Here the moon is "too spotty" and blemished to enter the celestial city and take its light therefrom.

1077–80. Rev. 22:2.

And alle in sute° her liurez wasse;° *to match/their garments were*
Tor° to knaw° þe gladdest chere.° *hard/know/face*
1110 Þe lombe° byfore° con° proudly passe, *lamb/in front/did*
Wyth hornez seuen of red golde cler;° *bright*
As praysed° perlez his wedez wasse. *valued*
Towarde þe throne þay trone a tras.° *made (their) way*
Þaȝ þay wern fele,° ne pres° in plyt,° *many/crowding/array*
1115 Bot° mylde as maydenez seme° at mas,° *but/maidens seemly/mass*
So droȝ° þay forth with gret delyt. *proceeded*
    Delyt þat hys come encroched° *coming brought*
To° much hit° were of for to melle.° *too/it/speak*
Þise aldermen,° quen he aproched,° *these elders/approached*
1120 Grouelyng to° his fete° þay felle. *prostrated at/feet*
Legyounes° of aungelez togeder uoched° *multitudes/angels/together summoned*

Þer kesten ensens° of swete° smelle. *scattered incense/sweet*
Þen glory and gle° watz nwe abroched,° *joy/anew issued*
Al songe° to loue° þat gay Iuelle.° *sang/praise/bright jewel*
1125 Þe steuen moȝt° stryke þurȝ° þe vrþe° to helle *sound might/through/earth*
Þat þe vertues of heuen° of° Ioye endyte.° *heaven/out of/joy utter*
To loue þe lombe his meyny° in melle° *company/among*
I-wyssc° I laȝt° a gret° delyt. *indeed/took/great*
    Delit þe lombe forto° deuise° *to/gaze upon*
1130 With much meruayle° in mynde went. *marvel*
Best watz he, blyþest° and moste to pryse,° *gentlest/prize*
Þat euer I herde° of speche spent;° *heard/words described*
So worþly whyt° wern wedez hys, *gloriously white*
His lokez symple,° hym self so gent. *expression meek/gracious*
1135 Bot a wounde ful° wyde and weete° con wyse° *very/wet/show*
An-ende° hys hert° þurȝ hyde to-rente.° *close to/heart/skin torn*
Of° his quyte° syde his blod out-sprent.° *from/white/blood gushed*
A-las! þoȝt° I, who did þat spyt?° *thought/wrong*
Ani breste for bale aȝt haf° for-brent,° *sorrow ought (to) have/burned up*
1140 Er° he þer-to hade° had delyt. *before/therein had*
    The lombe° delyt non lyste° to wene.° *lamb's/none cared/doubt*
Þaȝ° he were hurt and wounde hade, *though*
In his sembelaunt watz° neuer sene,° *face was (it)/seen*
So wern° his glentez° gloryous glade.° *were/looks/joyful*
1145 I loked° among his meyny schene° *saw/fair*
How þay wyth lyf° wern laste° and lade;° *life/loaded/filled*
Þen saȝ° I þer my lyttel quene, *saw*
Þat I wende° had standen° by me in sclade.° *supposed/stood/valley*

1111. *red golde:* Cf. above, p. 183, l. 47n.   **1130.** *in mynde went:* i.e., "my mind filled"

Lorde! much of mirþe watz° þat ho° made   *joy was (it)/she*
1150 Among her ferez° þat watz so quyt!   *companions*
Þat syȝt° me gart° to þenk° to wade   *sight/made/intend*
For luf-longyng° in gret delyt.°   *love/delight*

XX

Delyt me drof in yȝe° and ere,°   *entered through eye/ear*
My manez° mynde to maddyng° malte;°   *human/madness/gave way*
1155 Quen° I seȝ° my frely° I wolde° be þere,   *when/saw/fair (one)/wished (to)*
Byȝonde° þe water þaȝ ho were walte.°   *beyond/kept*
I þoȝt þat no þyng myȝt me dere,°   *hinder*
To fech° me bur° and take° me halte;   *fetch/(a) blow/make*
And to start in þe strem schulde° non me stere,°   *stream should/prevent*
1160 To swymme þe remnaunt,° þaȝ I þer swalte.°   *remainder/died*
Bot° of þat munt° I watz bi-talt;°   *but/purpose/shaken*
When I schulde° start in þe strem astraye,   *was about to*
Out of þat caste° I watz by-calt:°   *attempt/called back*
Hit° watz not at my pryncez paye.°   *it/pleasure*

1165 Hit payed° hym not þat I so flonc,°   *pleased/dashed*
Ouer meruelous merez° so mad arayde.°   *marvelous waters/madly disposed*
Of raas° þaȝ I were rasch and ronk,°   *in rush/impetuous*
Ȝet rapely° þer-inne I watz restayed;°   *quickly/restrained*
For ryȝt° as I sparred° vn-to þe bonc,°   *just/rushed/bank*
1170 Þat brathe° out of my drem° me brayde.°   *violence/dream/roused*
Þen wakned° I in þat erber wlonk;°   *awoke/arbor lovely*
My hede° vpon þat hylle° watz layde   *head/mound*
Þer as° my perle to grounde strayd.   *where*
I raxled° and fel in gret affray,°   *stretched/great dismay*
1175 And sykyng° to my self I sayd: *sighing*
"Now al be to þat pryncez paye."

Me payed ful° ille to be out-fleme°   *(it) pleased very/banished*
So sodenly of° þat fayre regioun,   *suddenly from*
Fro° alle þo° syȝtez so quykez° and queme.°   *from/those/lifelike/pleasing*
1180 A longeyng heuy° me strok in swone,°   *longing heavy/struck into (a) swoon*
And rewfully° þenne I con° to reme:°   *sorrowfully/began/lament*
"O perle," quod I, "of rych° renoun,   *said/glorious*
So watz hit me° dere þat° þou con deme°   *to me/precious what/tell*
In þys veray avysyoun!°   *true vision*
1185 If hit be ueray and soth sermoun°   *certain account*
Þat þou so stykez° in garlande gay,   *are set*
So wel is me° in þys doel-doungoun°   *happy am I/doleful dungeon*

1186. *garlande:* The garland is also seen in Dante's *Paradiso* (X, 91–93), in the circle of the blessed.

Þat þou art to þat prynsez paye."

  To þat pryncez paye hade° I ay° bente,

1190 And ȝerned° no more þen° watz me geuen,°

And halden me° þer in trwe entent,°

As þe perle me prayed° þat watz so þryuen,°

As helde° drawen° to Goddez present,°

To mo° of his mysterys I hade° ben dryuen;°

1195 Bot ay wolde man° of happe° more hente°

Þen moȝten° by ryȝt vpon hem clyuen.°

Þer-fore my ioye° watz sone° to-riuen,°

And I kaste° of kythez° þat lastez aye.

Lorde! mad hit arn° þat agayn þe stryuen,°

1200 Oþer proferen° þe oȝt° agayn þy paye;

  To pay þe prince oþer sete° saȝte°

Hit is ful eþe° to þe god krystyin;°

For I haf founden° hym, boþe day and naȝte,°

A God, a lorde, a frende ful fyin.°

1205 Ouer° þis hyul° þis lote° I laȝte,°

For pyty° of my perle enclyin,°

And syþen° to God I hit by-taȝte°

In krystez dere° blessyng and myn,°

Þat in þe forme of bred° and wyn°

1210 Þe preste vus schewez° vch a° daye;

He gef° vus to be his homly hyne°

Ande precious perlez vnto his pay.°

AMEN. AMEN.

---

had/ever

desired/than/granted

restrained myself/true intent

asked/fair

very likely/drawn/presence

more/would have/been brought

would men/happiness/take

might/right to them belong

joy/quickly/torn away

cast out/realms

they are/against you strive

or propose/anything

be/at peace

easy/good Christian

have found/night

noble

on/mound/fortune/received

sorrow/prostrate

then/it (i.e., the Pearl) committed

Christ's dear/mine

bread/wine

priest us shows/every

permitted/household servants

pleasure

DIDACTIC AND HAGIOGRAPHICAL LITERATURE

Literature written primarily for religious instruction in the Middle Ages was strong in numbers and generally weak in qualities of entertainment, but certain types can be mentioned as exceptions. The exempla were often-interesting little stories useful to preachers in illustrating their sermons, and there were whole collections of these, whereas the sermons themselves often seem very dull. Books of instruction were common but rarely attained the stylistic and personal warmth of the *Ancrene Riwle*. Miracles of the Virgin achieved great popularity, and approached the sensationalism of the saints' lives in appealing to mass interest. Both the *Legenda Aurea* and the *South English Legendary* were large collections of saints' legends and stories, often apocryphal, following the Church year. Most of this religious prose and verse was written in the thirteenth and fourteenth centuries, and the coming of the friars greatly stimulated its dissemination.

REFERENCES

D'Evelyn, C., and Mill, A., eds. *South English Legendary*. Oxford, 1956.

Gerould, G. H. *The Northern English Homily Collections*. Lancaster, Pa., 1902.

———. *Saints' Legends*. Boston, 1916.

Metcalfe, W. M. *Legends of Saints in Scottish of the Fourteenth Century*. Edinburgh, 1888–96.

Mosher, J. A. *The Exemplum in the Early Religious and Didatic Literature of England*. New York, 1911.

Owst, G. R. *Literature and Pulpit in Medieval England*. Cambridge, 1933.

———. *Preaching in Medieval England*. Cambridge, 1926.

Pantin, W. A. *The English Church in the Fourteenth Century*. Cambridge, 1955.

Pfander, Horace G. *The Popular Sermon of the Medieval Friar in England*. New York, 1937.

Didactic and hagiographical literature is treated in the General Introduction of this volume, pp. 11, 17–18, and 19.

from ANCRENE RIWLE

DATE: a. 1200. ◢ MANUSCRIPTS: Seventeen MSS are known—eleven English, four Latin, two French—the earliest written c. 1230. They are now in the British Library and various colleges of Cambridge University. The dialect is of the West Midlands. ◢ EDITIONS: James Morton, ed. and trans., *The Ancren Riwle, A Treatise on the Rules and Duties of Monastic Life* (London, 1853; rptd. as *The Nun's Rule*, The Medieval Library [New York, 1966]); this is the translation used in the present volume. The English text has been edited by A. C. Baugh, *The English Text of the Ancrene Riwle. Ed. from British Museum MS Royal 8 C.1.*, Early English Text Society, 232 (1956). See also C. D'Evelyn, ed., *The Latin Text of the Ancrene Riwle*, Early English Text Society, 216 (1944); J. A. Herbert, *The French Text of the Ancrene Riwle*, Early English Text Society, 219 (1944). The Early English Text Society is in the process of editing all the MSS, and a list of the works already completed can be had in the appendix to A. C. Baugh and Kemp Malone, *The Middle Ages*, Vol. I of *A Literary History of England*, ed. A. C. Baugh, 2d ed., 4 vols. (New York, 1967).

The *Ancrene Riwle* is one of the most important pieces of English prose between the time of Alfred the Great and the 16th century, for it not only links Old English stylistic features to later Middle English compositions, showing the continuity of English prose, but it also reflects a humanity, a warmth, and a common-sense wisdom rarely found in religious treatises of that time. The *Riwle* was written at the request of three sisters of noble birth who wished to retire to a contemplative, spiritual life. The author divides his work into eight sections; Book I treats devotional exercises, and the following sections discuss the senses as guardians of the spirit, the temptations of the flesh, and the advantages of a solitary life. Book VIII, given here, concerns external matters: food, clothing, the employment of servants, and the countless little things that make up everyday affairs. It is in this section on the outer rule more than the others that the author's kindly personality, his sense of humor, and his obvious sympathy for his young and delicate charges shines through. But elsewhere, too, the writer employs common sayings, beast fables, and poignant anecdotes, all of which made the *Riwle* relevant to the needs of his charges. To a certain extent, this relevance holds true today.

BOOK VIII

The Outer Rule

Biuoren, on erest, ich seide þet ȝe ne schulen nout, ase unwise, bihoten uorto holden none of þeo uttre

I said before, at the commencement, that ye ought not, like unwise people, to promise to keep any of

riwlen. Þet ilke ich sigge ȝete; ne non ne write ich ham, buten ou one. Ich sigge þis forði þet oðre ancren ne sigge nout þet ich, þuruh mine meistrie, makie ham neowe riwlen. Ne bidde ich nout þet heo holden ham; and ȝe ȝet moten chaungen ham, hwonse ȝe euer willeð, þeos for betere. Aȝean þinges þet beoð biuoren, of ham is lutel strencðe.

Of sihðe and of speche, and of þe oðre wittes is inouh i-seid. Nu is þeos laste dole, ase ich bihet ou on erest, to-deled and i-sundred o lutle seoue stucchenes.

Me let lesse deinté to þinge þet me haueð ofte; and forði ne schule ȝe beon, bute ase ure leawude breðren beoð, i-huseled wiðinnen tweolf moneð, bute viftene siðen—a mide-winteres dei; con-delmesse dei; tweolfte dei; a sunedei midwei bitweonen þet and ester, oðer ure lefdi dei, ȝif he is neih þene sunendei, uor þe heihnesse; ester dei; þene þridde sunendei þerefter; holi þursdei; hwitesunedei; and sumersdei; seinte Marie dei Magdaleine; þe assumciun; þe natiuité; seinte Mihaeles dei: alre halewune dei; seinte Andrewes dei. And aȝean alle þeos dawes, lokeð þet ȝe beon clenliche i-schriuen and nimeð disceplines; neuer þauh of none monne, buten of ou suluen. And forgoð enne dei our pitaunce. And ȝif out limpeð misliche þet ȝe beon nout i-huseled i þeos i-sette termes, ȝe muwen akoueren hit þene nexte

the external rules.[1] I say the same still; nor do I write them for any but you alone. I say this in order that other anchoresses may not say that I, by my own authority, make new rules for them. Nor do I command that they observe them, and ye may even change them, whenever ye will, for better ones. In regard to things of this kind that have been in use before, it matters little.

Of sight, and of speech, and of the other senses enough was said. Now this last part, as I promised you at the commencement, is divided and sepa-rated into seven small sections.

Men esteem a thing as less dainty when they have it often, and therefore ye should be, as lay brethren are, partakers of the holy communion only fifteen times a year: at Mid-winter; Candle-mas;[2] Twelfth-day;[3] on Sunday half-way between that and Easter, or our Lady's day,[4] if it is near the Sunday, because of its being a holiday; Easter-day; the third Sunday thereafter; Holy Thursday; Whitsunday;[5] and Midsummer day; St. Mary Magdalen's day;[6] the Assumption;[7] the Nativity; St. Michael's day;[8] All Saints' day;[9] St. Andrew's day.[10] And before all these days, see that ye make a full confession and undergo discipline; but never from any man, only from yourselves. And forgo your pittance for one day. And if any thing happens out of the usual order, so that ye may not have received the sacrament at these set times, ye

---

1. In the introduction to the *Riwle* the confessor states that the outer rule is variable, depending on the needs of individuals. The outer rule, teaching how people should eat, drink, sleep, and walk, concerns bodily exercise—which, according to the Apostle Paul (I Tim. 4:8), profits little and is "a branch of the science of mechanics" made only to serve the inner rule. "The other is as a lady; this is as her handmaid; for, whatever men do of the other outwardly, is only to direct the heart within." The outer rule also includes the whole formal—or, to use the author's word, *material*—side of religious life, such as the set prayers for the day or the season, fasting, times for receiving Communion, etc.

2. February 2, the day celebrating the Purification of the Virgin Mary, when candles are blessed.

3. January 6, the end of the medieval Christmas celebrations.

4. The Annunciation, March 25, when the angel Gabriel announced to Mary the incarnation of Christ.

5. The seventh Sunday after Easter, celebrating the descent of the Holy Spirit.

6. July 22.

7. A feast on August 15 celebrating the bodily assumption into heaven of the Virgin Mary.

8. September 29.

9. Nov. 1, a festival in honor of all the saints, also called Allhallows, the evening before being Allhallows Eve or Halloween.

10. November 30.

sunendei þerefter; oðer ȝif þe oðer terme is neih, abiden uort þeonne.

ȝe schulen eten urom ester uort þet þe holi rode dei, þe latere, þet is ine heruest, eueriche deie twie, bute uridawes and umbridawes and ȝoing dawes and uigiles. I þeos dawes, ne in þe aduent ne schulen ȝe eten nout hwit, bute ȝif neode hit makie. Þet oðer halue ȝer ȝe schulen uesten, al bute sunendawes one.

ȝe ne schulen eten vleschs ne seim buten ine muchele secnesse; oðer hwoso is euer feble eteð potage bliðeliche; and wunieð ou to lutel drunch. Noðeleas, leoue sustren, ower mete and ower drunch haueð iþuht me lesse þen ich wolde. Ne ueste ȝe nenne dei to bread and to watere, bute ȝe habben leaue. Sum ancre makeð hire bord mid hire gistes wiðuten. Þet is to muche ureondschipe, uor, of alle ordres þeonne is hit unkuindelukest and mest aȝean ancre ordre, þet is al dead to þe worlde. Me haueð i-herd ofte siggen þet deade men speken mid cwike men; auh þet heo eten mid cwike men ne uond ich neuer ȝete. Ne makie ȝe none gistninges; ne ne tulle ȝe to þe ȝete none unkuðe harloz; þauh þer nere non oðer vuel of bute hore meðlease muð, hit wolde oðer hwule letten heouenliche þouhtes.

Hit ne limpeð nout to ancre of oðer monne elmesse uorto makien hire large. Nolde me lauhwen ane beggare lude to bisemare þet bede men to feste? Marie and Marthe, boðe heo weren sustren; auh hore lif sundrede. ȝe ancren habbeð i-numen ou to Marie dole, þet ure Louerd sulf herede. "Maria optimam partem elegit." "Mar-

may make up for it the Sunday next following, or if the other set time is near, ye may wait till then.

Ye shall eat twice every day from Easter until the Holyrood day, the later,[11] which is in harvest, except on Fridays, and Ember days,[12] and procession days and vigils. In those days, and in the Advent, ye shall not eat any thing white,[13] except necessity require it. The other half year ye shall fast always, except only on Sundays.

Ye shall eat no flesh nor lard except in great sickness; or whosoever is infirm may eat potage without scruple; and accustom yourselves to little drink. Nevertheless, dear sisters, your meat and your drink have seemed to me less than I would have it. Fast no day upon bread and water, except ye have leave. There are anchoresses who make their meals with their friends outside the convent. That is too much friendship, because, of all orders, then is it most ungenial, and most contrary to the order of an anchoress, who is quite dead to the world. We have often heard it said that dead men speak with living men; but that they eat with living men, I have never yet found. Make ye no banquetings, nor encourage any strange vagabond fellows to come to the gate; though no other evil come of it but their immoderate talking, it might sometimes prevent heavenly thoughts.

It is not fit that an anchoress should be liberal of other men's alms. Would we not laugh loud to scorn a beggar who should invite men to a feast? Mary and Martha were two sisters, but their lives were different. Ye anchorites have taken to yourselves Mary's part, whom our Lord himself commended. "Mary hath chosen the best part.

---

11. The later Holyrood day, September 14, celebrates the Exaltation of the Holy Cross; the earlier Holyrood day, celebrating the Invention of the Holy Cross, falls on May 3.

12. Ember Days (OE *ymbrendæg*, from *ymbren*, "running around," the days occurring around the whole Church year) are times set apart in the four Church seasons for fasting and prayer.

13. Probably meant to pertain to delicate foods, like wastel bread of exceedingly fine white flour (such as Chaucer's Prioress fed her dogs) and white meat of any kind. The coarser, darker breads were more appropriate for these days.

the, Marthe," cweð he, "þu ert ine muchele baret. Marie haueð i-chosen betere, and ne schal hire noðing binimen hire dole." Husewifschipe is Marthe dole; and Marie dole is stilnesse and reste of alle worldes noise; þct noðing ne lette hire uorto i-heren Godes stefne. And lokeð hwat God seið—þet noðing ne schal binimen ou þeos dole. Marthe haueð hire mester; leteð hire i-wurðen, and sitte ʒe mid Marie ston-stille ed Godes fet, and hercneð him one. Marthe mester is uorto ueden and schruden poure men, ase huselefdi. Marie ne ouh nout uorto entremeten hire þerof; and ʒif ei blameð hire, God sulf oueral wereð hire þerof, ase holi writ witneð. An oðer half, non ancre ne ouh forto nimen bute gnedeliche þet hire to neodeð. Hwarof þeonne mei heo makien hire large? Heo schal libben bi elmesse ase neruhliche ase heo euer mei; and nout gederen uorto ʒiuen hit eft. Heo nis nout husewif; auh is a chirche ancre. Ʒif heo mei sparien eni poure schreaden, sende ham al derneliche ut of hire woanes. Vnder semblaunt of gode is ofte i-heled sunne. And hwu schulen þeos riche ancren þet beoð eorðe tilien, oðer habbeð rentes i-sette, don to psource neiheboures derneliche hore elmesse? Ne wilnen nout forto habben word of one large ancre; ne uorto ʒiuen muchel ne beo non þe grediure uorto habben more. Þeo gredinesse rote of hire bitternesse; alle beoð þe bowes bittre þet of hire springeð. Bidden hit, uorto ʒiuen hit nis nout ancre rihte. Of ancre kurtesie, and of ancre largesse, is i-kumen ofte sunne and scheome on ende.

Wummen and children þet habbeð i-swunken uor ou, hwatse ʒe sparieð on ou makieð ham to etene—nenne mon biuoren ou, bute ʒif he habbe neode; ne laðe ʒe to drinken nout. Ne ʒirne ich þet me telle ou hendi ancren. Et gode ureond nimeð al þet ʒe habbeð neode hwon heo beodeð hit ou; auh, for none bode, ne nime ʒe nout wiðuten neode,

Martha, Martha," said he, "thou art much cumbered. Mary hath chosen better, and nothing shall take her part from her."[14] Housewifery is Martha's part, and Mary's part is quietness and rest from all the world's din, that nothing may hinder her from hearing the voice of God. And observe what God saith, "that nothing shall take away this part from you." Martha hath her office; let her alone, and sit ye with Mary stone-still at God's feet, and listen to him alone. Martha's office is to feed and clothe poor men, as the mistress of a house. Mary ought not to intermeddle in it, and if any one blame her, God himself supreme defendeth her for it, as holy writ beareth witness. On the other hand, an anchoress ought to take sparingly only that which is necessary for her. Whereof, then, may she make herself liberal? She must live upon alms, as frugally as ever she can, and not gather that she may give it away afterwards. She is not a housewife, but a church anchoress. If she can spare any fragments for the poor, let her send them quite privately out of her dwelling. Sin is oft concealed under the semblance of goodness. And how shall those rich anchoresses that are tillers of the ground, or have fixed rents, do their alms privately to poor neighbours? Desire not to have the reputation of bountiful anchoresses, nor, in order to give much, be too eager to possess more. Greediness is the root of bitterness: all the boughs that spring from it are bitter. To beg in order to give away is not the part of an anchoress. From the courtesy of an anchoress, and from her liberality, sin and shame have often come in the end.

Make women and children who have laboured for you to eat whatever food you can spare from your own meals; but let no man eat in your presence, except he be in great need; nor invite him to drink any thing. Nor do I desire that ye should be told that ye are courteous anchoresses. From a good friend take whatever ye have need of when

---

14. Luke X : 38–42.

leste ʒe kecchen þene nome of gederinde ancren. Of mon þet ʒe misleueð ne nime ʒe nouðer lesse ne more—nout so much þet beo a rote gingiure. Muchel neode schal driuen ou uorte bidden out; þauh, edmodliche scheaweð to ower leoueste ureond ower meseise.

ʒe, mine leoue sustren, ne schulen habben no best, bute kat one. Ancre þet haueð eihte þuncheð bet husewif, ase Marthe was, þen ancre; ne none wise ne mei heð beon Marie, mid griðfulnesse of heorte. Vor þeonne mot heo þenchen of þe kues foddre, and of heorde-monne huire, oluhnen þene heiward, warien hwon me punt hire, and ʒelden, þauh, þe hermes. Wat Crist, þis is lodlich þing hwon me makeð mone in tune of ancre eihte. Þauh, ʒif eni mot nede habben ku, loke þet heo none monne ne eilie, ne ne hermie; ne þet hire þouht ne beo nout þeron i-uestned. Ancre ne ouh nout to habben no þing þet drawe utward hire heorte. None cheffare ne driue ʒe. Ancre þet is cheapild, heo cheapeð hire soule þe chepmon of helle. Ne wite ʒe nout in oure huse of oðer monnes þinges, ne eihte, ne cloðes; ne nout ne underuo ʒe þe chirche uestimenz, ne þene caliz, bute ʒif strencðe hit makie, oðer muchel eie; vor of swuche witunge is i-kumen muchel vuel oftesiðen. Wiðinnen ower woanes ne lete ʒe nenne mon slepen. Ʒif muchel neode mid alle makeð breken ower hus, þe hwule þet hit euer is i-broken, loke þet ʒe habben þerinne mid ou one wummon of clene liue deies and nihtes.

Uorði þet no mon ne i-sihð ou, ne ʒe i-seoð nenne mon, wel mei don of ower cloðes, beon heo hwite, beon heo **blake**; bute þet heo beon unorne and warme, and wel i-wrouhte—uelles wel

she offereth it to you; but for no invitation take any thing without need, lest ye get the name of gathering anchoresses. Of a man whom ye distrust, receive ye neither less nor more—not so much as a race of ginger. It must be great need that shall drive you to ask any thing; yet humbly shew your distress to your dearest friend.

Ye shall not possess any beast, my dear sisters, except only a cat. An anchoress that hath cattle appears as Martha was, a better housewife than anchoress; nor can she in any wise be Mary, with peacefulness of heart. For then she must think of the cow's fodder, and of the herdsman's hire, flatter the heyward,[15] defend herself when her cattle is shut up in the pinfold, and moreover pay the damage. Christ knoweth, it is an odious thing when people in the town complain of anchoresses' cattle. If, however, any one must needs have a cow, let her take care that she neither annoy nor harm any one, and that her own thoughts be not fixed thereon. An anchoress ought not to have any thing that draweth her heart outward. Carry ye on no traffic. An anchoress that is a buyer and seller selleth her soul to the chapman[16] of hell. Do not take charge of other men's property in your home, nor of their cattle, nor their clothes, neither receive under your care the church vestments, nor the chalice, unless force compel you, or great fear, for oftentimes much harm has come from such caretaking. Let no man sleep within your walls. If, however, great necessity should cause your house to be used, see that, as long as it is used, ye have therein with you a woman of unspotted life day and night.

Because no man seeth you, nor do ye see any man, ye may be well content with your clothes, be they white, be they black; only see that they be plain, and warm, and well made—skins well

---

15. An officer in charge of hedges and enclosures who watched that cattle did not break into the private lands from the village commons. When this happened, even anchoresses were not immune from penalty.

16. Merchant (i.e., the Devil, who barters for souls).

i-tauwed; and habbeð ase monie ase ou to-
neodeð, to bedde and eke to rugge.

Nexst fleshe ne schal mon werien no linene
cloð, bute ȝif hit beo of herde and of greate
heorden. Stamin habbe hwose wule; and hwose
wule mei beon buten. Ȝe schulen liggen in on
heater, and i-gurd. Ne bere ȝe non iren, ne here,
ne irspiles felles; ne ne beate ou þer mide, ne mid
schurge i-leðered ne i-leaded; ne mid holie, ne
mid breres ne ne biblodge hire sulf wiðuten
schriftes leaue; ne ne nime, et enes, to ueole
disciplines. Ower schone beon greate and warme.
Ine sumer ȝe habbeð leaue uorto gon and sitten
baruot; and hosen wiðuten uaumpez; and ligge
ine ham hwoso likeð. Sum wummon inouhreaðe
wereð þe brech of heare ful wel i-knotted, and þe
strapeles adun to hire uet, i-laced ful ueste. Ȝif
ȝe muwen beon wimpel-leas, beoð bi warme
keppen and þeruppon blake ueiles. Hwose wule
beon i-seien, þauh heo atiffe hire nis nout muchel
wunder; auh to Godes eien heo is lufsumere, þet
is, uor þe luue of him, untiffed wiðuten. Ring, ne
broche nabbe ȝe; ne gurdel i-menbred, ne glouen,
ne no swuch þing þet ou ne deih forto habben.

Euer me is leouere so ȝe don gretture werkes.
Ne makie none purses, uorte ureonden ou mide;
ne blodbendes of seolke; auh schepieð, and
seouweð, and amendeð chirche cloðes, and poure
monne cloðes. No þing ne schule ȝe ȝiuen wiðuten
schriftes leaue. Helpeð mid ower owune swinke,
so uorð so ȝe muwen, to schruden ou suluen and
þeo þet ou serueð, ase Seint Jerome lereð. Ne beo
ȝe neuer idel; uor anonrihtes þe ueond beot hire
his werc þet ine Godes werke ne wurcheðð; and he
tuteleð anonrihtes touward hire. Uor, þeo hwule
þet he isihð hire bisi, þencheð þus: vor nout ich

tawed; and have as many as you need, for bed
and also for back.

Next your flesh ye shall wear no flaxen cloth,
except it be of hards[17] and of coarse canvas.
Whoso will may have a stamin,[18] and whoso will
may be without it. Ye shall sleep in a garment and
girt.[19] Wear no iron, nor haircloth, nor hedgehog-
skins; and do not beat yourselves therewith, nor
with a scourge of leather thongs, nor leaded; and
do not with holly nor with briars cause yourselves
to bleed without leave of your confessor; and do
not, at one time, use too many flagellations. Let
your shoes be thick and warm. In summer ye are
at liberty to go and to sit barefoot, and to wear
hose without vamps, and whoso liketh may lie
in them. A woman may well enough wear drawers
of haircloth very well tied, with the strapples
reaching down to her feet, laced tightly. If ye
would dispense with wimples, have warm capes,
and over them black veils. She who wishes to be
seen, it is no great wonder though she adorn
herself; but, in the eyes of God, she is more lovely
who is unadorned outwardly for his sake. Have
neither ring, nor broach, nor ornamented girdle,
nor gloves, nor any such thing that is not proper
for you to have.

I am always the more gratified, the coarser the
works are that ye do. Make no purses, to gain
friends therewith, nor blodbendes[20] of silk; but
shape, and sew, and mend church vestments, and
poor people's clothes. Ye shall give nothing away
without leave from your father confessor. Assist
with your own labour, as far as ye are able, to
clothe yourselves and your domestics, as St.
Jerome teacheth. Be never idle; for the fiend
immediately offers his work to her who is not
diligent in God's work; and he beginneth directly
to talk to her. For, while he seeth her busy, he

---

17. (Also *hurds*) the coarser parts of flax and hemp.
18. According to the *OED* a coarse worsted cloth worn by ascetics as an undergarment.

19. (Also *girth*) belt.
20. Specially prepared bandages used in bloodletting to stop the bleeding.

schulde nu kumen neih hire; ne mei heo nout i-hwulen uorto hercnen mine lore. Of idelnesse awakeneð muchel flesshes fondunge. "Iniquitas Sodome saturitas panis et ocium": þet is, al Sodomes cweadschipe com of idelnesse and of ful wombe. Iren þet lið stille gedereð sone rust; and water þet ne stureð nout readliche stinkeð. Ancre ne schal nout forwurðen scolmeistre, ne turnen hire ancre hus to childrene scole. Hire meiden mei, þauh, techen sum lutel meiden, þet were dute of forto leornen among gromes; auh ancre ne ouh forto ȝemen bute God one.

ȝe ne schulen senden lettres, ne underuon lettres, ne writen buten leaue. ȝe schulen beon i-dodded four siðen iðe ȝere, uorto lihten ower heaued; and ase ofte i-leten blod; and oftere ȝif neod is; and hwoso mei beon þer wiðuten, ich hit mei wel i-ðolien. Hwon ȝe beoð i-leten blod, ȝe ne schulen don no þing, þeo þreo dawes, þet ou greue; auh talkeð mid ouer meidenes and mid þeaufule talen schurteð ou to-gederes. ȝe muwen don so ofte hwon ou þuncheð heuie, oðer beoð uor sume worldliche þinge sorie oðer seke. So wisliche witeð ou in our blod-letunge; and holdeð ou ine swuche reste þet ȝe longe þerefter muwen ine Godes seruise þe monluker swinken; and also hwon ȝe i-ueleð eni secnesse; vor muchel sotschipe hit is uorto uorleosen, uor one deie, tene oðer tweolue. Wascheð ou hwarse ȝe habbeð neode, ase ofte ase ȝe wulleð.

Ancre þet naueð nout neih hond hire uode, beoð bisie two wummen; one þet bileaue euer et hom, on oðer þet wende ut hwon hit is neod; and þeo beo ful unorne, oðer of feir elde; and bi þe weie ase heo geð go singinde hire beoden; ne ne holde heo nout non tale mid mon ne mid wummon; ne ne sitte ne ne stonde, bute þet leste þet heo mei, er þen heo kume hom. Nouhwuder elles ne go heo bute þider ase me sent hire. Wiðute leaue ne ete heo ne ne drinke ute. Þe oðer beo euer inne, ne wiðute þe ȝeate ne go heo wiðute leaue. Boðe beon obedient to hore dame in alle þinges, bute ine

thinketh thus: It would avail nothing if I were now to accost her, nor would she take time to listen to my teaching. From idleness ariseth much temptation of the flesh: "All the wickedness of Sodom came of idleness, and of a full belly." Iron that lieth still soon gathereth rust; and water that is not stirred soon stinketh. An anchoress must not become a schoolmistress, nor turn her anchoress-house into a school for children. Her maiden may, however, teach any little girl concerning whom it might be doubtful whether she should learn among boys, but an anchoress ought to give her thoughts to God only.

Ye shall not send, nor receive, nor write letters without leave. Ye shall have your hair cut four times a year to disburden your head; and be let blood as oft, and oftener if it is necessary; but if any one can dispense with this, I may well suffer it. When ye are let blood, ye ought to do nothing that may be irksome to you for three days; but talk with your maidens, and divert yourselves together with instructive tales. Ye may often do so when ye feel dispirited, or are grieved about some worldly matter, or sick. Thus wisely take care of yourselves when you are let blood, and keep yourselves in such rest that long thereafter ye may labour the more vigorously in God's service, and also when ye feel any sickness, for it is great folly, for the sake of one day, to lose ten or twelve. Wash yourselves wheresoever it is necessary, as often as ye please.

When an anchoress hath not her food at hand, let two women be employed, one who stays always at home, another who goes out when necessary; and let her be very plain, or of sufficient age; and, by the way, as she goeth let her go singing her prayers; and hold no conversation with man or with woman; nor sit, nor stand, except the least possible, until she come home. Let her go nowhere else, but to the place whither she is sent. Without leave, let her neither eat nor drink abroad. Let the other be always within, and never go out of the gate without leave. Let both be obedient to their

sunne one. No þing nabben heo þet hore dame hit nute; ne ne underuon no þing, ne ne ȝiuen wiðuten hire leaue. Nenne mon ne leten heo in; ne þe ȝungre ne speke mid none monne bute leaue; ne ne go nout ut of tune widuten siker uere; ne ne ligge ute. Ȝif heo ne con o boke, sigge bi Paternostres and bi auez hire vres; and wurche þet me hat hire wiðuten grucchunge. Habbe euer hire earen opene touward hire dame. Nouðer of þe wummen ne beren urom hore dame, ne ne bringed to hire none idele talen, ne neowe tiðinges; ne bitweonen hamsulf ne singen; ne ne speken none worldliche spechen; ne lauhwen, ne ne pleien so þet ei mon þet hit iseie muhte hit to vuel turnen. Ouer alle þing leasunge and luðere wordes hatien. Hore her beo i-koruen; hore heued cloð sitte lowe. Eiðer ligge one. Hore hesmel beo heie istihd; al wiðute broche. No mon ne i-seo ham unweawed, ne open heaued. Louh lokunge habben. Heo ne schulen cussen nenne mon, ne uor luue cluppen ne kuð ne unkuð; ne wasshen hore heaued; ne loken ueste o none monne; ne toggen mid him, ne pleien. Hore weaden beon of swuche scheape, and alle hore aturn swuch þet hit beo eðcene hwarto heo beoð i-turnde. Hore lates loken warliche, þet non ne edwite ham ne ine huse, ne ut of huse. On alle wise uorberen to wreððen hore dame; and ase ofte ase heo hit doð, er heo drinken oðer eten, makien hore uenie akneon adun to þer eorðe biuoren hire, and sigge "Mea culpa"; and underuon þe penitence þet heo leið upon hire, lutende hire louwe. Þe ancre neuer more þer efter þene ilke gult ne upbreide hire, uor none wreððe, bute ȝif heo eft sone ualle iðet ilke; auh do hit allunge ut of hire heorte. And ȝif eni strif ariseð bitweonen þe wummen, þe ancre make eiðer of ham to makien oðer venie akneon to þer eorðe, and eiðer rihte up oðer, and kussen ham on ende; and þe ancre legge on eiðer sum penitence; more upon þe ilke þet gretluker haueð agult. Þis is o

dame in all things, sin only excepted. Let them possess nothing unknown to their mistress, nor accept nor give any thing without her permission. They must not let any man in; nor must the younger speak with any man without leave; nor go out of town without a trusty companion, nor sleep out. If she cannot read her hours in a book, let her say them with Paternosters[21] and Ave Marias;[22] and do the work that she is commanded to do, without grudging. Let her have her ears always open to her mistress. Let neither of the women either carry to her mistress or bring from her any idle tales, or new tidings, nor sing to one another, nor speak any worldly speeches, nor laugh, nor play, so that any man who saw it might turn it to evil. Above all things, they ought to hate lying and ribaldry. Let their hair be cut short, their headcloth sit low. Let each lie alone. Let their hesmel[23] be high pointed: none to wear a broach. Let no man see them unveiled, nor without a hood. Let them look low. They ought not to kiss, nor lovingly embrace any man, neither of their acquaintance nor a stranger, nor to wash their head, nor to look fixedly on any man, nor to romp nor frolic with him. Their garments should be of such a shape and all their attire such that it may be easily seen to what life they are dedicated. Let them observe cautiously their manners, so that nobody may find fault with them, neither in the house nor out of the house. Let them, by all means, forbear to vex their mistress; and, whenever they do so, let them before they either eat or drink make obeisance on their knees bending to the earth before her and say, "Mea culpa;"[24] and accept the penance that she layeth upon them, bowing low. And let not the anchoress ever again thereafter upbraid her with the same fault, when vexed, except she soon afterwards fall into the same, but drive it entirely out of her heart. And if any strife ariseth between the women, let

---

21. Our Fathers, from the first words of the Lord's Prayer in Latin.

22. Hail Marys, prayers based on the angel Gabriel's salutation to the Virgin.

23. According to the *MED* a short cape covering the shoulders as part of the habit of a member of the Gilbertine Rule. It was evidently used generally by religious persons.

24. Latin, "by my fault."

þing, wute ȝe wel to soð, þet is God leouest—
seihnesse and some—and þe ueonde loðest; and
forði he is euer umbe to arearen sume wreððe.
Nu isihð þe deouel wel þet hwon þet fur is wel o
brune, and me wule þet hit go ut, me sundreð þe
brondes; and he deð al so onond þet ilke. Luue
is Jesu Cristes fur þet he wule þet blasie in vre
heorte; and þe deouel bloweð forto puffen hit ut;
and hwon his blowinge ne geineð nout, þeonne
bringeð he up sum luðer word, oðer sum nouh-
tunge hwar þuruh heo to-hurteð eiðer urommard
oðer; and þe Holi Gostes fur acwencheð, hwon
þe brondes, þuruh wreððe, beoð i-sundred. And
forði, holden ham ine luue ueste to-gederes, and
ne beo ham nout of hwon þe ueond blowe; and
nomeliche, ȝif monie beoð i-ueied somed, and wel
mid luue ontende.

Þauh þe ancre on hire meidenes uor openliche
gultes legge penitence, neuer þe later to þe preoste
schriuen ham ofte; auh euer þauh mid leaue. And
ȝif heo ne kunnen nout þe mete graces, siggen in
hore stude Pater noster and Aue Maria biuoren
mete, and efter mete also, and Credo moare; and
siggen þus on ende, "Veder and Sune and Holi
Gost and, on Almihti God, he ȝiue ure dame his
grace, so lengre so more; and leue hire and us
boðe nimen god endinge; and forȝelde alle þet us
god doð, and milce hore soulen þet us god i-don
habbeð—hore soulen and alle cristene soulen.
Amen." Bitweonen mele ne gruselie ȝe nout
nouðer frut, ne oðerhwat; ne ne drinken wiðuten
leaue; auh þe leaue beo liht in alle þeo þinges
þer nis sunne. Ette mete no word, oðer lut, and
þeo beon stille. Al so efter þe ancre cumplie uort
mid-morwen ne don no þing, ne ne siggen, hware
þuruh hire silence muwe beon i-sturbed. Non

the anchoress cause them to make obeisance to
each other kneeling to the earth, and the one to
raise up the other, and finally to kiss each other;
and let the anchoress impose some penance on
both, but more upon her who is most in fault. Be
ye well assured, this is a thing most pleasing to
God—peace and concord—and most hateful to
the fiend; and, therefore, he is always endeavour-
ing to stir up some strife. Now the devil seeth well
that when the fire is fairly blazing, and men wish
it to go out, they separate the brands: and he doth,
in regard to this, just the same thing. Love is
Jesus Christ's fire, which he would have to burn
in our hearts, and the devil bloweth that he may
puff it out; and when his blowing is of no avail, he
then bringeth up some insulting word, or some
other mark of contempt, whereby they are repelled
from each other, and the flame of the Holy Spirit
is quenched, when the brands, through anger, are
sundered. And therefore, keep them firmly united
in love, and be not away from them when the
fiend may blow; and especially, if there be many
joined together, and well kindled with love.

Though the anchoress impose penance on her
maidens for open faults, let them nevertheless
confess often to the priest; but always, however,
with permission. And if they cannot say the graces
at meals, let them say, instead of them, Paternoster
and Ave Maria, before and also after meat, and
the Creed over and above; and in conclusion say
thus, "May the Father, Son, and Holy Ghost, one
God Almighty, give our mistress his grace, always
more and more, and grant to her and us both to
have a good ending, and reward all who do us
good, and be merciful to the souls of them who
have done us good—to the souls of them and of all
Christians. Amen." Between meals, do not munch
either fruit or any thing else; and drink not without
leave; but let the leave be easily granted in all
those matters where there is no sin. At meat let
there be no talking, or little, and then be still. Also,
neither do nor say any thing after the anchoress'

ancre seruant ne ouhte, mid rihte, uorto asken i-sette huire, bute mete and cloð þet heo mei vlutten bi, and Godes milce. Ne misleue non god, hwat so bitide, of þe ancre, þet he hire trukie. Þe meidenes wiðuten, ȝif heo serueð þe ancre al so ase heo owen, hore hure schal beon þe eche blisse of heouene. Hwoso haueð eie hope touward so heie hure, gledliche wule heo seruen, and lihtliche alle wo and alle teone þolien. Mid eise ne mid este ne kumeð me nout to þer heouene.

ȝe ancren owen þis lutle laste stucchen reden to our wummen eueriche wikes enes, uort þet heo hit kunnen. And muche neod is ou beoðe þet ȝe nimen to ham gode ȝeme; vor ȝe muwen muchel þuruh ham beon i-goded, and i-wursed on oðer halue. Ȝif heo suneged þuruh ower ȝemeleaste, ȝe schulen beon bicleoped þerof biuoren þe heie demare; and forði, ase ou is muche neod, and ham is ȝete more, ȝeorneliche techeð ham to holden hore riulen, boðe uor ou and for ham suluen; liðeliche þauh, and luueliche; uor swuch ouh wummone lorc to beon—luuelich and liðe, and seldhwonne sturne. Boðe hit is riht þeo heo ou dreden and luuien; auh þer beo more euer of luue þen of drede. Þeonne schal hit wel uaren. Me schal helden eoli and win beoðc ine wunden, eftere godere lore; auh more of þe softe eolie þen of þe bitinde wine; þet is, more of liðe wordes þen of suwinde; vor þerof kumeð þinge best—þet is luue-eie. Lihtliche and sweteliche uorȝiueð ham hore gultes hwon heo ham i-knoweð and bihoteð bote.

compline,[25] until **prime**[26] next morning, whereby her silence might be disturbed. No servant of an anchoress ought, properly, to ask stated wages, except food and clothing, with which, and with God's mercy, she may do well enough. Let her not disbelieve any good of the anchoress, whatever betide, as that she may deceive her. The maidens out of doors, if they serve the anchoress in such a manner as they ought, shall have their reward in the eternal blessedness of heaven. Whoso hath any hope of so high a reward will gladly serve, and easily endure all grief and all pain. With ease and abundance men do not arrive at heaven.

Ye anchoresses ought to read these little concluding parts to your women once every week until they know it well. And it is very necessary for you both that ye take much care of them, for ye may be much benefited by them; and, on the other hand, made worse. If they sin through your negligence, ye shall be called to give account of it before the Supreme Judge; and, therefore, it is very necessary for you, and still more for them, that ye diligently teach them to keep their rule, both for your sake and for themselves; in a gentle manner, however, and affectionately; for such ought the instructing of women to be—affectionate and gentle, and seldom stern. It is right that they should both fear and love you; but that there should be always more of love than of fear. Then it shall go well. Both wine and oil should be poured into the wounds, according to divine instruction; but more of the soft oil than of the biting wine; that is, more of gentle than of vehement words; for thereof cometh that which is best—love-fear. Mildly and kindly forgive them their faults when they acknowledge them and promise amendment.

---

25. The last of the canonical hours, a night prayer, said before going to bed. It might have come after matins for the next day had been said in the evening.

26. After matins and lauds (the night and dawn prayers), the morning canonical hour, usually between 6 and 9 A.M.

Se uorð ase ȝe muwen of drunch and of mete and of cloð, and of oðer þinges þet neode of flesche askeð, beoð large touward ham, þauh ȝe þe neruwure beon and te herdure to ou suluen; vor so deð he þe wel bloweð—went þe neruwe ende of þe horne to his owune muðe, and utward þene wide. And ȝe don al so, ase ȝe wulleð þet ower beoden bemen and dreamen wel ine Drihtenes earen; and nout one to ower ones, auh to alle uolkes heale; ase ure Louerd leue, þuruh þe grace of himsulf, þet hit so mote beon. Amen!

O þisse boc redeð eueriche deie hwon ȝe beoð eise—eueriche deie lesse oðer more. Uor ich hopie þet hit schal beon ou, ȝif se ȝe redeð ofte, swuðe biheue þuruh Godes grace; and elles ich heuede vuele bitowen muchel of mine hwule. God hit wot, me were leouere uorto don me touward Rome þen uorto biginnen hit eft forto donne. And ȝif ȝe iuindeð þet ȝe doð al so ase ȝe redeð, þonkeð God ȝeorne; and ȝif ȝe ne doð nout, biddeð Godes ore, and beoð umbe þer abuten þet ȝe hit bet hol holden, efter ower mihte. Veder and Sune and Holi Gost, and on Almihti God, he wite ou in his warde! He gledie ou, and froure ou, mine leoue sustren, and, for al þet ȝe uor him drieð and suffreð, he ne ȝiue ou neuer lesse huire þen altogedere him suluen! He beo euer i-heied from worlde to worlde, euer on ecchenesse! Amen.

Ase ofte ase ȝe readeð out of þisse boc, greteð þe lefdi mid one Aue Marie, uor him þet maked þeos riwle, and for him þet hire wrot and swonc her abuten. Inouh meðful ich am, þet bidde so lutel.

As far as ye can, in regard to drink, and food, and clothing, and other things which the wants of the flesh require, be liberal to them, though ye be the more strict and severe to yourselves; for so doth he that bloweth well: He turneth the narrow end of the horn to his own mouth, and the wide end outward. And do ye the like, as ye would that your prayers may resound like a trumpet, and make a sweet noise in the ears of the Lord; and not to your own salvation only, but to that of all people; which may our Lord grant through the grace of himself, that so it may be. Amen.

In this book read every day, when ye are at leisure—every day, less or more; for I hope that, if ye read it often, it will be very beneficial to you, through the grace of God, or else I shall have ill employed much of my time. God knows, it would be more agreeable to me to set out on a journey to Rome, than to begin to do it again.[27] And, if ye find that ye do according to what ye read, thank God earnestly; and if ye do not, pray for the grace of God, and diligently endeavour that ye may keep it better, in every point, according to your ability. May the Father, and the Son, and the Holy Ghost, the one Almighty God, keep you under his protection! May he give you joy and comfort, my dear sisters, and for all that ye endure and suffer for him may he never give you a less reward than his entire self. May he be ever exalted from world to world, for ever and ever. Amen.

As often as ye read any thing in this book, greet the Lady with an Ave Mary for him who made this rule, and for him who wrote it, and took pains about it. Moderate enough I am, who ask so little.

---

27. Pilgrimages varied in difficulty and excitement. A trip to Canterbury might be considered a pleasurable outing, but one to Rome, either by sea or over the Alps, was accompanied by considerable perils and hardships. Yet, as the author of the *Riwle* implies, everything is relative.

from SOUTH ENGLISH LEGENDARY

DATE: 1280–90. ✦ MANUSCRIPTS: Bodleian Library, Oxford, Laud 108 (1280–90); British Library Harleian 2277 (c. 1300) Corpus Christi College, Cambridge, 145 (c. 1320); and others. The dialect of the Laud MS. is impure Southern (Southwest). ✦ EDITIONS: C. Horstmann, *Early South English Legendary*, Early English Text Society, 87 (London, 1887); Charlotte D'Evelyn and Anna J. Mill, *The South English Legendary*, 3 vols., Early English Text Society, 235, 236, 241 (London, 1956–59). Horstmann's edition of the Laud MS. is used here. The critical articles by Minnie E. Wells on the relationship of the *Legendary* to the *Legenda Aurea* (*PMLA*, 51 [1936], 337–60) and on the development of the *Legendary* (*Journal of English and Germanic Philology*, 41 [1942], 320–44) are of value. A. Jameson's *Sacred and Legendary Art*, 2 vols. (New York, 1896), is an excellent source book for the saints' legends.

Although the dialect of the *Legendary* is Southern, it is quite corrupt. We will not find, for instance, the usual initial *v* for *f*, though *u* for *eo* and *y* is occasionally present (*fullen* = *fell, pusse* = *this*). On the other hand, it is very important to recognize the various older pronoun forms: *heo*, "she"; *huy*, "they"; *is*, "his"; *him*, "himself"; *heom*, "themselves"; *heore*, "their." The following should also be noted: (1) ȝw stands for *w*, *wh* (*ȝwat* = *what*, *ȝweol* = *well*); (2) the prefix *i-* usually precedes a past participle (*i-writen*), and also at times a present plural form (*i-seoth* = *see*); (3) *-th* is the normal present plural ending of verbs (*seoth*, "they see," *beoth*, "they are"); (4) *u* and *v* are regularly interchanged (*pov* = *thou*, *liue* = *live*).

The *South English Legendary* is a collection of saints' lives and stories illustrating important seasons of the Church year, which grew with the contributions of many people over many decades. It was originally begun shortly before the *Legenda Aurea*, a similar anthology by Jacobus de Voragine, near the abbey of Gloucester by a Franciscan friar sometime before 1275. The numerous MSS attest to the popularity of this kind of literature, but the arrangement and contents of the various compositions show wide variations. A certain folk development of apocryphal literature can be noted throughout the whole. The legend of Saint George, for instance, is a humorless account of torture and survival. On the other hand, the story of Saint Martin of Tours is filled with interesting tidbits from popular tradition and contains a most revealing account of clerical pique. The legends are saintly but far from dull. Like the exempla of Robert Mannyng of Brunne, they appealed to "lewde men."

Saint George of Cappadocia

Seint° George þe holie man, ase° we findez i-write,°	*Saint/as/find written*
In þe londe° of Cappadoce he was i-bore° and bi-ȝite.°	*land/born/begotten*
Þe false godes° he for-sok° and tornede° to cristine-dom,°	*gods/forsook/turned/Christianity*
And louede Iesu° crist swiþe° wel and holi man bi-com.°	*loved Jesus/very/became*
5 Dacian, þe luþere° prince þat was in þulke stounde,°	*evil/that time*
Alle þe cristine° men þat he fond° he let bringue° to grounde.	*Christian/found/had brought*
A° day, ase he honourede is° false godes and oþere manie on,°	*one/honored his/others many (a) one*
Seint George i-saiȝ° al þis ase he cam þare-forth gon.°	*saw/came there traveling*
Þe signe he made of þe croiz° and blessede him° al-a-boute	*cross/himself/all over*
10 And armede° him þoruȝ þe holie gost with-inne and with-oute.	*armed/through*
He wende him° forth wel baldeliche° and wel loude bi-gan° to grede°	*turned/very boldly/began/call*
To Dacian and to alle his and þeose° wordes sede:°	*these/said*
"Alle false godes so beoth° deuelschine, i-wis;°	*are/devils, indeed*
For ore louerd° made heuene° ase in þe sautere° i-writen it is."	*our Lord/heaven/Psalter*
15 Þo° Dacian i-heorde° þis he grennede° and femde faste,°	*when/heard/bared his teeth/foamed greatly*
And lourede° with sori semblaunt,° and þeos wordes out he caste:	*glowered/angry face*
"Belamy, ȝwat° art þou þat so gret fol° art and so bold,	*what (i.e., who)/great fool*
Þat in ovre power and bi° ovre godes swuche° wordes hast i-told?°	*about/such/spoken*
Þov ne° dost us nouȝt one° schame, ase we alle i-seoth,°	*not/not alone/see*
20 Ake° ore godes and us, ȝwane° þou seist° þat huy deuelene° beoth.	*but/when/say/they devils*
Tel me sone of ȝwannes° þou art and ȝwat is þi riȝte° name,	*quickly from whence/right*
Þat darst° us° segge° and ore godes þus baldeliche swch° schame."	*dare/to us/say/such*
"Gcorge ich° hote,"° þis° oþur seide,° "and cristine man ich am,	*I/am called/the/said*
And out of þe lond of cappadoce hidere° to eov° ich cam."	*hither/you*
25 "Bel amy," seide Dacian, "torne° þi word a-non°	*change/quickly*
And honoure here ovre godes oþur° it schal an-oþur gon."°	*or/amiss go*

---

1. *Seint George:* The patron saint of soldiers and armorers, born in Cappadocia (Asia Minor) of Christian parents, was a tribune in the army of Diocletian. His legend here begins after he had slain the dragon and saved the princess Cleodolina in Libya—or, as some sources have it, in Lebanon. Diocletian's edict against Christians was posted at this time in the market-places. Saint George tore the proclamations down and spoke against idolatry, whereupon the proconsul Dacian ordered him to be tortured.

6. *bringue to grounde:* i.e., "put to death."

17. *Belamy:* OF, "good friend," considered by some to be an opprobrious form of greeting (cf. the Host's address to the Pardoner in Chaucer's *Canterbury Tales*).

"Beo° stille, þov fol," seint George seide;   "þou spext embe nou3t,°   *be/speak about nothing*

For ich habbe° on Iesu crist   i-fastned° al mi þou3t."°   *have/fastened/thought*

"A, traytour,"° seide Dacian,   "wolt° þov take° on so?   *ah, traitor/will/carry*

³⁰ Þov schalt in oþere ribaudies°   sone dai3es° beo i-do."°   *to other amusement/this day/put*

He liet° him hangi° up an hei3   in one-manere° rode°   *ordered/hanged/on high/on a kind (of)/cross*

And þare-to° him binde° faste al naked   with ropes strongue° and guode.°   *thereon/bound/strong/good*

With kene owles° þer-under   þe tormentores stode°   *sharp awls (i.e., nails)/stood*

And to-drowen° is holie lymes°   þat° faste huy ronne on blode;°   *tore/limbs/so that/ran with blood*

³⁵ Al huy to-teren° is tendre flesch;   þe peces fullen° to grounde;   *tore/pieces fell*

Brenninde eoyle° huy nomen sethþe°   and casten° in þe wounde.   *boiling oil/took then/threw*

Þo huy hadden° him so longue to-drawe°   þat reouþe° it was to seo,°   *had/long tortured/pity/see*

Huy bi-þou3ten heom° of° more wo°   and nomen him a-doun of° þe treo:°   *decided among themselves/on/evil/down off/tree (i.e., cross)*

With smarte° scourges huy leiden° on him   and wounde op-on oþur° made—   *painful/laid/on (the) other*

⁴⁰ To þe bare bon° þe scourgenc comen°   ase þe owles hadden i-wade;°   *bones/scourges came/gone in*

Þe woundene° huy selten° sethþe   and salt ful° þicke caste,   *wounds/salted/very*

And sethþe with a clout° of here°   roddeden° þe woundes faste.°   *rag/hair/reddened/much*

Louerd, muche was þe pine° þat he hadde,   ech ope° oþur þerc,   *sorrow/each upon*

Þo men selten so is quike° flesch   and roddeden so with here!   *sensitive*

⁴⁵ Reuþe° it was swuch pine to se,°   ho-so ou3t° of reuþe were;°   *pity/see/whoever anything/knew*

And euere° lay þe guode man   ase þei° him° noþing nere.°   *ever/as though (it)/to him/were not*

Þo Dacian i-sai3° þat he ne mi3te°   ouer-comen° him so,   *saw/might/overcome*

He let° binde þene° holie man   and in strongue prisone do.°   *had/the/put*

Þare° he lai al þe longue ni3t°   to° oþur wo þat he hadde.   *there/night/in addition to/woe*

⁵⁰ A-morewe° þe tormentores eft-sone°   bi-fore° Daciane him ladden.°   *in the morning/again soon/before/led*

In eche manere° huy fondeden þo°   3if° huy mi3ten tuyrne is þou3t.°   *every way/tried then/if/might change his mind*

Ake þo huy i-sei3en euerech-one°   þat it was al for nou3t,   *saw everyone*

Dacian let makie° a weol° of bras°   so° strong ase he mi3te,   *made/wheel/brass/as*

And scharpe sweordes wel° þicke a-boute   þare-on° faste he pi3te:°   *swords very/thereon/placed*

⁵⁵ He let nime° þis holie man   and þare-aboue° him do,   *taken/there above*

Þat þe swerdes scholden° is bodi to-rende°   and to-drawe al-so.°   *swords should/tear/torture so*

So sone° ase huy þis guode man   a-boue þusse ȝweole brouȝte,°   *soon/this wheel brought*

Þat ȝweol to-brac,° ase God it wolde,°   and to-bruysde° al-to° nouȝte;   *burst/wanted/broke/all to*

So þat þis holie man   harmles° þarof° he was.   *unharmed/by it*

60 Dacian was swiþe wroth°   þo° he i-saiȝ þat cas.°   *very angry/when/happening*

A forneis° he let maken° of bras   and fullen° it ful of led:°   *furnace/made/filled/lead*

He let maken a strong fuyr i-novȝ,°   ase he nam sone° is red.°   *fire enough/took quickly/counsel*

Þo þat led was al i-molte°   and boylede° swiþe faste,   *melted/boiled*

He let nimen° þis holie man   and riȝt a-middes° caste.   *taken/right/in the middle*

65   Seint° George nam° up is hond°   and þe croiz bi-fore him made,   *Saint/raised/hand/(sign of the) cross before himself*

And in þe wallinde° led   baldeliche° he gan° wade.   *boiling/boldly/did*

Þare-inne° he sat wel softe a-doun   ase þei him noþing nere,   *therein*

And leonede° to þe brerde° stille   ase þei he a-slepe° were;   *leaned/side/asleep*

He lai ase þei he in reste were   for-to° þat led atþe° laste   *until/at*

70 Was al in-to° þe colde i-turnd°   þat boylede er° so faste.   *to/turned/before*

Louerd, muche° is þi miȝte,   ase men miȝten þare i-seo,°   *Lord, great/see*

Þat ani man miȝte in þe wallinde led   so longue harmles beo!°   *be*

Þo Dacian þis i-seiȝ   his wit him° was neiȝ bi-nome;°   *he/nearly deprived of*

"Mahun,"° he seide,° "hov geth° þis?   ȝware° is novþe° þi miȝte bi-come?°   *Mohammed/said/how goes/where/ now/gone to*

75 ȝwane° I ne° may þis foule þeof°   ouer-come in þusse wise,°   *when (i.e., since)/not/thief/manner*

I schal bi-nime° him sone is lijf;°   þare he ne schal neuere° a-rise."   *deprive/(of) his life/never*

His dom° he gan to° ȝiue a-non,°   þat huy° seint George nome   *decree/did/give then/ they/take*

And drowen° him þoruȝ-ovt° al þe toun   for-to huy with-oute° come,   *drag/throughout/outside*

And þat huy smiten of° his heued°   with-oute þe toun atþe laste,   *smite off/head*

80 And is bodi þare in sum° foul place   to wilde bestes° it caste.   *some/beasts*

Þo þis dom was þus iȝyue°   hit° nas° nouȝt i-lete;°   *given/it/was not/not delayed*

Huy nomen° and drowen° þis holie man   villiche þoruȝ° þe strete,°   *took/dragged/vilely through/street*

Forto huy comen° with-oute toun   þare° huy wolden° is heued of smite.   *came/where/would*

Heore wepne° huy drowen° forth and ȝwetten hem°   kene forto° bite.   *their weapons/drew/whetted them/ sharp to*

---

62. *ase he nam . . . is red:* i.e., "as he was advised."

74. *Mahun:* Although this is an obvious anachronism, in medieval literature all evil and pagan characters swore by Mahound or Mohammed, who was often identified with the Devil himself.

85 "Leoue° breþren," seint George seide,   "one stounde a-bidez ȝuyte,°   *dear/moment wait yet*

For-to ich habbe° to Iesu° crist   mine bone i-bede° a luyte."°   *I have/Jesus/prayer addressed/little*

His hondene° he heold° up on heiȝ;°   a-doun° he sat on kneo,°   *hands/held/high/down/knee*

And seide, "Swete° louerd Iesu crist,   þat alle þing° miȝt i-seo,   *sweet/things*

Graunte° me, ȝif þi wille is,   þat, ho-so° in guode manere°   *grant/whoever/good manner*

90 Halewez° mine day in Aueril°   for mi loue on eorþe° here,   *hallows/April/earth*

Þat þare° ne falle in þat hous   no qualm° in al þe ȝere,°   *there/death/year*

Ne gret sijknesse° ne hongur° strong,   þat þerof° beo no fere;°   *nor great sickness/hunger/thereof/fear*

And ho-so in perile of þe se°   to me bit is° bone,   *sea/addresses his*

Oþur° in any oþur stude° perilous,   louerd, þov helpe heom° sone!"   *or/place/him*

95 Þo i-heorden° huy a voiz° in heuene°   þat to him seide, i-wis:°   *then heard/voice/heaven/indeed*

"Mi blessede child, cum° here forth to me;   þi bone i-heord is."   *come*

Þo is heued was of i-smite,°   ase° al þat folk i-seiȝ,°   *smitten/as/saw*

Aungles° nomen is swete soule   and to heuene beren° on heiȝ.   *angels/bore*

Þare he is in grete Ioye°   þat last with-outen° ende.   *great joy/lasts without*

100 Nov° God for seint Georges loue   late ore soule þudere wende.°   *now/let our souls there go*

Saint Martin

Seint° Martyn was i-bore°   in þe londe° of sabarie;   *Saint/born/land*

Wel ȝong° he was i-noriced°   in þe londe of papie.   *very young/nourished*

A noble knyȝht is fadur° was   and maister° of þe fierde;°   *knight his father/master/army*

Vnder Costantyn° þe Aumperour°   and al is ost° he stierde.°   *Constantine/emperor/host/led*

105 For into batayle° he brouȝhte° is ȝoungue sone°   þar-of° him to lere.°   *battle/brought/young son/thereof/teach*

None heorte° nadde° he þer-to   for huy heþene° were;   *no inclination/had not/they heathens*

---

90. *mine . . . Aueril:* Saint George's day of martyrdom and death was April 23, 303.

101. *Seint Martyn:* The patron saint of Tours, Lucca, and penitent drunkards was the son of a tribune of the army in the reign of Constantine the Great. *sabarie:* Saberia, formerly Steinamanger, now Szombathely in Hungary, near the Austrian border.

102. *papie:* probably the Roman province of Pannonia along the Danube.

103. *fierde:* The fyrd was in actuality the English militia under Alfred the Great and others, before the Norman Conquest. It was not a regular standing army, but a gathering of farmers called up in emergencies and for a limited time. When the set time was up, the fyrd often went home to reap the crops, causing logistical problems in battle of which the *Anglo-Saxon Chronicle* gives evidence. Here the English author probably means the regular Roman troops stationed in the province.

His heorte bar° him euere° to Iesu° crist   þei° he i-cristned° nere;°   *heart bore|ever|Jesus|although| christened|were not*

He i-saiȝh° þat heore bi-leue° nas° nauȝht° bi-lefden° þere.   þat huy   *saw|their belief|was not|nothing| believed*

To churche, þo° he was twelf ȝer° old,   stilleliche° he wende°   *when|twelve years|quietly|went*

110 And bi-het ore louerd° cristine° to beo°   ȝwane° he þe time him° sende.°   *promised our Lord|Christian|be| when|to him|announced*

Þe Aumperour het into° al þat lond   to euereche° olde kniȝte°   *commanded in|every|knight*

Þat heore sones scholden° into batayle comen°   and for heore faderes fiȝhte.°   *should|come|fathers fight*

So þat þe ȝungue° seint Martin   nas bote° of fiftene ȝer°   *young|but|fifteen years old*

Þo he þe armes in eche° bataile   for is fadere ber.°   *every|bore*

115 A° winter ase° þis child rod°   bi þe weye° al one,°   *one|as|knight rode|way|alone*

A miseise° man he mette naked,   sore sike° and grone.°   *beggar|bitterly sighing|groaning*

Seint Martyn drovȝ° out is swerd,°   ase we findeth in þe bok,°   *drew|sword|book*

And carf° is mantel half a-to,°   and þe pouere° manne it bi-tok.°   *cut|in two|poor|took*

Sone aftur-ward, ase he bi-heold°   to-ward heouene an heiȝh,°   *looked|heaven on high*

120 With is halue° mantel i-heled°   ore louerd crist he seiȝh:°   *half|covered|saw*

"Lo," he seide° to is aungles,°   þis ne° worth me° nouȝht° bi-reued;°   *said|angels|not|I shall be|not| deprived of*

Martin, þat is heþene ȝuyt,°   here-with me hath bi-weued."°   *yet|covered*

Þo Martin þis i-herde°   and ore louerd he saiȝh° þere,   *heard|saw*

Glad ne° bliþe nolde° he beo   are° he i-cristned° were.   *nor|would not|until|christened*

125   Eiȝhtetene° ȝer he was old   þo he i-cristned was;   *eighteen*

Þat he hadde so longue a-bide°   ofte he seide alas.   *long awaited*

Ake° al þe to° ȝer þare-afturward°   in-to batailes he wende   *but|two|afterward*

For is fader wide a-boute   ase þe Aumperor him sende.°   *sent*

Hit bi-fel of° a gret° bataile   þat þe Aumperor hadde i-nome,°   *it happened concerning|great| undertaken*

130 He° het alle is knyȝhtes in is lond   þat huy scholden to him come;   *(that) he*

He het Martyn with heom wende°   and armure° with him take.   *them (to) go|weapons*

"Certes,° sire," Martin seide, "þine armes ich habbe° for-sake;   *indeed|I have*

---

115. Saint Martin was sent to join the legion in Gaul. The winter of 332, when he was stationed at Amiens, was of such severity that men died of cold in the streets. *child:* the medieval term for knight (cf. above, p. 143, ll. 27–28*n*), though in this instance it may also refer to Saint Martin's extreme youth.

117. *bok:* i.e., the author's unknown source.

129. *Aumperor:* The emperor at this time was Julian the Apostate, and Saint Martin was forty.

Ich am Iesu cristes knyȝht   and so ich habbe i-beo°   *been/a long time*
longue,°

And none oþure armes bote° his   i-nelle° vnder-fonge."   *except/I will not/take up*

135 "Ei, couward,"° seide þe Aumperour,   nouþe° þou sparest°   *ah, coward/now/do you refuse/fear*
for fere°

For-to° fiȝhte with þine felawes°   ase þi riȝte° were?"°   *to/companions/right/would be*

"Sire," seide Martin þo,°   "þe soþe° þou schalt i-se:°   *then/truth/see*

Of° þine armes ne kepe° i nouȝt°   ake þe furste° ichulle°   *for/care/nothing/first/I shall*
beo

Al one bi-fore° al þi folk   naked to þe bataile;   *before*

140 Mine louerdes miȝhte° þou schalt i-seo,°   for he me nele°   *might/see/will not/not*
nouȝt° faile."

Þo þat ferd° al-ȝare° was,   seint Martin wende a-non°   *army/all ready/then*

Vn-armed with is° swerd a drawe°   among alle is fon.°   *his/drawn/foes*

Þo he a-mong hem° was i-come°   þare° nas of hem nouȝt on° *them/come/there/one*

Þat miȝhte ani more hebbe° up is hond°   þane° it were a   *raise/hand/than (if)/stone*
ston;°

145 Huy ȝolden° him þe maistrie a-non°   bote þat° he let° hem *yielded/mastery quickly/if only/*
a-liue.°   *(would) let/live*

Saint Martin clepede° is felawes   and het° hem hom wel   *called/ordered/home very quickly*
bliue.°

"Sire Aumperour,"° he seide, "nouþe þou sixt°   ȝwuch° is   *Emperor/see/how much*
mi louerdes miȝhte;

Are ȝe° alle it hadden þar-to i-brouȝht,°   longue ȝe mosten° *before you/had thereto brought/*
fiȝhte!   *would have had to*

Nov° þou hast alle þine fon i-wonne,°   þonke° God, and   *now/captured/thank*
nouȝht me,

150 And haue guod° day, for i-nelle   no lengore serui þe."°   *good/longer serve you*

He nam° is leue° and wende° forth   —he nolde no leng   *took/leave/went/longer stay*
a-bide—°

To þe holie bischop hyllari°   þat wonede° þare-bi-side.°   *Hilary/lived/nearby*

Of° him he was i-maud a-colite°   and dude° al bi is rede.° *by/made acolyte/did/counsel*

Ore louerd cam° to him a niȝht°   and þeos° wordes to him *our Lord came/one night/these*
seide:

155 "Ich hote° þe, Martin, þat þou go   wel ofte to þine   *command/kindred*
kunne,°

And spec° with hem, ȝif° þov miȝht   bringue° hem out of *speak/(and see) if/bring/sin*
sunne;°

Þei þat° huy heþene beon,°   ne let° heom nouȝt þare-fore,° *although/heathens are/discard/*
therefore

---

136. *þi riȝte:* i.e., "right for you."

141–45. Historically, the emperor placed Saint Martin under arrest with a guard for the night, intending to test him the next day, but the enemy in the morning asked for terms of capitula-tion, Saint Martin's faith thus winning out. The English author intensifies the miracle. *Vn-armed:* i.e., without protective armor or shield (cf. *naked*, l. 139).

152. *hyllari:* Saint Hilary was a 4th-century bishop of Poitiers.

For ech° guod man schal anouri° þat kun°   þat he was of   *every/honor/family/born*
i-bore.°

Ake gret a-nuy° þov schalt habbe   þe ȝwile° þou gest°   *trouble/while/go*
a-boute;

160 Þe ȝwyle þou mine grace hast   þe þarf° no-wiȝht° doute."°   *need/no man/fear*

Þis guode man, ase° ore louerd him het,°   to-ward is kun°   *as/commanded/kindred*
wende.

Strongue° outlawes bi þe wei° he mette;   heore bouwes   *strong/way/their bows quickly/bent*
sone° huy bende,°

Þis guode man huy nomen°   and maden° him mani a   *took/gave*
wounde;

Forth huy ladden° him for-to sle,°   is hondene° faste   *led/slay/hands/bound*
i-bounde.°

165 Þe outlawes axede° him ȝif he were   so sore a-drad euere.°   *asked/afraid ever*

"Nai, certes," quath° þis holie man,   "þat nas° ich   *certainly/said/was not/never*
neuere.°

"Ore louerdes help was euere neiȝh°   þe manne þat was   *near/(his) care*
in care:°

So muche is þar-to min° hope   þat I ne rechche° hou ich   *therein my/not care*
fare."

Of Ihesu° crist he tolde° so   with heom þat him nome,°   *Jesus/talked/captured*

170 Þat huy ful sone leten° him go   and cristine° for° him   *soon let/Christian/because of/*
bi-come.°   *became*

Ase þis guode man eode° forth al one°   þe deuel a-ȝein°   *went/alone/Devil toward*
him cam;

In faire manere° he axede him   ȝwodere þene° wei he nam.   *manner/whither the*

Þis guode man seide,° "Ichulle° go   ase mi louerd wole   *said/I shall/will lead*
lede° me."

"Ȝwodere° þou go," þe oþur seide,   "þe deuel wole aȝein°   *wherever/against/be*
þe beo."°

175 "Ȝe,"° seide þis guode man,   "þou most° wel al-so;°   *yea/may (do)/so*

For ȝwane° ore louerd is min help   I ne rechche ȝwat   *when/what others*
oþure° do."

Þis guode man eode a-mong is freond;   is moder° cristine he   *friends/mother*
made—

His fader° nolde° cristine be   for al þat huy him bede.°   *father/would not/begged*

Seint Martin fond° a ȝong° man ded°   þat swiþe wel° with   *found/young/dead/very friendly*
him was,

180 Þat bi-lefde° on ore louerd for him   ake i-cristned nouȝt°   *believed/but christened not*
he nas.

Gret deol° made þis holie man   þat he nadde° ibe°   *great sorrow/had not/been/before*
i-cristned er:°

To is burieles° he eode, and bad° for him   and weop wel°   *his burial/prayed/wept very/tear*
mani a ter.°

Þe dede° man bi-gan a-non°   fram deþe° arise to liue;°   *dead/did then/from death/life*

"Martin," he seide, "i-hered° beo þou   and ore louerdes   *praised*
     woundes fiue!

185   Mi soule was to helle i-lad°   ase alle beoth° of oure kuynde,°   *led/are/kind*

Ake tweye aungles þoruȝ° Godes grace   hadden° me in   *two angels through/had/mind*
     muynde°

And seiden° ore louerd þat ich° hadde   ouwer° desciple   *told/I/your/been*
     i-beo;°

Þare-fore ore louerd me dude° a-rise   for þe honour of þe   *made*

And dude mi soule to mi bodi   for þi loue hider° bringue.°   *here/be brought*

190   Cristine-dom par charite°   ich esche bi-fore° alle þingue.'"°   *Christianity/charity/ask before/*
     things

     Gret Ioye° hadde þis holie man   of þis swete cas;°   *joy/sweet happening*

He nolde departi° fram him nouȝt°   are° he i-cristned was.   *depart/not/until*

Þat folk nam sethþe seint° Martin,   for he was so guod,°   *took then Saint/good*

And maden° him bischop of turoyne°   muche a-ȝein is mod.°   *made/Tours/will*

195   To mile with-oute° þe cite°   an abbeye he liet a-rere;°   *two miles outside/city/had built*

Four-score monekes° of guode liue   him-sulf° he dude° þere.   *monks/himself/placed*

With heom° he wonede° al in pays°   ase° he heore soueren°   *them/lived/peace/as if/sovereign*
     were;

He ne wende° nouȝt out bote° ȝwane it neod° was   þat folk   *not traveled/except/there need/to*
     for-to lere.°—   *teach*

So holi lif° seint Martin ladde   þat he hadde to° is heste°   *life/at/bidding*

200   Fuyr,° and treo,° and þe kuynde° of worm,°   of foules° and   *fire/tree/family/snakes/birds/beasts*
     of beste.°

A strong wind blevȝ° a fuyr   þat° to seint Martines house it   *blew/so that*
     wende,

And are° þis guode man it onder-ȝete°   i barnd° was þat   *before/perceived/burned/completely*
     on ende.°

Seint Martyn hiet° a-godes° name   þat fuyr a-ȝein wiende:°   *commanded/in God's/again (to) turn*

For° is heste þat fuyr flevȝ°   a-non° a-ȝein° þe wynde   *at/flew/quickly/against*

205   To þe stude þare° it cam° fram   and ne bi-lefde° no-wiȝht°   *place where/came/remained/not a*
     bi-hinde,°   *bit/behind*

And dude° a-ȝein þe kuynde of fuyre   a-ȝein þe wynde   *acted/fly*
     to fle.°

Þare° was i-sene° þat fuyr ne miȝhte°   a-ȝein is heste be.°   *there/seen/might/remain*

     To is heste he hadde, ase° ich seide er,   þe kuynde of þe   *as/tree*
     tre,°

Ase ȝe mouwen° bi a fair miracle   of him nouþe i-seo.°   *you may/now see*

210   On a dai ase he stod° under a treo   to prechi° Godes lawe,   *stood/preach*

---

190. *par:* OF, "for,"

194. Saint Martin was elected bishop of Tours in 371. The original *chapel* (OF for Latin *capella*, "little cape") of Saint Martin at Tours was the sanctuary where the saint's cloak was kept.

195. The cell built two miles outside of Tours, between a rocky embankment and the Loire River, was the foundation of the monastery of Marmoutier, which became famous throughout Europe.

Þe luþere° men þat þare-bi stoden°   þouȝten° him bringue   *evil/nearby stood/intended/to kill*
of dawe:°

Huy° gunne° sawie° þat treo a-to°   toward þis holie   *they/started to/saw/in two*
manne,

Þat it scholde° ouer-falle° him—   for þare **nadde he**   *should/fall on/none*
freond nanne.°

Þoruȝ° noyse of þe crakeȝingue°   þe guode man i-heorde°   *through/cracking/heard*

215 Þat þut° treo fel touward° him.   A-ȝein wel sone° he it   *that/toward/very quickly/turned*
cherde;°

He het° þat treo a-godes name   opward° a-ȝein tuyrne.°   *commanded/upward/(to) turn*

Þat treo a-ros up-riȝht i-nouȝh°   for it nolde is heste werne,°   *arose upright enough/defy*

And ouer-ful° in þat oþur side   manie of is fon.°   *fell on/foes*

Huy þat leoueden, lieten heom sone°   cristni° euerech-on.°   *lived, left him soon/(as) Christians/*
every one

220 Þe worm dude° is heste al-so,   for ase he cam bi a wateres   *did/edge*
brimme,°

A lodlich naddre° he i-saiȝh°   stifliche aȝein° him come   *loathly adder/saw/fiercely toward/*
swymme.°   *swimming*

"Ich hote þe,"° seide° þis holie man,   "þat þow aȝeinward   *command you/said/back turn*
wende,°

Ant° þat þou neuereft° here ne come   ne nouȝwere° in þis   *and/never again/nor nowhere/region*
ende."°

Þis worm turnede a-ȝen° a-non   ase þis holie man him het,   *turned again*

225 And swam in-to an oþur° lond°   and þulke contreiȝe fur-let.°   *another/land/that country left*

Foules duden is° heste al-so,   for on a° time ase he gan gon,°   *did his/one/did go*

He saiȝh° douedoppene° fisches cachche°   and swolewen°   *saw/diving birds/catch/swallow*
heom in a-non.

"Alas!" seide þis guode man,   "þis is þe feondes manere,°   *fiend's (i.e., Devil's) way*

Gultlese þingus° and vnwarre°   to cachchen,° ase huy   *guiltless things/unwary/catch*
doth here,

230 And þing þat non° harm ne doth   bote wenth° in pays° to   *no/but wishes/peace/be*
beo;°

So farez° þe deuel, a-waytez euere°   for-to° he is preiȝe°   *does/Devil, waits ever/until/prey*
i-seo."

He het þe foules a-godes name   ech-one° þannes teo°   *every one/away (to) go*

And þat huy scholden° in-to wildernesse   out of þat watere   *should/fly*
fleo,°

Þat huy neuereft þare ne comen°   gultlese þingues° to take.   *come/things*

235 Þis° foules a-non with þis word   awei° huy gonne schake.°   *these/away/did move*

Bestes° duden al-so is heste,   for ase he wende° a-boute,   *beasts/traveled*

---

221. *naddre:* the Old English word for "snake" (cf. German *Natter*). Mod. Eng. *adder* is from the wrong division of *nadder* with the indefinite article: *a nadder > an adder*. The nouns *napkin–apron* and *nonpeer–umpire* show a similar development.

227. *douedoppene:* dive-dapper birds, according to the *MED*, are either water hens or moorhens.

Aftur ane° hare he saiȝh vrne°   grehoundes° a gret route;°   *a/running/greyhounds/great pack*

"Alas," he seide, "þis seli° best   þat no-þing ne doth a-mis°!   *good/amiss*

Þis foule houndes it wollez to-drawe,°   gultles ase it is."   *wish (to) kill*

240 He het° þe grehoundes a-bide a-non°   and ne° do þat best   *ordered/(to) stop immediately/not/*
no wo;°   *harm*

Huy at-stunten° a-non, and eoden a-ȝein°   and lieten° þat   *stopped/went away/let*
best forth go.

On atyme kene° houndes comen°   a-boute one of is   *one time fierce/came/men*
manne;°

He ne miȝhte him wite,° so kene huy were,   ne help nadde°   *himself guard/had not*
he nanne:

"Ich hote eov,"° he seide, "a-godes° name   and on seint°   *I order you/in God's/Saint*
Martines al-so,

245 Þat ȝe me laten° a-pais° wende,°   min erinde for-to° do."   *let/in peace/go/my errand to*

Þe houndes a-non with þat word   bi-gonne° to stonde° stille,   *began/stand*

And wenden euerech° in is wey°   to do seint Martines wille.   *turned each/way*

A kov° al-so þat was gidi°   a-boute orn° in þe londe,   *cow/mad/ran*

Þat fale° men slov,° and bestes al-so   ȝware heo fond° anie   *many/killed/where she found/*
stonde;°   *standing*

250 Hire° ne miȝhte° no-þing atstonde a-ȝein,°   so strong þat   *her/might/withstand*
foule þing was.

A-ȝein seint Martin heo cam eorne°   ase ore louerd° ȝaf   *came running/as our Lord/made it*
þat cas;°   *happen*

Sore weren° is men a-dradde.°   Þis guode° man hire het   *were/afraid/good*
a-non

A-godes name stonde° stille   and nane° fot forþere gon.°   *(to) stand/not a/foot farther (to) go*

Þat best, þei° it gidi were,°   a-non it gan a-bide.   *although/was*

255 Seint Martin þene° deuel i-saiȝ°   opon° hire rugge ride.°   *the/saw/on/back riding*

"Þov luþere° þing, ȝwat° dostþov° þer?   for euere þou   *ugly/what/do you/work for evil*
dost to quede.°

Ȝwy trauailest° þou þat selie° best   þat ne loueth no   *why trouble/poor/misdeed*
misdede?°

A-corsede° þing, þou wend a-wei   ne cum neiȝh° hire   *cursed/come near/no more*
non-morc!"°

Þe deuel wende° a-wei a-non   ȝeollinde suyþe sore—°   *went/yelling very bitterly*

260 He moste° nede° is heste° do   ase wel ase þe kov.   *must/of necessity/bidding*

Þo° heo of° him deliured° was,   ase ȝe i-hereth hov,°   *when/from/delivered/you hear how*

Mildeliche° heo eode° to seint Martyn;   to° is fet° heo feol°   *mildly/went/at/feet/fell/on her*
a-kneo° a-non,   *knees*

And schok° hire heued° to þonki° him;   he° nolde° fram°   *shook/head/thank/she/would not/*
him gon.   *from*

Seint Martin hire het a-risen° up   and to ire felawes°   *commanded (to) rise/her*
wende.   *companions*

265 Heo lottede on° him and eode forth   hom° to ire owene   *bowed to/home/own district*
ende.°

Seint Martin was apostlene pier,°   for þe holie gost   *apostles' peer/alighted*
    a-liȝhte°
In him ase in þe Apostles   in fourme° of fuyr wel briȝhte.°   *form/fire very bright*
A° dai ase þis guode man sat   allone° in is° celle,   *one/alone/his*
His priue men° a-biden° him þare-oute°   and heorden° him   *intimates/waited for/outside/heard/*
    loude telle;°   *speak*
270 Al-so ase þei° it wummen° were   huy° heorden with him   *though/women/they/speak*
    speke.°
Þare-of hem þouȝhte° wonder gret   ne dorsten° huy   *this they thought/dared/not/break*
    nouȝt° in breke.°
    Sethþe° þo þe guode man cam out   huy fullen a-doun°   *then/fell down/on their knees*
    a-kneo,°
And axeden° ȝwat þe speche° were   þat with him hadde   *asked/conversation/been*
    i-beo.°
Þe guode man seide,° "Ich may eou telle,   for ȝe me° beoz   *said/to me/are close*
    priue:°
275 It was ore lauedi° and seint Anneis°   þat þare-inne° weren   *Lady/Anne/therein*
    with me,
Of þe Ioye° of heouene° huy speken°   and ofte huy doth so.   *joy/heaven/spoke*
Seint petre° and seint powel°   to me comiez° ofte al-so."   *Peter/Paul/come*
Seint Martin at paray°   mette ane musel° bi cas.°   *Paris/a leper/chance*
He custe° him, and anon° aftur-ward   þe musel al hol° was.   *kissed/immediately/cured*
280   Men ne seiȝe° him neuere wroth°   ne liȝe no-þe-mo,°   *not saw/never angry/lie ever*
And ȝwat-so-euere° is men duden°   he wolde euere° bi   *whatever/did/would ever/himself*
    on° go.
In wel pouere wede° a day   he rod° out on ane° asse;   *poor clothes/rode/an*
Heiȝe° men he mette bi þe weie°   þat tolden of° him þe   *high-class/way/accounted/less*
    lasse.°
Heore hors° weren of him a-dradde   for° is pouere cloþes,   *their horses/because of*
285 And ornen a-bach,° and felden hem° a-doun.   Huy weren   *ran (i.e., reared) back/threw them/*
    with him ful wroþe;°   *very angry*
Huy sturten° up and nomen° þis holie man   and beoten°   *jumped/took/beat*
    him ful sore.
Euere he was stille and ne spak° no word;   for þi° huy   *spoke/therefore*
    beoten him þe more.
    Þo huy him hadden° so i-bete°   huy bi-lefden° him   *had/beaten/left/at the*
    atþen° ende
Ligginde þare,° and worþen° on heore hors   forth heore   *lying there/jumped/go*
    wei to wende.°
290 Ake° heore hors nolden° gon° of þe stude°   for al þat huy   *but/would not/go/place/do might*
    don miȝten,°

---

283. *tolden . . . lasse:* i.e., "considered him of little worth."

Ʒuyt° huy smiten° with ʒeorde° and with spore°   are þat°   *yet/struck/stick/spur/before/*
    huy a-liʒhten°   *alighted*

And criden merci° þis guode° man   þat huy him hadden   *asked pardon (of)/good/*
    mis-do.°   *mishandled*

Heore hors hem bere° forth a-non°   þo huy token on° so.   *carried/then/(had) done*

And in an hous þe ʒwile° it barnde°   he slep wit-oute° harm;   *while/burned/slept without*

295 His° cloþes fur-barnden° al-to° cole°   he ne fielde° it   *(although) his/burned up/all to/*
    no-þing° warm.   *coal/felt/not at all*

At a gret feste, ase° he scholde°   þe heiʒe° masse   *great festival, when/had to/high/*
    singe,°   *sing*

To churche he wende with is men;   men gunne° a-ʒein   *did/him encircle*
    him ringue.°

Ane pouere man he mette nake°   þat no schroud him°   *naked/garment himself/had not/*
    nadde° a-boue,°   *upon*

And bad° him sum-þing° to helien° him with   for ore   *asked/(for) something/ cover/our*
    louerdes° loue.   *Lord's*

300 Seint° Martyn bad is Ercedekne°   þat he him ʒeue sum°   *Saint/archdeacon/give some*
    cloth.

Þe Ercedekne tolde þarof luyte°   and nolde,° he swor is oth.°   *thought thereof little/would not/oath*

Seint Martin bote anne cuyrtel°   on him-sulf þo° nadde;   *but a tunic/himself then*

To þe pouere manne he hine ʒaf°   in an hous þare° he him   *it gave/where/led*
    ladde.°

He ne bi-lefde on him no cloth of wolle°   bote is cope   *wool/only*
    al-one.°

305 Þe masse ne miʒhte° he bi-guynne nouʒht°   þat° folk made   *might/begin not/so that/lament*
    þar-of mone.°

"Ʒwy° neltþou,"° seide þe Ercedekne,   "þine masse   *why/will you not*
    bi-guynne?"

"For þou most er° ane pouere manne   sum cloth to him   *must first/give*
    i-winne."°

"Nov° is þis," seide þe Ercedekne,   "gret a-nuy with þe,°   *now/annoyance from you*

For j-ne° seo° no pouere man   nouʒwere° a-boute þe be."   *I do not/see/nowhere*

310 "No," seide þis holie man,   it nele° faillie° þe nouʒht;   *will not/fail*

Al redi° þou findest a pouere man;   habbe° þou þat cloth   *ready/have/brought*
    i-brouʒth."°

Þe Ercedekne in grete wrathþe°   eode° into chepingue;°   *wrath/went/(the) market*

A lodlich° cloth he bouʒhte° for fif panes;°   to þe bischope   *loathly/bought/five pence/did/bring*
    he gan° it bringue.°

Þe bischop eode into þe vestiarie;   is° cope he gan of strepe.°   *his/off take*

315 He nadde° under is vestimenz°   to habbe on bote is Iuype;°   *had not (anything)/vestments/shirt*

Vnneþe° it heolede° is derne limes°   and nouʒht folliche° is   *hardly/covered/private parts/fully/*
    elbouwes;°   *elbows*

For is bare armes atþe° masse   þis guode man hadde gret   *at/felt very foolish*
    houwe°—

For þe uestimenz wide weren°   and is armes smale° and   *were/small/lean*
    lene;°

Laste° is armes nakede weren i-seiȝe°   he ne dorste hebbe   *lest/seen/dared raise up/hands*
    op° is hondene.°

320   Ake þo° he nedlingus° at þe sacrement   is hondene   *when/of necessity*
    hebbe up scholde,

An aungel schrudde° is nakede armes   with tweie sleuene°   *angel clad/two sleeves*
    of golde.

Þe ercedekne cride° and bi-hiet°   þat neuere-eft° mis-don°   *cried/promised/never again/wrong*
    him he nolde.

Þe deuel° hadde to° þis holie man   gret onde with-alle.°   *Devil/of/envy besides*

He cam° in a° time him to bi-traye°   in riche cloþus° of   *came/one/betray/clothes*
    palle,

325 With hosen° and schon° of briȝte° golde;   swyþe° fair he   *hose/shoes/bright/very*
    was of face.

"Martin," he seide,° "wel þe beo;°   i-founde° þou hast   *said/health to you/found*
    mine grace:

Ich° am þilke° þat þou seruest wel;   ichulle° me schewi°   *I/the one/I shall/myself show*
    to þe;

Þov most sone chaungi þi lif°   and bi-time° come to me."   *soon change/life/in due time*

Þis guode man sat in gret þouȝt;°   no word he ne sede.°   *thought/not said*

330 "Martyn," he seide, "ich am þi freond;°   ȝwar-of°   *friend/of what/have you/fear*
    hastþou° drede,°

Ȝwane þin owene° God spekez° with þe   here mouth with   *when your own/speaks*
    mouþe?

Euere° þou hast of guode bi-leue i-beo;°   ne lat° it nouȝt   *ever/good faith been/let/not fail/now*
    faili° þe nouþe!°

For ich blessi° alle þat on me bi-leuez°   þei huy° me nouȝht   *bless/believe/although they*
    ne seo,

And er° þis þei þov ne seiȝe° me nouȝht   in þulke   *before/saw/such blessing/would*
    blessingue° þou woldest° be."

335   "I nuste° neuere,"° quath° þis guode man,   "þat mi   *knew not/never/said*
    louerd euere sede

Þat he wolde on vrþe° come   in swuche° riche kingene wede;°   *earth/such/royal garments*

And bote° ich mouwe° of mine louerdes woundes   on þe   *unless/may/see*
    signe i-se°

Oþur° of is croyz,° inelle° i-leue°   þat þou mi louerd be."   *or/cross/I will not/believe*

Þe foule þing wende a-wey°   and was adrad° of ane boule;°   *went away/afraid/a falsehood*

340 Þe stude þare-aftur° swiþe longue°   stonk° of him riȝt   *place thereafter/very long/stank/*
    foule.°   *right foully*

    Þis guode man seide his ende-day°   him° was swyþe   *last day/to him/truly*
    wel° come.

---

324. *palle:* any rich material.

His desciples weopen° sore   and gret deol° to heom nome.°   *wept/great lament/him made*

"Leoue fader,"° huy seiden,° "ʒwat schulle° we do,   þat þov   *dear father/said/what shall/will*
us wolt° for-sake?

Vs fader-les° with-oute confort°   ʒwam° woltþu° bitake?°   *fatherless/comfort/whom/will you/*
                                                                                    put in charge of

³⁴⁵ Nov wollez° wilde wolues come   and alle þine schep   *now will/sheep kill*
a-spille."°

"Ich mot° nede,"° seide þis guode man,   "don° mine   *must/of necessity/do/Lord's*
louerdes° wille."

Of askene° and of is here° he made   a bed at is ende-day,   *ashes/hair shirt*

And þaron° feble° aʒen° is deþe°   opriʒht adoun him-   *on it/feeble/at the approach of/*
sulue° he lay;°   *death/straight down himself/*
                                                                                    laid

And toward heouene lokede ay°   so longue þat it° nas°   *heaven looked ever/there/was not/no*
non° ende.

³⁵⁰ His men þouʒhten° it dude° him harm   and wolden° him   *thought/did/wanted/(to) help/turn*
helpe° to wende.°

"Λ-bideth,"° seide þis holie man,   "ʒwy° wolle ʒe° don so?   *stop/why/you*

Latez° me ane ʒwyle bi-holde° þe stude   þat mi soule   *let/while behold/(go) to*
schal to!"°

Þo i-saiʒh° he þene° deuel aftur is soule   stonde þare° with   *then saw/the/standing there/*
is feren.°   *companions*

"A-wey," he seide, "þou luþere best;°   þou nast° nouʒt° to   *evil beast/have not/nothing*
don here!

³⁵⁵ With me nastþou° nouʒt to done,   for mi louerd me wole   *you have not/will receive*
onderfongue;°

In is° name to him ich wende°   þat bouʒhte° me swiþe   *his/go/redeemed/thoroughly*
strongue."°

With þusse° worde he ʒaf° þene gost—   aungles i-redie°   *this/gave (up)/ready*
were;

Þat folk heorde heore murie° song   ase° huy þe soule bere.°   *heard their merry/as/bore*

Four hondret ʒer° it was   and in þe six-and-sixtiþe° ʒere   *hundred years/sixty-sixth*

³⁶⁰ Aftur ore° louerdes buyrtyme°   þat þis guode man deide°   *our/death/died*
þere.

Four-score winter° he was old   are° he was ded° al-so.   *winters/before/dead*

God ʒiue° us part of þulke ioye°   þat is soule wende° to.   *give/that joy/went*

359–60. The English poet seems to be in error here: Saint
Martin died November 11, 397. The Martinmas goose is
roasted at this time in his honor.

from HANDLYNG SYNNE

Robert Mannyng of Brunne

DATE: 1303. ✔ MANUSCRIPTS: British Library Harleian 1701 (c.1350–75); Bodleian Library, Oxford, 415 (c. 1400). The dialect is of the Northeast Midlands. ✔ EDITION: F. J. Furnivall, ed., *Robert of Brunne's "Handlyng Synne,"* Early English Text Society, OS 119, 123 (London, 1901, 1903).

Northern influence (specifically Northeast Midland, Lincolnshire) appears in occasional *ā* for *ō* (*knawe = know*). The uninflected genitive in an Old English *r*-stem noun (*dohtyr = daughter's*) is a long-lived fossil throughout Middle English. The following points should also be noted. (1) Pronouns that might cause confusion are *hem*, "them," "themselves," and *here*, "their." Others are normal and will cause little trouble. (2) Plurals of nouns will be found in *-ys* instead of *-es* (*talys, wundys*). (3) The present participle is at times formed with *-and* (*karoland*). (4) Before nasals and liquids (*m, n, l, r*) *u* is normally found instead of *o* (*wurlde, cumpanye, tunge*).

Handlyng Synne by Robert Mannyng of Brunne is a free translation of William of Wadington's Anglo-Norman *Manuel de Pechiez*, a treatise on the commandments, sins, and sacraments. Mannyng, a canon of the Gilbertine order, lived in Bourne, Lincolnshire. His avowed purpose was to write of moral matters for unschooled men, and like John Gower later, he realized that a good story, often racy and sensational, will keep the attention of the tavern crowd, whereas sermons by their dullness might do more harm than good. Mannyng's treatise, therefore, consists of a series of exempla, secular stories with spiritual morals. He draws his illustrations from life around him, simple tales, often exaggerated but always to the point. His *Handlyng Synne*, therefore, becomes a handbook of life in medieval England, a series of very short anecdotes which today perhaps more delight us by their narrative crispness than they teach us of spiritual truths.

from Prologue (vss. 41–96)

Þat° may be weyl on° englyssh tolde,	*that (which)/well in*
To telle ȝow° þat, y° may be bolde;°	*you/I/emboldened*
For lewde° men y vndyr-toke°	*unschooled/undertook*
On englyssh tunge° to make þys boke.°	*tongue/book*
5 For many ben° of swyche manere,°	*are/such kind*
Þat talys and rymys wyl bleþly here;°	*happily hear*

Yn gamys, and festys,° and at þe ale,°   *feasts/tavern*
Loue men to lestene° troteuale:°   *listen to/idle talk*
Þat may falle ofte to vylanye,°   *into coarseness*
10 To dedly° synne, or oþer folye;°   *deadly/folly*
For swyche men haue y made þis ryme
Þat þey may weyl dyspende here° tyme,   *spend their*
And þere-yn sumwhat° for to here,   *something*
To leue° al swyche foul manere,°   *leave off/habit*
15 And for to kunne knowe° þerynne   *learn (to) know*
Þat þey wene° no synne be ynne.°   *believe/is in*
    To alle crystyn° men vndir° sunne,   *Christian/under*
And to gode° men of Brunne,°   *good/Bourn*
And speciali,° alle be° name,   *especially/by*
20 Þe felaushepe° of Symprynghame,°   *fellowship/Sempringham*
Roberd° of Brunne greteþ° ȝow   *Robert/greets*
In al godenesse° þat may to prow.°   *good will/be shown*
    Of Brunnewake yn Kesteuene,
Syxe myle be-syde° Sympryngham euene,°   *miles from/exactly*
25 Y dwelled yn þe pryorye
Fyftene ȝere° yn cumpanye,°   *years/company*
In þe tyme of gode dane Ione°   *Dan John*
Of Camelton, þat now ys gone:
In hys tyme was y þere ten ȝeres,
30 And knewe and herd° of hys maneres;°   *heard/(good) habits*
Syþyn° with dane Ione of Clyntone,   *then*
Fyue wyntyr° wyþ hym gan° y wone;°   *five winters/did/live*
Dane Felyp° was mayster° þat tyme   *Philip/master*
Þat y began þys englyssh ryme.
35 Þe ȝeres of grace fyl þan to be°   *were at that time*
A þousynd° and þre° hundred and þre.   *thousand/three*
    In þat tyme turnede° y þys   *translated*
On englyssh tunge out of frankys,°   *French*
Of° a boke as° y fonde ynne;°   *from/that/found (it) in*
40 Men clepyn° þe boke "Handlyng Synne."   *call*

---

11. The author frankly appeals to an unschooled audience, with interesting, often sensational stories told for a good end. This is the typical exemplum, devised so that the Devil would not have a monopoly on exciting narratives.

15–16. *knowe . . . ynne:* i.e., "to know from it the truth about things in which they believe there is no sin."

18: *Brunne:* Bourn in Lincolnshire.

20. The headquarters of Mannyng's order, that of the Gilbertines, was located at Sempringham.

23. *Brunnewake:* the village of Bourn, surnamed Wake for an important family living there, according to John W. Hales (*Academy*, 31 [1887], 27); *Kesteuene:* one of the three districts of Lincolnshire (the others being Lindsey and Holland).

27. *dane Ione:* The priors Dan John of Cameltoun and Dan John of Clyntoun (l. 31) governed the house in 1302–17. *Dan*, from Latin *dominus*, "lord," was a title of honor similar to *Master*.

33. *Dane Felyp:* Philip of Burton presided over the Gilbertines in 1298–1332.

35. *of grace:* i.e., after the birth of Christ.

In frenshe þer° a clerk hyt° sees,   *where (i.e., when)/scholar it*
He clepyþ hyt "Manuel de Pecches."
"Manuel" ys "handlyng with honde";°   *hand*
"Pecches" ys "synne," y vndyrstonde.°   *I understand*
45 Þese twey wurdys° þat beyn otwynne,°   *two words/are separated*
Do hem° to gedyr,° ys "handlyng synne."   *put them/together*
And weyl ys clepyd,° for þys skyle;°   *well (it) is named/reason*
And as y wote, ȝow shew° y wyle.°   *know, you show/will*
We handel synne euery day;
50 In wurde and dede,° al we may,   *deed*
Lytyl° or mochel,° synne we do,   *little/much*
Þe fend° and oure flesh tysyn° vs þerto;   *Fiend/entice*
For þys skyle hyt may be seyde°   *said*
"Handlyng synne" for oure mysbreyde;°   *misdeeds*
55 For euery day and euery oure°   *hour*
We synne þat shal we bye° ful soure.°   *pay for/very sorely*

The Tale of Zenon, the Would-Be Thief (vss. 2095–2142)

Þys yche° abbot, Zenon he hyght,°   *same/was called*
And wel° he was with° God almyght;°   *pious/toward/almighty*
Vppon a day he went hys wey°   *way*
60 To Palestyne, þat° ys an abbey,   *where*
To make hys vysytacyun°   *visitation*
As falleþ° yn relygyun;°   *happens/religious duties*
And as he went by° þe strete°   *along/street*
He behelde a fruyt ryȝt feyre° and swete.°   *fruit very fair/sweet*
65 Þys yche fruyt he desyred faste,°   *strongly*
And hys herte moche° þarto° he caste,°   *heart much/toward it/inclined*
"Gourdys" þus men clepe° þe name;   *call*
Þys gode° man þoght,° "Y° am to blame   *good/thought/I*
ȝyf° y take ouþer° mennys þyng°   *if/other/things*
70 Wyþ-oute leue° of any askyng.   *leave*
For soþe,° he seyde, þan° were° y a þefe°   *in truth/said, then/would be/thief*
And þefte ne° ys gode, ne gode° man lefe;°   *not/nor (to) good/fitting*
And ȝyf y stele,° y am a felun;°   *steal/felon*
Hanged y shal be, þurgh ryȝt resun.°   *by right reason*
75 Fyrst y wylle wyte° þe soþe certeyne,°   *know/certainly*

---

42. *Manuel de Pecches:* The *Manuel de Pechiez,* attributed to William of Wadington, was an Anglo-Norman handbook for confession.

57. *Zenon:* (possibly Zeno, bishop of Verona [died c. 375]) is from the *Vitae Patrum* (ed. Heribert Rosweyd, 2 vols. [Antwerp, 1607], Vol. I, p. 742).

61–62. Visitations of abbeys by bishops were inspection tours, often unannounced, by which they attempted to control clerical discipline in the houses. In many monasteries the rule was exceedingly relaxed.

3yf y may suffre° þat yche peyne°   *endure/pain*
Þat þefys° suffre for þeft° sake,   *thieves/theft's*
Ar° y wyl oght° of þe fruyt take;   *before/any*
And 3yf y may nat° suffre þat wo,°   *not/woe*
80 To þefte wyl y neuer go."

   Ryght° as he þoght, he dede eche dele;°   *just/did every thing*
He 3ede° and clambe° vpp on a pele,°   *went/climbed/perch*
And hyng° þeron by þe hond°   *hung/hand*
Nat by þe nekke,° y vndyrstonde°   *neck/understand*
85 For hyt° ys nat oueral° þe lawe   *it/everywhere*
For to do so, men to dawe.°   *try*
Fyue° days he hyng þere stylle°   *five/quietly*
A3ens° þe sunne by hys° wylle;   *in/his (own)*
And hyt was yn þe somerys tyde,°   *summertime*
90 Whan° þe hete° ys al yn pryde.°   *when/heat/strength*
Þan seyd he, to hymself þore,°   *there*
"Þys peyne wyl y suffre no more:
Þeftc," he seyde, "y here forsake;
Þys fruyt wyl y nat take.
95 Syn° y may nat suffre for grefe°   *since/grief*
Þe peyne þat befalleþ to a þefe."

   Þys ensample° were gode to kone,°   *example/know*
Alle° hem° þat to þefte hem wone;°   *for all/them/themselves accustom*
Þo° þat haue here° handys as lyme,   *they/their*
100 To hem were gode to here° þys ryme   *hear*
Þan myght þey wyte redly°   *immediately*
What shame þat þey were wurþy,°   *due*
And swych° gracc my3t° God hem sende   *such/might*
Þat þey þurgh° þys my3t hem amende.   *through*

The Tale of the Husband and Wife Coupled Together (vss. 8937–9014)

105 Þyr° was a man, and hyght° Rychere,   *there/called*
A ryche of pens° and of powere;   *rich (man) in pence*
Hyt° telleþ° algate° he hadde enmys,°   *it/is told/always/enemies*
Oþer° for° hys gode,° or for folys;°   *either/because of/good (deeds)/ foolish (ones)*

Of hem° hadde he swyche drede° and eye,°   *them/such dread/fear*
110 He fled and woned° yn an abbeye.   *lived*
   Þe abbot ded° hym a chambre werche°   *did/prepare*
For hys ese, fast° by þe cherche;°   *comfort, close/church*
And he and hyse° hadde here wonnyng,°   *his/their dwelling*
Wyfe and chylde, and ouþer þyng.°   *other things*

¹¹⁵ O nyȝt° þyr was,° he knewe hys wyfe — *one night/it happened*
Of flesshely dede,° as fyl° here lyfe; — *deed/it happened in*
And God was nat payd,° and wlde° hyt noȝt,° — *not pleased/wanted/not*
So ny° þe cherche swyche dede were wroȝt;° — *near/was done*
Þey myghte no more be broghte a-sondre° — *brought asunder*
¹²⁰ Þan dog and bych° þat men on wondre.° — *bitch/look*
Betydde a° shame, þey gun° to crye, — *when occurred the/began*
Þat wundyr fyl° on here folye.° — *(a) marvel fell/folly*
    Men asked sone° what was þat drede;° — *soon/terror*
At þe laste, hyt shewed° yn dede. — *showed*
¹²⁵ Sone oueral ȝede° þat fame;° — *everywhere went/news*
Ȝow þar° nat aske ȝyf° þey þoȝt° shame. — *you need/if/thought (it)*
    Þys man dyd° þe munkes° to kalle,° — *had/monks/called*
And specyaly besoghte° hem alle — *especially asked*
To praye for hem yn orysun° — *common prayer*
¹³⁰ Þat þey myghte be undoun.° — *separated*
"And largely° we wul° ȝow° ȝyue,° — *generously/will/to you/give*
And wurshyp° þys stede° whyl þat° we lyue;° — *honor/place/while/live*
Þat° God almyȝty graunte° hyt be so — *if/almighty grant*
Þat oure synne he wyl vndo."
¹³⁵ Þese munkes besoghte for hem a bone,° — *boon*
And God almyȝty graunted hyt sone.° — *quickly*
    Þere, þurgh° alle here ordynaunce,° — *through/ordinances*
Þey dede° to wryte° yn boke° þys chaunce,° — *ordered/be written/book/occurrence*
For to shewe hyt euer more,
¹⁴⁰ Þat ouþer myȝt° beware þar-fore.° — *others might/thereof*
    Þys chaunce fyl° nat for hem allone,° — *happened/alone*
But for to warne vs euerychone° — *every one*
Þat we shul° euermore drede° — *shall/beware*
Yn holy place to do þat dede.
¹⁴⁵ For moche° more dampnacyun° — *much/damnation*
Wyl falle of° fornycacyun,° — *(because) of/fornication*
And ȝyt° more for auowtrye° — *yet/adultry*
Of prestys° or wyues lecherye, — *priests/wives'*
Whan° God toke wreche,° þat many of spake,° — *when/took vengeance/spoke*
¹⁵⁰ For a dede þat was do° yn ryȝt° wedlake.° — *done/true wedlock*
    Þys yche° chaunce, to ȝow y° tolde, — *same/I*
For hyt° ys gode° yn herte° to holde, — *it/good/heart*
Namly° men of holy cherche,° — *especially/Church*
Þat þey þer-ynne no swyche° dede werche.° — *such/do*

119–20. These lines, and also ll. 129–30, are scratched and inked out in the Harleian MS. The clerical censor evidently felt that the point had been made too effectively.

¹⁵⁵ Karolles, wrastlynges,° or somour° games,	*wrestling/summer*
Who-so euer haunteþ° any swyche shames	*frequents*
Yn cherche, oþer° yn chercheȝerd,°	*or/churchyard*
Of sacrylage° he may be a-ferd;°	*sacrilege/afraid*
Or entyrludes,° or syngynge,	*interludes*
¹⁶⁰ Or tabure bete,° or oþer pypynge,	*drum beating*
Alle swyche þyng forbodyn es,°	*forbidden is*
Whyle þe prest stondeþ° at messe.°	*stands/mass*
Alle swyche to euery gode preste ys lothe,°	*hateful*
And sunner° wyl he make hym° wroth°	*sooner/become/angry*
¹⁶⁵ Þan he wyl þat haþ no wyt,	
Ne vndyrstondeþ nat° holy wryt;	*nor understands not*
And specyaly at hyghe tymes°	*holy seasons*
Karolles to synge and rede° rymys	*read*
Noght° yn none° holy stedes,	*not/no*
¹⁷⁰ Þat myȝt dysturble° þe prestes bedes,°	*disturb/prayers*
Or ȝyf° he were yn° orysun°	*if/at/common prayer*
Or any ouþer deuocyun,°	*other devotion*
Sacrylage ys alle hyt tolde,°	*called*
Þys and many oþer folde.°	*times*
¹⁷⁵ But for to leue° yn cherche to daunce,°	*leave off/dance*
Y shal ȝow telle° a ful grete chaunce,°	*you tell (of)/very great occurrence*
And y trow,° þe most þat fel°	*believe/happened*
Ys as soþ° as þe gospel;	*true*
And fyl° þys chaunce° yn þys londe,°	*happened/incident/land*
¹⁸⁰ Yn Ingland, as y vndyrstonde;	
Yn a kynges tyme þat hyght° Edward	*was called*
Fyl þys chaunce þat was so hard.°	*terrible*

The Tale of the Sacrilegious Carolers (vss. 9016–252)

Hyt° was vpp-on a crystemesse nyȝt°	*it/Christmas night*
Þat twelue folys° a karolle dyȝt;°	*fools/carol danced*

---

155. *somour games:* Summer games were sometimes specifically the midsummer pastimes enjoyed during the Eve of Saint John; but "summerings" in general were amusements, dances, and sports enjoyed during the warm season. *Karolles:* Carols were ring dances accompanied by songs, also the songs alone.

159. *entyrludes:* This is an early reference to dramatic productions in England. Interludes normally were short plays acted between the courses of a meal, but later any brief, light performance went by this name.

179–82. The curing of Saint Theodoric from the dance (cf. ll. 183–86n) occurred at the tomb of Saint Edith at the abbey of Wilton during the time of Edward the Confessor (1042–66), although the dance itself did not take place in England.

183–86. The famous dance supposedly occurred in Kölbigk, in Anhalt, Saxony, in the year 1021. William of Wadington's version came from the *Letter of Otbert* by a supposed survivor of the grim dance, but Mannyng greatly enlarged his source, using the Latin story of Saint Edith of Wilton for his text. This legend came from a letter by Theodoric, which cites Bruno, bishop of Tours (later Pope Leo IX), as the authority. The simulation of such disorders as Saint Vitus's dance was utilized by mendicants all over Europe for their profit.

185 Yn wodehed° as° hyt were yn cuntek°	*madness/as if/contest*
Þey come° to a tounne men calles Colbek;°	*came/Kölbigk*
Þe cherche° of þe tounne þat þey to come	*church*
Ys of seynt Magne° þat suffred martyrdome;	*Saint Magnus*
Of seynt Bukcestre hyt ys also,	
190 Seynt Magnes suster,° þat þey come to.	*sister*
Here° names of alle, þus fonde y wryte,°	*their/found I written*
And as y wote,° now shul ȝe wyte:°	*know/shall you learn*
Here lodes-man° þat made hem glew,°	*leader/them mirth*
Þus ys wryte, he hyȝte° Gerlew;	*was called*
195 Twey° maydens were yn here coueyne,°	*two/company*
Mayden Merswynde and Wybessyne;	
Alle þese come þedyr° for þat enchesone°	*there/purpose*
Of° þe prestes doghtyr° of þe tounne.	*for/priest's/daughter*
Þe prest° hyȝt Robert, as y kan ame;°	*priest/can guess*
200 Aȝone hyght° hys sone° by name;	*was called/son*
Hys doghter, þat þese men wulde haue,°	*desired*
Þus ys° wryte, þat she hyȝt Aue;	*(it) is*
Echoune° consented to o wyl,°	*everyone/with one mind*
Who shuld° go, Aue oute to tyl:°	*should/fetch*
205 Þey graunted° echone out to sende	*consented*
Boþe Wybessyne and Merswynde.	
Þese wommen ȝede° and tolled here° oute	*went/brought her*
Wyþ hem to karolle þe cherche aboute.	
Beune ordeyned° here karollyng;	*arranged*
210 Gerlew endyted° what þey shuld syng:	*composed*
Þys ys þe karolle þat þey sunge,°	*sang*
As telleþ þe latyn tunge,°	*tongue*
"Equitabat Beuo per siluam frondosam,	
Ducebat secum Merswyndam formosam,	
215 Quid stamus, cur non imus?"	
"By þe leued wode° rode Beuolyne,	*leafy wood*
Wyþ hym he ledde feyre° Merswyne;	*fair*
Why stonde° we? why go we noght?"	*stand/not*
Þys ys þe karolle þat Grysly wroght.°	*composed*
220 Þys songe sunge þey yn þe chercheȝerd°—	*churchyard*
Of foly° were þey no þyng° aferd°—	*folly/not at all/afraid*
Vn-to° þe matynes° were alle done,	*until/matins*
And þe messe° shuld° bygynne sone.°	*mass/was to/begin soon*

---

188. *seynt Magne:* the patron saint of the church at Kölbigk.

189. *seynt Bukcestre:* Saint Bukchester is unknown.

209. *Beune:* (also *Beuo* and *Beuolyne*) should be *Bovo*. It is useless to expect consistency of names.

219. *Grysly:* should be *Gerlew*.

222. *matynes:* the service for the first of the seven canonical hours, beginning usually at midnight but sometimes at daybreak.

Þe preste hym reuest° to begynne messe,   *himself robed*
225 And þey ne left° þerfore, neuer þe lesse,   *not stopped*
But daunsed furþe° as þey bygan;   *danced forth*
For alle þe messe þey ne blan.°   *ceased*
    Þe preste, þat stode° at þe autere°   *stood/altar*
And herde° here noyse and here bere,°   *heard/behavior*
230 Fro° þe auter down he nam,°   *from/came*
And to þe cherche° porche he cam,°   *church/came*
And seyd,° on Goddes behalue, y ȝow forbede°   *said/behalf, I you forbid*
Þat ȝe° no lenger° do swych dede;°   *you/longer/such deed*
But comeþ yn, on feyre manere,°   *in good manner*
235 Goddes seruyse° for to here,°   *service/hear*
And doþ at° Crystyn° mennys lawe;   *follow/Christian*
Karolleþ° no more for Crystys awe,°   *carol/reverence*
Wurschyppeþ° hym with alle ȝoure myȝt,°   *worship/might*
Þat of þe vyrgyne° was bore° þys nyȝt."°   *Virgin/born/night*
240   For alle hys byddyng, lefte þey noȝt,°   *not*
But daunsed furþ, as þey þoȝt.°   *wished*
Þe prest þarefore° was sore a-greued;°   *therefore/angered*
He preyd° God þat he on beleuyd,°   *prayed/believed*
And for seynt Magne,° þat he wulde so werche,°   *Saint Magnus/would bring (it) about*

245 Yn° whos wurschyp sette° was þe cherche,   *for/built*
Þat swych a veniaunce° were° on hem° sent   *vengeance/would he/them*
Are° þey oute of þat stede° were went,°   *before/place/gone*
Þat þey myȝt euer ryȝt° so wende°   *just/go*
Vnto þat tyme tweluemonth ende.°   *(a) year hence*
250 (Yn þe latyne þat y fonde þore,°   *found there*
He seyþ nat° "tweluemonth," but "euermore.")   *not*
He cursed hem þere alsaume°   *together*
As þey karoled on here gaume.°   *their game*
    As sone as þe preste° hadde so spoke,   *priest*
255 Euery hande yn ouþer° so fast was loke°   *other/locked*
Þat no man myȝt with no wundyr°   *miracle*
Þat tweluemonþe parte hem asundyr.
    Þe preste ȝede° yn, whan° þys was done,   *went/when*
And commaundcd° hys sone° Aȝone   *commanded/son*
260 Þat he shulde° go swyþe° aftyr Aue,   *should/quickly*
Oute of þat karolle algate° to haue.   *by all means*
But al to° late þat wurde° was seyd,   *too/word*
For on hem alle was þe veniaunce leyd.°   *laid*
    Aȝone wende weyl° for to spede;°   *thought well/succeed*
265 Vn-to þe karolle asswyþe° he ȝede;   *quickly*
Hys systyr° by þe arme he hente,°   *sister/grabbed*
And þe arme fro þe body wente.

Men wundred° alle þat þere wore,° — *wondered/were*
And merueyle mowe° ȝe here more,° — *marvel may/hear greater*
270 For seþen° he had þe arme yn hande, — *when*
Þe body ȝede furþ karoland;° — *forth caroling*
And noþer° body ne° þe arme — *neither/nor*
Bledde neuer blode,° colde ne warme, — *blood*
But was as drye, with al° þe haunche,° — *also/shoulder*
275 As° of° a stok° were ryue° a braunche.° — *as if/from/tree/torn/branch*
    Aȝone to hys fadyr° went, — *father*
And broght° hym a sory° present: — *brought/sorry*
"Loke,° fadyr," he seyd,° "and haue hyt° here, — *look/said/it*
Þe arme of þy doghtyr dere° — *daughter dear*
280 Þat was myn° owne syster Aue, — *my*
Þat y° wende y myȝt a saue.° — *I/have saved*
Þy cursyng, now sene° hyt ys — *seen*
With veniaunce on þyn° owne flessh; — *your*
Fellyche° þou cursedest, and ouer sone;° — *cruelly/too quickly*
285 Þou askedest veniaunce, þou hast þy bone."° — *request*
    Ȝow þar° nat aske ȝyf° þere was wo° — *you need/if/woe*
With þe preste and with many mo.° — *more*
    Þe prest þat cursed for° þat daunce,° — *because of/dance*
On some of hys fyl harde chaunce.° — *his (family) fell (a) terrible lot*
290 He toke° hys doghtyr° arme forlorn° — *took/daughter's/lost*
And byryed° hyt on þe morn; — *buried*
Þe nexte day, þe arme of Aue,
He fonde° hyt lyggyng° aboue þe graue. — *found/lying*
He byryed hyt on anouþer° day, — *another*
295 And eft° aboue þe graue hyt lay; — *again*
Þe þrydde° tyme he byryed hyt, — *third*
And eft was hyt kast oute of þe pyt.
Þe prest wulde° byrye hyt no more; — *priest would*
He dredde° þe veniaunce ferly° sore; — *feared/vengeance very*
300 Yn-to þe cherche° he bare° þe arme, — *church/bore*
For drede° and doute° of more harme; — *dread/fear*
He ordeyned° hyt for to be, — *arranged*
Þat euery man myȝt° with ye° hyt se.° — *might/eye/see*
    Þese men þat ȝede° so karolland — *went*
305 Alle þat ȝere° hand yn hand, — *year*
Þey neuer oute of þat stede° ȝede, — *place*
Ne° none myȝt hem þenne lede;° — *nor/them away lead*
Þere° þe cursyng fyrst bygan,° — *where/began*
Yn þat place, a-boute þey ran,
310 Þat° neuer ne° felte þey no werynes°— — *so that/not/weariness*
As many bodyes° for goyng dos°— — *(i.e., people)/from walking do*
Ne mete ete,° ne drank drynke, — *food ate*

Ne slepte onely a-lepy° wynke;   *even a single*
Nyȝt,° ne day, þey wyst° of none,   *night/knew*
315 Whan° hyt was come, whan hyt was gone;   *when*
Frost ne snogh,° hayle ne reyne,°   *snow/rain*
Of° colde ne hete,° felte þey no peyne;°   *from/heat/pain*
Heere° ne nayles neuer grewe,   *hair*
Ne solowed° cloþes, ne turned hewe;°   *soiled/changed color*
320 Þundyr ne lyȝtnyng° dyd hem no dere,°   *lightning/harm*
Goddes mercy dyd hyt fro° hem were;°   *it from/guard*
But sungge° þat songge þat þe wo wroȝt,°   *(they) sang/wrought*
"Why stonde° we, why go we noȝt?"°   *stand/not*
What man shuld þyr° be, yn þys lyue,°   *should there/life*
325 Þat ne wulde° hyt see,° and þedyr dryue?°   *wanted/(to) see/there go*
Þe Emperoure Henry come° fro Rome   *came*
For to see þys harde dome;°   *terrible judgment*
Whan he hem say,° he wepte sore   *saw*
For þe myschefe° þat he sagh þore;°   *distress/saw there*
330 He ded° come wryȝtes° for to make   *had/carpenters*
Coueryng° ouer hem, for tempest° sake;   *shelter/tempest's*
But þat° þey wroght,° hyt was yn veyn,°   *what/built/vain*
For hyt come to no certeyn;°   *nothing*
For þat þey sette° on oo° day,   *set (up)/one*
335 On þe touþer,° downe hyt lay;   *the other*
Ones, twyys, þryys,° þus þey wroȝt,°   *once, twice, thrice/built*
And alle here makyng° was for noȝt;°   *their building/nothing*
Myght no coueryng hyle° hem fro colde   *keep*
Tyl tyme of mercy, þat° Cryst hyt wolde.°   *when/would*
340 Tyme of grace fyl þurgh° hys myȝt°   *fell through/might*
At þe twelvemonth° ende, on þe ȝole° nyȝt,   *year's/Yule*
Þe same oure° þat þe prest° hem banned,°   *hour/priest/cursed*
Þe same oure atwynne° þey woned;°   *separated/were*
Þat houre þat he cursed hem ynne,°   *in*
345 Þat same oure þey ȝede atwynne:°   *walked apart*
And, as yn twynkelyng of an ye,°   *eye*
Yn-to þe cherche gun° þey flye,   *church did*
And on þe pauement þey fyl alle downe,
As° þey hade be dcde,° or fal° yn a swone.°   *as if/had been dead/fallen/swoon*
350 Þre° days, styl,° þey lay echone,°   *three/still/each one*
Þat° none steryd, oþer° flesshe or bone,   *so that/stirred, either*
And, at þe þre days ende,
To lyfe God grauntede hem° to wende.°   *granted them/come*

---

324. *yn þys lyue:* i.e., "alive."
326. *Emperoure Henry:* maybe Henry II, king of Germany and Holy Roman Emperor (1014–24).

Þey sette hem° vpp, and spak apert°   *sat themselves/spoke openly*
355 To þe parysshe prest, syre Robert:
    "Þou art ensample° and enchesun°   *occasion/reason*
    Of oure long confusyun;°   *distress*
    Þou maker° art of oure trauayle,°   *creator/hardship*
    Þat ys to many grete meruayle;   *(a) great marvel*
360 And þy traueyle° shalt þou sone° ende,   *travail/soon*
    For to þy long home sone shalt þou wende."°   *go*
        Alle þey ryse° þat yche tyde,°   *rose/same time*
    But Aue; she lay dede besyde;°   *beside (them)*
    Grete sorowe had here fadyr,° here broþer,   *her father*
365 Merueyle° and drede° had alle ouþer,°   *astonishment/fear/others*
    Y trow° no drede of soule dede,°   *I believe/for (her) soul's death*
    But with pyne° was broght° þe body dede.°   *suffering/brought/to death*
    Þe fyrst man was þe fadyr, þe prest,
    Þat deyd° aftyr þe doȝtyr nest;°   *died/daughter next*
370 Þys yche arme þat was of Aue,
    Þat none myȝt leye° yn graue,   *might lay*
    Þe emperoure dyd° a vessel werche°   *had/made*
    To do hyt° yn, and hange yn þe cherche,   *put it*
    Þat alle men myȝt se° hyt and knawe,°   *see/know*
375 And þenk° on þe chaunce° when men hyt sawe.   *reflect/misfortune*
        Þese men þat hadde go° þus karolland°   *gone/caroling*
    Alle þe ȝere,° fast hand yn hand,   *year*
    Þogh þat° þey were þan asunder,°   *although/then apart*
    Ȝyt° alle þe worlde spake° of hem wunder:°   *yet/spoke/(with) wonder*
380 Þat same hoppyng þat þey fyrst ȝede,°   *did*
    Þat daunce ȝede° þey þurgh° land and lede;°   *dance led/through/folk*
    And as þey ne° myȝt fyrst° be vnbounde,   *not/(at) first*
    So efte to-gedyr° myȝt þey neuer be founde,   *after together*
    Ne° myȝt þey neuer come aȝeyn°   *nor/again*
385 To-gedyr, to oo stede certeyn.°   *one spot certain*
        Foure ȝede° to þe courte of Rome,   *went*
    And euer hoppyng aboute þey nome;°   *went*
    With sundyr lepys come° þey þedyr,°   *sundry leaps came/there*
    But þey come neuer efte° to-gedyr;   *again*
390 Here° cloþes ne roted,° ne nayles grewe,   *their/rotted*
    Ne heere° ne wax,° ne solowed hewe,°   *hair/grew/paled (in) color*
    Ne neuer hadde þey amendement,°   *help*
    Þat we herde, at° any corseynt,°   *heard, from/saint*
    But at þe vyrgyne Seynt Edyght,°   *virgin Saint Edith*

---

394. *Seynt Edyght:* Saint Edith (d. 984), abbess of Wilton,
where the famous cure of Theodoric (Dietrich) took place.

³⁹⁵ Þere was he botened,° seynt Teodryght;°   *cured/Theodoric*
On oure lady° day, yn lenten° tyde,   *Lady's/Lent*
As he slepte here° toumbe° besyde,   *(i.e., Saint Edith's)/tomb*
Þere he hade° hys medycyne,   *had*
At seynt Edyght, þe holy vyrgyne.

⁴⁰⁰   Brunyng, þe bysshop of seynt° Tolous,   *holy*
Wrote þys tale so merueylous;°   *marvelous*
Seþþe° was hys name of more renoun,°   *since then/fame*
Men called hym þe pope Leoun;°   *Leo*
Þys at þe court of Rome þey wyte,°   *know*
⁴⁰⁵ And yn þe kronykeles° hyt ys wryte,°   *chronicles/written*
Yn many stedys be-ȝounde° þe see,°   *places beyond/sea*
More þan ys° yn þys cuntre;°   *(it) is/country*
Þarfor° men seye, an weyl° ys trowed,°   *therefore/say, and well/believed*
"Þe nere° þe cherche,° þe fyrþer fro° God."   *nearer/church/further from*
⁴¹⁰   So fare° men here by° þys tale: *act/in regard to*
Some holde hyt° but a troteuale;°   *it/idle talk*
Yn oþer stedys hyt ys ful dere,°   *much valued*
And for grete merueyle° þey wyl° hyt here;°   *great wonder/want/(to) hear*
A tale hyt ys of feyre shewyng,°   *good intent*
⁴¹⁵ Ensample° and drede aȝens° cursyng;   *example/warning against*
Þys tale y° tolde ȝow,° to make ȝow aferde^ᵁ   *I/you/afraid*
Yn cherche to karolle,° or yn cherche ȝerde,°   *carol/yard*
Namely aȝens° þe prestys° wylle;   *especially against/priest's*
Leueþ,° whan° he byddeþ^ᵁ ȝow be stylle. . . .   *leave off/when/asks*

---

400. Bruno Tullanus (bishop of Toul, not Toulouse) became Pope Leo IX (1049–54).

from PROSE TREATISES

Richard Rolle of Hampole

DATE: 1300–49. ✦ MANUSCRIPTS: Lincoln Cathedral Library, Thornton MS. (a. 1450); Cambridge University Library Dd. v. 64 (c. 1400), and others. The dialect is Northern, from Yorkshire. ✦ EDITIONS: Hope Emily Allen, *Writings Ascribed to Richard Rolle, Hermit of Hampole, and Materials for his Biography* (New York, 1927), and *English Writings of Richard Rolle Hermit of Hampole* (Oxford, 1931); George G. Perry, *English Prose Treatises of Richard Rolle de Hampole*, Early English Text Society, OS 20 (London, 1866).

The language of Richard Rolle has strong Northern characteristics. (1) OE $\bar{a}$ is kept instead of the normal *o* as in *haly, na, blawen* for *holy, no, blow*. (2) The present participle is formed with *-and* (*settand = sitting, doande = doing*). (3) *Till* is used for "into," "toward," and the first part of the infinitive. (4) Single *s* instead of *sh* is generally seen as in *sall = shall, sulde = should*. (5) Pronoun forms will seem normal, except for the feminine third-person singular *scho*. (6) Noun plurals are formed by *-is* or *-ys* in addition to the regular *-es* (*kindis*).

The great English mystic of the 14th century, Richard Rolle of Hampole, was born in 1300 at Thornton Dale, near York. After studying at Oxford, he forsook the scholastic life, dressed himself as a hermit, and lived in retirement—first with the Dalton family, then in the archdeaconry of Richmond near Ainderby, close to the recluse Margaret Kirby. We last hear of him remaining in seclusion at Hampole, southern Yorkshire, where he died of the plague in September, 1349.

Although Rolle's major mystical works were written in Latin, he dedicated three English works on the love of God—*Ego Dormio, Commandment of the Love of God*, and the *Form of Living*—to his feminine disciples, who regarded him as their spiritual confessor. In his best known writings, the *Incendium Amoris* and the *Emendatio Vitae*, Rolle has given autobiographical facts on his mystical experience. His style throughout all his compositions is deeply devotional, intense, and rhythmical. The selection on the bee and the stork included here will give evidence of his pleasure in parallel phrasing, repetition of particles, and general melody. Not only his style but his whole spiritual involvement is of a sensuous nature; in his meditations he feels an inner "heat." His work in general shows an aloofness and withdrawal from the world, a communion not with man but only with God.

The Nature of the Bee and the Stork

The bee has thre[1] kyndis.[2] Ane es,[3] þat scho[4] es neuer ydill,[5] and scho es noghte[6] with thaym[7] þat will noghte wyrke,[8] bot[9] castys thaym owte, and puttes thaym awaye. A-nothire[10] es, þat when scho flyes, scho takes erthe[11] in hyr fette[12] þat[13] scho be[14] noghte lyghtly[15] ouer-heghede[16] in the ayere of[17] wynde.[18] The thyrde es, þat scho kepes clene[19] and bryghte hire wingez.[20] Thus ryghtwyse[21] men þat lufes[22] God are never in ydyllnes, for owthire[23] þay ere[24] in trauayle, prayand,[25] or thynkande,[26] or redande,[27] or othere gude doande,[28] or withtakand[29] ydill men, and schewand[30] thaym worthy to be put fra[31] þe ryste[32] of heuen,[33] for thay will noghte trauayle. Here þay take erthe, þat es, þay halde[34] þam selfe[35] vile and erthely, that thay be noghte blawen[36] with þe wynde of vanyte[37] and of pryde. Thay kepe thaire[38] wynges clene, that es, þe twa[39] commandements of charyte[40] þay fulfill in gud concyens,[41] and thay hafe othyre vertus vnblendyde[42] with þe fylthe of syn and vnclene luste. Aristotill sais þat þe bees are feghtande agaynes[43] hym þat will drawe þaire hony fra thaym;[44] swa sulde[45] we do agaynes deuells[46] þat afforces tham[47] to reue[48] fra vs þe hony of poure[49] lyfe and of grace. For many are[50] þat neuer kane[51] halde[52] þe ordyre[53] of lufe ynesche[54] þaire frendys,[55] sybbe[56] or fremmede,[57] bot outhire[58] þay lufe þaym ouer mekill,[59] or thay lufe þam[60] ouer lyttill,[61] settand[62] thaire thoghte vnryghtwysely[63] on thaym, or þay lufe thaym ouer lyttill, yf þay doo noghte all as þey wolde till[64] þam. Swylke[65] kane noghte fyghte for thaire

---

1. three.
2. distinctive characteristics.
3. one is.
4. she.
5. idle.
6. not.
7. them.
8. work.
9. but.
10. another.
11. earth.
12. her feet.
13. so that.
14. is.
15. easily.
16. carried too high.
17. air by.
18. *when ... wynde:* from the *Historia Animalium* (ix, 40), attributed in the Middle Ages to Aristotle.
19. keeps clean.
20. her wings.
21. righteous.
22. love.
23. either.
24. they are.
25. labor, praying.
26. thinking.
27. counseling.
28. good doing.
29. reproaching.
30. showing.
31. from.
32. rest.
33. heaven.
34. hold.
35. themselves.
36. blown.
37. vanity.
38. their.
39. two.
40. charity.
41. good conscience.
42. have other virtues unmixed.
43. fighting against.
44. *Aristotill ... thaym: Historia Animalium,* ix, 27.
45. thus should.
46. devils.
47. try.
48. take.
49. poor.
50. (there) are.
51. can.
52. keep to.
53. order.
54. toward.
55. friends.
56. family.
57. strangers.
58. others.
59. much.
60. them.
61. little.
62. setting.
63. thought unjustly.
64. would to.
65. such.

hony, for-thy[66] þe deuelle turnes it to wormes, and makes þeire saules[67] ofte sythes full[68] bitter in angwys[69] and tene,[70] and besynes[71] of vayne thoghtes, and oþer wrechidnes, for thay are so heuy[72] in erthely frenchype[73] þat þay may noghte flee in-till[74] þe lufe of Ihesu[75] Criste, in þe wylke[76] þay moghte wele for-gaa[77] þe lufe of all creaturs lyfande[78] in erthe. Whare-fore, accordandly,[79] Arystotill sais þat some fowheles[80] are of gude flyghyng,[81] þat passes fra a[82] land to a-nothire; some are of ill flyghynge, for heuynes[82] of body and for[84] þaire neste es noghte ferre[85] fra þe erthe. Thus es it of thaym þat turnes þam[86] to Godes seruys[87]— some are of gude flyeghynge, for thay flye fra erthe to heuen, and rystes thaym thare[88] in thoghte, and are fedde in delite of Goddes lufe, and has thoghte of na[89] lufe of þe worlde. Some are

þat kan noghte flyghe fra þis lande, bot in þe waye late[90] theyre herte[91] ryste, and delyttes[92] þaym in sere[93] lufes of men and women, als[94] þay come and gaa,[95] nowe ane[96] and nowe a-nothire. And in Ihesu Criste þay kan fynde na swettnes,[97] or if þay any tym[98] fele oghte,[99] it es swa[100] lyttill and swa schorte, for othire thoghtes þat are in thaym,[101] þat it brynges thaym till[102] na stabylnes.[103] Or þay are lyke till a fowle þat es callede "strucyo" or storke,[104] þat has wenges,[105] and it may noghte[106] flye, for charge[107] of body. Swa þay hafe vnderstandynge, and fastes and wakes,[108] and semes haly[109] to mens syghte; bot thay[110] may noghte flye to lufe[111] and contemplacyone of God, þay are so chargede wyth othyre affeccyons[112] and othire vanytes.

The Girl in the Sepulcher

Alswa[1] Heraclides[2] þe clerke telles þat a mayden forsuke[3] hir cete,[4] and satte in a sepulcre, and tuke[5] hir mete[6] at a lyttill[7] hole, ten ȝere.[8] Scho

saghe[9] neuer man ne[10] woman, ne þay[11] hir face, bot stode[12] at a hole, and talde[13] why scho was enclosede, and said þat "a ȝonge[14] man was

---

66. therefore.
67. souls.
68. times very.
69. anguish.
70. distress.
71. occupation.
72. heavy.
73. friendship.
74. into.
75. Jesus.
76. which.
77. might well forgo.
78. living.
79. wherefore, accordingly.
80. birds.
81. flying.
82. one.
83. heaviness.
84. because.

85. far.
86. themselves.
87. service.
88. themselves there.
89. no.
90. let.
91. heart.
92. delight.
93. particular.
94. as.
95. go.
96. one.
97. sweetness.
98. time.
99. feel anything.
100. is so.
101. them.
102. to.
103. stability.
104. Obviously the ostrich, not the stork, is meant here. The Latin *struthio* can refer to either bird.
105. wings.
106. not.

107. weight.
108. keep vigils.
109. seem holy.
110. but they.
111. love.
112. affections.
1. also.
2. Heraclitus, the "weeping philosopher," c. 500 B.C. in Ephesus wrote a treatise on the transitory state of earthly things called *Concerning Nature*. The story of the entombed maiden, however, was widely circulated in medieval folklore.
3. forsook.
4. her city.
5. took.
6. food.
7. little.
8. years.
9. she saw.
10. nor.
11. they.
12. but stood.
13. told.
14. young.

tempede of[15] my fairehede;[16] for-thy me warre leuere[17] be, als lange[18] als I lyfe,[19] in þis sepulcre, þan[20] any sawle[21] þat es[22] made til[23] þe lyknes[24] of Gode suld perichse[25] by cause[26] of me." And when men askede hire[27] how scho myghte swa lyffe,[28] scho said, "Fra[29] the begynnynge of the day I gyfe me till praynge[30] till forthe dayes;[31] thane[32] I wyrke[33] with handes some thynge; and alswa I wyrke[34] in thoghtes,[35] by patryarkes,[36] prophetes, appostilles,[30] martyrs and confessours, and byhaldes þaire Ioye.[38] And aftyrwarde I take my mete. When euen[39] commys, with gret[40] Ioye I lofe[41] my lorde. The ende of my lyfe I habyde[42] in gude[43] hope and tholemodnes" :[44] and loo,[15] swa perfitly[46] a woman lyfede![47] Richard herymyte reherces[48] þis tale in ensampill.[49]

---

15. tempted by.
16. beauty.
17. therefore I would rather.
18. as long.
19. live.
20. than (that).
21. soul.
22. is.
23. in.
24. likeness.
25. should perish.
26. because.
27. her.
28. so live.
29. from.
30. give myself to praying.
31. late in the day.
32. then.
33. do.
34. work.
35. thought.
36. patriarchs.
37. apostles.
38. behold their joy.
39. evening.
40. great.
41. praise.
42. await.
43. good.
44. patience.
45. lo.
46. perfectly.
47. lived.
48. hermit tells.
49. as an example.

CLASSICAL LEGEND

O ne of the most popular genres of literature throughout the Middle Ages was classical legend—the stories, many with Eastern motifs and carried to Europe by Crusaders, having their sources in the tales of Troy, Thebes, Alexander, and the Roman emperors. These legends must be distinguished from the romances dealing with the Matter of Rome, as the former did not necessarily treat of chivalric themes with a classical background. Thus Chaucer's *Man of Law's Tale* of Constance and his *Physician's Tale*, and many of the episodes in the *Gesta Romanorum* and of Gower's *Confessio Amantis* can be termed classical legends. The Alexander story appeared early in England with the fictitious *Letters of Alexander to Aristotle* of the ninth century. In the eleventh century *Apollonius of Tyre*, a Greek romance, was translated into English. Themes of the Trojan War were supplied from Virgil's *Aeneid* and from the fraudulent accounts by Dictys Cretensis in the fourth century and by Dares Phrygius a hundred years later—the former showing the Greek perspective, the latter the Trojan. The wonders of the East, of old Rome, and of the pagan trio of the Nine Worthies—Hector, Alexander, and Julius Caesar—continued for centuries to fascinate a medieval audience.

REFERENCES

Cary, G. *The Medieval Alexander*. Cambridge, 1956.

Gough, A. B. *The Constance Saga*. Berlin, 1902.

Griffin, N. E. *Dares and Dictys: An Introduction to the Study of Medieval Versions of the Story of Troy*. Baltimore, 1907.

Herrtage, Sidney J. H., ed. *The Early English Versions of the Gesta Romanorum*. Early English Text Society, 33. London, 1879. Rpt. 1898, 1932, 1962.

Magoun, F. P., Jr. *The Gests of King Alexander of Macedon*. Cambridge, Mass., 1929.

Classical legend is treated in the General Introduction of this volume, pp. 17–18.

THE TALE OF FLORENT

John Gower

DATE: c. 1390. ☛ MANUSCRIPTS: Bodleian Library, Oxford, Fairfax 3; some forty MSS are extant, dated 1390 and 1392–93. The dialect is the court English of London. ☛ EDITION: G. C. Macauley, *The Complete Works of John Gower*, 4 vols. (Oxford, 1899–1902). The first critical treatment of the writer is by John H. Fisher, *John Gower: Moral Philosopher and Friend of Chaucer* (New York, 1964). Terence Tiller's translation of the *Confessio Amantis* (Baltimore, 1963) is readable and handy in format.

John Gower's London dialect is as easy to understand as the language of Chaucer. In general the student will find no special dialectal, scribal, or orthographic problems, but the following points should be noted. (1) The scribe occasionally runs articles and prepositions into the following nouns or verbs (*themperor, tobreke*). (2) In this text *ie* is the common spelling for *ē* (*chiere, lievest*). (3) Also frequent metathesis of *r* occurs (*thurgh = through*). (4) The pronouns *hem*, "them," *hir*, "her," and *him*, "himself," appear frequently, and the reflexive especially should be kept in mind.

John Gower, friend of Chaucer, courtier, and clerical benefactor, was a prolific and very dedicated writer. His three most famous works, the French *Speculum Meditantis* (*Mirour de l'Omme*) of 30,000 lines, the Latin *Vox Clamantis* of 10,000 lines, and the English *Confessio Amantis* of 30,000 lines, form the headrest of the stone effigy on his tomb. Born between 1327 and 1330 of a wealthy Kentish family, the poet was known both by Richard II and Henry IV and received from them lands and sinecures in Norfolk, Suffolk, and Kent. The priory of Saint Mary Overies in Southwark was his home for many years. He probably died in October, 1408.

Not without reason did Chaucer call his friend "moral Gower." Earnestness and dedication to moral right, law, order, and reform when it occurs within the establishment describe the message in Gower's poems. The *Confessio Amantis*, his most popular work, is a frame story ostensibly on the theme of the Seven Deadly Sins, but in reality a series of exempla, in the form of classical legends, illustrating various aspects and problems of courtly love. *The Tale of Florent* is not the best of these, but it is in many ways typical of Gower. As an analogue to Chaucer's *Wife of Bath's Tale* and the burlesque *Wedding of Sir Gawain and Dame Ragnell*, the poem is worthy of critical comparison. Gower was a hard worker and a fine craftsman, but his technique and didacticism often outweigh his genius.

from CONFESSIO AMANTIS, I, 1396–1861

Mi sone,° and I thee rede° this,	son/advise
What so befalle of° other weie,°	in/ways
That thou to loves heste° obeie	command
Als ferr° as thou it myht° suffise:°	as far/might/be able
5 For ofte sithe° in such a wise°	times/manner
Obedience in love availeth,	
Wher al a mannes strengthe faileth;	
Wherof, if that the list° to wite°	you wish/know
In a cronique° as it is write,°	chronicle/written
10 A gret ensample° thou myht fynde,	great example
Which now is come to my mynde.	
Ther was whilom be daies° olde	once in days
A worthi knyht,° and as men tolde	knight
He was nevoeu° to themperour°	nephew/the emperor
15 And of his court a courteour:°	courtier
Wifles° he was, Florent he hihte,°	wifeless/was called
He was a man that mochel myhte,°	much might (accomplish)
Of armes he was desirous,°	eager
Chivalerous and amorous,	
20 And for the fame of worldes speche,°	renown
Strange aventures° forte° seche,°	adventures/in order to/seek
He rod° the marches° al aboute.	rode/districts
And fell a° time, as he was oute,	(it) happened one
Fortune, which may every thred°	thread
25 Tobreke° and knette° of mannes sped,°	break/knot/success
Schop,° as this knyht rod in° a pas,°	ordained/at/pace
That he be° strengthe take° was,	by/taken
And to a castell thei him ladde,°	led
Wher that he fewe frendes hadde:	
30 For so it fell that ilke stounde°	same time
That he hath with a dedly° wounde	deadly
Feihtende° his oghne hondes° slain	(in) fighting (with)/own hands
Branchus, which to the capitain°	captain
Was sone and heir, whereof ben° wrothe	were
35 The fader° and the moder° bothe.	father/mother
That knyht Branchus was of his hond°	manner
The worthieste of al his lond,°	land
And fain° thei wolden° do vengance°	eagerly/wanted to/have vengeance

---

14. The tenuous reference to the Roman emperor categorizes this tale as a classical legend similar to the stories with Roman background in the *Gesta Romanorum*. Like these, *The Tale of Florent* is also an exemplum, but, unlike these, an amorous and not a moral one.

22. *marches:* the frontier borderlands of any nation.

Upon Florent, bot° remembrance	*but*
40 That thei toke° of his worthinesse	*had*
Of knyhthod° and of gentilesse,°	*chivalry/courtesy*
And how he stod° of cousinage°	*stood/kinship*
To themperour, made hem assuage,°	*them stop*
And dorsten noght slen° him for fere:°	*(they) dared not slay/fear*
45 In gret desputeisoun° thei were	*argument*
Among hemself,° what was the beste.	*themselves*
Ther was a lady, the slyheste°	*sliest*
Of alle that men knewe tho,°	*then*
So old sche myhte unethes go,°	*scarcely walk*
50 And was grantdame° unto the dede:°	*grandmother/dead (man)*
And sche with that began to rede,°	*counsel*
And seide° how sche wol° bringe him inne,°	*said/will/in*
That sche schal him to dethe winne°	*death bring*
Al only° of° his oghne grant,°	*entirely/by/consent*
55 Thurgh° strengthe of verray covenant°	*through/true agreement*
Withoute blame of eny wiht.°	*any person*
Anon° sche sende° for this kniht,°	*quickly/sent/knight*
And of hire sone° sche alleide°	*her son/mentioned*
The deth, and thus to him sche seide:	
60 "Florent, how so° thou be° to wyte°	*although/are/guilty*
Of Branchus° deth, men schal respite°	*Branchus's/desist*
As now to take vengement,°	*from taking vengeance*
Be so° thou stonde° in juggement°	*if/stand/judgment*
Upon certein condicioun,°	*certain condition*
65 That thou unto a questioun	
Which I schal axe° schalt ansuere;°	*ask/answer*
And over° this thou shalt ek swere,°	*beyond/also swear*
That if thou of the sothe° faile,	*true answer*
Ther schal non° other thing availe,°	*no/help*
70 That thou ne° schal thi deth receive.	*not*
And for° men schal thee noght deceive,	*so that*
That thou therof myht ben avised,°	*might be advised*
Thou schalt have day and tyme assised°	*assigned*
And leve saufly forto wende,°	*permission safely to go*
75 Be so° that at thi daies° ende	*on condition/(appointed) day's*
Thou come ayein° with thin avys."°	*again/your answer*
This knyht, which worthi was and wys,°	*wise*
This lady preith° that he may wite,°	*asks/know*
And have it under seales write,°	*written*
80 What questioun it scholde° be	*should*
For which he schal in that degree	
Stonde of his lif° in jeupartie.°	*life/jeopardy*

With that sche feigneth compaignie,°   *friendship*
And seith: "Florent, on love it hongeth°   *depends*
85 Al that to myn axinge longeth:°   *my question pertains*
What alle wommen most desire
This wole° I axe, and in thempire°   *will|the empire*
Wher as° thou hast most knowlechinge°   *wherever|best advice*
Tak conseil° upon this axinge."   *take counsel*
90   Florent this thing hath undertake,°   *undertaken*
The day was set, the time take,°   *appointed*
Under his seal he wrot° his oth,°   *wrote|oath*
In such a wise° and forth he goth   *manner*
Home to his emes° court ayein;   *uncle's*
95 To whom his aventure plein°   *adventure completely*
He tolde, of that° him is befalle.°   *what|befallen*
And upon that thei weren° alle   *were*
The wiseste of the lond° asent,°   *land|sent for*
Bot natheles of on° assent   *but nevertheless with one*
100 Thei myhte noght acorde plat,°   *not agree wholly*
On seide° this, on othre° that.   *said|another*
After the disposicioun°   *disposition*
Of naturel complexioun°   *temperament*
To som womman it is plesance,°   *pleasure*
105 That to an other is grevance;°   *annoyance*
Bot such a thing in special,°   *especially*
Which to hem° alle in general   *them*
Is most plesant,° and most desired   *pleasant*
Above alle othre° and most conspired,°   *others|sought after*
110 Such o° thing conne° thei noght finde   *one|can*
Be constellacion ne kinde:°   *by astrology nor nature*
And thus Florent withoute cure°   *remedy*
Mot stonde upon° his aventure,°   *must abide by|fortune*
And is al schape unto° the lere,°   *prepared for|hopeless task*
115 As in defalte° of his answere.   *default*
This knyht hath levere° forto dye°   *knight would rather|die*
Than breke° his trowthe° and forto lye°   *break|word|lie*
In place° ther as° he was swore,°   *(the) place|where|sworn*
And schapth him gon ayein° therfore.   *prepares himself (to) go again*
120 Whan° time cam° he tok° his leve,°   *when|came|took|leave*
That lengere wolde° he noght beleve,°   *longer would|remain*
And preith° his em he° be noght wroth,   *begs|uncle (that) he*
For that is a point of his oth,

---

111. *kinde:* i.e., "reason."

He seith, that noman° schal him wreke,°	*no one/avenge*
125 Thogh° afterward men hiere speke°	*though/hear (it) said*
That he par aventure deie.°	*by chance died*
And thus he wente forth his weie°	*(on) his way*
Alone as knyht aventurous,	
And in his thoght° was curious	*thought*
130 To wite° what was best to do:	*know*
And as he rod° al one° so,	*rode/alone*
And cam nyh° ther as° he wolde° be,	*near/where/wanted to*
In a forest under a tre°	*tree*
He syh° wher sat a creature,	*saw*
135 A lothly° wommannysch figure,	*loathly*
That forto speke° of fleisch° and bon°	*to speak/flesh/bone*
So foul yit° syh he nevere non.°	*yet/none*
This knyht behield° hir redely,°	*looked at/her quickly*
And as he wolde have passed by,	
140 Sche cleped° him and bad abide;°	*called/bade (him) stay*
And he his horse heved° aside	*pulled*
Tho torneth,° and to hire° he rod,	*then turns/her*
And there he hoveth° and abod,°	*tarries/waited*
To wite what sche wolde mene.°	*intend*
145 And she began him° to bemene,°	*for him/lament*
And seide:° "Florent be thi name,	*said*
Thou hast on honde° such a game,	*hand*
That bot° thou be° the betre avised,°	*unless/are/better advised*
Thi deth° is schapen° and devised,	*death/ordained*
150 That° al the world ne° mai the° save,	*so that/not/you*
Bot if that° thou my conseil° have."	*unless/counsel*
Florent, whan he this tale herde,°	*heard*
Unto this olde wyht° answerde	*person*
And of° hir conseil he hir preide.°	*for/begged*
155 And sche ayein to him thus seide:	
"Florent, if I for the so schape,°	*work*
That thou thurgh° me thi deth ascape°	*through/escape*
And take worschipe of° thi dede,°	*gain honor by/deed*
What schal I have to° my mede?"°	*for/reward*
160 "What° thing," quod° he, "that thou wolt axe."°	*whatever/said/will ask*
"I bidde° nevere a betre taxe,"°	*ask/nothing better*
Quod sche, "bot ferst, er° thou be sped,°	*but first, before/gone*
Thou schalt me leve° such a wedd,°	*leave/pledge*
That I wol° have thi trowthe° in honde°	*will/promise/hand*
165 That thou schalt be myn housebonde."°	*my husband*
"Nay," seith Florent, "that may noght° be."	*not*
"Ryd thanne° forth thi wey,"° quod sche,	*ride then/way*

"And if thou go withoute red,°   *counsel*
Thou schalt be sekerliche ded."°   *surely dead*
170 Florent behihte° hire good ynowh°   *promised/enough*
Of lond,° of rente, of park, of plowh,°   *land/plow*
Bot al that compteth° sche at noght.°   *counted/nothing*
Tho fell this knyht° in mochel thoght,°   *knight/deep thought*
Now goth he forth, now comth ayein,°   *again*
175 He wot° noght what is best to sein,°   *knows/say*
And thoghte, as he rod° to and fro,   *rode*
That chese° he mot on° of the tuo,°   *choose/must one/two*
Or forto° take hire to° his wif°   *either to/as/wife*
Or elles° forto° lese° his lif.°   *else/lose/life*
180 And thanne he caste° his avantage,°   *saw/advantage*
That sche was of so gret° an age,   *great*
That sche mai live bot a while,
And thoghte put hire° in an ile,°   *(to) put her/island*
Wher that noman° hire scholde° knowe,   *no one/should*
185 Til sche with° deth were overthrowe.°   *by/overcome*
And thus this yonge° lusti knyht   *young*
Unto this olde lothly° wiht   *loathly*
Tho seide:° "If that non° other chance   *then said/no*
Mai make my deliverance,
190 Bot only thilke° same speche°   *that/speech*
Which, as thou seist, thou schalt me teche,°   *teach*
Have hier° myn hond,° I schal thee wedde."   *here/hand*
And thus his trowthe° he leith° to wedde.   *word/gives*
With that sche frounceth° up the browe: *raises*
195 "This covenant I wol allowe,"
Sche seith: "if eny° other thing   *any*
Bot that° thou hast of° my techyng   *what/from*
Fro deth° thi body mai respite,°   *from death/save*
I woll thee of thi trowthe acquite,°   *pledge release*
200 And elles be° non other weie.°   *otherwise in/way*
Now herkne° me what I schal seie.°   *listen to/say*
Whan° thou art come into the place,   *when*
Wher now thei maken gret manace°   *menace you greatly*
And upon thi comynge abyde,°   *wait*
205 Thei wole anon° the same tide°   *will then/time*
Oppose° thee of° thin° answere.   *demand/from you/your*
I wot thou wolt° nothing forbere°   *will/hide*

---

183. Banishment of undesirable persons, political or familial, to islands in the Mediterranean was a common practice of the Roman emperors.

207–10. I.e., he will propose the best answers he has before resorting to hers.

Of that thou wenest be° thi beste,°　　*think are/best (answers)*
And if thou myht° so finde reste,°　　*might/respite*
210　Wel is,° for thanne° is ther nomore.　　*is (it)/then*
And elles this schal be my lore,°　　*teaching*
That thou schalt seie, upon this molde°　　*earth*
That alle wommen lievest wolde°　　*most desire*
Be soverein° of mannes love:　　*(to) be sovereign*
215　For what womman is so above,°　　*at advantage*
Sche hath, as who seith,° al hire wille;　　*is said*
And elles may sche noght° fulfille　　*not*
What thing hir° were° lievest° have.°　　*to her/(it) would be/most desirable/ (to) have*

With this answere thou schalt save
220　Thiself, and other wise noght.
And whan thou hast thin ende wroght,°　　*purpose accomplished*
Com hier ayein,° thou schalt me finde,　　*again*
And let nothing out of thi minde."
　　He goth him° forth with hevy chiere,°　　*goes/in sad mood*
225　As he that not° in what manere°　　*knows not/manner*
He mai this worldes joie atteigne:°　　*joy attain*
For if he deie,° he hath a peine,°　　*die/sorrow*
And if he live, he mot him° binde　　*must himself*
To such on° which of alle kinde　　*(a) one*
230　Of wommen is thunsemlieste:°　　*the ugliest*
Thus wot° he noght what is the beste:　　*knows*
Bot° be him lief° or be him loth,°　　*but/he willing/unwilling*
Unto the castell forth he goth
His full answere forto yive,°　　*to give*
235　Or° forto deie or forto live.　　*either*
Forth with his conseil cam° the lord,　　*council came*
The thinges stoden° of record,　　*stood*
He sende° up for the lady sone,°　　*sent/immediately*
And forth sche cam, that olde mone.°　　*mother*
240　In presence of the remenant°　　*group*
The strengthe° of al the covenant°　　*gist/agreement*
Tho° was reherced° openly,　　*then/repeated*
And to Florent sche bad forthi°　　*commanded then*
That he schal tellen° his avis,°　　*tell/answer*
245　As he that woot° what is the pris.°　　*knows/at stake*
Florent seith° al that evere he couthe,°　　*says/knew*

---

223. I.e., "forget nothing."　　**232.** *be . . . loth:* i.e., "for better, for worse."

Bot such word cam ther non° to mowthe,° *none/mouth*
That he for yifte° or for beheste° *gift/promise*
Mihte eny wise° his deth areste.° *might any way/death stop*
250 And thus he tarieth° longe and late, *tarries*
Til that this lady bad algate° *by all means*
That he schal for the dom° final *judgment*
Yive his answere in special° *specifically*
Of that° sche hadde him ferst opposed:° *for what/first demanded*
255 And thanne° he hath trewly° supposed *then/truly*
That he him may of nothing yelpe,° *boast*
Bot if so be° tho° wordes helpe, *unless/those*
Whiche as° the womman hath him tawht;° *which/taught*
Wherof° he hath an hope cawht° *from which/caught*
260 That he schal ben° excused so, *be*
And tolde out plein° his wille tho. *completely*
And whan that° this matrone herde° *when/heard*
The manere how this knyht ansuerde,° *knight answered*
Sche seide: "Ha treson, wo° thee be, *treason, woe*
265 That hast thus told the privite,° *secret*
Which alle wommen most desire!
I wolde° that thou were afire." *would*
Bot natheles° in such a plit° *nevertheless/manner*
Florent of his answere is quit:
270 And tho began his sorwe newe,° *sorrow anew*
For he mot gon,° or ben untrewe,° *must go/untrue*
To hire° which his trowthe° hadde. *her/pledge*
Bot° he, which alle schame dradde,° *but/dishonor hated*
Goth forth in stede° of his penance, *to the place*
275 And takth° the fortune of his chance, *takes*
As he that was with trowthe affaited.° *by (his) word bound*
    This olde wyht° him hath awaited *person*
In place wher as° he hire lefte: *where*
Florent his wofull heved° uplefte° *head/raised up*
280 And syh° this vecke° wher sche sat, *saw/old woman*
Which was the lothlieste what° *loathliest whatever*
That evere man caste on his yhe:° *eye*
Hire nose bass,° hire browes hyhe,° *low/high*
Hire yhen smale° and depe° set, *eyes small/deep*
285 Hire chekes ben° with teres° wet, *cheeks were/tears*
And rivelen° as an emty skyn *wrinkled*
Hangende° doun unto the chin, *hanging*
Hire lippes schrunken ben for° age, *from*
Ther was no grace in the visage,

²⁹⁰ Hir front° was nargh,° hir lockes hore,°   *her forehead/narrow/hoary*
Sche loketh° forth as doth a More,°   *looks/Moor*
Hire necke is schort, hir schuldres courbe,°   *shoulders bent*
That myhte° a mannes lust destourbe,°   *might/inhibit*
Hire body gret° and nothing° smal,   *great/not at all*
²⁹⁵ And schortly to discrive° hire al,   *describe*
Sche hath no lith° withoute a lak;°   *limb/fault*
Bot lich° unto the wollesak.°   *like/woolsack*
Sche proferth hire° unto this knyht,   *offers herself*
And bad° him, as he hath behyht,°   *commanded/promised*
³⁰⁰ So as° sche hath ben° his warant,°   *since/been/protection*
That he hire° holde covenant,°   *(with) her/keep agreement*
And be° the bridel sche him seseth.°   *by/seizes*
Bot Godd wot° how that sche him pleseth°   *knows/pleases*
Of° suche wordes as sche spekth:°   *by/speaks*
³⁰⁵ Him thenkth welnyh° his herte brekth°   *he thinks almost/heart breaks*
For sorwe° that he may noght fle,°   *sorrow/not flee*
Bot if° he wolde° untrewe be.   *unless/would*
   Loke,° how a sek° man for his hele°   *look/sick/health*
Takth baldemoine° with canele,°   *gentian/cinnamon*
³¹⁰ And with the mirre° takth the sucre,°   *myrrh/sugar*
Ryht° upon such a maner lucre°   *right/manner (of) gain*
Stant° Florent as in this diete:°   *stands/diet*
He drinkth the bitre° with the swete,°   *bitter/sweet*
He medleth° sorwe with likynge,°   *mixes/pleasure*
³¹⁵ And liveth, as who seith,° deyinge;°   *is said/dying*
His youthe schal be cast aweie°   *away*
Upon such on° which as the weie°   *(a) one/road*
Is old and lothly overal.°   *entirely*
Bot nede° he mot° that nede° schal: *needs/must/need (to)*
³²⁰ He wolde algate° his trowthe° holde,   *by all means/promise*
As every knyht° therto is holde,°   *knight/bound*
What happ so evere° him is befalle:°   *whatever chance/befallen*
Thogh° sche be the fouleste of alle,   *though*
Yet to thonour° of wommanhiede°   *the honor/womanhood*
³²⁵ Him thoghte° he scholde taken hiede;°   *thought/should take heed*
So that for pure gentilesse,°   *courtesy*
As he hire couthe° best adresce,°   *her could/approach*

---

291. *More:* Although the term refers specifically to the Muslim inhabitants of North Africa and/or the Saracen populace of medieval Spain, in a general context in the Middle Ages it designated any native inhabitant of black Africa.

297. Gower's humor is infrequent, and when it occurs it should be prized. Comparing the hag to a lumpy woolsack is not only graphic but very English: wool was England's staple export in the Middle Ages, and any Londoner who had ever been to the Thames embankment knew what a woolsack looked like.

319. *nede . . . schal:* i.e., "he must do as he has to."

In ragges, as sche was totore,°	*tattered*
He set hire on his hors tofore°	*in front*
³³⁰ And forth he takth his weie softe;°	*quietly*
No wonder thogh he siketh° ofte.	*sighs*
Bot° as an oule fleth° be nyhte°	*but/owl flies/night*
Out of alle othre briddes syhte,°	*birds' sight*
Riht° so this knyht on daies brode°	*just/in daylight broad*
³³⁵ In clos° him hield,° and schop° his rode°	*hidden/himself kept/planned/ journey*
On nyhtes° time, til the tyde°	*night/time*
That he cam there° he wolde abide;°	*came where/remain*
And prively° withoute noise	*secretly*
He bringth this foule grete° coise°	*gross/hag*
³⁴⁰ To his castell in such a wise°	*way*
That noman° myhte° hire schappe avise,°	*no one/might/shape see*
Til sche into the chambre cam:	
Wher he his prive conseil nam°	*secret counsel took*
Of suche men as he most troste,°	*trusted*
³⁴⁵ And tolde hem° that he nedes moste°	*them/must*
This beste° wedde to° his wif,°	*beast/as/wife*
For elles° hadde he lost his lif.°	*otherwise/life*
The prive wommen° were asent,°	*ladies-in-waiting/sent for*
That scholden ben° of his assent:°	*should be/agreeable to him*
³⁵⁰ Hire ragges thei anon of drawe,°	*quickly off pull*
And, as it was that time lawe,	
She hadde bath, sche hadde reste,	
And was arraied to° the beste.	*dressed in*
Bot with no craft° of combes brode	*skill*
³⁵⁵ Thei myhte hire hore° lockes schode,°	*hoary/divide*
And sche nc° wolde noght° be schore°	*not/would not/shorn*
For no conseil,° and thei therfore,	*argument*
With such atyr° as tho° was used,	*attire/then*
Ordeinen° that° it was excused,°	*contrived/so that/disguised*
³⁶⁰ And hid so craftelic he° aboute,	*skillfully*
That noman myhte sen hem oute.°	*notice them*
Bot when sche was fulliche° arraied	*fully*
And hire atyr was al assaied,°	*examined*
Tho was sche foulere on° to se:°	*upon/look*
³⁶⁵ Bot yit° may non other be,°	*yet/not otherwise (it) be*

334–37. Cf. *The Wedding of Sir Gawain and Dame Ragnell* (this volume, pp. 418–39): whereas Florent rides at night, Dame Ragnell insists on riding openly with Arthur to Carlisle.

338–41. Again, Florent hides the hag in the castle, whereas

Dame Ragnell is openly viewed by all the inhabitants of Carlisle as she enters. *coise:* (probably) OF *cuisse,* "thigh" (see *MED*). In this sense the meaning is certainly derogatory.

Thei were wedded in the nyht;
So wo begon° was nevere knyht°   *woebegone/knight*
As he was thanne° of° mariage.   *then/because of*
And she began to pleie° and rage,°   *play/make amorous advances*
370 As who seith,° I am wel ynowh;°   *(one) who says/good enough*
Bot he therof° nothing° ne lowh,°   *at that/not at all/laughed*
For sche tok thanne chiere on honde°   *acted in a gay manner*
And clepeth° him hire housebonde,°   *calls/her husband*
And seith, "My lord, go we to bedde,
375 For I to° that entente° wedde,   *with/intention*
That thou schalt be my worldes blisse":
And profreth° him with that to kisse,   *offers*
As° sche a lusti lady were.   *as if*
His body myhte wel be there,
380 Bot° as of thoght° and of memoire°   *but/thought/mind*
His herte° was in purgatoire.°   *heart/purgatory*
Bot yit for° strengthe° of matrimoine°   *because of/bond/matrimony*
He myhte° make non essoine,°   *might/no excuse*
That he ne mot algates plie°   *must wholly agree*
385 To gon° to bedde of compaignie:°   *go/together*
And whan° thei were abedde° naked,   *when/in bed*
Withoute slep° he was awaked;°   *sleep/kept awake*
He torneth° on that° other side,   *turns/the*
For that° he wolde hise yhen hyde°   *because/his eyes hide*
390 Fro lokynge° on that foule wyht.°   *from looking/person*
The chambre was al full of lyht,°   *light*
The courtins° were of cendal° thinne,   *curtains/silk*
This newe bryd° which lay withinne,   *bride*
Thogh° it be noght with his acord,°   *though/agreement*
395 In armes sche beclipte° hire lord,   *embraced*
And preide,° as he was torned fro,°   *begged/turned away*
He wolde him° torne ayeinward° tho;°   *would himself/toward her/then*
"For now," sche seith, "we ben° bothe on."° *are/one*
And he lay stille as eny ston,°   *any stone*
400 Bot evere in on° sche spak° and preide, *the same manner/spoke*
And bad° him thenke° on that° he seide,   *bade/think/what*
Whan that he tok° hire be° the hond.°   *took/by/hand*
    He herde° and understod° the bond,   *heard/understood*
How he was set to his penance,
405 And as it were a man in trance
He torneth him al sodeinly,°   *very suddenly*

---

366. Florent's wedding is secret and at night. This is exactly what Arthur and also Guinevere propose to Dame Ragnell, but the obstinate woman insists not only on a public wedding at a high mass but also that the ceremony be proclaimed in the shire and numerous guests invited.

And syh° a lady lay° him by | *saw/lying*
Of eyhtetiene wynter° age, | *eighteen winters*
Which was the faireste of visage
410 That evere in al this world he syh: |
And as he wolde have take hire° nyh,° | *taken her/to him*
Sche put° hire hand and be his leve° | *put (out)/leave*
Besoghte° him that he wolde leve,° | *besought/refrain*
And seith° that forto° wynne or lese° | *says/to/lose*
415 He mot on of tuo° thinges chese,° | *two/choose*
Wher° he wol° have hire such on nyht,° | *whether/will/at night*
Or elles upon daies° lyht, | *else in day's*
For he schal noght° have bothe tuo. | *not*
And he began to sorwe° tho, | *grieve*
420 In many a wise° and caste his thoght,° | *way/reflected*
Bot° for al that yit cowthe° he noght | *but/yet could*
Devise himself° which was the beste. | *decide*
And sche, that wolde° his hertes reste,° | *desired/heart's ease*
Preith that he scholde° chese algate,° | *should/quickly*
425 Til ate° laste longe and late | *at*
He seide: "O ye, my lyves hele,° | *life's salvation*
Sey° what you list° in my querele,° | *say/desire/debate*
I not° what ansucre° I schal yive:° | *know not/answer/give*
Bot evere whil° that I may live, | *while*
430 I wol° that ye be my maistresse,° | *desire/lady*
For I can noght miselve gesse° | *myself guess*
Which is the best unto my chois.° | *choice*
Thus grante I yow myn hole vois,° | *you my whole voice*
Ches° for ous bothen,° I you preie;° | *choose/us both/beg*
435 And what as evere that° ye seie,° | *whatever/say*
Riht° as ye wole° so wol I." | *just/wish*
    "Mi lord," sche seide, "grant merci,° | *thank you*
For of this word that ye now sein,° | *say*
That ye have mad° me soverein,° | *made/sovereign*
440 Mi destine° is overpassed,° | *(evil) fate/overcome*
That° nevere hierafter° schal be lassed° | *so that/hereafter/lessened*
Mi beaute,° which that I now have, | *beauty*
Til I be take into my grave;
Bot nyht and day as I am now
445 I schal alwey° be such to yow. | *always*
The kinges dowhter° of Cizile° | *daughter/Sicily*
I am, and fell° bot siththe awhile,° | *(it) happened/just a short while ago*
As I was with my fader° late, | *father*
That my stepmoder,° for an hate | *stepmother*
450 Which toward me sche hath begonne,° | *begun (to have)*
Forschop° me, til I hadde wonne | *transformed*

The love and sovereinete°   *sovereignty*
Of what knyht° that in his degre°   *whatever knight/rank*
Alle othre passeth of° good name: *others surpasses in*
455 And, as men sein, ye ben° the same,   *are*
The dede proeveth° it is so;   *deed proves*
Thus am I youres evermo."°   *evermore*
Tho° was plesance° and joye ynowh,°   *then/pleasure/enough*
Echon° with other pleide° and lowh;°   *each one/played/laughed*
460 Thei live longe and wel thei ferde,°   *fared*
And clerkes that this chance herde°   *event heard (of)*
Thei writen° it in evidence,   *write*
To teche° how that obedience   *teach*
Mai wel fortune° a man to love   *lead by chance*
465 And sette him in his lust° above,   *pleasure*
As it befell unto this knyht.

from GESTA ROMANORUM

DATE: C. 1440. ✦ MANUSCRIPTS: British Library Harley 7333 (c. 1440) and Additional 9066, of the same date; University Library, Cambridge, Kk, 1. 6., end of the 15th century. ✦ EDITION: Sidney J. H. Herrtage, *The Early English Versions of the Gesta Romanorum*, Early English Text Society, 33 (London 1879, rpt. 1898, 1932, 1962). Other works useful in connection with the *Gesta Romanorum* are Stith Thompson, *Motif-Index of Folk-Literature* rev. ed., 6 vols. (Bloomington, Ind., 1955–58); Antti Aarne, *The Types of the Folk-Tale*, rev. trans. by Stith Thompson (Helsinki, 1961, rpt. New York, 1971); and Stith Thompson, *The Folktale* (New York, 1951).

The language of the *Gesta Romanorum*, which is very late Middle English, should cause no difficulty in reading. (1) Past participles may have the *y-* prefix (*ydo,* "done") or may end in *-id* (*vallid, commaundid*). (2) The ending *-id/-yd* is found in the past tense. (3) Noun plurals and the third person singular of the present tense of the verb generally end in *-is/-ys*. (4) Generally *y* is used for *g* (*yeve = give*). (5) Pronouns are regular, although *here,* "their," may cause confusion.

The *Gesta Romanorum* is a vast collection of exempla—narratives in Latin from classical and Oriental sources—which was widely popular in Europe in the Middle Ages, as evidenced by over 165 MSS in English and Continental libraries. There is a wealth of folklore and traditional matter here, which serves as source material for Shakespeare, Chaucer, Boccaccio, and many others. The narratives were soon used for spiritual instruction by monks, and morals were appended which translated the secular tales into Christian terms, the stories thus becoming typical of the exempla used by contemporary preachers. It is thought that the Anglo-Latin *Gesta*, the direct source of the early English translations, was composed in the 13th century, and that the collection spread from England to the Continent, where Latin and German texts were numerous.

Of the Drunkards and the Innkeeper

Lenoppus was a wise Emperour, and regnyd[1] in Rome; and among all othir vertuys[2] he was mercifull; and for grete pyte he maade[3] a lawe, that euery man þat were blinde, shuld[4] haue an Cˢ.[5]

Hit happid,[6] þat xiiij felawis[7] were gon to-gedre[8] to þe Cite[9] of Rome out of þe cuntre,[10] for noon[11] oþer cause, but only for to drinke wyne. And whenne þei were sette in the tauerne, þei cessid[12]

Heading. *Of the Drunkards and the Innkeeper:* Motif J 1820 (Inappropriate Action through Misunderstanding), according to Thompson, *Motif-Index of Folk Literature.*

1. reigned. 2. virtues. 3. great pity he made.

4. should.
5. hundred shillings.
6. it happened.

7. fellows.
8. together.
9. city.

10. country.
11. no.
12. ceased.

neuer drinking by[13] þe space of iij days or iiij, and dronke[14] more be moch[15] þan þei hadde money to pay for. At þe last the tauernere askid his payment, and saide þat noon[16] of them shuld passe, til tyme þat he were payd. Thenne spake oon[17] of þe drinkers, and saide to his felowis, [18] "Seris,[19] I can tell you a goode conseil[20] in þis cas.[21] ȝe wete[22] wel, it is þe lawe of the Emperour þat euery blind man shuld haue to his tresour[23] an Cˢ; and þerfore, seris, lat[24] vs drawe cut,[25] and drawe out his yen,[26] on whom the cut wol[27] falle; and þenne he may go to þe palys,[28] and aske an Cˢ by þe Emperouris lawe, and qwite[29] vs all." And whenne the other men hurde[30] þis, they were right[31] glad, and seide,[32] þat it was goode conseil. And þei drowe[33] cut; and it fell vp on him þat ȝafe[34] þe conseil. Thenne his yen were don[35] out; and so he wente to þe Emperouris stiward,[36] and askid an Cˢ. "Nay," quoþ[37] þe senescal,[38] "for þou haddist goode siȝt ȝisterday;[39] nay, felowe, þou vndirstondiste[40] þe lawe wrong. The lawe is I-sette[41] for hem[42] þat ben[43] made blinde by infirmite,[44] or by þe will of God; and þou haddiste ij yen in þe tauerne, and nowe þou hast done hem out only by þi selfe. Go aȝen[45] to the tauernere, and accord[46] with him as þou may, for sothly[47] þou shult[48] of me haue neyther jᵈ,[49] ne obolus,[50] ne quadrans."[51] He ȝede[52] aȝen to his felowis, and tolde hem howe[53] the stiward seide to him. Whenne þe tauerner hurde þis, he spoiled[54] him of all his clothis,[55] and bette[56] him soore,[57] and so lete[58] hem all go with gret[59] confusion.

Moralite

Deere Frendis,[60] þis Emperour is our Lord iesu[61] crist, þe which hath maade a lawe, þat ech[62] man þat is blind, *scil.*[63] euery erþely[64] man that synnyth, by instigacion of þe devill, of þe wordle,[65] or of þe flesh, that if he be sory[66] for his synnys, as blind men ben for hire dorkenesse,[67] he shalle haue an Cˢ, þat is to sey,[68] an hundride sithis ioy[69] of victorie; as he seyithe,[70] *Centuplum accipietis, et vitam eternam possidebitis.*[71] And so is a synner callid blind. The felowis that comyth to þe tauerne er[72] synners, þat gon[73] ofte tyme to the tauerne of þe devill, and drinkith, *scil.* wastith and consumyth all þe vertuys þat þei receivid in baptisme; and so the devill spoilith hem of all the goodis[74] that they haue y-don.[75] They drowe[76] cut, *scil.* dilecacion,[77] and custome of synne; and þe sort[78] of synne fallith vp on[79] him that is with oute riȝtwissnesse[80] or mercy. Suche a man is wilfully blynde, as was Judas, that betrayed crist, his lord, withoute ony[81] suggestion; and þerfore his synne was þe moor.[82] And þerfore when such on[83] comith to þe stiwarde, *scil.* prelatis of holy chirch,[84] he may not liȝtly[85] haue grace—Why? For þey ben not in þe wey[86] to leve[87] hire synne. And þerfore late[88] vs not synne wilfully; but if we synne by sikenesse, or frailte, anoon[89] late vs with shrifte,[90] and contricion,[91] and fulfilling of penaunce, do[92] it away, to haue remission of our synnes, and ioy perdurable,[93] þat graunte[94] vs þe lord, *qui cum patre, et filio, et spiritu sancto.*[95]

---

13. for.	**29.** repay.	**45.** again.	**Heading.** *Moralite:* allegory.	**63.** namely (Latin *scilicet*).
14. drank.	**30.** heard.	**46.** agree.	**60.** dear friends.	**66.** sorry.
15. by much.	**31.** very.	**47.** truly.	**61.** Jesus.	**67.** their darkness.
16. none.	**32.** said.	**48.** shall.	**62.** each.	**68.** say.
17. spoke one.	**33.** drew.	**49.** one penny.	**64.** earthly (i.e., on earth)	**69.** times joy.
18. fellows.	**34.** gave.	**50.** nor obol [a Greek coin].	**65.** world.	**70.** says.
19. sirs.	**35.** put.	**51.** 1/6 drachma [a Greek coin].		

71. shall receive an hundred fold, and shall inherit everlasting life (Matt. 19:29).

20. counsel.	**36.** steward.	**52.** went.	
21. case.	**37.** said.	**53.** what.	**72.** are.
22. you know.	**38.** seneschal.	**54.** despoiled.	**73.** go.
23. for his treasure.	**39.** sight yesterday.	**55.** clothes.	**74.** good things.
24. let.	**40.** understand.	**56.** beat.	**75.** done.
25. lots.	**41.** made.	**57.** sorely.	**76.** draw.
26. eyes.	**42.** them.	**58.** let.	**77.** delectation.
27. will.	**43.** are.	**59.** great.	**78.** lot.
28. palace.	**44.** infirmity.		**79.** upon.

80. without righteousness.	**88.** let.	
81. any.	**89.** sickness, or frailty, then.	
82. greater.	**90.** confession.	
83. (a) one.	**91.** contrition.	
84. church.	**92.** penance, put.	
85. easily.	**93.** everlasting.	
86. way.	**94.** grant.	
87. leave.		

95. who with the Father, Son, and Holy Ghost.

How a Son Concealed His Father in His House, and How He Was Found Out

Adrianus[1] regned[2] a wys[3] emperoure in þe Cite[4] of Rome; þe which ordeined[5] for the lawe, þat euery knyght aftir þat he myght no more vse armys, for feblenesse,[6] he shuld[7] be put oute of the empire; and if þat he myght be founde within þe empire, aftir that he were impotent, he shuld be ded withoute pite.[8] There was a knyght named Porphirius, a wise man, and witty[9] in armys and in alle his werkys.[10] When he come in to[11] age, and loste his strengthe, he callid to him his sone,[12] that was a knyght, and seid,[13] "Dere[14] sone, thou knowest what is þe lawe of the emperoure; and now I am feble, and may no lenger[15] vse armys, I mote[16] be put oute of the empire, and þerfore I not[17] how I shalle lyve." Then seid his sone, "Fadir[18] if hit happe the[19] to dye,[20] I am redy[21] to dye with the. Neuertheles[22] in sight of all men thou shalt entry[23] in to a shippe, and at nyght I shal previlye[24] send aftir the; and then we shul duelle to-gidre[25] alle oure lyf,[26] and non[27] shal know þerof but I and my wif,[28] þat shal servy[29] the in my absence." Then spake[30] the fadir, and seid, "Sone, I thonke[31] the moche,[32] but if þou do so, I drede[33] that þou shalt be accused, and suffre deth[34] for me." Then spak the sone, "Fadir, drede the not; þou shalt abide with me, and I shall fynde[35] the all

the daies[36] of my lif." Then the fadir entrid in to a shippe, in sight of folke, as who seith,[37] "Now go I oute of the empire, aftir the lawe"; but in the nyght he come prevely agein[38] to his sones hous, and his sonnes wif servid him. And euer when eny counseill[39] shuld be ydo[40] in þe Empire, þe yong[41] knyght was callid þerto; and þere was non that yaf[42] better counseill[43] than the yong knyght did. At þe last, lordis of the empire had grete[44] envy of his wisdom, and thei seid to þe emperour, "Lord, wheþer[45] the sone of Porphirie,[46] þat yevith[47] so wise counseill, haue not þe wisdom of his old fader Porphirie? Sothely,[48] we trowith[49] þat he hath all of[50] his fadir, and þat he holdith him in þe empire in previte,[51] þough he ascendid in to ship; and if hit be founden[52] so, he were[53] worthi a foule deth." "Hold you still," quod[54] the Emperoure; "I trow[55] to come to soth[56] of this mater wele ynow."[57] Anon[58] he let calle[59] the sone of Porphirie. When he was come, the emperoure seid to him, "I commaund[60] the, vpon peyne[61] of thi lif, that þou bryng me thre[62] thynges to-morowe,[63] that is to sey,[64] thi best frend that þou haste[65] in the world; thi moste[66] comfort; and thi moste enemy." "Sir, hit shallbe[67] do,"[68] quod he. He yede[69] home to þe castel, but he wist[70] not

Heading. *How a Son Concealed His Father:* Motif K 2213.4 (Betrayal of Husband's Secret by Wife) and Motif J 151.1 (Wisdom of Hidden Old Man Saves Kingdom), according to Thompson, *Motif-Index.* The first motif is common in the lore of India.
1. Hadrian (Publius Aelius Hadrianus 76–138, Roman emperor 117–138). The names of the Roman emperors are not historically connected with the acts ascribed to them in the *Gesta Romanorum.*

2. reigned.
3. wise.
4. city.
5. ordained.
6. feebleness.
7. should.
8. dead without pity.

9. skillful.
10. works.
11. came into.
12. son.
13. said.
14. dear.
15. longer.
16. must.

17. know not.
18. father.
19. it befalls you.
20. die.
21. ready.
22. nevertheless.
23. enter.
24. secretly.

25. shall dwell together.
26. life.
27. none.
28. wife.
29. serve.
30. spoke.
31. thank.
32. much.
33. fear.
34. death.
35. care for.
36. days.
37. as (one) who says.
38. secretly again

39. any council.
40. called.
41. young.
42. gave.
43. counsel.
44. great.
45. i.e., does.
46. Porphyrius.
47. gives.
48. truly.
49. believe.
50. from.
51. secret.
52. found.
53. would be.
54. said.
55. trust.

56. (the) truth.
57. matter well enough.
58. then.
59. had called.
60. command.
61. pain.
62. three.
63. tomorrow.
64. say.
65. have.
66. greatest.
67. shall be.
68. done.
69. went.
70. knew.

how he myght haue suche thre. He yede to his fadir, as he was wonte to do, when he had any grete counseill to do, and he askid counseill in this mater. "A!"[71] quod þe fadir, "all þis is for me, for to know whethir þou holdist me or noo;[72] but take with the thi hound, thi litel[73] sone, and thi wif; and þou shalt make satisfaccion[74] to þe will of the emperoure." And so the knyght did; he toke tho[75] thre, the hound, the child, and his wife; and yede to the emperoure. Þo[76] seid the Emperoure, "Hast þou ydo[77] as I commaundid the?" "Yee,[78] sir," seid the knyght, "for, ser, the best frend þat I haue in this world is my hounde; and þis is my cause and my reason, for he woll[79] neuer faile me ne[80] forsake me, in wele[81] ne in wo;[82] and though I bete[83] him as sore as I can, yit[84] if I profre[85] him brede,[86] or any chere[87] do to him, he wol come to me ayene[88] with good chere;[89] and all nyght he woll rest by my bed, and kepe[90] me and my hous, þat[91] no man greve[92] vs; and ofte tymes I shuld haue be[93] robbid and yslayn,[94] ne had my hound ybe.[95] And, sir, here is my sone,[96] my moste comfort; and þis is my skile,[97] for when I am in moste anger or tribulacion, þer is no iogoloure[98] þat can make me so fast lawe,[99] as woll my sone; for he woll with his praty[100] wordis and pleys[101] make me foryete[102] my anger, þough I wer as hote[103] as fire. Also, ser, here I haue brought my most enemy, my wif;[104] for grete labour and thought I haue in diuers contres[105] and places for hir sustentacion,[106] as wele as for me and for my childryn, and yit she is euermore contrary to my will, and so is non[107] but she." When the wif herd[108] this, she cried, and seid[109] with a vois,[110] as[111] hit[112] had be an horne. "O! wrecche, clepist[113] þou me thi most enemy? Sir Emperoure, I pray you," she said, "Here[114] me, what I shal sey. This man, that is here present, susteyneþ[115] in thi empire his sire, aȝens[116] your lawe; and in his hous he hath duellid sith[117] the tyme that he was worthi to be put oute." And when she had put oute[118] her venemous hert[119] in this manere,[120] then seid the knyght, "Lo! ser," he seid, "what I told you; is she not my enemy, þat accusith me so hily?[121] Wherfore I myght be ded, but if[122] your grace ordeined[123] othir weys[124] for me." Then the emperour seid, "Ne[125] were[126] thi wif, I myght not haue know[127] þe soth,[128] and þerfore þou shalt lede[129] th lif[130] with thi enemy. Go thi wey; I woll not dampne the,[131] and as long as þou levist[132] susteyne thi fadir."[133] Thenne the knyght yeld thonkyng[134] to the emperoure, and yede home, and faire[135] ende made.

Moralite

Dere Frendis,[136] this emperour is the devill, þat makith lawe among synners, *scil*.[137] þat eche[138] knyght, aftir that he hath passid tyme of armys, *scil*. that eche good man þat truly hath levid, and kept him,[139] and servid God in all the tyme of his yongith,[140] þat he then in his elde[141] be put

---

71. ah.
72. not.
73. little.
74. satisfaction.
75. took those.
76. then.
77. done.
78. yea.
79. will.
80. nor.
81. happiness.
82. woe.
83. beat.
84. yet.

85. offer.
86. bread.
87. good.
88. again.
89. cheer.
90. guard.
91. so that.
92. harm.
93. should have been.
94. slain.
95. had it not been for my hound.
96. son.

97. reason.
98. juggler.
99. laugh.
100. pretty.
101. plays.
102. forget.
103. hot.
104. wife.
105. various countries.
106. her support.
107. none.
108. heard.
109. said.

110. voice.
111. as if.
112. it.
113. wretch, call.
114. hear.
115. sustains.
116. against.
117. dwelt since.
118. opened.
119. venomous heart.
120. manner.
121. strongly.
122. dead, unless.

123. ordained.
124. ways.
125. not.
126. were (it for).
127. known.
128. truth.
129. lead.
130. life.
131. condemn you.
132. live.
133. father.
134. gave thanks.
135. fair.

Heading. *Moralite*: allegory.
136. dear friends.
137. namely (Latin *scilicet*).
138. each.
139. himself.
140. youth.
141. age.

a-bak fro[142] þe kyngdome of heven,[143] by the vice of covetice.[144] For that vice is more redy[145] to an old man þan to a yong,[146] as we mowe se alday;[147] and þerfore seith Seneca,[148] *Cum omnia peccata senescunt, sola cupiditas iuvenescit,* this is to sey,[149] "When all vices wexith old, oonly covetise[150] wexith yong, þat is to sey, in an old man." The knyght, þat susteyneth his fader, is euery good Cristen[151] man, that is ybound[152] to susteyne in the hous of his hert, by meritory werkes,[153] oure Lord Ihesu[154] Crist, þe which heng[155] for vs vpon þe cros; but many puttith him oute by synne. Þe hounde, þat is þe moste[156] frend, is the tong[157] of a good Cristen man, þe which praieth continuelly, like a berkyng[158] hound: wherof seith holy Writ, *Breuis oracio,* scil. *iusti, penetrat celum,* þat is to sey, "A short orison[159] of the rightwis[160] man or of the iust[161] man thirlith[162] or perissheth[163] heuen." By the litell[164] child þat plcieth,[165] so we shulle vndirstond[166] a clene[167] soule, ywassh[168] by baptyme;[169] þe which pleieth and hath dilectation in penaunce,[170] by the which a man getith the loue of God, and þe ioy[171] of heuen, and by the which a man is deliuered oute of tribulacion and of angir; *vnde ieronymus,* "wherof, as seith Jerom," *Penitencia est secunda tabula post naufragium,* þat is to sey, "Penaunce is þe secunde table[172] aftir shipbreche."[173] By the wif[174] þat accusith the man, is vndirstond[175] the flesshe, þat bryngith many yuels[176] in to a man, and tiseth[177] him to synne; as seith the Appostill[178] Paul, *Datus est michi stimulus carnis mee, angelus sathane, vt me colaphizet,* þat is to sey, "There is yoven[179] to me a pryk[180] of my flessh, an aungell[181] of þe devylle, to turment[182] me"; and þerfore this flessh is to be chasticed, þat hit[183] be not founde in synne, in tyme of deth,[184] lest hit be founden[185] þi enemy. And þerfore let vs study for to norissh[186] our Fadir, and hold oure lord Ihesu Crist so within vs, þat the devill in þe day of dome[187] haue no þing to putte forth ayens[188] vs, þat may greve[189] our soulis; and then we shul veriliche[190] trust to come to þe kyngdom of heuen. To þe which he vs bring, *qui cum Patre, et filio, et spiritu sancto.*[191]

How an Emperor Bequeathed His Empire to the Most Slothful of His Sons

Polemius was an Emperoure in the cetee[1] of Rome, þe whiche hadde iij sonnes, that he moche[2] lovid. So as þis Emperoure laye in[3] a certeyne[4] night in his bedde, he thowte[5] to dispose his Empir,[6] and he thou3t to yeve[7] his kyngdome to the slowest of his sones.[8] He callid to him his sonnes, and saide,

---

142. away from.
143. heaven.
144. covetousness.
145. ready.
146. young.
147. may see every day.

148. Lucius Annaerus Seneca, (d. 65), Roman philosopher born in Spain, tutor to Nero, was ordered by the emperor to take his own life. Among his writings are works dealing with the Stoic philosophy and several tragedies which became a great influence on the Elizabethans in their so-called Senecan tragedies, or "tragedies of blood."

149. say.
150. grow old, only covetousness.
151. Christian.
152. bound.
153. works.
154. Jesus.
155. hung.
156. greatest.
157. tongue.
158. barking.
159. prayer.
160. righteous.
161. just.
162. pierces.
163. destroys.
164. little.
165. plays.
166. shall understand.
167. clean.
168. washed.
169. baptism.
170. delectation in penance.
171. joy.

172. *Tabula* really means "flooring" or "deck." The implication is that penance is the second firm support after the first, the ship, is wrecked.

173. shipwreck.
174. wife.
175. understood.
176. evils.
177. entices.
178. Apostle.
179. given.
180. prick.
181. angel.
182. torment.
183. chastised, so that it.
184. death.
185. found.
186. nourish.
187. judgment.
188. against.
189. harm.
190. shall verily.

191. who with the Father, Son, and Holy Ghost.

Heading. *How an Emperor Bequeathed His Empire to the Most Slothful of His Sons:* This is an extremely common tale in folklore, Motif W 111.1 according to Thompson, *Motif-Index,* and Type 1950 according to Aarne-Thompson, *Types of the Folktale.*

1. city.
2. much.
3. on.
4. certain.
5. thought.
6. empire.
7. thought to give.
8. sons.

"He that is the slowest of yow,[9] or most slewthe[10] is in, shall have my kungdom aftir my discese."[11] "Þenne shall I have hit,"[12] quod[13] the eldest sone; "for I am so slowe, and swiche[14] slewthe is in me, that me[15] hadde leuer late[16] my fote brynne[17] in the fyr,[18] whenne I sitte þer by, than to withdrawe, and save hit." "Nay," quod the secounde, "yit[19] am I mor worthi thanne þow;[20] for yf case[21] that my necke wer in a rope to be hongid;[22] and yf þat I hadde my two hondes[23] at wille, and in on[24] honde þe ende of þe rope, and in that[25] oþer honde a sharpe swerde,[26] I hadde levir dye[27] ande be hongid, þan I wolde styr myn[28] arme, and kitte[29] the rope, whereby I myte[30] be savid." "Hit is I," quod the thirde, "that shalle regne[31] aftir my syre, for I passe hem[32] bothe in slewthe. Yf I lygge[33] in my bedde wyde opyn,[34] and þe reyne[35] rayne vppon boþe myn yen, yee,[36] me hadde leuer lete[37] hit reyne hem oute of the hede,[38] than[39] I turnid me oþere[40] to the right syde, or to the lyfte[41] syde." Þenne the Emperoure biquathe[42] his Empir to the thirde sone, as for the slowist.

Moralitee

Dere frendes,[43] this Emperoure is the devil, that is kynge and fadir[44] a-bove al childerin[45] of pryde. By the first sone is vndirstonde[46] the man that dwellithe in a wickid sitee[47] or place, by the whiche a flavme[48] of fire, *scil.*[49] of synne, is stirte to[50] him; and yit it is moche I-sene,[51] that he hadde leuer brynne yn synne withe hem thanne remeve[52] from the companye. By the secounde sonne is he vndirstonde that knowithe welle him selve[53] to be fastenid in the cordes and bondes of synne, and wolle[54] not smyte hem aweye[55] with the swerde of his tonge;[56] and hadde leuer be hongid for hem in helle, thanne to be shriven her.[57] Bi the thirde sone, vpon whom water dropis, boþ of[58] the riȝt ye[59] and of the lyfte, is vndirstonde he that hurithe[60] the doctrine of the ioyes[61] of paradys, and of the paynis and tormentes of helle, and wolle not for[62] slownesse of wytte torne him[63] to the right syde, *scil.* to leve[64] synne for love of the Ioyes, ne[65] to the left, *scil.* to leeve synne for drede[66] of peynis,[67] but lithe[68] stille in synnys vnmevabely;[69] and swiche wolle have the kyngdom of helle, and not of hevene.[70] *A quo nos liberet, et ad quod nos perducat imperator semper iure regnans!*[71] Amen.

---

9. you.
10. sloth.
11. decease.
12. it.
13. said.
14. such.
15. I.
16. rather let.
17. foot burn.
18. fire.
19. yet.
20. you.
21. it happened.

22. hanged.
23. hands.
24. one.
25. the.
26. sword.
27. rather die.
28. would move my.
29. cut.
30. might.
31. reign.
32. surpass them.

33. lie.
34. awake.
35. rain.
36. eyes, yea.
37. let.
38. head.
39. than (that).
40. myself either.
41. left.
42. bequeathed.

Heading. *Moralitee:* allegory.
43. dear friends.
44. father.
45. children.
46. understood.
47. city.
48. flame.
49. namely (Latin *scilicet*).
50. has reached.

51. often seen.
52. remove.
53. himself.
54. will.
55. away.
56. tongue.
57. absolved here.
58. on.
59. right eye.
60. hears.

61. joys.
62. because of.
63. turn himself.
64. leave.
65. nor.
66. fear.
67. pains.
68. lies.
69. unmoving.
70. heaven.

71. From whatever he may free us, and wherever he may lead us, the ruler should always reign according to the law.

A Fable of a Cat and a Mouse

A mouse on a[1] tyme felle into a barell of newe ale, that spourgid,[2] and myght not come oute. The cate come[3] beside, and herde[4] the mouse crie in the barme,[5] "Pepe![6] pepe!" for she myght not come oute. The cate seide,[7] "Why cries thou?" The mouse seide, "For[8] I may not come oute." The catte saide, "If I delyuer the[9] this tyme, thou shalte come to me when I calle the." Þe mouse seide, "I graunte[10] the, to come when thou wilte." The catte seide, "Thou moste swere[11] to me," and the mouse sware[12] to kepe couenaunte.[13] Then the catte with his fote[14] drew oute the mouse, and lete[15] hym go. Afterward the catte was hongry,[16] and come to the hole of the mouse, and called and bade hire[17] come to hym. The mouse was aferde,[18] and saide, "I shall not come." The catte saide, "Thou

haste[19] made an othe[20] to me, for to come." The mouse saide, "Broþer, I was dronkyne[21] when I swarc, and therfore I am not holdyn[22] to kepe myn[23] othe." Right[24] so many a man and woman, when they were seke,[25] or in prison, or in perell,[26] they purposyn[27] for to leue here[28] synne, and amende here life with fastyng and prayere, and to do othere werkes[29] of penaunce;[30] but when sekenesse or perell is passyd from hem,[31] they make no force[32] to fullfill the othe or the be-heste[33] that they made, for they sayne,[34] they were in perell, and therfore they are not holdyn to kepe the othe ne[35] the be-heste that they madyn.[36] Of whom it is saide, vnto a[37] tyme they beleuyn,[38] and in tyme of temptacion they gon[39] a-way there fro.[40]

How Man's Works Are Weighed in a Balance

A man there was that was seke nere[1] to the dethe,[2] and sawe ij aungills,[3] a good, and a bad; the which ij wedyn in ballaunce[4] his werkes,[5] boþe good and bad. And when he sawe his good werkes were but fewe, then he seide,[6] "A![7] lorde Iesu[8] Criste, shall it not helpe me that thou deyeste[9] for me, and suffred thy pynefull[10] passion for me, and was

nayled to the Crosse for me?" And when he had seide thus, he wepte faste.[11] And anone[12] a grete[13] nayle felle into the balaunce, where his good werkes were; and than[14] they weyed mych[15] more than his badde; and this man was sauyd,[16] blessyd be God! deo gracias.[17] Amen.

Heading. *A Fable of a Cat and a Mouse:* The fable is found in the works of Odo de Cheriton, 12th century.

1. one.
2. fermented.
3. cat came.
4. heard.
5. hole.
6. peep.
7. said.
8. because.
9. you.
10. promise.
11. must swear.
12. swore.
13. keep (the) agreement.
14. foot.
15. let.
16. hungry.
17. her.
18. afraid.
19. have.
20. oath.
21. drunk.
22. forced.
23. my.
24. just.
25. sick.
26. peril.
27. intend.
28. leave their.
29. works.
30. penance.
31. them.
32. effort.
33. promise.
34. say.
35. nor.
36. made.
37. for a certain.
38. believe.
39. go.
40. from.

---

1. sick almost.
2. death.
3. angels.
4. weighed on (a) scale.
5. works.
6. said.
7. ah.
8. Jesus.
9. died.
10. sorrowful.
11. greatly.
12. at once.
13. great.
14. then.
15. weighed much.
16. saved.
17. To God be thanks.

How a King's Son Shared His Reward

Þere was a kyng some[1] tyme, that had ij sonys,[2] an eldre, and an yongere.[3] To the eldre he bequathe[4] his kyngdome, and gafe[5] it hym in his lyfe: and the yonger he sette to the[6] scole,[7] for to lere,[8] for he bequathe hym right nought.[9] The eldre brothere dwelled at home with his fadre[10] in solace;[11] the yonge sone beynge atte scole, spendid euyll[12] the money that was take[13] hym to[14] the vse of the scole. There come[15] a frende[16] to the kyng, and passyd by the scole, and he sawe how the yonge sone gafe hym[17] to no studie, ne[18] to his lyrnyng,[19] but spendid euyll his tyme, and tolde the kyng. The kyng sente for his sone, and askid why he wold[20] not lyrne. And he seide hit longed[21] not to hym, syne[22] he was a kynges sone. Then seide þe kyng to hym, "For[23] thou seyste[24] thy brothere be[25] with me at home in delites,[26] therfore thou woldiste lede[27] his lyfe; but wete wele,[28] thou may not; for when I am dede,[29] thy brothere hathe wherof[30] he may lyve, for I gafe hym all my kyngdome; and I putte the[31] to scole, that thou myght helpe thy selfe after my dethe."[32] But whan[33] the kyng perseyued[34] he wolde[35] not profite in scole, but that he wolde dwelle in his fadres house, with his eldre brothere, and not laboure, he sete[36] hym euery day atte mete[37] with his knaues.[38] The childe was ashamed, and prayde his fadre that he myght go a-gayne to the scole.

The kyng saide, "Nay." Then the childe wente, and prayde his frendes, that they wolde pray his fadre for hym, that he myght go to scole. And so they didden;[39] and the kynge graunted hem here[40] prayere, but he gafe hym not so large expenses as he did be-fore. On a[41] day he made the childe to go with hym in to a chambre, in the which were dyuerse cofers,[42] with money of the kynges. The kyng toke[43] the keyes of the cofers to the childe, and seide, "Opyn oon[44] of thes[45] chestes, which that[46] thou wilte;[47] and that[48] thou fyndes there in, thou shalte haue." He openyd a cheste, and fownde[49] xx[ti]s;[50] and he[51] saide, "For sothe[52] thou shalte haue no more of me." But the fadre loked[53] to the erthward,[54] and fownde a peny,[55] and gafe it hym, and seide, "Haue this penny, and now haste[56] thou xx[ti]s and a penny." The childe toke his money, and wente to the scole; and while he was in the way goyng, he mette a man beryng[57] at his back a panyere.[58] The child asked hym what he had in his panyere. He saide, a wonderfull fyshe, that had a goldyn hede,[59] and a syluer bodie, and a grene tayle. The childe sawe the fyshe, and asked whether he wolde sell it. He seide, "Yee."[60] "What shall it coste?" He seide, "xx[ti]s." Then the childe toke[61] hym xx[ti]s; and than lafte[62] no more with hym but a peny. And while the sellere tolde[63] his money, the childe bownde[64] the

---

Heading. *How a King's Son Shared His Reward:* The story of Sharing the Reward or the Blows Received is Type 1610 according to Aarne-Thompson, *Types of the Folktale*, and Motif K 187 according to Stith Thompson's *Motif-Index*.

1. one.	**10.** father.	**19.** learning.
2. sons.	**11.** comfort.	**20.** would.
3. younger.	**12.** spent ill.	**21.** said it pertained.
4. bequeathed.	**13.** given.	**22.** since.
5. gave.	**14.** for.	**23.** because.
6. placed at.	**15.** came.	**24.** see.
7. school.	**16.** friend.	**25.** is.
8. learn.	**17.** himself.	**26.** delights.
9. absolutely nothing.	**18.** nor.	**27.** wish (to) lead.

28. know well.	**40.** granted them their.	**52.** in truth.
29. dead.	**41.** one.	**53.** looked.
30. (that) with which.	**42.** several coffers.	**54.** ground.
31. you.	**43.** took.	**55.** penny.
32. death.	**44.** open one.	**56.** have.
33. when.	**45.** these.	**57.** carrying.
34. perceived.	**46.** whichever.	**58.** basket.
35. would.	**47.** wish.	**59.** head.
36. placed.	**48.** what.	**60.** yea.
37. (i.e., to eat).	**49.** found.	**61.** gave.
38. servant boys.	**50.** twenty shillings.	**62.** then (that) left.
39. did.	**51.** (i.e., the king).	**63.** counted.
		64. tied.

fyshe in the panyere. That sawe the sellere ande seide, "All thoge[65] I solde the þe fyshe, I solde the not the panyere; who so[66] shall haue þe panyere, shall gyve me a penny, for it is so worthe." The childe wiste wele[67] he myght not bere it with oute[68] a vessell, and gafe[69] hym a peny. Now, as ye han herde,[70] he hathe paide all his money that his fadre toke hym to[71] the scole.[72] And the childe toke the panyere with the fyshe, and bare it at his bak.[73] He sawe a litill be-side[74] a fayre manere,[75] and mette a man, and asked if any man dwelled there. He saide, "Yee, a grete[76] lorde and a gentill;[77] for there is non[78] that dothe any thing for hym, be it neuer so litill, but he yeldes[79] it hym wele a-gayne." The child wente to the courte, and fownde the porter, and said he wolde speke[80] with the lorde. The porter asked hym what he wolde with the lorde. The childe seide[81] he had a presente. The porter seide, "The maner[82] is in this courte that I shulde se[83] the presente or[84] it come to the lorde." And the child shewed[85] hym the gyfte. When the porter saw it, he seide, "This hede is myn;[86] for it is the maner, who so brynges a beste[87] or a fyshe for a presente, I shall haue the hede for my parte." The childe thought, "If the hede shuld be cutte of,[88] the presente shulde be the worse, and the more abhomynable." The childe seide, "I pray the, suffere,[89] and thou shalte haue halfe my mede."[90] The porter graunted.[91] Then wente the childe, and come[92] to the vshere[93] of the halle, that saide he shulde haue the bodie of the fyshe; for it was the maner of this courte. To whom the childe seide, "If thou wilte

be curteyse[94] as the porter was, to whome I graunted halfyndele[95] my mede, and that[96] shall be more[97] I shall gyfe[98] the the halfyndele." And he graunted[99] hym to entere. Then come the childe to the chambreleyne,[100] and he asked[101] the tayle, sayeng, "It is the custome of the courte that I shuld haue the tayle." To whome the childe seide, "I graunted the porter the halfyndele of my mede, and to the vshere halfe that lafte ouere,[102] and nowe I pray the, suffere me to entere, and I shall gyfe the parte of that[103] comythe[104] to me." The chambreleyne graunted, and lete[105] hym entere, hopyng, as his felawes didden,[106] to haue some grete thing. The childe come to the lorde, and gafe hym this presente, the which the lorde hely resseyued,[107] and saide, "This is a fayre gyfte; aske therfor some good thing, that I may gyve the; and if thou aske wisely, I shall gyve with that to the my doughter to[108] wife, with my kyngdome." This herden[109] the seruauntes.[110] Some cownseyled[111] hym to aske a maner, anothere cownsayled hym to aske gold or syluer; and othere tresoure.[112] This herde the childe, and seide to the lorde, "Lorde, these men cownseylen[113] me to aske a maner, golde and syluere, but I say[114] you, I will aske non of all these, but if ye gyfe me any thing, me moste[115] gyve the porter the halfeyndele, and to the vshere halfe that leuyth[116] ouer, and the chambreleyne moste haue a parte, as the cause is be-fore seide. But I pray you, lorde, that ye wolde[117] graunte me xij buffettes, of the which the porter shall haue the vj, the vshere iij, and the chambreleyne iij." And this was done.

---

65. although.
66. whoever.
67. knew well.
68. without.
69. gave.
70. have heard.
71. father gave him for.
72. school.
73. back.

74. little (way) off.
75. manor.
76. great.
77. noble.
78. none.
79. repays.
80. speak.
81. said.
82. custom.

83. should see.
84. before.
85. showed.
86. mine.
87. beast.
88. off.
89. you, allow (me to pass).
90. reward.
91. granted (it).

92. came.
93. usher.
94. courteous.
95. half.
96. (of) that (which).
97. left over.
98. give.
99. allowed.
100. chamberlain.

101. asked (for).
102. over.
103. what.
104. comes.
105. let.
106. fellows did.
107. nobly received.
108. daughter for.

109. heard.
110. servants.
111. advised.
112. treasure.
113. advise.
114. tell.
115. I must.
116. is left.
117. would.

The lorde sawe that slely[118] and so wisely he had asked, and gafe[119] his kyngdome with his doughter. This kyng is Criste, that had ij sonys.[120] Be[121] the eldre sone are vndirstondyn aungells,[122] to which is geuyn[123] the kyngdome that reigneth with the fadre, with oute[124] laboure. The yonge[125] sone is man, that is putte in to the worlde, that is full of wrechidnesse,[126] as vnto a scole,[127] for to lyrne[128] to loue God. Man is the fyshe; as the prophete witnesseth Abacuk,[129] *facies hominis quasi pisces maris*.[130] The porter is the worlde; and right[131] as by the porter so by the worlde we may transite.[132] The hede[133] of þe fyshe is the loue that he wolde haue, for right as golde is moste preciouse of all metalles, so is loue moste preciouse of all thing.[134] But gyfe the porter, that is, the worlde, vj buffettes, that is, vj werkes[135] of mercy. Be the vshere is vnderstonden the fleshe, that wil haue the body, be þe which are understondyn delites;[136] but gyfe hym iij buffettes, that are wakynges,[137] prayers, and fastynges. The chambreleyn is the deuyll,[138] that wil haue the grene tayle, that is, the lyfe; but gyfe hym iij buffettes, that is, mekenesse, charite,[139] and mercy. And so chesyng[140] and deuydyng,[141] the kyng, that is, Criste, shall gyfe[142] to the[143] his doughter, and the kyngdome, that is, the blisse of heuyn.[144] To the which bryng vs Iesu[145] Criste! Amen.

---

118. slyly.	**122.** understood angels.	**125.** young.	**131.** just.	**137.** vigils.	**141.** dividing.
119. gave.		**126.** wretchedness.	**132.** pass through.	**138.** Devil.	**142.** give.
120. sons.	**123.** given.	**127.** school.	**133.** head.	**139.** meekness, charity.	**143.** you.
121. by.	**124.** father, without.	**128.** learn.	**134.** things.		**144.** heaven.
			135. works.	**140.** choosing.	**145.** Jesus.
			136. delights.		

129. Habakkuk, eighth in the order of minor prophets.
130. "[Thou] makest man as the fishes of the sea."

PROSE—LORE AND ROMANCE

Aside from the prose romances, which began to be written after 1300, the fourteenth century saw the production of a greater quantity of secular prose, culminating in the great output of the fifteenth century. Thus Mandeville's *Travels*, a fictitious travelogue, was written between 1366 and 1371, and John Trevisa's translations of Higden's *Polychronicon* and the encyclopedia of Bartolomeus Anglicus were completed in 1387 and 1398 respectively. In the fifteenth century the reading public was larger and more demanding. Much so-called courtesy literature was produced, treatises on hawking (like the *Book of Saint Albans*), on education of the young (like the *Book of the Knight of La Tour-Landry*, translated into English in 1450); and from this period also come the *Paston Letters*, the correspondence of a famous Norfolk family, 1422–1509. Reginald Pecock (1395–1460) was the most prolific prose writer of the century, although undoubtedly Thomas Malory's *Morte Darthur* was the outstanding work. A wider literacy among the middle class and the establishment of a press in 1476 by William Caxton, who combined the role of printer with that of editor and translator, provided impetus for a greater creativity in prose and translation. Thus in many ways the fifteenth century seeded the literary soil of the English Renaissance.

REFERENCES

Bennett, H. S. *Chaucer and the Fifteenth Century*. London, 1947.
————. *The Pastons and Their England*, London, 1922.
Furnivall, F. J., ed. *The Babees Book*. London, 1868.
Letts, Malcolm. *Sir John Mandeville: The Man and His Book*. London, 1949.
Pollard, A. W. *Fifteenth Century Prose and Verse*. New York, 1964.
Vinaver, Eugène. *The Works of Sir Thomas Malory*. 3 vols. Oxford, 1947; 2d ed., 1967.

Prose—Lore and Romance, is treated in the General Introduction of this volume, pp. 26–27.

from THE TRAVELS
OF SIR JOHN MANDEVILLE

DATE: 14th century. ⚓ MANUSCRIPT: British Library Cotton Titus C. xvi (c. 1410–20). About three hundred MSS are extant. The dialect is of the Southeast Midlands. ⚓ EDITION: P. Hamelius, ed., *Mandeville's Travels*, Early English Text Society, OS 153, 154 (London, 1919–23). See also critical studies: Josephine W. Bennett, *The Rediscovery of Sir John Mandeville*, MLA Monograph Series, No. 19 (New York, 1954), which attacks the testimony of Jean d'Outremeuse and pleads for an Englishman as the author; Malcolm Letts, *Sir John Mandeville: The Man and His Book* (London, 1949), which retains the traditional views.

The Southeast Midland dialect is late and therefore quite easy to understand. (1) Personal pronouns are *þei*, "they," *hire*, "their," *hem*, "them," "themselves." (2) Demonstrative pronouns are *þo*, singular, and *þeise*, plural.

The mystery surrounding the author of Sir John Mandeville's *Travels* is extraordinary, especially since this work was one of the most popular books of the Middle Ages. Starting rather prosaically as a travel guide to the Holy Land, the account copies the work of Guillaume de Boldensele (1336) in the first part and then moves into fantastic descriptions of men and animals, customs and geography, flora and fauna of the Far East, much of it taken from evidence in the stories of Odoric de Pordenone (1330). The *Speculum Naturale* of Vincent de Beauvais (1250) was another source, and it can be seen that the famous *Travels* could have been written without the author's leaving home. They were probably composed in French in 1366–71 in Liège by a physician named Jehan de Bourgogne (alias John of Burgundy or John with the Beard) but were very soon translated into Latin and English. It may be that this John of Burgundy was actually an English physician, John de Mandeville, knight of Saint Albans, who, having killed a man in England and spent many years traveling to distant countries, retired to a secluded life in Liège in 1343 and died there in 1372. There is some circumstantial evidence supporting this identification and the epitaph on a tomb in Liège stating that a "Dominus Joannes de Montevilla Miles, alias dictus ad Barbam," English physician, was buried there in 1372. Also the note of Jean d'Outremeuse (1338–99) in Part IV of the *Myreur des Histoires*, unfortunately lost, stating that a Jean de Bourgogne confessed on his deathbed to being Mandeville, author of the *Travels*, has stirred the winds of confusion. The riddle of the author's identity may never be solved; but the characteristic identity of the work itself is, in the English translation, one of easy, fluent prose and, in the French original, one of vigorous imagination.

Of the Contrees and Yles Þat Ben Beȝonde the Lond of Cathay and of the Frutes Þere and of XXIJ Kynges Enclosed Withjn the Mountaynes

Now schall I seye ȝou[1] sewyngly[2] of contrees and yles þat ben beȝonde the contrees þat I haue spoken of. Wherfore I seye ȝou, in passynge be[3] the lond of Cathaye toward the high ynde[4] and toward Bacharye,[5] men passen[6] be a kyngdom þat men clepen[7] Caldilhe,[8] þat is a full[9] fair contre. And þere groweth a maner[10] of fruyt as þough it weren gowrdes,[11] and whan[12] þei ben rype men kutten hem a to[13] and men fynden[14] withjnne a lytyll best[15] in flesch, in bon[16] and blode,[17] as þough it were a lytill lomb withouten wolle.[18] And men eten[19] bothe the frut[20] and the best, and þat is a gret merueylle.[21] Of þat frute I haue eten[22] all þough it were wonderfull[23] but þat I knowe wel þat God is merueyllous in his werkes.[24] And natheles[25] I tolde hem of als[26] gret a merueyle to hem þat is a monges[27] vs and þat was of the bernakes.[28] For I tolde hem þat in oure contree weren trees þat baren[29] a fruyt þat becomen briddes fleeynge.[30] And þo[31] þat fellen[32] in the water lyuen,[33] and þei þat fallen[34] on the erthe dyen[35] anon;[36] and þei ben right gode to[37] mannes mete.[38] And here of[39] had þei als[40] gret meruaylle[41] þat summe[42] of hem trowed[43] it were[44] an jnpossible thing to be. In þat contre ben longe apples[45] of gode sauour, where of ben mo[46] þan an C[47] in a clustre and als manye in a noþer.[48] And þei han[49] grete longe leves[50] and large of ij fote[51] long or more and in þat contree and in oþer contrees þere abouten growen[52] many trees þat beren[53] clowe gylofres[54] and notemuges[55] and grete notes[56] of ynde and of canell[57] and of many oþer spices. And þere ben vynes þat beren so grete grapes þat a strong man scholde[58] haue ynow[59] to done[60] for to bere o[61] clustre with all the grapes. In þat same regioun ben the mountaynes of Caspye[62] þat men clepen Vber[63] in the contree. Betwene þo mountaynes the Iewcs[64] of x lynages[65] ben enclosed þat men clepen Goth and Magoth[66] and þei mowe[67] not gon[68] out on no syde. Þere weren

---

Heading. *contrees:* countries. *iles:* isles. *ben.* are. *lond:* land. *Cathay:* China.

1. tell you.
2. as follows.
3. by.
4. India.
5. ? Bactria (if so, then it refers to an ancient nation in Asia, between the Hindu Kush ["Killer"] Mountains and the Oxus River).
6. pass.
7. call.
8. Caldili or Caloy (a Tartar kingdom on the Volga).
9. very.
10. kind.
11. were gourds.
12. when.
13. cut them in two.
14. find.
15. little beast.
16. bone.
17. blood.
18. lamb without wool.
19. eat.
20. fruit.
21. great marvel.
22. eaten.
23. strange.
24. works.
25. nevertheless.
26. as.
27. among.
28. Vincent de Beauvais says that the *bartlathes* are birds growing on wood and commonly called *bernacae*. After they fall off they fly like other birds, but they cannot live if they do not soon find water. Their flesh is eaten in Lent since they are really transformed barnacles or shellfish. Thus we have the fabulous origin for our "barnacle goose."
29. bear.
30. becomes birds flying.
31. those.
32. fell.
33. live.
34. fall.
35. die.
36. at once.
37. very good for.
38. food.
39. at that.
40. such.
41. wonder.
42. some.
43. believed.
44. was.
45. plantains (a kind of bananas).
46. more.
47. hundred.
48. many in another.
49. have.
50. leaves.
51. two feet.
52. about grow.
53. bear.
54. clove gillyflowers.
55. nutmegs.
56. nuts.
57. cinnamon.
58. should.
59. enough.
60. do.
61. one.
62. Caucasus.
63. The Ubera Aquilonis ("Breasts of the North Wind") were two mountains which *Pseudo-Methodius* (a compilation, probably composed originally in Greek c. 676–78 in Syria, although falsely attributed to Bishop Methodius of Olympus and Tyrus [d. 311], of Alexander stories, revelations, and prophecies which were intended to prove the imminence of Doomsday) states came together at the request of Alexander the Great to entomb his enemies and lock them in with brazen gates (Ernst Sackur, ed., *Sibyllinische Texte und Forschungen* [Halle, 1898], pp. 73–74).
64. Jews.
65. tribes.
66. In the Alexander legends, Gog and Magog are allied to the Indian emperor Porus in resisting the advances of the Macedonian conqueror, and Alexander's great Caucasian wall contained them. Although occasionally thought to be of the Scythian tribes, Gog and Magog are mentioned in Ezekiel 38, 39, and Revelation 20:8 as the princes of Mesheck and Tubal. They represent the people deceived by Satan, the Tartars or the Ten Lost Tribes of Israel.
67. may.
68. go.

enclosed xxij kynges with hire peple,[69] þat dwelle-
den[70] betwene the mountaynes of Sychye.[71] Þere
kyng Alisandre chacede[72] hem betwene þo mountaynes and þere he thoughte for to enclose hem
þorgh[73] werk of his men. But whan he saugh[74] þat
he myghte not don it ne[75] bryng it to an ende, he
preyed[76] to God of nature þat he wolde parforme[77]
þat þat he had begonne.[78] And all were[79] it so þat
he was a payneme[80] and not worthi to ben herd,[81]
ʒit[82] God of his grace closed the mountaynes
togydre,[83] so þat þei dwellen[84] þere all faste
ylokked[85] and enclosed with high mountaynes
alle aboute, saf[86] only on o syde, and on þat
syde is the see[87] of Caspye.[88] Now may sum men
asken:[89] Sith[90] þat the see is on þat o syde, wherfore go þei not out on the see syde for to go where
þat hem[91] lyketh? But to this questioun I schal
answere: Þat see of Caspye goth out be londe[92]
vnder the mountaynes and renneth[93] be the desert
at o syde of the contree[94] and after it streccheth[95]
vnto the endes of Persie. And allþough it be clept[96]
a see, it is no see ne it toucheth to non[97] oþer see,
but it is a lake, the grettest[98] of the world. And
þough þei wolden putten hem[99] in to þat see, þei
ne wysten[100] neuer where þat þei scholde ar-
ryuen.[101] And also þei conen[102] no langage but
only hire owne þat noman[103] knoweth but þei,
and þerfore mowe þei not gon out. And also ʒee
schull vnderstonde[104] þat the Iewes han no propre
lond of hire owne for to dwellen jnne[105] in all the
world, but only þat lond betwene the mountaynes,
and ʒit þei ʒelden[106] tribute for þat lond to the
queen of Amazoine[107] the whiche þat maketh
hem[108] to ben kept in cloos full[109] diligently þat
þei schull not gon out on no syde but be the cost[110]
of hire lond, for hire lond marcheth[111] to þo
mountaynes. And often it hath befallen þat summe
of the Iewes han gon[112] vp the mountaynes and
avaled[113] down to the valeyes, but gret nombre[114]
of folk ne may not do so for the mountaynes ben[115]
so hye[116] and so streght[117] vp, þat þei moste[118]
abyde þere maugree[119] hire myght, for þei mowe
not gon out but be a littil issue[120] þat was made be
strengthe of men; and it lasteth wel a[121] iiij grete
myle.[122] And after is þere ʒit a lond all desert,
where men may fynde no water ne[123] for dyggynge
ne for non other þing, wherfore men may not
dwellen in þat place so is it full of dragounes, of
serpentes and of oþer venymous bestes[124] þat
noman dar[125] not passe but ʒif[126] it be be strong[127]
wynter. And þat streyt[128] passage men clepen[129]
in þat contree Clyron,[130] and þat is the passage
þat the queen of Amazoine maketh to ben kept.
And þogh[131] it happene sum of hem be fortune[132]
to gon[133] out, þei conen no maner[134] of langage but
Ebrew,[135] so þat þei can not speke[136] to the peple.[137]
And ʒit natheles[138] men seyn[139] þei schull gon out
in the tyme of Antecrist[140] and þat þei schull
maken[141] gret slaughter of cristene[142] men, and
þerfore all the Iewes[143] þat dwellen[144] in all londes

---

69. their people.
70. dwelt.
71. Scythia.
72. Alexander
chased.
73. through.
74. saw.
75. nor.
76. prayed.
77. would perform.
78. begun.
79. although was.
80. pagan.
81. be heard.

82. yet.
83. together.
84. dwell.
85. locked.
86. except.
87. sea.
88. Caspia.
89. ask.
90. since.
91. they.
92. by land.
93. runs.
94. country.
95. stretches.

96. called.
97. no.
98. greatest.
99. would place
themselves.
100. not knew.
101. arrive.
102. know.
103. no one.
104. you shall
understand.
105. in.
106. yield.

107. Amazonia. Among the signs of Doomsday were the reign
of a woman and the return of the Ten Lost Tribes (Rupert
Taylor, *The Political Prophecy in England* [New York, 1911],
p. 34).
108. them.   **109.** close very.   **110.** coast.

111. reaches.
112. have gone.
113. escaped.
114. numbers.
115. are.
116. high.
117. straight.

118. must.
119. in spite of.
120. little
opening.
121. a full.
122. long miles.
123. neither.

124. venomous
beasts.
125. dare.
126. unless.
127. in deep.
128. narrow.
129. call.

130. Identified by George F. Warner (*The Buke of John
Maundevill* [Westminster, 1889]) with the Direu of Brunetto
Latini (1220–94). According to Francis J. Carmody (ed.,
Li Livres dou Tresor de Brunetto Latini [Berkeley, 1948], Direu
was situated west of the Elburz Mountains on the Caspian Sea,
near a narrow gorge called "Les portes de Caspe" by Latini.

131. though.
132. fortunate.
133. go.
134. kind.
135. Hebrew.
136. speak.

137. people.
138. yet
nevertheless.
139. say.
140. See above, n. 107.

141. make.
142. Christian.
143. Jews.
144. dwell.

lernen[145] all weys[146] to speken[147] Ebrew, in hope þat whan[148] the oþer Iewes schull gon out, þat þei may vnderstonden hire speche[149] and to leden[150] hem in to cristendom for to destroye the cristene peple. For the Iewes seyn þat þei knowen[151] wel be[152] hire prophecyes þat þei of Caspye[153] schull gon out and spreden[154] þorgh out[155] all the world and þat the cristene men schull ben[156] vnder hire subieccioun als[157] longe as þei han ben[158] in subieccioun of hem. And 3if[159] þat 3ee wil wyte[160] how þat þei schull fynden[161] hire weye, after þat[162] I haue herd seye[163] I schall tell 3ou.[164] In the tyme of Antecrist a fox shall make þere his trayne[165] and mynen[166] an hole where kyng Alisandre leet make[167] the 3ates[168] and so longe he schall mynen and percen[169] the erthe[170] til þat he schall passe þorgh[171] towardes þat folk. And whan þei seen[172] the fox they schull[173] haue gret merueylle of[174] him be cause[175] þat þei saugh[176] neuer such a best, for of all oþere bestes þei han enclosed amonges hem, saf[177] only the fox. And þanne[178] þei schullen chaccn[179] him and pursuen[180] him so streyte,[181] till þat he come to the same place þat hc cam fro.[182] And þanne þei schullen dyggen[183] and mynen so strongly, till þat þci fynden the 3ates

þat kyng Alisandre leet make of grete stones and passynge[184] huge, wel symented[185] and made stronge for the maystrie.[186] And þo[187] 3ates þei schull breken[188] and so gon out be[189] fyndynge of þat issue.[190] Fro þat lond[191] gon men to ward[192] the lond of Bacharie,[193] where ben full yuele[194] folk and full cruell. In þat lond ben trees þat beren wolle[195] as þogh it were of scheep, where of men maken clothes and all þing[196] þat may ben made of wolle. In þat contree[197] ben many ypotaynes[198] þat dwellen somtyme in the water and somtyme on the lond and þei ben half man and half hors as I haue seyd[199] before, and þei eten[290] men whan þei may take hem. And þere ben ryueres[201] and watres þat ben full byttere,[202] þree sithes[203] more þan is the water of the see.[204] In þat contre ben many grirfounes[205] more plentee[206] þan in ony[207] other contree. Summen[208] seyn[209] þat þei han[210] the body vpward as an egle[211] and benethe[212] as a lyoun[213] and treuly[214] þei seyn soth[215] þat þei ben of þat schapp.[216] But o[217] griffoun hath the body more gret and is more strong þanne viij lyouns, of suche lyouns as ben o[218] this half,[219] and more gret and strongere þan an C[220] egles suche as wc han amonges vs. For o griffoun þere wil bere

---

145. learn.
146. always.
147. speak.
148. when.
149. understand their speech.
150. lead.
151. know.
152. by.
153. Caspia.
154. spread.
155. throughout.
156. be.
157. subjection as.
158. been.
159. if.
160. know.
161. find.
162. what.
163. heard said.
164. you.
165. strategy. The OF word is *taignere* (Mod. F. *tanière*), "den," but the translator took it as "stratagem" or "device." The occurrence of errors in meaning because of a mistranslation from the French is common in the English versions.
166. mine.
167. Alexander had made.
168. gates.
169. pierce.
170. earth.
171. through.
172. see.
173. shall.
174. great wonder at.
175. because.
176. saw.
177. among them, except.
178. then.
179. shall chase.
180. pursue.
181. closely.
182. came from.
183. dig.
184. surpassingly.
185. cemented.
186. exceedingly.
187. those.
188. break.
189. by.
190. opening.
191. land.
192. toward.
193. Bactria.
194. are very evil.
195. bear wool (the reference is to cotton plants).
196. things.
197. country.

198. hippopotamuses. It may be that the hippopotamus is here confused with the mythical hippocentaur, a creature half horse, half man—although the centaurs were normally found in the mountains of Thessaly. One of them, the wise Chiron, was the teacher of Achilles, and nourished a stable of many other Greek heroes. Vincent de Beauvais in his *Speculum Historiale* mentions that two hundred of Alexander's troops were eaten by hippopotamuses as they swam across a river. The reference below to the bitter water and the griffins is from the same source.
199. said.
200. eat.
201. rivers.
202. bitter.
203. times.
204. sea.
205. griffins: mythical animals having the head and wings of an eagle and the body and hind legs of a lion.
206. plentiful.
207. any.
208. some men.
209. say.
210. have.
211. eagle.
212. beneath.
213. lion.
214. truly.
215. truth.
216. shape.
217. one.
218. of.
219. The lions "of this half" are those of the city of Liège, probably meant facetiously. The griffins of Vincent de Beauvais fight Alexander's men in India.
220. hundred.

fleynge[221] to his nest a gret hors ȝif he may fynde him at the poynt[222] or ij oxen ȝoked togidere[223] as þei gon[224] at the plowgh. For he hath his talouns so longe and so large and grete vpon his feet as þough þei weren[225] hornes of grete oxen or of bugles[226] or of kyȝn,[227] so þat men maken[228] cuppes of hem to drynken[229] of. And of hire[230] ribbes and of the pennes[231] of hire wenges[232] men maken bowes full stronge to schote[233] with arwes[234] and quarell.[235] From þens[236] gon men be many iourneyes þorgh[237] the lond of Prestre Iohn[238] the grete Emperour of ynde,[239] and men clepen[240] his roialme[241] the yle[242] of Pentexoire.[243]

Of the Ryall Estate of Prestre Iohn and of a Riche Man þat Made a Merueylous Castell and Cleped It Paradys and of His Sotyltee

This Emperour Prestre Iohn holt full gret lond[1] and hath many full noble cytees[2] and gode[3] townes in his royalme[4] and many grete dyuerse yles[5] and large. For all the contree[6] of ynde[7] is deuysed in[8] yles for[9] the grete flodes[10] þat comen[11] from Paradys þat departen[12] all the lond in many parties.[13] And also in the see[14] he hath full manye[15] yles. And the beste cytee in the yle of Pentexoire[16] is Nyse[17] þat is a full ryall cytee and a noble and full riche. This Prestre Iohn hath vnder him many kynges and many yles and many dyuerse folk of dyuerse condiciouns. And this lond is full gode and ryche, but not so riche as is the lond of the grete Chane.[18] For the marchauntes[19] comen not thider[20] so comounly[21] for to bye[22] marchandises as þei don[23] in the lond of the gret Chane, for it is to fer[24] to trauaylle[25] to. And on[26] þat other partie, in the yle of Cathay[27] men fynden[28] all maner thing[29] þat is nede[30] to man: clothes of gold, of silk, of spycerye and all maner auere de poys,[31] and þerfore, all be it[32] þat men han[33] gretter chep[34] in the yle of Prestre Iohn, natheless[35] men dreden[36] the longe weye[37] and the grete periles in the see in þo[38] partyes. For in many places of the see

---

221. flying.
222. in first position.
223. together.
224. go.
225. were.
226. buffalo.
227. cows.
228. make.
229. drink.
230. their.
231. quills.
232. wings.
233. shoot.
234. arrows.
235. bolt.
236. thence.
237. journeys through.
238. In the Middle Ages, Prester John was thought to be a Christian king and priest ruling an enormous and wealthy theocracy in the Orient. Marco Polo in his *Travels* identifies him with Un-Khan (d. 1203), to whom the Tartars paid tribute but who was killed by Genghis Khan. Because of the knowledge of and interest in the Nestorian Christians of Abyssinia which reached Europe in the 15th century, Prester John was also identified with the king of Ethiopia.
239. India.
240. call.
241. realm.
242. isle.
243. In the French text of Odoric de Pordenone, whose authentic travel descriptions were used by Mandeville (Jean d'Outremeuse, *Ly Myreur des Histors*, ed. S. Bormans [Brussels, 1864], Vol. I, p. 139), Pentexoire is located near the Yellow River.

Heading. *ryall:* royal. *Iohn:* John. *merueylous:* marvelous. *cleped:* called. *sotyltee:* craftiness. On Prester John see above, n. 238.
1. controls very great land.
2. cities.
3. good.
4. realm.
5. various isles.
6. country.
7. India.
8. composed of.
9. because of.
10. rivers.
11. come.
12. separate.
13. parts.
14. sea.
15. many.
16. See above, n. 243.
17. Nysa, a city which the god Bacchus founded in India.
18. Khan (of Cathay).
19. merchants.
20. there.
21. commonly.
22. buy.
23. do.
24. too far.
25. travel.
26. in.
27. China.
28. find.
29. kinds (of) things.
30. necessary.
31. avoirdupois (i.e., weight).
32. although.
33. have.
34. trade.
35. nevertheless.
36. dread.
37. way.
38. those.

ben [39] grete roches[40] of stones of the Adamant,[41] þat of his propre nature draweth iren[42] to him,[43] and þerfore þere passen[44] no schippes þat han ouþer bondes[45] or nayles of iren within hem,[46] and ʒif[47] þer do anon[48] the roches of the Adamantes drawen[49] hem to hem, þat neuer þei may go þens.[50] I myself haue seen o ferrom[51] in þat see as þough it hadde ben[52] a gret yle full of trees and buscaylle[53] full of thornes and breres[54] gret plentee,[55] and the schipmen tolde vs þat all þat was of schippes þat weren drawen[56] thider be[57] the Adamauntes for the iren þat was in hem. And of[58] the roteness[59] and oþer thing[60] þat was within the schippes grewen[61] such buscaylle and thornes and breres and grene grass and such maner of thing, and of the mastes and the seyll ʒerdes[62] it semed[63] a grete wode[64] or a groue. And suche roches ben in many places þere abouten. And þerfore dur[65] not the marchantes passen þere but ʒif[66] þei knowen[67] wel the passages or ell[68] þat þei han gode lodesmen.[69] And also þei dreden the longe weye and þerfore thei gon[70] to Cathay for it is more nygh.[71] And ʒit[72] is it not so nygh but þat men moste ben[73] trauayllynge be see and lond xj monethes[74] or xij from Gene[75] or from Venyse or[76] he come to Cathy. And ʒit

is the lond[77] of Prestre Iohn more ferr be many dredfull iourneyes.[78] And the marchantes passen be the kyngdom of Persie and gon to a cytee[79] þat is clept[80] Hermes[81] for Hermes the Philosophre founded it, and after þat þei passen an arm of the see[82] and þanne[83] þei gon to another cytee þat is clept Golbach[84] and þere þei fynden marchandises and of popengayes[85] as gret[86] plentee as men fynden here of gees.[87] And ʒif þei wil passen ferthere[88] þei may gon sykerly jnow.[89] In þat contree[90] is but lytyll whete[91] or barly and þerfore þei eten ryʒs[92] and hony and mylk and chese[93] and frute. This Emperour Prestre Iohn[94] taketh allweys to[95] his wif[96] the doughter of the grete Chane[97] and the grete Chane also in the same wise the doughter of Prestre Iohn, for þeise[98] ij ben the grettest lordes vndir the firmament. In the lond of Prestre Iohn ben many dyuerse[99] things and manye[100] precious stones so grete and so large þat men maken[101] of hem vessell,[102] as plateres,[103] dissches and cuppes, and many oþer merueyles[104] ben þere þat it were to combrous[105] and to long to putten[106] it in scripture[107] of bokes.[108] But of the principall ylcs[109] and of his estate and of his lawe I schall telle ʒou[110] som partye.[111] This Emperour Prestre Iohn is cristene[112] and a

---

39. are.   **40.** rocks.

41. The Adamants were magnetized rocks which wrecked ships by attracting them through the iron in their structure or sank them by pulling all iron nails and bands out of their wood. Either way, they were very dangerous to shipping, and nautical engineers attempted to build ships completely of wood. Vincent de Beauvais places the lodestone rocks in the Indian Ocean, but the general vagueness of their position made them unchartable.

81. Hormuz or Ormuz, an island in the Strait of Hormuz, located between Iran and the northern tip of Trucial Oman. Hermes the philosopher is probably Hermes Trismegistus (Thrice Great) the Greek name for the Egyptian god of wisdom, Toth. Hermes was the reputed founder of alchemy, and to him were attributed after the 3rd century mystical works concerning Oriental and Greek philosophy. So-called "Hermetic" books treated geography, astronomy, myth, and medicine.

42. iron.	**55.** plenty.	**68.** else.	**82.** sea.	**92.** eat rice.	**103.** platters.
43. himself.	**56.** were drawn.	**69.** pilots.	**83.** then.	**93.** cheese.	**104.** marvels.
44. pass.	**57.** by.	**70.** go.	**84.** Cambaye, north	**94.** John.	**105.** would be too
45. either bands.	**58.** from.	**71.** near.	of Bombay.	**95.** always for.	cumbersome.
46. them.	**59.** rottenness.	**72.** yet.	**85.** parrots.	**96.** wife.	**106.** put.
47. if.	**60.** things.	**73.** must be.	**86.** great.	**97.** Khan.	**107.** writing.
48. at once.	**61.** grew.	**74.** months.	**87.** geese.	**98.** these.	**108.** books.
49. draw.	**62.** sail yards.	**75.** Genoa.	**88.** farther.	**99.** various.	**109.** isles.
50. thence.	**63.** seemed.	**76.** Venice before.	**89.** safely enough.	**100.** many.	**110.** you.
51. from afar.	**64.** wood.	**77.** land.	**90.** country.	**101.** make.	**111.** part.
52. been.	**65.** dare.	**78.** dreadful journeys.	**91.** little wheat.	**102.** vessels.	**112.** Christian.
53. shrubbery.	**66.** unless.	**79.** city.			
54. briars.	**67.** know.	**80.** called.			

gret partie of his contree also, but ʒit þei haue not all the articles of oure feyth[113] as wee hauen.[114] Þei beleuen[115] wel in the fader,[116] in the sone[117] and in the holy gost[118] and þei ben full[119] deuoute and right trewe on[120] to a nother[121] and þei sette[122] not be[123] no barettes ne by cawteles[124] ne of no disceytes.[125] And he hath vnder him lxxij prouynces and in euery prouynce is a kyng. And þeise kynges han[126] kynges vnder hem[127] and alle ben tributaries to Prestre Iohn. And he hath in his lordschipes[128] many grete merueyles, for in his contree is the see þat men clepen[129] the Grauely[130] See þat is all grauell and sond[131] withouten ony drope[132] of water. And it ebbeth and floweth in grete wawes[133] as oþer sees don.[134] And it is neuer stille ne in pes[135] in no maner cesoun[136] and noman[137] may passe þat see be navye[138] ne be no maner of craft and þerfore may no man knowe what lond is beʒond[139] þat see. And all be it[140] þat it haue no water ʒit[141] men fynden[142] þere in and on the bankes full gode[143] fissch of other maner of kynde[144] and schapp[145] þanne men fynden in ony other see and þei ben of right goode tast and delicyous to[146] mannes mete.[147] And a iij iourneys long fro[148] þat see[149] ben grete mountaynes out of the whiche goth out a gret flood[150] þat cometh out of Paradys and it is full of precious stones withouten ony drope of water and it renneth þorgh[151] the desert on þat o[152] syde, so þat it maketh the see grauely.

And it bereth[153] into þat see and þere it endeth. And þat flomme[154] renneth also iij dayes in the woke[155] and bryngeth with him grete[156] stones and the roches[157] also þerewith and þat gret plentee,[158] and anon[159] as þei ben entred in to the grauely see þei ben seyn[160] nomore, but lost for euermore. And in þo[161] iij dayes þat that ryuere[162] renneth noman dar entren[163] in to it, but in the oþer dayes men dar entren wel ynow.[164] Also beʒonde þat flomme, more vpward to the desertes is a gret pleyn[165] all grauelly betwene[166] the mountaynes. And in þat playn euery day at the sonne[167] risynge begynnen[168] to growe smale[169] trees and þei growen[170] til mydday berynge[171] frute. But noman dar taken[172] of þat frute for it is a thing of fayre.[173] And after midday þei discrecen[174] and entren aʒen[175] in to the erthe,[176] so þat at the goynge doun of the sonne þei apperen[177] no more and so þei don euery day and þat is a gret mervaylle.[178] In þat desert ben many wylde men þat ben hidouse[179] to loken[180] on for þei ben horned and þei speken nought[181] but þei gronten[182] as pygges. And þere is also gret plentee of wylde houndes, and þere ben manye popegayes[183] þat þei clepen psitakes[184] in hire langage.[185] And þei speken of hire propre nature[186] and saluen[187] men þat gon[188] þorgh the desertes and speken to hem als appertely[189] as þough it were a man. And þei þat speken wel han[190] a large tonge[191] and han v toos[192] vpon a fote.[193]

---

113. faith.
114. we have.
115. believe.
116. Father.
117. Son.
118. Ghost.
119. are very.
120. very true one.
121. another.
122. care.
123. for.
124. fraud nor for cunning.
125. deceits.
126. have.
127. them.
128. domains.
129. call.
130. Gravelly.
131. sand.
132. without any drop.
133. waves.
134. do.
135. peace.
136. kind (of) season.
137. no one.
138. by ship.
139. beyond.
140. although.
141. yet.
142. find.
143. good.
144. nature.
145. shape.
146. for.
147. food.
148. (days') journey's distance from.
149. sea.
150. river.
151. runs through.
152. one.
153. runs.
154. river.
155. week.
156. great.
157. rocks.
158. plenty.
159. then.
160. seen.
161. those.
162. river.
163. dares enter.
164. enough.
165. plain.
166. between.
167. sun.
168. begin.
169. small.
170. grow.
171. bearing.
172. take.
173. fairyland (these are the "ephemeral trees" of the Alexander romances). Fruit that is of *fayrye* (usually apples) must not be eaten, lest one be captured by the power of fairyland and never be able to return to the mortal world.
174. decrease.
175. again.
176. earth.
177. appear.
178. marvel.
179. hideous.
180. look.
181. speak not.
182. grunt.
183. are many parrots.
184. The bird *psitacus*, according to Vincent de Beauvais, is one of the marvels of India.
185. their language.
186. as it is their nature to speak.
187. greet.
188. go.
189. as openly.
190. have.
191. tongue.
192. toes.
193. foot.
194. little.

And þere ben also of oþer manere, þat han but iij toos vpon a fote and þei speken not or but litill[194] for þei cone not[195] but cryen.[196] This Emperour Prestre Iohn whan[197] he goth into bataylle aȝenst ony[198] other lord, he hath no baneres born[199] before him but he hath iij crosses of gold fyn,[200] grete and hye,[201] full of precious stones. And euery[202] of þo cross[203] ben sett in a chariot full[204] richely arrayed. And for to kepen[205] euery cros ben ordeyned x mill[206] men of armes and mo[207] þan an C M[208] men on fote in maner[209] as men wolde[210] kepe a standard[211] in oure contrees[212] whan þat wee[213] ben in lond of werre.[214] And this nombre[215] of folk is withouten[216] the princypall hoost[217] and withouten wenges[218] ordeynd for the bataylle. And whan he hath no werre, but rideth with a pryuy meynee þanne[219] he hath bore[220] before him but o cros of tree[221] withouten peynture[222] and withouten gold or siluer or precious stones in remembrance þat Ihesu[223] crist suffred deth[224] vpon a cros of tree. And he hath born before him also a plater[225] of gold full of erthe in tokene þat his nobless[226] and his myght and his flessch schall turnen[227] to erthe. And he hath born before him also a vessell of siluer full of noble iewelles of gold full riche and of precious stones in tokene of his lordschipe and of his nobless and of his myght. He duelleth comounly[228] in the cytee[229] of Suse[230] and þere is his principall palays[231] þat is so riche and so noble þat noman[232] wil trowe[233] it by estimacioun but[234] he had seen it. And abouen[235] the chief tour[236] of the palays ben ij rounde pomeles[237] of gold and in euerych[238] of hem[239] ben ij charboncles grete[240] and large þat schynen[241] full brighte vpon the nyght and the principall ȝates[242] of his palays ben of a precious ston[243] þat men clepen sardoyne.[244] And the bordure[245] and the barres ben of iuorye and the wyndowes of the halles and chambres ben of cristall and the tables whereon men eten[246] somme ben of emeraudes, summe[247] of amatyst[248] and somme of gold full of precious stones. And the pileres[249] þat beren[250] vp the tables ben of the same precious stones and the degrees[251] to gon vp to his throne where he sitteth at þe mete on[252] is of oniche,[253] anoþer is of cristall and anoþer of iaspre[254] grene, anoþer of amatyst, anoþer of sardyne,[255] anoþer of corneline.[256] And the vij þat he setteth onne his feet[257] is of crisolyte. And all þeise[258] degrees ben[259] bordured with fyn gold with the othere precyous stones sett with grete perles oryent. And the sydes of the sege[260] of his throne ben of emeraudes and bordured with gold full nobely and dubbed[261] with oþer precious stones and grete perles. And all the pileres in his chambre ben of fyne gold with precious stones and with manye[262] charboncles þat ȝeuen[263] gret lyght vpon the nyght[264] to all peple.[265] And all be it þat[266] the charboncle ȝeue lyght right ynow, natheles[267]

---

195. know nothing.
196. (to) cry.
197. John when.
198. battle against any.
199. banners borne.
200. fine.
201. high.
202. every (one).
203. crosses.
204. very.
205. guard.
206. ordered ten thousand.

207. more.
208. hundred thousand.
209. manner.
210. would.
211. standard.
212. countries.
213. we.
214. land at war.
215. number.
216. not counting.
217. host.
218. wings.

219. private retinue then.
220. borne.
221. (i.e., wood).
222. without paint.
223. Jesus.
224. death.
225. platter.
226. nobility.
227. turn.
228. lives usually.
229. city.
230. supposedly a town in India.

231. palace. The description that follows is very similar to that of the New Jerusalem in *Pearl* (cf. above, p. 747 ll. 985–1050).

232. no one.
233. believe.
234. hearsay unless.
235. above.
236. tower.
237. pommels.

238. each.
239. them.
240. carbuncles great.
241. shine.
242. gates.
243. stone.
244. call sardonyx.
245. border.

246. eat.
247. emeralds, some.
248. amethyst.
249. pillars.
250. bear.
251. steps.
252. meals one.
253. onyx.
254. jasper.

255. sard.
256. carnelian.
257. his feet rest on.
258. these.
259. are.
260. seat.
261. adorned.
262. many.
263. gives.

264. Many stones in the Middle Ages were thought to have the property of giving off light in the dark. Vincent de Beauvais states that diamonds light the dark and carbuncles also have such qualities. Whole rooms in Constantinople were said to have been illuminated in this way—as was the chamber when in 1898 Pierre and Marie Curie discovered the element radium, only modern counterpart to these lucent minerals of the Middle Ages.

265. people.   **266.** although.   **267.** enough, nevertheless.

at alle tymes brenneth[268] a vessell of cristall full of bawme[269] for to ȝeuen gode[270] smell and odour to the Emperour and to voyden awey[271] all wykkede eyres[272] and corrupciouns. And the forme of his bedd is of fyne saphires bended[273] with gold for to make him slepen[274] wel and to refreynen[275] him from lechrye.[276] For he will not lyȝe[277] with his wyfes[278] but iiij sithes[279] in the ȝeer[280] after the iiij cesouns,[281] and þat is only for to engendre children. He hath also a full[282] fayr palays and a noble at the cytee of Nyse[283] where þat he duelleth whan him[284] best lyketh.[285] But the ayr is not so attempree[286] as it is at the cytee of Suse. And ȝee schull vnderstonde[287] þat in all his contree ne[288] in the contrees þere all aboute men eten noght[289] but ones[290] in the day, as þat[291] men maken hem[292] in the court of the grete Chane.[293] And so þei eten euery day in his court mo[294] þanne xxx M[295] persones, withouten[296] goeres and comeres. But the xxx M persones of his contree ne of the contree of the grete Chane ne spenden noght[297] so moche gode[298] as don[299] xij M of oure contree. This Emperour Prestre Iohn[300] hath eueremore vij kynges with him to seruen[301] him and þei departen hire[302] seruice be certeyn monethes.[303] And with þeise kynges seruen all weys[304] lxxij dukes and ccc and lx erles. And all the dayes of the ȝeer þere eten in his houshold and in his court xij erchebysshoppes[305] and xx bisshoppes. And the Patriark[306] of seynt[307] Thomas is þere as is the Pope here. And the erchebisshoppes and the bisshoppes and the abbottes in þat contree ben alle kynges. And eueryche[308] of þeise grete[309] lordes knowen vel[310] ynow the attendance of hire seruyce. The on[311] is mayster[312] of his houshold, anoþer is his chambirleyn,[313] anoþer serueth him of[314] a dyssch, anoþer of the cuppe, anoþer is styward,[315] anoþer is mareschall,[316] anoþer is prynce of his armes; and þus is he full nobely and ryally[317] serued. And his lond dureth[318] in verry brede[319] iiij monethes iorneyes[320] and in lengthe out of mesure,[321] þat is to seyne,[322] all the yles[323] vnder erthe[324] þat wee supposen[325] to ben[326] vnder vs. Besyde the yle of Pentexoire þat is the lond of Prestre Iohn is a gret yle long and brode[327] þat men clepen[328] Milstorak[329] and it is in the lordschipe[330] of Prestre Iohn. In þat yle is gret plentee of godes.

Þere was dwellynge somtyme a riche man and it is not longe sithe[331] and men clept[332] him Gatholonabes[333] and he was full of cauteles[334] and of sotyll disceytes.[335] And he hadde a full fair castell and a strong in a mountayne, so strong and so noble þat noman[336] cowde devise[337] a fairere ne a strengere.[338] And he had let muren[339] all the mountayne aboute with a strong wall and a fair. And withjnne þo[340] walles he had the fairest gardyn þat ony[341] man myghte beholde and þerein were trees berynge[342] all maner[343] of frutes þat ony man cowde deuyse. And þerein were

---

268. burns.
269. balm.
270. good.
271. dispel.
272. bad odors.
273. bound.
274. sleep.
275. keep.
276. lechery.
277. lie.
278. wives.
279. times.
280. year.
281. seasons.
282. very.
283. Nysa.
284. when he.

285. pleases.
286. temperate.
287. you shall understand.
288. country nor.
289. not.
290. once.
291. as.
292. do.
293. Khan.
294. more.
295. thirty thousand.
296. not counting.
297. not spend not.
298. much money.
299. do.
300. John.

301. serve.
302. divide their.
303. by certain months.
304. always.
305. archbishops.
306. Patriarch.
307. Saint.
308. each.
309. great.
310. know well.
311. one.
312. master.
313. chamberlain.
314. from.
315. steward.
316. marshal.

317. royally.
318. land reaches.
319. true breadth.
320. journey.

321. measure.
322. say.
323. isles.
324. earth.

325. we suppose.
326. be.
327. broad.
328. call.

329. The name has many variants: *Mellestoire, Millestorte, Ministorte, Mileser,* etc. It is derived either from the Arabic *melahideh,* "infidels," "heretics," or from the town of Melazgherd in the province of Erzurum, north of Lake Van (eastern Turkey in the mountains of Armenia).

330. domain.
331. ago.
332. called.
333. The name is unexplained.
334. trickery.
335. subtle deceits.
336. no one.

337. could imagine.
338. stronger.
339. ordered walled.
340. those.
341. any.
342. bearing.
343. kinds.

also all maner vertuous[344] herbes of gode[345] smell and all oþer herbes also þat beren[346] faire floures.[347] And he had also in þat gardyn many faire welles, and beside þo welles he had lete make[348] faire halles and faire chambres depeynted[349] all with gold and azure. And þere weren[350] jn þat place many a[351] dyuerse thinges[352] and manye[353] dyuerse storyes.[354] And of bestes[355] and of bryddes[356] þat songen full delectabely[357] and meveden be craft,[358] þat[359] it semede[360] þat þei weren quyke.[361] And he had also in his gardyn all maner of foules[362] and of bestes þat ony man myghte thenke[363] on for to haue pley[364] or desport[365] to beholde hem.[366] And he had also in þat place the faireste damyseles[367] þat myghte ben founde vnder the age of xv ʒeer[368] and the faireste ʒonge[369] striplynges þat men myghte gete[370] of þat same age; and all þei weren clothed in clothes of gold full richely and he seyde[371] þat þo[372] weren aungeles.[373] And he had also let make iij welles faire and noble and all envyround[374] with ston[375] of jaspre, of cristall, dyapred[376] with gold and sett with precious stones and grete[377] orient perles. And he had made a

conduyt vnder erthe so þat the iij welles at his list on scholde renne[378] mylk, anoþer wyn[379] and anoþer hony;[380] and þat place be clept paradys. And whan[381] þat ony gode knyght þat was hardy and noble cam[382] to see this rialtee,[383] he wolde lede[384] him in to his paradys and schewen[385] him þeise[386] wonderfull thinges to[387] his desport and the merueyllous[388] and delicious song of dyuerse briddes and the faire damyseles and the faire welles of mylk, of wyn and of hony plentevous[389] rennynge. And he wolde let make[390] dyuerse jnstrumentes of musik to sownen[391] in an high tour[392] so merily þat it was ioye[393] for to here[394] and noman scholde see the craft[395] þere of. And þo he seyde[396] weren aungeles of God and þat place was paradys þat God had behight[397] to his frendes seyenge:[398] *Dabo vobis terram fluentem lacte et melle.*[399] And þanne wolde[400] he maken[401] hem to drynken[402] of a certeyn[403] drynk[404] whereof anon[405] þei scholden[406] be dronken.[407] And þanne wolde hem thinken[408] gretter delyt[409] þan þei hadden[410] before. And þan wolde he seye to hem þat ʒif[411] they wolde dyen[412] for him and for his

344. kinds (of) beneficial.
345. good.
346. bear.
347. flowers.
348. made.
349. adorned
350. were.
351. many.
352. various delights.
353. many.
354. pastimes.
355. beasts.
356. birds.
357. sang very delightfully.
358. moved through skill.
359. so that.
360. seemed.
361. alive.
362. birds.
363. think.
364. pleasure.
365. sport.
366. them.
367. damsels.
368. years.
369. young.
370. get.
371. said.
372. they.
373. angels.
374. surrounded.
375. stone.
376. adorned.
377. great.
378. pleasure one should run.
379. wine.
380. honey.
381. when.
382. came.
383. royal realm.
384. would lead.
385. show.
386. these.
387. for.
388. marvelous.
389. abundantly.
390. order made.
391. sound.
392. tower.
393. joy.
394. hear.

395. device. The French word is *menistriers*, "minstrels," misread and mistranslated as *mystère*, "craft," "guild," "mystery."
396. said.   **397.** promised.   **398.** saying.
399. "I shall give you a land flowing with milk and honey" Lev. 20:24).
400. then would.   **402.** drink.
401. make.   **403.** certain.

404. The *drynk* was the drug hashish (Indian hemp) by which members of the fanatical religious and political sect called the Assassins (a corruption of *hashish*, "hashish takers") were induced to have visions of paradise. The sect of Assassins, an offshoot of Islam and Magianism, was founded in 1090 by Hasan-ben-Sabbah (called the Old Man of the Mountain from his stronghold of Alamut south of the Caspian Sea), a Persian and a fellow student of Omar Khayyam in the academy of Nishapur. The spread of the movement to Lebanon coincided with political murders under the auspices of the Isma'ilite sect. Ritual religious murders were not new to the Orient, as evidenced by the 8th-century "Stranglers" of southern Iraq. The Assassins used only daggers, often consecrated, and there are poems praising their courage and loyalty. Stories of *houris* (maidens of paradise) and gardens of milk and honey are not substantiated in Isma'ilite sources, but Hasan commanded a huge, dedicated army of terrorists and spies and controlled many fortresses. Though his doctrine was successfully countered by Islamic orthodoxy in the universities, physical protection from his men was virtually impossible (cf. Bernard Lewis, "The Isma'ilites and the Assassins," in *A History of the Crusades, The First Hundred Years*, ed. Marshall W. Baldwin [Philadelphia, 1955]).

405. soon.   **408.** they think.   **411.** if.
406. should.   **409.** delight.   **412.** die.
407. drunk.   **410.** had.

loue þat after hire deth[413] þei scholde come to his paradys and þei scholden ben[414] of the age of þo[415] damyselles and þei scholde pleyen[416] with hem and ʒit[417] ben maydenes.[418] And after þat ʒit[419] scholde he putten[420] hem in a fayrere[421] paradys, where þat þei scholde see God of nature visibely in his magestee[422] and in his blisse. And þan wolde he schewe hem[423] his entent[424] and seye[425] hem þat ʒif þei wolde go sle[426] such a lord or such a man þat was his enemye or contrarious[427] to his list,[428] þat þei scholde not drede[429] to don[430] it and for to be slayn þerfore hem self,[431] for after hire deth he wolde putten hem in to anoþer paradys, þat was an C fold[432] fairere þan ony[433] of the tothere[434] and þere scholde þei dwellen[435] with the most fairest damyselles þat myghte be and pley with hem eueremore. And þus wenten[436] many dyuerse[437] lusty bacheleres[438] for to sle grete lordes in dyuerse contrees[439] þat weren[440] his enemyes and made hemself to ben slayn in hope to haue þat paradys. And þus often tyme he was revenged of his enemyes be[441] his sotyll disceytes[442] and false cawteles.[443] And whan the worthi men of the contree hadden perceyued[444] this sotyll falshod[445] of this Gatholonabes, þei assembled hem[446] with force and assayleden[447] his castell and slowen[448] him and destroyeden[449] all the faire places and all the nobletees[450] of þat paradys. The place of the welles and of the walles and of many oþer thinges ben ʒit apertly sene,[451] but the ricchesse[452] is voyded clene;[453] and it is not longes gon sith[454] þat place was destroyed.

---

413. their death.
414. be.
415. those.
416. play.
417. yet.
418. virgins.
419. further.
420. put.
421. fairer.
422. majesty.
423. show them.
424. intention.
425. tell.
426. slay.
427. contrary.
428. pleasure.
429. fear.
430. do.
431. themselves.
432. hundredfold.
433. any.
434. others.
435. dwell.
436. went.
437. various.
438. bachelors.
439. countries.
440. were.
441. by.
442. subtle deceits.
443. trickery.
444. perceived.
445. falsehood.
446. themselves.
447. assailed.
448. killed.
449. destroyed.
450. magnificence.
451. are yet plainly seen.
452. richness.
453. gone completely.
454. long ago since.

from MORTE DARTHUR

Sir Thomas Malory

DATE: 1460–70. ✦ MANUSCRIPTS: Aside from William Caxton's edition, which appeared July 31, 1485, a separate MS. (a. 1500) of Malory's works was found in 1934 in the Fellows' Library of Winchester College. The language of the works is late 15th century or very early Modern English. ✦ EDITIONS: Eugène Vinaver, *The Works of Sir Thomas Malory*, 3 vols. (Oxford, 1947; 2d ed., 1967), and a shorter one-volume edition published by the same press in 1954. The text is mainly from the Winchester MS.

In general Malory's early Modern English is very easy to read. Some confusion can be avoided if the following points are noted: (1) The word *and* often stands for *if* or *unless*. (2) The pronoun *hem* is the dative-accusative "them" but is often used reflexively as "themselves." (3) What seems like an interchange of *a* for *o* (*warke* = *work*, *warrse* = *worse*) and *a* for *e* (*harde* = *herde* "heard," *hart* = *herte*, "heart") is really an interchange of *a* for *e* before *r*. This is a late Middle English sound change, *er* becoming *ar*, resulting in some well-known differences between American and English pronunciation: *Derby*, *clerk*. (4) The plural of nouns is usually in *-is*/*-ys* (*talis* = *tales*, *swerdis* = *swords*).

There is much debate on the identification of Sir Thomas Malory, "knight-prisoner"; and the argument has been reopened recently by the interesting study of William Matthews (*The Ill-Framed Knight* [Berkeley, 1966]), which proposes a Yorkshire Malory who had seen military service in France. According to the accepted theory in the past, the author-translator-editor of the vast repository of Arthurian romances found in the French prose cycles was a Warwickshire knight, born c. 1405, active in his country's affairs—at times legally, at other times not. He served in France at Calais in 1436 and was a member of Parliament in 1445. After this he spent years in and out of jail, accused of ambushing the duke of Buckingham, robbing Coombe Abbey, forcing wives, raiding cattle herds. It may be that he was involved for political reasons, though the charges against him were extraordinarily numerous. His prison leisure was spent composing the *Morte*. He died there March 14, 1471, and was buried near Newgate. His turbulent career, dramatic escapes, and violent existence reflect the whole disorientation of 15th-century life caused by the Wars of the Roses.

Malory's contribution to English literature was a sharply paced prose style and the preservation of the Arthurian legend, which had lost vitality in France. His French sources were the *Suite du Merlin*, *Tristan de Léonois*, and the immense prose romance *Le Roman de Lancelot du Lac*, from which the section included here, Malory's book *The Most Piteous Tale of the Morte Arthur Saunz Guerdon*, is taken. The lengthy, cumbersome French plots were condensed by Malory. Tennyson's *Idylls of the King*, as well as all of our modern Arthurian treatments, must be traced to Malory, who truly helped

Arthur return from Avalon. But for him the reading public might today be as oblivious of the legends as Arthur himself was when he endured the blessed sleep. France has retained no interest in the stories; and neither Layamon nor Geoffrey of Monmouth nor the Alliterative *Morte Arthure* contain the whole poetic truth, the entire romance captured by Malory.

Slander and Strife

In May, whan[1] every harte floryshyth[2] and burgenyth[3] (for, as the season ys lusty to beholde and comfortable, so man and woman rejoysyth and gladith[4] of somer[5] commynge with his freyshe floures,[6] for wynter wyth hys rowghe[7] wyndis and blastis causyth lusty men and women to cowre and to syt by fyres), so thys season hit[8] befelle in the moneth[9] of May a grete angur[10] and unhappe[11] that stynted nat[12] tylle the floure of chyvalry of all the worlde was destroyed and slayn.

And all was longe uppon[13] two unhappy knyghtis whych were named sir Aggravayne and sir Mordred, that were brethirn[14] unto sir Gawayne. For thys sir Aggravayne and sir Mordred had ever a prevy[15] hate unto the quene, dame Gwenyver,[16] and to sir Launcelot; and dayly and nyghtly they ever wacched[17] uppon sir Launcelot.

So hyt myssefortuned[18] sir Gawayne and all hys brethirne were in kynge Arthurs chambir, and than[19] sir Aggravayne seyde[20] thus opynly,[21] and nat in no counceyle,[22] that manye[23] knyghtis myght here:[24]

"I mervayle[25] that we all be nat ashamed bothe to se[26] and to know how sir Launcelot lyeth dayly and nyghtly by the quene. And all we know well

that hit ys so, and hit ys shamefully suffird of[27] us all that we shulde[28] suffir so noble a kynge as kynge Arthur ys to be shamed."

Than spake[29] sir Gawayne and seyde,

"Brothir, sir Aggravayne, I pray you and charge you, meve[30] no such maters[31] no more afore[32] me, for wyte[33] you well, I woll[34] nat be of youre counceyle."[35]

"So God me helpe," seyde sir Gaherys and sir Gareth, "we woll nat be knowyn of[36] your dedis."[37]

"Than woll I!" seyde sir Mordred.

"I lyve[38] you well," seyde sir Gawayne, "for ever unto all unhappynes, sir, ye woll graunte.[39] And I wolde[40] that ye leffte all thys and make you[41] nat so bysy,[42] for I know," seyde sir Gawayne, "what woll falle of[43] hit."

"Falle whatsumever[44] falle may," seyde sir Aggravayne, "I woll disclose hit to the kynge!"

"Nat be[45] my counceyle," seyde sir Gawayne, "for, and[46] there aryse warre and wrake[47] betwyxte sir Launcelot and us, wyte you well, brothir, there woll many kynges and grete lordis holde with sir Launcelot. Also, brothir, sir Aggravayne," seyde sir Gawayne, "ye muste remembir how oftyntymes sir Launcelot hath rescowed[48] the kynge and the quene; and the beste of us all had

---

1. when.	**9.** month.	**17.** spied.	**25.** marvel.	**33.** know.	**41.** yourself.
2. heart flourishes.	**10.** great anger.	**18.** by ill fortune.	**26.** see.	**34.** will.	**42.** busy.
3. burgeons.	**11.** misfortune.	**19.** then.	**27.** allowed by.	**35.** counsel.	**43.** happen from.
4. are glad.	**12.** stopped not.	**20.** said.	**28.** should.	**36.** know about.	**44.** whatever.
5. for summer's.	**13.** because of.	**21.** openly.	**29.** spoke.	**37.** deeds.	**45.** by.
6. fresh flowers.	**14.** brothers.	**22.** council.	**30.** discuss.	**38.** believe.	**46.** if.
7. rough.	**15.** secret.	**23.** many.	**31.** matters.	**39.** consent.	**47.** hostility.
8. it.	**16.** Guinevere.	**24.** hear.	**32.** before.	**40.** would.	**48.** rescued.

bene full[49] colde at the harte-roote had nat sir Launcelot bene bettir than we, and that hathe preved[50] hymselff full ofte. And as for my parte," seyde sir Gawayne, "I woll never be ayenste[51] sir Launcelot for[52] one dayes dede, that was whan[53] he rescowed me frome[54] kynge Carados of the Dolerous Towre[55] and slew hym and saved my lyff.[56] Also, brother, sir Aggravayne and sir Modred, in lyke wyse sir Launcelot rescowed you bothe and three score and two frome sir Tarquyne.[57] And therefore, brothir, methynkis[58] such noble dedis and kyndnes shulde be remembirde."

"Do ye as ye lyste,"[59] seyde sir Aggravayne, "for I woll layne hit[60] no lenger."[61]

So wyth thes[62] wordis cam[63] in sir Arthur.

"Now, brothir," seyde sir Gawayne, "stynte[64] youre stryff."[65]

"That woll I nat,"[66] seyde sir Aggravayne and sir Mordred.

"Well, woll ye so?" seyde sir Gawayne. "Than God spede[67] you, for I woll nat here of youre talis, nothir[68] be of your counceile."

"No more woll I," seyde[69] sir Gaherys.

"Nother I," seyde sir Gareth, "for I shall never say evyll by[70] that man that made me knyght."

And therewythall[71] they three departed makynge grete dole.[72]

"Alas!" seyde sir Gawayne and sir Gareth, "now ys thys realme holy[73] destroyed and myscheved,[74] and the noble felyshyp[75] of the Rounde Table shall be disparbeled."[76]

So they departed, and than[77] kynge Arthure asked them what noyse they made.

"My lorde," seyde sir Aggravayne, "I shall telle you, for I may kepe[78] hit no lenger. Here ys I and my brothir sir Modred brake unto[79] my brothir sir Gawayne, sir Gaherys and to sir Gareth; for thys ys all, to make hit shorte: we know all that sir Launcelot holdith your quene, and hath done longe, and we be[80] your syster sunnes,[81] we may suffir[82] hit no lenger. And all we wote[83] that ye shulde[84] be above sir Launcelot, and ye ar[85] the kynge that made hym knyght, and therefore we woll[86] preve hit that he is a traytoure[87] to youre person."

"Gyff[88] hit be so," seyde the kynge, "wyte[89] you well, he ys non[90] othir. But I wolde[91] be lothe[92] to begyn such a thynge but[93] I myght have prevys[94] of hit, for sir Launcelot ys an hardy knyght, and all ye know that he ys the beste knyght amonge us all, and but if[95] he be takyn[96] with[97] the dede[98]

---

49. been very.   51. against.   53. when.
50. proved.   52. because of.   54. from.
55. Gawain was captured by the giant Carados of the Tour Douloureuse because he had supposedly murdered the giant's uncle; in the French prose *Lancelot* he is rescued from this predicament by Lancelot. In folklore, it may be remembered, the uncle-nephew relationship was closer than that of father-son (see below, Arthur's relationship with Gawain and Modred; cf. above, p. 77n).
56. life.
57. Sir Tarquin was the brother of Carados of the Tour Douloureuse, who was killed by Lancelot. In revenge Tarquin killed a hundred knights of the Round Table and imprisoned sixty-four, all of whom were released when Tarquin in turn was mortally wounded. Such was Tarquin's promise, and Lancelot kept him to his word.
58. I think.   63. came.   68. nor.
59. please.   64. stop.   69. said.
60. conceal it.   65. strife.   70. of.
61. longer.   66. not.   71. thereupon.
62. these.   67. prosper.   72. great lament.

73. wholly.   76. dispersed.   79. at odds with.
74. hurt.   77. then.   80. are.
75. fellowship.   78. keep.
81. sister's sons. There is a mix-up of sources here. In Geoffrey of Monmouth and other versions, Ambrosius Aurclianus is confused with his nephew Arthur; and Gawain and Modred are mistakenly called his nephews, whereas it is not his sister but Arthur's sister Anna, daughter of King Uther Pendragon, who marries King Loth of Lodonesia (Orkney) and Norway, from which union come Gawain and Modred, Arthur's nephews. However, Geoffrey also mentions Modred as the son of Arthur and his sister Anna, thus son and nephew alike. In Malory, Anna is named Morgawse, mother also of Gareth, Gaheris, and Agravain. It is not hard to become lost in the jungle of Arthurian family trees.
82. allow.   88. if.   94. proof.
83. know.   89. know.   95. unless.
84. should.   90. no.   96. caught.
85. are.   91. would.   97. in.
86. will.   92. loath.   98. act.
87. traitor.   93. unless.

he woll fyght with hym that bryngith up the noyse,[99] and I know no knyght that ys able to macch[100] hym. Therefore, and[101] hit be sothe[102] as ye say, I wolde that he were takyn with the dede."

For, as the Freynshe[103] booke[104] seyth, the kynge was full[105] lothe that such a noyse shulde be uppon[106] sir Launcelot and his quene; for the kynge had a demyng[107] of hit, but he wold nat here[108] thereoff, for sir Launcelot had done so much for hym and for the quene so many tymes that wyte you well the kynge loved hym passyngly[109] well.

"My lorde," seyde sir Aggravayne, "ye shall ryde to-morne an-huntyng,[110] and doute[111] ye nat, sir Launcelot woll nat go wyth you. And so whan[112] hit drawith towarde nyght ye may sende the quene worde that ye woll ly[113] oute all that nyght, and so may ye sende for your cookis. And than, uppon payne of deth,[114] that nyght we shall take hym wyth the quene, and we shall brynge hym unto you, quycke[115] or dede."[116]

"I woll well,"[117] seyde the kynge. "Than I counceyle[118] you to take with you sure felyshyp."[119]

"Sir," seyde sir Aggravayne, "my brothir sir Mordred and I woll take wyth us twelve knyghtes of the Rounde Table."

"Beware," seyde[120] kynge Arthure, "for I warne you, ye shall fynde hym wyght."[121]

"Lat[122] us deale!"[123] seyde sir Aggravayne and sir Mordred.

So on the morne kynge Arthure rode an-huntyng and sente worde to the quene that he wolde be oute all that nyght. Than sir Aggravayne and sir Mordred gate to[124] them twelve knyghtes and hyd hem-selff[125] in a chambir in the castell of Carlyle.[126] And thes[127] were their namys: sir Collgrevaunce, sir Mador de la Porte, sir Gyngalyne, sir Mellyot de Logris, sir Petipace of Wynshylsé, sir Galleron of Galoway, sir Melyon de la Mountayne, sir Ascomore, sir Gromoresom Erioure, sir Cursesalayne, sir Florence, and sir Lovell. So thes twelve knyghtes were with sir Mordred and sir Aggravayne, and all they were of Scotlonde,[128] other ellis[129] of sir Gawaynes kynne, othir well-wyllers[130] to hys brothir.

So whan the nyght cam[131] sir Launcelot tolde sir Bors how he wolde go that nyght and speke[132] wyth the quene.

"Sir," seyde sir Bors, "ye shall nat[133] go thys nyght be[134] my counceyle."

"Why?" seyde sir Launcelot.

"Sir, for I drede me[135] ever of sir Aggravayne that waytith uppon you dayly to do you shame and us all. And never gaff[136] my harte ayenste[137] no goynge[138] that ever ye wente[139] to the quene so much as now, for I mystruste[140] that the kynge ys oute thys nyght frome[141] the quene bycause peradventure[142] he hath layne[143] som wacche[144] for you and the quene. Therefore I dred me sore of som treson."[145]

"Have ye no drede,"[146] seyde sir Launcelot, "for I shall go and com agayne and make no taryynge."[147]

Sir," seyde sir Bors, "that me[148] repentis,[149] for I drede me sore that youre goyng thys nyght shall wratth[150] us all."

---

99. rumor.
100. match.
101. if.
102. true.
103. French.
104. This would be the prose *Lancelot* of the Vulgate cycle, although the section is not found there nor in any other source. Malory usually cites an authority to disguise his own contributions.
105. very.
106. about.
107. suspicion.
108. hear.
109. exceedingly.
110. tomorrow a-hunting.
111. doubt.
112. when.
113. stay.
114. death.
115. alive.
116. dead.
117. so desire it.
118. counsel.
119. (a) trusted group.
120. said.
121. tough.
122. let.
123. act.
124. got with.
125. themselves.
126. Carlisle in Cumberland is often confused with Caerleon-upon-Usk in Monmouthshire, site of the mythical Camelot.
127. these.
128. Scotland.
129. or else.
130. friends.
131. came.
132. speak.
133. not.
134. by.
135. am afraid.
136. was set.
137. heart against.
138. going (of yours).
139. made.
140. suspect.
141. from.
142. because perhaps.
143. laid.
144. trap.
145. treason.
146. fear.
147. delay.
148. I.
149. am sorry about.
150. harm.

"Fayre neveawe,"[151] seyd sir Launcelot, "I mervayle me[152] much why ye say thus, sytthyn[153] the quene hath sente for me. And wyte[154] you well, I woll[155] nat be so much a cowarde, but she shall undirstonde[156] I woll se[157] her good grace."

"God spede[158] you well," seyde sir Bors, "and sende you sounde and sauff[159] agayne!"

So sir Launcelot departed and toke[160] hys swerde[161] undir hys arme, and so he walked in hys mantell, that noble knyght, and put hymselff in grete jouparté.[162] And so he past[163] on tylle he cam to the quenys chambir, and so lyghtly[164] he was had[165] into the chambir.

For, as the Freynshhe[166] booke seyth, the quene and sir Launcelot were togydirs.[167] And whether they were abed other at other maner[168] of disportis,[169] me lyste[170] nat thereof make[171] no mencion,[172] for love that tyme was nat as love ys nowadayes.[173]

But thus as they were togydir there cam sir Aggravayne and sir Mordred wyth twelve knyghtes with them of the Rounde Table, and they seyde[174] with grete cryyng and scaryng[175] voyce,

"Thou traytoure,[176] sir Launcelot, now ar[177] thou takyn!"[178]

And thus they cryed wyth a lowde voyce, that all the courte myght hyre hit.[179] And thes[180] fourtene knyghtes all were armed at all poyntis, as[181] they shulde[182] fyght in a batayle.[183]

"Alas!" seyde quene Gwenyver,"[184] now ar we myscheved[185] bothe!"

"Madame," seyde sir Launcelot, "ys there here ony[186] armour within you that myght cover my body wythall?[187] And if there be ony, gyff[188] hit me and I shall sone stynte[189] their malice, by the grace of God!"

"Now, truly," seyde the quyne,[190] "I have none[191] armour nother helme, shylde,[192] swerde, nother speare, wherfore I dred me sore oure longe love ys com to a myschyvus[193] ende. For I here[194] by their noyse there be many noble knyghtes, and well I wote[195] they be[196] surely armed, and ayenst them ye may make no resistence. Wherefore ye ar lykly[197] to be slayne, and than[198] shall I be brente![199] For and[200] ye myght ascape[201] them," seyde the quene, "I wolde nat doute[202] but that ye wolde rescowe[203] me in what daunger that I ever[204] stood in."

"Alas!" seyde sir Launcelot, "in all my lyff[205] thus was I never bestad[206] that I shulde be thus shamefully slayne, for lake[207] of myne armour."

---

151. nephew.
152. wonder.
153. since.
154. know.
155. will.
156. understand.
157. see.
158. prosper.
159. safe.
160. took.
161. sword.
162. great danger.
163. passed.
164. easily.
165. received.
166. French.
167. together.
168. kind.
169. pastimes.
170. wish.
171. (to) make.
172. mention.

173. Malory did not understand the traditions and rituals of courtly love, the cult of *service d'amour* as shown in the old French romances. He considered it a nobler, more spiritual relationship than the physical love he himself observed in the hurly-burly 15th century, and he mourned for the good old days. His introductory passage to *The Knight of the Cart* is often quoted:

For lyke as wynter rasure doth allway arace and deface grene summer, so faryth hit by unstable love in man and woman, for in many persones there ys no stabylite. For we may se all day for a lytyll blaste of wyntres rasure, anone we shall deface and lay aparte trew love, for lytyll or nowght, that coste much thynge. Thys ys no wysedome nother stabylité, but hit ys feyblenes of nature and grete disworshyp whosomever usyth thys. . . .

But nowadayes men cannat love sevennyght but they must have all their desyres. That love may nat endure by reson, for where they bethe sone accorded and hasty, heete sone keelyth. And ryght so faryth the love nowadayes, sone hote sone colde. Thys ys no stabylyté. But the olde love was nat so. For men and women coude love togydirs seven yerys, and no lycoures lustis was betwyxte them, and than was love, trouthe and faythefulnes. And so in lyke wyse was used such love in kynge Arthurs dayes.

Wherefore I lykken love nowadayes unto somer and wynter. For lyke as the tone ys colde and the othir ys hote, so faryth love nowadayes. . . .

174. said.
175. frightening.
176. traitor.
177. are.
178. caught.
179. hear it.
180. these.
181. as if.
182. should.
183. battle.
184. Guinevere.
185. harmed.
186. any.
187. at all.
188. give.
189. soon stop.
190. queen.
191. no.
192. nor helmet, shield.
193. bad.
194. hear.
195. know.
196. are.
197. likely.
198. then.
199. burned (at the stake).
200. if.
201. escape.
202. would not doubt.
203. rescue.
204. whatever danger that I.
205. life.
206. hard pressed.
207. lack.

But ever sir Aggravayne and sir Mordred cryed, "Traytour knyght, come oute of the quenys chambir! For wyte thou wel thou arte besette so that thou shalt nat ascape."

"A,[208] Jesu mercy!" seyd sir Launcelot, "thys shamefull cry and noyse I may nat suffir,[209] for better were[210] deth[211] at onys[212] than thus to endure thys payne."

Than he toke the quene in hys armys and kyssed her and seyde,

"Moste nobelest Crysten[213] quene, I besech[214] you, as ye have ben[215] ever my speciall good lady, and I at all tymes your poure[216] knyght and trew[217] unto my power, and as I never fayled you in ryght nor in wronge sytthyn[218] the firste day kynge Arthur made me knyght, that ye woll[219] pray for my soule if that I be slayne. For well I am assured that sir Bors, my nevewe[220] and all the remenaunte[221] of my kynne, with sir Lavayne and sir Urré,[222] that they woll nat fayle you to rescow you from the fyer.[223] And therfore, myne owne lady, recomforte yourselff,[224] whatsomever[225] com[226] of me, that ye go with sir Bors, my nevew, and they all woll do you all the plesure[227] that they may, and ye shall lyve lyke a quene uppon my londis."[228]

"Nay, sir Launcelot, nay!" seyde the quene. "Wyte[229] thou well that I woll nat lyve longe aftir thy dayes. But and ye be slayne I woll take my dethe as mekely[230] as ever ded marter[231] take hys dethe for Jesu Crystes sake."

"Well, madame," seyde[232] sir Launcelot, syth[233] hit ys so that the day ys com that oure love muste departe,[234] wyte you well I shall selle my lyff as dere[235] as I may. And a thousandfolde," seyde sir Launcelot, "I am more hevyar[236] for you than for myselff! And now I had levir[237] than to be lorde of all Crystendom that I had sure armour uppon me, that men myght speke[238] of my dedys or[239] ever I were slayne."

"Truly," seyde the quene, "and hit[240] myght please God, I wolde that they wolde take and sle[241] me and suffir[242] you to ascape."

"That shall never be," seyde sir Launcelot, "God deffende me frome[243] such a shame! But Jesu Cryste, be Thou my shylde[244] and myne armoure!"

And therewith[245] sir Launcelot wrapped hys mantel aboute hys arme well and surely; and by than they had getyn[246] a grete[247] fourme[248] oute of the halle, and therewith they all russhed at the dore.

"Now, fayre lordys," seyde sir Launcelot, "leve[249] youre noyse and youre russhynge, and I shall sette opyn[250] thys dore, and than[251] may ye do with me what hit lykith[252] you."

"Com of,[253] than," seyde they all, "and do hit, for hit avaylyth the nat[254] to stryve ayenste[255] us all! And therefore lat[256] us into thys chambir, and we shall save thy lyff[257] untyll thou com to kynge Arthur."

Than sir Launcelot unbarred the dore, and with hys lyffte honde[258] he hylde[259] hit opyn a lytyll,[260] that but one man myght com in at onys. And so there cam[261] strydyng a good knyght, a much[262] man and a large, and hys name was

---

208. ah.
209. abide.
210. would be.
211. death.
212. once.
213. Christian.
214. beseech.
215. been.
216. poor.
217. true.
218. since.
219. will.
220. nephew.
221. rest.
222. Sir Urré of Hungary had been severely wounded in a tournament in Spain. He was cursed by the mother of a knight he had slain, so that his wounds would ever fester and bleed until they had been "searched" by the best knight in the world. Lancelot cured him, and Sir Urré remained faithful to Lancelot, eventually following him into exile. Sir Urré and Sir Lavayne, who married Urré's sister, had been made knights of the Round Table.
223. fire.
224. take courage again.
225. whatever.
226. become.
227. pleasure.
228. lands.
229. know.
230. meekly.
231. did martyr.
232. said.
233. since.
234. end.
235. dear.
236. sadder.
237. rather.
238. speak.
239. deeds before.
240. it.
241. slay.
242. allow.
243. from.
244. shield.
245. thereupon.
246. gotten.
247. great.
248. bench.
249. stop.
250. open.
251. then.
252. pleases.
253. on.
254. you not.
255. against.
256. let.
257. life.
258. left hand.
259. held.
260. little.
261. came.
262. great.

called sir Collgrevaunce of Goore. And he wyth a swerde streke[263] at sir Launcelot myghtyly, and so he put asyde[264] the streke,[265] and gaff[266] hym such a buffette upon the helmet that he felle grovelyng dede[267] wythin the chambir dore.

Than sir Launcelot with grete myght drew the knyght within the chambir dore. And than sir Launcelot, wyth helpe of the quene and her ladyes, he was lyghtly[268] armed in Collgrevaunce[269] armoure. And ever stood sir Aggravayne and sir Mordred, cryyng,

"Traytoure knyght! Come forthe oute of the quenys chambir!"

"Sires, leve youre noyse," seyde sir Launcelot, "for wyte you well, sir Aggravayne, ye shall nat preson[270] me thys nyght! And therefore, and[271] ye do be[272] my counseyle,[273] go ye all frome thys chambir dore and make you no suche cryyng and such maner[274] of sclaundir[275] as ye do. For I promyse you be my knyghthode,[276] and ye woll[277] departe and make no more noyse, I shall as to-morne appyere afore[278] you all and before the kynge, and than lat hit sene whych[279] of you all, other ellis[280] ye all, that woll depreve[281] me of treson.[282] And there shall I answere you, as a knyght shulde,[283] that hydir[284] I cam to the quene for no maner of male engyne,[285] and that woll I preve[285] and make hit good uppon you wyth my hondys."

"Fye uppon the, traytour,"[287] seyde[288] sir Aggravayne and sir Mordred, "for we woll have the magré[289] thyne hede[290] and sle the, and we lyste![291] For we let the wyte[292] we have the choyse of[293] kynge Arthure to save the other sle the."

"A,[294] sirres," seyde sir Launcelot, "ys there none other grace with you? Than kepe[295] youre-selff!"

And then sir Launcelot sette all opyn the chambir dore, and myghtyly and knyghtly[296] he strode in amonge them. And anone[297] at the firste stroke he slew sir Aggravayne, and anone[298] aftir twelve of hys felowys.[299] Within a whyle he had layde them down colde to the erthe,[300] for there was none of the twelve knyghtes myght stonde[301] sir Launcelot one buffet. And also he wounded sir Mordred, and therewithall[302] he fled with all hys myght. And than sir Launcelot returned agayne unto the quene and seyde,

"Madame, now wyte you well, all oure trew[303] love ys brought to an ende, for now wyll kyng Arthur ever be my foo.[304] And therefore, madam, and hit lyke[305] you that I may have you with me, I shall save you frome[306] all maner[307] adventures daungers."[308]

"Sir, that ys nat[309] beste," seyde the quene, "mesemyth,[310] for now ye have don so much harme hit woll be beste that ye holde you[311] styll with this. And if ye se[312] that as to-morne they woll putte me unto dethe,[313] than may ye res-cowe[314] me as ye thynke beste."

"I woll well,[315] seyde sir Launcelot, "for have ye no doute,[316] whyle I am a man lyvyng I shall rescow you."

And than[317] he kyste[318] her, and ayther[319] of hem gaff[320] othir a rynge, and so the quene he leffte there and wente untyll[321] hys lodgynge.

Whan[322] sir Bors saw sir Launcelot he was never so glad of hys home-comynge.

---

263. sword struck.
264. parried.
265. stroke.
266. gave.
267. dead.
268. quickly.
269. Collgrevaunce's.
270. imprison.
271. if.
272. act by.
273. advice.

274. kind.
275. slander.
276. knighthood.
277. will.
278. by tomorrow appear before.
279. seen which (one).
280. or else.
281. convict.
282. treason.

283. should.
284. hither.
285. evil designs.
286. prove.
287. traitor.
288. said.
289. in spite of.
290. warning.
291. please.
292. know.
293. from.

294. ah.
295. guard.
296. befitting a knight.
297. at once.
298. then.
299. companions.
300. earth.
301. stand.
302. thereupon.
303. true.

304. foe.
305. it pleases.
306. from.
307. manner (of).
308. perilous dangers.
309. not.
310. I believe.
311. yourself.
312. see.
313. death.

314. rescue.
315. will do so.
316. doubt.
317. then.
318. kissed.
319. either.
320. them gave.
321. to.
322. when.

"Jesu mercy!" seyde sir Launcelot, "why be ye all armed? What meanyth thys?"

"Sir," seyde sir Bors, "aftir ye were departed from us we all that ben[323] of your blood and youre well-wyllars[324] were so adretched[325] that som of us lepe[326] oute of oure beddis naked, and som in their dremys[327] caught naked swerdys[328] in their hondis.[329] And therefore," seyde sir Bors, "we demed[330] there was som grete stryff[331] on honde, and so we demed that we were betrapped with[332] som treson; and therefore we made us[333] thus redy, [334] what nede that ever[335] ye were in."

"My fayre nevew,"[336] seyde sir Launcelot unto sir Bors, "now shall ye wyte all that thys nyght I was more harde bestad[337] than ever I was dayes[338] of my lyff.[339] And thanked be God, I am[340] myselff ascaped[341] their daungere."[342] And so he tolde them all how and in what maner,[343] as ye have harde toforehande.[344] "And therefore, my felowys," seyde[345] sir Launcelot, "I pray you all that ye woll[346] be of harte[347] good, and helpe me in what nede that ever I stonde,[348] for now ys warre comyn[349] to us all."

"Sir," seyde sir Bors, "all ys wellcom that God sendyth us, and as we have takyn[350] much weale[351] with you and much worshyp,[352] we woll take the woo[353] with you as we have takyn the weale."

And therefore they seyde, all the good knyghtes,

"Loke[354] ye take no discomforte! For there ys no bondys[355] of knyghtes undir hevyn[356] but we shall be able to greve[357] them as muche as they us, and therefore discomforte nat yourselff by[358] no maner. And we shall gadir togyder[359] all that we love and that lovyth us, and what that ye woll have done shall be done. And therefore lat[360] us take the wo[361] and the joy togydir."

"Grauntmercy,"[362] seyde sir Launcelot, "of[363] youre good comforte, for in my grete distresse, fayre nevew, ye comforte me gretly. But thys, my fayre nevew, I wolde that ye ded,[364] in all haste that ye may or hit[365] ys far dayes paste:[366] that ye woll loke[367] in their lodgynge that ben lodged nyghe[368] here aboute the kynge, whych woll holde with me and whych woll nat.[369] For now I wolde[370] know whych were my frendis fro[371] my fooes."[372]

"Sir," seyde sir Bors, "I shall do my payne,[373] and or hit be seven of the clok[374] I shall wyte[375] of such as ye have dout fore,[376] who that woll holde with you."

Than[377] sir Bors called unto hym[378] sir Lyonel, sir Ector de Marys, sir Blamour de Ganys, sir Bleoberys de Ganys, sir Gahalantyne, sir Galyhodyn, sir Galyhud, sir Menaduke, sir Vyllyers the Valyaunte, syr Hebes le Renowne, sir Lavayne, sir Urré of Hungry,[379] sir Neroveus, sir Plenoryus (for thes[380] two were knyghtes that sir Launcelot wan[381] upon a brydge, and therefore they wolde never be ayenst[382] hym), and sir Harry le Fyz Lake, and sir Selyses of the Dolerous Towre, sir Mellyas de Lyle, and sir Bellangere le Bewse that was sir Alysaundir le Orphelyne sone;[383] bycause[384] hys modir[385] was Alys la Beale Pelleryn, and she

---

323. are.
324. friends.
325. perturbed.
326. leaped.
327. dreams.
328. swords.
329. hands.
330. believed.
331. great strife.
332. entrapped by.
333. ourselves.
334. ready.

335. (to meet) whatever need.
336. nephew.
337. pressed.
338. (in) days.
339. life.
340. have.
341. escaped.
342. threat.
343. manner.
344. heard before.
345. said.

346. will.
347. heart.
348. stand (in).
349. come.
350. received.
351. benefit.
352. honor.
353. woe.
354. see (that).
355. group.
356. heaven.
357. grieve.

358. in.
359. gather together.
360. let.
361. woe.
362. thank you.
363. for.
364. did.
365. before it.

366. past day.
367. see.
368. near.
369. not.
370. would.
371. from.
372. foes.
373. best.

374. clock.
375. know.
376. doubt about.
377. then.
378. himself.
379. Hungary.
380. these.
381. defeated.

382. against. Lancelot had met their challenge at a bridge, overcome them, and spared their lives. Many of those he had conquered swore eternal allegiance to Lancelot.
383. Orphelyne's son. **384.** because. **385.** mother.

was kyn unto sir Launcelot, he hylde[386] with hym. So cam[387] sir Palomydes and sir Saphir, hys brothir; sir Clegis, sir Sadok, sir Dynas and sir Clarryus of Cleremount.

So thes two-and-twenty knyghtes drew hem[388] togydirs, and by than[389] they were armed and on horsebak they promysed sir Launcelot to do what he wolde. Than there felle to[390] them, what[391] of Northe Walys and of Cornwayle, for sir Lamorakes sake and for sir Trystrames sake,[392] to the numbir of a seven score knyghtes. Than spake[393] sir Launcelot:

"Wyte you well, I have bene[394] ever syns[395] I cam to thys courte well-wylled[396] unto my lorde Arthur and unto my lady quene Gwenyver[397] unto my power. And thys nyght bycause my lady the quene sente for me to speke[398] with her, I suppose hit was made[399] by treson;[400] howbehit[401] I dare largely excuse her person, natwithstondyng[402] I was there be[403] a forecaste nerehond[404] slayne but as[405] Jesu provyded for me."

And than that noble knyght sir Launcelot tolde hem[406] how he was harde bestad[407] in the quenys chambir, and how and in what maner[408] he ascaped[409] from them:

"And therefore wyte you well, my fayre lordis, I am sure there nys[410] but warre unto me and to myne. And for cause[411] I have slayne thys nyght sir Aggravayne, sir Gawaynes brothir, and at the leste[412] twelve of hys felowis,[413] and for thys cause

now am I sure of mortall warre.[414] For thes knyghtes were sente by kynge Arthur to betray me, and therefore the kyng woll[415] in thys hete[416] and malice jouge[417] the quene unto brennyng,[418] and that may nat I suffir[419] that she shulde[420] be brente[421] for my sake. For and[422] I may be harde[423] and suffirde and so takyn,[424] I woll feyght[425] for the quene, that she ys a trew[426] lady untyll[427] her lorde. But the kynge in hys hete, I drede,[428] woll nat[429] take me as I ought to be takyn."

"My lorde, sir Launcelot," seyde[430] sir Bors, "be myne advyce, ye shall take the woo[431] wyth the weall.[432] And sytthyn hit[433] ys fallyn[434] as hit ys, I counceyle[435] you to kepe[436] youreselff, for and ye woll youreselffe there ys no felyshyp[437] of knyghtes crystynde[438] that shall do you wronge. And also I woll counceyle you, my lorde, that my lady quene Gwenyver, and she be in ony[439] distres, insomuch as she ys in payne for youre sake, that ye knyghtly rescow[440] her; for and ye ded[441] ony other wyse[442] all the worlde wolde[443] speke you[444] shame to the worldis ende. Insomuch as ye were takyn[445] with her, whether ye ded[446] ryght othir[447] wronge, hit ys now youre parte to holde wyth the quene, that she be nat slayne and put to a myschevous deth.[448] For and she so dye,[449] the shame shall be evermore youres."

"Now Jesu deffende me from shame," seyde sir Launcelot, "and kepe and save my lady the quene from vylany[450] and shamefull dethe, and

---

386. held.   **388.** themselves.   **390.** joined.
387. came.   **389.** when.   **391.** men.
392. Sir Tristram kept Isolde safe from the wrath of King Mark in Lancelot's castle of Joyeuse Garde (see below, nn: 482, 484), and Lancelot's hospitality in a time of need was remembered by Tristram's followers.
393. spoke.   **400.** treason.   **407.** pressed.
394. been.   **401.** although.   **408.** manner.
395. since.   **402.** nevertheless.   **409.** escaped.
396. friendly.   **403.** by.   **410.** is nothing.
397. Guinevere.   **404.** plot almost.   **411.** because.
398. speak.   **405.** except that.   **412.** least.
399. done.   **406.** them.   **413.** companions.

414. war to the death.   **426.** true.   **439.** any.
415. will.   **427.** unto.   **440.** chivalrously rescue.
416. anger.   **428.** fear.
417. doom.   **429.** not.   **441.** acted.
418. burning.   **430.** said.   **442.** way.
419. allow.   **431.** woe.   **443.** would.
420. should.   **432.** happiness.   **444.** of you.
421. burned.   **433.** since it.   **445.** caught.
422. if.   **434.** happened.   **446.** did.
423. heard.   **435.** counsel.   **447.** or.
424. accepted.   **436.** guard.   **448.** unfortunate death.
425. fight.   **437.** fellowship.   **449.** die.
     438. Christian.   **450.** villainy.

that she never be destroyed in[451] my defaute![452] Wherefore, my fayre lordys, my kyn and my fryndis,"[453] seyde sir Launcelot, "what woll ye do?"

And anone[454] they seyde all with one voyce, "We woll do as ye woll do."

"Than[455] I put thys case unto you," seyde sir Launcelot, "that my lorde, kynge Arthur, by evyll counceile woll to-morne[456] in hys hete put my lady the quene unto the fyre and there to be brente, than, I pray you, counceile me what ys beste for me to do."

Than they seyde all at onys[457] with one voice, "Sir, us thynkis[458] beste that ye knyghtly rescow the quene. Insomuch as she shall be brente, hit ys for youre sake; and hit ys to suppose,[459] and ye myght be handeled,[460] ye shulde have the same dethe, othir ellis[461] a more shamefuller dethe. And, sir, we say all that ye have rescowed her frome[462] her deth many tyms for other mennes quarels; therefore us[463] semyth[464] hit ys more youre worshyp[465] that ye rescow the quene from thys quarell,[466] insomuch that she hath hit for your sake."

Than sir Launcelot stood stylle and sayde, "My fayre lordis, wyte[467] you well I wolde be lothe[468] to do that thynge that shulde dishonour you or my bloode; and wyte you well I wolde be full[469] lothe that my lady the quene shulde

dye such a shamefull deth. But and hit be so that ye woll[470] counceyle me to rescow her, I must do much harme or[471] I rescow her, and peradventure[472] I shall there destroy som of my beste fryndis, and that shold moche repente[473] me. And peradventure there be som, and[474] they coude[475] wel brynge it aboute or disobeye my lord kynge Arthur, they wold sone[476] come to me, the whiche I were[477] loth to hurte. And if so be that I may wynne the quene away, where shall I kepe[478] her?"

"Sir, that shall be the leste[479] care of us all," seyde[480] sir Bors, "for how ded the moste noble knyght sir Trystram? By youre good wyll, kept nat[481] he with hym La Beall Isode[482] here three yere[483] in Joyous Garde,[484] the whych was done by youre althers avyce?[485] And that same place ys youre owne, and in lyke wyse[486] may ye do, and ye lyst,[487] and take the quene knyghtly[488] away with you, if so be that the kynge woll jouge[489] her to be brente.[490] And in Joyous Garde may ye kepe her longe inowe[491] untyll the hete[492] be paste[493] of the kynge, and than hit[494] may fortune[495] you to brynge the quene agayne to the kynge with grete[496] worshyp, and peradventure ye shall have than thanke[497] for your bryngyng home, whether othir[498] may happyn to have magré."[499]

"That ys hard for to do," seyde sir Launcelot, "for by sir Trystram I may have a warnynge: for whan[500] by meanys of tretyse[501] sir Trystram

451. through.
452. fault.
453. friends.
454. at once.
455. then.
456. tomorrow.
457. once.
458. we think.
459. be supposed.
460. captured.
461. else.
462. from.
463. to us.
464. (it) seems.
465. (to) your honor.
466. predicament.
467. know.
468. loath.
469. very.
470. will.
471. before.
472. perhaps.
473. should much grieve.
474. if.
475. could.
476. soon.
477. would be.
478. keep.
479. least.
480. said.
481. not.

482. La Belle Isolde, daughter of the king of Ireland, fell in love with Tristram as he was being cured of a wound. When Tristram returned to Cornwall, his uncle, King Mark, sent him back to Ireland, wishing to marry the beautiful Isolde himself. Tristram acted in good faith; but on the voyage back, both Tristram and Isolde by mistake partook of a love potion meant for King Mark. Although Mark and Isolde married, Tristram and his sovereign lady ran away and lived in an

adulterous love until they were betrayed and Tristram killed by Mark. Complications were added from other sources, such as the love of Tristram for Isolde of Brittany, also called Isolde of the White Hands: he married the second but loved both.
483. years.
484. In the prose *Lancelot*, the hero, fostered by the Lady of the Lake, engages in many adventures. One of them is the capture of the castle of the Douloureuse Garde, where he discovers his name on the tomb wherein he will be buried. After removing all the evil enchantments of the castle, Lancelot renames it the Joyeuse Garde and makes it his residence.
485. advice of you all.
486. manner.
487. please.
488. chivalrously.
489. doom.
490. burned.
491. enough.
492. anger.
493. passed.
494. it.
495. befall.
496. great.
497. thanks.
498. whether (or not) others.
499. ill will.
500. when.
501. agreement.

brought agayne La Beall Isode unto kynge Marke from Joyous Garde, loke[502] ye now what felle on[503] the ende, how shamefully that false traytour[504] kyng Marke slew hym as he sate[505] harpynge afore[506] hys lady, La Beall Isode. Wyth a grounden glayve[507] he threste[508] hym in behynde to the harte,[509] whych grevyth[510] sore me," seyde sir Launcelot, "to speke[511] of his dethe,[512] for all the worlde may nat fynde such another knyght."

"All thys ys trouthe," seyde sir Bors, "but there ys one thyng shall corrayge[513] you and us all: ye know well that kynge Arthur and kynge Marke were never lyke of condycions,[514] for there was never yet man that ever coude preve[515] kynge Arthur untrew of[516] hys promyse."

But so, to make shorte tale, they were all condiscended[517] that, for bettir othir[518] for wars,[519] if so were[520] that the quene were brought on that morne to the fyre, shortely they all wolde rescow here.[521] And so by the advyce of sir Launcelot they put hem[522] all in a bushement[523] in a wood as nyghe[524] Carlyle as they myght, and there they abode stylle[525] to wyte what the kynge wold do.

Now turne[526] we agayne, that whan sir Mordred was ascaped frome[527] sir Launcelot he gate[528] hys horse and cam[529] to kynge Arthur sore wounded and all forbled,[530] and there he tolde the kynge all how hit was, and how they were all slayne save hymselff alone.

"A,[531] Jesu, mercy! How may thys be?" seyde the kynge. "Toke[532] ye hym in the quenys chambir?"

"Yee,[533] so God me helpe," seyde sir Mordred,

"there we founde hym unarmed, and anone[534] he slew sir Collgrevaunce and armed hym[535] in hys armour."

And so he tolde the kynge frome the begynnyng to the endynge.

"Jesu mercy!" seyde[536] the kynge," he ys a mervaylous[537] knyght of proues.[538] And alas," seyde the kynge, "me[539] sore repentith[540] that ever sir Launcelot sholde[541] be ayenste[542] me, for now I am sure the noble felyshyp[543] of the Rounde Table ys brokyn for ever, for wyth hym woll[544] many a noble knyght holde. And now hit ys fallen[545] so," seyde the kynge, "that I may nat with[546] my worshyp[547] but my quene muste suffir dethe," and was sore amoved.[548]

So than[549] there was made grete ordynaunce[550] in thys ire, and the quene muste nedis[551] be jouged[552] to the deth. And the law was such in tho[553] dayes that whatsomever[554] they were, of what astate[555] or degré,[556] if they were founden[557] gylty of treson[558] there shuld[559] be none[560] other remedy but deth, and othir[561] the menour[562] other the takynge wyth[563] the dede[564] shulde be causer[565] of their hasty jougement.[566] And ryght[567] so was hit[568] ordayned for quene Gwenyver: bycause[569] sir Mordred was ascaped sore wounded, and the dethe of thirtene knyghtes of the Rounde Table, thes previs[570] and experyenses[571] caused kynge Arthur to commaunde[572] the quene to the fyre and there to be brente.[573]

Than spake[574] sir Gawayn and seyde,

"My lorde Arthure, I wolde counceyle[575] you nat to be over hasty, but that ye wolde put hit

---

502. see.
503. happened at.
504. traitor.
505. sat.
506. before.
507. sharp spear.
508. thrust.
509. heart.
510. grieves.
511. speak.
512. death.
513. encourage.
514. alike in character.

515. prove.
516. untrue to.
517. agreed.
518. or.
519. worse.
520. (it) were.
521. would rescue her.
522. them.
523. ambush.
524. near.
525. waited quietly.
526. return.

527. escaped from.
528. got.
529. came.
530. bleeding heavily.
531. ah.
532. took.
533. yea.
534. then.
535. himself.
536. said.
537. marvelous.
538. prowess.

539. I.
540. grieve.
541. should.
542. against.
543. fellowship.
544. will.
545. happened.
546. not (do otherwise) for.
547. honor.
548. moved.
549. then.
550. decree.

551. of necessity.
552. doomed.
553. those.
554. whatever.
555. condition.
556. rank.
557. found.
558. treason.
559. should.
560. no.
561. either.
562. behavior.
563. discovery in.

564. act.
565. cause.
566. immediate judgment.
567. just.
568. it.
569. because.
570. these proofs.
571. incidents.
572. command.
573. burned.
574. spoke.
575. counsel.

in respite, thys jougemente of my lady the quene, for many causis. One ys thys, thoughe hyt were so that sir Launcelot were founde in the quenys chambir, yet hit myght be so that he cam thydir[576] for none evyll. For ye know, my lorde," seyde sir Gawayne, "that my lady the quene hath oftyntymes ben gretely[577] beholdyn unto sir Launcelot, more than to ony[578] othir knyght; for oftyntymes he hath saved her lyff[579] and done batayle[580] for her whan[581] all the courte refused the quene. And peradventure[582] she sente for hym for goodness and for none evyll, to rewarde hym for his good dedys[583] that he had done to her in tymes past. And peravventure my lady the quene sente for hym to[584] that entente,[585] that sir Launcelot sholde a[586] com prevaly[587] to her, wenyng[588] that hyt had[589] be[590] beste in eschewyng[591] of slaundir; for oftyntymys we do many thynges that we wene for the beste be, and yet peradventure hit turnyth to the warste.[592] For I dare sey," seyde sir Gawayne, "my lady, your quene, ys to you both good and trew.[593] And as for sir Launcelot, I dare say he woll make hit good[594] uppon ony knyght lyvyng that woll put uppon[595] hym vylany[596] or shame, and in lyke wyse[597] he woll make good for my lady the quene."

"That I beleve well," seyde kynge Arthur, "but I woll nat that way worke with sir Launcelot, for he trustyth so much uppon[598] hys hondis[599] and hys myght that he doutyth[600] no man. And therefore for my quene he shall nevermore fyght, for she shall have the law. And if I may gete[601] sir Launcelot, wyte[602] you well he shall have as shamefull a dethe."[603]

"Jesu defende me," seyde[604] sir Gawayne, "that I never se[605] hit nor know hit."

"Why say you so?" seyde kynge Arthur. "For, perdé,[606] ye have no cause to love hym! For thys nyght last past he slew youre brothir sir Aggravayne, a full[607] good knyght, and almoste he had slayne youre othir brother, sir Mordred, and also there he slew thirtene noble knyghtes. And also remembir you, sir Gawayne, he slew two sunnes[608] of yours, sir Florens and sir Lovell."

"My lorde," seyde sir Gawayne, "of all thys I have a knowleche,[609] whych of her[610] dethis sore repentis[611] me. But insomuch as I gaff hem[612] warnynge and tolde my brothir and my sonnes aforehonde[613] what wolde falle on[614] the ende, and insomuche as they wolde nat do be[615] my counceyle, I woll[616] nat meddyll me[617] thereoff,[618] nor revenge me[619] nothynge[620] of[621] their dethys; for I tolde them there was no boote[622] to stryve with sir Launcelot. Howbehit[623] I am sory[624] of the deth of my brothir and of my two sunnes, but they ar[625] the causars[626] of their owne dethe; for oftyntymes I warned my brothir sir Aggravayne, and I tolde hym of the perellis[627] the which ben[628] now fallen."[629]

Than[630] seyde kynge Arthur unto sir Gawayne, "Make you redy,[631] I pray you, in youre beste armour, wyth youre brethirn,[632] sir Gaherys and sir Gareth, to brynge my quene to the fyre and there to have her jougement."[633]

"Nay, my moste noble kynge," seyde sir Gawayne, "that woll I never do, for wyte you well I woll never be in that place where so noble a quene as ys my lady dame Gwenyver[634] shall

---

576. there.	**586.** have.	**596.** (of) villainy.	**606.** by God.	**615.** act by.	**625.** are.
577. been greatly.	**587.** secretly.	**597.** manner.	**607.** very.	**616.** will.	**626.** causes.
578. any.	**588.** believing.	**598.** in.	**608.** sons.	**617.** meddle.	**627.** perils.
579. life.	**589.** would have.	**599.** hands.	**609.** knowledge.	**618.** therein.	**628.** are.
580. battle.	**590.** been.	**600.** fears.	**610.** their.	**619.** myself.	**629.** happened.
581. when.	**591.** avoiding.	**601.** get.	**611.** grieves.	**620.** not at all.	**630.** then.
582. perhaps.	**592.** worst.	**602.** know.	**612.** gave them.	**621.** for.	**631.** ready.
583. deeds.	**593.** true.	**603.** death.	**613.** before.	**622.** use.	**632.** brothers.
584. with.	**594.** avenge it.	**604.** said.	**614.** would happen at.	**623.** although.	**633.** judgment.
585. intent.	**595.** accuse.	**605.** see.		**624.** sorry.	**634.** Guinevere.

take[635] such a shamefull ende. For wyte you well," seyde sir Gawayne, "my harte[636] woll nat serve me for to se her dye,[637] and hit[638] shall never be seyde that ever I was of youre counceyle[639] for her deth."

"Than," seyde the kynge unto sir Gawayne, suffir[640] your brethirn sir Gaherys and sir Gareth to be there."

"My lorde," seyde sir Gawayne, "wyte you well they wyll be lothe[641] to be there present bycause[642] of many adventures that ys lyke[643] to falle, but they ar yonge[644] and full unable to say you nay."

Than spake[645] sir Gaherys and the good knyght sir Gareth unto kynge Arthur,

"Sir, ye may well commande us to be there, but wyte you well hit shall be sore ayenste[646] oure wyll. But and[647] we be there by youre strayte commaundement,[648] ye shall playnly holde us there excused: we woll be there in pesyble wyse,[649] and beare none harneyse[650] of warre uppon us."

"In the name of God," seyde[651] the kynge, "than make you redy, for she shall have sone[652] her jugemente."

"Alas," seyde sir Gawayne, "that ever I shulde[653] endure to se[654] this wofull[655] day!"

So sir Gawayne turned hym[656] and wepte hartely,[657] and so he wente into hys chambir. And so the quene was lad furthe without[658] Carlyle, and anone[659] she was dispoyled[660] into[661] her smokke.[662] And than her gostely fadir[663] was brought to her to be shryven[664] of her myssededis.[665] Than was there wepyng[666] and waylynge and wryngyng of hondis[667] of many lordys and ladyes; but there were but feaw[668] in comparison that wolde beare ony[669] armour for to strengthe[670] the dethe[671] of the quene.

Than was there one that sir Launcelot had sente unto that place, whych wente to aspye[672] what tyme the quene shulde go unto her deth. And anone[673] as he saw the quene dispoyled into her smok and shryvyn, than he gaff[674] sir Launcelot warnynge anone.[675] Than was there but[676] spurryng and pluckyng up of horse, and ryght[677] so they cam[678] unto the fyre. And who that[679] stoode ayenste them, there were they slayne; there myght none withstande sir Launcelot.

So all that bare[680] armes and withstoode them, there were they slayne, full[681] many a noble knyght. For there was slayne sir Bellyas le Orgulus, sir Segwarydes, sir Gryfflet, sir Braundyles, sir Agglovale, sir Tor; sir Gauter, sir Gyllymer, sir Raynold, three brethir,[682] and sir Damas, sir Priamus, sir Kay le Straunge, sir Dryaunt, sir Lambegus, sir Hermynde, sir Pertolyp, sir Perymones, two brethren whych were called the Grene Knyght and the Red Knyght.

And so in thys russhynge and hurlynge, as sir Launcelot thrange[683] here and there, hit[684] mysfortuned[685] hym to sle[686] sir Gaherys and sir Gareth, the noble knyght, for they were unarmed and unwares.[687] As the Freynshe[688] booke sayth, sir Launcelot smote sir Gaherys and sir Gareth uppon the brayne-pannes, wherethorow[689] that they were slayne in the felde.[690] Howbehit[691] in very trouth[692] sir Launcelot saw them nat.[693] And so were they founde dede amonge[694] the thyckyste of the press.[695]

Than[696] sir Launcelot, whan[697] he had thus done, and slayne and put to flyght all that wolde

---

635. receive.	**646.** against.	**656.** turned.	**666.** weeping.	**677.** just.	**687.** unwary.
636. heart.	**647.** if.	**657.** exceedingly.	**667.** hands.	**678.** came.	**688.** French.
637. die.	**648.** strict command.	**658.** led forth	**668.** few.	**679.** whoever.	**689.** skulls, whereby.
638. it.	**649.** peaceable	outside.	**669.** any.	**680.** bore.	**690.** field.
639. agreement.	manner.	**659.** then.	**670.** bring about.	**681.** very.	**691.** although.
640. allow.	**650.** no gear.	**660.** undressed.	**671.** death.	**682.** brothers.	**692.** truth.
641. loath.	**651.** said.	**661.** down to.	**672.** discover.	**683.** pressed.	**693.** not.
642. because.	**652.** soon.	**662.** smock.	**673.** as soon.	**684.** it.	**694.** dead in.
643. likely.	**653.** should.	**663.** father confessor.	**674.** gave.	**685.** happened	**695.** crowd.
644. young.	**654.** see.	**664.** confessed.	**675.** at once.	unluckily for.	**696.** then.
645. spoke.	**655.** woeful.	**665.** misdeeds.	**676.** (nothing) but.	**686.** slay.	**697.** when.

wythstonde[698] hym, than he rode streyt[699] unto quene Gwenyver[700] and made caste[701] a kurdyll[702] and a gown uppon her, and than he made her to be sette behynde hym and prayde her to be of good chere.[703] Now wyte[704] you well the quene was glad that she was at that tyme ascaped frome[705] the deth, and than she thanked God and sir Launcelot.

And so he rode hys way wyth the quene, as the Freynshe booke seyth,[706] unto Joyous Garde, and there he kepte her as a noble knyght shulde. And many grete[707] lordis and many good knyghtes were sente hym, and many full noble knyghtes drew unto hym. Whan they harde[708] that kynge Arthure and sir Launcelot were at debate many knyghtes were glad, and many were sory of[709] their debate.[710]

The Day of Destiny

As sir Mordred was rular of all Inglonde, he lete make[1] lettirs as thoughe that they had com frome[2] beyond the see,[3] and the lettirs specifyed that kynge Arthur was slayne in batayle[4] with sir Launcelot. Wherefore sir Mordred made[5] a parlemente,[6] and called the lordys togydir,[7] and there he made them to chose[8] hym kynge. And so was he crowned at Caunturbury,[9] and hylde[10] a feste[11] there fiftene dayes.

And aftirwarde he drew hym[12] unto Wynchester, and there he toke[13] quene Gwenyver,[14] and seyde[15] playnly that he wolde[16] wedde her (which was hys unclys wyff[17] and hys fadirs[18] wyff). And so he made redy[19] for the feste, and a day prefyxte[20] that they shulde[21] be wedded; wherefore quene Gwenyver was passyng hevy.[22]

But she durst nat discover[23] her harte,[24] but spake fayre,[25] and aggreed to sir Mordredys wylle.

And anone[26] she desyred of sir Mordred to go to London to byghe[27] all maner[28] thynges that longed[29] to the brydale.[30] And bycause[31] of her fayre speche[32] sir Mordred trusted her and gaff[33] her leve;[34] and so whan[35] she cam[36] to London she toke[37] the Towre of London, and suddeynly in all haste possyble she stuffed hit[38] with all maner of vytayle,[39] and well garnysshed[40] hit with men, and so kepte[41] hit.

And whan sir Mordred wyst[42] thys he was passynge wrothe[43] oute of[44] mesure.[45] And shorte tale to make, he layde a myghty syge[46] aboute the Towre and made many assautis,[47] and threw engynnes[48] unto them, and shotte grete[49] gunnes.

---

698. would withstand.	**702.** kirtle.	**706.** says.
699. straight.	**703.** heart.	**707.** great.
700. Guinevere.	**704.** know.	**708.** heard.
701. had thrown.	**705.** escaped from.	**709.** sorry about.

710. In the sections that follow, omitted here, Gawain swears to avenge his brothers and encourages Arthur to besiege Joyeuse Garde. The pope intercedes, and Guinevere is returned to Arthur, whereupon Lancelot retires across the sea to his French possessions. He is the son of King Ban of Benwick, and it is at the siege of Benwick by Arthur, who has followed him to France, that Lancelot and Gawain meet in combat. Lancelot defends himself mightily as Gawain's strength increases all the forenoon (he receives his mythical power from the sun), but after high noon Gawain's strength begins to wane and Lancelot wounds him in the head. Arthur, who while fighting Lancelot on the Continent has made Modred regent of England and put Guinevere in his charge, lifts the siege when he hears of Modred's treason.

1. had made.	**20.** set.	**36.** came.
2. from.	**21.** should.	**37.** occupied by force.
3. sea.	**22.** exceedingly sorrowful.	**38.** it.
4. battle.	**23.** dared not reveal.	**39.** food.
5. convened.	**24.** heart.	**40.** garrisoned.
6. parliament.	**25.** spoke pleasantly.	**41.** guarded.
7. together.	**26.** then.	**42.** knew.
8. choose.	**27.** buy.	**43.** angry.
9. Canterbury.	**28.** manner (of).	**44.** beyond.
10. held.	**29.** pertained.	**45.** measure.
11. feast.	**30.** wedding.	**46.** siege.
12. drew.	**31.** because.	**47.** assaults.
13. took.	**32.** speech.	**48.** (siege) engines.
14. Guinevere.	**33.** gave.	**49.** great.
15. said.	**34.** leave.	
16. would.	**35.** when.	
17. wife.		
18. father's.		
19. ready.		

But all myght nat prevayle, for quene Gwenyver wolde never, for fayre speache nother[50] for foule, never to truste unto sir Mordred to come in hys hondis[51] agayne.

Than cam the Bysshop of Caunturbyry, whych was a noble clerke[52] and an holy man, and thus he seyde unto sir Mordred:

"Sir, what woll[53] ye do? Woll ye firste displease God and sytthyn[54] shame youreselff and all knyghthode?[55] For ys nat kynge Arthur your uncle, and no farther but[56] youre modirs[57] brothir, and uppon her he hymselffe begate[58] you, uppon hys owne syster? Therefore how may ye wed youre owne fadirs wyff? And therefor, sir," seyde the Bysshop, "leve[59] thys opynyon,[60] other ellis[61] I shall curse you with booke, belle[62] and candyll."[63]

"Do thou thy warste,"[64] seyde[65] sir Mordred, "and I defyghe[66] the!"[67]

"Sir," seyde the Bysshop, "wyte[68] you well I shall nat feare me[69] to do that me[70] ought to do. And also ye noyse[71] that my lorde Arthur ys slayne, and that ys nat so, and therefore ye woll make[72] a foule warke[73] in thys londe!"[74]

"Peas,[75] thou false pryste!"[76] seyde sir Mordred, "for and[77] thou chauffe[78] me ony[79] more, I shall stryke of[80] thy hede!"[81]

So the Bysshop departed, and ded[82] the cursynge in the moste orguluste wyse[83] that myght be done. And than[84] sir Mordred sought the Bysshop off[85] Caunturbyry for to have slayne hym. Than the Bysshop fledde, and tooke parte of hys good[86] with hym, and wente nyghe[87] unto Glassyngbyry.[88] And there he was a presteermyte[89] in a chapel, and lyved in poverté[90] and in holy prayers; for well he undirstood that myschevous[91] warre was at honde.

Than sir Mordred soughte uppon[92] quene Gwenyver by lettirs and sondis,[93] and by fayre meanys and foule meanys, to have her to come oute of the Towre of London; but all thys avayled nought,[94] for she answerd hym shortely, opynly[95] and pryvayly,[96] that she had levir sle[97] herselff than to be maryed[98] with hym.

Than cam there worde unto sir Mordred that kynge Arthure had areysed[99] the syge frome[100] sir Launcelot and was commynge homwarde[101] wyth a greate oste[102] to be avenged uppon sir Mordred, wherefore sir Mordred made wryttes[103] unto all the baronny[104] of thys londe. And muche[105] people drew unto hym; for than was the comyn voyce[106] amonge them that with kynge Arthur was never othir lyff[107] but warre and stryff,[108] and with sir Mordrede was grete joy and blysse. Thus was kynge Arthur depraved,[109] and evyll seyde[110] off; and many there were that kynge Arthur had brought up of[111] nought, and gyffyn[112] them londis, that myght nat[113] than say hym a good worde.

---

50. speech nor.
51. hands.
52. cleric.
53. will.
54. then.
55. knighthood.
56. more distant than.
57. mother's.
58. begot.
59. abandon.
60. intention.
61. or else.
62. bell.
63. candle.
64. worst.
65. said.
66. defy.
67. you.
68. know.
69. fear.
70. what I.
71. spread rumors.
72. do.
73. deed.
74. land.
75. peace.
76. priest.
77. if.
78. anger.
79. any.
80. off.
81. head.
82. did.
83. forceful manner.
84. then.
85. of.
86. possessions.
87. near.
88. Glastonbury, in the 12th century a center of literary and political activity near the Bristol Channel, is surrounded by marchland and has been identified with the Isle of Avalon, to which Arthur was carried at his death (cf. below, n. 610). The supposed tombs of Arthur and Guinevere were discovered in Glastonbury in 1190 near the Lady Chapel, rebuilt after a fire in 1186. Although in the past it has been thought that the monks of Glastonbury (who in matters of Plantagenet policy were propagandistic agents of the crown) obligingly "discovered" the remains in order to support the campaign of Henry II against Celtic nationalism and to dispel the hopes of Arthur's return, recent archaeological evidence tends to support the identification. Geoffrey Ashe, in The Quest for Arthur's Britain (New York, 1968), has assembled all the findings and makes a strong case for Arthur's, if not Guinevere's, burial at Glastonbury.
89. priest-hermit.
90. poverty.
91. evil.
92. of.
93. messengers.
94. nothing.
95. openly.
96. secretly.
97. rather slay.
98. married.
99. raised.
100. from.
101. homeward.
102. host.
103. summons.
104. barons.
105. many.
106. general opinion.
107. life.
108. strife.
109. disparaged.
110. spoken.
111. from.
112. given.
113. not.

Lo, ye all Englysshemen, se[114] ye nat what a myschyff[115] here was? For he that was the moste[116] kynge and nobelyst knyght of the worlde, and moste loved the felyshyp[117] of noble knyghtes, and by hym they all were upholdyn,[118] and yet myght nat thes[119] Englyshemen holde them[120] contente with hym. Lo thus was the olde custom and usayges[121] of thys londe, and men say that we of thys londe have nat yet loste that custom. Alas! thys ys a greate defaughte[122] of us Englys-shemen, for there may no thynge us please no terme.[123]

And so fared the peple[124] at that tyme: they were better pleased with sir Mordred than they were with the noble kynge Arthur, and muche people drew unto sir Mordred and seyde[125] they wold abyde wyth hym for bettir and for wars.[126] And so sir Mordred drew with a greate oste to Dovir, for there he harde[127] sey[128] that kyng Arthur wolde aryve, and so he thought to beate hys owne fadir fro[129] hys owne londys. And the moste party[130] of all Inglonde hylde[131] with sir Mordred, for the people were so new-fangill.[132]

And so as sir Mordred was at Dovir with hys oste, so cam[133] kyng Arthur wyth a great navy of shyppis and galyes[134] and carykes,[135] and there was sir Mordred redy[136] awaytyng uppon hys londynge,[137] to lette[138] hys owne fadir to londe[139] uppon the londe that he was kynge over.

Than[140] there was launchyng of greate botis[141] and smale,[142] and full of noble men of armys; and there was muche slaughtir of jantyll[143] knyghtes, and many a full[144] bolde barown[145] was layde

full lowe, on bothe partyes.[146] But kynge Arthur was so curragious[147] that there myght no maner[148] of knyght lette hym to lande, and hys knyghtes fyersely[149] folowed hym. And so they londed magré[150] sir Mordredis hede[151] and all hys powere, and put[152] sir Mordred abak,[153] that[154] he fledde and all hys people.[155]

So whan[156] thys batayle[157] was done, kynge Arthure let serche[158] hys people that were hurte and dede.[159] And than was noble sir Gawayne founde in a greate boote, liynge[160] more than halff dede. Whan kyng Arthur knew that he was layde so low he wente unto hym and so fownde hym. And there the kynge made greate sorow oute of[161] mesure,[162] and toke[163] sir Gawayne in hys armys, and thryse[164] he there sowned.[165] And than whan he was waked, kyng Arthur seyde,

"Alas! sir Gawayne, my syster[166] son, here now thou lyghest,[167] the man in the worlde that I loved moste. And now ys my joy gone! For now, my nevew,[168] sir Gawayne, I woll[169] discover me[170] unto you, that in youre person and in sir Launcelot I moste had my joy and myne affyaunce.[171] And now have I loste my joy of you bothe, wherefore all myne erthely[172] joy ys gone fro me!"

"A, myn[173] uncle," seyde sir Gawayne, "now I woll[174] that ye wyte[175] that my deth-dayes be[176] com! And all,[177] I may wyte, myne owne has-tynes[178] and my wylfulnesse, for thorow[179] my wylfulnes I was causer[180] of myne owne dethe; for I was thys day hurte and smytten uppon myne olde wounde[181] that sir Launcelot gaff[182] me, and I fele[183] myselff that I muste nedis[184] be dede by

---

114. see.
115. misfortune.
116. greatest.
117. fellowship.
118. supported.
119. these.
120. themselves.
121. usage.
122. fault.
123. (length of) time.
124. people.
125. said.
126. worse.

127. heard.
128. (it) said.
129. father from.
130. part.
131. held.
132. fickle.
133. came.
134. galleys.
135. carracks.
136. ready.
137. landing.
138. stop.
139. from landing.
140. then.

141. boats.
142. small.
143. gentle.
144. very.
145. baron.
146. sides.
147. courageous.
148. manner.
149. fiercely.
150. in spite of.
151. desire.
152. turned.
153. back.
154. so that.

155. Compare the account of the sea battle in the Alliterative *Morte Arthure* (above, p. 108) for a more vigorous and detailed description.
156. when.
157. battle.
158. had searched (for).
159. dead.
160. boat, lying.
161. beyond.
162. measure.
163. took.
164. thrice.
165. swooned.
166. sister's.
167. lie.
168. nephew.
169. will.
170. reveal.
171. trust.
172. earthly.
173. ah, my.
174. desire.
175. know.

176. death-day is.
177. all (because of).
178. hastiness.
179. through.
180. cause.
181. Cf. above, p. 848, n. 710.
182. gave.
183. feel.
184. of necessity.

the owre[185] of noone. And thorow me and my pryde ye have all thys shame and disease,[186] for had that noble knyght, sir Launcelot, ben[187] with you, as he was and wolde have ben, thys unhappy warre had never ben begunne; for he, thorow hys noble knyghthode[188] and hys noble bloode, hylde all youre cankyrde[189] enemyes in subjeccion[190] and daungere.[191] And now," seyde[192] sir Gawayne, "ye shall mysse sir Launcelot. But alas that I wolde nat[193] accorde[194] with hym! And therefore, fayre unkle, I pray you that I may have paupir,[195] penne, and inke, that I may wryte unto sir Launcelot a letter wrytten with myne owne honde."[196]

So whan pauper, penne and inke was brought, than sir Gawayne was sette up waykely[197] by kynge Arthure, for he was shryven[198] a lytyll afore.[199] And than he toke hys penne and wrote thus, as the Freynshe[200] booke makith mencion:[201]

"Unto the,[202] sir Launcelot, floure[203] of all noble knyghtes that ever I harde[204] of or saw be[205] my dayes, I, sir Gawayne, kynge Lottis sonne of Orkeney, and systirs sonne unto the noble kynge Arthur, sende the gretynge, lattynge[206] the to have knowlecche[207] that the tenth day of May I was smytten upon the olde wounde that thou gaff me afore the cité[208] of Benwyke,[209] and thorow that wounde I am com to my dethe-day. And I woll that all the worlde wyte that I, sir Gawayne, knyght of the Table Rounde, soughte my dethe, and nat thorow thy deservynge, but myne owne sekynge.[210] Wherefore I beseche[211] the, sir Launcelot, to returne agayne unto thys realme and se[212] my toumbe and pray som prayer more other les[213] for my soule. And thys same day that I wrote the same sedull[214] I was hurte to the dethe, whych

wounde was fyrste gyffyn of thyn[215] honde, sir Launcelot; for of a more nobelar[216] man myght I nat be slayne.

"Also, sir Launcelot, for all the love that ever was betwyxte us, make no taryyng,[217] but com over the see[218] in all the goodly haste that ye may, wyth youre noble knyghtes, and rescow[219] that noble kynge that made the knyght, for he ys full straytely bestad wyth[220] an false traytoure[221] whych ys my halff-brothir, sir Mordred. For he hath crowned hymselff kynge, and wolde have wedded my lady, quene Gwenyver;[222] and so had he done, had she nat kepte[223] the Towre of London with stronge honde. And so the tenth day of May last paste[224] my lorde kynge Arthur and we all londed[225] uppon them at Dover, and there he put that false traytoure, sir Mordred, to flyght. And so hit[226] there mysfortuned[227] me to be smytten upon the strooke[228] that ye gaff[229] me of olde.

"And the date of thys lettir was wrytten but two owrys[230] and an halff afore my dethe,[231] wrytten with myne owne honde and subscrybed[232] with parte of my harte[233] blood. And therefore I requyre the, most famous knyght of the worlde, that thou wolte[234] se my tumbe."[235]

And than[236] he wepte and kynge Arthur both, and sowned.[237] And whan[238] they were awaked bothe, the kynge made sir Gawayne to resceyve[239] hys sacrament, and than sir Gawayne prayde the kynge for to sende for sir Launcelot and to cherysshe hym aboven[240] all othir knyghtes.

And so at the owre of noone sir Gawayne yelded up the goste.[241] And than the kynge lat entere[242] hym in a chapell within Dover castell.

---

185. hour.	**195.** paper.	**206.** greeting, letting.	**216.** nobler.	**226.** it.	**236.** then.
186. sorrow.	**196.** hand.		**217.** delay.	**227.** happened unluckily for.	**237.** swooned.
187. been.	**197.** weakly.	**207.** knowledge.	**218.** sea.		**238.** when.
188. knighthood.	**198.** confessed.	**208.** city.	**219.** rescue.	**228.** stroke.	**239.** receive.
189. evil.	**199.** little before.	**209.** Benwick.	**220.** very seriously threatened by.	**229.** gave.	**240.** above.
190. subjection.	**200.** French.	**210.** seeking.		**230.** hours.	**241.** up his spirit.
191. scorn.	**201.** mention.	**211.** beseech.	**221.** traitor.	**231.** death.	**242.** had buried.
192. said.	**202.** you.	**212.** see.	**222.** Guinevere.	**232.** signed.	
193. would not.	**203.** flower.	**213.** or less.	**223.** guarded.	**233.** heart's.	
194. make my peace.	**204.** heard.	**214.** letter.	**224.** past.	**234.** will.	
	205. in.	**215.** given by your.	**225.** landed.	**235.** tomb.	

And there yet all men may se the skulle of hym, and the same wounde is sene[243] that sir Launcelot gaff in batayle.[244]

Than was hit tolde the kynge that sir Mordred had pyght a new fylde[245] uppon Bareon[246] Downe. And so uppon the morne kynge Arthur rode thydir[247] to hym, and there was a grete[248] batayle betwyxt hem,[249] and muche people were slayne on bothe partyes.[250] But at the laste kynge Arthurs party stoode beste, and sir Mordred and hys party fledde unto Caunturbyry.[251]

And than the kynge let serche[252] all the downys for hys knyghtes that were slayne and entered them; and salved them with soffte salvys that full sore were wounded. Than much[253] people drew unto kynge Arthur, and than they sayde that sir Mordred warred uppon kynge Arthure wyth wronge.

And anone[254] kynge Arthure drew hym[255] wyth his oste[256] downe by the seesyde westewarde, towarde Salusbyry.[257] And there was a day assygned betwyxte kynge Arthur and Sir Mordred, that they shulde mete[258] uppon a downe bysyde[259] Salesbyry and nat[260] farre frome[261] the seesyde. And thys day was assynged on Monday aftir Trynyté Sonday,[262] whereof kynge Arthur was passyng[263] glad that he myght be avenged uppon sir Mordred.

Than sir Modred araysed[264] muche people aboute London, for they of Kente, Southsex[265] and Surrey, Esax,[266] Suffolke and Northefolke[267] helde the[268] moste party[269] with sir Mordred. And

many a full[270] noble knyght drew unto hym and also the kynge; but they that loved sir Launcelot drew unto sir Mordred.

So uppon Trynyté Sunday at nyght kynge Arthure dremed[271] a wondirfull dreme, and in hys dreme hym[272] semed[273] that he saw uppon a chafflet[274] a chayre, and the chayre was faste to a whele,[275] and thereuppon sate[276] kynge Arthure in the rychest clothe of golde that myght be made. And the kynge thought there was undir hym, farre from hym, an hydeous depe blak[277] watir, and therein was all maner[278] of serpentis and wormes and wylde bestis fowle[279] and orryble.[280] And suddeynly the kynge thought that the whyle[281] turned up-so-downe,[282] and he felle amonge the serpentis, and every beste toke[283] hym by a lymme.[284] And than[285] the kynge cryed as he lay in hys bed,

"Helpe! helpe!"

And than knyghtes, squyars[286] and yomen[287] awaked the kynge, and than he was so amased[288] that he wyste[289] nat where he was. And than so he awaked[290] untylle hit was nyghe[291] day, and than he felle on[292] slumberynge agayne, nat slepynge[293] nor thorowly[294] wakynge. So the[295] kyng semed verryly[296] that there cam[297] sir Gawayne unto hym with a numbir of fayre ladyes wyth hym. So whan[298] kyng Arthur saw hym he seyde,[299]

"Wellcom, my systers sonne, I wende[300] ye had bene dede![301] And now I se the[302] on lyve,[303] much am I beholdyn[304] unto Allmyghty Jesu.

---

243. seen.
244. battle. Caxton, in his preface to the 1485 edition of Malory's works, cites evidence of the truth of the Arthurian legend: "Fyrst, ye may see his sepulture in the monasterye of Glastyngburye ... item, in the castel of Dover ye may see Gauwayns skull and Cradoks mantel [cf. the ballad *The Boy and the Mantle*, this volume, pp. 497–504] at Wynchester, the Rounde Table; in other places Launcelottes swerde and many other thynges."

245. gathered his forces anew.
246. Barham.
247. there.
248. great.
249. them.
250. sides.
251. Canterbury.
252. searched.
253. many.
254. then.
255. drew.
256. host.
257. Salisbury.
258. should meet.
259. near.
260. not.
261. from.
262. Trinity Sunday.
263. exceedingly.
264. recruited.
265. Sussex.
266. Essex.
267. Norfolk.
268. (for) the.
269. part.
270. very.
271. dreamed.
272. to him.
273. (it) seemed.
274. platform.
275. wheel.
276. sat.
277. deep black.
278. manner.
279. beasts foul.
280. horrible.
281. wheel.
282. upside down.
283. took.
284. limb.
285. then.
286. squires.
287. yomen.
288. amazed.
289. knew.
290. lay awake.
291. it was almost.
292. into.
293. sleeping.
294. thoroughly.
295. to the
296. truly.
297. came.
298. when.
299. said.
300. thought.
301. been dead.
302. see you.
303. alive.
304. indebted.

A,[305] fayre nevew,[306] what bene thes[307] ladyes that hyder be[308] com with you?''

"Sir," seyde sir Gawayne, "all thes be ladyes for whom I have foughten[309] for, whan I was man lyvynge. And all thes ar tho[310] that I ded batayle fore[311] in ryghteuous[312] quarels, and God hath gyvyn hem[313] that grace at their grete[314] prayer, bycause I ded batayle for them for their ryght that they shulde brynge me hydder unto you. Thus much hath gyvyn me leve[315] God for to warne you of youre dethe:[316] for and[317] ye fyght as to-morne[318] with sir Mordred, as ye bothe have assygned, doute[319] ye nat ye shall be slayne, and the moste party of youre people on bothe partyes.[320] And for the grete grace and goodnes that All-myghty Jesu hath unto you, and for pyté of[321] you and many mo[322] other good men[323] there shall be slayne, God hath sente me to you of Hys speciall grace to gyff[324] you warnyng that in no wyse[325] ye do batayle as to-morne but that ye take[326] a tretyse for[327] a moneth-day.[328] And proffir you largely,[329] so that to-morne ye put in[330] a delay. For within a moneth[331] shall com sir Launcelot with all hys noble knyghtes, and rescow[332] you worshypfully,[333] and sle[334] sir Mordred and all that ever wyll holde wyth hym."

Than sir Gawayne and all the ladyes vanysshed, and anone[335] the kynge called uppon hys knyghtes, squyars, and yomen, and charged[336] them wyghtly[337] to fecche[338] hys noble lordis and wyse bysshoppis unto hym. And whan they were com the kynge tolde hem of hys avision,[339] that

sir Gawayne had tolde hym and warned hym that and he fought on the morn, he sholde[340] be slayne. Than the kynge commanded sir Lucan the Butlere[341] and hys brothir sir Bedyvere the Bolde, with two bysshoppis wyth hem, and charged them in ony wyse[342] to take a tretyse for a moneth-day with sir Mordred:

"And spare nat, proffir[343] hym londys[344] and goodys[345] as much as ye thynke resonable."[346]

So than[347] they departed and cam to sir Mordred where he had a grymme oste[348] of an hondred[349] thousand, and there they entretyd[350] sir Mordred longe[351] tyme. And at the laste sir Mordred was aggreed for to have Cornwale[352] and Kente by[353] kynge Arthurs dayes;[354] and afftir that all Inglonde,[355] after the dayes of kynge Arthur.

Than were they condescende[356] that kynge Arthure and sir Mordred shulde mete[357] betwyxte bothe their ostis, and everych[358] of them shulde brynge fourtene persons. And so they cam[359] wyth thys worde unto Arthur. Than seyde[360] he,

"I am glad that thys ys done," and so he wente into the fylde.[361]

And whan[362] kynge Arthur shulde departe he warned all hys hoost[363] that and they se[364] ony swerde drawyn,[365] "loke[366] ye com on fyersely[367] and sle that traytoure,[368] sir Mordred, for I in no wyse truste hym." In lyke wyse sir Mordred warned hys oste, "that and ye se ony maner[369] of swerde drawyn, loke that ye com on fyersely and so sle all that ever before you stondyth,[370] for

---

305. ah.
306. nephew.
307. are these.
308. hither are.
309. fought.
310. are those.
311. did battle for.
312. righteous.
313. granted them.
314. great.
315. leave.
316. death.
317. if.
318. by tomorrow.
319. arranged, doubt.
320. sides.
321. pity for.
322. more.
323. men (who).
324. give.
325. way.
326. make.
327. truce until.
328. this day one month hence.
329. offer generous terms.
330. achieve.
331. month.
332. rescue.
333. honorably.
334. slay.
335. at once.
336. ordered.
337. urgently.
338. fetch.
339. vision.
340. should.
341. Lit., "Bottler," i.e., the wine steward, or in the 14th- and 15th-century government service the man in charge of the wine duties and taxes for all the ports of England. Thomas Chaucer, the son of Geoffrey, was chief butler of England in the 15th century.
342. any manner.
343. not, offer.
344. lands.
345. possessions.
346. reasonable.
347. then.
348. host.
349. hundred.
350. treated with.
351. (for a) long.
352. Cornwall.
353. in.
354. lifetime.
355. England.
356. agreed.
357. should meet.
358. each.
359. came.
360. said.
361. field.
362. when.
363. host.
364. see.
365. sword drawn.
366. see (that).
367. fiercely.
368. traitor.
369. manner.
370. stand.

in no wyse I woll[371] nat truste for[372] thys tretyse."
And in the same wyse seyde sir Mordred unto hys
oste: "For I know well my fadir[373] woll be avenged
upon me."

And so they mette as their poyntemente[374] was,
and were agreed and accorded[375] thorowly.[376]
And wyne was fette,[377] and they dranke togydir.[378]
Ryght so[379] cam oute an addir of[380] a lytyll[381]
hethe-buysshe,[382] and hit stange[383] a knyght in
the foote. And so whan the knyght felt hym[384] so
stonge,[385] he loked[386] downe and saw the adder;
and anone he drew hys swerde to sle the addir, and
thought none[387] othir harme. And whan the oste
on bothe partyes[388] saw that swerde drawyn, than
they blewe beamys,[389] trumpettis, and hornys,
and shoutted grymly, and so bothe ostis dressed
hem[390] togydirs. And kynge Arthur toke[391] hys
horse and seyde,

"Alas, this unhappy day!" and so rode to hys
party, and sir Mordred in lyke wyse.

And never syns[392] was there never seyne[393] a
more dolefuller batayle[394] in no Crysten[395] londe,
for there was but russhynge and rydynge, foyn-
ynge[396] and strykynge, and many a grym worde
was there spokyn of aythir[397] to othir, and many
a dedely[398] stroke. But ever kynge Arthure rode
thorowoute[399] the batayle of[400] sir Mordred many
tymys and ded full[401] nobely, as a noble kynge
shulde do, and at all tymes he faynted never. And
sir Mordred ded hys devoure[402] that day and put
hymselffe in grete perell.[403]

And thus they fought all the longe day, and
never stynted[404] tylle the noble knyghtes were

layde to the colde erthe.[405] And ever they fought
stylle tylle hit was nere[406] nyght, and by than[407] was
there an hondred[408] thousand leyde[409] dede uppon
the erthe. Than was kynge Arthure wode wrothe[410]
oute of[411] mesure,[412] whan he saw hys people so
slayne frome[413] hym.

And so he loked aboute hym and cowde[414] se
no mo[415] of all hys oste[416] and good knyghtes leffte,
no mo on lyve[417] but two knyghtes: the tone[418] was
sir Lucan de Buttler and hys brother, sir Bedwere;[419] and yette they were full sore wounded.

"Jesu mercy!" seyde[420] the kynge, "where ar[421]
all my noble knyghtes become?[422] Alas, that ever
I shulde[423] se thys doleful day! For now," seyde
kynge Arthur, "I am com to myne ende. But
wolde[424] to God," seyde he, "that I wyste[425] now
where were that traytoure sir Mordred that hath
caused all thys myschyff."[426]

Than kynge Arthur loked aboute and was
ware[427] where stood sir Mordred leanyng uppon
hys swerde[428] amonge a grete hepe[429] of dede men.

"Now, gyff[430] me my speare," seyde kynge
Arthure unto sir Lucan, "for yondir I have
aspyed[431] the traytoure[432] that all thys woo[433] hath
wrought."

"Sir, latte[434] hym be," seyde sir Lucan, "for he
ys unhappy. And yf ye passe[435] this unhappy day
ye shall be ryght well revenged. And, good lord,
remembre ye of your nyghtes dreme[436] and what
the spyryte of sir Gawayne tolde you to-nyght,
and yet God of Hys grete goodnes hath preserved
you hyddirto.[437] And for Goddes sake, my lorde,
leve of[438] thys, for, blyssed[439] be God, ye have

---

371. will.	**383.** stung.	**395.** Christian.	**407.** then.	**418.** the one.	**429.** heap.
372. in.	**384.** himself.	**396.** thrusting.	**408.** hundred.	**419.** Bedevere.	**430.** give.
373. father.	**385.** stung.	**397.** by either.	**409.** laid.	**420.** said.	**431.** spied.
374. appointment.	**386.** looked.	**398.** deadly.	**410.** angry.	**421.** are.	**432.** traitor.
375. in accord.	**387.** no.	**399.** throughout.	**411.** beyond.	**422.** gone.	**433.** woe.
376. thoroughly.	**388.** sides.	**400.** with.	**412.** measure.	**423.** should.	**434.** let.
377. fetched.	**389.** clarions.	**401.** acted very.	**413.** around.	**424.** would.	**435.** survive.
378. together.	**390.** advanced.	**402.** did his duty.	**414.** could.	**425.** knew.	**436.** dream.
379. just then.	**391.** took.	**403.** great peril.	**415.** more.	**426.** misfortune.	**437.** up to now.
380. from.	**392.** since.	**404.** stopped.	**416.** host.	**427.** aware.	**438.** leave off.
381. little.	**393.** seen.	**405.** earth.	**417.** alive.	**428.** sword.	**439.** blessed.
382. heath bush.	**394.** battle.	**406.** nearly.			

won the fylde;[440] for yet we ben[441] here three on lyve, and with sir Mordred ys nat[442] one of lyve.[443] And therefore if ye leve of now, thys wycked day of Desteny ys paste!"[444]

"Now tyde me[445] dethe,[446] tyde me lyff,"[447] seyde the kyng, "now[448] I se[449] hym yondir alone, he shall never ascape[450] myne hondes![451] For at a bettir avayle[452] shall I never have hym."

"God spyede[453] you well!" seyde sir Bedyvere.

Than the kynge gate[454] his speare in bothe hys hondis, and ran towarde sir Mordred, cryyng and saying,

"Traytoure, now ys thy dethe-day com!"

And whan[455] sir Mordred saw kynge Arthur he ran untyll[456] hym with hys swerde drawyn[457] in hys honde, and there kynge Arthur smote sir Mordred undir the shylde,[458] with a foyne[459] of hys speare, thorowoute[460] the body more than a fadom.[461] And whan sir Mordred felte that he had hys dethys wounde he threste[462] hymselff with the myght that he had upp to the burre[463] of kyng Arthurs speare, and ryght[464] so he smote hys fadir,[465] kynge Arthure, with hys swerde hold-ynge[466] in both hys hondys, uppon the syde of the hede,[467] that[468] the swerde perced[469] the helmet and the tay[470] of the brayne. And therewith Mordred daysshed[471] downe starke dede[472] to the erthe.[473]

And noble kynge Arthure felle in a swoughe[474] to the erthe, and there he sowned[475] oftyntymys, and sir Lucan and sir Bedwere offtetymys hove[476] hym up. And so waykly[477] betwyxte them they lad[478] hym to a lytyll[479] chapell nat farre frome[480] the see,[481] and whan the kyng was there, hym thought hym resonabely eased.[482]

Than harde[483] they people crye in the fylde.[484]

"Now go thou, sir Lucan," seyde[485] the kyng, "and do[486] me to wyte[487] what betokyns[488] that noyse in the fylde."

So sir Lucan departed, for he was grevously[489] wounded in many placis; and so as he yode[490] he saw and harkened by the moonelyght how that pyllours[491] and robbers were com into the fylde to pylle[492] and to robbe many a full[493] noble knyght of brochys[494] and bees[495] and of many a good rynge and many a ryche juell.[496] And who that[497] were nat dede all oute,[498] there they slew them for their harneys[499] and their ryches.

Whan sir Lucan undirstood thys warke[500] he cam[501] to the kynge as sone[502] as he myght, and tolde hym all what[503] he had harde and seyne.[504]

"Therefore be[505] my rede,"[506] seyde sir Lucan, "hit[507] ys beste that we brynge you to som towne."

"I wolde[508] hit were so," seyde the kynge, "but I may not stonde,[509] my hede worchys[510] so.... A,[511] sir Launcelot!" seyde kynge Arthure, "thys day have I sore myssed the![512] And alas, that ever I was ayenste[513] the! For now have I my dethe, whereof sir Gawayne me warned in my dreame."

Than sir Lucan toke[514] up the kynge the tone[515] party[516] and sir Bedwere the othir parte, and in the lyfftyng up the kynge sowned, and in the

---

440. battle (cf. above, p. 73, n. 608).
441. are.
442. not.
443. alive.
444. past.
445. befall.
446. death.
447. life.
448. now (that).
449. see.
450. escape.
451. hands.
452. advantage.
453. prosper.
454. got.
455. when.
456. to.
457. drawn.
458. shield.
459. thrust.
460. through.
461. cubit.
462. thrust.
463. The burr of the spear was the metal sleeve or ring which protected the hand and covered the forearm in jousting.
464. just.
465. father.
466. held.
467. head.
468. so that.
469. pierced.
470. membrane.
471. fell.
472. dead.
473. earth.
474. swoon.
475. swooned.
476. raised.
477. weakly.
478. led.
479. little.
480. from.
481. sea.
482. he felt himself reasonably comfortable.
483. then heard.
484. field.
485. said.
486. cause.
487. know.
488. means.
489. grievously.
490. went.
491. scavengers.
492. plunder.
493. very.
494. brooches.
495. bracelets.
496. jewel.
497. whoever.
498. outright.
499. armor.
500. business.
501. came.
502. soon.
503. that.
504. seen.
505. by.
506. advice.
507. it.
508. would.
509. stand.
510. swims.
511. ah.
512. you.
513. against.
514. took.
515. the one.
516. side.

lyfftynge sir Lucan felle in a sowne, that parte of hys guttis felle oute of hys bodye, and therewith[517] the noble knyght hys harte braste.[518] And whan the kynge awoke he behylde[519] sir Lucan, how he lay fomyng[520] at the mowth and parte of his guttes lay at hys fyete.[521]

"Alas," seyde the kynge, "thys ys to me a fulle hevy[522] syght, to se[523] thys noble deuke[524] so dye[525] for my sake, for he wold have holpyn[526] me that had more nede[527] of helpe than I! Alas, that he wolde nat complayne hym,[528] for hys harte was so sette to helpe me. Now Jesu have mercy uppon hys soule!"

Than sir Bedwere[529] wept for the deth[530] of hys brothir.

"Now leve[531] thys mournynge and wepyng, jantyll[532] knyght," seyde the kyng, "for all thys woll[533] nat avayle me. For wyte thou well, and[534] I myght lyve myselff, the dethe of sir Lucan wolde greve[535] me evermore. But my tyme passyth on faste," seyde the kynge. "Therefore," seyde kynge Arthur unto sir Bedwere, "take thou here Excaliber, my good swerde,[536] and go wyth hit to yondir watirs[537] syde; and whan[538] thou commyste there, I charge[539] the throw[540] my swerde in that water, and com agayne and telle me what thou syeste[541] there."

"My lorde," seyde sir Bedwere, "youre commaundement[542] shall be done, and lyghtly brynge[543] you worde agayne."

So sir Bedwere departed. And by the way he behylde that noble swerde, and the pomell and the haufte[544] was all precious stonys. And than he seyde[545] to hymsclff, "If I throw thys ryche swerde in the water, thereof shall never com good,

but harme and losse." And than[546] sir Bedwere hyd Excalyber undir a tre,[547] and so[548] as sone as he myght he cam agayne unto the kynge and seyde he had bene[549] at the watir and had throwen[550] the swerde into the watir.

"What sawe thou there?" seyde the kynge.

"Sir," he seyde, "I saw nothyng but wawis[551] and wyndys."

"That ys untruly seyde of[552] the," seyde the kynge. "And therefore go thou lyghtly agayne, and do my commaundemente; as thou arte to me lyff[553] and dere, spare[554] nat, but throw hit[555] in."

Than sir Bedwere returned agayne and toke the swerde in hys honde;[556] and yet hym thought[557] synne and shame to throw away that noble swerde. And so effte[558] he hyd the swerde and returned agayne and tolde the kynge that he had been at the watir and done hys commaundement.

"What sawist thou there?" seyde the kynge.

"Sir," he seyde, "I saw[559] nothynge but watirs wap[560] and wawys wanne."[561]

"A, traytour[562] unto me and untrew,"[563] seyde kyng Arthure, "now hast thou betrayed me twyse![564] Who wolde wene[565] that thou that hast bene to me so leve[566] and dere, and also named so noble a knyght, that thou wolde betray me for the ryches of thys swerde? But now go agayn lyghtly; for thy longe taryynge[567] puttith me in grete jouperté of my lyff,[568] for I have takyn colde. And but if[569] thou do now as I bydde the,[570] if ever I may se[571] the, I shall sle[572] the myne[573] owne hondis, for thou woldist for my rych swerde se me dede."[574]

Than sir Bedwere departed and wente to the swerde and lyghtly toke[575] hit up, and so he wente

---

517. thereupon.
518. heart burst.
519. beheld.
520. foaming.
521. feet.
522. very sad.
523. see.
524. duke.
525. die.
526. helped.
527. need.

528. not complain.
529. Bedevere.
530. death.
531. stop.
532. weeping, noble.
533. will.
534. if.
535. grieve.
536. sword.

537. I.e., lake's.
538. when.
539. order.
540. (to) throw.
541. see.
542. commandment.
543. (I shall) quickly bring.
544. haft.
545. said.
546. then.

547. tree.
548. then.
549. been.
550. thrown.
551. waves.
552. by.
553. beloved.
554. dear, hesitate.
555. it.
556. hand.

557. he thought (it a).
558. again.
559. saw.
560. lapping.
561. dark.
562. ah, traitor.
563. untrue.
564. twice.
565. would believe.

566. beloved.
567. delay.
568. my life in great jeopardy.
569. unless.
570. you.
571. see.
572. slay.
573. (with) my.
574. dead.
575. took.

unto the watirs syde. And there he bounde the gyrdyll[576] aboute the hyltis,[577] and threw the swerde as farre into the watir as he myght. And there cam[578] an arme and an honde above the watir, and toke hit and cleyght[579] hit, and shoke[580] hit thryse[581] and braundysshed,[582] and than vanysshed with the swerde into the watir.

So sir Bedyvere cam agayne to the kynge and tolde hym what he saw.

"Alas," seyde the kynge, "helpe me hens,[583] for I drede me[584] I have taryed over[585] longe."

Than sir Bedwere toke the kynge uppon hys bak and so wente with hym to the watirs syde. And whan[586] they were there, evyn faste[587] by the banke hoved[588] a lytyll[589] barge wyth many fayre ladyes in hit, and amonge hem[590] all was a quene, and all they had blak hoodis. And all they wepte and shryked[591] whan they saw kynge Arthur.

"Now put me into that barge," seyde[592] the kynge.

And so he ded sofftely,[593] and there resceyved[594] hym three ladyes with grete[595] mournyng. And so they sette hem[596] downe, and in one of their lappis kyng Arthure layde hys hede.[597] And than[598] the quene sayde,

"A, my dere brothir! Why have ye taryed so long from me? Alas, thys wounde on your hede hath caught overmuch coulde!"[599]

And anone[600] they rowed fromward[601] the londe,[602] and sir Bedyvere behylde[603] all tho[604] ladyes go frowarde[605] hym. Than sir Bedwere[606] cryed and seyde,

"A, my lorde Arthur, what shall becom of me, now ye go frome[607] me and leve[608] me here alone amonge myne enemyes?"

"Comforte thyselff," seyde the kynge, "and do as well as thou mayste, for in me ys no truste for to trust in. For I muste[609] into the vale of Avylyon[610] to hele me[611] of my grevous[612] wounde. And if thou here[613] nevermore of me, pray for my soule!"

But ever the quene and ladyes wepte and shryked, that hit[614] was pité[615] to hyre.[616] And as sone[617] as sir Bedwere had loste the syght of the barge he wepte and wayled, and so toke[618] the foreste and wente all that nyght.

And in the mornyng he was ware,[619] betwyxte two holtis hore,[620] of a chapell and an ermytage.[621] Than was sir Bedwere fayne,[622] and thyder[623] he wente, and whan he cam into the chapell he saw where lay an ermyte grovelynge on all four,[624] faste thereby a tumbe[625] was newe gravyn.[626] Whan the ermyte saw sir Bedyvere he knew hym well, for he was but lytyll tofore[627] Bysshop of Caunturbery[628] that sir Mordred fleamed.[629]

"Sir," seyde sir Bedyvere, "what man ys there here entyred[630] that ye pray so faste fore?"[631]

"Fayre sunne,[632] seyde the ermyte, "I wote

---

576. belt.
577. hilt.
578. came.
579. seized.
580. shook.
581. thrice.
582. brandished (it).
583. hence.
584. fear.
585. too.
586. when.
587. quite close.

588. floated.
589. little.
590. them.
591. shrieked.
592. said.
593. did gently.
594. received.
595. great.
596. sat.
597. head.
598. then.
599. cold.

600. then.
601. away from.
602. land.
603. beheld.
604. those.
605. away from.
606. Bedevere.
607. from.
608. leave.
609. must (go).

610. The Isle or Vale of Avalon is the Celtic "Isle of the Blessed," where Arthur is taken after his death. The classical Fortunate Isles, a similar place of repose for the dead, lay west of the Pillars of Hercules. Geoffrey of Monmouth connects the name of the island with Welsh *aval*, "apple," and Welsh

sources call the place *ynys avallach*. The other explanation is that Avalloc ruled the island with his daughter Morgan la Fay, *ynys avallach* therefore being simply the "island of Avalloc." The second explanation seems more correct, especially since *avallach*, "orchard," is a ghost word. An extensive discussion of Avalon and its connection with Glastonbury is found in Roger Sherman Loomis's article "The Legend of Arthur's Survival," in his collection and edition *Arthurian Literature in the Middle Ages* (Oxford, 1959).

611. heal myself.
612. grievous.
613. hear.
614. (so) that it.
615. pity.
616. hear.
617. soon.
618. took (to).

619. aware.
620. copses old.
621. hermitage.
622. glad.
623. there.
624. fours.
625. tomb.
626. newly dug.

627. before.
628. Canterbury.
629. put to flight.
630. buried.
631. fervently for.
632. son.

nat[633] veryly[634] but by demynge.[635] But thys same nyght, at mydnyght, here cam[636] a numbir of ladyes and brought here a dede corse[637] and prayde me to entyre hym. And here they offird an hondred tapers, and they gaff[638] me a thousande besauntes."[639]

"Alas!" seyde sir Bedyvere, "that was my lorde kynge Arthur, whych lyethe here gravyn[640] in thys chapell."

Than sir Bedwere sowned,[641] and whan he awooke[642] he prayde the ermyte that he myght abyde with hym stylle, there to lyve with fastynge and prayers:

"For from hens woll[643] I never go," seyde sir Bedyvere, "be[644] my wyll, but all the dayes of my lyff[645] here to pray for my lorde Arthur."

"Sir, ye ar[646] wellcom to me," seyde[647] the ermyte, "for I know you bettir than ye wene[648] that I do: for ye ar sir Bedwere the Bolde, and the full[649] noble duke sir Lucan de[650] Butler was your brother."

Than[651] sir Bedwere tolde the ermyte all as ye have harde[652] tofore, and so he belaffte[653] with the ermyte that was beforehande Bysshop of Caunturbyry. And there sir Bedwere put uppon hym poure clothys,[654] and served the ermyte full lowly[655] in fastyng and in prayers.

Thus of Arthur I fynde no more wrytten in bokis[656] that bene auctorysed, nothir[657] more of the verry sertaynte[658] of hys deth[659] harde I never rede,[660] but thus was he lad[661] away in a shyp wherein were three quenys; that one was kynge Arthur[662] syster, quene Morgan le Fay,[663] the tother[664] was the quene of North Galis,[665] and the thirde was the quene of the Waste Londis.[666]

(Also there was dame Nynyve,[667] the chyff[668] lady of the laake,[669] whych had wedded sir Pellyas, the good knyght; and thys lady had done muche for kynge Arthure. And thys dame Nynyve wolde[670] never suffir[671] sir Pelleas to be in no place where he shulde be in daungere of hys lyff,[672] and so he lyved unto the uttermuste[673] of hys dayes with her in grete[674] reste.)

Now more of the deth of kynge Arthur coude[675] I never fynde, but that thes[676] ladyes brought hym to hys grave, and such one was entyred there whych the ermyte bare wytnes[677] that sometyme was Bysshop of Caunterbyry. But yet the ermyte knew nat in sertayne[678] that he was veryly[679] the body of kynge Arthur; for thys tale sir Bedwere,[680] a knyght of the Table Rounde, made hit[681] to be wrytten.

Yet som men say in many partys of Inglonde[682] that kynge Arthur ys nat dede, but had[683] by the wyll of oure Lorde Jesu into another place; and men say that he shall com agayne, and he shall wynne the Holy Crosse. Yet I woll nat[684] say that hit shall be so, but rather I wolde sey: here

---

633. know not.
634. for certain.
635. guessing.
636. came.
637. dead corpse.
638. gave.
639. (a kind of coin).
640. buried.
641. swooned.
642. awoke.
643. hence will.
644. by.
645. life.
646. are.
647. said.
648. believe.
649. very.
650. the.
651. then.
652. heard.
653. remained.
654. himself poor clothes.
655. humbly.
656. books.
657. are composed, nor.
658. true certainty.
659. death.
660. read.
661. led.
662. Arthur's.
663. Morgan la Fay is a villainess in most of the Arthurian legends. She is one of Arthur's sisters, married to King Uriens; she is also at times identified as the Lady of the Lake, confused with Nimue or Vivien. All these women may go back to one original Lake Lady: Morgan, daughter of Avalloc, the ruler of the island. Thus Morgan is at times a sympathetic character, depending on the setting.
664. other. **665.** Wales. **666.** Lands.
667. Nynyve or Nimue or Vivien (scribal errors confusing the same name) is the Lady of the Lake, who supposedly raised Lancelot, gave Arthur the sword Excalibur, and received it back. She marries Pelleas and through magic beguiles an adoring Merlin into doting on her. After she makes him do all kinds of foolish things, she finally lures him under a rock and buries him.
668. chief.
669. lake.
670. would.
671. allow.
672. his life should be in danger.
673. end.
674. great.
675. could.
676. these.
677. hermit bore witness.
678. for certain.
679. truly.
680. Bedevere.
681. it.
682. England.
683. was carried.
684. not.

in thys worlde he chaunged[685] hys lyff. And many men say that there ys wrytten uppon the tumbe[686] thys:

HIC IACET ARTHURUS,
REX QUONDAM REXQUE FUTURUS[687]

And thus leve[688] I here sir Bedyvere with the ermyte that dwelled that tyme in a chapell besydes[689] Glassyngbyry;[690] and there was hys ermytage. And so they lyved in prayers and fastynges and grete abstynaunce.[691]

And whan[692] quene Gwenyver[693] undirstood that kynge Arthure was dede[694] and all the noble knyghtes, sir Mordred and all the remanaunte,[695] than she stale[696] away with fyve ladyes with her, and so she wente to Amysbyry,[697] and there she lete make[698] herselff a nunne, and wered whyght[699] clothys and blak, and grete penaunce[700] she toke[701] uppon her,[702] as ever ded[703] synfull woman in thys londe. And never creature coude make her myry,[704] but ever she lyved in fastynge, prayers, and almes-dedis,[705] that[706] all maner[707] of people mervayled[708] how vertuously she was chaunged.

---

685. changed.
686. tomb.
687. "Here lies Arthur, the once and future king."
688. leave.
689. near.
690. The Lady Chapel of Glastonbury Abbey (cf. above, n. 88).

691. abstinence.
692. when.
693. Guinevere.
694. dead.
695. rest.
696. stole.

697. Almesbury.
698. had made.
699. wore white.
700. (as) great penance.
701. took.
702. herself.

703. did.
704. merry.
705. almsgiving.
706. so that.
707. manner.
708. marveled.

THE DRAMA

Medieval drama falls into two categories. The earlier group, the miracle plays, were probably at first dramatizations of the miracles of saints, but then developed into biblical stories acted by the guilds (cf. above, p. 19). The second group consists of the later morality plays.

The miracle plays, which entertained the townspeople and taught the Bible, evidently originated in the enactment of church pageants during the festivals of Easter and Christmas. Performed at first by the choir in the nave, they soon outgrew their limits and were produced on the church porch. In the fourteenth century the guilds presented them in cycles on Corpus Christi Day, and the plays of York, Wakefield, and Chester are the most famous still extant.

The morality plays, in which allegorical characters such as Everyman, Death, and Conscience appeared, started with the fourteenth-century Paternoster plays acted by crafts in York, Lincoln, and Beverley. They treated subjective, moral, and ethical themes—the summons of Death, the salvation of man, the fall of pride teaching spiritual lessons in abstract terms. The *Pride of Life* (c. 1400), concerning a king's duel with Death, is the earliest of the extensive *memento mori* type, whereas the longest morality is the fifteenth-century *Castle of Perseverance*. Although the origins of these plays are obscure, the seeds of the form can be found in homiletic and debate literature and the theme of the Dance of Death. The classic morality play is of course *Everyman*, perhaps a translation of the Dutch *Elckerlijk* (c. 1495), known in German as *Jedermann*. The play is definitely "good theater," and in the production of Hugo von Hofmannsthal it has been performed since 1920 in Salzburg and elsewhere.

REFERENCES

Adams, J. Q. *Chief Pre-Shakespearean Dramas*. Boston, 1924.

Bevington, David. *Medieval Drama*. Boston, 1975.

Chambers, E. K. *English Literature at the Close of the Middle Ages*. Chap. 1, "Medieval Drama." New York, 1947.

———, *The Mediaeval Stage*. 2 vols. Oxford, 1903.

Craig, H. *English Religious Drama of the Middle Ages*. Oxford, 1955.

Manly, J. M. *Specimens of the Pre-Shakespearean Drama*. 2 vols. Boston, 1897.

Salter, F. M. *Medieval Drama in Chester*. Toronto, 1955.

Southern, Richard W. *The Medieval Theatre in the Round: A Study of the Staging of "The Castle of Perseverance" and Related Matters.* London, 1957.

Stratman, C. J. *A Bibliography of Medieval Drama.* Berkeley, 1954.

Wickham, Glynn. *Early English Stages*, 1300–1600. 2 vols. New York, 1959, 1962.

Young, K. *The Drama of the Medieval Church.* 2 vols. Oxford, 1933.

The drama is treated in the General Introduction of this volume, pp. 19–20.

from THE YORK CYCLE

DATE: 14th century. ✦ MANUSCRIPT: British Library Addit. 35290, c. 1430–40, or possibly c. 1475. The dialect is Northern (Yorkshire). ✦ EDITION: L. Toulmin-Smith, ed., *York Mystery Plays* (Oxford, 1885).

The York cycle, like that of Wakefield (the Towneley Plays), shows typical Northern characteristics. (1) The present participle ends in *-and* (*falland, fayland*), and the past participle in *-id, -yd* (*callid*). (2) Terminal *s* in the third person singular verb forms and in noun plurals is commonly extended to *-is/-ys* (*biddis, thynkis, hillis, knyghtis*). (3) Quite often *s* stands alone for *sh* (*sall*, "shall," *sulde*, "should"). (4) Replacing *wh* is *qw* (*qwen = when*), a common Northern and Scottish orthographic trait. We also find *ā* for *o* in other dialects (*calde, lange*) and *k* for *ch* (*swilke*, "such"), both specific Northern elements. (5) Doubling of consonants is common (*gyffis = gives, lyff = life, itt = it*). (6) Lexical variations to be considered are: *sho*, "she"; auxiliaries *gon, gan*, "do," "make," *mon*, "must."

The York cycle of forty-eight guild pageants performed on wagons throughout the whole city on Corpus Christi Day is the longest of the mystery cycles, and performances were already mentioned in 1378 as being traditional. The city fathers often attempted to assign appropriate crafts to the various plays (later only occasionally, since the crafts too frequently insisted on inserting commercial announcements into their performances); thus the fishers and sailors performed the story of Noah and the Flood, and the pin makers (*pynneres*) and painters acted out the Crucifixion. The humor in these plays ranges from domestic squabbling to macabre raucousness. The general tone is obviously meant to appeal to the taste and temperament of a medieval bourgeois audience.

The play of Noah follows Gen. 5: 28–31; 7: 6–8, 20; 9: 8–17. The play of the Crucifixion follows Matt. 27: 33–35; Luke 23: 33–37; Mark 25: 22–32.

NOAH AND HIS WIFE, THE FLOOD AND ITS WANING

(THE FYSSHERS AND MARYNARS)

[DRAMATIS PERSONAE

NOAH	(*Noe or Noye*)
NOAH'S WIFE	(*Vxor*)
THREE SONS OF NOAH	(*1, 2, 3 filius*)
THREE DAUGHTERS OF NOAH	(*1, 2, 3 filia*)]

[SCENE I: *The Ark in the forest where it was built*]

NOYE.   That Lord þat leves° ay lastand° lyff,°　　　　*lives/everlasting/life*
I loue þe° euer with hart° and hande,　　　　　　*you/heart*
That me wolde rewle be° reasonne ryffe,°　　　　*would order with/abounding*
Sex hundereth yere° to lyffe° in lande.　　　　　*six hundred years/live*
5　Thre semely° sonnes and a worthy wiffe°　　　　*three handsome/wife*
I haue euer at my steven° to stande;　　　　　　*call*
Bot° nowe my cares aren° keen as knyffe,°　　　　*but/are/knife*
By-cause° I kenne° what is commannde.°　　　　　*because/know/commanded*
Thare° comes to ilke contre,°　　　　　　　　　*there/every country*
10　　　　3a,° cares both kene° and calde.°　　　　*yea/sharp/cold*
For God has warned me,
Þis worlde wastyd shalle be,
And certis° þe sothe° I see,　　　　　　　　　*certainly/truth*
As forme fadres° has talde.°　　　　　　　　　*ancestors/told*

15　My fader° Lamech, who likes to neven,°　　　　*father/mention*
Heere° in this worlde þus lange° gon lende,°　　　*here/long/did dwell*
Seuene° hundereth yere seuenty and seuene,　　　*seven*
In swilke° a space his tyme he spende.°　　　　　*such/spent*
He prayed to God with stabill steuene,°　　　　　*steady voice*
20　Þat he to hym a sone shuld° sende,　　　　　*son should*
And at þe laste þer come° from heuen°　　　　　*came/heaven*
Slyke hettyng° þat hym mekill amende;°　　　　　*such promise/greatly comforted*
And made hym grubbe° and graue,°　　　　　　　*dig/plow*
　　　　And ordand° faste be-forne,°　　　　　　*prepare (everything)/ahead*
25　For he a sone shulde haue,
As he gon aftir° crave;　　　　　　　　　　　*for*
And as God vouchydsaue°　　　　　　　　　　　*promised*
　　　　In worlde þan° was I borne.°　　　　　　*then/born*

When I was borne Noye° named he me,　　　　　*Noah*
30　And saide þees° wordes with mekill wynne,°　　*these/great joy*
"Loo,"° he saide, "þis ilke° is he　　　　　　　*lo/same*
That shalle be comforte to man-kynne,"°　　　　*mankind*
Syrs, by þis wele witte° may ye,　　　　　　　*good (fact) know*
My fadir knewe both more and mynne,°　　　　　*less*
35　By sarteyne° signes he couthe wele° see,　　　*certain/could well*
That al þis worlde shuld synke° for synne.　　　*drown*

---

4. Noah lived for 350 years after the Flood, dying at the age of 950.
5. Noah begot Ham, Shem, and Japheth.

15. Lamech was the son of Methuselah.
23–24. God made Lamech till the soil and prepare the crop to sustain his enlarged family.

Howe God shulde vengeaunce° take,　　*vengeance*
　　As nowe is sene sertayne,°　　*seen certainly*
And hende° of mankynde make,　　*end*
40　That synne would nouȝt° for-sake　　*not*
And howe þat it shuld slake,°　　*abate*
　　And a worlde waxe° agayne.　　*grow*

I wolde God° itt wasted were,　　*would (to) God*
Sa° þat I shuld nott tente þer-tille.°　　*so / have to worry about it*
45　My semely° sonnes and doughteres dere,°　　*good / daughters dear*
Takis ȝe entent° vn-to my skylle.°　　*pay you attention / reason*
1 FIL.　Fader, we are all redy° heere,　　*ready*
Youre biddyng baynly° to fulfille.　　*directly*
NOE.　Goos° calle youre modir,° and comes nere,°　　*go / mother / come near*
50　And spede vs° faste þat we nouȝt spille.°　　*let us hurry / perish*
1 FIL.　Fadir, we shal nouȝt fyne°　　*stop*
　　To° youre biddyng be done.　　*until*
NOE.　Alle þat leues° vndir lyne,°　　*live / linen*
Salle sone,° son, passe to pyne.°　　*shall soon / sorrow*

[SCENE II:　*Noah's home. First son enters.*]

55　1 FIL.　Where are ye, modir myne?
　　Come to my fadir sone.°　　*father quickly*

VXOR.　What sais þou? Sone?
1 FIL.　　　　　　　Moder, certeyne
My fadir thynkis to flitte full ferre.°　　*flee very far*
He biddis you haste with al youre mayne°　　*might*
60　Vnto hym, þat no thyng° you marre.°　　*nothing / harm*
VXOR.　Ȝa!° good sone, hy þe° faste agayne,°　　*yea / son, hurry / (back) again*
And telle hym I wol° come no narre.°　　*will / nearer*
1 FILIUS.　Dame, I wolde do youre biddyng fayne,°　　*eagerly*
But yow bus wende, els° bese° it warre.°　　*you must go, else / will be / worse*
65　VXOR.　Werre!° þat wolde I witte.　　*worse*
　　We bowrde° al wrange,° I wene.°　　*jest / wrong / think*
1 FILIUS.　Modir, I saie° you yitte,°　　*tell / definitely*
My fadir is bowne° to flitte.°　　*ready / get out*
VXOR.　Now, certis,° I sall nouȝt sitte,°　　*certainly / rest*
70　Or° I se° what he mene.°　　*until / see / intends*

───────────

53. A generally inclusive phrase meaning "everyone" (cf. above, p. 311, l. 1814*n*).

[SCENE III: *The Ark, as before.*]

1 FILIUS.   Fadir, I haue done nowe as ye comaunde,°   *commanded*
My modir comes to you this daye.
NOE.   Scho° is welcome, I wele warrande,°   *she/promise*
This worlde sall sone be waste° awaye.   *wasted*
        [*Wife comes in.*]
75 VXOR.   Wher arte þou, Noye?°   *Noah*
NOE.   Loo!° here at hande,   *lo*
Come hedir° faste, dame, I þe° praye.   *here/you*
VXOR.   Trowes° þou þat I wol leue° þe harde° lande,   *think/leave/dry*
And tourne° vp here on toure deraye?°   *come/tower (of) confusion*
Nay, Noye, I am nouȝt bowne
80   To fonde° nowe ouer þere fellis,°   *go/the hills*
Doo,° barnes,° goo we° and trusse to° towne.   *get ready/children/let us go/pack for*
NOE.   Nay certis, sothly þan mon° ye drowne.   *truly then must*
VXOR.   In faythe þou were als goode° come downe,   *might as well*
     And go do som what° ellis.°   *something/else*

85 NOE.   Dame, fowrty° dayes are nerhand° past   *forty/nearly*
And gone sen° it be-gan to rayne;   *since*
On lyffe° salle noman° lenger° laste   *alive/no one/longer*
Bot° we allane,° is nought to layne.°   *but/alone/it cannot be concealed*
VXOR.   Now Noye, in faythe þe fonnes° full faste.   *grow silly*
90 This fare° wille I no lenger frayne;°   *business/ask about*
Þou arte nere woode,° I am agaste.°   *nearly crazy/aghast*
Fare-wele,° I wille go home agayne.   *farewell*
NOE.   O! woman, arte þou woode?
     Of my werkis° þou not wotte;°   *work/know*
95 All þat has ban° or bloode   *bone*
Salle° be ouere flowed° with° þe floode.   *shall/drowned/by*
        [*Detains her.*]
VXOR.   In faithe, þe were als° goode   *so*
     To late° me go my gatte.°   *let/way*

We owte!° herrowe!°   *look out/help*
NOE.   What now! what cheere?°   *what's up*
100 VXOR.   I wille° no narre for no kynnes nede.°   *will (go)/kind (of) need*
NOE.   Helpe, my sonnes, to holde her here!
For tille° her harmes she takes no heede.   *to*
2 FILIUS.   Beis mery, modir,° and mende° youre chere;°   *be happy, mother/change/mood*
This worlde beis° drowned with-outen drede.°   *will be/without doubt*

83–84. Noah is working on top of the ark. Mrs. Noah doesn't   **100.** *no kynnes nede:* i.e., "anything."
understand her husband's sudden obsession with carpentry.

105 VXOR.   Allas!° þat I þis lare shuld lere.° *alas/lesson should learn*
    NOE.   Þou spilles° vs alle, ille myght þou speede!° *destroy/prosper*
    3 FILIUS.   Dere° modir, wonne° with vs; *dear/stay*
        Þer shal no-þyng you greue.° *grieve*
    VXOR.   Nay, nedlyngis° home me bus,° *of necessity/I must (go)*
110 For I haue tolis° to trusse. *utensils*
    NOE.   Woman, why dois° þou þus, *do*
        To make vs more myscheue?° *trouble*

    VXOR.   Noye, þou myght haue leteyn° me wete;° *let/know*
    Erly and late þou wente þer outte,° *out there*
115 And ay° at home þou lete° me sytte, *ever/let*
    To loke° þat nowhere were wele° aboutte. *see/well*
    NOE.   Dame, þou holde me excused of itt;
    It was Goddis wille with-owten doutte.° *doubt*
    VXOR.   What? Wenys° þou so for to go qwitte?° *think/quit*
120 Nay, be° my trouthe,° þou getis° a clowte.° *by/troth/get/blow*
        [Strikes him.]
    NOE.   I pray þe,° dame, be stille *you*
        Thus God wolde° haue it wrought.° *would/done*
    VXOR.   Thow shulde haue witte° my wille,° *asked/opinion*
    Yf I wolde sente° þer tille,° *agree/to it*
125 And Noye,° for þat same skylle° *Noah/reason*
        Þis bargan° sall be bought.° *bargain/paid for*

    Nowe at firste° I fynde and feele° *for the first time/understand*
    Wher° þou hast to þe forest soght;° *why/gone*
    Þou shuld haue tolde me for oure seele° *happiness*
130 Whan° we were to slyke bargane broght.° *when/such state brought*
    NOE.   Now, dame, þe thar noȝt drede° adele° *need not fear/at all*
    For till accounte° it cost þe noght;° *in accounting/nothing*
    A hundereth wyntyr,° I watte° wele, *hundred winters/know*
    Is wente sen° I þis werke° had wrought.° *gone since/work/begun*
135 And when I made endyng,
        God gaffe° me mesore° fayre *gave/measure*
    Of euery-ilke a° thyng; *every*
    He bad° þat I shuld bryng *commanded*
    Of beestis° and foules ȝynge,° *beasts/birds young*
140   Of ilke a° kynde, a peyre.° *each/pair*

    VXOR.   Nowe, certis, and° we shulde skape fro skathe,° *certainly, if/escape from harm*
    And so be saffyd° as ye saye here, *saved*

---

116. I.e., "not knowing of anything."   126. *Þis bargan:* i.e., "what you have done."

My commodrys° and my cosynes bathe,°   *companions/cousins both*
Þam° wolde I wente with vs in feere.°   *(that) they/together*
145 NOE. To wende° in þe watir it were° wathe,° *go/would be/dangerous*
Loke° in and loke with-outen were.° *look/fear*
VXOR. Allas!° my lyff° me° is full lath;° *alas/life/to me/very hateful*
I lyffe ouere lange° þis lare° to lere.° *live too long/lesson/learn*
1 FILIA. Dere modir, mende° youre moode, *dear mother, change*
150 For we sall° wende you with.   *shall*
VXOR. My frendis þat I fra yoode° *from went*
Are ouere flowen° with° floode.   *drowned/by*
2 FILIA. Nowe thanke we God al goode
  That he has grauntid grith.° *granted (us) safe conduct*

155 3 FILIA. Modir, of þis werke nowe wolde ye noȝt wene,° *believe*
That alle shuld worthe° to watres wan.° *should be turned/water gloomy*
2 FILIA. Fadir,° what may þis meruaylle mene?° *father/marvel mean*
Wher-to° made God medilerth° and man? *why/middle-earth*
1 FILIA. So selcouthe° sight was never non° seene, *wondrous/none*
160 Sen firste þat God þis worlde began.
NOE. Wendes° and spers° youre dores be-dene!° *go/bar/immediately*
For bettyr counsell none I can.°   *know*
Þis sorowe is sente for° synne;   *because of*
  Therfore to God we pray,
165 Þat he oure bale wolde blynne.° *sorrow would stop*
3 FILIUS. The kyng of al man-kynne° *mankind*
Owte of þis woo° vs wynne,°   *woe/save*
  Als° þou arte lorde, þat maye.° *as/may (do so)*

1 FILIUS. Ȝa!° lorde, as þou late° vs be borne° *yea/let/born*
170 In þis grete° bale, som bote° vs bede.° *great/remedy/give*
NOE. My sonnes, se ȝe,° myd day and morne *look you*
To thes catelles takes° goode hede.° *of this cattle take/care*
Keppes þam wele° with haye and corne; *keep them well*
And, women, fanges° þes foules and feede, *catch*
175 So þat þey be noȝt lightly lorne,° *not easily lost*
Als longe as we þis liffe sall lede.° *lead*
2 FILIUS. Fadir, we ar° full fayne° *are/eager*
  Youre biddyng to fulfille.
Ix monethes paste er playne°   *months passed are fully*
180 Sen° we wer° putte to peyne.°   *since/were/pain*

---

158. *medilerth:* i.e., the world. In Norse mythology Midgard is below Asgard, the home of the gods, and above Nydgard, the region of fog.

179. *Ix monethes:* Gen. 8:5,6 mentions eleven months. Perhaps *Ix* is a mistake for *xI*, but "nine" agrees with l. 251.

3 FILIUS.   He þat is most of mayne°   *greatest in might*
   May mende° it qwen° he wyll.   *amend/when*

NOE.   O! barnes,° it waxes clere° aboute,   *children/grows clear*
Þat may ʒe see ther wher ʒe sitte.
185 1 FILIUS.   Leffe° fadir, ye loke° þare owte,°   *dear/see/outside*
Yf þat þe water wane ought° ʒitt.°   *at all/yet*
NOE.   That sall I do with-owten dowte,°   *without doubt*
For be° the wanyng may we witte.°   *by/know*
A!° lorde, to þe° I love° and lowte.°   *ah/you/praise/bow down*
190 The catteraks° I trowe be knytte;°   *cataracts/believe are closed*
Beholde, my sonnes al three,
   Þe clowdes are waxen° clere.   *become*
2 FILIUS.   A! lorde of mercy free,°   *generous*
   Ay louyd° myght þou be.   *ever praised*
195 NOE.   I sall assaye° þe see,°   *shall plumb/sea*
   How depe° þat it is here.   *deep*

VXOR.   Loved be that lord þat giffes° all grace,   *gives*
Þat kyndly þus oure care wolde kele.°   *cool*
NOE.   I sall caste leede° and loke° þe space,   *lead/observe*
200 Howe depe þe watir is ilke a° dele.°   *each/part*
   [*Casts the lead.*]
Fyftene cubittis° of highte° itt hase°   *cubits/height (i.e., depth)/has*
Ouere° ilke a hille fully to feylle,°   *over/to be felt*
Butte beese° wel comforte° in þis casse;°   *be/comforted/case*
It is wanand,° þis wate° I wele.   *waning/know*
205 Ther-fore a fowle° of flight   *bird*
   Full sone° sall I forthe sende   *very quickly*
To seke° if he haue sight,   *find out*
Som lande vppon to light;
Þanne° may we witte° full right   *then/know*
210   When oure mornyng° sall mende.   *grief*

Of all þe fowles þat men may fynde,
The raven is wighte,° and wyse is hee.°   *sturdy/he*
Þou arte ful crabbed and al thy kynde;°   *tribe*
Wende° forthe þi° course I comaunde° þe,   *go/(on) your/command*
215 And werly watte° and yþer° þe wynd,°   *warily know/hither/return*
Yf þou fynde awdir° lande or tree.   *either*
   [*Sends forth the raven.*]
Ix monethes here haue we bene pyned,°   *been pained*

---

188. *witte:* i.e., "know whether the weather is clearing."

But when God wyll, better mon bee.°	*may (we) be*
1 FILIA. Þat lorde þat lennes° vs lyffe,°	*grants/life*
220 To lere° his lawes in lande,	*learn*
He mayd° bothe man and wyffe,°	*made/woman*
He° helpe to stynte° oure striffe.°	*(may) he/stop/trouble*
3 FILIA. Oure cares are kene° as knyffe,°	*sharp/knife*
God graunte° vs goode tydand.°	*grant/news*
225 1 FIL. Fadir,° þis foule° is forthe° full lange;°	*father/bird/gone/long*
Vppon sum° lande I trowe he lende,°	*some/landed*
His foode þerfore to fynde and fange,°	*catch*
That makis hym be a fayland° frende.	*failing*
NOE. Nowe sonne, and yf he so forthe gange,°	*went*
230 Sen° he for all oure welthe gon° wende,	*since/well-being did*
Then be he for his werkis wrange°	*wrongdoing*
Euermore weried with-owten° ende.	*cursed without*
And sertis° for to see	*certainly*
Whan° oure sorowe salle sesse,°	*when/shall cease*
235 A nodyr° foule full free°	*another/good*
Owre° messenger salle be.	*our*
Þou doufe,° I comaunde þe°	*dove/you*
Owre comforte to encresse.°	*increase*
A faithfull fewle° to sende art þow,°	*bird/you*
240 Of alle with-in þere wauys° wyde.	*the waves*
Wende forthe, I pray þe, for owre prowe,°	*profit*
And sadly seke° on ilke a° side	*seriously search/every*
Yf þe floodes be falland° nowe,	*falling*
Þat þou on þe erthe may belde° and byde;°	*reach cover/remain*
245 Bryng vs som tokenyng° þar° we may trowe°	*sign/by which/know*
What tydandes° sall of° vs be-tyde.°	*tidings/to/befall*
[*Sends forth the dove.*]	
2 FILIA. Goode lorde! on vs þou luke,°	*look*
And sesse oure sorow sere,°	*sorrows many*
Sen we al synne for-soke°	*forsook*
250 And to thy lare vs toke.°	*teaching ourselves took*
3 FILIA. A twelmothe bott° xij weke°	*year minus/weeks*
Have we be houerand° here.	*been waiting*
NOE. Now barnes,° we may be blithe and gladde,	*children*
And lowe° oure lord of heuenes° kyng.	*reverence/heaven*
255 My birde has done as I hym badde;°	*asked*
An olyue braunche° I se° hym brynge.	*olive branch/see*
Blyste° be þou, fewle þat neuere° was fayd,°	*blessed/never/doomed*
That in thy force° makis no faylyng.	*power*

Mare joie° in herte° never are° I hadde;   *more joy/heart/before*
260 We mone° be saued, now may we synge!   *will*
Come hedir,° my sonnes, in hye;°   *here/quickly*
    Oure woo° away is wente.°   *woe/gone*
I see here certaynely
    Þe hillis of hermonye.°   *Armenia*
265 1 FILIUS.   Lovyd° be þat lord for-thy°   *praised/therefore*
    That vs oure lyffes hase lente.°   *lives has granted*

VXOR.   For wrekis° nowe þat we may wynne,°   *from punishment/get away*
Oute of þis woo þat we in wore.°   *were*
But Noye,° where are nowe all oure kynne,°   *Noah/kin*
270 And companye we knewe before?
NOE.   Dame, all ar° drowned, late be° thy dyne,°   *are/stop/noise*
And sone° þei boughte° þer synnes sore.   *quickly/paid for*
Gud lewyn latte° vs be-gynne   *good living let*
So þat we greue° oure God nomore;   *grieve*
275 He was greved in degre,°   *to (a) degree*
    And gretely° moved in mynde,   *greatly*
For synne as men may see,
Dum dixit penitet me.
Full° sore for-thynkyng° was he   *very/repentant*
280   That euere° he made mankynde.   *ever*

That makis vs nowe to tole° and trusse,°   *work/prepare*
But sonnes, he saide, I watte wele° when,   *know well*
Arcum ponam in nubibus,
He sette his bowe clerly° to kenne,°   *rainbow clearly/recognize*
285 As a tokenyng by-twcnc° hym and vs   *bond between*
In knawlage tille° all cristen° men.   *knowledge to/Christian*
That fro° þis worlde were fynyd° þus,   *when/ended*
With wattir wolde° he neuere wastyd° þen.   *would/destroy (it)*
Þus has God, most of° myght,   *greatest in*
290   Sette his senge° full clere°   *sign/clearly*
Vppe in þe ayre of heght;°   *on high*
The rayne-bowe it is right,
As men may se, in sight,
    In seasons° of þe yere.°   *certain times/year*

295 2 FIL.   Sir, nowe sen° God oure souerand syre°   *since/sovereign lord*

---

264. Noah's ark supposedly rested on Mount Ararat in Armenia, now eastern Turkey. The ark has been the object of several unsuccessful search expeditions, although Mandeville says it could easily be seen on a clear day!

278. "Until he said, 'I repent.'"

283. "I shall place an arc (i.e., rainbow) in the clouds."

Has sette his syne° þus in certayne,°   *sign/certainty*
Than° may we wytte° þis worldis empire   *then/know*
Shall euermore laste, is noȝt to layne.°   *it cannot be concealed*
NOE.   Nay, sonne, þat sall° we nouȝt° desire,   *shall/not*
300 For and° we do we wirke° in wane,°   *if/labor/vain*
For it sall ones° be waste with° fyre,   *once/destroyed by*
And never worþe to° worlde agayne.   *become a*
VXOR.   A!° syre, owre hertis° are feere° for° þes sawes°   *ah/our hearts/afraid/because of / these sayings*

That ȝe° saye here,   *you*
305 That myscheffe mon° be more.   *trouble will*
NOE.   Beis noȝt aferde° þerfore;   *be not afraid*
ȝe sall noght lyffe þan yore,°   *not live then anymore*
Be° many hundereth yhere.°   *by/hundred years*

1 FILIUS.   Fadir,° howe sall þis lyffe° be ledde,   *father/life*
310 Sen non° ar in þis worlde but we?   *none*
NOE.   Sones,° with youre wiffes° ȝe salle be stedde,°   *sons/wives/put to work*
And multyplye youre seede salle ȝe.
ȝoure barnes° sall ilkon° othir wedde,   *your children/each*
And worshippe God in gud degre;°   *good measure*
315 Beestes° and foules° sall forthe be bredde,   *beasts/birds*
And so a worlde be-gynne to bee.°   *be*
Nowe travaylle° salle ȝe taste   *hardship*
To wynne you° brede° and wyne,   *for yourself/bread*
For alle þis worlde is waste;
320 Theȝ° beestes muste be vnbraste,°   *the/unloosed*
And wende° we hense° in haste,   *go/hence*
In Goddis blissyng° and myne.°   *blessing/remembrance*

CRUCIFIXIO CRISTI

(THE PYNNERES AND PAYNTERS)

[DRAMATIS PERSONAE
JESUS
FOUR SOLDIERS (*1, 2, 3, 4 Miles*)]

[SCENE: *Golgotha, afterwards Mount Calvary.*]

1 MILES.   Sir knyghtis, take heede° hydir° in hye,°   *look/here/quickly*
This dede° on-dergh° we may noght° drawe;°   *deed/without trouble/not/carry out*
ȝee woote° youre selffe als wele° as I   *you know/as well*

Howe lordis and leders° of owre° lawe   *leaders/our*
5 Has geven dome° þat þis doote° schall dye.°   *given judgment/fool/die*
  2 MIL.   Sir, alle þare counsaile° wele we knawe;°   *their counsel/know*
Sen° we are comen° to Caluarie,   *since/come*
Latte ilke° man helpe nowe as hym awe.°   *let each/he ought*
  3 MIL.   We are all redy, loo,°   *ready, lo*
10 Þat forward° to fulfille.   *agreement*
  4 MIL.   Late° here howe we schall doo,°   *let's (see)/do*
And go we tyte° þer tille.°   *directly/to it*

  2 MIL.   It may noȝt° helpe her° for to hone,°   *not/here/delay*
If we schall any worshippe° wynne.   *praise*
15 2 MIL.   He muste be dede° nedelyngis° by none.°   *dead/of necessity/noon*
  3 MIL.   Þan° is goode tyme þat we begynne.   *then*
  4 MIL.   Late dynge° hym doune, þan is he done;   *let's knock*
He schall nought dere° vs with his dynne.°   *not hurt/noise*
  1 MIL.   He schall be sette° and lerned sone,°   *placed/taught quickly*
20 With care° to hym and all his kynne.°   *sorrow/kin*
  2 MIL.   Þe foulest dede° of all   *death*
Shalle he dye for his dedis.
  3 MIL.   That menes crosse° hym we shall.   *means crucify*
  4 MIL.   Behalde° so right he redis.°   *behold/counsels*

25 1 MIL.   Thanne to þis werke vs° muste take heede,°   *work we/pay attention*
So þat oure wirkyng° be noght wronge.   *working*
  2 MIL.   None° othir noote° to neven° is nede,°   *no/matter/mention/necessary*
But latte vs haste hym for to hange.
  3 MIL.   And I haue gone for gere,° goode speede,°   *gear/quickly*
30 Bothe hammers and nayles large and lange.°   *long*
  4 MIL.   Þanne may we boldely do þis dede;
Commes° on, late kille þis traitoure strange.°   *come/strong*
  1 MIL.   Faire° mygȝt ȝe falle° in feere,°   *good fortune/ you befall/together*
Þat has wrought on° þis wise.°   *acted in/manner*
35 2 MIL.   Vs nedis° nought for to lere°   *need/learn*
Suche faitoures° to chastise.   *deceivers*

  3 MIL.   Sen ilke a° thyng es° right arrayed,°   *every/is/arranged*
The wiselier° nowe wirke may we.   *better*
  4 MIL.   Þe crosse on grounde is goodely graied,°   *prepared*
40 And boorede° even as it awith° to be.   *bored/ought*
  1 MIL.   Lokis° þat þe ladde on° lengthe be layde,   *see/fellow at (full)*
And made° me° þane vnto° þis tree.°   *placed/for me/then on/(i.e., beam)*

---

35. *for to lere:* i.e., "to be taught."

2 MIL. For alle his fare° he schalle be flaied;°	*doings/frightened*
That one assaie sone° schalle ye see.	*trial soon*
45 3 MIL. Come forthe, þou cursed knave;	
Thy comforte sone schall kele.°	*cool*
4 MIL. Thyne hyre° here schall þou haue.	*wages*
1 MIL. Walkes oon,° now wirke° we wele.°	*walk on/do/well*
JESUS. Almyghty God, my Fadir free,°	*Father generous*
50 Late þis materes° be made° in mynde.°	*let these matters/put/remembrance*
Þou badde° þat I schulde buxsome° be,	*bade/should humble*
For Adam plyght° for to be pyned.°	*Adam's sin/suffer*
Here to dede I obblisshe me°	*obligate myself*
Fro° þat synne for to saue mankynde,	*from*
55 And soueraynely° be-seke° I þe,°	*above all/beseech/you*
That þai° for° me may fauoure fynde;	*they/because of*
And fro þe fende þame fende,°	*Devil them defend*
So þat þer saules° be saffe,°	*souls/saved*
In welthe withouten° ende;	*bliss without*
60 I kepe nought ellis° to craue.	*care nothing else*
1 MIL. We!° herke,° sir knyghtis, for mahoundis° bloode!	*hey/listen/by Mohammed's*
Of Adam-kynde° is all his þoght.°	*Adam's kin/thought*
2 MIL. Þe warlowe° waxis° werre° þan woode;°	*wicked man/is getting/worse/mad*
Þis doulfull dede ne dredith° he noght.°	*grievous death not fears/not*
65 3 MIL. Þou schulde haue mynde, with mayne° and moode,°	*might/thought*
Of wikkid werkis° þat þou haste wrought.°	*wicked deeds/have done*
4 MIL. I hope° þat he had bene as° goode	*think/been so*
Haue sesed of sawes° þat he vppe sought.°	*(to) have ceased in sayings/brought*
1 MIL. Thoo° sawes schall rewe hym° sore	*those/repent he*
70 For all his saunteryng sone.°	*babbling soon*
2 MIL. Ille spede° þame° þat hym spare	*luck/to them*
Tille he to dede be done!	
3 MIL. Haue° done belyue,° boy, and make þe bounc,°	*get/quickly/yourself ready*
And bende þi bakke° vn-to þis tree.	*back*
[*Jesus lies down.*]	
75 4 MIL. Byhalde,° hym-selffe has laide hym° doune,	*behold/himself*
In lenghe° and breede° as he schulde bee.°	*length/breadth/be*
1 MIL. This traitoure here teynted of° treasoune,	*tainted with*
Gose° faste and fette° hym þan, 3e thre.°	*go/fetch/then, you three*
And sen° he claymeth kyngdome with croune,	*since*

---

61. *for mahoundis bloode:* The soldiers, as representatives of infidels and the religious enemy best known to contemporary Christendom, swear by Mohammed—one of several anachronisms in the play.

80 Even as a kyng here haue° schall hee.°   *have (it)/he*
   2 MIL.   Nowe, certis,° I schall noȝt feyne°   *certainly/not stop*
   Or° his right hande be feste.°   *before/fastened*
   3 MIL.   Þe lefte hande þanne is myne;
   Late° see who beres° hym beste.   *let's/carries*

85 4 MIL.   Hys lymmys on° lenghe þan schalle I lede,°   *limbs at (full)/place*
   And even vnto þe bore° þame bringe.   *nail hole*
   1 MIL.   Vnto his heede° I schall take hede,°   *head/pay attention*
   And with myne hande helpe hym to hyng.°   *hang*
   2 MIL.   Nowe sen we foure shall do þis dede,
90 And medill° with þis vnthrifty° thyng,   *meddle/ill-thriving*
   Late° no man spare° for° speciall speede,   *let/be sparing/of*
   Tille þat we haue made endyng.
   3 MIL.   Þis forward° may not faile,   *agreement*
   Nowe are we right arraiede.°   *prepared*
95 4 MIL.   This boy° here in oure baile°   *fellow/? power*
   Shall bide full° bittir brayde.°   *suffer very/torment*

   1 MIL.   Sir knyghtis, saie,° howe wirke° we nowe?   *say/work*
   2 MIL.   Ȝis,° certis, I hope° I holde þis hande.   *yes/expect*
   3 MIL.   And to þe boore° I haue it brought,   *nail hole*
100 Full boxumly with-outen bande.°   *obediently without rope*
   4 MIL.   Strike on þan harde, for hym þe boght.°   *(who) you redeemed*
   1 MIL.   Ȝis, here is a stubbe will stiffely° stande;   *nail (that) will strongly*
   Thurgh° bones and senous° it schall be soght.°   *through/sinews/brought*
   This werke° is well,° I will warande.°   *work/good/warrant*
105 2 MIL.   Saie, sir, howe do we þore?°   *there*
   Þis bargayne° may not blynne.°   *affair/stop*
   3 MIL.   It° failis° a foote and more,   *(the body)/is short*
   Þe senous are so gone ynne.°   *shrunk*

   4 MIL.   I hope þat marke a-misse be° bored.   *was wrongly*
110 2 MIL.   Þan muste he bide in bittir bale.°   *sorrow*
   3 MIL.   In faith,° it was ouere skantely scored;°   *truly/too short marked*
   Þat makis it fouly° for to faile.°   *badly/in error*
   1 MIL.   Why carpe° ȝe so? Faste° on a corde,   *chatter/tie*

---

80. The line refers to a statement in the previous play in the cycle, *Christ Led Up to Calvary* by the shearers, that the cross was made out of a tree called the "king's tree." This is fitting for someone who calls himself king.

101. *for . . . boght:* The irony of this tag would not have gone unnoticed by the audience.

111. In the previous play of the cycle, the third soldier specifically mentions that he has measured the cross correctly. Since the plays followed each other in pageant wagons on the streets, the audience could easily remember and link the speeches of one play to those in the following production. This linkage and resulting unification of the plays justifies the general title of the York cycle as *The Play of Corpus Christi.*

And tugge hym to, by toppe and taile.
115 3 MIL.   3a,° þou comaundis lightly° as a lorde;   *yea/command (as) easily*
Come helpe to haale,° with ille haile.°   *haul/bad luck (to you)*
1 MIL.   Nowe certis þat schall I doo,°   *do*
Full suerly° as a snayle.   *surely*
3 MIL.   And I schall tacche° hym too,°   *tack/on*
120 Full nemely° with a nayle.   *nimbly*

Þis werke will holde, þat dar° I heete,°   *dare/promise*
For nowe are feste faste° both his handis.   *fastened strongly*
4 MIL.   Go we all foure þanne° to his feete;   *then*
So schall oure space° be spedely spende.°   *time/quickly spent*
125 2 MIL.   Latte° see, what bourde° his bale myght beete;°   *let's/jest/remedy*
Tharto° my bakke° nowe wolde° I bende.   *thereto/back/would*
3 MIL.   Owe!° Þis werke is all vnmeete;°   *oh/unfit*
This boring muste all be amende.°   *corrected*
1 MIL.   A!° pees,° man, for mahounde;°   *ah/be quiet/Mohammed*
130 Latte° noman° wotte° þat wondir.°   *let/no one/find out/calamity*
A roope° schall rugge° hym doune,   *rope/pull*
Yf° all synnous go a-soundre.°   *(even) if/sinews tear apart*

2 MIL.   Þat corde full kyndely° can I knytte,°   *easily/knot*
Þe comforte of þis karle° to kele.°   *churl/cool*
135 1 MIL.   Feste° on þanne faste þat° all be fytte;°   *fasten/so that/fitted*
It is no force° howe felle° he feele.°   *matter/sharply/feels (it)*
2 MIL.   Lugge° on 3e° both a litill 3itt.°   *tug/you/little more*
3 MIL.   I schalle nought sese,° as I haue seele.°   *not stop/bliss (in heaven)*
4 MIL.   And I schall fonde° hym for to hitte.   *try*
140 2 MIL.   Owe, haylle!°   *haul*
4 MIL.   Hoo° nowe, I halde° it wele.°   *ho/hold/well*
1 MIL.   Haue° done, dryue in þat nayle,   *get*
So þat no faute° be foune.°   *fault/found*
4 MIL.   Þis wirkyng° wolde no3t° faile,   *job/not*
Yf foure bullis here were boune.°   *bound*

145 1 MIL.   Ther° cordis haue evill encressed° his paynes,   *the/badly increased*
Or° he wer tille° þe booryngis° brought.   *before/were to/nail holes*
2 MIL.   3aa, assoundir° are both synnous and veynis,   *yea, apart*
On ilke a° side, so° haue we soughte.°   *each/as/looked*
3 MIL.   Nowe all his gaudis° no thyng° hym gaynes;   *tricks/nothing*
150 His sauntering° schall with bale° be bought.   *babbling/sorrow*

---

118. The snail's progress is sure. Our present idea of the slow "snail's pace" is probably not implied here.

138. *as ... seele:* a tag (though here an ironic one) similar to *for the nonys* (l. 219) and *so motte I thryve* (l. 246).

4 MIL.   I wille goo saie° to oure soueraynes° — *go say/sovereigns*
Of all þis werkis° howe we haue wrought.° — *work/done*
1 MIL.   Nay, sirs, a nothir° thyng — *another*
Fallis firste to youe me;° — *(and) me*
155 Þai badde° we schulde° hym hyng° — *they bade (that)/should/hang*
On heghte° þat men myght see. — *high*

2 MIL.   We woote° wele so ther° wordes wore,° — *know/their/were*
But sir, þat dede° will do vs dere.° — *deed/be hard for us*
1 MIL.   It may° not mende° for to moote° more; — *will/do/argue*
160 Þis harlotte° muste be hanged here. — *recreant*
2 MIL.   The mortaise° is made fitte þerfore.° — *mortise/for it*
3 MIL.   Feste on° youre fyngeres° þan, in feere.° — *grab on (with)/fingers/together*
4 MIL.   I wene° it wolle neuere° come þore.° — *think/will never/there*
We foure rayse it noȝt right, to yere.° — *this year*
165 1 MIL.   Say, man, whi carpis° þou soo?° — *chatter/so*
Thy liftyng was but light.° — *weak*
2 MIL.   He menes° þer muste be moo° — *means/more*
To heve° hym vppe on hight.° — *heave/high*

3 MIL.   Now certis,° I hope it schall noght° nede° — *certainly/not/be necessary*
170 To calle to vs more companye.
Me-thynke° we foure schulde do þis dede, — *I think*
And bere° hym to ȝone° hille on high. — *carry/yonder*
1 MIL.   It muste be done, with-outen drede.° — *without doubt*
Nomore,° but loke° ȝe be redy,° — *no more/see/ready*
175 And þis parte schalle I lifte and leede;° — *lead*
On lenghe° he schalle no lenger° lie. — *at (full) length/longer*
Therfore nowe makis you boune;° — *make yourselves ready*
Late° bere hym to ȝone hill. — *let's*
4 MIL.   Thanne° will I bere° here doune, — *then/push*
180 And tente° his tase° vntill.° — *attend/toes/to*

2 MIL.   We twoo schall see tille aythir° side, — *(the) other*
For ellis° þis werke° will wrie° all wrang.° — *else/work/turn/wrong*
3 MIL.   We are redy, in° Gode, sirs, abide,° — *by/wait*
And late° me first his fete° vp fang.° — *let/feet/take*
185 2 MIL.   Why tente ȝe° so to tales þis tyde?° — *listen you/(at) this time*
　　　　　　[*All lift the cross together.*]
1 MIL.   Lifte vppe!
4 MIL.　　　　　Latte° see! — *let's*
2 MIL.　　　　　　　　Owe!° lifte a-lang.° — *oh/along*
3 MIL.   Fro° all þis harme he schulde hym hyde,° — *from/should (be able) himself (to) hide*

And° he war° God. — *if/were*

4 MIL. þe deuill hym hang!	
1 MIL. For grete° harme haue I hente;°	great/come to
190 My schuldir° is in soundre.°	shoulder/asunder
2 MIL. And sertis° I am nere schente,°	certainly/nearly ruined
So lange° haue I borne vndir.	long
2 MIL. This cross and I in twoo muste twynne,°	part
Ellis° brekis° my bakke° in sondre sone.°	(or) else/will break/back/soon
195 4 MIL. Laye doune agayne and leue° youre dynne,°	stop/noise
þis dede for° vs will neuere be done.	by
[They lay it down.]	
1 MIL. Assaie,° sirs, latte se° yf any gynne,°	try/see/contrivance
May helpe hym vppe, with-outen hone;°	delay
For here schulde wight° men worschippe° wynne,	sturdy/praise
200 And noght with gaudis° al day to gone.°	foolishness/waste
2 MIL. More wighter men þan we	
Full° fewe I hope° ʒe fynde.°	very/think/(will) find
2 MIL. þis bargayne° will noght bee,°	business/be
For certis me° wantis° wynde.	I/am out of/breath
205 4 MIL. So wille of° werke neuere° we wore;°	at a loss about/never/were
I hope þis carle° some cautellis caste.°	churl/tricks played
2 MIL. My bourdeyne satte° me wondir soore;°	burden sits/wondrous sore
Vnto þe hill I myght noght laste.	
1 MIL. Lifte vppe, and sone he schall be þore;°	there
210 Therfore feste on° your fyngeres faste.°	hold on (with)/fingers hard
[They take up the cross again.]	
3 MIL. Owe lifte!	
1 MIL. We,° loo!°	hey/good
4 MIL. A litill° more.	little
2 MIL. Holde þanne!	
1 MIL. Howe nowe!	
2 MIL. þe werste° is paste.°	worst/past
3 MIL. He wcycs° a wikkid wcght.°	weighs/mean weight
2 MIL. So may we all foure saie,	
215 Or° he was heued° on heght,°	before/heaved/high
And raysed in þis array.°	manner
4 MIL. He made vs stande as any stones,	
So boustous° was he for to bere.°	huge/carry
1 MIL. Nowe raise hym nemely° for þe nonys,°	nimbly/at this time
220 And sette hym be° þis mortas° heere.	in/mortise
And latte° hym falle in alle at ones,°	let/once

For certis þat payne schall haue no pere.°   *equal*

3 MIL.   Heue vppe!

[*The cross is reared.*]

4 MIL.   Latte doune, so all his bones

Are a-soundre° nowe on sides seere.°   *asunder/several*

225 1 MIL.   Þis fallyng was more felle°   *painful*

Þan all the harmes he hadde,

Nowe may a man wele telle°   *count*

Þe leste lith° of þis ladde.°   *smallest joint/fellow*

3 MIL.   Me thynkith þis cross will noght abide,°   *not stay*

230 Ne° stande stille in þis morteyse ʒitt.°   *nor/mortise yet*

4 MIL.   Att° þe firste tyme° was it made ouere° wyde;   *from/the first/too*

Þat makis it wave, þou may wele witte.°   *notice*

1 MIL.   Itt schall be sette on ilke a° side,   *each*

So þat it schall no forther flitte.°   *further move*

235 Goode wegges° schall we take þis tyde,°   *wedges/time*

And feste° þe foote; þanne° is all fitte.   *fasten/then*

2 MIL.   Here are wegges arraied°   *placed*

For þat, both grete° and smale.°   *great/small*

3 MIL.   Where are oure hameres° laide,   *hammers*

240 Þat we schulde wirke° with all?°   *should work/with*

4 MIL.   We haue þem here euen° atte oure hande.°   *just/at hand*

2 MIL.   Gyffe° me þis wegge; I schall it in dryue.   *give*

4 MIL.   Here is anodir° ʒitt ordande.°   *another/made ready*

3 MIL.   Do take° it me hidir belyue.°   *bring/here quickly*

245 1 MIL.   Laye on þanne faste.

3 MIL.   ʒis,° I warrande.°   *yes/warrant*

I thryng þame same,° so motte° I thryve.   *(will) press them together/may*

Nowe will þis crosse full° stabely stande;   *very*

All° yf he raue þei will noght ryve.°   *even/tear*

1 MIL.   Say, sir, howe likis° þou nowe,   *like (it)*

250 Þis werke° þat we haue wrought?°   *work/done*

4 MIL.   We praye youe sais° vs howe   *tell*

ʒe fele,° or faynte ʒe ought?°   *you feel/at all*

JESUS.   Al men þat walkis by waye° or strete,°   *road/street*

Takes tente° ʒe schalle no trauayle tyne;°   *take heed/labor lose*

255 By-holdes myn heede,° myn handis, and my feete,   *behold my head*

And fully feele nowe or° ʒe fyne°   *before/stop*

Yf any mournyng° may be meete°   *grief/equal*

Or myscheue mesured° vnto myne.   *sorrow measured*

My fadir,° þat alle bales° may bete,° — *Father/cares/remedy*
260 For-giffis þes° men þat dois° me pyne.° — *forgive these/cause/pain*
What þai wirke wotte° þai noght; — *they do know*
Therfore, my Fadir, I craue
Latte neuere þer° synnys be sought,° — *(that you) let never their/sought (out)*

But see° þer saules° to saue. — *look/souls*

265 1 MIL.   We!° Harke! He jangelis° like a jay. — *hey/chatters*
   2 MIL.   Me° thynke he patris° like a py.° — *I/patters/magpie*
   3 MIL.   He has ben doand° all þis day, — *been doing (it)*
And made grete meuyng of° mercy. — *plea for*
   4 MIL.   Es° þis þe same þat gune° vs say° — *is/did/tell*
270 That he was Goddis sone° almyghty? — *son*
   1 MIL.   Therfore he felis full felle affraye,° — *badly frightened*
And demyd° þis day for to dye.° — *doomed/die*
   2 MIL.   Vah!° Qui destruis templum. — *ah*
   3 MIL.   His sawes wer° so, certayne.° — *words were/certainly*
275 4 MIL.   And sirs, he saide to some
He myght rayse it agayne.

   1 MIL.   To mustir° þat he hadde no myght, — *show*
For all the kautelles° þat he couthe kaste,° — *tricks/could do*
All yf° he wer in worde so wight,° — *although/strong*
280 For all his force nowe he is feste.° — *bound*
   Als° Pilate demed is° done and dight,° — *as/decreed (it) is/prepared*
Therfore I rede° þat we go reste. — *advise*
   2 MIL.   Þis race mon° be rehersed° right, — *deed must/told*
Thurgh° þe worlde both este° and weste. — *through/east*
285 3 MIL.   3aa, late° hym hynge° here stille, — *yea, let/hang*
And make mowes on° þe mone.° — *faces at/moon*
   4 MIL.   Þanne° may we wende° at wille. — *then/go*
   1 MIL.   Nay, goode sirs, noght° so sone.° — *not/soon*

For certis° vs° nedis° anodir note;° — *certainly/for us/is necessary/another matter*

290 Þis kirtill wolde° I of you craue. — *robe would*
   2 MIL.   Nay, nay, sir, we will loke be° lotte — *see by*
Whilke° of vs foure fallis° to to haue. — *which/(it) falls*
   3 MIL.   I rede we drawe cutte° for þis coote;° — *straws/coat*
Loo, se° howe sone alle sidis° to saue.° — *lo, see/parties/are protected*

259–61. Luke 23:34.
273. "Thou that destroyest the temple" (Matt. 27:40).

291–2. John 19:23, 24.

²⁹⁵ 4 MIL.   The schorte cutte schall wynne, þat wele ȝe woote,°   *well you know*
Whedir° itt falle to knyght or knave.°   *whether/boy*
1 MIL.   Felowes,° ȝe thar° noght flyte,°   *fellows/need/scold*
For this mantell is myne.
2 MIL.   Goo° we þanne hense tyte;°   *go/away quickly*
³⁰⁰ Þis trauayle° here we tyne.°   *labor/lose (? forget)*

THE SECOND SHEPHERDS' PLAY

DATE: a. 1500. ✦ MANUSCRIPT: from Towneley Hall in Lancashire, now in the Huntington Library, San Marino, California. The dialect is Northern (Yorkshire). ✦ EDITIONS: G. England and A. W. Pollard, eds., *The Towneley Plays*, Early English Text Society, ES 71 (London, 1897); J. M. Manly, *Specimens of the Pre-Shakespearean Drama* (Boston, 1897). One may also consult Millicent Carey, *The Wakefield Group in the Towneley Cycle*, Hesperia Ergänzungsreihe, XI (Baltimore, Göttingen, 1930).

Typical Northernisms found in the text are: (1) *-is/-ys* is used for the present third person singular and plural of verbs (*walkys, commys*) and the plural of nouns (*nyghtys*). (2) The Northern interchange of *wh* for *qu* (*whik = quick*) and *qw* for *wh* (*qwy = why*) is common. (3) OE *a* is kept before nasals (*sang = song, lang = long*). (4) In the vocabulary, the following forms will recur frequently: *till*, "to," *gar*, "make," *lyg*, "lie," *ilk*, "each." In general, the glosses should eliminate further difficulties.

The Second (and also the inferior *First*) *Shepherds' Play* is the work of the anonymous Wakefield Master, the genius of medieval comic drama. The play was the thirteenth in the Towneley cycle of guild plays performed in Wakefield during the 15th century. With its high humor and its references to exploited laborers, husbands, and wives, this miracle play has obvious audience appeal; and as a brilliant, if impudent, parody of a religious scene, the comedy is continually astonishing in its boldness.

[DRAMATIS PERSONAE

FIRST SHEPHERD (*Primus Pastor*)   MAK   ANGEL (*Angelus*)
SECOND SHEPHERD (*Secundus Pastor*) JILL, HIS WIFE (*Gyll, uxor ejus*) JESUS
THIRD SHEPHERD (*Tercius Pastor*)   MARY (*Maria*)]

PRIMUS PASTOR. Lord, what these weders ar° cold! and I am yll happyd;°	*how this weather is/dressed*
I am nere hande° dold° so long haue I nappyd;	*almost/numbed*
My legys thay° fold, my fyngers ar° chappyd;	*they/are*
It is not as I wold,° for I am al lappyd°	*wish/wrapped*
5 In sorow.	
In stormes and tempest,	
Now in the eest,° now in the west,	*east*
Wo° is hym° has neuer rest	*woe/him (that)*
Myd day nor morow!	

¹⁰ Bot° we sely shepardes° that walkys on the moore,   *but/poor shepherds*
In fayth we are nere handys outt° of the doore;   *(put) out*
No wonder as it standys if we be poore,
For the tylthe° of oure landys lyys° falow as the floore,   *produce/lies*
    As ye ken.°   *know*
¹⁵ We ar so hamyd,°   *crippled*
  For-taxed° and ramyd,°   *overtaxed/driven*
  We ar mayde hand-tamyd,°   *made tame*
    With thyse gentlery° men.   *by these gentle*

Thus thay refe° vs oure° rest, oure lady theym wary!°   *deprive/(of) our/them curse*
²⁰ These men that ar lord fest° thay cause the ploghe tary.°   *lords' servants/plow (to) stick*
That men say is for the best we fynde it contrary;
Thus ar husbandys opprest,° in pointe to myscary°   *farmers oppressed/danger of*
        suffering
    On° lyfe.   *in*
Thus hold thay vs hunder,°   *under*
²⁵ Thus thay bryng vs in blonder;°   *disaster*
It were° greatte wonder,   *would be*
    And° euer shuld° we thryfe.°   *if/should/thrive*

For may° he gett a paynt slefe° or a broche° now on dayes,°   *if/an embroidered sleeve/brooch/*
        nowadays
Wo is hym that hym grefe° or onys° agane says!°   *grieves/anything/gainsays*
³⁰ Dar° noman° hym reprefe° what mastry° he mays,°   *dares/no one/reprove/wrong/*
        may (do)
And yit° may noman lefe oone° word that he says,   *yet/believe one*
    No letter.
He can make purveance,°   *get provision*
  With boste° and bragance,°   *boast/bragging*
³⁵ And all is thrugh mantenance°   *through support*
    Of men that are gretter.°   *greater*

Ther shall com a swane° as prowde as a po,°   *man/peacock*
He must borow my wane,° my ploghe also.   *wagon*
Then I am full fane° to graunt or° he go.   *very happy/grant before*
⁴⁰ Thus lyf° we in payne, anger, and wo,   *live*
    By nyght and day;
He must haue if he langyd,°   *wants (it)*
If° I shuld forgang° it.   *(even) if/should forgo*

---

20. *These ... fest:* The shepherd's complaint is evidently directed at stewards and reeves, those men permanently in the service of a lord.

39. I.e., he must appear to be happy to give his wagon and plow.

I were° better be hangyd   *would*

45   Then oones° say hym nay.   *than once*

It dos° me good, as I walk thus by myn oone,°   *does/myself*
Of this warld° for to talk in maner° of mone.°   *world/(a) kind/complaint*
To my shepe° wyll I stalk and **herkyn anone,°**   *sheep/listen then*
Ther abyde° on a balk or sytt on a stone   *wait*

50   Full soyne.°   *soon*
For I trowe,° perde,°   *believe/in faith*
Trew° men if thay° be,   *true/they*
We gett more compane°   *company*
          Or it be noyne.°   *noon*

55 SECUNDUS PASTOR.   Benste and dominus! what may this   *mean*
          bemeyne?°
Why fares this warld thus? Oft haue we not sene.°   *seen*
Lord, thyse weders ar spytus° and the windys° full kene.° *this weather is spiteful/winds/ sharp*

And the frostys so hydus° thay water myn eeyne,°   *hideous/my eyes*
          No ly.°   *lie*

60 Now in dry, now in wete,°   *wet*
Now in snaw,° now in slete,°   *snow/sleet*
When my shone freys° to my fete,°   *shoes freeze/feet*
          It is not all esy.°   *easy*

Bot° as far as I ken° or yit as I go,   *but/know*

65 We sely° wedmen° dre mekyll wo.°   *poor/married men/suffer much woe*
We haue sorow then° and then; it fallys° oft so.   *over/happens*
Sely capyle,° oure hen, both to and fro   *silly Coppel*
          She kakyls;°   *cackles*
Bot begyn° she to crok,°   *(if) begins/croak*

70 To groyne° or to clok,°   *grunt/cluck*
Wo is hym° is oure cok,°   *woeful/cock*
          For he is in the shekyls.°   *shackles*

These men that ar° wed haue not all thare° wyll,   *are/their*
When they ar full hard sted° thay sygh full styll.°   *pressed/constantly*

75 God wayte° thay ar led full hard and full yll.   *knows*
In bower° nor in bed thay say noght° ther tyll.°   *chamber/nothing/thereto*
          This tyde°   *time*
My parte haue I fun,°   *learned*

---

49. *balk*: the narrow strip of grassland dividing two plowed parts of the commons (the land owned and used by all the inhabitants of a town).

55. *Benste*: contraction of Latin *benedicite*, "bless us"; *dominus*: Latin, "Lord."

I know my lesson.
80 Wo is hym that is bun,°   *bound*
    For he must abyde.°   *remain*

Bot now late in oure lyfys° a meruell° to me,   *lives/marvel*
That° I thynk my hart ryfys sich° wonders to see.   *so that/heart stops such*
What that° destany dryfys° it shuld° so be: *whatever/drives/must*
85 Som men wyll have two wyfys° and som men thre,°   *wives/three*
    In store;
Some are wo that has any
Bot so far can° I,   *know*
Wo is hym that has many,
90   For he felys° sore.   *feels (it)*

Bot yong° men of wowyng,° for God that you boght,°   *young/wooing/redeemed*
Be well war° of wedyng° and thynk in youre thoght,°   *very wary/wedding/thought*
"Had I wyst"° is a thyng it° seruys° of noght;°   *known/that/serves/no use*
Mekyll styll mowrnyng° has wedyng home broght,°   *sorrow/brought*
95   And grefys,°   *griefs*
With many a sharp showre,°   *pain*
For thou may cach° in an owre°   *catch/hour*
That° shall savour fulle sowre°   *what/taste very sour*
    As long as thou lyfys.°   *live*

100 For, as euer red° I pystyll° I haue oone to° my fere°   *read/Epistle/one for/mate*
As sharp as a thystyll,° as rugh° as a brere;°   *thistle/rough/briar*
She is browyd° lyke a brystyll° with a sowre loten chere;°   *eyebrowed/bristle/appearing look*
Had she ooncs° wett hyr whystyll° she couth° syng full clere°   *once/her whistle/could/clearly*
    Hyr pater noster.
105 She is as greatt as a whall,°   *whale*
She has a galon of gall:
By hym that dyed° for vs all,   *died*
    I wald° I had ryn to° I had lost hir.°   *wish/run till/her*

PRIMUS PASTOR.   God looke° ouer the raw!° Full defly° ye   *watch/company/deaf*
    stand.
110 SECUNDUS PASTOR.   Yee,° the dewill° in thi maw so tariand.° *yea/Devil/belly (for) so tarrying*
Sagh° thou awre° of Daw?°   *saw/anything*
PRIMUS PASTOR.   Yee, on a ley land°   *fallow field*
Hard° I hym blaw;° he commys° here at hand,   *heard/blow (pipes)/comes*
    Not far;
Stand styll.

---

100. *as ... pystyll.* a tag meaning "in truth," "certainly."   **104.** *pater noster:* (Latin, "our father") the Lord's Prayer.

SECUNDUS PASTOR. Qwhy?°	*why*
115 PRIMUS PASTOR. For he commys, hope I.	
SECUNDUS PASTOR. He wyll make° vs both a ly°	*trick/(with) a lie*
Bot if° we be war.	*unless*

TERCIUS PASTOR. Crystys crosse me spede° and sant° Nycholas!	*help/Saint*
Ther of had I nede,° it is wars then° it was:	*need/worse than*
120 Whoso couthe° take hede° and lett the warld pas,°	*could/heed/world pass*
It is euer in drede° and brekyll° as glas,°	*doubt/brittle/glass*
And slythys.°	*slides (away)*
This warld fowre° neuer so,	*fared*
With meruels mo° and mo,	*marvels more*
125 Now in weyll,° now in wo,°	*happiness/woe*
And all thyng wrythys.°	*things turn*

Was neuer syn Noe° floode sich° floodys seyn;°	*since Noah's/such/seen*
Wyndys and ranys° so rude° and stormes so keyn;°	*rains/rough/keen*
Som stamerd,° som stod° in dowte,° as I weyn;°	*stammered/stood/doubt/think*
130 Now God turne all to good, I say as I mene,°	*mean*
For ponder:°	*pondering*
These floodys so thay° drowne,	*they*
Both in feyldys° and in towne,	*fields*
And berys° all downe,	*carry*
135 And that is a wonder.	

We that walk on° the nyghtys oure catell° to kepe,°	*in/cattle/guard*
We se sodan° syghtys when othere men slepe.°	*see strange/sleep*
Yit me° thynk my hart lyghtys;° I se shrewys pepe.°	*yet I/heart leaps/rascals peep*
Ye ar two all-wyghtys;° I wyll gyf° my shepe°	*monsters/give/sheep*
140 A turne.	
Bot full yll° haue I ment.°	*but very badly/planned*
As I walk on this bent,°	*field*
I may lyghtly° repent,	*easily*
My toes if I spurne.°	*stub*

145 A,° sir, God you saue and master myne!	*ah*
A drynk fayn wold° I haue and somwhat° to dyne.°	*eagerly would/something/eat*
PRIMUS PASTOR. Crystys curs,° my knaue,° thou art a ledyr hyne!°	*curse/boy/bad fellow*
SECUNDUS PASTOR. What! the boy lyst° rave; abyde vnto syne;°	*likes to/wait until later*
We haue mayde° it.	*made*

---

149. I.e., "we have finished eating."

¹⁵⁰ Yll thryft° on thy pate!°   curse/head
    Though the shrew cam° late,   came
      Yit is he in state
        To dyne, if he had it.

TERCIUS PASTOR.   Sich seruandys° as I that swettys° and   servants/sweat/toil
    swynkys°
¹⁵⁵ Etys° oure brede full dry° and that me forthynkys;°   eat/bread very dry/think wrong
    We ar° oft weytt° and wery° when master-men wynkys,°   are/wet/weary/masters sleep
    Yit commys° full lately° both dyners° and drynkys.   come/late/dinners
      Bot nately°   thoroughly
Both oure dame and oure syre,
¹⁶⁰ When we haue ryn° in the myre,   run
    Thay can nyp at° oure hyre,°   cut/wage
      And pay vs full lately.

Bot here° my trouth,° master, for the fayr° that ye make,°   hear/promise/fare/give
I shall do therafter wyrk° as° i take;°   work/according to what/get
¹⁶⁵ I shall do a lytyll,° sir, and emang° euer lake,°   little/in between/play
For yit lay my soper° neuer on my stomake°   supper/stomach
    In feyldys.
Wherto shuld° I threpe?°   why should/argue
With my staf can I lepe,°   run away
¹⁷⁰ And men say "lyght chepe°   cheap bargain
    Letherly for-yeldys."°   poorly pays off

PRIMUS PASTOR.   Thou were° an yll lad to ryde on wowyng°   would be/a-wooing
With a man that had bot lytyll of° spendyng.   (money) for
SECUNDUS PASTOR.   Peasse,° boy, I bad° no more Iangling,°   peace/ask/quarreling
¹⁷⁵ Or I shall make the° full rad,° by the heuen's° kyng, you (quiet)/quickly/heaven's
    With thy gawdys°—   tricks
Wher ar oure shepe, boy?—we skorne.°   (that we) scorn
TERCIUS PASTOR.   Sir, this same day at morne
I thaym° left in the corne,   them
¹⁸⁰   When thay rang lawdys;°   lauds

Thay° haue pasture good, thay can not go wrong.   they
PRIMUS PASTOR.   That is right, by the roode!° Thyse° nyghtys   cross/these
    ar long,
Yit° I wold, or° we yode, oone gaf° vs a song.   yet/before/went, one gave

---

180. *lawdys:* the second (or if sung with matins, the first) of the canonical hours, in monasteries usually rung at dawn. A monastic house is evidently in the neighborhood, perhaps the cell of Augustinian or Black Canons at Woodkirk, four miles north of Wakefield.

SECUNDUS PASTOR.   So I thoght° as I stode° to myrth° vs   *thought/stood/make mirth/among*
    emong.°

185 TERCIUS PASTOR.   I grauntt.°   *agree*
PRIMUS PASTOR.   Lett me syng the tenory.°   *tenor*
SECUNDUS PASTOR.   And I the tryble° so hye.°   *treble/high*
TERCIUS PASTOR.   Then the meyne° fallys to me;   *middle*
    Lett se° how ye chauntt.°   *let's see/sing*

Tunc intrat Mak, in clamide se super togam vestitus.   ***Then Mak enters, with a cloak over his tunic***

190 MAK.   Now Lord, for thy naymes sevyn,° that made both   *names seven/moon/stars*
    moyn° and starnes°
Well mo then° I can neuen,° thi will, Lorde, of° me tharnys;°   *much more than/name/concerning/ is lacking*

I am all vneuen,° that° moves oft my harnes.°   *disturbed/so that/brains*
Now wold° God I were in heuen, for there wepe° no barnes°   *would/weep/children*
    So styll.°   *continually*
195 PRIMUS PASTOR.   Who is° that pypys° so poore?   *is (it)/pipes*
MAK.   Wold God ye wyst° how I foore!°   *knew/suffer*
Lo, a man that walkys on the moore,
    And has not all his wyll!

SECUNDUS PASTOR.   Mak, where has thou gon? Tell vs   *news*
    tythyng.°
200 TERCIUS PASTOR.   Is he commen?° Then ylkon° take hede to°   *come/everyone/care of/property*
    his thyng.°

Et accipit clamidem ab ipso.   *He takes the coat from him.*

MAK.   What! ich be° a yoman,° I tell you, of the king;   *I am/yeoman*
The self and the same sond° from a greatt lordyng,°   *messenger/lord*
    And sich.°   *such*
Fy° on you! Goyth° hence.   *fie/go*
205 Out of my presence!
I must haue reuerence;
    Why, who be ich?

PRIMUS PASTOR.   Why make ye it° so qwaynt?° Mak, ye do   *act/strange/wrong*
    wrang.°
SECUNDUS PASTOR.   Bot,° Mak, lyst° ye saynt?° I trow° that ye   *but/want/(to) show off/believe/ like to*
    lang.°

---

201. *yoman:* The *OED* defines *yeoman* as a servant of a royal or noble household, in rank between page and squire or between groom and sergeant.

209. *lyst ye saynt?* lit., "do you want to play the saint?"

²¹⁰ TERCIUS PASTOR. I trow the shrew° can paynt,° the dewyll°	*rascal/deceive/Devil*
myght hym hang!	
MAK. Ich shall make complaynt and make you all to thwang°	*be flogged*
At a worde,	
And tell euyn how° ye doth.	*even what*
PRIMUS PASTOR. Bot, Mak, is that sothe?°	*true*
²¹⁵ Now take outt that sothren tothe,°	*Southern tooth*
And sett° in a torde!°	*set (it)/turd*
SECUNDUS PASTOR. Mak, the dewill in youre ee,° a stroke	*eye/give*
wold I leyne° you.	
TERCIUS PASTOR. Mak, know ye not me? By God I couthe	*could vex*
teyn° you.	
MAK. God looke° you all thre!° Me° thoght I had sene° you;	*look (after)/three/I/seen*
²²⁰ Ye ar° a fare compane.°	*are/fair company*
PRIMUS PASTOR. Can° ye now, mene° you?	*know (us)/think*
SECUNDUS PASTOR. Shrew, pepe!°	*villain, look*
Thus late as thou goys,°	*go*
What wyll men suppos?°	*suppose*
And thou has an yll noys°	*reputation*
²²⁵ Of stelyng° of shepe.°	*for stealing/sheep*
MAK. And I am trew° as steyll,° all men waytt,°	*true/steel/know*
Bot a sekenes° I feyll° that haldys° me full haytt;°	*sickness/feel/seizes/very severely*
My belly farys not weyll,° it is out of astate.°	*well/condition*
TERCIUS PASTOR. Seldom lyys° the dewyll dede° by the gate.°	*lies/dead/way*
²³⁰ MAK. Therfor	
Full sore am I and yll;	
If° I stande stone styll,	*may*
I° ete° not an nedyll°	*(if) I/have eaten/needle (morsel)*
Thys moneth° and more.	*month*
²³⁵ PRIMUS PASTOR. How farys thi wyff?° By my hoode, how	*wife/she*
farys sho?°	
MAK. Lyys walteryng,° by the roode,° by the fyere,° lo!	*sprawling/cross/fire*
And a howse° ful of brude.° She drynkys well to;	*house/children*
Yll spede° othere good that she wyll do!	*succeed*
Bot sho	

215–16. The antagonism between Northerners and Southerners is shown here. Chaucer's Parson says, "But trusteth wel, I am a Southren man,/I kan not geeste 'rum, ram, ruf,' by lettre," referring to the Northern habit of alliterating in verse. To the Northern shepherds, a *sothren tothe* may be identical with a lying tongue. Also, as Mossé pointed out, Mak may be imitating the Southern pronunciation of the court, since he passes himself off as a royal officer.

229. The Devil is always active and rarely does us the favor of being *hors de combat*; the same goes for Mak.

²⁴⁰ Etys° as fast as she can,   *eats*
And ilk yere° that commys° to man   *each year|comes*
She bryngys furth° a lakan,°   *forth|baby*
    And som yeres two.

Bot were I not more gracyus° and rychere befar,°   *kind|richer by far*
²⁴⁵ I were° eten outt of howse and of harbar;°   *would be|home*
Yit° is she a fowll dowse° if ye com nar:°   *yet|foul harlot|near*
Ther is none that trowse° nor knowys a war°   *believes|worse*
    Then ken° I.   *than know*
Now wyll ye se° what I profer?°   *see|offer*
²⁵⁰ To gyf° all in my cofer°   *give|coffer*
To morne at next° to offer   *tomorrow morning*
    Hyr hed-maspenny.°   *funeral donation*

SECUNDUS PASTOR.   I wote° so forwakyd° is none in this shyre: *believe|sleepy*
I wold slepe if° I takyd les to° my hyere.°   *would sleep (even) if|received less*
                                                for|wage

²⁵⁵ TERCIUS PASTOR.   I am cold and nakyd and wold haue a
    fyere.
PRIMUS PASTOR.   I am wery,° for-rakyd° and run in the myre.   *weary|worn out by walking*
    Wake thou!
SECUNDUS PASTOR.   Nay, I wyll lyg° downe by,°   *lie|by (you)*
For I must slepe truly.
²⁶⁰ TERCIUS PASTOR.   As good a man's son was I
    As any of you.

Bot, Mak, com heder!° Betwene° shall thou lyg downe.   *here|between (us)*
MAK.   Then myght I lett° you bedene of that° ye wold   *hinder|indeed from what|whisper*
    rowne,°
    No drede.°   *doubt*
²⁶⁵ Fro° my top to my too,°   *from|toe*
Manus tuas commendo,
Poncio Pilato,
    Cryst° crosse me spede!°   *Christ's|help*

Tunc surgit, pastoribus dormientibus, et dicit: *Then he rises, while the shepherds*
                          sleep, and says:

Now were tyme for a man that lakkys° what he wold°   *lacks|wants*
²⁷⁰ To stalk preuely than° vnto a fold,   *secretly then*

250–52. "I would give all I have if she were dead and tomorrow morning I could offer a mass for her soul."
266. "I commend thy hands to Pontius Pilate" (cf. Luke 23:46). The un-Christian aspect of Mak's character is ironically portrayed by his altered version of the biblical passage.

And neemly° to wyrk° than and be not to° bold, *nimbly/act/too*
For he might aby° the bargan° if it were told *rue/bargain*
  At the endyng.
Now were tyme for to reyll;° *set about*
275 Bot° he nedys° good counsell *but/needs*
That fayn wold° fare weyll,° *would like (to)/well*
  And has bot lytyll° spendyng.° *little/to spend*

Bot abowte° you a serkyll° as rownde° as a moyn,° *about/circle/round/moon*
To° I haue done that I wyll tyll that it be noyn,° *until/noon*
280 That ye lyg stone styll to that I haue doyne,° *done*
And I shall say thertyll° of good wordys a foyne.° *thereto/few*
  "On hight° *high*
Ouer youre heydys° my hand I lyft, *heads*
Outt go youre een;° fordo° your syght." *eyes/do away with*
285 Bot yit I must make better shyft,
  And° it be right. *if*

Lord! what thay° slepe hard! that may ye all here;° *how they/hear*
Was I neuer a shepard,° bot now wyll I lere.° *shepherd/learn*
If the flok° be skard yet° shall I nyp nere,° *flock/scared yet/creep near*
290 How!° Drawes hederward!° Now mendys° oure chere° *hey/come here/amends/mood*
  From sorow:
A fatt shepe, I dar° say, *dare*
A good flese° dar I lay.° *fleece/trap*
Eft-quyte° when I may, *repay*
295   Bot this will I borow.

  [*Mak goes home.*]

How, Gyll,° art thou in? Gett vs som lyght. *Jill*
VXOR EIUS. Who makys sich dyn° this tyme of the nyght? *such noise*
I am sett for to spyn; I hope° not I myght *think*
Ryse a penny to wyn,° I shrew° them on hight! *earn/curse*
300   So farys
A huswyff° that has bene° *housewife/been*
To be rasyd° thus betwene:° *raised (i.e., interrupted)/from her work*

Here may no note° be sene° *(completed) work/seen*
  For° sich small charys.° *because of/chores*

278–84. Mak, who has been identified as a devil before, uses a magic incantation (in contrast to the mock blessing of l. 266) to make the shepherds sleep.

300–4. It is important to keep the audience participation in mind: after the husbands have complained of their lot, the wives are given a chance to reciprocate. This appeal to the women in the audience is especially emphasized in ll. 416ff.

MAK.   Good wyff,° open the hek!° Seys° thou not what I   *wife/gate/see*
     bryng?
VXOR.   I may thole the dray° the snek.° A,° com in, my   *allow you (to) draw/latch/ah/sweet*
     swetyng!°
MAK.   Yee,° thou thar° not rek of° my long standyng.   *yea/need/care about*
VXOR.   By the nakyd nek° art thou lyke° for to hyng.°   *neck/likely/hang*
MAK.   Do way:°   *go on*
310 I am worthy my mete,°   *food*
For in a strate° can I gett   *pinch*
More then° thay that swynke° and swette°   *than/toil/sweat*
          All the long day.

Thus, it fell to my lott, Gyll; I had sich grace.°   *luck*
315 VXOR.   It were° a fowll° blott to be hanged for the case.   *would be/foul*
MAK.   I haue skapyd,° Ielott,° oft as hard a glase.°   *escaped/little Jill/blow*
VXOR.   "Bot° so long goys° the pott to the water," men says,   *but/the longer goes*
     "At last
Comys it home broken."
320 MAK.   Well knowe I the token,°   *meaning*
Bot let it neuer be spoken;
          Bot com and help fast.

I wold° he were flayn.° I lyst° well ete:°   *would/skinned/like/(to) eat*
This twelmothe° was I not so fayn° of oone° shepe mete.°   *year/eager/for a/sheep's meat*
325 VXOR.   Com° thay or° he be slayn and here the shepe blete?°   *(what if) come/before/bleat*
MAK.   Then myght I be tane,° that were a cold swette!   *caught*
     Go spar°   *lock*
The gaytt° doore.   *gate*
VXOR.   Yis,° Mak,   *yes*
For and° thay com at thy bak?°   *what if/back*
330 MAK.   Then myght I by, for° all the pak,°   *buy (i.e., get), from/pack*
     The dewill° of the war.°   *Devil/worse*

VXOR.   A good bowrde° haue I spied° syn° thou can° none.   *trick/thought up/since/know*
Here shall we hym hyde to thay be° gone,   *until they are*
In my credyll abyde;° lett me alone,   *cradle (let it) lie*
335 And I shall lyg° besyde in chylbed,° and grone.°   *lie/childbed/groan*
MAK.   Thou red;°   *advise (well)*
And I shall say thou was lyght°   *delivered*
Of a knaue° childe this nyght.   *boy*
VXOR.   Now well is me° day bright,   *happy am I (for the)*
340   That euer was I bred.°   *born*

This is a good gyse° and a far cast;°   *disguise/clever trick*
Yit° a woman avyse° helpys at the last.   *yet/woman's advice*

I wote° neuer who spyse;° agane° go thou fast.	*know/spies/back*
MAK. Bot° I com or thay ryse els blawes° a cold blast!	*unless/then blows*
345 I wyll go slepe.°	*sleep*

[Mak returns to the shepherds, and resumes his place.]

Yit slepys all this meneye,°	*group*
And I shall go stalk preuely,°	*slip in secretly*
As° it had neuer been° I	*as if/been*
That caryed thare° shepe.	*stole their*

350 PRIMUS PASTOR. Resurrex a mortruus! haue hald° my hand.	*take hold (of)*
Iudas carnas dominus! I may not well stand:	
My foytt° slepys, by ihesus,° and I walter° fastand.°	*foot/Jesus/totter/for hunger*
I thoght° that we layd vs° full nere yngland.°	*thought/lay/very near England*
SECUNDUS PASTOR. A ye!°	*ah yea*
355 Lord! what° I haue slept weyll;°	*how/well*
As fresh as an eyll,°	*eel*
As lyght I me feyll°	*myself feel*
As leyfe° on a tre.°	*leaf/tree*

TERCIUS PASTOR. Benste be here in! So my hart qwakys,°	*heart quakes*
360 My hart is outt of skyn, what so° it makys.°	*whatever/causes*
Who makys all this dyn?° So my browes blakys,°	*noise/brow darkens*
To the dowore° wyll I wyn.° Harke felows, wakys!°	*door/move/fellows, wake*
We were fowre:°	*four*
Se° ye awre° of Mak now?	*see/anything*
365 PRIMUS PASTOR. We were vp or° thou.	*before*
SECUNDUS PASTOR. Man, I gyf° God a vowe,	*give*
Yit yede° he nawre.°	*went/nowhere*

TERCIUS PASTOR. Me° thoght he was lapt° in a wolfe skyn.	*I/dressed*
PRIMUS PASTOR. So are many hapt° now, namely within.°	*dressed/especially underneath*
370 SECUNDUS PASTOR. When he had long napt° me thoght with a gyn°	*napped/trick*
A fatt shepe he trapt, bot° he mayde° no dyn.	*trapped, but/made*
TERCIUS PASTOR. Be styll:	

---

350. *Resurrex a mortruus:* corruption of Latin *resurrexit a mortuis,* "resurrected from the dead."

351. *Judas carnas dominus:* corrupt Latin, "Judas (in)carnate Lord."

353. The shepherds are logically in Palestine, but dream that they are in England—where, of course, they really are. The "time warp" in the play, the trinity of present, future (the Mak/ Gill episode of the devilish incarnation of Anti-Christ fore-

shadows the Second Coming), and past is encapsuled in this dream. Basically there is no time measurement in God's eternity (cf. Miceál F. Vaughan, "The Three Advents in the *Secunda Pastorum,*" *Speculum,* 55 [1980], pp. 484–504).

359. *Benste:* Cf. l. 55n.

366. *gyf . . . vowe:* i.e., "swear to God."

369. Their inner selves are "wolfish."

Thi dreme° makys the woode:°   *dream|you crazy*
It is bot fantom,° by the roode.°   *phantom|cross*
375 PRIMUS PASTOR.   Now God turne all to good,
    If it be his wyll.

SECUNDUS PASTOR.   Ryse, Mak, for shame! Thou lygys right   *lie too long*
    lang.°
MAK.   Now Crystys holy name be vs emang!°   *among*
What is this? For sant Iame° I may not well gang!°   *by Saint James|go*
380 I trow° I be° the same. A! My nek° has lygen wrang°   *hope|am|neck|lain wrong*
    Enoghe;°   *enough*
Mekill thank.° Syn yister euen,°   *much thanks|since yesterday*
                        evening

Now, by sant Stevyn,°   *Stephen*
I was flayed with° a swevyn°—   *frightened by|dream*
385   My hart out of sloghe.°   *jumped out of my skin*

I thoght Gyll° began to crok° and trauell° full sad,°   *Jill|groan|be in labor|hard*
Welner° at the fyrst cok,° of a yong° lad,°   *almost|cock|young*
For to mend° oure flok;° then be I neuer glad.   *enlarge|flock*
I haue tow° on my rok° more then° euer I had.   *wool|distaff|than*
390   A, my heede!°   *head*
A house full of yong tharmes,°   *bellies*
The dewill knok° outt thare harnes!°   *Devil knock|their brains*
Wo° is hym has° many barnes,°   *woe|(that) has| children*
    And therto lytyll brede!°   *little bread*

395 I must go home, by youre lefe,° to Gyll as I thoght.°   *leave|intended*
I pray you looke° my slefe° that I steyll noght:°   *look (at)|sleeve|steal nothing*
I am loth° you to grefe° or from you take oght.°   *loath|grieve|anything*
TERCIUS PASTOR.   Go furth,° yll myght thou chefe!° Now   *forth|succeed|would|looked (to see)*
    wold° i we soght,°
    This morne,
400 That we had all oure store.
PRIMUS PASTOR.   Bot I will go before;
Let vs mete.°   *meet*
SECUNDUS PASTOR.   Whore?°   *where*
TERCIUS PASTOR.   At the crokyd° thorne.   *crooked*

MAK.   Vndo this doore! Who is here? How long shall I
    stand?

---

403. Near Wakefield there was at this time a thorn tree called   (see l. 455*n*), where shepherds used to let their sheep graze on
the Shepherds' Thorn, in Mapplewell, not far from Horbury   the moor (England and Pollard, p. xiv).

405 VXOR EIUS. Who makys sich° a bere?° Now walk in the	*such/noise/waning moon*
wenyand.°	
MAK. A,° Gyll, what chere?° It is I, Mak, youre husbande.	*ah/cheer*
VXOR. Then may we se° here the dewill° in a bande,°	*see/Devil/noose*
Syr Gyle;°	*Guile*
Lo, he commys° with a lote°	*comes/sound*
410 As° he were holden in° the throte.°	*as if/held by/throat*
I may not syt at my note°	*work*
A hand lang while.°	*length's time*
MAK. Wyll ye here° what fare° she makys to gett hir° a	*hear/fuss/herself/excuse*
glose,°	
And des noght bot lakys° and clowse hir toose.°	*does nothing but play/scratch her*
	toes
415 VXOR. Why, who wanders, who wakys, who commys, who	*goes*
gose?°	
Who brewys, who bakys? What makys me thus hose?°	*hoarse*
And than°	
It is rewthe° to beholde,	*pity*
Now in hote,° now in colde,	*heat*
420 Full wofull° is the housholde	*very woeful*
That wantys a woman.	
Bot what ende has thou mayde° with the hyrdys,° Mak?	*made/shepherds*
MAK. The last worde that thay° sayde when I turnyd	*they/back*
my bak,°	
Thay wold looke that thay hade° thare shepe° all the pak.°	*had/sheep/pack*
425 I hope° thay wyll nott be well payde° when thay thare	*think/pleased/lack*
shepe lak,°	
Perde.°	*in faith*
Bot how so° the gam° gose,	*however/game*
To° me thay wyll suppose,°	*of/be suspicious*
And make a fowll° noyse,	*foul*
430 And cry outt apon° me.	*upon*
Bot thou must do as thou hyght.°	*promised*
VXOR. I accorde me° thertyll.°	*agree/to it*
I shall swedyll° hym right in my credyll;°	*swaddle/cradle*
If it were a gretter slyght yit couthe° I help tyll.°	*greater trick still could/in it*
I wyll lyg° downe stright;° com hap° me;	*lie/right away/wrap*
MAK. I wyll.	

---

405. *Now . . . wenyand:* The waning moon was considered an   **412.** *hand lang:* i.e., "short."
unlucky time.

435 VXOR.   Behynde!
Com° Coll and his maroo,°   *(if) come/friend*
Thay will nyp° vs full naroo.°   *catch/close*
MAK.   Bot I may cry "out, haroo,"°   *help*
The shepe if thay fynde.
440 VXOR.   Harken ay° when thay call; thay will come onone.°   *listen ever/right away*
Com and make redy° all and syng by thyn oone;°   *ready/yourself alone*
Syng lullay° thou shall, for I must grone,°   *lullaby/groan*
And cry outt by the wall on Mary and Iohn,°   *John*
For sore.°   *pain*
445 Syng lullay on fast°   *quickly*
When thou heris° at the last;   *hear*
And bot° I play a fals cast,°   *if/false trick*
Trust me no more.

TERCIUS PASTOR.   A,° Coll, goode morne. Why slepys° thou   *ah/sleep*
nott?
450 PRIMUS PASTOR.   Alas, that euer was I borne!° We haue a   *born*
fowll blott.°   *shame*
A fat wedir° haue we lorne.°   *wether/lost*
TERCIUS PASTOR.   Mary, Godys forbott!°   *marry, God forbid*
SECUNDUS PASTOR.   Who shuld° do vs that skorne?° That   *should/wrong/would be*
were° a fowll spott.
PRIMUS PASTOR.   Some shrewe.°   *rascal*
I haue soght° with my dogys   *searched*
455 All horbery shrogys,°   *Horbury Shrogs*
And of fifteyn° hogys°   *fifteen/young sheep*
Fond° I bot oone° ewe.   *found/but one*

TERCIUS PASTOR.   Now trow° me, if ye will, by sant°   *believe/Saint*
Thomas of Kent,
Ayther° Mak or Gyll° was at that assent.°   *either/Jill/an accomplice*
460 PRIMUS PASTOR.   Peasse,° man, be still! I sagh° when he   *peace/saw*
went;
Thou sklanders° hym yll; thou aght° to repent   *slander/ought*
Goode spede.°   *quickly*
SECUNDUS PASTOR.   Now as euer myght I the,°   *prosper*
If I shuld euyn° here de,°   *even/die*

---

447. *cast:* as in dice.
451. *Mary:* "Marry" = "by Mary."
455. The topographical allusions can be precisely identified:
Horbury is a village just a few miles south of Wakefield; *shrog*, a Northern term, is any rough ground covered with brushwood (England and Pollard, p. xiv).

⁴⁶⁵ I wold° say it were° he   *would/was*
    That dyd that same dede.°   *deed*

TERCIUS PASTOR.   Go we theder,° I rede,° and ryn° on oure   *there/advise/run*
    feete.
Shall I neuer ete brede° the sothe to° I wytt.°   *eat bread/truth until/know*
PRIMUS PASTOR.   Nor drynk in my heede° with hym tyll   *head (i.e., mouth)/meet*
    I mete.°

⁴⁷⁰ SECUNDUS PASTOR.   I wyll rest in no stede° tyll that I   *place/greet*
    hym grete,°
    My brothere.
Oone° i will hight:°   *one (thing)/promise*
Tyll I se° hym in sight   *see*
Shall I neuer slepe one nyght
⁴⁷⁵   Ther° I do anothere.   *where*

TERCIUS PASTOR.   Will ye here° how thay hak?° Oure syre   *hear/jangle/sire (i.e., Mak)*
    lyst croyne.°   *likes (to) croon*
PRIMUS PASTOR.   Hard° I neuer none crak° so clere° out of   *heard/bawl/clearly/tune*
    toyne;°
Call on hym.
SECUNDUS PASTOR.   Mak! Vndo youre doore soyne.°   *quickly*
MAK.   Who is° that spak,° as° it were noyne,°   *is (it)/spoke/as if/noon*
⁴⁸⁰   On loft?°   *above*
Who is that, I say?
TERCIUS PASTOR.   Goode felowse,° were it° day.   *fellows/would that it were*
MAK.   As far as ye may,
    Good, spekys° soft,   *good (friend), speak*

⁴⁸⁵ Ouer a seke° woman's heede° that is at° mayll easse;°   *sick/head/in/distress*
I had leuer° be dede or° she had any dyseasse.°   *rather/dead than (that)/discomfort*
VXOR.   Go to an othere° stede; I may not well qweasse.°   *another/breathe*
Ich fote° that ye trede goys thorow° my nesc°   *each step/tread goes through/nose*
    So hee.°   *high*
⁴⁹⁰ PRIMUS PASTOR.   Tell vs, Mak, if ye may,
How fare ye, I say?
MAK.   Bot ar ye in this towne to day?
    Now how fare ye?

Ye haue ryn in the myre and ar weytt yit:°   *are wet still*

---

475. I.e., "where I have slept before."   **485.** *mayll easse:* specifically, in childbed.

⁴⁹⁵ I shall make you a fyre if ye will syt.
   A nores° wold I hyre. Thynk ye on° yit?°   *nurse/do you remember/yet*
   Well qwytt° is my hyre;° my dreme° this is itt,   *paid/wage/dream*
      A seson.°   *in season*
   I haue barnes,° if ye knew,   *babies*
⁵⁰⁰ Well mo then enewe,°   *much more than enough*
   Bot we must drynk as we brew,
      And that is bot reson.°   *right*

   I wold ye dynyd or° ye yode.° Me° thynk that ye swette.°   *before/went/I/sweat*
   SECUNDUS PASTOR.   Nay, nawther mendys° oure mode°   *neither calms/mind/food*
      drynke nor mette.°
⁵⁰⁵ MAK.   Why, sir, alys° you oght bot° goode?   *ails/anything but*
   TERCIUS PASTOR.   Yee,° oure shepe° that we gett,°   *yea/sheep/tend*
   Ar stollyn° as thay° yode; oure los° is grette.°   *stolen/they/loss/great*
   MAK.   Syrs, drynkys!°   *drink*
   Had I bene thore,°   *been there*
   Som shuld° haue boght° it full° sore.   *should/paid for/very*
⁵¹⁰ PRIMUS PASTOR.   Mary,° som men trowes° that ye wore,°   *marry/believe/were*
      And that vs forthynkys.°   *bothers*

   SECUNDUS PASTOR.   Mak, som men trowys that it shuld be° ye.   *was*
   TERCIUS PASTOR.   Ayther° ye or youre spouse, so say we.   *either*
   MAK.   Now if ye haue suspowse to Gill° or to me,   *suspicion of Jill*
⁵¹⁵ Com and rype° oure howse° and then may ye se°   *ransack/house/see*
      Who had hir,°   *her*
   If I any shepe fott,°   *took*
   Ayther cow or stott;°   *bullock*
   And Gyll, my wyfe, rose nott
⁵²⁰   Here syn° she lade hir.°   *since/laid herself (down)*

   As I am true and lele° to God here I pray   *honest*
   That this be° the fyrst mele° that I shall ete° this day.   *is/meal/eat*
   PRIMUS PASTOR.   Mak, as haue I ceyll,° avyse the,° I say;   *(bliss in) heaven/reflect*
   He lernyd tymely° to steyll° that couth° not say nay.   *in time/steal/could*
⁵²⁵ VXOR.   I swelt!°   *die*
   Outt, thefys, fro° my wonys!°   *thieves, from/dwelling*
   Ye com to rob vs for the nonys.°   *right now*
   MAK.   Here° ye not how she gronys?°   *hear/groans*
      Youre hartys° shuld melt.   *hearts*

⁵³⁰ VXOR.   Outt, thefys, fro my barne!° Negh° hym not thor.°   *child/(come) near/there*

---

498. I.e., "right on time."   **505.** *alys . . . goode?* i.e., "is there anything wrong?"

MAK.   Wyst° ye how she had farne,° youre hartys wold °
    be sore.   *knew/fared/would*

Ye do wrang,° I you warne, that thus commys° before   *wrong/come*
To a woman that has farne°—bot I say no more.   *been in labor*
VXOR.   A,° my medyll!°   *ah/middle*

535 I pray to God so mylde,
If euer I you begyld,°   *beguiled*
That I ete this chylde
    That lygys° in this credyll.°   *lies/cradle*

MAK.   Peasse,° woman, for Godys payn and cry not so: *peace*
540 Thou spyllys° thy brane° and makys me full wo.°   *destroys/wits/much woe*
SECUNDUS PASTOR.   I trow° oure shepe be° slayn. What   *think/is/think*
    finde° ye two?
TERCIUS PASTOR.   All wyrk° we in vayn; as well may we go.   *work*
    Bot hatters!
I can fynde no flesh,
545 Hard nor nesh,°   *tender*
Salt nor fresh,
    Bot° two tome platers.°   *but/empty platters*

Whik catell° bot this, tame nor wylde,   *live cattle*
None, as haue I blys,° as lowde° as he smylde.°   *joy/strong/smelled*
550 VXOR.   No, so God me blys° and gyf° me ioy° of my chylde!   *bless/give/joy*
PRIMUS PASTOR.   We haue merkyd amys;° I hold vs begyld.°   *aimed amiss/deceived*
SECUNDUS PASTOR.   Syr, don.°   *completely*
Syr, oure Lady hym saue,
Is youre chyld a knaue?°   *boy*
555 MAK.   Any lord myght hym haue
    This chyld to° his son.   *for*

When he wakyns he kyppys,° that ioy is to se.°   *grabs/see*
TERCIUS PASTOR.   In good tyme° to hys hyppys° and in ccle.° *fortune/hips/happiness*
Bot who was his gossyppys° so sone rede?°   *godparents/soon ready*
560 MAK.   So fare fall thare lyppys!°   *fair befall their lips*
PRIMUS PASTOR.   Hark now, a le!°   *lie*
MAK.   So God thaym° thank,   *them*
Parkyn, and Gybon Waller, I say,
And gentill Iohn° Horne, in good fay,°   *good John/faith*

---

543. *hatters:* lit., "by God's clothing" (cf. above, p. 472, l. 596*n*).

540. *Whik . . . this.* "no live cattle but this child."

551. This line is, of course, dramatic irony: they are truly deceived!

558. I.e., "Good health [or "luck" or "fortune"] to him!"

560. *So . . . lyppys:* i.e., "May they have joy."

563–65. John Horne, with the long legs, is a shepherd in *The First Shepherds' Play.* He and Gyb quarrel over an imaginary flock of sheep.

He made all the garray,°	*fuss*
565 With the greatt shank.°	*long legs*

SECUNDUS PASTOR.   Mak, freyndys° will we be, for we ar° all   *friends/are/together*
    oone.°
MAK.   We? Now I hald° for me,° for mendys° gett I none.   *agree/myself /amends*
Fare well all thre.° All glad° were ye gone.   *three/glad (would I be)*

[*The shepherds leave.*]

TERCIUS PASTOR.   Fare wordys may ther be, bot luf° is ther   *love*
    none.
570   This yere.°   *year*
PRIMUS PASTOR.   Gaf° ye the chyld any thyng?   *gave*
SECUNDUS PASTOR.   I trow° not oone° farthyng.   *believe/one*
TERCIUS PASTOR.   Fast agane° will I flyng,°   *back/run*
    Abyde° ye me there.   *await*

[*Goes back to the house.*]

575 Mak, take it to no grefe° if I com to thi barne.°   *harm/child*
MAK.   Nay, thou dos° me greatt reprefe,° and fowll° has   *do/shame/badly/behaved*
    thou farne.°
TERCIUS PASTOR.   The child will it not grefe,° that lytyll°   *grieve/little/daystar*
    day starne.°
Mak, with youre leyfe° let me gyf youre barne   *permission*
    Bot° six pence.   *just*
580 MAK.   Nay, do way:° he slepys.°   *go away/sleeps*
TERCIUS PASTOR.   Me° thynk he pepys.°   *I/peeps*
MAK.   When he wakyns he wepys.°   *weeps*
    I pray you go hence.

[*The other shepherds come back.*]

TERCIUS PASTOR.   Gyf me lefe° hym to kys° and lyft vp the   *permission/kiss/cloth*
    clowtt.°

[*Seeing the sheep.*]

585 What the dewill° is this? He has a long snowte.°   *devil/snout*
PRIMUS PASTOR.   He is merkyd amys.° We wate° ill abowte.°   *deformed badly/wait/about*

---

577. *day starne:* a foreshadowing reference to the Star of Bethlehem; in l. 727 the Christ Child is also addressed as "little daystar." It is obvious that the Mak story (the guardian shepherd, the baby-lamb motif, the miracle of how such a mother could give birth to such a child, etc.) is a direct parody of the manger scene in Bethlehem, as well as being the devilish counterpart to the divine conception (ll. 603–4). Folk variations and burlesques of biblical themes were common in the Middle Ages. The story of the begetting of Merlin by an incubus as a result of the Devil's Parliament, to counteract the Incarnation, was also widely known. It must not be supposed that these parts of the cycle plays were considered sacrilegious, even though the drama by this time was completely secularized.

586. *wate ill abowte:* i.e., "waste our time."

SECUNDUS PASTOR. Ill spon weft, Iwys, ay commys foull owte.° — *spun web, certainly, ever comes badly out*
Ay, so!
He is lyke to oure shepe!° — *sheep*
590 TERCIUS PASTOR. How, Gyb! may I pepe?
PRIMUS PASTOR. I trow, kynde° will crepe° — *(human) nature/creep*
Where it may not go.° — *walk*

SECUNDUS PASTOR. This was a qwantt gawde° and a far cast.° — *cunning deception/clever trick*
It was a hee frawde.° — *great fraud*
TERCIUS PASTOR. Yee,° syrs, wast.° — *yea/(it) was*
595 Lett bren° this bawde and bynd hir° fast. — *let's burn/her*
A fals skawde hang° at the last; — *false scold hangs*
So shall thou.
Wyll ye se° how thay swedyll° — *see/they swaddle*
His foure feytt° in the medyll?° — *feet/middle*
600 Sagh° I neuer in a credyll° — *saw/cradle*
A hornyd lad or° now. — *before*

MAK. Peasse byd° I. What! Lett be youre fare;° — *peace ask/fuss*
I am he that hym gatt,° and yond° woman hym bare.° — *begot/yonder/bore*
PRIMUS PASTOR. What dewill shall he hatt,° Mak? Lo, God, — *be called/heir*
Makys ayre.°
605 SECUNDUS PASTOR. Lett be all that. Now God gyf° hym care, — *give*
I sagh.° — *saw*
VXOR. A pratty° child is he — *as pretty (a)*
As syttys on a waman's kne;° — *woman's knee*
A dyllydowne,° perde,° — *darling/in faith*
610 To gar° a man laghe.° — *make/laugh*

TERCIUS PASTOR. I know hym by the eere° marke; that is a — *ear/sign*
good tokyn.°
MAK. I tell you, syrs, hark! Hys noyse° was brokyn. — *nose*
Sythen° told me a clerk that he was forspokyn.° — *afterwards/bewitched*
PRIMUS PASTOR. This is a fals wark;° I wold fayn° be — *work/would gladly/avenged*
wrokyn:°
615 Gett wepyn.° — *weapon*
VXOR. He was takyn with° an elfe, — *taken by*
I saw it myself.

---

587. A traditional proverb, as also ll. 591–92, 596.

604. The first shepherd is the most gullible and tolerant of the three. In ll. 623–28 he is the one who mitigates Mak's punishment.

616. Jill's excuse is that the child was a "changeling." Elves customarily would steal a new born baby and put one of their own ugly spawn in the cradle.

When the clok stroke twelf°   clock struck twelve
  Was he forshapyn.°   transformed

620 SECUNDUS PASTOR.   Ye two ar° well feft sam° in a stede.°   are/endowed together/one place
  TERCIUS PASTOR.   Syn° thay manteyn thare° theft, let do   since/maintain their/put them/death
    thaym° to dede.°   again, cut off /head
  MAK.   If I trespas eft, gyrd of° my heede.° again, cut off /head
  With you will I be left.   I leave it up to you
  PRIMUS PASTOR.   Syrs, do° my reede.°   take/advice
    For this trespas
625 We will nawther ban ne flyte,°   neither curse nor reprove
  Fyght nor chyte,°   chide
  Bot° haue don as tyte,°   but/quickly as possible
    And cast hym in canvas.

         [*They toss Mak in a sheet.*]

  Lord! What° I am sore,° in poynt for° to bryst.°   how/tired/about/burst
630 In fayth I may no more; therfor wyll I ryst.°   rest
  SECUNDUS PASTOR.   As a shepe° of sevyn skore° he weyd° in   sheep/seven score/weighed
    my fyst.
  For to slepe ay whore° me° thynk that I lyst.°   anywhere/I/would like
  TERCIUS PASTOR.   Now I pray you,
  Lyg° downe on this grene.   lie
635 PRIMUS PASTOR.   On these thefys yit° I mene.°   thieves yet/think
  TERCIUS PASTOR.   Wherto shuld° ye tene?°   why should/bother
    Do as I say you.

   Angelus cantat "*gloria in exelsis*" : *postea dicat:*   An angel sings "Gloria in Exelsis,"
                                                          and then says :

  ANGELUS.   Ryse, hyrd men° heynd!° For now is he borne°   shepherds/gracious/born
  That shall take fro° the feynd that° Adam had lorne:°   from/Fiend what/lost
640 That warloo° to sheynd° this night is he borne.   sorcerer/destroy
  God is made youre freynd° now at this morne,   friend
    He behestys.°   promises
  At Bedlem° go se°   to Bethlehem/see
  Ther lygys° that fre°   where lies/noble (one)
645 In a cryb full° poorely,   very
    Betwyx° two bestys.°   between/beasts

---

629. *What . . . sore:* i.e., "how sore I am."

631. *sevyn skore:* 140 pounds.

643. *Bedlem:* Bethlehem was corrupted in colloquial speech to

Bedlem. The word survives today in *bedlam*, from the London hospital for the insane, Saint Mary of Bethlehem.

PRIMUS PASTOR.   This was a qwant stevyn that° euer yit°   *as strange (a) voice as/ yet/heard*
  I hard.°

It is a meruell° to neuyn,° thus to be skard.°   *marvel/name/scared*

SECUNDUS PASTOR.   Of Godys son of heuyn° he spak° vpward.°   *heaven/spoke/ from above*

650 All the wod on° a leuyn° me thoght° that he gard   *forest in/ flash of light/thought/*
    Appere.°   *made appear*

TERCIUS PASTOR.   He spake of a barne°   *child*

In Bedlem, I you° warne.°   *to you/declare*

PRIMUS PASTOR.   That betokyns yond starne.°   *means yonder star*

655   Let vs seke° hym there.   *seek*

SECUNDUS PASTOR.   Say, what was his song? Hard ye not   *sang*
  how he crakyd° it?

Thre brefes° to a long.   *three breves*

TERCIUS PASTOR.   Yee, mary,° he hakt° it.   *yea, marry/trilled*

Was no crochett° wrong nor no thyng° that lakt it.°   *crochet (i.e., quarter note)/*
    nothing/was lacking

PRIMUS PASTOR.   For to syng vs emong right° as he knakt° it,   *among just/trilled*
660   I can.

SECUNDUS PASTOR.   Let° se how ye croyne.°   *let's/croon*

Can ye bark at the mone?°   *moon*

TERCIUS PASTOR.   Hold youre tonges,° haue done!   *tongues*

PRIMUS PASTOR.   Hark after, than.°   *then*

665 SECUNDUS PASTOR.   To Bedlem he bad° that we shuld gang:°   *bade/go*

I am full fard° that we tary to lang.°   *afraid/wait too long*

TERCIUS PASTOR.   Be mcry° and not sad; of myrth is oure sang.°   *merry/song*

Euer lastyng° glad to mede° may we fang,°   *everlasting/gladness for reward/*
    Withontt noyse.   *receive*

670 PRIMUS PASTOR.   Hy° we theder° for thy,°   *hurry/there/therefore*

If° we be wete° and wery,°   *(even) if /wet/weary*

To that chyld and that lady;

    We haue° it not to lose.°   *must/ forget*

SECUNDUS PASTOR.   We fynde by the prophecy—let be°   *stop/noise*
  youre dyn°—

675 Of Dauid and Isay° and mo then° I myn,°   *Isaiah/more than/remember*

Thay prophecyed by clergy° that in a vyrgyn   *they **prophesied** by doctrine*

---

657. *Thre ... long:* "The relation of *longa* to *brevis* (usually *modus perfectus*: one to three) had been settled by Franco of Cologne in the 13th century and the *ars nova* (14th and 15th centuries) was chiefly concerned with the mensuration of smaller note values: only the tenors in masses and motets of the 15th century used the *modus perfectus* in their *cantus firmi* of slow-moving, long-held notes over which elaborate polyphonic structures were erected. ... At any rate, the shepherds are overwhelmed by the angel's music, because it represents a type of artistic, learned music more recherché than the simple polyphony in descant style which probably constituted their own performances" (N. C. Carpenter, "Music in the Secunda Pastorum," *Speculum*, 26 [1951] p. 698).

Shuld° he lyght° and ly° to slokyn° oure syn   *should/alight/lie/quench*
    And slake° it,   *relieve*
Oure kynde° from wo;°   *nature/woe*
680 For Isay sayd so:
Ecce virgo
    Concipiet a chylde that is nakyd.

TERCIUS PASTOR. Full glad may we be and abyde° that day   *await*
That lufly° to se,° that all myghtys may.°   *gracious (one)/see/power controls*
685 Lord, well° were° me° for ones° and for ay,°   *happy/would be/I/once/ever*
Myght I knele° on my kne° som word for to say   *kneel/knee*
    To that chylde.
Bot° the angell sayd   *but*
In a cryb was he layde;
690 He was poorly arayd,°   *arrayed*
    Both mener° and mylde.   *humble*

PRIMUS PASTOR. Patryarkes° that has bene° and prophetys   *patriarchs/been/in the past*
    beforne,°
Thay desyryd to haue sene° this chylde that is borne.°   *seen/born*
Thay ar° gone full clene.° That haue thay lorne.°   *are/absolutely/lost*
695 We shall se hym, I weyn, or° it be morne,   *think, before*
    To tokyn.°   *as (a) sign*
When I se hym and fele,°   *feel*
Then wote° I full weyll°   *know/well*
It is true as steyll°   *steel*
700   That° prophetys haue spokyn: *what*
To so poore as we ar that he wold appere,°   *would appear*
Fyrst fynd,° and declare by his messyngere.°   *find (us)/messenger*
SECUNDUS PASTOR. Go we° now, let vs fare; the place is vs nere.°   *let us go/near*

TERCIUS PASTOR. I am redy° and yare;° go we in fere°   *ready/eager/company*
705   To that bright.°   *bright (child)*
Lord, if thi wylles° be—   *will*
We ar lewde° all thre°—   *ignorant/three*
Thou grauntt° vs somkyns° gle°   *grant/some kind (of)/mirth*
    To comforth° thi wight.°   *comfort/son*

    [*They enter the stable.*]

710 PRIMUS PASTOR. Hayll, comly° and clene!° Hayll, yong°   *comely (one)/pure/young*
    child!
Hayll, Maker, as I meyne, of° a madyn° so mylde!   *mean, (born) of/maiden*

681–82. *Ecce virgo Concipiet:* "Behold, a virgin shall conceive."
713. Cf. *Piers Plowman*, where Guiler is a synonym for Satan/ Devil. The phrase here refers back to l. 408 and links Mak to the Fiend.

Thou has waryd,° I weyne,° the warlo° so wylde;   *conquered/think/Fiend*
The fals gyler of teyn,° now goys° he begylde.°   *false malignant deceiver/goes/*
                                                                      beguiled

    Lo, he merys;°   *smiles*
715 Lo, he laghys,° my swetyng.°   *laughs/sweet*
    A wel fare metyng.°   *happy meeting*
    I haue holden° my hetyng.°   *kept/promise*
      Haue a bob° of cherys.°   *bunch/cherries*

SECUNDUS PASTOR.   Hayll, sufferan Sauyoure!° For thou has   *sovereign Savior/sought*
    vs soght.°
720 Hayll, frely foyde° and floure,° that all thyng° has wroght!°   *noble child/ flower/things/made*
Hayll, full of fauoure, that made all of noght!°   *nothing*
Hayll! I kneyll° and I cowre.° A byrd haue I broght°   *kneel/bow/brought*
    To my barne.°   *child*
Hayll, lytyll tyné mop!°   *little tiny baby*
725 Of oure crede° thou art crop:°   *faith/(the) head*
I wold drynk on° thy cop,°   *from/cup*
    Lytyll day starne.°   *daystar*

TERCIUS PASTOR.   Hayll, derlyng dere,° full of godhede!°   *darling dear/Godhead*
I pray the° be nere when that I haue nede.°   *you/need*
730 Hayll! Swete° is thy chere!° My hart° wold blede°   *sweet/look/heart/bleed*
To se° the sytt here in so poore wede,°   *see/clothing*
    With no pennys.
Hayll! Put furth° thy dall!°   *forth/hand*
I bryng the bot° a ball: *but*
735 Haue and play the with all,°   *with it*
    And go to the tenys.°   *tennis*

MARIA.   The Fader° of heuen,° God omnypotent,   *Father/heaven*
That sett° all on seuen,° his Son has he sent.   *made/in seven (days)*
My name couth° he neuen° and lyght or° he went.   *did/name/alighted (in me) before*
740 I conceyuyd° hym full euen° thrugh myght,° as he ment,°   *conceived/entirely/through (his)*
                                                                    power/planned

    And now is he borne.°   *born*
He kepe° you fro wo!°   *(may) he keep/ from woe*
I shall pray hym so;
Tell° furth as ye go,   *tell (this)*
745   And myn on° this morne.   *remember*

---

726. The reference is to the Eucharist.

736. The gift of the ball to "go to the tennis" is proof of the shepherds' ignorance (to which they confess in ll. 706–9), but at the same time it amuses the audience (God's "wights")—an effect which they had also asked for indirectly in the same lines.

This provides a clever theatrical conclusion to the comic-serious section. *The First Shepherds' Play* by the Wakefield Master does not have the tennis reference, nor the request of "lewde" men to provide "somkyns gle."

PRIMUS PASTOR.   Farewell, lady so fare° to beholde,   *fair*
With thy childe on thi kne!°   *knee*
SECUNDUS PASTOR.   Bot he lygys full° cold.   *lies very*
Lord, well is me!° Now we go, thou behold.   *happy am I*
TERCIUS PASTOR.   For sothe° all redy° it semys° to be told   *truly/already/seems*
750   Full oft.
PRIMUS PASTOR.   What grace we haue fun.°   *found*
SECUNDUS PASTOR.   Com furth; now ar° we won.°   *are/saved*
TERCIUS PASTOR.   To syng ar we bun:°   *ready*
        Let° take on loft.°   *let's/raise our voices*

Explicit pagina Pastorum.   *Here ends the pageant of the*
                                                                          shepherds.

EVERYMAN

DATE: 1500. ✦ MANUSCRIPT: Four printed copies, all between 1508 and 1537, but no MSS are extant. The earliest complete edition, by John Skot c. 1530, is the copy from Britwell Court Library, reprinted by W. W. Greg and used here. In addition there is another Skot copy from the A. H. Huth Library (England) and the two fragments printed by Pynson (1493–1530) one in the British Library, the other being the Douce fragment in the Bodleian Library, Oxford. All copies have been reprinted by W. W. Greg. The spelling is early Modern English. ✦ EDITION: W. W. Greg, ed., "Everyman," in *Materialien zur Kunde des älteren Englischen Dramas*, IV (Leipzig, London, 1904). The spelling has been kept, but certain phrasings and assignments of speeches to characters have been changed, as in other editions, when these were obvious errors and would lead to confusion. Punctuation has been added.

The language of *Everyman* is quite modern and should pose no difficulty. Two points might be noted: (1) The word *and* is quite often equivalent to "if." (2) *u* and *v*, *y* and *i* are interchanged: *gyue* = *give*, *lyuynge* = *living*.

Different from the craft-guild (miracle) plays of biblical stories performed in cycles in such cities as York and Wakefield, *Everyman* is a morality play, and the finest of the small extant group. The moralities, performed occasionally by guilds but more often by wandering professional players, or perhaps actors permanently attached to noble houses, were plays of a didactic, ethical nature, whose characters personified human traits. Thus life, with its various drives—for money, power, kinship, love—is treated in allegorical terms. The Dutch play *Elckerlijk*, the equivalent of *Everyman*, may or may not be an earlier composition, and there has been much debate on which play is the translation; both were written before the end of the 15th century. Hugo von Hofmannsthal's modern version of the Old German *Jedermann* is performed frequently.

Everyman is a stark play, simple and direct. In this it has the emotional impact of other folk literature (for example, the ballad). A certain fatalism surrounds the man who is wealthy in worldly goods and friends but poor in spirit and good deeds. Slowly he is stripped naked to the bare soul; and only when this is mortified is it pure. The allegory of dying is realistic: man stops; life goes on by. The end for every man is lonely, and only faith in eternal salvation can ease the passage. To a medieval audience, for whom death was a common and vivid phenomenon, suddenly and frighteningly appearing in war and pestilence, the depiction of Everyman's agony on the stage must have been a grim experience.

HERE BEGYNNETH A TREATYSE HOW YE HYE FADER OF
HEUEN SENDETH DETHE TO SOMON EUERY CREATURE TO
COME AND GYUE ACOUNTE OF THEYR LYUES IN THIS
WORLDE, AND IS IN MANER OF A MORALL PLAYE.

[DRAMATIS PERSONAE

GOD

MESSENGER	KNOWLEDGE (*Knowlege*)
DEATH (*Dethe*)	CONFESSION (*Confessyon*)
EVERYMAN (*Eueryman*)	BEAUTY (*Beaute*)
FELLOWSHIP (*Felawshyp*)	STRENGTH (*Strengthe*)
KINDRED (*Kynrede*)	DISCRETION (*Dyscrecion*)
COUSIN (*Cosyn*)	FIVE WITS (*Fyve Wyttes*)
GOODS (*Goodes*)	ANGEL (*Aungell*)
GOOD DEEDS (*Good Dedes*)	DOCTOR (*Doctour*)]

MESSENGER.   I pray you all gyue your audyence°   *attention*
And here° this mater° with reuerence,   *hear/matter*
By fygure° a morall playe.   *in form*
The Somonynge° of Eueryman called it is,   *summoning*
5 That of our lyues and endynge shewes°   *shows*
How transytory we be all daye.°   *always*
This mater is wonders° precyous,   *wondrous*
But the entent° of it is more gracyous   *meaning*
And swete° to bere° awaye.   *sweet/bear*
10 The story sayth: man, in the begynnynge
Loke° well and take good heed to the endynge,   *look*
Be you neuer so gay.
Ye thynke synne in the begynnynge full° swete,   *very*
Whiche in the ende causeth the soul to wepe°   *weep*
15 Whan° the body lyeth° in claye   *when/lies*
Here shall you se° how Felawshyp° and Iolyte,°   *see/Fellowship/Jollity*
Bothe Strengthe, Pleasure, and Beaute,°   *Beauty*
Wyll fade from the° as floure° in Maye.   *you/flower*
For ye shall here how our heuen° kynge   *heaven's*
20 Calleth Eueryman to a generall rekenynge.°   *reckoning*
Gyue audyence and here what he doth saye.
GOD.   I perceyue° here in my maieste°   *perceive/majesty*
How that all creatures be to me vnkynde,°   *disobedient*
Lyuynge° without drede° in worldely prosperyte.°   *living/fear/prosperity*
25 Of ghostly° syght the people be so blynde,   *spiritual*

---

1. The Messenger enters as a Prologue, onto the apron of the stage. The discussion between God and Death is similar to that of Der Herr (God) and Mephistopheles in Goethe's *Faust* and that of God and Satan in the Book of Job; all involve the testing of mankind.

Drowned in synne they know me not for theyr God;
In worldely ryches is all theyr mynde;
They fere° not my ryghtwysnes,° the sharpe rood.°   *fear/righteousness/rod*
My lawe° that I shewed whan I for them dyed°   *law/died*
30 They forgete clene° and shedynge° of my blode rede.°   *forget clean/shedding/blood red*
I hanged bytwene° two, it can not be denyed;   *between*
To gete° them lyfe I suffred to be deed.°   *give/dead*
I heled° theyr fete;° with thornes hurt was my heed.°   *healed/feet/head*
I coude° do no more than I dyde° truely,   *could/did*
35 And nowe I se° the people do clene forsake me.   *see*
They vse° the seuen deedly synnes dampnable,°   *practice/damnable*
As Pryde, Coueytyse,° Wrathe, and Lechery   *Avarice*
Now in the worlde be° made commendable,   *are*
And thus they leue° of aungelles° the heuenly° company.   *leave/angels/heavenly*
40 Eueryman lyueth so after his owne pleasure,
And yet of theyr lyfe they be nothinge° sure.   *not at all*
I° se the more that I them forbere°   *forbear*
The worse they be fro yere° to yere.   *from year*
All that lyueth appayreth° faste;   *worsens*
45 Therfore I wyll in all the haste
Haue a rekenynge of Euerymannes persone.
For and° I leue the people thus alone   *if*
In theyr lyfe and wycked tempestes,°   *tumults*
Veryly° they wyll become moche° worse than beestes,°   *truly/much/beasts*
50 For now one wolde by° enuy another vp ete;°   *would from/eat*
Charyte° they do all clene forgete.   *charity*
I hoped well that Eueryman
In my glory shulde° make his mansyon,   *should*
And therto° I had them all electe.°   *for that/chosen*
55 But now I se, lyke traytours deiecte,°   *traitors/debased*
They thanke me not for the pleasure that I to° them ment,°   *for/intended*
Nor yet for theyr beynge that I them haue lent.
I profered° the people grete° multytude of mercy,   *offered/great*
And fewe there be that asketh it hertly.°   *sincerely*
60 They be so combred° with worldly ryches,   *encumbered*
That nedes° on them I must do Iustyce°   *of necessity/justice*
On Eueryman lyuynge without fere.
Where arte thou, Deth,° thou myghty messengere?   *Death*
DETHE.   Almyghty God, I am here at your wyll,

---

31. Christ was crucified between two thieves, members of brigand bands against which the Roman procurators had to wage continual police action. The men probably expected to die with Barabbas, as participants in his insurrection. One of them repents on the cross.

35–38. Gluttony, Envy, and Sloth complete the list of the Seven Deadly Sins, for a graphic and lively personification of which see *Piers Plowman* (above, pp. 693–709).

⁶⁵ Your commaundement° to fulfyll.   *commandment*

GOD.   Go thou to Eueryman

And shewe° hym in my name   *tell*

A pylgrymage he must on hym take

Which he in no wyse° may escape   *way*

⁷⁰ And that he brynge with hym a sure rekenynge°   *reckoning*

Without delay or ony taryenge.°   *any tarrying*

DETHE.   Lorde, I wyll in the worlde go renne° ouer all°   *run everywhere*

And cruelly out serche° bothe grete and small.   *search*

Eueryman wyll I beset that lyueth° beestly°   *lives/beastly* (i.e., *like a beast*)

⁷⁵ Out of Goddes lawes and dredeth° not foly.°   *fears/folly*

He that loueth rychesse° I wyll stryke with my darte,   *riches*

His syght to blynde and from heuen to departe,°   *separate*

Excepte that° almes be his good frende,   *unless*

In hell for to dwell, worlde without ende.

⁸⁰ Loo,° yonder I se° Eueryman walkynge.   *lo/see*

Full lytell° he thynketh on my comynge;   *very little*

His mynde is on flesshely lustes and his treasure,

And grete payne it shall cause hym to endure

Before the Lorde, heuen° kynge.   *heaven's*

⁸⁵ Eueryman, stande styll; whyder° arte thou goynge   *whither*

Thus gayly? Hast thou thy Maker forgete?°   *forgotten*

EUERYMAN.   Why askest thou?

Woldest thou° wete?°   *do you wish/(to) know?*

DETHE.   Ye,° syr, I wyll shewe you: *yea*

⁹⁰ In grete hast° I am sende° to the°   *haste/sent/you*

Fro° God out of his mageste.°   *from/majesty*

EUERYMAN.   What, sente to me?

DETHE.   Ye, certaynly.

Thoughe thou haue forgete hym here,

⁹⁵ He thynketh on the in the heuenly spere,°   *sphere*

As or° we departe thou shalte knowe.   *before*

EUERYMAN.   What desyreth God of me?

DETHE.   That shall I shewe the:

A rekenynge he wyll nedes haue

¹⁰⁰ Without ony lenger respyte.°   *longer delay*

EUERYMAN.   To gyue° a rekenynge longer layser° I craue;   *give/leisure*

This blynde mater° troubleth my wytte.°   *dark matter/reason*

DETHE.   On the° thou must take a longe Iourney;°   *yourself/journey*

Therfore thy boke° of counte° with the thou brynge,   *book/accounts*

---

85. The manner of handling entrances and exits should be imagined by the reader. Usually Everyman is seen at the opposite side of the stage from Death. He may be thought of as staggering in drunkenly as he is accosted, his reaction being one of befogged surprise. Or a wild banquet scene, with the characters all present as guests can be imagined for the whole play: Goods may be seen tied up in a corner; Good Deeds lies weakly on the floor, etc.

¹⁰⁵ For turne agayne thou can not by no waye.
And loke° thou be sure of thy rekenynge,　*see*
For before God thou shalte answere and shewe°　*tell*
Thy many badde dedes° and good but a fewe,　*deeds*
How thou hast spente thy lyfe and in what wyse°　*manner*
¹¹⁰ Before the chefe° Lorde of paradyse.　*chief*
Haue ado° we were° in° that waye,　*get ready (so that)/would be/on*
For wete° thou well thou shalte make none attournay.°　*know/appoint no attorney*
EUERYMAN.　Full vnredy° I am suche rekenynge° to gyue.　*unready/reckoning*
I knowe the not. What messenger arte thou?
¹¹⁵ DETHE.　I am Dethe,° that no man dredeth;°　*Death/fears*
For euery man I rest° and no man spareth,　*arrest*
For it is Goddes commaundement°　*commandment*
That all to me sholde° be obedyent.　*should*
EUERYMAN.　O Deth, thou comest whan° I had the leest° in　*when/least*
　　mynde!
¹²⁰ In thy power it lyeth° me to saue,　*lies*
Yet of my good° wyl I gyue the yf thou wyl be kynde　*goods*
Ye, a thousande pounde° shalte thou haue;　*pounds*
And dyfferre° this mater tyll an other° daye.　*defer/another*
DETHE.　Eueryman, it may not be by no waye.
¹²⁵ I set° not by° golde, syluer, nor rychesse,°　*care/for/riches*
Ne° by pope, emperour, kynge, duke ne prynces　*nor*
For and° I wolde receyue° gyftes grete°　*if/would receive/great*
All the worlde I myght gete,°　*get*
But my custome is clene° contrary.　*quite*
¹³⁰ I gyue the° no respyte; come hens° and not tary.°　*you/hence/tarry*
EUERYMAN.　Alas, shall I haue no lenger respyte?
I may saye Deth geueth° no warnynge.　*gives*
To thynke on the it maketh my herte seke,°　*heart sick*
For all vnredy is my boke of rekenynge.
¹³⁵ But° xii yere° and I myght haue a bydynge°　*(of) only/years/delay*
My countynge° boke I wolde make so clere°　*accounting/clear*
That my rekenynge I sholde not nede° to fere.°　*need/fear*
Wherfore, Deth, I praye the, for Goddes mercy,
Spare me tyll I be prouyded of° remedy.　*provided with*
¹⁴⁰ DETHE.　The auayleth° not to crye, wepe,° and praye;　*(it) avails/weep*
But hast the° lyghtly,° that thou were gone° that Iournaye,°　*make haste/quickly/gone (on)/ journey*

And preue° thy frendes yf thou can.　*test*
For, wete thou well, the tyde° abydeth° no man,　*time/waits for*

---

111. *Haue ado:* i.e., "let's get moving."
112. *thou . . . attournay:* i.e., "you can deputize no one to make this journey for you."

And in the worlde eche lyuynge° creature   *each living*
145 For Adams synne must dye of° nature.   *die (by force) of*
    EUERYMAN.   Dethe, yf I sholde this pylgrymage take
    And my rekenynge suerly° make,   *surely*
    Shewe° me, for saynt charyte,°   *tell/holy charity*
    Sholde I not come agayne shortly?
150 DETHE.   No, Eueryman, and thou be ones° there,   *are once*
    Thou mayst neuer more come here,
    Trust me veryly.°   *truly*
    EUERYMAN.   O gracyous God in the hye sete° celestyall,   *high seat*
    Haue mercy on me in this moost° nede.   *greatest*
155 Shall I haue no company fro° this vale terestryall°   *from/terrestrial*
    Of myne acqueynce,° that way me to lede?°   *acquaintance/lead*
    DETHE.   Ye,° yf ony° be so hardy°   *yea/any/brave*
    That wolde go with the and bere° the company.   *bear*
    Hye the,° that thou were gone to Goddes magnyfycence,   *hasten*
160 Thy rekenynge° to gyue° before his presence.   *reckoning/give*
    What, wenest° thou thy lyue° is gyuen the   *believe/life*
    And thy worldely gooddes also?
    EUERYMAN.   I had wende° so veryle.°   *thought/truly*
    DETHE.   Nay, nay, it was but lende° the,   *lent*
165 For as soone as thou arte go°   *gone*
    Another a whyle shall haue it and than° go ther fro   *then*
    Euen as thou hast done.
    Eueryman, thou arte made;° thou hast thy wyttes fyue°   *mad/five*
    And here on erthe wyll not amende thy lyue;
170 For sodeynly° I do come.   *suddenly*
    EUERYMAN.   O wretched caytyfe, wheder° shall I flee,   *villain, whither*
    That I myght scape° this endles° sorowe?   *escape/endless*
    Now gentyll Deth,° spare me tyll to morowe,°   *good Death/tomorrow*
    That I may amende me°   *myself*
175 With good aduysement.°   *counsel*
    DETHE.   Naye, therto I wyll not consent,
    Nor no° man wyll I respyte,°   *(for) no/delay*
    But to the herte° sodeynly I shall smyte   *heart*
    Without ony aduysement.°   *warning*
180 And now out of thy syght I wyll me hy;°   *hasten*
    Se° thou make the redy° shortely,   *see/yourself ready*
    For thou mayst saye this is the daye
    That no man lyuynge may scape awaye.
    EUERYMAN.   Alas, I may well wepe° with syghes depe°   *weep/deep*
185 Now haue I no maner° of company   *manner*

---

145. *of nature:* i.e., "naturally."

To helpe me in my Iourney° and me to kepe,° *journey/protect*
And also my wrytynge° is full° vnredy. *account book/very*
How shall I do now for to excuse me?
I wolde° to God I had neuer be gete.° *would/been born*
190 To my soule a full grete° profyte it had° be, *great/would have*
For now I fere° paynes huge and grete. *fear*
The tyme passeth, Lorde helpe that all wrought,° *created*
For though I mourne it auayleth nought.° *not*
The day passeth and is almoost ago;° *almost gone*
195 I wote° not well what for to do. *know*
To whome were I best my complaynt to make?
What and° I to Felawshyp° therof spake° *if/Fellowship/spoke*
And shewed° hym of this sodeyne chaunce° *told/unexpected chance*
For in hym is all myne affyaunce.° *trust*
200 We haue in the worlde so many a daye° *days*
Be good frendes in sporte and playe.
I se hym yonder certaynely.
I trust that he wyll bere me company;
Therfore to hym wyll I speke° to ese° my sorowe. *speak/ease*
205 Well mette, good Felawshyp, and good morowe.
FELAWSHIP.   Eueryman, good morowe by° this daye. *on*
Syr, why lokest° thou so pyteously? *look*
If ony° thynge be amis° I praye the° me saye,° *any/amiss/you/tell*
That I may helpe to remedy.
210 EUERYMAN.   Ye,° good Felawshyp, ye, *yea*
I am in greate ieoparde.° *trouble*
FELAWSHIP.   My true frende, shewe to me your mynde;
I wyll not forsake the to my lyues° ende, *life's*
In the waye of good company.
215 EUERYMAN.   That was well spoken and louyngly.° *lovingly*
FELAWSHIP.   Syr, I must nedes° knowe your heuynesse.° *of necessity/grief*
I haue pyte° to se you in ony dystresse. *pity*
If ony haue you wronged, ye shall reuenged be,
Thoughe I on the grounde be slayne for the,
220 Though that I knowe before that I sholde dye.° *should die*
EUERYMAN.   Veryly,° Felawshyp, gramercy.° *truly/thanks*
FELAWSHIP.   Tusshe, by° thy thankes I set° not a strawe; *for/care*
Shewe me your grefe° and saye no more. *grief*
EUERYMAN.   If I my herte° sholde to you breke° *heart/open*
225 And than° you to tourne° your mynde fro° me *then/turn/from*
And wolde not me comforte whan° ye here° me speke, *when/hear*
Than sholde I ten tymes soryer° be. *sorrier*
FELAWSHIP.   Syr, I saye as I wyll do in dede.° *indeed*
EUERYMAN.   Than be° you a good frende at nede;° *are/in need*
230 I haue founde you true here before.

FELAWSHIP.   And so ye shall euermore,
For, in fayth, and thou go to hell
I wyll not forsake the by the waye.
EUERYMAN.   Ye speke lyke a good frende; I byleue° you well.   *believe*
235 I shall deserue° it and I may.   *repay*
FELAWSHIP.   I speke of no deseruynge, by this daye,
For he that wyll saye and nothynge do
Is not worthy with good company to go.
Therfore shewe° me the grefe of your mynde   *tell*
240 As to your frende mooste° louynge and kynde.   *most*
EUERYMAN.   I shall shewe you how it is.
Commaunded° I am to go a iournaye,°   *commanded/journey*
A long waye, harde and daungerous,°   *dangerous*
And gyue° a strayte counte° without delaye   *give/strict account*
245 Before the hye Iuge° Adonay;   *high judge*
Wherfore I pray you bere° me company,   *bear*
As ye haue promysed, in° this iournaye.   *on*
FELAWSHIP.   That is mater° in dede. Promyse is duty,   *(a) problem*
But and° I sholde take suche a vyage° on me,°   *if/trip/myself*
250 I knowe it well it shulde° be to my payne.   *should*
Also it make° me aferde certayne.°   *makes/afraid certainly*
But let vs take counsell here as well as we can,
For your wordes wolde fere° a stronge man.   *would frighten*
EUERYMAN.   Why, ye sayd yf I had nede,
255 Ye wolde me neuer forsake, quycke ne deed,°   *alive nor dead*
Thoughe it were to hell truely.
FELAWSHIP.   So I sayd, certaynely,
But suche pleasures be set asyde, the sothe° to saye,   *truth*
And also yf we toke° suche a iournaye,   *took*
260 Whan sholde° we come agayne?   *should*
EUERYMAN.   Naye, neuer agayne tyll the daye of dome.°   *doom*
FELAWSHIP.   In fayth, than wyll not I come there.
Who hath you these tydynges brought?
EUERYMAN.   In dede Deth° was with me here.   *Death*
265 FELAWSHIP.   Now by God that all hathe bought,°   *redeemed*
If Deth were the messenger,
For no man that is lyuynge° to daye°   *living/today*
I wyll not go that lothe° iournaye,   *loathsome*

---

245. *Adonay:* It is interesting to note how pagan-Judaic-Christian themes are used by the *Everyman* author. Everyman hopes to impress his friends according to their position in the ethical and spiritual scheme of things. Fellowship is not a specifically Christian term, nor does it have pagan overtones; therefore Everyman cites Adonai (the Old Testament Jehovah) to Fellowship in order to make his point with greatest urgency. In l. 407, however, when speaking to Goods—i.e., Mammon, the Aramaic "riches," personifying avarice—Everyman hopes to impress him with the highest pagan divinity, Jupiter. Finally, in l. 494, the Christian concept of Good Deeds is emphasized by reference to the Messiah, king of Jerusalem.

Not for the fader° that bygate° me.	*father/begot*
270 EUERYMAN. Ye promysed other wyse,° parde.°	*otherwise/by God*
FELAWSHIP. I wote° well, I sayd so truely,	*know*
And yet yf thou wylte ete° and drynke and make good chere°	*eat/cheer*
Or haunt to° women the lusty company,	*keep of*
I wolde not forsake you whyle the daye is clere,°	*bright*
275 Truste me veryly.°	*truly*
EUERYMAN. Ye,° therto ye wolde be redy.°	*yea/ready*
To go to myrthe, solas,° and playe	*pleasure*
Your mynde wyll soner° apply°	*sooner/be ready*
Than to bere me company in my longe iournaye.	
280 FELAWSHIP. Now in good fayth I wyll not° that waye,	*not (go)*
But and thou wyll murder or ony° man kyll,	*any*
In that I wyll helpe the° with a good wyll.	*you*
EUERYMAN. O that is a symple aduyse° in dede.°	*foolish advice/indeed*
Gentyll felawe,° helpe me in my necessyte.°	*good fellow/necessity*
285 We haue loued longe and now I nede,°	*need*
And now, gentyll Felawshyp, remembre me.	
FELAWSHIP. Wheder° ye haue loued me or no,	*whether*
By saynt John I wyll not with the go.	
EUERYMAN. Yet I pray the take° the labour and do so moche°	*undertake/much*
for me,	
290 To brynge me forwarde,° for saynt charyte°	*accompany me/holy charity*
And comforte me tyll I come without° the towne.	*outside*
FELAWSHIP. Nay, and° thou wolde gyue° me a newe gowne	*if/would give*
I wyll not a fote° with the go,	*foot*
But and thou had taryed° I wolde not haue lefte the so;	*tarried*
295 And as° now, God spede° the in° thy Iournaye,°	*so/speed/on/journey*
For from the I wyll departe as fast as I maye.	
EUERYMAN. Wheder° awaye, Felawshyp? Wyll thou	*whither*
forsake me?	
FELAWSHIP. Ye, by my faye.° To God I betake° the.	*faith/entrust*
EUERYMAN. Farewell, good Felawshyp; for the my herte° is	*heart*
sore.	
300 Adewe° for euer;° I shall se° the no more.	*adieu/forever/see*
FELAWSHIP. In fayth, Eueryman, fare well now at the ende.	
For you I wyll remembre that partynge is mournynge.	*parting*
EUERYMAN. Alacke, shall we this° departe in dede°—	*thus/indeed*
A,° Lady, helpe—without ony more comforte?	*ah*
305 Lo, Felawshyp forsaketh me in my moost° nede.	*greatest*
For helpe in this worlde wheder shall I resorte?°	*turn*

---

304. *Lady:* The Virgin Mary is the intercessor between man and Christ. In the Middle Ages Mary was often asked to plead to her Son for man's salvation in moments of trial (cf. *Sir Gawain and the Green Knight*, above, p. 278, ll. 736–39).

Felawshyp here before with me wolde mery° make,   *merry*
And now lytell° sorowe for me dooth° he take.°   *little/does/have*
It is sayd in prosperyte° men frendes may fynde   *prosperity*
310 Whiche in aduersyte be full° vnkynde.   *adversity are very*
Now wheder for socoure° shall I flee   *help*
Syth° that Felawshyp hath forsaken me?   *since*
To my kynnesmen I wyll truely,
Prayenge° them to helpe me in my necessyte.   *begging*
315 I byleue° that they wyll do so,   *believe*
For kynde° wyll crepe° where it may not go.°   *kinship/creep/walk*
I wyll go saye,° for yonder I se them go.   *try*
Where be ye now, my frendes and kynnesmen?
KYNREDE.   Here be we now at your commaundement.°   *command*
320 Cosyn,° I praye you shewe° vs your entent°   *Cousin/tell/intent*
In ony wyse° and not spare.°   *any manner/do not hesitate*
COSYN.   Ye,° Eueryman, and to vs declare   *yea*
Yf ye be dysposed to go ony whyder,°   *anywhere*
For wete° you well, we wyll lyue° and dye togyder.°   *know/live/die together*
325 KYNREDE.   In welth° and wo° we wyll with you holde,   *wealth/woe*
For ouer° his kynne a man may be bolde.°   *upon/make demands*
EUERYMAN.   Gramercy,° my frendes and kynnesmen kynde.   *thanks*
Now shall I shewe you the grefe° of my mynde: *grief*
I was commaunded° by a messenger   *commanded*
330 That is a hye° kynges chefe° offycer.   *high/chief*
He bad° me go a pylgrymage, to my payne,   *bade*
And I knowe well I shall neuer come agayne.
Also I must gyue° a rekenynge strayte,°   *give/reckoning strict*
For I haue a grete° enemy° that hath me in wayte,°   *great/(i.e., Satan)/lies in wait*
          for me
335 Whiche entendeth me for to hynder.
KYNREDE.   What accounte is that whiche ye must render?
That wolde° I knowe.   *would*
EUERYMAN.   Of all my workes I must shewe,
How I haue lyued and my dayes spent,
340 Also of yll dedes° that I haue vsed°   *deeds/done*
In my tyme syth lyfe was me lent
And of all vertues that I haue refused.
Therfore I praye you go thyder° with me   *there*
To helpe to make myn° accounte, for saynt charyte.°   *my/holy charity*
345 COSYN.   What, to go thyder? Is that the mater?°   *case*
Nay, Eueryman, I had leuer fast brede° and water   *rather fast (on) bread*

---

316. The family will hold together in hardship: "Blood is thicker than water."

All this° fyue yere° and more.   *the next/ five years*

EUERYMAN.   Alas, that euer I was bore,°   *born*

For now shall I neuer be mery°   *merry*

350 If that you forsake me.

KYNREDE.   A,° syr, what? Ye be° a mery man;   *ah/are*

Take good herte° to you and make no mone.°   *heart/moan*

But one thynge I warne you, by saynt Anne,

As for me, ye shall go alone.

355 EUERYMAN.   My Cosyn, wyll you not with me go?

COSYN.   No, by our lady, I haue the crampe in my to.°   *toe*

Trust not to me, for, so God me spede,°   *help*

I wyll deceyue° you in your moost nede.°   *deceive/greatest need*

KYNREDE.   It auayleth not vs to tyse.°   *entice*

360 Ye shall haue my mayde with all my herte;

She loueth to go to feestes° there to be nyse°   *feasts/foolish*

And to daunce° and abrode° to sterte.°   *dance/about/run*

I wyll gyue her leue° to helpe you in that Iourney°   *permission/journey*

If that you and she may agree.

365 EUERYMAN.   Now shewe° me the very effecte° of your mynde.   *tell/cast*

Wyll you go with me or abyde behynde?

KYNREDE.   Abyde behynde? Ye,° that wyll I and° I maye.   *yea/if*

Therfore farewell tyll another daye.

EUERYMAN.   Howe sholde° I be mery or gladde?   *should*

370 For fayre promyses men to me make,

But whan° I haue moost° nede they me forsake.   *when/most*

I am deceyued; that maketh me sadde.

COSYN.   Cosyn Eueryman, farewell now,

For veryly° I wyll not go with you.   *truly*

375 Also of myne owne an vnredy rekenynge°   *unready reckoning*

I haue to accounte; therfore I make taryenge.°   *delay*

Now God kepe the,° for now I go.   *protect you*

EUERYMAN.   A Iesus,° is all come here to?°   *Jesus/to this*

Lo, fayre wordes maketh fooles fayne;°   *happy*

380 They promyse and nothynge wyll do certayne.°   *certainly*

My kynnesmen promysed me faythfully

For to abyde with me stedfastly,

And now fast awaye do they flee.

Euen so Felawshyp° promysed me.   *Fellowship*

385 What frende were best me of° to prouyde?   *myself with/provide*

I lose my tyme here longer to abyde,

Yet in my mynde a thynge there is:

All my lyfe I haue loued ryches.

If that my Good° now helpe me myght   *Goods*

390 He wolde° make my herte full° lyght.   *would/very*

I wyll speke° to hym in this dystresse.   *speak*

Where arte thou, my Gooddes and ryches?

GOODES.   Who calleth me? Eueryman? What, hast thou haste?

I lye° here in corners trussed° and pyled so hye,°   *lie/bound/high*

395 And in chestes I am locked so fast,

Also sacked in bagges, thou mayst se° with thyn° eye   *see/your*

I can not styre;° in packes lowe I lye.   *stir*

What wolde ye haue? Lyghtly° me saye.   *quickly*

EUERYMAN.   Come hyder,° Good, in al the hast° thou may,   *hither/haste*

400 For of counseyll° I must desyre° the.   *for counsel/entreat*

GOODES.   Syr, and ye in the worlde haue sorowe or aduersyte,°   *adversity*

That can I helpe you to remedy shortly.

EUERYMAN.   It is another dysease° that greueth° me.   *trouble/grieves*

In this worlde it is not, I tell the so.

405 I am sent for an other° way to go,   *another*

To gyue° a strayte counte° generall   *give/strict accounting*

Before the hyest Iupyter° of all,   *Jupiter (i.e., God)*

And all my lyfe I haue had Ioye° and pleasure in the;   *joy*

Therfore I pray the go with me,

410 For parauenture° thou mayst before God almyghty   *perhaps*

My rekenynge helpe to clene° and puryfye,   *clean*

For it is sayd euer amonge°   *about*

That money maketh all right that is wronge.

GOODES.   Nay, Eueryman, I synge an other songe.

415 I folowe no man in suche vyages;°   *trips*

For and° I wente with the,   *if*

Thou sholdes° fare moche° the worse for me,   *should/much*

For bycause° on me thou dyd set thy mynde   *because*

Thy rekenynge° I haue made blotted and blynde,°   *reckoning/unreadable*

420 That° thyne accounte thou can not make truly   *so that*

And that hast thou for the loue of me.

EUERYMAN.   That wolde greue me full sore

Whan° I sholde° come to that ferefull° answere.   *when/should/fearful*

Vp, let vs go thyther to gyder.°   *together*

425 GOODES.   Nay, not so. I am to brytell;° I may not endure.   *too brittle*

I wyll folowe no man one fote,° be ye sure.   *foot*

EUERYMAN.   Alas, I haue the° loued and had grete° pleasure   *you/great*

All my lyfe° dayes on° good and treasure.   *life's/in*

GOODES.   That is to thy dampnacyon, without lesynge,°   *damnation/lie*

430 For my loue is contrary to the loue euerlastynge,

But yf thou had me loued moderately durynge°   *all this time*

As to the poore to gyue parte of me,

Than° sholdest thou not in this dolour° be   *then/sadness*

Nor in this grete sorowe and care.

435 EUERYMAN.   Lo, now was I deceyued or° I was ware,°   *deceived before/aware*

And all I may wyte° mysspendynge of tyme.   *blame on*

GOODES.   What, wenest° thou that I am thyne?   *believe*

EUERYMAN.   I had went° so.   *thought*

GOODES.   Naye, Eueryman, I saye no.

440   As for a whyle I was lente the;

A season thou hast had me in prosperyte.°   *prosperity*

My condycyon° is mannes soule to kyll;   *nature*

Yf I saue one, a thousande I do spyll.°   *destroy*

Wenest thou that I wyll folowe the?

445   Nay, fro° this worlde not, veryle.°   *from/truly*

EUERYMAN.   I had wende° otherwyse.   *believed*

GOODES.   Therfore to thy soule Good° is a thefe°   *Goods/thief*

For whan thou arte deed,° this is my gyse,°   *dead/custom*

Another to deceyue in this same wyse°   *manner*

450   As I haue done the and all to his soules represe.°   *shame*

EUERYMAN.   O false Good, cursed may thou be,

Thou traytour° to God, that hast deceyued me   *traitor*

And caught me in thy snare.

GOODES.   Mary,° thou brought thy selfe in care,   *marry*

455   Wherof I am gladde.

I must nedes° laugh; I can not be sadde.   *of necessity*

EUERYMAN.   A,° Good, thou hast had longe my hertely° loue.   *ah/true*

I gaue the that whiche sholde be the Lordes aboue.

But wylte thou not go with me in dede?°   *indeed*

460   I praye the trouth° to saye.   *truth*

GOODES.   No, so God me spede.°   *help*

Therfore fare well and haue good daye.

EUERYMAN.   O to whome shall I make my mone°   *lament*

For to go with me in° that heuy Iournaye?°   *on/sad journey*

465   Fyrst Felawshyp° sayd he wolde° with me gone;°   *Fellowship/would/go*

His wordes were very plesaunte° and gaye,   *pleasant*

But afterwarde he lefte me alone.

Than spake° I to my kynnesmen all in despayre,   *spoke*

And also they gaue me wordes fayre;

470   They lacked no fayre spekynge,°   *speech*

But all forsake° me in the endynge.   *forsook*

Than wente I to my Goodes, that I loued best,

In hope to haue comforte, but there had I leest°   *least*

For my Goodes sharpely dyd me tell

475   That he bryngeth many in to hell.

Than° of my selfe I was ashamed,   *then*

And so I am worthy to be blamed.

Thus may I well my selfe hate.

---

454. *Mary:* "Marry" = "by Mary."

Of whome shall I now counseyll° take?	counsel
480 I thynke that I shall neuer spede°	have success
Tyll that I go to my Good Dede,°	Deeds
But alas, she is so weke°	weak
That she can nother go° nor speke;°	neither walk/speak
Yet wyll I venter° on her now.	gamble
485 My Good Dedes, where be° you?	are
GOOD DEDES. Here I lye,° colde in the grounde.	lie
Thy synnes hath me sore bounde	
That° I can not stere.°	so that/stir
EUERYMAN. O Good Dedes, I stande in fere.°	fear
490 I must you pray of° counseyll,	for
For helpe now sholde° come ryght well.	should
GOOD DEDES. Eueryman, I haue vnderstandynge	
That ye be somoned° a counte° to make	summoned/account
Before Myssyas° of Iherusalem° kynge.	Messiah/Jerusalem
495 And° you do by me,° that Iournay with you wyll I take.	if/follow my advice
EUERYMAN. Therfore I come to you my moone° to make.	lament
I praye you that ye wyll go with me.	
GOOD DEDES. I wolde full fayne° but I can not stande, veryly.°	very eagerly/truly
EUERYMAN. Why, is there ony thynge° on° you fall?°	anything/to/happened
500 GOOD DEDES. Ye,° syr, I may thanke you of all.	yea
Yf ye had parfytely chered° me,	perfectly cheered
Your boke° of counte full redy° had° be.°	book/completely ready/would have/been
Loke° the bokes of your workes and dedes eke;°	see/also
Behold how they lye vnder the fete,°	feet
505 To your soules heuynes.°	sorrow
EUERYMAN. Our Lorde Iesus helpe me,	
For one° letter here I can not se.°	(not even) one/see
GOOD DEDES. There is a blynde rekenynge° in tyme of dystres.°	unreadable reckoning/distress
EUERYMAN. Good Dedes, I praye you helpe me in this nede°	need
510 Or elles° I am for euer° dampned° in dede.°	else/forever/damned/indeed
Therfore helpe me to make rekenynge	
Before the redemer° of all thynge°	redeemer/things
That kynge is and was and euer shall.°	shall (be)
GOOD DEDES. Eueryman, I am sory° of your fall,	sorry
515 And fayne wolde° I helpe you and I were able.	would
EUERYMAN. Good Dedes, your counseyll I pray you gyue° me.	give
GOOD DEDES. That shall I do veryly.	
Thoughe that on my fete I may not go.	
I have a syster that shall° with you also	shall (go)
520 Called Knowlege whiche shall with you abyde	
To helpe you to make that dredefull° rekenynge.	fearful
KNOWLEGE. Eueryman, I wyll go with the° and be thy gyde°	you/guide

In thy moost° nede to go by thy syde. — *greatest*
EUERYMAN.   In good condycyon I am now in euery thynge° — *everything*
525 And am hole° content with this good thynge, — *wholly*
Thanked by° God my Creature.° — *be/Creator*
GOOD DEDES.   And whan° he hath brought you there — *when*
Where thou shalte hele the° of thy smarte,° — *cure yourself/hurt*
Than° go you with your rekenynge and your Good Dedes — *then/Deeds together*
togyder°
530 For to make you Ioyfull° at herte° — *yourself joyful/heart*
Before the blessyd Trynyte.° — *Trinity*
EUERYMAN.   My Good Dedes, gramercy.° — *thank you*
I am well content certaynly
With your wordes swete.° — *sweet*
535 KNOWLEGE.   Now go we togyder louyngly° — *lovingly*
To Confessyon, that clensyng ryuere.° — *cleansing river*
EUERYMAN.   For Ioy° I wepe;° I wolde we were there. — *joy/weep*
But I pray you gyue me cognycyon° — *information (about)*
Where dwelleth that holy man Confessyon.
540 KNOWLEGE.   In the hous of saluacyon;° — *salvation*
We shall fynde hym in that place
That shall vs comforte by Goddes grace.
Lo, this is Confessyon! Knele° downe and aske mercy, — *kneel*
For he is in good conceyte° with God almyghty. — *esteem*
545 EUERYMAN.   O gloryous fountayne that all vnclennes° doth — *uncleanness/purify*
claryfy,°
Wasshe fro° me the spottes of vyce vnclene° — *from/unclean*
That on me no synne may be sene.° — *seen*
I come with Knowledge for my redempcyon,° — *redemption*
Redempte° with herte and full contrycyon,° — *redeemed/contrition*
550 For I am commaunded° a pylgrymage to take — *commanded*
And grete° accountes before God to make. — *great*
Now I praye you, Shryfte, moder° of saluacyon, — *Confession, mother*
Helpe my Good Dedes for my pyteous exclamacyon.° — *exclamation*
CONFESSYON.   I knowe your sorowe well, Eueryman.
555 Bycause° with Knowlege ye come to me — *because*
I wyll you comforte as well as I can,
And a precyous Iewell° I wyll gyue° the — *jewel/give*
Called penaunce, voyder° of aduersyte.° — *penance, remover/adversity*
Therwith shall your body chastysed be
560 With abstynence and perseueraunce° in Goddes seruyce. — *perseverance*
Here shall you receyue° that scourge of me — *receive*
Whiche is penaunce stronge that ye must endure,
To remembre thy Sauyour° was scourged for the — *Savior*
With sharpe scourges and suffred it pacyently.° — *patiently*
565 So must thou, or° thou scape° that paynful pylgrymage. — *before/escape*

Knowlege, kepe° hym in this vyage°	*protect/trip*
And by that tyme Good Dedes wyll be with the.°	*you*
But in ony wyse° be seker° of mercy	*every way/sure*
For your tyme draweth° fast. And° ye wyll saued be	*draws (near)/if*
570 Aske God mercy and he wyll graunte° truely;	*grant*
Whan° with the scourge of penaunce man doth hym° bynde,	*when/himself*
The oyle° of forgyuenes° than shall he fynde.	*(i.e., balm)forgiveness*
EUERYMAN. Thanked be God for his gracyous werke,°	*work*
For now I wyll my penaunce begyn.	
575 This hath reioysed° and lyghted° my herte°	*rejoiced/lightened/heart*
Though the knottes° be paynfull and harde within.	*knots (of the penance scourge)*
KNOWLEGE. Eueryman, loke° your penaunce that ye fulfyll,	*see*
What payne that euer it to you be,	
And Knowlege shall gyue you counseyll° at wyll	*counsel*
580 How your accounte ye shall make clerely.°	*clearly*
EUERYMAN. O eternall God, O heuenly° fygure,	*heavenly*
O way of ryghtwysnes,° O goodly vysyon,	*righteousness*
Whiche descended downe in a vyrgyn pure	
Bycause he wolde° euery man redeme°	*would/redeem*
585 Whiche Adam forfayted° by his dysobedyence,	*forfeited*
O blessyd Godheed,° electe and hye deuyne,°	*Godhead/high divinity*
Forgyve my greuous° offence.	*grievous*
Here I crye the mercy in this presence.	
O ghostly° treasure, O raunsomer° and redemer,	*spiritual/ransomer*
590 Of all the worlde hope and conduyter,°	*guide*
Myrrour of Ioye, foundatour° of mercy,	*joy, founder*
Which enlumyneth° heuen and erth therby,	*illuminates*
Here° my clamorous complaynt though it late be.	*hear*
Receyue my prayers vnworthy in this heuy° lyfe.	*sorrowful*
595 Though I be a synner moost abhomynable,°	*most abominable*
Yet let my name be wryten° in Moyses table.°	*written/Moses' Tablets*
O Mary, praye to the Maker of all thynge°	*things*
Me for to helpe at my endynge	
And saue me fro° the power of my enemy,	*from*
600 For Deth° assayleth me strongly.	*Death*
And Lady, that I may by meane° of thy prayer	*means*

---

576. "Although the knotted whip is hard on the body (i.e., senses)." Flagellation was a common form of penance among men and women in the Middle Ages. Whole groups of Flagellants would wander about the countryside, weeping and singing, though in 1349 Clement VI condemned the practice and ordered those penitents unlicensed by the apostolic see to be imprisoned. Nails were often added to the whip knots to induce greater bleeding, pain, and sympathy.

595. *abhomynable:* The spelling was used from Wyclif to the 17th century to show the presumed origin of the word: "away from man," i.e., "unnatural." The original source is Latin *abominabilis,* "deserving imprecation."

596. *Moyses table:* The Tablets of Moses contained the names of baptized and penitent sinners.

Of your sones glory to be partynere°   *partner*
By the meanes of his passyon I it craue.
I beseche° you helpe my soule to saue.   *beseech*
⁶⁰⁵ Knowlege, gyue° me the scourge of penaunce;°   *give/penance*
My flesshe therwith shall gyue acqueyntaunce.°   *make acquaintance*
I wyll now begyn yf God gyue me grace.
    KNOWLEGE.   Eueryman, God gyue you tyme and space.
Thus I bequeth° you in° the handes of our Sauyour.°   *bequeath/into/Saviour*
⁶¹⁰ Now may you make your rekenynge° sure.   *reckoning*
    EUERYMAN.   In the name of the Holy Trynyte,°   *Trinity*
My body sore punysshyd shall be:
Take this, body, for the synne of the flesshe!
Also° thou delytest° to go gay and fresshe   *as/delight*
⁶¹⁵ And in the way of dampnacyon° thou dyd me brynge,   *damnation*
Therfore suffre now strokes of punysshynge.
Now of penaunce I wyll wade the water clere
To saue me° from purgatory, that sharpe fyre.   *myself*
    GOOD DEDES.   I thanke God now I can walke and go
⁶²⁰ And am delyuered of° my sykenesse° and wo.°   *delivered from/sickness/woe*
Therfore with Eueryman I wyll go and not spare.
His good workes I wyll helpe hym to declare.
    KNOWLEGE.   Now, Eueryman, be mery° and glad.   *merry*
Your Good Dedes° cometh; now ye may not be sad.   *Deeds*
⁶²⁵ Now is your Good Dedes hole° and sounde,   *whole*
Goynge vpryght vpon the grounde.
    EUERYMAN.   My herte° is lyght and shalbe° euermore.   *heart/shall be*
Now wyll I smyte° faster than I dyde° before.   *smile (myself)/did*
    GOOD DEDES.   Eueryman, pylgryme, my specyall frende,
⁶³⁰ Blessyd be thou without ende.
For the° is preparate° the eternall glory.   *you/prepared*
Ye haue me made hole and sounde;
Therfore I wyll byde by the in euery stounde.°   *hour*
    EUERYMAN.   Welcome, my Good Dedes. Now I here° thy voyce   *hear*
⁶³⁵ I wepe° for very swetenes° of loue.   *weep/sweetness*
    KNOWLEGE.   Be no more sad, but euer reioyce.°   *rejoice*
God seeth thy lyuynge in° his trone° aboue.   *life on/throne*
Put on this garment to thy behoue°   *advantage*
Whiche is wette with your teres°   *tears*
⁶⁴⁰ Or elles° before God you may it mysse   *else*
Whan° ye to your iourneys° ende come shall.   *when/journey's*
    EUERYMAN.   Gentyll° Knowlege, what do ye it call?   *good*
    KNOWLEGE.   It is a garmente of sorowe;
Fro° payne it wyll you borowe.°   *from/release*
⁶⁴⁵ Contrycyon° it is   *contrition*
That getteth forgyuenes;°   *forgiveness*

He pleasyth God passynge° well.   *exceedingly*
GOOD DEDES.   Eueryman, wyll you were° it for your hele?°   *wear/salvation*
EUERYMAN.   Now blessyd be Iesu,° Maryes sone,°   *Jesus/son*
650 For now haue I on true contrycyon.
And lette vs go now without taryenge.°   *tarrying*
Good Dedes, haue we clere° our rekenynge?°   *clear/reckoning*
GOOD DEDES.   Ye,° in dede,° I haue° here.   *yea/indeed/have (it)*
EUERYMAN.   Than° I trust we nede° not fere°   *then/need/fear*
655 Now, frendes, let vs not parte in twayne.°   *from one another*
KNOWLEGE.   Nay, Eueryman, that wyll we not certayne.°   *certainly*
GOOD DEDES.   Yet must thou led° with the   *lead*
Thre° persones of grete° myght.   *three/great*
EUERYMAN.   Who sholde° they be?   *should*
660 GOOD DEDES.   Dyscrecyon° and Strength they hyght,°   *Discretion/are called*
And thy Beaute° may not abyde behynde.   *Beauty*
KNOWLEGE.   Also ye must call to mynde
Your Fyue° Wyttes as for your counseylours.   *Five*
GOOD DEDES.   You must haue them redy° at all houres.   *ready*
665 EUERYMAN.   Howe shall I gette them hyder?°   *here*
KNOWLEGE.   You must call them all togyder°   *together*
And they wyll here you incontynent.°   *immediately*
EUERYMAN.   My frendes, come hyder and be present,
Dyscrecyon, Strengthe, my Fyue Wyttes, and Beaute.
670 BEAUTE.   Here at your wyll we be all redy.
What wyll ye that we sholde do?
GOOD DEDES.   That ye wolde° with Eueryman go   *would*
And helpe hym in his pylgrymage.
Aduyse you,° wyll ye° with him or not in that vyage?°   *take counsel/you (go)/trip*
675 STRENGTHE.   We wyll brynge hym all thyder°   *all (the way) there*
To his helpe and comforte, ye may beleue° me.   *believe*
DYSCRECION.   So wyll we go with hym all togyder.
EUERYMAN.   Almyghty God, loued myght thou be.
I gyue the° laude that I haue hyder brought   *give you*
680 Strength, Dyscrecyon, Beaute and Fyue Wyttes; lacke I nought°   *nothing*
And° my Good Dedes,° with Knowlege clere,   *if/Deeds*
All be in my company at my wyll here.
I desyre no more to° my besynes.°   *for/affairs*
STRENGTHE.   And I, Strength, wyll by you stande in dystres,°   *distress*
685 Though thou wolde in batayle° fyght on the grounde.   *battle*
FYUE WYTTES.   And though it were thrugh° the worlde rounde,   *through*
We wyll not departe for swete ne° soure.   *sweet nor*
BEAUTE.   No more wyll I vnto dethes° houre,   *until death's*
What so euer° therof befall.   *whatever*
690 DYSCRECION.   Eueryman, aduyse you fyrst of all;
Go with a good aduysement° and delyberacyon.°   *counsel/deliberation*

We all gyue you vertuous monycyon°	*good prediction*
That all shall be well.	
EUERYMAN. My frendes, harken° what I wyll tell:	*listen to*
695 I praye God rewarde you in his heuen spere.°	*heavenly sphere*
Now herken,° all that be here,	*hearken*
For I wyll make my testament	
Here before you all present.	
In almes halfe my good° I wyll gyue with my handes twayne°	*goods/two*
700 In the way of charyte° with good entent,°	*charity/intent*
And the other halfe° styll shall remayne	*half (which)*
In queth° to be retourned there° it ought to be.	*bequest/returned where*
This I do in despyte of the fende° of hell	*Fiend*
To go quyte° out of his perell°	*free/peril*
705 Euer after and this daye.	
KNOWLEGE. Eueryman, herken° what I saye:	*listen to*
Go to presthode,° I you aduyse,°	*priesthood/advise*
And receyue° of hym in ony wyse°	*receive/at all costs*
The holy sacrament and oyntement° togyder.°	(i.e., *extreme unction*)/*together*
710 Than° shortly se° ye tourne° agayne hyder;°	*then/see (that)/turn/hither*
We wyll all abyde° you here.	*wait for*
FYUE WYTTES. Ye,° Eueryman, hye you° that ye redy° were.°	*yea/hasten/ready/would be*
There is no Emperour, Kinge, Duke, ne Baron	
That of God hath commycyon°	*commission*
715 As hath the leest preest° in the worlde beynge,°	*least priest/existing*
For of the blessyd sacramentes pure and benygne	
He bereth° the keyes and therof hath the cure°	*bears/care*
For mannes redempcyon,° it is euer sure,	*redemption*
Whiche God for our soules medycyne	
720 Gaue vs out of his herte° with grete° payne,	*heart/great*
Here in this transytory lyfe for the° and me.	*you*
The blessyd sacramentes vii there be:°	*are*
Baptym, confyrmacyon,° with preesthode° good,	*baptism, confirmation*/(i.e., *ordination*)
And the sacrament of Goddes precyous flesshe and blod,°	*blood*
725 Maryage,° the holy extreme vnccyon,° and penaunce.°	*marriage/unction/penance*
These seuen be good to haue in remembraunce,°	*remembrance*
Gracyous sacramentes of hye deuynyte.°	*high divinity*
EUERYMAN. Fayne wolde° I receyue that holy body,	*gladly would*

---

705. Cf. the expression "forever and a day."

716–17. The priesthood received the power of the keys from Saint Peter. In Matt 16:19, Christ granted Peter the power to loosen or lock in heaven everything that was so done on earth. These then are the keys of the kingdom, and Saint Peter is the gatekeeper. The crossed keys are the symbol of the Vatican and the pope, as well as the medieval pilgrim's sign that he had made a trip to Rome. Giving the key, as in England when certain officers at their installation receive a golden key, has for generations been the symbol that the person is entrusted with an important charge.

And mekely° to my ghostly fader° I wyll go.   *meekly/spiritual father*
730 FYUE WYTTES.   Eueryman, that is the best that ye can do;
God wyll you to saluacyon° brynge,   *salvation*
For preesthode excedeth° all other thynge.°   *exceeds/things*
To vs holy scrypture they do teche°   *teach*
And conuerteth man fro° synne heuen° to reche.°   *from/heaven/reach*
735 God hath to them more power gyuen°   *given*
Than to ony aungell° that is in heuen.   *any angel*
With v wordes he may consecrate
Goddes body in flesshe and blode to make
And handeleth his Maker bytwene° his hande.°   *between/hands*
740 The preest byndeth and vnbyndeth all bandes.°   *bonds*
Both in erthe and in heuen;
Thou mynystres° all the sacramentes seuen.   *administers*
Though we kyste° thy fete° thou were worthy.   *kissed/feet*
Thou arte surgyon° that cureth synne deedly.°   *surgeon/deadly*
745 No remedy we fynde vnder God
Bute° all onely° preesthode.   *except/only*
Eueryman, God gaue preests that dygnyte°   *dignity*
And setteth them in his stede° amonge vs to be;   *place*
Thus be they aboue aungelles in degree.
750 KNOWLEGE.   If preestes be good, it is so, suerly.°   *surely*
But whan Iesu° hanged on þe crosse with grete smarte,°   *when Jesus/great pain*
There he gaue out of his blessyd herte
The same sacrament in grete tourment;°   *torment*
He solde them not to vs, that Lorde omnypotent.
755 Therefore saynt Peter the apostell° dothe saye   *apostle*
That Iesus° curse hath all they   *Jesus'*
Whiche God theyr Sauyour° do by° or sell   *Savior/buy*
Or they for ony° money do take or tell.°   *anything/count out*
Synfull preest° gyueth the synners example bad.   *priest*

---

737. *v wordes:* i.e., "For this is my body."

740–41. Cf. ll. 716–17n.

742–44. Here Five Wits is addressing priesthood directly. It may be that there is a nonspeaking character present, though he is not mentioned in the dramatis personae.

749. Everyman exits here.

754–58. Giving or receiving money for the sacraments was condemned by the Church as simony, so called after Simon Magus, a sorcerer living in the apostolic age. Born at Giton in Samaria and educated in the Gnostic school at Alexandria, he became interested in Christianity through the preaching and miracles of Saint Philip and was baptized in 36 or 37. When Peter and John achieved success by the laying on of hands, Simon, known by this time for his magical powers, wished to buy that gift from Peter, who denounced him severely. Simon, bent on revenge, followed Peter to Rome without success. He died there, after being buried alive at his own request: he was sure he would rise on the third day. See Acts 8:9–24, and Hippolytus ([c. 170–236,] ecclesiastical writer and doctor, the most important 3d-century theologian of the Roman church), in E. Miller, ed., *Origenis Philosophumena* (Oxford, 1851), Book VI.

759. Cf. the General Prologue to Chaucer's *Canterbury Tales* (A 501–4):

For if a preest be foul, on whom we truste,
No wonder is a lewed man to ruste;
And shame it is, if a prest take keep,
A shiten shepherde and a clene sheep.

760 Theyr chyldren sytteth by other mennes fyres, I haue harde,°   *heard*
And some haunteth° womens company   *keep*
With vnclene° lyfe, as lustes of lechery.   *unclean*
These be° with synne made blynde.   *are*
FYUE WYTTES.   I trust to God no suche may we fynde.

765 Therfore let vs preesthode° honour   *priesthood*
And folowe theyr doctryne for our soules socoure.°   *succor*
We be theyr shepe,° and they shepeherdes° be   *sheep/shepherds*
By whome we all be kepte in suerte.°   *safety*
Peas,° for yonder I se° Eueryman come   *peace/see*

770 Whiche hath made true satysfaccyon.°   *satisfaction*
GOOD DEDES.   Me° thynke it is he in dede.°   *I/indeed*
EUERYMAN.   Now Iesu be your alder° spede.°   *of you all/salvation*
I haue receyued° the sacrament for my **redempcyon**°   *received/redemption*
And than° myne extreme vnccyon.°   *then/unction*

775 Blessyd be all they that counseyled° me to take it.   *counseled*
And now, frendes, let vs go with out longer respyte.°   *delay*
I thanke God that ye haue taryed° so longe.   *tarried*
Now set eche° of you on this rodde° your honde°   *each/cross/hand*
And shortely folowe me.

780 I go before there° I wolde° be. God be our gyde.°   *where/would/guide*
STRENGTHE.   Eueryman, we wyll not fro° you go   *from*
Tyll ye haue done° this vyage° longe.   *finished/trip*
DYSCRECION.   I, Dyscrecyon, wyll byde by you also.
KNOWLEGE.   And though this pylgrymage be neuer° so stronge°   *ever/hard*

785 I wyll neuer parte you fro.
Eueryman, I wyll be as sure° by the°   *surely/you*
As euer I dyde° by Iudas Machabee.°   *did (i.e., was)/Judas Maccabaeus*
EUERYMAN.   Alas, I am so faynt I may not stande;
My lymmes° vnder me doth folde.   *limbs*

790 Frendes, let vs not tourne° agayne to this lande,   *turn*
Not for all the worldes golde,
For in to this caue must I crepe°   *creep*
And tourne to erth and there to slepe.°   *sleep*

---

760. The illegitimate children of priests were adopted into other families (cf. Chaucer's *Reeve's Tale* for a parson's daughter).

787. *Iudas Machabee:* Judas Maccabaeus (the Hammer) was the most prominent member of a heroic Jewish family that fought against Antiochus Epiphanes, Seleucid king of Syria, who had banned monotheistic worship in Jerusalem. When Mattathias, father of Judas, died in 166 B.C., his son took over the leadership of the war of independence and won Jerusalem. Judas died in battle at Eleasa in 160 B.C., fighting against great odds, and was succeeded by two brothers. The four Books of the Maccabees passed into the Vulgate, and two were accepted by the Council of Trent as canonical; they now form part of the Apocrypha. If Knowledge here represents acquaintance with the law of God, then the reference is to I Maccabees 3:5–6: "Those who disobeyed the Law, he pursued and dispersed. . . . They all feared him who disobeyed the Law, and they who broke the Law were dismayed. . . ." The fact that knowledge is obviously not equivalent to mystical, spiritual insight but only represents the literary perception of God's word is seen later, at the graveside.

BEAUTE.   What, in to this graue, alas?

795 EUERYMAN.   Ye,° there shall ye consume,° more and lesse.   *yea/decay*

BEAUTE.   And what, sholde° I smoder° here?   *should/smother*

EUERYMAN.   Ye, by my fayth, and neuer more appere.°   *appear*

In this worlde lyue° no more we shall   *live*

But in heuen° before the hyest° lorde of all.   *heaven/highest*

800 BEAUTE.   I crosse out all this; adewe,° by saynt Iohan.°   *adieu/John*

I take my cap in my lappe and am gone.

EUERYMAN.   What, Beaute, whyder° wyll ye?   *Beauty, whither*

BEAUTE.   Peas, I am defe;° I loke° not behynde me,   *deaf/look*

Not and° thou woldest gyue° me all the golde in thy chest.   *if/give*

805 EUERYMAN.   Alas, wherto° may I truste?   *whom*

Beaute gothe° fast awaye fro me;   *goes*

She promysed with me to lyue and dye.°   *die*

STRENGTHE.   Eueryman, I wyll the also forsake and denye;

Thy game lyketh° me not at all.   *pleases*

810 EUERYMAN.   Why than, ye wyll forsake me all?

Swete° Strength, tary a lytell space.°   *sweet/little while*

STRENGTHE.   Nay, syr, by the rode° of grace,   *cross*

I wyll hye me° from the fast   *hasten*

Though thou wepe° tyll thy herte° to-brast.°   *weep/heart/break*

815 EUERYMAN.   Ye wolde euer byde by me, ye sayd.

STRENGTHE.   Ye, I haue you ferre ynoughe conueyde.°   *far enough accompanied*

Ye be° olde ynoughe, I vnderstande,   *are*

Your pylgrymage to take on° hande.   *in*

I repent me° that I hyder° came.   *am sorry/hither*

820 EUERYMAN.   Strength, you to dysplease° I am to blame,   *for displeasing you*

Yet promyse is dette,° that ye well wot.°   *debt/know*

STRENGTHE.   In fayth, I care not.

Thou arte but a foole to complayne.

You spende your speche° and wast° your brayne.   *speech/waste*

825 Go thryst the° in to the grounde.   *thrust yourself*

EUERYMAN.   I had wende° surer I shulde° you haue founde.   *believed/should*

He that trusteth in his Strength

She hym deceyueth° at the length.°   *deceives/end*

Bothe Strength and Beaute forsaketh me,

830 Yet they promysed me fayre and louyngly.°   *lovingly*

DYSCRECION.   Eueryman, I will after Strength be gone.

As for me, I will leue° you alone.   *leave*

EUERYMAN.   Why, Dyscrecyon,° wyll ye forsake me?   *Discretion*

DYSCRECION.   Ye, in fayth, I wyll go fro the,°   *from you*

835 For whan° Strength goth before   *when*

---

795. *more and lesse:* i.e., "all of you."   **801.** *take . . . lappe:* i.e., "I doff my cap low."

I folowe after euer more.

EUERYMAN.   Yet I pray the for the loue of the Trynyte,° *Trinity*

Loke in my graue ones° pyteously. *once*

DYSCRECION.   Nay, so nye° wyll I not come. *close*

840 Farewell euerychone.° *everyone*

EUERYMAN.   O all thynge° fayleth saue God alone, *things*

Beaute, Strength, and Dyscrecyon!

For whan Deth° bloweth his blast *Death*

They all renne° fro me full° fast. *run/very*

845 FYUE WYTTES.   Eueryman, my leue now of the I take.

I wyll folowe the other,° for here I the forsake. *others*

EUERYMAN.   Alas, than° may I wayle and wepe, *then*

For I toke° you for my best frende. *took*

FYUE WYTTES.   I wyll no lenger° the kepe;° *longer/protect*

850 Now fare well, and there an ende.

EUERYMAN.   O Iesu,° helpe! All hath forsaken me! *Jesus*

GOOD DEDES.   Nay, Eueryman, I wyll byde with the.

I will not forsake the in dede.° *indeed*

Thou shalte fynde me a good frende at nede.° *need*

855 EUERYMAN.   Gramercy,° Good Dedes,° now may I true *thank you/Deeds/see*

frendes se.°

They haue forsaken me, euerychone.° *every one*

I loued them better than my Good Dedes alone.

Knowlege, wyll ye forsake me also?

KNOWLEGE.   Ye,° Eueryman, whan ye to Deth shall go, *yea*

860 But not yet for no maner° of daunger.° *manner/danger*

EUERYMAN.   Gramercy, Knowlege, with all my herte.ᵛ *heart*

KNOWLEGE.   Nay, yet I wyll not from hens° departe *hence*

Tyll I se where ye shall be come.

EUERYMAN.   Me° thynke, alas, that I must be gone *I*

865 To make my rekenynge° and my dettes° paye *reckoning/debts*

For I se my tyme is nye° spent awaye. *nearly*

Take example, all ye that this do here° or se, *hear*

How they that I loue best do forsake me

Except my Good Dedes that bydeth truely.

870 GOOD DEDES.   All erthly thynges is but vanyte;° *vanity*

Beaute,° Strength, and Dyscrecyon do man forsake; *Beauty*

Folysshe° frendes and kynnesmen that fayre spake,° *foolish/spoke*

All fleeth saue Good Dedes, and that am I.

EUERYMAN.   Haue mercy on me, God moost° myghty, *most*

875 And stande by me, thou moder° and mayde, holy Mary! *mother*

GOOD DEDES.   Fere° not, I wyll speke° for the.° *fear/speak/you*

---

863. *where . . . come:* i.e., "what shall become of you."

EUERYMAN. Here I crye God mercy.	
GOOD DEDES. Shorte° oure ende and mynysshe° our payne.	*shorten/diminish*
Let vs go and neuer come agayne.	
880 EUERYMAN. In to thy handes, Lorde, my soule I commende;	
Receyue° it, Lorde, that it be not lost.	*receive*
As thou me boughtest,° so me defende	*redeemed*
And saue me from the fendes boost,°	*Fiend's boast*
That I may appere° with that blessyd hoost°	*appear/host*
885 That shall be saued at the day of dome,°	*doom*
In manus tuas, of myghtes moost,°	*most mighty*
For euer° *Commendo spiritum meum*.	*forever*
KNOWLEGE. Now hath he suffred that° we all shall endure;	*what*
The Good Dedes shall make all sure.	
890 Now hath he made endynge.	
Me thynketh that I here aungelles° synge	*angels*
And make grete Ioy° and melody	*great joy*
Where Euerymannes soule receyued shall be.	
AUNGELL. Come, excellente electe° spouse to Iesu.°	*chosen/Jesus*
895 Here aboue thou shalte go	
Bycause° of thy synguler vertue.°	*because/special virtue*
Now the soule is taken the body fro,°	*from*
Thy rekenynge is crystall clere.°	*clear*
Now shalte thou in to° the heuenly spere°	*(go) into/heavenly sphere*
900 Vnto the whiche all ye shall come	
That lyueth° well before the daye of dome.	*live*
DOCTOUR. This morall men may haue° in mynde	*keep*
Ye herers,° take it of worth,° olde and yonge°	*listeners/cherish it/young*
And forsake Pryde, for he deceyueth° you in the ende,	*deceives*
905 And remembre Beaute, Fyue Wyttes, Strength, and	
Dyscrecyon;°	*Discretion*
They all at the last do Eueryman forsake;	
Saue° his Good Dedes° there dothe he take.	*only/Deeds*
But beware, and° they be small,	*if*
Before God he hath no helpe at all.	
910 None° excuse may be there for Eueryman.	*no*
Alas, how shall he do than?°	*then*
For after dethe° amendes may no man make,	*death*
For than mercy and pyte° doth hym forsake.	*pity*
If his rekenynge° be not clere whan° he doth come,	*reckoning/when*

---

886. *In manus tuas:* "into thy hands."

887. *Commendo spiritum meum:* "I commend my spirit."

894. *spouse:* At this point Everyman and Good Deeds descend into the grave. The soul is often personified as the Bride of Christ (cf. *Pearl*).

902. At this point a wise doctor of theology explains the moral of the play to the audience.

915 God wyll saye, *Ite maledicti in ignem eternum.*
    And he that hath his accounte hole° and sounde   *whole*
    Hye° in heuen he shall be crounde,°   *high/crowned*
    Vnto whiche place God brynge vs all thyder°   *there*
    That we may lyue body and soule togyder.°   *together*
920 Therto helpe the Trynyte.°   *Trinity*
    Amen, saye ye, for saynt charyte.°   *holy charity*

FINIS

---

915. *Ite . . . eternum:* "Go, cursed one, into eternal fire."

SCOTTISH LITERATURE

With the exception of John Barbour, the nationalistic author of the epic-romance *The Bruce* (1376), all of the best-known fifteenth-century Scottish writers were Chaucerians who wrote primarily in the allegorical tradition of Machaut, Deschamps, and Guillaume de Lorris that Geoffrey Chaucer imitated during his so-called "French Period." King James I of Scotland, long imprisoned in England, studied his English master and produced the autobiographical love poem *The Kingis Quair* (1423), a dream-vision allegory describing his courtship of Jane Beaufort. The "rhyme royal" in which this poem was written was first used by Chaucer. Robert Henryson (c. 1425–1506) was perhaps the most vigorous of the Scottish Chaucerians, his harsh *Testament of Cresseid* being a sequel to Chaucer's story. Gavin Douglas (c. 1475–1522) and Sir David Lindsay (1490–1555) were lesser poets; the latter, because of his preceptorial duties at court, wrote in a didactic vein. Finally, William Dunbar (c. 1465–c. 1530) must be cited as one of the strongest figures in a century admittedly weak in poetry. In satire and realism, in allegory and religious elegy, he approached his English master more closely than any of his compatriots.

REFERENCES

Elliott, Charles, ed. *Robert Henryson: Poems*. Oxford, 1963.

Henderson, T. F. *Scottish Vernacular Literature*. 3d ed. Edinburgh, 1910.

Mackenzie, W. Mackay, ed. *The Kingis Quair*. London, 1939.

Murison, W. *Sir David Lindsay, Poet and Satirist of the Old Church in Scotland*. Cambridge, 1938.

Skeat, W. W., ed. John Barbour's *The Bruce*. 4 vols. Early English Text Society, ES 11, 21, 29, 55. London, 1870, 1874, 1877, 1889.

Smith, G. G. *Scottish Literature: Character and Influence*. London, 1919.

Stearns, Marshal W. *Robert Henryson*. New York, 1949.

Taylor, R. A. *Dunbar, the Poet and his Period*. London, 1931.

Scottish authors are treated in the General Introduction of this volume, p. 12.

from THE BRUCE

John Barbour

DATE: 1375. ✔ MANUSCRIPTS: Saint John's College, Cambridge, G 23 (1487); and Advocates' Library, Edinburgh (1489). The dialect is Northern English (Lowland Scottish). ✔ EDITION: W. W. Skeat, *The Bruce*, 4 vols., Early English Text Society, ES 11, 21, 29, 55 (London, 1870, 1874, 1877, 1889).

The Northern English (Lowland Scottish) dialect has certain pronounced characteristics which should be noted: (1) As elsewhere, often *u* and *v* are interchanged (*vnlikly* = *unlikely*, *preuely* = *privately*), and also *v* and *w* (*vode* = *wode*, "wood," *vachit* = *wachit*, "watched"). (2) *Quh* always replaces *wh* (*quhat* = *what*, *quhyll* = *while*). (3) OE *ā* remains where normally *o* has taken its place (*banes* = *bones*, *nan* = *none*). (4) The third person singular verb and noun plural forms regularly end in *-is*/*-ys* (*takis* = *takes*, *frendis* = *friends*). The preterite inflection and the past participle are represented by *-it* and *-yt* (*assayit* = *assayed*, *enterit* = *entered*). (6) Such Northernisms as *til(l)* for *to*, *swa* for *so*, *sic* for *such* and *ta* for *take* must be watched. (7) *Ch* replaces *gh* (*mycht* = *might*).

Andrew Wyntoun (? 1350–? 1420), a chronicler, states that *The Bruce* was written by John Barbour (1320–95), archdeacon of Aberdeen. Barbour dated his work 1375. *The Bruce* is a highly nationalistic poem—part epic, part romance, and much chronicle —of 13,549 lines, twenty books of rhymed octosyllabic couplets (the common romance meter: cf. *Havelok the Dane*). It recounts the deeds of Robert Bruce in Scotland and Ireland from his crowning to his death. The adventures of James Douglas are also told with vigor and often brutal realism.

from Book V

Douglas Celebrates Palm Sunday, Captures His Castle, and Enjoys the "Douglas Larder" (vss. 255–428)

Now takis Iames° his viage°	*James/journey*
Toward Douglas, his heritage,°	(i.e., *ancestral castle*)
Vith twa ʒhomen, forouten ma;°	*with two yeomen, without more*
That ves° a sympill stuff° to ta,°	*was/simple equipment/take*
5 A land or castell for to vyn!°	*win*
The quhethir° he ʒarnit° to begyn,	*nevertheless/yearned*
To bryng his purpos till° ending,	*to*

For gude° help is in begynnyng.	*good*
For gude begynnyng and hardy,	
10 And° it be followit vittely,°	*if/wisely*
May ger oftsiss vnlikly° thing	*cause often unlikely*
Cum° to full conabill° endyng.	*(to) come/very suitable*
Sa° did it her;° bot° he wes viss°	*so/here/but/was wise*
And saw he mycht, on nakyn wiss,°	*might, in no way*
15 Warray° his fais° vith evyn° mycht;	*fight/ foes/equal*
Tharfor° he thoucht° to virk° with slicht.°	*therefore/thought/work/sleight*
In Douglasdaill, his awn cuntre,°	*own country*
Apon ane evynnyng° enterit he,	*upon an evening*
And vith a man wonnit thar-by,°	*lodged thereby*
20 That wes of° frendis rycht mychty,°	*in/very strong*
And rich of mwbill° and catell,°	*goods/property*
And had beyn° till his fader lele;°	*been/father loyal*
And till him-self in his ȝoutheid°	*youth*
He had done mony **thankfull deid**.°	*many (a) praiseworthy deed*
25 Thom Dicson wes his name, perfay;°	*in faith*
Till **him he** send,° and can° him pray	*sent/did*
That he wald° cum all anerly,°	*would/alone*
For to spek° with hym preuely.°	*speak/privately*
And he but danger° till him gais;°	*without difficulty/goes*
30 But fra° he tald° him quhat° he wes,	*from (the time)/told/what (i.e., who)*
He gret° for Ioy° and for pite,°	*wept/joy/pity*
And hym richt till° his **houss had he**;	*immediately into*
Quhar,° in a chalmer preualy,°	*where/chamber secretly*
He held him and his cumpany,°	***company***
35 That° nane° of him had persaving.°	*so that/none/knowledge*
Of mete° and drink, and othir thing,°	*food/things*
That mycht **thame eiss, thai**° **had plente**.°	*them comfort, **they**/**plenty***
Swa wroucht° he than throu sutelte,°	*so wrought/then through/subtlety*
That all the leill° men of the land,	*loyal*
40 That with his fader wes duelland,°	*dwelling*
This **gud man gert**° **cum ane and**° ane,	*got to/one by*
And mak° him manrent° euirilkane,°	*do/homage/every one*
And he him-self first homage maid.°	*did*
Douglas in hert gret **blithnes**° had,	*heart great happiness*
45 That the gud men of his cuntre	
Wald swa-gat° bundin° till him be.	*in such manner/bound*
He sperit° the cowyn of° the land,	*asked/group (of his followers) about*

---

17. *Douglasdaill:* Douglas-dale in Kircudbrightshire (near Solway Firth in southern Scotland).

20. *wes . . . mychty:* i.e., "had many friends."

22. Lord William Douglas had been helped by Thomas Dickson (see l. 25) to capture the castle of Sanwheire, also by stratagem.

And quha° the castell had in hand, *who*
And thai him tald all halely,° *entirely*
50 And syne emang° thame preualy **then among**
Thai ordanit° that he still suld° be *decided/should*
In hyddillis° and in preuate,° *hiding/secret*
Till Palmesonday° that ves neir° hand, *Palm Sunday/was near (at)*
The thrid° day eftir followand.° *third/after following*
55 For than the folk of the cuntre
Assemblit at the kirk vald° be, *church would*
And thai that in the castell were
Vald als° be thar thar° palmys to bere,° *also/there their/carry*
As folk that had na dreid° of ill, *no fear*
60 For thai thoucht° all wes° at thar will. *thought/was*
Than suld he cum° with his twa° men; *come/two*
Bot, for° that men suld nocht° him ken,° *but, so/not/know*
He suld a mantill haf, ald° and bare, *mantle have, old*
And a flaill, as° he a taskar ware;° *as if/thresher were*
65 Vndir the mantill, nocht-for-thi,° *however*
He suld be armyt preualy;
And quhen° the men of his cuntre,° *when/country*
That suld all bown° befor him be, *ready*
His ensenзhe° mycht heir° him cry, *war cry/might hear*
70 Than suld thai, full enforsaly,° *very strongly*
Richt° in myddis° the kirk assale° *right/middle of/attack*
The ynglis° men vith° hard battale,° *English/with/battle*
Swa° that nane mycht eschap thaim fra;° *so/escape them from*
For thar-throu trowit° thai to ta° *thereby thought/take*
75 The castell, that besyde wes neir.
And quhen this, that I tell зow her,° *you here*
Wes deuisit and vndirtane,° *undertaken*
Ilkane° till° his houss is gane;° *each one/to/gone*
And held the spek° in preuate, *conversation*
80 Till the day of thair assemble.° *their assembly*

The folk apon° the Sononday° *upon/Sunday*
Held° to Sanct Brydis° kirk thar way; *took/Saint Bride's (or Bridget's)*
And thai° that in the castell were *they*
Yschit° out, bath less° and mare,° *issued/both less/more*
85 And went thair palmys for to bere;
Outane° a cuke° and a portere.° *except for/cook/doorkeeper*
Iames° of Douglas of thare cummyng, *James*

---

53. *Palmesonday:* March 19, 1307. **84.** *less and mare:* i.e., "poor and rich."
60. *at thar will:* i.e., "as they wanted it."

And quhat° thai war,° had vittering;° — *what (i.e., who)|were|knowledge*
And sped him° to the kirk in hy.° — *hurried|haste*
90 Bot or° he com, to hastely° — *before|came, too hastily*
Ane° of his° cryit, "Douglass! Douglass!" — *one|his (men)*
Thomas Dicsone, that nerest° was — *nearest*
Till thame° that war of the castel, — *them*
That war all innouth° the chancell, — *inside*
95 And quhen° he "Douglas" sa herd° cry, — *when|so heard*
Drew out his suerd,° and felloly° — *sword|fiercely*
Ruschit emang° thame to and fra,° — *rushed among|fro*
And ane othir forouten ma;° — **without more**
Bot thai in hy° war left lyand.° — *quickly|lying (dead)*
100 Vith that Douglass com rycht° at hand, — *immediately*
That than° enforsit° on thame the cry, — *then|raised loudly*
Bot° thair chancer° full sturdely° — *but|chancel|stoutly*
Thai held, and thaim° defendit weill,° — *themselves|well*
Till of thair men war slane° sumdeill.° — *slain|a part*
105 Bot the Douglas so weill him bare° — *himself bore*
That all the men that with hym ware° — *were*
Had confort of° his weill-doing, — *comfort from*
And he him sparit na kyn° thing, — *no **manner** (of)*
Bot prufit swa° his fors° in ficht,° — *proved so|strength|fight*
110 That throu° his vorschip° and his mycht° — *through|bravery|might*
His men sa kenly° helpit he than, — *strenuously*
That thai the chanser on° thame van.° — *chancel from|won*
Than dang° thai on thame sa hardely,° — *struck|vigorously*
That in schort tym° men mycht se ly° — *time|see lie*
115 The twapart ded,° or than deand.° — *two-thirds dead|**dying***
The laiff° war sesit soyn° in hand; — *remainder|seized soon*
Swa that of **xxx** wes levit nane° — *was left none*
Na° thai war slane ilkane,° or tane.° — *but|every one|taken*

Iames of Douglas, quhen° this ves° done, — *when|was*
120 The presoners° has tane alsone;° — *prisoners|very soon*
And, vith° thame of his cumpany,° — *with|company*
Towart° the castell went in hy, — *toward*
Or ony° noyss or cry suld riss.° — *before any|should rise*
And for° he vald° thame soyn suppriss,° — *because|wanted|(to) surprise*
125 That levit in the castell were, —
That war bot twa forouten mare,° — *two without more*
Fiffe° men or sex° befor send° he, — *five|six|sent*
That fand° all oppyn° the entre;° — *found|open|entry*

---

98. Dickson is slain.

And enterit, and the portar tuk°	doorkeeper seized
130 Rycht° at the ʒat,° and syne° the cuk.°	right/gate/then/cook
Vith that Douglas com° to the ʒet,°	came/gate
And enterit in forout debat,°	argument
And fand the met° all reddy grathit,°	food/ready prepared
Vith burdis° set and clathis° laid.	tables/(table)cloths
135 The ʒettis than he gert thame spare,°	had them locked
And sat and ete° at all lasare.°	ate/leisure
Syne all the gudis tursit thai,°	valuables trussed they
Thai thoucht° that thai mycht haf avay,°	thought/carry away
And namly vapnys° and armyng,°	namely weapons/armor
140 Siluer, tresour,° and ek clething.°	treasure/also clothing
Vittalis,° that mycht nocht° **tursit be,**	food/not
On° this maner distroit° he.	in/manner destroyed
All the vittale, outakin° salt,	**food, except for**
As quhet,° flour, meill,° and malt,	wheat/meal
145 In the vyne-sellar° gert he bryng,°	wine cellar/brought
And sammyn° on the flure° all flyng,°	together/floor/thrown
And the presoners that he had tane,	
Richt tharin gert° he hed° ilkane.	right therein did/behead
Syne of the tunnys° the hedis° out-strak,°	wine barrels/heads/**struck off**
150 A foull melle thair can° he mak;°	foul mixture **there did/make**
For meill, malt, blude,° and vyne°	blood/wine
Ran all to-gidder° in a mellyne,°	together/hodgepodge
That wes vnsemly° for to se;	unpleasant
Tharfor° the men of that cuntre,°	therefore/country
155 For sic° thingis thar mellit° were,	such/there mixed
Callit it "the Douglas lardenere."°	larder
Syne tuk° he salt, as I herd° tell,	took/heard
And ded horss,° and fordid° the well,	dead horses/spoiled
And syne brynt° all, outakyn stane;°	burned/stone
160 And is furth° with his menʒhe gane°	**forth/company** gone
Till° his reset,° for him° thocht weill,°	to/place of hiding/he/well
Gif° hc had haldiɴ° the casteill,°	if/held/castle
It suld° haue beyn assegit rath,°	should/been besieged quickly
And that him thoucht to mekill vath;°	too much risk
165 For he na hop° had of reskewing,°	no hope/being rescued
And it is to perelouss° thing	perilous
In castell till assegit° be,	besieged
Quhar° that ane° vantis of° thir thre,°	where/one/lacks/these three (things)

134. *burdis set:* Movable tables ("boards") were set on trestles in the hall and removed when the feast was over. These were in contrast to the *tables dormant* (of which Chaucer's Franklin in the General Prologue to the *Canterbury Tales* boasted). The latter were permanently set and loaded with food for any unexpected guests such as hunting parties, which often arrived en masse.

Vittale, or men with thair° armyng,   *their*
170 Or than gud° hop of reskewing.   *then good*
And for° he dred° thir thingis suld fale,°   *because/feared/fail*
He chesit forthward° to travale,°   *chose out/travel*
Quhar he mycht° at his largess° be,   *might/at large*
And sua° driff furth° his destane.°   *so/continue/destiny*

from BOOK VII

The Bruce Meets Three Traitors (vss. 400–87)

175 Swa hapnyt° it that on a° day,   *so happened/one*
He vent till hwnt,° for till assay°   *went to hunt/test*
Quhat gammyn wes° in that cuntre;°   *what game was/country*
And sa° hapnyt that day that he   *so (it)*
By a vode-syde° to sett° is gane,°   *woodside/sit/went*
180 Vith° his twa hundis hym allane;°   *with/two hounds (by) himself alone*
Bot° he his swerd ay° vith hym bare.°   *except/sword always/carried*
He had bot° schort quhill syttyn thare,°   *but (a)/while sat there*
Quhen° he saw fra° the vode cumand°   *when/from/coming*
Thre° men vith bowis in thar° hand,   *three/their*
185 That toward hym com spedely,°   *came quickly*
And he persauit° that in hy,°   *perceived/haste*
Be thair effeir° and thair havyng,°   *by their behavior/manner*
That thai lufit° hym na kyn thyng.°   *they loved/not at all*
He raiss° and his leysche° till him drew he,   *rose/leash*
190 And leit° his houndis gang° all fre.°   *let/go/free*
God help the kyng now for° his mycht!°   *with/might*
For, bot° he now be viss° and vicht,°   *unless/wise/brave*
He sall° be set in mekill press.°   *shall/great trouble*
For thai° thre men, vithouten less,°   *those/without lie (i.e., truly)*
195 War° his fayis° all vtrely,°   *were/foes/completely*
And had vachit° so besaly,°   *watched/carefully*
To se° quhen thai vengeans° mycht tak°   *see/vengeance/take*
Of° the kyng for Iohne Cwmynys sak,°   *on/John Comyn's sake*

Heading: There are many versions of the story of Bruce and the traitors: (1) Two Macindrossers and a third man attack Bruce on horseback; all are killed. (2) A once-eyed man and his two sons plan to kill Bruce for forty pounds; Bruce is warned, as he often is by women he has known. They attack Bruce and his page; all traitors are slain. (3) Five of John of Lorne's men attack Bruce and his foster brother; Bruce kills all. (4) Three men carrying a wether meet Bruce and pass the night with him and his foster brother. Bruce suspects them, but his foster brother falls asleep during his watch and the men attack; all the traitors and the foster brother are slain. (5) Three traitors are slain by Bruce and his hounds.

188. An example of litotes (cf. above, p. 50, ll. 24–25n).

198. *Iohne Cwmynys:* On February 10, 1306, Bruce murdered Sir John Comyn before the altar of the Grey Friars church at Dumfries. The story is told in Book II, ll. 25ff.

That° thai thoucht than° thai laser° had;	*as/thought then/opportunity*
200 And sen° he hym allane wes stad,°	*since/situated*
In hy thai thoucht thai suld° him sla,°	*should/slay*
And gif° that thai mycht cheviss° swa,	*if/achieve*
Fra that° thai the kyng had slayn,	*after*
That thai mycht vyn° the vode agayn,	*reach*
205 His men, thai thoucht, thai suld nocht dreid.°	*not fear*
In hy towart° the kyng thai ȝeid,°	*toward/went*
And bend° thair bowis quhen thai var neir;°	*bent/were near*
And he, that dred° in gret maneir°	*feared/great way*
Thair arowis,° for he nakit° was,	*arrows/unarmed*
210 In hy ane spekyng° to thame mais,°	*(a) speech/them makes*
And said, "ȝhe aucht° to shame,° perde,°	*you ought/be ashamed/by God*
Syn° I am ane° and ȝhe ar° thre,	*since/one/are*
For to schut° at me on fer!°	*shoot/from afar*
Bot haf ȝhe° hardyment, cum ner°	*if you have/(the) courage, come near*
215 Vith ȝour° swerdis, me till assay;°	*your/attack*
Wyn° me on sic viss,° gif ȝhe may;	*win (against)/in such manner*
ȝhe sall weill mair° all prisit° be."	*much more/praised*
"Perfay,"° quod° ane than of the thre,	*in faith/said*
"Sall no man say we drede the swa,°	*fear you so*
220 That we vith° arrowis sall the sla."	*with*
With that thair bowis avay° thai kest,°	*away/cast*
And com on fast but langer frest.°	*without longer delay*
The kyng thame met full hardely,°	*very bravely*
And smat° the first so rigorusly,	*smote*
225 That he fell ded° doun on the greyn.°	*dead/green*
And quhen° the kyngis hounde has seyn°	*when/saw*
Thai men assale° his mastir swa,	*attack*
He lap till° ane and can° hym ta°	*leaped on/did/take*
Richt be° the nek° full felonly,°	*right by/neck/fiercely*
230 Till top our taill° he gert° hym ly.°	*head over tail/made/lie*
And the kyng, that his swerd° vp had,	*sword*
Saw° he so fair succour hym maid,°	*(when he) saw/given*
Or° he that fallyn wes mycht ryss,°	*before/was might rise*
Had hym assalȝeit° on sic wiss°	*attacked/(a) manner*
235 That he the bak strak evyn° in twa.°	*back broke evenly/two*
The thrid° that saw his fallowis° swa	*third/fellows*
Forouten° recoueryng be slayne,	*without*
Tuk till° the vod° his vay agane.	*took to/wood/way again*
Bot° the kyng followit spedely;°	*but/quickly*
240 And als° the hound that wes hym by,	*also*

---

209. *nakit:* i.e., "without protective armor."

Quhen he the man saw gang hym fra,°   *escaping him*
Schot° till hym soyn,° and can hym ta   *dashed/quickly*
Richt be the nek, and till hym dreuch;°   *drew*
And the kyng, that ves° neir eneuch,°   *was/enough*
²⁴⁵ In° his risyng sic rowt° hym gaf,°   *on/(a) blow/gave*
That stane-ded° till the erd° he draf.°   *stone-dead/earth/fell*
The kyngis menȝe° that war neir,°   *retainers/were near*
Quhen at° thai° saw on sic maneir°   *when/they/manner*
The kyng assalit sa suddandly,°   *so suddenly*
²⁵⁰ Thai sped thame° toward hym in hy,°   *hurried/haste*
And askit how that cass° befell.   *affair*
And he all haly° can thaim° tell,   *entirely/them*
How thai assalȝeit hym all thre.°   *three*
"Perfay," quod thai, "we may weill se°   *well see*
²⁵⁵ That it is hard till vndirtak°   *undertake*
Sic mellyng° vith ȝow° for to mak,°   *such combat/you/make*
That so smertly° has slayn thir° thre   *vigorously/these*
Forouten hurt." "Perfay,"° said he,   *in faith*
"I slew bot ane° forouten° ma,°   *one/and no/more*
²⁶⁰ God and my hound has slane° the twa.   *slain*
Thair tresoune cumrit thame° perfay,   *their treason hindered them*
For richt vicht° men al thre var° thai."   *very brave/were*

THE TESTAMENT OF CRESSEID

Robert Henryson

DATE: Late 15th century. ✧ MANUSCRIPTS: No early MSS are extant. A MS copy of the poem is found in Saint John's College, Cambridge, at the end of a 15th-century copy of Chaucer's *Troilus and Criseyde*. Henryson's poem was first printed in William Thynne's edition of Chaucer (London, 1532), and under the author's name by Henry Charteris (Edinburgh, 1593). A copy is in the British Library. The dialect is Northern (Lowland Scottish). ✧ EDITIONS: G. Gregory Smith, *The Poems of Robert Henryson* 3 vols. Scottish Text Society, 55, 58, 64, (Edinburgh, 1906–14); H. Harvey Wood, *The Poems and Fables of Robert Henryson*, 2d ed. (Edinburgh, 1958); W. W. Skeat, *Chaucerian and Other Pieces*, Supplement to *The Complete Works of Geoffrey Chaucer* (Oxford, 1897). A recent edition is that by Denton Fox in Thomas Nelson's Medieval and Renaissance Library (London, 1968). Other works and articles are mentioned in A. C. Baugh and Kemp Malone, *The Middle Ages*, Vol. I of *A Literary History of England*, ed. A. C. Baugh, 2d ed., 4 vols. (New York, 1967), bibliographical supplement.

The Lowland Scottish dialect is very similar to Northern English. The following points especially might be kept in mind. (1) The past participle and the preterite of verbs usually end in *-it* instead of *-ed* (*causit, honourit*); the present participle usually ends in *-and* instead of *-ing* (*glitterand, shaikand*). (2) The present singular and plural of verbs end in *-is* instead of *-es, -s* (*cummis, listis*); the same is true for the plural of nouns (*thornis, spycis*). (3) *Qu/quh* is used for *w* and *wh* (*quhen* = *when, quha* = *what, quilk* = *which*). (4) The OE *ā* is retained for *ō* (*knawledge, name, stan, ane*). (5) *U, ui* is interchanged for *oo* (*blud, gud, tuik*). (6) We find *s* instead of *sh* (*sall* = *shall, suld* = *should*). (7) These variations occur frequently: *fra*, "from," *can*, "did," "does," *ane*, "a," "an," "one," *sa*, "so," *sho*, "she," *til*, "to." (8) The palatal *ch* replaces *gh* (*nocht* = *nought, brocht* = *brought, licht* = *light*). (9) *I* is much used to indicate a long vowel (*bair*, "bare," *shaikand*, "shaking," *raid*, "rode," *weip*, "weep," *cloisit*, "closed," *luik*, "look"). (10) The late Middle English sound change *ar* for *er* is frequent (*warld*, "world," *nar* [from earlier *nerre*] "nearer"). The different pronounciation of such words as *derby* and *clerk* in England and America is a result of this change, the American articulation being, as always, the older one.

Robert Henryson (c. 1425–1506), master of the Benedictine Abbey Grammar School at Dunfermline and in 1462 a member of the new University of Glasgow, was the most famous of the Scottish Chaucerians, those men who wrote in imitation (in this case with a spark of genius) of their master Chaucer. Henryson was the author of some lively fables and various moral, allegorical poems. *The Testament of Cresseid*, a sequel to

Chaucer's *Troilus and Criseyde,* shows his best effort. Its harsh yet intensely pathetic message is, with Chaucer's work, a literary precursor to Hogarth's graphic *Harlot's Progress.*

Ane dooly sesoun° to ane cairfull dyte°	*a dreary season/sorrowful song*
Suld° correspond, and be equivalent.	*should*
Richt sa° it wes quhen° I began to wryte	*just so/was when*
This tragedy; the wedder richt fervent,°	*weather very stormy*
⁵ Quhen Aries, in middis° of the Lent,	*(the) middle*
Shouris° of haill can fra° the north discend;°	*showers/did from/(cause to) descend*
That scantly° fra the cauld° I micht defend.°	*scarcely/cold/might (myself) protect*
Yit° nevertheles, within myn orature°	*yet/my oratory*
I stude,° quhen Tytan° had his bemis bricht°	*stood/(i.e., the sun)/beams bright*
¹⁰ Withdrawin° doun and sylit° under cure;°	*drawn/covered/(his) care*
And fair Venus, the bewty° of the nicht,°	*beauty/night*
Uprais,° and set unto° the west full richt°	*uprose/over against/just exactly*
Hir° goldin face, in oppositioun°	*her/opposite*
Of° god Phebus direct discending doun.	*to*
¹⁵ Throwout° the glas° hir bemis brast° sa fair	*through/window/burst*
That I micht see, on every syde me by,	
The northin° wind had purifyit the air,	*northern*
And shed° the misty cloudis fra the sky.	*swept*
The froist freisit,° the blastis bitterly	*frost froze*
²⁰ Fra pole Artyk come quhisling° loud and shill,°	*Arctic came whistling/shrill*
And causit me remuf aganis° my will.	*(to) withdraw against*
For I traistit° that Venus, luifis° quene,	*hoped/love's*
To quhom sum-tyme° I hecht° obedience,	*whom once/promised*
My faidit hart of luf sho wald mak° grene;	*faded heart with love she would make*
²⁵ And therupon, with humbil reverence,	
I thocht° to pray hir hy° magnificence;	*thought/high*
But for greit cald° as than° I lattit° was,	*great cold/then/hindered*
And in my chalmer° to the fyr° can pas.°	*chamber/fire/go*
Thocht° luf be hait,° yit in ane man of age	*though/hot*

5. *Aries:* the Ram, the first sign of the zodiacal year, which the sun enters about March 12. It is the beginning of spring. In the General Prologue to Chaucer's *Canterbury Tales* we find the pilgrimage starting when "the yonge sonne/Hath in the Ram his halve cours yronne."

³⁰ It kendillis nocht° sa sone° as in youthheid,°   *kindles not/soon/youth*
Of quhom the blude° is flowing in ane rage;°   *blood/passion*
And in the auld° the curage douf° and deid,°   *old/ardor dull/dead*
Of quhilk° the fyr outward is best remeid,°   *for which/remedy*
To help be phisik **quhair° that nature failit**;   *by medicine where*
³⁵ I am expert, for baith° I have assailit.°   *both/tried*

I mend° the fyr, and beikit me° about,   *mended/warmed myself*
Than tuik° ane drink **my spreitis° to comfort,**   *took/spirits*
And armit me weill° fra the cauld thairout.°   *well/outside*
To cut the winter-nicht, and mak it short,
⁴⁰ I tuik ane quair,° and left all uther° sport,   *book/other*
Writtin be worthy Chaucer glorious,
Of fair Cresseid° and lusty Troilus.   *Cressida*

And thair° I fand, efter° that Diomeid°   *there/found, **after/Diomedes***
Ressavit° had that lady bricht of hew,°   *received/hue*
⁴⁵ How Troilus neir° out of wit abraid,°   *almost/(his) wits went*
And weipit soir,° with visage paill° of hew;   *wept bitterly/pale*
For quhilk wanhope° his teiris can° renew,   *despair/tears did*
Quhill esperans rejoisit° him agane:°   *until hope rejoiced/again*
Thus quhyl° in joy he levit,° quhyl in pane.°   *sometimes/lived/pain*

⁵⁰ Of° hir behest° he had greit comforting,   *from/promise*
Traisting° to Troy that sho suld° mak retour,°   *trusting/should/return*
Quhilk he desyrit maist° of eirdly thing,°   *desired most/earthly things*
For-quhy° sho was his only paramour.   *because*
Bot quhen° he saw passit baith day and hour   *but when*
⁵⁵ Of hir gaincome,° than sorrow can oppres°   *her return/oppress*
His woful° hart in cair° and heviness.°   *woeful/care/heaviness*

Of his distres me neidis° nocht reheirs,°   *distress I need/tell*
For worthy Chaucer, in the samin buik,°   *same book*
In guidly° termis and in joly veirs°   *goodly/pleasant verse*
⁶⁰ Compylit hes° his cairis, quha° will luik.°   *has/whoever/look*
To brek° my sleip° ane uther° quair I tuik,   *break/sleep/another*
In quilk° I fand the fatall desteny°   *which/destiny*
Of fair Cresseid, that endit wretchitly.°   *wretchedly*

Quha wait gif° all that Chauceir wrait° was trew?°   *who knows if/wrote/true*

32–34. For older men the fire in the hearth is a better remedy than the inner fire of passion.
43–44. The Greek Diomedes led Cressida away after she had been exchanged for the prisoner Antenor. Cressida promised to return to Troilus but was seduced by Diomedes.
50. *hir behest:* Cressida had said she would return by the tenth day.

⁶⁵ Nor I wait nocht gif this narratioun   *authorized/imitated after/new*
   Be authoreist,° or fenyeit of° the new°   *(style)*

   Be sum poeit, throw° his inventioun,   *some poet, through*
   Maid° to report the lamentatioun   *made*
   And woful end of this lusty° Cresseid,   *worthy*
⁷⁰ And quhat° distres sho thoillit,° and quhat deid.°   *what/she suffered/death*

   Quhen Diomed had all his appetyt,°   *appetite*
   And mair,° fulfillit of this fair lady,   *more*
   Upon ane uther he set his haill delyt,°   *whole delight*
   And send° to hir ane lybel° of repudy,°   *sent/a bill/divorce*
⁷⁵ And hir excludit fra° his company.   *from*
   Than desolait° sho walkit up and doun,   *then desolate*
   And, sum men sayis, into the court commoun.°   *common*

   O fair Cresseid! the flour° and *A-per-se*   *flower*
   Of Troy and Grece, how was thou fortunait,°   *the victim of fortune*
⁸⁰ To change in° filth all thy feminitee,°   *into/womanliness*
   And be with fleshly lust sa maculait,°   *so spotted*
   And go amang° the Greikis air° and lait°   *among/Greeks early/late*
   Sa giglot-lyk, takand° thy foull plesance!°   *harlotlike, taking/pleasure*
   I have pity° thee° suld fall sic° mischance!   *pity (that)/on you/such*

⁸⁵ Yit° nevertheles, quhat-ever men deme° or say   *yet/judge*
   In scornful langage° of thy brukilnes,°   *language/frailty*
   I sall° excuse, als far-furth° as I may,   *shall/as much*
   Thy womanheid,° thy wisdom, and fairnes,°   *womanhood/beauty*
   The quilk Fortoun° hes put to sic distres   *Fortune*
⁹⁰ As hir pleisit,° and na-thing° throw the gilt°   *(it) pleased/not/guilt*
   Of thee, throw wikkit° langage to be spilt.°   *wicked/destroyed*

   This fair lady, in this wys° destitut   *manner*
   Of all comfort and consolatioun,
   Richt prively, but° fellowship, on fut°   *very secretly, without/foot*
⁹⁵ Disgysit passit° far out of the toun   *disguised went*
   Ane myle or twa,° unto ane mansioun   *two*
   Beildit full gay, quhair hir° father Calchas,   *built very fair, where (was) her*
   Quhilk° than amang the Greikis dwelland° was.   *who/dwelling*

---

65. *this narratioun:* i.e., the story he is about to tell. It was a literary fashion in the Middle Ages to ascribe to another one's own creation. Chaucer says he heard the Troilus story from "Lollius," a fictitious informant.

74. *lybel of repudy:* Matt. 19:7 has a "libellum repudii."

77. *into . . . commoun:* i.e., became a prostitute.

78. *A-per-se:* "A-by-itself" (i.e., "number one," "best").

97–98. *Calchas:* the Trojan priest of Apollo (not of Venus, as ll. 107–9 have him) who after hearing at Delphi the warning that Troy would fall has defected to the Greeks.

Quhan° he hir saw, the caus he can inquyr° — *when/did ask*
100 Of hir cuming;° sho said, syching° full soir,° — *coming/sighing/bitterly*
"Fra° Diomeid° had gottin his desyr° — *as soon as/Diomedes/desire*
He wox wery,° and wald° of me no moir!"° — *grew weary/wanted/more*
Quod° Calchas, "Douchter, weip thow° not thairfoir;° — *said/daughter, weep you/therefore*
Peraventure° all cummis° for the best; — *perhaps/comes*
105 Welcum° to me; thow art full deir ane° gest."° — *welcome/a very dear/guest*

This auld° Calchas, efter° the law was tho,° — *old/as/then*
Wes° keeper of the tempill,° as ane preist,° — *was/temple/a priest*
In quhilk° Venus and hir son Cupido° — *which/Cupid*
War° honourit; and his chalmer° was thaim° neist;° — *were/chamber/to them/next*
110 To quhilk Cresseid,° with baill aneuch° in breist,° — *Cressida/sorrow enough/breast*
Usit to pas,° hir prayeris for to say; — *go*
Quhill° at the last, upon° ane solempne° day, — *until/on/holy*

As custom was, the pepill° far and neir,° — *people/near*
Befoir the none,° unto the tempill went — *before noon*
115 With sacrifys devoit° in thair maneir.° — *sacrifice devout/their manner*
But still Cresseid, hevy° in hir intent,° — *heavy/heart*
In-to the kirk wald° not hir-self present, — *church would*
For° giving of° the pepil ony deming° — *to avoid/to/any knowledge*
Of hir expuls fra° Diomeid the king: — *expulsion from*

120 But past° into ane secreit orature° — *went/a secret oratory*
Quhair sho micht weip° hir wofull desteny.° — *where she might bemoan/woeful destiny*

Behind hir bak° sho cloisit° fast the dure,° — *back/closed/door*
And on hir kneis bair° fell down in hy.° — *knees bare/directly*
Upon Venus and Cupid angerly° — *angrily*
125 Sho cryit out, and said on° this same wys, — *in*
"Allas!° that ever I maid yow° sacrifys! — *alas/made you*

"Ye gave me anis° ane devyn responsaill° — *once/divine response*
That I suld° be the flour° of luif° in Troy; — *should/flower/love*
Now am I maid an unworthy outwaill,° — *outcast*
130 And all in cair translatit° is my joy. — *into care transformed*
Quha sall° me gyde?° Quha sall me now convoy,° — *who shall/guide/accompany*
Sen° I fra Diomeid and nobill° Troilus — *since/noble*
Am clenc° excludit, as abject° odious? — *wholly/outcast*

"O fals° Cupide, is nane° to wyte bot° thow — *false/(there) is none/blame but*

¹³⁵ And thy mother, of luf° the blind goddes!° — *love/goddess*
Ye causit me alwayis understand° and trow° — *(to) understand/believe*
The seid° of luf was sawin° in my face, — *seed/sown*
And ay° grew grene throw° your supply° and grace. — *ever/through/nourishment*
But now, allas! that seid with froist° is slane,° — *by frost/slain*
¹⁴⁰ And I fra luifferis° left, and all forlane!"° — *by lovers/forlorn*

Quhen° this was said, doun in ane extasy,° — *when/ecstasy*
Ravishit in spreit, intill° ane dream sho fell; — *deprived of spirit, into*
And, be apperance,° hard,° quhair sho did ly,° — *it seemed/heard/lie*
Cupid the king ringand° ane silver bell, — *ringing*
¹⁴⁵ Quhilk men micht heir° fra hevin° unto hell; — *hear/heaven*
At quhais° sound befoir° Cupide appeiris° — *whose/before/appears*
The sevin° planetis, discending° fra thair spheiris,° — *seven/descending/spheres*

Quhilk hes° power of° all thing generabill° — *which have/over/things created*
To reull° and steir, be° thair greit° influence, — *rule/steer, by/great*
¹⁵⁰ Wedder° and wind and coursis variabill.° — *weather/variable*
And first of all Saturn gave his sentence,° — *judgment*
Quhilk gave to Cupid litill° reverence, — *little*
But as ane busteous° churl, on his maneir, — *rough*
Com crabbitly,° with auster luik° and cheir.° — *came crabbedly/austere look/ countenance*

¹⁵⁵ His face fronsit,° his lyr° was lyk° the leid,° — *was wrinkled/complexion/like/lead*
His teith° chatterit and cheverit° with the chin; — *teeth/(he) trembled*
His ene drowpit, how, sonkin° in his heid,° — *eyes drooped, hollow, sunk/head*
Out of his nois° the meldrop° fast can rin;° — *nose/rheum/did run*
With lippis bla,° and cheikis leine° and thin; — *livid/cheeks lean*
¹⁶⁰ The yse-shoklis° that fra° his hair doun hang — *icicles/from*
Was wonder° greit, and as ane speir als lang.° — *wondrous/a spear as long*

Atour° his belt his lyart lokkis° lay — *about/gray locks*
Felterit unfair, ourfret° with froistis hoir;° — *tangled unpleasantly, covered/hoary*
His garmound° and his gyte full gay° of gray; — *garment/mantle very elegant*
¹⁶⁵ His widderit weid° fra him the wind out woir.° — *tattered clothes/blew*
Ane busteous° bow within his hand he boir;° — *huge/carried*

---

135. Normally Cupid/Eros is portrayed as blind—not his mother Venus/Aphrodite.
147. *sevin planetis:* The seven "planets" of the Ptolemaic system—Saturn, Jupiter, Mars, Sun, Venus, Mercury, and Moon—are named in order of the magnitude of their orbits around the earth.
155. *leid:* the metal of Saturn. A "saturnine" countenance is gloomy, dark, and angry.

Under his gyrdil° ane flash° of felloun flanis°   *belt/sheaf/sharp arrows*
Fedderit° with yse,° and heidit° with hail-stanis.°   *feathered/ice/headed/hailstones*

Than° Juppiter richt° fair and amiabill,°   *then/very/amiable*
170 God of the starnis° in the firmament,   *stars*
And nureis° to all thingis generabill,   *nurse*
Fra his father Saturn far different,
With burely° face, and browis bricht° and brent;°   *handsome/bright/smooth*
Upon his heid ane garland wonder gay
175 Of flouris° fair, as° it had been in May.   *flowers/as if*

His voice was cleir,° as cristal wer° his ene;   *clear/were*
As goldin wyr sa glitterand° was his hair;   *wire so glittering*
His garmound and his gyte full gay of grene,
With goldin listis° gilt on every gair;°   *borders/fold*
180 Ane burely brand° about his middill bair.°   *goodly sword/middle (he) wore*
In his right hand he had ane groundin° speir,   *sharpened*
Of his father the wraith° fra us to weir.°   *anger/ward off*

Nixt efter° him com Mars, the god of ire,   *next after*
Of stryf, debait,° and all dissensioun;   *strife, argument*
185 To chyde and fecht,° als feirs° as ony fyr;°   *fight/fierce/any fire*
In hard harnes, hewmound° and habirgeoun,°   *armor, helmet/coat of mail*
And on his hanche° ane rousty fell° fachioun:°   *hip/rust-colored wicked/curved sword*
And in his hand he had ane rousty sword,
Wrything° his face with mony° angry word.   *twisting/many (an)*

190 Shaikand° his sword, befoir° Cupide he com   *shaking/before*
With reid° visage and grisly glowrand° ene;   *red/glowering*
And at his mouth ane bullar stude° of fome,°   *bubble stood/foam*
Lyk to ane bair quhetting° his tuskis kene°   *boar whetting/sharp*
Richt tuilyour-lyk, but° temperance in tene;°   *quarrelsome, without/anger*
195 Ane horn he blew, with mony bosteous brag,°   *(a) boisterous blast*
Quhilk° all this warld° with weir lies maid° to wag.° *which/world/war has made/move*

Than fair Phebus, lanterne and lamp of licht°   *light*
Of man and beist, baith frute° and flourishing,°   *beast, both fruit/flowering*

---

173. *burely*: from OE *borlice*, "excellently," "nobly." Middle English spellings *bur-*, *bour-* indicate an association with ME *bour*, "bower"; thus by folk etymology a *burely* (Mod. Eng. *burly*) man was supposedly one strong, handsome, etc.

187–88. *rousty*: The word here probably does not imply "old," "corroded," but "rust-colored"; cf. the oft-recurring phrase "brown-edged sword" in Old English epic poetry, and "burnished [by metathesis from *brun*, "brown"] blade." The "browning" of the sword was a method of treating the steel. Hadley Tremaine, "Beowulf's 'Ecg Brun' and Other Rusty Relics," *Philological Quarterly*, 48 [1969], 145–50.)

Tender nureis, and banisher of nicht,°   *night*
200 And of° the warld causing, be° his moving   *in/creating, by*
And influence, lyf° in all eirdly thing;°   *life/earthly things*
Without comfort of quhom, of force° to nocht°   *whom, by necessity/naught*
Must all ga dy,° that in this warld is wrocht.°   *go die/created*

As king royall he raid° upon his chair,°   *rode/chariot*
205 The quhilk Phaeton gydit sum-tyme unricht;°   *guided once wrongly*
The brichtnes° of his face, quhen° it was bair,°   **brightness/when/bare**
Nane micht behald° for° peirsing° of his sicht.°   *none might behold/to avoid/dazzling/*
                                                                                                                          sight

This goldin cart with fyry bemes° bricht   **fiery beams**
Four yokkit steidis, full° different of hew,°   *yoked steeds, very/color*
210 But bait° or tyring throw° the spheiris° drew.   *pause/through/spheres*

The first was soyr,° with mane als° reid as rois,°   *sorrel-colored/as/rose*
Callit Eoy, in-to° the orient;°   *(meaning) in/east*
The second steid to° name hecht° Ethios,   *by/was called*
Quhytly° and paill,° and sum-deill ascendent;°   *whitish/pale/somewhat rising*
                                                                                                               (above the horizon)
215 The thrid° Peros, richt hait° and richt fervent;°   *third/very hot/spirited*
The feird° was blak,° callit Philegoney,   *fourth/black*
Quhilk rollis Phebus down in-to the sey.°   *sea*

Venus was thair° present, that goddes° gay,   *there/goddess*
Hir sonnis querrel° for to defend, and mak°   *her son's quarrel/make*
220 Hir awin° complaint, cled° in ane nyce° array,   *own/clad/an extravagant*
The ane° half grene, the uther° half sabill-blak;   *one/other/sable black*
Quhyte° hair as gold, kemmit° and shed abak;°   *fair/combed/flowing behind*
But in hir face semit greit° variance,   *seemed great*
Quhyles perfit treuth,° and quhyles inconstance.°   *sometimes **perfect truth/inconstancy***

225 Under smyling sho° was dissimulait,°   *(her) smiling she/full of dissimula-*
                                                                                                                  tion
Provocative with blenkis° amorous;   *looks*
And suddanly° changit and alterait,°   *suddenly/altered*
Angry as ony° serpent venemous,°   *any/venomous*
Richt pungitive° with wordis odious.   *sharp*
230 Thus variant° sho was, quha list tak keip,°   *variable/whoever wishes (to) take*
                                                                                                                  heed

---

205. *Phaeton:* Phaëthon could not control the horses of the sun when he stole the chariot of his father Apollo for a day's ride. **211–17.** According to Ovid (*Metamorphoses*, II, 153), the horses were called Eous, Aethon, Pyröeis, and Phlegm. The four horses follow the progress of the sun from dawn to evening.

With ane eye lauch,° and with the uther weip°—	*laughs/weeps*
In taikning° that all fleshly paramour,°	*as a sign/love*
Quhilk Venus hes in reull° and governance,	*rule*
Is sum-tyme sweit,° sum-tyme bitter and sour,	*sometimes sweet*
235 Richt unstabill,° and full of variance,	*unstable*
Mingit° with cairfull° joy, and fals plesance;°	*mixed/sorrowful/false pleasure*
Now hait, now cauld;° now blyth,° now full of wo;°	*cold/happy/woe*
Now grene as leif,° now widderit° and ago.°	*(a) leaf/withered/gone*
With buik° in hand than com° Mercurius,	*book/then came*
240 Richt eloquent and full of rethory;°	*rhetoric*
With polite termis° and delicious;	*phrases*
With pen and ink to report all redy;°	*ready*
Setting sangis,° and singand merily.°	*composing songs/singing merrily*
His hude° was reid, heklit atour° his croun,°	*hood/red, drawn over/head*
245 Lyk° to ane poeit° of the auld fassoun.°	*like/poet/old style*
Boxis he bair° with fine electuairis,°	*carried/electuaries*
And sugerit syropis° for digestioun;	*sugared syrups*
Spycis belangand° to the pothecairis,°	*belonging/apothecaries*
With many hailsum° sweit confectioun;	*many (a) wholesome*
250 Doctour in phisik,° cled in scarlot° goun,	*of medicine/scarlet*
And furrit° weill,° as sic° ane aucht° to be,	*trimmed with fur/well/such (a)/ ought*
Honest and gude,° and not ane word coud le.°	*good/could lie*
Nixt efter° him com lady Cynthia,	*next after*
The last of all, and swiftest in hir spheir,°	*orbit*
255 Of colour blak, buskit° with hornis twa,°	*adorned/two*
And in the nicht° sho listis° best appeir;°	*night/likes/(to) appear*
Haw° as the leid,° of colour na-thing cleir.	*dull/lead/not clear*
For all hir licht° sho borrowis at° hir brothir	*her light/from*
Titan; for of hir-self sho hes nane° uther.	*has no*
260 Hir gyte° was gray, and full of spottis blak;°	*mantle/black*
And on hir breist ane churl° paintit ful evin,°	*breast an (old) man/very evenly*

244–5. Perhaps Henryson has in mind the image of Chaucer as he was known to his friends and as he was drawn in the MS. *De Regimine Principum* of Thomas Hoccleve, "to putte othir men in remembraunce of his persone."

246. *electuairis:* Electuaries were medicines mixed with honey or syrup into a sweet paste.

250–5. *cled . . . goun:* Chaucer's Doctor of Physic is dressed this way.

261. *ane churl:* This is the man in the moon, who, according to one story, stole a bunch of thorns or firewood; in another version he was caught working on a Sunday. As punishment he is not allowed to approach heaven but must spend eternity on the moon.

Beirand ane° bunch of thornis on his bak,°   *bearing a/back*
Quhilk° for this thift micht clim na nar° the hevin.°   *which/theft might climb no nearer/*
   heaven

Thus quhen° they gadderit war, thir° goddis sevin,°   *when/gathered were, those/seven*
265 Mercurius they cheisit° with ane° assent   *chose/one*
To be foir-speikar° in the parliament.   *first speaker*

Quha had ben thair,° and lyking for° to heir°   *been there/wanted/hear*
His facound toung° and termis exquisyte,   **eloquent tongue**
Of rhetorik the praktik° he micht leir,°   *practice/learn*
270 In breif sermone° ane pregnant sentence wryte.   *short speech*
Befoir° Cupide vailing° his cap a lyte,°   *before/lowering/little*
Speiris° the caus of that vocacioun;°   *inquires/convocation*
And he anon shew° his intencioun.°   *quickly showed/intention.*

"Lo!" quod° Cupide, "quha° will blaspheme the name   *said/whoever*
275 Of his awin° god, outhir° in word or deid,°   *own/either/deed*
To all goddis he dois baith° lak° and shame,   *does both/reproach*
And suld° have bitter panis to° his meid.°   *should/pains for/reward*
I say this by° yonder wretchit Cresseid,°   *about/wretched Cressida*
The quhilk throw° me was sum-tyme flour° of lufe,°   *through/once flower/love*
280 Me and my mother starkly can reprufe.°   *harshly did reprove*

"Saying, of hir greit infelicité°   *great unhappiness*
I was the caus; and my mother Venus,
Ane blind goddes° hir cald,° that micht not see,   *goddess/(she) called*
With slander and defame° injurious.   *defamation*
285 Thus hir leving unclene° and lecherous   *life unclean*
Sho wald returne° on me and on my mother,   *she would blame*
To quhom° I shew° my grace abone° all uther.°   *whom/show/above/others*

"And sen° ye ar° all sevin deificait,°   *since/are/deified*
Participant of devyn sapience,°   *divine wisdom*
290 This greit injury don to our hy estait°   **high estate**
Me-think° with pane we suld mak° recompence;   *I intend/make*
Was never to goddis don sic° violence.   *such*
As weill° for yow° as for myself I say;   *well/you*
Thairfoir ga° help to revenge, I yow pray."   *therefore go*

295 Mercurius to Cupid gave answeir,°   *answer*
And said, "Shir° king, my counsall° is that ye   *sir/counsel*
Refer yow° to the hyest planeit heir,°   *yourself/planet here*
And tak to° him the lawest° of degre,°   *take with/lowest/degree*
The pane° of Cresseid for to modify;°   *punishment/determine*

³⁰⁰ As god Saturn, with him tak Cynthia."
"I am content," quod he, "to tak thay twa."°   *those two*

Than° thus proceidit° Saturn and the Mone,°   *then/proceeded/Moon*
Quhen thay° the mater rypely° had degest;°   *they/matter thoroughly/considered*
For the dispyt° to Cupid sho had done,   *wrong*
³⁰⁵ And to Venus oppin° and manifest,   *open*
In all hir lyf° with pane to be opprest°   *her life/oppressed*
And torment sair,° with seiknes incurabill,°   *sore/sickness incurable*
And to all lovers be abominabill.°   *abominable*

This dulefull° sentence Saturn tuik on° hand,   *sorrowful/took in*
³¹⁰ And passit° doun quhair cairfull° Cresseid lay;   *went/where sad*
And on hir heid° he laid ane° frosty wand,   *head/a*
Than lawfully on this wyse° can he say;   *manner*
"Thy greit fairnes,° and al thy bewty° gay,   *loveliness/beauty*
Thy wantoun blude,° and eik° thy goldin hair,   *sportive blood/also*
³¹⁵ Heir I exclude fra° thee for evermair.°   *from/evermore*

"I change thy mirth into melancholy,
Quhilk° is the mother of all pensivenes;°   *which/pensiveness*
Thy moisture and thy heit in cald° and dry;   *heat into cold*
Thyne insolence, thy play and wantones°   *wantonness*
³²⁰ To greit diseis:° thy pomp and thy riches   *great misery*
In mortall neid;° and greit penuritie°   *need/poverty*
Thow° suffer sall,° and as ane beggar die."   *you/shall*

O cruel Saturn, fraward° and angry,   *willful*
Hard is thy dome,° and to° malicious!   *judgment/too*
³²⁵ On fair Cresseid quhy hes° thow na° mercy,   *Cressida why have/no*
Quhilk° was sa sweit, gentill,° and amorous?   *who/so sweet, gentle*
Withdraw thy sentence, and be gracious
As thow was never; so shawis° thow thy deid,°   *show/deed*
Ane wraikfull° sentence gevin° on fair Cresseid.   *vengeful/given*

³³⁰ Than Cynthia, quhen° Saturn past° away,   *when/went*
Out of hir sait discendit° down belyve,°   *seat descended/quickly*
And red° ane bill on Cresseid quhair sho° lay,   *read/where she*
Contening° this sentence diffinityve:°   *containing/definitive*
"Fra heil° of body I thee now depryve,   *of health*
³³⁵ And to° thy seiknes sal be na recure,°   *from/recovery*

---

318. Heat and moisture were characteristics of the sanguine
temperament, cold and dryness of the melancholic.

But in dolour thy dayis to indure.°   *endure*

"Thy cristall ene minglit° with blude I mak,°   *eyes stained/make*
Thy voice sa cleir unplesand, hoir,° and hace;°   *clear unpleasing, old/hoarse*
Thy lusty lyre ourspred° with spottis blak,°   *pleasant face covered/black*
340 And lumpis haw appeirand° in thy face.   *dull appearing*
Quhair thow cummis, ilk° man sall flee the place;   *come, every*
Thus sall thou go begging fra hous to hous,
With cop° and clapper, lyk° ane lazarous."°   *cup/like/leper*

This dooly° dream, this ugly visioun   *dreary*
345 Brocht° to ane° end, Cresseid fra it awoik,°   *brought/an/awoke*
And all that court and convocatioun°   *assembly*
Vanischit away. Than rais° sho up and tuik   *then rose*
Ane poleist glas,° and hir shaddow coud luik;°   *polished mirror/her image did see*
And quhen sho saw hir face sa deformait,°   *deformed*
350 Gif° sho in hart° was wa aneuch,° God wait!°   *if/heart/woeful enough/knows*

Weiping full sair,° "Lo! quhat° it is," quod° she,   *weeping very bitterly/what/said*
"With fraward langage° for to mufe° and steir°   *angry language/move/stir*
Our crabbit° goddis, and sa is sene on° me!   *crabbed/seen in*
My blaspheming now have I bocht° full deir;°   *bought (i.e., paid for)/dearly*
355 All eirdly° joy and mirth I set areir.°   *earthly/behind (me)*
Allas,° this day! Allas, this wofull tyde,°   *alas/sorrowful time*
Quhen I began with my goddis to chyde!"

Be° this was said, ane° child com fra° the hall   *when/a/came from*
To warn° Cresseid the supper was redy;°   *advise/ready*
360 First knokkit° at the dure,° and syne° coud call: *knocked/door/then*
"Madame, your father biddis you cum in hy;°   *immediately*
He has mervell° sa lang° on grouf° ye ly,°   *wonder (that)/long/prostrate/lie*
And sayis, 'Your prayers been° to lang sum-deill;°   *are/much too long*
The goddis wait all your intent full weill.'"°   *well*

365 Quod sho, "Fair child, ga° to my father deir,°   *go/dear*

---

337. *minglit with blude:* i.e., "bloodshot."

343. Lepers in Europe carried a cup for their own use, and a clapper to announce their coming and also beg victuals from others. Since the disease was thought to be contagious (and specifically of venereal origin), lepers were isolated outside the city walls and placed in special hospitals. The "venereal disease" of medieval Europe has therefore been thought to be leprosy, since according to some older medical authorities syphilis was not known in Europe until it was brought back from the New World by Columbus's men on their return from the voyage of 1492. However, it is known today that true leprosy can be transferred only after years of contact, and that medieval "leprosy" was an inclusive term, for a myriad of skin diseases probably including endemic syphilis. The problem is very complicated (see T. J. Garbáty "The Summoner's Occupational Disease," *Medical History*, 7 [October 4, 1963], 348–58), but in the case of Cressida, and according to medieval science, it is obvious that Henryson means to have the punishment fit the crime.

And pray him cum to speik° with me anon."°   *speak/quickly*
And sa° he did, and said, "Douchter,° quhat cheir?"°   *so/daughter/news*
"Allas!" quod she, "father, my mirth is gon!"
"How sa?" quod he; and sho can° all expone,°   *did/explain*
370 As I have tauld,° the vengeance and the wrak,°   *told/punishment*
For hir trespas,° Cupide on hir coud tak.°   *sin/take*

He luikit° on hir ugly lipper° face,   *looked/leper*
The quhilk° befor was quhyte° as lilly-flour;°   *which/white/lily flower*
Wringand° his handis, oftymes he said, Allas!   **wringing**
375 That he had levit° to see that wofull hour!   *lived*
For he knew weill that thair° was na° succour   *there/no*
To° hir seiknes;° and that dowblit° his pane;°   *for/sickness/doubled/pain*
Thus was thair cair° aneuch betwix tham twane.°   *care/between them two*

Quhen thay togidder murnit° had full lang,   *when they together mourned*
380 Quod Cresseid,° "Father, I wald° not be kend;°   *Cressida/want/(to) be recognized*
Thairfoir° in secreit wyse° ye let me gang°   *therefore/secret manner/go*
To yon hospitall at the tounis end;
And thidder sum meit,° for cheritie,° me send   *there some food/charity*
To leif° upon; for all mirth in this eird   *live*
385 Is fra me gane;° sik° is my wikkit weird."°   *gone/such/wicked fate*

Than in ane mantill° and ane bevar° hat,   *mantle/beaver*
With cop° and clapper, wonder prively,°   *cup/very secretly*
He opnit° ane secreit yet,° and out thairat°   *opened/gate/therefrom*
Convoyit hir,° that° na man suld espy,°   *brought her/so that/should see*
390 Unto ane village half ane myle thairby;°   *away*
Deliverit hir in at the spittail-hous,°   *hospital*
And dayly sent hir part of his almous.°   *alms*

Sum knew hir weill, and sum had na knawlege°   *knowledge*
Of hir, becaus sho° was sa deformait°   *she/deformed*
395 With bylis blak,° ourspred° in° hir visage,°   *boils black/spread about/on*
And hir fair colour faidit° and alterait.°   *faded/altered*
Yit° thay presumit, for° hir hy regrait°   *yet/because of/intense grief*
And still° murning, sho was of nobill kin;°   *silent/noble family*
With better will thairfoir they tuik° hir in.   *took*

400 The day passit, and Phebus went to rest,
The cloudis blak ourquhelmit° all the sky;   *overwhelmed*

---

385. *weird:* OE *wyrd,* "fate." The term, found often in Old English poetry and also Layamon's *Brut,* is the origin of our modern word *weird,* denoting anything strange or mystifying, a happening to be understood only as a result of the incomprehensible workings of fate.

God wait gif° Cresseid was ane° sorrowful gest,° *knows if/a/guest*
Seeing that uncouth fair° and herbery.° *strange fare/shelter*
But° meit or drink sho dressit hir° to ly° *without/prepared herself/lie*
405 In ane dark corner of the hous allone;° *alone*
And on° this wyse, weiping,° sho maid° hir mone.° *in/weeping/made/moan*

The Complaint of Cresseid

"O sop of sorrow sonken° into cair! *sunk*
O caytive° Cresseid! now and ever-mair° *wretched/evermore*
  Gane is thy joy and all thy mirth in eird;° *earth*
410 Of all blyithnes° now art thow blaiknit bair;° *happiness/rendered bare*
Thair is na salve may saif° thee of° thy sair!° *save/from/sore*
  Fell° is thy fortoun,° wikkit is thy weird; *harsh/fortune*
  Thy blis° is baneist,° and thy baill° on° breird!° *bliss/banished/bale/up to the/brim*
Under the eirth° God gif° I gravin wer,° *earth/would to God/buried were*
415   Quhar nane° of Grece nor yit of Troy micht heird!° *where none/might pass*

"Quhair° is thy chalmer, wantounly besene° *where/chamber, luxuriously decked*
With burely° bed, and bankouris browderit bene,° *goodly/seats ornamented well*
  Spycis and wynis to° thy collatioun;° *for/repast*
The cowpis° all of gold and silver shene,° *cups/shining*
420 The swete meitis° servit in plaittis clene,° *sweetmeats/platters bright*
  With saipheron sals° of ane gude sessoun;° *saffron sauce/good seasoning*
  Thy gay garmentis, with mony° gudely goun, *many (a)*
Thy plesand lawn° pinnit with goldin prene?° *pleasant lawn (kerchief)/brooch*
  All is areir° thy greit° royall renoun! *gone/great*

425 "Quhair is thy garding,° with thir greissis° gay *garden/those plants*
And fresshe flouris, quhilk° the quene Floray° *flowers, which/Flora*
  Had paintit plesandly° in every pane,° *pleasingly/bed*
Quhair thou was wont full merily° in May *very merrily*
To walk, and tak° the dew be° it was day, *gather/when*
430   And heir° the merle° and mavis mony ane;° *hear/blackbird/thrush many (a) one*
With ladyis fair in carrolling to gane,° *go*
And see the royal rinkis° in thair° array *folk/their*
  In garmentis gay, garnischit° on every grane?° *decorated/particular*

"Thy greit triumphand° fame and hy° honour, *triumphant/high*

---

421. Saffron was much used in the medieval menu, which was heavily spiced for purposes of conservation as well as taste. Most meat was pounded into a mush and the original taste hidden by sharp sauces; the art of the cook lay in his ability to disguise food.

428–29. Dew gathered in May for washing beautified the complexion.

435 Quhair° thou was callit of eirdly wichtis flour,°	*whereby/creatures (the) flower*
All is decayit; thy weird° is welterit° so,	*fate/overturned*
Thy hy estait° is turnit in **darknes**° dour!	*estate/into **darkness***
This lipper ludge tak° for thy burelie bour,°	*leper lodge take/pleasant chamber*
And for thy bed tak now ane bunch of stro.°	*straw*
440 For waillit° wyne and meitis° thou had tho,°	*choice/food/then*
Tak mowlit breid, peirry,° and syder° sour;	*moldy **bread, perry**/cider*
Bot° cop° and clapper, now is all ago.°	*except for/cup/gone*

"My cleir° voice and my courtly carrolling,	*clear*
Quhair I was wont with ladyis for to sing,	
445 Is rawk° as ruik,° full hiddeous, hoir,° and hace;°	*raucous/rook/old/hoarse*
My plesand port° all utheris precelling,°	*bearing/others excelling*
Of lustines° I was held maist conding;°	*in/pleasingness/most excellent*
Now is deformit the figour° of my face;	*features*
To luik° on it na leid° now lyking hes.°	*look/no youth/has*
450 Sowpit° in syte,° I say with sair siching°—	*drenched/sorrow/sore sighing*
Lugeit amang° the lipper-leid°—'Alas!'	*lodged among/leper folk*

"O ladyis fair of Troy and Grece, attend°	*heed*
My misery, quhilk nane may comprehend,	
My frivoll fortoun,° my infelicitie,°	*fickle fortune/unhappiness*
455 My greit mischief,° quhilk na man can amend.	*distress*
Be war° in tyme, approchis neir° the end,	*warned/approaches near*
And in your mynd ane° mirrour mak° of me.	*a/make*
As I am now, peradventure that° ye,	*perhaps*
For all your micht,° may cum° to that same end,	*might/come*
460 Or ellis war,° gif ony° war may be.	*else worse, if any*

"Nocht° is your fairnes bot° ane faiding° flour,	*naught/beauty but/fading*
Nocht is your famous laud and hy honour	
Bot wind inflat° in uther mennis eiris;°	*blown/ears*
Your roising reid° to rotting sall retour.°	*rosy red/shall return*
465 Exempill° mak of me in your memour,°	*example/mind*
Quhilk° of sic° thingis wofull witnes beiris.°	*who/such/woeful witness bears*
All welth in eird° away as wind it weiris;°	*earth/wears*
Be war thairfoir;° approchis neir the hour;	*therefore*
Fortoun is fikkil, quhen sho° beginnis and steiris."°	*fickle, when she/governs*

470 Thus chydand° with her drery desteny,°	*chiding/dreary destiny*
Weiping,° sho woik° the nicht fra° end to end,	*weeping/waked/night from*

---

441. *peirry:* either the fermented liquor of pears or a kind of stew (from OF *porée*).

But all in vane;° hir dule,° hir cairfull° cry | *vain/her grief/sorrowful*
Micht nocht remeid,° nor yit° hir murning° mend. | *remedy/yet/mourning*
Ane lipper-lady rais,° and till° hir wend,° | *rose/to/turned*
475 And said, "Quhy spurnis° thou aganis° the wall, | *why dash (yourself)/against*
To sla° thyself, and mend na-thing° at all? | *slay/nothing*

"Sen° that thy weiping dowbillis bot° thy wo,° | *since/only doubles/woe*
I counsall° thee mak vertew° of ane neid,° | *counsel/(to) make (a) virtue/*
                                                     necessity

To leir° to clap thy clapper to and fro, | *learn*
480 And live efter° the law of lipper-leid." | *according to*
Thair° was na buit,° bot forth with thame° sho yeid° | *there/help/(for it)/them/went*
Fra place to place, quhill cauld° and hounger sair° | *while cold/hunger sore*
Compellit hir to be ane rank beggair.° | *beggar*

That samin° tyme, of Troy the garnisoun,° | *same/garrison*
485 Quhilk° had to chiftane° worthy Troilus, | *which/as chief*
Throw jeopardy° of weir° had strikkin° doun | *through chance/war/struck*
Knichtis° of Grece in number mervellous.° | *knights/wondrous*
With greit° triumph and laud victorious | *great*
Agane° to Troy richt° royally thay raid° | *again/very/they rode*
490 The way quhair Cresseid° with the lipper baid.° | *where Cressida/lepers waited*

Seing° that company cum, all with ane stevin° | *seeing/one voice*
They gaif° ane cry, and shuik coppis° gude speid;° | *gave/shook cups/vigorously*
Said, "Worthy lordis, for Goddis lufe° of hevin,° | *love/heaven*
To us lipper part° of your almous-deid."° | *give/almsgiving*
495 Than to thair° cry nobill° Troilus tuik heid;° | *then of their/noble/took heed*
Having pity, neir° by the place can pas° | *near/did pass*
Quhair Cresseid sat, nat witting quhat° sho was. | *not knowing who*

Than upon him sho kest° up baith° her ene,° | *cast/both/eyes*
And with ane blenk° it com° in-to his thocht° | *a look/came/thought*
500 That he sum-tyme° hir face befoir° had sene;° | *once/before/seen*
But sho was in sic ply° he knew hir nocht.° | *such plight/not*
Yit than hir luik° in-to his mind it brocht° | *look/brought*
The sweit° visage and amorous blenking° | *sweet/glances*
Of fair Cresseid, sumtyme his awin° darling. | *own*

505 Na° wonder was,° suppois° in mynd that he | *no/(it) was/to think*
Tuik hir figure sa sone,° and lo! now, quhy? | *image so soon*
The idole° of ane thing in cace° may be | *image/(a certain) case*

505–6. *in mynd* . . . *Tuik:* i.e., "remembered."

Sa deip imprentit° in the fantasy,   *deeply imprinted*
That it deludis the wittis° outwardly,   *reason*
510 And sa appeiris° in forme and lyke estait°   *appears/state*
Within the mynd as it was figurait.°   *figured*

Ane spark of lufe than till his hart coud° spring,   *heart did*
And kendlit° all his body in ane fyre;   *kindled*
With hait° fevir ane **sweit°** and **trimbilling°**   *hot/a sweat/trembling*
515 Him tuik, quhill° he was redy° to expyre;   *until/ready*
To beir° his sheild° his breist° began to tyre;   *bearing/shield/breast*
Within ane whyle° he changit mony hew,°   *(short) while/color much*
And nevertheles not ane ane-uther° knew.   *the other*

For knichtly° pity and memoriall°   *knightly/memory*
520 Of fair Cresseid, ane girdill can° he tak,°   *belt did/take*
Ane purs° of gold and mony° gay jowall,°   *purse/many (a)/jewel*
And in the skirt of Cresseid doun can swak;°   *throw*
Than raid away, and not ane word he spak,°   *spoke*
Pensive in hart, quhill he com to the toun,
525 And for greit cair oft-syis almaist° fell doun.   *grief often almost*

The lipper-folk° to Cresseid than can draw,   *lepers*
To see the equall distribucioun°   *distribution*
Of the almous;° but quhan° the gold they saw,   *alms/when*
Ilk° ane to uther prevely° can roun,°   *each/other secretly/whisper*
530 And said, "Yon° **lord hes mair°** affectioun,   *that/has more*
However it be, unto yon lazarous°   *leper*
Than to us all; we knaw be° his almous."   *know by*

"Quhat° lord is yon," quod sho,° "have ye na feill,°   *what/said she/knowledge*
Hes° don to us so greit **humanitie?"°**   *(who) has/great kindness*
535 "Yes," quod a lipper-man, "I knaw him weill;°   *well*
Shir° Troilus it is, gentill° and free."°   *Sir/noble/generous*
Quhen Cresseid understude° that it was he,   *when **Cressida** understood*
Stiffer° than steill thair stert° ane **bitter** stound°   *harder/steel there started/**pang***
Throwout hir° hart, and fell° doun to the ground.   *through her/(she) fell*

540 Quhen sho ourcom,° with syching sair° and sad,   *recovered/sighing sore*
With mony cairfull° cry and cald:° "**Ochane!**   *sorrowful/called out*
Now is my breist with stormy stoundis stad,°   *beset*
Wrappit in wo,° ane° wretch full will of wane,"°   *woe/a/wholly astray from hope*
Than swounit° sho oft or° sho coud refrane,°   *then fainted/before/could stop*

---

541. *Ochane:* the Irish (Gaelic) lament "O hone!"   **543.** *will of wane:* i.e., "hopeless."

545 And ever in hir swouning cryit sho thus:
    "O fals° Cresseid, and trew° knicht Troilus!   *false/true*

    "Thy luf,° thy lawtee,° and thy gentilnes°   *love/loyalty/nobility*
    I countit small in my prosperitie;
    Sa elevait° I was in wantones,°   *so raised/wantonness*
550 And clam° upon the fickill quheill° sa hie;°   *climbed/fickle wheel/high*
    All faith and lufe° I promissit to thee   *love*
    Was in the self° fickill° and frivolous;   *itself/fickle*
    O fals Cresseid, and trew knicht Troilus!

    "For lufe of me thou keipt gude countinence,°   *kept up a good appearance*
555 Honest and chaist° in conversatioun;   *sober*
    Of all wemen° protectour and defence   *women*
    Thou was, and helpit thair opinioun.°   *defended their repute*
    My mynd, in fleshly foull affectioun,
    Was inclynit to lustis lecherous;
560 Fy!° fals Cresseid! O, trew knicht Troilus!   *fie*

    "Lovers, be war,° and tak° gude heid° about   *warned/take/heed*
    Quhom° that ye lufe, for quhom ye suffer paine;   *whom*
    I lat yow wit,° thair is richt° few thairout°   *let you know/very/about*
    Quhom ye may traist,° to have trew lufe againe;°   *trust/in return*
565 Preif° quhen ye will, your labour is in vaine.   *try*
    Thairfoir° I reid° ye tak thame° as ye find;   *therefore/advise/them*
    For they ar sad° as widdercock° in wind.   *are constant/weathercock*

    "Becaus I knaw the greit unstabilnes°   *instability*
    Brukkil° as glas, into° my-self, I say°   *brittle/glass, unto/say (that)*
570 Traisting° in uther als° greit unfaithfulnes,   *(I) expect/others as*
    Als unconstant, and als untrew of fay.°   *faith*
    Thocht sum° be trew, I wait° richt few ar thay.°   *though some/know/they*
    Quha° findis treuth,° lat him his lady ruse;°   *whoever/truth/praise*
    Nane° but my-self, as now, I will accuse."   *none*

575 Quhen this was said, with paper sho° sat doun,   *she*
    And on° this maneir maid° hir TESTAMENT: *in/manner made*
    "Heir° I beteich° my corps° and carioun°   *here/commit/body/flesh*
    With° wormis and with taidis° to be rent;   *by/toads*
    My cop° and clapper, and myne ornament,   *cup*
580 And all my gold, the lipper-folk sall° have,   *lepers shall*

---

550. *fickill quheill:* The "fickle wheel" is the Wheel of Fortune, one of the
central motifs of Chaucer's *Troilus and Criseyde* (e.g., IV, 6–7, 11).

Quhen° I am deid,° to bury me in grave. — *when/dead*

"This royall ring, set with this ruby reid,° — *red*
Quhilk° Troilus in drowry° to me send,° — *which/as dowry/sent*
To him agane° I leif° it quhan° I am deid, — *again/leave/when*
585 To mak° my cairfull deid° unto him kend.° — *make/sorrowful death/known*
Thus I conclude shortly, and mak ane° end. — *an*
My spreit° I leif to Diane, quhair° sho dwellis, — *soul/where*
To walk with hir° in waist woddis° and wellis.° — *her/waste woods/rills*

"O Diomeid!° thow hes baith broche° and belt — *Diomedes/you have both brooch*
590 Quhilk Troilus gave me in takinning° — *token*
Of his trew lufe!"° And with that word sho swelt.° — *true love/died*
And sone ane° lipper-man tuik of° the ring, — *quickly a/took off*
Syne° buryit hir withoutin tarying.° — *then/without delay*
To Troilus furthwith° the ring he bair,° — *forthwith/carried*
595 And of Cresseid° the deith° he can declair.° — *Cressida/death/did announce*

Quhen he had hard° hir greit infirmité,° — *heard/great infirmity*
Hir legacy and lamentatioun,
And how sho endit in sik poverté,° — *such poverty*
He swelt° for wo,° and fell doun in ane swoun;° — *fainted/woe/swoon*
600 For greit sorrow his hart° to birst° was boun.° — *heart/burst/ready*
Syching full° sadly, said,° "I can no moir;° — *sighing very/(he) said/more*
Sho was untrew, and wo is me thairfoir!"

Sum said, he maid ane tomb of merbell° gray, — *marble*
And wrait° hir name and superscriptioun,° — *wrote/inscription*
605 And laid it on hir grave, quhair that sho lay,
In goldin letteris, conteining° this ressoun:°— — *containing/declaration*
"Lo! fair ladyis, Cresseid of Troyis° toun, — *Troy*
Sumtyme° countit the flour° of womanheid,° — *once/flower/womanhood*
Under this stane,° late lipper, lyis° deid!" — *stone/(a) leper, lies*

610 Now, worthy wemen,° in this ballet° short, — *women/ballad*
Made for your worship° and instructioun, — *honor*
Of cherité° I monish° and exhort, — *in charity/admonish*
Ming° not your luf° with fals° deceptioun. — *mix/love/false*
Beir° in your mynd this short conclusioun° — *bear/sudden end*
615 Of fair Cresseid, as I have said befoir;° — *before*
Sen sho° is deid, I speik° of hir no moir. — *since she/speak*

589–91. In Chaucer's *Troilus and Criseyde* Criseyde gives Diomede a brooch that Troilus had given her as a token. Troilus recognizes it on the armor which he has captured from Diomede (V, 1660–66, 1669, 1688–91). The belt is Henryson's addition.

APPENDIX A

Index According to Chronology (Page number in parentheses)

JRTEENTH CENTURY

Early 14th century

	Interludium de Clerico et Puella (475)
1300—49	Richard Rolle of Hampole, *Prose Treatises* (794)
1303	Robert Mannyng of Brunne, *Handlyng Synne* (782)
c. 1325	*Sir Orfeo* (349)
c. 1370—80	The Alliterative *Morte Arthure* (92)
1375	John Barbour, *The Bruce* (934)
c. 1376—87	William Langland, *Piers Plowman* (676)
1380—1400	*Pearl* (721)
c. 1390	*Sir Gawain and the Green Knight* (254)
c. 1390	Geoffrey Chaucer, *Sir Thopas* (398)
c. 1390	Geoffrey Chaucer, *The Miller's Tale* (455)
c. 1390	John Gower, *The Tale of Florent* (800)
a. 1400	Thomas Chestre, *Sir Launfal* (365)
c. 1400	Geoffrey Chaucer, *Complaint to His Purse* (408)
c. 1400	*The Debate of the Body and Soul* (603)

14th century

The Travels of Sir John Mandeville (824)

14th century

The York Cycle: Noah and His Wife (863)

Crucifixio Cristi (872)

14th century Lyrics:

Nou Skrinketh Rose (639)
Annot and Iohon (642)
Alysoun (645)
A Wayle Whyt (647)
Lenten Is Come with Love to Town (649)
When the Nightingale Sings (651)
The Man in the Moon (653)
The Irish Dancer (655)
All Night by the Rose (656)
Maiden in the Moor Lay (657)

FIFTEENTH CENTURY

1400—40	*The Tournament of Tottenham* (410)
? c. 1403	Thomas Clanvowe, *The Cuckoo and the Nightingale* (620)

c. 1440   *Gesta Romanorum* (813)

c. 1450   *The Wedding of Sir Gawain and Dame Ragnell* (418)

1460—70   Sir Thomas Malory, *Morte Darthur* (835)

Late 15th century

Robert Henryson, *The Testament of Cresseid* (942)

a. 1500   *The Wakefield Cycle: The Second Shepherds' Play* (882)

1500   *Everyman* (907)

15th Century Lyrics:

Complaint to a Pitiless Mistress (659)
I Sing of a Maiden (661)
Jolly Jankyn (662)
Jack, the Nimble Holy-Water Clerk (664)
The Servant Girl's Holiday (667)
Sir John Doth Play (669)
The Smiths (671)
The Fox and the Goose (672)
The False Fox (673)

15th century Ballads:

Saint Stephen and Herod (492)
The Marriage of Sir Gawain (505)

post-15th century Ballads:

Lord Randal (484)
Edward (486)
Hind Horn (489)
The Three Ravens (494)
The Twa Corbies (496)
The Boy and the Mantle (497)
Thomas Rymer (514)
Sir Patrick Spens (518)
The Unquiet Grave (520)
The Knight and Shepherd's Daughter (522)
Johnie Cock (527)
Robin Hood and the Butcher (531)

APPENDIX B

Index According to Dialect (Page number in parentheses)

c. 1250   *The Bestiary* (East) (538)

c. 1285   *Havelok the Dane* (East) (181)

13th century Ballad:

Judas (Southwest) (481)

1303   Robert Mannyng of Brunne, *Handlyng Synne* (East) (782)

c. 1325   *Sir Orfeo* (Southeast) (349)

c. 1376—87   William Langland, *Piers Plowman* (Southwest) (676)

1380—1400   *Pearl* (Northwest) (721)

c. 1390   *Sir Gawain and the Green Knight* (Northwest) (254)

c. 1400   *The Debate of the Body and Soul* (West) (603)

14th century

The Travels of Sir John Mandeville (Southeast) (824)

14th century Lyrics (West) (639— 58)

c. 1450   *The Wedding of Sir Gawain and Dame Ragnell* (East) (418)

NORTHERN

1300—49   Richard Rolle of Hampole, *Prose Treatises* (794)

Early 14th century

Interludium de Clerico et Puella (475)

c. 1370—80   The Alliterative *Morte Arthure* (92)

1375   John Barbour, *The Bruce* (Lowland Scottish) (934)

14th century

The York Cycle: Noah and His Wife (863)
Crucifixio Cristi (872)

1400—40   *The Tournament of Tottenham* (410)

a. 1500   *The Wakefield Cycle: The Second Shepherds' Play* (882)

Late 15th century

Robert Henryson, *The Testament of Cresseid* (Lowland Scottish) (942)

15th century and post-15th century Ballads (Lowland Scottish) (485—535)

LONDON

c. 1390   Geoffrey Chaucer, *Sir Thopas* (398)

c. 1390   Geoffrey Chaucer, *The Miller's Tale* (455)

c. 1390   John Gower, *The Tale of Florent* (800)

c. 1400   Geoffrey Chaucer, *Complaint to His Purse* (408)

? c. 1403   Thomas Clanvowe, *The Cuckoo and the Nightingale* (620)

EARLY MODERN

c. 1440   *Gesta Romanorum* (813)

1460—70   Sir Thomas Malory, *Morte Darthur* (835)

15th century Lyrics (659—74)

1500   *Everyman* (907)

APPENDIX C

Index According to Mode—Courtly, Popular, Religious (Page number in parentheses)

Note: This index is organized according to the predominant audience and content material of the various works. Cross-references are given when two or three modes are involved, as in Chaucer's *The Miller's Tale,* where the content is popular but the attitude and audience clearly courtly, or in *Havelok the Dane* and *Sir Launfal,* where the reverse is true. A work like *The Owl and the Nightingale* is full of folklore but debates courtly and moral themes, and the audience was probably a clerkly, educated, or noble one. Thus the network of Middle English literature can here be seen at a glance.

COURTLY

14th century Lyrics (also Popular):

> *Annot and Iohon* (642)
> *Alysoun* (645)
> *A Wayle Whyt* (647)
> *Lenten Is Come with Love to Town* (649)
> *When the Nightingale Sings* (651)

c. 1400	Geoffrey Chaucer, *Complaint to His Purse* (408)
? c. 1403	Thomas Clanvowe, *The Cuckoo and the Nightingale* (620)
c. 1450	*The Wedding of Sir Gawain and Dame Ragnell* (also Popular) (418)
1460—70	Sir Thomas Malory, *Morte Darthur* (835)

Late 15th century

> Robert Henryson, *The Testament of Cresseid* (942)

15th century Lyric:

> *Complaint to a Pitiless Mistress* (659)

15th century Ballad (also Popular):

> *The Marriage of Sir Gawain* (505)

post-15th century Ballads (also Popular):

> *Lord Randal* (484)
> *Edward* (486)
> *Hind Horn* (489)
> *The Three Ravens* (494)
> *The Twa Corbies* (496)
> *The Boy and the Mantle* (497)
> *Sir Patrick Spens* (518)

POPULAR

a. 1200	*The Owl and the Nightingale* (also Courtly and Religious) (556)
c. 1250	*The Bestiary* (also Religious) (538)
1280—90	*South English Legendary* (also Religious) (767)
c. 1285	*Havelok the Dane* (also Courtly) (181)
a. 1300	*Dame Sirip* (also Courtly) (442)
a. 1300	*The Fox and the Wolf* (545)

13th century Ballad (also Religious):

> *Judas* (481)

13th century Lyrics:

> *Sumer Is Icumen In* (633)
> *Mirie It Is While Sumer Ilast* (634)
> *Foweles in the Frith* (635)

1303   Robert Mannyng of Brunne, *Handlyng Synne* (also Religious) (782)

Early 14th century

Interludium de Clerico et Puella (also Courtly) (475)

c. 1376—87   William Langland, *Piers Plowman* (also Religious) (676)

c. 1390   Geoffrey Chaucer, *The Miller's Tale* (also Courtly) (455)

14th century Lyrics:

Nou Skrinketh Rose (639)
The Man in the Moon (653)
The Irish Dancer (655)
All Night by the Rose (656)
Maiden in the Moor Lay (657)

14th century Lyrics (also Courtly):

Annot and Iohon (642)
Alysoun (645)
A Wayle Whyt (647)
Lenten Is Come with Love to Town (649)
When the Nightingale Sings (651)

14th century

The Travels of Sir John Mandeville (824)

14th century

The York Cycle: Noah and His Wife (also Religious) (863)
Crucifixio Cristi (also Religious) (872)

a. 1400   Thomas Chestre, *Sir Launfal* (also Courtly) (365)

1400—40   *The Tournament of Tottenham* (also Courtly) (410)

c. 1440   *Gesta Romanorum* (also Religious) (815)

c. 1450   *The Wedding of Sir Gawain and Dame Ragnell* (also Courtly) (418)

a. 1500   *The Wakefield Cycle: The Second Shepherds' Play* (also Religious) (882)

1500   *Everyman* (also Religious) (907)

15th century Ballad (also Religious):

Saint Stephen and Herod (492)

15th century Lyrics:

Jolly Jankyn (662)
Jack, the Nimble Holy-Water Clerk (664)
The Servant Girl's Holiday (667)
Sir John Doth Play (669)
The Smiths (671)
The Fox and the Goose (672)
The False Fox (673)

post-15th century Ballads:

> *Thomas Rymer* (514)
> *The Unquiet Grave* (520)
> *The Knight and Shepherd's Daughter* (522)
> *Johnie Cock* (527)
> *Robin Hood and the Butcher* (531)

RELIGIOUS

a. 1200   *The Owl and the Nightingale* (also Courtly and Popular) (556)

a. 1200   *The Ancrene Riwle* (756)

c. 1250   *The Bestiary* (also Popular) (538)

1280—90   *South English Legendary* (also Popular) (767)

13th century Lyric (also Courtly):

> *Edi Beo Thu, Heuene Quene* (636)

13th century Ballad (also Popular):

> *Judas* (481)

1300—49   Richard Rolle of Hampole, *Prose Treatises* (794)

1303   Robert Mannyng of Brunne, *Handlyng Synne* (also Popular) (782)

c. 1376—87   William Langland, *Piers Plowman* (also Popular) (676)

1380—1400   *Pearl* (721)

14th century

> *The York Cycle: Noah and His Wife* (also Popular) (863)
>   *Crucifixio Cristi* (also Popular) (872)

c. 1400   *The Debate of the Body and Soul* (603)

a. 1500   *The Wakefield Cycle: The Second Shepherds' Play* (also Popular) (882)

1500   *Everyman* (also Popular) (907)

15th century Lyric:

> *I Sing of a Maiden* (661)

15th century Ballad (also Popular):

> *Saint Stephen and Herod* (492)

APPENDIX D

Index According to Themes and Motifs (Page number in parentheses)

ARTHURIAN MATTER

CHASTITY TEST

post-15th century Ballad:

> *The Boy and the Mantle* (497)

LOATHLY LADY—FALSE APPEARANCE, SEDUCTION OF GAWAIN

    c. 1390   *Sir Gawain and the Green Knight* (254)

    c. 1390   John Gower, *The Tale of Florent* (800)

    c. 1450   *The Wedding of Sir Gawain and Dame Ragnell* (418)

15th century Ballad:

> *The Marriage of Sir Gawain* (505)

post-15th century Ballad:

> *The Knight and Shepherd's Daughter* (522)

FAIRY LOVE—SEDUCTION

    c. 1175   Marie de France, *Lanval* (340)

    c. 1325   *Sir Orfeo* (349)

    c. 1390   Geoffrey Chaucer, *Sir Thopas* (398)

    a. 1400   Thomas Chestre, *Sir Launfal* (365)

post-15th century Ballad:

> *Thomas Rymer* (514)

EXILE AND RETURN

    c. 1250   *King Horn* (also False Steward, Love Token) (142)

    c. 1285   *Havelok the Dane* (also False Steward, King's Mark) (181)

    c. 1325   *Sir Orfeo* (also Loyal Steward, Beasts Charmed with Music, Rash Promise, Boon) (349)

15th century Ballad:

> *Hind Horn* (489)

ADULTEROUS LOVE—SEDUCTION

    c. 1175   Marie de France, *Lanval* (340)

    a. 1200   *The Owl and the Nightingale* (556)

    a. 1300   *Dame Siriþ* (442)

Early 14th century

> *Interludium de Clerico et Puella* (475)

    c. 1390   *Sir Gawain and the Green Knight* (254)

c. 1390   Geoffrey Chaucer, *The Miller's Tale* (455)

a. 1400   Thomas Chestre, *Sir Launfal* (365)

14th century Lyrics:

> *All Night by the Rose* (656)
> *Maiden in the Moor Lay* (657)

15th century Lyrics:

> *Jolly Jankyn* (662)
> *Jack, the Nimble Holy-Water Clerk* (664)
> *The Servant Girl's Holiday* (667)
> *Sir John Doth Play* (669)

post-15th century Ballad:

> *The Knight and Shepherd's Daughter* (522)

BEAST ELEMENT

937   *The Battle of Brunanburg* (49)

a. 1200   *The Owl and the Nightingale* (556)

c. 1250   *The Bestiary* (538)

1280—90   *South English Legendary: Saint Martin* (771)

a. 1300   *The Fox and the Wolf* (545)

1300—49   Richard Rolle of Hampole, *Prose Treatises:*
The Nature of the Bee and the Stork (795)

c. 1376—87   William Langland, *Piers Plowman:*
Belling the Cat/The Council of Rats and Mice (682)

? c. 1403   Thomas Clanvowe, *The Cuckoo and the Nightingale* (620)

c. 1440   *Gesta Romanorum: A Fable of a Cat and a Mouse* (819)

15th century Lyrics:

> *The Fox and the Goose* (672)
> *The False Fox* (673)

post-15th century Ballads:

> *The Three Ravens* (494)
> *The Twa Corbies* (496)

LYRIC COMPLAINTS

c. 1400   Geoffrey Chaucer, *Complaint to his Purse* (408)

15th century Lyric:

> *Complaint to a Pitiless Mistress* (659)

DREAM VISION

THE EXCHANGE OF GIFTS

3 4 5 6 7 8 9 0